Tolley's TAXWISE I
2006-07

Income Tax
National Insurance
Corporation Tax
Capital Gains Tax and Stamp Duty

Authors:
John Clube MA CA CTA
Keith Gordon MA (Oxon) ACA CTA Barrister
Peter Gravestock FCA CTA (Fellow) ATT

LexisNexis®
Tolley

Members of the LexisNexis Group worldwide

United Kingdom	LexisNexis Butterworths, a Division of Reed Elsevier (UK) Ltd, Halsbury House, 35 Chancery Lane, London, WC2A 1EL, and RSH, 1–3 Baxter's Place, Leith Walk Edinburgh EH1 3AF
Argentina	LexisNexis Argentina, Buenos Aires
Australia	LexisNexis Butterworths, Chatswood, New South Wales
Austria	LexisNexis Verlag ARD Orac GmbH & Co KG, Vienna
Benelux	LexisNexis Benelux, Amsterdam
Canada	LexisNexis Canada, Markham, Ontario
Chile	LexisNexis Chile Ltda, Santiago
China	LexisNexis China, Beijing and Shanghai
France	LexisNexis SA, Paris
Germany	LexisNexis Deutschland GmbH, Munster
Hong Kong	LexisNexis Hong Kong, Hong Kong
India	LexisNexis India, New Delhi
Italy	Giuffrè Editore, Milan
Japan	LexisNexis Japan, Tokyo
Malaysia	Malayan Law Journal Sdn Bhd, Kuala Lumpur
Mexico	LexisNexis Mexico, Mexico
New Zealand	LexisNexis NZ Ltd, Wellington
Poland	Wydawnictwo Prawnicze LexisNexis Sp, Warsaw
Singapore	LexisNexis Singapore, Singapore
South Africa	LexisNexis Butterworths, Durban
USA	LexisNexis, Dayton, Ohio

© Reed Elsevier (UK) Ltd 2006
Published by LexisNexis Butterworths

A CIP Catalogue record for this book is available from the British Library.

ISBN 10: 0 7545 2959 2

ISBN 13: 9 780754 529590

Typeset by Letterpart Ltd, Reigate, Surrey
Printed and bound in Great Britain by William Clowes Limited, Beccles, Suffolk
Visit LexisNexis Butterworths at www.lexisnexis.co.uk

About this book

For over 30 years Tolley's Taxwise I has provided practitioners with a practical means of keeping up to date with changing legislation by way of worked examples. The publication is updated annually to show the changes introduced by the Finance Acts.

The publication is useful as a manual for staff and practitioners giving guidance as to the layout of computations and notes explaining both the law and practice relating to taxation issues. In addition, the worked examples provide a comprehensive study aid to students of taxation, allowing the testing of theoretical knowledge on practical examples of a style that could well form the basis of an examination question for professional qualifications.

Coverage

A selection of taxation examples based on the legislation current for 2006/07, complete with annotated solutions.

The examples are preceded by a summary commencing on page (xv) of the main provisions of the Finance Act 2006, which received Royal Assent on 19 July 2006.

The book is not an exhaustive work of reference but it shows the treatment of all the points that are most likely to be encountered.

The contents list starting on page (v) shows the broad coverage of each example. In addition, there is a general index at the back of the book to assist in the location of specific points.

References to ITTOIA 2005 are to the Income Tax (Trading and Other Income) Act 2005.

The authors

John Clube, MA, CA, CTA, Director, John Clube & Co Ltd; Keith Gordon, MA (Oxon), ACA, CTA, Barrister; Peter Gravestock, FCA, CTA (Fellow), ATT, Past President of the Association of Taxation Technicians, tax lecturer and author, continuing the original work of Arnold Homer, FCA, CTA, TEP, and Rita Burrows, MBA, ACIS, CTA.

Companion publications

Tolley's Taxwise II 2006-07 (covering Inheritance Tax and Taxation of Trusts and Estates)

iv

Contents

PERSONAL TAX RATES

1. Income tax is chargeable on taxable income, ie that part of income which remains after all allowable deductions, including personal allowances, have been made. The rates of tax for 2005/06 and 2006/07 are:

	2005/06			2006/07		
	Rate	On	Tax on full band	Rate	On	Tax on full band
		£	£		£	£
Non-savings income:						
Starting rate	10%	2,090	209.00	10%	2,150	215.00
Basic rate	22%	30,310	6,668.20	22%	31,150	6,853.00
Basic rate limit		32,400	6,877.20		31,400	7,068.00
Higher rate on excess over basic rate limit	40%					

Savings income (taxed as top slice of income, with dividend income as highest part of slice) (rates for 2005/06 and 2006/07):

Non-dividend savings income	10% (starting rate) up to starting rate limit, 20% (lower rate) up to basic rate limit, 40% thereafter
Tax-credit inclusive dividends	10% (dividend ordinary rate) up to basic rate limit, 32½% (dividend upper rate) thereafter.

For 2006/07 Class 4 national insurance contributions for self-employed persons are payable at 8% of profits between £5,035 and £33,540 plus 1% on all profits above £33,540 (8% of profits between £4,895 and £32,760 for 2005/06 with 1% on all profits above £32,760). They are included in half-yearly payments on account and balancing payments under self-assessment. See page (ix) for other national insurance contribution rates.

2. Discretionary and accumulation and maintenance trusts are charged on non-dividend income at a single rate, called 'the rate applicable to trusts'. For 2005/06 and 2006/07 the rate is 40%. For 2006/07 a standard rate band of £1,000 (£500 for 2005/06) applies to the first slice of income chargeable at the rate applicable to trusts. Trustees of other trusts are liable at the basic rate of 22% on the trust non-savings income and at the lower rate of 20% on the non-dividend savings income.

The rate of tax for discretionary and accumulation and maintenance trusts on dividend income, called 'the dividend trust rate', is 32.5%, for 2005/06 and 2006/07. Trustees of other trusts pay tax on dividend income at 10%.

From 6 April 2004 trusts for vulnerable people can elect to be taxable as if the income of the trust were the income of the beneficiary.

3. Personal allowances for 2005/06 and 2006/07 are:

	2005/06 £	2006/07 £
Personal allowance:		
Under 65	4,895	5,035
65 to 74*	7,090	7,280
75 and over*	7,220	7,420
* Excess allowance over basic amount of	4,895	5,035
reduced by £1 for every £2 by which income exceeds	19,500	20,100
Age-related married couple's allowance (tax saving thereon 10%)†		
Elder born before 6 April 1935 and under 75**	5,905	6,065
Elder 75 or over**	5,975	6,135
**Excess allowance over basic amount of	2,280	2,350
reduced by £1 for every £2 by which income exceeds	19,500	20,100

† Reduced in tax year of marriage by 1/12th for each complete month (running from 6th day of one month to 5th day of next) in that year prior to the date of marriage

3. Personal allowances for 2005/06 and 2006/07 (continued)

	2005/06 £	2006/07 £
Blind person's relief (available to each blind person, whether single or married)	1,610	1,560

Life assurance relief as a deduction of 12½% from premiums payable where the life assurance contract was entered into before 14 March 1984.

Maximum allowable premiums either:

(a)   one-sixth of total income, or

(b)   £1,500

whichever is greater.

4. Tax credits for 2005/06 and 2006/07 are:

Credit element	Annual amount, 2005/06 £	2006/07 £
Family element of CTC	545	545
Baby element of CTC	545	545
Child element of CTC	1,690	1,765
Disability element of CTC[1]	2,285	2,350
Severe disability element of CTC[1]	920	945
Basic element of WTC	1,620	1,665
Couple's or lone parent element of WTC[2]	1,595	1,640
30 hour element of WTC	660	680
Disability element of WTC[4]	2,165	2,225
Severe disability element of WTC[4]	920	945
50-plus return to work element of WTC[2,3,4]	1,110	1,140
50-plus return to work element of WTC, 30 hour rate[3,4]	1,660	1,705
For both working credit and child tax credit		
– first income threshold	5,220	5,220
– first withdrawal rate	37%	37%
– second income threshold	50,000	50,000
– second withdrawal rate	1 in 15	1 in 15
– first threshold (those entitled to child tax credit only)	13,910	14,155
Childcare element		
Percentage of eligible costs	70%	80%
Maximum eligible costs (weekly)	£	£
– one child	175	175
– two or more children	300	300

1. The disability element of CTC is paid for each child for whom a Disability Living Allowance (DLA) is due or if the child is registered blind. If the higher care component of DLA is due then the severe disability element is paid.

2. The 16-29 hours 50-plus element is not payable in addition to the couple's element unless the claimant is responsible for a child or qualifies for the disability element of WTC.

3. The two 50-plus elements are mutually exclusive ie a claimant working 18 hours gets the £1,140; a claimant working 30 hours gets £1,705, both being paid in addition to the other elements.

4. If both claimants in a joint claim are disabled or entitled to the 50-plus element then the award will include two elements per couple.

TAXATION OF DIRECTORS AND OTHERS IN RESPECT OF CARS

INCOME TAX CAR BENEFITS CHARGES

Car benefits charge is based on CO_2 emissions and ranges from 15% to 35% of list price (for details see Example 11). The taxable benefit for cars registered after 31 December 1997 with no CO_2 emissions figures is 15%, 25% or 35% of list price depending on engine size (the 15% and 25% rates being increased by 3% for diesel cars). The taxable benefit for pre 1 January 1998 cars is 15%, 22% or 32% of list price depending on engine size. The taxable benefit for cars with no cylinder capacity is 35% of list price (32% for pre 1 January 1998 cars), except for electric cars, for which the charge is 9%. Special provisions apply to very low emission diesel cars and environmentally friendly cars, such as those running wholly or partly on road fuel gas.

The list price is restricted to a maximum of £80,000, and is reduced by up to £5,000 in respect of a capital contribution from the employee.

For cars 15 years old or more at end of tax year with a market value of £15,000 or more, market value (up to £80,000) is substituted for list price if higher.

The benefit is reduced proportionately if the car is not available for part of the year.

CAR FUEL BENEFIT SCALES

	2003/04 to 2006/07
	Petrol and Diesel
Cylinder capacity: 1,400 or less Over 1,400 up to 2,000 Over 2,000 Any car with no cylinder capacity:	£14,400 multiplied by the % figure used to calculate the car benefit

VAT ON FUEL FOR PRIVATE USE

From 1 May 2006 Quarterly returns	Petrol scale charge	VAT 7/47	Diesel scale charge	VAT 7/47
	£	£	£	£
1,400cc or less	273	40.66	260	38.72
Over 1,400cc up to 2,000cc	346	51.53	260	38.72
Over 2,000cc	508	25.66	331	49.30
Monthly returns	Petrol scale charge	VAT 7/47	Diesel scale charge	VAT 7/47
	£	£	£	£
1,400cc or less	91	13.55	86	12.81
Over 1,400cc up to 2,000cc	115	17.13	86	12.81
Over 2,000cc	169	25.17	110	16.38

From 1 May 2005 Quarterly returns	Petrol scale charge	VAT 7/47	Diesel scale charge	VAT 7/47
	£	£	£	£
1,400cc or less	246	36.64	236	36.15
Over 1,400cc up to 2,000cc	311	46.32	236	75.15
Over 2,000cc	457	68.06	331	44.65
Monthly returns	Petrol scale charge	VAT 7/47	Diesel scale charge	VAT 7/47
	£	£	£	£
1,400cc or less	82	12.21	78	11.62
Over 1,400cc up to 2,000cc	103	15.34	78	11.62
Over 2,000cc	152	22.64	110	16.38

TAX FREE REVENUE APPROVED MILEAGE RATES FOR BUSINESS USE OF OWN TRANSPORT FOR 2003/04 TO 2006/07

	First 10,000 business miles	Additional business miles
Cars and vans	40p	25p
Motor cycles	24p	24p
Bicycles	20p	20p
Passenger payments, car or van only, per passenger	5p	5p

NATIONAL INSURANCE CONTRIBUTIONS

National insurance contribution rates from 6 April 2006 are as follows:

Class 1 contributions

Lower earnings limit:	£84	a week	(previously £82)
Earnings threshold (employers and employees):	£97	a week	(previously £94)
Upper earnings limit (employees only):	£645	a week	(previously £630)

Employees

11% of weekly earnings between £97 and £645 (previously £94 and £630)

Reduced rate for married women and widows with valid certificate of election   4.85% on weekly earnings as above

For both categories of employees an additional 1% is chargeable for 2006/07 on the balance of earnings over £645 (£670 for 2005/06) per week.

Employers   12.8% on all earnings over £97 per week (previously 12.8% and £94)

Contracted out employees

Reduction in 'not contracted out' contributions, applicable to weekly earnings from £97 to £645:

	Salary related schemes	Money purchase schemes
Employees	1.6%*	1.6%*
Employers	3.5%*	1%*
	(unchanged)	(unchanged)

* Employees and employers also receive these rebates on earnings between £84 and £97 a week, on which they do not pay contributions. If an employee's rebate exceeds his contributions, the excess rebate goes to the employer.

Employers' Class 1A and Class 1B contributions   12.8%

Class 2 contributions

Self-employed flat rate	£2.10	a week	(previously £2.10)
Small earnings exception	£4,465	a year	(previously £4,345)

Class 3 contributions

Voluntary contributions	£7.55	a week	(previously £7.35)

Class 4 contributions

8% of profits between £5,035 and £33,540 (previously 8% on profits between £4,895 and £32,760)

and 1% of all profits above £33,540 (2005/06 £32,760).

CAPITAL GAINS TAX

Total net gains of individuals for 2006/07 not exceeding £8,800 (2005/06 £8,500) are exempt. The remaining gains are taxed as if they were the top slice of income at non-dividend savings income rates, ie at the starting rate of 10% up to the starting rate limit, the lower rate of 20% up to the basic rate limit and at 40% thereafter.

Personal representatives are entitled to the annual exemption, currently £8,800, for the year of death and the next two years. Gains not covered by the exemption are taxed at 40%.

Gains of trusts in which the settlor retains an interest are taxed as the settlor's gains. For other trusts, the trustees are entitled to an annual exemption of £4,400 (2005/06 £4,250), divided equally between trusts created by the same settlor, subject to a minimum exemption of £880 for each trust (2005/06 £850). Gains in excess of the exemption are charged at 40% for both discretionary trusts (including accumulation and maintenance trusts) and for other trusts.

CAPITAL GAINS TAX ACTUARIAL TABLE FOR LEASES (TCGA 1992 Sch 8)

Years	Percentage	Years	Percentage
50 (or more)	100.000	24	79.622
49	99.657	23	78.055
48	99.289	22	76.399
47	98.902	21	74.635
46	98.490	20	72.770
45	98.059	19	70.791
44	97.595	18	68.697
43	97.107	17	66.470
42	96.593	16	64.116
41	96.041	15	61.617
40	95.457	14	58.971
39	94.842	13	56.167
38	94.189	12	53.191
37	93.497	11	50.038
36	92.761	10	46.695
35	91.981	9	43.154
34	91.156	8	39.399
33	90.280	7	35.414
32	89.354	6	31.195
31	88.371	5	26.722
30	87.330	4	21.983
29	86.226	3	16.959
28	85.053	2	11.629
27	83.816	1	5.983
26	82.496	0	0
25	81.100		

If the duration of the lease is not an exact number of years, find the percentage for the number of whole years and add to it for each extra month one-twelfth of the difference between that percentage and the next higher percentage (counting an odd fourteen days or more as one month).

INDEXATION ALLOWANCE

Indexation allowance is based on the retail prices index, and is calculated to three decimal places (which means to one decimal place when expressed as a percentage), except for calculations in respect of the post 31 March 1982 holding of quoted securities, which are not rounded. After April 1998 indexation allowance is relevant only for companies, since it is available only to April 1998 for non-corporate taxpayers.

The retail prices index was re-based to 100 in January 1987. To avoid complications where two different bases are used, the examples in this book are based on the following table, in which the figures for months before January 1987 have been re-calculated to the new base. This does, however, give some differences from the precise figures because of rounding. The precise figures are published monthly by HMRC and in various other publications.

	1982	1983	1984	1985	1986	1987	1988	1989
January		82.61	86.84	91.2	96.25	100.0	103.3	111.0
February		82.97	87.2	91.94	96.6	100.4	103.7	111.8
March	79.44	83.12	87.48	92.8	96.73	100.6	104.1	112.3
April	81.04	84.28	88.64	94.78	97.67	101.8	105.8	114.3
May	81.62	84.64	88.97	95.21	97.85	101.9	106.2	115.0
June	81.85	84.84	89.2	95.41	97.79	101.9	106.6	115.4
July	81.88	85.3	89.1	95.23	97.52	101.8	106.7	115.5
August	81.9	85.68	89.94	95.49	97.82	102.1	107.9	115.8
September	81.85	86.06	90.11	95.44	98.3	102.4	108.4	116.6
October	82.26	86.36	90.67	95.59	98.45	102.9	109.5	117.5
November	82.66	86.67	90.95	95.92	99.29	103.4	110.0	118.5
December	82.51	86.89	90.87	96.05	99.62	103.3	110.3	118.8

	1990	1991	1992	1993	1994	1995	1996	1997
January	119.5	130.2	135.6	137.9	141.3	146.0	150.2	154.4
February	120.2	130.9	136.3	138.8	142.1	146.9	150.9	155.0
March	121.4	131.4	136.7	139.3	142.5	147.5	151.5	155.4
April	125.1	133.1	138.8	140.6	144.2	149.0	152.6	156.3
May	126.2	133.5	139.3	141.1	144.7	149.6	152.9	156.9
June	126.7	134.1	139.3	141.0	144.7	149.8	153.0	157.5
July	126.8	133.8	138.8	140.7	144.0	149.1	152.4	157.5
August	128.1	134.1	138.9	141.3	144.7	149.9	153.1	158.5
September	129.3	134.6	139.4	141.9	145.0	150.6	153.8	159.3
October	130.3	135.1	139.9	141.8	145.2	149.8	153.8	159.5
November	130.0	135.6	139.7	141.6	145.3	149.8	153.9	159.6
December	129.9	135.7	139.2	141.9	146.0	150.7	154.4	160.0

	1998	1999	2000	2001	2002	2003	2004	2005
January	159.5	163.4	166.6	171.1	173.3	178.4	183.1	188.9
February	160.3	163.7	167.5	172.0	173.8	179.3	183.8	188.9
March	160.8	164.1	168.4	172.2	174.5	179.9	184.8	190.5
April	162.6	165.2	170.1	173.1	175.7	181.2	185.7	191.6
May	163.5	165.6	170.7	174.2	176.2	181.5	186.5	192.0
June	163.4	165.6	171.1	174.4	176.2	181.3	186.8	192.0
July	163.0	165.1	170.5	173.3	175.9	181.3	186.8	192.2
August	163.7	165.5	170.5	174.0	176.4	181.6	187.4	192.6
September	164.4	166.2	171.7	174.6	177.6	182.5	188.1	193.1
October	164.5	166.5	171.6	174.3	177.9	182.6	188.6	193.3
November	164.4	166.7	172.1	173.6	178.2	182.7	189.0	193.6
December	164.4	167.3	172.2	173.4	178.5	183.5	189.9	194.1

	2006
January	193.4
February	194.2
March	195.0
April	196.5
May	197.7
June	198.5

CAPITAL GAINS TAX TAPER RELIEF FOR INDIVIDUALS, PERSONAL REPRESENTATIVES AND TRUSTEES

Gains on disposals of business assets on or after 6 April 2002*			Gains on disposals of non-business assets on or after 6 April 1998		
Whole yrs in qualifying period	% reduction available	% of gain chargeable	Whole yrs in qualifying period	% reduction available	% of gain chargeable
1	50	50	1	–	–
2 or more	75	25	2	–	–
			3	5	95
			4	10	90
			5	15	85
			6	20	80
			7	25	75
			8	30	70
			9	35	65
			10 or more	40	60

For non-business assets, an extra year is included in the qualifying period if the asset was owned before 17 March 1998 (except where anti-avoidance provisions apply).

* For business assets owned before 17 March 1998, the taper relief rates were 7.5% for disposals in 1998/99, 15% for disposals in 1999/2000, 25% for disposals in 2000/01 and 50% for disposals in 2001/02.

CORPORATION TAX RATES

Financial years

(ie beginning 1 April)	2000	2001	2002	2003	2004	2005	2006
Corporation tax full rate (%)	30	30	30	30	30	30	30
Small companies' rate (%)	20	20	19	19	19	19	19
Marginal relief limits (£000's)							
lower	300	300	300	300	300	300	300
higher	1,500	1,500	1,500	1,500	1,500	1,500	1,500
Marginal relief calculation (M – P) x I/P x fraction	1/40	1/40	11/400	11/400	11/400	11/400	11/40
Effective marginal rate	32.5%	32.5%	32.75%	32.75%	32.75%	32.75%	32.75%

Starting rate (%)	10	10	0	0	0	0	
Marginal relief limits (£000's)							
lower	10	10	10	10	10	10	
higher	50	50	50	50	50	50	
Marginal relief calculation (R2 – P) x I/P x fraction	1/40	1/40	19/400	19/400	19/400	19/400	
Non-Corporate Distribution Rate					19%	19%	
Effective marginal rate	22.5%	22.5%	23.75%	23.75%	23.75%	23.75%	

SUMMARY OF MAIN INCOME TAX, CORPORATION TAX, CAPITAL GAINS TAX AND STAMP DUTY PROVISIONS OF FINANCE ACT 2006

Finance Act 2006 reference		*Example*
s 23	*Income Tax – rates for 2006/07*	
	The starting, basic and higher rates for 2006/07 are unchanged at 10%, 22%, and 40% respectively. The rate bands have been increased by statutory indexation as shown on page (vii).	1
	Personal allowances	
	These were increased by the rate of inflation to the rates shown on page (vii).	2–4
	Rates of income tax and personal allowances for the over 65s for 2006/07 were set as shown on page (vii).	
s 24	*Corporation tax – rates for the financial year 2007*	
	The main rate of corporation tax for the financial year 2007 will remain at 30% as for financial year 2006.	48
s 25	*Small companies rate and fraction for the financial year 2006*	
	The small companies rate for the financial year 2006 remains at 19%, with a marginal relief and fraction of 11/400, but see s 26 below for the abolition of the starting rate and the non-corporate distribution rate.	49
s 26	*Abolition of starting rate and non-corporate distribution rate*	
	The starting rate of 0% on the first £10,000 of profit, and the non-corporate distribution rate, are abolished with effect from 1 April 2006. Profits for periods straddling 1 April 2006 are to be apportioned. The effect is that, from 1 April 2006, the minimum rate of corporation tax is 19%.	49
s 27 and Sch 1	*Group relief extension to EEA subsidiaries*	
	Following the European Court of Justice decision in the M&S case, group relief is extended to losses of 75% subsidiaries of UK companies established in EEA countries, subject to conditions. The loss must first be utilised against any other foreign profits and must be of a nature that would qualify for UK group relief. Relief is restricted to the lesser of the loss calculated according to UK tax laws and foreign tax laws. The effective date is 1 April 2006.	63
ss 28 and 29	*Research and development*	
	Payments made to volunteers in clinical trials will qualify for R&D reliefs from a date to be approved by the European Commission. Claims for enhanced deductions must be made on the company's tax return for periods ending on or after 31 March 2006, with transitional rules requiring claims by 31 March 2008 for prior periods.	51
s 30	*FYA increase for small enterprises*	
	For small enterprises only, FYA is increased from 40% to 50% for one year. This is effective from 6 April 2006 for unincorporated businesses, and from 1 April 2006 for companies.	18

ss 69 to 72   *Capital losses anti-avoidance*

From 5 December 2005, where there has been a change of ownership of a company whose main purpose was to obtain a tax advantage, capital losses will not be allowable. Schemes to convert to capital to use capital losses are also blocked.

These measures are not intended to catch genuine commercial transactions.

s 73   *Capital redemption policies anti-avoidance*

From 5 December, relief for losses generated by certain types of insurance policies are blocked.

s 74   *CGT 'Bed and Breakfasting' anti-avoidance*

The 30-day asset matching rules will not apply in the case of non-residence from 22 March 2006, to counter schemes of avoidance.

s 75 and Sch 5   *Film partnership interest*

From 10 March relief is restricted to 40% of the eligible interest, to counter schemes of avoidance.

s 76 and Sch 6   *Avoidance involving financial arrangements*

A number of measures block notified tax-avoidance schemes, or clarify legislation on profit measurement issues, to ensure that interest or interest-like income is taxed. It specifies that certain instances of the phrase 'fairly represents . . . all profits . . .' in the Taxes Acts overrule accounting treatment.

s 77   *Intangible fixed assets*

Certain avoidance schemes intended to take advantage of provisions of the intangibles regime are blocked.

s 78   *Controlled foreign companies*

Companies not within the CFC legislation by reason of migration before 1 April 2002 are brought within the rules in respect of UK subsidiaries acquired from 22 April 2006.

s 79 and Sch 7   *Transfer of assets abroad*

The anti-avoidance rules on transfer of assets abroad are refined, clarifying the circumstances of exemption and apportionment.

s 80   *Pre-owned assets*

Avoidance of the pre-owned assets charge is blocked in respect of interest in possession trusts. An election may be made for IHT treatment of the assets, in place of the pre-owned asset charge.

s 81 and Schs 8 to 9   *Long funding leases of plant and machinery*

For funding leases finalised from 1 April 2006 capital allowances will be given to the lessee, not the lessor. A funding lease is a finance lease exceeding five years in length. The lessee may claim capital allowances under this regime, or continue to deduct lease costs as at present. There are transitional provisions, and certain exclusions, such as plant supplied with land.

ss 82 to 85   *Sale of lessors*

These provisions curb the use of lessor companies for exploiting capital allowances, and sheltering profits.

Companies must be UK resident quoted companies, and the ring-fenced rental trade must comprise at least 75% of total activity. There is a charge of 2% on the market value of assets entering the new rental business, which must rent out at least three properties, none comprising more than 40% of rental income. Borrowing costs may not exceed 80% of rental income.

The profits of the rental trade, and gains on rental properties, are exempt from corporation tax provided that 90% of profits are distributed to shareholders as income subject to withholding of income tax. This income is treated as rental income in the hands of the recipient.

s 169   *Company reorganisations – SDLT*

SDLT will not be chargeable in reorganisations not involving change of ownership.

ss 173 to 176   *International tax enforcement*

These measures allow for sharing of tax information with other territories, and cover indirect taxes in addition to direct taxes that were previously covered. They also allow for the recovery of certain foreign tax debts in UK, under the terms of reciprocal agreements to be made with other territories.

50

PROVISIONS NOT COVERED IN THE SUMMARY

ss 1 to 22	Excise duties and VAT
ss 99 to 100	Nuclear decommissioning
ss 147 to 155	Oil taxation
ss 156 to 158	Inheritance tax
s 171	Landfill tax
ss 172 to 173	Climate Change Levy
s 177	Disclosure of information

Christopher Thackery, aged 50, is married to Helen, aged 39, and they have a son, Mark, aged 14. Their respective incomes are as follows:

Christopher Thackery:	£
(i) Salary as a sales representative for year ending 5.4.2007 (tax deducted under PAYE £6,244)	29,665
(ii) Bonus based on the company profits for the accounting year to:	
31 March 2006 (paid 1 June 2006)	4,600
31 March 2007 (paid 1 June 2007)	4,750

(iii) Investment income	*Year ended 5 April 2007* £
Dividends received from UK companies (exclusive of dividend tax credits)	1,701
Net interest received from Midwest Bank	976
National Savings Bank interest (Easy Access Savings)	1,600
Interest on National Savings Certificates	815
Interest arising on overseas bank accounts	180
Rental income	4,930

Helen Thackery:	£
(i) Profits from hairdressing business operated since 1993	
Year to 31.7.2006	5,640
Year to 31.7.2007	7,500
(ii) Building society interest – net amount received in year ended 5.4.2007	732

Mark Thackery:

Mark has a building society account, the source of capital being gifts from his father. The interest for the year ended 5.4.2007 was £24. The account has been registered for interest to be paid gross. He also has dividends of £360 on shares given to him by his grandfather.

Outgoings year ended 5 April 2007

Christopher paid mortgage interest of £4,320 on a home loan of £84,000. He also paid £3,000 interest on a loan to buy the rented property, which had been let throughout the year at a full rent. The couple do not incur any childcare costs and Helen is nominated as the main carer of Mark.

(i)   Compute the income tax due (or repayable) for each family member for the year 2006/07 and show what tax credits are due, based on Helen and Christopher's 2006/07 income.

(ii) State the tax treatment and reduction in liability arising if Christopher Thackery paid £780 net in 2006/07 into a personal pension plan, and compare that treatment with a similar contribution by Helen Thackery.

Ignore foreign taxation.

(i)   **Income Tax Computations 2006/07**

	£	£
Christopher Thackery		
Non-savings income:		
Salary	29,665	
Bonus (paid 1 June 2006)	4,600	34,265
Rental income (4,930 less interest paid 3,000)		1,930
		36,195
Non-dividend savings income		
National Savings Bank	1,600	
Midwest Bank interest (976 + tax deducted 244)	1,220	
Foreign bank interest	180	3,000
Dividend income		
UK dividends received (1,701 + dividend tax credit 189)		1,890
		41,085
Personal allowance		5,035
Taxable income		36,050

Tax thereon: On non-savings income			
Starting rate	2,150 @ 10%	215	
Basic rate	29,010 @ 22%	6,382	
	31,160		
On savings income other than dividends			
Lower rate	2,140 @ 20%	428	
	33,300		
Higher rate	860 @ 40%	344	
	34,160		
On dividend income			
Upper rate	1,890 @ 32½%	614	
	36,050		
Tax liability			7,983
Less: Tax deducted – under PAYE		6,244	
– by Midwest Bank		244	
Tax credits on UK dividends		189	6,677
Tax due			1,306

	£	£
Helen Thackery		
Business profits (yr ended 31 July 2006)		5,640
Building society interest (732 + tax deducted 183)		915
		6,555
Personal allowance		5,035
Taxable income		1,520
Tax thereon @ 10%		152
Less: Tax deducted		183
Tax repayable		31

Tax Credits

Helen, as carer, will receive child tax credit in respect of Mark. The relevant income for tax credits being:

	£
Christopher (as above)	41,085
Helen (as above)	6,555
	47,640
Less: Investment income disregard	300
	47,340

As this is less than £50,000 the amount due is £545, the family element only. This is paid four weekly to Helen (with Child Benefit) during the year, assuming Helen and Christopher made a joint claim by 31 August 2006 and their income for 2005/06 was at a similar level. For more detail on tax credits see Example 5.

Mark Thackery

Mark's building society interest of £24 is covered by his personal allowance, so he has no income tax liability, hence his entitlement to receive gross interest. His dividend income is similarly covered by his personal allowance. Tax credits on dividends are not, however, repayable, so he will effectively suffer the notional tax credit of $(1/9 \times 360 =)$ £40 shown on the dividend voucher.

(ii) **Payment of a personal pension premium**

Christopher Thackery's personal pension premium of £780 is net of basic rate tax. The gross premium is therefore £1,000. Providing the payment is within the limits allowed, no tax relief is withdrawn from such a payment even if the payer has no tax liability. Since 6 April 2006, the amount of relievable contribution has not been dependent on the contributor's age. Relief is available on the amount up to the individual's earnings for the year (subject to an over all minimum of £215,000 for 2006/07). For someone like Christopher who is liable to higher rate tax, the extra relief over and above the basic rate tax retained at source is given by extending the basic rate limit by the amount of the premium, so that in Christopher's case the revised limit is £34,300. The position would therefore be as follows:

	£	£
Taxable income as in (i)		36,050

			£	£
Tax thereon:	On non-savings income			
	Starting rate		2,150 @ 10%	215
	Basic rate		29,010 @ 22%	6,382
			31,160	
	On non-dividend savings income			
	Lower rate		3,000 @ 20%	600
	On dividend income			
	Ordinary rate		140 @ 10%	14
			34,300	
	Upper rate		1,750 @ 32½%	569
			36,050	7,780
Less: Tax deducted and dividend tax credits as before				6,677
Tax due				1,103

Thus the effect of paying a pension premium of £1,000 gross, £780 net, is to give relief of:

Reduction of tax due (1,306 – 1,103)	203
Tax relief given by deduction from premium	220
	£ 423

The relief is more than 40% because the effect of increasing the basic rate band by £1,000 in this case is to move £172 of non-dividend savings income out of the higher rate band into the lower rate band, saving 20% = £31, plus £860 of dividend income into the ordinary rate band, saving 22½% = £140 giving a total reduction of tax of (172 + 31 =) £203, plus the tax of £220 deducted from the payment. The effective rate of tax saving on the premium is 42.3%.

Helen Thackery would also pay the premium of £1,000 net of basic rate tax. Since she is not a higher rate taxpayer the premium would not affect her tax liability and she would retain the £220 deducted at source, even though only £152 tax was charged on her income. If the premium had instead been paid gross rather than net her position would have been:

	£	£
Business profits	5,640	
Less: Retirement annuity premium	1,000	4,640
Non-dividend savings income		915
		5,555
Personal allowance		5,035
Taxable income		520
Tax thereon @ 10%		52
Tax deducted from savings income		183
Tax repayable		131

Thus the tax saving from paying a retirement annuity premium of £1,000 would be (£31 previously repayable compared with £131 now repayable =) £100, ie only 10% since that is the rate of tax payable on the top £1,000 of her income.

The payment of £1,000 (gross) to a pension plan by either Helen or Christopher would make no difference to their tax credits entitlement. Even with the pension deduction their income is too high to receive anything but the family element.

Explanatory Notes

Scope of income tax charge

1.   Income tax is charged broadly on the world income of UK residents, subject to certain deductions for earnings abroad and for individuals who are not ordinarily resident or not domiciled in the UK (see Examples 6 and 8). Non-residents are liable to income tax only on income that arises in the UK. The UK excludes the Channel Islands and the Isle of Man. The introduction of a Scottish Parliament has brought with it the right for that Parliament to increase or decrease the basic rate of income tax by up to 3%. It is intended that any Scottish variable rate would apply only in place of the *basic* rate of tax and would not affect the starting, lower, higher or dividend rates of tax for income tax purposes. There would also be some circumstances where income would be charged at the normal basic rate instead of the Scottish rate. As capital gains are charged at starting, lower or higher rates the Scottish rate would not affect the tax liability on such gains.

Certain aspects of UK tax are affected by the provisions of the European Union, EU law taking precedence over UK law. The EU treaty limits the right of member states to impose taxes, and requires that the laws of member states do not discriminate against members of other states. Furthermore the UK tax legislation must be compatible with the European Convention on Human Rights and, from October 2000, the Human Rights Act 1998.

From 1 January 1999 businesses may pay their taxes in euros, although liabilities will still be calculated in sterling and under- or overpayments may arise because of exchange rate fluctuations before payments are actually credited by the tax authorities. SI 1998/3177 prevents unintended tax consequences arising in the UK as a result of the adoption of the euro by other EU states.

Taxable income

2.   An individual's income for tax purposes is called his total income. (Income and Corporation Taxes Act 1988 (TA 1988) s 835). It is the sum of all income of that person computed in accordance with the provisions of the Income Tax Acts. In addition to provisions within the Taxes Act 1988 trading and other income (eg property) is computed under the Income Tax (Trading and Other Income) Act 2005 (ITTOIA 2005). Under the legislation expenses can often be deducted from income in arriving at the taxable amount. In the case of dividends the taxable amount is the amount received plus the related tax credit (equal to 1/9 of the dividend received). Earnings and pensions are taxed in accordance with the Income Tax (Earnings and Pensions) Act 2003 (ITEPA 2003).

After totalling all chargeable income, certain payments are deducted to arrive at total income, namely patent royalties and allowable interest (see note 5). Where relevant, trading losses are also deducted. Part (ii) of the example illustrates that retirement annuity premiums reduce earnings, and thus total income, whereas personal pension contributions do not. Gift aid donations to charity or to registered community amateur sports clubs do not reduce total income, relief being given in the same way as for personal pension contributions, but see Example 3 explanatory note 1 for the special personal pension contributions and gift aid rules in relation to age allowance and Example 95 part (c) for the different treatment of personal pension contributions and gift aid donations for top slicing relief on life insurance policies. See also Example 2.

Income exempt from tax

3.   Certain income is exempt from tax, the principal items being as follows:

Interest and bonuses on National Savings Certificates.

Income from TESSA Only Special Savings Accounts (TOSSAs), Personal Equity Plans (PEPs) and Individual Savings Accounts (ISAs).

Terminal bonuses on Save As You Earn (SAYE) contracts.

Prizes (including Premium Bond prizes) and bettings winnings.

The stipulated capital element of a purchased life annuity.

Statutory redundancy payments (and certain other payments on termination of employment).

Educational grants and scholarships.

Maintenance payments.

Qualifying sickness and unemployment insurance payments (such as benefits paid from permanent health insurance policies, income protection insurance, mortgage payment protection insurance, and insurance to meet loan repayments or domestic bills).

Damages and compensation for personal injury (whether received as a lump sum or by periodic payments).

Some state benefits, including wounds and disability pensions, war widows' pensions, disability living allowance, child benefit, attendance allowance, severe disablement allowance, income support (except to the unemployed and to strikers), jobfinder's grant, payments and training vouchers under the Jobmatch programme, tax credits, housing benefit, pensioners' Christmas bonus, pensioners' winter allowance and pension credits (see Example 10 for details of taxable state benefits).

Tax is not normally payable on cashbacks and rebated commissions received by someone as an ordinary retail customer (see Revenue Statement of Practice 4/97).

Charging income to tax

4.   The tax year runs from 6 April to 5 April. Income is taxed on a 'current year basis', which means that the taxable income is always that of the tax year (except for business income, for which the taxable income is normally the profits of the accounting year ending in the tax year).

Employment earnings are charged to tax when they are received, regardless of the year in which they were earned. Christopher's bonus received in June 2006 is thus charged in 2006/07, even though it was earned in the previous tax year.

5.   In working out how much tax is payable, certain payments, eg patent royalty payments, pension premiums (see explanatory note 11), donations to charity (see explanatory note 12), and allowable interest payments under headings (i) to (vi) in explanatory note 13, qualify for tax relief at the taxpayer's highest tax rate, although in the case of personal pension premiums the minimum tax saving is the tax of 22% deducted from the premium, as illustrated in part (ii) of the example in relation to Helen Thackery. Patent royalties are also paid net of basic rate tax (except where paid by one company to another – see Example 6 part (a)), but in this case the relief may not be retained by a non-taxpayer (see explanatory note 12). Certain qualifying investments, such as under the Enterprise Investment Scheme or Venture Capital Trust Scheme (see Example 94), give relief at 20% and 30% respectively of the investment. Qualifying investments in Community Development Finance Institutions give relief at 5% of the investment for up to five years (see Example 94).

6.   As well as being able to save tax on certain payments, taxpayers may claim various tax allowances (see pages (vii) and (viii)). From 6 April 2000, married couple's allowance is available only to a couple one of whom was born before 6 April 1935.

The age-related personal allowance and the increased married couple's allowance for the over 75s first apply in the tax year in which the taxpayer (or for married couple's allowance, the elder of the two) reaches the relevant age (or would have reached that age if he/she had not died earlier in the tax year). For detailed notes see Example 3. The personal allowance and blind person's relief, where relevant, reduce statutory income and save tax at the payer's highest tax rate. Married couple's allowance and maintenance relief for the over 65s save tax at 10% for 2005/06. The tax saving is given by reducing the tax payable by the appropriate amount. See Example 9 for the way this is done through the PAYE system. Although still called the married couple's allowance, the allowance is also available to members of a registered civil partnership provided that at least one of the partners was born before 6 April 1935.

In addition, a family unit or a single person may be able to claim tax credits. These are payable if the claimant(s) have low income or a child. For details see Example 5.

7.   Life assurance relief is given at 12½% of premiums on qualifying policies taken out up to 13 March 1984. It is not given on policies taken out after that date. The relief is obtained by paying the premium net. The maximum amount of premiums qualifying for relief on pre 13 March 1984 policies is £1,500 or one sixth of total income whichever is the *greater*. It is therefore possible for a non-taxpayer to obtain relief on premiums up to £1,500. For detailed notes on life assurance see Example 95.

Rates of tax

8.   On income other than savings income, tax is payable for the tax year 2006/07 at the starting rate of 10% on the first £2,150, then the basic rate of 22% on the next £31,150, and the higher rate of 40% on income above £33,300 (the basic rate limit). (Tax rates are shown on page (vii).)

Different rates apply to savings income, the main items of which are dividend income, interest from banks and building societies, interest on company debentures and government stocks, the income element of a purchased life annuity (see Example 4 explanatory note 3) and accrued income charges on the sale/purchase of interest-bearing securities (see Example 7) (TA 1988 ss 1A, 1B). Savings income is taxed as the top slice of income (except for termination payments – see Example 12 explanatory note 9, and life policy gains – see Example 95 explanatory note 6). Savings income is subdivided into dividends and other savings income, with dividends being treated as the top slice of the savings income. Tax is payable on savings income other than dividends at the starting rate of 10% until the £2,150 limit is used then at the lower rate of 20% on income up to the basic rate limit of £33,300 and at 40% thereafter. Dividend income is taxed at the dividend ordinary rate of 10% on income up to the basic rate limit and the dividend upper rate of 32½% thereafter. The rates on dividends and other savings income apply not only to UK income but also to foreign savings income (except for income charged to tax on a remittances basis, to which the normal non-savings income rates apply – see Example 6). Relief is available for foreign tax deducted. The savings income rates do not apply to other investment income, such as rents or to annuities (other than purchased life annuities), or to other taxable income even if the underlying source is savings income (see Example 2 part (b)).

Tax at the 20% rate is deducted from UK building society and bank interest received (except National Savings Bank interest) unless a non-taxpayer (or in this example, his parent on his behalf) has registered to receive interest in full. For details see Example 6.

Shareholders receive a tax credit of 1/9th on UK dividends (representing 10% of the tax credit inclusive amount). The maximum credit that can be set against the tax payable is, however, restricted to 10% of taxable income (ITTOIA 2005 s 397). See Example 4 explanatory note 9 for the effect of this restriction on a higher rate taxpayer whose income consists wholly of dividends. Non-taxpayers cannot recover the tax credits on dividends, although credits could be claimed up to 5 April 2004 by managers of Individual Savings Accounts and Personal Equity Plans (see Example 93) and by friendly societies (see Example 2 part (b)(ii)). Tax deducted from other savings income is repayable.

The self-employed pay Class 4 national insurance contributions based on their profits, Class 4 contributions being collected along with income tax (see page (xi)).

Taxation of the family

9.   Income and capital gains of a married couple are taxed on each of them separately. Each is entitled to a personal allowance and annual exemption. The age-related married couple's allowance goes to the husband, unless an election is made to transfer all or half of it to the wife. In any event, any unused tax saving may be transferred to the other spouse if income is too low to use it. For the detailed provisions see Example 3.

Although still called the married couple's allowance, the allowance is also available to members of a registered civil partnership provided that at least one of the partners was born before 6 April 1935. For claims for married couples age allowance after that date, the income of the higher earner will be used (as opposed to that of the husband for couples married before that time).

By contrast entitlement to tax credits is dependent upon the total income of the couple computed in accordance with the rules for tax credits. For the detailed provisions see Example 5.

10.   The income of unmarried children under 18 is treated as the parent's, if it derives from funds transferred to the child or settled on the child by the parent. There are certain exceptions, including income of up to £100 a year, which covers Mark's building society interest in this example. For further details see Example 2.

Personal pension premiums and retirement annuity premiums

11.   UK residents under 75 may pay contributions to buy themselves a pension. The detailed provisions are in Examples 37 and 38. Generally, people paying under pre 1 July 1988 contracts (retirement annuity contracts) may pay the premiums gross and obtain tax relief at their marginal rate by deducting the premiums from their taxable earnings. However, they may now be paid net of basic rate tax like other pension premiums, including stakeholder pension premiums, and higher rate relief where relevant is given in the payer's self-assessment or coding notice. The extra higher rate relief is given by extending the basic rate band by the amount of the payment, as shown in part (ii) of the example for Christopher Thackery.

(For further details, see Example 37).

National insurance contributions are not deducted in calculating earnings for pension contribution purposes (FA 2004 s 182(2)), and pension scheme payments (either under personal, stakeholder, retirement annuity or occupational schemes) are not deducted in calculating earnings or profits on which national insurance contributions are calculated (SSCBA 1992 Sch 2.3).

Position of non-taxpayers in relation to tax relief deducted from payments

12.   The tax deducted from personal pension premiums may be retained by both taxpayers and non-taxpayers.

Where tax has been deducted at source from patent royalties and other annual payments, then in order to retain the tax deducted, the payer must pay tax at 22% (or more) on an equivalent gross amount, even if the income would otherwise be within the starting or lower rate band (TA 1988 ss 3 and 348). If the payer pays insufficient tax to cover the tax deducted, the shortfall should be paid over to HMRC, who should issue an assessment for the amount due (TA 1988 s 350). The strict rules for payment of the shortfall may not be enforced, but HMRC will take the tax due into account if the payer is claiming a tax refund.

Where tax has been deducted at source from gift aid donations to charity then the taxpayer needs to have paid sufficient tax to cover the amount deducted. The tax paid for this purpose includes income tax, non-repayable tax credits on dividends and capital gains tax (see Example 91).

Allowable interest

13.   Before 6 April 2000 relief was available to someone aged 65 or over who had taken out a loan to buy a life annuity, the loan being secured on the only or main residence of the borrower/annuitant. The relief was at the then basic rate of 23% on the first £30,000 of a qualifying loan. Relief for such loans remains available (under the Mortgage Interest Relief At Source (MIRAS) scheme where appropriate) for loans taken out before 9 March 1999 (or for which a written offer had been made before that date), providing the property was the borrower's main residence immediately before that date. Despite the reduction in the basic rate to 22%, relief for home annuity loans continues at 23% (TA 1988 ss 353(1G), 369(1A)). If the taxpayer leaves the property, eg to move into a nursing home, or remortgages the property, or moves to a different property, the relief will continue so long as the loan or replacement is still outstanding (TA 1988 s 365). Relief is no longer available from 6 April 2000 on any other home loans.

Relief at the payer's marginal rate is available for interest on loans under the following headings.

(i)   Loans to buy plant or machinery, for example an office machine, for use in a partnership or in one's employment (s 359). Relief in this case is restricted to interest payable not later than three years after the end of the tax year in which the loan was made. Where there is part private use, relief is restricted to the business proportion of the interest. Employees cannot claim relief for plant and machinery unless it is *necessarily* provided for use in their employment (TA 1988 s 359 & CAA 2001 s 36).

(ii) Loans to buy shares in or lend money to a close company that is a trading or property investment company, providing the borrower either owns more than 5% of the ordinary share capital, or owns some share capital and has worked for the greater part of his time in the management or conduct of the company in the period since obtaining the loan to the time the interest is paid (ss 360, 360A). The loan interest does not qualify for relief if either income tax relief or capital gains deferral relief has been given in respect of the shares under the enterprise investment scheme (see Example 94).

(iii) Loans to a partner to buy an interest in a partnership or to lend money to it, providing the borrower is still a partner when the interest is paid and providing he is not a limited partner or a partner in an investment limited liability partnership (see Example 27) (s 362).

(iv) Loans to personal representatives to pay inheritance tax on a deceased person's personal property (ie property other than freehold land and buildings), in respect of interest paid within one year from the making of the loan (s 364).

(v) Loans for the purchase of shares in unquoted employee-controlled trading companies by their full-time employees or spouses (s 361).

(vi) Loans to acquire a share or shares in a co-operative (s 361).

In no circumstances can bank overdraft interest be deducted from *total* income, no matter for what purpose the overdraft is used. Relief is only available for bank overdraft interest where it is paid in connection with a business and is thus deductible as a business expense under the trading rules where it relates to let property (see Example 98).

Where the claim for allowable interest relates to trading purposes then if the interest cannot be offset within the tax year it may be added to trading losses carried forward (see Example 29) or included in a terminal loss claim (see Example 32) (TA 1988 s 390).

Self-assessment

14. Around one third of taxpayers are technically required to 'self-assess' the amount of income tax and capital gains tax payable, although HMRC will still work out the tax if the taxpayer wants them to, providing returns are sent in early enough or filed via the internet. Most taxpayers, however, account for their tax under PAYE and by deduction at source. HMRC issue assessments themselves in some circumstances, in particular where they discover that tax has been underpaid because the taxpayer has failed to disclose relevant information.

If Christopher Thackery receives a self-assessment tax return, then he is required to compute his 'tax due for 2006/07 before payments on account'. This will be the tax liability less tax deducted at source (ie PAYE tax, tax deducted by banks and building societies etc and dividend tax credits).

Note that the reduction of the tax liability in respect of dividend tax credits is restricted to 10% of the income actually charged to tax (see Example 4 explanatory note 9).

In Christopher Thackery's case, the tax due arises because National Savings Bank Easy Access Savings Account interest, rental income and foreign bank interest have been received without deduction of tax, and higher rate tax is due on £2,750 of investment income. The actual liability will always be slightly different from the exact figure because of the rounding of allowances and rates under the PAYE system, and the possible offset of untaxed interest against allowances under PAYE (see Example 9 explanatory note 1).

Because of the nature of Christopher's income no payments on account will have been made. Provided Christopher files his tax return by 30 September 2007, or electronically by 30 December 2007 (Internet), HMRC will collect the amount due by way of an adjustment to his PAYE code number in 2008/09 (see Example 9 explanatory note 13). If the return is filed too late for a coding adjustment, the tax due must be paid by 31 January 2008. For detailed notes on self-assessment see Example 40.

(a)   Mr Victor, a married man aged 55, has the following income for 2006/07:

	£
Non-savings income (gross)	25,910
Savings income (dividends of £10,800 + dividend tax credits £1,200)	12,000

His two children, Arthur aged 23 and Brian aged 15, are beneficiaries under an accumulation and maintenance trust set up by Mr Victor in 1992, under which the children are entitled to the income at age 18. The trust's investments comprise interest-bearing securities. In 2006/07 the income of the trust was £4,000, the trustees paying £2,000 gross in respect of each of the children and deducting tax therefrom at the appropriate rate. Brian has no other income. Arthur is a post graduate student at university and in addition to the trust income he has vacation earnings of £800 (from which no tax has been deducted) and a research grant.

Mrs Victor does not work, her only income being savings income of £14,850 (gross).

Show the tax position of Mr Victor and his children for 2006/07, assuming that the family income for tax credits for 2005/06 amounted to £60,000, and a claim for tax credits was made in 2005/06, showing Mrs Victor as the main carer of Brian.

(b)   Outline:

    (i)   the broad principles of the income tax treatment of trusts;

    (ii)   tax-effective transfers by parents to their infant children;

    (iii)   tax planning possibilities for husband and wife.

(c)   Set out the tax treatment relating to:

    (i)   financial support to adopters;

    (ii)   receipts from foster care.

(a)   **Mr Victor and his children – Income tax computations 2006/07**

Arthur's income from the trust is his in his own right and tax will have been deducted by the trustees at the savings income rate of 20%. Brian's income will be treated as his father's income, taxable not as savings income but as miscellaneous income (ITTOIA s 629). The trustees will have deducted tax at 40% (see part (b)(i) note 4 of the example). The tax position is therefore as follows:

Mr Victor

		£
Non-savings income, including Brian's income from the trust		27,910
Savings income (dividends)		12,000
		39,910
Personal allowance		5,035
Taxable income		34,875
Tax thereon:		
On non-savings income	2,150 @ 10%	215
	20,725 @ 22%	4,560
	22,875	4,775
On dividend income (part)	10,425 @ 10%	1,042
	33,300	
On dividend income (balance)	1,575 @ 32½%	512
	34,875	
Tax liability		6,329
Less: Tax deducted – by trustees	800	
Tax credits on dividends	1,200	2,000
Tax payable		4,329

Brian

Brian has no taxable income, his only income being treated as his father's under the parental settlement rules, since he is under 18 and unmarried.

Arthur

Arthur's trust income is not treated as his father's because he is over 18.

His research grant is exempt from tax. His trust income of £2,000 plus his vacation earnings of £800 are below his personal allowance of £5,035, so he can recover from HMRC the tax of £400 deducted from the trust income.

Tax Credits

Mrs Victor, as carer, will be entitled to tax credits for the couple, the amount being computed on their joint income for 2005/06 adjusted to actual for 2006/07 provided a claim had been made by 31 August 2006. In this case a claim was made and the initial award notice would show nil.

When final details of income were filed that claim would be amended to:

	£
Income	
Mr Victor (as above)	39,910
Mrs Victor	14,850
	54,760
Less: Disregard	300
	54,400
Family element award	545
Less: Excess income (54,400 – 50,000 =) 4,400 × 6.67%	293
Tax credits payable	252

(b)   (i)   **Tax treatment of trusts**

The tax treatment of trusts is dealt with in detail in the companion to this book, Tolley's Taxwise II 2006/07. The broad principles are as follows:

1. The settlor remains liable for income tax on the trust income if he or his spouse/civil partner has retained an interest in the settlement or where the settlement transfers income but not capital. Spouse/civil partner does not include a future, former or separated spouse/civil partner or the settlor's widow(er) or surviving civil partner (ITTOIA 2005 s 624).

   These provisions do not apply to annual payments made for commercial reasons in connection with an individual's business. There are also exceptions for outright gifts between spouses/civil partners, and for various arrangements made on separation or divorce. For trust income arising on or after 6 April 2000, there is no charge on the settlor to the extent that the trust income is given to charity (see Example 91 explanatory note 5).

   All income treated as the settlor's income under ITTOIA 2005 s 624 other than dividend income is taxed as non-savings income. Dividend income is charged at 10% or 32½% of the tax credit inclusive amount as the case may be.

2. Even if a settlement is of capital in which the settlor does not retain an interest, if income of the settlement is paid to or for the benefit of an unmarried child of the settlor who is under 18, it is treated as the settlor's income, subject to the exceptions in part (b)(ii) of the example (ITTOIA 2005 ss 626–627). The tax deducted by the trustees from the payment counts as tax paid by the settlor (s 687(2)(a)). If the settlor has to pay any further tax he is entitled to recover it from the trustees, or from the person who received the income (ITTOIA 2005 s 646), (but see part (b)(ii) of the example). The income charged as the settlor's income under s 660B is treated as miscellaneous income and it does not count as savings income. This applies even if the income is derived from dividends, because such income comes from the general pool of income in the trust.

3. Where someone has an interest in possession in a trust, ie the right to income (usually a life interest), the trustees are liable to tax at the dividend ordinary rate of 10% on tax credit inclusive dividend income, the lower rate of 20% on other savings income and at the basic rate on other trust income (without any deduction for their expenses) and they deduct tax at the appropriate rate from income payments to the life tenant. Non-taxpaying beneficiaries can claim repayment of the tax deducted, except that the tax credits on dividend income are not repayable. Arthur in part (a) of the example would not therefore have been able to reclaim tax if the trust's income had been dividend income.

4. Where the trust is a discretionary trust (including accumulation and maintenance trusts), the trustees are liable to tax at the trust dividend rate of 32½% on tax credit

inclusive dividend income (of which the tax credit covers 10%) and at 40% on other income, after deducting trust expenses (ITTOIA 2005 s 568). With effect from 6 April 2005 the first £500 of discretionary trust income is instead liable at the rates set out at 3 above, that is dividends 10%, other savings income 20%, non-savings income 22% (FA 2005 s 14). Even though tax on dividends is paid at only 32½%, the trustees deduct tax at 40% on payments to beneficiaries (and non-taxpaying beneficiaries may claim repayment of the tax deducted), but the trustees cannot treat the tax credits on the trust's dividend income as covering part of the tax at 40% to be accounted for by them on the payments to the beneficiaries (s 687).

5.   Special rules apply from 2004/05, by election, where it is a trust with a vulnerable beneficiary. In order to qualify the beneficiary must be entitled to all of the income and the property must be held for the vulnerable beneficiary absolutely. If the beneficiary qualifies as a minor he/she must be absolutely entitled to the property at 18. A vulnerable person is either a disabled person who is incapable of administering their affairs by reason of a mental disorder, or a person in receipt of attendance allowance, or disability living allowance (higher or middle rate), or a minor (under 18) where one or both parents have died. The election enables the tax liability of the trust to be computed using the tax rates and allowances applicable to the vulnerable beneficiary. The treatment extends to capital gains tax. For full details see Tolleys Taxwise II 2006/07.

(ii)   **Tax-effective transfers by parents to infant children**

Children are taxpayers in their own right, no matter how young they are, and they are entitled to the personal allowance against their income. This does not apply to certain income from their parents, as indicated in (i) above. The following items are not caught by the parental settlement rules:

1.   Income deriving from funds provided by the parent if it is less than £100 a year. The £100 income limit applies separately to each parent.

2.   National Savings Children's Bonus Bonds for children under 16. The maximum holding per child is £3,000 in the current issue plus earlier issues of the Bonds. All interest and bonuses are tax-free, but no further returns are earned after the child's 21st birthday.

3.   Premiums of up to £270 a year on a qualifying friendly society life assurance policy for a child under 18. The returns under the policy are exempt from tax, but friendly societies are not able to reclaim dividend tax credits.

4.   From 6 April 2001, contributions of up to £3,600 a year to a personal pension policy on behalf of a child, such contributions being paid net of basic rate tax, which is retained whether or not the child is a taxpayer. The contributions would probably be exempt from inheritance tax under the rules for regular gifts out of income (inheritance tax is dealt with in detail in the companion to this book, Tolley's Taxwise II 2005/06). The child cannot draw pension benefits from the fund until he/she reaches age 55.

Parents can also establish accumulation and maintenance settlements for their children, the income from which is not treated as theirs unless and to the extent that it is used for the maintenance or education of children who are under 18 and unmarried, as illustrated in part (a) of the example.

The effect of Brian's trust income of £2,000 being treated as Mr Victor's income in part (a) of the example is to make part of Mr Victor's income liable to higher rate tax liability and to reduce the family's claim for child tax credit. As stated in (i) note 2, the settlor has the right to recover from the trustees any additional tax payable by him. Section 660C(3) states that the settlement income is regarded as the top slice of the settlor's income. This is, however, overridden by TA 1988 s 1A requiring savings income to be treated as the top slice of income.

Although the settlement income is in fact savings income, it is not treated as such in Mr Victor's hands. The effect for Mr Victor is that the settlement income falls within the basic rate tax band.

In fact, the inclusion of the trust income increases his overall **tax** liability by £794, because the trust income is charged to tax at 22%, costing £440, and it moves £1,575 of his dividend income that would have been charged at 10% into the 32½% rate band, costing £354. Mr Victor is entitled to treat the tax at 40% deducted by the trustees from the trust income (£800) as paid by him (see (i) note 2). The loss of tax credits, £2,000 @ 6.67% = £133, is not recoverable from the trustees.

Before 9 March 1999, a simple alternative to an accumulation and maintenance trust was for the parent to set up a bare trust, under which the child beneficiary had an absolute right to the property and income, but the trustee (who could be the parent) was the legal owner and held the property effectively as nominee. The income of such a trust was treated as the child's income (against which the child's personal allowance could be used if available) unless the income was actually paid to or for the benefit of the child while the child was unmarried and under 18. In that event the income was treated as the parent's under ITTOIA 2005 s 629. The rules have changed for new bare trusts created by parents in favour of their children under 18 on or after 9 March 1999, and for income from funds added to existing trusts on or after that date. Income of such trusts will be taxed as that of the parent, unless covered by the £100 limit dealt with above.

Bare trusts created under a parent's will are still effective, and also bare trusts created by other relatives, although it is not possible to make a reciprocal arrangement for someone to create a trust for his relative's children and for the relative to do the same for his children. A disadvantage of bare trusts is that the child cannot be prevented from having the property put into his own legal ownership at age 18.

Bare trusts created by parents are still effective for capital gains purposes, so that it is possible to use such trusts to acquire investments for children that produce capital growth rather than income.

From 6 April 2001 it is possible for a child aged 16 or 17 to hold a cash ISA. It should be noted that if the funds used for that ISA are provided by the parents then the interest arising within the ISA will be taxable on the parent (subject to the £100 limit referred to at 1 above).

(iii)   **Tax planning for married couples and civil partners**

As far as capital gains tax is concerned, each member of a couple is entitled to the annual capital gains tax exemption. Losses of one may, however, not be set against gains of the other. Transfers of assets between them in tax years when they are living together for all or part of the year are made on a no loss/no gain basis. See Example 76.

It may be sensible for a couple to rearrange their affairs in order to obtain the maximum benefit from being taxed separately, for example if one party has insufficient income to use his/her personal allowance. Care should be taken with dividends as the tax credits are not repayable. However it may be possible to transfer part or all of the age-related married couple's allowance to increase the tax payable by one partner in order to use up dividend tax credits that would otherwise be lost.

It is not possible for one party to give the other the right to part of his/her income without transferring the capital, but outright transfers of capital, with no right for the transferring party to control the capital or derive a benefit from it, are tax effective (ITTOIA 2005 s 624). (The fact that the individual who gave the asset away later gets it back on the other's death, or as a gift, does not make the transfer ineffective providing the initial gift was not made with any express or implied stipulation as to what the receiving individual could do with it.) An attempt by two directors owning all the shares in a company to increase their wives' income by issuing them with preference shares (for which the wives paid a nominal amount) carrying rights to

30% of the profits but no voting rights nor rights to participate in surplus assets was treated as an income settlement, and thus ineffective in Young v Pearce, Young v Scrutton (1996).

In Tax Bulletin 64 (April 2003) the Revenue (now HMRC) issued further guidance on the settlements legislation and how they felt it could apply to individuals and businesses in non-trust situations. They listed factors they would consider in deciding whether the settlements legislation should be applied:

–   A main earner draws a low salary leading to enhanced dividends paid to shareholders who are family members.

–   Disproportionately large returns on capital investments.

–   Different classes of shares enabling payment of dividends only to shareholders paying lower rates of tax.

–   Waiver of dividends to enable higher dividends to be paid to those liable at lower rates of tax.

–   Income being transferred from a person making most of the business profits to a friend or family member who pays a lower rate of tax.

Common situations which HMRC felt could invoke the settlement rules were:

–   Shares are issued that carry only restricted rights.

–   Shares are gifted that carry only restricted rights.

–   Income of a company is derived mainly from a single employee but shares are held by others.

–   A share in a partnership is gifted or transferred at below market value.

–   Dividend waivers occur.

–   Dividends are only paid on certain classes of shares.

–   Dividends are paid to a settlor's minor children.

HMRC confirms that ITTOIA 2005 s 624 will not apply if there is no 'bounty' or if the gift is to a spouse/civil partner and is an outright gift which is not wholly, or substantially, a right to income, eg a gift of shares in a quoted company.

The Tax Bulletin article gives various examples of where the Revenue consider that the settlements legislation will apply. Their view was upheld in the case of Jones v Garnett (2005) where shares were held by husband and wife and the main earner (Mr Jones) drew a salary below the going rate for the work he had done. As a result the dividend paid to Mrs Jones was deemed to arise from the 'bounty' created by the failure to draw a salary at the going rate. Therefore, under s 660A (now ITTOIA 2005 s 624), that dividend income was taxable on Mr Jones. So far HMRC has not issued guidance on how a taxpayer determines what is the 'going rate' of salary. The Court of Appeal has since disagreed with the HMRC view and held that there was no bounty provided when Mrs Jones acquired her share in the company as she had acquired it at its then market value. Whilst that represents the current legal position, it should be noted that the case is due to be heard by the House of Lords late 2006 or early 2007.

Where capital transfers are made, and the property consists of mortgaged property, one point that needs watching is that if the liability to pay the mortgage is taken over by the transferee, stamp duty land tax is payable (unless the transfer is certified as not liable to duty because the consideration is £125,000 or less for residential property, £150,000 or less for non-residential).

Spouses and civil partners are normally treated as owning joint property as 'joint tenants', which means each has equal rights over the property and when one dies it goes automatically to the other. The joint tenancy can, however, be severed and replaced by a 'tenancy in common' in which the share of each is separate, and may be unequal, and may be disposed of in lifetime or on death as the individal wishes. Where property is in joint names, it is deemed to be owned equally for income tax purposes unless it is actually owned in some different proportions and a joint declaration is made to that effect (TA 1988 ss 282A and 282B). Declarations apply to income arising on or after the date of the declaration. For a declaration to be valid, notice must be given to HMRC (on Form 17) within the period of sixty days beginning with the date of the declaration. The form only covers the assets listed on it. Any new assets must be covered by a separate form. Tax Bulletin 63 (February 2003) makes it clear that normally bank and building society joint accounts are held in such a way that each owner is equally entitled to the whole account. Form 17 can only be used for these accounts if the parties have formally changed the legal basis on which the account is held.

With effect from 6 April 2004 the provisions of TA 1988 s 282A deeming joint ownership do not apply if the property is shares in a close company. Instead the income from the shares must be divided between husband and wife in accordance with their actual ownership rights in the shares.

The deemed equal ownership is not relevant for capital gains purposes. The actual underlying beneficial ownership determines the capital gains treatment (see Example 76 part (a)).

(c)   (i)   **Financial support to adopters**

Where a family receives financial support from a local authority or adoption agency the amount received is free of income tax under ITTOIA 2005 s 744. Prior to 6 April 2003 some adoption payments were exempt from tax under Revenue Concession A40.

(ii)   **Foster carers (ITTOIA 2005 part 7 chapter 2)**

From 6 April 2003 a new tax relief for foster carers was introduced, together with an optional simplified method of computing taxable profits for those foster carers whose income exceeds the new relief.

The exempt limit is the sum of

–   £10,000, per residence, per full tax year (s 808), plus

–   £200 per week for a child aged under 11, and £250 per week for a child aged 11 or older (s 811).

Where a foster carer's gross receipts exceed the above limits, then, instead of computing their business profits using the normal rules, they can elect to deem their profit as being the excess of gross receipts from foster care over the exempt limits. The election must be made by the first anniversary of the 31 January after the year of assessment, or such longer period as HMRC may allow (s 818). (There is statutory provision for the deadline to be extended if there is a late adjustment to the profits from the provision of foster care (s 819).) A carer who is exempt or using the simplified method of computing profits is not entitled to capital allowances (s 826). No balancing charge or balancing allowance arises when they become exempt or elect to go into the simplified scheme. If the foster carer goes back to using the normal method of computing profits he or she can claim capital allowances on assets still held at the start of that period, including assets purchased during the periods when he or she was exempt or using the simplified scheme (ss 824–827).

If a taxpayer ceases to trade as a foster carer whilst within the exempt limit, then any overlap relief due on cessation is given as a loss (s 828).

(a)   Richard White is a single man aged 68 with pension income of £20,100, building society income of £2,600 (gross) and dividend income of £180 plus dividend tax credits of £20. He paid a gift aid payment of £780 (net) to his local church during the year.

Calculate the income tax payable for 2006/07.

(b)   John Brown, aged 74, married Ann Old, aged 72, on 10 May 2006. Their incomes for 2006/07 are as follows:

John Brown:	Pension	13,500	
	Building society interest	11,000	£24,500
Ann Old:	Pension	12,900	
	Dividends (inc tax credits)	12,000	£24,900

Calculate the income tax payable by each of them for 2006/07.

(c)   John and Jane Stone were divorced in 1987. Since that time John (who has remarried) has paid maintenance of £3,000 pa to Jane (who has not remarried). They are both aged 73. Their income in 2006/07 is as follows:

	John £	Jane £
Pension	29,180	6,160
Building society interest (amounts received)	2,480	240
Dividends (amounts received)	5,850	855

Compute the net tax payable by or repayable to John and Jane for 2006/07.

(d)   D Partid died on 10 June 2006 aged 70. He would have been 71 in September 2006. His income for the period from 6 April 2006 to the date of his death was as follows:

State pension	£2,020
Dividends (cash amount received)	£1,800
Building society interest credited	£800

He left a widow aged 45 and a child aged ten. Mrs Partid, who does not work, had income for 2006/07, including building society interest (net of 20% tax) of £1,600 and taxable state benefits following her husband's death, amounting to £10,080 (gross) in total.

Show the tax and tax credits position of Mr and Mrs Partid for 2006/07 assuming they made a joint claim to child tax credit before Mr Partid died, and Mrs Partid made a single claim by 11 September 2006. Assume that both Mr Partid's, and Mrs Partid's, income for 2006/07 was greater than the income for 2006/07 and show only the final award tax credits figure.

(e)   Julia Jones, a single lady, will be 60 on 28 December 2006. She is entitled to a state pension of £100 per week. She will continue to work for at least one year at a salary of £52,000 pa. She has savings income of £1,000 pa. gross but no other pension provision.

Set out the tax liability (using 2006/07 allowances and rates throughout) arising on the state pension on the assumption that Julia:

(i)   Takes the pension of £100.00 per week from her 60th birthday.

(ii)   Defers her pension until she ceases employment on her 61st birthday where she will receive a pension of £110 per week.

(iii)   As in (ii) but Julia takes a lump sum of £5,500 with an ongoing pension of £100 per week.

(iv)   Continues to work until her 65th birthday then taking a lump sum of £32,825 plus a pension of £100 per week.

(v)   Indicate what would happen if Julia died before she took her deferred pension.

(a)   **Income tax payable by Richard White for 2006/07**

	£	£
Pension		20,100
Building society interest (2,080 + 520)		2,600
Dividends (180 + 20)		200
		22,900

	£		
Personal allowance (age 68)		7,280	
Reduced by:			
Income	22,900		
Less: Gift aid donation (gross)	1,000		
	21,900		
Age allowance income limit	20,100		
One half of excess of	1,800	900	6,380
Taxable income			16,520

Tax thereon:		
On non-savings income	2,150 @ 10%	215
	11,570 @ 22%	2,545
	13,720	
On non-dividend savings income	2,600 @ 20%	520
On dividend income	200 @ 10%	20
	16,520	
Tax payable		3,300

Notes   (i)   As tax payable of £3,300 exceeds the tax on the gift aid payment of £220 no adjustment is required for that tax.

(ii)   Where gift aid payments are made by taxpayers entitled to age allowance, total income for age allowance purposes is reduced by the gross gift (TA 1988 ss 257 and 257A; FA 1990 s 25(9A)). Richard paid a net gift of £780 on which tax of £220 (£780 × 22/78) is deemed deducted, giving a gross gift of £1,000. Thus the restriction of allowances by one-half of excess income over £20,100 is based on the reduced income of £21,900 not the actual income of £22,900.

(iii)   If Richard makes annual payments under gift aid of £780 (£1,000 gross), he could consider electing to carry back part of his 2007/08 gift aid payment to 2006/07. Provided that payment is made and the election is made before the tax return for 2006/07 is filed and before 31 January 2008 in any event, a carry back of £1,000 would further reduce income for age allowance to £20,900, thus reducing the restriction by a further £500 and saving tax of £500 @ 22% = £110. See Example 91 at explanatory note 8 for the effect on any payments on account.

(b)   **Tax position of John Brown and Ann Old for 2006/07**

John Brown		£	£
Pension		13,500	
Building society interest		11,000	24,500
Personal allowance (age 70)		7,280	
Reduced by ½ x (24,500 – 20,100)		2,200	(5,080)
Taxable income			19,420

Tax thereon:			
On non-savings income	2,150 @ 10%	215	
	6,270 @ 22%	1,379	
On non-dividend savings income	11,000 @ 20%	2,200	
Tax payable			3,794

Ann Old		£	£
Pension		12,900	
Dividends		12,000	24,900
Personal allowance (Additional age-related allowance of £2,245 forgone due to income level)			(5,035)
Taxable income			19,865

Tax thereon:			
On non-savings income	2,150 @ 10%	215	
	5,715 @ 22%	1,257	
On dividends	12,000 @ 10%	1,200	2,672
Less: Married couple's allowance (elder aged 74)		6,065	
Reduced by ½ x (24,900 – 20,100)	2,400		
Less reduction in personal allowance	2,245	155	
		5,910	
Less 1/12th of £5,910		493	
		5,417	
Tax saving at 10%			542
Tax payable			2,130

Notes (i)   Only claimant's income affects married couple's allowance, even if it is given by reason of other spouse's/civil partner's age.

(ii)   The married couple's allowance is reduced by half the excess of the claimant's income over £20,100, less the restriction already made to the personal allowance, before being reduced by 1/12th for each tax month before the date of marriage.

(iii)   Tax would be saved if income-producing assets were transferred from the claimant to the other spouse/civil partner to avoid the claimant's allowances being affected by the income limit. However, this should be done carefully as the other spouse/civil partner might end up with more income in the year and so would be the individual entitled to the allowance. This is less of an issue for couples who *married* before 5 December 2005 (see note (iv) below). See also explanatory note 4.

(iv)   If the marriage had taken place in May 2005 instead of May 2006 then married couple's age allowance would be given to the husband. Thus, John would receive the tax saving which would have been reduced

Married couples allowance (elder aged 74)		6,065
Reduced by ½ × (24,500 – 20,100)	2,200	
Less reduction in personal allowance	2,200	NIL
		6,065
Tax saving @ 10%		607

This is a difference of £65 in married couple's allowance.

The difference can be explained by John having an additional entitlement to age allowances of £155 (at 10%) plus the fact that a full-year's married couple allowance is available rather than merely 11/12ths (worth an additional £493 at 10%).

(c)   **Net tax payable by or repayable to John and Jane Stone for 2006/07**

John Stone   £   £

Pension		29,180
Building society interest (2,480 + tax deducted 620)		3,100
Dividends (5,850 + tax credits 650)		6,500
		38,780
Personal allowance (age 73, but see note (i))		5,035
Taxable income		33,745

Tax payable thereon:

On non-savings income	2,150 @ 10%	215
	21,995 @ 22%	4,839
	24,145	
On non-dividend savings income	3,100 @ 20%	620
On dividends (part)	6,055 @ 10%	606
	33,300	
On dividends (balance)	445 @ 32½%	145
	33,745	6,425
Less: Married couple's age allowance (basic amount – see note (i))	2,350	
Relief for maintenance to former wife (see note (ii))	2,350	
	4,700 @ 10%	470
Tax payable		5,955

Jane Stone   Income   Tax deducted
                                                                              £   £

Pension	6,160	
Building society interest (240 + tax deducted 60)	300	60
Dividends (855 + non-repayable dividend tax credits 95)	950	
	7,410	
Personal allowance (age 73)	7,280	
Taxable income	130	

Tax payable thereon:

On dividends	130 @ 10% 13	
Less: Dividend tax credits, restricted to 10% of taxable income of £130 (see note (iii))	13	–
Tax repayable		60

Notes   (i)   John is aged 73, but his income is too high for him to benefit from the increased personal allowance of £7,280. He is, however, entitled to the basic married couple's allowance of £2,350 regardless of his income (see explanatory notes 1 and 2).

(ii)   Maintenance received is not taxable. Maintenance relief is only available for payers who satisfy the relevant conditions (see explanatory notes 5 and 6) and one of the parties to the marriage was born before 6 April 1935. The relief is 10% of maintenance paid to a maximum of 10% of £2,350.

(iii)   Dividend credits can be used to reduce tax payable (up to a maximum of 10% of taxable income – see Example 1 explanatory note 8), but are not repayable.

(d)   **Tax position of Mr and Mrs Partid for 2006/07**

	Income £	Tax deducted £
Mr Partid		
State pension	2,020	
Building society interest (800 + 200)	1,000	200
Dividends (1,800 + 200 non-repayable tax credit)	2,000	–
	5,020	200
Personal allowance (over 65)	(7,280)	–
Tax repayable		200

Personal representatives will notify HMRC that married couple's allowance of £6,065 is to be transferred to the widow.

Mrs Partid		£	£
Total income, including savings income of (1,600 + 400) = 2,000			10,080
Personal allowance			5,035
Taxable income			5,045
Tax thereon: Non-savings income			
2,150 @ 10%		215	
895 @ 22%		197	
Non-dividend savings income			
2,000 @ 20%		400	812
Less: Married couple's age allowance (transferred from husband)	6,065 @ 10%		606
Tax due			206
Tax deducted at source			600
Tax repayable			394

Tax Credits – Mr and Mrs Partid (joint claim)

Award period   6 April 2006 to 10 June 2006 = 66 days
Eligibility   WTC – No
                Childcare – No
                CTC – Yes
                Family element – Yes

Income – 2006/07	Mr Partid £		Mrs Partid £			Total £
State taxable benefits	–		8,080			8,080
Other income (including state pension)	5,020	+	2,000	– 300 =		6,720
Income for Tax Credits – Mr & Mrs Partid						14,800
Income for award period 66/365 x 14,800						2,676

Income – 2006/07		Mr Partid	Mrs Partid £		Total £
Maximum claim					
CTC			4.63		
Family element			1.50		
		66 days			
Relevant period		x	6.13	=	404
Restricted by					
Income			2,676		
Income threshold	66/365 x 14,155		2,560		
37% x			116		43
Tax Credits payable					361

Tax Credits – Mrs Partid (single claim)
Award period   11 June 2006 to 5 April 2007 = 299 days
Eligibility – CTC and Family element
Income – 2006/07

			Mrs Partid		Total
Employment (state taxable benefits)			8,080		
Other income	(2,000 – 300)		1,700		
			9,780		
Income for award period	299/365 x 9,780				8,011
Maximum claim			£		
CTC			4.63		
Family element			1.50		
		299 days			
Tax Credits payable		x	6.13		1,833

Amount is not restricted as income £8,011 is below the threshold income level of 299/365 x 14,155 = £11,595.

(e)   **Deferral of state pension**

   (i)   *Tax liability on state pension – commencing 2006/07*

Julia has income of (£52,000 + £1,000) £53,000 before drawing her state pension and is therefore a 40% taxpayer. Her tax liability on state pension is

State pension –	
14 weeks @ £100 = £1,400 @ 40% =	£560

2007/08
Julia will have other income of at least (£38,000 + £1,000) in 2007/08
and is still a higher rate taxpayer
Liability on state pension

52 weeks @ £100 = £5,200 @ 40% =	£2,080

2008/09
Assuming Julia ceased paid employment in December 2007 her liability
in 2008/09 (aged 61) is

	£	
State pension	5,200	
Other income	1,000	
	6,200	
Personal allowance	(5,035)	
Liable at 10%	1,165	= £117

When Julia reaches age 65 in December 2011 her age allowance will exceed her income and she will have no liability from 2011/12 onwards.

   (ii)   *Deferral for one year*

If Julia defers her state pension then her liability on pension becomes

2007/08

	£
State pension (income as in (i) above)	
14 weeks @ £110 = £1,540 @ 40% =	616

2008/09, 2009/10 and 2010/11

	£	
State pension	5,720	
Other income	1,000	
	6,720	
Personal allowance	(5,035)	
Liable at 10%	1,685	= £,169

From 2011/12 onwards Julia's age allowance will exceed her income and she will have no liability to tax.

   (iii)   *Drawing a lump sum*

If Julia opts to take the lump sum of £5,500 that amount is taxable when received at the rate applicable to her total income

	£
2007/08	
Earnings	38,000
Other income	1,000
	39,000

Rate applicable (£39,000 is greater than the personal allowance plus the
basic rate limit of £33,300) is 40%

Tax on lump sum £5,550 @ 40%	2,220
Tax on state pension 14 weeks @ £100 = £1,400 @ 40%	560
Tax liability on state benefits	2,780

However, Julia may elect to receive the lump sum on 6 April 2008 instead of 28 December 2007. (She could also delay receiving her state pension to 6 April 2008 which would increase the lump sum payable.)

In 2007/08 the resultant tax liabilities would be

On state pension (as above) £1,400 @ 40% = £560

In 2008/09 the tax liabilities would be

	£
State pension	5,200
Other income	1,000
Total income before lump sum	6,200

Rate applicable (£6,200 is greater than the starting rate limit of £2,150 but less than the basic rate limit) is 22%.

Tax on lump sum £5,500 @ 22%	1,221
Tax on total income (as in (i) above) £1,165 @ 10% =	117
	1,338

(iv)   *Drawing pension at age 65*

Similar rules would apply at age 65, ie tax at 40% would be due on the lump sum unless Julia deferred receiving the amount until 6 April 2012 when 22% would apply.

(v)   *Death*

If Julia dies after deferring her state pension, but before opting to take the lump sum or increased pension, no amount would be payable to her estate as she is single. (See note (c) below.)

Notes

(a)   The Pensions Act 2004 has amended Schedule 5 to the Social Security Contributions and Benefits Act 1992 with effect from 5 April 2005 to increase the subsequent pension payable following deferment and also to enable the deferred pension to be taken as a lump sum with no increase in state pension. State pension includes Basic Pension, SERPS, S2P and Graduated Pensions (SSCBA 1991 Sch 5.A1).

Deferral must be for a minimum period of five weeks and gives an uprating of pension of 1% for each five weeks of deferral (10.4% pa uplift) (SSCBA 1992 Sch 5.2A).

To take a lump sum the minimum deferral period is one year. The lump sum is the pension foregone increased by Bank Base Rate plus 2% compounded. At a bank rate of 4.75% that gives an increase of 6.75% pa (SSCBA 1992 Sch 5.3B).

(b)   The lump sum is not treated as income but is taxed at a flat rate based upon total income (excluding the lump sum) for the year (F(No2)A 2005 s 7).

If total income (excluding lump sum) for 2005/06 is

NIL	the rate is	0%
£1 to £2,150	the rate is	10%

£2,151 to £33,300	the rate is 22%
£33,301 upward	the rate is 40%

The limits being, the starting rate (£2,150) and basic rate limits (£33,300) for the relevant years.

Total income is defined in TA 1988 s 835 as being before the deduction of allowances. It is not known whether this is the intention of the legislation. The above example has used total income as defined in s 835 ie gross before deductions of allowances.

Because it is likely that the pensioner will have other income in the year of retirement, provision is made for the deferral of the lump sum to the first day of the following fiscal year (F(No2)A 2005 s 8(5)). This would reduce the tax rate for Julia from 40% to 22%. In practice it will often be more advantageous also to defer taking the state pension until the first day of the new tax year. The lump sum would then be further increased by the additional pension deferred which otherwise for Julia would have been taxed at 40%.

(c)   If a state pension is deferred and the taxpayer dies before opting to take a lump sum or enhanced pension then the benefits are lost unless there is a surviving spouse or civil partner. If the deceased taxpayer had a spouse or civil partner then, provided the period of deferment is at least twelve months, the surviving spouse (partner) may elect to receive a lump sum based upon basic state pension plus one-half of the additional pension deferred (SSCBA 1992 Sch 5 3C). Alternatively, the surviving spouse (partner) may take an enhanced pension of an amount equal to the increase the deceased would have been entitled to had deferment ceased on the date of death. This applies after five weeks of deferment.

(d)   Deferral will reduce a claimant's income for the purpose of drawing benefits or council tax benefit. However, when the increased pension is drawn entitlement to such benefits may be reduced. To mitigate the effects of taking a lump sum the amount received (net of tax) is disregarded in calculating such benefits.

(e)   A lump sum is taxable in the applicable year of assessment, that is the tax year in which the first pension payment date falls, or if the pensioner dies before the beginning of that year, the tax year in which the pensioner dies (F(No 2)A 2005 s 8(2)). The actual date of payment of the lump sum is not relevant (s 8(8)).

If a surviving spouse elects for a lump sum the applicable year of assessment is the tax year in which their spouse dies (s 8(4)).

If the lump sum is not payable until the following tax year then it is taxed in the following year unless the pensioner dies before the start of the following tax year in which case it is taxed in the year of death (s 8(6)).

Explanatory Notes

Age-related allowances

1.   Each of a married couple (or members of a registered civil partnership) is entitled to a personal allowance based on their own age. Higher allowances apply to someone aged 65 or over in the tax year, the allowances for 2006/07 being £7,280 for someone aged 65 to 74 and £7,420 for someone aged 75 or over. The higher age-related allowances are reduced by half of the excess of the net total income over a certain limit (£20,100 for 2006/07) and this limit applies to each spouse/civil partner separately.

The allowances are not, however, reduced below the basic personal allowance (£5,035 for 2006/07).

The net total income for the purpose of age allowances is after deducting charges on income such as patent royalties and other annual payments (and where relevant, trading losses). Retirement annuity premiums paid under the pre 1 July 1988 rules are deducted from relevant earnings and therefore also reduce total income. This no longer applies in respect of personal pension contributions. Relief for such contributions is given by deducting and retaining basic rate tax at source, higher rate relief where relevant being given by extension of the basic rate limit (see Example 1 part (ii)) and total income is not affected. However, by Revenue Concession A102 total income for age allowances is reduced by the gross amount of the pension premium as for gift aid payments (as to which see part (a) note (ii) of the example).

2. The married couple's allowance is no longer available unless at least one spouse or civil partner was born before 6 April 1935. Where available, the allowance is given as a reduction of tax payable, rather than as a deduction from taxable income, and saves tax at 10%. For 2006/07 the allowance is £6,065 where the elder is over 71 on 6 April 2006 and £6,135 where the elder is 75 or over at any time in the tax year. The allowance is reduced if the claimant's total income is over £20,100, the reduction being equal to half of the excess over £20,100, but not so as to reduce the allowance below a basic allowance of £2,350 (TA 1988 s 257A). See note 1 for the definition of total income.

    The allowance was previously always given in the first instance to the husband. A married woman is, however, entitled as of right to half the basic allowance, ie £1,175, if she makes a claim (on form 18) to that effect. Alternatively the couple may jointly claim for the *whole* of the basic allowance of £2,350 to be given to the wife. In either case, the claim must be made *before* the beginning of the relevant tax year, ie before 6 April 2007 for 2007/08 (except in the year of marriage, when the claim may be made within that tax year). The allowance will then be allocated in the chosen way until the claim is withdrawn, or where a joint claim has been made for the whole of the basic allowance to go to the wife, until the husband makes a fresh claim for half of that amount. The withdrawal or husband's claim must also be made before the beginning of the tax year for which the revised allocation is to take effect (TA 1988 s 257BA).

    The husband is entitled to any extra allowance over the basic £2,350, and it is his income level that determines how much of the extra allowance is available.

    Following the introduction of the Civil Partnership Act 2004, civil partners are also allowed the allowance with effect from 2005/06 provided that at least one partner was born before 6 April 1935. For such couples, the allowance is initially allocated to the partner with the higher total income in the year. This allocation also applies to married couples whose marriage is on or after 5 December 2005 (TA 1988 s 257AB).

    If the tax payable by either spouse/civil partner is too low to use the tax saving to which he/she is entitled on the married couple's allowance, that spouse/civil partner may notify HMRC (on the tax return or on form 575) that the excess is to be transferred to the other spouse/civil partner (s 257BB). The time limit for making the claim is five years from the 31 January following the end of the relevant tax year.

    Where there are other deductions from tax payable, the married couple's allowance is treated as the last deduction (except for double taxation relief on foreign income) (TA 1988 s 256(3)), thus maximising the amount that is available to be transferred to the other spouse/civil partner.

    Allowing a wife to claim half of the basic married couple's allowance by right gives greater equity, although more than four fifths of the allowance still goes to the husband unless he agrees for the wife to claim a further £1,175. There would be a cash flow benefit from transferring the allowance if the wife is an employee paying tax weekly or monthly on her earnings and the husband is self-employed paying tax on his business profits as part of his half-yearly payments on account and balancing payments under self-assessment.

    In addition, although where a husband claims the allowance, any unused tax relief may be transferred to the wife, relief for the basic allowance would be given earlier by making the advance claim to transfer it if it was known that the husband would not be paying enough tax to use it.

It should be noted that a claim to transfer half or all of married couple's allowance to the spouse/civil partner prior to the start of the tax year may save tax if the transferor is likely to have unused non-repayable tax credits on dividends. The increase in the transferor's taxable income because of the transfer of allowances may enable the dividend credits to be used, with the transferee using the transferred allowance against his/her own liability.

3.   The effect of the restriction of the age-related personal allowance when income exceeds the limit is to increase the taxable income by 1½ times the extra income. The marginal rate of tax on the extra income depends on the mix of dividend income, other savings income and non-savings income. If there is no savings income the marginal rate is 33% (ie 1½ x 22%). If there is non-dividend savings income the marginal rate will be somewhere between 30% (ie 1½ x 20%) and 33% depending on the respective amounts of non-dividend savings income and non-savings income. Where the income includes dividend income, or income liable at the starting rate, the marginal rate will be between 15% (ie 1½ × 10%) and 33%, depending on the income mix.

If the reduction is high enough to cause a restriction in married couple's age allowance, as in part (b) of the example, the marginal tax rate on that part of the excess income is only 5% higher than the normal rate, since the reduction affects the married couple's allowance that saves tax at only 10%.

Married couple's allowance – year of marriage/entering into a civil partnership

4.   The married couple's allowance remains available after 5 April 2000 to those born before 6 April 1935, even if they did not get married or register the civil partnership until after 5 April 2000, or if they become single after that date and later remarry or enter into a civil partnership.

In the year of marriage or registration, the allowance is reduced by 1/12th for each complete tax month (ending on the 5th) before the wedding/registration date (TA 1988 ss 257A and 257AB).

Where a party's income is sufficiently above the income limit for the married couple's allowance to be affected (his personal allowance first having been reduced to the normal £5,035 level), the income restriction is applied first, and the resulting allowance is then reduced according to the date of marriage/registration, as shown in part (b) of the example.

The effect of the income limit for age allowances on marginal tax rates is stated in note 3 above. Ann Old's marginal rate in part (b) of the example is 22% on non-savings income, 10% on dividend income and 20% on non-dividend savings income (unless taxable income exceeds the basic rate limit of £33,300).

Suppose Ann Old had received some shares from her husband resulting in an increase of dividend income (including the tax credits) of £1,000 (and a corresponding decrease in her husband's income). This would have reduced the value of the married couple's allowance by (£500 x 11/12 at 10% =) £46.

John Brown, however, would have regained an additional £500 of his age-related personal allowance. With income being taxed at 22%, this would have saved him an additional £110.

Year of separation – married couple's allowance and maintenance payments

5.   For a couple one or both of whom was born before 6 April 1935, the married couple's allowance is given in full in the tax year of separation, but it is not available in later tax years except where someone born before 6 April 1935 remarries or enters into a civil partnership (or a younger person marries or enters into a civil partnership with a person who *was* born before 6 April 1935).

6.   All maintenance payments are exempt from tax in the hands of the recipient and they are received in full without tax being deducted (ITTOIA 2005 s 727). Where either of a separated or divorced couple was born before 6 April 1935 the payer may claim a deduction from his/her tax liability at 10% on up to £2,350 (index linked) of maintenance paid to the spouse/civil partner (either for the recipient's own maintenance or for the benefit of a child under 21) (TA 1988 s 347B). Relief is not

available if payments are expressed to be payable direct to a child, even though actually paid to the wife (Billingham v John 1997). The maintenance relief is not increased where there is more than one ex-spouse/civil partner receiving maintenance.

The full maintenance relief is given in the year of separation, as well as the married couple's allowance. Payments due after the recipient remarries do not qualify for relief. If the payer remarries or enters into a civil partnership he/she will still be entitled to maintenance relief as well as any married couple's allowance.

The above provisions also apply to maintenance paid under court orders and written agreements the proper law of which is that of a part of a European Community member state, or a member state of the European Free Trade area forming part of the European Economic Area. For a list of the relevant countries see Revenue Manual, Relief Instructions Re 1190 (TA 1988 s 347B).

No relief is available for payments which are voluntary and not made under a legal obligation.

Child Support Agency

7. Maintenance assessed by the Child Support Agency qualifies for tax relief in the same way as maintenance under a court order (TA 1988 s 347B), and maintenance collected by the Agency for a divorced or separated spouse qualifies for relief as if it had been paid direct to the spouse. Maintenance paid to the Department for Work and Pensions for a spouse/civil partner who receives income support also qualifies for relief as if it had been paid to the spouse/civil partner.

Life assurance relief

8. Husband and wife continue to get relief for life assurance premiums on each other's lives even after they are divorced (TA 1988 Sch 14.1) provided that the policies were issued before 14 March 1984. The relief of 12.5% of the premiums is given by deduction at source and does not affect the tax payable.

Age-related allowances in year of death

9. The higher allowances for someone aged 65 or over (or 75 or over) are available in the tax year in which the relevant birthday falls, even if the person dies earlier in the tax year.

    Married couple's allowance, where available, is given to the husband unless a claim has been made for all or half of the basic allowance to go to the wife. The full allowance is available in the year of death of either husband or wife.

    The surviving spouse may have transferred to him/her any part of the allowance claimed by the other spouse that the other's income is too low to use, providing the personal representatives notify HMRC accordingly (TA 1988 s 257BB).

    All the allowances available to a wife in the year of her husband's death are available against *any* of her income for the full tax year.

    (See note 2 above for civil partners and marriages after 4 December 2005.)

Dealing with the deceased's estate

10. When someone dies, the tax position of the deceased for the year of death must be dealt with by the personal representatives, who also have a tax liability in respect of transactions carried out by them in completing the administration of the estate. Under self-assessment, the normal time limit for enquiring into a tax return is twelve months from the due date for the return, ie for 2006/07, one year from 31 January 2008 (see Example 40 note 12). To minimise delays in winding up estates and trusts, and in distributing estate or trust property, HMRC have announced that they will, on request, issue tax returns before the end of the tax year of death, or of winding up an estate or trust, and will give early confirmation if they do not intend to enquire into the return.

The personal representatives will not usually be able to settle the deceased's tax liabilities until probate is obtained. The deceased's tax district should be asked to arrange for the HMRC Accounts Office not to issue any further Statements of Account in the meantime. By HMRC Concession A17, interest on tax falling due after death will not start to run until thirty days after the grant of probate.

11.   For further provisions on taxation of spouses and civil partners see Example 2.

Tax Credits

12.   The claim for tax credits for the period to date of death will be based upon the joint income of the claimants. It would appear that the calculation is based upon their income for the whole tax year (SI 2002/2006 reg 3(1)) apportioned to the award period of 66 days (SI 2002/2008 reg 8(3) Step 3).

For the period after date of death Mrs Partid is a sole claimant. Again, it is her income for the whole of the tax year that is relevant. This time the £300 disregard applies wholly to her income. The result is then apportioned to the award period of 299 days.

Because Mr and Mrs Partid do not work the income threshold for CTC is used, £14,155 per year.

State retirement pension counts as 'pension income' for tax credit purposes and benefits from the £300 disregard. Other taxable state benefits are counted in full along with employment income, student income and miscellaneous income (see Step 2, SI 2002/2006 reg 3(1)).

If Mr and Mrs Partid had been entitled to any payment of non-taxable pension credit then the income threshold does not apply and full CTC is payable.

For further details about tax credits see Example 5.

(a)   Doreen, a widow since 1995, is aged 73. Her income in the year ended 5 April 2007 consisted of:

	£
Retirement pension	4,266
Building society interest – cash amount received*	2,347
3½% War Loan interest (£2,000 of the stock was sold March 2007)	105
National Savings Bank interest	85
Purchased life annuity (gross amount, including agreed capital element £632)	790
Dividends received from UK companies	630

*   Doreen has not registered to receive interest gross.

Doreen's grandchildren, James aged 17 (still at school) and Bertha aged 13, have lived with her and been maintained by her since their parents were killed in an aeroplane crash in 1997. They have an interest in a discretionary trust set up by the wills of their parents and during 2006/07 the trustees paid the sum of £990 to help with an educational trip abroad for Bertha. Bertha does not have any other sources of income.

Calculate the amount of Doreen's and Bertha's income tax repayments for 2006/07 together with tax credits payable to Doreen, assuming that Doreen's income for tax credits in 2005/06 amounted to £7,685, and Doreen made a claim to tax credits by 31 August 2006.

(b)   In 2006/07 John, a single man aged 60, has pension income of £3,410 (no tax deducted under PAYE). He also has building society interest of £4,800 (cash amount received). He made a gift aid payment to the local church amounting to £390.

Calculate John's income tax repayment for 2006/07.

(c)   Nigel, a widower aged 50, makes a single gift aid donation to a registered community amateur sports club of £780 in 2006/07. Show the tax saving arising from the payment if Nigel's income is:

	(i) £	(ii) £	(iii) £
Salary	40,000	21,000	21,000
Building society interest (gross amount)	3,000	20,000	11,000
Dividends (including dividend tax credits)	1,000	3,000	12,000
	44,000	44,000	44,000

(a)   **Doreen – Income tax repayment 2006/07**

	£	Income £	Income tax paid £
Non-savings income			
Retirement pension		4,266	
Savings income other than dividends			
Building society interest (2,347 + 587)	2,934		587
3½% War Loan interest (see explanatory note 1)	105		
National Savings Bank interest	85		
Income element of annuity (see explanatory note 3)	158	3,282	32
Savings income – dividends			
630 + dividend tax credit 70		700	
Net total income		8,248	619
Personal allowance (65 to 74)		7,280	
Taxable income		968	
Income tax thereon (see explanatory note 5):			
On non-dividend savings income	268 @ 10%	27	
On dividends	700 @ 10%	70	
		97	
Less: Tax credits on dividends		70	
Tax payable			27
Repayment due			592

Bertha – Income tax repayment 2006/07

	Income £	Income tax paid £
Non-savings income		
Income from discretionary trust (see explanatory note 12) (990 + (40/60) 660)	1,650	660
Personal allowance (£5,035, but restricted to income)	1,650	
	–	
Tax repayable		660

Tax Credits – Doreen

Initial award 2006/07

Eligibility	WTC – No
	Childcare – No
	CTC – Yes
	Family element – Yes

Income – 2005/06
(below threshold) £7,685

	£
Maximum claim applies	
CTC – 2 children, £4.63 x 2 x 365	3,380
Family element, £1.50 x 365	545
Tax credits payable	3,925

Income for 2006/07		
As for Income Tax	8,248	
Less: Disregard	300	£7,948

Less than £25,000 increase – no adjustment

However, the tax credit rates have increased for 2006/07. Therefore, Doreen is entitled to the following elements:

	£
CTC – 2 children, £4.84 x 2 =	9.68
Family element, £1.50 =	1.50
	11.18

As income below threshold of £14,155 a daily amount of £11.18 will be payable until James leaves school.

(b) **John – income tax repayment 2006/07**

	Income £	Income tax paid £
Non-savings income		
Pension	3,410	–
Savings income other than dividends		
Building society interest (4,800 + 1,200)	6,000	1,200
	9,410	1,200
Personal allowance	5,035	
Taxable income	4,375	
Income tax thereon: 2,150 @ 10%	215	
2,225 @ 20%	445	660
4,375		
Repayment due		540

Note: As tax chargeable of £660 exceeds the tax of £110 retained on the charitable gift (390 net + 110 tax @ 22% = £500 gross), the repayment is not restricted.

(c) **Nigel – tax relief on gift aid donation 2006/07**

Nigel is a higher rate taxpayer, so his basic rate threshold is increased from £33,300 to £34,300 as a result of the gift aid payment of £780 net, £1,000 gross. Where a higher rate taxpayer has income from a number of sources, the effect of extending the basic rate band is to give relief at 22% plus the marginal rate otherwise chargeable on the slice of income that moves below the basic rate threshold as a result of the extension.

The position in Nigel's case is therefore as follows:

	(i) £	(ii) £	(iii) £
Salary	40,000	21,000	21,000
Building society interest	3,000	20,000	11,000
Dividends	1,000	3,000	12,000
	44,000	44,000	44,000
Personal allowance	5,035	5,035	5,035
Taxable income	38,965	38,965	38,965

Tax due without gift

Non-savings income:

	(i)	(ii)	(iii)
2,150 / 2,150 / 2,150 @ 10%	215	215	215
31,150 / 13,815 / 13,815 @ 22%	6,853	3,039	3,039
1,665 / – / – @ 40%	666	–	–
34,965 15,965 15,965			

Non-dividend savings income:

	(i)	(ii)	(iii)
– / 17,335 / 11,000 @ 20%	–	3,467	2,200
3,000 / 2,665 / – @ 40%	1,200	1,066	–
37,965 35,965 26,965			

Dividends:

	(i)	(ii)	(iii)
– / – / 6,335 @ 10%	–	–	633
1,000 / 3,000 / 5,665 @ 32½%	325	975	1,841
38,965 38,965 38,965	9,259	8,762	7,928

Tax due with gift

Non-savings income:

	(i)	(ii)	(iii)
2,150 / 2,150 / 2,150 @ 10%	215	215	215
32,150 / 13,815 / 13,815 @ 22%	7,073	3,039	3,039
665 / – / – @ 40%	266	–	–
34,965 15,965 15,965			

Non-dividend savings income:

	(i)	(ii)	(iii)
– / 18,335 / 11,000 @ 20%	–	3,667	2,200
3,000 / 1,665 / – @ 40%	1,200	666	–
37,965 35,965 26,965			

Dividends:

	(i)	(ii)	(iii)
– / – / 7,335 @ 10%	–	–	733
1,000 / 3,000 / 4,665 @ 32½%	325	975	1,516
38,965 38,965 38,965	9,079	8,562	7,703

	(i)	(ii)	(iii)
Saving of higher rate/upper rate tax	180	200	225
Basic rate tax retained out of gift aid payment	220	220	220
Tax saving	400	420	445
Representing a tax saving of	40%	42%	44.5%

This is because the £1,000 income that has moved below the basic rate threshold is:

(i)   Salary, giving tax saving of 22% + 18% = 40%

(ii)   Building society interest, giving tax saving of 22% + 20% = 42%

(iii)   Dividends, giving tax saving of 22% + 22.5% = 44.5%

Explanatory Notes

Interest on Government Stocks and National Savings Bank accounts

1.   Interest on 3½% War Loan is always paid gross (half yearly in June and December). By selling some of her stock in March 2007, Doreen effectively received three months' interest (ie from December 2006) as part of her capital proceeds. There are 'accrued income scheme' provisions to treat such amounts that accrue on any marketable securities other than shares as income. The provisions do not, however, apply where the nominal value of all securities held does not exceed £5,000. This exception applies in Doreen's case, since £105 represents interest on £3,000 stock (£2,000 of which has now been sold), so the provisions would not apply to her March 2007 sale. For details of the scheme see Example 7.

2.   Interest on National Savings Bank accounts is received in full without tax being deducted. For details see Example 6.

Purchased life annuities

3.   When a life annuity is purchased for a lump sum, part of the annual payment is deemed to be a return of the capital and is not taxable. The rate of tax deducted at source on the income element is the lower rate of 20%. The capital element is determined by HMRC, with the usual rights of appeal (ITTOIA 2005 Part 6 Chapter 7). Doreen will receive a cash sum of £758, being £158 income less £32 tax = £126 plus £632 capital.

Income from a discretionary trust

4.   The payment towards Bertha's educational trip counts as her income and since it is paid from a discretionary trust its value is after tax of 40% not 22% (TA 1988 s 687 – see Example 2 part (b)(i) note 4). An income tax repayment claim can be made on behalf of Bertha to recover the £660 tax deducted since her income is covered by her personal allowance. See note 12 below as to why vulnerable trust treatment does not apply.

Order of deductions

5.   A taxpayer may offset allowances and reliefs against income of different descriptions in the most advantageous order unless the legislation provides otherwise (TA 1988 s 835). As far as tax rates are concerned, the legislation provides that savings income is to be treated as the highest part of income, and that dividend income is to be treated as the highest part of the savings income (TA 1988 s 1A). As the starting rate applies to both non-savings income and non-dividend savings income, the most advantageous way of offsetting the personal allowance will normally be first against non-savings income, then non-dividend savings income, then dividend income. Married couple's allowance, where available, is given as a reduction of tax payable rather than being offset against income. Any surplus married couple's allowance may be transferred to a spouse/civil partner. The legislation provides for the allowance to be treated as the last deduction, except for double taxation relief on foreign income, thus maximising the unused amount available to be transferred (TA 1988 s 256 – see Example 3 explanatory note 2).

Dividends carry a non-repayable dividend tax credit at 1/9th of the amount received, ie 10% of the tax credit inclusive amount. The dividend tax credits are set against the tax chargeable (rather than being deducted in arriving at it) (ITTOIA 2005 s 397). They are therefore taken into account after reliefs and allowances that reduce the tax chargeable.

Age-related allowances – income restriction

6. The personal allowance is increased where a person is sixty-five years of age or over at any time in the year of assessment, and is further increased in the tax year in which the person reaches seventy-five years of age. The allowance is reduced by one half of the excess of net total income over £20,100, but cannot be reduced below the normal personal allowance of £5,035 (TA 1988 s 257). Age-related married couple's allowance is similarly reduced by half the excess income over £20,100 less any reduction made in the personal allowance, but the allowance is not reduced below £2,350.

7. Note that net total income for the purpose of the age allowance income limit means income after deducting gross gifts to charities (TA 1988 ss 257 and 257A, FA 1990 s 25(9A)) and personal pension contributions (FA 2004 s 192(5)) (see Example 3 explanatory note 1). See Example 91 for the detailed provisions on charitable gifts and gifts to amateur sports clubs and Examples 37 and 38 for the treatment of pension contributions.

Repayment claims

8. Repayments arise where tax is deducted at source from some income and other income is too low to utilise available allowances. Someone whose income is expected to be covered by available allowances can register to receive bank and building society interest in full (see Example 6). This would have benefited Doreen in part (a) of the example, although she would still have had to claim repayment of the tax deducted from the life annuity. A claim however is not available to Doreen because a claim to receive interest in full cannot be made where income is expected to exceed allowances, even where a repayment is due. HMRC will, however, refund overpaid tax of £50 or more before the end of the relevant tax year (see HMRC leaflet IR 110). Repayment claims may be made outside the self-assessment system. HMRC do not require the claims to be supported by tax vouchers, although they may call for extra information if they cannot calculate the repayment from the information shown on the claim form.

    Where someone is taxed under PAYE, an overpayment of £10 or less is not repaid unless a specific claim is made. It will usually be dealt with by a coding adjustment in the following year (SP 6/95). (For detailed notes on PAYE see Example 9.)

9. John in (b) and Nigel in (c) could not have registered to receive building society interest gross as both have income chargeable to tax.

    Nigel should submit a self-assessment return as a higher rate taxpayer. If his income had been wholly subject to PAYE, the income tax deducted would amount to £9,334 and he would be entitled to a repayment of (40% – 22%, ie) £180 because of the gift aid payment. Accordingly all higher rate taxpayers making qualifying gift aid donations to charity will need to request a self-assessment return to obtain the higher rate relief if one is not sent automatically each year.

    Note that if Nigel's income of £44,000 had been wholly dividend income, his tax position taking into account the gift aid payment of £1,000 gross would be:

	£
Dividend income (including non-repayable dividend tax credits of £4,400)	44,000
Personal allowance	5,035
Taxable income	38,965
Tax thereon: 34,300 @ 10%	3,430
4,665 @ 32½%	1,516
Tax due	4,946
Less: Dividend credits (restricted*)	3,896
Tax remaining payable	1,050

   *   The maximum tax credits that may be set against taxable income are 10% of the dividends brought into charge to tax, ie the taxable income of £38,965. The tax remaining payable is thus 22½% of £4,665.

10. If Nigel in part (c) of the example had income in 2005/06 liable to higher rate tax, and the marginal income was dividend income whereas in 2006/07 it is salary, then it would be advantageous to make a carry back claim for the Gift Aid donation. The gift to the community amateur sports club would have to have been made before 31 January 2007 and before submission of the 2005/06 tax return. The relief against dividend income in 2005/06 would give a tax saving at 44.5%, whereas against salary in 2006/07 the saving would only be at 40%. There would also be a cash-flow advantage in the carry back.

11. Where a taxpayer is entitled to a tax repayment then it is possible to specify on the self assessment return (but not on a repayment claim) a charity to receive part or all of that repayment. It is necessary to enter the charity code at box 19A.3. This is obtained from the website (www.hmrc.gov.uk/charities/charities-search.htm) or by ringing 0845 9000 444. Furthermore, by ticking box 19A.4, the repayment will be increased by the basic rate tax deemed deducted. If John at (b) above had received a self-assessment tax return and had nominated his church to receive the repayment, the amount paid to the church would be $£540 \times \dfrac{100}{78} = £692$. This would also be a deemed gift aid donation made by John at the date the amount is paid to the church, say December 2007, and higher rate tax relief could be claimed in 2007/08 of £692 × 18% = £125 (assuming John was a higher rate taxpayer in 2007/08).

No claim is possible to relate the amount back to the previous year as by the very process the gift cannot be made until the 2006/07 tax return is filed and processed. It is a requirement of the gift aid carryback claim that the claim is made prior to the filing of the relevant tax return, therefore the relevant date has passed at the time the gift is made to the charity.

12. Although special tax treatment is available for trusts with vulnerable beneficiaries these rules cannot apply to Bertha or James in part (a).

In order to claim special treatment the beneficiary must be a disabled person or a relevant minor. A disabled person is a taxpayer who is incapable of administering his/her own property by reason of a mental disorder or a person in receipt of attendance allowance or disability living allowance (higher or middle rate). A relevant minor is a person under 18 where one or both of the parents have died. Bertha and James are therefore relevant minors. In addition the trust must also qualify. To do so the property must be held for the benefit of the vulnerable person absolutely. The beneficiary must be entitled to all of the income, and where the beneficiary is a minor they must be entitled to the property at 18. In the case of Bertha and James the trust is a discretionary trust and therefore does not qualify. In the same way if the trust had been an accommodation and maintenance trust for the children where they become entitled at age 25, again Bertha and James would not have been able to claim vulnerable trust treatment.

Where special treatment is claimed, available by election from 2004/05 onwards, the tax liability of the trust is computed in the normal way. The trustees then make a claim to reduce that liability to the amount due treating the trust income and capital gains as being the income or gains of the vulnerable beneficiary computed by adding those amounts to the actual income and gains of the beneficiary. The increase in the liability of the individual is the trusts tax liability. See Tolleys Taxwise II for a computation of such a claim.

A.   (a)   Outline the basic principles of tax credits, setting out the criteria to be satisfied for eligibility for

(i)   Working tax credit (WTC)

(ii)   Childcare element of WTC

(iii)   Child tax credit (CTC).

(b)   How is 'income' computed for tax credits?

(c)   What changes in circumstances must be reported to HMRC, and by what date?

(d)   What is an 'award period', and why are separate calculations required for each 'relevant period' within the award period?

(e)   What information must be provided at the end of each fiscal year and how will underpayment/overpayment of tax credits be dealt with?

B.   (a)   Brian and Angela Smith are married. Brian is self-employed preparing accounts to 31 December each year. Angela is employed. Both usually work more than 30 hours per week. They have one child, Joanna, date of birth 30 June 2001. She attends an approved nursery costing £165 per week. Because Angela is pregnant she has increased the time Joanna spends at the nursery and from 5 January 2007 the cost increases to £200 per week. On 1 March 2007 Colin was born. No nursery costs were incurred for Colin in 2006/07. Angela was still on statutory maternity leave at 5 April 2007.

Their income for 2005/06 per their tax returns was:

	Brian	Angela
Self-employment	18,810	
Per P60		22,000
Per P11D – Car		2,160
– Medical		640
Investment income (gross)	180	520

Brian pays £130 per month (net) to a personal pension policy and Angela pays £39 (net) per month under gift aid to the local church.

Their income for 2006/07 per their tax returns was:

	Brian	Angela
Self-employment		
(Accounts y/e 31/12/06) – Loss	(2,800)	
Per P60		16,100
Per P11D – Car		2,160
– Medical		700
Investment Income (gross)	20	140

Included in Angela's P60 for 2006/07 is Statutory Maternity Pay of £2,326 for 10 weeks and Statutory Sick Pay of £193. Brian will make a claim under TA 1988 s 380 to carry his loss back to 2005/06.

A renewal claim for tax credits for 2005/06 was filed by Brian and Angela on 30 July 2005 and renewal information provided on 6 July 2006. Notification of increase in nursery costs and the birth of Colin was given on 5 May 2007.

Compute the tax credits payable to Angela or Brian during 2006/07 (the provisional award), and the under/overpayment arising for 2006/07 after calculation of the final award.

(b)   Re-compute the position on the assumption that instead of a loss the accounts of Brian for the year ended 31 December 2006 showed a profit of £35,000.

A.   (a)   *Basic principles*

Tax credits were introduced as a form of 'negative income tax' with effect from 6 April 2003. The primary legislation is the Tax Credits Act (TCA) 2002 which is supplemented by numerous statutory instruments. The aim of the legislation is to provide help to those on low income who are working and those with children. The method of award is based upon the family unit. If this is a married couple living together and not permanently separated, or, a man and a woman living together as husband and wife, the claim is based upon the joint income of the couple. From 5 December 2005 a same-sex couple also count as a family unit, whether or not that couple form a civil partnership and their joint income is used for tax credits If the claimant is a lone parent or someone who is aged 25 or over and working at least 30 hours per week, then the claim is based on the income of that person. Special rules apply to those with a disability which puts them at a disadvantage in getting a job.

An award is made per day. The elements of tax credits are computed by dividing the yearly amount by the number of days in the tax year (SI 2002/2008 regs 6-9) and rounding up to the nearest penny. All days with the same entitlement within the award period are aggregated and are known as a 'relevant period'.

Income is based upon broadly the taxable income of the fiscal year. That is again divided by the number of days in the tax year and applied to the relevant periods.

The first award of tax credits is provisional and is based on the income of the preceding year, ie for 2006/07 the claim is initially based upon the income of 2005/06. From 6 April 2006 the income increase disregard is increased to £25,000 (SI 2006/963 reg 4). This will have the effect, for most claimants, of making the relevant income for tax credits the lower of the income of the preceding year, or, the income of the current year, ie for a 2006/07 claim (assuming income has not increased by more than £25,000 when comparing 2005/06 income with 2006/07 income) the award is based on the lower of the income for 2005/06 or 2006/07.

Because claims have to be made within three months of the commencement of the year, to prevent loss of credits, protective claims are necessary for any claimants who think that their income for the current year could be low enough to make them qualify. Claims should be made by 6 July in the tax year. This could apply to claimants with:

(i)   children,

(ii)   self-employed income, or

(iii)   employment where income may significantly reduce within the fiscal year.

For some awards the amount of credits will be constant, providing income falls between certain bands (this will apply to many entitled to the 'family element' of CTC only). For this type of award a claimant will receive on automatic renewal pack at the year-end and the claim will continue. Any changes of circumstances, or income falling outside the levels set out in the pack, must be notified to HMRC by 31 August.

The claim must be made at the time that eligibility arises; an award can only be backdated up to three months prior to the date of submitting a completed claim. Thus to claim tax credits for 2006/07 in full a claim must be made by 6 July 2006. If, for example, a claim was submitted on 2 August 2006 then the award period would commence on 2 May 2006 and only 340 days of credits would be payable for 2006/07.

An award in payment at 5 April 2006 will continue to be paid until the renewal pack is returned, or 31 August if earlier. Any alteration to existing claims will be backdated to 6 April provided the information is provided by 31 January.

If the forms are not returned by 31 August then tax credit payments will cease.

If the forms are not returned by 31 January then increased claims based on the renewal information will only be backdated three months. Furthermore HMRC will institute proceedings to recover tax credit payments made between 6 April and 31 August.

All other claimants will file details of income at the year-end. This will be used to correct the claim to 'actual' and also form the basis of claim for the following year. A return will be required by 31 August 2006 for 2005/06 (30 September 2005 for 2004/05). If income is not known at that time an estimate should be used with the return being corrected by the following 31 January ie in the above example by 31 January 2007.

Any underpaid credit will be paid to the claimant and any overpaid amount is recovered by HMRC. In computing overpayments, the first £25,000 (£2,500 for years up to 5 April 2006) increase in income between the preceding year and the current year is ignored.

Eligibility for tax credits are set out below.

(i)   *Working Tax Credit (WTC)*

A person is entitled to Working Tax Credit if they are working at the date of claim, or will commence work within seven days and are:

– aged at least 16, and working for not less than 16 hours per week and have a child for whom he or his partner is responsible, or

– aged at least 16, working for not less than 16 hours per week, and have a disability that puts him at a disadvantage in getting a job and satisfy either the 'qualifying benefit test' or the special 'fast-track' rules to qualify for a disability element, or

– aged at least 25, and working not less than 30 hours per week, or

– aged at least 50, returning to work on or after 6 April 2003 after qualifying for certain out-of-work benefits for at least the previous six months and working not less than 16 hours per week.

Work must be expected to continue for at least four weeks, and must be for payment.

In arriving at hours normally worked customary or paid holiday and unpaid time allowed for meals, etc is disregarded.

A person is treated as engaged in qualifying remunerative work for any period during which they are on statutory maternity, paternity or adoption leave providing that they were in qualifying work before they went on leave. This also applies to the self-employed providing that they would have qualified for statutory maternity, paternity or adoption leave if they had been an employee. Any additional non-statutory leave does not count as a period in work eg unpaid additional maternity leave.

In the same way, a person is treated as being in qualifying remunerative work if they are receiving Statutory Sick Pay or various other benefits because of illness. This provision is also applied to the self-employed as appropriate.

The disability element of WTC is paid if the claimant has a physical or mental disability which puts them at a disadvantage in getting a job, eg seeing, hearing, communicating with people, mobility, mental disability, or exhaustion and pain, and satisfies the 'qualifying benefit' test or the special 'fast-track' rules.

There are three 'qualifying benefit' tests. Either the claimant is receiving one of the following:

– Disability Living Allowance

– Attendance Allowance

- Industrial Injuries Disablement Benefit with Constant Attendance Allowance (CAA)

- War Disablement Pension with CAA or Mobility Supplement

- A vehicle provided under the Invalid Vehicle Scheme

or they must have received one of the following in the previous six months:

- Incapacity Benefit at the short-term higher rate or the long-term rate

- Income based Jobseeker's Allowance*

- Income Support*

- Severe Disablement Allowance

- Council Tax Benefit*

- Housing Benefit*

* This must include a Disability Premium or a Higher Pensioner Premium

or they have been training for work in the last eight weeks following a period of receiving certain disability benefits.

There is also a set of fast-track rules for those who are finding it hard to stay in work because of a disability. They allow a claimant to qualify for the disability element earlier than under the 'qualifying benefit' tests above.

The Severe Disability element is payable if the claimant is entitled to a Disability Living Allowance (Highest Care Component) or Attendance Allowance (Higher Rate).

For more detail on all these disability elements see *WTC2 Child Tax Credit and Working Tax Credit A Guide* or SI 2002/2005 regs 9 and 17 (as amended).

All WTC payments are made by HMRC directly to the claimant.

The annual income threshold is £5,220 (£5,060 for 2003/04 and 2004/05) with credits being reduced by 37p for every £ of income over the threshold. The credits available for 2006/07 are shown in the rates and allowances on page (v).

(ii)   *Childcare element of WTC*

A claimant is entitled to claim for childcare if they are eligible for WTC even if, because of the 37% tapering, the amount payable is nil. The claimant(s) must have one or more children and pay for registered or approved childcare. The childcare element is 80% (2005/06 70%) of the amount payable with a maximum cost of £175 per week for one child or £300 per week for two or more children. If the claim is by a couple both partners must work at least 16 hours unless one partner is incapacitated or is an in-patient at a hospital or is in prison.

Payment of this element of WTC is made to the main carer with the Child Tax Credit (CTC).

Approved care is care provided for a child by a registered childminder or an accredited organisation. Childcare can be claimed until the Saturday following the 1 September following a child's 15th birthday, or a further year if the child is disabled.

To compute the average weekly childcare costs one of the following methods is used depending on the method of payment:

If the charges are for a fixed weekly amount take the weekly amount for the last four weeks and divide by 4;

If the charges are for a fixed monthly amount multiply that amount by 12 and divide by 52;

If the charges vary take the amount paid in the last 52 weeks (or the last 12 months) and divide by 52;

If childcare costs have not yet commenced, or have started in the last 52 weeks then an estimate of the costs for the next 52 weeks (divided by 52) is used.

If payment of childcare is expected to last for less than 52 weeks then the estimated total is divided by the expected weeks of provision.

If costs decrease for at least four weeks in a row by £10 per week or more, or childcare ceases, then notification of this change in circumstance is required within three months (one month from April 2007). The method of calculation of the new average weekly cost is determined by the original method used. If that was the same amount paid weekly then the new average weekly cost is the amount to be paid in the next four weeks divided by 4. In all other cases the new average weekly cost is the estimated amount payable over the next 52 weeks divided by 52 (use the expected number of weeks of payment in both places in the above calculation if provision is for less than 52 weeks).

If one of the claimants is on statutory maternity, paternity or adoption leave they are still treated as being in work for the purposes of having qualifying childcare costs, but only in respect of any existing children of the family for whom they incur childcare costs. They cannot claim childcare for the new child.

Approved child care means care provided by:

- registered childminders, nurseries and play schemes

- out-of-hours clubs on school premises run by a school or a local authority

- childcare schemes run by school governing bodies under the 'extended schools' scheme

- childcare schemes run by approved providers

- in England and Scotland certain approved childcare provided in the claimants' home.

A claim cannot be made for childcare provided in the claimants' home by a relative, or for the child's education.

With effect from 6 April 2005 where childcare is provided in the home of a relative then that relative must also provide care to children who are not related. Thus a relative (eg aunt or grandparent) will not normally be able to qualify for looking after the relative's child in their own home even if they are an approved childcare provider. In order to make a claim the relative would also need to look after a non-related child. (SI 2005/93).

(iii)   *Child Tax Credit (CTC)*

CTC brings together most of the previously available support for families with children, including the child element of Income Support, Jobseeker's Allowance, WFTC, DPTC and the Children's Tax Credit including the Baby Rate. CTC is paid directly to the main carer, usually the mother.

In order to claim CTC it is necessary to be responsible for a child or qualifying young person.

A child is a person who has not attained the age of 16 and they remain a child for tax credit purposes until immediately before the 1 September following their 16th birthday.

A qualifying young person is a person aged under 20 (19 until 5 April 2006) who is either in full-time non-advanced education or is under 18, has ceased full-time education, and has registered for work or training with the Careers Service, Connexions Service or the Department of Employment and Learning. CTC continues for a further 20 weeks after he ceases full-time education.

If a child or young person dies the entitlement ceases eight weeks following death (but not beyond the date when the qualifying young person would have reached age 20).

If the child or qualifying young person has a child of their own, only one claim for CTC can be made in respect of that newborn child. If the intermediate parent is under 16 then the grandparents would claim for both 'children' as no claim by the intermediate parent would be possible. If the intermediate parent was 16 or over then the claim could be made by the parent and the grandparent would not then be able to claim for their 'young person'. This would require the intermediate parent to be supporting the child however. If that was not the case then the grandparent could continue to claim for both providing that the intermediate parent still qualified as a young person.

Being responsible for a child (or qualifying young person) means that the child must normally live with the claimant. If the child lives with more than one potential claimant(s), the claim is to be made by the person or couple having 'main responsibility' for the child. Parties can jointly elect which of them satisfies the main responsibility test. In the absence of such an agreement HMRC make the decision and in order to do so they will ask questions to discover:

–   which address does the child give as a contact address, or for mail

–   where the child spends most nights, goes to after school

–   who keeps clothes/toys/belongings

–   who buys their clothes, food, underwear, provides pocket money

–   which is the registered address for healthcare, social worker, health visitor

–   whether there are any court orders determining responsibility.

The various elements of CTC, available for 2006/07, are shown in the rates and allowances on page (vi). Most of the credits are tapered in the same way as they are for WTC, ie a reduction of 37p for every £ of income over the threshold. If the claimant is also entitled to WTC the threshold remains at £5,220 (£5,060 for 2004/05). Taper will reduce WTC (excluding childcare) before CTC. It then reduces childcare and finally CTC. If the claimant is only entitled to CTC, eg the claimant is not working, or is a student or student nurse, the threshold is £14,155 (£13,910 for 2005/06).

The family element of CTC is tapered last and at a different rate. The full £545 pa (or £1,090 for the 12 months after birth) is payable until income exceeds the higher of income at which the 37% taper ceases (see table at note 7 below), or the second threshold of £50,000 pa. At which point family element is tapered away at the rate of £1 for every £15 of further income, a withdrawal rate of 6.67%. This gives a cut off point of around £58,000 or £66,000 in year of birth. (These thresholds can alter if there are more than two children and maximum childcare costs and/or disability elements in the claim.)

Child Tax Credit is paid in addition to Child Benefit of £17.45 per week for the first child and £11.70 per week for every other child. For a lone parent the first child rate is increased to £17.55 per week.

Claimants in receipt of income support or income based jobseeker's allowance are automatically entitled to the maximum amount of WTC and CTC (TCA 2002 s 7 and SI 2002/2008 reg 4).

Claimants in receipt of pension credit who are also responsible for a child will be entitled to the full amount without the taper provisions applying (SI 2003/2170).

(b)   *Income for tax credits*

Income for tax credits is computed for the claimant, or joint claimants, for the fiscal year. The amounts to include or exclude are set out in SI 2002/2006 as amended. The legislation requires the income to be computed in the following manner.

Step 1

Add together

–   Pension Income

–   Investment Income, including Chargeable Event Gains (before top-slicing relief)

–   Property Income

–   Foreign Income

–   Notional Income

If the result is £300 or less, treat as nil. If the result is more than £300 only the excess is included. The £300 applies on a per claim basis ie the income of a couple is added together and the £300 deducted from the sum.

Step 2

Add together

–   Employment Income

–   Social Security Income

–   Student Income (ie certain student dependant grants)

–   Miscellaneous Income.

Step 3

–   Add together Steps 1 and 2.

Step 4

Add trading income to Step 3 or deduct a trading loss of the year from Step 3. This could be the trading loss of a partner.

From the above is deducted

–   Gift Aid payments (gross)

–   Pension payments (gross).

Where a Gift Aid contribution is carried back by election, then it is deductible for tax credits in the fiscal year of payment.

Employment Income

Employment income means:

–   Any earnings received in the tax year, including any money's worth (see below)

–   Any expense payment chargeable to income tax

–   Any non-cash voucher, credit token or cash voucher, chargeable to income tax (excluding childcare vouchers)

–   Any termination payment chargeable to income tax

- Any SSP

- Any SMP, SPP or SAP to the extent that it exceeds £100 per week per person (note the rate of SMP for 2006/07 is £108.85 per week)

- Benefit in kind on cars and car fuel and the taxable part of any mileage allowances

- Any amount subject to tax by ITEPA 2003 s 225 (restrictive undertakings)

- Any strike pay.

The definition appears to exclude all other taxable benefits in kind but those earning £8,500 or more are taxed on the full cost of any assets transferred to them rather than on the second-hand value so that the figures returned on the P11D are used.

Employment income does not include:

- Pension income

- Qualifying removal expenses (under £8,000)

- Payments covered by most ITEPA 2003 expenses claims (travelling costs, professional fees etc)

- Items covered by specific concessions eg staff suggestion schemes

- Deemed earnings under IR 35

- Employer provided childcare vouchers.

From employment income may be deducted:

- Travel expenses

- Fees and subscriptions to professional bodies

- Employee liability insurance

- Entertainers expenses

- Fixed sum deductions

- Personal security assets and services

- Give As You Earn donations

- Allowable expense claims

- Allowable claims for mileage allowance relief (ie where the employer has paid less than the mileage allowance rates).

Pension Income

This includes pensions paid by

- The Crown

- Annuities under a Retirement Benefit Scheme, Superannuation Scheme, etc, Unapproved Pension Payments.

- Lump sums payable where state pension has been deferred.

- Taxable lump sums arising from commutation of trivial pension policies.

Trading Income

This is the profit or loss for the year disregarding averaging.

Student Income

This means any grant under the Education (Student Support) Regulations 2002 other than

– A grant for a dependent child,

– A grant for books, travel or equipment.

Investment Income

This is investment income as calculated for income tax but without top-slicing relief for chargeable events.

Property Income

This is as for income tax (ie excluding non-taxable rent a room income). It is the amount chargeable to tax ie after deduction of losses brought forward (box 5.47 on SA tax return).

Foreign Income

This means income arising outside the UK which is **not**

– Employment income

– Trading income

– Investment income.

Foreign income is computed on an income arising basis whether or not remitted. The 10% relief for certain foreign pensions is given.

Foreign income includes any income arising or income that has been excluded from UK liability by a double taxation agreement.

Notional Income

Notional income means income, which a claimant is treated as having, but which he does not in fact receive.

This includes amounts treated as income under ITTOIA 2005, including:

–	s 277	Premium on rent
–	s 409	Stock dividends
–	s 415	Release of a loan to a participator by a close company
–	s 624	Income rising under a settlement where the settlor retains an interest
–	s 629	Payments to unmarried minor children of the settlor
–	s 633	Sums paid to settlor otherwise than as income
–	s 652	Income from the residue on an estate
–	TA 1988 ss 714 & 716	Accrued income scheme
–	FA 2004 s 84 & Sch 15	Benefit charge on pre-owned assets

If a claimant has deprived himself of income for the purpose of securing entitlement to, or increasing the amount of, a tax credit he is treated as having that income. This could include dividends not received because of a dividend waiver.

If income would become available to a claimant upon making an application for that income he is treated as having that income.

If a claimant provides a service for less than full value to another person who could afford to pay, then trading income or employment income is deemed to include the full value. This does not apply where the claimant is a volunteer, or is engaged to provide the service by a charitable or voluntary organisation and the Board are satisfied that it is reasonable for the claimant to provide the service free of charge.

Miscellaneous Income

This includes any other income chargeable not already included above, such as an amount taxable on change of accounting basis (including UITF 40).

(c)   *Changes in circumstances*

The tax credits rules require a claimant to notify within three months (one month from April 2007) any changes in

(i)   the claiming unit (eg starting to live with a partner or separating from a partner), including being part of a same-sex unit from 5 December 2005,

(ii)   childcare payments where certain reductions in payments occur, or

(iii)   ceasing to be 'in the UK' (see explanatory note 4).

From November 2006 a claimant is also required to notify

(iv)   changes in hours worked where the level decreases below 30, or 16 hours per week,

(v)   changes in the number of children eligible for the tax credits within the claiming unit.

Failure to notify can result in a penalty not exceeding £300.

Other changes in circumstances, which would result in an increase in credits, should be notified within three months because the entitlement to the new element of the claim can only be backdated for three months.

Changes which have to be notified, and which carry the potential £300 penalty, are:

– Date of marriage (if claiming as a single person)

– Date of commencement to live as a couple

– Date ceased to live as a couple (including death)

– Decrease in childcare payments to nil or by £10 a week or more

– Claimant leaves the UK for 8 weeks or more at the beginning of a temporary absence of 52 weeks or less (the period is extended to 12 weeks in circumstances of illness or bereavement)

– Claimant leaves the UK for a period which will be more than 52 weeks

– Partner of claimant returns to the UK after period of absence during which they were treated as not being 'in the UK' (see explanatory note 4 for more detail on these 'residence rules').

– Birth or Death of a child

– Change in the 'main responsibility' for a child

– Child ceases full-time education after 1 September following their 16th birthday

– Changes to the number of working hours.

Other changes in circumstances which should be notified at some time are:

– Increase in childcare of £10 a week or more lasting four weeks in a row

– Changes to entitlement to disability elements

It is also obviously useful to tell HMRC about changes of employer, address, bank account or childcare provider.

Changes in income can be notified in year, or at the year-end. If there is an increase in excess of £25,000 pa over the income of the previous year the tax credit award will be recalculated and an overpayment of tax credits may have to be returned to HMRC.

If income decreases then it is advisable to notify the reduction to HMRC. This will increase the tax credits award. From April 2007 the recalculated daily rate will be paid from the date of notification, but the increase from the previous 6 April to date of notification will not be paid until the final award notice is issued after notification of actual income for the year.

Tax Credits interact with Housing Benefit and Council Tax benefits, so it is necessary to notify the Local Authority of any change in the level of award.

(d) *Award periods and relevant periods*

An award period is normally a fiscal year, however if eligibility first arises in the year, eg on birth of first child, it is the period from the date of eligibility (or three months before date of claim if later) to the end of the fiscal year. If eligibility ceases before the end of the year then the award period ceases on that day.

Within the award period each day is considered separately, however all days with the same entitlement are aggregated and that period is known as a 'relevant period'.

In all instances the average income of the year of claim is used. This is normally the lower of the income for the fiscal year, or, for the preceding fiscal year, as computed for Tax Credits, divided by the number of days in the year and multiplied by the number of days in the relevant period to give the income for the relevant period.

The same principle is used to calculate the maximum award for a relevant period although the childcare credit rules are slightly different to allow for the fact that there are weekly, rather than daily, maxima.

(e) *Year-end procedures*

A claimant is required to provide such information as will enable HMRC to confirm the claim made and to continue payments for the following year. In many instances this will only require notification if the income of the family unit was not within certain limits.

Where a recomputation applies the renewal information will require a declaration of actual income by 31 August. If actual income is not known estimates must be provided and the form marked to show an estimate has been used. The actual figures must be filed by 31 January following.

If income has reduced and additional tax credits are due the amount will be paid directly to the claimants.

If income has increased by £25,000 (£2,500 for 2005/06 and earlier years) or less no adjustment will be made to the income part of the claim for the year under review. The increased income will be used in recomputing the provisional award for the following year, ie the award now being paid.

If income has increased by more than £25,000 the excess over £25,000 is taken into account resulting in an overpayment of credits at the rate of 37% of the excess (or, if a claim for family element only, 6.67%). The excess payments will be recovered from future tax credit awards wherever possible (see note 6). Otherwise direct payment will be required. The amount is recovered as tax and is due within 30 days of the notice. On application overpayments may be repaid by 12 monthly instalments without interest. TCA 2002 s 37 provides for interest to be charged on overpayments of tax credits but only where the overpayment is attributable to the fraud or neglect of any person. In cases of hardship application may be made to arrange for repayment of the overpayment over a period in excess of 12 months.

TCA 2002 s 29(5) also provides for overpayments to be recovered through the PAYE system but currently HMRC are unable to use this provision.

In the case of a joint claim, both members of the family unit are required to sign claim forms and both have to repay any excess ie there is a joint and several liability (TCA 2002 s 28(4)).

B.(a)   **Brian and Angela Smith – Tax Credits Claim 2006/07**

Initial award based on 2005/06 income

Award period

Date of renewal claim	–	30 July 2005
Date of eligibility (made prior to 30 September)	–	6 April 2005
Renewal pack returned	–	6 July 2006

Award period 6 April 2006 to 5 April 2007   (365 days)
Relevant period – initially the whole year   (365 days)

Initial eligibility

WTC	–	Yes both work full time
Childcare	–	Yes
CTC	–	Yes for one child (not under one)
Family element	–	Yes

Income

	£	£
Investment income		
Brian	180	
Angela	520	
	700	
Less:	300	400
Self-employment		
Brian	18,810	
Less: Personal pension ($£1,560 \times \dfrac{100}{78}$)	2,000	16,810
Employment		
Angela – P60	22,000	
Car	2,160	
	24,160	
Less: Gift Aid ($£468 \times \dfrac{100}{78}$)	600	23,560
Base income on PY basis for 2006/07		40,770

Maximum claim (per day)

	£		
WTC – Basic	4.56		
Second adult	4.49		
30 hours	1.86		
CTC – One child	4.84		
– Family element	1.50		
Relevant period = 365 days ×	17.25	=	6,296
Childcare, £165 × 80% × 52			6,864
			13,160

Restricted by			
Income	40,770		
Income threshold	5,220		
37% ×	35,550	=	13,153
But not below Family element 365 × 1.50		=	£545

Payable at the rate of £10.50 pw (£42.00 per 4 week) to Angela

Award revised to actual, calculation of final award

Award period 6 April 2006 to 5 April 2007 (365 days)

Relevant periods

Changes   –   Childcare from 5 January 2007, but not notified
              until 5 May 2007, therefore increase claim from
              5 February 2007
          –   Birth of Colin – 1 March 2007 (notified 5 May
              2007 ie within 3 months)

6 April 2006 to 4 February 2007	305 days
5 February 2007 to 28 February 2007	24 days
1 March 2007 to 5 April 2007	36 days

Income

	£	£	£
Investment income			
Brian	20		
Angela	140		
	160		
Less: £300 restricted to	160		–
Employment			
Angela – P60	16,100		
Less: SMP 10 weeks @ £100	1,000		
	15,100		
Car	2,160		17,260
Less: Trading loss		2,800	
Personal pension		2,000	
Gift Aid		600	5,400
Income for tax credits 2006/07			11,860

	6/4/06 – 4/2/07	5/2/07 – 28/2/07	1/3/07 – 5/4/07
Maximum claim (per day)			
	£	£	£
WTC – Basic	4.56	4.56	4.56
Second adult	4.49	4.49	4.49
30 hours	1.86	1.86	1.86
CTC – Child	4.84	4.84	9.68
– Family element	1.50	1.50	2.99
	17.25	17.25	23.58
× days in relevant period	305	24	36
	£	£	£
	5,261	414	849
Childcare (per relevant period):			
£165 × 52 × 305/365 × 80%	5,736		
£175/7 = £25 × 24 × 80%		480	
£175/7 = £25 × 36 × 80%			720
Maximum credits due	£13,460	10,997	894	1,569

		£	£	£
Restricted by				
Income £11,860		9,910	780	1,170
Threshold £5,220		4,362	343	515
		5,548	437	655
× 37%	£2,457	2,053	162	242

Payment of claim (calculation of under payment)

– *As WTC to worker*

	£
Maximum	
(4.56 + 4.49 + 1.86) × 365	3,982
Less restriction	2,457
To Brian or Angela per claim	1,525

– *As WTC and CTC to carer*

	£
Balance of TC (13,460 – 3,982)	9,478
Paid in year	545
Payable to Angela	8,933

Angela and Brian's initial award for 2007/08 will be based on 2006/07 income and their circumstances at the time of renewal. It will be necessary to know whether Angela is going back to work after her period of statutory maternity leave because this will determine whether the couple can continue to claim the childcare element. If she does return to work, and incurs childcare costs for both children, a different maximum of £300 per week will apply. The higher family element of £1,090, £2.99 per day, will be payable up to 28 February 2008. If Brian believes that he will make a profit in the year to 31 December 2007 of a similar level, to year ending 31 December 2005 then it would be advisable to notify HMRC of the increased earning levels so that an overpayment does not arise from 6 April 2008.

(b) **Revised Income 2006/07**

	£	£
Investment income – as above		–
Employment – as above	17,260	
Less: Gift Aid (600)	600	16,660
Self-employment	35,000	
Less: Personal pension	2,000	33,000
		49,660
Original income		40,770
As increase is less than £25,000 – ignore		8,890

Claim is recomputed using the actual circumstances of the year but still using the income figure of £40,770.

Maximum claim	6/4/06 – 4/2/07	5/2/07 – 28/2/07	1/3/07 – 5/4/07
As above:	£	£	£
Maximum credits due £13,460	10,997	894	1,569
Income: £40,770	34,068	2,681	4,021
Threshold	4,362	343	515
	29,706	2,338	3,506
× 37%	10,991	865	1,297

Credits due:
Family element only
£1.50 per day   £457 (x 305)   £36 (x 24)
Family element £2.99 per day (x 36)
£107, but actual credits greater
£1,569 less £1,297   £272

Total credits due £765 (457 + 36 + 272), less paid in year £545 = £220 payable to Angela (representing increased family element and some child element payable because of the increased childcare costs).

Explanatory Notes

Eligibility

1. The above sets out the main criteria for eligibility. Reference should be made to 'WTC2 – Child Tax Credit and Working Tax Credit' a Revenue booklet which sets out the rules for eligibility in detail with more information on childcare, disability, severe disability and fast track claims. Help can also be obtained from the Helpline on 0845 300 3900 or 0845 603 2000 (Northern Ireland).

Claims

2. Agents must file a Form 64-8 (New Version) signed by each of the claimants in order to receive information about tax credits from HMRC. Copies of claim forms can be obtained from 01772 235 623.

Trading Losses

3. If a taxpayer suffers a trading loss then *three* separate loss claims will be required ie:

   (a) Income Tax – Claim under s 380 or s 381 or s 385 or s 386 or s 388 or against gains under FA 1991 s 72 (see Examples 30–33).

   (b) Class 4 NIC – Claim against income liable to Class 4 only (SSCBA 1992 Sch 2.3(4)) (see Example 47.5).

   (c) Tax Credits – Claim against income of the *couple* or single claimant for year of loss only (SI 2002/2006 reg 3(1)). Any amount not used in this way may be deductible from trading income from the same source of the claimant in subsequent years. Uncommercial losses are not relievable.

Separate schedules will be needed to compute the carried forward amount for each claim.

In the case of tax credits the surplus loss of 2001/02 was carried forward to 2003/04. In subsequent years the surplus loss is used against the next available profits of the same source. A loss of 2002/03 cannot be used in a tax credit claim.

It is not clear how to compute the loss carryforward where the taxpayer with the loss has had more than one relevant period within the year. It is thought that the loss is restricted by the relevant days of the claims made. Where a loss claim (or gift aid or pension claim) is made a form TC 825 is completed and filed with HMRC. In circumstances where a couple have parted HMRC will notify the loss to be used in future years, eg Alan lived with Beth until 30 July 2006. They parted, and on 6 February 2007 he moved in with Carol. In 2006/07 Alan had a loss of £14,000. Beth's income (for tax credits) is £17,000 and Carol £10,000.

The income calculation is always for the full fiscal year.

	Alan & Beth £	Alan £	Alan & Carol £	
Alan	Nil	Nil	Nil	
Partner	17,000		10,000	
Less: Loss	14,000	–	10,000	
	3,000		Nil	
Days in relevant period	116	190	59	
Loss used				
(116/365 × 14,000)	4,448	Nil		
(59/365 × 10,000)			1,616	
Loss for year				14,000
Used re Alan and Beth			4,448	
re Alan			Nil	
re Alan and Carol			1,616	6,064
Loss to carry forward				7,936

Loss claims should be made after claims for Gift Aid or pension payments as any excess loss can be carried forward.

Being 'in the UK' and Temporary Absences

4.   When computing *income* for tax credits the income tax definitions of Resident, Ordinarily Resident and Domicile are used although this is not of much practical relevance since virtually all worldwide income counts for tax credit purposes.

When considering entitlement (ie whether someone can claim tax credits) different rules are relevant.

TCA 2002 s 3(3) requires the claimant(s) to be 'in the UK'. This requires physical presence in the UK on the days of entitlement.

The Tax Credits Residence Regulations (SI 2003/654) state that a person shall not be treated as being 'in the UK' if they are not ordinarily resident here, although this does not apply to a Crown servant posted overseas or his partner. Certain EC workers are treated as being ordinarily resident, as are certain persons in the UK as a result of compulsion by law. CTC is a family benefit under EC law and some claimants will qualify regardless of the requirements of these regulations.

Persons who are ordinarily resident for tax credit purposes (see HMRC Manual at TCTM 02003 as to what ordinary residence means for tax credit purposes) can also be treated as being 'in the UK' for certain periods of temporary absence. This is an absence which is not expected to be for more than 52 weeks in total. In this situation the first 8 weeks of absence are ignored. This is extended to 12 weeks if the absence or continued absence is due to the illness of the claimant or the illness/death of his partner, or his or his partner's child or qualifying young person, or a close relative of his or his partner.

It follows that if a claimant, who is part of a couple, works abroad for a temporary period, then for the first 8 weeks they will still be treated as a couple and a joint tax credit claim will be available. After 8 weeks the partner in the UK must notify the absence of the other (within three months) and the partner remaining in the UK will become a single claimant. This *may* increase the claim as only the UK partner's income will be counted. (If there are no children the claimant remaining in the UK would lose the couple's element of WTC assuming that they were working themselves and therefore entitled to WTC.)

Unfortunately the provision that deems a person as being resident for up to 8 or 12 weeks of absence does not also deem them to be working in the UK. This means that a parent remaining in the UK with children will lose their entitlement to claim childcare credits during that period. This is because the tax credits claim is by a couple, but one member (the parent overseas) is not working in the UK.

On the return of the overseas worker a further notification will be required (within three months) and the claim must revert to a joint claim. If the claimant was not part of a couple the only notification which has to be made is their own lengthy or permanent departure from the UK. When the individual returns to the UK they will have a choice as to whether they make a new claim to tax credits. They will obviously have to do so within three months of qualifying in order to get the maximum entitlement.

Penalties

5.   There is a penalty for fraudulently or negligently making incorrect statements etc in connection with tax credit claims, or notifications of changes in circumstances, limited to a maximum of £3,000 per offence.

There is a maximum penalty of £300 initially and £60 per day thereafter for failure to provide information when required.

There is a separate penalty for failure to notify certain changes in circumstances within three months (one month from April 2007):

–   Changes in the claiming unit (eg starting to live with a partner or separation), or ceasing to be 'in the UK'.

–   Falls in childcare costs to nil or by £10 per week or more for four or more weeks.

–   Ceasing to be 'in the UK'.

–   Changes in hours worked (decrease below 30 or 16).*

–   Changes in eligible children.*

(*Apply from November 2006).

Any changes in income arising from an enquiry for income tax may have a corresponding effect upon a claim for tax credits. In the same way any agreed alteration of income for tax credits may affect income tax and possibly national insurance.

Overpayments

6.   Where HMRC become aware of an overpayment in a year, eg notification of change in circumstances or increase in income, they will automatically recover the amount from the tax credits due to be paid for the remainder of the year. If this causes hardship then the claimant may apply for a top-up payment, however, such amounts will be recovered by becoming an overpayment at the year-end.

To determine 'hardship', HMRC will use the same maximum deduction rates as for year-end recoveries.

For year-end overpayments and, from April 2006, in-year overpayments, the maximum deduction from future awards of tax credits will be:

If claiming maximum WTC/CTC   –   10% of current tax credit award
If claiming family element of CTC only –   100% of current tax credit award
In all other cases   –   25% of current tax credit award.

In the first instance the restriction applies to a tax credits award of the same type. Therefore if the overpayment is WTC the maximum recoverable will be 10% (or 25%) of the WTC payable only. If no WTC is payable for the year then the restriction applies to CTC payable in the year.

In exceptional circumstances HMRC will not recover an overpayment. This will be where the overpayment was due to an HMRC mistake and the claimant believed that the award was correct. See Code of Practice 26 for further details.

For joint claims both parties remain liable for overpayments even if they no longer live together. However, HMRC will take into account the circumstances of the individual case in deciding how to take proceedings to recover the overpayment. This can include asking for one former partner to pay all or most of the amount due, or by taking different forms of action against each partner.

Employer provided childcare vouchers

7.   From 6 April 2005 an employer can provide his employees with childcare vouchers to the value of up to £50 per week. From 6 April 2006 the maximum became £55 per week. Such vouchers do not count as income for tax credits and are not liable to income tax or national insurance. (See Example 10 Explanatory Note 24 for the conditions attached to the vouchers in order to obtain tax free status.)

Care must be taken when claiming tax credit childcare to ensure that the amount of childcare claimed is net of the cost covered by such vouchers.

Although this would appear a generous tax-free perk, in fact in most cases where 37% taper applies no benefit will arise as most employers will restrict salary by an amount equal to the tax-free voucher provided. The adverse effect on net income being per week

	£	£	£
Before voucher			
Childcare		55	
Covered by tax credits – 80%		44	
Net cost (from net pay)			11.00
With Voucher			
Childcare £55 – £55 voucher		Nil	
Loss of salary		(55.00)	
Net of Tax @ 22%	12.10		
NI @ 11%	6.05	18.15	
		36.85	
Less increase in tax credits			
£55 (reduction in income) @ 37%		20.35	16.80
Difference in net income – Loss			(5.50)

In the same way a claimant with a 10% tax rate would be better off receiving salary than a voucher.

However, in the first year of change there is a further complication of the £25,000 income disregard. If the employee had the choice between a £55 per week rise or a £55 per week tax-free childcare voucher and tax rates were as above then it would cost the employee £1,344 to take the voucher. This is because the taper would not apply to the increase in pay assuming that the family unit had no other alteration in income.

	£	£	£
Increase in salary		2,860	
Less Tax @ 22%	629		
NI @ 11%	315	944	
		1,916	
Increase in income less than £25,000 – no clawback			
Childcare costs		2,860	
Tax credits 80%		2,288	572
Net increase in pay			1,344

	£	£	£
Compared with			
Childcare voucher		2,860	
Childcare costs		2,860	Nil

At maximum childcare costs, 37% taper applies until a couple's income is as below:

No of Children	1	2	3	4	5
2005/06	37,476	54,342	58,909	63,422	68,409
2006/07	40,436	59,260	64,030	68,800	73,570

Enquiries

8. For interaction of tax credits and self-assessment see Example 45.

Other examples showing tax credits

9. For further examples of tax credits see

Example 2	–	Restriction of family element
Example 3(d)	–	Year of death
Example 4(a)	–	Use of previous year income
Example 8 explanatory note 13	–	Absence from UK
Example 9	–	Employers and WTC
Example 10	–	Benefits
Example 29	–	Trading losses
Example 30	–	Opening years – choice of accounting period
Example 33	–	Averaging claims
Example 91	–	Charitable giving
Example 95	–	Chargeable event gains

(a) Outline the sources of income chargeable to tax as savings and other income, indicate how income tax is collected and when income tax is deducted at source from such income.

(b) In relation to the information given for each person shown below state the basis of assessment under which the income will be chargeable to UK income tax.

Ignore double taxation relief.

(i) B Nice, who was born in England (as were his parents and grandparents) emigrated to Canada in 1991 when he was twenty-five years of age. On 1 May 2003 he returned to England for an extended holiday to visit relatives and expects to stay for at least five years. In December 2003 he instructed his Canadian bankers to remit his debenture interest from Jackboots (Montreal) Ltd to his temporary London bank account and continue this until further notice. The debentures have been held since 1993.

(ii) M Layber, a Spaniard, has been staying with friends in England for the last five years and has transferred his share of the profits from a Spanish partnership to provide his living expenses.

(iii) Fred Senior now permanently resides in England and is entitled to a pension from his previous employers in Germany. He has not remitted any of his pension during the past five years, during which it was paid into a current account overseas.

(iv) Romeo, who is domiciled, resident and ordinarily resident in the UK, receives interest from a foreign government which is payable through a London paying agent. He also receives dividends from various foreign companies. Both sources of income have been held for many years.

(a) *Income assessable*

Under ITTOIA 2005 part 4 interest and investment income is chargeable to income tax as savings income on the income paid in the fiscal year. This includes

Chapter 2	Interest
Chapter 3	Dividends – UK companies
Chapter 4	Dividends – non-UK companies
Chapter 5	Stock dividends
Chapter 6	Release of a loan to a participator in a close company
Chapter 7	Purchased life annuities
Chapter 8	Profits from deeply discounted securities
Chapter 9	Gains from contracts for life assurance
Chapter 10	Distributions from unauthorised unit-trusts
Chapter 11	Transactions in deposits
Chapter 12	Futures and options
Chapter 13	Sales of foreign dividend coupons

In addition tax is charged as non-savings income by part 5 of ITTOIA 2005 on

Chapter 2	Receipts from intellectual property
Chapter 3	Films and sound recordings
Chapter 4	Telecommunication rights
Chapter 5	Settlements
Chapter 6	Income from estates
Chapter 7	Annual payments
Chapter 8	Income not otherwise charged to tax

Employment income, employment related annuities (retirement annuities) and pensions are chargeable under the Income Tax (Earnings and Pensions) Act 2003 (ITEPA 2003) as non-savings income (see Examples 8–13).

Trading income is charged as non-savings income under ITTOIA 2005 part 2, and property income under ITTOIA 2005 part 3.

The other parts of ITTOIA 2005 deal with

Part 6	Exempt income
Part 7	Rent-a-room and foster carers
Part 8	Special rules for foreign income
Part 9	Partnerships

Tax is chargeable on the sum of income from all sources liable to UK tax subject to allowable deductions and reliefs.

Self-assessment

A taxpayer is required to self assess their personal liability to tax (see Examples 40 and 41). Having computed their liability under self-assessment, subject to certain de minimis limits, provisional payments on account of the income tax on all sources of income are payable half-yearly on 31 January in the tax year and 31 July following, based on the net income tax liability of the previous tax year (after deducting PAYE tax and tax at source). The payments on account and the amounts of tax deducted at source and under PAYE are compared with the final income tax and capital gains tax liability for the tax year, and a balancing payment is made or repayment claimed on or before the following 31 January (see Example 40).

The rate of tax on income up to the basic rate limit (currently £33,300) is 22% on non-savings income, 20% on savings income other than dividends and 10% on dividends, the rates applicable to income above that limit being 40% and 32½% on dividend income. These rates apply to both UK and foreign savings income, except for any foreign income that is taxed on a remittances basis, to which the non-savings tax rates apply.

Deduction of tax at source

Tax is deducted at source from many sources of savings and other income, the rate of tax deducted from interest being the lower rate of 20% and the rate of tax deducted from patent royalties and annual payments being the basic rate of 22%. Tax is not deducted at source from most National Savings interest (see explanatory note 5). Nor is tax deducted from interest, patent royalties and annuities paid by a company to another company that the paying company reasonably believes to be liable to corporation tax on the amount received or is an EU company, and payments by and to local authorities. The range of people to whom companies and local authorities may pay such amounts gross includes bodies exempt from tax, such as charities, pension funds, and those managing ISAs, TESSAs and PEPs (TA 1988 ss 349A–349D). See explanatory note 10 re special provisions for royalty payments by companies to certain recipients entitled to double tax relief. Tax is not deducted at source from copyright royalties unless they are paid to non-residents (see explanatory note 8). Retirement annuities and other employment-related annuities have basic rate tax deducted at source by virtue of ITEPA 2003 Sch 6.50 and 6.51. From 6 April 2007 such annuities will be brought within the PAYE scheme.

From 6 April 1998, interest on all gilt edged securities (other than bearer gilts) acquired on or after that date is paid gross, unless the holder applies to receive it net (TA 1988 s 50(A1)). (Interest on 3½% War Loan is always paid gross.) Those already holding stocks on 6 April 1998 are treated as having applied for net payment, but may apply at any time for gross payment. The provisions for paying interest gross also apply to bearer gilts (TA 1988 s 50(A1)). Many government stocks can be purchased by post, using forms obtainable at a post office or from the Bank of England.

Company debenture interest is paid net of tax except when paid to another company etc as indicated above or where the debenture stock is a listed security (see later in this note). The same applies to interest paid by banks other than the National Savings Bank, or by licensed deposit takers (specified by Treasury order) or building societies, unless it is paid to an individual who can register to receive the interest in full (see below) or the interest comes within a specified exception, the main exceptions being as follows (TA 1988 ss 477A, 480A, 481, 482, SIs 1990/2231, 1990/2232):

(i) Certificates of deposit (including certificates issued in 'paperless' form) and sterling or foreign currency time deposits, providing the loan is not less than £50,000 and is repayable within five years.

(ii) General client deposit accounts with building societies or banks operated by solicitors and estate agents.

(iii) Accounts held at overseas branches of UK and foreign banks and building societies. (See explanatory note 13.)

(iv) Bank and building society accounts and accounts with other deposit holders, where the account holder is not ordinarily resident in the UK and has provided a declaration to that effect (see Example 36 explanatory note 7).

(v) Bank and building society accounts in the names of charities.

(vi) Bank and building society accounts in the names of companies, clubs and societies.

(vii) Accounts held by Individual Savings Account and Personal Equity Plan managers (see Example 93).

(viii) Interest on cash received by a building society in respect of an agreement for the sale and repurchase of securities.

There is a general requirement in TA 1988 s 349(2) to deduct tax at source from interest paid to a non-resident, subject to any express provisions to the contrary. There are such express provisions for certain bank and building society interest (see (iv) above), and exemption from tax is sometimes provided under a double tax agreement. See Example 36 for further details.

Interest on all quoted eurobonds is paid gross to both individuals and companies (TA 1988 s 349). A quoted eurobond is any interest-bearing security issued by a company that is listed on a recognised stock exchange. 'Company' for this purpose includes a building society, so that building society permanent interest-bearing shares (see Example 62 explanatory note 1) are within the definition of eurobond.

Where a taxpayer is not ordinarily resident in the UK (see below) tax is not deducted on UK government stocks. Nor is tax deducted where the recipient is exempt from tax, such as interest paid to UK charities (TA 1988 s 505). TA 1988 s 350A gives HMRC power to make specific regulations relating to the deduction of tax on Government stocks that are not within the gross payment provisions.

Under FA 2005 s 51 returns from alternative finance arrangements are to be treated as interest for the purposes of ITTOIA 2005. This will include returns from arrangements that do not involve the receipt or payment of interest in adherence with Shari'a law. Such agreements and returns are economically equivalent to conventional banking product interest. However, they were not previously taxed as interest. Under this legislation the profit is taxed as savings income.

Registering to receive interest in full

An individual may register to receive bank and building society interest and interest on deposits with local authorities in full if he expects his total taxable income to be below his available allowances (TA 1988 ss 477A & 480B, SIs 1990/2231, 1990/2232). The relevant forms (R85) may be obtained from banks, building societies and local authorities or from tax offices. A separate form is needed for each account. A parent can register the account of a child under 16 if the child's total income will be less than the personal allowance (£5,035 for 2006/07), providing not more than £100 income arises from parental gifts (a separate £100 limit applying to income from gifts from each parent).

The account holder must tell the bank or building society straight away if his circumstances change so that he is no longer eligible to receive interest in full, and he should contact his tax office about any tax he may have to pay. Where tax has been underpaid it is collected either by adjustment to a PAYE coding or in the taxpayer's self-assessment. A penalty of up to £3,000 may be imposed if someone fraudulently or negligently certifies that he is entitled to register to receive interest in full, or if he fails to notify that he is no longer entitled to receive interest in full (TMA 1970 s 99A). HMRC is notified by banks and building societies of amounts of interest credited.

It is not possible to register to receive gross interest on some accounts and not on others, and those who expect to have some taxable income cannot register, even though they will be entitled to a refund. It is, however, possible to claim a refund before the end of the tax year if it amounts to £50 or more. Smaller refunds will only be made after the end of the year.

Interest on late paid debts

Under the Late Payment of Commercial Debts (Interest) Act 1998 statutory interest is payable where payment is delayed on certain contracts for the supply of goods or services. Such interest is not annual interest and is brought into tax as a trading receipt under ITTOIA 2005. The interest is paid gross and will normally be an allowable deduction for trading concerns. Similar tax treatment applies to interest payable under the terms of a trading contract. In the case of a company interest is included in the loan relationships regime. If interest for late payment is received by an individual other than in the course of business then it will be taxable at the savings rate (20%).

Remittance basis

Where a taxpayer is not domiciled in the UK, or not ordinarily resident in the UK, then they may claim to be liable to tax on relevant foreign income on a remittance basis (ITTOIA 2005 s 831). This does not apply to income arising in the Republic of Ireland.

Tax will be due on the full amount received in the UK within the tax year without deductions.

Relevant foreign income is set out in ITTOIA 2005 s 830. It includes income arising from an overseas source such as

–   trading profits

–   property income

–   interest

–   dividends

–   pensions (ITEPA 2003 s 575(3)).

(b)   (i)   **B Nice**

Since it was B Nice's intention to remain in England for at least five years on his return in May 2003, he would have been regarded as resident and ordinarily resident from the date of his return and treated as a new permanent resident. He has a UK domicile of origin which will have been retained unless he acquired a domicile of choice in Canada, but such a change requires a high standard of proof. This will depend partly upon whether B Nice has settled permanently in one particular Canadian province.

His debenture interest from Jackboots (Montreal) Ltd will be assessable in the UK.

If he has retained his UK domicile the basis of assessment will be the full amount of interest arising in the current tax year (whether remitted to the UK or not).

If he had acquired a Canadian domicile, however, he would be charged only on a remittance basis and the source would be treated as acquired when income was first remitted, the assessable income in each tax year being the amount remitted in that year.

The 20% tax rate on non-dividend savings income up to the basic rate threshold applies to savings income from abroad, unless the income is charged on a remittance basis, in which case the tax rates for non-savings income apply.

(ii)   **M Layber**

M Layber is not domiciled in the UK, but he is resident here. He is accordingly chargeable to tax on that part of his Spanish profits that is remitted to the UK, according to the remittances basis rules outlined in (i) above, but the income is non-savings income liable at 22%. The 20% rate would not apply whether or not M Layber was charged on the remittance basis.

(iii)   **Fred Senior**

Fred Senior is resident and ordinarily resident in the UK. If he is also domiciled here he will be charged to tax on his German pension under ITEPA 2003 s 573 whether he remits it to the UK or not, but subject to a deduction of 10% (the basis of assessment being the same as indicated in (i) above). If he is not domiciled in the UK he will not be charged to tax on the pension at all unless it is remitted. If it is remitted, he will be charged on the full amount of the remittance with no percentage deduction according to the rules outlined in (a) above. The 20% tax rate does not apply in any event since the income is not savings income.

(iv)   **Romeo**

Since Romeo is resident, ordinarily resident and domiciled in the UK, the interest will be taxed at 20% and the dividends at 10%, to the extent that his income does not exceed the basic rate limit.

Explanatory Notes

Interest received by companies

1. For companies, all interest payable and receivable, including interest from abroad, is brought into account under loan relationship rules calculating the company's income, together with profits and losses on disposals. The detailed provisions are in Example 62. Tax is not deducted from interest paid by a company to a company within the charge to corporation tax or to certain other recipients, or from interest on listed company securities, as indicated in part (a) of the example.

Maintenance payments

2. Certain maintenance payments between separated and divorced couples used to be charged to tax but from 6 April 2000 all maintenance is exempt from tax.

Basis of assessment

3. Income tax is charged on all amounts computed under ITEPA 2003 and ITTOIA 2005. On interest the amount is the full amount of interest arising in the tax year (ITTOIA 2005 s 370).

4. Interest 'arises' on the date it is received. In the case of a bank account the interest arises when it is credited to the account. For non-corporate taxpayers there are no adjustments to take account of interest that is merely accruing. Different rules apply to companies (see Example 62).

National Savings investments, ISAs and TESSAs

5. National Savings and Investments offer a wide range of investments. Income bonds (including pensioners' guaranteed income bonds) carry interest which is paid without deduction of tax monthly. Capital bonds carry guaranteed interest that is credited gross each year. The interest is accumulated until the bond is cashed in, but tax is charged on the interest when credited. Fixed rate savings bonds pay interest net of tax annually at rates fixed a year at a time, and the bonds can be cashed at any anniversary date without interest penalty. Higher rate taxpayers will have extra tax to pay and those liable at less than the lower rate may claim a refund. National Savings Certificates, which may be fixed-interest or index-linked, carry interest which is accumulated until they are repaid, and the interest is free of all taxation. Premium bonds earn no interest at all, and any prizes are free of all taxation. For children under 16, National Savings Children's Bonus Bonds are available, under which all interest and bonuses are tax-free. For details see Example 2 part (b)(ii) note 2.

6. Interest on the cash component of Individual Savings Accounts (ISAs) and on Tax Exempt Special Savings Accounts (TESSAs) is exempt from tax providing the rules of the schemes are satisfied. For details see Example 93.

Accrued income scheme

7. For sales of interest bearing securities (but not shares), the accrued income provisions of TA 1988 ss 710 to 722 apply. These are illustrated in Example 7.

The accrued income provisions prevent income tax being avoided by selling securities just before an interest payment date, thus receiving the interest as part of the capital proceeds. The rules do not apply if the nominal value of all the securities held by an individual in the tax year in which the next interest payment on the securities falls due or in the previous tax year does not exceed £5,000.

Deduction of tax at source from copyright and patent royalties

8. Where copyright royalties are paid, basic rate tax is not deducted at source unless:

    (a) the owner's usual place of abode is outside the UK (TA 1988 s 536) (and even then, tax is not deducted if the royalties are paid to a non-resident professional author)

    or

    (b) the copyright is held as an investment and the royalties are deemed to be annual payments subject to deduction of tax under TA 1988 ss 348 and 349.

Copyright royalties that are paid in full are a normal trading expense. If they are paid net by individuals they are deducted from total income.

9. The treatment of patent royalties is different from that of copyright royalties, because TA 1988 ss 348 and 349 require that basic rate tax is deducted at source from them (unless they are paid by a company or local authority to another company including an EU company or local authority or to a tax-exempt body as indicated in part (a) of the example). When paid by an individual such payments are deducted from total income.

This does not apply where the payments are for overseas patents unless the royalties are 'pure income profit' in the hands of the receiver. It is common for agreements to provide that the person paying the patent royalties is kept informed of any developments relating to the patent, so that the income would not be 'pure income profit' and tax would not have to be deducted. If the payments were made gross, they would be a normal trading expense.

Treatment of royalties in computing income

10. For companies patents and copyrights are dealt with under the rules for intangible assets, and are brought into account either as trading income or non-trading income. For details see Example 65.

A company paying royalties to a non-resident may pay gross, or deduct tax at a reduced rate according to the provisions of the relevant double tax treaty, if it believes the recipient to be entitled to double tax relief (TA 1988 s 349E). If the company's belief turns out to be incorrect, however, the company will have to account for the tax that should have been deducted, plus interest and possibly penalties.

11. Where copyright royalties are received by individual authors, composers etc, the income is income of their profession. Royalty receipts from purchased copyrights will be intellectual property charged under ITTOIA 2005 s 579.

12. The position of patent royalties received by individuals is similar. Where they are received by the inventor, the receipts are taxed as earned income (TA 1988 s 833(5)(5B)).

Where patents are held as investments, that is they have been purchased then the income is not earned income (TA 1988 s 833(5C)).

Foreign Income

13. Income from abroad is taxed in the UK as illustrated in part (b) of the example. These rules may, however, be affected by double tax agreements, which in many cases provide for the normal statutory rules to be varied.

Non-residents are not liable to tax on foreign income. UK residents who are not domiciled in the UK and citizens who are resident but not ordinarily resident in the UK are charged to tax only when foreign income is brought into the UK, known as the remittance basis.

Other UK residents are charged on the income arising abroad, whether it is remitted or not. If the income is a foreign pension, the taxable amount is only 90% of the amount arising (TA 1988 s 65(2) as applied by ITEPA 2003 s 575(2)). (This also applies to a foreign public service pension taxed under the pension income rules – ITEPA 2003 s 617.) Pensions payable by the governments of Germany and Austria to victims of Nazi persecution are, however, totally exempt from tax (ITEPA 2003 s 642).

Where income that is charged on the 'arising' basis has not been brought into the UK, it is converted into sterling at the exchange rate on the date it arises. Where there are frequent credits, an average exchange rate for the year may be used, using rates published by HMRC, providing the amounts are not materially affected and the averaging basis is adopted consistently.

For detailed notes on the meaning of residence and ordinary residence see Example 8. Someone's country of domicile is broadly the country in which he has his permanent home. Under UK law a child acquires his father's domicile as his domicile of origin at birth, unless he is illegitimate, in which case he acquires his mother's domicile. The domicile of origin may be changed to a domicile of choice, but a very high standard of proof is required to show a change of domicile. Consultation is taking place on possible changes to the law of domicile.

14.   Relief for foreign trading losses is given only against the foreign trading profits (TA 1988 ss 391 & 393).

Foreign rental income of individuals is taxed in broadly the same way as UK rental income, and the same rules apply in general to companies (see Example 98). The 'furnished holiday letting' provisions do not apply to overseas property. Losses on foreign lettings are deducted from total letting income from overseas property, any unrelieved amount being carried forward to set against later overseas letting income.

Relief is available for foreign tax suffered on overseas income taxed in the UK. For details see Example 36.

Foreign partnerships

15.   The partnership business in part (b) (ii) is apparently controlled and carried on abroad. Even so, the profit shares of partners who are resident, ordinarily resident and domiciled in the UK are charged in the UK. For a UK resident partner who, like M Layber, is not domiciled and/or not ordinarily resident in the UK, however, it is only profits earned in the UK that are charged. Profits earned abroad are taxed on the remittances basis, as indicated in part (b) (ii) of the example.

Foreign business profits are not liable to Class 4 national insurance contributions (SSCBA 1992 s 16).

Tax Credits

16.   For tax credits foreign income is computed on an arising basis whether or not remitted or excluded from UK liability by a double taxation agreement. There is an exception for unremittable income (SI 2002/2006 reg 3(3)). The 10% relief for foreign pensions is given (SI 2002/2006 reg 12(3)(b), as amended by SI 2003/732), as are the equivalent exemptions for victims of Nazi persecution, foreign social security payments, and the exemptions in various Extra Statutory Concessions (see Reg 12(3)(c) for further details). It appears that relief for foreign trading losses could be set against total tax credit income of the claimants under Step 4 of Reg 3 (see Example 5(b)) but no relief is available for a loss arising on a property let overseas.

Special withholding tax

17.   Where a UK taxpayer has savings in Austria, Belgium or Luxembourg a special withholding tax may be applied (but not before 1 January 2005). This can be avoided by authorising any paying agent to report information about the income to HMRC authorities or by obtaining a certificate from HMRC. Such a certificate will be valid for up to three years.

If 'special withholding tax' is suffered then full credit will be given against the individual's income tax or capital gains tax liability with any excess being repayable (unless relief has also been obtained in another jurisdiction). Relief will be given for foreign tax before special withholding tax so as to maximise the benefit of double taxation relief.

A.   Briefly set out the basic principles of the Accrued Income Scheme giving details of:

     (a)   securities affected by the scheme;

     (b)   persons affected by the scheme;

     (c)   how the accrued income scheme works.

B.   Interest on 8½% Treasury Stock is paid half yearly on 25 January and 25 July, the stock going ex-dividend on 18 January and 18 July.

     Mr Pinter bought £100,000 nominal stock ex-dividend for settlement on 21 January 2007. He sold the stock cum-dividend for settlement 11 June 2007.

     Show the accrued income adjustments arising from these transactions.

A. The accrued income scheme was originally introduced as an anti-avoidance measure to prevent the process known as 'bond-washing'. 'Bond-washing' was a practice whereby holders of securities (such as government stocks or corporate bonds) would dispose of their stocks immediately prior to the date on which interest became payable. The price obtained for the security included the 'accrued interest' on the stock, but the profit on the security was taxed under the capital gains rules rather than being treated as income (as it would have been had the interest actually been received).

This practice was particularly prevalent at a time when CGT rates were lower than those applying to income tax. It also allowed taxpayers to use capital gains tax exemptions and reliefs against profits which would otherwise have been treated as income.

The accrued income scheme provisions are in TA 1988 ss 710–722. They were brought in to deal with disposals and acquisitions by taxpayers of certain securities and set out how to compute accrued interest on a sale or purchase of stocks and bonds.

(a) *Securities affected by the scheme (TA 1988 s 710)*

The accrued income scheme applies to interest-bearing marketable stocks and bonds including:

- British Government securities ('gilts');

- building society permanent interest bearing shares (PIBS);

- local authority bonds; and

- company debentures and loan stock.

The scheme does not apply to ordinary or preference shares in a company, units in a unit trust, bank deposits or National Savings Certificates.

(b) *Persons affected by the scheme*

The accrued income scheme does not apply to companies (TA 1988 s 710 (1A)). Any profits made by companies on the sale and acquisition of securities are dealt with under the 'loan relationships' rules (see Example 62).

The scheme applies to individuals, trusts and estates. However the vesting of securities in personal representatives on a person's death is not subject to the accrued income scheme provisions (TA 1988 s 710(5)), nor is a transfer to a legatee by the personal representatives in the interest period in which death occurs (TA 1988 s 721(2)).

Individuals are not caught by the accrued income scheme if the nominal value of their total holdings does not exceed £5,000 at any time in both:

- the tax year in which the next interest date falls; and

- the previous tax year.

Individuals are not caught by the scheme if they are not resident and not ordinarily resident in the UK (TA 1988 s 715(1)(f)).

For individuals who are resident in the UK but are not UK domiciled, the scheme only applies to UK securities.

The scheme does not apply to traders in securities, for whom these transactions represent trading profits.

(c) *How the accrued income scheme works*

To make the required tax adjustments under the accrued income scheme it is necessary to determine whether a sale or purchase was 'cum-dividend' or 'ex-dividend'. The term 'cum' means 'with' and 'ex' means 'without', therefore a transaction with the right to the next dividend is 'cum-dividend' and a deal without the right to the next dividend is 'ex-dividend'.

It is common practice to use the terms 'ex-div' and 'cum-div' even though the return on the investment is in fact interest and perhaps the terms 'ex interest' and 'cum interest' would be more appropriate. The HMRC guidance on this area uses the terms 'ex-div' and 'cum-div'.

All stocks will have an ex-div date. Most stocks pay interest every six months (although some pay annually and some pay quarterly). If an investor holds stock at the ex-div date, the investor will be entitled to receive the next interest payment, even if the investor disposes of the stock before the actual date on which the interest is paid. There may be a few weeks between the ex-div date and the date on which the interest is physically paid.

Once the ex-div date has passed, the market price for the stock will go down. This is because a purchaser will not thereafter have a right to the net interest payment and will therefore offer a lower amount to purchase the stock.

The price of the stock will vary for many reasons, one of which is that the purchase price will or will not include the right to the next interest payment. A transaction cum-div will be priced to include the right to receive the next interest payment in full even though the stock will have been owned for less than the full interest period.

All securities have a 'nominal value'. This is the value on which interest payments are calculated. The nominal value is also the value at which the stocks will be redeemed. However, the 'nominal value' is unlikely to be the same as the market value of the stock. All accrued income will be calculated on nominal values. Market values are irrelevant for income tax.

The accrued income scheme calculates the 'accrued interest' every time stock is bought and sold and allocates this interest between buyer and seller. The accrued income is effectively the increase or reduction in the price of the stock depending on whether the stock has been purchased or sold 'cum-div' or 'ex-div'.

In practice, most taxpayers who buy and sell stock will receive a contract note and details of any accrued income will be shown on that contract note.

The way in which the accrued interest scheme works depends on whether:

- the taxpayer is the buyer or seller; and

- if the stock is being transferred 'cum-div' or 'ex-div'.

There are therefore four possible scenarios:

1.   A person selling stock cum-div.

2.   A person selling stock ex-div.

3.   A person buying stock cum-div.

4.   A person buying stock ex-div.

1.   A person selling stock cum-div.

Selling 'cum-div' means that the buyer will be entitled to the next interest payment. Therefore the price of the stock will be increased by accrued interest. This accrued interest, known as the 'accrued income charge', is taxable on the seller at the time of the next interest payment.

The accrued interest is calculated on a daily basis from the date of the previous interest payment through until the date of settlement based upon the gross interest payable.

It is taxed as 'miscellaneous income' and is entered on an individual's self-assessment tax return at boxes 10.12 and 10.14.

The income is taxed in the tax year in which the next interest date falls. For instance, if the next interest date following settlement is 30 April 2007, the accrued income charge is taxed in 2007/08.

2. A person selling stock ex-div.

    Selling 'ex-div' means that the seller will be entitled to the next interest payment, therefore the price of the stock will be decreased by accrued interest. That amount is known as the 'accrued income allowance' and is a deduction from the next interest payment on that security before entering onto the self-assessment tax return.

3. A person buying stock cum-div.

    A purchaser of securities 'cum-div' will be entitled to the full amount of interest payable on the next interest date, therefore the price paid will be increased by the accrued interest. That amount is the 'accrued interest allowance' because it represents the return of the investor's own funds when the interest is paid. It is deducted from the amount paid before inclusion in the self-assessment tax return.

4. A person buying stock ex-div.

    When buying 'ex-div' there is no entitlement to the next interest payment therefore the price paid is reduced by the 'accrued interest charge'. That amount is taxed at the date of the next interest payment by inclusion in the self-assessment tax return (box 10.12 and 10.14 for individuals).

B. **Mr Pinter – purchase and sale of 8½% Treasury Stock**

    Treatment of the purchase for settlement on 21 January 2007

    This is a purchase ex-div, therefore the seller will receive the full half-year interest to 25 January 2007 of £4,250. The purchase price will have been reduced to take into account the interest due from 22 January 2007 (the day after the settlement date) and 25 January 2007. This amounts to:

    Days from 22 January to 25 January 2007 $\dfrac{4}{365} \times £8,500 = £93.15$

    The seller is entitled to an accrued income allowance of £93.15 to reduce his taxable income for 2006/07 (in which the next interest payment date, 25 January, falls) and Mr Pinter will have an accrued income charge on the same amount for that year.

    Treatment of the sale for settlement on 11 June 2007

    This is a sale cum-div therefore the buyer will receive the full half-year interest to 25 July 2007. The purchase price will have been increased to take into account the interest due between 26 January 2007 and 11 June 2007. This amounts to:

    Days from 26 January to 11 June 2007 $\dfrac{137}{365} \times £8,500 = £3,190.41$

    Mr Pinter will have an accrued income charge of £3,190.41 in 2007/08 (in which 25 July 2007 falls) and the buyer is entitled to an accrued income allowance of the same amount for that year.

    The accrued income allowance reduces the taxpayer's savings income, and thus saves a basic rate taxpayer 20%. Accrued income charges are taxed at the savings rate (TA 1988 s 1A).

    If Mr Pinter is a basic rate taxpayer he will be taxed in 2006/07 at 20% on £93.15 and in 2007/08 at 20% on £3,190.41. If the other parties are basic rate taxpayers, they will get relief at 20% in each case. If anyone is a higher rate taxpayer then the applicable rate will be 40%.

Explanatory Notes

Capital Gains Tax

1. Capital gains tax (CGT) essentially charges tax on the profit made by an investor on the sale of an asset. The disposal of a security could therefore give rise to a CGT charge as well as an accrued income adjustment.

The contract note for the sale and purchase of securities will normally detail the amount of any accrued income. For CGT, exclude any accrued income allowance from acquisition cost and add any accrued income charge to acquisition cost as otherwise there will be an element of double counting or double taxation. On sale, deduct any accrued income charge and add any accrued income allowance to sale proceeds.

Most securities liable to the accrued income scheme, such as British Government stock, qualifying corporate bonds and building society PIBS, are exempt from CGT, however some securities, such as non-sterling loan stocks, are chargeable to CGT.

Tax credits and tax treatment of accrued income

2.   Accrued income charges and allowances are taken into account in computing income for tax credits (SI 2002/2006 reg 14(2)(ix)). The charge increases income of the tax year in which the next income payment, after the settlement date, falls. Accrued income allowances reduce the interest received on the next interest date. Charges and allowances are not netted off unless they relate to the same stock with the same interest payment date.

Discounted securities

3.   Taxpayers other than companies are subject to special rules dealing with discounted securities (ITTOIA 2005 ss 427–460). The accrued income scheme does not apply to such securities. The discounted security rules apply where the issue price is lower than the redemption price by more than ½% per year between issue and redemption, or, if that period exceeds 30 years, by more than 15%. Investors are charged to income tax in the tax year of disposal, at savings rate, on the profit. If a loss arises on securities acquired before 27 March 2003 then that loss may be offset against the total income of the year, (for trustees against income from discounted securities only) otherwise loss relief is not available (ITTOIA 2005 s 454).

On death there is a deemed disposal at market value with tax charged accordingly. Transfers from the personal representatives to legatees are also deemed disposals with income tax being charged on the estate on the difference between value at death and value at transfer.

A.   (i)   Explain in the context of income tax what is meant by the term 'resident and ordinarily resident in the UK', indicating the factors to be taken into account in deciding whether an individual is so resident and ordinarily resident.

    (ii)   When would an individual's employment income be taxed on the 'remittance' basis?

B.   Your client Dance is a British subject who until now has been resident, ordinarily resident and domiciled in the UK. He proposes to take a contract of employment with a UK company where most of his duties will be performed outside the UK. The contract will initially be for a period of two years but if he enjoys working abroad Dance anticipates that on its expiry he will either extend the contract or obtain other employment outside the UK.

He is uncertain if income from employment in these circumstances will be charged to UK income tax and he has asked you to write to him explaining the rules which will determine the position. He has also asked you specifically to answer the following questions:

(1)   Will interest on the savings which he makes from employment abroad be taxable in the UK?

(2)   If his wife goes with him, and takes up employment in the foreign country where he is based, will her income be taxable in the UK?

(3)   If he lets his house whilst he is abroad will the income from that be liable to UK taxation?

Write to Dance explaining the assessability to UK income tax of his income in the circumstances he outlines and answering the specific questions that he has raised.

C.   To what extent is the following income taxable in the UK?

(a)   Salary of C Sawyer, who is resident and ordinarily resident in the UK and is employed by a UK company. Some of the duties are performed abroad in each tax year. He is not a seafarer.

(b)   Salary of F Aristo, who is not ordinarily resident in the UK and works for a UK company, the duties being performed mainly abroad.

(c)   Salary of Y D Dandy, who is domiciled in the USA. He has lived and worked in the UK for 10 years, his employer throughout having been an American company. During 2006/07 he was given three months' unpaid leave to undertake a special employment contract with a German company. He has left his earnings from the employment in a German bank account to use on holiday trips.

D.   On 1 June 2006 Soames, who works full time for Glasnost plc, was sent by the company to set up their Moscow operation. During his tour of duty in Russia he has returned to the UK on leave from time to time. The inclusive dates of his visits to the UK are as follows:

10 August 2006 to 22 August 2006
11 December 2006 to 10 January 2007
29 August 2007 to 12 September 2007

On the basis of the above information write a memorandum indicating the earliest date on which he could return permanently to the UK in order to qualify as a non-resident for the period of absence.

A. (i) **Residence and ordinary residence**

The question of whether someone is resident and/or ordinarily resident in the UK is always considered in relation to a tax year. The two concepts are quite separate, and someone can be resident without being ordinarily resident and vice versa. By Revenue Concession A11, the year of arrival in the UK and the year of departure may be split into 'resident' and 'non-resident' periods (for further details see Example 35).

In order to be regarded as resident in a particular tax year, the individual must normally be present in the UK for at least part of that year. Under TA 1988 s 334, a UK citizen who goes abroad for some temporary purpose is, however, treated as remaining resident in the UK, and in the case of Reed v Clark 1985 it was not ruled out that such a person could be regarded as resident even though he was absent from the UK throughout the year. Conversely, a visitor who is in the UK for a *temporary* purpose and not with the intention of establishing his residence here is not treated as resident in a tax year unless his visits amount in the aggregate to 183 days (days of arrival and departure normally being ignored in counting days in UK). Having UK accommodation available for use is ignored in deciding whether someone is in the UK for such a temporary purpose (TA 1988 s 336).

Someone who comes to the UK with the intention of remaining for at least three years, or to work for at least two years, is regarded as resident from the outset, the tax year being split as indicated above (concession A11). (This would be reviewed if the circumstances changed.) If that did not apply, the person would be regarded as a short-term visitor.

A visitor will also be regarded as resident (and ordinarily resident) if he makes regular, substantial visits to the UK. HMRC normally regard an average of 91 days a year over four tax years or more as constituting such visits. In this event the individual is regarded as resident (and ordinarily resident) from the fifth tax year onwards, or from any earlier year in which it was clear that such regular, substantial visits were to be made.

Any days spent in the UK because of circumstances beyond the individual's control are disregarded for the purpose of the 'regular, substantial visits' provisions, but not for the 183 days rule (SP 2/91).

Ordinary residence can be regarded as the country where someone is habitually resident. The position regarding regular visitors is indicated above. Those who come to the UK with the intention of staying for at least three years are regarded as ordinarily resident from the outset. Otherwise, they are regarded as ordinarily resident from the beginning of the tax year after the third anniversary of their arrival (SP 17/91). If, however, they remain in the UK and buy property in the UK, or lease property for three years or more, or form a firm intention to stay for at least three years, ordinary residence commences from the tax year in which that event occurs, or from the day of arrival if it occurs in the tax year of arrival.

Former UK residents who have gone to live abroad are subject to these UK visits rules in the same way as foreigners, but it would be sensible for someone who has gone to live abroad to remain away for a whole tax year to demonstrate a clear break with the UK.

Someone who is employed or self-employed full-time abroad for a period spanning at least a complete tax year is normally regarded as non-resident from the day after the date of departure and as a new permanent resident from the date of returning to the UK, providing interim UK visits are less than 183 days in any tax year and less than 91 days a year on average (taken over a period of up to four years). The same applies to someone who accompanies or later joins their spouse/civil partner, whether or not they are working full-time abroad.

Someone who goes to live abroad permanently, or for at least three years, without taking up full-time work will still be regarded as non-resident from the date of leaving providing the absence covers a complete tax year and UK visits average fewer than 91 days a tax year.

See also the Revenue's Tax Bulletin of April 2001 for their views on the interpretation of the residence rules in relation to mobile workers.

Under self-assessment, individuals certify their own residence/ordinary residence status in their tax returns, and HMRC will no longer give prior rulings, although they may make enquiries about residence status as part of an enquiry into a return, in which case supporting evidence will probably be called for. Evidence of leaving the UK permanently could be selling the UK home and buying one abroad. If someone who was not working full time abroad continued to own UK property, he would need to be able to show that this was consistent with his stated intention of living abroad for three years or more.

(ii)   **Remittance basis**

ITEPA 2003 provides that the 'remittance' basis applies to assessable earnings in the following circumstances.

Section 21 provides that the earnings of an employee who is resident, ordinarily resident but not domiciled in the UK are chargeable to UK tax except to the extent that they are 'chargeable overseas earnings',

Section 22 then applies tax to 'chargeable overseas earnings' that are remitted to the UK, and

Section 23 defines 'chargeable overseas earnings' as earnings from employment with a foreign employer where the duties are performed wholly outside the UK.

Section 25 applies for any tax year to someone who is resident but not ordinarily resident in the UK, charging earnings from UK duties to tax. Section 26 applies to non-UK duties which are charged to tax only where the earnings are remitted to the UK.

Remittances are charged in the tax year in which they are made even if the employment is no longer held in that year.

B.   **Non-residence and income arising abroad**

15 October 2006

Dear Mr Dance,

With reference to your proposed contract of employment under which most of your duties will be performed abroad during a two year period, which will possibly be extended, I give below an outline of the income tax position that will arise.

If you work full-time abroad for a period which includes a full tax year, you will be treated as not resident and not ordinarily resident from the day following your departure, unless your UK visits during your term abroad amount to 183 days or more in any one tax year, or 91 days or more per annum on average over a period of up to four tax years. If you eventually returned to the UK, you would be treated as a new permanent resident from the date of your return (but not for the earlier part of that tax year). If your wife accompanied you (or later joined you) she would be treated in the same way, whether or not she was employed abroad.

So long as you and your wife are treated as non-resident, you will not be liable to UK tax on any of your income abroad, either from employment or interest on savings. You would, however, remain liable on any earnings from employment in the UK (unless regarded as merely incidental to your earnings abroad), on the rent from your UK house and (subject to certain exceptions) on any investment income arising in the UK. If the rent from the UK house is paid to you outside the UK the payer will be required to deduct basic rate tax and account for it to HMRC unless you agree with HMRC to include any tax due in your self-assessment. As a non-resident British subject you would be entitled to claim personal allowances against the income liable to UK tax.

If the nature of your UK duties is such that your contract cannot be regarded as full-time employment abroad, your two year absence would probably be insufficient for you to be regarded as non-resident.

In that event both your UK and foreign income would remain liable to UK tax. Your wife would still be regarded as non-resident if she was employed full-time abroad for a period spanning a full tax year.

This area of tax law is complex and can also be affected by the double tax treaty between the UK and the other country. It would be helpful for us to go into the details fully before you finalise your arrangements. If you will telephone my office I will be happy to arrange a meeting.

Yours sincerely,
A.N. Adviser

C. **Taxable Earnings**

(a) Since C Sawyer is resident and ordinarily resident in the UK, he is taxable on his earnings, for both UK and foreign duties, with a UK employer.

(b) F Aristo is taxable in respect of earnings for his UK duties (unless the employment is one which is in substance performed abroad and the UK duties are regarded as merely incidental to the foreign duties). If he is resident, even though not ordinarily resident, in the UK then he will also be liable in respect of any earnings from abroad which he *remits* to the UK.

(c) Since Y D Dandy has lived in the UK for 10 years he is undoubtedly regarded as resident and ordinarily resident. His UK earnings are therefore taxable.

As a non-UK domiciled person, however, he is not taxed on any earnings from an employment with a non-UK resident employer if all the duties of the employment are performed outside the UK. This applies to his contract with the German company. As long as the earnings are kept outside the UK, he will not be charged to tax on them. He will, however, be liable to tax if he remits the earnings to the UK in a later year, even if the employment is not held in that year.

D. **Memorandum re overseas tour of duty by Soames for Glasnost plc**

1. In order to qualify as a non-resident, Soames must be employed full time abroad for a period covering at least one complete tax year. Visits to the UK are permitted provided they are less than 183 days in a tax year and less than 91 days a year on average. By Revenue Concession A11 the tax years of departure and return may be split into resident and non-resident periods.

2. Soames's visits to the UK are clearly less than the allowable 91 days on average and he is employed full time in Russia. However, he will not complete one full tax year of absence until 6 April 2008. Provided he does not return permanently to the UK before that date he will be treated as non-resident from 1 June 2006 and his salary whilst in Russia will not be liable to UK tax. Otherwise he will remain UK resident and fully liable to UK tax on his overseas earnings.

3. If Soames is liable to both UK tax and Russian tax, double tax relief will be available. Reference should also be made to the double tax treaty between the countries, which overrides the normal legislation.

Explanatory Notes

Income Tax (Earnings and Pensions) Act 2003

1. The detailed rules relating to employment income chargeable to tax are contained in Part 2 with overseas provisions in Chapter 5 (ss 20-41).

2. ITEPA 2003 s 15 applies to the earnings for any tax year in which the person holding the employment is resident, ordinarily resident and domiciled in the UK. (See Example 6 explanatory note 13 for the meaning of domicile.)

The charge covers the full amount of the earnings received in the tax year, whether they are earned in the UK or abroad. Earnings of seafarers during a 'long absence' abroad qualify for a 100% deduction (see note 8).

3.   ITEPA 2003 s 27 applies to UK earnings for any tax year in which the person holding the employment is not resident in the UK. The section provides that the amount chargeable to tax is the earnings in respect of duties performed in the UK.

4.   The charge on *remittances to the UK* consists of:

   (i)   Earnings from an employment wholly abroad with a foreign employer by an employee who is resident, ordinarily resident but not domiciled in the UK (ITEPA 2003 s 22). The amount taxable is known as 'chargeable overseas earnings' (ITEPA 2003 s 23).

   (ii)   Earnings for the non-UK duties of someone resident but not ordinarily resident in the UK (ITEPA 2003 s 26).

5.   Where earnings are for a tax year before an employment starts, they are treated as being for the first tax year of the employment, and earnings for a tax year after an employment ends are treated as earnings for the last tax year of the employment (ITEPA 2003 s 17).

6.   Taxable earnings are based on the amount *received in* the tax year (ITEPA 2003 ss 18 and 19, and ss 31 and 32). This applies even if the employment is no longer held in the tax year in which the emoluments are received (ITEPA 2003 ss 17 and 30). Where earnings are received after someone dies, however, they are treated as income of the deceased before his death. Tax is charged on the personal representatives and is a debt payable out of the deceased's estate (ITEPA 2003 s 13).

Earnings during absences abroad

7.   The circumstances in which someone is regarded as becoming non-UK resident are outlined in part A(i) of the example. Where an absence does not establish non-residence, there is no longer any deduction in respect of earnings abroad except for those who qualify as 'seafarers', as indicated in note 8.

8.   (a)   A 100% deduction is available to seafarers in respect of earnings during a 'long absence' abroad. The definition of seafarers explicitly excludes those employed on offshore installations for oil/gas exploration or extractions (ITEPA 2003 ss 378-385 as amended by FA 2004). A jack-up drilling rig used in the offshore oil and gas industry is now treated as an offshore installation overturning the decision in Perks v Clark and other cases, CA 2001.

     (b)   To qualify for the 100% deduction, the duties of an employment or successive employments must be performed wholly or partly abroad during a *qualifying period* of at least 365 days. The emoluments for a period of leave immediately following a qualifying period also qualify for the 100% deduction but the final leave cannot be regarded as forming *part of* the qualifying period, so that it is necessary to establish the 365 day period first.

     A *qualifying period* must either consist entirely of days of absence or consist partly of such days and partly of days included by reason of the following:

     Where a period consisting entirely of days of absence ends, it may be linked to an earlier qualifying period to make a single qualifying period providing that there are no more than 183 intervening days and that the total days spent in the United Kingdom do not exceed one half of the total number of days *in the whole period*. Note that the one half rule must not be overstepped when looking at the position at the end of *each* absence abroad.

     (c)   A person is not regarded as absent from the UK on any day unless he is absent at the end of it (ITEPA 2003 s 378(4)).

     (d)   Emoluments qualifying for the 100% relief are calculated *after* pension contributions, capital allowances and allowable expenses (ITEPA 2003 s 381). Charitable donations under the payroll deduction scheme are not, however, on the list of items to be deducted.

(e) Where an employment is partly in the UK and partly abroad, the emoluments must be apportioned to arrive at the amount qualifying for the 100% deduction on the basis of 'the proportion . . . . that is reasonable having regard to the nature of and time devoted to the duties performed outside and in the United Kingdom, and all other relevant circumstances' (ITEPA 2003 s 380(2)).

9. Where the duties of an employment are substantially performed abroad, then any UK duties which are merely incidental to the performance of the foreign duties are regarded as performed abroad (ITEPA 2003 s 39). This rule was rigidly interpreted in the case of Robson v Dixon 1972, where a British airline pilot employed by KLM Dutch Airlines and based at Amsterdam (commuting thereto from London), who performed less than 5% of his total take-offs and landings at Heathrow, was held not to be within this provision because it was the *quality* and not the *quantity* of the UK duties that had to be taken into account.

However, one should note the case of Shepherd v HMRC (2006). There an individual claimed to have left the UK for Cyprus and kept his visits to the UK below the 91-day and 183-day thresholds. However, the Court held that he had not sufficiently left the UK in the first place (his work as a pilot was based in London) and therefore he was held to have remained UK-resident and ordinarily resident.

Travelling and board and lodging expenses

10. Certain expenses which might not normally satisfy the ITEPA 2003 s 336 expenses rule (see Examples 10 and 13) are allowable in the case of employments abroad. These are:

(i) *Travelling expenses (ITEPA 2003 ss 341 and 342)*

Where the employee is resident and ordinarily resident in the UK, and the duties of the employment are performed wholly outside the UK, and if the employer is a foreign employer the employee is domiciled in the UK, a deduction is allowed for the expenses of:

(a) Travelling from the UK to take up the employment and returning to the UK at the end of the employment. Where the travel expenses are only partly attributable to the taking up or termination of the employment the deduction is restricted accordingly (ITEPA 2003 s 341).

(b) Travelling between the UK and foreign places of employment, where the employee has two or more employments and performs the duties of one or more abroad (the deduction being restricted as in (a) if the travel is only partly for the purposes of the employment) (ITEPA 2003 s 342).

(ii) *Travel expenses in other circumstances*

Where the employee is resident and ordinarily resident in the UK a deduction is allowed against the benefits charge where certain travel costs are met, or reimbursed, by the employer. The rules allow for any number of visits to and from the UK. This only applies where the employee is absent from the UK wholly and exclusively for the purpose of performing the duties of one or more employments *or* the duties are performed partly outside the UK and the journey is made wholly and exclusively for the purpose of performing them or returning after performing them (ITEPA 2003 s 370).

Relief would be available both for travelling and subsistence expenses under the general expenses rule in ITEPA 2003 s 336 for an employee who performed part of his duties abroad, whether the expenses were borne by the employer or the employee (see Example 13).

(iii) *Board and lodging expenses (ITEPA 2003 s 376)*

Where the employee is resident and ordinarily resident in the UK, and the duties of the employment are performed wholly outside the UK, and if the employer is a foreign employer the employee is domiciled in the UK, a deduction is allowed against the benefits charge when foreign accommodation and subsistence costs are met, or reimbursed by, the employer. If the accommodation or subsistence is only partly for the purpose of enabling the employee to perform the duties of the employment, the deduction is restricted accordingly.

(iv)   *Family visits* (ITEPA 2003 s 371)

The travelling expenses of not more than two visits in any one tax year by the employee's spouse/civil partner and children (under 18 at the beginning of the outward journey) to the employee are allowed as a deduction, providing the employee is absent for a continuous period of at least sixty days (either in a single tax year or straddling two tax years), and providing the payments are met or reimbursed by the employer (the deduction thus offsetting the benefits charge). As in (iii) this relief is given where the employee is resident and ordinarily resident in the UK.

There is also a special exemption for the payment or reimbursement by the employer of personal incidental expenses of up to £10 a night (ITEPA 2003 s 241(3)(b)).

Travelling expenses of employees not domiciled in the UK (ITEPA 2003 ss 373–375)

Reliefs similar to those given to UK resident and ordinarily resident employees are available to expatriate employees working in the UK. Non-UK domiciled employees may claim a deduction from their UK earnings for expenses paid or reimbursed by the employer in respect of unlimited journeys to and from the UK by the employee, and up to two return journeys per tax year for spouse/civil partner and children (subject to the same sixty day rule as in (iv) above). The reliefs are, however, only available where the employee was either not resident in the UK in either of the two tax years before the tax year of arrival in the UK, or was not in the UK at any time during the two years immediately preceding his arrival, and they are limited to a period of five years from the date of arrival in the UK. Relief is restricted where only part of the journey is for the specified purpose.

Self-assessment and non-residence

11.   Self-assessment has posed problems for employees who start an absence abroad during the tax year. They will not be able to claim to be non-resident in their tax return due on the following 31 January since they will not qualify at that time, so they will have to make the claim after the return is submitted. They would usually have arranged not to pay tax under PAYE from the start of the absence, but this would be reflected in an underpayment for the year. If the underpaid amount is not paid, it appears that interest will first be charged and then refunded when the non-residence conditions are satisfied.

Rent payable to non-resident

12.   Non-residents are broadly liable to UK tax on income arising in the UK. Where rent is paid direct to someone outside the UK, it must be paid net of basic rate tax unless the non-resident has agreed with HMRC to settle his tax liability directly (TA 1988 s 42A – see Example 98 explanatory note 11). Non-resident British subjects are entitled to claim UK personal allowances. For further details see Example 35.

Tax Credits

13.   In order to claim tax credits it is normally necessary to be 'ordinarily resident' and 'in the UK'. Ordinary residence for this purpose has a different meaning from the one for income tax. For definitions and detailed rules see Example 5 at explanatory note 4.

If a claimant leaves the UK permanently then notification is required within three months of departure. If the claimant leaves the UK temporarily but the absence exceeds eight weeks then notification is required within three months of the end of the eight weeks of absence. A penalty of up to £300 may be levied for failure to notify. (The eight-week rule may be extended to twelve weeks in certain circumstances.)

In the same way if the claimant who has left the UK was claiming tax credits as part of a couple, notification will be required within three months of return.

In the situation where one member of a couple goes abroad to work for periods in excess of 8/12 weeks, a family will have to make both joint and single claims to tax credits during the fiscal year. For the joint claims the income will be that of the couple. For the single claim the income will be that of the individual remaining in the UK.

For example, John and Joan have one child aged 12. John works overseas on a three months on, one month off basis. He is not a Crown servant. He earns £36,600 pa. Joan does not work and they have no other taxable income. During 2006/07 he was in the UK from:

6 April 2006 to 30 April 2006
2 August 2006 to 7 September 2006
24 December 2006 to 24 January 2007.

John and Joan claim tax credits on 10 February 2006. Joan notifies John's departures and returns within three months of the relevant dates, and establishes her entitlement to make single claims at the same time.

John and Joan – Award periods:

6 April 2006 to 25 June 2006 (8 weeks after 30 April)	81 days
2 August 2006 to 2 November 2006 (8 weeks after 7 September)	93 days
24 December 2006 to 20 March 2007 (8 weeks after 24 January)	87 days

Claim is for family element only of £1.50 per day (John's income for these periods is too high to entitle John and Joan to any fast taper credits).

261 days @ £1.50 =   £391

Joan – Award periods:

26 June 2006 to 1 August 2006	37 days
3 November 2006 to 23 December 2006	51 days
21 March 2007 to 5 April 2007	16 days

Claim is	£	
CTC	4.84	
Family element	1.50	
	6.34	per day

104 days @ £6.34 =   £659

Note: Joan has no income and therefore the claim cannot be restricted. In order to claim the child must normally live with Joan in the UK. There is no entitlement to WTC as Joan does not work. See Example 5 at note 4 for the unexpected restriction to WTC childcare claims during periods of temporary absence.

The example assumes John's work is outside the European Economic Area. The situation for those with rights under EC legislation can be more complicated.

A.   Your firm has recently been instructed to act as advisers to a newly incorporated manufacturing company, Byrd Ltd.

Mr Tallis, the managing director of Byrd Ltd, has requested you to write to him summarising the major points in the operation of a Pay As You Earn (PAYE) scheme in order that he can ensure his new part time accounts assistant is operating the scheme correctly and maintaining the necessary records.

You have established that the staff complement comprises two full time working directors, one employee earning £8,400 per annum (plus substantial reimbursed expenses), the accounts assistant, who is a graduate, earning £16,000 per annum and several part time employees each earning approximately £80 per week.

Write to Mr Tallis setting out the information requested and ensuring that your letter covers the following specific points:

(a)   requirements on employees joining and leaving,

(b)   records required for operation of PAYE, NI and other employer obligations,

(c)   calculation of pay and payment of monies to HMRC, and

(d)   end of year returns and forms.

Note: Ignore the requirements of the statutory sick pay, statutory maternity pay, statutory adoption pay and statutory paternity pay schemes.

B.   In connection with the HMRC form P11D explain:

(a)   the purpose of this form,

(b)   when, by whom, and in respect of whom, it is necessary to complete and submit the form,

(c)   the major contents of the form.

Outline the purpose and contents of form P9D.

A.   **Operating PAYE**

Smith & Co,
Old Street, Newtown.

1 October 2006

Mr Tallis
Managing Director, Byrd Ltd.

Dear Mr Tallis,

As requested I summarise below the major points in the operation of a Pay As You Earn (PAYE) scheme and other payroll responsibilities.

(1)   Basic documentation – A New Employer's Starter Pack is available from the HMRC helpline on 0845 60 70 143. This includes tax and national insurance tables and employers' help books, together with an order form for obtaining relevant forms and employers' guides explaining the scheme. The Employer's CD ROM contains most employer forms, guidance and tables and includes calculators, forms to fill in on-screen and step-by-step help for people new to running basic payroll. The accounts assistant should familiarise himself with the workings of the scheme and refer to the employers' guides on points of difficulty. Help for existing employers is available from the helpline on 0845 71 43 143. It is also possible to obtain PAYE forms from the Employer's Forms and Online Order Service at www.hmrc.gov.uk/menus/formmenu.htm. There is also an internet service for PAYE at www.hmrc.gov.uk (see (11) below).

(2)   All new employees should be asked for parts 2 and 3 of form P45 given to them by previous employers or by the Benefit Office if they have been drawing jobseeker's allowance. For employees who produce form P45 a deductions working sheet should be made out according to the instructions in the employer's day-to-day payroll help book, and part 3 of the P45 sent to HMRC. Part 2 is retained. This procedure must be followed whether or not the employee's pay with you will exceed the tax and national insurance thresholds, so it is particularly important in relation to the part-time employees. Care must be taken to check whether the employee is subject to a student loan repayment deduction. This is shown in Box 5 on form P45 by the inclusion of the letter Y (see (10) below).

(3)   If a new employee does not produce form P45, the employers' day-to-day payroll helpbook specifies the action to be taken. In the case of the part-time employees earning below the tax and national insurance thresholds, if they certify on form P46 that the employment with you is their only or main employment and that they do not receive a pension, HMRC do not have to be notified but the form P46 must be retained, and records must be kept of the employee's name, address and pay.

(4)   When an employee for whom a deductions working sheet is in use leaves, form P45 must be completed, the top copy sent to HMRC and the bottom three copies (including part 1A which is the employee's copy) handed to the employee.

(5)   Records should be kept of the name, address, national insurance number and date of birth of each employee for whom a deductions working sheet has been prepared, and it would be advisable to have this information available for all employees even if a deductions working sheet is not in use.

(6)   On each pay day the details of pay and the tax and employer's and employee's national insurance thereon, together with any student loan deduction (calculated in each case from the tables) must be recorded on the tax deduction sheets. The accounts assistant will need a summary sheet of the total pay and the total tax and national insurance due. Within fourteen days after the end of each tax month, ie by the 19th, a cheque for the total amount due for the month must be received by HMRC Accounts Office with an accompanying payslip (supplied by HMRC).

(7)   Details of what counts as pay are given in the employers' guides. Broadly it covers all cash payments and also benefits in kind if they can be readily converted into cash. There are more stringent rules relating to directors and to employees earning £8,500 per annum or more. Reimbursed expenses are included under these stricter provisions unless HMRC grant a dispensation allowing the expenses to be ignored, in which case they do not have to be recorded on form P11D (see 8 below). Details of the nature of any expenses reimbursed should be supplied to the tax office and a dispensation requested. In any event, reimbursed expenses do not count as pay for deduction purposes, but must be recorded on form P11D if a dispensation is not granted. An employee will not be included in a dispensation if it would have the effect of reducing his taxable earnings (not just pay) below £8,500, so a dispensation will not be available for the employee who earns £8,400.

Certain amounts will be included in gross pay for national insurance, but not for income tax. These amounts are liable to Class 1 national insurance contributions when paid but are treated as benefits for PAYE and included on form P11D. See Chapter 5 of CWG2 'Employer's Further Guide to PAYE and NICs' for the detail on these payments.

(8)   At the end of the tax year you will be required to send year-end documents to HMRC. Forms P14, which are in three parts, must be completed for each employee in respect of whom entries were required on the tax deduction card (form P11). A form P14 must be completed if an employee has earned £84 or more in any pay week even though no deductions are shown. Two parts of form P14 are for HMRC and the third part constitutes the form P60 (details of pay and tax deducted) for the employee. Form P35 must be completed showing the tax and national insurance for each employee, and the totals should reconcile with the wages records. The completed form P35 and two copies of each P14 should be sent to HMRC by 19 May. Forms P60 must be issued to employees by 31 May.

A form P11D must be completed for each director and employee earning £8,500 or more, showing details of all benefits provided other than anything already included as pay on the deduction sheets or covered by a dispensation or in respect of which you have entered into a PAYE settlement agreement with HMRC to settle the tax liability for all relevant employees. The boxes on the form that are relevant for Class 1A national insurance contributions (see (9) below) are colour coded. If expenses payments in excess of £25 to non-P11D employees have not been treated as pay (other than reimbursed business expenses and expenses paid in accordance with a scale agreed with the tax office), or certain benefits have been provided to non-P11D employees, form P9D must also be completed. Forms P11D and P9D should be sent to HMRC by 6 July and copies must be provided by that date to anyone employed at 5 April. If an employee has left after 5 April, the copy may be sent to his last known address. You are not *required* to give copies to employees who leave *during* the year unless they make a written request, but it would be sensible and helpful to the employee to do so. This could be done either at the time the employee leaves or when issuing copies to other employees at the year-end.

(9)   Class 1A employers' national insurance contributions, currently at 12.8% of the cash equivalent of benefits, are payable annually in arrear on the provision of all taxable benefits (except child care). The amount due is calculated annually from the P11D entries and is payable to the Accounts Office using the special payslip by 19 July 2007 for 2006/07. The payment is shown on form P11D(b) which must be filed with the PAYE tax office by 6 July. Interest is charged from the day after the 19 July due date on any late payment.

When cars and fuel are first provided, and when changes are made, HMRC must be notified on form P46 (Car) within 28 days after each quarter to 5 July, 5 October, 5 January and 5 April.

(10) Where a student took a student loan as a new borrower after August 1998 then repayment of those loans will be collected by way of a deduction from salary. You are not required to take any action unless you receive a start notice (SL1). The first deduction date will be

approximately six weeks later. For new employees 'Y' in the SL box on form P45 triggers the deduction. The repayment is 9% of the excess of earnings over £288 per week (£1,250 per month). Deductions must continue until a stop notice (SL2) is received. Earnings will be the amount computed for national insurance purposes.

(11)   HMRC encourage the use of the internet to submit forms P14, P35, P11D, P11D(b), P9D, P45 and P46. Employers may also receive forms such as P6 (coding details) and P9 (code amendments) via the internet.

From 2004/05 an employer with more than 250 employees must use electronic communications with HMRC for PAYE/NI. This was extended from 6 April 2005 to employers with more than 50 employees. It is anticipated that all employers will be required to use electronic communications from 2009/10. However, if small businesses (50 or fewer employees) use electronic communications earlier, cash incentive payments will be made. These started at £250 for 2004/05, reducing to £75 by 2008/09.

From April 2004 a large employer (250+ employees) is obliged to pay PAYE/NI and associated amounts electronically. If any employer pays PAYE/NI electronically, or through the bank, the cleared payment must arrive by the 22nd of the month (or the previous bank working day if the 22nd is a bank holiday or falls on a weekend). A large employer will be charged a surcharge if they pay late or do not pay electronically.

(12)   Interest is charged on PAYE, NIC, student loan and CIS deductions that remain outstanding 14 days after the end of the tax year, ie from 19 April 2007 for 2006/07, except for Class 1A contributions, where interest runs from the due date of payment, ie 19 July 2007 for 2006/07. There are also penalties if you are late sending in forms P14, P35, P11D, P11D(b) or P9D, or if you fraudulently or negligently provide incorrect information in a P11D, P11D(b) or P9D or in relation to a PAYE return or a return under the CIS scheme. For student loan deductions there are penalties for fraudulently or negligently making incorrect deductions, or making or receiving incorrect payments. For tax credits there are penalties for refusing or repeatedly failing to make payments to an employee and, by reason of fraud or neglect, for not paying the correct amount. Such interest and penalties are not deductible in computing the tax liabilities of the employer.

(13)   If your company failed to pay national insurance contributions because you had been fraudulent or negligent, you could be held personally liable for the failure. It is essential that you make sure that the payroll is properly administered and that all liabilities are paid by the due date.

(14)   As you have more than four people on your payroll, you will be obliged to designate a 'stakeholder pension provider' within three months of starting business, after discussion with your employees. If employees so wish, you are required to make the pension deductions from their pay. You must stop deductions when asked to do so, but you need not accept instructions from any employee to change contributions more than once in any six-month period. The contributions, which are net of basic rate tax, are deducted from net pay. They do not affect the amount of national insurance contributions payable. Employers are not obliged to contribute to the scheme. The amounts deducted must be paid to the stakeholder provider not later than the 19th of the following month. If you fail to do so, a report will be sent to the regulatory authority. Persistent offences will result in fines being imposed upon the company.

You might have heard about employers paying working tax credits on behalf of the Government. You will not need to worry about this as this stopped by April 2006 and all tax credits are paid direct by HMRC.

This is only an outline of the main points of the PAYE scheme, and if there are any points of difficulty I will be happy to discuss them with you.

Yours sincerely,
A N Other

B. **Form P11D**

(a) The purpose of form P11D is to give HMRC details of expenses payments and benefits provided in the tax year to directors or to employees earning at the rate of £8,500 per annum or more. The form also enables the employer to compute his liability to Class 1A national insurance on benefits. A copy must be provided to employees and directors to enable them to complete their self-assessment tax returns and, if they wish, to work out their own tax. The form must show not only payments and benefits provided by the employer himself but also by anyone else where the employer has arranged for that other person to provide the payments or benefits. Insignificant private use of assets and services mainly used for work purposes is exempt from tax (and national insurance contributions) and is not included on forms P11D (ITEPA 2003 s 316). The exemption does not apply to potentially high value items, such as motor vehicles, boats, aircraft, and alterations to living accommodation. The Treasury have the power to issue regulations exempting minor benefits (ITEPA 2003 s 210).

(b) Form P11D is required to be completed by employers and sent to HMRC, with a copy to the employee/director, by 6 July after the end of the tax year. There are penalties if the forms are submitted late, or if the employer fraudulently or negligently provides incorrect information in the form.

A form has to be completed for each director and for each employee earning £8,500 per annum or more, except those for whom no expenses payments or benefits have been provided, when employers are simply required to confirm to HMRC on form P11D(b) that all the necessary forms P11D have been completed and returned. (Form P11D(b) is also used to notify the amount of Class 1A contributions due, as indicated in part A of the example at note (9).) The due date for form P11D(b) is the same as for form P11D, ie 6 July following the tax year.

The definition of 'director' includes every director except one who

(i) earns less than £8,500 per annum, and

(ii) owns not more than 5% of the ordinary share capital of the company, and

(iii) either works full time or works for a charitable or non-profit making body.

In determining whether or not the £8,500 earnings limit is reached all expenses payments and the cash equivalent of all benefits must be included (computed according to the special rules for directors and employees earning £8,500 or more). Where a car is provided all payments reimbursed by the employer in respect of the car as well as the benefits charge for the car and (if private fuel is provided) for car fuel must also be included (although the reimbursements do not form part of the taxable pay since they are covered by the charges for car and car fuel provision). Only certain deductions can be made from this total figure (eg payroll giving, contributions to an employer's pension scheme, free-standing AVCs). For the full list see ITEPA 2003 s 218(4).

A third party who has provided expenses payments or benefits to an employee or director other than by arrangement with the employer must provide details of the cash equivalents to the employee/director by 6 July following the end of the tax year. This does not apply to corporate hospitality unless the provision was in return for services rendered by the employee/director or the provision was directly or indirectly procured by the employer, or by someone connected with him. Nor does it apply to gifts costing not more than £250 in total from the same donor (ITEPA 2003 s 324). Tips and items included in a Taxed Award Scheme are also excluded, although they are taxable. (Under the Taxed Award Scheme the third party is already required to provide information to the employee – see explanatory note 8.) The third party does not have to provide information to HMRC unless required to complete a return under TMA 1970 s 15.

(c) The major contents of form P11D are details of the provision of cars and car fuel for private use, beneficial loans, relocation expenses, excess mileage allowances for use of the employee's own car (see Example 10 explanatory note 20), vans made available for private use, private medical etc treatment and insurance, general expenses allowances for business travel, travelling and subsistence, entertainment, home telephone benefits, subscriptions, services supplied, vouchers and credit cards, assets given or transferred to the director/employee, or placed at his disposal, nursery provision and educational assistance, provision of living accommodation, and income tax paid for a director and not deducted from his wages. Except where HMRC have given a dispensation (see part A(7)) or the tax liability has been settled by the employer under a Taxed Award Scheme or by a PAYE Settlement Agreement (see explanatory notes 8 and 9), all other expenses payments and benefits must also be shown, including payments made on the employee's behalf and not repaid.

Payments include those made by credit card or any other means. HMRC view is that the figures quoted must include value added tax where appropriate. Dispensations would most commonly be given for travelling and subsistence expenses, professional subscriptions and entertainment.

Employers must calculate and show on the form the cash equivalent of all the benefits. The amounts reported by the employer do not take into account any reduction for allowable expenses, for which the employee must make his own claims (see below). Employers may obtain from HMRC optional working sheets for living accommodation, cars and fuel, vans, beneficial loans and relocation expenses.

The cash equivalent of benefits is normally the marginal cost to the employer of providing them, less any amount made good by the employee.

The cash equivalent for cars is based upon the list price of the car and its carbon dioxide emissions figure and the fuel benefit is calculated by applying the percentage based upon the emissions figure to £14,400 pa. A fixed charge may apply for private use of a van. (See Example 10 at note 18.)

The provision of living accommodation attracts a charge equivalent to its annual value less any rent paid, plus an additional charge if the cost of the accommodation exceeds £75,000, plus a further charge in respect of running costs if applicable.

Where other assets are provided for the employee's use the cash equivalent is 20% of the market value at the time the asset is first provided, proportionately reduced if the asset is also used for business purposes. For computer equipment first made available before 6 April 2006, the first £2,500 of market value is ignored.

The cash equivalent of beneficial loans is the difference between the interest paid by the director/employee, if any, and interest calculated at a rate prescribed by statutory instrument. Loans to buy the main residence are within the beneficial loans rules (see Example 57 explanatory note 5).

If any of the expenses included on the form are incurred 'wholly, exclusively and necessarily in the performance of the duties of the employment' the director/employee may submit a claim under ITEPA 2003 s 336 for an appropriate deduction.

Taxable benefits are liable to Class 1A national insurance and must be shown separately from expenses. For example, if an employer provides private medical insurance for an employee or his family, that is a benefit on which tax and Class 1A NI contributions are due. However, if the insurance is to cover medical risks whilst working overseas for the employer, that is an expense not giving rise to a tax or NI liability. Whereas if the contract is made by the employee but paid by the employer, that is a payment made on behalf of the employee liable to Class 1 NIC (employer's and employee's contributions). It must also be shown on form P11D and is liable to income tax. See explanatory note 8 re benefits provided under the Taxed Award Scheme.

Form P9D

The purpose of form P9D is to give HMRC details at the end of the tax year of taxable benefits and expenses payments for employees earning less than £8,500 and to provide those details to the employees so that they may enter the amounts in their self-assessment tax returns if they receive them. The time limits for sending in the forms and the penalties for late submission and incorrect information are the same as for forms P11D. No Class 1A national insurance liability arises on benefits shown on form P9D.

The main contents of the form are expenses payments totalling more than £25 for the tax year (other than those wholly for business purposes, or for which relief is available, such as the first £8,000 of relocation expenses), payments made on the employee's behalf, gifts (at second-hand value), non-cash vouchers (including the excess of luncheon vouchers over 15p a day), and living accommodation.

Explanatory Notes

PAYE codings

1.   The foregoing covers the main features of the PAYE scheme and the requirements for completing forms P11D and P9D. The PAYE regulations are in SI 2003/2682. The tax calculation is made using code numbers notified by HMRC on form P6. The code represents the tax allowances and deductions the employee is entitled to, reduced by amounts needed to cover other adjustments, such as benefits charges for cars and fuel, or to avoid too much income being charged at the starting rate/basic rate where someone has more than one employment. Another adjustment is the Allowance Restriction to restrict the tax saving to 10% on age-related married couple's allowance. Where the employee has untaxed income from other sources it is frequently deducted from the employee's allowances to avoid tax having to be accounted for separately on that other income. Inevitably, coding adjustments will often be based on estimates and will not result in the exact amount of tax due being collected, so that year-end adjustments or adjustments to the next year's coding may have to be made. In Blackburn v Keeling the Court of Appeal held that a loss likely to arise in 2003/04 could not be included in a 2002/03 code. The taxpayer was a name in various Lloyd's syndicates and claimed carryback relief for losses to be declared in May 2003.

2.   The code number is the amount of the allowances less the last digit, so that the code for a single person entitled to the personal allowance of £5,035 is 503L. Most codes are three numbers followed by a suffix. For example, suffix L denotes personal allowance, V age-related personal and married couple's allowances for someone aged 71 to 74, P age-related allowance for someone aged 65 to 74 and Y age-related allowance for someone aged 75 or older. The suffixes enable HMRC to implement changes in these allowances by telling employers to adjust the codes by a specified amount. Some codes have a prefix instead of a suffix, eg prefix D which is used to collect higher rate tax, and prefix K which is used to collect tax on an excess of an employee's taxable benefits or a pensioner's state pension over available allowances. The maximum tax deducted from any payment of earnings under K codes is, however, restricted to 50%. Other codes are BR, which means basic rate tax applies, OT, which means no allowances are available, NT, which means no tax is to be deducted and T, which means the code is only to be changed if a specific notification is received from the tax office.

3.   The tax tables work on a cumulative basis, so that the allowances are spread evenly over the tax year, unless for some reason it would be inappropriate for the cumulative basis to apply in a particular case, for example, where a coding is reduced to take account of an increase in a separate source of untaxed income and to apply the tax tables on a cumulative basis would result in a very large decrease in take-home pay for one particular week/month. In such cases, the deductions for the remainder of the tax year are made on a non-comulative or week 1/month 1 basis which means that one week's or month's proportion of the allowances due for the tax year is given against each week's/month's pay. When this basis is used it is shown in the code, eg '503L Wk 1'.

Employees joining and leaving

4. The P45/P46 procedure enables the cumulative basis to be continued from one employment to another where appropriate. Form P45 has a separate part 1A for the employee and the form shows a separate figure for the pay and tax in that employment if it differs from the cumulative figures (ie if pay from a previous employer is included in the totals). Where a new employee does not produce form P45, then the employer must fill in a form P46 and ask the employee to certify either that he is a school leaver who has not drawn jobseeker's allowance or income support for the unemployed or that the employment is his only or main employment. He must also state whether he receives a pension, and give information about other employments in the previous 12 months.

   The treatment of completed forms P46 depends on the circumstances. For employees who state that they receive a pension, the forms must be sent to HMRC and tax must be deducted at the basic rate. Otherwise, the forms are not sent to HMRC if the employee's earnings do not exceed the PAYE earnings threshold (£97 a week for 2006/07), although if the employee's earnings are at or above the national insurance lower earnings limit (£84 a week for 2006/07) a deductions working sheet must be prepared in order to record the amount paid, and to account for tax and national insurance contributions as and when pay exceeds the earnings threshold. The forms P46 must be retained, together with details of the employee's name, address and amount of pay. For employees earning more than the earnings threshold, forms P46 are sent to HMRC and tax is deducted on the normal cumulative basis for school leavers and on a week 1 or month 1 basis for other employees using code 489L until a code number is received.

   If the employee does not complete any of the statements on form P46, then the form as completed by the employer is sent to HMRC and tax deducted at basic rate until further instructions are received.

   Where an employee is retiring on a pension paid by the employer, the employer completes form P160 instead of form P45, sending one copy to HMRC and giving the other to the employee. Tax on the pension is then deducted using the existing code but on a week 1/month 1 basis until further instructions are received.

Accounting for PAYE

5. Employers do not have to use the deductions working sheets and year end forms P14 supplied by HMRC, and may use their own substitutes for either or both. The substitutes can be in the form of computerised records, and employers may transmit information via the internet (see part A note (11) of the example).

6. Employers who expect their average total monthly payment for PAYE, national insurance and student loan deductions (and taking into account sub-contractors' deductions for those in the construction industry where appropriate), to be less than £1,500 may pay quarterly to 5 July, 5 October, 5 January and 5 April instead of monthly. New employers must notify HMRC accordingly but existing employers need not do so unless they receive a demand from the Collector (SI 2003/2682).

Car and car fuel provision

7. The calculation and treatment of benefits in kind for directors and employees earning £8,500 or more is dealt with in detail in Example 10. Where employees are provided with cars and/or fuel, or changes are made to the car/fuel provision, employers have to provide details to HMRC on form P46 (Car) within 28 days after each quarter to 5 July, 5 October, 5 January and 5 April. For company cars and fuel details see Example 11.

Taxed Award Schemes

8. Where employers or third parties have entered into a 'Taxed Award Scheme' with HMRC, under which the scheme providers agree to pay the tax on non-cash incentive awards at either basic rate or basic and higher rate, certificates showing the entries to be made in tax returns are given to employees by scheme providers separately from forms P11D, and relevant information is also provided separately to HMRC. Class 1 national insurance contributions are payable on the tax paid

by scheme providers, but not on the prizes themselves. Where the benefits are provided by a third party, Class 1A rather than Class 1 contributions are payable. Where the employer has not arranged for the awards to be provided, the third party *must* pay both the Class 1A contributions and the associated tax.

PAYE Settlement Agreements (PSAs)

9. Some employers enter into PAYE settlement agreements (PSAs) with HMRC under which they pay a lump sum to cover the tax liability of their employees on expenses and benefits that are minor or irregular, or where it would be impracticable to apply PAYE (for example where benefits are shared) (ITEPA 2003 ss 703–707). Items covered by the PSA need not be shown on forms P35, P14, P11D and P9D, nor are they shown on employees' tax returns. Once a PSA has been negotiated with HMRC, it may be carried forward to later years, subject to adjustment for changed circumstances. The employer's payment under the PSA is due by 19 October following the end of the tax year. Class 1B national insurance contributions are payable for 2006/07 at 12.8% on the benefits etc taxed under the PSA, to the extent that there would have been a national insurance liability under Class 1 or Class 1A. In addition a Class 1B liability of 12.8% is due on the tax payable under a PSA (Social Security Act 1998 and SI 2001/1004 regs 41, 42). The Class 1B contributions are payable by employers at the same time as they pay the tax on the PSAs. The imposition of the national insurance charge on the employer's tax payment may result in employers who are able to monitor and report individual benefits withdrawing from a PSA.

Interest is charged on overdue tax and Class 1B contributions from the 19 October due date.

Penalties for late and incorrect employer returns

10. Employers need to be fully aware of the requirements of the PAYE scheme, because there are penalties for late filing of year-end forms, and interest is charged where the tax and national insurance due for a tax year has not been received by HMRC by 19 April or 22 April if tax paid electronically (SI 2003/2682 reg 82). Interest on Class 1A contributions runs from the day after the 19 July due date (see part A note (9) of the example). See note 9 above re interest on late paid income tax and Class 1B contributions under PSAs.

The statutory penalty for late or incorrect forms P14 and P35 is £100 for every 50 employees (or part of 50) for each month or part month the return is late. In practice the penalty is limited to the *higher* of £100 and the total of the tax and national insurance contributions for the year that should be shown on the return. The initial penalty for each late form P11D or P9D is up to £300, and there is a further penalty of up to £60 a day if the failure continues. For fraudulent or negligent forms P35 a penalty of up to the underpaid amount may be charged. The penalty for fraudulently or negligently providing incorrect information in a P11D or P9D is up to £3,000. The same penalty applies for fraudulently or negligently providing incorrect information in relation to student loans or working tax credit.

The monthly penalties stated above for late forms P14 and P35 also apply to late P11D(b) Class 1A returns (due date 6 July as indicated in note (9) of part A of the example). The automatic penalty is not charged if forms P35 and P14 are received by HMRC within seven days of 19 May, and for P11D and P11D(b) when received by 19 July (filing date 6 July). For fraudulent or negligent Class 1A returns a penalty up to the underpaid amount may be charged.

HMRC also have power to visit employers' premises to undertake PAYE audits, and as well as the PAYE audit teams they have compliance officers who concentrate particularly on expenses payments and benefits for P11D employees. PAYE audits and the penalty and interest provisions are dealt with in Example 44.

Date when earnings regarded as paid

11. ITEPA 2003 s 686 lays down rules to determine when a payment of, or on account of, employment income is to be regarded as being made for the purpose of applying PAYE, so that the definitions of payment for PAYE purposes and receipt for assessment purposes match.

The general rule is that PAYE must be applied at the date income is paid.

Payment is deemed to occur on the earliest of:

(a)   the date on which the payment is made;

(b)   the date on which an employee becomes entitled without restriction to remuneration;

(c)   the date on which sums on account of director's remuneration are credited in the company's records;

(d)   the end of a period during which a director's remuneration is determined;

(e)   the time when a director's remuneration is determined, if that is after the end of the period to which the remuneration relates.

Any restriction on the right to draw money is ignored.

Normally directors' remuneration is determined by the company in a general meeting. HMRC will therefore treat the date of the annual general meeting at which the accounts are approved as the date of legal entitlement.

Pay in the form of readily convertible assets

12.   Under provisions in ITEPA 2003 ss 696 and 702 relating to income tax and SI 2001/1004 Schedule 3 relating to national insurance contributions, PAYE tax and Class 1 national insurance contributions must be accounted for when an employee is provided with marketable assets such as stocks and shares, gold bullion, futures and commodities, assets subject to a fiscal warehousing regime, assets that give rise to cash without any action being taken by the employee, assets in the form of debts owed to the employer that have been assigned to the employee, and assets for which trading arrangements exist or are likely to come into existence. The convertible assets provisions apply equally where vouchers and credit tokens are used to provide the assets, and the legislation has been strengthened to ensure that the vouchers provisions operate as intended. It has also been made explicit that the convertible assets provisions apply to agency workers and to those working for someone in the UK but employed and paid by someone overseas.

Benefits chargeable under the convertible assets provisions are treated as notional pay for PAYE, and the tax and national insurance due is deducted from actual cash payments made either when the notional payment is made or later in the same income tax month. If there is insufficient pay, the employer must still pay over the amount due with his remittance for that month, the payment then being treated as tax paid by the employee (ITEPA 2003 s 710). If the employee does not then make good that amount to the employer within 90 days of the provision of the asset, he is treated as having received further pay of that amount (ITEPA 2003 s 222), such pay being shown on year-end forms P11D and P9D.

PAYE/NI applies where pay is provided in the form of the enhancement of the value of an asset owned by the employee (such as paying premiums to increase the value of an employee-owned life policy).

PAYE/NI also applies where an employee is taxable on the exercise, assignment or release of a share option, or when a risk of forfeiture is lifted, or when shares are converted into shares of a different class, if the shares can be readily realised for cash. These provisions are mirrored in the national insurance legislation. See Example 87 for further details. Employers and employees can jointly elect for the liability for employer's Class 1 national insurance contributions to be transferred from the employer to the employee, with the amount payable being a deduction from the taxable amount arising on an unapproved share option (see Example 47 explanatory note 14).

Self-assessment

13.   Under self-assessment, those who pay all their tax through PAYE are not required to self-assess, although if they wish to do so they may require HMRC to send them a return. The time limit for making this demand is 5 years from 31 October following the end of the tax year, eg by 31 October

2012 for 2006/07 (ITEPA 2003 s 711). If an employee's return shows an underpayment of less than £2,000, then providing the return is submitted by *30 September* (or if filed electronically by 30 December) following the tax year, eg by 30 September 2007 for 2006/07, the underpayment will be dealt with by a PAYE coding adjustment unless the employee wishes to pay it directly. Where paper returns are filed before the end of November HMRC will also attempt to code in such underpayments, but cannot guarantee to do so. Where there is an overpayment of PAYE tax, those who do not self-assess will still be able to make a repayment claim outside the self-assessment system. See Example 42 for the position regarding coding claims under self-assessment and HMRC's power to enquire into such claims.

14.   Even if employees do not have to fill in tax returns under self-assessment, they must still keep records relating to their tax liabilities. Records must be retained for 22 months from the end of the tax year, unless the employee is also self-employed or receives rents from property letting, in which case the retention period is 5 years 10 months. If HMRC enquire into the employee's tax affairs, records must be retained until the end of the enquiry if later than the normal period (TMA 1970 s 12B). Relevant records include forms P60, P11D or P9D, P45 or P160 for pensioners, information to support expenses claims and coding notices. Such records should also be retained for tax credit claims.

Charitable donations under payroll deduction scheme

15.   Participating employers may arrange for their employees to have deductions made from their pay for donation to charities of the employee's choice through an agent or agency charity (ITEPA 2003 s 713). The earnings are taken into account net of the deduction for PAYE purposes, so that the figure of pay on the year-end form P60 is after making the deduction (but the deduction does not reduce earnings for national insurance purposes). The deduction must be made under a scheme authorised by HMRC and subject to regulations made by statutory instrument (SI 1986/2211).

The employer may deduct as an expense against profits any expenses incurred in operating a payroll giving scheme, including payments to an approved agency to meet the agency's expenses in running a scheme (TA 1988 s 86A and ITTOIA 2005 s 72).

For detailed notes on charitable donations see Example 91.

Miscellaneous points

16.   Where someone receives incapacity benefit, the benefit is tax-free for the first 28 weeks (or if it was first received before 13 April 1995) but is taxable otherwise. For those liable to tax under PAYE (eg on an occupational pension), tax on the incapacity benefit is collected by a coding adjustment. Those not subject to PAYE on other income have tax deducted directly from the benefit by the Department for Work and Pensions under a simplified form of PAYE.

17.   For the detailed provisions on employers' and employees' national insurance contributions, see Example 47.

18.   When fixing employees' pay, employers are required to comply with the requirements of the National Minimum Wage Act 1998 and the National Minimum Wage Regulations 1999 (SI 1999/584). There are also various burdens imposed on employers in order to implement aspects of Government policy. As indicated in the example, employers are required to collect repayments of student loans through PAYE. They will also be required to give paid time off for studying or training to employees satisfying stipulated criteria. Employers who do not either have an occupational pension scheme that all employees are eligible to join within one year of starting work or provide employees with access to a personal pension scheme satisfying various conditions (in particular that the employer contributes an amount equal to at least 3% of the employee's earnings), must offer access to a registered stakeholder pension scheme if they have five or more employees, of whom at least one meets the conditions to be provided with such access (see Example 38 for details of personal pension schemes).

If a Scottish variable rate is introduced, it will affect employers in England if one of their workers is classed as a Scottish resident. In that event, an 'S' indicator will be shown on coding notices and HMRC will notify employers when to start and stop applying the Scottish variable rate.

Help for new and small businesses is provided by HMRC Business Support teams, who will give general advice on tax and national insurance and run workshops to help employers to comply with PAYE obligations. Electronic communication is being encouraged as indicated in Part A note (11) of the example.

19. Employers may make special PAYE arrangements for foreign national employees (known as tax equalisation) under which the employers meet all or part of the employees' tax and provide a professional adviser to deal with employees' UK tax affairs. A guide to tax equalisation is provided in Revenue Help Sheet 212 – see HMRC's Tax Bulletins of October 1997, June 1998 and June 2002.

20. Shares purchased as partnership shares by an employee under an approved Share Incentive Plan (previously referred to as an All Employee Share Ownership Plan) are bought out of salary before the deduction of PAYE or NI, the maximum amount being the lower of £1,500 pa or 10% of salary. For full details see Example 87.

21. For details of the employers responsibility to deduct PAYE on tips and gratuities together with the national insurance liability on such payments, see Example 47 at part (d).

Honiton is employed by International Megabytes plc, and has a gross salary for 2006/07 of £46,000 before deducting pension contributions of 5%. In June 2005 the company required him to transfer to the Newcastle office so that he could supervise the installation of a new reporting system in that area. It is anticipated that this assignment will last for two years and at the conclusion of that period he will return to work in the head office in Swindon.

During his stay in Newcastle he is living with his wife and youngest child in a company house, which cost £80,000 in 1994 and has an annual value of £700. His older children are remaining at the family home in Swindon. The company paid certain of the household bills for the Newcastle house, which for the year ended 5 April 2007 were as follows:

	£
Electricity	330
Gas	410
Gardener	240
Redecoration	680

In addition the company furnished the house at a cost of £6,400. Honiton pays the company £70 per month by way of contribution towards the cost of his accommodation.

The company provides him with a car (CO_2 figure 190 grams per kilometre) which had a list price of £15,600 when purchased new in August 2004. He pays for all petrol but is reimbursed by the company for the full amount, including private petrol amounting to £1,120. The car is fitted with a car phone, which is used mainly, but not wholly, for business, and he does not pay for private calls. For the duration of his stay in Newcastle his wife has been provided with a car (CO_2 figure 143 grams per kilometre) bought new in February 2003, list price £9,200. Honiton contributes £35 per month towards the provision of this car. His wife pays for all her petrol.

Other benefits provided are:

(i) Medical insurance costing £1,480 under a company scheme. This included £300 for additional medical cover for Mr Honiton for periods spent outside the UK on company business. (Mr Honiton received hospital treatment during the year, for which the insurance company paid £750.)

(ii) Meals in the company's staff dining room. The dining room, which is open to all staff at the Newcastle office, provides subsidised lunches at £1.50 against an estimated cost of £4. On the basis of 240 working days the subsidy is worth £600 in a full year.

(iii) The Newcastle office runs a creche for the children of staff. Honiton's daughter, age 3, attends the creche twice a week. The cost, which is borne by the company, is £250.

(iv) During the year the company paid Mr Honiton's travelling expenses amounting to £6,750 and reimbursed entertaining incurred by him of £1,560. These amounts relate wholly to company activities.

In July 2006 Honiton and his family went on holiday to Minorca as a prize in the company's productivity increase scheme. The cost of the holiday was £2,200.

The company operates a staff loan scheme at 2% per annum interest. In December 2005 Honiton borrowed £6,000 for personal expenditure. The loan is for a period of five years with no repayment for the first two years. The official rate of interest has been 5% since 6 January 2002. Assume the rate remains unchanged for the remainder of 2006/07.

Honiton received an award of £250 for passing the examinations of the Computer Institute.

(a) Compute the amount assessable as employment income for 2006/07, setting out the amounts on which Class 1 and Class 1A national insurance contributions are payable.

(b) Comment on any differences between Mr Honiton's remuneration for income tax: for Class 1 national insurance purposes and for tax credits.

(a) **Honiton – amount assessable as employment income for 2006/07**

	£	£	£
Salary		46,000	
Less: Pension contributions 5%		2,300	43,700

Taxable benefits:

	£	£	£
Provision of living accommodation –			
Annual value	700		
Running expenses (330 + 410 + 240 + 680)	1,660		
Use of furniture 20% x 6,400	1,280		
Additional charge on accommodation costing more than £75,000			
(80,000 – 75,000) = £5,000 @ 5%	250		
	3,890		
Less: Contribution	840	3,050	
Provision of car –			
Car charge 15,600 x 25%		3,900	
Fuel scale charge 14,400 x 25%		3,600	
Provision of car phone		–	
Provision of car for wife –			
9,200 x 15%	1,380		
Less: Contribution (providing this is paid as a condition			
of the car being available for private use)	420	960	
Medical insurance	1,480		
Less: re Overseas business trips	300	1,180	
Travel and subsistence	8,310		
Less: Incurred wholly for company activities	8,310	–	
Prize – holiday in Minorca		2,200	
Interest on beneficial loan of £6,000 @ 5%	300		
Less: Amount paid (2%)	120	180	
Award for passing Computer Institute exams		250	15,320
			59,020

Class 1 and Class 1A national insurance contributions

	£	£
Class 1 contributions		
Salary	46,000	
Cash award	250	
	46,250	
Primary (employee's) contributions		
11% x (33,540 – 5,035)	3,135	
plus		
1% x (46,250 – 33,540)	127	3,262
Secondary (employer's) contributions		
12.8% x (46,250 – 5,035)		5,275

	£	£
Class 1A (employer's) contributions on taxable benefits		
Benefits as above	15,320	
Less: Cash award	250	
	15,070	
Contributions due 19 July 2007		
12.8% x 15,070		1,929

(b) **Differences between pay for tax, for national insurance and for tax credits**

Pay for national insurance purposes is broadly the same as pay for income tax, but it is taken before deducting the employee's occupational pension (or stakeholder/personal pension scheme) contributions and charitable payments under the payroll giving scheme. Payments in kind are excluded from pay for Class 1 national insurance unless they are specifically chargeable under the provisions of SI 2001/1004 reg 25 and Sch 3. These charging provisions also cover vouchers which may be exchanged for any of the relevant items. The payments in kind that are specifically treated as pay are gilt-edged stock, company loan stock, futures, options, certificates of deposit, units in authorised unit trusts, company shares, marketable assets such as gold or commodities, gemstones and certain alcoholic liquor, amounts taxed on employees in respect of payments into Funded Unapproved Retirement Benefits Schemes (FURBS), relocation expenses in excess of £8,000, and *any* asset (including a voucher) for which trading arrangements exist to enable it to be exchanged for an equivalent amount (see Example 9 explanatory note 12).

HMRC National Insurance Contributions Office takes the view that payments in kind are to be regarded as pay for Class 1 national insurance purposes if they can be turned into cash by mere surrender, rather than needing to be sold, so premium bonds would count as pay for Class 1 but the gift of a television set would not. Cash vouchers and vouchers exchangeable partly for cash count as pay for Class 1.

Although payments in kind escape a Class 1 national insurance charge except as indicated above, employers have to pay a separate charge – Class 1A contributions – on virtually all benefits provided to P11D employees that are not charged to PAYE tax and Class 1 contributions (see note 24 about the provision of childcare). The amounts chargeable to Class 1A contributions are the amounts of the taxable benefits and are taken from the entries on forms P11D. The charge does not apply if the benefit is *wholly* offset by a matching deduction for tax purposes. Where, however, there is both business and private use, Class 1A contributions are payable on the full amount, even though employees are entitled to a deduction for the business proportion for tax purposes. Class 1A contributions are payable annually in arrear, the payment for 2006/07 being due by 19 July 2007.

The Class 1A chargeable amount includes the amounts of the car and car fuel benefits that are charged to income tax for employees' private use. Class 1A contributions are similarly payable on the taxable amounts for private use of employer-provided vans.

If an employer provides private fuel for an employee's own car or van, Class 1A rather than Class 1 contributions are payable if the employer provides the fuel directly, or pays for it by way of credit card, agency card etc providing the fact that the fuel was being bought on behalf of the employer was explained in advance. There is no reduction in the chargeable amount for business use. If fuel is provided in any other circumstances, Class 1 employer's and employee's contributions are payable on the full amount, except to the extent that records are available to identify the business mileage. Class 1 contributions would also be payable in these circumstances on private fuel for employer-provided vans. Instead of paying for private and business fuel for employees' own vans, it is more tax-efficient for a business mileage allowance to be paid using HMRC authorised mileage rates (see note 20).

Pay for tax credits includes earnings received in the year together with taxable amounts relating to cars and car fuel, readily convertible assets, non-cash vouchers, credit tokens, cash vouchers and any amounts paid to settle a pecuniary liability of an employee. The amount is reduced by allowable contributions to pension schemes and give as you earn charitable donations.

Honiton would therefore include the following employment income in any claim for tax credits.

	£	£
Salary (net of pension)		43,700
Car – self	3,900	
– wife	960	
Fuel	3,600	
Award re exams	250	8,710
		52,410

Assuming that Mr and Mrs Honiton have no other income in 2006/07 and that the base year (2005/06) income was more than £52,410 their entitlement to a family element of CTC would be:

	£	£
Family element		545
Restricted by		
Income	52,410	
Income threshold	50,000	
6.67% x	2,410	160
		385

providing that they made a claim by 31 August 2006.

(See Example 5 for further details of income for Tax Credits.)

Explanatory Notes

Assessable income

1.   The tax charge under ITEPA 2003 covers earnings from employment and also pensions, both from employers and from the State, and some other social security benefits.

Taxable social security benefits include:

- Bereavement allowance

- Carer's allowance

- Incapacity benefit

- Income support

- Jobseeker's allowance

- Statutory adoption pay

- Statutory maternity pay   } Where paid by the DWP

- Statutory paternity pay

- Statutory sick pay

Non-taxable social security benefits include:

- Long term incapacity benefit which began before 13 April 1995

- Short-term incapacity benefit

- Increases in taxable benefits in respect of a child

- Attendance allowance

- Child benefits

- Tax credits

- Council tax benefit

- Disability living allowance

- Housing benefit

- Industrial injuries benefit

- Pensioner's Christmas bonus and winter fuel allowance

- Pension credits

- State maternity allowance

- Bereavement payments (lump sum)

2.   Employees are taxed on their earnings, which includes any salary, wage or fee, any gratuity or other profit or benefit of any kind (ITEPA 2003 s 62). To be earnings from the employment, the remuneration must be in return for the employee 'acting as or being an employee' (Hochstrasser v Mayes, HL 1959). It broadly means something that is a reward for services rendered in the employment, but the case of Hamblett v Godfrey (1986) showed that the test is wider, and covered payments made to employees at GCHQ Cheltenham to compensate them for giving up their right to be in a trade union, because the rights were connected with the employer/employee relationship. (A payment to compensate an employee for loss of rights under a share option scheme on his ceasing to be eligible following a management buy-out was, however, held to be not taxable in Wilcock v Eve 1994.)

   A payment by the employer for a debt for which the employee is legally responsible (referred to as meeting a pecuniary liability of the employee) counts as pay both for tax and national insurance. Class 1 national insurance contributions are payable at the time of payment, but tax is not deducted under PAYE and the payments are reported on forms P11D and P9D at the year-end (see Example 9 part B). This rule applies to payments for home telephone bills if the *employee* is the subscriber, unless the employer does no more than meet the cost of business calls excluding rental. It does not apply if the *employer* is the subscriber. In either case there would be a charge on P11D employees (see notes 11 and 12), subject to a claim for a deduction for the cost of the business calls. Where there is no Class 1 charge there will be a Class 1A charge on the full amount of the bill, unless the telephone is only available for business use.

3.   Where employees receive commissions and discounts from their employers, the commissions count as pay even if paid to or passed on to the customer or invested for the customer's benefit. HMRC have, however, stated that where the transaction is at arm's length and is a normal part of the employer's business, the employee will usually be able to claim a deduction under the 'wholly, exclusively and necessarily' expenses rule (see note 5). Commissions on employees' own transactions also count as pay, unless the same commissions are available to the general public. Discounted prices for an employee's own transactions as distinct from commission sacrifices do not normally result in a tax charge, but if the cost to the employer exceeds the price paid, P11D employees are charged to tax on the excess. 'Cashbacks' as inducements to employees to enter into transactions are not taxable if they are available on the same terms to the general public. For further details see Revenue Tax Bulletin February 1998.

4.   The charge is on taxable earnings *received* in the tax year (ITEPA 2003 s 15). Earnings are treated as received on the earliest of the following (s 18):

(a)   when actual payment is made of, or on account of, the earnings

(b)   when a person becomes entitled to payment of, or on account of, the earnings

and in the case of directors

(c)   when sums on account of the earnings are credited in the company's accounts or records (whether or not there are any restrictions on the director's right to draw the earnings)

(d)   the end of a period, where the earnings for the period are determined before it ends

(e)   the time when the earnings for a period are determined, if that is after the end of the period.

Normally directors' remuneration is determined by the company in general meeting unless the shareholders agree on some other occasion to remunerate the directors with certain sums. HMRC therefore usually treat the date of the annual general meeting at which the accounts are approved as the date of legal entitlement.

There are parallel rules to determine when income is deemed to be paid for PAYE (ITEPA 2003 s 686) (see Example 9 explanatory note 11).

Allowable expenses

5.   Certain expenses may be deducted from the emoluments to arrive at the taxable pay. The general expenses rule is in ITEPA 2003 s 336, which provides that if an employee is 'obliged to incur and pay out of earnings . . . qualifying travelling expenses, or any amount (other than qualifying travelling expenses) incurred wholly, exclusively and necessarily in the performance of the duties of the employment' he may claim a deduction for those expenses. For detailed notes on travelling expenses see Example 13.

Some expenses that are not covered by the general rule in s 336 are specifically allowed by statute, such as contributions to approved pension schemes, most professional subscriptions that are relevant to the employment (ITEPA 2003 ss 343 and 344), and charitable donations under the payroll giving scheme (ITEPA 2003 ss 713–715).

To avoid unnecessary work, payments by employers in respect of expenses for which the employee could obtain a deduction are not normally treated as pay under the PAYE scheme, so that the employee does not have to make an expenses claim, but there are special rules for those earning £8,500 per annum or more and for directors (see below at note 11 onwards).

Provision of living accommodation

6.   The annual value of accommodation provided for an employee is specifically chargeable to tax (less any rent paid), no matter how little he earns, except where it is provided in the performance of his duties (ITEPA 2003 s 99). This exception does not apply to a director unless he owns not more than 5% of the ordinary share capital and either works full-time or works for a charitable or non-profit making company. If the employer pays the employee's council tax and water charges, the payments count as taxable benefits unless the accommodation is necessary for the performance of the employee's duties, in which case the payments escape tax (and also national insurance contributions (SI 2001/1004 Sch 3 Part VIII para 10)).

Where the cost of the accommodation provided exceeds £75,000 an additional charge is made, even if the employee escapes the annual value charge by paying rent to cover it. The additional charge is calculated as follows:

Cost plus improvements less £75,000 @ beneficial loan interest rate at *beginning* of tax year (6 April 2006 – 5% as used in the example).

If the employee is paying rent in excess of the annual value of the property, the excess reduces the additional charge. Employees exempt from the charge on annual value because the accommodation is provided in the performance of their duties are also exempt from the additional charge. (S 99 disapplies the whole of Chapter 5 of Part 3 of ITEPA 2003 which includes the additional charge.)

Both the charge on annual value and the additional charge are scaled down pro rata if the accommodation is provided for only part of the year, and are also reduced to the extent that part of the property is used exclusively for business.

Annual values for UK properties are based on rateable values, even though domestic rates have been abolished. Where no annual value is available, or where there is a material change of circumstances, employers should estimate what the annual value would have been under the rating system. Special rules apply in Scotland.

For properties outside the UK the annual value will be the rent that could be obtained for the property let on an annual basis, unfurnished, on the assumption that the landlord meets costs of repairs and insurance and the tenant meets all other costs customarily borne by the tenant (HMRC Manual EIM 11441).

If the employee earns £8,500 per annum or more, or is a director, the cost of the provision of services in relation to the accommodation (ie heating, lighting, cleaning, repairs, maintenance, decoration and the provision of furniture) is chargeable as a benefit in addition to the provision of the accommodation itself. This applies even if the employee is provided with the accommodation in the performance of his duties, although in that case the charge for the provision of services cannot exceed 10% of the employee's emoluments excluding the value of those services (ITEPA 2003 s 315) (see Example 57 part (c) for an illustration).

There is specific legislation in ITEPA 2003 ss 64 and 109 which prevents salary sacrifice schemes being used to reduce the tax charge for the provision of living accommodation.

Relocation expenses

7. When an employee is relocated and his existing home is not within reasonable travelling distance of his new workplace, qualifying removal expenses and benefits are exempt up to a maximum of £8,000 per move so long as they are paid or provided in the period from the date of the job change to the end of the next following tax year (or the end of a later tax year if HMRC grant an extension). Allowable expenses include expenses of disposing of the old property and buying another, removal expenses, providing replacement domestic goods, travelling and subsistence (including temporary accommodation), and bridging loan expenses (ITEPA 2003 Part 4 Chapter 7). A payment to an employee to compensate him for a fall in value when he sells his home does not qualify and is fully taxable. The company house in Newcastle is Honiton's permanent location for the duration of his assignment, rather than temporary accommodation while he seeks a permanent home, and it does not therefore qualify under the relocation expenses provisions. If Honiton had incurred expenses in moving to the Newcastle house they would have qualified up to the £8,000 limit.

Where an employee sells his home to the employer or to a relocation company on terms that give him the right to share in any later surplus, there would be a taxable benefit if the value of that right plus the amount initially paid to the employee exceed the open market value of the property.

Employers do not have to operate PAYE on qualifying relocation payments, but qualifying expenses payments and benefits in excess of £8,000, and all non-qualifying expenses and benefits, must be reported on year-end returns. The taxable benefit is liable to Class 1A national insurance contributions for P11D employees. Both PAYE and Class 1 national insurance contributions are payable on non-qualifying expenses payments.

For the capital gains treatment where an employee sells his home to a relocation company see Example 82 explanatory note 15.

Employee liability insurance etc

8. The cost of employee liability insurance, professional indemnity insurance and work-related uninsured liabilities is not a taxable benefit if paid by the employer and is an allowable expense if paid by the employee (ITEPA 2003 s 346). National insurance contributions are not payable on such benefits. Relief can continue for six years after the year in which the employment ceased (ITEPA 2003 ss 555–564).

Vouchers

9. Cash vouchers are treated as pay and are chargeable to tax (and Class 1 national insurance contributions) at the time of receipt (ITEPA 2003 s 81). Non-cash vouchers (other than certain

childcare vouchers – see note 24 below) are also treated as pay, but are dealt with by year-end notification on forms P11D/P9D (except where they are used in connection with the provision of assets that can be readily converted into cash, in which case they are also charged to tax and Class 1 national insurance contributions under PAYE – see Example 9 note 12).

The benefit is the cost of the voucher plus the cost of the goods and services for which it may be exchanged (ITEPA 2003 s 87). Vouchers are sometimes used in connection with incentive award schemes (see SP 6/85 for the costs to be taken into account and see Example 9 explanatory note 8 for notes on such schemes). There is a specific exemption for vouchers used to obtain a car parking space (ITEPA 2003 s 266(1)(a)). Class 1 national insurance contributions are charged on most non-cash vouchers, subject to certain exceptions that mainly mirror income tax provisions but also including qualifying childcare vouchers (SI 2001/1004 Sch 3 Part V). For detailed notes on the national insurance position on vouchers see Example 47 part (b).

Non-P11D employees – salary sacrifice arrangements etc

10. For employees and directors who are not within the special rules outlined in note 11 below, the charging rules of ITEPA 2003 do not apply to benefits in kind except where:

   (a) A specific amount of salary has been sacrificed for the benefit, in which case under the principle established in Heaton v Bell 1969 the amount forgone is taxable (subject to what is said in note 6 re living accommodation), or

   (b) The benefit can be converted into cash, in which case the taxable amount is the second-hand value.

P11D employees/directors

11. Special rules apply to the computation of benefits of lower paid employees, that is, those earning less than £8,500 per annum (ITEPA 2003 Part 3 Chapter 11). All employees earning £8,500 per annum or more are subject to the normal rules. Directors who do not own more than 5% of the ordinary share capital and either work full-time or work for a charitable or non-profit making company are subject to the special rules if they earn less than £8,500 per annum. All other directors are included in the normal rules whatever they earn (ITEPA 2003 s 216).

   Earnings for the purpose of the £8,500 rule are calculated inclusive of expenses payments and benefits and *before* deducting any allowable expenses other than employees' contributions to the employer's pension scheme and some other reliefs (ITEPA 2003 s 218).

   The expenses payments made by an employer for his employee are notified annually to HMRC on form P11D (see Example 9). Employers may ask HMRC to grant a dispensation (notice of nil liability) under ITEPA 2003 s 65 in relation to expenses that would be allowable under the ITEPA 2003 s 336 'wholly, exclusively and necessarily' rule or other rules allowing deductions from employment income. If the dispensation is granted the expenses do not have to be shown on the form P11D, so that they are not treated as pay. Dispensations are most frequently given for travelling and subsistence expenses, professional subscriptions and entertainment. They do not apply to a particular employee if the effect would be to reduce the employee's earnings below the £8,500 limit. Dispensations are also effective for national insurance contributions. Forms P11D do not need to show items covered by a PAYE settlement agreement (see Example 9 explanatory note 9), nor details of non-cash incentives under 'Taxed Award Schemes', to which special provisions apply (see Example 9 explanatory note 8). From 6 April 2002 no entries are required for mileage allowance payments that do not exceed the statutory limits (see explanatory note 20).

   See Example 9 explanatory note 14 for the record-keeping responsibilities of employees under self-assessment.

12. Virtually all benefits received are chargeable to tax as earnings, but the employee/director may then make a claim for expenses incurred 'wholly, exclusively and necessarily' in the performance of his duties. The benefits provisions apply not only to benefits provided to the employee himself, but also

benefits to his 'family or household', defined as his spouse/civil partner, children and their spouses/civil partners, parents, and his servants, dependants and guests (ITEPA 2003 s 721(4) & (5)).

Benefits consisting of the private use of assets and services used for performing the duties of the employment are, however, exempt, if the private use is insignificant, except for motor vehicles, boats, aircraft and alterations to living accommodation (ITEPA 2003 s 316 – see Example 9 part B(a)). Under ITEPA 2003 s 210 HMRC have the power to exempt minor benefits. They have used this power to exempt from 9 July 2002 any private use of hearing aids and other equipment, services or facilities provided to disabled people under the Access to Work Programme or Disability Discrimination Act 1995 to enable them to do their work (but this still does not include the 'excluded benefits' as given in ITEPA 2003 s 316(5) and listed above).

The effect of the benefits provisions is to treat all amounts arising from the employee's or director's employment as taxable (unless they are specifically exempt) and to place the onus of an expenses claim on him. This is mitigated by the provisions for dispensations and PAYE settlement agreements. This example illustrates many of the provisions. Other points are covered in Example 57.

The employee/director is charged on the 'cash equivalent' of the benefit. This normally means the cost to the employer (including VAT where appropriate in the view of HMRC, whether recovered or not) less any amounts made good by the employee. In the case of Pepper v Hart, HL 1992, concerning a schoolmaster who paid reduced fees for his son, it was confirmed that cost for in-house benefits means the additional cost of providing the benefit, ie its marginal cost, and not a proportion of total costs.

Special rules apply where an asset has been used by an employee before it is given to him (see note 21) and to the calculation of the benefit of cheap loans and private use of cars and vans (see notes 26, 13 and 18 respectively).

Virtually the only benefits that escape tax for employees earning £8,500 or more and directors are mobile telephones (ITEPA 2003 s 319 – see note 19), free canteen meals (see note 23), certain computer equipment available to employees generally and first made available before 6 April 2006 (ITEPA 2003 s 320 – see note 27), employers' contributions to an approved pension fund (ITEPA 2003 s 307) or to an employee's personal pension plan (ITEPA 2003 s 308), the provision of a parking space for a car, van, motor cycle or bicycle (or voucher to obtain one) at or near the place of work or reimbursement of an employee's expense in obtaining such a parking space near his work (ITEPA 2003 s 237), works bus services (ITEPA 2003 s 242) and subsidised public transport (ITEPA 2003 s 243) (see note 28), provision of cycles and safety equipment for use mainly for travel to work or for business journeys (ITEPA 2003 s 244 – see note 29), the provision of services or assets to protect the employee from a special security threat, such as from terrorists (ITEPA 2003 s 377), the provision of creche facilities or, from 6 April 2005, approved child care or child care vouchers of up to £55 per week (£50 before 6 April 2006) (ITEPA 2003 ss 270A and 318–318D – see note 24), certain entertainment and gifts (ITEPA 2003 ss 264 and 265 – see note 31), stress counselling and outplacement counselling for redundant employees (ITEPA 2003 s 310), welfare counselling services available to employees generally (SI 2000/2080), in-house sports facilities (ITEPA 2003 s 261); the payment or reimbursement by the employer of personal expenses such as newspapers and phone calls up to a VAT-inclusive amount of £5 a night (£10 if outside the UK) where an employee is away from home overnight on business (ITEPA 2003 s 240). HMRC have confirmed that no benefit charge arises where an employee uses recreational facilities or canteen facilities on the premises of another employer where the employees of that employer work at the same site and use the same facilities. See also notes 8 and 35.

Private use of cars

13. The private use of a car provided by the employer attracts a benefits charge, unless the car qualifies as a 'pool car' under ITEPA 2003 s 167 or as an 'emergency vehicle' under ITEPA 2003 s 248A. A pool car is one that is used by more than one employee, is not normally garaged at an employee's home, and where the private use, if any, is merely incidental to the business use (see SP 2/96 for

HMRC's interpretation of incidental private use). An emergency vehicle is a car made available to a member of the fire, police or ambulance service to enable them to respond quickly to emergencies by taking the vehicle home.

The charge for private use of cars other than pool/emergency cars is based on the list price (up to a maximum of £80,000) (ITEPA 2003 Part 3 Chapter 6). The value includes accessories supplied with the car (other than mobile phones) and any accessory costing £100 or more that is added later, but not including accessories for disabled employees. Replacement accessories only increase the taxable value of the car to the extent, if any, that they are superior to the old ones, ie they cost more than accessories that are equivalent to the old ones.

The list price is the manufacturer's, importer's or distributor's list price of an individual car at the time of first registration (including delivery and VAT, but excluding road tax), not the price actually paid. Cars valued at more than £15,000 and at least 15 years old at the end of the tax year are taxed according to their open market value if more than the list price. An employee contribution of up to £5,000 towards the initial cost of a car reduces the cost on which the tax charge is based (ITEPA 2003 s 132).

The charge is a percentage of price graduated according to the level of the car's carbon dioxide emissions (see Example 11 part (a) for the relevant percentages).

The taxable benefit covers all benefits connected with the provision of the car including the London Congestion Charge except private fuel (see below) and the provision of a chauffeur (ITEPA 2003 s 239(5)).

Where the employee makes a payment to the employer as a condition of the car being available for private use, this sum reduces the taxable benefit (ITEPA 2003 s 144).

Provision of private fuel

14. There is a separate additional charge for the provision of private fuel in an employer-provided car, based on the percentage used for the car benefit (see Example 11), whether the cost of the fuel is reimbursed or paid directly (ITEPA 2003 ss 149–153).

    The fuel charge is not varied according to the level of business mileage. It is not reduced by any contribution made by the employee unless the employee makes good to the employer the whole cost of the fuel for his private use, in which case there is no assessable benefit.

    The fuel charge is calculated by applying the percentage applicable to the car benefit to £14,400. Where free fuel ceases to be provided during the tax year, the benefit is reduced pro rata (unless fuel is again provided later in the same tax year, in which case a full year's charge will apply).

    HMRC has issued advisory fuel rates for company cars that can be used from 2001/02 to charge employees for fuel provided by the employer for private miles travelled in the company car, or to reimburse employees for fuel used for business miles travelled in the company car. If the employer prefers he may provide evidence of actual costs and substitute them for the advisory rates. Without such evidence any excess payment will be liable to PAYE and Class 1 national insurance contributions (but the fuel scale will not apply). Failure to charge for fuel provided for all private miles will result in the scale charge being applied.

    Company cars – advisory fuel rates for company cars from 1 July 2005

    These rates apply to all journeys on or after 1 July 2005 until further notice:

Engine Size	Petrol		Diesel		LPG	
	To 30.6.06	From 1.7.06	To 30.6.06	From 1.7.06	To 30.6.06	From 1.7.06
1400cc or less	10p	11p	9p	10p	7p	7p
1401cc to 2000cc	12p	13p	9p	10p	8p	8p
Over 2000cc	16p	18p	13p	14p	10p	11p

These rates are taken from the HMRC website.

From 6 April 2004 to 30 June 2005 the notes were the same except for engines over 2000cc when the rates were 14p (petrol), 12p (diesel) and 10p (LPG).

The rates are acceptable to HMRC for VAT purposes (see note 20).

Change of car and periods of unavailability

15. Where the car is not available for part of the year, the car charge and fuel charge are reduced proportionately. It is treated as not available for any day if it was not made available until after that day, or ceased to be available before that day, or if it was incapable of being used at all for not less than 30 consecutive days. Where a car is unavailable for less than 30 days, a temporary replacement of similar quality is ignored and the same car is regarded as provided throughout.

    Employers have to give HMRC details of new and changed arrangements for the provision of cars and car fuel to employees on form P46 (Car). The form must be submitted within 28 days after each quarter to 5 July, 5 October, 5 January and 5 April. Details are also required on year-end forms P11D.

VAT and national insurance on cars and fuel

16. In addition to the income tax charges, the employer has to pay VAT on the provision of fuel for private use. VAT is not payable on the provision of the car itself, even if the employee makes a payment for private use, unless the employer recovered all of the input tax on the acquisition of the car, or leases it from a lessor who reclaimed all the input tax on it, in which case a payment by the employee would attract VAT. Employer's Class 1A national insurance contributions are payable both on the provision of fuel in a car provided by the employer and the provision of the car itself (see part (b) of the example and also Example 47). The national insurance charges are based on the income tax figures, taking into account any reduction for any employee contributions for the use of the car.

    Unlike the income tax and national insurance charges, the VAT scale charges apply to all employees who are provided with fuel no matter what they earn, and no matter whether the car is owned by the employer or the employee, except where an employee has paid for the fuel in full, including VAT, in which case the output VAT has to be accounted for. The VAT fuel scale charges are shown at the front of the book.

    See note 19 re VAT on mobile phones.

Cars or cash

17. Because of the increased levels of scale charges for income tax, and the added burden of VAT and national insurance, it is often more cost effective for an employer not to provide fuel for private use. Furthermore from 6 April 2002 it may be more effective not to provide a car but to pay the employee for use of his own car using the mileage allowance rates (see note 20). Because the employee will not have the option of claiming for actual costs this method will be most useful in the case of older cars which have high list prices. In most other cases the facility to claim actual costs against the employer's profits will outweigh any increase in the taxable benefit in kind for the employee.

    Some employers may offer employees extra salary in place of private use of the company car and/or fuel. Non-P11D employees are taxed on the salary forgone. P11D employees are charged to tax and national insurance on what they actually get, either car or cash (ITEPA 2003 s 119).

Private use of vans

18. A fixed tax charge applies for private use of vans with a laden weight of 3.5 tonnes or less (ITEPA 2003 ss 154–166). The taxable amount is reduced by any payment by the employee for private use.

    Since 6 April 2005 there has been no charge where a van is primarily provided to an employee for business purposes but the employee is permitted to take the vehicle home (ordinary commuting). All other private use of the vehicle must be disallowed. However, the legislation does permit other private use if it is insignificant. It is understood that this would cover the use of the van to take rubbish to the tip as part of a normal commuting journey.

Where the above exemption does not apply the taxable amount is a fixed charge of £500 per annum where an employee has exclusive private use of a van (including where relevant the provision of private fuel). The charge is reduced to £350 if the van is four years old or more at the end of the tax year. The taxable benefit is reduced proportionately if the van is not provided for the whole year, or is unavailable for thirty consecutive days or more, or for periods when the van is a shared van (see below).

Where vans are shared between several employees, the total fixed charges at £500 or £350 are calculated and split evenly between those employees, regardless of variations in private use, but with no employee being taxed on more than £500. The benefit is not reduced if the employee has the use of a shared van for only part of the year (for example if he joins or leaves during the year). An employee may, however, elect to be taxed on £5 for each day of private use instead of the normal calculation.

If an employee has both exclusive and shared use in the same tax year, the charges are calculated separately and aggregated, but if the employee at no time had the use of more than one van, the total taxable benefit is restricted to £500 (before reduction by any employee contribution).

If a van is accepted as a van for VAT purposes then it will normally be treated in the same way by HMRC for income tax. A twin cab vehicle with a load area of more than one tonne will be treated as a van. Car derived vans will be treated as cars unless they meet the technical criteria specified by Customs. A list of such car derived vans is available on www.hmrc.gov.uk/business/vat/motor-trade.htm

A van charge is reduced proportionately if the vehicle is not available for a period of not less than 30 consecutive days. If a van is provided part way through a year, or available only for part of the year, then again a pro-rata charge applies.

Where the van is made available concurrently to more than one employee for private use by the same employer then the cash equivalent is worked out as if the van was not shared and then that charge is reduced on a just and reasonable basis to apportion the charge between the users.

Where it is a condition of the van being made available for private use, that the employee is required to pay for, and does pay for, that use, the cash equivalent is reduced.

The charge includes any private fuel usage.

From 6 April 2007 the discount for older vans is removed and the scale charge increased to £3,000. In addition where fuel is provided the charge will be increased by a further £500 to £3,500.

Mobile phones

19. From 2006/07 the provision of tax-free mobile phones has been limited to one per employee. However, no charge will be imposed in respect of any mobile phones provided for the employee's use before 6 April 2006 (ITEPA 2003 s 319).

     Despite the income tax exemption, private use by employees affects the input VAT that employers may recover. HMRC have, however, announced that input VAT may be recovered on the cost of the phones and on standing charges and also on call charges if private use is not permitted. If the employer charges employees for private use, input VAT on calls may be recovered in full but output VAT must be accounted for in the charges to employees. If no charge is made input VAT must be apportioned appropriately.

Business use of own vehicle, motor cycle or bicycle

20. Where an employee uses his own transport for business purposes, he is entitled to relief for the business use (ITEPA 2003 ss 229–236).

The fixed rates are as follows:

Cars and vans: First 10,000 miles in tax year	40p per mile
Each additional mile	25p per mile
Motor cycles	24p per mile
Bicycles	20p per mile

Payments by the employer up to the fixed rates for business mileage in an employee's own transport are not liable to tax or Class 1 national insurance. Any excess is liable to Class 1 NI (see below) and for tax purposes the excess will be shown on forms P11D and on forms P9D if it exceeds £25.

If the employer does not pay mileage allowances, or pays less than the fixed rates, the employee may claim an appropriate expenses deduction (mileage allowance relief) in his tax return. Employees are no longer able to make a claim based on actual costs, and the fixed rate cannot be increased by relief for loan interest paid or capital allowances.

Class 1 national insurance contributions are charged on business mileage allowances for cars and vans only to the extent, if any, that they exceed the authorised rates applicable to the first 10,000 miles, ie 40p per mile. If, instead of paying a mileage allowance, the employer reimburses the employee's fuel costs, the reimbursement counts as pay for Class 1 contributions, excluding the business proportion providing this is supported by mileage records. Class 1A rather than Class 1 contributions would be payable if an employer's credit card or agency card was used, as indicated in part (b) of the example.

In addition to the mileage allowance payment, an employer may also pay up to 5p per passenger per mile free of tax and national insurance for fellow employees carried in the employer's or employee's car or van where the journey constitutes business travel for both driver and passengers. The employee cannot claim any relief if the employer does not pay the passenger rate.

Employers have to pay the VAT scale charges on private fuel provided for employees' own cars. They currently can reclaim the input tax if they reimburse the cost to the employees, and can claim input tax on the fuel element of a mileage allowance, but not on the part of the allowance that is for repairs etc. The advisory rates in note 14 should be used for this purpose. This recovery of VAT paid by an employee has been ruled illegal by the European courts and revised rules will be issued shortly.

Use of employer-provided assets other than cars, vans or living accommodation

21. Where an employee has the use of an asset other than a car, van or living accommodation, the cash equivalent of the benefit is 20% of the market value of the asset at the time of its first provision plus the full amount of any expense incurred in providing the asset (hence the charge on Honiton for the use of the furniture in the company house). The cash equivalent is reduced proportionately where there is part business use of the asset, and is also reduced pro rata if the asset is only provided for part of the year. If the ownership of the asset is subsequently transferred to an employee then he is charged to tax at that time on the *higher* of:

   (a) The market value of the asset at the time of the transfer of ownership.

   (b) The market value at the time of the original provision less the total amounts charged on any employee as benefits under the benefits code of ITEPA 2003 for the use of the asset.

This calculation does not apply to the transfer of previously-loaned computers if the computer was first made available to the employee before 6 April 2006 or bicycle to an employee at market value (ITEPA 2003 s 206(6)).

Medical insurance

22. The cost of medical insurance is assessable on directors and employees earning £8,500 or more under the general charging provisions of the benefits code (ITEPA 2003 Part 3 Chapter 10). The cost of any medical treatment paid by the insurance scheme is irrelevant. The measurement of the benefit is *what*

it cost to buy that insurance. There is an exception for both tax and national insurance for the cost of insurance and/or medical treatment while an employee is working abroad (ITEPA 2003 s 325 and SI 2001/1004 Sch 3 Part VIII).

Meals and luncheon vouchers

23. Employees are not taxed on the benefit of free or subsidised meals if the meals are provided for the staff generally on the employer's own premises or in a canteen located elsewhere (but if a public restaurant was used, there would have to be an area separate from that open to the general public), or where using the canteen situated at the place of employment run by another employer where the facilities are not taxable on that employer's staff. (ITEPA 2003 s 317). Where companies do not have such separate facilities, the provision of luncheon vouchers is covered by the voucher provisions of ITEPA 2003 s 89 (see note 9), but luncheon vouchers of 15p per day are not chargeable. If their value exceeds 15p per day, the excess is chargeable on all employees and is reported at the year-end on forms P11D/P9D. The same value is treated as pay for Class 1 national insurance contributions. The full cost of the vouchers is allowable as an expense to the employer.

Child care

24. The provision of child care facilities for children aged under 18 is exempted from the employee benefits charging provisions (ITEPA 2003 s 318). The exemption does not cover supervised activity provided primarily for educational purposes.

    The facilities may be provided jointly with other employers, voluntary bodies or local authorities, but each employer must be partly responsible for finance and management. The premises must be registered where required by law, and they cannot be domestic premises. In addition the exemption covers another employer's staff, who work at the providing employer's premises, when using the childcare facilities.

    The exemption does *not* cover cash allowances, the provision of vouchers or the payment by the employer of the employee's child care bills. Such provision for child care expenses is liable to Class 1 national insurance as for tax.

    With effect from 6 April 2005 an employer may provide vouchers for qualifying child care to a value not exceeding £55 per week to employees (or £50 per week before 6 April 2006). Such vouchers are free of tax and national insurance (employers and employees). The employer may also pay the voucher provision costs. The vouchers must be accessible to all employees or to all persons working at the location where the scheme operates. A similar relief is available on employer contracted child care. Both father and mother can receive vouchers to the value of £55 per week under this provision for the same child. See also booklets IR115 and E18 (2005) (ITEPA 2003 ss 318–318D). It is possible to combine the provision of child care with equivalent salary sacrifice.

    For details of tax credits claimable in respect of qualifying child care costs and details of when it is disadvantageous to receive tax free child care vouchers see Example 5.

Examination prizes

25. The definition of earnings under the benefits code will catch a cash prize paid at the employer's discretion to an employee. This is also counted as earnings for tax credits. If the payment is in kind then it will be liable to Class 1A NI instead of Class 1 and excluded for tax credits.

Beneficial loans

26. P11D employees who have interest free or favourable interest rate loans from their employers are taxed on the shortfall of the interest charged compared with the official rate (ITEPA 2003 Part 3 Chapter 7). From 6 April 1999 the official rate is normally fixed for the whole tax year, although there is provision for the rate to be reduced if interest rates fall significantly during the year. The rate from 6 January 2002 is 5%. There is no tax charge on loans made to employees on commercial terms by employers who lend to the general public or if the loan is a qualifying loan for interest relief (see

Example 1 explanatory note 13). Nor is there any charge if the total of all beneficial loans does not exceed £5,000 at any time in the tax year. See Example 57 for further notes and a detailed illustration of the beneficial loans rules.

Computers used at home

27.   Where an employee has private use of a computer, the benefit is calculated as in 21 above ie based on 20% of the cost of the computer (including VAT) plus related expenditure, eg insurance and maintenance. Where computer equipment was first made available to employees generally before 6 April 2006 (including members of their family or household), the benefit is chargeable only to the extent that the cash equivalent (*before* reduction for business use etc) exceeds £500. The exemption does not apply where the equipment is only available to directors, or the equipment is made available to directors on more favourable terms than to other employees.

Computer equipment includes printers, scanners, modems, disks and other peripheral devices connected to and inserted into the computer and also software. However, the use of a telephone with the modem will give rise to a separate benefit in kind (ITEPA 2003 s 320).

The transfer of ownership of the computer will not give rise to the charge set out in 21 above provided the employee pays full market value and provided it was first made available before 6 April 2006.

Subsidised transport

28.   There is no benefit in kind charge on the provision by an employer of a free or low cost works bus service, free or subsidised travel on local public stopping bus services used by employees to travel to or from work, or employer financial or other support for other bus services used for such journeys providing in this latter case that the employees do not obtain the service on more favourable terms than other passengers (ITEPA 2003 s 242). A works bus must have 9 or more passenger seats, be used for qualifying journeys, and must be available to the employees generally. It may be used for limited purposes during a working day without the employees incurring a benefit, eg to take them shopping in the lunch break.

Bicycles

29.   Workplace parking for bicycles and motor cycles is free of tax and national insurance (ITEPA 2003 s 237). Furthermore an employer may provide a cycle (and safety equipment) for commuting and business journeys (ITEPA 2003 s 244). The equipment must be available to the employees generally and used mainly for qualifying journeys. Transfer of ownership at market value will not give rise to a tax charge (as set out in 21 above). Alternatively an employee may provide his own cycle for business journeys, claiming an allowance of 20p per business mile as indicated in note 20 above. If the employer pays less than 20p per business mile the employee may make a tax claim for the shortfall.

To encourage employees to travel to work by cycle, employers may provide 'cyclist breakfasts' without a tax charge on the employee. This is available even if only part of the employee's journey to work is by bicycle.

Car sharing arrangements

30.   Where employees car share and the arrangements break down in exceptional circumstances (eg the driver is required to return home during working hours because of illness of spouse/children) then the employer may provide transport to take the employees home without a charge to tax.

Entertaining expenses (including staff entertaining) and gifts

31.   If an employee receives amounts specifically for entertaining, or is specifically reimbursed for entertaining expenses he has incurred (such as the £1,560 received by Honiton in this example), those expenses are deductible in calculating taxable income (ITEPA 2003 s 357). They are disallowed in the employer's computation of taxable profit and employers who are trading organisations must tick a box on form P11D to indicate that this has been done. If an employee pays entertaining expenses out

of his salary or out of a round sum allowance not specifically earmarked for entertaining, he is assessed on the full salary or allowance and may not claim any deduction, but the employer is allowed to deduct the full salary or allowance paid to the employee in his profit computation.

The benefit arising from entertaining provided to employees by third parties is not charged to tax, unless it has been procured by the employer or it relates to services performed or to be performed in the employment (ITEPA 2003 s 265). Gifts to employees from third parties of up to £250 in a tax year are exempt (ITEPA 2003 s 324), unless they are procured by the employer or relate to services that are part of the employee's normal duties. S 264 provides that employees are not charged on the benefit of one or more annual parties etc that are open to staff generally, providing the cost to the employer for each person attending (including employees' guests) does not exceed £150 a year (VAT-inclusive). If the total cost per person for all annual functions exceeds £150 the exemption can be claimed on one or more of the functions for which the total cost does not exceed £150. For the treatment of entertaining expenses for the employer see Example 15 explanatory note 7.

Scholarships and training courses

32. Although income in the form of scholarships and educational grants is exempt from tax for the recipient under ITTOIA 2005 s 776, scholarships awarded to children of employees are assessable on the parent (ITEPA 2003 ss 211–215) unless they are fortuitous awards paid from a trust fund or scheme under which not more than 25% of the total payments relate to employees (whether P11D employees or not).

33. An employee is not taxed on the payment or reimbursement by his employer of the cost of a training course providing it satisfies stipulated criteria (ITEPA 2003 Part 4 Chapter 4). The provisions cover not only directly job-related training but also training in health and safety and to develop leadership skills. As well as the direct costs, the exemption covers learning materials, examination fees and registration of qualifications. Travelling and subsistence expenses are allowed to the same extent as they would be for employment duties.

Where employees are retrained in new work skills when they are about to leave or have left their present jobs, they are not taxed on the benefit of the expenses of retraining which are paid for or reimbursed by the employer, and the employer is able to deduct the cost in calculating taxable profits (ITEPA 2003 s 311).

Employees on full-time and sandwich courses at universities and colleges lasting 1 year or more may receive pay of up to £15,000 a year tax free while they are on the course from 1 September 2005 (previously £7,000 pa) (Revenue Statement of Practice 4/86 updated 16 March 2005).

Long service awards

34. An employer may make a non-taxable award in kind to an employee to mark not less than 20 years service. The award must have a value not exceeding £50 per year of service and awards cannot be made at intervals of less than 10 years (ITEPA 2003 s 323).

Homeworkers' expenses

35. Payments by the employer for reasonable additional household expenses incurred in carrying out duties of the employment at home under home-working arrangements are exempt from income tax under ITEPA 2003 s 316A. To minimise the need for record keeping employers can pay up to £2 per week (£104 per year) without supporting evidence of the costs the employee has incurred.

National insurance

36. For detailed notes on national insurance contributions see Example 47. For the special rules relating to marketable assets such as gold and commodities see Example 9 explanatory note 12.

Pre-owned assets

37. From 6 April 2005 a free-standing income tax charge arises where a taxpayer has the use or enjoyment of land, chattels or intangible assets previously owned by them or financed by gifts made by the taxpayer in the previous seven years. For detailed notes see Example 92.

Tips and gratuities

38.   See Example 47 part (d) for the tax and national insurance treatment of gratuities.

Pension provision

39.   HMRC have confirmed that tax-efficient pension contributions will be relievable by employers as deductible business expenses if the overall remuneration level is reasonable for the work done.

(a)   Explain the method of calculation of the cash equivalent of the benefit applicable to a motor car used privately.

(b)   Set out the method to be used if the vehicle does not have a CO_2 emissions figure.

(c)   John Hodges is employed by Cecil Ltd. He travels 7,000 business miles and 8,000 private miles per annum in his company car, which he will change early in 2007. His employer has offered John a choice of car from the following list:

Car	CO_2 emissions figure	Fuel type	Expected list price plus accessories £
VW Passat 2.3 V5	223	Petrol	19,905
VW Passat 1.9 TDI Sport	154	Diesel	20,900
BMW 740 (1997 model)	–	Petrol*	39,875**
Ford Galaxy	242	Petrol	19,460

   * 4,398 cc
  ** Second-hand price in 2007 £10,000

Advise John of the amounts on which income tax would be charged in 2007/08 in respect of each car assuming the car was available from 6 April 2007.

(d)   Comment on the advisability of Cecil Ltd providing fuel for John to use privately in the company car.

(a)   **Computation of cash equivalent of car benefit**

Carbon dioxide emissions figure

Where a car is provided by an employer to an employee or member of his family or household from 6 April 2002, the cash equivalent of the benefit is based on the published carbon dioxide (CO_2) emissions figure (in grams per kilometre) for a given car. That figure is determined by the manufacturer using an EU standard test.

Many aspects affect the emissions figure, including the size and efficiency (state of tune) of the engine, fuel used, transmission (manual, automatic, two or four wheel drive) and accessories (eg air conditioning). Each model variant will have a separate emissions figure. From 1 March 2001 that figure appears in the car 'log book', to which reference should be made or on the internet at www.vca.gov.uk. For cars registered between 1 January 1998 and 1 March 2001 the emissions figure can be obtained from a booklet published by the Vehicle Certification Agency, 1 The Eastgate Office Centre, Eastgate Road, Bristol, BS5 6XX or on the internet at www.smmt.co.uk

The emissions figure is rounded down to the nearest whole 5 grams below, eg CO_2 emissions figure 187 becomes 185, and is then converted to a percentage using the HMRC table shown below. Cars are expected to become more environmentally friendly and the scale figures are being progressively reduced.

The maximum percentage to be applied to the list price of the car is 35%. In calculating the benefit, the list price is capped at £80,000 (see Example 10 explanatory note 13 for detailed notes on the meaning of list price).

CO_2 Emissions Figure – Cars registered from 1.1.98

CO_2 emissions in grams per km

2002–2003	2003–2004	2004–2005	2005–2006 to 2007–2008	2008–2009 onwards	Percentage of car's price taxed
165	155	145	140	135	15
170	160	150	145	140	16
175	165	155	150	145	17
180	170	160	155	150	18
185	175	165	160	155	19
190	180	170	165	160	20
195	185	175	170	165	21
200	190	180	175	170	22
205	195	185	180	175	23
210	200	190	185	180	24
215	205	195	190	185	25
220	210	200	195	190	26
225	215	205	200	195	27
230	220	210	205	200	28
235	225	215	210	205	29
240	230	220	215	210	30
245	235	225	220	225	31
250	240	230	225	230	32
255	245	235	230	235	33
260	250	240	235	240	34
265	255	245	240	235	35

From 2008/09 qualifying low emisions cars will have a percentage of 10%.

Special provisions for particular circumstances

Diesel cars have a low CO_2 figure but produce other emissions. To maintain an environmental balance with petrol vehicles, the percentage is increased by 3% (up to the maximum 35%). The 3% surcharge does not apply to diesel cars first registered before 1 January 2006 that meet Euro Standard 4 (ultra low emission diesel cars).

Disabled drivers who are required to use an automatic car because of their disability may use the CO_2 figure of the equivalent manual car.

If a normally fuelled car is converted to use gas, the cost of conversion is excluded from list price. However, a car designed to use gas or bi-fuels at manufacture receives no reduction from list price in cases where the car benefit is taxed by reference to the CO_2 emissions figure. Such cars benefit from a lower % rate – see below.

Electric cars are taxed on 9% of list price. Gas cars have a CO_2 figure. Bi-fuel cars have two CO_2 figures, the lower (invariably the gas figure) being used to calculate the relevant percentage. For gas cars and bi-fuel cars the charge is reduced by a discount of 1% of list price, and if the CO_2 figure is below the qualifying level for the minimum 15% charge for the year, there is an additional discount of 1% of list price for each 20 grams per km that the emissions figure is below the qualifying level. In the case of hybrid cars (electric/petrol), the charge is reduced by a discount of 2% of list price plus an extra 1% for each 20 grams that the CO_2 figure is below the qualifying level for the 15% charge. Rotary engined cars have a percentage of 35%.

From 6 April 2006 the above discounts are simplified and become:

– Cost of conversion is disregarded for bi-fuel gas and petrol cars where conversion is after type approval.

– 2% discount for bi-fuel gas and petrol cars where manufacture of or converted before type approval.

– 3% discount for hybrid electric and petrol cars.

– 6% discount for electric only cars.

Periods of unavailability, business mileage, older cars etc

A reduction for periods of unavailability of at least 30 consecutive days is available. The charge is reduced by capital contributions made by an employee not exceeding £5,000. There are no discounts for business use or for the age of the vehicle. Where the car provided is more than 15 years old at the end of the tax year (classic cars) and has a market value exceeding £15,000 then market value is substituted for list price, up to the maximum figure of £80,000.

Second cars are charged at the same rate as first cars.

(b)   **Computation of cash equivalent where CO_2 figure is unavailable**

Cars registered before 1 January 1998 do not have a CO_2 emissions figure computed to the relevant standard. The percentage will continue to be based on engine size, but with no discounts for age or business use, as follows:

Engine size (cc)	*Percentage of car's price taxed*
0–1400	15%
1401–2000	22%
2001 and over	32%
Cars without a cylinder capacity (eg rotary engined petrol cars)	32%

A limited number of cars produced on or after that date will also not have a CO_2 figure, eg kit cars, imports of specialised cars from outside the EU, home-built cars. The percentage to be used is then:

Engine size (cc)	Percentage of car's price taxed
0–1400	15%*
1401–2000	25%*
2001 and over	35%
Cars without a cylinder capacity (eg rotary engined petrol cars)	35%

* Plus 3% supplement for diesel cars.

(c) **John Hodges – cash equivalent of benefits**

	List price		2007/08	
	£	%		£
VW Passat 2.3 V5	19,905			
CO_2 figure 223 = 220		31		6,170
VW Passat 1.9 TDI Sport	20,900			
CO_2 figure 154 = 150				
(17% + 3% diesel supp)		20		4,180
BMW 740 (used 1997 model)	39,875			
Over 2000 cc		32		12,760
Ford Galaxy	19,460			
CO_2 figure 242 = 240		35		6,811

Thus the most expensive car in the schedule (the VW Passat 1.9 TDI, the cost of the BMW being £10,000) gives the lowest tax charge (£4,180) and the cheapest car (the BMW) gives the highest tax charge (£12,760).

Because 'perk cars' have the same charge as business cars, it may be very tax-efficient to provide a perk car, especially where the emissions percentage is low (say 21% or lower). The provision of a car where the percentage is high (say 29% or higher) is unlikely to be cost-effective. The provision of a business car may continue to be tax-effective if the emissions figure is low or private miles are high, or for most high business mileage users. The provision of an employee's own car and payment of mileage allowances is likely to be more tax-efficient in the case of older, larger cars such as the BMW above where the taxable benefit is over 127% of the second-hand cost of the car.

(d) **Provision of fuel for private use**

In most circumstances, the provision of fuel for private use is not cost-effective. An increase in salary to compensate for the employees buying their own fuel can be at a lower figure than the cost of the fuel purchased. The price of fuel and the advisory fuel scale will alter over the life of the car, but the principle can be illustrated using current figures. In the case of John Hodges he would have a tax charge on a benefit for 2006/07 as follows (annual amounts, pro-rata to actual dates car provided):

VW Passat 2.3 V5	14,400 x 31%	£4,464
VW Passat 1.9 TDI Sport	14,400 x 20%	£2,880
BMW 740	14,400 x 32%	£4,608
Ford Galaxy	14,400 x 35%	£5,040

Cecil Ltd could use the advisory fuel rates for company cars (see Example 10 explanatory note 14) or actual costs.

Assuming fuel consumption as shown below, and assuming the price of fuel to be petrol 99p per litre = £4.49 per gallon, diesel 101p per litre = £4.59 per gallon, the position would be:

		Actual cost per mile	Advisory scale rate to 30/6/06	Advisory scale rate from 1/7/06
VW Passat 2.3 V5	31.4 mpg	14p	16p	18p
VW Passat 1.9 TDI Sport	55.1 mpg	8p	9p	11p
BMW 740	24.2 mpg	18p	16p	18p
Ford Galaxy	27.7 mpg	16p	16p	18p

Assuming that John Hodges is a basic rate taxpayer, the salary increase required and overall savings to Cecil Ltd might be:

If Cecil Ltd provides private fuel for VW Passat 1.9 TDI Sport

	£	£
Fuel cost to Cecil Ltd for 15,000 miles		
272 gallons @ £4.59	1,248	
Class 1A NI on fuel charge £2,880 x 12.8%	368	1,616
Cost to John		
Tax on £2,880 @ 22%	633	

If John buys fuel and charges Cecil Ltd for 7,000 business miles, using advisory fuel scale rates

Fuel cost (as above)	1,248	
Less: business use 7,000 miles @ 11p	770	
Net cost to John	478	
Tax saved as above	633	
Saving to John	155	
Cost of business fuel to Cecil Ltd		770
Saving to Cecil Ltd		846

	£	£
If Cecil Ltd provides private fuel for BMW		
Fuel cost to Cecil Ltd for 15,000 miles		
620 gallons @ £4.49	2,784	
Class 1A NI on scale charge £4,608 x 12.8%	590	3,374
Cost to John		
Tax on £4,608 @ 22%	1,013	

If John buys fuel and charges Cecil Ltd for 7,000 business miles, using actual costs

Fuel cost (as above)	2,784	
Less: business use 7,000 miles @ 18p	1,260	
Net cost to John	1,524	
Tax saved as above	1,013	
Extra cost to John	511	
Extra salary required to compensate:		763
Less: Tax @ 22%	168	
NI @ 11%	84	252
		511

	£	£
Cost of business fuel to Cecil Ltd	1,260	
Salary increase to John	763	
Employer's NI on additional salary @ 12.8%	98	2,121
Saving to Cecil Ltd		1,253

The calculations are assumed to be VAT neutral. Similar, smaller savings would apply to the other cars considered.

(a) Explain the tax treatment of lump sum payments made when an employee takes up employment (sometimes called 'golden hellos' or 'golden handcuffs').

(b) On 31 December 2006 Gordon Jones retired from his employment with Widgets International plc after 30 years' service, the first 12 of which were at the company's overseas branch. He received a lump sum ex gratia payment of £100,000.

Show how much of the £100,000 is taxable.

(c) Mrs Baines retired from her employment on 31 October 2006 because of a permanent disability. She was awarded an ex gratia lump sum payment of £40,000 on that day.

Show how much of the £40,000 is taxable.

(d) Mrs Juliette Brassington, managing director of T & S Textiles Ltd, was made redundant on 5 September 2006. She received £25,000 as compensation for loss of office and was also given her company car at its agreed value of £5,000.

Show the amount on which she is taxable in respect of the redundancy package.

(e) Gerry Scattergood was made redundant from Shillingford in 2006/07 after many years service.

Upon leaving he was paid a lump sum of £40,000 which has been accepted by HMRC as compensation for loss of office. He also received £2,000 statutory redundancy pay.

Gerry's taxable income for 2006/07, before considering the £40,000, amounted to £25,300, none of which was savings income.

Calculate the tax payable on the £40,000 termination payment.

(f) Supposing the statutory income of £25,300 of Gerry Scattergood for 2006/07 in part (e) had included jobseeker's allowance totalling £600, state how this will have been dealt with for tax purposes.

(a)   Where a lump sum payment is made to a prospective employee, it is necessary to decide whether the payment is taxable under the general earnings rules as remuneration for future services, or whether it represents compensation for some right or asset given up on taking up the employment, in which case it escapes a general earnings charge. These are essentially questions of fact to be decided by the Commissioners, with the usual rights of appeal.

In Jarrold v Boustead 1964 a signing-on fee to a Rugby football player to compensate him for giving up his amateur status was held not to be taxable. The same applied to an allotment of shares to an accountant to compensate him for giving up his position as senior partner in his own firm and taking on employment as managing director with a former client company (Pritchard v Arundale 1971). But in the case of Glantre Engineering Ltd v Goodhand 1983, a payment to the company's accountant when he took on the role of financial director with the small, dynamic but relatively new company was held to be an inducement to take up the employment rather than compensation for leaving his previous employment with a nationally known firm of accountants. Similarly, a payment by Nottingham Forest Football Club to Peter Shilton when he was transferred to Southampton was held to be an inducement to join Southampton rather than an ex gratia payment on leaving Nottingham Forest (Shilton v Wilmshurst, HL 1991). It is clear therefore that great care needs to be taken when considering the tax treatment of such payments.

Sometimes a lump sum is paid in return for the individual agreeing to restrict his conduct or activities in some way, for example agreeing not to leave to take up employment with a competitor within a certain period of time (often called a 'golden handcuff'). All payments in respect of such restrictive covenants are taxed as pay in the normal way, and the employer is allowed to deduct them as an expense (ITEPA 2003 s 225). If an employee makes such an agreement in return for a non-cash benefit, the value of the benefit still counts as pay for tax and national insurance contributions (ITEPA 2003 s 226). HMRC do not regard s 225 as applying where the only undertaking by the employee is that he will not pursue an action against the employer concerning the termination of his employment (Statement of Practice SP 3/96).

(b)   **Gordon Jones**

HMRC may take the view that the ex gratia payment represents an arrangement to provide a benefit from an unapproved retirement benefits scheme and is therefore taxable in full under ITEPA 2003 Part 6 Chapter 2, in which case none of the provisions granting full or partial exemption relating to overseas service (ITEPA 2003 ss 413, 414) or the £30,000 exemption (ITEPA 2003 s 403(1)) will be available. In so far as the amount falls within the tax-free lump sum maximum limits, when added to any such sum received from a pension fund, there will be no tax liability. Any excess will be liable to income tax. Normally a tax-free lump sum on retirement can only be paid from an approved pension scheme. HMRC Savings, Pensions, Share Schemes (HMRC SPSS) will, however, approve a single lump sum payment where there was no scheme in force and the payment satisfies the normal requirements for a tax-free lump sum. Approval is not necessary for a payment of up to £8,800 that satisfies the requirements (see explanatory note 5).

If the payment is not regarded as caught under ITEPA 2003 s 394 (non-approved pension payments), the position will be as follows:

	£
Ex gratia sum on retirement – 31 December 2006	100,000
Less: Exemption under ITEPA 2003 s 403	30,000
	70,000
Less: Exemption for overseas service (see note 6(c) (ii)) 12/30ths	28,000
Taxable part of £100,000	42,000

(c)   **Mrs Baines**

Mrs Baines's ex gratia lump sum is wholly exempt from tax under the 'golden handshake' provisions because it arises through her disability (ITEPA 2003 s 406). Unless the disability was the result of an accident, however, the payment will possibly be regarded as being received under an unapproved retirement benefits scheme, in which case it will be chargeable to tax in full under ITEPA 2003 Part 6 Chapter 2, subject to the possibility of obtaining approval for a lump sum payment as indicated in (b) above.

(d) **Mrs Juliette Brassington**

The golden handshake provisions apply both to cash payments and benefits in kind, but only if they are not otherwise chargeable to tax. If an ex gratia payment or benefit represents a reward for past services, it will be charged to tax under the general earnings provisions, in which case national insurance will also be due, Class 1 on the cash and Class 1A on the benefit. If it is not, it may be regarded as a benefit from an unapproved retirement benefits scheme (see (b) above). HMRC have, however, stated that this will not normally apply to a straightforward redundancy package. Unless the car is regarded as a reward for past services, therefore, its value will be exempt from tax under ITEPA 2003 s 403(1), along with the compensation payment of £25,000. In view of the amounts involved it would have been more straightforward if Mrs Brassington had been given a redundancy payment of £30,000, then allowed to buy the car from the company at the market value of £5,000.

(e) **Gerry Scattergood – Tax payable on lump sum termination payment – 2006/07**

	£		£
Termination payment			40,000
Exempt under ITEPA 2003 s 403(1)	30,000		
Less: Required to cover statutory redundancy	2,000		28,000
Taxable portion remaining			12,000
Less unused part of basic rate band (33,300 – 25,300)			8,000
Taxable at the higher rate			4,000
Tax payable:	8,000	@ 22%	1,760
	4,000	@ 40%	1,600
	12,000		£ 3,360

(f) The jobseeker's allowance of £600 received by Gerry Scattergood, although taxable, will have been paid to him in full, and if he was still unemployed at the end of the tax year the benefit office will have worked out his tax position by reference to his coding and sent him any refund due. If he has underpaid tax the underpayment will normally be collected by a coding adjustment for a later year. If he had started work again before the end of the tax year, the benefit office would have refunded any tax overpaid to that point and given him a form P45 to produce to his new employer. Compensation payments do not prevent an unemployed person getting unemployment credits for national insurance purposes for the period covered by the compensation.

Explanatory Notes

Golden handcuffs

1. The rules in relation to lump sum payments on commencement of employment are explained in part (a) of the example on page 12.2.

Termination payments and benefits

2. A payment or benefit received in connection with the termination of the holding of an office or employment or any change in its functions or earnings, whether made in pursuance of any legal obligation or not is, if not otherwise chargeable to tax, chargeable to tax under ITEPA 2003 Part 6 Chapter 3. Special rules do, however, apply to the calculation of the taxable amount.

Section 403 can apply to a termination payment received in the UK by a taxpayer who is neither resident nor ordinarily resident in the UK in the tax year and who did not perform any UK duties in that year. The exemption and reliefs in note 6(c) will apply where appropriate.

3. Tax is charged in the tax year or years in which payments and benefits arise, after applying the reliefs and exemptions in note 6 below. The £30,000 exemption is allocated to the earliest payments and benefits received. If both payments and benefits are received in the same tax year, the exemption is used first against cash payments then against benefits. Benefits are valued using the benefits code, or if an asset has appreciated since the employer acquired it, the market value at the relevant time using the 'money's worth' principle (ITEPA 2003 s 415(2)(a)). Where the benefit is a beneficial loan, the taxable amount is treated as interest paid (ITEPA 2003 s 416), so that relief is available if the loan is a qualifying loan (see Example 1 explanatory note 13).

4. The proviso 'This chapter does not apply to any payment chargeable to income tax apart from this Chapter' in ITEPA 2003 s 401(3) is a reminder that a lump sum payment is not automatically exempt from the normal rules of taxing remuneration. The test is broadly whether the lump sum payment arises from *cessation of the employment or duties*, rather than a payment for services already performed or to be performed in the future.

   If it can be seen to relate to services already performed (eg contract of service provides for a twelve months' employment at £300 per month and a lump sum of £6,400 at the cessation of the twelve months' employment) or to services to be performed (eg the employee is currently paid £20,000 per annum, and he agrees to accept £15,000 per annum for the next five years in consideration of a lump sum of £20,000 now), the payment will be caught as general earnings and liable to Class 1 national insurance contributions in the normal way.

   HMRC have sought to treat enhanced redundancy payments as liable to tax and national insurance contributions in the normal way where the arrangements had become part of the terms of the contract of employment. This was held not to be correct in the case of Mairs v Haughey 1993, the House of Lords deciding that the relevant factor was whether the payments were for services rendered by the employees or because their jobs had ceased to exist. It can be argued that the same reasoning should apply to all compensation for loss of office, whether it is contractual or not. It is important, however, that any payment must not be specifically provided for in the employment contract (even if the payment is discretionary), or be part of an established practice on the part of the employer. Such payments would be regarded as made under the terms and conditions of the employment and would be liable to both tax and national insurance. The Revenue won the case of EMI Group Electronics Ltd v Coldicott in the High Court in 1997 (confirmed by the Court of Appeal in 1999) on the grounds that pay in lieu of notice in that case was a contractual substitution for earnings, whereas in the Mairs v Haughey case the payment was a contractual substitution for a redundancy payment. The Revenue also won the case of Richardson v Delaney in 2001, which related to compensation based on a compromise agreement varying a taxable provision within the contract of employment.

   If a contract of employment provides for pay in lieu of notice it will always be liable to tax and national insurance. Where the contract does not so provide, and the employer requires the employee to leave immediately, he will be in breach of the contract of employment and the payment will represent compensation for that breach. Care should, however, be taken with the consequential employment law implications of the employer failing to honour the terms of the employment contract. See Tax Bulletin 63 February 2003 for HMRC view on the tax treatment of payments in lieu of notice.

Benefits under employer-financed retirement benefits schemes

5. Certain payments and benefits received on termination of employment are treated as benefits under an employer-financed retirement benefits scheme rather than being taxed under the provisions of ITEPA 2003 Part 6 Chapter 3. This applies where there are 'arrangements' to provide relevant benefits, so that tax is chargeable under ITEPA 2003 s 394. Before 6 April 2006 schemes were known as unapproved retirement benefits schemes. Now unregistered schemes are known as employer-

financed retirement benefits schemes. Generally, the taxation post-6 April 2006 is the same but transitional rules apply for some former unapproved retirement benefits schemes in respect of certain payments on or after that date. The general rule is that relevant benefits received from the scheme will be charged to tax as employment income under ITEPA 2003 s 394.

The key difference is that the meaning of relevant benefits differs for unapproved schemes.

Generally, a relevant benefit is any pension, lump sum, gratuity or other like benefit given:

(a)   on retirement or on death, or

(b)   in anticipation of retirement, or

(c)   after retirement or death in connection with past service, or

(d)   on or in anticipation of or in connection with any change in the nature of the employee's service, or

(e)   by virtue of a pension sharing order or provision.

For unapproved schemes, only cash benefits count as 'relevant benefits'. For employer-financed schemes, both cash and non-cash benefits count as 'relevant benefits'.

However, it does not include benefits provided solely by reason of an employee's disablement or death by accident occurring whilst he or she is in the employer's service nor benefits provided on ill-health.

In addition, relevant benefits (for employer-financed schemes) do not include

(i)   pension income within Part 9 ITEPA 2003, or

(ii)   benefits chargeable under Schedule 34 FA 2004.

There must be a 'scheme' for a charge to arise under the non-approved or employer-financed retirement benefits scheme legislation.

The definition for both schemes is essentially the same and states that it 'includes a deed, agreement, series of agreements or other arrangements' providing for relevant benefits. SP13/91 explained that a scheme may be quite informal. It includes, for example:

–   A decision at an employer's meeting

–   A decision by an employee with delegated authority or in accordance with a policy

–   The making of a payment under a plan, pattern, policy, practice or decision-making process or custom.

Although SP13/91 has been withdrawn with effect from 6 April 2006 because of the introduction of the simplified pensions regime, that does not affect HMRC's interpretation of 'scheme'.

Under SI 2006/210 and ITEPA 2003 s 393B, there is no tax charge on the payment of a lump sum by an employer-financed retirements benefit scheme under the rules that were in place before 6 April 2006.

Where the benefits include a beneficial loan, the amount taxable under ITEPA 2003 s 394 in respect of the loan is treated as interest paid (ITEPA 2003 s 399), so that relief is available if the loan is a qualifying loan (see Example 1 explanatory note 13).

Reliefs and exemptions

6.   If it can be established that a payment is not otherwise chargeable to tax and therefore falls to be treated under the special rules for lump sum payments, ITEPA 2003 s 403 et seq gives certain exemptions and reliefs as follows:

(a)   Certain amounts received are wholly exempt, viz:

Payments and benefits for entering into a restrictive covenant (since caught specifically under ITEPA 2003 s 225, as shown in part (a) of the example).

Payments made in connection with the employee's death, injury or disability.

Benefits under registered pension schemes.

(b)   In addition, the first £30,000 of other sums received does not attract tax (any statutory redundancy payments being included in this figure (ITEPA 2003 s 403)).

(c)   If part of the service in the employment is performed overseas, then the following rules apply:

  (i)   *No tax at all is charged* where the foreign service comprises:

    In any case, three-quarters of the whole period of service; or

    the whole of the last ten years, if the service exceeded ten years; or

    if the service exceeded twenty years, half of the period of service including any ten out of the last twenty years (ITEPA 2003 s 413).

  (ii)   *If the foreign service is not covered under the above provisions* the taxable amount is reduced by the proportion of foreign service to total service (ITEPA 2003 s 414).

  (iii)   Any lump sum benefits from an overseas pension scheme are exempt from tax in the same way as other amounts received if (i) above applies, and are proportionately chargeable as in (ii) if (i) does not apply (Revenue concession A10).

Legal costs

7.   If an employee incurs costs in obtaining a termination payment they do not reduce the taxable amount. Where, however, an employer pays an employee's legal costs in obtaining the payment, HMRC will not treat the payment of costs as a taxable benefit if the payment is made direct to the employee's solicitor following an out of court settlement, or if it is made to the employee under a Court Order (Revenue Concession A81).

Way in which tax is collected and reporting requirements

8.   To the extent that a termination payment exceeds £30,000 it is treated as pay for PAYE purposes if it is paid before the employee leaves, and is entered on the tax deduction working sheet and form P45, with PAYE being applied in the normal way. If the payment is not made until after the employee has left and been issued with form P45, the payment is still taxed under PAYE, but the employer is required to deduct tax at the basic rate. Class 1 national insurance is not payable on the termination payment.

Where the taxable amount relates to a benefit rather than a cash payment, tax will not be deducted by the employer.

The employee will pay the whole of the tax on benefits, and any higher rate tax due on cash payments, in his self-assessment, or claim a refund if appropriate. The due date of payment is 31 January after the end of the tax year, eg 31 January 2008 for 2006/07, and interest on underpaid tax, if relevant, would run from that date. Although making the payment after the employee has left defers the payment of tax for a higher rate taxpayer, it may result in increased payments on account for the following year, since the balance of tax payable forms part of the tax paid directly rather than through PAYE.

As far as the employer is concerned, unless the termination settlement is wholly cash, or the total value of the settlement including benefits is estimated not to exceed £30,000, the employer must provide details to HMRC not later than 6 July following the end of the tax year in which the termination settlement was awarded (copies being provided to employees to enable them to complete their tax returns). The details should cover the total value of the settlement, the amounts of cash and the nature of the benefits to be provided and their cash equivalents, indicating which, if any, amounts and benefits are to be provided in later years. No further report needs to be submitted unless, exceptionally, there is a subsequent variation increasing the value of the termination settlement by more than £10,000, in which case a report must be sent to HMRC by 6 July following the tax year of variation. If a report is not submitted because the value is originally estimated not to exceed £30,000, but it subsequently exceeds that amount, a report and employee copy must be provided by 6 July following the tax year in which the value is increased. The employer is liable to a penalty of up to £300 if he fails to submit a report, plus up to £60 a day from the time the £300 penalty is imposed until the report is submitted. If an incorrect report is submitted fraudulently or negligently the maximum penalty is £3,000.

Top slicing rules

9. Where the income of the year in which a termination payment is received includes savings income, then although the savings income is treated as the top slice of income for all other purposes (except in relation to tax charges on life assurance policies), it is taken into account before termination payments (TA 1988 ss 1A(5)(6), 833(3)).

In part (e) of the example, therefore, if Gerry Scattergood's other income of £25,300 had included non-dividend savings income of £5,000, the rates of tax payable by him would have been:

On non-savings income	2,150	@ 10%
	18,150	@ 22%
On non-dividend savings income	5,000	@ 20%
	25,300	
On compensation (as before)	8,000	@ 22%
	40,000	@ 40%
	12,000	

If the normal rules had applied and the non-dividend savings income of £5,000 had been treated as the top slice of income, a further £5,000 of the compensation payment would have been taxed at 22%, giving an increase in tax payable of £5,000 @ (22 − 20)% = £100.

If the savings income of £5,000 had been dividends, the increase in tax payable would have been £225 without the special rule, ie:

Increase of £5,000 @ (22 − 10)% =	600
Less Saving of £5,000 @ (40 − 32½)% =	375
	£225

Where practicable, the termination of employment should be timed so as to reduce the employee's liability at the higher rate. If the employee's income will fall after he leaves, for example, it would be better to make the termination payment at the beginning of a new tax year so that little or none of his employment earnings are included in his income.

Jobseeker's allowance

10. Jobseeker's allowance is means tested after the first six months and is not payable in any event to those over pensionable age.

The receipt of a termination payment does not affect entitlement to non-means tested jobseeker's allowance except to the extent that it represents pay in lieu of notice. However, it does affect entitlement to the means tested allowance if the taxpayer then has more than £3,000 capital, and if capital exceeds £8,000 the means tested allowance is not available.

Jobseeker's allowance is chargeable to tax as social security income under Part 10 of ITEPA 2003, as indicated in part (f) of the example. In most cases an overpayment rather than an underpayment will arise, because the amount received is usually less than the available personal allowance. The taxpayer does not get a refund, however, until he starts work again, or until the end of the tax year if he remains unemployed.

If employees are on strike, they may be able to claim income support. Employers cannot make tax refunds to employees while they are on strike. (Refunds would normally be due because no wages would be paid to utilise the tax free pay the employee is entitled to each week.) Even if the strike continues beyond the end of the tax year the employee will not receive any refund from the employer. The employer will give him a statement at the tax year end showing any refund due for that tax year and the refund will be made by the tax office when his position for the year is finalised.

Tax Credits

11.   Because entitlement to WTC and CTC is based upon actual income for the whole fiscal year redundancy can have the effect of reducing average earnings and increasing entitlement. However, a claim can be backdated by only three months. It may be considered appropriate to put in a protective claim by 6 July in any tax year if redundancy is a possibility, or as soon as loss of employment may occur, to maximise credits. Any amount taxable under Chapter 3 of Part 6 of ITEPA 2003 will be income for tax credits (ie amounts in excess of £30,000 etc) as will any payment for entering a restrictive covenant to which ITEPA 2003 s 225 applies. Strike pay counts as income for tax credit purposes. However, benefits under Chapter 2 of Part 6 of ITEPA 2003 are not included as income.

(a)   Mark, who runs a garage business providing vehicle repairs, has written to you asking for advice about the mechanics who work in his garage. They wish to be treated as self-employed, and Mark has asked for your views on whether or not this is possible, the tax implications for him of their being so treated, and the potential risk to him if he treats them as self-employed and subsequently HMRC deem them to be employees.

    Prepare brief notes for a meeting with Mark to discuss the matter.

(b)   Wanda, a single woman, has recently returned to the UK after working overseas for a number of years. She is undecided whether to accept an offer of full-time employment from a company located near her home, or to set up her own consultancy business using her home as the base for her business.

    You have advised her that the rules governing the deductibility of expenses for employees differ from the rules for self-employed persons. Wanda has now asked for a report summarising the position.

    Prepare the report for Wanda, covering the basic rules for allowable expenditure, and their application in particular to travelling expenses (both within and outside the UK), subscriptions, and clothing.

(c)   Ken Brown is employed as a clerk in the local factory, but has for many years been interested in antiques and he has pursued this as his hobby in most of his spare time.

    In order to finance a holiday in the Bahamas, however, Ken had recently started buying and selling antiques for which he charged less than the normal retail price but nevertheless made a reasonable profit. When discussing this with a friend, he was told that he would have to pay income tax on this income as he was in fact carrying on a trade.

    Consider whether or not Ken is carrying on a trade, giving your reasons fully and referring to leading cases in this area.

(a) *Notes for meeting with Mark on employed or self-employed status of mechanics*

1. The main distinction between trading income from self-employment taxable by ITTOIA 2005 part 2 and employment taxable under ITEPA 2003 is that the former is a contract for services and the latter a contract of service (ITEPA 2003 s 4(1)(a)). HMRC has issued a booklet IR56 giving guidelines to help in the decision. (A separate booklet IR148 is available for those in the construction industry.)

2. Factors pointing to employment are that the individual works wholly or mainly for one business, that he needs to carry out the work in person, to take orders as to when and how to do it, to work at the premises of those providing the work, or at a place determined by them, and to work set hours at an hourly, weekly or monthly rate, and that he is paid for overtime, sickness and holidays. An entitlement to a pension through the contributions of those for whom he works is also persuasive.

3. Factors pointing to self-employment are that the individual risks his own capital and bears any losses arising, that he controls whether, how, when and where he does the work, provides his own equipment, is free to employ others to do the work he has undertaken, and is required to bear the cost of correcting faulty work.

4. None of the factors is in itself conclusive in one direction or the other, and all the circumstances need to be taken into account. Nevertheless, two factors pointing towards self-employment are usually persuasive (if not determinative of the issue). First, the unrestricted right for the person to select a substitute to do the work. Alternatively, the lack of mutual obligation between the worker and the person requesting the work. However, these contractual terms have to be genuine and not merely included in a contract in order to satisfy the tax authorities. Written evidence, such as contracts, invoices, VAT registration, will have a considerable bearing on the decision.

5. If the mechanics were treated as self-employed, Mark would pay for their services in full and they would be liable for tax and Class 2 and Class 4 self-employed national insurance contributions. If their turnover was high enough they would have to register for VAT. Alternatively, they could voluntarily register for VAT.

6. Applying the general principles of what constitutes self-employment, however, it seems likely that HMRC would regard the mechanics as employees. If Mark treats them as self-employed without seeking a ruling in advance, and they are later deemed to be employees, he will be liable for tax and national insurance contributions. If the charge is based upon the amount paid being the gross pay then no deduction will be allowable in computing Mark's profits for the tax and employees' NI. That amount might not be recoverable from the employee. A deduction will be allowed for employer's NI. If the tax and NI due is calculated on the basis that the amounts paid were net of deductions (ie by grossing up the net payments to find the gross wages), the amount of tax and national insurance paid by Mark will be allowed in computing his own profits for the period in which they are paid. There is also the possibility of penalties if the failure is considered to be wilful. There is no deduction available against Mark's profits for the penalties. HMRC would not collect the tax from the mechanics unless they were held to have known that Mark had wilfully failed to deduct tax.

    A recent case heard by the Special Commissioners (Demibourne Limited v HMRC (2005)) highlights the difficulties of getting a worker's status wrong. In that case, a worker was treated as self-employed. He was therefore paid gross and he declared his earnings on his self-assessment return (and paid the tax accordingly). Subsequently, HMRC queried the worker's status on a PAYE enquiry. They considered that the worker was in fact an employee and raised a determination on the company under SI 2003/2682 reg 80 for the PAYE due but unpaid. By this time it was too late for the worker to reclaim his tax from HMRC and the employer had no right of recovery from the employee.

The Special Commissioner agreed that the worker was an employee and therefore that the reg 80 determination should be upheld. However, he realised that this would have meant HMRC receiving the tax twice (once from the worker and once from the employer) at the expense of the employer. He suggested that HMRC gave a credit for the tax already accounted for although such a request could not be binding on HMRC.

7. HMRC have one person at each of their tax offices nominated to deal with questions on an individual's status. Mark should contact either his local tax or national insurance contributions office to ask for a ruling.

8. From 6 April 2000 tax and NI contributions are charged on deemed salary when personal services are provided through an intermediary such as a partnership or limited company. The charge is on the intermediary, therefore the client cannot be liable for the tax and national insurance of the worker where an intermediary is used. Mark could safeguard his position by insisting that his workers can only provide services to him other than as an employee if a partnership or limited company is used as an intermediary.

(b) To: Wanda

From: A N Adviser   17 October 2006

Rules governing the deductibility of expenses for employees compared with the rules for self-employed persons

1. The main difference in the expenses treatment for employees compared with the self-employed is that employees are allowed to deduct expenses that are wholly, exclusively and necessarily incurred in the performance of the duties of their employment, whereas the self-employed are allowed to deduct expenses that are incurred wholly and exclusively for the purpose of their trade, profession or vocation, without any requirement that the expenses should be necessary.

2. Dealing first with employees, the general expenses rule is found in ITEPA 2003 s 336, which provides that an employee is allowed to deduct expenses wholly, exclusively and necessarily incurred in performance of his duties. Sections 337 to 342 of ITEPA 2003 give relief for certain travelling expenses, with additional provisions for overseas travel in ss 370 to 375.

3. (i) Travel expenses are allowed where they are either in the performance of the duties of the employment or for 'necessary attendance' (ITEPA 2003 ss 337–340).

   The full cost of travelling on business direct from home and associated subsistence expenses is allowed, unless the journey is ordinary commuting to/from your permanent workplace. From 6 April 2002 fixed mileage allowance payment rates must be used if the travel is in your own vehicle.

   If you are temporarily sent from your normal workplace to a different workplace for up to 24 months, returning to your normal place of work thereafter, you are allowed relief for the related travelling, accommodation and subsistence expenses. This will not apply if the temporary posting is expected to exceed 24 months. If it does in fact exceed or looks as if it will exceed 24 months the expenses are allowable up to the time that fact became known.

   (ii) If *part* of the duties of an employment are performed abroad, it is specifically provided by ITEPA 2003 s 370 that travel expenses *paid or reimbursed by the employer* for any journey from any place in the UK to the overseas destination and back again are allowed, providing the duties can only be performed abroad and that the 'wholly and exclusively' rule is satisfied (see s 370(4) and (5)). The provisions of ITEPA 2003 s 338 outlined in (i) above would, however, give relief for the expenses of travelling abroad wholly for business whether the cost was borne by the employer or the employee, and would in addition give relief for subsistence expenses. ITEPA 2003 s 371 also provides relief for up to two journeys a tax year by a spouse and children to visit an employee working abroad for 60 days or more, but this is not relevant in your case. Similarly if *all* the duties of your employment are performed abroad, you are entitled to a deduction for the expenses of travelling abroad to take up the appointment and returning to the UK thereafter if your earnings include an amount in respect of such travel (ITEPA 2003 s 370(1)(2)(3)) ie they are again paid or reimbursed by your employer. You are also allowed relief for board and lodging expenses in similar circumstances (ITEPA 2003 s 376).

(iii)   If *all* the duties of one or more employments are performed abroad and providing you are resident and ordinarily resident in the UK (and domiciled here if your employer is a foreign employer), you are entitled to a deduction for the expenses of travelling abroad to take up the appointment, travelling between the appointments, and returning to the UK thereafter. For this relief there is no requirement for the payments first to have been met by your employer (ITEPA 2003 ss 341, 342). You are entitled to deduct an appropriate part of the expenses if the travelling is only partly for the purposes of the employment (ITEPA 2003 ss 341(5) and 342(8)).

(iv)   Where someone makes a dual purpose visit (eg a business trip combined with a holiday), either in the UK or abroad, this will not deny relief for the expenses providing the journey had to be made in the performance of the duties of the employment. If, however, a deduction is being claimed under ITEPA 2003 s 370 to balance an expenses payment by an employer (as in (ii) above), it will be denied if the journey has both a business and a private purpose. The cost of any journey that was specifically private would obviously be disallowed (for example, if your employer required you to go to Paris, but you went to the South of France on holiday first).

4.   Subscriptions that are payable in order to be able to carry on particular employments, for example, that of an architect, health professional or teacher (ITEPA 2003 s 343), are specifically allowable by statute. This also applies to other professional subscriptions to bodies of persons approved by HMRC, providing the activities of the body are relevant to the employment (ITEPA 2003 s 344).

Subscriptions other than approved professional subscriptions must satisfy the general rule that they be 'wholly, exclusively and necessarily incurred' and very few subscriptions would qualify. A list of subscriptions may be obtained at www.hmrc.gov.uk/list3

5.   The expense of clothing is not allowed unless it is protective clothing or a uniform. This is so even if the clothing is worn only at work.

6.   Turning now to the position of the self-employed, the general rule is found in ITTOIA 2005 Chapter 4, which provides that a self-employed person cannot deduct expenses unless they are 'wholly and exclusively laid out or expended for the purposes of the trade, profession or vocation' (s 34), and that the expenditure must be of an income and not a capital nature (s 33).

7.   As far as travelling expenses are concerned, the cost of travel from home to work base is not allowed, and journeys that are partly for business and partly for private purposes are disallowed. There is no distinction between travelling expenses in the UK and abroad, unless the trade, profession or vocation is carried on wholly abroad, in which case the cost of travelling abroad and back again, and between two separate foreign businesses, is allowed, providing the absence is wholly and exclusively for the purpose of performing the functions of one or more of the businesses (ITTOIA 2005 ss 92–94).

Where a self-employed person's work base is his home, all business travelling from the home base is allowed, even if there is only one person for whom work is done. But merely doing some of your work at home does not enable you to claim the cost of travelling from home to the main work base.

8. Subscriptions to trade associations, although not usually satisfying the general expenses rule, are allowed providing the association has entered into an agreement with HMRC to pay tax on the excess of their receipts over their allowable expenses. Other subscriptions would need to satisfy the general rule.

9. As far as clothing is concerned, the self-employed are in no better position than employees, and unless clothing is special or protective clothing the cost is not 'wholly and exclusively' for the purposes of the business.

   The position is different for value added tax, because there is no 'wholly and exclusively' requirement. Input tax can be recovered if the clothing is for business purposes, with an apportionment if there is part private use.

10. To summarise, although the requirements for expenditure to be allowable in an employment are more stringent than for the self-employed, there are a large number of areas, in particular those dealt with in this report, where the treatment is broadly the same.

(c) In order to decide whether activities constitute trading, the starting point is the basic definition of a trade in TA 1988 s 832, which states that the word trade 'includes every trade, manufacture, adventure or concern in the nature of trade'.

On its own the definition is not very helpful, but it has been given legal interpretation in many cases that have come before the courts.

In 1955 the Royal Commission on the Taxation of Profits and Income established six 'badges of trade', which represent the major considerations to be taken into account in deciding whether or not a trade is being carried on. These were:

(1) The subject matter of the realisation

(2) The length of the period of ownership

(3) The frequency or number of similar transactions by the same person

(4) Supplementary work on or in connection with the property realised

(5) The circumstances that were responsible for the realisation

(6) Motive.

Some or all of these would usually be present in trading activities, although the absence of any one or more would not necessarily indicate that a trade was not being carried on.

In relation to subject matter, it was considered in CIR v Fraser (1942) that there were only three reasons for purchasing an article: for own use or consumption, as an investment possibly to yield income, or for resale at a profit, ie for the purpose of trading. The very nature of some assets will point towards trading rather than investment or own use. In CIR v Rutledge (1929), for example, there was an isolated purchase of 1 million rolls of toilet paper. And in Wisdom v Chamberlain (1969), concerning the short-term purchase and resale of silver bullion as a hedge against devaluation, it was clear that the asset itself gave the owner no aesthetic pleasure or pride of ownership. In both cases the profits were held to be assessable as trading profits.

A long period of ownership may indicate investment rather than trading. Obviously many assets appreciate in value with the passage of time, and holding assets to realise capital gains rather than buying and selling short-term to realise income has been widespread practice among those liable to income tax at higher rates. A quick sale, on the other hand, may not necessarily indicate trading, for example, when an asset is received as an inheritance and is disposed of shortly afterwards.

An isolated profitable transaction has been held to be trading, as in the case of CIR v Rutledge (above). Frequent repetition of transactions obviously constitutes even stronger evidence of trading, and it may be particularly important where the nature of the asset is not such as to be usually regarded as trading stock, eg Leach v Pogson (1962), where the taxpayer was held to be trading in establishing and selling driving schools. But there is a prima facie presumption against trading for speculative dealings in securities, and making 200 such transactions in about three years was held not to be trading in Salt v Chamberlain (1979).

Where an asset is resold after being processed or worked on in some way, this may indicate trading, eg buying in bulk and breaking down into smaller saleable units. A leading case in this area is Cape Brandy Syndicate v CIR (1921), where a syndicate imported brandy, blended it, re-casked it and resold it.

A need for ready money to meet a sudden emergency would be clear evidence of the absence of a trading motive on the sale of an asset.

The lack of a profit motive is not conclusive evidence against trading (re Duty on Estate of Incorporated Council of Law Reporting for England and Wales, 1888). But clearly the existence of a profit motive is a very strong indicator that a trade exists.

Applying these general considerations to the circumstances of Ken Brown's activities, it is clear that he will almost certainly be held to be carrying on a trade.

His original activity of purchasing antiques as a hobby, and presumably owning them for lengthy periods and reselling some of them from time to time, would be regarded as investment rather than trading. Antiques would give him pride and pleasure in their ownership, and their appreciation in value over time would give the opportunity to realise a profit on his investment. But the nature of his activities has changed with the commencement of short-term buying and selling. It was stated in the case of Hawes v Gardiner (1957), that what started as a hobby may develop into a trade, and that is almost certainly the case here. Ken's intention of holding for personal enjoyment and investment has changed to frequent buying and selling short-term to make an immediate profit.

As a result of the change of Ken's hobby to a trade, there is also a liability to Class 2 national insurance. Ken must notify the change within three months of the month in which his intention altered by submitting form CWF1 to HMRC's National Insurance Contributions Office at Newcastle upon Tyne or by calling the helpline on 08459 15 45 15. Failure to notify within the time limit will result in a penalty of £100 (SI 2001/1004 reg 87). The penalty will not be charged if throughout the period of failure to notify Ken would have been able to claim exemption from Class 2 NI because his expected earnings were below the small earnings exemption limit (£4,465 for 2006/07).

It is advisable for Ken to obtain the Revenue booklet P/SE/1 'Thinking of working for yourself' and also a 'Starting up in business' guide from the helpline.

Explanatory Notes

Employment or self-employment

1. The distinction between employment and self-employment is often hard to draw. It is not set out in the legislation. Instead it is a question of fact based upon a series of tests developed from case law. A number of different elements have to be considered and a picture needs to be drawn from all the relevant factors. The question was well summarised by Mummery J in Hall v Lorimer, the summary being approved by Nolan LJ when the case went to the Court of Appeal (1993): 'In order to decide whether a person carries on business on his own account it is necessary to consider many different aspects of that person's work activity. This is not a mechanical exercise of running through a check list to see whether they are present in, or absent from, a given situation. The object of the exercise is to paint a picture from the accumulation of detail. The overall effect can only be appreciated by standing back from the detailed picture which has been painted, by viewing it from a distance and by making an informed, considered, qualitative appreciation of the whole.'

   The difficulty is determining what weight to give to any individual item and what conclusion to draw from the whole. Very few tests or facts give a conclusive answer. The strongest single indicator of self-employment is the exercised ability to provide a substitute. A contract of service (employment) cannot exist unless it contains an obligation on the part of the employee to provide his/her services personally. In the case of Express & Echo Publications Ltd v Taunton (1999), it was made clear that if a worker did not have to perform the duties personally then he could not be an employee. However, the reverse, ie the requirement to undertake the duties personally, does not automatically make the worker an employee (McManus v Griffiths (1997)), but will be a strong pointer.

The courts use the test of 'mutual obligations' extensively. If no obligations exist there can be neither a contract of service nor a contract for services. Thus where a person may, but need not, be asked to perform a service and, if asked, is free to decline to provide the service asked for, there exists no mutuality of obligation and thus no contract of service. Note, however, mutual obligations may be created by custom and habit, which in turn may give rise to an enforceable contract of service.

The other major factor to take into account is the 'economic reality'. Is the worker really in business on his own account? Does he have the ability to subcontract work to others? Is he responsible for his own actions? In summary, can he gain or lose by his own actions?

In any given case all of the factors will not be relevant. Each case must be determined on its own facts. The factors include:

–   Mutual obligations

–   Substitution, the ability to subcontract work

–   Financial risk

–   Is there a written (or unwritten) contract of service

–   Business management, own office, notepaper etc

–   Number of providers of work

–   Provision of business and public liability or professional indemnity insurance

–   A proper accounting system

–   Contract for fixed term or job

–   Basis of remuneration

–   Capital invested in business

–   Equipment – who provides major items

–   Control

–   Place of duties

–   Provision of benefits, sick pay, holiday pay or pension scheme

–   Organisation (integration with client's business).

2.   In recent years HMRC has taken a different view in relation to various activities, and have succeeded in some cases taken before the courts, eg Sidey v Phillips (1987), where a non-practising barrister who lectured part-time on legal subjects and had two other separate sources of earnings was held to be an employee, and Walls v Sinnett (1987), where a part-time lecturing appointment held by a professional singer was also held to be an employment. They had succeeded in the much earlier (1973) case of Fall v Hitchen, where a dancer on a six-month Equity contract was held to be an employee. They have, however, now decided that self-employment will usually be more appropriate for most people in the performing arts. Employment treatment will be restricted to cases where someone receives a regular salary to perform in a series of productions, with a period of notice required to end the contract, such as permanent members of orchestras, and of opera, ballet and theatre companies. Where entertainers are taxed as employees they may claim a deduction for agent's fees up to a maximum of $17\frac{1}{2}\%$ of their earnings in the relevant tax year (ITEPA 2003 s 352).

HMRC has lost some other recent cases, including the case of McMenamin v Diggles (1991), in which a barrister's senior clerk had changed his contractual arrangements to bring himself into the self-employed category, and Hall v Lorimer mentioned in 1 above (CA 1993), concerning a vision mixer who undertook short-term engagements for various production companies. The Revenue won the case of Barnett v Brabyn (1996), where they successfully argued that the taxpayer was self-employed despite only working for one client, but lost the case of Andrews v King (1991), where they argued that a gangmaster should be treated as self-employed. The court disagreed, holding that Andrews was selecting workers and hiring on behalf of his employers.

3. The same treatment should apply both to tax and national insurance, but someone (in any business) who has been reclassified as self-employed has the option of not claiming a refund of Class 1 contributions, so that the contributions will remain on his record for the purpose of earnings-related pension. Employers will be able to reclaim their share of the Class 1 contributions wrongly paid for such self-employed workers, subject to SSA 1998 s 54, which provides for a two year time limit. Earlier contributions are deemed to have been correctly paid irrespective of the employment status. This also applies to Class 1A and 1B contributions. Where contributions have been wrongly paid in the belief that someone was an employee, then after the end of the next following tax year (eg after 5 April 2008 for contributions paid in respect of 2006/07) the contributions will be treated as having been correctly paid for the relevant period, which means there will be no need for the HMRC National Insurance Contributions Office (NICO) to amend the contribution record of the worker concerned or to make repayments. The rules on NIC for entertainers is different – see Tax Bulletin 65 June 2003 for the latest position.

4. Contractors in the construction industry were required to have completed a review of the status of their workers by 5 April 1997 and to have commenced PAYE deductions of tax and national insurance contributions for those who should properly be treated as employees. If contractors are subsequently found not to have done so, arrears will be payable back to 5 April 1997, but not earlier unless there is clear evidence of evasion. Construction workers whose services are supplied by employment agencies are taxed as employees.

5. From 6 April 2000, under the 'IR35' rules, the provision of personal services, such as construction labour, through a partnership or limited company are 'looked through' and the individual is treated as an employee (see Example 88 for full details).

However, the application of these rules has been thrown into some doubt following the employment case of Cable and Wireless v Muscat CA (2006). In that case an individual was held to have been an employee even though engaged through a personal services company.

6. The main points of difference between employment and self-employment are dealt with in part (a) of the example, and part (b) illustrates some of the consequences in terms of allowable expenditure.

Travelling and subsistence expenses

The treatment of employees' travelling expenses is dealt with in ITEPA 2003 ss 337–342. Relief is given for travelling expenses, that is, amounts necessarily expended on travelling in the performance of the duties of the employment, or other travelling expenses which are attributable to the necessary attendance of the employee at any place in the performance of his duties and are not expenses of ordinary commuting or private travel.

Ordinary commuting broadly means travel from home to the permanent workplace. Private travel means travel between home and a place that is not a workplace, or between two places neither of which is a workplace. A permanent workplace is a workplace that is not a temporary workplace, and a temporary workplace is a workplace the employee attends to perform a task of limited duration or for some other temporary purpose. A workplace is not a temporary workplace if the employee works there continuously for a period of more than 24 months or if the employment itself is expected to last for 24 months or less.

Work at a particular place is regarded as continuous if the duties of the employment fall to be performed to a significant extent at that place (significant being regarded by HMRC as 40% or more). Site-based employees with no permanent workplace are allowed the cost of travelling to and from home and subsistence while away providing the job at the site is expected to and does last for not more than 24 months. As and when it becomes clear that the job will last for more than 24 months, travel and subsistence expenses are taxable from that time. Site-based employees are not allowed relief for subsistence expenses if they have no permanent home, because subsistence expenses must be attributable to the business travel.

Employees are entitled to relief for the full amount of qualifying travelling expenses. The full cost of meals and accommodation while travelling or staying away on business is allowable as part of the cost of travel. Business travel includes travelling on business from home where the journey is to (or from) a temporary workplace, or where the nature of the employment requires the employee to carry out his duties at home (but doing work at home for convenience rather than because of the nature of the job does not turn the home into a workplace). Where a journey has both a business and a private purpose, the expense will be allowed if the journey is substantially for business purposes.

As far as national insurance contributions are concerned, the rules are the same as for income tax, except that mileage payments may be made at 40p for every mile without NIC becoming due whereas for income tax there is a 10,000 mile limit before the lower rate of 25p applies. Contributions will normally be payable only if the employer makes a payment to the employee that exceeds the cost of a business journey.

Relevant cases concerning travelling expenses for the self-employed are Horton v Young (1971), where the expenses of travelling from home to the sites of the main contractor by a bricklaying subcontractor were allowed, and Newsom v Robertson (1953), where a barrister's expenses of travelling between his home, where he did some of his work, and his London chambers were disallowed. In the recent High Court case of Powell v Jackman (2004) the Court found that a milkman's business base was not his home, where he kept his business records, nor his depot where he kept his milk float, but that he had a defined area of business being his milk round. This reversed the decision of the Special Commissioners.

Clothing

As far as clothing is concerned, it has been held in various cases concerning employees (Woodcock v IRC (1977), Hillyer v Leeke (1976)) that clothing is 'partly for cover and comfort' and thus does not come within the 'wholly and exclusively' rule. The same rules were applied in the case of Mallalieu v Drummond (1983), relating to a self-employed barrister.

Nature of a trade

7.   Part (c) of the example indicates the main considerations in determining whether or not a trade exists. Where there are one or more isolated transactions it has to be decided whether they are 'in the nature of trade' or merely the conversion of capital in one form into capital in another. A purchase and sale is either a trading transaction or a capital transaction. There is no other interpretation, and a charge could not, for example, be raised under the 'miscellaneous profits or gains' provisions.

8.   The badges of trade mentioned in part (c) of the example were reviewed in the case of Marson v Morton 1986, in which it was held that the sale of land originally bought as an investment to be held for a year or two but in fact sold only a few months later was not 'an adventure in the nature of trade'. The following points were made, which re-state and in some respects add to the indicators listed by the Royal Commission:

     (i)   Although not conclusive, lack of repetition is a pointer that may indicate something other than a trade.

     (ii) Is the transaction related to the taxpayer's existing trade or trades?

     (iii) Was the subject matter a typical trading commodity which can only be turned to advantage by realisation?

     (iv) Was the transaction carried out in a typical trading way for that type of commodity?

(v) If the item was bought with borrowed money, that points to an intention to short-term re-sale.

(vi) Was the item re-sold in one lot or broken down into smaller lots?

(vii) What was the intention of the purchaser at the time of purchase?

(viii) Did the item yield either enjoyment or pride of ownership, or produce income, any of which would point to investment rather than trading?

The judge stated that 'in 1986 it is not any longer self-evident that unless land is producing income it cannot be an investment'.

Mutual trading

9. Where there is mutual trading, so that the people carrying on the trade and the customers are the same persons, as with members' clubs, any resulting surplus is not taxable as a trading profit, because it represents an excess of the members' contributions over the association's expenditure. This does not extend to trading with those who are not members, since the principle of mutuality does not then apply. Care must be taken to put into place a system to clearly identify the turnover attributable to members, so as to eliminate the non-taxable proportion. Many 'club licences' no longer restrict bar sales only to members. The club would also be taxable on any other profits, such as investment income and capital gains, and as an unincorporated association other than a partnership it would be liable to corporation tax rather than income tax and/or capital gains tax (see Example 48 explanatory note 1). Banks and building societies are able to pay interest to clubs without deducting tax, so the clubs will be due to account for corporation tax on the full amount of the interest at the appropriate rate. HMRC may be prepared to treat a club as dormant if it is mainly for recreational and other non-commercial purposes, even though there is strictly a small tax liability. Unless HMRC have given written notification of dormant status, however, clubs must complete returns and account for tax under the self-assessment system. Where dormant status has been granted, clubs must notify HMRC within twelve months after the end of the relevant accounting period if their circumstances change, or if chargeable assets are likely to be disposed of (see HMRC's Guide to corporation tax self-assessment CTSA/BK2). See also HMRC's booklet IR46 *Clubs, societies and voluntary associations*.

The introduction of a £10,000 per annum nil rate band for corporation tax from 1 April 2002 meant that most small clubs do not have any tax liability even where limited trading with non-members takes place, or there is interest received. However, the reintroduction of a 19% rate from 1 April 2006 has removed this saving. See also Example 91 part B and explanatory notes 10 to 12 for the tax exemptions for registered amateur sports clubs.

Illegal trading

10. It is established case law that profits of illegal trading are nonetheless taxable. The unlawful nature of the contracts cannot be used as a defence to avoid paying tax on the proceeds. Hence the profits from illegal gambling machines were assessable in Mann v Nash (1932), from illegal street betting in Southern v AB (1933) and from prostitution in CIR v Aken (1988). As to betting, it was held in Partridge v Mallandaine (1886) that a racecourse bookmaker's profits were assessable as the profits of a vocation even though he could not at law enforce the wagering contracts. In contrast someone whose means of livelihood was betting on horses from his private address at starting prices was held not to be carrying on a trade (Graham v Green, 1925).

Trading or investment

11. The general conclusion to be drawn from the legislation and case law is that in cases where an activity is not clearly established as a trade at the outset, there may nonetheless come a point where its character is such that it may be challenged as a trading activity. An example is buying and selling Krugerrands. Occasional purchases and sales of Krugerrands with fairly lengthy intervening periods of ownership would be treated as capital transactions subject to capital gains tax. If, however, the scale and frequency of the transactions became such as to indicate a trading motive they would be challenged by HMRC as assessable as trading income.

12. Individuals pay tax on gains at non-dividend savings income rates, and companies pay tax at the same rates on both income and gains. There are, however, significant differences between the treatment of income and gains that need to be borne in mind, particularly the following.

   Capital profits of companies are reduced by an indexation allowance. For individuals the indexation allowance is available only for periods up to April 1998 and taper relief is available thereafter. Capital profits may also be eligible for some relief or even exemption, including, for individuals, an annual exemption of (currently) £8,800. Income profits, on the other hand, may be reduced or eliminated by paying pension premiums, or acquiring tax-efficient investments. Trading losses may be set against total income and capital gains, whereas capital losses may only be set against capital gains (except for losses on shares subscribed for in an unquoted trading company – see Example 77 explanatory note 10).

Define capital expenditure and revenue expenditure and receipts and explain how they are treated differently for tax purposes.

Capital and revenue expenditure

The terms capital and revenue expenditure are not defined in the legislation. However, profits must be calculated in accordance with generally accepted accounting practice (GAAP) (ITTOIA 2005 s 25). For accounting periods from 1 January 2005 this will be UK GAAP or, where appropriate, international accounting standards (IAS) apply. There are provisions to prevent groups of companies gaining a tax advantage by one company using IAS and another UK GAAP. The normal accounting distinction between capital and revenue expenditure is that expenditure that is going to affect only the current accounting period is revenue expenditure, whereas expenditure that is going to give benefit to the business over more than one accounting period is capital expenditure.

Interest is a revenue item whatever the nature of the loan (ITTOIA 2005 s 29). Capital expenditure (s 33) and capital receipts (s 96) are excluded from profits unless specifically included by legislation. For example, the deduction of part of a short lease premium is spread over the term of the lease and revenue profits are reduced by capital allowances on certain capital assets. Capital expenditure that does not qualify for capital allowances forms part of the allowable cost for capital gains purposes, but on certain assets, such as leases, the expenditure is deemed to waste away over the tax life of the asset, so that no tax relief at all is given for the expenditure that is so treated. The same applies to any revenue expenditure that is specifically disallowed, such as entertaining expenses.

The tax treatment of capital and revenue expenditure has been varied for companies in recent years, with certain items being taken out of the capital gains area and brought into the computation of revenue profits. The main areas are the treatment of loan relationships (see Example 62) and the treatment of goodwill and intangible assets (see Example 65). In other instances, companies are entitled to deduct a greater amount from profits than the expenditure incurred, in particular in relation to research and development expenditure (see Example 51). These differences need to be borne in mind when considering what follows.

In determining the treatment of expenditure as revenue or capital, guidance can be obtained from the cases that have come before the courts. These cases often give conflicting opinions however. Lord Wilberforce, in the 1979 case of Tucker v Granada Motorway Services Ltd said that 'reported cases are the best tools that we have, even if they may sometimes be blunt instruments'. It is important to remember that the cases are only a guide, and each new situation must be considered on its own facts. In the case of Vodafone Cellular Ltd v Shaw (CA 1997 – see below) the judge in the High Court said that the decision involved 'a measure of gut reaction' in an area with 'an over-abundance of case law and the danger of over-citation'.

A recent case that considered the distinction between capital and revenue was CIR v John Lewis Properties plc (2003). In that case the Court of Appeal set out certain tests to determine whether an item is capital or revenue:

1. If the item is long lasting it is more likely to be a capital item. On the other hand, if it is appropriate to classify the item as part of the fixed, rather than the circulating capital of the business, then it will be a capital item even though it has a brief life. The context is therefore important.

2. The value of the asset is important, the higher the relative value the more likely the item is capital.

3. The fact that a payment causes a diminution in value of the asset is important but this diminution need not be permanent. It should be judged at the time of the disposal, and the size of the reduction is material.

4. A single lump sum payment is more likely to be capital and a series of recurring payments revenue.

5. Where a disposal of an asset is accompanied by the transfer of risk this indicates a capital transaction.

In some of the older cases, two different tests emerged. The first was the distinction between fixed and circulating capital (essentially the difference between the fixed and current assets of a business) and the second was the 'enduring benefit' test stated in Atherton v British Insulated and Helsby Cables Ltd (1926): 'When an expenditure is made not only once and for all, but with a view to bringing into existence an asset or an advantage for the enduring benefit of a trade, I think that there is very good reason (in the absence of special circumstances leading to an opposite conclusion) for treating such an expenditure as properly attributable, not to revenue, but to capital'. This case was cited by the Revenue in the Vodafone case mentioned above, the Revenue contending that a cancellation payment by Vodafone to escape from a requirement to pay 10% of their profits by way of annual fees to an American company holding 15% of Vodafone's shares yielded an enduring benefit to Vodafone and was therefore a capital payment. This was rejected by the court, but the Commissioners and the High Court found against Vodafone on the grounds that the payment, although accepted as revenue expenditure, benefited not only the parent company but its subsidiaries as well, so that it failed the 'wholly and exclusively' test in TA 1988 s 74(1)(a) (the provision applicable for companies). This decision was reversed by the Court of Appeal, which held that the *purpose* of the payment was to remove a liability from Vodafone and it did exclusively benefit that company, even though the *effect* was to benefit the other companies in the group as well.

In the Tucker case mentioned above, the House of Lords considered that the first step was to decide on what asset the expenditure had been incurred. (So if it was a current asset, such as a motor vehicle for resale by a car dealer, sums spent on putting it into saleable condition would be revenue expenditure.) If the asset was a capital asset, it was then necessary to consider the nature of the expenditure, so that expenditure linked to its acquisition or disposal (such as legal expenses on buying or selling a property) would be capital expenditure, whereas expenditure on maintaining and repairing it would be revenue. This general principle has been extended to the treatment of liabilities, particularly in the field of exchange losses, where it was held by the House of Lords in Beauchamp v Woolworth 1989 that capital borrowing was something that is to be borrowed once and for all and income borrowing is going to recur every year. The company's exchange losses on repaying substantial sums that it had borrowed for a five-year period were therefore capital losses and could not be deducted in calculating income profits. (Special rules apply to the treatment of exchange gains and losses relating to companies – see Example 62 explanatory note 2.)

Repairs or improvements

One of the key areas where the distinction is important is that of repairs. There are two aspects, first the treatment of repairs to newly acquired assets, and second the question of whether an item is a repair and thus allowable or an improvement or renewal and thus not allowable.

Where a newly acquired asset is repaired, the expenditure will not be allowed for tax purposes if the repairs must be done in order to bring the asset into use in the business (Law Shipping v CIR (1924)). If the asset is usable and commercially viable in its existing state, the subsequent repair expenditure will be allowable (Odeon Associated Theatres Ltd v Jones (1972)).

As far as improvements are concerned, the essential question is whether you are left with what you had originally or whether you have something extra. Money spent by a railway company in increasing the number of sleepers under each rail was capital expenditure, but expenditure on replacing worn rails and sleepers was revenue expenditure (Rhodesia Railways Ltd v Income Tax Collector of Bechuanaland Protectorate 1933). This case also raises the question of renewals. What needs to be decided is what is the entirety. If you incur expenditure on renewing a subsidiary part of an asset, you have repaired the asset. If you replace the entire asset, you have incurred capital expenditure. Thus the cost of demolishing and rebuilding a colliery chimney was held to be capital expenditure, since the chimney was the entirety (O'Grady v Bullcroft Main Collieries Ltd (1932)), whereas the cost of removing and replacing a factory chimney was a repair to part of the factory building and was allowable (Samuel Jones & Co (Devondale) Ltd v CIR (1951)).

Provisions

The 1998 case of Jenners Princes Street Edinburgh Ltd v CIR raised the question of when a sum is expended for repairs. The departmental store had carried out a survey relating to external repairs and at the year-end was in the process of granting contracts to carry out the repair work. The actual work was done in the following two years. The Special Commissioners agreed with the company that a specific provision had been made, that it accorded with sound commercial accounting principles and therefore the amount had been 'expended' in the accounting sense even though not paid out.

In the 1999 case of Herbert Smith v Honour the High Court held that the expected future loss on a lease of vacated premises was an allowable deduction in the year of vacating the property, the provision being required under Financial Reporting Standard 12 (FRS 12) issued September 1998, which states that 'if an entity has a contract that is onerous, the present obligation under the contract should be recognised and measured as a provision'.

Under FRS 12, provisions must be made, and can only be made, when at the balance sheet date 'a business has a present obligation (legal or constructive) as a result of a past event, it is probable that expenditure will be required to settle the obligation, and a reliable estimate can be made of the obligation'.

In addition, post balance sheet events must be considered in arriving at the quantification of the provision. For example, a stock obsolescence provision cannot value stock at an amount below that subsequently achieved on an actual sale, ie its net realisable value. In the same way a provision cannot be made against a debt which has subsequently, but before the finalisation of the accounts, been paid in full. If settled at a reduced amount then the provision is restricted to the actual loss (FRS 21).

All profits realised by the balance sheet date must be included even if invoiced after that date. However, the profits of a sole trader or partner are not realised until the service is completed (see Example 25(b)).

The Revenue set out their views in Tax Bulletin 44 issued December 1999 and Working Together Issue 13, published June 2003. A provision will be deductible provided it is a revenue amount, the provision is required by generally accepted accounting principles, does not conflict with statute and can be accurately quantified.

Goodwill and intangible assets

Another Accounting Standard that has a particular bearing on tax computations is FRS 10 – Goodwill and intangible assets. FRS 10 broadly requires *purchased* goodwill and intangible assets (but not internally created goodwill and intangibles) to be written off over the expected economic life of the asset. In some cases the tax law prescribes a different treatment, for example, expenditure incurred by individuals on goodwill is wholly capital expenditure and a deduction against profits cannot be made. FRS 10 does, however, affect the tax treatment of some payments for intangible assets, a particular example being transfer fees for football (and other sports) players. The fees are now written off over the term of the player's contract (FA 1999 s 63). As indicated above, the treatment of goodwill and intangible assets for companies has changed from 1 April 2002, the treatment now being largely as prescribed by accounting standards.

Capital profit or trading income

Similar principles to those outlined above are used to distinguish receipts which are part of the trading income from capital profits. Receipts of the trade form part of income, whereas capital receipts are dealt with under the capital gains rules.

The disposal of trading stock clearly gives rise to trading income, whereas the amount received for disposal of a fixed asset is a capital receipt. Particular difficulty arises in relation to compensation payments. Lump sums are not necessarily capital receipts. It depends on whether the compensation is to make good damage to, or for the physical destruction of, a capital asset of the business.

Compensation relating to the cancellation of trading contracts, including agency contracts, is usually treated as a trading receipt, unless the contract is so dominant that its loss accounts for substantially the whole of the company's trade (Barr Crombie and Co Ltd v CIR (1945)), or the contract regulates the whole structure or framework of the trade (Van den Berghs Ltd v Clark, (HL 1935)). The Van den Berghs decision was followed in the case of Sabine v Lookers Ltd (1958), where the Court of Appeal held that compensation for a material variation of a 'continuity clause' that had previously given a car distributor an ongoing option to renew its main distributorship was a capital receipt because the agreement 'governed Lookers' whole trade and was not merely one of several contracts or engagements'.

Supplementary notes

1. In the absence of a specific statutory provision, the trading rules would not permit a deduction for expenses incurred prior to the commencement of trade. Such expenses are, however, specifically dealt with in ITTOIA 2005 s 57, which provides that pre-trading expenditure incurred by an individual

within seven years prior to the commencement of a trade, which would have been allowable expenditure if it had been incurred after the commencement, is treated as incurred on the first day of trading and is thus allowable as an expense of the first accounting period. The same applies to companies, except for pre-trading interest, for which different rules apply (see Example 48 explanatory note 6).

2. Legal charges on acquiring an asset such as a lease are part of the capital cost and are not allowed in computing taxable profits. HMRC will by concession allow the cost of *renewing* a short lease (ie one with fifty years or less to run) but not the cost of the original acquisition.

3. For full details of the tax treatment of intangible assets for companies see Example 65.

D E Flour is a wholesale merchant who has been in business for many years, making up his accounts to 31 March each year. The following is a summary of his Profit and Loss Account for the year to 31 March 2007:

			£
Sales			897,251
Less: Cost of sales			782,359
Gross profit after warehouse wages etc			114,892
Rent from temporary letting of surplus warehouse space			10,000
Bank interest			90
Profit on sale of equipment			78
Dividend on holding of shares in Export and Import plc			314
			125,374
Less: Salary – Mrs Flour		10,000	
Other salaries		39,846	
Rates and insurances		3,200	
Light and heat		2,000	
Telephone		1,520	
Repairs		6,250	
Motor car expenses:			
Flour's own car	3,000		
Warehouse manager's car	1,600	4,600	
Bank interest		90	
Loan interest		2,250	
Bad and doubtful debts		138	
Legal and professional expenses		1,206	
General expenses		2,810	
Depreciation		800	
Business use of home		456	
Management salary – D E Flour		12,000	87,166
Net profit			38,208

The following further information is available:

1. Mrs Flour assists with the book-keeping and other clerical duties. Her salary was paid monthly at the rate of £720, a further £1,360 bonus being paid at the end of April 2007 and included in creditors.

2. Mrs Doe (Mrs Flour's widowed mother) lives on the premises and it has been agreed that one-quarter of the insurance, light and heat relate to the living accommodation. She does not act as caretaker.

3. Rates and insurance comprise:

	£
Business rates	2,100
Council tax (Mrs Doe)	620
Insurances	480
	3,200

4. The telephone is used mainly for business, but there is an extension in the living accommodation and it has been agreed that one-tenth of the expenditure relates to private use.

5. Repairs comprise:

	£
Work on staff toilets	400
Redecoration of showroom	850
Division of large room into three private offices	5,000
	6,250

The toilets although usable were in a very bad state of repair when the premises were purchased in March 2006.

Had the large room not been converted into three private offices, the ceiling would have required repairing at a cost of £1,000.

6. The expenses for Flour's car are the total running expenses for the year. Flour's mileage in the year to 31 March 2007 was as follows:

Home to business	4,000
Purely private journeys	4,000
Purely business journeys	10,000
Trip to south of England	
(Flour spent the week there, two	
days at the annual conference of	
Wholesalers' Trade Association and	
the remaining five days on holiday	
travelling round the region)	2,000
	20,000 miles

The warehouse manager's car had been purchased new in the year for £10,000. He uses the car 50% for private purposes. No private petrol is provided.

7. The premises from which trade was carried on were purchased at the beginning of the year, having previously been rented. The loan interest relates to the purchase thereof. The premises are larger than Flour currently needs, so he has let a small part on a monthly basis until his business expands.

8. The bad debts account was:

	£			£
Trade debts written off	390	Specific debt reserve } B/F		230
		2% of debtors reserve }		800
Loan to customer written off	54			
		Debts recovered		
Specific debt reserve } C/F	250	(previously charged and allowed		
2% of debtors reserve }	1,000	in computing trading profits)		526
		Profit and loss account		138
	1,694			1,694

9. Legal and professional expenses were:

	£
Legal costs – debt collection	250
negotiation of loan re premises	316
Accountancy	640
	1,206

10. (a) General expenses comprise:

	£
Printing and stationery	500
Annual payment under deed of covenant to local hospital (gross)	40
Subscription – trade association	70
Gift to local charity	30
Entertaining expenses and gifts (see below)	2,120
Donation to the Hospital Saturday Fund to which all the employees belong	50
	2,810

(b) Entertaining expenses and gifts were made up as follows:

	£
Entertaining customers	550
Christmas gifts to staff	366
Gift to employee on marriage	50
Gifts to customers	
One pocket diary to each customer at Christmas – cost £3.40 each	850
Expenses of staff dinner at Christmas	304
	2,120

11. Flour maintains an office at his home. He has been charged business rates on the office amounting to £306, and the lighting and heating costs are estimated at £150.

12. (a) Mr Flour has taken various goods for his own use or consumption, the selling price being £864 and the cost price £558. He has paid for these goods at cost price, £558 being included in his sales for the year.

(b) His mother owns a small grocery shop. Flour has in June 2006 professionally valued her stock for which he would normally charge a fee of £500 since this is one of the activities of his trade. He did not, however, make any charge.

13. All amounts are adjusted appropriately for VAT.

Using the Standard Accounts Information format, compute the trading profit for tax purposes (before deducting capital allowances).

Computation of Net Business Profit for tax purposes for the year ended 31 March 2007

	£	£	*Explanatory Note*
Turnover		897,251	
Less: Cost of sales	782,359		
Construction industry subcontractor costs	–		
Other direct costs	–	782,359	
Gross profit (loss)		114,892	
Other income/profits		10,404	2
		125,296	

	Disallowable £	£	*Explanatory Note*
Less: Employee costs		49,846	4
Premises costs (3,200 + 2,000 + 456)	1,240	5,656	3(a),15
Repairs	5,000	6,250	3(b),5
General administrative expenses			⎰3(a)(d),
(1,520 (telephone) + 2,810 – 2,120 (entg.))	192	2,210	⎱6,8
Motor expenses	1,500	4,600	14
Travel and subsistence	–	–	
Advertising, promotion and entertainment	550	2,120	7
Legal and professional costs	79	1,206	10
Bad debts	254	138	3(c)
Interest (90 + 2,250)	562	2,340	9
Other finance charges	–	–	
Depreciation and loss/(profit) on sale	722	722	3(e)
Other expenses	12,000	12,000	4
Total expenses		87,088	
Net profit/(loss)		38,208	
Add: Disallowable expenses	22,099		
Goods etc taken for personal use and other adjustments (apart from disallowable expenses) that increase profits	306		13
Total additions to net profit		22,405	
(deduct from net loss)			
		60,613	
Deductions from net profit (add to net loss) [receipts that are either not taxable or are not business profits]		404	2
Net business profit for tax purposes		60,209	

Explanatory Notes

All references in these notes are to ITTOIA 2005 unless otherwise stated.

Self-assessment – Standard Accounts Information

1.   For tax purposes, the profit shown in a trader's accounts has to be adjusted in accordance with the tax rules to arrive at the taxable profit (or allowable loss) for the accounting period. Section 25 requires profits for a trade to be calculated in accordance with generally accepted accounting

practice, subject to any adjustment required or authorised by law. For information on the effect of Accounting Standards on tax computations see Example 14.

Under self-assessment, the accounts figures must be shown in tax returns in a standardised format (known as Standard Accounts Information), except for certain very large partnerships – see Example 41 note 5. The headings under which information must be given are those shown in the example. Taxpayers whose accounts include a balance sheet are also required to show the balance sheet details on the return in a standard format. Those whose turnover is less than £15,000 are not required to show a balance sheet, nor to complete accounts information. They need only show their turnover, purchases and expenses, and net profit, although if annual turnover is usually close to £15,000, it may be better to submit full accounts to lessen the possibility of an HMRC enquiry (see Example 40 note 12).

The net business profit arrived at after the various tax adjustments is reduced by capital allowances to arrive at the taxable profit.

Non-trading income

2. The 'other income' comprises rent of £10,000, bank interest of £90 and the dividend of £314. The profit on sale of equipment of £78 is not included because it is netted off against the depreciation figure (see note 3(e)). The interest and dividends are excluded from the taxable income because they are taxable under other provisions. The same should strictly apply to the rent from letting, but where a small part of business premises is let because it is temporarily surplus to requirements and is likely to be used by the business within three years, the rent may be treated as part of the trading income.

Expenditure 'wholly and exclusively' for the trade

3. Unless it is covered by a specific statutory provision, expenditure is not allowable in computing profits unless it is wholly and exclusively for the purposes of the trade (s 34). A payment that satisfies the general rule is even so not allowable if it is a criminal payment, such as a bribe or protection money to terrorists, or a payment made in response to threats, menaces, blackmail and other forms of extortion. This restriction includes any payment made overseas which, if it were made in the UK, would constitute a criminal offence (s 55).

    A distinction is drawn between expenditure incurred in the capacity of trader, and in the capacity of taxpayer, the latter being an appropriation of profit and not allowable. So the expenses of an appeal against business rates would be allowable, since they relate to the trade, whereas the expenses of an appeal against a tax assessment would not, because they are incurred in the capacity of taxpayer. In the case of accountancy expenses, some of the expense is clearly related to the agreement of the tax liability on the profits, but by HMRC practice the full amount is allowable. This does not extend to the expense of preparing self-assessment returns and calculating capital gains, but HMRC accepts that the additional costs are likely to be minimal for someone whose personal tax affairs are straightforward. The relief for accountancy expenses does not apply to additional accounting charges relating to an in-depth investigation of the trader's affairs by HMRC. Such expenses are only allowed if no adjustment to profit results from the investigation, or where there is an adjustment to the current year only and the additional profits do not arise out of negligent or fraudulent conduct (Statement of Practice SP 16/91). Under self-assessment, HMRC is able to undertake random audits under the 'enquiry' procedure, in addition to their powers to investigate cases of fraudulent or negligent conduct or inadequate disclosure (see Example 40 notes 12 and 15). HMRC has confirmed that they will apply their stated practice to self-assessment enquiries and that accountancy expenses arising out of HMRC enquiries will be allowable if the enquiry results in no addition to profits, or only in an adjustment to the year of enquiry that does not arise out of negligent or fraudulent conduct.

    The wholly and exclusively provision in s 34 is interpreted in practice in the following way:

    (a) Living expenses and private payments are not allowable as they are not for the purpose of the trade. Therefore the expenses of the living accommodation occupied by Flour's mother-in-law are not allowable. The accommodation expenses would be allowable if she were acting as caretaker and therefore occupying the accommodation as an employee.

The council tax relating to Mrs Doe is also a private payment. If she had been an employee, then unless the accommodation was necessary for her to do her job the payment would have been treated as part of her wages for both tax and national insurance contributions, and would be reported on form P11D for employees earning £8,500 per annum or more and for directors, or on form P9D for other employees (for details of the PAYE provisions see Example 9). In these circumstances it would be an allowable deduction from Mr Flour's profits.

The disallowed premises costs of £1,240 comprise ¼ of the insurance and light and heat (£120 and £500 respectively) and the council tax of £620. 1/10th of the telephone costs, ie £152, is part of the disallowance of £192 on general administrative expenses (the other £40 relating to the charity covenant – see note 3(d)).

(b) Nothing can be allowed for repairs which might have been but have not been carried out. The £1,000 which would have been spent on the large room ceiling repair is therefore not allowable and the whole cost of dividing the room into offices is capital expenditure (see note 5).

(c) Debts cannot be written off except for bad debts that were incurred wholly and exclusively for the purpose of the trade, doubtful debts to the extent that they are respectively estimated to be bad and debts released by the creditor in a voluntary arrangement under the 1986 Insolvency Act. (The debtor in a voluntary arrangement will not have to bring into his trading profit debts that have been released in this way, but debts released other than under such arrangements must be treated as a trading receipt – ITTOIA 2005 s 97.) A general bad debts provision is therefore disallowed when it is made. If it is subsequently increased the increase is disallowed, and if it is decreased, the decrease is excluded from the profit. For detailed notes on deductibility of provisions see Example 14.

Writing off a loan to a customer is not allowable unless lending money is part of the taxpayer's trade, since it was not for trading purposes. The disallowance of £254 comprises the increase of £200 in the general reserve and the loan of £54 written off. Writing off a loan to an employee where the loan was made by reason of the employment would (in the absence of special circumstances) be an allowable expense to the employer – but the employee would usually be liable to tax on the amount so released. The employer would need to show that the loss was connected with or arose out of the trade. For the detailed provisions on employee loans see Example 57.

(d) Patent royalties (s 51), or payments such as pension contributions for the sole trader or under the 'gift aid' scheme (personal donations – see Example 91 for details) are not allowed as trading expenses.

(e) Any capital items and expenses connected with the acquisition or disposal of capital items are not allowable (the depreciation of equipment of £800 is thus not allowable and the profit on sale of equipment of £78 is not included in the taxable profit, giving a net disallowance of £722). By concession, the legal costs of *renewing* a short lease (ie for 50 years or less) are allowable. See Example 14 for the tests that apply to determine capital expenditure.

Family wages and drawings

4. Mrs Flour's salary and bonus are allowable provided they can be shown to be commercially justifiable (ie wholly and exclusively for the trade). Earnings that are paid after the end of the account to which they relate may only be taken into account in that period if paid within nine months after it ends. Otherwise they are deducted in the period in which they are paid (s 36). These provisions do not affect Mrs Flour's bonus since it is paid within one month. The bonus will form part of Mrs Flour's income for 2007/08 (in which it is received).

The payment described as a management salary to Mr Flour actually represents drawings of profit and is not allowed. The same applies to profit shares allocated to partners that are described as salaries, interest, etc.

Repairs

5. The repair work on the staff toilets and indeed the decorating of the showroom is allowable since there was no question of their not being usable at the time of acquisition (Odeon Associated Theatres Ltd v Jones (1972)). If repairs are necessary before an asset can be used in a business, they are part of the capital cost. Expenditure on extensions, improvements and additions is capital expenditure and is not allowable, as in the case of the division of a room into three offices in the example. Capital allowances will be available on disallowed repair expenditure if the building is a qualifying building (see Example 21 part A).

Entertaining, gifts, donations and subscriptions

6. The donation to the Hospital Saturday Fund is allowable since it is for the benefit of employees.

7. Expenditure on entertaining and gifts is covered by s 45 which disallows expenditure on entertaining and gifts except for the following:

   (a) Gifts carrying a conspicuous advertisement, not consisting of food, drink or tobacco and not exceeding £50 per person per annum (s 47(3)). This covers Flour's expenditure on diaries.

   (b) Gifts for employees (s 47(4)). The wedding gift will come under this heading. It may escape tax in the hands of the employee if it can be regarded as having been made on personal grounds (even though there is a link between the payment and the employment), but not if it is regarded as paid as a reward for or in return for acting as or being an employee.

   Expenditure on staff entertaining (s 46(3)), although allowable to the employer as being for the benefit of staff, will result in a benefits charge on a director or P11D employee, unless covered by the £150 exemption (see Example 10 explanatory note 31). The VAT position on staff entertaining costs is that input tax can be recovered on the proportion relating to employees only and not that relating to other guests (since entertaining expenses other than those relating to staff are disallowed – see note 16).

   (c) Gifts to charities (s 47(5)) (other than gift aid payments – see 3(d)), providing they are *wholly* and *exclusively* for the purposes of the trade. It will usually be difficult to show a trading motive for a gift to a charity. The trader may be able to show that being known as a subscriber to the charity benefits his trade. A modest gift to a charity with which the trader has a direct connection could usually be justified on 'wholly and exclusively' grounds. It has been assumed that this applies to Flour's gift to the local charity. HMRC has stated that subscriptions to hospitals, churches, chapels etc are not normally regarded as admissible except in a small community where the trader is the dominant employer and the employees are the predominant users of the facilities. There are separate provisions to allow relief for gifts of trading stock to charities and educational establishments (s 108). For details see Example 48 explanatory note 4(vi) and Example 91.

   Where a business makes sponsorship payments of a revenue nature, they are allowed providing they satisfy the 'wholly and exclusively' rule, ie the purpose must be to provide the payer with a commensurate benefit, usually in the form of advertising.

8. Subscriptions to trade associations are normally allowable, the association bearing tax on any excess of its subscription income over its allowable expenses. Any other subscriptions need to be considered under the 'wholly and exclusively' rule.

Finance costs

9.   Whilst disallowing capital expenditure in computing profits, s 29 and s 34 permit the deduction of interest paid wholly and exclusively for the trade. The loan interest has therefore been allowed, except for the proportion relating to the mother-in-law's living accommodation (assumed to be one-quarter).

10.   The incidental costs of raising loan finance (excluding stamp duty) are allowed providing that the interest on the loan qualifies as a deduction from profits (so the private proportion of ¼, ie £79, is disallowed) (s 58). HMRC has stated that if a life policy is taken out as a condition of obtaining loan finance, the premiums would not be 'incidental costs' of obtaining the finance, although any incidental costs of taking out the policy would be.

11.   Interest paid (or received) on delayed payment on contracts for the supply of goods or services will be a revenue expense (or trading receipt). The interest is not subject to deduction of tax at source (see Example 6 part (a)).

Security expenditure

12.   Expenditure to meet a special threat to the personal security of a sole trader or partner, such as from terrorists, is allowable subject to various restrictions (s 81). Revenue expenditure, such as on bodyguards, is allowed as a business expense. Capital expenditure, such as on alarm systems and bullet resistant windows, qualifies for capital allowances (see Example 18 part (a)). Where expenditure is incurred in relation to employees, there are parallel provisions to exempt the employee from any benefits charge on the security assets and security services provided.

Goods and services for own use

13.   Own goods are generally thought to be accounted for at selling price (Sharkey v Wernher (1956)), whilst there is no rule requiring services to be accounted for at any greater figure than the charge made (Mason v Innes 1967). It has been suggested by a number of leading commentators that the decision in Sharkey v Wernher is no longer appropriate. Nevertheless, HMRC still continue to apply it. VAT is due on the price paid by the business.

Motor expenses

14.   Motor expenses are capable of division into a part which is wholly and exclusively for the purposes of the trade and a part which is not, the former part being allowable on an apportionment basis (s 34(2)). Private motoring includes home to business travelling even though there are some duties undertaken at the private residence for which an allowance is made in computing profits (Newsom v Robertson (1953)). Half of the expenses on Flour's car have been disallowed on the basis of 10,000 private miles. Expenses that are *partly* for business are not allowed. The essential point is whether the trader had only a business purpose in mind when incurring the expenditure. If so the expenditure would be allowable, even if some incidental private benefit was obtained. But if there was more than one purpose, even if the trading purpose was the main one, the whole of the expenditure is strictly disallowed. For this reason the trip to the south of England, having both a private and a business purpose, is disallowed. HMRC may be prepared to accept a claim for a proportion of travelling expenses for a mixed purpose journey on the basis of the time spent on business. This could not be done on a mileage basis for Flour's trip, because he has clearly covered extra miles during his holiday. Under self-assessment, a trader's assessment of such a business element would only be questioned if HMRC enquired into his return or later made a discovery that there had been fraud, negligence or insufficient disclosure. In addition to claiming the appropriate proportion of running expenses, Flour will be able to claim the same proportion of capital allowances (see Example 20 explanatory note 12). For those whose turnover does not exceed the VAT threshold (£61,000 from 1 April 2006), HMRC allow traders to use the HMRC Authorised Mileage Allowance Rates (see page (viii)) to compute allowable motoring expenses, capital allowances then not being claimable in addition. The trader can only change the basis of claim to actual costs on a change of motor vehicle.

Private use by *employees* does not cause any restriction either in allowable running expenses or in capital allowances. If the employee earns £8,500 or more or is a director, the private use will be the subject of a benefits charge (see Example 10).

If a trader leases a motor car, and its retail price when new exceeded £12,000, then the allowable hire charge is restricted (s 48) (see Example 20 explanatory note 14).

Business use of home

15. Where a room at home is used for business purposes, a deduction may be claimed for the additional costs of the business use, such as light and heat. Where part of a property is used for business purposes, business rates are payable if the business use prevents the continued domestic use of that part of the property. This means strictly that there must always be mixed use to avoid a business rates charge, and where a room is exclusively set aside as an office business rates should be payable. Where business rates are not paid, the appropriate part of the council tax may be deducted as a business expense. The inclusion of £456 in the premises costs covers the home expenditure on rates, light and heat.

Value added tax

16. As a VAT registered trader Flour will account for VAT on his sales (including the sale of equipment), less a deduction for allowable input VAT he has suffered. He cannot claim a deduction for the VAT on business entertaining. It was, however, decided in the case of Thorn EMI plc v C & E (1994) that input tax should be apportioned where expenditure is partly for business entertaining and partly for other business purposes. He will have to pay a VAT scale charge for his private car fuel and this is similarly not deductible. If he had provided private fuel to employees, he would have to pay VAT scale charges for each employee, but the amounts charged would have been included as part of his deductible car expenses. As far as the car bought for the warehouse manager is concerned (and any other cars bought, but not commercial vehicles) Flour will not be able to reclaim the input VAT, but he can claim capital allowances on the VAT-inclusive amount. The VAT-inclusive cost is presumably £10,000, since the example states that amounts have been adjusted appropriately for VAT and no adjustment is appropriate in this instance.

As far as cars that are leased rather than purchased are concerned, leasing companies are entitled to reclaim input VAT in full on cars acquired for leasing. (The same applies to other businesses that use cars wholly for business purposes, such as self-drive hire firms and driving schools.) Where the leasing company has recovered the input VAT, the lessee may recover only 50% of the input VAT on the leasing charges if there is any use of the car for private purposes. The disallowed input VAT forms part of the deductible leasing charges in computing profit (subject to any restriction for private use by a sole trader or partner).

Where a VAT registered trader makes a gift of business goods costing more than £50, VAT output tax will be due based upon input tax claimed on the goods. However, if the gift is to a charity for resale in a charity shop the supply will be zero-rated.

A non-VAT registered trader includes VAT as part of his allowable expenses or capital costs, subject to the disallowance of VAT on business entertaining and on any private use proportion. A partly exempt trader may recover any non-deductible input VAT in a similar way. Some approximation may be necessary in allocating the VAT to the various items of expenditure and this will be accepted by HMRC providing it is reasonable.

For the treatment of VAT where small business flat rate scheme is used see Tax Bulletin 64. Expenses should then be shown as VAT inclusive and the amount payable to HMRC can either be deducted from the VAT inclusive turnover or shown as an expense in 'other expenses' on the tax return.

National insurance

17. As an employer, Flour will have to pay employers' Class 1, Class 1A (and if appropriate Class 1B) national insurance contributions, which are deductible in arriving at his taxable profit (see Example 47 for details). He will also have to pay self-employed Class 2 and Class 4 contributions, but these are not tax deductible (see Example 47).

Interest surcharges and penalties on income tax and VAT paid late

18.   These are not deductible in arriving at the taxable figure of business profits, this includes interest on late paid CIS deductions, NI and student loan repayments (s 54).

Miscellaneous

19.   This example deals with the treatment of most common items of expenditure. For the treatment of expenditure incurred prior to the start of a trade, see Example 14 supplementary note 1. For the treatment of premiums paid on short leases, see Example 100 part (h). Other points are dealt with in Example 48.

In (a) and (b) below, all calculations are to be taken to the nearest month.

(a) Show the assessments arising in the following four examples, assuming that the traders all started in business on 1 January 2006 and made profits (net of capital allowances) as shown:

(i)	Year to 31 December 2006	£12,000
	Year to 31 December 2007	£18,000
(ii)	Six months to 30 June 2006	£3,000
	Year to 30 June 2007	£17,000
(iii)	15 months to 31 March 2007	£3,750
	Year to 31 March 2008	£16,000
(iv)	16 months to 30 April 2007	£4,400
	Year to 30 April 2008	£18,000

(b) Show the assessments for the final tax year for the businesses in (a) if they had all continued to make up accounts annually to the dates shown and had ceased on 31 August 2011, the profits for each of them in the final two years being at the rate of £5,000 a month and the final accounting periods being:

(i) 8 months from 1.1.2011 to 31.8.2011

(ii) 14 months from 1.7.2010 to 31.8.2011

(iii) 5 months from 1.4.2011 to 31.8.2011

(iv) 16 months from 1.5.2010 to 31.8.2011

(c) (i) State how trading stock is valued on discontinuance of a business.

(ii) State how post cessation receipts and expenditure are treated.

References in this example are to the Income Tax (Trading and Other Income) Act 2005 (ITTOIA 2005) unless otherwise stated.

(a) Although s 203(3) states that apportionments should be made in days, all calculations in the example have been taken to the nearest month in accordance with s 203(4) which permits apportionments either in days, or months, or months and fractions of months, providing the chosen method is used consistently. The 2005/06 profit in part (i) of the example works out at £3,000 when apportioned in months, with the overlap profit being the same amount. It would be 95/365 of £12,000, ie £3,123 if apportioned in days, and the overlap profit would then be £3,123.

Where a business makes up accounts to 31 March, HMRC is prepared to treat an apportionment of profit for a period of 5 days or less as nil in accordance with s 209. On this basis, a business that started on 1 April 2006 and made up accounts to 31 March 2007 would have no assessable profit in 2005/06 and would pay tax in each succeeding year on the profit of the year to 31 March; overlap profits would not arise unless the accounting date was changed. HMRC is similarly prepared to treat a change of accounting date to 31 March as being equivalent to a change to 5 April (per s 220(5)), all existing overlap relief being deducted at the time of the change (see Example 28 part (c) for an illustration).

					£
(i)	2005/06	1.1.06 – 5.4.06	3/12 x	12,000	3,000
	2006/07	Yr to 31.12.06			12,000
	2007/08	Yr to 31.12.07			18,000
	Overlap profit 1.1.06 – 5.4.06 (3 months)			£3,000	
(ii)	2005/06	1.1.06 – 5.4.06	3/6 x	3,000	1,500
	2006/07	1.1.06 – 31.12.06			
		1st 6 mths		3,000	
		6/12 x 17,000		8,500	11,500
	2007/08	Yr to 30.6.07			17,000
	Overlap profit:	1.1.06 – 5.4.06 3/6 x 3,000		1,500	
		1.7.06 – 31.12.06 6/12 x 17,000		8,500	
	Total overlap profit (9 months)			£10,000	
(iii)	2005/06	1.1.06 – 5.4.06	3/15 x	3,750	750
	2006/07	1.4.06 – 31.3.07	12/15 x	3,750	3,000
	2007/08	Yr to 31.3.08			16,000
	Overlap profit 5 days from 1.4.06 – 5.4.06			–	
(iv)	2005/06	1.1.06 – 5.4.06	3/16 x	4,400	825
	2006/07	6.4.06 – 5.4.07	12/16 x	4,400	3,300
	2007/08	1.5.06 – 30.4.07	12/16 x	4,400	3,300
	2008/09	1.5.07 – 30.4.08			18,000
	Overlap profit 1.5.06 – 5.4.07 (11 months)			£3,025	

Relief for the overlap profits is given either when the business ceases or on an earlier change of accounting date if more than 12 months' profits is being taxed in one year.

(b) If the businesses in (a) closed down on 31 August 2011, the tax year of cessation would be 2011/12. The profits of the final accounting period would be:

In (a)(i)	8 months to 31.8.11	£40,000
In (a)(ii)	14 months to 31.8.11	£70,000
In (a)(iii)	5 months to 31.8.11	£25,000
In (a)(iv)	16 months to 31.8.11	£80,000

The final assessments would be as follows:

(i)	Profits 1.1.11 to 31.8.11	40,000	
	Less overlap relief	3,000	£37,000
(ii)	Profits 1.7.10 to 31.8.11	70,000	
	Less overlap relief	10,000	£60,000
(iii)	Profits 1.4.11 to 31.8.11		
	(No overlap relief)		£25,000
(iv)	Profits 1.5.10 to 31.8.11	80,000	
	Less overlap relief	3,025	£76,975

(c) (i) *Valuation of trading stock*

The valuation of stock and work in progress is dealt with in Chapter 12.

Any unsold trading stock at the date of discontinuance of a business is treated as follows:

1. Any stock sold to an unconnected UK trader who can deduct the cost of it in his computation of assessable trading profits is brought into the final accounts or computations at the amount for which it is sold (s 173). Where stock is transferred with other assets, the consideration is apportioned on a just and reasonable basis.

2. Any stock sold to a UK trader who is connected with the vendor (eg through a family link, or as companies in the same group), is treated as sold for an arm's length price (s 177). If, however, that amount is greater than both the actual sale price and the cost of the stock, the two parties may make a claim to use the higher of cost and sale price instead of arm's length value. The claim must be made within two years after the end of the chargeable period (ie tax year or company accounting period) in which the trade ceased (s 178).

3. Any other stock (eg stock given away or retained for private purposes) is adjusted in the final income tax computation to reflect the amount it would have realised if it had been sold in the open market at the discontinuation of the trade (s 175(4)).

4. The provisions of notes 1 to 3 do not apply where a business ceases because of the death of the sole proprietor (s 173(4)), and the closing stock is valued at the lower of cost and market value. Its acquisition value for executors or beneficiaries is, however, its market value at the date of death, both for capital gains purposes and for income tax purposes if they carry on the business.

    Work in progress is valued at consideration received, or at market value if no consideration (s 184). In the case of a profession the taxpayer may elect for work in progress to be valued at cost. An excess amount subsequently received being treated as a post-cessation receipt (s 185). The election must be made within one year from 31 January following the tax year of cessation.

(ii) *Post-cessation receipts*

Where income is received after a business has ceased, and it has not been included in the final accounts, it is charged to tax under Chapter 18, at s 242. The taxable amount may be reduced by any expenses, capital allowances or losses that could have been set against it if it had been received before the business ceased (s 254). The taxable amount is treated as earned income of the tax year in which it is received. If, however, the income is received in a tax year beginning not later than six years after the cessation date, an election may be made to have it taxed as if it had been received on the date of cessation (s 257). The election must be made within one year from 31 January following the tax year in which the amount is received. Although the tax adjustment from backdating is calculated by reference to the earlier year, the claim is treated as relating to the tax year in which the amount is received and is given effect by increasing the tax payable for that later tax year. The additional tax is not, however, treated as part of the tax *assessed* for the later year and does not therefore affect payments on account for the next following year (see Example 42).

The treatment of post cessation receipts is particularly relevant to barristers within the first seven years of practice, because they normally prepare their accounts on the basis of cash received rather than on an earnings basis. See Example 25(b) for details of the withdrawal of the cash basis of accounting other than for new barristers and the special 'catching up charge' arising as a result of bringing work in progress into the accounts.

Post-cessation expenditure

Where qualifying payments are made within seven years after cessation (or debts for which provision was not made in the final accounts become irrecoverable), then unless there are post-cessation receipts against which the amounts may be set, a claim may be made to set them against the total income and capital gains of the tax year in which the payment is made (or the debt proves to be irrecoverable) (TA 1988 s 109A(1)). The claim must be made within 12 months after 31 January following the end of the relevant tax year.

Qualifying payments are those made wholly and exclusively for professional indemnity insurance, or to remedy defective work, goods or services, or paid by way of damages in respect of such defects, including related legal and other professional expenses, or in respect of debt recovery costs.

The relief for post cessation expenses does not apply for corporation tax purposes, nor is any relief given when computing income for tax credit purposes.

Explanatory Notes

Current year basis of assessment

1. Trading profits are charged to tax on the 'current year basis', which broadly means the profits of the accounting year ending in the current tax year. The detailed rules are given below. Businesses commencing on or after 6 April 1994 have used the current year basis from the outset. For businesses already in existence at that date the current year basis took effect from 1997/98, with 1996/97 being a transitional year.

Current year basis rules and overlap relief

2. The current year basis rules are contained in Chapter 15. The essence of the rules is that businesses will be taxed over their lifetime on the taxable profits made. Although overlaps occur on commencement and possibly on changes of accounting date, they are dealt with by calculating the amount of profit that has been double charged (overlap profit) and allowing that amount as a deduction either when the business ceases or on an earlier change of accounting date if and to the extent that more than 12 months' profit is being taxed in one year. It is possible, however, that tax will be charged overall on more than the profits earned, for example where there are insufficient profits and/or other income against which to set overlap profits (see note 5).

    A record needs to be kept not only of the amount of any overlap profits but also the length of the overlapping period. If an overlap period shows a loss, it must be recorded as an overlap of nil for the appropriate period. This is important because overlap relief is given at the time of a change of accounting date if and to the extent that more than 12 months' profit would otherwise be chargeable in one year (see Example 28 part (c)). Self-assessment returns provide for entries to be made for overlap profits brought forward and carried forward.

Opening years

3. The rules for the opening tax years are as follows (ss 199 to 201):

   Year 1   Profit from date of commencement to the end of the tax year

   Year 2 (a) If there is an account of at least 12 months ending in year 2, profits of 12 months to the end of that account (as in (a)(i) and (iii) in the example)

   (b) Where the first account ends in year 2 but is for less than 12 months, profits of 12 months from commencement (as in (a)(ii) in the example)

   (c) Where no account ends in year 2, profits of the tax year itself (as in (a)(iv) in the example)

   Year 3 on-wards   Normally profits of accounting year ending in the tax year, but with special rules for changes of accounting date, under which the basis period will never be less than 12 months but may be longer. (Changes of accounting date are dealt with in Example 28.)

   If, however, the tax year is the first year in which there is an accounting date not less than 12 months after commencement (as in the third year 2007/08 in part (a)(iv) of the example), the profits of *12* months to the accounting date are taken, even though the accounting period itself is longer.

   Where there are losses, a loss that would otherwise be taken into account in two successive years is not included in the computation for the second year (see Example 30 for an illustration).

4. When a taxpayer acquires a new source of income, details must be shown in his return for the tax year in which income first arises. If the taxpayer does not receive a tax return for that tax year, he must notify HMRC within 6 months after the end of the year that he is chargeable to tax, otherwise interest and penalties may arise (TMA 1970 s 7 – see Example 40 note 5). This is particularly important for new businesses. However, for Class 2 national insurance a new business must be notified within three calendar months after the calendar month of commencement. In this example the businesses commenced in January 2006 and notification would be required by 30 April 2006. Failure to notify gives rise to a penalty of £100 (SI 2001/1004 reg 87) – see Example 13 part (c). All the businesses in part (a) of the example have taxable profits for 2005/06, even though their first accounts would not have been available until 2006/07 or later. Even though accounts may not be available in time, the tax finally found to be due for any year attracts interest from the original due date. It is important, therefore, to make estimated payments in order to avoid the interest charge (see Example 17). The legislation does not stipulate the length of the first account (or of subsequent accounts) but clearly the interest provisions discourage taxpayers from preparing a very long account to delay their tax liabilities.

Cessation of business

5. The basis period for the tax year in which a business ceases is from the end of the basis period for the previous tax year to the date of cessation, unless the business ceases in the second tax year, in which case the basis period for that tax year is from 6 April to the date of cessation (s 202). This means that there will often be two accounts that together form the final basis period, for example if in part (b) of the example the trader in part (a)(iv), instead of making up a 16 month account, had made up an account for the year to 30 April 2011 and a final 4 month account to 31 August 2011.

   Any overlap profit for which relief has not already been given is deducted in full from the assessable profit of the last *tax year* (as distinct from the profit of the final period of account), and if that results in a loss, the normal loss reliefs will be available. See Example 32, in particular explanatory note 5.

6. Part (b) of the example shows how overlap relief is dealt with on cessation. It should be noted that choosing an accounting year-end of 30 April still has the cash flow benefit of delaying the assessment of profits while the business continues, as shown in parts (a)(iii) and (iv) of the example, in which profits are broadly being earned at the same rate in both cases but are being taxed a year later in part (iv). However, on cessation this results in a final basis period that includes 11 months of the previous tax year.

This is illustrated in part (b)(iv) of the example, where the basis period is 16 months, even though the business ceases only 5 months into the tax year. Although the available overlap relief covers 11 months' profits, the overlap profits were at a much lower rate than those being earned on cessation, hence the difference between the final assessment on the business with the 31 March year end (£25,000) and that on the business with the 30 April year end (£76,975). If there had been a loss in the first accounting period there may be no overlap relief at all.

Capital allowances

7.   Capital allowances are treated as a trading expense of the accounting period. If the accounting period is shorter or longer than 12 months, the annual writing down allowances are reduced or increased proportionately (see Example 18 part (b)).

Transitional overlap relief

8.   Under the previous year basis of assessment, profits were charged more than once when a business started, and sometimes on a change of accounting date, balanced by profits escaping tax for an equivalent length of *time* when the business ceased. Under the current year basis, profits may also be charged more than once at the start and on changes of accounting date, but the balancing adjustment when the business ceases is equal to the *amount* of profits that were double charged (see note 2).

On the replacement of the previous year basis by the current year basis, all profits up to 5 April 1997 were treated as having been taxed under the previous year basis rules, but the profit for the period from the end of the basis period for 1996/97 to 5 April 1997 was also included in the taxable profits for 1997/98 under the current year basis. This profit therefore represents a transitional overlap profit, for which relief will be given as in note 2, ie when the business ceases, or possibly earlier if the accounting date is changed. Unlike normal overlap profits, transitional overlap profits were calculated *before* capital allowances. Where, as a result of a change of accounting date, further overlap profits arise, these will be merged with transitional overlap profits to form a single figure.

On 31 January 2005 David, a supervisor with a building supplies company, was made redundant. During the next twelve months he applied for many jobs, and attended a number of interviews but without success. On 1 February 2006, he set up his own business as a self-employed plumber providing services to local houseowners. He is a single man and has income from other sources of around £6,000 per annum.

His turnover for the first three months was £2,000 per month which David expects to rise by £200 per month in each quarter to a turnover of £2,800 per month in the quarter to April 2007. He estimates his turnover in future years to increase above the April 2007 level of £8,400 per quarter by approximately 10% per annum.

David estimates that his profits, adjusted for tax purposes, will be approximately 80% of his turnover.

He is considering preparing his first accounts either for the year to 31 January 2007 and annually thereafter, or for the 15 months to 30 April 2007 and annually thereafter.

(a)   What are the tax consequences of David's accounts being prepared annually to 30 April, rather than 31 January?

(b)   State whether David is *required* to register his business for VAT purposes and irrespective of whether David is required to register or not, whether he is *able* to register if he so wishes, and the advantages or disadvantages of registration.

(a)   David's anticipated turnover and resulting estimated profits for the alternative accounting dates are:

	Turnover £		Profits (80%) £
Year to 31 January 2007			
1st quarter 3 x 2,000	6,000		
2nd quarter 3 x 2,200	6,600		
3rd quarter 3 x 2,400	7,200		
4th quarter 3 x 2,600	7,800	27,600	22,080
Year to 31 January 2008			
Turnover: To 30.4.06 3 x 2,800	8,400		
For next 3 quarters @			
(8,400 x 110% =) 9,240	27,720		
	£ 36,120	Say 36,000	28,800
15 months to 30 April 2007			
1st 12 months	27,600		
5th quarter 3 x 2,800	8,400	36,000	28,800
Year to 30 April 2008			
Turnover (8,400 x 4) x 110%	£36,960	Say 37,000	29,600

The taxable profits arising are:

Accounts to 31 January annually		£
2005/06	1.2.06 – 5.4.06 2/12 x 22,080	3,680
2006/07	1.2.06 – 31.1.07	22,080
2007/08	1.2.07 – 31.1.08	28,800
		54,560

Overlap profits 1.2.06 – 5.4.06   £ 3,680

Accounts to 30 April annually		£
2005/06	1.2.06 – 5.4.06 2/15 x 28,800	3,840
2006/07	6.4.06 – 5.4.07 12/15 x 28,800	23,040
2007/08	1.5.06 – 30.4.07 12/15 x 28,800	23,040
		49,920

Overlap profits 1.5.06 – 5.4.07
11/15 x 28,800   £ 21,120

In each case the overlap profits represent the difference between the profits earned and the profits charged to tax, ie (54,560 – 3,680 =) £50,880 with a 31 January year-end and (49,920 – 21,120 =) £28,800 with a 30 April year-end.

If David makes up accounts to 30 April, therefore, there is a reduction in the taxable profits of the first three years of (54,560 – 49,920) = £4,640. If profits continue to rise, there will be an ongoing benefit of paying tax each year on earlier, lower profits. With a year-end of 31 January the taxable profits are very little different from the profits of the tax year itself, whereas with a year-end of 30 April nearly all the taxable profit relates to the previous year.

Unless there are losses for which relief is unavailable, however, the profits eventually charged to tax under the current year basis are the same as the profits earned. Paying tax each year on lower profits than have actually been earned is therefore effectively building up an amount of deferred profits on which tax must be paid when the business ceases. Furthermore, there is no inflation proofing of the overlap relief.

Say David ceased business on 31 January 2009, not having changed his accounting date in the meantime. The position in the final year would be:

Accounts to 30 April annually
2008/09   Profits of 21 months from 1.5.07 to 31.1.09 less overlap relief of £21,120

Accounts to 31 January annually
2008/09   Profits of 12 months from 1.2.08 to 31.1.09 less overlap relief of £3,680

Clearly if the rate of profits in 2008/09 is much higher than when the business started, the final assessment with the 30 April year-end will be very much higher than with the 31 January year-end.

As well as giving lower taxable profits when profits are rising, so long as the business continues, a 30 April year-end gives more time for preparation of accounts and tax computations. Under self-assessment, tax returns are due by 31 January following the tax year, eg by 31 January 2007 for 2005/06. This normally allows 21 months' preparation time with a 30 April year-end, compared with 12 months with a 31 January year-end. This might be of particular relevance if the tax return filing window is reduced as per the current Government proposals. The 30 April year-end, however, makes the calculation of tax bills more difficult at the start of the business.

In addition, a 30 April year-end could be beneficial for a tax credits claimant. Knowledge of the profits to the 30 April in the tax year will alert a claimant to the possibility of a claim for credits and this can then be more easily made by the 31 August deadline. A 30 April year-end could also mean that actual figures are available by 31 August following a year-end to complete any tax credits renewal form.

No matter which year-end is chosen, David has taxable profits for 2005/06, the tax on which is due for payment on 31 January 2007. Since the accounts will not be finalised by that date with either year-end, he will have to estimate the amount due, and will be charged interest from that date if his estimate falls short of the actual figure. (If he overestimates, he will receive a much lower rate of interest on the repayment than is charged on an underpayment.) He will know the exact amount of his profits sooner if he makes up accounts to 31 January. Furthermore, any tax due for 2005/06 will affect payments on account for 2006/07, unless it is covered by the de minimis limits, interest being payable from the half-yearly due dates of 31 January 2007 and 31 July 2007 based on the final figure of tax due for 2005/06. Estimated payments on account may therefore also be required, although in David's case the 2005/06 tax may be below the de minimis limits of £500 or 20% of the tax due.

Where taxable profits are lower as a result of the choice of year-end there will also be a saving in Class 4 contributions if the profits fall within the slice on which contributions are charged at the full rate. This would be the case for David in 2006/07, and probably in 2007/08 as well.

(b)   As far as VAT registration is concerned, David is required to register at any time if his turnover in the next *thirty days* is expected to exceed the VAT threshold (currently £61,000). He is also required to register at the end of any *month* if his turnover in the year ended on the last day of that month exceeded the threshold, unless HMRC is satisfied that his turnover in the coming year will not exceed (from 1 April 2006) £59,000.

Clearly David's turnover is expected to be below these limits for at least the first few years. He may register voluntarily if he wishes. This will not be to his advantage, because he would have to charge VAT to the houseowners for whom he works, and they would not be able to recover it, and he would also have to comply with the administrative requirements for keeping records and accounting to HMRC for the VAT charged to his customers (less a set-off for VAT he has suffered) although this could be simplified by using the Flat Rate Scheme.

If he remains non-registered, the VAT that he incurs forms part of the cost of the item concerned. If the item is an allowable deduction against his profit, such as his purchases of materials, he will save tax on the VAT suffered. If it is not, it may qualify for capital allowances, in which case the VAT forms part of the cost on which allowances are given. Where the asset is a chargeable asset for capital gains tax, any VAT not recovered forms part of the allowable expenditure taken into account when the asset is disposed of. Some VAT is not recoverable at all, such as on business entertaining.

Explanatory Notes

Choice of accounting date

1. For the detailed provisions on opening and closing years' assessments, see Example 16. Self-assessment is dealt with in Example 40.

2. Under the current year basis, the profits earned are normally taxed over the life of the business, any overlaps at the outset and on changes of accounting date being reflected in overlap relief when the business ceases. The effect of high inflation, however, could mean that overlap relief is of limited value in real terms. A year-end of 30 April has an ongoing cash flow benefit where profits are rising and also a benefit in the time for preparing accounts and computations, as indicated in the example.

    If a year-end of 31 March is chosen, no overlap relief arises, since HMRC is prepared to treat the accounting year as equivalent to the tax year (see Example 16 part (a)), so there is no adverse effect from inflation. If a business with a different year-end faces falling profits, switching to a 31 March year-end would trigger any available overlap relief and would reduce the ongoing assessments (see Example 29 part (c)).

Notifying liability and sending in returns

3. Not all taxpayers regularly receive tax returns for completion. By TMA 1970 s 7, a taxpayer is required to notify HMRC if he is liable to tax for any tax year, the notification being required to be made not later than six months from the end of that tax year (TMA 1970 s 7 – see Example 40 note 5). In David's case, if he does not get a return, he needs to notify HMRC that he has taxable income for 2005/06 not later than 5 October 2006.

4. Penalties arise both for failure to send in a return on time (TMA 1970 s 93) and for failure to notify liability to tax (TMA 1970 s 7). For the interest provisions see Example 43 and the penalty provisions Example 45.

Class 2 and 4 national insurance contributions

5. A self-employed person is liable to pay Class 2 and Class 4 national insurance contributions. Class 2 contributions are due if earnings are expected to exceed the exemption limit (£4,465 for 2006/07). It is necessary to notify liability within three calendar months after the calendar month of commencement of self-employment (see Example 13 part (c)). Notification for Class 2 also acts as notification for income tax, although a separate penalty of £100 applies for failure to notify for Class 2 in addition to the income tax penalty mentioned at 4 above.

    Class 4 national insurance contributions are calculated on profits net of capital allowances. Under self-assessment, they are calculated by HMRC if the taxpayer does not wish to calculate his own tax and submits his return by 30 September following the end of the tax year, and otherwise by the taxpayer. The Class 4 contributions are payable at the same time as income tax, so they are included in half-yearly payments on account. See Example 47 for detailed notes on national insurance contributions.

(a)   Where assets qualify for capital allowances, explain what expenditure may be taken into account, and state the date on which the expenditure is treated as incurred.

(b)   Explain the way in which capital allowances are given to traders and investors.

(c)   Explain the meaning of the expression 'connected person' in relation to capital allowances, and outline the treatment of transactions between connected persons.

All figures in the following examples are as adjusted for VAT purposes.

(d)   AB, whose business qualifies as small, is a long established trader making up accounts annually to 30 September. Using the following information relating to the years to 30 September 2005 and 2006, show the capital allowances claimable on the plant and machinery main pool for 2005/06 and 2006/07. All additions qualify for first year allowance.

	£
Pool written down value brought forward at 30.9.04	150,000

	Additions £
Year to 30 September 2005 –	
General plant (November 2004)	35,000
Computer (June 2005)	17,000
Year to 30 September 2006 –	
General plant (September 2006)	23,000

Disposals totalled £15,000 in the year to 30 September 2005 and £9,500 in the year to 30 September 2006.

(e)   C and D, whose business qualifies as small, had been in business for many years, making up accounts annually to 5 April and sharing profits 3:1. The following information relates to their plant and machinery in the year ended 5 April 2007:

Written down values brought forward at 6.4.06:

	£
Main pool	47,000
Car used by C	5,600
Car used by D	21,000

Disposal proceeds during period (no items sold for more than cost):

Van	3,500
Car used by works manager	4,000
C's car	6,500

Additions during period:

October 2006	Car to replace that used by works manager	11,500
December 2006	Replacement van	13,000
January 2007	New fixtures	8,500
March 2007	Replacement car for C	23,000

The partners' cars were used privately to the extent of one third. The works manager's car was used one quarter privately. None of the cars qualifies as one with low CO_2 emissions.

An amount of £1,200 relating to an electric sign bought in May 2006 had been disallowed in computing trading profit.

(i)   Compute the maximum capital allowances available for 2006/07.

(ii)   Without making computations, state what the position would be if the motor cars were owned personally by C and D.

(iii)   Comment on the treatment of capital allowances for partnerships.

References in this example are to the Capital Allowances Act 2001 (CAA 2001) unless otherwise indicated.

(a) *Qualifying expenditure*

On assets that qualify for capital allowances, the expenditure that may be taken into account is qualifying capital expenditure incurred in the *chargeable period* (s 6 – see (b) below). If expenditure is funded by borrowing, it is still treated as having been incurred, although interest on the borrowing is allowed as a business expense and not as part of the capital cost (Ben-Odeco Ltd v Powlson (1978)). Where there is a long lease of an industrial building, the landlord and tenant may jointly agree that the premium be treated as the purchase price for the building, so that the tenant may claim allowances (s 290 – see Example 21 explanatory note 8). If a tenant incurs capital expenditure on a qualifying building he may claim allowances on that expenditure. If expenditure for the purposes of the trade on repairs to a building is disallowed in computing income because it is regarded as capital expenditure, it is treated as capital expenditure for capital allowances purposes (s 272).

It is specifically provided by s 25 that expenditure on alterations to an existing building incidental to the installation of plant or machinery is treated as expenditure on plant or machinery. Where plant and machinery is moved from one site to another, the cost of removal and re-erection, if not allowed as an expense, may be treated as expenditure on plant and machinery for capital allowances. Where plant and machinery is demolished and replaced, the net cost of demolition is treated as expenditure on the replacement plant and machinery. If the plant and machinery is not replaced, the demolition cost is treated as qualifying expenditure for the period in which it is incurred (s 26).

Where someone brings into a trade plant and machinery that has been given to him, the plant and machinery is treated as having been bought at that time for its open market value (s 14). The same applies where plant and machinery that has previously been used other than for trading purposes is brought into a trade, except that if the cost is less than market value, the cost figure is substituted (or, for connected persons transactions, the cost to the connected person if less) (s 13).

Where a building is constructed and plant and machinery is installed therein, it will be necessary to apportion ancillary expenses such as professional fees of architects, surveyors and engineers and overhead costs between the building and the plant. Since such expenses often form a significant part of the cost, it is important to ensure that the allocation is appropriate and supported by the facts.

Certain expenditure that would not otherwise qualify as expenditure on plant is specifically treated as such, namely:

–   Expenditure on adding thermal insulation to an industrial building (s 28)

–   Fire safety expenditure required by a fire authority following an application for a fire certificate under the Fire Precautions Act 1971 (s 29). (NB This does not give relief for fire safety expenditure relating to nursing homes, which are covered by the Registered Homes Act 1984.)

–   Expenditure on safety at sports grounds (ss 30 to 32)

–   Expenditure on security assets, such as alarm systems and bullet-proof windows, to improve the personal security of those under *special* threat, eg from terrorists (s 33)

In all these cases, the disposal value in respect of such expenditure is treated as nil (s 63).

Coversely, expenditure on plant or machinery is not qualifying expenditure if incurred for leasing under a long-funding lease (s 34A).

If a trader other than a finance lessor acquires plant and machinery on hire purchase, the full capital cost is treated as incurred as soon as the asset is brought into use (s 67). The hire purchase charges are a revenue expense allowed over the term of the contract. Where plant and machinery is acquired under a lease, except for long-funding leases it is the lessor and not the lessee who is entitled to the allowances, whether the lease is an operating lease or a finance lease. Special anti-avoidance provisions apply to finance leases (see Example 20 part (a)).

Where a third party (for example, the Government, or a local authority) makes a contribution or subsidy towards cost, that amount is excluded from the qualifying expenditure (subject to certain exceptions) (s 532). Where such contributions are paid by traders or investors, the payer can claim allowances even though he does not strictly have an interest in the asset (ss 537 to 541).

Date expenditure treated as incurred

Section 5 provides that expenditure is deemed to be incurred on the date on which the obligation to pay becomes unconditional, but if any part of the payment is not due until more than four months after that date, that part of the expenditure is regarded as incurred on the due date of payment. The due date of payment is also substituted where the unconditional obligation to pay is earlier than normal commercial usage and the sole or main benefit is that expenditure would be treated as incurred in an earlier chargeable period. The date when the obligation to pay becomes unconditional depends on the terms of the contract. It will usually be either the invoice date or the delivery date. Where ownership is transferred in one chargeable period but the obligation becomes unconditional in the first month of the next, the obligation is regarded as having arisen in the earlier period. (This sometimes happens on a large construction contract, where the ownership of the asset is transferred, but the obligation to pay does not become unconditional until, for example, an architect's certificate is presented.)

Where expenditure on plant and machinery is incurred prior to the commencement of a trade, it is deemed to be incurred on the first day of the trade (s 12).

Allowances on leased assets

Capital allowances on plant and machinery are not normally available unless the plant and machinery belongs to the taxpayer at some time in the relevant period (s 11). Allowances are, however, available for expenditure incurred by a tenant on lifts, heating and ventilating equipment, etc, even though in law such items become landlord's fixtures. Where such fixtures are not bought outright but are acquired on lease, either by a landlord or a tenant, there are provisions to enable the allowances to be given to the equipment lessor, instead of to the landlord or the tenant as the case may be. These provisions are dealt with in more detail in Example 20.

Long funding leases

Since 1 April 2006 expenditure on assets acquired for the purpose of long-funding leasing have ceased to qualify for plant and machinery allowances (s 34A). Instead, the lessee is entitled to be treated as the owner of the expenditure (s 70A).

A long-funding lease is, broadly, a lease longer than seven years. Leases of between five and seven years are long-funding leases if:

(a)   they are treated as finance leases under GAAP;

(b)   the residual value of the plant or machinery is 5% or less of the market value at the commencement;

(c)   the total rentals due in the first year (if less than those due in the second year) are between 90% and 100% of the second year's rentals; and

(d)   the total rentals due in any year after the second (if greater than those due in the second year) are between 100% and 110% of the second year's rentals.

Certain leases of plant or machinery for a building or leased with land are excluded (ss 70G, 70R and 70U).

(b)   Some capital allowances are given in taxing a trade, profession, employment or property business following a claim in a tax return and others are given by a claim made other than in a return (s 3).

Capital allowances given in taxing a trade etc or property business

Capital allowances given in taxing a trade, profession, employment or property business are treated as an expense of the relevant *chargeable period*, both for individuals and companies. The meaning of chargeable period is as follows (s 6):

Chargeable period – companies:

For a company the chargeable period is the company's accounting period. An accounting period for corporation tax cannot exceed twelve months (TA 1988 s 12(3)), so a period of account that exceeds twelve months is split into a twelve month chargeable accounting period or periods and the remainder.

Chargeable period – individuals:

For sole traders and partners, the chargeable period is the period of account. A period of account is a period for which accounts are made up. The legislation prescribes rules for overlaps and gaps in periods of account, but in practice these will virtually never arise, because it would be very unusual for a business to produce more than one set of accounts for the same period, or to have a period for which accounts were not made up at all.

If a period of account is longer or shorter than 12 months, annual writing down allowances are proportionately increased or reduced. But if a period of account exceeds 18 months it is regarded for the purpose of computing allowances as being split into successive 12 month periods plus the balance (s 6(6)). The aggregate allowances for the separate periods are then treated as a business expense of the whole period. This prevents undue advantage being gained as a result of the long account, as follows:

For a medium-sized company – account made up for 26 months to 31.12.2006

If s 6(6) had not been enacted:

		£
Plant and machinery expenditure brought forward		100,000
Writing down allowance 25% x 26/12		54,167
		45,833
Additions November 2006	20,000	
First year allowance 40%	8,000	12,000
Written down value carried forward		57,833

Applying s 6(6):

		£
Plant and machinery expenditure brought forward		100,000
Writing down allowance 25% for first 12 months		25,000
		75,000
Writing down allowance 25% for next 12 months		18,750
		56,250
Writing down allowance 25% x 2/12		2,344
		53,906
Additions November 2006	20,000	
First year allowance 40%	8,000	12,000
Written down value carried forward		65,906

The s 6(6) rule restricts the allowances for the period to £54,094 instead of £62,167.

Where qualifying expenditure is incurred by an employee, or by an individual investor (including landlords of let property), the chargeable period for allowances is the tax year itself. The chargeable period for company investors is the accounting period, as for trading companies. As indicated on page 18.3, capital allowances in connection with let property (including capital allowances on leased plant and machinery where the lettings are in the course of carrying on a property business) are treated as an expense of the property business (s 248).

Capital allowances given by a claim made other than in a return

Allowances are given by a separate claim where plant and machinery is leased other than in the course of a 'qualifying activity', for example, a trade or property letting (see Example 20 explanatory note 1). Such leasing is referred to in the legislation as 'special leasing' (s 19). Leasing in such circumstances will be extremely rare. For income tax, relief for any such item of let plant and machinery is given against income from similar special leasing activities, unless the *lessee* does not use it for a trade etc throughout the relevant accounting period, in which case the set-off in that period is restricted to the time proportion of the accounting period that the plant and machinery has been leased (s 258). Excess allowances are carried forward to set against similar leasing income in later years. Similar rules apply for corporation tax, except that a claim may be made for excess allowances to be surrendered in a group relief claim (TA 1988 s 403ZB), or carried back against previous accounting periods for an equivalent period of time to that in which the excess occurred, unless the plant and machinery had not been used by the *lessee* for a trade etc for the whole of the relevant accounting period, in which case the treatment of the allowance is the same as for income tax (ss 259, 260).

Capital allowances claims

Claims for capital allowances by both traders and investors (other than claims relating to 'special leasing', as indicated above) are made in tax returns. For details see Example 42.

Treatment of excess allowances

Excess allowances relating to a trade form part of a trading loss for which the usual loss reliefs are available.

Where an individual makes a claim for capital allowances on assets used in his employment, then in the unlikely event that the allowances exceed his employment income, the excess is available for a loss claim against other income under TA 1988 s 380 (s 262 and annex to Explanatory Notes to the Act).

The treatment of excess allowances for which relief is available by a special claim is indicated above.

For individuals carrying on a 'property business', excess allowances form part of a UK property business loss. A claim may be made, for the tax year of loss or the following tax year, to set an amount equal to the capital allowances included in the loss against total income (TA 1988 s 379A). The time limit for the claim is one year from 31 January following the end of the tax year. Any loss not relieved in this way is carried forward against future rent income.

A corporate investor's capital allowances are similarly incorporated within the company's UK property business loss but no separate claim relating to excess allowances may be made. Relief for a company's UK property loss is given against the total profits of the same accounting period. A claim may be made (within two years after the end of the accounting period) for any remaining loss to be surrendered to another company in the same group under the group relief provisions (see Example 63). Otherwise it is carried forward to set against the *total* profits of later accounting periods.

(c)   *Connected persons – definition*

The basic definition of connected persons in TA 1988 s 839 covers close family, trustees, partners, and companies one of which controls the other or under common control. Close family means spouse, relatives, and relatives' spouses (relative being brother, sister, ancestor or lineal descendant). As far as partners are concerned, however, s 839 provides that partners are *not* connected with fellow partners and their spouses and relatives in relation to acquisitions or disposals of partnership assets pursuant to bona fide commercial arrangements. An expanded definition of connected persons is used in relation to *plant and machinery* in s 266, however, which brings partnership transfers within its scope.

Effect on plant and machinery allowances

First year allowances (see Example 20 explanatory note 2) are not available on assets acquired from a connected person (s 217).

When plant and machinery is disposed of, the disposal value to be brought into account is normally the net sale proceeds, except that it cannot exceed the original cost (or, where plant has been transferred between connected persons, the highest price paid by any of the connected persons – ss 61 and 62). Where, however, the plant and machinery is sold for less than its open market value, open market value is substituted unless the buyer's expenditure will be taken into account for capital allowances or there will be a benefit taxable on an employee under the benefits code (ss 61, 63(1)). Normal intra-group transfers can therefore be made at the price paid on the transfer if the companies so wish, but there is no provision to use written down value. Intra-group transfers relating to £12,000+ cars must, however, be treated as made at open market value (or the expenditure incurred or treated as incurred if less) (s 79).

Where a *trade* is transferred between connected persons (as defined in s 266 and TA 1988 s 839), the disposal value for plant and machinery is the open market value, but first year allowances are not available (s 265(4)). An election may, however, be made within two years of the transfer for a deemed disposal value such as gives no balancing allowance or balancing charge. The transferor then gets no allowances in the period of transfer, and the transferee stands in the transferor's shoes as regards allowances and balancing charges (ss 266, 267). The main instances when this applies are on incorporation of a business, or on a transfer of trade between companies in the same group (but see below under *Reconstructions* where there is 75% common ownership). Partnership changes are not treated as a cessation of the business, so the capital allowances computation is not affected.

Effect on other allowances

Where property other than plant and machinery is transferred between connected persons, or between bodies one of whom controls the other or controlled by the same persons, the property is treated as having been sold at open market value (ss 567, 568). An election may however, be made not later than two years after the transfer, for the transfer of industrial and enterprise zone buildings, hotels and research and development assets to be treated as made at written down value, so that balancing adjustments do not have to be made (s 569). This is relevant, for example, where a business is incorporated, or where assets are transferred from one group company to another.

Reconstructions

The above provisions relating to plant and machinery and other property transferred between connected persons are not relevant where a trade is transferred from one company to another, and at some time within one year before and two years after the transfer, the same persons own three quarters or more of the trade. This is treated by TA 1988 s 343 as a reconstruction of a company without a change of ownership. As far as the capital allowances computation for the period of transfer is concerned, first year allowances on plant and machinery are claimed by whoever incurred the expenditure and balancing adjustments are made on the company carrying on the trade at the time of the disposal. Writing down allowances are split on a time basis. TA 1988 s 343 also provides for trading losses to be carried forward into the successor company, subject to anti-avoidance provisions in TA 1988 s 344 if the successor company does not take over the predecessor's unpaid liabilities.

Tax avoidance schemes

Where a business enters into artificial transactions which depress the market value of an asset prior to its sale to a connected person then the balancing allowance on disposal is blocked. However, the acquirer can only claim allowances on the reduced price. This provision applies in relation to any balancing event occurring on or after 27 November 2002 and only applies where there is a tax avoidance scheme.

(d) **AB – Capital Allowances Computation 2005/06 and 2006/07**

	Main pool £	Total allowances £
2005/06 (1.10.04 to 30.9.05)		
Written down value brought forward	150,000	
Disposals	(15,000)	
	135,000	
WDA 25%	(33,750)	33,750
Additions (general plant) 35,000		
FYA 50% (17,500)	17,500	17,500
Additions (computer June 2005) 17,000		
FYA 40% (6,800)	10,200	6,800
	128,950	58,050
2006/07 (1.10.05 to 30.9.06)		
Disposals	(9,500)	
	119,450	
WDA 25%	(29,863)	29,863
Additions (general plant September 2006) 23,000		
FYA 50% (11,500)	11,500	11,500
Written down value carried forward	101,087	41,363

(e) **C and D**

(i) **Capital Allowances Computation 2006/07**

	Main pool £	C's first car £	C's second car (£12,000+) £	D's car (£12,000+) £	Total allow-ances £
Bf from 2005/06 (period ended 5.4.06)	47,000	5,600		21,000	
2006/07 (period ended 5.4.07)					
Additions – cars not qualifying for FYA	11,500		23,000		
Disposals					
Van	(3,500)				
Cars	(4,000)	(6,500)			
Balancing charge		900 (2/3= 600)			BC £600
	51,000		23,000	21,000	
WDA 25%	(12,750)		(Max) (3,000) (2/3= 2,000)	(3,000) (2/3= 2,000)	12,750 4,000
cf	38,250		20,000	18,000	16,750

	Main pool £	C's first car £	C's second car (£12,000+) £	D's car (£12,000+) £	Total allow-ances £
bf	38,250		20,000	18,000	16,750
Additions qualifying for FYA @ 50%: Elec sign May 2006, van Dec 2006 and fixtures Jan 2007 (1,200 + 13,000 + 8,500)	22,700				
FYA 50%	(11,350)	11,350			11,350
Cf to 2007/08		49,600	20,000	18,000	28,100

The capital allowances as computed will be deducted from the assessable profits, the balancing charge will be added to the profits, and the resulting amount will be divided three quarters to C and one quarter to D.

(ii)   If instead of the motor cars being partnership assets they had been owned personally by C and D, then the allowances on them would have been computed separately but still claimed by the partnership. They would not have been taken into account in computing the partnership profit divisible between the partners in the profit sharing ratio but would instead have been deducted separately from each partner's profit share. The total capital allowances, including those on the partners' cars, would be shown on the partnership self-assessment tax return and the share of profits after capital allowances (both partnership and individual) on the partnership statement. The net figure is then transferred to the tax returns of C and D respectively. For example, in 2006/07 the adjusted profit of the year to 5 April 2007 would be reduced by the first year and writing down allowances on the main pool totalling £21,830, the balance being split three quarters to C and one quarter to D. D's share would then be reduced by his capital allowances of £2,000 and C's share would be reduced by net allowances of (2,000 – 600) = £1,400.

(iii)   Partnership capital allowances are treated as a trading expense of a period of account and are deducted in arriving at taxable profits. Partners are taxed separately on their shares of the profit as if it had arisen from a separate individual trade. Allowances on assets that are partnership assets reduce the overall profit and allowances relating to a partner's own property reduce his share of the profit as indicated in (ii) above, but in both cases the allowances must be claimed in the partnership return and cannot be claimed separately by an individual partner.

Explanatory Notes

Chargeable periods

1.   For detailed notes on chargeable periods for capital allowances see part (b) of this example and for the allowances for plant and machinery in detail, including the first year allowances available to small and medium-sized businesses, see Example 20. For provisions on disclaiming capital allowances see Example 19.

2.   Capital allowances for individuals relate to the period of account, and writing down allowances are proportionately reduced or increased if the period of account is less than or more than 12 months, subject to special rules for periods exceeding 18 months (see part (b)) and for finance lessors (see Example 20 part (a)).

Private use

3.   Note in part (e) of the example that the private use restriction for the use of cars applies only to the cars used by the partners. Private use of assets by *employees* does not require any restriction of the capital allowances. The employees are charged on the benefit under the benefit code provisions of ITEPA 2003.

Business use of partner's own assets

4.   Where partners own assets personally and use them in the business, the same capital allowances are available as if the partnership owned them (CAA 2001 s 264), but the allowances are deducted in arriving at each partner's assessable profit, as indicated in part (e)(ii) of the example.

First year allowances

5.   First year allowances are now generally available to small and medium-sized enterprises at a rate of 40%. However, small enterprises are occasionally allowed to claim 50% first-year allowances. This was the case for expenditure incurred in 2004/05 (or the financial year 2004 for companies) and again for expenditure incurred in 2006/07 (or the financial year 2006 for companies).

(a) Lindley, L J in Yarmouth v France (1887) said 'Plant . . . . . . includes whatever apparatus is used by a businessman for carrying on his business – not his stock in trade which he buys or makes for sale, but all goods and chattels, fixed or moveable, live or dead, which he keeps for permanent employment in his business'.

Discuss in the light of later cases and legislation how far this statement can be said to be true today.

(b) Margaret was made redundant by Hi Fi plc on 31 March 2005. On 1 May 2005 she registered for VAT and commenced a trade as a producer and distributor of musical records and tapes. Her first accounts covered the seventeen months to 30 September 2006 and accounts were made up annually to 30 September thereafter.

Capital expenditure on and disposals of business assets up to 30 September 2007 were as follows (all amounts stated being VAT exclusive, other than the cost of the car, which is VAT inclusive):

9 April 2005	Jaguar 3600cc car costing £18,400. Business use has been provisionally agreed at 70%.
1 May 2005	Office fixtures and fittings costing £5,000.
2 November 2006	Installation of computerised musical and recording equipment costing £20,000.
23 March 2007	A computer costing £10,000.
11 May 2007	Computer used as a music design system costing £14,500.
4 June 2007	New mixing deck costing £10,000. This amount was after deducting a part-exchange allowance of £2,000 for a mixing deck bought in December 2006 for £2,800.
18 August 2007	Video equipment costing £7,000.

Prepare capital allowances computations for the first two accounting periods, assuming Margaret wishes to claim allowances as early as possible, and indicate how relief will be given. State any elections required and the time limit by which they should be made.

(c) Calculate the optimum capital allowances claims for the relevant income tax year or chargeable accounting period, in respect of the following businesses (the figures quoted being as adjusted for VAT).

If any options or elections are available these should be indicated and explained.

   (i) Falstaff is a single man entitled to a personal allowance of £5,035 in 2006/07. For the year ended 30 November 2006 his adjusted business profits before capital allowances were £8,350.

   The written down value brought forward of assets on which capital allowances are claimed was £10,500.

   On 7 April 2006 he purchased new plant costing £8,000.

   He has no income other than from the business.

   (ii) B Wise Ltd, a manufacturing company, has adjusted profits (before capital allowances) of £80,000 for its accounts year ended 31 December 2006.

   The written down value of the capital allowances pool as at 1 January 2006 was £42,500.

   In the year ended 31 December 2006:

1 January 2006	Purchased new plant costing £132,500
1 March 2006	Sold plant for £6,000 (it had cost £7,500)

   B Wise Ltd has a subsidiary company and this company has incurred a trading loss in the corresponding accounting period which results in group relief being available of £42,800. The subsidiary is not able to carry back the loss and is not expected to trade profitably for some years to come.

   The group is not small/medium-sized for Companies Act purposes.

(d)   A Part and D Lot, two unconnected, long established traders whose businesses qualify as small enterprises and who make up accounts to 31 December, each have sufficient profits in the year to 31 December 2006 to take advantage of the maximum capital allowances claimable. The following information relates to their VAT adjusted purchases and disposals of plant and machinery in the main pool in that year:

	A Part £	D Lot £
Written down value bf	20,000	65,000
Purchases qualifying for first year allowance:		
February 2006	30,000	30,000
May 2006	65,000	65,000
Disposal proceeds (no plant sold for more than cost)	60,000	60,000

Show the capital allowances each should claim.

(e)   (i)   B Green (London) Ltd, a trading company, has adjusted profits (before capital allowances) of £15,000 for its accounting year ended 31 March 2007. The company does not have any associated companies. The written down value of the capital allowances plant pool at 1 April 2006 was £6,400. On 1 May 2006 the company purchased a new car costing £14,000 with a carbon dioxide emissions figure of 119 grams.

            Show the optimum claim for capital allowances for the year to 31 March 2007.

    (ii)   Show the revised optimum claim for capital allowances in (i) above if B Green (London) Ltd had losses of £10,000 brought forward from the accounting year ended 31 March 2006.

(a) The meaning of the words 'plant' and 'machinery' has been considered by the courts on many occasions. 'Machinery' is given its ordinary meaning, but no definition of 'plant' that can be regarded as all embracing has been arrived at. Many of the cases described below have treated parts of buildings and structures as plant. CAA 2001 ss 21 to 23 attempt to clarify the boundary between plant and buildings, and to limit any further additions to the 'plant' category, while not disturbing the effect of existing case law. The legislation specifically states that an asset cannot be plant if its principal purpose is to insulate or enclose the interior of the building or provide an interior wall, floor or ceiling intended to remain permanently in place.

For many years books in a professional library were held not to be plant following Daphne v Shaw (1926), but this was overruled in Munby v Furlong (1977), since when the professional libraries of solicitors etc have been accepted as plant.

The case of Yarmouth v France was heard in 1887 and it concerned not taxation but employer's liability. An employee who had been injured by his employer's horse claimed under the workers' compensation provisions that he had been injured by his employer's 'plant', and the courts found in his favour.

The statement made by the judge in that case still forms the basis of the accepted definition of plant, and it was expanded in the war damage compensation case of J Lyons & Co Ltd v AG (1944) to emphasise that the basic distinction is between apparatus *with* which the trade is carried on and the setting *in* which it is carried on. This was echoed in the case of Jarrold v John Good & Sons Ltd (1962), where expenditure by a firm of shipping agents on moveable office partitioning which was used in order to give them maximum continuing flexibility in relation to the subdivision of their floor space was held to be on plant. Similarly, expenditure by a ship repairing company on the concrete work used in the construction of a dry dock and on excavating the land for the dock was held to be expenditure on plant (IRC v Barclay, Curle & Co Ltd (1969)), as was expenditure on a swimming pool at a caravan site (Cooke v Beach Station Caravans Ltd (1974)).

On the other hand, the 'setting' argument was used to disallow prefabricated moveable buildings used as a laboratory and gymnasium in a school (St John's School v Ward (1975)), the canopy over a petrol station (Dixon v Fitch's Garages Ltd (1975)), a false ceiling in a restaurant (Hampton v Fortes Autogrill Ltd (1980)), a floating ship used as a restaurant (Benson v Yard Arm Club Ltd (1979)), a fan-inflated polythene tennis court cover in a tennis coaching business (Thomas v Reynolds (1987)), car wash halls and sites (Attwood v Anduff Car Wash Ltd CA (1997)) and the structure of an electrical substation (only the equipment within it qualifying as plant – Bradley v London Electricity plc (1996)).

Two cases heard during 2004 show how subtle the distinction can be between plant and setting. In Shove v Lingfield Park, the Court of Appeal, overturning the finding of the Special Commissioner, held that an artificial surface on a racetrack allowing racing throughout the year was part of the setting. On the other hand, the Scottish Court of Session held that the construction of a five-a-side pitch could qualify for allowances (CIR v Anchor International Limited).

Several cases have gone partly for and partly against the taxpayer. In Cole Bros v Phillips (1980), the electrical switchboard and most of the electrical equipment in a department store were held to be plant, but not certain light fittings whose only function was to provide light in areas with few windows. The court held in that case that items had to be considered individually and not as a single installation. In the case of Carr v Sayer (1992), it was held that permanent quarantine kennels were not plant but temporary, moveable, quarantine kennels *were* plant. In two 1992 cases heard together concerning single storey warehouses (Hunt v Henry Quick Ltd and King v Bridisco Ltd), it was held that platforms erected to increase the floor space in the warehouses were plant, but lighting beneath the platforms was not. A glasshouse constructed as a 'planteria' to protect plants and create an appropriate growing environment, but without any mechanical controls, was not plant (Gray v Seymours Garden Centre (CA 1995)). HMRC accepts, however, that glasshouses that incorporate a sophisticated, probably computerised, system to control and monitor temperature, humidity etc, will usually qualify as plant, and they confirmed in their Tax Bulletin of June 1998 that such glasshouses will not normally be 'long life assets' (as to which see Example 20 explanatory note 16).

Although the question of what is and what is not plant is broadly a functional test, some of the cases involving buildings used by the public have held that various items forming part of the setting created atmosphere and thus performed the function of making the premises more attractive to customers. This has been applied to decor, murals, light fittings etc in hotels (IRC v Scottish and Newcastle Breweries Ltd (1981)) and to decorative screens in the shop front windows of building societies (Leeds Permanent Building Society v Proctor (1982)). But in Wimpy International Ltd v Warland (1988), only expenditure on light fittings was held to be plant on this criterion. Expenditure on shopfronts, floor and wall tiles, suspended ceilings, and mezzanine and raised floors was all disallowed, with the exception of one ceiling made of metal strips with gaps for visual interest. The Court of Appeal emphasised in that case that the starting point was the decision of the Appeal Commissioners. They considered there were two tests, the premises test and the business use test, and the business use test was only considered if the premises test was satisfied. Under the premises test, something which becomes part of the premises, instead of merely embellishing them, is not plant, except in the rare cases where the premises are themselves plant, like the dry dock in Barclay Curle, and the computerised glasshouses mentioned above. Under the business use test, if the item is not part of the premises and is not stock in trade, it is plant if it is used in carrying on the trade. (Although initial expenditure on a shopfront is disallowed, HMRC allows the cost of a subsequent replacement as a trading expense, except to the extent that the replacement does more than merely replace the original, ie any improvement element is disallowed.)

It can be seen, therefore, that although the statement in Yarmouth v France, as expanded in J Lyons & Co Ltd v AG, still forms the essence of the currently accepted definition of plant, the extent of its application is frequently contested before the courts and often some very narrow distinctions are drawn.

(b) **Margaret – capital allowances computations**

	Main pool	Computer (short life asset)	Computer (short life asset)	Jaguar (30% private)		Total allowances
	£	£	£	£		£
Period to 30 September 2006						
Purchases 9.4.05, 1.5.05	5,000			18,400		
FYA 40%	(2,000)					2,000
WDA 3,000 × 17/12				(4,250)	(× 70% = 2,975)	2,975
WDV	3,000			14,150		4,975
Year to 30 September 2007						
Disposal 4.6.07	(2,000)					
	3,800					
WDA 25%	(950)			(3,000)	(× 70% = 2,100)	950
Additions – pre 6/4/07						
– pool	20,000					
– short life			10,000			
FYA 50%	(10,000)	10,000	(5,000)			15,000
Additions – post 5/4/07						
– pool	19,000					
– short life			14,500			
FYA 40%	(7,600)	11,400	(5,800)			13,400
	24,250	5,000	8,700	11,150		31,450

The capital allowances will be deducted as trading expenses in arriving at the trading profit or loss of each accounting period. Assuming Margaret makes profits, the profits will be charged to tax as follows:

2005/06	Profit from 1.5.05 to 5.4.06	= 11/17 x 1st profit
2006/07	Profit from 1.10.05 to 30.9.06	= 12/17 x 1st profit
	Overlap profits 1.10.05 to 5.4.06 (6 months)	
2007/08	Profit for year to 30.9.07	

The effect of the overlapping income tax basis periods for 2005/06 and 2006/07 is that over the two years relief will be given for 23/17 of the capital allowances of £4,975 = £6,731. The extra relief of £1,756 is, however, reflected in a similar reduction in the overlap relief available in respect of the six months to 5 April 2006.

An election to treat the computers bought on 23 March 2007 and 11 May 2007 as short life assets must be made within the self-assessment time limit of one year from 31 January following the tax year in which the relevant accounting period ends, ie period to 30 September 2007 ends in 2007/08 giving a date of 31 January 2010.

(c)   (i)   **Falstaff – 2006/07**   £

	£
Falstaff's assessable profits are	8,350
and he has a personal allowance of	(5,035)
which leaves him with income unabsorbed of	3,315

He should therefore claim capital allowances for 2006/07 of £3,315 only, in order to reduce his income to the point where it is fully absorbed by his personal allowance (see explanatory note 3).

Capital allowances computation for year to 30 November 2006

	Pool £	Total Allowances £
WDV brought forward at 1 December 2005	10,500	
Additions 7 April 2006 (FYA not claimed)	8,000	
	18,500	
Writing down allowance (25% x £18,500 = £4,625) restricted to	3,315	3,315
WDV carried forward to account commencing 1 December 2006	15,185	

Alternatively Falstaff could consider leaving £2,150 into charge at 10% (plus 8% Class 4 national insurance) by restricting his writing down allowance to £1,165. This would give a tax saving if he is likely to be paying tax in the near future at basic rate (say 22% for 2007/08) plus Class 4 national insurance contributions (say 8% in 2007/08) or tax at 40% plus Class 4 contributions of 1%. £2,150 @ 18% = £387 paid now could give relief subsequently of £2,150 @ 30% = £645 or @ 41% = £882.

A variation would be to claim FYA of 50% restricted to £3,315 (or in order to leave £2,150 in charge, to claim FYA of £1,165) with no WDA, but the tax savings would be the same.

(ii)   **B Wise Ltd – Chargeable accounting period to 31 December 2006**

	£
B Wise Ltd has profits before capital allowances of	80,000
against which group relief is available of	42,800
which would leave unabsorbed profits of	37,200

The capital allowances claim should therefore be restricted to this figure (see explanatory notes 3 and 6). The computation will be as follows:

	Pool £	Total Allowances £
WDV brought forward at 1 January 2006	42,500	
Additions	132,500	
	175,000	
Sale proceeds	(6,000)	
	169,000	
Writing down allowance (25% x £169,000 = £42,250) restricted to	37,200	37,200
WDV carried forward at 31 December 2006	131,800	

(d)   **A Part and D Lot – Capital allowances claims for year ended 31 December 2006**

	A Part Main pool £	D Lot Main pool £
WDV bf at 1 January 2006	20,000	65,000
Purchases on which FYA not claimed	40,000	
Disposal proceeds	(60,000)	(60,000)
		5,000
WDA 25%		(1,250)
Purchases qualifying for FYA		95,000
less taken into account above (95,000 less 40,000)	55,000	
FYA 40% x 0/30,000		12,000
FYA 50% x 55,000/65,000	27,500	32,500
WDV cf	27,500	54,250

If A Part had claimed the full first year allowance of 40% on £30,000 and 50% on £65,000, it would have amounted to £44,500, but there would have been a balancing charge of (60,000 – 20,000 =) £40,000, giving him a net allowance of £4,500 compared with £27,500 as shown. D Lot has a sufficient balance of qualifying expenditure to cover his disposal proceeds, so he should claim the available FYA in full.

(e)   (i)   **B Green (London) Ltd – Chargeable accounting period to 31 March 2007**

Capital allowances computation	Pool	Car	Total Allowances
WDV brought forward at 1 April 2006	6,400		
Additions		14,000	
First year allowances (100%) – restricted		(13,400)	13,400
Writing down allowances (25%)	(1,600)		1,600
WDV carried forward at 31 March 2007	4,800	600	15,000

Alternatively, the company could have claimed all the first year allowance and made a partial claim for the writing down allowances. However, that would subsequently increase the potential balancing charge on the disposal of the car.

On the other hand, it might be more likely that a balancing charge would first arise on the disposal of plant and machinery in the main pool. In this case, it might be more appropriate to take a full first year allowance in respect of the car.

The company could also have claimed up to 100% FYA on the low emissions car.

		£
(ii)	B Green (London) Ltd has profits before capital allowances of	15,000
	The amount of profits covered by the loss brought forward is	10,000
	Leaving profits to be covered by capital allowances of	5,000

Capital allowances computation	Pool £	Total allowances £
WDV brought forward at 1 April 2006	6,400	
Additions 1 May 2006 (100% FYA not claimed)	14,000	
	20,400	
Writing down allowance (25% x 20,400 = 5,100) restricted to	5,000	5,000
WDV carried forward at 31 March 2006	15,400	

Explanatory Notes

Basis period for capital allowances

1. Capital expenditure on plant and machinery is taken into account according to the chargeable period in which it is incurred (CAA 2001 ss 2 and 6). Capital expenditure incurred before a trade starts is treated as incurred on the first day of trading, as with Margaret's expenditure in April 2005 prior to commencing trading in May 2005 in part (b) of the example (CAA 2001 s 12).

    See Example 18 part (b) for detailed notes on the chargeable period rules. Where a period of account exceeds 12 months but does not exceed 18 months, writing down allowances are proportionately increased, as shown in part (b) of the example.

2. For a further detailed illustration of the application of the plant and machinery provisions and detailed notes on other aspects, including the provisions for allocating assets to pools, the treatment of short life and long life assets and the availability of 100% first year allowance for computers, cleaner cars, etc, see Example 20.

Capital allowances claims and disclaimer

3. Both individuals and companies must make a specific claim for capital allowances, claims being made in tax returns (CAA 2001 s 3). Where the individual or company does not wish to claim all the plant and machinery allowances they are entitled to, the claim may be restricted to the amount required (CAA 2001 ss 52(4) and 56(5)). See also Example 21 explanatory note 5 re reduced claims to industrial buildings allowances. Allowances may be left unclaimed to avoid wasting personal allowances or other reliefs, as shown in part (c) of the example. The availability of first year allowances on certain expenditure (see Example 20 explanatory note 2) provides another reason for partial claims, as shown in part (d) of the example. If there would otherwise be a balancing charge, all or the appropriate part of expenditure on which a first year allowance is available may instead be included in the pool to cover a balancing charge (CAA 2001 s 58(5)).

4. Following CAA 2001, all writing down allowances may now be claimed wholly or only in part. For agricultural buildings allowances, however, partial claims for allowances will rarely if ever be advantageous (see Example 22 explanatory note 2).

5. Under income tax self-assessment capital allowances are subject to the same time limits as other entries in a return, ie any amendment must normally be made within 12 months after the 31 January filing date for the return.

    Companies are able to make, vary and withdraw capital allowances claims up to two years after the end of their accounting period. If the profits are not finally settled by that time, later time limits apply.

For detailed notes on claims procedures see Example 42.

6. If B Wise Ltd in part (c)(ii) of the example had claimed the full available allowances of £42,250 its profits would have been reduced to (£80,000 – £42,250 =) £37,750 and group relief restricted to that amount. The subsidiary company would then have been left with an unrelieved loss of £5,050 to carry forward, with no prospect of early relief in view of its anticipated unprofitable trend.

Value added tax

7. Value added tax is not taken into account as part of the expenditure for capital allowances if it is recoverable through the VAT system (see Example 15 note 16). Similarly, output VAT on disposals is excluded from disposal proceeds. VAT on cars is not normally recoverable, and in that event it forms part of the cost for capital allowances, as shown in this example. On the sale of a car VAT is not normally due but there are special rules for second-hand car dealers and in some other circumstances.

Special rules also apply for items of plant costing £2,000 or more (VAT inclusive) where the trader has elected to use the small business flat rate scheme. In those cases VAT input tax is recoverable and capital allowances are only due on the net cost. On the sale of these items output tax at 17.5% is payable but only the net sale proceeds are included in the capital allowances pool. For capital assets costing less than £2,000, under the flat rate scheme both output and input VAT-inclusive figures are used in the capital allowances computation. The only exception to this rule is where the asset was purchased before the trader joined the scheme in which case the VAT-exclusive price is deducted from the pool on sale. (Where the VAT-exclusive price is shown in the capital allowances pool, the sale is not included in the turnover for the purposes of the flat rate scheme and the output tax at 17.5% must be accounted for separately.)

(A) Alley plc, a company that qualifies as medium-sized, carries on a trade of multiple retailing. The company has traded for many years making up accounts to 31 December annually.

The company acquired some lorries under a finance lease for a two year period, 1 September 2006 to 31 August 2008. The lease rental payments are £485,000 per annum and the lorries have been capitalised in the accounts at £750,000, that amount being the cost of the lorries to the lessor company on 1 September 2006. Alley plc has charged depreciation on the lorries and the interest element of the rental payments in its accounts. The lessor company makes up accounts to 30 November annually.

The company made the following purchases and sales of plant and machinery in the two years ended 31 December 2007:

(a) 4 January 2006 purchased computer equipment costing £150,000, together with computer software costing £30,000.

(b) 12 January 2006 purchased three vans for £60,000.

(c) 21 March 2006 purchased a desk and office furniture for £1,600.

(d) 7 June 2006 purchased a motor car for use by the chairman for £16,000.

(e) 19 June 2006 sold two motor cars for £3,000 each, which had previously cost £9,500 each in 2002.

(f) 31 March 2007 purchased shop fittings for £20,000.

(g) 14 May 2007 disposed of the car purchased for use by the chairman for £7,000. It was replaced by the acquisition on lease of a new Jaguar with a retail value of £28,000, on which lease payments of £4,500 were made in 2007. These were charged in arriving at the operating profit.

(h) 1 August 2007 purchased shop fittings for £25,000.

In October 2007 the company spent £100,000 on making building alterations incidental to the installation at the beginning of 2008 of a new computerised control system.

The written down value at 1 January 2006 for the main pool was £104,100.

(a) Show the treatment of the leased lorries and the leased Jaguar car for Alley plc and also indicate the capital allowances treatment of the lorries for the lessor company.

(b) Compute the capital allowances on plant and machinery for the two years ended 31 December 2007, assuming that the maximum reliefs are claimed as early as possible.

Assume that the current law remains unaltered in 2007 and 2008.

(B) IJ, a sole trader, prepares accounts to 30 June annually. On 31 July 2004 he acquired patents having ten years to run at a cost of £5,000. The patents were sold outright for £6,000 on 30 April 2007.

Show the tax position for all the years.

(C) KL, a sole trader, has been in business for many years and makes up accounts to 30 September annually. In December 2006 he incurred capital expenditure of £100,000 on research and development. He also gave £20,000 to the South Riding University in June 2006 to be used for scientific research connected with his trade.

Show how these payments will be treated for tax purposes.

(D) MN makes up accounts annually to 30 April. In May 2004 he paid £8,400 for know-how for use in his trade. On 31 August 2006 he ceased trading. The business was not transferred to anyone else but he sold the know-how for £9,000.

Show the capital allowances available to him.

(A) **Alley plc**

(a) **Tax treatment of leased items**

Lorries under finance lease

The lorries acquired by Alley plc under the finance lease, although capitalised in the company's accounts, are not treated as purchased for tax purposes. Instead the rental payments of £485,000 per annum are treated as a trading expense. The payments must be allocated to periods of account under the accruals concept. Where the Accounting Standard SSAP 21 has been applied, Revenue Statement of Practice (SP3/91) permits the charge to comprise a mixture of the finance charge element and the accounting depreciation charge.

Finance leases are subject to detailed anti-avoidance provisions (see explanatory note 17). As far as the lessor company is concerned, the expenditure of £750,000 on the lorries qualifies for a restricted writing down allowance covering the three-month period from 1 September 2006 to 30 November 2006. The legislation puts this into effect by restricting the allowable expenditure in the first period, but the whole of the remaining expenditure goes into the pool at the end of that period, so it is more straightforward to apply the restriction to the writing down allowance. The position is therefore as follows:

Lessor company's year to 30 November 2006 – relevant entries in plant and machinery pool

	£
Cost of lorries 1 September 2006	750,000
WDA 25% x 3/12ths	46,875
Written down value carried forward	703,125

Jaguar car leased for use by chairman

Alley plc is entitled to a deduction from its profits in respect of the Jaguar car lease payment in the year to 31 December 2007. Since the car cost the leasing company more than £12,000, Alley plc cannot deduct the full amount paid of £4,500. The allowable deduction is:

$$£4,500 \times \left[\frac{12,000 + 28,000}{2 \times 28,000} = \frac{40,000}{56,000} \right] = £3,214$$

so £1,286 will be disallowed (see explanatory note 14).

(b)   Alley plc – Capital allowances on plant and machinery for two years ended 31 December 2007

	Main pool	Car £12,000+	Short life asset computer (1)	Short life asset computer (2)	Total Allces
Yr ended 31.12.2006	£	£	£	£	£
WDV bf 1.1.06	104,100	–	–		–
Additions not qualifying for FYA:					
Car (7.6.06)		16,000			
Sales proceeds (19.6.06)	(6,000)				
	98,100				
WDA 25%	(24,525)	(3,000)			27,525
Additions qualifying for FYA:					
Computer equipment (4.1.06)			150,000		
Computer software (4.1.06)			30,000		
Vans (12.1.06)	60,000				
Furniture (21.3.06)	1,600				
	61,600		180,000		
FYA 40%	(24,640)	36,960	(72,000)		96,640
	110,535	13,000	108,000		124,165
Yr ended 31.12.2007					
Sale proceeds (14.5.07)		(7,000)			
Balancing allowance		(6,000)			6,000
WDA 25%	(27,634)		(27,000)		54,634
Additions qualifying for FYA:					
Shop fittings (31.3.07)	20,000				
Shop fittings (1.8.07)	25,000				
	45,000				
FYA 40%	(18,000)	27,000			
Alterations to buildings incidental to installation of computer (Oct. 2007)	100,000				
FYA 40%	(40,000)			60,000	58,000
WDV cf 31.12.07	109,901		81,000	60,000	118,634

(B)   **IJ – Patents Allowances**

			£
2005/06	Year ended 30 June 2005	Cost	5,000
		WDA 25%	1,250
			3,750
2006/07	Year ended 30 June 2006	WDA 25%	938
			2,812
2007/08	Year ended 30 June 2007		
	Sale proceeds 30 April 2007 (limited to original cost)		5,000
	Balancing charge		2,188

The capital profit of £1,000 is taxed (ITTOIA 2005 ss 587–599) over six years commencing with the year in which it is received, ie 2007/08 (unless IJ elects under s 590(3) to have all the tax charged in one sum in 2007/08).

(C) **KL – Research and development**

December 2006 capital expenditure qualifies for capital allowances of £100,000 in 2007/08 (chargeable period year to 30 September 2007).

June 2006 gift of £20,000 to South Riding University is treated as a trading expense of the accounting year to 30 September 2006, reducing the assessable profit in 2006/07.

(D) **MN – Know-how**

			£
2005/06	Year ended 30 April 2005	Cost	8,400
		WDA 25%	2,100
			6,300
2006/07	Year ended 30 April 2006	WDA 25%	1,575
			4,725
2007/08	1 May 2005 to 31 August 2007		
	Sale proceeds		9,000
	Balancing charge (not restricted to allowances given)		£ 4,275

Explanatory Notes

All references in these notes are to CAA 2001 unless otherwise stated.

Qualifying expenditure and qualifying activities

1. For a company, the entitlement to capital allowances depends on qualifying expenditure incurred in the chargeable accounting period. Expenditure on a building preparatory to the installation of plant and machinery counts as expenditure on plant and machinery (s 25). For detailed notes on the expenditure qualifying for relief and the timing of reliefs, including the chargeable period provisions relating to allowances for income tax purposes, see Example 18.

    Plant and machinery allowances are available to those carrying on 'qualifying activities'. The main examples of qualifying activities are trades, professions, vocations and employments, property letting businesses, including furnished holiday lettings businesses, and special leasing businesses (as to which see Example 18 part (b) under *Capital allowances given by a claim made other than in a return*) (s 15). Allowances must be calculated separately for each qualifying activity (s 11).

    FA 2006 has brought some changes to the availability of capital allowances in respect of leased assets. They apply to leases longer than seven years (in some cases to leases longer than five years).

Allowances available

2. The allowances available are first year allowances, writing down allowances and balancing allowances. In some instances a balancing charge is made to take away allowances previously given. Writing down allowances and balancing allowances and charges are dealt with under a 'pooling' system, as outlined later in these notes. This note and notes 3 to 5 deal with first year allowances (FYAs). Where claimed, FYAs are given instead of the first year's writing down allowance.

    Although expenditure incurred before a trade starts is normally treated as incurred on the first day of trading (s 12), the actual date of the expenditure is the relevant date for FYAs. Where available, FYAs are given in full regardless of the length of the chargeable period (unless they are not or only partly claimed – see explanatory note 6).

FYAs are not available on transactions between connected persons (see Example 18 part (c)), or where obtaining allowances was the sole or main benefit of the sale (ss 213 to 217). Under the provisions of s 46, FYAs are not available on expenditure incurred in the period in which the trade ceases, nor on cars or taxis (other than low emission vehicles as indicated in note 5), motor cycles, ships, railway assets, most long life assets (see note 16), and machinery and plant for leasing or letting on hire, whether in the course of a trade or otherwise (subject to what is said in note 4). FYAs are also not available if there was a change in the nature or conduct of a trade carried on by someone other than the person who incurred the expenditure and obtaining an FYA was one of the main benefits that could be expected to arise from the change (s 46).

Under ss 44 and 52, small and medium-sized businesses as defined may claim FYA of 40% for the chargeable period in which qualifying expenditure is incurred. For the year commencing 1 April 2006 (6 April 2006 for a non-incorporated business) a small enterprise can claim FYA of 50%.

A small/medium-sized business is defined by reference to the Companies Act definition, adapted to apply to unincorporated businesses as well (ss 47 to 49). To qualify for financial years ending on or after 30 January 2004, the business must satisfy two of the following conditions in the current or previous year (and for companies in a group, the group must be small/medium-sized when the expenditure is incurred):

–   Turnover must not be more than £22.8 million (previously £11.2 million)

–   Assets must not total more than £11.4 million (previously £5.6 million)

–   There must not be more than 250 employees

To qualify as 'small' a business must satisfy at least two of the following criteria in the current or previous year (and if a company is a member of a group, the group must also be 'small'):

–   Turnover not more than £5.6 million (previously £2.8 million)

–   Assets not more than £2.8 million (previously £1.4 million)

–   Not more than 50 employees.

UK company members of a foreign group will not qualify unless the foreign group is small/medium-sized.

First year allowances are available at 100% for expenditure on energy saving and environmentally beneficial plant and machinery and plant and machinery for gas refuelling stations (see note 4), and electric and low emission cars (see note 5).

Computers

3.   For expenditure incurred in the four years to 31 March 2004, a small business as defined in ss 47 and 48 (see note 2) was able to claim 100% FYAs on investment in information and communications technology.

Qualifying expenditure comprises:

(a)   Computers (but not computerised control or management systems or other systems that are part of a larger system whose principal function is not processing or storing of information), peripheral devices designed to be connected to a computer, such as keyboards, printers etc, cabling and dedicated electrical systems for computers

(b)   Next generation mobile phones and devices designed to connect television to receive and transmit information to and from data networks such as the internet

(c)   Software for use with equipment within (a) and (b) (including new software for computers bought before 1 April 2000).

Computer software is an intangible asset, but it is specifically provided that capital expenditure on licensed software (except where acquired with a view to sub-licensing) and electronically transmitted software qualifies for plant and machinery allowances (s 71). Software is usually either developed 'in house' or acquired on lifetime licence for a particular user or users rather than being purchased outright. If licensed software is acquired on rental, the rentals are charged against profit over the life of the software. Where a lump sum is paid, HMRC normally takes the view that the cost of software with an expected life of less than two years may be treated as a revenue expense and deducted from profit. Otherwise it will usually be treated as capital expenditure for which plant and machinery allowances may be claimed (under the short life asset rules if appropriate). The treatment of in-house software is broadly similar, being either treated as capital or revenue depending on the expected period of use. HMRC has stated that expenditure on modifications in connection with EMU and the introduction of the Euro will normally be revenue expenditure.

From 1 April 2002 separate rules apply for companies in relation to intangible assets. Computer software treated as part of the cost of the related hardware is not affected by these rules. Software that is not so treated will be dealt with under the intangible assets provisions unless the company makes an election for capital allowances to apply. The election must be made within two years after the end of the accounting period in which the expenditure was incurred. Once made the election is irrevocable. For the detailed provisions on intangible assets see Example 65.

Energy saving and environmentally beneficial plant and machinery

4.   From 6 April 2001 (1 April 2001 for companies) 100% FYAs are available on new plant and machinery that is energy-efficient (ss 45A–45C). From 1 April 2003 this is extended to include environmentally beneficial plant and machinery. The FYA is available for qualifying expenditure on combined heat and power plant, boilers, motors, variable speed drives, lighting systems, refrigeration equipment, pipe insulation, heat pumps, radiant and warm air heaters, compressed air equipment, solar thermal systems, environmentally beneficial machinery and thermal screens. Qualifying products are listed on the UK Energy Technology List, which is available on the internet at www.eca.gov.uk. Businesses purchasing relevant products may establish whether the 100% FYA is available by obtaining a certificate from the manufacturers, or alternatively via the website.

The rules for fixtures in ss 172 to 204 (see note 21) have been adapted to enable energy service companies to claim the 100% first year allowances on qualifying energy saving plant and machinery as outlined above where the plant and machinery is provided and becomes a fixture on a client business's premises, and the plant and machinery is operated by the energy service company under an energy services agreement.

Under s 45E, 100% first year allowances may be claimed for expenditure incurred between 17 April 2002 and 31 March 2008 inclusive on new plant and machinery for gas refuelling stations.

From 17 April 2002 the general exclusion from FYAs of plant for leasing (see note 2) does not apply to plant and machinery for leasing that is energy-saving plant and machinery (s 45A), low emission cars (s 45D – see note 5), gas refuelling equipment (s 45E) or from 1 April 2003 environmentally beneficial plant (s 45H).

Low emission cars

5.   Expenditure on certain new cars purchased between 17 April 2002 and 31 March 2008 inclusive is eligible for 100% FYAs (s 45D). The eligible cars are those with a carbon dioxide emissions figure of 120 grams or less, bi-fuel cars where the lower emissions figure is 120 grams or less, and electric cars. 'Car' for this purpose includes a taxi but does not include a motor cycle.

Such cars are also excluded from the restrictions relating to cars costing more than £12,000 (see notes 13 and 14).

Partial claims for allowances

6.   Individuals and companies *need not claim* the full allowances available on plant and may instead claim the amount which gives the most favourable tax position taking all other circumstances into account (ss 52(4), 56(5)). The main reason for making partial claims for allowances is to enable the

taxpayer to claim other reliefs or allowances that cannot be claimed in a later period. As far as first year allowance is concerned, allowances may sometimes be higher if it is only partly claimed. For an illustration see Example 19.

Pooling

7. Expenditure on plant and machinery is pooled for the purposes of writing down allowances, balancing allowances and balancing charges (s 53). There are three kinds of pool, single asset pools, class pools and the main pool. Where someone carries on more than one qualifying activity, separate pools are required in relation to each activity.

    Single asset pools (which contain only one asset) are required for:

    (i)   A car costing more than £12,000 (other than a low emission car) (s 74) (see note 13).

    (ii)   A short life asset (s 86) (see note 15).

    (iii) An asset used privately by the proprietor (s 206) (see note 12).

    Class pools (which may contain more than one asset) are required for:

    (i)   Long life assets (see note 16).

    (ii)   Expenditure on assets leased outside the UK (s 109) (see note 20).

    All other qualifying expenditure goes into the main pool.

Writing down allowances and balancing adjustments

8. The calculation of the capital allowances position on the pool depends on whether the disposal proceeds are more than or less than the available qualifying expenditure (s 55), ie the unallowed expenditure brought forward, plus additional qualifying expenditure in the current period (other than expenditure on which FYA is claimed), less any disposal proceeds. (Businesses are not in fact *required* to bring expenditure into the pool in the earliest available period, so that if for example some of the expenditure was omitted in error it could be brought in when the error was discovered.) If the proceeds *exceed* the unallowed expenditure, a balancing charge is made to withdraw the excess allowances (but see note 10 re the limit on the disposal proceeds). This may occur either while the business is continuing or on cessation. Where the proceeds are less than the available expenditure, the available allowance is either a writing down allowance of 25% per annum on the reducing balance method (see note 9 re accounting periods of more or less than 12 months), or a balancing allowance if the period is the 'final chargeable period'. For a single asset pool, the final chargeable period is the period in which the asset is disposed of. For the main pool and class pools the final chargeable period is that in which the qualifying activity is permanently discontinued (s 65), although this is varied slightly for assets leased abroad (see note 20). A balancing allowance does not arise other than in the final chargeable period even if, say, the whole plant in the main pool were destroyed by fire and the compensation fell short of the balance on the pool. In those circumstances, the pool balance after deducting the compensation would continue to attract writing down allowances.

    Where a claim for first year allowance is made, the balance of expenditure (including a nil balance) is strictly not allocated to a pool until (at earliest) the commencement of the following period, unless the asset is also disposed of in the period in which it is acquired. In practice it is sensible to bring the balance of the expenditure into the relevant pool at the end of the period of expenditure, so that it forms part of the opening figure for the next period.

    The practical working order in respect of a pool for periods other than the final chargeable period is as follows (although some steps are clearly not relevant for single asset pools):

	£
Written down value (WDV) brought forward	?
Add: Expenditure not qualifying for FYA or on which FYA not claimed	?
Less: Disposal proceeds	(?)
	X
WDA on X (or balancing charge if X is a negative figure)	(?)
	?

Expenditure qualifying for FYA	?	
FYA	(?)	
Balance of expenditure allocated to pool		?
WDV carried forward		?

In the final chargeable period, if the qualifying activity is discontinued in that period, first year allowance is not available (see note 2) and there would be a balancing allowance rather than a writing down allowance if X was positive. On a single asset pool, if an asset was disposed of in the period in which it was acquired for less than its cost, there would be a balancing allowance on the shortfall. If it was disposed of in that period for more than cost, it would not be brought into account for capital allowances at all and the capital profit would be dealt with under the capital gains legislation (see Example 96).

Accounting periods of more than or less than 12 months (s 56)

9. If a company's chargeable accounting period is less than 12 months the writing down allowance is proportionately reduced.

    Under the income tax rules, capital allowances are treated as a trading expense of a period of account, which may be more or less than 12 months. Writing down allowances are proportionately decreased where the accounting period is less than 12 months and increased where the accounting period exceeds 12 months (but there are special rules for accounts exceeding 18 months – see Example 18 part (b)).

    For both companies and individuals, the writing down allowance is proportionately reduced if a qualifying activity has been carried on for only part of the accounting period (s 56).

Limit on disposal proceeds

10. If plant is disposed of for more than its cost, the disposal proceeds brought into the computation are limited to the original value placed into the pool, except when the plant was acquired from a connected person, in which case the limit of disposal proceeds is the highest price paid by one of the connected persons (s 62). For the connected persons rules see Example 18 part (c).

    A capital profit is dealt with under the capital gains legislation (see Example 96).

Hire purchase

11. Hire purchase does not prevent allowances being given as though there were an outright purchase at the time of the first use of the relevant asset, except for finance lessors (see note 17) (s 67). The cash price is therefore brought in at that time and the subsequent instalments of capital ignored, the interest element being charged in arriving at taxable profit (see also note 14).

Private use

12. Where directors or employees are allowed to use company assets, such as cars, for private purposes, this does not affect the employer's allowances. The employee is charged on the benefit under the benefits code of ITEPA 2003, if he is a director or an employee earning £8,500 pa or more. The reason for keeping the car used by the chairman separate from the car pool in this example is that it cost more than £12,000, so that allowances have to be restricted, as indicated in note 13. If it had cost £12,000 or less it would have been included in the pool in the usual way.

It is only where business assets are used partly for private purposes by the *proprietor* of the business (ie by a sole trader or by partners) that the capital allowances are restricted. In these circumstances the asset is kept separate in a single asset pool (s 206). The asset is written down by allowances calculated on the full cost, but only the business fraction is allowed in calculating taxable profits. When the asset is sold there is a final adjustment by way of balancing charge or balancing allowance (again restricted to the business fraction). If more than one asset is used privately then a separate single asset pool is set up for each asset (s 54). For an illustration see Example 18 part (e).

£12,000+ cars

13. Where a car, other than a low emission car, costs more than £12,000 a single asset pool is set up for it (s 74). 'Car' for this purpose is defined as a mechanically propelled road vehicle (including a motor cycle) other than one primarily suited for carrying goods or a vehicle not commonly used as a private vehicle and unsuitable to be so used. Qualifying hire cars (ie cars normally hired to the same person for less than 30 consecutive days and less than 90 days in any twelve months and cars let to someone receiving the mobility component of disability living allowance or a mobility supplement) are not subject to the £12,000 restriction and they go into the main pool.

The writing down allowance is restricted to £3,000 per annum and where there is private use (see note 12), to the business fraction of £3,000 (ss 75, 77). Once the written down value falls to the £12,000 level or less WDAs are calculated at 25% per annum in the usual way, but the car remains in the single asset pool until it is disposed of. There is no limit on a balancing allowance, as shown in the example in relation to the sale of the chairman's car on 14 May 2007.

Leased cars

14. Where a car is hired, if its retail price when new exceeds £12,000 and it is not a low emission car, the allowable hire charge that may be deducted in computing profits is restricted by applying the fraction

$$\frac{12,000 + P}{2P}$$

where P is the retail price when new (ITTOIA 2005 s 48). If there is a subsequent rebate of rentals, the amount brought in as a taxable receipt is reduced in the same proportion (s 48(4)). The retail price of a car when new is either the actual price paid by the lessor for the car when new, if known, or the manufacturer's list price less any generally available discount (Revenue Tax Bulletin April 2000). The allowable deduction may be further reduced where there is private use as set out in note 12.

Although a hire purchase agreement is an agreement for hire, with an option to purchase, it is expressly provided by ITTOIA 2005 s 49(2) that the hire charge restriction does not apply to a hire purchase agreement under which the option to purchase is exercisable on payment of an amount not exceeding 1% of the retail price of the car when new.

Short life assets

15. Where a trader purchases machinery or plant for use wholly and exclusively for the purposes of the trade, an election may be made to treat the machinery or plant as a short life asset (s 85). The asset is then kept in a single asset pool. The scheme is intended to apply when a trader expects to dispose of an item of machinery or plant at less than its written down value within four years from the year of its acquisition, and it is particularly relevant for assets with a high rate of obsolescence, such as computers. (The normal 40% FYA plus 25% WDA system takes seven years to write off approximately 90% of any expenditure.)

The election for short life asset treatment is to be made by companies within two years after the end of the chargeable period in which the capital expenditure was incurred (or, where the capital expenditure was incurred on different dates, as is the case with the building expenditure preparatory to the installation of the computerised control system in this example, within two years after the end of the period in which the first expenditure was incurred). For individuals the time limit is one year from 31 January following the tax year in which the relevant accounting period ends. When a short life asset is sold within four years after the end of the period in which the capital expenditure was incurred (or the first capital expenditure if it was incurred on different dates), there is a final adjustment by way of a balancing charge or balancing allowance.

However, if the short life asset is not sold within that time its written down value is transferred to the main pool and thereafter dealt with as if it had never been in a single asset pool.

Example

EF makes up accounts annually to 31 December. In April 2005 he acquired plant costing £10,000. On the basis that a short life asset election was made, show the capital allowances available in the following cases (ignoring the possibility of first year allowances):

(1)   The plant is sold in the year ended 31 December 2007 for (i) £3,000 and (ii) £6,000; and

(2)   The plant is not sold by 31 December 2009.

EF – Short life asset election

(1)   *Plant sold in yr ended 31 December 2007*

			(i) For £3,000 £	(ii) For £6,000 £
2005/06	Year ended 31.12.05	Cost	10,000	10,000
		WDA 25%	2,500	2,500
			7,500	7,500
2006/07	Year ended 31.12.06	WDA 25%	1,875	1,875
			5,625	5,625
2007/08	Year ended 31.12.07	Sale proceeds	3,000	6,000
Balancing allowance (charge)			2,625	(375)

(2)   *Plant not sold by 31 December 2009*

			£
WDV after allowance for 2006/07 as above			5,625
2007/08	Year ended 31.12.07	WDA 25%	1,406
			4,219
2008/09	Year ended 31.12.08	WDA 25%	1,055
			3,164
2009/10	Year ended 31.12.09	WDA 25%	791
WDV transferred to main pool			2,373

For further illustrations of the short life assets provisions see Examples 19 part (b).

Short life asset treatment does not apply to machinery or plant otherwise dealt with outside the main pool, as detailed in notes 7, 12 and 13 above.

Long life assets

16.   Special rules apply to long life assets (ss 90 to 104). These rules apply to expenditure on or after 26 November 1996. Expenditure on a second-hand asset is included if the special rules applied to the vendor in respect of that asset.

Long life assets are those with an expected economic life of 25 years or more. The provisions do not apply to machinery or plant in dwelling houses, retail shops, showrooms, hotels or offices, nor to cars (nor to certain ships and railway assets bought before the end of 2010). There is also a de minimis limit of £100,000 a year (reduced pro rata for companies with associated companies). There are various provisions to prevent the de minimis limit being exploited.

Assets within the provisions are pooled in a separate class pool and writing down allowances are given at 6% per annum on the reducing balance method. A first year allowance is not normally claimable unless the expenditure is on energy saving plant (s 45A); plant and machinery for gas refuelling stations (s 45E) or environmentally beneficial plant and machinery (s 45H). A balancing adjustment does not arise on disposal unless the trade has also ceased. In many cases the expenditure would alternatively qualify for industrial buildings allowances, and businesses may choose which allowances to claim.

Example

GH Ltd incurred the following expenditure on long life assets in its accounting years to 30 September 2005 and 2006. It had not previously acquired any long life assets.

1 January 2005	£200,000
1 September 2005	£150,000
30 August 2006	£250,000

Show the capital allowances claim in respect of these assets.

GH Ltd – capital allowances on long life assets – years to 30 September 2005 and 2006

	Long life assets pool £
Year to 30 September 2005	
Purchases (not qualifying for FYA)	350,000
WDA 6%	(21,000)
	329,000
Year to 30 September 2006	
Additions	250,000
	579,000
WDA 6%	34,740
WDV carried forward	544,260

The Revenue have given guidance on the long life assets rules in their Tax Bulletin of August 1997. See also the HMRC manuals at CA 23781.

Finance leases

17. For accounting purposes assets acquired under operating leases are treated as owned by the lessor, whereas assets acquired under finance leases are treated as owned by the lessee. Complex anti-avoidance provisions relating mainly to finance leases are included in ss 213 to 233. These rules have been augmented by Finance Act 2004 with additional restrictions on certain sale/lease and leaseback schemes to prevent double benefits accruing.

The main targets of the legislation are finance leases involving lower rentals with compensating capital payments (the capital sums being taxed at lower rates or possibly not at all, either through indexation allowance or by using a separate leasing company in which the shares are sold rather than the asset), and finance leases with back loaded payments, ie with rents concentrated towards the end of the lease. The provisions align the tax treatment more closely with the recognised accounting treatment. The receipt of a 'major lump sum' is treated as a disposal for capital allowances purposes and the rental income for tax purposes is normally the higher of the actual rent and the earnings recognised in the lessor's commercial accounts.

The first writing down allowance for finance lessors is restricted on a time basis according to the period from the date the expenditure is incurred to the end of the accounting period, as illustrated in part (a) of the example (s 220). Where a finance lessor obtains an asset on hire purchase, he will be entitled to capital allowances only as and when the capital expenditure is incurred, rather than being entitled to allowances on the full capital cost at the outset as indicated in note 11 (s 229). There are rules to prevent unused past allowances being transferred to finance lessors through sale and leaseback arrangements (ss 221 to 228). Provisions also limit the amount of lease rentals that may be deducted by the lessee where there has been a sale or lease followed by a finance leaseback (ss 228A to 228G). The term 'finance lease' is defined in s 219 as meaning arrangements which are, according to generally accepted accounting practice, treated as a finance lease or a loan in the books of one or more of the parties.

First year allowances are not available on plant and machinery for leasing, as indicated in note 2.

FA 2006 has introduced some anti-avoidance measures – particularly looking at the sale of lessor companies and the use of losses by leasing partnerships. New CAA 2001 s 228K removes the restriction on the disposal value where the lessor is required to bring in a disposal value but remains entitled to some or all of the rentals payable after that time. Even where the limit would not have applied, the disposal value is the actual consideration plus the net present value of these amounts to which the lessor remains entitled.

For HMRC's interpretation of various aspects of the rules on finance leases, see their Tax Bulletin of April 1997 and their manuals at CA28600.

Leasing plant and machinery together with land and buildings

18. Where plant and machinery is leased out as part of a letting of land and buildings, the property lettings are treated as a qualifying activity for plant and machinery allowances both for income tax and corporation tax (ss 15, 16). The effect is that a landlord's expenditure on plant and machinery is pooled, and relief is given when expenditure is incurred rather than when the particular letting commences (except for expenditure before the first property is let, which is treated as incurred when the first letting starts – s 12). Except as indicated in note 21, allowances are not available on furniture and furnishings in dwelling houses, for which a wear and tear allowance is usually given instead (see Example 98 explanatory note 6). For the way in which relief is given for excess allowances see Example 18 part (b). See also note 19 for the restriction on loss claims by an individual with excess allowances on leased plant and machinery and note 21 for the special rules relating to fixtures.

19. There are special provisions in s 19 relating to machinery and plant let other than in the course of a qualifying activity, but these circumstances will rarely arise (see Example 18 part (b)).

Where equipment leasing is a trade, the capital allowances are treated as a trading expense, and can therefore create or increase a trading loss. There is no restriction on the relief available for such a loss incurred by a company. If such a loss is incurred by an individual, however, the relief available is restricted to set-off against later rental income, rather than being set against other income under TA 1988 ss 380 and 381 (see Examples 29 and 30), unless the trade is carried on by the individual for a continuous period of at least six months in, or beginning or ending in, the tax year of loss, and the individual devotes substantially the whole of his time to that trade (TA 1988 s 384(6)). See also note 17 re finance leases and note 21 re fixtures. There are some anti-avoidance provisions relating to leasing in TA 1988 s 384A concerning partnerships with one or more company members.

20. Plant and machinery leased to non-residents for use overseas usually attracts writing down allowances of only 10% on the reducing balance basis, with all such expenditure being kept in a separate class pool (s 109). The final chargeable period for the pool is the period at the end of which there can be no more disposal receipts in any later period (s 65).

Fixtures

21. Sections 172 to 204 contain special rules relating to fixtures, ie plant and machinery that in law is treated as part of the building in which it is installed or otherwise fixed. The main intention of the provisions is to enable allowances to be claimed by whoever incurs capital expenditure on fixtures, whether or not that person has an interest in the land or buildings. The provisions are lengthy and complex, and what follows is only a brief summary.

As indicated in note 18, landlords may claim relief for expenditure on fixtures (other than in dwelling houses). Allowances on fixtures may also be claimed by a tenant if he incurs the expenditure (s 176).

Where fixtures are provided by equipment lessors, a joint election may be made by the equipment lessor and the equipment lessee (who may be the owner or tenant of the property) for the equipment lessor to claim the allowances (s 177). Equipment lessors cannot claim allowances on fixtures in dwelling houses, nor can they claim allowances on fixtures leased to non-taxpayers, such as charities. An exception is made for expenditure by equipment lessors incurred between 28 July 2000 and 31 December 2007 on boilers, radiators, heat exchangers and heating controls installed in low income homes under the Government's affordable warmth programme (s 180).

Allowances are not available on any amount in excess of the original cost of the fixtures when new plus any costs of installation (s 185). Vendors and purchasers may make a joint election (within two years of the date of the contract) fixing how much of the purchase price of a building relates to fixtures, the agreed amount being limited, however, to the vendor's original cost (s 198). Strictly elections should be made in respect of each fixture, but HMRC will accept a single election covering all the fixtures in a single property. Where a claim in a tax return becomes incorrect, for example, because of such an election, the claimant must notify an amendment to the return within three months after becoming aware of that fact (s 203). In the absence of an election under s 198, s 562 requires a 'just apportionment' of the purchase price between building and fixtures. See Example 18 part (a) for comments on apportionment.

There are anti-avoidance provisions to prevent double allowances and to prevent allowances on fixtures being artificially accelerated.

See note 4 re the special provisions to enable energy service providers to claim 100% allowances on energy saving plant and machinery that becomes a fixture.

VAT capital goods scheme

22.   For value added tax, a capital goods scheme applies to items of computer equipment with a tax-exclusive value of £50,000 or more per item, and land and buildings with a tax-exclusive value of £250,000 or more. Under the scheme, adjustments may be made over a period of five years for computers and buildings on a ten-year or shorter lease and over ten years for other land and buildings where the VAT exempt/taxable use of the asset varies during the adjustment period, VAT being payable or repayable accordingly.

Any VAT adjustments are reflected in capital allowances computations, extra expenditure being treated as incurred when any additional VAT is paid and VAT refunds being taken into account when received. Where an additional VAT liability relates to expenditure that qualifies for first year allowance, the FYA is also available on the additional VAT amount.

The date the VAT is treated as paid or repaid for the purpose of deciding in which capital allowances period the adjustment has to be made will normally be six months after the end of the taxpayer's VAT year. The adjustment to the plant and machinery pool therefore occurs in the period in which that date falls. If the adjustment relates to a building qualifying for capital allowances, the VAT adjustment is added to or deducted from the residue of expenditure at that date and writing down allowances are recomputed over the remainder of the building's life. Very few buildings that qualify for capital allowances are affected by VAT capital goods scheme adjustments. The main instance is enterprise zone buildings.

Renewals basis

23.   As an alternative to claiming capital allowances on plant and machinery, the renewals basis may be used. The original cost of an item does not qualify for any relief, but as and when it is replaced, the full cost of the replacement is charged against profit, excluding any amount representing additions or improvements. A trader may change from the renewals basis to capital allowances for all items in a particular class of plant and machinery by bringing their commercial written down value into the pool (Revenue Concession B1).

Patents

24. Where a trader incurs expenditure on devising and patenting an invention etc or in connection with a rejected patent application, the expenditure is allowable in computing trading profits (ITTOIA 2005 s 89). Where a trader purchases patent rights, he is entitled to capital allowances of 25% per annum on a reducing balance basis for expenditure.

Balancing adjustments are made on sale. If the sales proceeds exceed original cost, the capital profit is *not* charged to capital gains tax. It is charged over six years commencing with the tax year of receipt, unless the trader elects to have the whole amount charged in the year of receipt (ITTOIA 2005 ss 587–599).

For companies, the treatment of patents has changed from 1 April 2002. Capital allowances will not normally apply in respect of patent rights acquired on or after that date and the acquisition and disposal of the rights, and royalty payments on them, will be dealt with under the intangible assets rules. For details see Example 65. Capital allowances will continue to be available in respect of patents already owned by companies on 1 April 2002.

Research and development

25. Following FA 2000 s 68 and Sch 19, the term 'scientific research' has been largely replaced in the legislation by 'research and development', which is defined as covering activities that are treated as such in accordance with generally accepted accounting practice, subject to HMRC having power to issue regulations to include/exclude specified activities.

Where a trader incurs capital expenditure on research and development related to his trade he is entitled to a capital allowance equal to the full amount of that expenditure (CAA 2001 ss 437–451). The normal rules for chargeable periods apply. Expenditure on land is, however, excluded. Expenditure on dwellings is also excluded, except that where a building is used partly as a dwelling and partly for scientific research and not more than one quarter of the expenditure on the building relates to the dwelling, the whole of the expenditure is allowable.

Balancing adjustments are made upon the asset ceasing to belong to the trader. For this purpose, disposal value is taken into account rather than sale proceeds. Disposal value is defined as:

(a)   the proceeds of sale, if the asset is sold at open market value or higher;

(b)   the deemed proceeds of sale if the asset is deemed to be sold because of its destruction; it is treated as sold immediately before its destruction for any insurance proceeds, compensation, demolition proceeds etc (any demolition costs being added to the expenditure);

(c)   open market value, in any other event (CAA 2001 ss 443–445.).

See Example 51 for the treatment of revenue expenditure on research and development, including enhanced deductions and tax credit payments available to companies in certain circumstances.

Know-how

26. Know-how allowances are dealt with in CAA 2001 ss 452 to 463. Know-how means industrial information and techniques of assistance in manufacturing or processing goods or materials, working (or searching for) mineral deposits or carrying out agricultural, forestry or fishing operations. HMRC considers that the term does not include commercial know-how, such as information about marketing, packaging or distributing a product.

If know-how is sold as part of a business that is being disposed of, the payment is treated both as regards the seller and the buyer as a payment for *goodwill*, unless they jointly elect (within two years of the disposal) for it to be treated as a payment for know-how (ITTOIA 2005 s 194). If the election is made, or if know-how is disposed of other than as part of a business, capital allowances are available by way of annual writing down allowances of 25% on a reducing balance basis. Any additional expenditure is added to the written down value and any sale proceeds deducted before the writing down allowance is calculated. A balancing charge is made if know-how is sold for more than the written down value, and either a balancing charge or allowance is made when the trade ceases. Unlike balancing charges on other types of assets, a balancing charge is not restricted to the allowances that have been given in respect of the know-how, so if it is sold for more than cost, the excess is charged to tax within the balancing charge (CAA 2001 s 462).

For acquisitions by companies on or after 1 April 2002, know-how is dealt with under the rules for intangible assets. See Example 65 for details.

A. Set out when an industrial buildings allowance is available and briefly explain what comprises 'qualifying trade' and 'qualifying expenditure' for industrial buildings allowances.

B. Define a 'qualifying hotel'.

C. Explain the differences between allowances given for industrial buildings and hotels constructed:

(a) in 'enterprise zones', and

(b) elsewhere.

D. Calculate the capital allowances and/or balancing charges arising in the following cases (assuming, except in (d), that the annual accounting date is not changed):

(a) Arthur, a manufacturer of storage tanks, has been in business for several years, preparing accounts to 31 October annually. In the year ended 31 October 2006 he purchased land costing £100,000 and spent £300,000 on construction costs of a building for use in his trade. The building was not, however, used in that year, being first brought into use in November 2006.

(b) Arthur, instead of purchasing the land and constructing the building himself, purchased the land and building from a builder for £500,000 on 1 March 2007; £100,000 being applicable to the land. The building was brought into use immediately. The cost of construction to the builder was £350,000.

(c) Arthur, rather than building himself or purchasing from a builder, takes advantage of a trade depression to acquire an unused factory unit from Unfortunate Ltd, who had incurred construction costs of £200,000 in 2006 on land costing £100,000, intending to use the factory itself, but then had to dispose of the factory because of financial difficulties, selling to Arthur in December 2006 for £350,000 (including land £120,000). Arthur brought the building into use immediately.

(d) Roy took a ninety-nine year lease of an industrial building from the Barchester District Council, paying a premium of £110,000 in January 2006 in his first accounting period of fifteen months to 31 March 2007. The building was immediately brought into use in his trade of manufacturing ships tackle. The construction costs to the local authority were £120,000 excluding the land in the six months to June 2005 and Roy is to pay an annual rent of £3,000. Roy and the local authority each signed within the appropriate period the election under CAA 2001 s 290.

(e) Spares Ltd, a UK company that manufactures components for the motor industry and makes up accounts annually to 31 October, incurred capital expenditure as shown below on a new freehold factory in the year to 31 October 2006, the factory being immediately brought into use for manufacturing.

	£	£
Land		36,000
Levelling land and digging foundations		24,000
Building – Factory	208,000	
Drawing office	28,000	
Factory canteen	32,000	
Sales office	52,000	320,000
Sports pavilion		20,000
		400,000

(f) Benedict is a manufacturer making up his accounts to 31 December in each year. In March 2007 an industrial building, which originally cost Benedict £100,000 excluding land and on which allowances had been given resulting in a residue of expenditure at 31 December 2006 of

£70,000, was destroyed by fire. Receipts from sales of scrap amounted to £2,500; the cost of demolition was £4,000 and insurance proceeds were £125,000.

(g)   Honey, who makes up accounts to 31 March annually, built a factory for use in his manufacture of leather goods, the construction being completed in October 1989 and the factory brought into use on 31 March 1990. The construction cost was £320,000. He sold the factory in March 2006 for £500,000 excluding land.

(h)   Facts as in (g) except that the sales proceeds excluding land were:

    (i)   £40,000

    (ii)   £240,000.

(i)   Ivor was the purchaser from Honey. Calculate the allowances due to him on the alternative sales proceeds indicated in (g) and (h), that is £500,000, £40,000 and £240,000 respectively excluding land.

(j)   Pennicot, who prepares accounts to 31 December, sold four buildings on 31 December 2006 to Herbert, an unconnected manufacturer who also makes up accounts to 31 December. Herbert uses all four buildings for industrial purposes.

Details of the buildings are as follows:

1st Building

Building completed September 1962 at cost of £30,000 excluding land and brought into use 31 December 1962. Rate of initial allowance 5% and rate of writing down allowance 2%. Consistently used for industrial purposes except for a period of temporary disuse throughout 1971. Insulation against loss of heat added December 1988 at cost of £12,500. Sales proceeds (excluding land) £100,000 plus £10,000 for heat insulation.

2nd Building

Building completed 1973 at cost of £75,000 excluding land and brought into use 31 December 1973. Rate of initial allowance 40%. Used for industrial purposes until September 1999. Used as offices from that date until the date of sale. Sale proceeds (excluding land) £240,000.

3rd Building

Built 1985 at cost of £300,000 excluding land. Rate of initial allowance 25%. Date of first use 31 December 1985. Used for industrial purposes apart from a period of non-industrial use from 1 October 1992 to 31 March 1995. Sale proceeds (excluding land) £272,000.

4th Building

Built 1994 at cost of £1,000,000 excluding land. Date of first use 1 October 1994. Used as industrial building until 30 June 1999. Used for non-industrial purposes from 1 July 1999 to date of sale. Sale proceeds (excluding land) £500,000.

Show the allowances or charges that will arise to Pennicot for all relevant years and the allowances available to Herbert for 2006/07.

(k)   Lauderdale, who makes up accounts to 30 June each year, purchased a freehold interest in land in an enterprise zone on 10 August 2005 for £24,000. He entered into a contract on 5 October 2005 for the construction of a factory and offices on the site. Payments were made on architect's certificates and totalled £280,000 by 30 June 2006 (£228,000 relating to the factory and £52,000 to the offices) and the remaining £84,000 by 31 March 2007 (£38,000 relating to the factory and £46,000 to the offices). The factory was brought into use on that day. The construction had been financed by means of a bank loan, on which interest of £16,000 had been paid on each of 30 June 2006 and 31 March 2007. The loan interest had been capitalised. On 31 December 2007 Lauderdale sold the factory for £360,000 to another manufacturer, who makes up accounts to 31 March annually. Both claim maximum allowances.

1. Show the allowances or charges that will arise to Lauderdale for all relevant years.

2. State what allowances are available to the second-hand purchaser, and indicate what allowances would be available to a subsequent purchaser of the building.

(l) Maurice in 2005/06 incurs construction expenditure of £200,000 on a building which is situated in an enterprise zone and which he lets to Maurice Rest Homes Ltd from 24 June 2006 at a commercial rent.

The construction costs include:

	£
Fire safety expenditure	20,000
Thermal insulation	12,000

What relief is available against his general or rent income and in what years?

(m) Northern Hotels Ltd entered into a contract with a builder on 1 May 2006 for an extension of 20 bedrooms and made a stage payment of £180,000 at the end of its accounting period on 31 December 2006, but the extension was not by then habitable. Northern Hotels Ltd opens throughout the year offering full residential and restaurant facilities to commercial travellers and holidaymakers.

Show the allowances available on the expenditure assuming the extension was habitable by the end of 2007.

E. Outline the allowances available in respect of the conversion of redundant space over business premises into flats.

F. When may tax relief be claimed for the renovation of business premises in disadvantaged areas?

A. **Industrial buildings allowances – qualifying expenditure**

Industrial buildings allowances are available if expenditure has been incurred on the construction of a building or structure for use:

–   for a qualifying trade,

–   as a qualifying hotel,

–   as a qualifying sports pavilion, or

–   as a commercial building or structure in an enterprise zone.

All such buildings are defined as industrial buildings (CAA 2001 s 271).

A qualifying trade is defined in CAA 2001 s 274, the most common qualifying trades being manufacturing or processing goods or materials, but including a variety of other undertakings such as those concerned with transport, sewerage, water, electricity, hydraulic power, tunnels, bridges, mines, highways, agricultural operations on land occupied by someone else and fishing. Buildings used to store goods and materials before and immediately after manufacture or processing are included, as are buildings to store goods and materials on arrival in the UK by any means of transportation. It was held in the case of Girobank v Clarke (CA 1997) that the cheques and other documents processed at a data processing centre were not goods and materials, so the centre did not qualify. Nor did a cash and carry wholesale warehouse, although some minor processing activities were carried on (Bestway (Holdings) Ltd v Luff (1998)). By HMRC practice, buildings used for warehousing and storage by traders and wholesalers where the goods are to be used for an industrial process are included provided the storage forms a significant, separate and identifiable part of the trade and is conducted as a trade in its own right. No allowance will be due if the activity is a necessary and transitory incident of the conduct of the wholesale business (Revenue's Tax Bulletin December 1999).

Buildings are not used for the purposes of a qualifying trade if they are used as retail shops, showrooms, hotels, offices, or for purposes ancillary to those purposes (CAA 2001 s 277). In the case of Sarsfield v Dixons Group plc, a distribution warehouse operated as a separate undertaking by an associated company of a major retailer was held to be ancillary to the retail trade and did not qualify as a transport undertaking (CA 1998). Works offices are treated as in use for a qualifying trade as a result of the decision in CIR v Lambhill Ironworks Ltd (1950) and buildings used for the maintenance or repair of goods and materials are included (unless they are, or are part of, a retail business, or are used by a non-industrial business to maintain or repair goods or materials employed in that business). HMRC treats a motor dealer's vehicle repair workshop as an industrial building if it is completely separate from the vehicle sales area, does not have a reception, and public access is discouraged. Allowances would be restricted to the extent that vehicles for resale were repaired in the workshop.

There is a specific provision to include buildings provided for the welfare of workers in a qualifying trade, such as canteens (CAA 2001 s 275). A sports pavilion qualifies if it is provided for the welfare of workers in *any* trade (CAA 2001 s 280).

Where part of a building is outside the definition of industrial building, the whole building qualifies for relief providing the expenditure on the non-industrial part does not exceed 25% of the total cost. This only applies where the non-industrial part is housed within the same building, not where it is a separate building (CAA 2001 s 283).

Where a building qualifies as an industrial building, the expenditure that qualifies for relief is the capital expenditure on the construction of the building, excluding the cost of the land (CAA 2001 s 272), but including the cost of preparing the site for building, such as cutting, tunnelling and levelling (CAA 2001 s 273). Any subsequent capital expenditure on extensions and improvements to the building qualifies for relief as if it were a separate building. Revenue expenditure does not qualify, but it is expressly provided that where repair expenditure on an industrial building has not been allowed as a trading expense, the expenditure is treated as having been incurred on the construction of an addition to the building (CAA 2001 s 272(2)(3)). The relief is available to the person who incurs the construction expenditure, and there may be several people claiming relief on the same building, for example, the original owner in respect of the original expenditure, and a subsequent lessee or sub-lessee who incurs further capital expenditure on the building.

B.   Qualifying hotels

A qualifying hotel is a building of a permanent nature open at least four months in the seven months from April to October inclusive, with at least ten letting bedrooms. The bedrooms must be available to the public generally and must not normally be in the same occupation for more than one month. Services provided should include breakfast, evening meal, cleaning rooms and making beds. The hotel must be used for the purposes of the trade throughout the 12 months ending with the last day of the chargeable period (or throughout 12 months from the date of first use). The rules outlined in part A apply in respect of up to 25% of non-qualifying expenditure and buildings for the welfare of workers (CAA 2001 ss 279, 283).

C.   Enterprise Zones

(a)   Industrial buildings allowances are available on *any* building constructed in an enterprise zone except a dwelling house, and the building does not have to be used for a particular trade, nor does a hotel need to be a 'qualifying' hotel (CAA 2001 s 271). However, this will soon cease to be of practical relevance as the last designation of an enterprise zone expires in October 2006.

Where buildings (other than dwellings) are constructed in enterprise zones (or expenditure thereon is contracted for) within ten years from the designation of the zone, the allowances available to the person who incurs the expenditure on the construction of the building and anyone who buys the building within two years from the date of first use are an initial allowance of 100%, which may be disclaimed wholly or in part, and writing down allowances at the rate of 25% per annum on a straight line basis until the expenditure is fully relieved (CAA 2001 ss 305 and 310). Balancing charges and allowances are made on a sale (CAA 2001 s 314). A second-hand purchaser buying after the first two years of use is entitled to writing down allowances on the unrelieved balance of the expenditure, spread over the remainder of the 25-year life of the building (CAA 2001 s 311).

The fact that a balancing charge is made when an enterprise zone building is sold means that a sale in the early years results in the seller losing all or a large part of the benefit of the 100% allowances. To prevent a balancing charge being avoided by leasing rather than selling, the granting of a lease for a capital sum is treated as a sale, triggering a balancing charge, if it takes place within seven years after the date of the contract to acquire the interest in the building. This treatment does not apply to leases granted after more than seven years. If, however, there is a guaranteed exit arrangement, the seven-year period does not apply and a balancing charge will be made on the granting of a lease at any time within the building's 25-year life (CAA 2001 ss 327 to 331).

(b)   Where industrial buildings and hotels that are qualifying hotels as indicated in B above are constructed other than in enterprise zones, the allowances available to the first owner are writing down allowances at the rate of 4% per annum on a straight line basis. When the building is sold, there is a balancing adjustment on the seller and the buyer is entitled to allowances for the remaining expenditure over the balance of the building's 25-year life.

D. (a) **Arthur – Construction**

	£
Cost of land – not available for relief	–
Construction costs – year ended 31 October 2006	300,000

	£
Writing down allowance not available in 2006/07 since building not in use at end of basis period for that year (ie at 31 October 2006)	–
Writing down allowances 2007/08 to 2031/32 inclusive @ 4% = £12,000 per annum for 25 years	300,000

(b) **Arthur – Purchase from builder**

The cost to the builder is irrelevant, but the value of the land must still be eliminated. Allowances are therefore due on £400,000. The building is not in use at the end of the basis period for 2006/07 (year ended 31 October 2006), and writing down allowances will be given at 4%, ie £16,000 per annum, from 2007/08 to 2031/32 inclusive.

(c) **Arthur – Purchase of unused building**

Value of land must be eliminated.

Lower of cost of construction £200,000 or price paid for building £230,000 available for relief; therefore relief given on £200,000 @ 4% = £8,000 per annum for 25 years from 2007/08 to 2031/32 inclusive.

(d) **Roy – Purchase of long lease**

Premium paid on grant (less than construction costs) January 2005	£ 110,000

Roy will get writing down allowances at 4% per annum, ie £4,400, commencing in the chargeable period in which the interest in the building is acquired, ie the period to 31 March 2007. The writing down allowance is proportionately reduced *or increased* if the chargeable period is less than or more than one year. Roy's allowance for the 15-month period to 31 March 2007 is therefore 15/12 x £4,400 = £5,500. He will then get allowances at £4,400 per annum for subsequent periods (reduced or increased proportionately if the accounting date is changed) until the expenditure is written off (see explanatory note 2).

(e) **Spares Ltd – Qualifying expenditure**

	£
Levelling land and digging foundations	24,000
Building (sales office included since not more than 25% of (£320,000 + £24,000))	320,000
Sports pavilion	20,000
Expenditure qualifying for allowances	364,000

Since the building is brought into use in the year to 31 October 2006, writing down allowances will commence in that year. They will be given at the rate of 4% per annum, ie £14,560, for 25 years. The allowance will be scaled down proportionately for an accounting period of less than 12 months. Unlike the provisions for individuals outlined in (d) above, corporation tax chargeable accounting periods never exceed 12 months (see Example 51 explanatory note 2).

(f) **Benedict – Demolition costs – surplus on sale**

		£
Residue at 31 December 2006		70,000
Demolition cost		4,000
		74,000
Received during year ended 31 December 2007		
Scrap	2,500	
Insurance claim	125,000	127,500
Surplus on sale		53,500
Balancing charge year to 31 December 2007 (limited to allowances given of 100,000 – 70,000)		£ 30,000

(Remaining surplus liable to capital gains tax in 2006/07, subject to available reliefs, including indexation allowance to April 1998 and business assets taper relief.)

(g) **Honey – Sale of industrial building**

		£
1990/91 Construction cost year ended 31 March 1990		320,000
No initial allowance as post 31.3.86	–	
WDA 4%	12,800	
	12,800	
1991/92 to 2004/05 WDAs 4% for 14 years	179,200	192,000
Residue of qualifying expenditure at 31 March 2005		128,000
Sold during year ended 31 March 2006 (2005/06)		500,000
Surplus on sale		372,000
2005/06 Balancing charge – limited to allowances given		£ 192,000

The remainder of the surplus on sale of £180,000 represents the excess of the proceeds over cost. The sale is a chargeable disposal in 2005/06 for capital gains tax, and the computation will be based on the proceeds for both the land and the building, compared with their cost plus indexation allowance to April 1998, and subject to business assets taper relief of 75%.

(h) **Honey – Sale of industrial building**

	(i) £	(ii) £
Residue of qualifying expenditure at 31 March 2005 (basis period for 2005/06)	128,000	128,000
Sale in 2005/06 (year ended 31 March 2006)	40,000	240,000
Balancing allowance/(charge)	88,000	(112,000)

(i)   **Ivor – Purchase of second-hand industrial building**

	(g) £	(h) (i) £	(h) (ii) £
Residue of qualifying expenditure before sale	128,000	128,000	128,000
Add: Balancing charge	192,000		112,000
Less: Balancing allowance		88,000	
Residue of qualifying expenditure after sale	320,000	40,000	240,000
Divided by 9 years of life remaining out of 25 (ie from March 2006 to March 2015)			
Writing down allowance per annum	£ 35,556	£ 4,444	£ 26,667

Thus Ivor gets relief on the lower of the cost to the original user (from (g)) or the cost to him (from (h) (i) and (ii)).

(j)   **Pennicot – Temporary disuse and non-industrial use**

			£
1st Building			
Cost 1962			30,000
1963/64	Initial allowance 5%	1,500	
	WDA 2%	600	2,100
			27,900
1964/65 to 2005/06	WDAs 2% for 42 years (temporary disuse in 1971 ignored – note 12)		25,200
Residue of qualifying expenditure before sale			2,700
Sale proceeds – 31.12.06 £100,000			
Balancing charge 2006/07 – limited to allowances given			(27,300)

December 1988 expenditure of £12,500 on heat insulation qualified for allowances as plant and not as part of the industrial building expenditure. The proceeds of sale relating to the heat insulation expenditure are ignored (see explanatory note 7).

			£
2nd Building			
Cost 1973			75,000
1974/75	Initial allowance 40%	30,000	
	WDA 4%	3,000	
1975/76 to 1987/88	WDAs 4% for 13 years	39,000	
1988/89	WDA (balance)	3,000	75,000

Since the building is 25 years old at December 1998, the period of non-industrial use after that date is irrelevant, there will be no balancing charge on Pennicot when he sells the building and no allowances are available to Herbert.

			£
3rd Building			
Cost 1985			300,000
1986/87	Initial allowance 25%	75,000	
	WDA 4%	12,000	87,000
			213,000
1986/87 to 1993/94	WDAs 8 years at 4%		96,000
			117,000
1994/95 to 1996/97	Notional WDAs 3 years at 4%		36,000
			81,000
1997/98 to 2002/03	WDAs 6 years at 4%		72,000
2003/04	WDA (balance)		9,000
Residue of qualifying expenditure before sale			–

	£
Adjusted net cost of building	
Cost	300,000
Sale proceeds – 31.12.06	272,000
	28,000
Less: Proportion applicable to non-industrial use 2½/21 (ie 1.10.92 – 31.3.95 = 2½ yrs out of 21 yrs from 31.12.85 – 31.12.06)	3,333
	24,667

Allowances given	
£300,000 less notional allowances £36,000	264,000
Adjusted net cost as above	24,667
Balancing charge 2006/07	(239,333)

		£
4th Building		
Cost 1994		1,000,000
1995/96 to 1998/99	WDAs 4 years at 4%	160,000
		840,000
1999/00 to 2005/06	Notional WDAs 7 years at 4%	280,000
Residue of qualifying expenditure before sale		560,000

	£
Adjusted net cost of building	
Cost	1,000,000
Sale proceeds – 31.12.06	500,000
	500,000
Less: Proportion applicable to non-industrial use (7.5/12.25)	306,122
(October 1994 to June 1999, 4.75 years, being for industrial use)	193,878

	£
Allowances given	
1995/96 to 1998/99	160,000
Adjusted net cost as above	193,878
Balancing allowance 2006/07	33,878

Herbert	1st building £	3rd building £	4th building £
Residue of qualifying expenditure before sale	2,700	–	560,000
Balancing charge (allowance)	27,300	239,333	(33,878)
	30,000	239,333	526,122
Reduce to sale proceeds where applicable			(26,122)
Residue of expenditure after sale	30,000	239,333	500,000
Divided by unexpired life at date of sale	6 yrs*	4 yrs**	12.75 yrs***
WDAs to Herbert	£ 5,000	£ 59,833	£ 39,216

*   31.12.06 – 31.12.12 = 6 years
**   31.12.06 – 31.12.10 = 4 years
*** 31.12.06 – 30.9.19 = 12.75 years

(k)   **Lauderdale – enterprise zone factory**

1.   *Lauderdale – allowances and charges*

	£
2006/07 (yr to 30.6.06)	
Expenditure incurred	280,000
Initial allowance 100%	280,000
2007/08 (yr to 30.6.07)	
Expenditure incurred (no 25% restriction on office expenditure since building in enterprise zone)	84,000
Initial allowance 100%	84,000
Residue of qualifying expenditure before sale	–
Sale proceeds	360,000
Balancing charge	360,000

Note: Although the interest on the bank loan had been capitalised in the accounts, it is deducted from profit as a revenue expense for tax purposes.

The expenditure qualifies for the 100% allowance even though the zone's status has since expired.

2.   *Allowances to second-hand purchaser*

Purchase on 31 December 2007 is within two years from date of first use, 31 March 2007, so purchaser can claim allowances on the lower of the original expenditure of £364,000 and the amount he paid for the building, ie £360,000, as follows:

2007/08 (yr to 31.3.08)	£
Allowable expenditure	360,000
Initial allowance 100%	360,000

Since the written down value of the building is nil, there would be a balancing charge on a later sale or grant of a lease equal to the capital amount received, up to a maximum of the £360,000 allowance claimed. A subsequent purchaser would be able to claim writing down allowances on the lower of the amount paid by him and £360,000, spread over the remainder of a 25-year life calculated from 31 December 2007.

(l)   **Maurice – Relief against general or rent income**

Enterprise zone allowance is deductible as a trading expense from any rent income in the year of the expenditure 2005/06. This is nil unless Maurice has rent income from other properties.

He may therefore either carry forward the property business loss created by the allowance or claim relief against his general income in 2005/06. If that income is insufficient, the balance of the loss will be set against his rent income in 2006/07, and again he may claim to set the capital allowances element of any unrelieved loss against his other income of that year (see explanatory note 16), any remaining balance being carried forward against subsequent rent income.

Relief available is:	£		£
Fire safety	20,000		
Thermal insulation	12,000		
Other construction costs	168,000		
Enterprise zone buildings initial allowance	200,000	x 100% =	200,000

Instead of claiming the initial allowance of 100%, Maurice could claim writing down allowances at 25% of cost, ie £50,000, each year for four years, commencing in the tax year in which the building is brought into use, ie 2006/07. As a third alternative he could claim whatever part of the 100% available initial allowance he wished in 2005/06, and the balance would then be allowed from 2006/07 at £50,000 a year (or any lower amount claimed – see explanatory note 5) until reduced to nil. The way in which relief is given for writing down allowances is the same as for the initial allowance.

None of the expenditure would have qualified for allowances if the building had not been in an enterprise zone. The building itself is not a qualifying building, thermal insulation does not qualify unless it is in an industrial building used for a trade (see explanatory note 7) and fire safety expenditure in a nursing home does not qualify (see Example 18 part (a)).

(m) **Northern Hotels Ltd**

The expenditure of £180,000 on the hotel extension does not qualify for a writing down allowance in the year to 31 December 2006 because the extension was not in use at the end of the period. Writing down allowances at 4% per annum will be given for 25 years commencing with the year to 31 December 2007, not only on the stage payment but also on all further qualifying expenditure on the building in 2007.

E. **Conversion of redundant space over business premises into flats**

Provisions in CAA 2001 ss 393A to 393W give relief for expenditure incurred on or after 11 May 2001 on converting parts of business premises into flats. The conversion must take place within the existing boundaries of the building, except as is required to provide access to the new flats.

Allowances available

An initial allowance of 100%, which may be claimed wholly or in part, is available to owners and occupiers of qualifying properties for expenditure on the renovation or conversion of redundant space above shops or offices into qualifying flats for residential letting (s 393H). On any amount not claimed as initial allowance, a writing down allowance of 25% per annum of the original qualifying expenditure may be claimed, which again can be reduced to a specified amount (CAA 2001 ss 393J and 393K). The initial allowance will be withdrawn if the flat fails to qualify, or is sold before being let (s 393I).

Qualifying properties are defined as those meeting the following requirements (s 393C):

– The property must have been built before 1980

– There must be not more than four floors above the ground floor (excluding attics unless used as dwellings or part dwellings)

– The upper floors must have been constructed primarily for use as dwellings and must either be unoccupied or used only for storage within the year before conversion

    −   The ground floor must be authorised for business use within rating classes A1, A2, A3, B1 or D1(a), which broadly means retail shops, financial and professional services, food and drink, other offices, research and development and light industrial use, and medical etc services, such as doctors' and dentists' surgeries.

Qualifying flats (s 393D)

Each flat must be self-contained with external access separate from the ground floor premises.

Each flat must have no more than four rooms, excluding kitchen, bathroom, cloakroom and hallways.

The flat must be held for short-term letting (ie not more than five years), and must not be let to a person connected with the person who incurred the conversion expenditure.

The flat must not be a high value flat as defined by s 393E (ie with expected rental values in excess of specified limits, higher limits applying to flats in Greater London).

Balancing adjustments

A balancing adjustment will be made if the flat is sold, a long lease (exceeding 50 years) is granted, the person who incurred the expenditure dies, the flat is demolished or destroyed, or the flat ceases to be a qualifying flat. Since the available initial allowance is 100% the adjustment will normally be a balancing charge, which cannot exceed the allowances given. There will be no balancing adjustment if the balancing event occurs more than seven years after the time when the flat was first available for letting. Allowances are not transferable to a purchaser.

Way in which allowances are given

Allowances are treated as expenses of a property business. For the treatment of excess allowances see Example 18 part (b).

F.   **Renovation of business premises in disadvantaged areas**

Finance Act 2005 Schedule 6 introduced a new business premises renovation allowance (BPRA) from a date to be announced for a period of five years. This will give tax relief on 100% of the cost of renovating or converting business property where the building has been unused for one year and is situated in one of the 1997 designated disadvantaged areas.

BPRA will be available as a capital allowance to an individual or company being an initial allowance of up to 100% of the qualifying expenditure (CAA 2001 s 360G). If any part of the initial allowance is disclaimed a writing down allowance of up to 25% of the qualifying expenditure is available in subsequent years until costs are fully claimed (CAA 2001 s 360J). No balancing charge or allowance will occur providing there is no disposal event within seven years of the premises being brought back into use (s 360M). No allowance is available to the purchaser of the renovated building.

Qualifying expenditure means any capital expenditure, including fixtures, used on the repair, conversion or renovation of the building into a qualifying business premise (s 360B).

The building must have been last used for the purpose of a trade or profession, or as an office. It must have been unused for at least one year before the expenditure is incurred and situated in one of the voting list wards designated as disadvantaged for stamp duty (FA 2003 Sch 6). It must not have been used wholly or partly as a dwelling (s 360C).

The renovated building must be a qualifying business premises, that is, premises used or available for use for the purpose of a trade, profession or vocation or as an office. It must not be used wholly or in part as a dwelling (s 360D).

The initial allowance is available in the chargeable period in which the qualifying expenditure is incurred (s 360G) but will be withdrawn if the building is sold before first letting or use. (s 360H).

A balancing allowance or charge occurs if the building is disposed of within seven years of being available for use. Normally sale price (or market value) is compared with the unclaimed residue to arrive at the adjustment, any balancing charge to be restricted by restricting proceeds to cost. In the case of death proceeds are to equal the residue of unclaimed expenditure (s 360O).

Explanatory Notes

Definition of industrial building

1.   Following CAA 2001, the term 'industrial buildings' covers not only buildings in use for qualifying trades but also qualifying hotels, qualifying sports pavilions, and commercial buildings or structures in an enterprise zone (CAA 2001 s 271). Note that for the 'qualifying trades' part of the definition, the building must be *in use* for a qualifying trade, the most common of which are indicated in part A of the example. Note also that part of an industrial building may be outside the definition, provided that the expenditure on that part does not exceed 25% of the total cost of the building (10% for expenditure before 16 March 1983). Where a building was in an enterprise zone, there is no restriction on the use to which it may be put, except that a private dwelling does not qualify (see note 13).

   See Example 18 part (a) re apportioning expenditure between the building and any plant and machinery within it.

Allowances available

2.   Industrial buildings allowances are given as follows:

   (a)   Initial allowance (when available) in respect of expenditure in a chargeable period.

   (b)   Writing down allowance where the building is an industrial building at the end of the relevant period (CAA 2001 s 309).

   The writing down allowance is scaled down proportionately if a corporation tax accounting period is less than 12 months. For income tax, allowances are given for periods of account, and are proportionately increased or reduced if the account is for more or less than 12 months (CAA 2001 s 310) (see part D(d) of the example and Example 18 part (b)).

3.   The initial allowance is not currently available (except for buildings in enterprise zones – see note 13), but it has been available at various rates over the years, the most recent rates being as follows:

Date expenditure incurred	Initial allowance
13 November 1974 to 10 March 1981	50%
11 March 1981 to 13 March 1984	75%
14 March 1984 to 31 March 1985	50%
1 April 1985 to 31 March 1986	25%
1 November 1992 to 31 October 1993	20%

   Where a building has qualified for initial allowance and there is an additional VAT liability under the capital goods scheme which is treated as additional expenditure on the building (see note 18), the initial allowance is available on the additional expenditure.

4.   Writing down allowances where expenditure was incurred after 5 November 1962 are a flat 4% of cost (2% for expenditure on or before that date) to the original claimant, except for enterprise zone buildings (see note 13) (CAA 2001 s 310 & Sch 3.66).

   A second-hand purchaser does not get the same rate of relief as the original claimant. He gets allowances on the residue of qualifying expenditure after the sale (which usually means the amount he pays or the original building cost, whichever is lower) divided by the part of the tax life remaining at the date of purchase. The tax life of a building runs from the date the building was first used for 50 years for expenditure incurred on or before 5 November 1962, and for 25 years for expenditure after that date (CAA 2001 s 311 and Sch 3.67). If a building that has previously been used other than as an industrial building is acquired by an industrial user, the industrial user can claim writing down allowances over the remainder of the building's 25 (or 50) year life. Notional allowances are taken into account for the years when the building was not in industrial use (see note 12). The change to the current year basis for income tax does not affect the calculation of the writing down allowance for a second-hand purchaser, since it is based on the balance at the purchase date of the 25 (or 50) year period from the date the building was first used.

Partial claims for allowances

5. The initial allowance may be only partially claimed by both individuals and companies (CAA 2001 s 306). As stated above, the allowance is presently available only for enterprise zone buildings.

   It is also possible to disclaim a writing down allowance wholly or in part (CAA 2001 s 309). This could be done to avoid wasting other reliefs and allowances, as shown in Example 19 parts (c) to (e). The effect of disclaiming industrial buildings writing down allowance would be that the writing down period would be extended until the expenditure was fully written off, unless the building was sold in the meantime. Balancing adjustments cannot be made after the end of the 25 (or 50) year writing down period (see note 9), but this does not prevent writing down allowances continuing after the end of that period for someone whose ownership started before the writing down period expired.

Cost of construction

6. Allowances are given in respect of the cost of *construction* of the building. The cost of construction includes the costs of preparing the site. Where the site preparation includes demolishing existing buildings, then unless the buildings had been used for industrial purposes so that the demolition costs are taken into account in the balancing adjustment (see note 9), the demolition costs form part of the construction costs. Where a newly erected building is bought unused, the purchaser gets allowances on the cost of construction or the price he pays, whichever is the lower (unless he buys from the builder, in which case he gets allowances on the full purchase price – CAA 2001 ss 294 to 297). Since the allowances are given on the construction of the building no relief is available for the land (CAA 2001 s 272). Where capital expenditure is incurred on extensions and additions it is treated as expenditure on a separate building with its own writing down life and allowances are given to whoever incurred the expenditure, so that allowances may go to a lessee, or sub-lessee, as indicated in part A of the example.

   Where plant and machinery is purchased with a building, the purchase price needs to be apportioned and plant and machinery allowances can then be claimed on the appropriate part of the purchase price (see Examples 18 part (a) and 20 explanatory note 21).

Thermal insulation

7. If expenditure is incurred, either by the occupier or by a landlord, *in adding* any insulation against loss of heat in an industrial building in use for a qualifying trade, this qualifies as expenditure on plant and machinery and attracts allowances as such. When the building is sold, the disposal value of the thermal insulation expenditure is treated as nil, so that any sale proceeds are ignored. A purchaser does not get any relief on a payment to the vendor in respect of the insulation, since the legislation refers to expenditure in *adding any insulation*, whereas the insulation is already part of the building when a purchaser acquires it (CAA 2001 ss 27 and 28).

   See note 14 re thermal insulation in enterprise zone buildings.

Lease premiums

8. A trader who pays a premium on a *short* lease (not exceeding fifty years) can deduct, in computing his profits over the period of the lease, the amount assessable on the landlord as additional rent (see Example 100 explanatory note 11). No such relief is available for the payment of a premium on a *long* lease, which is regarded wholly as a capital matter. If the lessor and lessee so elect, however, the grant of the long lease can be treated as the sale of the building, with any capital sum paid being treated as the sale proceeds. The election must be made in writing within two years from the date on which the lease takes effect. This provision is aimed mainly at giving relief where a public body builds new factories to encourage local industries, but it applies to any long lease of an industrial building (CAA 2001 s 290). It is not, however, available for transactions between connected persons (CAA 2001 s 291). For the meaning of 'connected persons' see Example 18 part (c).

Balancing adjustments on disposal

9. When a building that is, or has been, an industrial building is sold during its 25-year (or 50-year) life, a balancing adjustment is made (CAA 2001 s 314). The demolition cost of a building is added to the residue of qualifying expenditure before the sale, for the purposes of calculating the balancing allowance or charge (CAA 2001 s 340). See note 6 re demolition costs incurred on a non-industrial building.

    If a building is sold after its writing down life, there is no balancing adjustment on the seller, and no allowances are available to the purchaser, as shown in part D(j) of the example in relation to the 2nd building. Even though the benefit of the capital allowances is retained by the seller, they are not deducted from the cost/31 March 1982 value in the capital gains computation when computing a gain.

10. The balancing adjustment on the seller is calculated as follows (CAA 2001 ss 318 to 320):

     (a) If the building has been in industrial use (or used for scientific research) throughout the period of ownership, the balancing charge or allowance is the difference between the sale proceeds and the written down value (residue of qualifying expenditure) before the sale, except that a balancing charge cannot exceed the allowances given, any capital profit being dealt with under the capital gains rules (CAA 2001 ss 318 & 320).

     In arriving at the residue of qualifying expenditure, initial allowances are treated as written off at the time of the expenditure (s 333) and writing down allowances at the end of the chargeable period (s 334). In part D (k) of the example relating to the enterprise zone building, both the additional expenditure qualifying for initial allowance and the sale of the building occur in the year to 30 June 2007. For 2007/08 there is therefore both an initial allowance of £84,000 and a balancing charge of £360,000 in the same year, giving a net addition to taxable profits of £276,000.

     (b) If the building has not been in industrial use (or used for research and development) throughout the period of ownership s 319 applies:

          (i) Where the sale, insurance, salvage or compensation moneys are *not less than* the capital expenditure, a balancing charge is made equal to the allowances given.

          (ii) Where the proceeds are *less than* the capital expenditure or are nil:

               A. If the adjusted net cost of the building exceeds the allowances given, a balancing allowance is made equal to the excess

               B. If the adjusted net cost of the building is less than the allowances given, a balancing charge is made equal to the shortfall.

          'Adjusted net cost' means the capital expenditure on the building less the disposal proceeds, reduced by the proportion of the period of ownership which the non-qualifying use bears to the whole, as illustrated in part D (j) of the example.

11. As indicated in note 4, a purchaser of a second-hand industrial building gets relief on the residue of qualifying expenditure after the sale. This is defined as (CAA 2001 s 313):

     The residue of qualifying expenditure before the sale

     Less any amount by which the sale proceeds fall short of that residue (s 337(2)), or

     Plus the balancing charge made on the seller, but not so as to give a residue of expenditure after the sale any greater than the sale proceeds (s 337(3) and (4)).

     In arriving at the residue of qualifying expenditure before the sale, notional allowances for a period of use for non-industrial purposes must be taken into account – s 336.

     Put simply, where there has been no non-industrial use the purchaser gets allowances on the original building cost or the amount he pays, whichever is less. Where there has been a period of non-industrial use the purchaser gets allowances on the seller's residue of qualifying expenditure before the sale plus the balancing charge, or the amount he pays, whichever is less, as illustrated in part D (j) of the example.

Temporary disuse

12. Temporary disuse as an industrial building does not prevent the continuity of allowances (CAA 2001 s 285). But if the building is put to other non-industrial use when not being used as an industrial building then no writing down allowances are given during that time and notional allowances have to be taken into account.

    The notional allowances affect the residue of qualifying expenditure that is taken into account in the calculation of a second-hand purchaser's writing down allowance (see note 11). They are not, however, brought into the calculation of the balancing adjustment on the seller, because the period of non-industrial use is taken into account by reducing the total amount for which allowances are available to the seller in proportion to the period of non-industrial use (see note 10).

Enterprise zone buildings

13. When the site of the building is in an area designated by the Secretary of State as an *enterprise zone* and construction expenditure is incurred (or contracted for) not more than ten years after the site was first included in the zone, the allowances available are:

Initial allowance	100% maximum (CAA 2001 s 306)
Writing down allowance	25% of cost per annum instead of 4% (CAA 2001 s 310)

    The last designations as an enterprise zone took place on 21 October 1996. Enterprise zone allowances cannot, however, be claimed on expenditure incurred more than 20 years after the site was included in the enterprise zone, no matter when the contract was entered into (CAA 2001 s 298).

    The initial and writing down allowances may be claimed wholly or in part by both individuals and companies. See note 5 re partial claims for writing down allowance.

    As indicated in note 1, qualifying buildings in enterprise zones include not only buildings in use for qualifying trades and qualifying hotels but any other commercial buildings or structures used for a trade, profession or vocation (including hotels that are not qualifying hotels) or as offices, but excluding a dwelling house or part of a dwelling house (CAA 2001 s 281).

    The 25% de minimis rule (see note 1) applies in determining whether any non-qualifying expenditure has to be excluded, but this will only be relevant to any private dwelling element since all commercial buildings qualify for the allowance (CAA 2001 s 283).

    If the first sale after an enterprise zone building is brought into use occurs within two years from that time, the purchaser is treated as if he had bought an unused building, so that he can claim the 100% initial allowance or 25% writing down allowance as indicated above on his qualifying expenditure (CAA 2001 s 301). If there is more than one sale in the first two years, this only applies to the first of them.

    Where a partly completed enterprise zone building is sold during the life of the enterprise zone, the purchaser will normally be entitled to the 100% relief both on the amount paid for the construction to date and for the completion of the building, but care needs to be taken with the contractual arrangements (see Revenue Tax Bulletin June 1998). Where part of the expenditure on a building was incurred neither within the ten-year life of the enterprise zone, nor under a contract entered into within the ten-year period, that part of the expenditure qualifies only for the normal level of buildings allowances, or not at all if it is a non-qualifying building (CAA 2001 s 298 and ss 302 to 304).

    Although the whole of the expenditure on an enterprise zone building less than two years old can be written off immediately, or in any event within four years, the building is still deemed to have a 25-year life, and if it is sold during that 25-year period, a balancing adjustment is made on the seller. Unless the sale occurs in the first two years, the buyer gets writing down allowances on any of the original expenditure that remains unrelieved, spread over the remainder of the 25-year life. If, however, someone purchased the building within the first two years of its life, the 25-year life of the building runs from the date of that purchase as shown in part D(k) of the example.

The rules outlined in part C (a) of the example impose a balancing charge on someone who owns an interest in an enterprise zone building if he grants a lease for a capital sum in the first seven years (or at any time if there are guaranteed exit arrangements). There would not, however, be any allowance to the lessee if the lease was a short lease (see note 8). In the case of a long lease, the lessor could elect with the lessee to treat the grant of the lease as a sale under the provisions outlined in note 8, which would not prevent the balancing charge on the lessor but would enable the lessee to claim allowances on his payment (or on the building cost if less).

Where a building is transferred between connected persons (for example, husband and wife – see Example 18 part (c)), they may elect to treat the transfer as being at written down value so that the transferor would not lose the benefit of the higher enterprise zone allowances which had already been given.

Enterprise zone allowances may be claimed both by traders and investors, as shown in part D (l) of the example.

14. Thermal insulation in buildings in enterprise zones may be treated as part of the building, giving rise to a claim for initial allowance of up to 100%. On sale of the building within 25 years a balancing charge may arise. Alternatively, a claim may be made as indicated in note 7 for the expenditure to be treated as expenditure on plant, with allowances at 25% on the reducing balance. No balancing adjustment in relation to the thermal insulation expenditure would then arise on disposal of the building.

Capital Allowances – Hotels

15. (a) Relief is available for expenditure incurred after 11 April 1978 on the construction of a qualifying hotel, using broadly the same rules as those that apply to industrial buildings in use for qualifying trades.

(b) *Qualifying Hotel (CAA 2001 s 279)*

Buildings of a permanent nature open at least four months in the seven months from April to October inclusive. The building must have at least ten letting bedrooms which are available to the public generally and not normally in the same occupation for more than one month. Services should normally include breakfast, evening meals, cleaning rooms and making beds.

(c) The hotel must be used for purposes of trade (i) throughout the twelve months ending with the last day of the relevant accounting period; or (ii) if the hotel was first used on a date after the beginning of those 12 months, by reference to 12 months beginning with the date of first use.

A hotel that does not qualify under (i) because it has less than ten letting bedrooms can qualify under (ii) from the date of having at least ten letting bedrooms, as if that date were the date of first use.

(d) Qualifying expenditure includes that on any building provided for the welfare of hotel workers (CAA 2001 s 275).

(e) Expenditure incurred by an individual trader or a partnership does not qualify for relief if it relates to accommodation which during the time the hotel is open in the season (April – October) is normally used as a dwelling by that trader or a partner or by their family or household. As with other industrial buildings, however, this does not apply if the dwelling part of the building does not exceed 25% (previously 10%) (CAA 2001 s 283).

(f)   Allowances available (except for hotels in enterprise zones – see note 13) are:

Initial allowance 20% for expenditure incurred before 1 April 1986 or contracted for in the year to 31 October 1993 – in the chargeable period or basis period when the expenditure is incurred.

Writing down allowance – 4% to first user. Residue of qualifying expenditure after the sale (as with other industrial buildings) to a purchaser who did not himself incur the expenditure, spread over remainder of 25-year tax life.

Balancing allowances and charges apply. There may be a restriction on a balancing adjustment if during the tax life of the hotel it qualified for part but not all of the time.

(g)   Where the building ceases to qualify as a hotel because of a change of use but a sale is not made, there is a deemed sale at market value two years after the time when it ceased to qualify and a balancing allowance or charge will arise (CAA 2001 s 317).

Temporary disuse does not, however, mean that the building ceases to qualify or that the deemed sale at market value is to apply; but the temporary disuse cannot extend beyond two years after the end of the chargeable period in which the disuse commences.

Way in which allowances are given on let property

16.   The various buildings allowances are available to the owner of a building in respect of expenditure he has incurred on a building which is to be let under a lease or tenancy. (If the lessee or tenant himself incurs capital expenditure on extensions, additions etc, he will be entitled to allowances on that expenditure.) Occupation by a licensee of the owner or tenant is treated as occupation by the owner/tenant.

Any available initial allowance (which presently applies only to enterprise zone expenditure) is given when the expenditure is incurred (CAA 2001 ss 5 and 305), and writing down allowances commence when the building is brought into qualifying use (CAA 2001 s 309). The chargeable period for a lessor is the tax year itself (or company chargeable accounting period) (CAA 2001 s 6).

For both individuals and companies, the allowances are treated as an expense of a property business (CAA 2001 s 353 – see Example 18 part (b), which also deals with the treatment of excess allowances). An individual may claim to set a property business loss created by capital allowances against any other income of the year to which the loss relates, or of the following year, as indicated in part D(l) of the example (Maurice Rest Homes), with any balance remaining being carried forward against later rent income (TA 1988 s 379A). The time limit for the claim against general income is one year from 31 January following the tax year to which the claim relates.

Sale after cessation of trade

17.   Where an industrial building is sold after a trade ceases and a balancing charge arises, the charge is treated in the same way as a post-cessation receipt under TA 1988 s 103 or 104(1) for the purpose of enabling unrelieved losses, expenses and capital allowances to be set against it (CAA 2001 s 354). For notes on post-cessation receipts and expenses see Example 16 part (c)(ii).

VAT capital goods scheme

18.   Where a qualifying building costing £250,000 or more is used by a VAT partly exempt business (such as an office in an enterprise zone used by a bank), VAT adjustments may be required under the capital goods scheme, and those adjustments are reflected in the capital allowances computation. For details see Example 20 explanatory note 22.

Conversion of redundant space over shops and offices into flats

19.   The 100% allowances for the conversion of redundant space over shops and offices into flats for short-term letting dealt with in part E of the example were introduced as part of the Government's measures to regenerate Britain's towns and cities. The provisions are very detailed, and care needs to be taken to make sure the rules are complied with.

(a) (i)   Outline the way in which agricultural buildings allowances are given to individuals.

(ii) Archer commenced farming on 1 July 2003, making up accounts annually to 30 June. He incurred qualifying capital expenditure of £100,000 on agricultural buildings in March 2004. On 30 September 2006 he transferred the farm to Oakes, a farmer who makes up accounts annually to 31 March. No election was made for a balancing adjustment. Show the allowances available to each of Archer and Oakes assuming no further changes are made and neither of them changes his accounting date.

(b) (i)   Nicholas, a farmer who has made up his accounts to 30 April for many years, incurred £50,000 of expenditure on the construction of a barn on 1 January 2007 which was brought into use immediately.

Calculate the allowances due in respect of the expenditure.

(ii) Show the position if the barn in (i) above were sold for £45,000 on 1 October 2009 to Reginald, an established farmer who makes up accounts to 31 January.

Assume that neither Nicholas nor Reginald changes his accounting date during the writing down period.

(c) Somerset acquired the freehold of a farm on 1 April 2001 paying £350,000 for the land and buildings. No agricultural buildings allowances remain available on the buildings purchased. The farm is let to Essex for £6,000 per annum payable half yearly in advance on 1 April and 1 October. Essex makes up his farm accounts to 31 March in each year. Somerset incurred the following further capital expenditure on the farm:

		£
10 June 2001	Grain store	22,000
31 March 2002	Fencing	3,000

Essex incurred capital expenditure on the farm as follows:

25 July 2001	Drainage system	15,000
10 January 2002	Extension to farmhouse	33,000

On 1 October 2006 Kent took over the tenancy of the farm from Essex, paying £40,000 to Essex in respect of his capital expenditure. They did not elect for a balancing adjustment on the sale. Kent makes up accounts to 30 June annually.

On 1 August 2007 Somerset sold his freehold interest in the farm to Cornwall for £500,000, Kent continuing as tenant. No election was made for a balancing adjustment.

(i)   What agricultural buildings allowances are due to each person concerned (none of whom is connected in any way with any of the others)?

(ii) Calculate the chargeable gain on the sale of the freehold by Somerset.

(d) Rufus, a single man who owns the freehold of a farm property, incurred capital expenditure of £300,000 on new farm buildings (not including a farmhouse) in October 2006. He leased the buildings to a farming tenant from 1 May 2007, the tenant paying rent of £15,000 a year quarterly in advance. Rufus has no other agricultural income, but his income from other sources in 2006/07 is £30,000 (none of it being rents). Show his taxable income for that year and for 2007/08 (assuming that Rufus's income continues at the same level).

(a) **Agricultural buildings allowances**

(i) Agricultural buildings allowances of 4% per annum on a straight line basis are available in respect of capital expenditure on agricultural buildings and works (see explanatory note 1). The allowances are given over a writing down period of 25 years commencing at the start of the period of account (for income tax) or chargeable accounting period (for corporation tax) in which the expenditure is incurred.

Where the allowances are claimed by traders, they are treated as trading expenses of the period of account. If the period of account is shorter or longer than 12 months (but not exceeding 18 months), the allowance is decreased or increased proportionately. If a period of account exceeds 18 months it is split into successive periods of 12 months plus the balance for calculating allowances, the aggregate amount for the separate periods then being treated as a business expense of the whole period. Although the result of the first trading period may be used to arrive at the assessable profits for the first two tax years, effectively giving relief for the capital allowances more than once, the treatment of overlap relief means that the business is charged over its life on the profits made, so there is no double relief.

Where agricultural buildings are sold and the accounting year-ends of seller and buyer differ, the allowances may have been given in full before the writing down period expires. No balancing adjustment occurs on sale unless the vendor and purchaser jointly elect for such an adjustment.

In the year of sale the vendor is entitled to a final writing down allowance based upon the period to the date of sale divided by the length of the period of account. In the year of purchase the second (and subsequent) owner is also entitled to a writing down allowance based upon the period from the date of purchase to the end of the period of account divided by the length of the period of account.

For individuals who are investors rather than traders, the capital allowances period of account is the tax year itself (CAA 2001 s 6). Agricultural buildings allowances (and other allowances) are deducted as expenses of the investor's 'property business'. To the extent that a property business loss represents unrelieved capital allowances, it may be set against any other income of the same tax year or the total income of the next following year, or both years if the loss is large enough (see note 3).

(ii) **Archer and Oakes**

The writing down period is the 25 years from the beginning of Archer's period of account in which the expenditure is incurred, ie from 1 July 2003 to 30 June 2028. Allowances will be given as follows:

Archer

	£
Qualifying expenditure (March 2004)	100,000
WDAs 3 yrs to 30.6.06 @ £4,000 per annum	(12,000)
WDA to 30.9.06 (yr to 30.6.07) 3/12 x 4,000	(1,000)
WDV transferred to Oakes	87,000

Oakes

	£
WDV transferred from Archer	87,000
WDA yr to 31.3.07 (from 1.10.06) 6/12 x 4,000	(2,000)
WDAs for 21 yrs to 31.3.28	(84,000)
WDA to 30.6.28 (balance remaining)	(1,000)

(b)   **Nicholas**

(i)   Expenditure of £50,000 on barn in January 2007 is in the period of account to 30 April 2007. The writing down period is therefore the 25 years from 1 May 2006 to 30 April 2031.

The expenditure will be written off by writing down allowances of £2,000 per annum over the 25-year period. The first allowance, being due in 2007/08, amounts to £2,000.

(ii)   Unless the former and new owners elect for a balancing adjustment, writing down allowances will continue at £2,000 per annum until the expenditure is fully relieved. The allowances to Nicholas will cease in the tax year 2010/11 (the sale taking place in the chargeable period for that year, ie in the year to 30 April 2010). Nicholas will be entitled to a final writing down allowance proportionate to the length of the chargeable period to the date of sale, ie 1.5.09 – 1.10.09 = 5/12 x £2,000 = £833. The total allowances to Nicholas will therefore be 2007/08 to 2009/10 = 3 years @ £2,000 + £833 in 2010/11 = £6,833, leaving unrelieved expenditure of £43,167.

Reginald will be entitled to allowances on the balance of £43,167, commencing in 2009/10, based on his accounting year to 31 January 2010 and ending (if there is no earlier sale) not later than the period of account in which the last day of the writing down period (30 April 2031) falls, ie in the year to 31 January 2032, affecting the tax year 2031/32. The first allowance will be proportionate to the part of the period of account falling after the date of sale, ie from 1.10.09 – 31.1.10 = 4/12 x £2,000 = £667. Reginald will then get writing down allowances of £2,000 per annum for 21 years = £42,000, with a final allowance of £500 in 2031/32, making total allowances to him of £43,167 (see note 5).

If Nicholas and Reginald elect for a balancing adjustment, the position will be as follows:

Nicholas	£
Cost 1 January 2007	50,000
2007/08 to 2009/10 WDAs 4% per annum	6,000
Residue of qualifying expenditure before sale	44,000
Year to 30.4.10 (tax year 2010/11)	
Sale proceeds October 2009	45,000
Balancing charge (trading receipt of accounting year to 30.4.10)	1,000

Reginald	
Year to 31.1.10 (tax year 2009/10)	
Residue of qualifying expenditure before sale	44,000
Add balancing charge on vendor	1,000
	45,000

Divided by balance of writing down period at date of sale, ie 21 yrs 7 mths (the chargeable period starting on 1.5.06 – see (i)) from 1.10.09 to 30.4.31, = WDA of £2,085 per annum. Reginald will get a writing down allowance for the 4 months from 1.10.09 to 31.1.10 = 4/12 of £2,085, ie £695, then allowances at £2,085 per annum for 21 years from the year ended 31 January 2011 to the year ended 31 January 2031, with a final allowance of £520 in the year to 31 January 2032 (in which the writing down period ends).

(c)   (i)   **Somerset**

Writing down period for the expenditure in June 2001 and March 2002 is 25 years from 6.4.2001 to 5.4.26 (basis period for an investor is the tax year itself).

			Allowances available
		£	£
2001/02	Grain store	22,000	
	Fencing	3,000	
		25,000	
	WDA 4%	1,000	1,000
		24,000	
2002/03 to 2006/07	WDAs 4% per annum for 5 years	5,000	5,000
		19,000	
2007/08	WDA 4% to 1.8.07 = 4 mths	333	333
	WDV transferred to Cornwall	18,667	

Cornwall

		£	£
2007/08	WDV transferred from Somerset	18,667	
	WDA 4% from 1.8.07 to 5.4.08 = 8 mths	667	667
	WDV carried forward	18,000	

Allowances will continue at £1,000 per annum until the expenditure is written off.

Essex

Writing down period is 25 years from 1.4.2001 to 31.3.2026.

			Allowances available
		£	£
2001/02	(yr to 31.3.02)		
	Drainage system	15,000	
	One third farmhouse extension (£33,000)	11,000	
		26,000	
	WDA 4%	1,040	1,040
		24,960	
2002/03 to 2005/06	WDAs 4% per annum	4,160	4,160
		20,800	
2006/07	WDA 4% from 1.4.06 to 30.9.06 = 6/12	520	520
	WDV transferred to Kent	20,280	

Kent

		£	£
2007/08	(yr to 30.6.07)		
	WDV transferred from Essex	20,280	
	WDA 4% from 1.10.06 to 30.6.07 = 9/12	780	780
	WDV carried forward	19,500	

If Kent continues as tenant to the end of the writing down period (and does not change his accounting date), his allowances will be:

2008/09 to 2025/26 18 years @ £1,040 per annum	18,720
2026/27 (based on year to 30 June 2026, in which the writing down period ends) WDA (balance of allowances)	780
Total allowances given	26,000

(c) (ii) **Chargeable gain on sale of farm by Somerset in 2007/08**

	£	£
Sale proceeds August 2007		500,000
Cost of land and buildings April 2001	350,000	
Expenditure June 2001	22,000	
Expenditure March 2002	3,000	
		375,000
		125,000

(iii) The farm will attract non-business asset taper relief until 5 April 2004 and business asset taper relief thereafter. The gain is divided over the relevant period ie 1 April 2001 to 1 August 2007 = 76 months

Non-business taper gain			
36/76 × £125,000	=	59,211	
taper relief (6 years)	20%	11,842	47,369
Business taper gain			
40/76 × £125,000		65,789	
taper relief (6 years)	75%	49,341	16,448
Gain after taper relief			63,817

(d) **Rufus – tax position 2006/07 and 2007/08**

If Rufus claims the maximum agricultural buildings allowances, and elects to set the allowances against his total income in 2006/07 and 2007/08 (see note 3), the position will be:

Agricultural buildings allowances	£
2006/07	
Expenditure	300,000
WDA 4%	12,000
	288,000
2007/08	
WDA 4%	12,000
WDV carried forward	276,000

Tax position 2006/07	
	£
Non-agricultural income	30,000
Property business loss (agricultural buildings allowance – see note 3)	12,000
	18,000
Personal allowance	(5,035)
Taxable income	12,965

Tax position 2007/08

			£
Profits of property business (see note 3):			
Farm rent 1.5.07 to 5.4.08:			
3 qrs @ £3,750	11,250		
1.2.08 to 5.4.08 65/90 x 3,750	2,708	13,958	
Less: agricultural buildings allowance		12,000	1,958
Other income			30,000
			31,958
Personal allowance (say)			(5,155)
Taxable income			26,803

If any property business loss in the form of unused allowances had remained after setting against total income in 2006/07 (and if necessary 2007/08), it could only have been set against income from the property business in later years (see note 3).

Explanatory Notes

Expenditure qualifying for allowances

1. Agricultural buildings allowances are available where the owner or tenant of agricultural land incurs capital expenditure on farmhouses, farm buildings, cottages, fences or other works. The expenditure must be for the purposes of 'husbandry' (CAA 2001 s 361). The meaning of husbandry given in s 362 does not actually define the term, but it effectively means farming. Husbandry is explicitly stated in s 362 to include intensive rearing of livestock or fish for human consumption and the cultivation of short rotation coppice. HMRC allow relief for a farm shop, except to the extent that stock is bought in rather than produced on the farm. Where the expenditure is on a farmhouse, not more than one third qualifies for relief. The allowance of up to one third of the expenditure is provided for by CAA 2001 s 369. The same fraction cannot be used for the part of the establishment charges of the farmhouse that are deducted from the farming profit. The claim in respect of these charges must be based on the extent of business use of the farmhouse.

   Allowances are not available in respect of buildings and works on forestry land.

Allowances available and writing down period

2. For expenditure after 31 March 1986, the allowances available are annual writing down allowances at 4% over 25 years (CAA 2001 s 373), except for expenditure under a contract entered into between 1 November 1992 and 31 October 1993, for which a 20% initial allowance was also available providing the buildings or works were brought into use before 1 January 1995. Allowances may be disclaimed wholly or in part. Any balancing allowance will, however, take into account all allowances that have been or *could have been* claimed. Furthermore no claim is available after the end of the 25-year period. It is therefore highly unlikely to be advantageous to disclaim a writing down allowance.

   The initial allowance was given for the chargeable period related to the incurring of the expenditure. The first writing down allowance was not given in the same period as the initial allowance unless the buildings or works were brought into use by the end of that period. Unless there is a sale on which a balancing adjustment is made (see below), the 25-year writing down period will be shortened according to how much of the initial allowance was claimed.

   Where there is no initial allowance, the first writing down allowance is given in the chargeable period relating to the incurring of the expenditure, the 25-year writing down period running from the first day of that period. The chargeable period for traders is the period of account for income tax and the chargeable accounting period for corporation tax (CAA 2001 s 6) (see note 3 for the chargeable period for investors).

Chargeable period for investors

3. For investors the chargeable period for the allowances is the tax year for income tax and the chargeable accounting period for corporation tax. For individuals, any available agricultural buildings allowances are treated as an expense of the individual's property business (as to which see Example 98). If no such business exists (ie if no letting has commenced), the individual is nonetheless treated as if he were carrying on such a business (CAA 2001 s 392). To the extent that an individual's capital allowances exceed property income from all sources in any tax year, a claim may be made for the excess to be set against the total income of that tax year or the following tax year or, if the loss is large enough, both tax years (TA 1988 s 379A). The time limit for the claim is one year from 31 January following the tax year. For further points on the way allowances are given to investors, including the provisions relating to companies, see Example 18 part (b).

Disposal of agricultural buildings

4. Where agricultural buildings are disposed of, the former and new owners may jointly elect for a balancing adjustment (CAA 2001 ss 381 and 382), and in the event of demolition or destruction the election is by the former owner. The election must be notified to the inspector by individuals within one year from 31 January following the end of the tax year. The time limit for companies is two years from the end of the chargeable accounting period (CAA 2001 s 382(6)(b)).

   The balancing adjustment is calculated by taking the residue of qualifying expenditure before the sale and comparing it with the sale, insurance, salvage etc moneys. A balancing charge cannot exceed the allowances given. The new owner gets writing down allowances based on the residue of qualifying expenditure before the sale plus any balancing charge or less any balancing allowance.

   That amount is divided by the unexpired part of the writing down period, to arrive at the annual writing down allowance. It is therefore necessary to calculate how much of the 25-year period from the first day of the chargeable period related to the incurring of the expenditure remains at the date of sale. This then determines the annual rate of writing down allowance, which will be proportionately increased or reduced for accounting periods of more or less than 12 months. Thus in part (b) of the example, following an election for a balancing adjustment, Reginald gets his first allowance for the four months from 1.10.09 (the date of sale) to 31.1.10 (the end of his accounting period).

5. Where an election is not made as outlined in note 4 above, the former owner gets a final writing down allowance for the chargeable period in which the sale occurs, the allowance being proportionate to the period from the start of that period to the date of sale. The new owner is entitled to relief for the balance of the expenditure, and he similarly gets his first allowance reduced according to the period from the date of sale to the end of *his* chargeable period (CAA 2001 s 375). The tax year in which the event is taken into account may be different for seller and purchaser where the accounting dates differ. For example, the last allowance to Nicholas in part (b) is given in 2010/11, whereas the first allowance to Reginald is in 2009/10.

6. The whole of the claimant's interest in the land has to be transferred for the allowances to be given to the purchaser. Thus an owner cannot transfer the allowances to a tenant by granting him a leasehold interest, as distinct from selling the freehold. Likewise a tenant must transfer his tenancy (like Essex did to Kent in the example) and not grant a sub-lease in order to pass the allowances on to the new tenant. Where an interest in land is a tenancy and the tenant transfers his interest, it is deemed to have been transferred:

   (a)   to the incoming tenant if he makes any payment to the outgoing tenant in respect of assets representing the expenditure in question,

   (b)   in any other case, to the landlord (CAA 2001 s 368).

The allowances also revert to the landlord if the tenant surrenders his lease without taking a new lease.

Thus if in this example Kent had made no payment to Essex upon taking over the tenancy, the remaining allowances would have accrued to the then owner Somerset. On the transfer of his interest to Cornwall, Somerset would in turn have passed on the agricultural buildings allowances remaining to be given.

Capital gains tax

7.   Capital allowances are not taken into account in computing a gain for capital gains tax (TCGA 1992 s 41). The main reason is that the allowances are normally withdrawn by balancing adjustments, but the section makes no special provision for situations where that does not apply, for example, where no election is made for a balancing adjustment on the sale of agricultural buildings (and also where industrial buildings are disposed of after their writing down life has expired).

In the calculation of the gain to Somerset in part (c)(ii) of the example, there is accordingly no restriction of the allowable expenditure by reference to the allowances he has received, even though no income tax balancing adjustment was made.

Because Somerset did not use the farm for the purpose of a trade (farming) carried on by him, he will only be entitled to the non-business assets rate of taper relief until 5 April 2004. This is computed for complete years from 1 April 2001, giving six complete years. The non-business assets rate of taper relief available is therefore 20%. From 6 April 2004 Somerset can claim business asset taper relief as the farm is *used* for the purpose of a trade. The previous restriction to personal usage is removed by FA 2003 s 160. The gain has therefore to be apportioned over the whole relevant period ie the period since 1 April 2001. The two rates of taper relief are given to each part based upon the length of the total relevant period in complete years. So even though only 40 months of the period relate to business use relief is given based upon six years ie 75% (see Example 74 part (a)(i) for the detailed taper relief provisions).

Kay, a single woman aged 45, is an author who has written many books.

Her income as an author fluctuates and for recent years her results have been:

Year ended 30 April 2003	Loss	(£3,650)
(Fully relieved against 2002/03 assessable profits under TA 1988 s 380)		
Year ended 30 April 2004	Loss	(£11,760)
Year ended 30 April 2005	Profit	£90,400
Year ended 30 April 2006	Profit	£32,550

Kay has no other income. Her income from appearances and talks is included in her literary accounts.

Show the tax and Class 4 national insurance contributions payable by Kay for each year, assuming all available reliefs are claimed.

Tax and Class 4 national insurance contributions payable

Assessable profits	£	£	£
2003/04			
Year ended 30.4.2003			Nil
(Loss carried back to 2002/03)			
2004/05			
Year ended 30.4.04 – Loss	(11,760)		
2005/06			
Year ended 30.4.05 – Profit	90,400		
Claim for averaging with 2004/05 made by 31.1.08:			
Year ended 30.4.04		–	
Year ended 30.4.05		90,400	
Average		45,200	
Revised assessments:			
2004/05			
Average profits		45,200	
Less: s 380 loss claim re year to 30.4.04		(11,760)	33,440
2005/06			
Average profits	45,200		
2006/07			
Year ended 30.4.06	32,550		
Difference	12,650		
Averaging by claim made by 31.1.09:			
75% of higher profit = £33,900			
70% of higher profit = £31,640			
Averaging adjustment is:			
3 × 12,650		37,950	
Less 75% × 45,200		33,900	
Deduct from higher and add to lower		4,050	
Revised assessments:			
2005/06 (45,200 – 4,050)			41,150
2006/07 (32,550 + 4,050)			36,600
(subject to any claim to average with 2007/08)			

Tax payable	£	£	£
2003/04			Nil
2004/05 Schedule D Case II		33,440	
Personal allowance		4,745	
Taxable income		28,695	
Tax thereon: 2,020 @ 10%		202	
26,675 @ 22%		5,869	
28,695		6,071	
Class 4 NIC (31,720 – 4,745) @ 8%	2,158		
(33,440 – 31,720) @ 1%	17	2,175	8,246

			£	£	£
2005/06	Trading income			41,150	
	Personal allowance			4,895	
	Taxable income			36,255	
	Tax thereon:	2,090 @ 10%		209	
		30,310 @ 22%		6,669	
		3,855 @ 40%		1,542	
		36,255		8,420	
	Class 4 NIC	(32,760 – 4,895) @ 8%	2,229		
		(41,150 – 32,760) @ 1%	84	2,313	10,733
2006/07					
	Trading income			36,600	
	Personal allowance			5,035	
	Taxable income			31,565	
	Tax thereon:	2,150 @ 10%		215	
		29,415 @ 22%		6,471	
		31,565		6,686	
	Class 4 NIC	(33,540 – 5,035) @ 8%	2,280	2,311	8,997
		(36,600 – 33,540) @ 1%	31		
			2,311		

Explanatory Notes

Averaging profits of creative artists

1. Provisions enabling the profits of 'creative artists' to be averaged are contained in ITTOIA 2005 part 2 Chapter 16. The provisions apply for 2000/01 and later years (so that the first years that could be averaged are 2000/01 and 2001/02). Previous provisions enabling backward and forward spreading of certain copyright and similar payments were repealed in respect of payments receivable on or after 6 April 2001. The rules are now the same as those applying to farmers (see Example 33).

2. A 'creative artist' is someone whose profits are:

   (a) derived wholly or mainly from literary, dramatic, musical or artistic works, or from designs, created by the taxpayer personally or by someone in partnership with the taxpayer, and

   (b) chargeable to income tax as trading income.

   'Artistic works' would include paintings and sculpture. The inclusion in profits of appearance fees and speaking fees would not prevent a claim for averaging.

Averaging calculation

3. A claim may be made to average the profits of two consecutive tax years provided the lower profit is not more than 70% of the higher profit (losses being treated as nil in the calculation, with normal loss reliefs being available). If the lower profit is more than 70% but less than 75% of the higher profit, then each profit figure may be adjusted by a figure calculated as three times the difference between the two figures less 75% of the higher figure. This is illustrated in the averaging claim for 2005/06 and 2006/07 in the example. No claim may be made for the tax year in which the taxpayer begins or ceases to carry on the business.

It should be noted that the tax saving from the averaging claim is affected by the Class 4 national insurance contributions position, so that in many cases the saving will be the difference between the higher rate tax of 41% and a charge of 30%, being 22% basic rate tax and 8% Class 4 national insurance.

4. An averaging claim cannot be made for an earlier period if the profits of the later period have already been the subject of an averaging claim. So the averaged profits of 2004/05 of £45,200 could not then be averaged again with the nil profits of 2003/04 to use the personal allowance of the earlier year.

Time limits for claims and effect of carryback claims

5. The time limit for claims under ITTOIA 2005 s 221 is one year from 31 January following the second tax year to which the claim relates (s 222(5)). Claims may be made by individuals and by partners, but not by companies.

   Special rules apply under TMA 1970 Sch 1B to claims for relief involving two or more tax years (see Example 42). Any tax adjustments arising from backdating amounts such as those covered in this example are *calculated* by reference to the earlier tax year, but they are *given effect* in the later tax year. Interest on overdue or overpaid tax would run from the 31 January following the later tax year.

Tax Credits

6. When computing income for tax credits the amount included is *before* averaging ie the original taxable profits for each accounting period. There are special rules for the relief of losses (see Example 5).

Link with farmers' averaging

7. The creative artists' averaging provisions are now identical to those applying for farmers, which are illustrated in Example 33. The effect of an averaging claim on payments on account is set out in detail in that example. Explanatory note 5 of that example also applies to this example.

(a) The partnership of A, B and C commenced on 1 September 2004, accounts being made up annually to 31 August. They shared profits A one half, B one third, C one sixth after a salary of £6,000 to C. The profits for the first two years, net of capital allowances on partnership assets, were as follows:

	£
Year to 31 August 2005	42,000
Year to 31 August 2006	48,000

In addition each partner uses his own car for the business, capital allowances being due as follows:

	Yr to 31.8.05	Yr to 31.8.06
	£	£
A	2,500	2,500
B	1,800	1,350
C	2,000	1,833

Show the tax position of each partner arising out of the above, and state what the situation would be if C left the partnership on 31 October 2007, A and B sharing profits in the same ratio as before.

(b) Partners D and E have been in business for fifteen years, sharing profits equally and making up accounts annually to 30 April. F joined as an equal partner on 1 January 2006.

Profits net of capital allowances around the time F joined were as follows:

Year to 30 April 2006	£36,000
Year to 30 April 2007	£45,000

Show the assessable income arising to each partner in respect of these profits and indicate their position regarding overlap relief.

(c) G, H and J have been in partnership for many years, making up accounts annually to 30 June and sharing profits and losses equally. The partners were entitled to transitional overlap relief of £25,500 each. G retired on 30 September 2006. H and J continued as equal partners. Recent profits were as follows:

		£
Year to 30 June 2006		84,000
Year to 30 June 2007:		
1 July 2006 to 30 September 2006	25,650	
1 October 2006 to 30 June 2007	51,300	76,950

Show the assessable income arising to each partner in respect of these profits and the treatment of overlap relief.

(d) K and L have traded in partnership since 2001 as consultants, making up accounts to 5 April. They work on the basis of hourly billing, but have experienced delays in invoicing and billing. Due to loss of contracts, profits are expected to decrease over the coming years, as follows:

Year to	Profit before capital allowances £	Capital Allowances £
05/04/2006	50,000	6,000
05/04/2007	40,000	7,000
05/04/2008	30,000	4,000
05/04/2009	20,000	5,000
05/04/2010	20,000	3,000

As at 5 April 2005 the reasonably estimated billable time in unfinished work amounted to £20,000 over and above work in progress valued at cost. As a result of adoption of UITF 40, the profit element is recognised for the first time in the accounts to 5 April 2006.

Calculate

- profits assessable to tax for all years, and

- state what the position would be had the business ceased on 5 April 2007.

(e)   Outline the treatment of partnership non-trading income.

(a) **Partnership of A, B and C**

Division of profits:

	Total £	A £	B £	C £
Year to 31.8.05				
Salary	6,000			6,000
Balance 3:2:1	36,000	18,000	12,000	6,000
	42,000	18,000	12,000	12,000
Less capital allowances on partners' cars	6,300	2,500	1,800	2,000
	35,700	15,500	10,200	10,000
Year to 31.8.06				
Salary	6,000			6,000
Balance 3:2:1	42,000	21,000	14,000	7,000
	48,000	21,000	14,000	13,000
Less capital allowances on partners' cars	5,683	2,500	1,350	1,833
	42,317	18,500	12,650	11,167

Assessments on individual partners:

	A £	B £	C £
2004/05			
1.9.04 – 5.4.05			
7/12 x profit share for yr to 31.8.05 (which constitute overlap profits eligible for subsequent relief)	9,042	5,950	5,833
2005/06			
1.9.04 – 31.8.05	15,500	10,200	10,000
2006/07			
1.9.05 – 31.8.06	18,500	12,650	11,167

If C left the partnership on 31 October 2007, the profit of the year to 31 August 2008 would be split as to the first 2 months between A, B and C according to their profit sharing arrangements and the remaining 10 months between A and B according to their profit sharing arrangements.

C's 2007/08 income from the partnership would comprise his share of the profit of the year to 31 August 2007 and his 2 months' share of the profit of the year to 31 August 2008, reduced by overlap relief of £5,833. A and B would continue to be taxed each year on their shares of the profits, and would get their overlap relief when they left the business or on an earlier change of accounting date if and to the extent that more than 12 months' profit was charged to tax in one year.

(b) **Partnership of D, E and F**

Individual profit shares:

	Total £	D £	E £	F £
Year to 30.4.2006				
1.5.05 – 31.12.05 (8 mths)	24,000	12,000	12,000	
1.1.06 – 30.4.06 (4 mths)	12,000	4,000	4,000	4,000
	36,000	16,000	16,000	4,000
Year to 30.4.07	45,000	15,000	15,000	15,000

D and E will be taxed on their shares in 2006/07 and 2007/08. They are entitled to transitional overlap relief on their shares of the profits (*before* capital allowances) for the 11 months from 1 May 1996 to 5 April 1997 (the full 12 months to 30.4.97 being assessed in 1997/98).

F will be taxed as follows:

			£
2005/06	1.1.06 – 5.4.06		
	3/4 x 4,000		3,000
2006/07	1.1.06 – 31.12.06:		
	1.1.06 – 30.4.06	4,000	
	1.5.06 – 31.12.06		
	8/12 x 15,000	10,000	14,000
2007/08	Yr to 30.4.07		15,000

F will be entitled to overlap relief on the following profits (which are *after* capital allowances):

1.1.06 – 5.4.06	3,000	
1.5.06 – 31.12.06	10,000	£13,000

(c) **Partnership of G, H and J**

Taxable profits and overlap relief

Ignoring differences between taxable profits and actual profits, the profits of the two years to 30 June 2007 will be divided between the partners as follows:

	Total £	G £	H £	J £
Yr to 30.6.06	84,000	28,000	28,000	28,000
Yr to 30.6.07:				
To 30.9.06	25,650	8,550	8,550	8,550
To 30.6.07	51,300		25,650	25,650
	76,950	8,550	34,200	34,200

Assessments

	Total £	G £	H £	J £
2006/07 (yr to 30.6.06)	84,000	28,000	28,000	28,000
On retirement of G,				
period to 30.9.06		8,550		
Less overlap relief		(25,500)		
		11,050	28,000	28,000
2007/08 (yr to 30.6.07)	76,950			
Less allocated to G	(8,550)			
	68,400		34,200	34,200
Overlap relief cf			25,500	25,500

(d)   **Partnership of K and L, and UITF 40 spreading**

As the uplift arose from adoption of UITF 40 in a year ending on or after 22 June 2005, it may be spread over a maximum of six years, as follows:

Adjustment profit (UITF 40 amount)   £20,000

		(a)	(b)	(c)	
Tax the lesser of:	Profit before capital	1/3 of adjustment	1/6 of profits before capital	Balance	
Year to	allowances	profits	allowances	Remaining	Add the lesser
05/04/2006	50,000	6,667	8,333	–	6,667
05/04/2007	40,000	6,667	6,667	13,333	6,667
05/04/2008	30,000	6,667	5,000	6,666	5,000
05/04/2009	20,000		3,333	1,666	1,666
05/04/2010	20,000		3,333	0	0

	Profit before capital	Capital	Profits after capital	Adjustment	
Taxable Profits	allowances	allowances	allowances	income	Assessable
2005/06	50,000	6,000	44,000	6,667	50,667
2006/07	40,000	7,000	33,000	6,667	39,667
2007/08	30,000	4,000	26,000	5,000	31,000
2008/09	20,000	5,000	15,000	1,666	16,666
2009/10	20,000	3,000	17,000	–	17,000

If the business had ceased on 5 April 2007, spreading would still be available, but the criterion of one-sixth of profit disappears, so the result would be as follows:

Adjustment profit   £20,000

		(a)	(b)	(c)	
Tax the lesser of:	Profit before capital	1/3 of Adjustment	1/6 of Profit before capital	Balance	
Year to	allowances	profit	allowances	Remaining	Add the lesser
05/04/2006	50,000	6,667	8,333	–	6,667
05/04/2007	40,000	6,667	6,667	13,333	6,667
05/04/2008	–	6,667	–	6,666	6,666

	Profit before capital	Capital	Profit after capital	Adjustment	
	allowances	allowances	allowances	income	Assessable
2005/06	50,000	6,000	44,000	6,667	50,667
2006/07	40,000	7,000	33,000	6,667	39,667
2007/08	–	–	–	6,667	6,667

See note 5 for details of changes in accounting basis.

Class 4 National Insurance does not apply to the adjustment income.

(e)   **Partnership non-trading income**

Non-trading partnership income, such as rents and interest, is taxed separately on each partner (ITTOIA 2005 s 851). The way in which each partner's taxable income is arrived at depends on whether the income has been taxed at source.

If the income is taxed at source (or, in the case of dividends, is accompanied by a tax credit), then although it is divided according to the sharing arrangements of the partnership accounting period, each partner must show the income relating to each tax year in his own self-assessment. Shares of taxed income, together with the tax thereon, are therefore shown in partnership tax returns for the tax year rather than for the accounting period (see Example 41).

As far as untaxed income is concerned, it is treated as if it arose in a separate notional trade that started when the partner joined the firm (not when he started business on his own if he was a sole trader before becoming a partner) and ceased when he left (even if he continues as a sole trader, and even if the source of income actually ceased much earlier). A partner will therefore be entitled to overlap relief in respect of untaxed non-trading income in the same way as for trading profits when he joins the firm. The overlap relief will be given by reducing his share of the non-trading income when he leaves the firm (unless it has been given on an earlier change of accounting date), even if he then carries on business alone (s 854). This is different from overlap relief relating to the trade (see explanatory note 3). If the partner's share of non-trading income in the relevant tax year is less than the overlap relief to be deducted, the balance is relieved against other income of that tax year (s 856). Relief for any transitional overlap profits arising on the change to the current year basis of assessment is given in the same way as for normal overlap profits.

Explanatory Notes

Basis of assessment

1. Businesses starting on or after 6 April 1994 are taxed under the current year basis rules, which are dealt with in Example 16.

Taxation of trading profits

2. The trading profits of the accounting period are shared between the partners according to their sharing arrangements, and each partner's share is regarded as his profit from a separate business (ITTOIA 2005 s 853). A new partner is therefore treated as commencing a new business when he joins (as illustrated in part (b) of the example), unless he had previously carried on the business as a sole trader, and a partner is treated as ceasing business when he ceases to be a partner (as illustrated in parts (a) and (c) of the example), unless he continues the business as a sole trader. Unless given on an earlier change of accounting date, overlap relief is given when the partner leaves the partnership, or if he continues the business as a sole trader, when the sole trade ceases (s 856). The partnership itself is not treated as discontinued on a change of partners except where none of the old partners continue.

    Although partners are taxed separately on their profit shares, there will still have to be overall agreement by the partners as to the amount of partnership profit and the division of the profits.

Non-trading income

3. Non-trading partnership income is divided according to the sharing arrangements in the accounting period (ss 850 and 851). If it is *untaxed* income, it is taxed as if it arose from a separate deemed trade, which is treated as having started when the partner joined the firm and ceased when a partner leaves the firm (*not* when the source of income ceases) (ss 849 and 851). The rules for overlap relief apply equally to untaxed non-trading income.

    In a tax year in which overlap relief on non-trading income is to be deducted (ie usually in the year when the partner leaves the firm, but possibly earlier if the accounting date is changed), then if it exceeds the partner's non-trading income it may be set against any other income of that year (s 856(3)). There is, however, no provision for carrying any excess back to an earlier year.

    There are no overlap problems with income that is taxed at source and dividends carrying tax credits. Such income is allocated to the appropriate tax year as indicated in part (e) of the example.

Calculation of overlap relief

4. The detailed rules on the calculation of overlap relief are in Example 16. Even though partners may share profits and losses equally, their overlap relief may have been calculated at different times, so

that the amounts of profits on which each has paid tax more than once are different. On a cessation of business, therefore, the profits assessable on each equal partner will reflect the differences in the overlap relief available. In part (c) of the example G, H and J became equal partners at the same time and each is entitled to the same amount of overlap relief. In part (b), although D, E and F are equal partners, the overlap relief available to D and E is based on their profit shares for the 11 months to 5 April 1997, whereas that for F is based on his profit shares for the 3 months to 5 April 2006 and the 8 months to 31 December 2006.

UITF 40 and changes in accounting basis

5.   UITF 40 was issued by the Accounting Standards Board on 10 March 2005 to clarify existing UK accounting standards, particularly FRS 5 and Application note G. It is concerned with recognising at the year-end an element of profit that has not yet been realised, but where a right to remuneration has accrued. Work under a letter of engagement providing for remuneration at hourly rates would normally give rise to such an element of profit, as the right to remuneration builds up by the hour. UITF 40 is effective for all accounting periods beginning on or after 22 June 2005, and is applicable to all contracts for services, not just financial services.

Adoption of FRS 5 will have resulted in businesses including a credit for work in progress in their accounts in earlier years. However, this will often be valued at the lesser of cost and net realisable value. The accounts should therefore already contain a credit for costs on partially completed work, such as staff time and overheads. It will usually have excluded any element of profit, or the remuneration of partners or sole practitioners that is a component of profit. UITF 40 requires that the profit earned by the year-end, but not realised until after the year end, should be accrued as revenue in the accounts.

This will result in accelerated recognition of profit in some businesses providing services, generating a one-off uplift in the year that the new interpretation of policy is adopted.

An argument could be made to claim that not all businesses are affected by UITF 40, perhaps by reason of adopting a version of FRSSE. HMRC clearly expect all entities to adopt UITF 40, and UK accountancy bodies give no support to non-adoption. The measures for spreading the uplift are limited to accounting periods ending on or after 22 June 2005, and beginning before that date.

As the uplift in profit in the first year could be substantial, FA 2006 provides measures to identify the profits to be spread, and to specify to which year they should be spread. The profit that may be spread is limited to that arising from UITF 40 (or IAS equivalent), and not from any other change of accounting policy.

As businesses should already have included work in progress in their accounts, movements on work in progress may not be included in spreading. Only accrued revenue that is recognised for the first time may be spread, so it must be identified separately, and movements on work in progress must be excluded.

The legislation does not provide guidance of how to calculate the profit uplift, which remains entirely the province of accounting standards. The profit element will be reduced by foreseeable future under-recoveries, over-runs or additional costs, but if any profit remains, the proportion earned by the year end must be included in the accounts as accrued income. Quantification of the amount derives from accounting standards and judgement. Guidance has been issued by ICAEW entitled 'Guidance on the application of UITF 40 "Revenue recognition and service contracts" ' at http://www.icaew.co.uk/index.cfm?route=135435.

The uplift is incorporated into the accounts as a prior year adjustment, and is therefore the uplift at the *beginning* of the year, not at the end. The adjustment to be included in the 5th April 2006 accounts is the value of work at 5 April 2005. The adjustment to be spread is the value of work as revised for UITF 40, less the value of WIP originally in the 5 April 2005 accounts, which will now be eliminated.

The adjustment is not trading profit, but is taxed as 'adjustment income'. It is not liable to Class 4 National Insurance Contributions, but counts as income for purposes of tax credits and as relevant earnings for registered pension schemes.

The self-assessment Help Sheet IR238 as amended, which is available from the HMRC website, explains HMRC's view of the procedure.

The uplift may be deferred for tax by spreading over up to six years according to the following rules:

Year	The amount to be charged is
1	Lesser of: 1/3 of original amount or 1/6 of profit
2	Lesser of: 1/3 of original amount or 1/6 of profit
3	Lesser of: 1/3 of original amount or 1/6 of profit
4	Lesser of: 1/3 of original amount or 1/6 of profit or remainder
5	Lesser of: 1/3 of original amount or 1/6 of profit or remainder
6	The whole remaining amount

Unless the UITF uplift is more than 50% of normal profits, or unless profits decline, the spread will be over three years rather than six. As additional taxable income will increase payments on account, the payment of tax will be spread over an even shorter period. The tax and accountancy bodies are making representations on this issue.

The profit for the purposes of this calculation must exclude capital allowances, and any spreading adjustments available under other legislation.

An election may be made to accelerate the spreading in any year. Any amount accelerated also reduces the 'original amount' in the calculation above. The election must be made by all partners jointly, except in the case of cessation when they may elect individually. This may be useful for utilising allowances or flattening fluctuations in income. The election must be made within one year of the normal tax return filing date.

If the business ceases completely, the spreading may continue on the basis of one-third of the original amount.

Effect of ITTOIA 2005 s 25 on changes in the basis of accounting adopted by a business

Accounting periods beginning after 6 April 1999

For periods of account beginning after 6 April 1999, business profits must be computed in accordance with generally accepted accounting practice, subject to any statutory taxation adjustments required (FA 1998 s 42 now ITTOIA 2005 s 25). The effect of the section was that debtors cannot be excluded in calculating profits. Thus, cash basis was no longer acceptable and all businesses that had not already done so were required to adopt an accruals basis of accounting. There is an exception for new barristers, who may continue to exclude debtors for periods of account ending not more than seven years after commencement (ITTOIA 2005 s 160). They must then include it thereafter, and will be subject to the catching-up charge outlined below, which may be spread over ten years as indicated.

Under the provisions of FA 1998 s 44 and Sch 6 (now ITTOIA 2005 part 2 Chapter 17), if debtors were not already included in accounts, they had to be brought in and treated as income arising on the first day of the first accounting period beginning after 6 April 1999, tax being payable under Schedule D Case VI (now adjustment income) on the amount of the adjustment (known as the 'catching-up charge') over a maximum of ten years starting in 1999/2000 (unless accounts were made up to 5 April, in which case the first year was 2000/01). This adjustment must be excluded from profit for purposes of calculating the amount of UITF 40 uplift to be spread.

The catching-up charge is limited to 1/10th of the profit before capital allowances in the first nine years, with the balance taxable in the tenth year. The charge in each year is made on the partners in that year according to their profit shares in the accounting year before the anniversary of the date on which debtors were brought in. This means that, unless appropriate adjustments are made between them, partners leaving the partnership during the ten-year period will escape tax and partners joining will pay tax on part of the charge.

If the business ceases, the charge continues for the remainder of the ten-year period without restriction by reference to profits. Where the cessation relates to a partnership, the subsequent annual charges are split between the former partners according to the profit sharing arrangements of the period prior to the cessation.

An election may be made to pay all or part of the charge earlier, for example to utilise the basic rate band, or if there are allowable losses which can be set off If the election relates to a partnership, it must be made by all who were partners in the relevant twelve-month period, unless the partnership has ceased, in which case it is made by each former partner separately.

Whether debtors are brought in compulsorily or by earlier choice, the amount charged to tax counts as relevant earnings for the purposes of calculating registered pension scheme contributions. It does not, however, attract Class 4 national insurance contributions.

If, exceptionally, the change resulted in a reduction of profits, that amount could be taken wholly in 1999/2000.

The provisions of ITTOIA 2005 part 2 Chapter 17 deal not only with a change of accounting basis, but also where there is a change, either in law or practice, in the way accounts are adjusted for tax purposes. The revised provisions apply for changes occurring in a period of account ending on or after 1 August 2001. All changes in the basis of accounting or computation for receipts, expenses, valuation of stock and WIP, and of depreciation if relevant, are adjusted for. The aggregate adjustment is brought into account as adjustment income or adjustment expense, arising on the last day of the first period of account to which the new basis applies.

Partnership self-assessment

6. For the self-assessment provisions as they relate to partnerships see Example 41.

Limited liability partnerships

7. From 6 April 2001 a further type of commercial structure known as a 'limited liability partnership' (LLP) is available. An LLP has limited liability as though it were a limited company but its members are taxed as though it were a partnership. For details see Example 26.

The partnership of Pipe and Ross has traded for many years in the business of chartered architects and decided to merge with another long-standing partnership of architects, Simpson, Taylor and Venables, to form the new firm of Pipe Simpson with effect from 6 October 2006. Pipe and Ross have made up their accounts to 5 July each year and Simpson, Taylor and Venables have made up accounts to 5 May each year. The recent tax adjusted profits and sharing arrangements have been as follows:

	Pipe & Ross £		Simpson, Taylor & Venables £
Year to 5 July 2006	58,400	Year to 5 May 2006	85,600
Period to 5 October 2006	23,750	Period to 5 Oct 2006	33,250

	Profit share %	Overlap relief bf £		Profit share %	Overlap relief bf £
Pipe	60	21,870	Simpson	40	28,600
Ross	40	14,580	Taylor	30	21,450
			Venables	30	21,450

No formal notices of change of accounting date have been or are being given in respect of the accounts to 5 October 2006.

From the partnership merger accounts are to be made up to 5 July and profits are to be shared as detailed below:

To 5 July 2007
First slice of £10,000 per annum to each partner.
Balance split:

Pipe	22%
Ross	16%
Simpson	22%
Taylor	20%
Venables	20%

From 6 July 2007
Profits shared equally.

The profit for the period 6 October 2006 to 5 July 2007 amounted to £121,000 and for the year to 5 July 2008 £200,000.

(a)   Compute the taxable profits for the years 2006/07 to 2008/09, the division between the partners and the overlap relief to be carried forward at 5 April 2009.

(a) **Assessable profits – Schedule D Case II**

Individual assessments

Partners are individually assessable on their shares of the profits for the accounting period ended in the tax year as follows:

	Pipe £	Ross £	Simpson £	Taylor £	Venables £	Total £
2006/07						
(yr to 5.7.06)	35,040	23,360				58,400
(yr to 5.5.06)			34,240	25,680	25,680	85,600
2007/08 (period to 5.7.07 – merger on 6.10.06)						
6.7.06 to 5.10.06	14,250	9,500				23,750
6.5.06 to 5.10.06			13,300	9,975	9,975	33,250
6.10.06 to 5.7.07:						
First slice (9/12)	7,500	7,500	7,500	7,500	7,500	37,500
Balance	18,370	13,360	18,370	16,700	16,700	83,500
						121,000
Less 2 months' overlap relief (Simpson, Taylor & Venables only) 2/11 (see explanatory note 2)			(5,200)	(3,900)	(3,900)	
	40,120	30,360	33,970	30,275	30,275	
2008/09 (yr to 5.7.08)	40,000	40,000	40,000	40,000	40,000	200,000
Overlap relief cf	21,870	14,580	23,400	17,550	17,550	

Note: Strictly there is a later accounting date in 2006/07 for each of the old partnerships (5 October 2006). The temporary use of a new date need not, however, trigger the change of accounting date rules unless the taxpayers choose to notify the change under ITTOIA 2005 s 217. If no notification is made, the old date continues to apply (see Example 28 at page 28.2).

Explanatory Notes

New firm or continuing firm

1. This example is somewhat different from the normal one involving admission of a new partner or retirement of a partner, in that it involves the merger of two businesses to form one new business. This does not cause the cessation of a trade or commencement of a new one for any partner who is a member of both the old and new businesses unless the new business is different in nature from either of the two previous businesses. In that event it would be advisable to seek the view of HMRC as to whether the merger can be regarded as the continuation of an existing business or whether it has resulted in a new business emerging, in which case all partners in the previous firms would be regarded as having ceased trading (with the full amount of any available overlap relief being given) and having recommenced in a new venture.

Overlap relief

2. Since the partnerships are old-established businesses who have made up accounts regularly to the same accounting date each year, transitional overlap relief will have arisen on the change to the current year basis of assessment (see Example 16 explanatory note 8). The transitional overlap period

for Pipe and Ross was the period from 6 July 1996 to 5 April 1997, ie 9 months, and for Simpson, Taylor and Venables the period from 6 May 1996 to 5 April 1997, ie 11 months. Since the 2007/08 basis period for Simpson, Taylor & Venables runs for the 14 months from 6 May 2006 to 5 July 2007, each partner is entitled to deduct a two months' proportion of his available overlap relief, ie 2/11ths as shown in part (a) of the example.

Self-assessment returns

3.   The basic rules for dealing with self-assessment for partners are in Example 41. This example deals with a merger, and accordingly no individual ceases to trade. Therefore the cessation provisions do not apply even though the old partnerships cease.

As indicated in the example, the old firms need not notify HMRC of a change of accounting date to 5 October, but accounts have even so been made up to 5 October 2006, which ends in 2006/07. In view, however, of 5 October not having been formally adopted as a new accounting date, the partners' shares of the profits of that period do not form part of their individual assessments for 2006/07. Those profits to 5 October 2006 instead form part of their 2007/08 income.

Simpson, Taylor and Venables have changed their accounting date from 5 May to 5 July consequent upon the merger, but the accounts to 5 July 2007 are made up by the new merged firm.

It is necessary for a partnership return to be completed by the new merged firm for 2006/07. The position regarding returns is as follows:

2006/07

Pipe and Ross:

Partnership return will be required to the date of cessation on 5 October 2006. The return will include accounting details for the year to 5 July 2006 and a second set of trading income pages for the period 6 July 2006 to 5 October 2006 (with a comment in the additional information box that the profit of this period will form part of the taxable profits to 5 July 2007).

There will be two partnership statements, one covering the year to 5 July 2006 and the other covering the period 6 July 2006 to 5 October 2006. The statements will also include taxed interest etc for the period 6 April 2006 to 5 October 2006.

Simpson, Taylor and Venables:

Again, a return with two sets of trading statements and partnership statements will be required, covering the year ended 5 May 2006 and the period 6 May 2006 to 5 October 2006.

Pipe, Ross, Simpson, Taylor and Venables:

This partnership will have a separate unique tax reference number and the return will not include accounts, as no accounts ended in the year to 5 April 2007. The return will show a start date of 6 October 2006 and the partnership statement will include details of taxed interest etc for the period 6 October 2006 to 5 April 2007.

2007/08

No returns will be required from the former partnerships.

Pipe, Ross, Simpson, Taylor and Venables:

A partnership return will be required, including the accounting details for the period 6 October 2006 to 5 July 2007. The partnership statement will cover the same period for trading and untaxed non-trading income. The taxed income will be for the year ended 5 April 2008.

Note: In the personal returns for 2007/08, the individual partners will complete separate partnership supplementary pages for each business, eg Pipe will complete a partnership page for the income from Pipe and Ross for the period 6 July 2006 to 5 October 2006 and a further partnership page for the income from Pipe, Ross, Simpson, Taylor and Venables for the period

6 October 2006 to 5 July 2007. However, no entry will be required for a commencement or a cessation, as each individual has continued to trade throughout the year. Presumably the overlap profits will be brought forward on the pages for Pipe and Ross and carried forward on the pages for Pipe, Ross, Simpson, Taylor and Venables.

(a) The Ben Williams Partnership carries on a retail trade and is UK resident. Its partners to 30 June 2006, all of whom are UK resident, are Ben Williams Limited, Henderson Traders Limited and John Wilson. The first £100,000 profit is allocated to John Wilson and the remaining profits are shared:

Ben Williams Limited	56%
Henderson Traders Limited	42%
John Wilson	2%

The partnership was formed in January 1991, at which time the two companies commenced trading. The partnership prepares its accounts to 31 December, as do the two corporate partners. John Wilson has transitional overlap relief brought forward of £46,700.

On 1 July 2006 Daniel Grant joined the partnership. He is entitled to a prior charge share of profits of £30,000 plus 1% of profits, Henderson Traders Ltd's share of profits reducing to 41% from that date.

Assume that profits and capital allowances, both for income tax and corporation tax purposes, are as follows:

Year to	Profits (before capital allowances) £	Capital allowances £
31.12.2005	5,200,000	70,000
31.12.2006	5,000,000	65,000
31.12.2007	5,500,000	76,000

Show the amounts assessable on each partner in respect of the three years concerned, and state when tax will be payable.

Ignore Class 4 national insurance contributions.

(b) Sharon Smith and Daniel Brown propose to commence trading on 1 January 2007 as S and D LLP, a limited liability partnership of chartered surveyors. Write brief notes for them setting out the legal and taxation aspects of an LLP.

(a) Where partnerships have both individual and corporate partners, separate computations have to be made for income tax and corporation tax, the computations being made *before* deducting shares of capital allowances according to the partnership agreement (see explanatory note 2). The total partnership profits for corporation tax purposes may therefore differ from those for income tax purposes. The example assumes, however, that profits are the same in each case. The division of the capital allowances, and the profit shares taking the capital allowances into account, are therefore as follows:

	Total	Ben Williams Limited	Henderson Traders Limited	John Wilson	Daniel Grant
Division of capital allowances	£	£	£	£	£
Year to 31.12.2005	70,000	39,200	29,400	1,400	
Year to 31.12.2006					
To 30.6.06	32,500	18,200	13,650	650	
To 31.12.06	32,500	18,200	13,325	650	325
	65,000	36,400	26,975	1,300	325
Year to 31.12.2007	76,000	42,560	31,160	1,520	760
Division of profits					
Year to 31 December 2005					
First allocation	100,000			100,000	
Share of balance					
(56:42:2)	5,100,000	2,856,000	2,142,000	102,000	
	5,200,000	2,856,000	2,142,000	202,000	
Less: Capital allowances	70,000	39,200	29,400	1,400	
	5,130,000	2,816,800	2,112,600	200,600	
Year to 31 December 2006					
1.1.06 to 30.6.06					
First allocation	50,000			50,000	
Share of balance					
(56:42:2)	2,450,000	1,372,000	1,029,000	49,000	
	2,500,000	1,372,000	1,029,000	99,000	
1.7.06 to 31.12.06					
First allocation	65,000			50,000	15,000
Share of balance					
(56:41:2:1)	2,435,000	1,363,600	998,350	48,700	24,350
	5,000,000	2,735,600	2,027,350	197,700	39,350
Less: Capital allowances	65,000	36,400	26,975	1,300	325
	4,935,000	2,699,200	2,000,375	196,400	39,025
Year to 31 December 2007					
First allocation	130,000			100,000	30,000
Share of balance					
(56:41:2:1)	5,370,000	3,007,200	2,201,700	107,400	53,700
	5,500,000	3,007,200	2,201,700	207,400	83,700
Less: Capital allowances	76,000	42,560	31,160	1,520	760
	5,424,000	2,964,640	2,170,540	205,880	82,940

Amounts assessable on partners

The corporate partners are assessable on their shares as shown above.

The assessable profits of the individual partners are as follows:

John Wilson

John Wilson will be assessable on his shares as shown above in 2005/06, 2006/07 and 2007/08, the assessments being based on the accounting period ending in the tax year.

Daniel Grant

2006/07	1.7.06 – 31.12.06		39,025	
	1.1.07 – 5.4.07	3/12 × 82,940	20,735	£59,760
2007/08	Yr to 31.12.07			£82,940

Overlap relief:
3 mths from 1.1.07 – 5.4.07 as above   £20,735

Due date of payment of tax liabilities

Self-assessment applies both for income tax and corporation tax (see note 8). Ben Williams Ltd and Henderson Traders Ltd will be required to make quarterly payments on account of corporation tax if their profits are £1.5 million or above.

John Wilson and Daniel Grant will include their profits in their self-assessment returns. Payments on account will be made on 31 January and 31 July each year, based on the partner's *total* net income tax liability for the previous year, with a balancing payment (or claim for a refund) on the next 31 January.

The self-assessment returns will show overlap relief carried forward of £46,700 for John Wilson and £20,735 for Daniel Grant.

(b) **Limited liability partnerships**

Under the Limited Liability Partnerships Act 2000, from 6 April 2001 it is possible to carry on a business with a view to profit through the medium of a limited liability partnership (LLP). This is achieved by two or more persons registering an incorporation document with the Registrar of Companies. The subscribers are known as members. Thereafter new members can be added by agreement of existing members, and members may leave as long as at least two remain. There is no upper limit. Broadly a member will have limited liability as if operating through a limited company.

The members have the functions of both shareholders and directors of limited companies. The internal organisation of the LLP is similar to a partnership and is governed by agreement (formal or otherwise) of the members. There is no minimum capital requirement. Members can be obliged to contribute to the assets of the LLP on winding up. Normally each member will be required to provide capital and it may be appropriate for the agreement to provide that any undrawn profits will be added to capital. Accounts will be required as for a limited company, as will an audit (except for certain small LLPs), and filing requirements are as for limited companies.

Normally a member's liability will be restricted to capital provided plus undrawn profits. If this is below a specified amount, a member may be required to contribute on winding up. An individual can, however, still remain personally liable under the law of tort where a duty of care to another exists. This particularly applies to professional firms. Furthermore, members can be sued for wrongful or fraudulent trading and can be disqualified from being a member of an LLP.

Taxation aspects of LLPs

Members of an LLP are basically taxed as if they were members of a partnership (ITTOIA 2005 s 863 and TCGA 1992 s 59A). All activities of the LLP are treated as carried on by the members and property is held by the members. All references to a partnership in the tax legislation include an LLP. On liquidation, however, the transparency of the LLP is lost and instead the LLP is treated for income and capital gains purposes as a company.

The transfer of a partnership to an LLP will be tax neutral, eg no balancing adjustments for capital allowances, the existing overlap relief of a partner continues, no capital gains charges or stamp duty. National insurance Class 2 and 4 contributions are payable as before. A single partnership tax return can be made for the tax year of change. It is not possible to re-register a limited company as an LLP or to convert an LLP to a limited company.

Anti-avoidance legislation applies to LLPs that are property investment or investment LLPs (defined in TA 1988 s 842B) to prevent abuse. No interest relief is available on loans used to buy an interest in, or lend money to, such partnerships (TA 1988 s 362). Other provisions affect pension funds, insurance companies and friendly societies.

An LLP is treated as a limited company for VAT, registration being by form VAT1. The LLP can become part of a VAT group.

Tax treatment of trading and professional losses

Where professional partnerships, such as S and D LLP chartered surveyors, operate through an LLP, loss relief will be due as for a normal partnership. Where the LLP carries on a trade, however, relief for losses will be restricted to a member's subscribed capital. Undrawn profits will normally be regarded as a debt of the LLP rather than part of a member's capital unless the members' agreement provides otherwise. Where the restriction causes losses to be unrelieved, the unrelieved amount will be carried forward and treated as a loss available for relief against other income under TA 1988 ss 380 and 381 in later years, subject to the 'subscribed capital' restriction in those years (TA 1988 s 117 as extended by ss 118ZB to 118ZD).

It is a question of fact as to whether the business is a trade or profession. It is accepted that law, medicine and the church are professions. This clearly also applies to chartered surveyors, qualified accountants and similar persons exercising intellectual skill rather than carrying out commercial operations. Until a body of case law is available, care must be taken with activities within the grey area, eg financial advisers, recruitment consultants, or estate agents who only act for the purchase or sale of property.

Winding-up

When a liquidator is appointed (or, if earlier, when a winding-up order is made), the tax treatment changes. Any income will thereafter belong to the LLP and will be taxed as that of a corporate body. Any chargeable gains will be computed by reference to the date the asset was acquired by the LLP and taxed on the LLP. Members will then be taxed (or obtain relief) on the gain/loss arising on their capital interest, the base cost being determined by the historical capital contribution made by the member to the LLP as if it had been a limited company. This treatment does not apply on an informal winding-up without the appointment of a liquidator.

Where, in respect of the acquisition of a share in an LLP asset, a member had claimed business assets rollover relief under TCGA 1992 ss 152, 153, or gains on depreciating assets had been held over under TCGA 1992 s 154, or the acquisition cost had been reduced by gifts holdover relief under TCGA 1992 s 165 or s 260, then on appointment of a liquidator the postponed gain will become chargeable without taper relief (TCGA 1992 s 156A and s 169A).

Explanatory Notes

Treatment of partnerships with company members

1.   Where a partnership has company members, the normal income tax rules of ITTOIA 2005 part 9 apply to partners who are individuals (see Example 24), but special rules in TA 1988 s 114 apply to corporate partners.

Computation of profits

2. Two computations are made, one for income tax using income tax principles and one for corporation tax using corporation tax principles. The reason for having two separate computations is that there are various points of difference in the computations, in particular:

    (a) Interest paid by a company is dealt with under the loan relationships rules rather than as a charge on income, whether or not tax is deducted at source, and if it relates to the trade it is taken into account (usually on an accruals basis) in arriving at the trading profit. (See Example 62 for full details of loan relationships rules.)

    (b) Different rules apply in relation to transactions in financial instruments (see Example 62) and the treatment of intangible assets (see Example 65).

    (c) The rules for calculating rental income of individuals and companies are broadly the same, but there are some differences that affect the computation.

Deduction of tax from payments of interest and patent royalties

3. Companies no longer deduct tax from interest or patent royalties in many circumstances (see Example 6 part (a)). Where tax is deducted, it is deducted at 20% from interest. Companies should strictly account for any tax deducted on the normal quarterly basis, but their shares may not be known at the appropriate time. Unless HMRC agrees to special arrangements, the company would have to account for tax on an estimated basis and adjust it later. Individuals would retain the tax deducted at source and any higher rate relief due would be given in calculating the tax due under self-assessment.

Treatment of company's share of profits

4. The share allocated to each company partner is reduced by the capital allowances and charges allocated to that company. The company's share of interest paid will be taken into account on an accruals basis either as a trading expense or in arriving at a Schedule D Case III surplus or deficit (see Example 48 explanatory note 5). The company's share of patent royalties paid will also be taken into account on an accruals basis under the intangible assets rules (see Example 65). The profit is charged to corporation tax as if it arose from a separate trade carried on by the company. Each corporate partner must include its share of the profits in its own corporation tax return. If the accounting periods of the company and partnership are different, the partnership share is time apportioned to the accounting periods of the company. If a loss arises the normal loss reliefs are available, subject to some anti-avoidance provisions in TA 1988 s 116.

Treatment of individual partners' profit shares

5. The share of the capital allowances relating to the individual partners is treated as a trading expense and deducted from the profit, each individual partner's share then being dealt with according to the normal rules. Each individual will include his share of the profits in the partnership pages of his own self-assessment return (see note 8).

6. Daniel Grant is entitled to overlap relief as shown in respect of the profits taxable both in 2006/07, when he joined the partnership, and 2007/08. John Wilson's transitional overlap relief brought forward relates to the changeover to the current year basis of assessment in 1997/98, and was based on the profits from the end of the 1996/97 basis period to 5 April 1997, ie from 1 January 1997 to 5 April 1997. Overlap relief is given on a change of accounting date if more than twelve months' profits would otherwise be chargeable, or when the partner ceases in business.

Changes of partner

7. As far as changes of partner are concerned, the firm is not treated as ceasing when an individual partner joins or leaves. Similarly, changes in the corporate partners do not have any effect on the continuance of the partnership business, unless a change occurs in which none of the company partners continues but one or more new company partners joins the partnership. In that event the trade is treated as having been transferred to a different company.

Self-assessment

8. Self-assessment was introduced for income tax purposes from 1996/97 and for corporation tax for accounting periods ending after 30 June 1999. Under the self-assessment provisions, partnerships are required to send in partnership returns (TMA 1970 s 12AA). This applies even if there are no individual partners in the partnership. Where all the partners are companies, accounts and computations must be submitted with the partnership return, and the 'Standard Accounts Information' does not have to be completed (see Example 41 note 5).

   If all the partners are individuals, the due date for sending in the partnership return is 31 January following the end of the tax year. If all partners are companies, the return is due 12 months after the end of the accounting period. In both cases where notice to submit a return is received late, the due date becomes 3 months from the date the notice is received.

   For partnerships with both company and individual members, the due date for the partnership return is the later of the company date and the date for individuals, the date in this example for the accounting year to 31 December 2006 being the later of 31 December 2007 and 31 January 2008, ie 31 January 2008. If accounts had instead been made up for the year to 31 March 2007, the return would have been due by the later of 31 January 2008 and 31 March 2008, ie 31 March 2008.

   The individuals and companies also have to file their separate returns, the due dates for those separate returns being the same as stated above for partnerships of all individuals or all companies.

Limited partnerships

9. Under the provisions of the Limited Partnership Act 1907, it is possible for one or more partners to restrict liability for partnership debts to the amount of the limited partner's agreed capital contribution, providing there is at least one general partner with unlimited liability. The limited partner cannot take part in the management of the partnership, and his share of partnership profits would normally rank as unearned income.

   A company could act as either a limited partner or a general partner in such a partnership, and if a limited company is the general partner this effectively limits the liability of that general partner.

10. Certain reliefs available to a limited partner cannot exceed the amount of the partner's agreed capital contribution plus undrawn profits (TA 1988 ss 117, 118). The main items concerned are reliefs for trading losses (including capital allowances) against the partner's income (or company profits) other than trading income, group relief for companies and interest paid in connection with the trade by an individual. A limited partner is also not entitled to relief for interest on a loan to buy an interest in a partnership, or lend money to it (see Example 1 explanatory note 13 (iii)).

11. The national insurance treatment of limited partners who are individuals depends on the circumstances. Class 2 national insurance contributions are payable by someone who is 'gainfully employed' otherwise than as an employee (SSCBA 1992 s 2(1)(b)). Class 4 contributions are payable where profits are 'immediately derived' from carrying on a trade, profession or vocation (SSCBA 1992 s 15(1)). Although a limited partner cannot take part in managing the business, he may participate in a lesser capacity, and if he does, contributions will be payable.

Limited liability partnerships

12. As indicated in part (b) of the example, the Limited Liability Partnerships Act 2000 enables partnerships to adopt a structure that limits the liability of members, without the restriction on taking part in the business that applies to limited partners under the provisions outlined in note 9 above. Similar restrictions apply as in note 10 above in relation to the reliefs available to partners in LLPs. The restriction on relief for interest on loans to buy an interest in, or lend money to, the partnership applies, however, only to partners in investment and property investment LLPs. The loss relief provisions are also different, in that undrawn profits cannot be included in the amount up to which loss relief may be claimed unless the members' agreement provides otherwise, but unrelieved losses may be carried forward and treated for the purposes of ss 380 and 381 as if they had been incurred in the next period. For an illustration see Example 34 part (d).

13. Also as indicated in part (b) of the example, certain rolled over or heldover gains are deemed to be made by members of an LLP when a liquidator is appointed. Such gains do not qualify for taper relief, because the member is *treated* as if a chargeable gain equal to the relevant amount had been made by the member immediately before the start of the formal liquidation, but there is no deemed *disposal* of the asset, so the taper relief provisions of TCGA 1992 s 2A do not apply.

14. For information on how an LLP is formed see example 27 at explanatory note 5.

Computer Aids
Lower Place
North Westock
Devon

25 July 2006

Mr T Jones
Brown Jones & Co
Taxation Practitioners
2 High Street
London

Dear Mr Jones,

As you know I have traded personally for some years selling electronic parts.

The recent interest in micro electronics has resulted in a substantial increase in turnover and, hopefully, profits.

I do not wish to transfer my business to a limited company as I understand this will require a number of legal formalities and extra costs. However, I would be grateful for any tax planning advice you may be able to offer me. I would be happy to pay my wife a very substantial salary or to have her as a partner in the business if this was advisable. Her participation has, in fact, increased significantly as a result of the growth of the business.

Yours sincerely,

I N Putt

Your files show that the tax adjusted profits for the last few years were:

Year ended 31 March 2004	£30,000
Year ended 31 March 2005	£38,000
Year ended 31 March 2006	£45,000

The profits for the year to 31 March 2007 are expected to be £70,000 and to increase to £100,000 for the following year, with further increases as the business expands.

Mrs Putt is employed by her husband. Her salary has been limited to £4,500 per annum paid monthly while the business was being established and she and her husband have no other sources of income.

Mr and Mrs Putt were both born in 1972. Neither has made any pension provision. They do not have children.

Write to Mr Putt comparing the tax position if his wife remains as his employee at an appropriately increased salary with the position if she joins him in partnership, setting out the steps you advise him to follow and briefly mentioning any other tax planning points you consider appropriate.

Brown Jones & Co
Taxation Practitioners
2 High Street
London

15 August 2006

Mr I N Putt
Computer Aids
Lower Place
North Westock
Devon

Dear Mr Putt,

Thank you for your letter of 25 July asking me to advise you in connection with your micro electronics business.

It is clear that your anticipated current profits will give you a significant tax liability at the higher rate and unless action is taken to adopt a more tax effective structure this will get worse as profits increase. A saving in higher rate tax could be made if your wife's income was increased and your own reduced since your wife has the same level of tax allowances and starting/basic rate bands as you do.

You could pay your wife an increased salary for the year to 31 March 2007 so long as it was paid before 31 December 2007 and included as a creditor in your accounts. If the salary was increased substantially, however, the increased amount would need to be justifiable as being 'wholly and exclusively for the purposes of the trade' and a salary of say half your expected profit would clearly be open to challenge. Under self-assessment HMRC will accept the figures shown in your return unless they open an enquiry into the return, but if such an enquiry was raised and it was eventually decided that the salary was not justifiable, your profits could be retrospectively amended and you would be liable to tax, interest, and possibly penalties on the additional profits if you were considered to have been negligent.

Even if such a large increase could be supported in view of your wife's increased participation in the business activities, the extra salary would result in a substantial amount of extra national insurance contributions for both yourself as employer and your wife. The increased salary would be taxed as your wife's income under PAYE at the time of payment and employer's and employee's national insurance contributions would also be payable. The reduction in your profits as a result of the increased salary would affect your tax payable for 2006/07. Your part of the national insurance cost as employer would also reduce your taxable profits, while the total contributions may enhance the potential social security benefits to which Mrs Putt is entitled.

It is possible to increase your wife's salary to the personal allowance limit (currently £97 per week, £420 per month) without attracting employer's or employee's national insurance. As you pay monthly you could increase Mrs Putt's pay from August to £420, without a national insurance cost. In a full year this would use all her personal allowance but not her starting rate band of tax, or basic rate band.

You should be aware that if you pay your wife more than £84 per week (£364 per month) then you are obliged to open a PAYE scheme and complete year end returns even though no amount is deductible from your wife's salary or payable by you as employer. Failure to do so could result in your wife receiving a reduced state pension.

If instead you formed a partnership with your wife, the following points should be noted:

(1)   Providing her profit share was not out of all proportion to her contribution to the business in terms of time, skill, financial investment or acceptance of risk, it should not be vulnerable to attack by HMRC as an arrangement for the avoidance of tax.

(2)   Although as a partner your wife would have to pay both Class 2 national insurance contributions at a fixed weekly rate, and Class 4 contributions on her profit share, these would amount to far less than the combined employer/employee contributions on an equivalent salary.

(3)   If a partnership is formed say from 1 September 2006, then an equal split of profits may be realistic from a tax point of view for the period to 31 March 2007, although allocating a slightly higher share to your wife would eliminate your higher rate tax for the year. It would be important to be able to show that her share of income was fair and reasonable and commercial, so that HMRC could not argue that there was any element of bounty. The extent to which your wife invests in the business, and takes on risks of liabilities as a partner, are important here. You and your wife may be able to vary the profit sharing agreement in subsequent years to make sure that optimum use was made of personal allowances and starting/basic rate bands, again providing the arrangement was commercially justified and could not be shown to be pure bounty.

A partnership with your wife will be more tax effective in your circumstances than increasing her salary, but there are some disadvantages to the formation of a partnership as follows:

(1)   As a partner your wife will join you in bearing full legal liability for the debts and liabilities of the business. In the extreme this means that you could both be made bankrupt if the firm's debts could not be met. In the present healthy state of your business this does not present a problem. If this matter causes you concern please let me know and I will provide full details of a limited liability partnership which may then be more suitable, but it has substantially the same administrative and legal burdens as a limited company.

(2)   Self-employed national insurance contributions do not give entitlement to jobseeker's allowance and the self-employed do not get earnings-related pension when they retire.

If you decide to form a partnership, it will be advisable to have a properly drawn partnership agreement, and I will be happy to assist you in arranging for this to be done. Your wife should be named on the letterheading and a partnership bank account should be opened. The change needs to be notified to your VAT office within 30 days, but a change of VAT number will not usually be necessary. Your wife needs to contact the national insurance contributions office within three months of the change to make arrangements to pay flat rate Class 2 contributions. These can be paid either by monthly direct debit or on a quarterly basis on receipt of a bill from the national insurance contributions office. The Class 4 contributions are calculated by reference to her profit share, and are payable to HMRC along with income tax.

The partnership will have to file a partnership return with HMRC, the profit allocation for the year ending 31 March 2007 assessable in 2006/07 being reflected in each of your personal self-assessment returns.

As I have previously suggested to you, it would be sensible for you and your wife to make provision for pensions by paying contributions to a registered pension plan.

From 6 April 2006 the amount you can contribute will effectively only be limited by your taxable earnings in any year. The individual yearly contributions limit of £215,000 and the lifetime fund limit of £1,500,000 are unlikely to cause a restriction for the next few years. Under the new rules the relevant income is that of the actual fiscal year and there are no provisions to carry premiums backwards or forwards. The premiums continue to be paid net of basic rate tax and higher rate relief given by self-assessment.

When you have had a chance to consider my proposals, I shall be happy to meet you to discuss them in further detail and to deal with the necessary documentation.

Yours sincerely,

T Jones

Explanatory Notes

Forming a partnership

1.   HMRC will not accept that a partnership exists merely because the parties say so. There must be an agreement, which should preferably although not necessarily be in writing, and there must be evidence that the agreement has been acted on. See Example 26 re limited liability partnerships.

Although partners are free to divide profits in whatever way they wish according to the provisions of the partnership agreement, the division being accepted as valid for tax purposes, the settlements provisions of ITTOIA 2005 part 5 Chapter 5 are wide enough to catch artificial partnership arrangements between husband and wife where a spouse joining a partnership takes a profit share out of all proportion to the contribution made. See Tax Bulletin 64 April 2003 for HMRC's current view on this.

It is therefore possible for many husband/wife partnerships to decide on profit shares for tax saving reasons providing the arrangements are not a sham. (The important factor to consider is that a deserted spouse may be left to meet the firm's liabilities.) A salary, on the other hand, must be wholly and exclusively for the purposes of the trade, and there is also a significant difference in terms of national insurance contributions, there being no upper ceiling for employer's contributions (at 12.8%) (see note 2).

National insurance contributions

2. National insurance contributions are a very significant consideration when comparing the tax position of an employee and a partner. The contributions of a self-employed person earning £33,540 for 2006/07 are £2,390, compared with £6,784 combined employer/employee contributions on the same level of earnings. Above £33,540 the self-employed pay 1% whereas the combined employer and employee rate is 13.8%. The comparison is affected by the employer's contributions in respect of his employees being tax deductible, whereas the contributions of a self-employed person are not tax deductible, but the difference remains high. This point is also relevant when considering at what profits level it would be advantageous to incorporate a business, because directors pay national insurance contributions as employees. See Example 47 for further details. See also Example 90 re choice of business medium.

Registered pension premiums

3. A registered pension premium within the permitted limits is paid net of basic rate tax, and the tax relief may be retained whether or not the payer is a taxpayer (FA 2004 ss 188 to 195). Mrs Putt could therefore pay a premium on or before 5 April 2007 of up to £4,700, deducting tax therefrom (or £5,040 if the salary is increased). Alternatively Mr Putt, as employer, could make a payment for her of up to any amount, subject to being able to show that the total remuneration package is commercial. (See Example 37 at 37.3). This would be paid gross, but would attract tax relief at the rate applicable to the business profits, which might be higher rate. The contract would still be in the name of Mrs Putt, and the resultant pension taxed on her.

In the same way Mr Putt could pay up to 100% of his share of profits for 2006/07 into a registered pension fund, obtaining basic rate tax relief by deduction and higher rate relief via his tax return. Premiums paid in year do reduce the payments on account for the following year.

Although pension funds are exempt from tax, they can no longer recover the tax credits on dividends, so that the value of an individual's personal pension fund is reduced accordingly. The pension legislation changed on 6 April 2006, all previous provisions were abolished and a new concept of a registered pension introduced. This does not affect the benefits accrued under the previous provisions. For the detailed provisions on registered pension plans from 6 April 2006 see Example 37.

Potential tax position of Mr & Mrs Putt for 2006/07

4. If no action is taken, Mr Putt's estimated 2006/07 income of £70,000 would be reduced by his personal allowance of £5,035 to £64,965, so that £31,665 would be taxable at 40% (the higher rate threshold being £33,300).

If Mr Putt took his wife into partnership on 1 September 2006, his wife being entitled to half of the profits from that date, then assuming the profits for the year to 31 March 2007 were £72,742 (being the estimated profits of £70,000 plus the wife's salary for seven months saved by taking her into partnership), the position would be:

	Husband £	*Wife* £
Salary to 31.8.06 5/12 x 4,700		1,958
Profit share:		
1.4.06 – 31.8.06 5/12 x 72,742	30,309	
1.9.06 – 31.3.07 7/12 x 72,742 = 42,433, split equally	21,216	21,217
	51,525	23,175
Personal allowance	5,035	5,035
Taxable income	46,490	18,140

Mr Putt's income in the higher rate band would be reduced from £31,665 to £13,190 (which may be further reduced if he paid a registered pension contribution), while Mrs Putt would pay tax at starting and basic rates. Mr Putt would pay self-employed national insurance contributions of around £2,569, while Mrs Putt would pay seven months' Class 2 contributions = £64 plus Class 4 contributions at 8% on (21,217 – 5,035 =) £16,182 = £1,295, giving a total of £1,359.

By comparison, if Mr Putt continued as a sole trader his national insurance liability would have been:

		£
Class 2	52 × £2.10	109
Class 4	33,540 – 5,035 = 28,505 @ 8%	2,280
	70,000 – 33,540 = 36,460 @ 1%	365
		2,754

National insurance has therefore increased by (2,569 + 1,359 – 2,754) =	1,174

Whereas income tax has decreased by

		£	£	
Mr Putt	31,665 – 13,190 = 18,475 × 40%		7,390	
Less Mrs Putt increase	2,150 × 10%	215		
	15,990 × 22%	3,518	3,733	3,657
	18,140			
Overall saving				2,483

(Previously Mrs Putt was unable to use £335 (5,035 – 4,700) of her personal allowance.)

Limited Liability Partnership

5.   A Limited Liability Partnership (LLP) is formed by completing the necessary documentation available from Companies House, website www.companieshouse.gov.uk, and filing it with the appropriate signatures and fee. Its name must end with 'LLP' or 'Limited Liability Partnership', and names are subject to the same restrictions as company names. LLPs may not choose a name closely similar to an existing company's name, and vice versa. Publications giving the details of formation and management of LLPs are available from the Companies House site.

The LLP has similarities to a company in that it is a separate legal entity contracting in its own right, it provides limitation on individuals' liability, and has accounting and administrative burdens similar to those of companies. It has similarities with traditional partnerships in that the partners (always referred to as 'members', not 'partners') are taxed on a very similar basis to that for traditional partnerships. Unless salaried, the members are taxed under the same income tax rules as partners, the basis periods are as for partnerships, and benefits in kind rules do not apply to assets such as cars. On liquidation, however, the LLP becomes subject to corporation tax.

LLP administration

The disclosure requirements for LLPs are similar to those for companies, although the LLP does not have a Memorandum of Association.

The LLP must have at least two members, and members' names must be notified to Companies House in the prescribed form, as for officers in the case of limited companies. A minimum of two members must be designated as 'designated members', who are in particular responsible for the filing and compliance obligations, in a manner akin to that of a limited company's Company Secretary. The LLP must complete an annual return, and notify changes of members details, of accounting periods, and place details of mortgages or charges on record.

The LLP has very similar arrangements for setting an Accounting Reference Date, appointing auditors, for filing accounts, and similar penalties for non-compliance, as a limited company. Although abbreviated accounts are available to small LLPs, accounts are placed in the public domain, and the privacy available to traditional partnerships is lost.

Limited liability

In comparison to a traditional partnership, the LLP carries an increased administrative burden, so its attraction is likely to lie in the limitation of liability.

As the LLP is a separate legal entity which contracts and holds property in its own right, in the case of a prudently run LLP, its liabilities should be limited to its assets. The individual partners are therefore not jointly and severally liable for all business debts as in a traditional partnership. As for companies, in the case of an individual acting negligently or in contravention of professional guidelines, a legal challenge may seek to look through the corporate veil and hold an individual personally responsible. A liquidator may seek to recover any funds (eg loans, profit, expenses) or property withdrawn from the LLP within two years of commencement of winding-up if the member knew or had reasonable grounds for believing that the firm would be made insolvent by the withdrawal.

The members should therefore consider the solvency of the LLP before withdrawing funds. The LLP offers significant limitation of liability in comparison with traditional partnerships.

State the rules for arriving at assessable profits following a change of accounting date, and show the computation of the assessable profits for all relevant years for the following traders, assuming they made up accounts to the dates shown (having not previously changed their accounting dates), and earned profits net of capital allowances as stated:

(a)   *Franky Flew*

   (business started in 1986)

	£	
Year ended 31 August 2005	12,000	
8 months ended 30 April 2006	28,800	
Transitional overlap profit	19,025	(217 days)

(b)   *Harlech*

   (business started 1 January 1997)

	£	
Year ended 31 December 2004	21,600	
16 months ended 30 April 2006	32,000	
Overlap profit	4,200	(3 months)

(c)   *Baines*

   (business started in 1975)

	£	
Year ended 30 April 2006	70,000	
11 months ended 31 March 2007	45,540	
Transitional overlap profit	63,343	(340 days)

(d)   *Duffryn*

   (business started in 1990)

	£	
Year ended 31 July 2004	45,600	
20 months ended 31 March 2006	70,000	
Year ended 31 March 2007	39,600	
Transitional overlap profit	36,011	(248 days)

Indicate what the position would have been if, instead of making up the 20-month account, Duffryn had made up accounts for:

   (i)   12 months to 31 July 2005, making a profit of £42,000 and 8 months to 31 March 2006, making a profit of £28,000, or

   (ii)   18 months to 31 January 2006, making a profit of £63,000, or

   (iii) 21 months to 30 April 2006, making a profit of £73,500.

Change of accounting date

Under ITTOIA 2005 s 214, an accounting change, ie a change from one accounting date to another, is treated as made in the first tax year in which accounts are not made up to the old date, or are made up to the new date, or both. In order for the change to become effective at the time it is made, then unless the change takes place before the end of the third tax year, the following rules must be satisfied (s 217):

1. The first account to the new date does not exceed 18 months.

2. Notice of the change is given to HMRC by 31 January next following the tax year of change.

3. Either:

    (a) No earlier change has been made in any of the 5 previous tax years

    or

    (b) The notice sets out the reasons for the change and HMRC either accept that the change is for bona fide commercial reasons or do not notify their dissatisfaction within 60 days of receiving the notice. (Obtaining a tax advantage is not a bona fide commercial reason.) If HMRC object to the change, the taxpayer has a right of appeal.

The fact that (apart from in the second and third tax year) HMRC does not recognise a change of accounting date unless the change is notified to them means that accounts may be made up to an intermediate date for commercial reasons, for example when a partner leaves, without the annual accounting date being altered (see explanatory note 2).

The provision that the new accounts period must not exceed 18 months does not prevent a longer account being made up. It merely prevents the account being recognised until the change of accounting date conditions can be satisfied, as illustrated in part (d) of the example. Thus, if the rules are not satisfied for the first relevant year, the change to the new date is treated as made in the next following year and so on until the rules are satisfied (s 219). (See Example 16 explanatory note 4 re the effect of making up a long first account in a new business, such an account not, of course, being covered by the change of accounting date rules.)

Where the change of date occurs in the second or third tax year, or the provisions of s 217 apply, the basis period for the tax year in which the change occurs depends on the 'relevant period', ie the period from the end of the basis period for the previous tax year to the new accounting date in the current tax year. (Note that depending on the periods for which accounts are made up, there may not be an account made up to the new date in the current year – see (b) below.) If the relevant period is less than 12 months the basis period for the tax year of change is 12 months to the new date. If the relevant period is more than 12 months, the basis period is that longer period. What this means is that if the new date is *earlier* in the tax year than the old date, the basis period will be 12 months and profits will be double charged, for which overlap relief will be available in due course. If the new date is *later* in the tax year than the old date, more than 12 months' profit will be charged in the tax year of change, but the assessable profit will be reduced by the appropriate proportion of any available overlap profits according to the excess of the basis period over 12 months compared with the length of the period in which the overlap profits arose (see (c) and (d) below).

Taxpayers need to maintain a running computation of overlap relief and the period to which it relates. The overlap period may be calculated in days, months, or months and fractions of months. For businesses in existence at 5 April 1994, transitional overlap relief on the changeover to the current year basis of assessment was maximised by calculating the overlap period in days. If that was done, it would then be necessary to work out overlap relief in days during the life of the business. Where a change of accounting date creates further overlap relief, the relevant period and amount are added to existing overlap relief to give a new single period and amount. Where a change of accounting date uses up some overlap relief, this reduces the period and amount of overlap relief carried forward. Where there is a loss in an overlap period it must be counted as a profit of nil for the appropriate period (see Example 31 for illustrations).

Assuming that transitional overlap relief had been calculated in days in parts (a), (c) and (d) and new business overlap relief in months in part (b) of the example, and also assuming that the rules in 2 and 3 above are satisfied, the position is as follows:

(a) *Franky Flew*

The change of accounting date takes place in 2006/07. The 'relevant period' is 1.9.05 to 30.4.06, which is less than 12 months, so the basis period for 2006/07 is the *year* to 30.4.06, giving assessable profits of:

1.5.05 – 31.8.05 123/365 x 12,000	4,044	
8 mths to 30.4.06	28,800	
	£ 32,844	

The profits of £4,044 have also been taxed in 2005/06, so they are added to the transitional overlap profit, the combined amount of (19,025 + 4,044 =) £23,069 then relating to a period of (217 + 123 =) 340 days. The overlap profit will qualify for relief on a later change of accounting date to the extent that more than 12 months' profits is being charged, or otherwise on cessation.

The change of accounting date does not affect any other tax year.

(b) *Harlech*

The change of accounting date takes place in 2005/06, since accounts are not made up to the old date in that year (or in fact to the new date, since no account ends in 2005/06). Assessments before 2005/06 are not affected, the 2004/05 assessment being as follows:

2004/05 (1.1.04 – 31.12.04)	£21,600
Overlap relief 1.1.97 – 5.4.97 (3 months)	£ 4,200

The 'relevant period' is 1.1.05 to 30.4.05 (ie the date of the new year-end in 2005/06). Since that period is less than 12 months, the assessable profit is based on 12 months to the new date. This gives the following results for 2005/06 and 2006/07:

2005/06	Yr to 30.4.05			
	1.5.04 – 31.12.04	8/12 x 21,600	14,400	
	1.1.05 – 30.4.05	4/16 x 32,000	8,000	£22,400
2006/07	Yr to 30.4.06	12/16 x 32,000		£24,000

The profits of £14,400 for 8 months have also been taxed in 2004/05, so they will be added to the initial overlap profit of £4,200, with the total amount of £18,600 covering an overlap period of 11 months qualifying for relief in a later year.

(c) *Baines*

The change of accounting date takes place in 2006/07, since accounts are made up to the new accounting date in that year, and the 'relevant period' is 1.5.05 to 31.3.07. As that period exceeds 12 months, it is the basis period for 2006/07.

On the change of accounting date to 31 March, the transitional overlap relief is given in full against the 2006/07 assessment, since 31 March may be regarded as equivalent to the tax year (see Example 16 part (a)).

The assessment is therefore as follows:

		£	£
2006/07	Yr to 30.4.06	70,000	
	11 months to 31.3.07	45,540	
		115,540	
	Less Transitional overlap relief	63,343	52,197

The change of accounting date does not affect any other tax year.

(d) *Duffryn*

The first year affected by Duffryn's change of accounting date is 2005/06. Since the change involves an account of more than 18 months, however, it cannot satisfy the conditions of s 217, so assessments continue to be based on the old accounting date until the conditions are satisfied. The assessment for 2005/06 is therefore based on the year to 31.7.05, ie 365/609 x £70,000 = £41,954.

The s 217 conditions can be satisfied for 2006/07, since they are considered in relation to the account of 12 months to 31 March 2007. The 'relevant period' is the 20 months from 1.8.05 to 31.3.07, so the 2006/07 assessment is as follows:

244/609 x £70,000	28,046
Yr to 31.3.07	39,600
	£ 67,646

Where an accounting date is changed to 31 March, all overlap relief is given at that time as indicated in (c) above, so that the transitional overlap relief of £36,011 will be given against the 2006/07 assessable profit, reducing it to £31,635.

If Duffryn had made up accounts for 12 months to 31.7.05 and 8 months to 31.3.06

The change would take place in 2005/06 and two accounts would be made up to dates within that tax year. The s 217 conditions would be satisfied and the relevant period would be 1.8.04 to 31.3.06, covering 20 months. The position and comparison with the single 20-month account would therefore be as follows:

		Two accounts £	20 month account £
2005/06	Yr to 31.7.05	42,000	
	1.8.05 to 31.3.06	28,000	
		70,000	
	Less: Transitional overlap relief	36,011	
		33,989	41,954
2006/07	Yr to 31.3.07	39,600	31,635

If Duffryn had made up accounts for 18 months to 31.1.06

The s 217 conditions would not be breached and the relevant period would be the 18 months from 1.8.04 to 31.1.06. Since that period exceeds 12 months, it would be the basis period for 2005/06. Duffryn has transitional overlap relief of £36,011 for 248 days. Since the basis period for 2005/06 would exceed 12 months by 184 days, 184/248 of the overlap relief of £36,011, ie £26,718, would be given against the 2005/06 assessable profit, leaving 64 days of overlap relief amounting to £9,293 to be given in the future. The position would therefore be as follows:

2005/06 18 mths to 31.1.06	63,000
Less: Transitional overlap relief	26,718
	£ 36,282

If Duffryn had made up accounts for 21 months to 30.4.06

The conditions of s 217 would again be broken, and it would take a further year before they could be satisfied, because in 2006/07 the account that ends in that year is the 21-month account, so the accounting change would be ignored and the basis period would be the year to 31.7.06. The change would be effective in 2007/08, since the 12-month account to 30 April 2007 can satisfy the s 217 conditions. The relevant period would then be 1.8.06 to 30.4.07, and since this is less than 12 months, the basis period for 2007/08 would be 12 months to 30.4.07. The position would therefore be as follows:

2005/06	Yr to 31.7.05 365/639 x £73,500	£ 41,984
2006/07	Yr to 31.7.06	
	274/639 x £73,500 + 92/365 x profits of year to 30.4.07	
2007/08	Profits of yr to 30.4.07	

The profits of the 92 days from 1.5.06 to 31.7.06 would be overlap profits which would be added to the transitional overlap profits, the combined amount qualifying for later relief then relating to a period of (248 + 92 =) 340 days.

Explanatory Notes

Changes of accounting date

1.   As indicated in the example, where accounts are made up to an earlier date in the tax year, this results in profits being charged more than once. The amount double charged represents an overlap profit, for which relief is available either on a further change of accounting date if more than 12 months' profit would otherwise be taxed in one year or on cessation. Where on a change of date the new date is later in the tax year, more than twelve months' profit will be charged, as indicated in parts (c) and (d) of the example, and an appropriate proportion of earlier overlap profits will be deducted.

Part (d) of the example illustrates that if profits of a business with overlap relief start to fall, the ongoing assessments may be reduced by switching to a 31 March year-end. The extended basis period that results from changing to the 31 March accounting date is offset by the fact that the profits are reduced by the whole of the overlap relief.

Notification of changes

2.   As indicated in the example, changes of accounting date are not recognised unless they are notified to HMRC, except where they occur in the second or third tax year (ITTOIA 2005 ss 200 and 215).

Where a business ceases and accounts to the date of cessation are to a date other than the annual accounting date, the cessation provisions of s 202 override the change of accounting date provisions for the final tax year. Depending on the dates to which accounts are made up, the change of accounting date rules may apply for the penultimate year, but this may be overcome by not notifying HMRC of the change as indicated above.

Where, however, a business is of very short duration, and a long account is made up to the date of cessation, a change of accounting date might technically occur in the second or third tax year for which no notification is required. HMRC has, however, stated that they will not object if computations are submitted on the basis that the old date continues to apply. For example:

Business starts 1 July 2004 and makes up accounts to 30 November 2005. The business ceases on 31 May 2007 and accounts are made up for the 18 months to that date. The basis periods are:

2004/05	1.7.04 – 5.4.05 (9/17 x 1st accounts)
2005/06	1.12.04 – 30.11.05
2006/07	Technically the change of accounting date rules should apply to give a basis period of the 12 months to 31.5.06, but HMRC will allow basis period to be left at:
	1.12.05 – 30.11.06 (12/18 x 2nd accounts)
2007/08	1.12.06 – 31.5.07 (6/18 x 2nd accounts)

Overlap relief would be computed on profits of 4 months from 1.12.04 – 5.4.05 and relieved in 2007/08.

William Smith, a married man aged 50, whose wife is aged 45, has been trading for some years preparing accounts to 31 December each year. He made a trading profit of £10,000 for the year to 31 December 2005 and a trading loss of £16,000 for the year to 31 December 2006. He has reorganised the business and expects to show a profit of around £11,000 in 2007, increasing in later years. Capital allowances have been taken into account in these figures.

His unearned income for 2005/06 and 2006/07 was as follows:

	2005/06 £	2006/07 £
Rental income	3,840	4,390
Bank interest (gross amounts)	880	655

Smith's wife's income is £10,000 per annum from full-time employment.

In 2005/06 Smith had sold some shares he had inherited many years ago and made a chargeable gain of £10,600 (after taper relief of 30%). He had no capital losses brought forward and he had no capital transactions in 2006/07.

Class 4 national insurance contributions are payable between:

2005/06	£4,895 and £32,760 @ 8% plus 1% on the excess over £32,760
2006/07	£5,035 and £33,540 @ 8% plus 1% on the excess over £33,540

Indicate what claims are available to Smith in respect of the 2006 loss and state the time limits involved.

Show the availability of a claim for tax credits and the effect of a claim made on

(a)   1 July 2006, or

(b)   1 July 2007

The couple do not have any children.

Loss claims available to William Smith in respect of 2006 loss

The loss of £16,000 in the year to 31 December 2006 is treated as the loss of the tax year 2006/07 (see explanatory note 1(b)). The loss claims available to Mr Smith are as follows:

(i)   He may carry forward the loss to set against his first available later profits from the same trade (TA 1988 s 385).

(ii)   He may claim to set the loss against his total income of 2006/07 or 2005/06, or, if he wishes, of both years (TA 1988 s 380).

(iii)   He may claim to set the balance of the loss after a s 380 claim (and after any other claims, such as under s 380 for the previous year) against his capital gains for the tax year(s) of the s 380 claim (FA 1991 s 72).

The time limit for the s 385 carry forward claim is five years from 31 January following the tax year (TMA 1970 s 43). Once the loss claim has been established, relief is given automatically against the first available later trading profits.

The time limit for claims under s 380 and against capital gains is one year from 31 January after the tax year of loss (s 380(1), FA 1991 s 72(1)), ie by 31 January 2009 for a 2006/07 loss.

The effect of the different claims would be as follows:

(i) Carry forward under TA 1988 s 385

The loss would be set against the trading profit of the year to 31 December 2007. If this is £11,000 as expected, there would still be an unrelieved loss of £5,000 to carry forward to a later year. Smith's other income currently covers his personal allowance, although this might not be the case in 2007/08. The claim would reduce or eliminate the tax and Class 4 national insurance contributions for 2007/08, which is payable by way of payments on account on 31 January 2008 and 31 July 2008, with a balancing payment (or repayment) on 31 January 2009. Tax would remain payable for 2005/06 and 2006/07.

(ii) and (iii) Claim under s 380 against total income of 2006/07 and/or 2005/06, and possibly against 2005/06 capital gains

Smith's income tax position for the relevant years before loss claims is as follows:

2006/07

	£
Trading income (loss in yr to 31.12.06)	–
UK property income	4,390
Savings income	655
	5,045
Personal allowance	(5,035)
Taxable income	10
Tax thereon at 10%	1

2005/06   £

Trading income					10,000
UK property income					3,840
Savings income					880
					14,720
Personal allowance					(4,895)
Taxable income					9,825
Tax thereon: On non-savings income	2,090		@ 10%	209	
	6,855		@ 22%	1,508	
On savings income	880		@ 20%	176	1,893
	9,825				
Class 4 national insurance contributions					
(10,000 – 4,895 =)	5,105		@ 8%		408
					2,301

His capital gains tax liability in 2005/06 is (10,600 – annual exemption 8,500) =
£2,100 @ 20% =   £ 420

Clearly a claim in 2006/07 would not be appropriate, since his personal allowance would be wasted and very little tax would be saved.

His income of 2005/06 does not fully cover the loss, so if he makes a claim for that year he cannot avoid wasting his personal allowance. The claim would save tax and Class 4 national insurance of £2,301 and leave an unrelieved loss of (16,000 – 14,720 =) £1,280, which could be carried forward under s 385 against later trading profits. Relief would be obtained at the basic rate in 2007/08 if his anticipated profit is realised. The loss carried forward for Class 4 national insurance purposes would be £6,000 being loss of £16,000 relieved against trading income only of £10,000 (see explanatory note 4). The effect of the loss claim would be to leave the starting rate band of £2,020 available for the capital gain, so that the tax on the gain would be reduced by £2,090 @ (20 – 10)% = £209, giving tax payable of (420 – 209 =) £211. This would increase the tax saved as a result of the loss claim to £2,512.

Alternatively, Smith could set the balance of the loss of £1,280 against his 2005/06 capital gains of £10,600. The gains *before* taper relief are £15,143 (the amount of £10,600 being after 30% taper relief). The loss of £1,280 would reduce the gains to £13,863, on which taper relief of 30% would be £4,159, giving chargeable gains of £9,704 less annual exemption £8,500 = £1,204. Tax thereon would be at the starting rate of 10%, amounting to £120, so that the extra tax saved through the claim would be (211 – 120 =) £91. (See Example 74 for the capital gains taper relief and tax rate provisions.)

Optimum loss claim(s)

Claiming the maximum relief under s 380, including relief against capital gains, means that the 2005/06 personal allowance is wasted and a part of the remainder of the loss saves tax at only 10% or 20%.

Furthermore, under self-assessment, carried back losses do not affect the calculation of payments on account either for the loss year or the next following year (see explanatory note 5), and interest on tax and Class 4 national insurance contributions refunded as a result of the loss claim is payable only from 31 January following the loss year. Assuming Smith made a s 380 claim for 2005/06 (possibly extended to capital gains), his tax position would be as follows:

2005/06   Income tax, Class 4 national insurance and capital gains tax totalling £2,512 refunded; a further capital gains tax refund of £91 made if loss set against gains. No interest on refund unless made after 31 January 2008 (balancing payment date for 2006/07).

2006/07	Payments on account would be based on tax/national insurance of (2,301 – 176 on savings income =) £2,125 payable directly for 2005/06. He would be entitled to a refund of (2,125 – 1 =) £2,124, unless he had claimed to reduce payments on account. Repayment supplement would be payable on the overpaid payments on account from the payment dates.
2007/08	Payments on account would not be required, because the 2006/07 tax of £1 is below the de minimis level of £500.

If the loss is carried forward under s 385, tax might be saved at the basic rate, depending on the level of his 2007/08 income, and there could be further relief in a later year if his 2007/08 trading profits do not fully cover the loss.

Smith may be able to delay the decision on what loss claim(s) to make until he is reasonably certain of the level of his 2007/08 income. On the other hand, he may need to make the s 380 claim in order to obtain immediate cash repayments.

Tax Credits and trading loss

William Smith and his wife have tax credits income for 2005/06 of £24,420 ([14,720 – 300] + 10,000).

They are eligible for WTC as both work full-time and are over 25. However, the award would be 'nil' based on this level of income; they are not entitled to child tax credit or the childcare element of WTC.

In 2006/07 William incurs a trading loss of £16,000.

For tax credits this is offset against the family income giving income for tax credits for 2006/07 of:

Investment income		
William	5,045	
Less:	300	4,745
Employment		
Mrs Smith		10,000
		14,745
Less: Trading loss		(16,000)
Unrelieved trading loss carried forward		(1,255)
Income for tax credits		nil
WTC claim (per day)		
Basic	4.57	
Second adult	4.50	
30 hours	1.87	
365 days ×	10.94	£3,993

Providing a claim is made by 6 July 2006 (ie 6 months before the end of the accounting period in which the loss occurs) the full tax credit will be payable, otherwise the claim is backdated 3 months from the actual date of claim.

Mr and Mrs Smith will therefore receive:

(a)	Claim on 1 July 2006	£3,993
(b)	Claim on 1 July 2007 backdated to 1 April 2007 ie 5 days × £10.94 =	£55

A provisional award would also be made for 2007/08 at the rate of £10.94 per day. However, when the actual income is known for 2007/08 it is possible that no award may be due and much of the £10.94 per day paid for 2007/08 is potentially repayable. However, for 2006/07 increases of income up to £25,000 are disregarded so some tax credit would be due provided income does not exceed £41,012.

The unrelieved 'tax credit' loss of £1,255 will be carried forward and relieved against the first available profits of William Smith from the same business. Income for 2007/08 for tax credits might then become:

	£	£
Investment income (say)	5,045	
Less:	300	4,745
Employment income – Mrs Smith		10,000
Trading income (say)	11,000	
Less trading loss b/f	1,255	9,745
		24,490

This would result in a 'nil' award for 2008/09 but would not affect the provisional payments made for 2007/08.

	£
Income 2007/08	24,490
Income disregard threshold 2006/07	25,000
Income for tax credits 2007/08 (as 2006/07)	Nil

Explanatory Notes

Loss reliefs available – income tax

1.   The reliefs available for a trading loss are as follows:

(a)   The loss may be carried forward to set against the first available later profits from the *same trade* (TA 1988 s 385). Where part of a loss remains unrelieved after other loss claims, the balance is carried forward under this section. The amount will include any allowable interest, relieved outside the accounts, incurred for trading purposes and not utilised in the year (TA 1988 s 390).

(b)   The loss of a tax year may be set against the net total income of that tax year, or of the previous tax year, or, if the loss is large enough and the claimant so wishes, of both tax years (TA 1988 s 380). Where s 380 claims are to be made for both available years, relief may be given in the order specified by the claimant. The trade does not have to have been carried on in the previous year. If relief is claimed in a tax year both for a loss of that year and a loss carried back from the following year, the current year's loss is relieved first (s 380(2)).

Losses are calculated using the *same basis periods* as are used for calculating profits, for claims under ss 380 and 381 (s 382(3)). Where a loss would otherwise enter into the calculations for two tax years, for example in the first year of business or on a change of accounting date, it is taken into account only in the first year. For an illustration see Example 31, which also deals with the calculation and treatment of overlap relief where losses are involved.

A claim may not be made under s 380 unless the trade is being carried on on a commercial basis with a view of profits (TA 1988 s 384).

(c)   For new businesses, relief may be claimed under TA 1988 s 381 where losses are incurred in the first four tax years. For details see Example 30.

(d)   A s 380 claim may be extended to include set-off against capital gains, in either or both of the tax year of loss and the previous year (FA 1991 s 72). The claim against income of the claim year must be made first (personal allowances therefore being wasted) and the loss available to set against capital gains is also reduced by any other loss relief claimed, for example under s 380 in the previous year or by carry back under s 381 in a new business. The amount of capital gains *available* to relieve the trading loss is the amount of the capital gains of the relevant year after deducting current and brought forward capital losses (FA 1991 s 72(4)), ignoring any later claim that affects the chargeable gains for the year (s 72(5)). Having identified the amount *available* for relief in this way, that amount is then treated as an allowable capital loss of the relevant year and is therefore relieved *in priority* to brought forward capital losses, and before taper relief.

Where there are no losses brought forward, the claim may mean wasting all or part of the annual capital gains exemption and taper relief. Where there are capital losses brought forward this will sometimes avoid wasting annual exemption, but in some cases there would be no immediate tax saving and it would be a question of whether the taxpayer wanted to have unrelieved trading losses carried forward or unrelieved capital losses carried forward.

In most instances it would probably be preferable to have unrelieved trading losses carried forward rather than capital losses, but if the business had closed down, the reverse would apply. If a later claim, such as a claim to business assets rollover relief, reduces the amount of the gains against which s 72 relief has been claimed, the s 72 losses which thereby become unrelieved are carried forward for relief against later gains, but they cannot be relieved in any tax year after the tax year in which the trade ceases (s 72(6)). Such losses must therefore be separately identified in the amount of unrelieved capital losses carried forward (see Example 96 explanatory note 11).

Capital gains are charged at non-dividend savings income rates of income tax. This includes the starting rate to the extent that it has not been used against income. The basic rate band will be extended by gross gift aid payments and personal pension contributions. For further notes see Example 74 explanatory note 1.

(e) Where a business has ceased, terminal loss relief may be claimed under TA 1988 s 388 in respect of the loss of the last twelve months (see Example 32).

Time limits for claims etc

2. A valid loss claim must state the source of the loss, the year of loss, and either the year of claim or the statutory reference under which the relief is claimed. The time limit for loss claims under ss 380 and 381 is one year from 31 January following the tax year of loss. The time limit for claims under ss 385 and 388 is 5 years from 31 January following the tax year of loss/cessation. Late claims cannot be accepted, but in very limited circumstances HMRC may grant relief as if a claim had been made within the time limit (see Tax Bulletin December 1994).

HMRC has stated that where claims are made under s 380 both against the current year's and the previous year's income, the loss will be dealt with according to the order in which the claims are made, so that if the claim relating to the previous year were made first, the loss would be set against the previous year's income first. If both claims were made together the loss would be set off according to the order specified by the claimant. Where, however, relief is claimed in one tax year in respect of a loss both of the current year and of the following year, the current year's loss is relieved first (s 380(2)).

Capital allowances

3. Capital allowances are automatically included in loss claims, since they are deducted as trading expenses in arriving at the trading result. There is some flexibility, in that some capital allowances may be wholly or partly disclaimed. In practice this applies mainly to writing down allowances on plant and machinery (CAA 1990 s 24(3) – see Example 19 explanatory notes 3 and 4).

Class 4 national insurance contributions and trading losses

4. Class 4 national insurance contributions are payable on profits above the personal allowance, as indicated in the example, and they are included in the calculation of payments of account and balancing payments (or repayments) under self-assessment. Although a trading loss may be set against non-trading income following a claim under TA 1988 s 380, it reduces only trading profits for the purpose of calculating Class 4 national insurance contributions. Mr Smith's future profits for Class 4 will therefore be reduced by any part of the loss set against non-trading income under the

s 380 claims. The self-assessment return provides a working sheet to calculate the appropriate adjustment to be made in the return. For detailed notes on national insurance contributions see Example 47.

Effect of carryback claims on payments on account and repayment supplement

5. Carrying back a loss for relief in an earlier year has an unwelcome effect on payments on account. The tax saving from the carryback claim is *calculated* by reference to the tax rates of the earlier year, but relief is given *in relation to* the later year. Since the tax of the earlier year is not altered, the claim does not affect payments on account for the loss year (although the refund flowing from the loss claim may enable those payments to be discharged or repaid). Nor does it affect the payments on account for the next following year, which are based on the tax *assessed* for the loss year.

Similarly, repayment supplement on any repayment arising out of a carryback claim does not relate to the payment dates for the carryback year. Supplement is not payable unless the claim is given effect after 31 January following the loss year, and in that event it runs from that 31 January (see Example 43 for an illustration).

Losses and registered pension scheme contributions

6. See Example 37 explanatory note 15 for the effect of loss claims on earnings for registered pension scheme contributions.

Losses and tax credits

7. This example illustrates the need for all self-employed persons, working full-time and over 25, to make a protective claim for tax credits each year. When William Smith made a claim in July 2006 it is probable that he expected to make a profit for 2006 and therefore was not entitled to tax credits. In the event the business incurred a loss and an award of £3,993 is payable. If he had waited until the loss was quantified then the award is only paid from three months prior to claim ie for a claim on 1 July 2007 payment is only made from 1 April 2007 to 5 April 2007. Thus William Smith has lost £3,938 by not making a protective claim.

The initial claim for trading loss relief under tax credits is always against the joint income of the claimants (Mr & Mrs Smith) in the year of loss. There are no provisions for carry back.

Any remaining trading loss for tax credits is carried forward and relieved against the first available later profits for tax credits from the same trade (SI 2003/2815). This will not normally be the same amount carried forward as for TA 1988 s 385 (see note 1 above). William Smith has excess trading loss for tax credits of £1,255 in 2006/07 which is carried forward to 2007/08 and relieved against expected trading profits of £11,000. This would apply regardless of the claim made for loss relief for income tax or capital gains. Thus if William Smith had decided to make a s 385 claim only the carry forward to 2007/08 would be £16,000 relieved as to £11,000 in that year with a further carry forward of (say) £5,000, for income tax but the tax credit claim would be as above.

The loss claims for income tax, Class 4 national insurance and tax credits are all stand-alone claims. In this example William Smith may obtain relief for his trading loss as to:

	£
Income tax (say without CGT) 2005/06	2,512
2007/08 £1,280 @ 22% – Income tax	281
£6,000 @ 8% – Class 4 NIC	480
Tax Credits (claim made 1 July 2006)	3,993
Tax Credits 2007/08	3,993
	11,259

An effective rate on a loss of £16,000 of 70%.

You have been consulted by R Bridges, aged 30, who commenced business as an engineering consultant on 1 August 2005. He had previously been employed, his taxable salary being:

2002/03   £36,000

2003/04   £26,000

2004/05   £26,000

He was unemployed from 6 April 2005 to 1 August 2005, receiving taxable benefits of £1,785.

He has a part-time bookkeeper who has prepared a draft profit and loss account to 31 March 2007 covering the first twenty months' trading which showed:

	£	£
Fees receivable		27,384
Less: Office rent, rates and insurance	9,344	
Office salaries	7,527	
Travelling expenses	1,210	
Motor expenses	4,740	
Stationery, postages and telephone	2,079	
Professional indemnity insurance	2,400	
General expenses	385	27,685
Loss for the period		(301)

You ascertain:

(i)   On 1 August 2005 Bridges bought a motor car for £15,400 which he used both for business and private purposes as to three-quarters and one-quarter respectively.

(ii)   At the same time he bought a computer and printer for £1,400 and subsequently purchased a scanner in August 2006 for £600. The scanner has been included in Stationery in the accounts.

(iii)   Although expenses accrued evenly over the entire period, of the total fees receivable only £5,617 related to the first eight months. Fees receivable and expenses are estimated to be the same for April 2007, but profits are now increasing strongly and are expected to reach £35,000 in the year to 31 March 2008 and to continue to rise thereafter.

(iv)   Bridges is a single man. His savings income has been:

	Building society interest (gross amounts)	Dividends (including dividend tax credits)
	£	£
2002/03	2,100	1,300
2003/04	1,400	600
2004/05	1,000	920
2005/06	2,500	1,100
2006/07	1,400	300

Assume the savings income remains the same for 2007/08 to 2009/10 ie Interest £1,400 gross Dividends and tax credits £300.

(v)   Bridges is registered for VAT and all amounts are shown net of recoverable input tax.

(vi)   Bridges informed the tax and national insurance offices of his self-employment in October 2005. He has paid Class 2 contributions from commencement. He received a 2005/06 tax return in April 2006, but has not yet completed it.

(vii)   You have agreed with Bridges to advise on the optimum tax claims, and will prepare accounts either to 31 March 2006 (and 2007) or for twenty months to 31 March 2007.

Tax data:

	2002/03 £	2003/04 £	2004/05 £	2005/06 £	2006/07 £
Personal allowance	4,615	4,615	4,745	4,895	5,035

Tax rates:

10% on	1,920	1,960	2,020	2,090	2,150
Basic rate	22%	22%	22%	22%	22%
Basic rate limit	29,900	30,500	31,400	32,400	33,300
Savings rate on income up to basic rate limit	20%	20%	20%	20%	20%
Dividend rate on income up to basic rate limit	10%	10%	10%	10%	10%

40% higher rate tax thereafter, or dividend upper rate of 32.5%.

Advise Bridges on how to finalise his draft accounts for submission to HMRC, and on his optimum loss claim(s), and compute the tax payable or repayable for 2005/06 and 2006/07.

Comment on the availability of a claim for tax credits for 2006/07.

The alternatives suggested are to complete accounts for two separate periods of eight and twelve months, or to complete accounts for twenty months to 31 March 2007.

The profits or losses and tax payable under each alternative are:

(1)   **Two Accounts**

	£	8 months to 31.3.06 £		12 months to 31.3.07 £
Fee income		5,617		21,767
Expenses	27,685			
Less: Scanner	(600)			
One-quarter car expenses	(1,185)			
Divisible 8 : 12	25,900	(10,360)		(15,540)
Capital allowances (see below)		(2,060)		(2,760)
		Loss (6,803)	Profit	3,467

Capital allowances	Car £		Pool £	Total allowances £
Period 1.8.05 to 31.3.06:				
Purchases	15,400		1,400	
WDA (8/12 × 3,000 max)	(2,000)	× 75%		1,500
FYA 40%			(560)	560
	13,400		840	2,060
Period 1.4.06 to 31.3.07:				
WDA	(3,000)	× 75%	(210)	2,460
Addition Aug 2006			600	
FYA 50%			(300)	300
WDV cf	10,400		930	2,760

Assessable profits				£
2005/06 (1.8.05 to 31.3.06)				–
Loss in basis period			6,803	
S 381 loss claim 2002/03			(6,803)	
2006/07 (yr to 31.3.07)				3,467

Tax repayable

Taxable income:				2002/03 £	2005/06 £	2006/07 £
Employment income				36,000	1,785	–
Trading income						3,467
Building society interest				2,100	2,500	1,400
Dividends (including tax credits)				1,300	1,100	300
				39,400	5,385	5,167
Less: Loss relief under s 381				(6,803)		
				32,597		
Less: Personal allowance				(4,615)	(4,895)	(5,035)
				27,982	490	132

Tax repayable following loss claim:

			Tax without Loss Claim £	Tax with Loss Claim £
Taxable Income (27,982 + 6,803)			34,785	27,982

Without Loss	*With Loss*	*Tax Rate*		
1,920	1,920	@ 10%	192	192
–	1,300	@ 10%		130
–	2,100	@ 20%		420
27,980	22,662	@ 22%	6,156	4,986
1,300	–	@ 32½%	422	
3,585	–	@ 40%	1,434	
Saving	£2,476		8,204	5,728
Tax repayable following loss claim				(2,476)

				2005/06	2006/07
Tax @ 10%				49	13
Less: Non-repayable tax credits				(49)	(13)
Tax due				–	–
Tax deducted at source on building society interest @ 20%				(500)	(280)
Tax repayable				(500)	(280)

Total repayable: (2,476 + 500 + 280) 3,256

Notes: Although Bridges has earnings below the Class 2 national insurance contributions exemption limits (2005/06 £4,345), repayment for 2005/06 had to be claimed by 31 December 2006. It is possible that Bridges would prefer to maintain a full national insurance record for maximum benefits.

No Class 4 contributions are due, but as the loss has been fully relieved against non-trading income, an equivalent loss can be carried forward for Class 4 purposes from 2005/06 to 2006/07. After deducting £3,467 in that year (on which no contributions would in fact have been payable), £3,336 of the loss remains to be carried forward to 2007/08.

(2)   **One Set of Accounts**

20 months to 31.3.07
£

Loss per draft accounts	(301)
Scanner	600
One-quarter car expenses	1,185
	1,484
Capital allowances (see below)	(4,750)
Revised loss	(3,266)

Capital allowances	Car		Pool	Total allowances
	£		£	£
Period 1.8.05 to 31.7.06:				
Purchases	15,400		1,400	
WDA (max)	(3,000)	× 75%		2,250
FYA 40%			(560)	560
	12,400		840	
Period 1.8.06 to 31.3.07:				
WDA (8/12)	(2,000)	× 75%	(140)	1,640
Addition Aug 06			600	
FYA 50%			(300)	300
WDV cf	10,400		1,000	4,750

Assessable profits		£	£
2005/06 (1.8.05 to 5.4.06)			–
Loss in basis period 8/20 × £3,266		1,306	
S 381 loss claim 2002/03		(1,306)	
2006/07 (yr to 31.3.07)			–
Loss in basis period 12/20 × £3,266		1,960	
S 381 loss claim 2003/04		(1,960)	

Tax repayable	2002/03	2003/04	2005/06	2006/07
	£	£	£	£
Employment income	36,000	26,000	1,785	–
Trading income			–	–
Building society interest	2,100	1,400	2,500	1,400
Dividends (including tax credits)	1,300	600	1,100	300
	39,400	28,000	5,385	1,700
Less: Loss relief under s 381	(1,306)	(1,960)		
	38,094	26,040		
Less: Personal allowance	(4,615)	(4,615)	(4,895)	(5,035)
	33,479	21,425	490	–
Tax repayable:				
1,306 @ 40%	(522)			
1,960 @ 22%		(431)		
Tax payable @ 10%			49	
Less: Non-repayable tax credits			(49)	
			–	

Tax repayable		*2005/06*	*2006/07*
		£	£
Tax deducted at source repayable to Bridges			
Building society interest @ 20%		(500)	(280)
Total repayable: (522 + 431 + 500 + 280)			£1,733

Note: Similar comments apply re Class 2 national insurance contributions as for separate accounts. For Class 4, again the loss has not been relieved against trading income, the loss carried forward being £3,266.

Tax Credits

	£	£
Income for base year (2004/05)		
Employment income		26,000
Investment income – Building Society	1,000	
– Dividends	920	
	1,920	
Less:	300	1,620
		27,620

Eligibility

R Bridges worked full-time throughout and is aged over 25. He is eligible but the award based on 2004/05 income will be nil, as his income is too high.

When he commenced self-employment on 1 August 2005 he should have claimed working tax credits (WTC) within three months ie by 2 November 2005. If he had done so he would have been entitled to WTC for the period 1 August 2005 to 5 April 2006 at the rate of:

WTC claim (per day)			
Basic	4.44		
30 hours	1.81		
248 days ×	6.25	=	£1,550

Although income for 2004/05 is too high, the revised income based upon actual income for 2005/06, gives a full award.

Income – 2005/06 (two sets of accounts)		
Taxable benefits		1,785
Building society interest	2,500	
Dividends (including tax credits)	1,100	
	3,600	
Less	300	3,300
		5,085
Less: Loss (two accounts)		(6,803)
Loss to achieve in 2006/07		(1,718)
Income for tax credits		nil
or		
One set of accounts		
Income as above		5,085
Less: Loss		(1,306)

		3,779
Loss Income threshold		5,220
no restriction of WTC		nil

If the claim is made after 7 July 2006, and therefore no WTC is payable for 2005/06, the loss is still deemed to have been used in 2005/06 as set out above.

If he had made a provisional claim for tax credits for 2006/07 by 7 July 2006, then his claim for 2006/07 would be:

(i)   **Two Accounts – 2006/07**

	£	£
Self-employment		3,467
Investment income – Building Society	1,400	
– Dividends	300	
	1,700	
Less:	300	1,400
		4,867
Less: loss brought forward		(1,718)
		3,149
WTC claim (per day)		
Basic	4.57	
30 hours	1.87	
365 days ×	6.44	£2,350

As income is below £5,220 no restriction.

(ii)   **One Account – 2006/07**

	£	£
Self-employment		nil
Investment income (as above)		1,400
		1,400
Less: Loss for year	1,960	
Loss carried forward	(560)	(1,400)
WTC – as above		£2,350

For 2007/08 the tax credits income will be provisionally based upon 2006/07 and a full award will be made.

However, when the income for that year is known the award will be withdrawn in part depending upon the profits for that year as follows:

		Two Accounts £	One Account £
Profit for y/e 31.3.08		35,000	35,000
Investment income – Building Society	1,400		
Dividends	300		
	1,700		
Less:	300	1,400	1,400
		36,400	36,400
Less: Loss brought forward			(560)

	Two Accounts £	One Account £
	36,400	35,840
Income disregard	25,000	25,000
	11,400	10,840
Threshold	5,220	5,220
	6,180	5,620
× 37%	£2,287	£2,079
As the maximum WTC (using 2006/07 rates) is:		
366 × £6.44	2,357	2,357
Reused award	70	278

The difference in tax credit award between one set of accounts or two is therefore not likely to exceed £208.

Overall conclusion on accounts submission

As the income tax repayment is 3,256 – 1,733 = £1,523 lower with one account compared with two accounts, it is advisable to submit separate accounts to HMRC, even though the tax credits award may be £208 lower on that basis.

Explanatory Notes

Notifying new sources of income and sending in tax returns

1. The rules for opening years' assessments do not prevent a taxpayer deciding the period covered by the first accounts. If a tax return is not received, however, HMRC must be notified not later than 5 October following the tax year that a new source of income has been acquired, ie by 5 October 2006 in the case of Bridges. For further details see Example 16 explanatory note 4. For Class 2 national insurance, a business is required to notify HMRC immediately. A penalty of £100 is payable if notification is not made within three calendar months after the calendar month of commencement unless profits are below the small earnings exemption limit (SI 2001/1004 reg 87 – see Example 47 part (a) for details). Notification for national insurance is also regarded as notification for tax purposes.

    Although Bridges notified HMRC in good time, he should have sent in his 2005/06 tax return by 31 January 2007. Failure to send in the return normally attracts a fixed penalty of £100, rising after six months (see Example 40 note 11), but the fixed penalty cannot exceed the tax payable for the year, which in this case is nil (and in fact Bridges is entitled to a refund of the tax deducted from his savings income).

Effect of basis periods: overlap relief, tax credits, cessation

2. For the basis periods in the opening years see Example 16 explanatory note 3.

    Where accounts are made up to 31 March annually, the problem of overlap profits does not arise. If accounts are made up other than to 31 March (or 5 April), and the accounts for the opening period show a loss, then it is probable that the overlap relief available will be nil. For example, if Bridges had made up accounts for the 21 months to 30 April 2007 showing a loss of £3,266, his assessments would be:

2005/06 (1.8.05 to 5.4.06)		Nil
S 381 loss available 8/21 (carryback to 2002/03) =	£1,244	
2006/07 (6.4.06 to 5.4.07)		Nil
S 381 loss available 12/21 (carryback to 2003/04) =	£1,866	
2007/08 (yr to 30.4.07)		Nil
S 381 loss available 1/21 (carryback to 2004/2005) =	£156	

(Overlap period 1.5.06 to 5.4.07 = 11 mths shows loss, therefore overlap relief nil. There is no doubling up of losses and the loss for the period 1.5.06 to 5.4.07 is allowed in 2006/07 only.)

As a consequence of the above, Bridges would waste most of his personal allowance in 2007/08, he would not use his starting rate band, and he would not be able to set off his dividend tax credits. He would, however, have no tax liability in that year and his claim for tax credits would be significantly increased.

With a 30 April year-end full tax credits (as calculated for 2006/07 above) would be claimable (subject to claim by 6 July within the tax year) for:

2006/07	£2,345
2007/08 (using 2006/07 rates)	£2,345

If, for example, Bridges had ceased business on 31 March 2010, having made profits as follows, assuming the same profits for years/periods to 31 March or 30 April for simplicity:

Year to 31 March or 30 April 2008	£30,000
Year to 31 March or 30 April 2009	£36,000
Year or 11 months to 31 March 2010	£27,500

With 31 March year-end, he would have been taxed on those profits in 2007/08, 2008/09 and 2009/10, amounting to £93,500, with possibly a small higher rate tax liability in 2008/09.

With 30 April year-end, he would have assessable profits as follows:

			£
2007/08			–
2008/09			30,000
2009/10	Yr to 30.4.2009	36,000	
	11 mths to 31.3.2010	27,500	
		63,500	
	Less overlap relief	–	63,500
			93,500

Although the total assessable profits are the same with either year-end, it is clear that a significant amount of higher rate tax would be payable for 2009/10 with the 30 April year-end. This would need to be set against the benefit of paying no tax in 2007/08, paying less tax in 2008/09 and the increased tax credits in 2007/08 as above. The effect on Class 4 national insurance contributions also needs to be considered (see note 7 below).

Relief under TA 1988 s 381 for losses in early years

3.   Where a loss is incurred in any of the first four tax years of a new business, relief may be claimed under TA 1988 s 381 against the *total income* of the previous three tax years, *earliest* first. TA 1988 s 382(3) provides that losses for s 381 (and s 380) are not only *calculated* in the same way as profits, but for the *same periods*. This is subject to subsection (4) of s 382, which provides that where a loss would otherwise enter into the computations for two successive tax years, it is not taken into account in the second year.

4.   As with TA 1988 s 380, relief cannot be claimed under s 381 unless the trade is conducted on a commercial basis with a view of profit, and under s 381 it is also necessary to show that a profit could reasonably have been expected in the loss period or within a reasonable time thereafter.

Capital allowances

5.   Capital allowances are treated as trading expenses of the accounting period and writing down allowances are proportionately reduced or increased if the period is less than or more than 12

months. If, however, the period exceeds 18 months, it is split into a 12 month period plus the remainder, as illustrated in the example in relation to the twenty month account (see Example 18 part (b)).

Repayment supplement

6. For losses, repayment supplement on repayments arising from carryback claims is payable from 31 January following the loss year (TMA 1970 Sch 1B). It runs to the date the repayment order is issued (see Example 43).

National insurance

7. The amounts payable (using 2006/07 rates for later years) with a 31 March year-end would be:

31 March y/e		2005/06	2006/07	2007/08	2008/09	2009/10
		£	£	£	£	£
Class 2		109*	109*	109	109	109
Class 4		–	–			
(30,000 – 3,266 – 5,035) @ 8%				1,736		
(33,540 – 5,035) @ 8%					2,280	
(36,000 – 33,540) @ 1%					25	
(27,500 – 5,035) @ 8%						1,797
Total	£6,383	109	109	1,845	2,414	1,906

* Subject to a claim for repayment for small earnings exemption if made. Whereas with a 30 April year-end the liability would be:

30 April y/e		2005/06	2006/07	2007/08	2008/09	2009/10
		£	£	£	£	£
Class 2		109*	109*	109*	109	109
Class 4						
(30,000 – 3,266 – 5,035) @ 8%					1,736	
(33,540 – 5,035) @ 8%						2,280
(63,500 – 33,540) @ 1%						300
Total	£4,861	109	109	109	1,845	2,689

* Subject to a claim for repayment for small earnings exemption if made.

Giving a saving of £1,522 (6,383 – 4,861).

Effect of accounting date on loss claims

8. There are points for and against making up accounts to a date early in the tax year (see notes 2 and 7 above and Example 17). Where losses are concerned, making up accounts to 30 April restricts the losses that may be taken into account in s 381 claims where successive losses are made in the early years of a new business. For example, if such a business started on 1 May 2004, the first accounts being either for the 11 months to 31 March 2005 or for the 12 months to 30 April 2005, the position regarding s 381 claims would be:

	Accounts to 31 March	Accounts to 30 April
2004/05	Loss of 11 months to 31.3.05	11/12 x loss to 30.4.04
2005/06	Loss of yr to 31.3.06	1/12 x loss to 30.4.05
2006/07	Loss of yr to 31.3.07	Loss of yr to 30.4.06
2007/08	Loss of yr to 31.3.08	Loss of yr to 30.4.07

The s 381 loss claims would cover 47 months with the 31 March year-end and only 36 months with the 30 April year-end.

Overall, if there is a loss in the opening period which will cause personal allowances and lower rate bands to be wasted, and it is expected that significant amounts of higher rate tax will be payable in the near future, it is advisable to use a 31 March (or 5 April) year-end. The position on tax credits (see explanatory note 2) and national insurance (see explanatory note 7) should also be considered.

Anti-avoidance provisions

9.   TA 1988 s 381 contains anti-avoidance provisions to prevent husband and wife transferring a trade from one to the other after the first four years of assessment and effectively starting again.

TA 1988 ss 118ZE to 118ZK restrict the relief for trading losses in the first four years of assessment to capital contributions made by the partner where the claimant is a partner who does not spend a significant amount of time personally engaged in the trade. See Example 34 part (e).

Miscellaneous

10.   Bridges needs to show his accounting results in his tax returns in 'Standard Accounts Information' format. For an illustration see Example 15. For capital allowances on plant see Example 20, for the disclaimer rules see Example 19 and for the rules on VAT registration see Example 17 part (b). For rules on tax credits see Example 5.   .

(a)   Hamilton commenced trading on 1 January 2005, making up accounts annually to 31 December. He made a loss of £18,000 in the year to 31 December 2005. Show how the loss will be taken into account for tax purposes.

What would be the overlap relief position if Hamilton made up an account of 18 months from 1 January 2007 to 30 June 2008, having made a profit of £36,000 in the previous 12 months. Assume the change of accounting date complies with the requirements of the legislation.

(b)   Riddell started a new business on 1 December 2005 and had the following results:

6 months from 1 December 2005 to 31 May 2006	Profit	£9,000
Year to 31 May 2007	Loss	£20,400
Year to 31 May 2008	Profit	£16,200

Show the alternative ways in which Riddell could obtain relief for his loss, assuming that he has enough other income to obtain full relief for any loss claimed under TA 1988 s 380 or s 381.

(c)   Raleigh, a single man, commenced business on 1 July 2005, making up accounts annually to 30 June. He had been employed at a salary of £10,000 per annum up to that date, but his business became his only source of income. His profits for the year to 30 June 2006 were £36,000. His early profitability was not sustained, and subsequent results were as follows, Raleigh having decided to change his accounting date to 31 December in 2008:

Year to 30 June 2007	Profits	£28,000
18 months to 31 December 2008	Profits	£13,000

Show Raleigh's taxable business profits for all relevant years and indicate what claims are available to him.

(d)   Drake, a single man who had been in business for many years, making up accounts to 30 April, had the following results (after capital allowances) in recent years:

Year to 30 April 2004	Profit	£30,000
Year to 30 April 2005	Profit	£24,000
Year to 30 April 2006	Loss	£18,000

His transitional overlap profit was £34,000, the overlap period being 340 days. He has no other sources of income.

(i)   Show his tax position for the relevant years;

(ii)   Show what the position would have been if he had changed his accounting date to 31 March, and had made a loss of £16,500 in the 11 months to 31 March 2006.

For tax rates and allowances see Example 30.

Class 4 national insurance contributions are payable on the following profits:

2004/05	£4,745 to £31,720 @ 8% and 1% thereafter
2005/06	£4,895 to £32,760 @ 8% and 1% thereafter
2006/07	£5,035 to £33,540 @ 8% and 1% thereafter

(a) **Hamilton – losses and overlap relief**

Loss of £18,000 in first year to 31 December 2005 will be taken into account as follows:

2004/05   1.1.05 – 5.4.05   Loss, therefore assessment nil. 3/12 x £18,000 = £4,500 loss
available for relief under s 380 and/or s 381.

2005/06   1.1.05 – 31.12.05   Loss, therefore assessment nil. Balance of loss, ie £13,500, available for relief under s 380 and/or s 381.

Any part of the loss of £18,000 not relieved under s 380 or s 381 would be carried forward under s 385.

For overlap relief purposes, even though there is a loss in the first 12 months, there is an overlap from 1.1.05 to 5.4.05, ie 3 months to the nearest month, with an overlap profit of nil. This must be aggregated with any subsequent overlap to establish the amount of overlap profit and the period to which it relates.

The 18 month account to 30 June 2008 would result in the following basis periods (see Example 28):

2006/07   Year to 31 December 2006
2007/08   Year to 30 June 2007
2008/09   Year to 30 June 2008

There is therefore a 6 months' overlap from 1.7.06 to 31.12.06 with overlap profits of £18,000. This is aggregated with the previous overlap to give a total overlap period of 9 months with a total overlap profit of (nil + £18,000 =) £18,000. If at a later date Hamilton changed his accounting date back to 31 December (again complying with the requirements of the legislation), he would be taxed on 18 months' profits at that time, reduced by *6/9ths* of the overlap profits of £18,000, ie £12,000, leaving overlap profits of £6,000 for 3 months to carry forward.

(b) **Riddell – losses and overlap relief**

2005/06   1.12.05 – 5.4.06
            4/6ths x £9,000 profit   £6,000

2006/07   Since no 12 month account ends in the second year, the
            basis period is 1.12.05 to 30.11.06:
            Profit to 31.5.06   9,000
            Loss 1.6.06 – 30.11.06 (6/12 x £20,400)   (10,200)

            Loss available for relief   £ (1,200)

            Profit   nil

            Profit of £9,000 is offset by an equivalent amount of loss in arriving at nil assessment. £6,000 of the profit of £9,000, ie for the 4 months from 1.12.05 to 5.4.06, is an overlap profit for which overlap relief will be available (see explanatory note 1).

2007/08   Basis period is 1.6.06 to 31.5.07 but cannot include loss to 30.11.06 since already taken into account in 2006/07. Since there is still a loss in the remainder of the period, the assessment is nil and the loss available for relief is 6/12 x £20,400 = £10,200.

            There is a further overlap period of 6 months from 1.6.06 to 30.11.06 with an overlap profit of nil (since there is a loss in the period). This is aggregated with the previous 4 month overlap period to give a total overlap period of 10 months with an overlap profit of (6,000 + nil =) £6,000.

2008/09   Assessable profit £16,200.

£9,000 of the loss was offset against profit in arriving at the nil assessment for 2006/07. If relief for the 2006/07 loss of £1,200 and the 2007/08 loss of £10,200 has been claimed against other income, the loss will therefore have been fully relieved. If no claims have been made against other income, there will be losses of £11,400 brought forward to set against the 2008/09 assessment.

(c)   **Raleigh's tax position**

Assessable business profits are as follows:

				£
2005/06	1.7.05 – 5.4.06	9/12 x 36,000		24,000
2006/07	Yr to 30.6.06			36,000
(overlap profits 1.7.05 to 5.4.06 £24,000)				
2007/08	Yr to 30.6.07			28,000
2008/09	1.7.07 – 31.12.08		13,000	
	Less: overlap profits			
	6/9 x 24,000		16,000*	
	Loss		3,000	
	Therefore assessable profit			nil

* 3 months' overlap relief amounting to £8,000 carried forward.

Raleigh has a loss of £3,000 for 2008/09, for which s 380 relief may be claimed against his total income of 2008/09 or 2007/08. Since the 2008/09 income is nil, the claim will be made for 2007/08. Before loss relief his tax position for 2007/08 is:

			£
Business profits			28,000
Personal allowance			5,035
Taxable income			22,965
Tax thereon (using 2006/07 rates):	2,190	@ 10%	219
	20,775	@ 22%	4,571
	22,965		4,790

The loss of £3,000 will therefore save tax of £3,000 @ 22% = £660.

There will also be a saving in Class 4 national insurance contributions because the profits of £28,000 are below the upper earnings limit of £33,540 (2006/07 rates), so that the reduction to £25,000 gives a saving of £3,000 @ 8% = £240.

Although *calculated* by reference to Raleigh's 2007/08 tax position, the loss relief will be given in relation to the tax year of loss, ie 2008/09. If he has made any 2008/09 payments on account, they will be refunded, as will the tax saving of £900 from the loss claim (see explanatory note 3).

(d)   **Drake's tax position – loss with change of accounting date**

(i)   *Tax position for relevant years*

		£
2004/05 (yr to 30.4.04)		30,000
2005/06 (yr to 30.4.05)		24,000
2006/07 (yr to 30.4.06)		nil
Loss available for relief	£18,000	

Relief for the loss could be claimed in 2006/07 or in 2005/06. Assuming no other income, the carryback to 2005/06 would be preferable unless Drake is likely to be a higher rate taxpayer in 2007/08 (yr to 30.4.07).

Tax position	2004/05	2005/06 before loss	2005/06 after loss	2006/07
	£	£	£	£
Trading income	30,000	24,000	24,000	nil
Less: S 380 loss claim			(18,000)	
			6,000	
Less: Personal allowance	(4,745)	(4,895)	(4,895)	
	25,255	19,105	1,105	
Tax: 2,020/2,090/1,105 @ 10%	202	209	110	
23,235/17,015 @ 22%	5,112	3,743	–	
	5,314	3,952	110	
Class 4 NIC:				
8% × (30,000 – 4,745)	2,020			
8% × (24,000/6,000 – 4,895)		1,528	88	
	7,334	5,480	198	nil
Tax and NIC repayable			£5,282	

(ii)   *With change of accounting date to 31 March 2006*

Assessments	£	£
2004/05 – as above		30,000
2005/06 (1.5.04 to 31.3.06)		
yr to 30.4.05 Profit	24,000	
period ended 31.3.06 Loss	(16,500)	
	7,500	
Less: overlap relief	(34,000)	nil
Loss available for relief	(26,500)	

The loss may be relieved in 2005/06 or 2004/05. Assuming no other income, the carryback to 2004/05 would be preferable unless Drake is likely to be a higher rate taxpayer in 2006/07 (ie accounts year ended 31 March 2007).

Tax position	2004/05 before loss	2004/05 after loss	2005/06
	£	£	£
Trading income	30,000	30,000	nil
Less: S 380 loss claim		(26,500)	
		3,500	
Less: Personal allowance	(4,745)	(3,500)	
	25,385	nil	
Tax and NIC (as above)	7,334	nil	nil
Tax and NIC repayable		£7,334	(and no liability in 2005/06)

By changing his accounting date to a date nearer to 5 April, Drake has increased his available loss by means of overlap relief. In this example he has fully used the available overlap relief, as the change is to 31 March, and as a result has wasted part of his personal allowances. A change to 28 February would give an estimated repayment of:

	£
2005/06 (1.5.04 to 28.2.06)	
yr to 30.4.05	24,000
period ended 28.2.06 (say)	(14,000)
	10,000
Less: overlap relief 309/340 × 34,000	(30,900)
Loss available for relief	(20,900)

	2004/05 after loss £
Trading income	30,000
Less: S 380 loss claim	(20,900)
	9,100
Less: Personal allowance	(4,745)
	4,355
Tax: 2,020 @ 10%	202
2,335 @ 22%	514
	716
Class 4 NIC (9,100 – 4,745) @ 8%	348
	1,064

With a February year-end the loss of £1,500 in March (and £1,500 in April) would reduce the assessable profits of 2006/07 (yr ended 28.2.07) and overlap relief of £34,000 – £30,900 = £3,100 would be carried forward at the cost of £1,064 payable for 2004/05. This is not as favourable as the position with the 31 March year-end.

Explanatory Notes

Overlap profits and overlap period

1. Under the current year basis, care needs to be taken in the calculation of overlap profits and the overlap period.

   ITTOIA 2005 s 204 defines an overlap profit as profits which arise in a period which falls within two basis periods (HMRC has stated that overlap periods may be calculated in days, months, or months and fractions of months providing the chosen method is used consistently). The Revenue's booklet SAT 1 paragraph 4.6 states that any overlap period must be identified as such, even if it shows a loss, and the period must be aggregated with any subsequent overlap period, as illustrated in parts (a) and (b) of the example. This affects the amount of overlap relief that may be claimed where more than 12 months' profit is being taxed in one year because of a change of accounting date.

2. Transitional overlap profits qualifying for relief on the change to the current year basis (see Example 16 explanatory note 8) are treated as overlap profits (ITTOIA 2005 Sch 2.52).

3. As indicated in Example 29 explanatory note 1(b), s 380 losses under the current year basis are calculated for the same periods as profits (TA 1988 s 382(3)). Where, therefore, there is an account of more than 12 months showing a loss, the loss is the loss of the tax year in which that account ends. The loss in such an extended basis period is increased by the appropriate amount of overlap relief.

In part (c) of this example, the long account does not in itself show a loss, but the profit is turned into a loss by the overlap relief deduction. In part (d) of the example the change of accounting date to a date nearer to 5 April enhances the available loss relief, and also has the effect of turning a profit into a loss.

See Example 42 for the way in which relief arising from carryback loss claims is given and the position regarding repayment supplement.

National insurance contributions

4. National insurance contributions are dealt with in Example 47.

Tax Credits

5. Examples 5, 29 and 30 set out the rules for tax credits and the interaction with trading losses. It should be noted that any loss relieved under income tax provisions by way of carryback does not apply for tax credits. The unreduced profits and income of the earlier year are included in the computation of income for tax credits. The loss as computed for a fiscal year is initially offset against the joint income for tax credits of the claimants, any remaining trading loss for tax credits is then carried forward and relieved against the first available profits of the same trade for tax credits only.

(a)   Sewell has been trading as a sole trader for many years, making up accounts to 30 September each year. As a result of serious decline in trade he decided to cease trading at 31 January 2007.

His results after capital allowances for the last few periods of trading have been:

Profit (loss)	£
Year ended 30 September 2003	21,000
Year ended 30 September 2004	15,000
Year ended 30 September 2005	6,000
Year ended 30 September 2006	5,000
4 months to 31 January 2007	(20,000)

Overlap relief available was £11,579.

   (i)   Compute the amount of losses arising and show how these losses may be relieved.

   (ii)   State what alternative form of relief is available to Sewell if the trade were to be transferred to a limited company solely in exchange for shares in the company.

(b)   From the following details of the income of Waterloo, a sole trader who has been carrying on the business of light engineering since 1970, show details of all taxable profits covered by the figures given and how relief for the loss on cessation may be obtained.

Tax adjusted profits or losses (after capital allowances):

		Profit	*Loss*
		£	£
Year ended 30 June	2004	10,500	
	2005	13,200	
	2006	8,000	
10 months to 30 April (when business ceased)	2007		9,600

Overlap relief available was £9,900.

Patent royalties of £500 (gross amount) per half year were payable on 31 March and 30 September annually. The last payment was made on 31 March 2007.

Waterloo is a single man and he has no income other than from the business.

(c)   Trafalgar, a single man, ceased business on 30 June 2006. His results in the period leading up to the cessation were as follows:

Year to 31 December 2003	Profit	£8,000
Year to 31 December 2004	Profit	£13,000
Year to 31 December 2005	Profit	£4,000
6 months to 30 June 2006	Loss	£19,200
Overlap relief available was		£5,800

Trafalgar had previously had no other sources of income, but he took up employment after ceasing trading and earned £15,000 in 2006/07.

Show the alternative loss claims available to Trafalgar and calculate his tax position for the relevant years. For tax allowances and rates for years before 2006/07 see Example 30, for Class 4 national insurance rates see Example 31, and for earlier years.

2003/04   £4,615 to £30,940 @ 8% and 1% thereafter

2004/05   £4,745 to £31,720 @ 8% and 1% thereafter

(a)   (i)   **Sewell – terminal loss relief**

The position before loss relief is as follows:

			£
2003/04	(yr to 30.9.03)		21,000
2004/05	(yr to 30.9.04)		15,000
2005/06	(yr to 30.9.05)		6,000
2006/07	(1.10.05 to 31.1.07)		
	To 30.9.06	5,000	
	To 31.1.07	(20,000)	
	Loss	(15,000)	

The whole of any available overlap relief is included in the terminal loss of the final tax year (see explanatory note 5).

The losses available for relief are calculated as follows (see explanatory notes 1 to 5):

TA 1988 s 380

Loss of 2006/07 comprises the loss of £15,000 in the 16 months to 31 January 2007, augmented by the overlap relief of £11,579, giving a loss of £26,579.

TA 1988 s 388 terminal loss

£5,000 of the loss has already been relieved against the profit of the year to 30 September 2006 in arriving at the 2006/07 nil assessment and cannot be included in the terminal loss. The terminal loss is therefore as follows:

Loss	1.2.06 – 5.4.06:	
	Profit therefore	–
Loss	6.4.06 – 31.1.07:	
	To 30.9.06 6/12 x 5,000 profit	(2,500)
	To 31.1.07 (20,000 – 2,500 loss already	
	relieved against balance of profit)	17,500
	Overlap relief	11,579
		£ 26,579

The same amount is thus available for relief both under s 380 and s 388.

If Sewell has no other income the terminal loss would be relieved against trading profits as follows:

2006/07		–
2005/06		6,000
2004/05		15,000
2003/04	(reducing assessable profit to £15,421)	5,579
		£ 26,579

Had any loss remained unrelieved after setting against the 2003/04 profit, no further relief would be available.

Personal allowances of 2004/05 to 2005/06 would be wasted.

If Sewell has other income, the s 380 claim would be against the *total* income of 2006/07 and/or 2005/06. Unless the other income is very substantial, however, the terminal loss claim would still be preferable, because it would leave the other income to cover personal allowances.

(ii) **Alternative relief available to Sewell**

If the trade were transferred to a limited company solely in exchange for shares, then so long as the shares continued to be held, the loss could be carried forward and relieved against income received by Sewell from the company, both earned income (eg director's fees) and unearned income (eg dividends) (see explanatory note 7).

(b) **Waterloo – Assessable profits and relief for losses**

The tax position before relief for the loss on cessation is as follows:

		£
2004/05	(yr to 30.6.04)	10,500*
2005/06	(yr to 30.6.05)	13,200*
2006/07	(yr to 30.6.06)	8,000*
2007/08	(10 months to 30.4.07 being loss of £9,600)	nil

* In each of 2004/05, 2005/06 and 2006/07 Waterloo's net total income is £1,000 less than the assessable profits, because he has to account for the tax deducted from the patent royalties. The amount available for loss relief in each year is reduced accordingly.

Claims under TA 1988 s 380 are not relevant, since Waterloo has no income other than from the business. The position is therefore as follows:

Terminal loss relief under s 388			£
Loss 1.5.06 – 5.4.07:			
1.5.06 – 30.6.06	Profit 2/12 x 8,000	(1,333)	
1.7.06 – 5.4.07	Loss 9/10 x 9,600	8,640	7,307
Loss 6.4.07 – 30.4.07	1/10 x 9,600	960	
	Overlap relief (see explanatory note 5)	9,900	10,860
Terminal loss available for relief			18,167
Set against:			
2006/07 profits (8,000 – 1,000 re patent royalties)			(7,000)
2005/06 profits (balance)			(11,167)
			–

Leaving profits assessable in 2005/06 of (13,200 – 11,167) = £2,033, which cover the patent royalties of £1,000 paid in that year.

(c) **Trafalgar – loss relief available on cessation of business**

Before loss relief claims Trafalgar's taxable profits are as follows:

		£
2003/04 (yr to 31.12.03)	Profit	8,000
2004/05 (yr to 31.12.04)	Profit	13,000
2005/06 (yr to 31.12.05)	Profit	4,000
2006/07 (6 mths to 30.6.06)	Loss	–

If terminal loss relief is claimed under TA 1988 s 388, followed by s 380 claim

Terminal loss relief   £

Loss 1.7.05 – 5.4.06:
    Profit 1.7.05 – 31.12.05 6/12 x 4,000   (2,000)
    Loss 1.1.06 – 5.4.06 3/6 x 19,200   9,600   7,600

Loss 6.4.06 – 30.6.06 3/6 x 19,200   9,600
    Add overlap relief (see explanatory note 5)   5,800   15,400

Terminal loss available for relief   23,000

Since there are no trading profits in 2006/07, the terminal loss will be relieved as follows:

	£
2005/06	4,000
2004/05	13,000
2003/04	6,000
	23,000

Leaving assessable profits in 2003/04 of (8,000 – 6,000 =) £2,000.

Relief under s 380

Loss of 2006/07 (19,200 + overlap relief 5,800)   25,000
Less already relieved   23,000

Loss available for relief   2,000

Trafalgar's 2006/07 income of £15,000 will be reduced to £13,000.

If loss relief is claimed under TA 1988 s 380, followed by s 388 claim

Relief under s 380   £

Loss of 2006/07 (19,200 + overlap relief 5,800)   25,000
Set against 2006/07 employment income   15,000

Loss remaining unrelieved   10,000

There would be no point in making a s 380 claim for 2005/06 since there is no non-trading income and the terminal loss claim is available against the trading profits.

Terminal loss relief

The part of the terminal loss relieved under s 380 is regarded as being (15,000 – 2,000) = £13,000, since £2,000 of the s 380 loss is not included in the terminal loss (see explanatory notes 2 and 4(b)). The terminal loss is therefore as follows:

Loss 1.7.05 – 5.4.06:   £
    Profit 1.7.05 – 31.12.05   (2,000)
    Loss 1.1.06 – 5.4.06 3/6 x 19,200   9,600

                            7,600
    Less already relieved under s 380   (7,600)   –

Loss 6.4.06 – 30.6.06 as above   15,400
    Less already relieved under s 380 (13,000 – 7,600)   (5,400)   10,000

Terminal loss available for relief   10,000

This will be set against the 2005/06 profits of £4,000 and £6,000 of the 2004/05 profits of £13,000, leaving £7,000 assessable for that year.

Tax position with alternative loss claims

Taxable income after loss claims	Terminal loss relief first £	S 380 claim first £
2003/04	2,000	8,000
2004/05	–	7,000
2005/06	–	–
2006/07	13,000	–
	15,000	15,000

Tax and Class 4 NIC payable				
2003/04	(2,000 – 4,615)		–	
	(8,000 – 4,615)	= 3,385 @ 10%/22% + 8%		781
2004/05	(7,000 – 4,745)	= 2,255 @ 10%/22% + 8%	–	434
2006/07	(13,000 – 5,035)	= 7,965 @ 10%/22% + 8%	2,131	–
			2,131	1,215

There is therefore a reduction of £916 in the tax and Class 4 NICs payable if the s 380 claim is made first. Under self-assessment there is no longer any repayment supplement advantage from carryback claims, and there is a disadvantage in terms of payments on account (see Example 29 explanatory note 5).

Explanatory Notes

Calculation of losses available for relief

1. Under the current year basis rules, losses under ss 380 and 381 are calculated not only in the same way as profits but also for the *same periods* (subject to excluding any loss already included in a previous tax year where basis periods overlap) (TA 1988 s 382(3)). The terminal loss rules have not, however, been properly adapted to fit in with the accounting period treatment, and terminal losses still have to be calculated separately for the parts of the last twelve months falling up to and after the end of the tax year. This may restrict the terminal loss available for relief where there is a profit in part of the last twelve months (see note 4(a)), eg in part (c) of the example £2,000 of the loss of £19,200 in the last six months does not form part of the terminal loss, although Trafalgar does in fact get relief for it under s 380 because he has other income in 2006/07 (see note 2).

2. Where more than one loss claim is available in respect of a loss, the strict position is that losses that reduce trading profits (such as terminal losses) take priority over losses that reduce total income (such s 380 losses). If, however, relief under s 380 has become final before relief is given under s 388, the s 380 relief will not be altered. The HMRC Manuals state that in practice a taxpayer may choose which claim he wishes to become final first.

    The effect of making alternative claims is shown in part (c) of the example. The calculation of the terminal loss where the s 380 claim is made first is not clear. The view has been taken that the amount of relief given under s 380 may be regarded as covering first that part of the loss that is excluded from the terminal loss because of the way in which the terminal loss is calculated. This enables relief to be given overall for the full amount of the loss in that example. It is considered that this approach would be acceptable to HMRC.

Calculation of terminal loss and relief available

3. The terminal loss is calculated in two stages as follows (TA 1988 s 388):

    (a) (i) Trading loss in tax year in which business ceases, calculated from 6 April to date of cessation.

(ii) That part of any *trade charges* of the year of cessation on which tax has been paid under TA 1988 s 350 (ie charges that could have been carried forward as a trading loss under TA 1988 s 387 had the business continued – see explanatory note 6).

(b) (i) Fraction of trading loss of penultimate year which when added to the period in (a)(i) makes up a twelve month period.

(ii) The same fraction as in (b)(i) of any s 350 assessment on trade charges in that year.

4. The following points should be noted:

(a) If 3 (a) or (b) is a profit it is treated as nil in the computation – it is *not* deducted from the terminal loss, as shown in part (a) of the example. If, however, there is a profit for *part* of the period concerned, it is taken into account in *arriving at* the loss for (a) or (b), as shown in parts (a) and (b) of the example.

(b) The terminal loss cannot include any loss for which relief has already been obtained (eg under s 380 or s 385). See note 2 regarding the interpretation of this provision.

If a terminal loss claim is made, the loss is set first against the trading profits of the final tax year and then against the trading profits of the three previous tax years, latest first.

Overlap relief

5. ITTOIA 2005 s 205 provides for overlap relief to be taken into account in computing the result of the *tax year of cessation*. This means that it does not need to be apportioned over the last 12 months in the terminal loss calculation. This is confirmed by paragraph 4.30 of the Revenue's self-assessment guide SAT 1. For the calculation of transitional overlap relief see Example 16 explanatory note 8.

Treatment of charges

6. Where charges have been paid out of which tax has been retained at source, they reduce the amount of profits available to be used in a s 380 or terminal loss claim, as indicated in part (b) of the example. Where profits have been used to pay *non-trade* charges in a year in which terminal loss relief is given, the terminal loss for which relief may be obtained for earlier years must be reduced by the same amount (TA 1988 s 388(5)). As charges on income are now seldom encountered for income tax purposes, terminal loss restriction in relation to non-trade charges will rarely apply.

If the charges *exceed* the available profits, basic rate tax on the excess has to be paid under TA 1988 s 350. Where the charges are wholly and exclusively for the purposes of the trade, however, the amount on which tax has been paid under s 350 can be regarded as a *trading loss* to carry forward (TA 1988 s 387), or where appropriate, as part of a *terminal loss* to carry back, as indicated in note 4 (s 389). As for non-trade charges, trade charges will now rarely be encountered, and these reliefs will rarely apply.

Transfer of a business to a company

7. Where a business is transferred to a company by a sole trader or partners in exchange solely or mainly for shares in the company, then it is provided by TA 1988 s 386 that any income from the company, such as director's fees and dividends, can be regarded as trading income for the purposes of a s 385 loss claim, providing that the business has been carried on and the shares held throughout the tax year for which the claim is made (or in the tax year in which the transfer takes place, for the whole of the remainder of that year). In practice HMRC give the relief providing at least 80% of the shares are retained.

A. Rodney Rogers is a single man who has been farming in England since 1970 and has interest on savings of £6,000 (gross) per year.

His recent results (after capital allowances) have been:

Year ended	Profit (loss)
	£
30 April 2002	30,000
30 April 2003	20,000
30 April 2004	18,000
30 April 2005	(9,000)
30 April 2006	21,000

(a) State the original assessable profits for all relevant tax years, assuming that a s 380 loss relief claim was made for the first available year, and

(b) State the amended profits for all years assuming that Rodney makes claims for 'averaging relief' wherever possible and assuming that a s 380 loss relief claim is made for the most advantageous year.

(c) Comment on the effect of the averaging adjustments, and include a summary of Rodney's tax credit position.

B. Harold Pendragon had farmed Tintrim Farm for many years.

In 2004 Harold moved from Tintrim Farm to Bishops Farm, but the move was unsuccessful, so he moved in April 2005 to Green Leasowes Farm.

His recent farming results (after capital allowances) were as follows, accounts always having been prepared to 30 April:

				£
9 months ended 31 January 2004	Tintrim Farm	Profit	54,200	
3 months ended 30 April 2004	Bishops Farm	Loss	(12,000)	42,200
11 months ended 31 March 2005	Bishops Farm	Loss	(11,000)	
1 month ended 30 April 2005	Green Leasowes	Profit	2,450	(8,550)
Year ended 30 April 2006	Green Leasowes	Profit		40,000

Harold, who is a single man, has savings income taxed at source of £3,000 gross per annum (none of it being dividends).

(i) Calculate Harold's income for all years affected by the above trading results, making averaging and loss claims to the best advantage, and show the effect on Class 4 national insurance contributions.

(ii) Show the effect of the averaging claims on payments on account, assuming claims are made to reduce such payments based upon the most favourable averaging/loss choice.

Relevant allowances and tax bands are as follows:

	Starting rate band 10% £	Basic rate threshold £	Personal allowance £	Income limit for higher rate tax £
2002/03	1,920	29,900	4,615	34,515
2003/04	1,960	30,500	4,615	35,115
2004/05	2,020	31,400	4,745	36,145
2005/06	2,090	32,400	4,895	37,295
2006/07	2,150	33,300	5,035	38,335

Class 4 national insurance contributions are payable at the rates indicated on profits between the following limits:

2002/03	@ 7% on	£4,615 to £30,420
2003/04	@ 8% on	£4,615 to £30,940 and 1% thereafter
2004/05	@ 8% on	£4,745 to £31,720 and 1% thereafter
2005/06	@ 8% on	£4,895 to £32,760 and 1% thereafter
2006/07	@ 8% on	£5,035 to £33,540 and 1% thereafter

A.   **Rodney Rogers**

(a)   *Original assessable profits for 2002/03 to 2006/07 assuming s 380 claim made for first available year*

		£	£
2002/03	(yr to 30.4.02)		30,000
2003/04	(yr to 30.4.03)		20,000
2004/05	(yr to 30.4.04)	18,000	
	Less s 380 claim re loss of yr to 30.4.05	(9,000)	9,000
2005/06	(yr to 30.4.05) Loss, therefore		–
2006/07	(yr to 30.4.06)		21,000

(b)   *Amended assessments for 2002/03 to 2006/07 assuming averaging relief claimed wherever possible and assuming s 380 claim made for most advantageous year*

Assessments before loss claims are:

		£		£
2002/03	(7/10ths = £21,000)	30,000	becomes	25,000
2003/04		20,000	becomes	25,000
		50,000		50,000
2003/04	(7/10ths = £17,500, 3/4 = £18,750)	25,000	becomes	22,750
2004/05		18,000	becomes	20,250
	Difference	7,000		

		£
x 3 =		21,000
Less 3/4 x £25,000		18,750
Deduct from higher and add to lower		2,250

		£		£
2004/05	(7/10ths = £14,175)	20,250	becomes	10,125
2005/06		–	becomes	10,125
		20,250		20,250
2005/06		10,125	becomes	15,562
2006/07	(7/10ths = £14,700)	21,000	becomes	15,563
		31,125		31,125

It will be better to claim loss relief in 2005/06 rather than 2004/05 (see part (c)). Assessments after loss claims will therefore be as follows:

		£	£
2002/03			25,000
2003/04			22,750
2004/05			10,125
2005/06		15,562	
	Less s 380 claim re loss of yr to 30.4.05	(9,000)	6,562
2006/07	(subject to any averaging claim re 2007/08)		15,563

(c)   *Effect of averaging adjustments*

Where an averaging adjustment decreases the income of an earlier year, this does not result in any change to the self-assessment of that year, because although the *tax saving* is calculated according to the tax position of the earlier year, the claim is *given effect* for the later year (see explanatory note 6).

Averaging 2002/03 and 2003/04 is worthwhile because it eliminates the higher rate tax in 2002/03. However, had it exceeded the Class 4 NIC threshold of £30,420 for 2002/03, it would have increased the NIC liability (subject to further averaging).

Averaging 2003/04 and 2004/05 does not, in fact, achieve any immediate tax saving because no higher rate tax was payable in either year.

Without an averaging claim for 2004/05 and 2005/06, there would be no trading income in 2005/06 because of the loss. There is £6,000 of non-trading income. Averaging brings income into 2005/06 to cover the balance of the starting rate band. Claiming relief for the 2005/06 loss in 2004/05, however, would reduce the trading income of that year to only £1,125, thus wasting most of the nil rate Class 4 band. It would be better to make the loss claim for 2005/06, at the same time making an averaging claim for 2005/06 and 2006/07 to increase the 2005/06 trading income to £15,562 (time limit for loss claim 31 January 2008). After setting off the loss of £9,000, there is then sufficient income remaining (trading income £6,562 plus savings income £6,000) to cover the personal allowance nil rate Class 4 NIC and starting rate bands. If 2005/06 and 2006/07 were not averaged, the trading income of £10,125 plus savings income of £6,000 would be reduced to £7,125 after the loss claim, so that part of the Class 4 nil rate band would be wasted.

The effect of averaging on Class 4 contributions payable by Rodney is as follows:

Class 4 NICs payable:

	No averaging		Averaging	
	Profit	Class 4	Profit	Class 4
	£	£	£	£
2002/03	30,000	1,777	25,000	1,427
2003/04	20,000	1,231	22,750	1,451
2004/05	9,000	340	10,125	430
2005/06	–	–	6,562	133
2006/07	21,000	1,277	15,563	842
		4,625		4,283

From 2002/03 to 2006/07 there is a net reduction of £342.

Tax credits

For tax credits the farming income is before averaging. For 2003/04 that would amount to £20,000 and a nil award would be made. Assuming Rodney had made a protective claim by 7 July 2005 he would be entitled to tax credits in 2005/06 of:

Eligibility – working full-time and aged over 25. Yes.

	£	£
Income: Investment income	6,000	
Less	300	5,700
Trading loss (y/e 30.04.05)		(9,000)
Unrelieved trading loss carried forward		(3,300)
WTC (per day)		
Basic	4.44	
30 hours	1.81	
365 days ×	6.25	£2,281

For 2006/07 his provisional claim will be based upon the income of 2005/06, ie nil, and Rodney Rogers would receive a tax credit award of:

WTC claim (per day)

Basic	4.57	
30 hours	1.87	
365 days ×	6.44	£2,350

His actual income for 2006/07 for tax credits would be:

		£
Investment income (or above)		5,700
Trading income (y/e 30.04.06)	21,000	
Loss brought forward	(3,300)	17,700
Tax credits income for 2006/07		23,400
Provisional income for 2006/07 (based on 2005/06)		nil
Disregard first £25,000 of increase		23,400
		23,400
		nil

Rodney will keep the WTC paid in 2006/07 of £2,350 but in computing a claim for 2007/08 his income will be provisionally based upon the 2006/07 income of £23,400 and therefore no award is due for 2007/08.

B. Harold Pendragon

(i) Total income and Class 4 national insurance contributions

(a) *Assessable profits, subject to averaging* (see explanatory note 8)

		£
2004/05	yr to 30.4.04	42,200
2005/06	yr to 30.4.05 (Loss of £8,550)	–
2006/07	yr to 30.4.06	40,000

Relief for the loss of £8,550 for 2005/06 may be claimed under s 380 in 2005/06 or 2004/05, or the loss may be carried forward to 2006/07.

(b) *Possible farmer's averaging adjustments*

		£		£
Profits if all three years	2004/05	42,200	becomes	21,100
are averaged	2005/06	–	becomes	21,100
		42,200		42,200
	2005/06	21,100	becomes	30,550
	2006/07	40,000	becomes	30,550
		61,100		61,100
Profits if only 2004/05	2004/05			21,100
and 2005/06 are averaged	2005/06			21,100
	2006/07			40,000

(c) *Total income, taking into account averaging and loss claims*

Averaging all three years will eliminate the higher rate tax for 2004/05 and 2006/07. Relief for the loss should then be claimed in 2005/06, thus reducing the tax of that year and reducing the payments on account required for 2006/07. If losses are carried back, the tax saving from the loss claim does not reduce payments on account for *any* year (see explanatory note 6).

Higher rate tax could be substantially eliminated by averaging only 2004/05 and 2005/06, and carrying the loss forward to reduce the profits of 2006/07. This would, however, result in more tax being paid at an earlier stage and increase the payments on account required for 2006/07. Furthermore there would be less Class 4 NICs saving because the loss would reduce profits above the NICs 8% ceiling of £33,540.

The best overall position is achieved by averaging all three years and claiming relief for the 2005/06 loss against the income of that year. This gives the following results:

	2004/05 £	2005/06 £	2006/07 £
Farm profits (a)	42,200	–	40,000
Averaging adjustments (b)	(21,100)	30,550	(9,450)
Case I assessable profits	21,100	30,550	30,550
Savings income	3,000	3,000	3,000
	24,100	33,550	33,550
Loss relief under s 380		(8,550)	
Total income	24,100	25,000	33,550

(d) *Effect on Class 4 national insurance contributions*

		2004/05 £	2005/06 £	2006/07 £
Profits before averaging, with 2005/06 loss set against 2004/05 profits (i)		33,650	–	40,000
Profits after averaging and loss claim (ii)		21,100	22,000	30,550
Contributions payable				
(i)	31,720 – 4,745 @ 8% ⎱	2,177		
	33,650 – 31,720 @ 1% ⎰			
(ii)	21,100 – 4,745 @ 8%	1,308		
(i)	–		–	
(ii)	22,000 – 4,895 @ 8%		1,368	
(i)	33,540 – 5,035 @ 8% ⎱			
	40,000 – 33,540 @ 1% ⎰			2,345
(ii)	30,550 – 5,035 @ 8%			2,041
Increase/(decrease)		(869)	1,368	(304)

There is thus a net increase in national insurance contributions of £195.

(ii) **Effect of averaging claims on payments on account**

(a) *Before averaging claims*

		£	Tax £
2004/05	Trading income	42,200	
	Savings income	3,000	600
		45,200	
	Personal allowance	4,745	
		40,455	
Tax thereon:	31,400 @ starting and basic rates	6,666	
	9,055 @ 40%	3,622	
	40,455	10,288	
Class 4 NIC	(31,720 – 4,745) @ 8%		
	(42,200 – 31,720) @ 1%	2,263	12,551

Tax due by payments on account 31.1.05
and 31.7.05 with balancing payment 31.1.06 — 11,951

Note It is not possible to reduce this amount because of the loss/averaging claim to be made for 2005/06. The amount will be repayable in part when the 2005/06 return is filed.

2005/06	Payments on account due on each of 31.1.06 and 31.7.06 – half of £11,951	5,976

(b) *Following averaging claims re 2004/05 and 2005/06 and s 380 loss claim*

		£	Tax £
2004/05	Trading income	21,100	
	Savings income	3,000	600
		24,100	
	Personal allowance	4,745	
		19,355	
Tax thereon:	Non-savings income –		
	2,020 @ 10%, 14,335 @ 22%	3,356	
	Savings income 3,000 @ 20%	600	
		3,956	
Class 4 NIC (21,100 – 4,745) @ 8%		1,308	5,264
			4,664
Paid for year (as in (a))			11,951
Repayment given effect for 2005/06 on filing 2005/06 return			7,287
2005/06	Trading income	21,100	
	Savings income	3,000	600
		24,100	
	Less s 380 claim re loss of year	(8,550)	
		15,550	
	Personal allowance	4,895	
		10,655	

			£	*Tax* £
Tax thereon: Non-savings income				
2,090 @ 10%, 5,565 @ 22%			1,433	
Savings income				
3,000 @ 20%			600	
			2,033	
Class 4 NIC (21,100 − 8,550 − 4,895) @ 8%			612	2,645
				2,045
Payments on account due 31.1.06 and 31.7.06 as in (a)			11,951	
Reduced to actual following claim on form SA 303			9,906	2,045
2006/07	Payments on account due on each of			
	31.1.07 and 31.7.07 − half of £2,045			1,022

(c)   *Following averaging claim re 2005/06 and 2006/07*

		£	*Tax* £
2005/06	Trading income	30,550	
	Savings income	3,000	600
		33,550	
	Less s 380 claim re loss of year	(8,550)	
		25,000	
	Personal allowance	4,895	
		20,105	
Tax thereon:	Non-savings income −		
	2,090 @ 10%, 15,015 @ 22%	3,512	
	Savings income 3,000 @ 20%	600	
		4,112	
Class 4 NIC (22,000 − 4,895) @ 8%		1,368	5,480
			4,880
Paid for year (as in (b) above)			2,045
Due with 2006/07 liability			2,835

		£	*Tax* £
2006/07	Trading income	30,550	
	Savings income	3,000	600
		33,550	
	Personal allowance	5,035	
		28,515	
Tax thereon:	Non-savings income −		
	2,150 @ 10%, 23,365 @ 22%	5,355	
	Non-dividend savings income 3,000 @ 20%	600	
		5,955	
Class 4 NIC (30,550 − 5,035) @ 8%		2,041	7,996
			7,396
Payments on account per (b)			2,045
			5,351
Due for 2005/06 re averaging claim as above			2,835
Payable re 2006/07 on 31.1.08			8,186

| 2007/08 | Payments on account due on each of 31.1.08 and 31.7.08 – half of £7,396 | | 3,698 |
| | Total payable 31.1.09 | | 11,884 |

Summary of payments due

		£	£
2004/05	Total due by 31.1.06		11,951
2005/06	Due 31.1.06 (1st payment on account)	5,976	
	Reduced by claim	4,953	
	Revised amount due 31.1.06		1,023
	2nd payment on account due 31.7.06		1,022
2006/07	Due 31.1.07		1,022
	Due 31.7.07		1,023
	Balance due 31.1.08	8,186	
2007/08	1st payment on account due 31.1.08	3,698	11,884
Repayable re 2004/05 by claim with 2005/06 tax return			(7,287)

Tax Credits

As trading results are always taken before farmer's averaging Harold would be entitled to a payment of tax credits for 2005/06 of £2,281 (see above in part A(c) for computation) providing a protective claim was made by 7 July 2005. This is based upon a trading loss for 2005/06 of £8,550 and savings income of £3,000. There would be no claim for 2006/07 as trading profits for year ended 30 April 2006 (2006/07) amounted to £40,000 before averaging. Any provisional tax credits paid for 2006/07 between 6 April 2006 and date of notifying actual income for 2006/07 would be repayable.

Explanatory Notes

Averaging claims

1.   ITTOIA 2005 s 221 gives averaging relief for individuals and partnerships who are farmers or creative artists who make a claim in their tax return or an amended return. It need not be claimed unless required. Profits to be averaged are taken into account *after* capital allowances. The amount of capital allowances *claimed* may be varied using the disclaimer provisions (see Example 19). The profits taken into account for averaging are before deducting losses.

Time limits for claims

2.   The time limit for making averaging claims is 12 months from the 31 January following the end of the second tax year (eg by 31 January 2007 for an averaging claim for 2003/04 and 2004/05).

The averaging adjustment

3.   The averaging rules provide that if, in respect of consecutive years of assessment, profits in either year do not exceed 7/10ths of the other year or are nil, a claim may be made for the profits of each year to be adjusted so that one-half of the profits for the two years taken together, or for the year for which there are profits, is assessed in each year.

Where profits are nil because there is a loss, any independent claim for loss relief is not affected and in calculating available losses the original results and not the averaged results are used.

4.   Marginal relief is available where profits for either year exceed 7/10ths but are less than three-quarters of the profit for the other year. Profits for each year may then be adjusted by adding to those that are lower and deducting from those that are higher three times the difference between them less three-quarters of the higher profits. This is illustrated in part A(b) of the example in relation to the 2003/04 and 2004/05 assessments.

Once an averaging calculation has been done, the average itself is the figure to use if the next year's profits are to be averaged.

No claim can be made for the first and last years of assessment.

5.   A claim is nullified if profits for either year are adjusted for any other reason (for example because of a change of accounting date, or cessation of trade), but any further claim in respect of the profits as adjusted is not out of time if made before one year from 31 January following the tax year in which the adjustment is made.

Carryback claims under self-assessment

6.   The treatment under self-assessment of claims that affect an earlier year is that although the effect of the adjustment is *calculated* by reference to the tax position in the earlier year, the adjustment is *given effect* in the later year (TMA 1970 Sch 1B). The adjustment does not, however, affect the tax *assessed* for the later year. For taxpayers who are calculating their own tax, the amount of any tax underpaid for the earlier year is shown in box 18.4 on the return and any overpayment is shown in box 18.5.

Carried back amounts do not affect payments on account for the first of the two years that are averaged, because the tax of the earlier year is not adjusted. The payments on account for the second of the averaged years will initially be based on the unaveraged profits of the first year. Once the liability for the second year can be accurately ascertained, based on the averaged profits, a claim can be made to reduce payments on account if appropriate. The change to the assessable profit of the second year affects the payments on account for the next following year, which are based on the tax *assessed* for the second year.

The treatment of averaging claims under self-assessment means that even if an averaging adjustment which reduces the profits of the current year does not save any tax overall, because it is balanced by an increase of the same amount in the tax payable for the previous year, a cash flow advantage will still arise. This is because the reduction in the current year's tax reduces the payments on account for the next following year. Furthermore, if the reduction of the current year's liability reduces the amount payable below the payments on account made for that year, repayment supplement will be payable on the overpaid amounts as at 31 January in the tax year and 31 July following, even though the overpayment will be balanced by an underpayment for the previous year, that underpayment being payable by 31 January following the current year.

Thus in part B(ii) of the example, the repayment based on 2004/05 does not alter the payments for that year, or payments on account for 2005/06, but is repayable after any outstanding tax (and tax due within 35 days) is settled. Once the revised liability for 2005/06 is known, a claim may be made to reduce payments on account for that year to the revised liability, repayment supplement being paid where appropriate. Following the next claim to average 2005/06 with 2006/07, this increases the liability for 2005/06, the increase being added to the tax due for 2006/07 (ie on 31 January 2008) but the adjustment does not affect the payments on account for any year, nor does it affect the tax *assessed* for 2006/07, so that the payments on account for 2007/08 are based on the 2006/07 tax due of £7,996 less the tax of £600 deducted at source.

Interest on overdue or overpaid tax is charged from 31 January following the second year. There is therefore no interest benefit from an adjustment that reduces the tax of the earlier year as in 2004/05 in B(ii) above. On the other hand there is no interest disadvantage from an averaging adjustment that increases the tax of the earlier year as in 2005/06 in B(ii) above. And where the tax of the second year is reduced as a result of the adjustment, then interest will be paid on overpaid payments on account for the second year as indicated above. For detailed notes on carryback claims see Example 42.

Partnerships

7.   Under the current year basis, averaging claims are made by individual partners in respect of their shares of the profit and not in respect of the partnership as a whole.

Farming treated as one trade

8. In part B of the example, Harold's trade is treated as continuing notwithstanding his change of farms, since all farming carried on by any particular person is treated as one trade (ITTOIA 2005 s 9). Where the trade is carried on by a firm then that trade is separate from any farming trade carried on by an individual who is a partner of the firm (s 859).

Restrictions on relief for farming losses

9. The farmers in both parts of this example have made intermittent profits and losses. There are special rules where farmers sustain losses over a long period. A loss in the sixth tax year of a consecutive run of farming and market gardening losses (calculated before capital allowances) cannot be relieved other than by carrying forward against later profits of the same trade. The same applies to a loss in a company accounting period following a similar five-year run of losses (before capital allowances). The restriction does not apply if a competent farmer or market gardener could not have expected a profit until after the six-year loss period. If losses are required to be carried forward, any related capital allowances are similarly treated (TA 1988 s 397).

    Although under the current year basis rules, capital allowances are treated as trading expenses, and are thus part of a trading loss, losses are still calculated before capital allowances for the purpose of s 397.

National insurance contributions

10. For detailed notes on national insurance contributions see Example 47.

Tax Credits

11. For detailed notes on tax credits see Example 5 and for interaction with losses Example 29.

(a) Somerton, Tiverton and Dulverton have been in partnership for many years sharing profits and losses after charging interest on capital and salaries in the proportions of one-half, one-fifth and three-tenths respectively, drawing up accounts to 30 April annually. Interest on capital amounts to £3,200, £2,260 and £940 respectively. Dulverton is entitled to a salary of £16,000 and Somerton to a salary of £8,000.

The partnership results for the years to 30 April 2005 and 2006 are as follows:

		Profit (loss)
		£
Year to 30 April	2005	18,600
	2006	(9,600)

Show the tax allocation of trading profits and losses for the two years, and show what s 380 claims may be made assuming that the partners have substantial other income.

(b) John, Paul and George have been partners in a firm of turf accountants for many years, making up accounts annually to 31 July and sharing profits and losses in the ratio 40:35:25. The accounts for recent periods, as adjusted for tax purposes, have shown the following profits and losses:

	£
Year to 31 July 2005	53,200
Year to 31 July 2006	11,800
Period to 31 January 2007	(43,920)
Total of partners' overlap profits	
for 8 months from 1 July 1996 to 5 April 1997	19,867

On 31 January 2007 John retired due to ill health.

Calculate the assessable profits for 2005/06 and 2006/07 and show the allocation of these profits among the partners. Show also how the loss to 31 January 2007 is treated and indicate the loss claims available to each partner.

Ignore capital allowances.

(c) Greely is a limited partner in a partnership and under the partnership agreement his share of the profits or losses of the business is 25%. His capital introduced was £10,000.

During the year to 31 March 2007 the partnership suffered a loss of £60,000.

Calculate Greely's share of the loss for income tax purposes.

(d) Victoria became a member of Posh LLP, a trading limited liability partnership, on 6 April 2004, introducing capital of £10,000 into the LLP. The LLP makes up accounts annually to 5 April. During the year ended 5 April 2007 Victoria made a further capital contribution of £6,000. Victoria has sufficient other income to claim full loss relief under TA 1988 s 380 in all years.

The losses attributable to Victoria are as follows:

	£
Year to 5 April 2005	6,000
Year to 5 April 2006	6,000
Year to 5 April 2007	3,000

Set out the amounts of s 380 loss relief available for each year.

(e) Richard and Judy commence trading as property developers on 6 April 2006. The partnership is funded by capital introduced of:

Richard	£500,000
Judy	£10,000

It is agreed that Richard be entitled to a salary of £50,000 and profits and losses be divided equally. Richard works full time in the business but Judy only works five hours per week, on average, for the partnership.

The results for the first three years are:

	Profit (loss) £
Year to 5 April 2007	(100,000)
Year to 5 April 2008	(30,000)
Year to 5 April 2009	80,000

On 31 March 2009 Judy contributes further capital of £20,000. Both Richard and Judy have sufficient other income to utilise their share of losses for all relevant years. They have made no capital withdrawals from the partnership.

Set out the amount of s 380 or s 381 loss relief available for Richard and Judy for each year and the amount of loss relief carried forward after making maximum claims against other income.

(a) **Somerton, Tiverton and Dulverton**

Profit of year to 30 April 2005

	Total £	Somerton £	Tiverton £	Dulverton £
Interest on capital	6,400	3,200	2,260	940
Salaries	24,000	8,000	–	16,000
Balance ½, 1/5, 3/10	(11,800)	(5,900)	(2,360)	(3,540)
	18,600	5,300	(100)	13,400
Eliminate Tiverton's 'loss' 5,300:13,400		(28)	100	(72)
Division of assessable profit	18,600	5,272	–	13,328

The partners are individually assessable on their profit shares in 2005/06.

Loss of year to 30 April 2006 available for relief under s 380

	Total £	Somerton £	Tiverton £	Dulverton £
Interest on capital	6,400	3,200	2,260	940
Salaries	24,000	8,000	–	16,000
Balance ½, 1/5, 3/10	(40,000)	(20,000)	(8,000)	(12,000)
	(9,600)	(8,800)	(5,740)	4,940
Eliminate Dulverton's 'profit' 8,800:5,740		2,990	1,950	(4,940)
Final division of loss	(9,600)	(5,810)	(3,790)	–

Each partner's share of the loss is a loss of 2006/07 for s 380 claims, relief for which may be claimed against total income of 2006/07 and/or 2005/06 (see explanatory note 2). Since they have substantial other income, they will be able to obtain full relief in either year. If relief is claimed against 2005/06 income, Somerton's share of £5,810 would eliminate his profit share of £5,272 and the balance of £538 would be set against his other income. Since Tiverton's 2005/06 profit share was nil, his share of the loss, ie £3,790, would all be set against his other income. (The losses set against non-trading income would still be available to reduce the partners' later profit shares for calculating Class 4 national insurance contributions.)

Carrying back losses does not, however, reduce the tax of the earlier year (see Example 42 for details). Relief is *calculated* by reference to the earlier year but is *given effect* in relation to the loss year. Furthermore, the tax saving through the carryback claim does not affect the calculation of payments on account for any year (although the refund flowing from the loss claim may enable payments on account to be discharged or repaid). Somerton and Tiverton may prefer to claim relief against their 2006/07 income, providing the rate of tax saved was the same. This would then reduce the tax *assessable* for that year, enabling 2006/07 payments on account to be discharged or repaid and affecting the calculation of payments on account for 2007/08.

(b) **Assessments on John, Paul & George 2005/06 and 2006/07**

Under the current year basis, each partner is treated as if he carried on a separate notional trade, which ceases when he leaves the partnership, unless he continues the business on his own, in which case the actual date of cessation is taken. When John retires on 31 January 2007, therefore, his business is treated as having ceased and he can claim terminal loss relief if appropriate.

The accounting date has been changed by making up accounts to 31 January. Unless the partnership choose to notify the change to the Revenue, the accounts to 31 January 2007 could be regarded as interim (see Example 28). The next accounts could be made up for the six months to 31 July 2007 and the two sets of results amalgamated as far as Paul and George are concerned. On the assumption that the accounting date is in fact changed permanently, the position would be as follows:

Individual assessments 2005/06

The 2005/06 assessments are based on the profit of the year to 31 July 2005, which is divided as follows:

Total	*John (40%)*	*Paul (35%)*	*George (25%)*
£	£	£	£
53,200	21,280	18,620	13,300

Position for 2006/07

There will be nil assessments in 2006/07, since the basis period runs from 1.8.05 to 31.1.07 and the combined result of the accounts of that period shows losses for each partner as follows:

	Total	*John (40%)*	*Paul (35%)*	*George (25%)*
	£	£	£	£
Yr to 31.7.06	11,800	4,720	4,130	2,950
6 mths to 31.1.07	(43,920)	(17,568)	(15,372)	(10,980)
Loss in basis period		(12,848)	(11,242)	(8,030)

Division of overlap profits

	Total	*John (40%)*	*Paul (35%)*	*George (25%)*
	£	£	£	£
	19,867	7,947	6,953	4,967

As indicated in the example, the overlap relief covers the 8 months from 1 July 1996 to 5 April 1997. John's share of the overlap relief would be taken into account in full on the cessation of his business. Since the 2006/07 basis period spans 18 months, Paul and George would include in their allowable losses for 2006/07 a 6 months' proportion of their overlap relief, ie 6/8ths = £5,215 and £3,725 respectively, leaving overlap profits carried forward of £1,738 and £1,242 respectively.

Share of 2006/07 losses for s 380 claims

Under the current year basis, losses are calculated for the same periods as profits for s 380 claims. Available losses are therefore as follows.

	John (40%)	*Paul (35%)*	*George (25%)*
	£	£	£
Loss as above	12,848	11,242	8,030
Overlap relief	7,947	5,215	3,725
	20,795	16,457	11,755

Relief is available against the *total* income of 2006/07 and/or 2005/06. Although the partners' other income is not known, each has sufficient *trading* income in 2005/06 to obtain full relief for his loss share, although unless there is other income some of their personal allowance would be wasted. In addition to the tax saving, the loss claim would eliminate the 2005/06 Class 4 national insurance contributions. If loss relief was claimed against other income in 2006/07, John would lose the benefit of reducing Class 4 contributions, but Paul and George would be able to set the losses against later *trading* income for Class 4 purposes. If Paul and George did not wish to claim relief under s 380 their shares would be carried forward under s 385 to set against later trading profits.

John's loss for s 388 terminal loss claim

John's terminal loss is the loss from 1.2.06 to 31.1.07, excluding any loss for which relief has already been obtained, and including the *whole* of any available overlap relief. John had a loss of £12,848 in the 18 months' basis period for 2006/07, and the whole of his share of the profit of the year to

31 July 2006, ie £4,720, was taken into account in arriving at that amount. His loss of £17,568 has therefore been relieved to that extent, so that only £12,848 can be included in the terminal loss claim. This is then augmented by the overlap relief of £7,947 to give a terminal loss of £20,795, which is the same as under s 380. Since John has no trading income in 2006/07, this could be fully relieved against his 2005/06 trading profit. Had the loss been larger it could have been carried back against his 2004/05 profits and then his 2003/04 profits.

Effect of carryback claims

As indicated in part (a), carryback claims are *calculated* by reference to the tax position of the earlier year but are *given effect* for the later year (see Example 42 for details).

(c)   **Greely**

Greely's share of the loss of £60,000 for the year to 31 March 2007 is £15,000. Since his capital contribution is only £10,000, however, and he is a limited partner, he may not claim loss relief against income other than from the business on any amount in excess of £10,000, plus the amount of his undrawn profits, less any part thereof that has been offset by earlier losses.

(d)   **Victoria, partner in Posh LLP**

As a member of Posh LLP, Victoria is entitled to s 380 relief for her share of losses arising, subject to maximum loss claims not exceeding her subscribed capital. This restriction would not apply if the LLP carried on a profession.

Her s 380 loss claims are as follows:

2004/05	£6,000	(capital remaining £4,000)
2005/06	£4,000	(capital remaining nil, loss carried forward £2,000)
2006/07	£5,000	(capital contributed £6,000 of which £5,000 used, leaving £1,000 carried forward)

In 2006/07 her actual loss of £3,000 can be increased by the unrelieved loss of £2,000 brought forward. Because she has introduced further capital of £6,000, the full loss of £5,000 can be relieved under a s 380 claim for 2006/07 (TA 1988 s 118ZD).

(e)   **Richard and Judy**

Loss of year to 5 April 2007

	Total £	Richard £	Judy £
Salary	50,000	50,000	
Balance equally	(150,000)	(75,000)	(75,000)
	(100,000)	(25,000)	(75,000)

The 2006/07 assessments will be *nil* for both partners. Relief will be available under s 380 in 2006/07 or 2005/06 or under s 381 in 2003/04 against other income as follows:

	Richard £	Judy £
Loss as above	25,000	75,000
s 380/s 381 relief		
Restricted to contribution to trade	25,000	10,000
Restricted loss carried forward	–	65,000

Loss of year to 5 April 2008

	Total £	Richard £	Judy £
Salary	50,000	50,000	–
Balance equally	(80,000)	(40,000)	(40,000)
	(30,000)	10,000	(40,000)
Element of Richard's profit	–	10,000	10,000
	(30,000)	–	(30,000)

The 2007/08 assessments will be *nil* for both partners. Richard does not have a share of loss to use in a s 380/s 381 claim.

Judy has fully used her 'contribution to trade' and therefore can only add the loss of £30,000 to the amount of restricted loss brought forward of £65,000 to carry forward £95,000 to 2008/09.

Profit of the year to 5 April 2009

	Total £	Richard £	Judy £
Salary	50,000	50,000	–
Balance equally	30,000	15,000	15,000
	80,000	65,000	15,000

Richard will be assessed on profits of £65,000 in 2008/09.

Judy for 2008/09 has:

	£
Profits	15,000
Restricted loss brought forward	95,000
Available restricted loss	80,000
s 380/s 381 loss claim (being contribution to trade)	20,000
Restricted losses carried forward	60,000

Her assessment will be nil with relief for £20,000 given under s 380 in either 2008/09 or 2007/08, or under s 381 in 2005/06.

Explanatory Notes

Commencement and cessation

1. Each partner is treated as starting a new business when he joins a partnership (unless he previously carried on the business as a sole trader) and as ceasing business when he leaves, unless he continues the business on his own, in which case he will not be treated as ceasing until that business is permanently discontinued (ITTOIA 2005 s 852).

    As and when a partner is treated as ceasing business, he may claim terminal loss relief if appropriate (TA 1988 s 389(4)) (see part (b) of the example, and also Example 32).

    Losses are personal to the partners, so if anyone retires or dies with unrelieved losses, the losses cannot be transferred to the other partners.

Losses for s 380 claims

2. Under the current year basis rules, loss relief under s 380 is given against the income of the current and/or previous tax years.

Losses carried forward

3.   In calculating a loss available to carry forward under s 385, any loss that has been relieved in some other way must be excluded. This includes not only relief by way of another loss claim but also relief by aggregating the loss with a profit in arriving at the assessable result for a year. Hence the restriction on the losses available to be carried forward by Paul and George in part (b) of the example.

Unusual profit/loss allocations

4.   It is not possible for one partner to show a loss for tax purposes whilst there is an overall profit, and vice versa.

Hence the elimination of Tiverton's minus share in the year to 30 April 2005 and Dulverton's plus share in the year to 30 April 2006 in part (a) of the example. The amount that has to be eliminated is split between the other partners in the ratio of their shares of the original allocation.

If, exceptionally, the partnership agreement provides that losses are to be shared in a different proportion to profits and the accounting results show a profit whereas the taxable amount is a loss then the partnership agreement applies to the accounting results even if the effect is to divide the loss for taxation in a different proportion to that provided for by the partnership agreement.

In both of the above cases it would be possible to provide in the partnership agreement for a tax indemnity for any tax costs arising to a partner due to the taxable division being different to that provided for by the profit share in the partnership agreement.

Non-active partners

5.   From 10 February 2004 further restrictions on s 380, FA 1991 s 72 and s 381 claims are introduced for non-active general partners and non-active members of a limited liability partnership (TA 1988 s 118ZE to s 118ZK).

A claim under s 380, s 381 or s 353 (relief for payment of interest) is restricted to the individual's contribution to the trade where the individual did not personally work for a significant amount of time in the trade and the year is the year of commencement or one of the three following years of assessment (s 118ZE). This restriction does not apply to Lloyds Underwriters.

An 'individual's contribution to the trade' is defined in s 118ZG as the sum of

–   amounts subscribed (capital introduced) to the partnership

–   profits of the trade not withdrawn, and

–   amounts contributed to the partnership on its winding up

–   *less* capital withdrawn directly or indirectly within five years.

The test applies at the end of the year of assessment. There are anti-avoidance provisions to prevent the contribution to the trade being withdrawn shortly after loss relief has been claimed.

A 'significant amount of time' is defined in s 118ZH as an average of at least ten hours per week personally engaged in activities carried on for the purpose of the trade. The test applies for a relevant period, ie the basis period for the assessment, or if that period is less than six months (eg date of commencement to following 5 April or where basis period of cessation is less than six months) then the six months commencing from starting date or six months to date of cessation.

Any losses not claimable under s 380/s 381/s 353 because of the above restrictions can be carried forward as unrelieved losses of a non-active partner known as a 'restricted loss'. Relief is then available under s 380 (or s 381 in the first four years of trading) in a subsequent year of assessment in which the individual makes a contribution to the partnership or on its winding up (s 118ZI). This will include a year of assessment when the partner does contribute a significant amount of time to the partnership, and is not restricted to the first four years of trading.

The new rules apply where the basis period for the year of assessment includes 10 February 2004 and for subsequent basis periods. Where the basis period includes 10 February 2004 the loss relating to the period before that date is not affected by these provisions, and the balance of the loss is only claimable under s 380/s 381 insofar as it does not exceed the individual's contribution to the trade at the end of the year of assessment (s 118ZJ). In determining the apportionment of the loss it is deemed that the partnership drew up a set of accounts as at 9 February 2004 and that the claim for capital allowances arose at the time the capital expenditure was incurred.

Special relief is available for individuals who became a partner between 10 February 2004 and 25 March 2004 and who would be entitled to access a share of the loss arising before 10 February 2004 (s 118ZJ(8)).

Film partnership

6. Anti-avoidance legislation is introduced from 10 December 2003 and extended from 2 December 2004 to counter schemes where an investor in a film tax relief partnership seeks to convert a tax deferral into a permanent tax gain.

Limited partners

7. For detailed notes on limited partners and the treatment of their shares of losses, see Example 27 explanatory notes 9, 10 and 11.

Limited liability partnerships

8. For detailed notes on limited liability partnerships see Example 26 part (b) and explanatory notes 12 and 13.

National insurance contributions

9. For detailed notes on national insurance contributions see Example 47.

A. Harding, a married man born in 1954, is a British subject who is not resident in the UK.

His income for 2006/07 is:

	£
UK rental income (net amount after basic rate tax)	3,510
Interest (gross) from 3½% War Loan	1,500
Earnings from employment abroad	60,000
Interest from Canada (gross)	150

His employment is with a company resident outside the UK for whom he has worked for seven years and none of the duties are performed in the UK. The country in which he works is outside the European Community and he is not a servant of the Crown.

His wife accompanied him abroad, but is not working there, and she returns to their UK home for the main school holidays when their children aged 17 and 14 are home from boarding school (approximately two months each year). Both husband and wife are regarded as neither resident nor ordinarily resident in the UK. Mrs Harding has UK building society interest of £4,000 per annum (received in full), an annuity from a family trust of £4,500 per annum (from which basic rate tax is deducted), and interest of £250 on a foreign bank account.

Compute the amount of UK income tax payable by or repayable to Mr and Mrs Harding for the year 2006/07 assuming that any available relief is claimed.

Ignore double taxation.

B. Mr Carey, a single man, is a British subject who is domiciled, resident and ordinarily resident in the United Kingdom. He is taking up employment in France on 1 August 2006 and plans to make his permanent home there.

Relevant details of his tax position are as follows:

	2006/07 (to 31.7.06) £
Salary	7,200
Tax paid under PAYE	1,455
UK bank interest – amount received	24

The following additional information is available:

(a) He will retain the bank account and expects the interest credited on 31 December 2006 to be £100.

(b) He is renting out his house furnished and will get £180 per week (for twenty-eight weeks in 2006/07), which will be collected by an agent. The agent will deduct tax at the basic rate from the net rents and pay it over to HMRC.

Expenses are estimated at £1,500 for 2006/07, including mortgage interest from 1 August 2006.

(i) State what action Mr Carey should take in relation to his UK tax position before he leaves.

(ii) Show Mr Carey's estimated tax position for 2006/07, indicating the amount of tax refund which is likely to arise.

(iii) Show how Mr Carey's tax position would alter if he did not settle in France and returned to live in England in February 2008.

A. **United Kingdom income tax position 2006/07**

	UK income £	UK tax paid £
Mr Harding		
UK rental income (3,510 + 990)	4,500	990
Personal allowance	(4,500)	
Taxable income	–	
Tax repayable		990
Mrs Harding	£	£
UK annuity	4,500	990
UK building society interest	4,000	–
	8,500	990
Personal allowance	5,035	
Taxable income	3,465	
Tax thereon: 2,150 @ 10%	215	
1,315 @ 20%	263	478
Tax repayable		512

B. (i) **Action to be taken by Mr Carey before emigration**

(a) Arrange for agent to receive rental moneys and pay tax quarterly to HMRC on the net rental income.

(b) Write to notify HMRC that he is emigrating and asking for a self-assessment return to be sent in due course to enable him to claim a tax refund.

(c) Inform bank of his change in status and commence to receive interest gross.

(ii) **Estimated income tax position for 2006/07**

	£	£	Tax deducted £
Salary		7,200	1,455
Rental income (see explanatory notes 6 and 8)*		3,036	668
Bank interest**			
To 31.7.06 (24 + tax deducted 6)	30		6
December 2006	100	130	
		10,366	2,129
Personal allowance		5,035	
Income chargeable to tax		5,331	
Tax thereon: On non-savings income 2,150 @ 10%		215	
3,051 @ 22%		671	
On savings income 130 @ 20%		26	912
Refund due			1,217
* Rental income (28 weeks at £180)		5,040	
Less: Estimated expenses	1,500		
Wear and tear allowance			
10% of £5,040	504	2,004	
Amount assessable		3,036	

** £24 bank interest received to 31.7.06 is after deduction of 20% tax. £100 interest in December 2006 is received gross.

(iii)   **If Mr Carey resumed UK residence in February 2008**

If Mr Carey is absent from the UK only from 1 August 2006 to January 2008 his absence will not have spanned a tax year and he will be regarded as having remained resident and ordinarily resident in the UK throughout. He will be liable to UK tax on his earnings in France, subject to double tax relief for tax suffered in France. Since his UK income will have been fully charged to tax (see explanatory note 6) there will be no other change to his tax position (unless other income had arisen to him while he was in France). Tax will again be deducted at source from his bank interest.

Mr Carey should have submitted his 2006/07 tax return by 31 January 2008, but may not have received the calculated refund at the time he returns to the UK. He will need to notify an amendment to the return to bring the French earnings into charge and the tax position will need to be recalculated. Depending on the tax deducted by the French authorities he may still have overpaid tax for 2006/07. If not, however, he will be charged interest on any underpayment from 31 January 2008.

Explanatory Notes

Personal allowances for non-residents

1.   Non-residents are not entitled to UK personal allowances unless they qualify under the provisions of TA 1988 s 278, or under the terms of a double taxation agreement. The main categories of qualifying non-resident under s 278 are citizens of the UK, Commonwealth or Republic of Ireland, residents of the Isle of Man or Channel Islands and EEA nationals (the EEA covers the European Union plus Iceland, Liechtenstein and Norway). Non-residents will not normally be able to register as blind and will not therefore be entitled to blind person's allowance. The available allowances may be set against any of the person's income which is liable to tax in the UK (TA 1988 s 278).

To qualify for tax credits Mr or Mrs Harding have to be 'in the UK' (physically present here) and ordinarily resident within the meaning of the Tax Credits legislation (see TCTM02003 of the HMRC's Tax Credit Technical Manual as to how HMRC interpret ordinary residence for this purpose). It is unlikely that either Mr Harding or Mrs Harding would qualify as ordinarily resident under the tax credits tests so no entitlement to CTC will arise. If Mrs Harding was able to establish ordinary residence for the future she would make a claim for tax credits as a single person based on the number of days she was 'in the UK' (ignoring certain periods of temporary absence – see SI 2003/654 reg 4). Only her income would count in the tax credits claim.

Government 'FOTRA' securities

2.   Government securities are not liable to UK income tax whilst in beneficial ownership of persons not ordinarily resident in the UK (ITTOIA 2005 s 713). Such securities are referred to as FOTRA securities (Free Of Tax to Residents Abroad). The exemption does not, however, apply where the interest is received as part of a trade carried on in the UK.

UK dividend tax credits

3.   Non-residents are not automatically entitled to a tax credit on UK dividends (ITTOIA 2005 s 397). A person who claims UK personal allowances under TA 1988 s 278 is, however, entitled to a tax credit (s 397(4)). Sometimes a double tax agreement may provide for income that is not exempt from UK tax to be charged at a reduced rate, for example interest may be taxed only at 10%. Tax credits for non-residents are provided for in most double taxation agreements (TA 1988 s 788) and the agreement may provide that the UK tax is not to exceed 15% of the tax credit inclusive amount. Now that the UK tax credit rate is only 10% such a restriction is not relevant.

Although UK dividend tax credits are not repayable to UK residents, non-residents are still entitled to repayment under double tax agreements if the credit exceeds the rate under the agreement, but the reduction of the UK tax credit rate to 10% means that repayments will rarely arise.

Where a dividend is received by a non-resident who is neither within the categories entitled to UK allowances as in note 1, nor entitled to relief under a double tax agreement, he is liable to tax only on the tax credit exclusive amount and then only to the extent, if any, of higher rate tax over lower rate tax (ITTOIA 2005 ss 399 and 400).

Working/living abroad

4.   Someone who is working full-time abroad for a period spanning a complete tax year is treated as non-resident from the date of leaving the UK to the date of return, providing that UK visits during the absence are less than 183 days in any tax year, and average less than 91 days in a tax year (taken over a maximum of 4 years).

Be The residence status of a husband and wife is determined independently. Where, however, someone who satisfies the above conditions is accompanied or later joined abroad by his/her spouse, the same treatment applies to the accompanying/joining spouse, whether or not he/she works full-time abroad.

See Example 8 part A(i) for the treatment of those who leave the UK without taking up full-time employment abroad.

Split year treatment

5.   Strictly the question of whether a person is resident or not resident in the United Kingdom ought to be decided for the tax year as a whole. By Concession A11, however, the Revenue splits the year for a person either coming to the UK for permanent residence, or leaving the UK for permanent residence abroad. This concession also applies to someone going to take up full-time employment abroad, providing they are away for a complete tax year, the employment lasts throughout that tax year, and interim UK visits during the absence do not amount to 183 days or more in any tax year or an average of 91 days or more in a tax year (taken over a maximum period of 4 years). A further concession (A78) extends the same treatment to a non-working spouse accompanying or later joining his or her spouse who is working full-time abroad. For the split year rules in relation to capital gains tax see Example 73 part (c).

Where the tax year is split under Concession A11, the limit on income chargeable on non-residents outlined in note 6 does not apply for that tax year. Even though income for each part of the year is calculated according to whether the individual is, or is not, resident, full personal allowances are available for that tax year.

As Mr Carey emigrates in 2006/07 in part B of the example, therefore:

(a)   His income arising in 2006/07 after the date of emigration will be assessed as if he were not resident, ie no liability on his foreign income (his French salary) but liability on income arising in the UK (his rental income and bank interest).

(b)   Full personal allowances will be available for 2006/07.

(c)   From 2007/08 the provisions in note 6 will apply.

Taxation of non-residents

6.   There is a general requirement for tax at the 20% savings rate to be deducted from interest paid to a person whose usual place of residence is outside the UK (TA 1988 s 349(2)), but this is subject to various exceptions (see Example 6 part (a)). One of the exceptions covers banks and building societies, who will pay interest gross to deposit holders who provide them with a declaration that they are not ordinarily resident in the UK, and give their address abroad (TA 1988 s 481(5)(k)(i)).

Since 6 April 2001 banks, building societies etc have been required to provide information to HMRC on interest paid to depositors whether or not ordinarily resident in the UK. Paying and collecting agents who handle interest and dividends from abroad are included in the provisions.

In addition, FA 2006 replaced the existing arrangements for exchange of information with overseas jurisdictions with more extensive arrangements that will cover not only the exchange of information with overseas tax authorities in both directions, but will also allow for enforcement of foreign taxes in the UK, and of UK taxes abroad.

In April 2006, HMRC were successful in obtaining a disclosure order requiring Barclays Bank to provide details of accounts held overseas by customers with UK addresses. It is expected that further such orders will be obtained against other banks, and that much undeclared income will come to light.

In addition to being exempt from tax on interest on government stocks, and possibly on other sources of income under a double tax agreement (see notes 2 and 3), non-residents may receive social security benefits and investment income other than rents in full, even though such income is not exempt. The *maximum* tax payable by a non-resident is the tax, if any, deducted at source from such income plus the tax on any other income, calculated as if personal allowances were not available (FA 1995 s 128). If a claim is made for UK personal allowances, however, any non-exempt income is taken into account, which effectively means that the allowances are set against the untaxed social security benefits and investment income first.

Thus in part A of the example, both Mr and Mrs Harding have taxed UK income of £4,500. Mr Harding's only other UK income is *exempt* interest on government stocks, so his tax refund following his claim for UK allowances is the full amount of tax deducted, ie £990. Mrs Harding's building society interest, on the other hand, although received gross and not in itself chargeable to UK tax, has to be taken into account in the repayment claim, so she can only reclaim £512 of the £990 deducted from her annuity.

By comparison, if Mrs Harding's UK building society interest had amounted to £9,000, it would have been beneficial for her to forgo personal allowances and exclude the interest from her tax computation, thus having a repayment of:

		UK income £	UK tax paid £
UK annuity		4,500	990
Tax thereon:	2,150 @ 10%	215	
	2,350 @ 22%	517	732
Tax repayable			258

Had personal allowances been claimed the computation would have been:

		UK income £	UK tax paid £
UK annuity		4,500	990
UK building society interest		9,000	
		13,500	
Personal allowance		5,035	
		8,465	
Tax thereon:	2,150 @ 10%	215	
	6,315 @ 20%	1,263	1,478
Tax payable			488

In part B of the example, if Mr Carey remained non-resident, the bank interest would escape tax from 2007/08 if he did not claim allowances under TA 1988 s 278. In view of the level of his rental income, however, it is probable that he would make a claim for allowances, so that the bank interest would be taken into account in arriving at the UK tax payable.

A non-resident who carries on a trade in the UK (on his own or in partnership) is taxed on his profits that relate to the UK trade, measured on an arm's length basis.

This example sets out the basic principles of the taxation of non-residents. Reference must always be made to any relevant double tax agreements, the provisions of which override the tax legislation of the respective countries.

Temporary absences

7. If the absence abroad is not permanent and does not span a complete tax year, a person is regarded as remaining resident and ordinarily resident in the UK throughout. In part B(iii), Mr Carey's French salary would therefore be taxable as earnings, for details of which see Example 8.

Income from property letting

8. Although Mr Carey is letting furnished accommodation in his own home, the rent is not exempt under the rent a room relief provisions of ITTOIA 2005 part 7 Chapter 1, because the property will not have been his main residence at any time during the rental period (see Example 98 explanatory note 14). If, however, Mr Carey had shared occupation with the tenant before 1 August 2006 then a claim under the rent a room provisions would be available for 2006/07 only.

    Where rent is paid to someone who usually lives abroad, tax is normally deducted at the basic rate, as shown in the example, although tax need not be deducted in certain circumstances. For further details see Example 98 explanatory note 11.

Self-assessment

9. HMRC sometimes makes a provisional repayment to someone who emigrates if they have no continuing sources of UK income. This does not apply to Mr Carey in part B of the example, who will receive UK rents and bank interest.

    The self-assessment return contains a non-residence section which is aimed at enabling individuals to work out their own residence status. For further details see Example 8 part A(i). Using the form, Mr Carey would have worked out that he was entitled to split-year treatment for 2006/07, ie to be treated as non-resident from his date of departure, since he intended to be away until after 5 April 2008. He would therefore have excluded his French earnings from the return, and based on his expected liability for 2006/07 a repayment would have been due to him. If he returned in February 2008, however, the liability would change and he would need to notify an amendment to the return, as indicated in the example. The time limit for notifying an amendment is one year from the filing date for the return, ie by 31 January 2009 for the 2006/07 return.

Centre for Non-Residents

10. There is a separate HMRC Centre for Non-Residents which deals with operational and technical work (including compliance) relating to non-resident individuals, non-resident trusts and certain non-resident companies. Its operations include dealing with non-resident landlords and double tax relief claims, and providing advice to individuals on their residence and domicile status.

Payment of tax or national insurance in Euros

11. Any tax or national insurance can be paid in Euros. There is a helpline on 01274 539 630. The payment is converted at the current rate of exchange. Any overpayment is repaid in sterling.

(a)   During 2006/07 Johnson, a single man who is resident and ordinarily resident in the UK, has the following income:

	£
Salary from employment	35,495
UK bank interest (tax deducted £348)	1,740
Dividends	
From UK companies	810
From Ruritanian company	255
From Utopian company	385

The following foreign tax had been deducted from the overseas dividends before receipt:

Ruritanian company	45
Utopian company	315

and additionally the following underlying (indirect) tax had been suffered:

Ruritanian company	60
Utopian company	50

No double taxation agreements exist between either country and the United Kingdom and relief is given unilaterally.

Showing the workings of overseas credits, compute the amount of United Kingdom income tax remaining to be paid by Johnson for the year 2006/07 presuming that his salary had been subject to deduction of tax under PAYE of £6,443.

(b)   In 2006/07 Boswell, a married man aged 71 who is resident and ordinarily resident in the UK, had UK income comprising state pension £4,769, UK building society interest (gross) of £5,371, gross foreign interest from Ruritania of £2,000 on which the foreign tax was £300 and gross foreign interest from Narnia of £1,000 on which the foreign tax was £100.

Show his liability to UK tax if he claims double tax relief where appropriate. His wife is aged 66.

(a) **Income tax payable by Johnson for 2006/07**

					£
Salary					35,495
Bank interest					1,740
Dividends –	United Kingdom	(810 + 90)			900
	Ruritania	(255 + 45)			300
	Utopia	(385 + 315)			700
					39,135
Personal allowance					5,035
					34,100

Income tax thereon:

On non-savings income	2,150	@ 10%	215	
	28,310	@ 22%	6,228	
	30,460			
On savings income (non-dividend)	1,740	@ 20%	348	
	32,200			
On dividends (part)	1,100	@ 10%	110	
	33,300			
On dividends (balance)	800	@ 32½%	260	7,161
	34,100			

Less: PAYE deductions				6,443	
Tax credit on United Kingdom dividends				90	

Tax credit on foreign dividends
(treating Utopian dividend as top slice of income)

Utopian company

Lower of:	Foreign tax				315	}		
	UK tax	700	@ 32½%		228	}	228	

Ruritanian company

Lower of:	Foreign tax				45	}		
	UK tax	100	@ 32½%	32		}		
		200	@ 10%	20	52	}	45	6,806
		300						

Tax remaining to be paid					£	355

(b) **Boswell's income tax liability for 2006/07**

Claiming double tax relief on dividends and interest

	£
State pension	4,769
UK interest	5,371
Foreign interest – Ruritania	2,000
– Narnia	1,000
	13,140
Personal allowance (over 65)	7,280
Taxable income	5,860

				£
Tax thereon: 2,150 at starting rate of 10%				215
3,710 at savings rate of 20%				742
				957
Less age-related married couple's allowance 6,065 @ 10%				607
				350

Less double tax relief:

On interest – Ruritania				
Lower of foreign tax	300	}		
and UK tax 2,000 @ 20% = £400 restricted by allowances to	350	} 300		
On interest – Narnia				
Lower of foreign tax	100	}		
and UK tax (350 – 350)	Nil	} –	300	

UK tax payable	50

Claiming double tax relief only on interest from Ruritania

	£
State pension	4,769
UK interest	5,371
Foreign interest – Ruritania	2,000
Foreign interest net of foreign tax – Narnia	900
	13,040
Personal allowance (over 65)	7,280
Taxable income	5,760

	£
Tax thereon: 2,150 @ 10%	215
3,610 @ 20%	722
	937
Less age-related married couple's allowance 6,065 @ 10%	607
	330
Less double tax relief on interest – Ruritania:	
Lower of £300 and £330	300
UK tax payable	30

Tax payable is £20 less through not claiming double tax relief on foreign interest from Narnia.

Explanatory Notes

Tax on savings income

1. The tax rate on both UK and foreign savings income, excluding dividends, is 20% if the savings income, as the top slice of income, does not exceed the basic rate limit, and 40% on any excess over the basic rate limit. Any unused starting rate at 10% is also available against savings income (TA 1988 s 1A). The tax rate on both UK and foreign dividend income is 10% if the dividend income, when treated as the top slice of savings income, does not exceed the basic rate limit and 32½% on any excess (TA 1988 s 1B).

    These rates do not apply to foreign savings income that is charged on a remittances basis (ie where it is received by someone who is not ordinarily resident and/or not domiciled in the UK). Such income is taxed at non-savings rates.

Double tax relief

2. Where the same income and capital gains are liable to tax in more than one country, relief for the double tax is given either under the provisions of a double tax treaty or unilaterally (TA 1988 ss 788-791, TCGA 1992 s 277).

    Where there is a double tax treaty, it may provide for certain income and gains to be wholly exempt, or for tax to be deducted at a reduced rate (see Example 35 explanatory note 3). Income that is not exempt is charged to UK tax, but a credit is given for the lower of the overseas tax and the UK tax.

    Where there is no treaty, unilateral relief may be claimed against the UK tax at the lower of the overseas tax and the UK tax.

    To counter tax evasion both nationally and internationally, HMRC has the power to obtain relevant tax information from taxpayers and third parties and for such information to be exchanged with, or obtained for, other EU states and countries with whom the UK has made either a double taxation agreement or a tax information exchange agreement (TA 1988 ss 815C and 816). FA 2006 contains powers to cancel existing arrangements, and replace them with more comprehensive information exchange arrangements, and also powers to recover tax in overseas courts.

3. Double tax relief is available only for direct foreign taxes on the income and where the income is dividend income, no credit is available for the underlying tax on the profits out of which the dividend is paid (TA 1988 s 790). Where the overseas country operates a similar system to the UK imputation system of corporation tax, under which dividends have tax credits attached and withholding tax is not deducted, the tax credits represent underlying tax and are not eligible for double tax relief unless specifically provided for by the double tax agreement. Where the treaty does not so provide, the net dividend paid is the amount charged to UK tax.

4. Sources of overseas income may be taken in the order most advantageous to the taxpayer (TA 1988 s 796); if the Ruritanian dividend had been regarded as the top slice of income in part (a) of the example, the credits would have been less advantageous, as follows:

    Ruritanian company

Lower of:	Foreign tax			45	£ 45	(same)
	UK tax	300	@ 32½%	97		

    Utopian company

Lower of:	Foreign tax				315	£183	(compared with £228)
	UK tax	500	@ 32½%	163		
		200	@ 10%	20	183	
		700				

5. If following a double tax claim, the amount of foreign tax payable is later adjusted, the amount of double tax relief claimed must be similarly adjusted. If an adjustment to foreign tax results in too much relief having been claimed, HMRC must be notified within one year after the adjustment (TA 1988 s 806).

Not claiming double tax relief

6. If double tax relief is not claimed, the income or gain is charged to UK tax net of the overseas tax suffered (TA 1988 s 811, TCGA 1992 s 278). This will rarely be more beneficial, except where the net overseas income is covered by allowances, or tax arising is reduced by other deductions, such as age-related married couple's allowance, as shown in part (b) of the example in relation to the foreign interest. If double tax relief is claimed on both sources of foreign interest, then after treating the Ruritania interest as the top slice of the income, attracting tax of £400, but restricted by claim for age-related married couple's allowance to £350, no UK tax relates to the Narnia interest, so that the double tax relief on that interest is nil. By not claiming double tax relief on the Narnia interest, the tax payable of £330 relates wholly to the Ruritania interest and no tax is suffered on the UK income

and the Narnia interest. Although the UK tax on the Ruritania interest is reduced from £350 to £330, this does not reduce the double tax relief because the credit is limited to the foreign tax of £300 in any event.

Basis of assessment of foreign income

7.   For notes on the basis of assessment of foreign income, see Example 6 for saving income and Example 8 for employment income. Where income is charged on the basis of the amount arising abroad, and the income has not been brought into the UK, it is converted into sterling at the exchange rate on the date it arises. Where there are frequent items, an average exchange rate for the year may be used, using rates published by HMRC, providing it is used consistently and does not materially affect the taxable amounts. Income chargeable on the remittances basis should be converted at the rate on the date the income is received in the UK.

Summarise the legislation relating to pension contributions applicable from 6 April 2006, giving brief details of the limits on contributions and the options and benefits available on retirement and death.

Pensions from 6 April 2006

With effect from 6 April 2006 all previous legislation relating to pension contributions was abolished. From that date all registered pension schemes operate under the rules introduced by Finance Act 2004 Part 4, Finance Act 2005 Part 5 and related regulations.

Where taxpayers had better rights under the previous schemes than under the new rules then existing rights as at 6 April 2006 were broadly preserved (FA 2004 Sch 36).

Previously there was a problem of interaction between the varying sets of rules. This was particularly apparent where a taxpayer was a member of more than one scheme concurrently. From 6 April 2006 an individual can belong to, or contribute to, as many schemes as they wish at any time, basically without restriction (FA 2004 s 188).

The previous rules enabled pension contributions to be carried back in certain circumstances, some rules allowed carry forward of unused reliefs, whereas others were based purely upon the fiscal year. The new rules give tax relief on contributions paid in a fiscal year with no carry back or carry forward rules. See note 4 as to the way relief is given for contributions made by individuals. In the case of contributions paid by an employer tax relief will be given in the accounting period in which contributions are paid (FA 2004 s 196(2)).

In order to restrict tax relief in any tax year two tests apply.

Annual allowance (FA 2004 ss 227 to 238)

The first test compares the 'total pension input' for a fiscal year with its annual allowance. The annual allowance is fixed for the first five years at (FA 2004 s 228)

2006/07 – £215,000
2007/08 – £225,000
2008/09 – £235,000
2009/10 – £245,000
2010/11 – £255,000

Total pension input (FA 2004 s 229)

In order to be able to have one set of rules it is necessary to compute in each year 'total pension input'. This is the sum of the contributions made to pension policies in the fiscal year plus the value of defined pension increase in benefits accrued during the year. See note 2 below as to the method of computing the value of pension input from defined benefits schemes.

If exceptionally an individual has 'total pension input' in excess of their annual allowance then there will be a tax charge on the individual of 40% on any amount of pension inputs over the annual allowance (s 227(4)).

Tax relief on pension contributions (FA 2004 ss 186 to 203)

The second test restricts the tax relief available to an individual to the amounts shown below.

Previously each type of pension scheme had its own maximum pension contribution. Those limits are abolished and there is only one limit, that is

–   Contributions paid by an individual in the fiscal year, to the higher of

   •   100% of UK earnings chargeable to tax, or

   •   £3,600 (provided relief at basic rate is given at source)

(FA 2004 s 190).

Contributions are normally paid net of basic rate tax. However, if contributions are paid in excess of the above limits the excess amount will be allowed to remain within the pension fund, but the excess will be deemed to be a gross contribution. For example, John, who is normally a higher rate tax payer, makes a pension contribution of £7,800 pa each year being a gross contribution of £10,000 less tax relief of £2,200.

In 2006/07 John's UK earnings only amounted to £3,000. He will, therefore, have a tax deductible premium of (£2,808 net + £792 tax =) £3,600 being the maximum allowed plus a non-tax allowable contribution of (£7,800 − £2,808) = £4,992 giving a total increase in his pension fund of £8,592.

An individual is entitled to tax relief on pension contributions paid in a tax year provided they are a 'relevant' UK individual (s 188(1)). A relevant UK individual is defined in s 189 as an individual who

–   has UK earnings chargeable to UK income tax, or

–   was resident in the UK at some time during the tax year, or

–   was resident in the UK when they joined the pension scheme and has been resident in the UK during part of the last five years, or

–   the individual or their spouse (or civil partner) has earnings from overseas Crown employment subject to UK tax.

The contributions may be paid directly to the pension provider or paid via an employer sponsored scheme. Relief is also available where the contribution is in the form of a transfer of eligible shares, ie those acquired under a SAYE option scheme or approved share incentive plan (s 195). Such transfers must be made within 90 days of exercising the SAYE option (when the shares are appropriated to the employee). The shares will be treated as a contribution equal to their market value at the date of transfer. Normally contributions are made net of tax and therefore tax relief is given on the grossed up value.

Where pension contributions are made by the employer then the full amount paid in the accounting period will be allowed subject to the usual restriction that the deduction must be for a payment made 'wholly and exclusively' for the purpose of the trade (FA 2004 s 196). (See HMRC manuals at BIM 46001 for further guidance).

In order for pension contributions paid to be allowable they must form part of a normal remuneration package. They are not considered as a stand-alone amount. It follows that a salary sacrifice will not prevent a tax deduction. Contributions will be allowable if the overall salary package is a normal commercial amount.

It is likely that HMRC will disallow any amount identifiable as relating to a non-trade purpose, for example, as part of arrangements to dispose of a business where the payment represents part of the sale proceeds, or of exceptional size. This would be of issue if the employer was not carrying on a trade eg a property holding company. The main focus of disallowance is likely to be in respect of directors who are controlling shareholders or their relatives/friends, and where the salary package has been significantly increased, eg where funds previously taken as dividends are now taken as a pension contribution.

Where exceptionally the employer makes special contributions and those contributions are in excess of £500,000 then the special contribution will be spread over two, three or four years. (FA 2004 s 197). (See Example 72 at note 25 as to the calculation of the special contribution and detailed rules on spreading.)

Where an individual has UK earnings in excess of the annual allowance then tax relief will be granted upon all the contributions made, but the actual tax relief will be limited by the annual allowance charge (FA 2004 s 227).

In so far as the contributions are in excess of the annual allowance, an 'annual allowance charge' of 40% will apply to the excess. This will effectively restrict relief to the lower of

–   taxable earnings, or

–   contributions

to a maximum of

•   annual allowance (2006/07 – £215,000).

Lifetime allowance (FA 2004 ss 214–226)

Benefits from money purchase schemes are based upon amounts paid in plus the growth in value of the fund. However defined benefit schemes have benefits based upon final salary and years of service. Both of these principles are restricted by a lifetime limit.

A fund will not be tested during its accumulation periods. The member can have as many different funds as he wishes. The lifetime limit only applies when withdrawals are made. If the fund value on which a withdrawal is to be made exceeds the remaining lifetime allowance then there will be a tax charge. The lifetime allowance is fixed for the first five years at

2006/07	£1,500,000
2007/08	£1,600,000
2008/09	£1,650,000
2009/10	£1,750,000
2010/11	£1,800,000

(FA 2004 s 218)

Benefit crystallisation event (FA 2004 s 216 and Sch 32)

When a withdrawal is made from any fund, other than a transfer to another approved fund or pension splitting, this is known as a 'benefit crystallisation event'. (FA 2004 s 216).

At that stage the withdrawal is valued and if it exceeds the available lifetime allowance then the excess will be subject to a lifetime allowance charge. If the amount to be used is lower than the remaining lifetime allowance then no tax charge arises but that proportion of the lifetime allowance that has been used will be noted and only the remaining percentage will be available on subsequent benefit crystallisation events (s 219).

Where the amount being used for a benefit crystallisation event exceeds the lifetime allowance then the excess is subject to a lifetime allowance charge (s 215) of

–   25% if the balance is used to buy a pension, or

–   55% if taken as a lump sum.

Pension benefits (FA 2004 ss 164 to 171 and Sch 28 and 29)

Benefits can be taken from most pension schemes from age 50 under current legislation. That will continue until 6 April 2010, thereafter the pension age is raised to a minimum of 55.

Previously early retirement from an Occupational Pension Scheme required the pensioner to leave service. That restriction was removed from 6 April 2006, subject to the rules of the scheme permitting early retirement.

From 6 April 2006 part of the benefit crystallisation can be taken as a tax free lump sum to a maximum of 25% of the fund being crystallised, restricted by the lifetime allowance, and the scheme rules. This gives an effective maximum for 2006/07 of 25% × £1.5 million = £375,000. Under the new rules all funds have a lump sum availability. (Subject to the rules of the specific scheme).

In the case of a money purchase scheme the lump sum is up to 25% of the fund. In the case of a defined benefit scheme, the scheme pension is multiplied by 20, and any entitlement to a lump sum added, to give a notional value, 25% of which is the maximum lump sum (FA 2004 Sch 29.3(6)).

Where a member of a money purchase scheme uses the fund to buy a scheme pension (defined benefits rules then apply) shortly before retirement, then the tax free lump sum is restricted to 25% of the original fund. (FA 2006 Sch 23(22)).

The tax free lump sum cannot be recycled into pension funds, any such recycling will constitute an unauthorised payment (see note 22 as to the tax consequences). This provision applies even if the pension contribution is made before the lump sum is drawn. It does not apply if the total lump sums received in a 12 month period does not exceed 1% of the lifetime limit (2006/07 £15,000) or where the increase in pension contributions do not exceed 30% of the lump sum (Sch 29 para 3A, inserted by FA 2006).

The balance of the fund must be used to buy a pension for the life of the member, or this can be provided by the fund. The annuity can be written for the joint lives of the member and spouse (including civil partner) and for a term certain not exceeding ten years.

The pension may be

– level,

– increasing (including one-off increases),

– linked (eg to RPI or based upon a with profit fund),

– with lump sum death benefits.

Where a pension is purchased with a death benefit then the death benefit must be payable on a death (before age 75) and will be subject to a tax charge of 35%. The death benefit must represent the difference between the amounts paid in lifetime and the original amount paid for the annuity policy. Such a policy is to be known as a 'value protected annuity'.

Where the pension is drawn before aged 75 it may be used as follows

– unsecured pension, or

– part of the fund used to buy a short term annuity (up to five years).

By age 75 the fund must have been used to buy a pension, or, where the member has a particular aversion to buying an annuity, to provide an 'alternatively secured pension' (ASP).

An ASP has the attributes of an unsecured pension (income withdrawal). That is to say the fund is not used to buy an annuity but instead the annuity is paid from the fund. However the balance of the 'alternatively secured pension' fund is not available for withdrawal on death. At that time the fund must be used to provide an unsecured pension for spouse, civil partner or dependant, if any, (or ASP if spouse/civil partner is aged 75 or older).

On the death of the spouse, civil partner or dependant or on the death of the member (if no dependants) the remaining alternatively secured pension fund must be gifted to a nominated charity or transferred to another member of the same pension scheme, at which time inheritance tax will be payable. This is calculated by treating the remaining fund as being the top slice of the estate of the member which is then charged to inheritance tax. That tax is payable by the pension scheme administrator. If the rates of inheritance tax have reduced since the death of the member then the liability is calculated as though the rates applicable at the date of death of the spouse/civil partner (the reduced rates) were in force at the date of the original death (IHTA 1984 Sch 2 para 6A, as added by FA 2006). No liability arises on a gift to charity (IHTA 1984 s 151A and s 151B).

Death benefits (FA 2004 s 167 and Schs 28 and 29)

From 6 April 2006 the whole of the fund may be paid as a death benefit, with no tax, providing death occurs before age 75, before crystallisation and the total of all of the funds does not exceed the lifetime allowance. Therefore the previous restriction to four times final salary for death in service is replaced by the provision that the maximum amount paid including contributions and growth in value and any insured or uninsured benefits payable on death cannot exceed the lifetime allowance.

After benefits have crystallised in an unsecured pension any remaining amounts on death drawn as cash will be subject to a tax charge of 35%. Such payments can only be made providing death occurs before age 75.

After age 75 the fund must have been used to buy an annuity or to have changed to an ASP which cannot pay a death benefit.

Further details

See notes 1 to 11 below for examples of maximum pension contributions, annual allowance charge and lifetime allowance charge. The notes also give more details on how tax relief will be given, transitional provisions, unsecured pension, alternatively secured pensions and term assurance.

See note 12 for the rules applicable to pension contributions in 2005/06 and earlier year. Notes 14 to 27 give details of the interactions with other legislation, such as national insurance, losses, divorce and tax credits.

Explanatory Notes

Pensions simplification

1. From 6 April 2006 the previous tax provisions relating to occupational and personal pension schemes were replaced by a single scheme for all registered pension schemes. The limits on contributions, the earnings cap, the 2/3rds of final remuneration limit for occupational schemes, and the lump sum restrictions no longer apply. Occupational schemes can now offer flexible retirement, enabling employees to draw benefits while continuing to work for the employer.

   The previous requirements for obtaining approval for schemes have been replaced by a simpler process of scheme registration. Individuals are now able to contribute to as many schemes as they wish. There are no provision to enable carrying contributions back or forward. Pension providers are able to invest in many types of investment, excluding residential property, and tangible moveable property where the policy holder can influence investment decisions (FA 2004 Sch 29A inserted by FA 2006). The borrowing limits are restricted, normally to a maximum of 50% of the fund value. The minimum pension age will rise from 50 to 55 on 6 April 2010 (earlier retirement still being permitted on ill health grounds).

   The following notes set out some of the terms used with examples of how maximum contributions are calculated and the effect of excess contributions. The lifetime limit is shown with examples of the lifetime allowance charge. Unsecured and alternatively secured pensions are reviewed. Finally the protection rules for existing pension benefits as at 5 April 2006 are briefly considered.

Pension inputs (FA 2004 s 229)

2. A pension input is the amount contributed to a pension policy in a fiscal year plus the increase in value of defined pension benefits. Where the amounts contributed are in cash or equivalent they are easily valued. Where the pension scheme provides a defined benefit then the scheme administrator will compute the increase in value of the pension benefits using the formula

(Opening Benefits × 10) + Lump Sum =	X
(Closing Benefits × 10) + Lump Sum =	Y
Increase	Z

   If a member does not accrue any rights under the arrangement during the fiscal year (typically because the member is no longer an employee of the sponsoring employer) then the opening value (X) is to be increased by the greater of 5% or RPI inflation for the fiscal year.

   The administrator of each fund will produce a figure for each member. Where exceptionally the difference is a decrease the amount will be deemed to be nil. Therefore all positive increases are aggregated with the contributions paid by the member, or others (eg his employer) to the defined contribution fund. The sum is known as 'total pension input'. This is used to test against the annual allowance (see note 3 below).

   There is no pension input if, before the end of the tax year, the member has died, or taken all of the benefits available from that fund, ie the benefits have crystallised.

Example

John is entitled to a pension on 1/60th of final salary plus 3/80ths lump sum. He has 5 years service as at 6 April 2006 and a salary of £210,000 per annum. By 6 April 2007 his salary has increased to £240,000 per annum. His P60 shows salary for the year of £225,000. John's pension input is

		£	£
Opening value	5/60ths × £210,000 × 10	175,000	
	15/80ths × £210,000	39,375	214,375
Closing value	6/60ths × £240,000 × 10	240,000	
	18/80ths × £240,000	54,000	294,000
Pension input			79,625
Annual limit			215,000
Maximum other contributions in year before 'Annual allowance charge' applies			135,375

John is entitled to obtain tax relief on contributions paid to all schemes to the maximum of his earnings for the year chargeable to UK tax, (£225,000). However, if his contributions exceed £135,375 (excluding contributions to the defined benefit scheme) he will attract an annual allowance charge of 40% on the excess. In practice John would not wish to pay a premium greater than the amount chargeable at 40% tax, or an amount that would exceed his pension input maximum. Because the calculation of pension inputs cannot be made until after the end of the year John will have to estimate his pension input from defined benefits scheme to determine the amount he wishes to contribute.

Annual allowance – excess contributions (FA 2004 s 227)

3. Where 'total pension inputs' are in excess of the annual allowance for the fiscal year, then the excess is subject to the 'annual allowance charge' of 40%.

Example

Jill has paid £50,000 in 2006/07 to a registered pension scheme.

Subsequently she is notified by the scheme administrators of her defined benefits pension scheme that the 'pension input' for the year 2006/07 is £180,000.

When Jill completes her Self Assessment Tax Return for 2006/07 she will have to enter an annual allowance charge computed as

	£
Total pension input (£50,000 + £180,000)	230,000
Annual allowance	215,000
Excess chargeable @ 40%	15,000

However, when she completes her Self Assessment Tax Return, she will claim tax relief on the £50,000 paid to a pension scheme. This will be allowable providing she has sufficient taxable earnings. Assuming her earnings were £250,000 her tax return would show

		£
Relief for pensions paid	50,000 @ 40%	20,000
Less annual allowance charge	15,000 @ 40%	6,000
Actual relief	35,000 @ 40%	14,000

It should be noted that the total pension input on which tax relief is being granted then equals the annual allowance ie value of pension inputs on increase in defined benefits £180,000 plus tax relief on £35,000 = £215,000.

The way tax relief is given (FA 2004 ss 190 to 201)

4. The way in which tax relief is granted depends upon the way in which the contributions are paid.

Members' own contributions are normally paid net of basic rate tax (s 192). Relief is therefore granted as follows:

Basic rate – at source
Higher rate – Self-Assessment Tax Return (or PAYE coding notice)

Higher rate relief is obtained by increasing the basic rate band for income tax or capital gains by the gross pension contribution (s 192(4)). When calculating income for age allowance purposes only, the gross pension payment is deducted from income (s 192(5)). Relief is therefore given as for personal pensions prior to 6 April 2006.

If a member pays a contribution via the employer then the contribution is paid to the insurance company gross. Tax relief is granted via the net pay scheme (s 193). This means that the gross pension contributions are deducted from earnings for PAYE (but not NI) and relief given accordingly.

Because employer-deducted contributions are excluded from earnings, relief for higher rate tax is given automatically. If an employer deducted contribution cannot be relieved by deduction from earnings (eg payment made after month 12 payroll has been processed) or where earnings are not liable to PAYE, such as benefits, then the employee makes a claim on the self-assessment tax return, and earnings are reduced by the unrelieved premiums paid.

Retirement Annuity Premium (RAP) contributions continue to be paid gross under the new scheme (s 194).

Relief for premiums paid gross is given by reducing earnings by the pension contributions made when computing total income (s 194(1)). The claim is normally made in the tax return.

Where a member contributes up to £3,600 pa (gross) to a pension scheme but has no taxable income then tax relief will still be given where the contribution has been paid net. There will be no recovery of the tax relief given.

If contributions in excess of the annual allowance are paid then the excess is clawed back by the 'annual allowance charge' of 40%. This charge does not apply when all pension benefits for the scheme crystallise in the same year as the contribution is made. In that final year 'pension input' for that scheme will be nil. However the maximum tax relief obtainable will of course be restricted to the amount of tax due.

Where tax is deducted at source on an amount in excess of £3,600, and earnings are nil (or less than £3,600 pa), then the first £2,808 of the payment will be deemed to be a net pension contribution and the excess will be deemed to be a gross pension payment on which no tax relief is available. The following example illustrates how such a situation can occur.

Jack, a self-employed builder, pays a net pension contribution of £500 per month. His accounts for the year ended 31 January 2007 show a tax adjusted net profit of £2,800. He has no other earnings.

Jack is entitled to tax relief in 2006/07 on the higher of

– 100% earnings =	2,800
– or	3,600

In 2006/07 Jack has paid pension contributions (net) of

12 × 500 =	6,000
Maximum allowable (£3,600 × 100/78 =)	2,808
Gross pension contribution (no relief available)	3,192
Total pension contribution paid by Jack (net)	6,000
Tax repaid to pension scheme (£8,600 × 22%)	792
Amount added to Jack's pension scheme	6,792

Lifetime limit (FA 2004 ss 214 to 226)

5. When pension benefits, other than State Pensions, are drawn there is a 'benefit crystallisation event'. At that time it is necessary to check the amount of pension funds used against the lifetime limit. If the amount is below the lifetime limit then full benefits can be paid with no additional tax charge. If a previous 'benefit crystallisation event' has used part of the lifetime limit then only the remaining percentage of the limit for the current year can be applied.

Example of one fund and one crystallisation

George has a pension fund of £2 million and is aged 75 next week. He wishes to take the maximum amount as a lump sum using the balance to buy a pension. The lifetime limit for 2006/07 is £1.5 million. Ignore transitional rules.

	£	£
Value of fund	2,000,000	
Maximum tax-free lump sum		
25% × £1.5 million	375,000	375,000
	1,625,000	
Balance of lifetime limit used to buy a pension (75% × 1.5 million)	1,125,000	
Excess	500,000	
Lifetime allowance charge		
Taken as lump sum – 55%	275,000	225,000
Maximum lump sum		600,000

If George had not wished to take the excess as a lump sum but instead wished to buy a pension then the tax charge would be as follows:

	£
Excess of fund	500,000
Lifetime allowance charge – 25% of £500,000	125,000
Available to buy pension	375,000

Effectively the tax charge will be identical as when the pension is taken it will be taxable income liable at say 40% therefore the tax due on the pension will be:

	£
40% × £375,000 (assumed pension received)	150,000
Lifetime allowance charge @ 25%	125,000
Giving total of	275,000

Thus the total tax collected by HMRC is 55% of £500,000 in each instance.

In practice very few members will have only one fund, or will draw the whole of their fund on one occasion. Where there are multiple withdrawals then the test has to be done each time benefits crystallise. The percentage of the fund that has been used is calculated and only the remaining percentage of the later year lifetime allowance will be available for later benefits.

Example of two crystallisations

William has a 'benefit crystallisation event' in 2006/07 using £1 million of his pension funds.

He has a further 'benefit crystallisation event' in 2010/11 using £700,000 of his pension fund. The lifetime allowance limit in 2010/11 is £1,800,000

2006/07 Lifetime limit	£1.5 million
'Benefits crystallisation event' fund used	£1 million (i.e. 66.67% of lifetime limit)

	£
2010/11 Lifetime limit	1,800,000
Used in 2006/07 66.67% × £1.8 million	1,200,000
Available lifetime allowance	600,000
Crystallised 2010/11	700,000
Lifetime allowance excess chargeable	100,000

There will be no charge on any other pension funds held until they have a 'benefit crystallisation event'. Then, as the whole 100% of the lifetime allowance has been used, the fund value on crystallisation will be chargeable.

It should be noted that William may believe that he does not have any charge to pay as his total crystallisation is £1 million plus £700,000 and the lifetime allowance in 2010/11 is £1.8 million whereas in reality there will be a deduction of £55,000 from funds taken in cash or £25,000 from funds taken used to buy a pension.

Pensions in payment as at 6 April 2006

If an individual had a pension in payment as at 6 April 2006 then immediately before the first 'benefit crystallisation event' occurring there is a deemed 'benefit crystallisation event', the amount of the lifetime limit used is

25 × existing annual pension in payment

If the individual has a pre 6 April 2006 income withdrawal then the existing pension is deemed to be 120% of the standard annuity (see note 6) regardless of the amount actually drawn.

If the individual has taken a tax free lump sum prior to 6 April 2006 then that amount when aggregated with the lump sum to be taken must not exceed 25% of the lifetime allowance.

In practice many individuals with existing vested policies or pensions in payment will use the transitional provisions (see note 8 below). Enhanced protection is available if no pension contribution, or increases in benefit rights, occur after 5 April 2006 even if the 'A day value' of the funds is below £1,500,000. This enables the benefits to be taken after 5 April 2006 without consideration of the lifetime allowance.

Unsecured pensions (FA 2004 s 165)

6.   The rules are very similar to the previous income withdrawal rules. Unsecured pension withdrawal will be available from age 50 (55 from 2010) until the pensioner is aged 75. On commencing withdrawal there is a benefit crystallisation event. At that time tax free cash can be taken up to 25% of the fund. The amount designated as available to pay the unsecured pension plus the tax-free cash taken is treated as the amount crystallised (s 216(1b)(1)). When the balance of the fund is used to buy an annuity, to convert to an alternatively secured pension or on death, the funds then available must

also be tested against the remaining lifetime limit as a 'benefit crystallisation event' has occurred (s 216(1b)(1)(4)(7)). However, the amount crystallised is reduced by the amount previously tested against the lifetime limit (Sch 32.3 and 4, as amended).

The balance of the fund must then be used to pay a pension each year. The pension will be taxable and subject to PAYE. There is no minimum withdrawal and the maximum withdrawal is 120% of the government standard annuity. The amount taken can be varied each year.

At five yearly intervals the standard annuity will be revalued thereby giving a new maximum amount.

Alternatively the fund can buy a short term annuity for a period not exceeding five years (and ending before the pensioner is aged 75).

If the pensioner dies before age 75 and before a pension is bought then the fund can be used

- to buy a pension for spouse or other dependant, or

- to provide an unsecured pension for spouse, if they are under age 75, or

- 35% of the fund can be paid as tax with the balance taken as a lump sum.

Alternatively secured pension ('ASP') (FA 2004 Sch 28)

7. These are available from 6 April 2006 for pensioners aged 75. They are designed for those who have conscientious objections to buying annuities. Instead of buying an annuity the member crystallises their benefits as for unsecured pensions. If the fund has not previously been used to take a tax free lump sum then up to 25% of the fund (subject to lifetime limit) can be used to provide a cash sum.

The balance of the fund must be used to provide a taxable pension. The maximum amount that can be drawn is 70% of the standard annuity payable to an annuitant aged 75 of the same sex.

In the case of alternatively secured pensions the pension must be reviewed every year using an annuity rate for an annuitant aged 75 applied to the then fund value.

The member can however agree with the pension's administrator that the agreed annuity will be paid for a term certain not exceeding ten years.

On the death of the alternatively secured pensioner the remaining fund must be used to provide a pension for their spouse, civil partner or other dependant. If the recipient is under 75 unsecured pension rules will apply. From aged 75 the alternatively secured pension rules will apply.

When the last recipient dies then the balance of the fund will be gifted to a nominated charity. Alternatively the last pensioner can nominate another member of the same pension scheme to have the transfer value of the remaining fund. The amount transferred will be after the payment of inheritance tax. The tax is computed by treating the value of the fund as the top slice of the estate of the original member, and the rates used will be those applicable at the date of the death of the last recipient of pension. The liability to pay the tax rests with the pension scheme administrator.

Example

Peter retires aged 60, when his pension funds are worth £1,000,000. He takes £250,000 as tax free cash, the lifetime limit being £1,500,000. He also takes unsecured pension within the limits, for the next 15 years. The remaining fund is now worth £800,000. The lifetime limit is now £2,400,000. He transfers to the ASP rules. His wife dies and he nominates the pension fund to his daughter. On the death of Peter the fund is worth £1,200,000. His daughter is aged 53, she has no pension fund other than a fund of £10,000 with the same provider who managed Peter's ASP. The annual limit for the year of Peter's death is £400,000 and the lifetime limit £3,000,000. Peter's estate exceeds the nil rate band for inheritance tax. Inheritance tax rate is 40%.

There is no lifetime charge on Peter's transfer to ASP. The benefit crystallisation at age 60 was £1,000,000 of a limit of £1,500,000 ie 66.67%.

On transfer to ASP of £800,000 the benefit crystallisation was:

Value of fund	£800,000
Less crystallised on commencement of unsecured pension (£1,000,000 less lump sum £250,000)	750,000
Increase in value	50,000
Remaining lifetime limit (100 − 66.67 =) 33.33% × £2,400,000	800,000

As there are no other funds to crystallise there is no excess.

Death is not a benefit crystallisation event unless a lump sum is payable.

On the death of Peter his chargeable estate for inheritance tax will be increased by the value remaining in the ASP, £1,200,000. Inheritance tax at 40%, £480,000, is payable leaving £720,000 to transfer to the pension funds of daughter.

Transitional provisions (FA 2004 Sch 36)

8. Existing pension rights, as at 6 April 2006, may be preserved by using the following provisions from Finance Act 2004.

Primary protection (Sch 36.7)

(a) Primary protection is given to any pension member who has a fund valued in excess of £1.5 million as at 6 April 2006. The pension member is required to give notice to HMRC. Notice must be given by 6 April 2009.

Where notice has been given then there will be an enhancement to the lifetime limit. This is calculated as

$$\frac{\text{Fund value @ 6 April 2006} - \text{£1.5 million}}{\text{£1.5 million}} \times \text{Lifetime Limit}$$

For example if Alison has a fund of £2 million as at 6 April 2006 then the lifetime limit enhancement will be

$$\frac{\text{£2 million} - \text{£1.5 million}}{\text{£1.5 million}} = 33\tfrac{1}{3}\% \text{ (expressed as a percentage)}$$

Therefore in a later year, say 2010/11, the lifetime limit for Alison would be the actual limit of £1.8 million × 133⅓% = £2.4 million.

Enhanced protection (Sch 36.12)

(b) Where a pension fund member has relevant pension arrangements that became registered pension schemes on 6 April 2006 and had ceased active membership of all registered pension schemes then enhanced protection is available from 6 April 2006. There is no minimum fund value to claim enhanced protection.

If the member has **any** pension input then the value of enhanced protection is lost and only primary protection is available. This applies to contributions made or benefits uprating received on or after 6 April 2006.

Where the member has elected for enhanced protection then there will be no lifetime charge when a pension and tax-free lump sum are drawn. The tax-free lump sum is still restricted to 25% of the fund value.

If the member makes any contribution, or his benefits are enhanced or the member wishes to withdraw his notice then enhanced protection may be replaced by primary protection.

Valuation of funds at 6 April 2006 for protection

(c) In order to compute the value of a pension fund as at 6 April 2006 it is necessary to add the value of all uncrystallised funds, ie the monetary value of defined contribution funds, plus the annual rate of pension to which the member is entitled × 20, plus the lump sum to which the member is entitled. To which is added the value of all crystallised pensions ie pensions in payment (for this purpose the annual pension is multiplied by 25 to take into account the lump sum already taken) plus an amount equal to the value of benefits that have been taken prior to 6 April 2006 wholly or mainly in the form of a tax free lump sum. Where the taxpayer is making income withdrawals the pension used is the maximum available under the arrangements.

Retirement before age 50 (Sch 36.21–36.23)

(d) If the pension member has the right to draw their pension because of their profession before age 50 (eg sportsmen) then that right will be preserved providing it is in place as at 6 April 2006.

Lump sums (Sch 36.24–36.36)

(e) Protection is provided for an accrued right to a lump sum in excess of £375,000 as at 6 April 2006.

This right is preserved by increasing the maximum lump sum accrued as at 6 April 2006 by the pro-rata increase in the lifetime limit.

Justin is entitled to a lump sum as at 6 April 2006 of £600,000. He crystallises his pension in 2010/11 when the lifetime limit is £1.8 million. His maximum lump sum would then be

$$\frac{£1.8 \text{ million (2010/11 limit)}}{£1.5 \text{ million (2006/07 limit)}} \times £600,000 = £720,000$$

A further protection is available if under an occupational pension scheme the member is entitled to a lump sum that exceeds 25% of the uncrystallised rights as at 6 April 2006. This protection works by computing the accrued lump sum as at 6 April 2006 and increasing that figure in line with the increasing lifetime limit as above. To that amount may be added 25% of the value of benefits that have accrued since 6 April 2006. If benefits are transferred from the scheme then protection is lost and only 25% of the fund is available as a lump sum.

Carry-back of RAP payments in 2005/06 to earlier years (Sch 36.39)

(f) The new pension rules do not allow the carry forward of unclaimed relief or the carry-back of premiums paid. All such provisions are abolished from 6 April 2006.

Because of the abolition of those rules it was necessary to legislate in order to allow the carry-back of a retirement annuity premium paid in 2005/06 to an earlier year. The Finance Act 2004 provides that the election must be made by 31 January 2007.

Funded unapproved retirement benefit scheme (FURBS)

9. (a) Where contributions to an existing FURBS (funded unapproved retirement benefits scheme) have been taxed on the employee and the income and gains of the scheme have been taxed on the trustees *and* no further contributions are added from 6 April 2006 then any amounts paid out as a lump sum will be tax free.

If contributions are added to the FURBS after 5 April 2006 only the value on 5 April 2006 increased by RPI will be tax free.

Unfunded unapproved retirement benefit schemes

(b) It would appear that promised benefits under unfunded unapproved retirement benefit schemes do not constitute a pension input and do not give rise to a benefits in kind charge (because no payments are made into the scheme). When any benefits are drawn they will be taxable as pension income immediately. The employer (or former employer) only obtains tax relief when taxable benefits are paid.

Employer contributions to non-registered pension schemes are not tax deductible until the benefit is paid out to the employee.

Term assurance

10. Under the new provisions there is no specific limit upon the amount of term assurance that can be written under the pension rules. Tax relief will be given on such premiums provided the life insurance ceases before age 75. The premiums will be pension inputs counting towards the annual limit.

Because the policy is a registered pension scheme the proceeds will count towards the lifetime limit. Tax will be charged if the total proceeds plus other pension fund values exceed the lifetime limit (at 55% of the excess).

The previous limit for Occupational Pension Schemes of four times final salary is abolished from 5 April 2006. The new limits will normally be more valuable than the old limits, although those with pension funds worth in excess of £1,500,000 on 6 April 2006 will find that the value of their death in service cover will have been reduced by 55% of the excess of total pension and life cover provision over the lifetime limit (or enhanced limit).

Others may wish to vary their entitlement from 6 April 2006 so that instead of having benefits on death in service of a dependant's pension plus a lump sum, the whole of the value of the entitlement to benefits becomes a tax free lump sum (to the lifetime limit of £1,500,000 for 2006/07 rising in future years).

Commutation of Trivial Pensions

11. To reduce the possibility of very small pension funds having to buy annuities at poor rates because of the administrative costs involved it is possible, from 6 April 2006, to withdraw the whole amount on vesting. The amount taken in excess of the tax-free sum is treated as pension income and is liable to income tax. This facility is only available where

    –   the total value of *all* pensions for that individual is less than 1% of the Lifetime Allowance (£15,000 for 2006/07),

    –   the individual is aged between 60 and 75,

    –   the whole of all funds are withdrawn within a 12-month period,

    –   all rights are extinguished by the payment from the fund.

Pension contributions in 2005/06

Retirement Annuity Contracts and Personal Pension Contracts

12. Pension contracts taken out between 1 July 1988 and 5 April 2006 will be 'personal pension contracts'. Contracts made before that date were 'retirement annuity contracts' and those with such contracts may continue to pay premiums into them. From 6 April 2001 some pension contracts are known as 'stakeholder pensions'. This means that the terms of the contract meet the government's 'CAT' standard as to costs, access and terms. For taxation these policies are treated as personal pension contracts. (See note 24).

The maximum allowable premiums that qualified for relief under a retirement annuity contract for someone aged under 51 were 17½% of net relevant earnings, higher limits applying if the taxpayer was 51 or over at the beginning of the tax year. The 17½% limit also applied to a personal pension contract for someone aged under 36, higher limits applying to older taxpayers (see (b) below). An earnings cap applied for personal pension contributions (PPCs) only. For retirement annuity premiums (RAPs), it was possible to carry forward any unused relief for use in any of the next six years after using the annual allowable limit for the year concerned. It was also possible to treat RAPs paid in one tax year as paid in the previous tax year (TA 1988 s 619(4)), the provisions and time limits being as indicated in (e) below. PPCs could also be carried back to the previous tax year, but the provisions were more restrictive. The pension contribution to be carried back must be paid by 31 January in the tax year and the election to carry back made at or before the time the contribution was paid (TA 1988 s 641) – see (e) below.

The different age limits for RAPs and PPCs, and the fact that PPCs were subject to an earnings cap whereas RAPs were not, made the calculation of maximum available premiums tricky in some cases where someone paid both RAPs and PPCs.

To work out the maximum RAPs payable, the unused RAP relief brought forward was added to the maximum RAP for the year. Any RAP paid used up the current year's maximum first, then unused relief brought forward, earliest first. If a PPC was also paid, it reduced the amount of unused RAP relief to carry forward.

To work out the maximum PPCs for a year see (b) below. The PPC limit for the year was the allowable maximum as reduced by any RAPs paid in the year.

It should be noted that RAPs paid in any year reduced the maximum available PPC *for that year*, whereas PPCs paid reduced the unused RAP relief *carried forward*. The most straightforward approach was to deal with RAPs first, and then to deal with PPCs as a separate exercise.

If a taxpayer paid a PPC in 2005/06, to carry it back to 2004/05, the premium must have been *paid* by 31 January 2006 and an election to carry back must have been made at or before the time the premium was paid (s 641A). If the premium paid was a RAP then the premium could be paid at any time during 2005/06 and the election to carry back must be made by 31 January 2007 (FA 2004 Sch 36.39).

Where premiums were carried back to an earlier year, then although the tax saving was *calculated* by reference to the tax position of the earlier year, the claim was *given effect* in relation to the later year by set-off or repayment of tax *payable in* that later year, but the payment against which the set-off is made is not restricted to tax payable *for* that year and could be a payment in respect of the previous year's tax. The treatment depends on when the claim is made. A carryback claim may either be made in a tax return or as a stand-alone claim (see Example 42). HMRC will not, however, give effect to the claim until the return for the earlier year has been submitted.

Relief for pension premiums

(a)   The taxpayer obtains relief for his premiums at his top tax rate. An allowable PPC, paid net of tax, receives tax relief on the gross amount even if the member is a non-taxpayer. However any contribution paid in excess of the maximum allowable must be returned by the pension provider. Excess RAPs do not have to be refunded.

Claims for relief are normally made in tax returns, but may be made by way of a stand-alone claim under the provisions of TMA 1970 Sch 1A (see Example 42). Taxpayers no longer have to provide evidence of payments with their claims, although the contribution certificates from the pension provider need to be retained as part of the taxpayer's records, since they may be called for in an HMRC enquiry.

Maximum allowable premiums

(b)   The maximum allowable premiums that qualified for relief are the following percentage of the individual's net relevant earnings, depending on the individual's age at the beginning of the tax year (TA 1988 s 626 RAPs, s 640 PPCs) or £3,600 for PPCs if higher:

	RAPs	%		PPCs	%
Age	50 and under	17.5	Age	35 and under	17.5
	51 to 55	20		36 to 45	20
	56 to 60	22.5		46 to 50	25
	61 and over	27.5		51 to 55	30
				56 to 60	35
				61 and over	40

Net relevant earnings for PPC relief are capped at £102,000 for 2004/05 and £105,600 for 2005/06.

Where someone has both RAP and PPC contracts, the PPC limit for the current year is reduced by any RAP payments.

From 6 April 2001 the maximum allowable PPCs became the greater of:

(a)   £3,600

(b)   The maximum allowable contribution computed as above.

Furthermore, the net relevant earnings for (b) are the highest of such earnings for the current year and any of the preceding five years. If the earnings ceased, then contributions could continue to be paid for the tax year of cessation and the five following years (but not later than 2005/06), based upon the highest net relevant earnings of the year of cessation and the previous five years. If appropriate, the earnings were subject to the cap for the year of use. The relevant percentage is based upon the taxpayer's age at the commencement of the year of use, as shown above. Personal pension contributions could also be paid by an employee who was in an occupational scheme, subject to a limit for employee/employer contributions of £3,600 per annum, providing the employee was not a controlling director and had not been a controlling director in any tax year in the last five years (counting only years from 2000/01 onwards), and had earned £30,000 or less in at least one of the last five tax years (counting only years from 2000/01 onwards).

The provisions enabled a taxpayer with no earnings to contribute £3,600 per annum to a personal pension contract and obtain basic rate tax relief by retaining it out of the contribution (higher rate relief also being given if investment income is high enough), providing that he was resident in the UK. Non-taxpayers were able to retain the benefit of the basic rate relief.

An employee, who was unable to make a PPC because he was a member of an occupational scheme and either earning over £30,000 pa or was a controlling director, who had other net relevant earnings could make a PPC of up to £3,600 pa (TA 1988 s 632A and s 639(1B)).

If premiums in excess of the maximum available limit were paid, the excess premiums were not deductible for tax purposes, and excess PPCs (not RAPs) must be refunded (TA 1988 s 638(3)).

Net relevant earnings

(c)   Net relevant earnings are defined as (RAPs s 623, PPCs s 646):

Earnings from self-employment or non-pensionable employment

Plus Balancing charges

Less Capital allowances
Losses*
Employment income expenses allowable against non-pensionable earnings
Excess of business charges over other sources of income

*   Losses need not be set against current relevant earnings if there is other income to cover them. If a loss is set against other income, however, later relevant earnings are reduced by the amount of the loss (TA 1988 s 623(7) and s 646(5)).

There does not appear to be any restriction of relevant earnings where losses have been offset against capital gains under FA 1991 s 72.

For PPCs, relevant earnings exclude amounts treated as earnings under share option and incentive schemes and termination payments (TA 1988 s 644(4)). This restriction does not apply to RAPs. For both PPCs and RAPs, relevant earnings *include* amounts deducted from an employee's pre-tax pay to buy partnership shares under an approved share incentive plan (FA 2000 Sch 8.83).

Relevant earnings cannot include a director's remuneration from a company whose income consists wholly or mainly of investment income and which is controlled by its present and/or past directors, where the director in question owns some (for RAP contracts, more than 5%) of the ordinary share capital of the company (PPCs TA 1988 s 644, RAPs TA 1988 ss 623 & 624). (Hence such director's fees do not qualify as relevant earnings.)

Relevant earnings for PPC contracts exclude the earnings of a director who controls 20% or more of the company's ordinary share capital (or has done at any time in the previous ten tax years) if he has taken early retirement from an occupational scheme but then works for the same or an associated company.

Carrying forward unused RAP relief

(d)   Where the maximum allowable RAP was not paid in any year, the amount that could have been paid, which is called 'unused relief', may be carried forward for six years but not beyond 5 April 2006 (s 625). Any premium paid is regarded as using first the allowable limit for the year in which it is paid, then unused relief for the previous six years, earliest first.

Carrying premiums back

(e)   A taxpayer could pay an RAP in one tax year and claim to have the premium treated as though it had been paid in the previous tax year, whether or not he could have obtained relief against the relevant earnings of the tax year of payment. If there were no net relevant earnings in that earlier year, the premium may be treated as paid in the year before that. The six year carry forward of unused relief provisions in (d) above then apply as if the premium had been paid in the year to which the premium has been carried back (s 619(4)). For PPCs, s 641A provides a more limited carryback relief from 2001/02 onwards.

Under the RAP provisions, claims must be made by 31 January following the tax year in which the premium is paid. For 2005/06 the claim must be made by 31 January 2007. For PPCs the claim must have been made at or before the time the premium was paid, and payment must be made by 31 January within the tax year. Premiums and claims must have been made by 31 January 2006 to carry back to 2004/05.

The carryback claim may either be made in the 2005/06 return or separately. The *tax saving* resulting from backdating is worked out by reference to the tax position of the earlier year, but the claim is treated as relating to the later year, and effect is given to it in that later year by set-off or repayment (TMA 1970 Sch 1B). Depending on when the claim for relief is made, the set-off may be against tax payable in the later year that relates to the earlier year. HMRC will not, however, give effect to a carryback claim until the tax return for the earlier year has been submitted. The claim should not give rise to a tax *repayment* unless the tax for the earlier year has been paid in full. Where the liability for *any* year is outstanding, or will become due within 35 days from the date the claim is processed, relief should be given by set-off. Where there are no outstanding liabilities, relief will be given by repayment.

National insurance contributions

13. Registered pension premiums are not deducted from profits for Class 4 national insurance purposes (SSCBA 1992 Sch 2.3). Nor do they reduce earnings for employers' and employees' Class 1 contributions (SI 2001/1004 para 24), although an *employer's* pension contributions to an employee's policy do not count as earnings for Class 1 purposes (see note 18).

Losses

14. Where relief for losses is claimed under TA 1988 s 380 or s 381, the loss is set against total income, and no set-off order is specified. A s 380/s 381 claim may therefore be regarded for pension purposes as reducing non-trading income in priority to trading income, thus enabling relevant earnings of the claim year to be left at a higher level.

Contracting out of S2P

15. Unless an employee is already in a registered scheme that is contracted out of the State Second Pension Scheme (S2P – see note 16), he may himself elect to contract out, still, however, contributing for a basic retirement pension. The part of the pension funded by these means can only be paid from age 60 onwards and must be drawn by age 75. It can normally be commuted for a lump sum and it must include provision for widows'/widowers' pensions. Employees and employers still pay full national insurance contributions, and HMRC pays the combined employer/employee contracting-out rebate plus tax relief at the basic rate on the gross equivalent of the employee's share of the rebate to the pension provider after the end of the tax year (see Example 47 part (e)(i)). The employee may contract out in this way whether or not the employer has a non-contracted-out registered scheme. Where there is no registered scheme, any premium paid by the employee is paid net of basic rate tax and HMRC pays the tax into the plan.

    The state pension age is to be equalised for men and women at 65, the change being phased in from 2010 to 2020. Women born before 6 April 1950 will still qualify at 60 but women born on or after 6 March 1955 will be subject to the 65 age limit.

Replacement of SERPS by S2P

16. From 6 April 2002 the State Earnings Related Pension Scheme (SERPS) was replaced by the State Second Pension Scheme (S2P). All existing benefits under SERPS are retained and the new scheme provides a better pension for those earning under £28,700 pa (for 2006/07).

    The S2P scheme gives enhanced benefits to the lower paid (under £12,500 pa (Social Security Pensions (Low Earnings Threshold) Order, SI 2006/500)), certain carers and those with long term disabilities. Contributions continue to be a percentage of earnings above the earnings threshold.

    The change to the funding basis makes the decision whether or not to contract out very evenly balanced. The treatment of national insurance and rebates to S2P is set out in note 15 above.

Employer contributions

17. An employer can contribute to the registered pension plan of an employee. As with employers' contributions to company schemes, the employer's contribution to an employee's registered pension scheme is not treated as the employee's earnings (ITEPA 2003 s 308), nor is it liable to employer's national insurance contributions (Social Security (Contributions) Regulations SI 2001/1004 para 24 and Sch 3 Part VI).

    In view of the fact that employers' pension contributions are not liable to national insurance, whereas there is no national insurance saving on an employee's pension contributions, it could be tax-efficient for a salary sacrifice to be made by the employee, and for the employer to pay a pension contribution of the sacrificed amount boosted by the employer's national insurance saving. The cost to the employer would be the same. For example if a basic rate taxpayer paid £78 a month into his personal pension the gross pension contribution would be £100. If he made a salary sacrifice of £115 per month, his net pay would reduce by the same amount, ie:

Gross pay		115	
Tax @ 22%	25		
Class 1 NI @ 11%	12	37	£78

His employer could then contribute £115 plus the employer's NI of £115 @ 12.8% = £15, giving a gross pension contribution of (115 + 15 =) £130 per month.

Commissions on pension policies

18. HMRC has issued a statement of practice SP 4/97 on their view of the tax treatment of commission, cashbacks and discounts. As far as pension policies are concerned, care must be taken to ensure that commission arrangements do not jeopardise the tax approval of the fund (as to which see note 21). The main point is that the commission arrangements must be under a separate contract. The pension contribution will be treated as the net amount paid if the commission is deducted from the contribution or a discounted premium is paid. If the contribution is paid in full and the commission is received separately, tax relief will be given on the full amount. A pension scheme's tax approval may be withdrawn if commission paid as a result of transfers between schemes represents an unauthorised payment.

The income position for the recipient of the commission is that it does not count as income if it is received by an ordinary member of the public. Commission passed on to customers by agents or employees of pension providers will count as part of the agent's or employee's income, but there will usually be an offsetting expenses deduction. Commission on an employee's own contracts will not count as employment income if it is available on the same basis to the general public. Similar treatment will apply by concession to the self-employed.

Transfers between funds

19. Someone with a registered pension plan who enters pensionable employment may transfer his pension fund to the employer's scheme or to another registered scheme (see Example 72 explanatory note 6).

Missold personal pension plans

20. Some employees were wrongly advised to opt out of their employers' schemes and take out personal pension plans funded by their own contributions. Where compensation is received for such wrong advice, the compensation is exempt from tax. Furthermore, special provisions apply for employees who rejoin their employers' schemes. For details see Example 72 explanatory note 20.

Unauthorised payments

21. Tax is charged at 40% on any unauthorised payments including recycled tax free lump sums, non-arm's length transactions with a member, or employer (s 208), or on deregistration of the fund by HMRC (s 242). The tax is payable by the member (or employer) or, on deregistration, by the scheme administrator.

Where the total unauthorised payments in any twelve month period exceeds 25% of the value of member's rights in the fund a further surcharge of 15% will apply (ss 209–213).

A further penalty known as a 'Sanction Charge' will be imposed on the administrator at the rate of 40% of the relevant transaction. This applies where a fund borrows more than 50% of the fund value, or makes unauthorised payments (other than benefits in kind chargeable to income tax by FA 2004 s 173). Where the sanction charge applies as well as the unauthorised payment charge then the charge is reduced by the lower of the unauthorised payment charge or 25% of the chargeable figure, giving an effective rate of 15% (ss 239–241).

If Alan's pension fund was valued at £1,000,000 and the administrator made an unauthorised payment of £50,000 to Alan the charges would be:

		£
– On Alan 40% × £50,000 (s 208)		20,000
– On the Administrator		
40% × £50,000 (s 239)	20,000	
Less tax paid by Alan restricted to		
25% × £50,000	12,500	7,500
Effective rate of tax is 55%		27,500

If the payment had been £251,000 to Alan then there would be a surcharge on Alan of 15% (£5,209) giving a total charge of 70% (ie £251,000 × 70%=) £175,700.

Pension splitting on divorce

22.   A pension fund can be split on divorce without affecting the tax approved status of the fund. A divorcing couple will not be *required* to share pensions, but all schemes (whenever they were approved) are regarded as including pension sharing provisions. Where the pension is shared, the spouse/civil partner in a pension scheme will get reduced pension rights (a 'pension debit') and rights will be allocated to the other spouse/civil partner (a 'pension credit'). The pension credit received will count towards the lifetime allowance at a benefits crystallisation event. If the pensions credit is a pension in payment then that pension will already have been applied against the other party's lifetime allowance. To prevent double counting, the recipient's lifetime allowance will be increased by an appropriate factor to reflect the value of the pension arising from the pension credit (FA 2004 s 220). The pension credit to the transferee spouse/civil partner must be administered in the same way as for any other approved pension scheme. Benefits may be taken between ages 50 and 75 with the usual options for a lump sum, unsecured pension etc. The pension splitting legislation applies to all types of pension arrangements other than the basic state pension.

Stakeholder pensions

23.   From 6 April 2001 a further type of registered pension known as a stakeholder pension was introduced. For a pension to qualify as a stakeholder pension, the costs must be restricted to 1% of the fund per annum. For those joining from 6 April 2005 the charges can be up to 1.5% of the fund value per year for the first 10 years and 1% thereafter. The investment fund can be chosen by the policyholder or be the default investment. That default may have a lifestyle feature allowing the insurer to move funds into low risk products as retirement approaches (SI 2005/577). The premiums must be able to be started or stopped at will and the minimum premium cannot exceed £20. From 8 October 2001 all employers with five or more employees must provide employees with access to a registered stakeholder scheme, except as indicated below. Those who operate a qualifying salary-related occupational scheme that all relevant employees are eligible to join within one year of starting work, and those who offer a group registered pension to all relevant employees which has no exit charges, that is available after no more than thirteen weeks' service and to which the employer contributes at least 3% of earnings, will not have to offer a stakeholder scheme. Relevant employees are all employees employed in the UK except those whose earnings were below the lower earnings limit (£84 per week in 2006/07) at any time in the previous three months, those under 18 or within five years of normal pension age, employees who have been offered membership of an occupational pension scheme and have declined to join and non-residents without UK net relevant earnings. If employees of non-exempt employers join a scheme, employers must deduct the net contributions from net pay if the employee so requests and forward them to the scheme provider by the 19th of the following month.

Waiver of premiums

24.   From 6 April 2001 new policies that provide for waiver of premium contributions will not obtain tax relief on the cost of that benefit. If a claim is made, however, the proceeds may be used to buy a pension net of basic rate tax.

Non-cash contributions to schemes from 6 April 2001

25.   Under the pension scheme rules applicable from 6 April 2001, a provision may be made for contributions to be made not only in cash but by way of transfer of shares received under SAYE share option schemes, approved share incentive plans (previously called all-employee share ownership plans) and approved profit sharing schemes (as to which see Example 87). Such transfers must be made within 90 days of exercising the SAYE option or of shares being appropriated to the employee. The shares will be treated as contributions equal to their market value at the date of the transfer. Tax relief will then be given on the contributions in the same way as for cash contributions.

Tax credits

26.   Income for tax credits is reduced by tax deductible pension contributions paid by the claimant or partner. The amount of the deduction is the gross allowable premium paid.

Dr Jolly is a medical practitioner who is in general practice. He makes his accounts up to 31 December in each year. In the year to 31 December 2006 his profits, adjusted for taxation (except for superannuation payments made) amounted to £112,500. He has other income in 2006/07 of:

Bank Interest Received	£480
Dividends Received	£270

He made a donation under Gift Aid to a national charity of £1,000 and paid (net) a pension contribution of £7,800.

Dr Jolly's staff are members of the NHS superannuation scheme. The employer's contribution for the year to 31 December 2006 amounted to £11,900.

As well as receiving NHS income, Dr Jolly is a police surgeon, has a consultancy with a leading engineering firm, undertakes insurance and HGV medical examinations and signs death certificates, passport applications, etc.

Your examination of Dr Jolly's superannuation account within his records provides the following information:

		£	£
01.01.06	Creditors – superannuation due		7,486
31.01.06	Quarterly payment	2,965	
30.04.06	Quarterly payment	2,965	
20.05.06	Settlement for 2005/06	3,983	
31.07.06	Quarterly payment	3,113	
30.10.06	Quarterly payment	3,113	
31.12.06	Creditors – superannuation due	6,221	
	Charged in accounts		
	Employers Contribution		10,424
	Employees Contribution		4,468
		22,360	22,360
01.01.07	Creditors – superannuation due		6,221
31.01.07	Quarterly payment	3,113	
02.04.07	Settlement for 2006/07	3,975	
30.04.07	Quarterly payment	3,113	

In May 2007 the NHS scheme administrator informs Dr Jolly that his pension input for the year 2006/07 amounted to £33,483.

You are required to:

(a)   adjust the taxable profits for the year ended 31 December 2006 for superannuation paid;

(b)   indicate how relief is given for superannuation paid by Dr Jolly; and

(c)   compute Dr Jolly's 2006/07 tax liability.

(a) **Dr Jolly adjusted profits of year to 31 December 2006**

	£	£
Profits before superannuation adjustments		112,500
Add Charged in accounts for Dr Jolly		
Employers contribution	10,424	
Employees contribution	4,468	14,892
Net profit for tax purposes		127,392

Note

No adjustment is required for staff superannuation provided the amount charged in the accounts is equal to the amount paid in the accounting period (FA 2004 s 196).

(b) **Relief for superannuation paid**

Dr Jolly is a member of the National Health Service Pension Scheme, which is a registered pension scheme. Relief is, therefore, available for contributions paid within the fiscal year.

In the year 2006/07 the amount paid was:

		£
30.04.06	Quarterly payment	2,965
20.05.06	Settlement for 2005/06	3,983
31.07.06	Quarterly payment	3,113
30.10.06	Quarterly payment	3,113
31.01.07	Quarterly payment	3,113
02.04.07	Settlement for 2006/07	3,975
Claim in 2006/07 tax return (box 14.10)		20,262

(c) **Tax Liability of Dr Jolly for 2006/07**

		£	
Self-employed earnings		127,392	
Bank interest received (480 + 120)		600	
Dividends (270 + 30)		300	
		128,292	
Superannuation paid		20,262	
		108,030	
Personal allowance		5,035	
Taxable income		102,995	
Tax thereon:			
On non-savings income,	2,150 @ 10%	215	
	31,150 @ 22%	6,853	
	11,282 @ 22%*	2,482	
	57,513 @ 40%	23,005	
On savings income	600 @ 40%	240	
	300 @ 32½ %	97	32,892
Class 4 National Insurance			
On 33,540 − 5,035 @ 8%		2,280	
On 127,392 − 33,540 @1%		939	3,219
Total Liability			36,111

*Basic rate band is extended by:

Gross pension contributions (paid net)	
7,800 x 100/78	10,000
Gross Gift Aid payments	
1,000 x 100/78	1,282
	11,282

Explanatory Notes

Pension inputs: annual allowance charge

1. To confirm that Dr Jolly is not liable to an annual allowance charge it is necessary to compare total pension inputs with the annual allowance for 2006/07.

	£
Pension Inputs	
Defined benefits scheme (NHS)	
– per administrator	33,483
Defined contribution scheme	
– own pension (gross)	10,000
	43,483

As £43,493 is less than the annual allowance for 2006/07 of £215,000 no annual allowance charge is payable.

It should be noted that the pensions input on a defined benefits scheme is calculated by reference to the increase in the benefits accruing, not on the amount paid into the scheme. See example 37 at note 2 for details of the calculation. In practice such calculations are undertaken by the pension scheme administrator.

Relief for contributions paid

2. Tax relief is available for contributions paid, restricted to earnings of the year (see example 37 at note 4). Where contributions are paid net of basic rate tax the basic rate band is extended by the grossed up pension contribution.

    Normally contributions to a defined benefits scheme are paid via the employer and the net pay scheme is used to give relief (FA 2004 s 193). However, a GP doctor is self-employed and, therefore, relief cannot be given in that way. Instead the contributions actually paid in the fiscal year are deducted in arriving at taxable income. Relief is claimed on the self-assessment tax return by way of an entry into box 14.10. No deduction is permitted for any pension contribution of the taxpayer in computing the Class 4 National Insurance contributions.

Contributions by retired GP's

3. Tax relief is only due provided the payer has UK earnings. Because GP's pay superannuation on account with a settlement when the annual return is submitted it is possible for payment of the final superannuation contribution to be made in the fiscal year after retirement. Insofar as the contribution exceeds earnings in that year, no relief will be given.

    Should the final adjustment be a refund of contributions that should be credited against the actual payments made and an amended tax return filed, normally for the year of retirement.

Contributions in 2004/05 and 2005/06 by GP's

4. For tax years 2004/05 onwards, GP doctors have been liable to pay both the employers (14%) contributions and the employees (6%) contributions to the NHS pension fund. Their NHS income has been increased to reflect the increased costs. Neither contribution is allowable as a deduction

against taxable profits, but a claim for relief for the actual amount paid in a fiscal year can be made in the Self-Assessment Tax Return. No claim can be made in respect of Class 4 National Insurance.

Normally, the maximum deductible pension contribution for 2004/05 and 2005/06 for occupational pension contributions is 15% of salary. For GP's for 2004/05 and 2005/06 only that limit is increased to 20% plus any additional voluntary contributions made to the same scheme to a maximum of 9%.

For those years it was possible to apply Extra Statutory Concession A9 to waive relief on NHS pension contributions and to claim relief under the normal pension rules. (See example 37 at note 12 for details.) In most cases such a claim would not now be tax efficient. HMRC have agreed that GP's may reclaim the contributions paid to other pension funds and revoke the election to use ESC A9.

ECS A9 has been withdrawn from 6 April 2006. As the new rules allow for contributions to more than one scheme any amounts repaid in respect of 2004/05 or 2005/06 could now be reinvested with tax relief in the current tax year. For further details see HMRC website www.hmrc.gov.uk/pensionschemes/esca9.htm

Mr and Mrs Norton, who are resident, ordinarily resident and domiciled in the United Kingdom, have previously dealt with their own tax affairs. In May 2006 they instructed you to prepare their income tax returns, and compute all tax liabilities, for the year ended 5 April 2006.

You have not received any documents from them other than their tax returns for 2005/06 but at your initial meeting you were informed that their personal circumstances were as follows:

(1) They are married and Mrs Norton has one child, James, from a previous marriage. Mr Norton was born on 11 May 1961 and Mrs Norton on 5 October 1965. James was born on 7 June 1993.

(2) Mr Norton is the overseas purchasing manager of Rumwell plc, a London department store, and receives gross remuneration of approximately £45,000 per annum. A car is provided by his employer.

(3) He has a bank deposit account.

(4) He pays an annual subscription to his professional association and gift aid payments to his local church.

(5) He has a mortgage of £30,000 on their private house in London.

(6) Mrs Norton is a director (working part time only) of Priddy Ltd, undertakers. She receives gross remuneration of between £2,500 and £10,000 per annum, depending upon results, and receives mileage allowance for use of her own car. As this is her family company, she also receives a dividend on her shareholding based upon the tax planning requirements of the company.

(7) She has stock exchange investments and building society deposits.

(8) She paid a premium under a personal pension plan in the year ended 5 April 2006.

(i) Prepare schedules to be sent to Mr and Mrs Norton listing documents and information that you will require for completion of their tax returns and computation of tax liabilities for the year ended 5 April 2006.

(ii) It is your office policy to undertake a review of the file of each personal taxation client before the end of each tax year. Explain why this is advisable and outline the matters which you would include in your review in February 2007.

(i) **Schedules to be sent to Mr and Mrs Norton listing documents and information required to complete tax returns and to compute liabilities for year to 5 April 2006**

Schedule to be sent to Mr Norton

1. *Earnings*

   (a) The following are required in respect of Rumwell plc for 2005/06:

   P60 year-end certificate of pay and tax deducted

   Coding notices issued for 2005/06 (and also coding notice for 2006/07) (forms P2), together with details of any underpayments brought forward from 2003/04 or 2004/05 to 2005/06, or amounts carried forward to 2006/07 in respect of 2005/06

   Form P11D (details of benefits and expenses received), together with any additional schedules provided by the employer

   Details of any expense payments received from the employer not included on form P11D (eg those covered by a dispensation)

   Expenses incurred in performance of duties of the employment to be itemised for expenses claim

   Details of car, including list price when new, CO_2 emissions figure, whether any capital contribution made and whether private fuel provided

   Details of share options and incentives, with particulars of any options exercised during 2006/07

   Details of any amounts received, other than from Rumwell plc in respect of the employment

   Confirmation of whether Mr Norton is a member of Rumwell's pension scheme.

   (b) Confirmation that there are no earnings from other sources. If there are any such earnings, details required of amount, source and date of payment. If employment changed in the year, form P45 (part 1A) is required.

   (c) National insurance number (if not shown on P60 code number or tax return).

2. *Bank deposit account*

   Details of the interest credited during the year to 5 April 2006. The name of the deposit taker and account number. Confirmation that the account is a UK based account and that interest is after deduction of lower rate tax. Tax vouchers for such interest.

3. *Professional subscription*

   Amount paid and name of professional association.

4. *Details of gift aid payments*

   Amounts actually paid to church in year with confirmation that Mr Norton has signed a gift aid declaration.

   Confirmation that Mr Norton did not make any other covenanted payments or charitable gifts from which he deducted basic rate tax during the year ended 5 April 2006.

   Details of any gift aid payments made since 5 April 2006, so that consideration may be given to a claim to carry such payments back to 2005/06.

5. *Information for tax credits*

   Child's full name, confirmation that James's father cannot make any child's tax credit claim in respect of James. If he could make such a claim, consider surrendering the child's tax credit to him if Mr and Mrs Norton are unable to make a full claim because of the level of their income.

Confirmation that Mr & Mrs Norton have made a claim for tax credits for 2005/06. This claim is based upon income for 2004/05 and then adjusted to actual income for 2005/06. It is possible that a claim will be due for 2005/06 as their joint income after deduction of professional subscription, gift aid payments, pension premiums and the £300 disregard for non-earnings, could be less than £58,000. If their income in 2004/05 was lower their final entitlement will also benefit from the £2,500 disregard. Their income is probably too high to qualify for childcare credit.

6. *Other income and outgoings, and capital transactions*

   Details of any other income and outgoings, or changes therein, and capital assets acquired or disposed of. (Details of capital assets acquired are not required for the tax return, but are essential for the adviser's file.)

   Confirmation that no investments in James's name were provided by Mr Norton.

7. *2004/05 tax calculation working sheet*

   Copies of the working sheet for 2004/05, or of HMRC's calculation of liability, together with a copy of the 2004/05 self-assessment tax return.

8. *2005/06 payments on account*

   Copies of any payments on account notices and summary of payments statements already issued for 2005/06. Details of any claim made to reduce payments on account (forms SA 303).

9. *Form 64-8*

   Signed form 64-8 giving authority to HMRC to issue copies of formal notices to agent and to discuss all taxation, national insurance and tax credit issues.

Schedule to be sent to Mrs Norton

1. *Earnings*

   P60 from Priddy Ltd for 2005/06, together with coding notices issued for 2005/06 and 2006/07 (forms P2) and details of any benefits and expenses received (form P11D, together with any additional schedules provided by the employer, and details of any expenses or benefits received not included on P11D).

   Expenses incurred in performance of duties.

   Details of business mileage undertaken in her own car and the amount paid by her employer.

   Amount, source and date of payment of any earnings in the year other than those included on form P60.

   National insurance number (if not shown on P60 code notices or tax return).

2. *Investments*

   Dividend vouchers for dividends paid by Priddy Ltd during 2005/06.

   Dividend and interest vouchers on stock exchange investments and contract notes covering any purchases and sales of securities.

   Details of original acquisitions of investments and whether any capital gains tax elections are in force.

   Details of building society accounts including account numbers and interest credited in the year. Confirmation that they are UK based accounts and interest is credited net of lower rate tax. Tax vouchers for such interest.

3. *Personal pension policy*

    Name of insurance company to which personal pension premium paid and amount thereof, form PPCC or other evidence of payment, and confirmation that the premium was paid net of basic rate tax.

    Previous retirement annuity or personal pension premium payments and earnings from Priddy Ltd or elsewhere during previous six years in order to ascertain the amount of any unused relief available to increase the limit of allowable retirement annuity premiums based on the 2005/06 earnings and the maximum permitted personal pension contributions.

    Confirmation that Priddy Ltd has not included her in a company pension scheme.

    Has an election been made to have any part of the 2005/06 premium treated as paid in 2004/05?

4. *Covenants and gifts*

    Confirmation that no covenanted payments or gifts under deduction of basic rate tax were made during the year to 5 April 2006 or since 5 April 2006.

5. *Provision for James*

    Details of any investments in James's name provided by Mrs Norton.

6. *Self-assessment details for 2004/05 and payments on account for 2005/06*

    Copies of any payments on account notices and summary of payments statements already issued for 2005/06, and of the tax calculation working sheet, or HMRC calculation of liability, for 2004/05, together with a copy of the 2004/05 tax return.

7. *Other income and outgoings, and capital transactions*

    Details of any other income and outgoings or changes therein, and capital assets acquired or disposed of.

8. *Form 64-8*

    Signed form 64-8 giving authority to HMRC to issue copies of formal notices to agent and to discuss all taxation, national insurance and tax credit issues.

(ii) **Year end review to be undertaken in February 2007**

Need for annual review

An annual review is essential in order that opportunities for tax mitigation are considered and any necessary action may be taken before the end of the tax year.

A record of the review should be kept in the file of each personal taxation client, and also those for whom one prepares accounts and agrees business taxation liabilities in so far as the personal taxation aspect of their affairs is concerned.

The main areas to be covered in the review are:

Areas relevant to Mr and Mrs Norton

1. *Pension provision*

    The schedule received from Mr Norton re 2005/06 will confirm whether Rumwell plc operates a pension scheme of which he is a member. Assuming that this is the case, consider whether any additional pension contributions are appropriate.

    Mrs Norton's pension provision should similarly be reviewed, including the possibility of paying £3,600 pa even if that is more than her earnings.

    The effect of the charge to pension rules from 6 April 2006 should be considered.

It is unlikely that Mr and Mrs Norton have exceeded the lifetime limit, but if they have then an election to protect their rights is required by 5 April 2009. It is possible that if Mr Norton is a member of an occupational pension scheme that he has rights to a lump sum in excess of 25% of the fund. If so that right will be preserved providing he does not transfer funds from that scheme before drawing benefits.

2. *Is income sufficiently large to utilise personal allowances, loss etc claims, and the starting and basic rate bands of each spouse and child?*

   Mr Norton clearly uses his available allowances. The position for Mrs Norton and her child should be checked. If allowances etc are not being used there may be nothing that can be done. If possible Mrs Norton should receive salary and benefits of an amount which, together with her savings income other than dividends, equals at least £5,035 before receiving dividends from Priddy Ltd and other investments, as the tax credit on dividends is not repayable.

3. *Gifts to charities*

   As well as ensuring that a gift aid declaration has been made for all charities to whom amounts are given, should additional gifts be made in favour of charities and a payment made before 6 April, relief at the higher rate then being available if appropriate? (Payments made after 5 April but before filing the tax return and before 31 January may also be carried back to the previous year.)

   Check that gifts are made by the spouse with the highest marginal rate of tax, ie Mr Norton unless Mrs Norton's investment income is substantial. If gifts were made by Mrs Norton, and she was a non-taxpayer, she would have to account for basic rate tax if insufficient tax credits were available on her dividend income to cover the amount deemed to be deducted (see Example 91).

4. *Potential capital gains tax position*

   Has Mrs Norton made sufficient gains to utilise the annual exemption (£8,800 for 2006/07)? If gains above that level have already been realised, are there assets standing at a loss which should be sold before 6 April 2007 in order to reduce the chargeable gains? Remember that the contract date is the date of disposal for capital gains tax. It should be borne in mind that in later life state aid for nursing care will be affected by the resulting holdings of assets.

5. *Transfers between spouses and inheritance tax planning*

   It appears that Mr Norton has no investments. Consider whether it would be appropriate for Mrs Norton to transfer some investments to him to utilise his annual exemption for capital gains tax, or into joint ownership (see supplementary note 4). Such transfers must be absolute gifts to be effective.

   When reviewing the investment position, a review of current wills could be made, incorporating a calculation of the potential inheritance tax liability. Any necessary advice about new wills and mitigation of potential inheritance tax liabilities by insurance, use of trusts, or other means could then be given.

   If appropriate, Mr and Mrs Norton should be made aware of the inheritance tax provisions for small gifts, gifts out of income and annual exemptions, and the facility to make potentially exempt transfers.

Areas for consideration generally

6. *Maximising allowances, starting rate band and reliefs*

   Consider whether justifiable payments for one spouse assisting in the other's business can be made before 6 April where appropriate. This is relevant not only for trades, professions and vocations but also in relation to a UK property business and for occupations such as clergymen and examiners. PAYE regulations (completion of form P46, deduction at source if appropriate etc) must be followed. The national insurance implications should also be considered. In 2006/07 a spouse could be paid £97 a week without attracting national insurance contributions. Pay at or above £84 makes the year a qualifying year for benefits purposes (including state pension). On the other hand, if a spouse's pay was at a much higher level (in order to use the basic rate band) the national insurance cost would be substantial.

In the case of discretionary trusts or deceased's estates, should a distribution be made before 6 April?

Where there is a family company, should a dividend be paid by the company before 6 April rather than after 5 April? Conversely would the tax position of the recipient be improved by delaying a dividend or indeed other income until a later tax year if that is possible? Since tax credits on dividends are not repayable, dividends are not effective in enabling personal allowances to be used.

For those near or over 65, the effect of bunching of income on age-related allowances should be borne in mind.

7. *Relief for the amount of a qualifying investment under the Enterprise Investment Scheme (TA 1988 s 306)*

The claim for relief must be made within five years after 31 January following the tax year in which the qualifying investment is made, but not earlier than four months after the company commenced to trade.

A decision should be made as to whether up to half of the amount subscribed before 6 October in any tax year should be carried back to the previous year (maximum carry-back £50,000 from 6 April 2006, previously £25,000). If so, this should be stated in the claim.

Supplementary Notes

Notifying HMRC of agent's appointment

1. Upon receiving instructions the agent should file Form 64-8 with the Central Agent Authorisation Team at Longbenton, Newcastle-upon-Tyne, NE98 1ZZ. It would be usual to write to the Area Office informing them of the instructions to act for Mr and Mrs Norton, asking them to supply copies of formal notices etc, and asking for:

    (a) Copies of the last tax returns of Mr and Mrs Norton.

    (b) Copies of the notice of calculation of tax liability for 2004/05.

    (c) Confirmation that there was no outstanding correspondence requiring attention, open appeals, or contentious matters under discussion or enquiry.

    (d) Details of any PAYE coding adjustments affecting 2005/06 or 2006/07.

    HMRC will usually supply this information/documents upon processing the Form 64-8, but otherwise they will do so on receipt of a letter from Mr and Mrs Norton.

    It should be noted that Form 64-8 is not sent to CAAT for

    –   Cases dealt with by Claims Offices,

    –   Complex personal returns,

    –   Expatriates,

    –   Companies, or

    –   Where there is also a CIS registration card application to accompany the Form 64-8.

    These 64-8 forms should be sent to the appropriate area office. If the agent files electronically, or uses a computer produced tax return, then the client will no longer receive a tax return for completion, but a formal notice requiring the submission of a completed return by the relevant date.

Pension provision

2.   Mrs Norton will pay personal pension premiums net of basic rate tax. Her employment income is low, but if her investment income is high enough to take her income above the basic rate limit, further relief will be due on the premiums.

    As an alternative, it may be possible to get Mrs Norton's employer (Priddy Ltd) to make the payments to the personal pension. Employer contributions are paid gross. The pension contribution is deductible for trading income purposes to the extent that it is incurred wholly and exclusively for the purpose of the trade. However, it is the remuneration package in total that must be wholly and exclusively for the purposes of the trade, and HMRC has stated that the proportion that the pension contribution bears to salary will not affect the deduction.

    The pension contribution is paid from funds that have not been reduced by national insurance contributions. It is, therefore, possible to effect a salary sacrifice of an amount that would have been liable to national insurance contributions, and enhance the contribution (and, therefore, total remuneration) by the amount of the national insurance saved. This can increase the value of the amount invested into the pension by up to 31%.

3.   All files should be reviewed each year in time for appropriate action to be taken in relation to pension contributions before 6 April 2007. If Mr Norton is not a member of an occupational scheme, a personal pension plan would be appropriate.

Transferring assets between spouses

4.   Rather than transferring assets outright, spouses may prefer to put them into joint ownership. In that event the income will be divided 50:50 for tax purposes regardless of the actual ownership proportions (TA 1988 s 282A). This provision does not apply to close company shares from 6 April 2004. In that case the division of income always follows the actual ownership.

    If the taxpayers prefer, a declaration may be made of the true beneficial ownership of the investment. Provided HMRC is notified (on form 17) within 60 days of the date of the declaration, the true division of income will apply from the date the declaration was made (TA 1988 s 282B). In Tax Bulletin 63 (February 2003) HMRC made it clear that joint bank and building society accounts are held equally and cannot be the subject of a s 282B election unless the parties have changed the legal basis on which the account is held, for example, by way of deed.

5.   Where action is being contemplated to reduce the income of the main earner from a family company full regard must be given to the anti-avoidance legislation relating to settlements in ITTOIA 2005 part 5 chapter 5. If an element of bounty is provided, then the income remains taxable on the main earner. The decision in Young v Pearse, Young v Scrutton (1996) should be noted. In this case, preference shares without voting rights were issued to wives, entitling them to dividends of 30%. It was held that the preference dividends remained assessable on the husbands under ITTOIA 2005 s 626 since the property given was wholly or substantially a right to income. HMRC has given their views as to when the settlement provisions will apply in Tax Bulletin 64 (April 2003).

    HMRC will review cases where it appears that:

-   the main earner draws a low salary leading to enhanced dividends paid to other family members or friends

-   dividends represent disproportionally large returns on capital investments

-   there are different classes of shares enabling dividends to be directed to shareholders only paying the lower rate of tax

-   there are dividend waivers in favour of shareholders who only pay at the lower rate of tax

-   there is income transferred from the earner to other members of the family or friends who pay tax at a lower rate.

Commonly, the settlements legislation will be considered to apply where:

– shares are subscribed for that carry only restricted rights

– shares are gifted that carry only restricted rights

– shares are subscribed for at par in a company where the income is derived mainly from the earnings of a single employee

– a share in a partnership is transferred at below market value

– there are dividend waivers

– dividends are only paid on certain classes of share

– dividends are paid to a settlor's minor children.

The test case of Jones v Garnett has gone through a series of appeals, some decisions favouring the taxpayer, some decisions favouring HMRC. In this instance, the main earner was paid a salary well below the going rate, which provided funds that could be distributed equally between husband and wife by a way of a dividend. A decision in 2005 confirmed that taking a salary below the market rate provided bounty, and therefore the dividend declared to the wife was taxable on the husband. This decision has since been reversed, but it still represents the view of HMRC, and the reversal of the decision is going to appeal in the House of Lords.

National insurance

6. A client's national insurance position needs to be considered when a business commences or any additional activities are undertaken. Notification of commencement of business should be made by telephone or on form CWF1 within three calendar months of the calendar month of commencement.

A certificate of deferment should be applied for if a client is expected to pay more than the overall maximum contributions under Classes 1, 2 or 4. The first application should normally be made by *14 February* before the relevant tax year (see Example 47). Renewal forms will be sent by the National Insurance Contributions Office for later years. If a deferment certificate is not held, a repayment should be applied for.

Those with small earnings from self-employment (under £4,465 for 2006/07) may apply for a certificate of exception from Class 2 contributions. Exception must be claimed no later than 31 December following the end of the relevant tax year. The certificate needs to be renewed each year. It may well be thought advisable for a client to pay the contributions in any event, in order to maintain a contributions record (the alternative voluntary Class 3 contributions being £5.45 a week higher).

Employees have entitlement to benefits if their earnings exceed the lower limit (£84 per week in 2006/07). Their contributions are 11% of earnings over £97 per week to a maximum of the upper earnings limit of £645 per week and 1% thereafter. Employers' contributions of 12.8% commence on earnings above £97 per week. Accordingly an employee could have earnings of £5,044 per annum without attracting any national insurance contributions. A PAYE scheme would be needed to establish the employee's entitlement to benefits.

Inheritance tax and taxation of trusts and estates

7. For detailed provisions see companion book Tolley's Taxwise II 2006/07.

Tax credits

8. All taxpayers with a qualifying child, or who work 30+ hours per week and are aged 25 or over should consider making a protective claim for tax credits by 6 July in a tax year. Any later claim can only be backdated by three months. Because an award is eventually based upon income for the actual year it will not be known, by 6 July, whether or not an amount will be payable. If the claimant waits until the award can be quantified it will often be too late to make any claim. See Example 5 for full details.

Outline the self-assessment provisions that apply to individuals.

Outline of self-assessment provisions for individuals

1.　　(a)　*Requirement to send in a return*

Self-assessment applies for income tax and capital gains tax from 1996/97. On receipt of a notice from HMRC requiring a return to be made, those taxpayers who wish to work out their own tax must send in their return, together with supporting schedules, by 31 January following the end of the tax year, ie by 31 January 2008 for 2006/07 (or, if the notice is given after 31 October following the tax year, three months from the date of the notice) (TMA 1970 ss 8 and 9). Taxpayers may produce returns using a personal computer if they wish and appropriate software is commercially available. If a taxpayer only needs to complete the basic form plus the employment, self-employment, individual partnership and land and property pages, the form is available on the HMRC website. HMRC cannot accept a return on disk. Filing via the internet is available to those who register with HMRC's internet filing website (accessible from www.hmrc.gov.uk). HMRC has been recommended by the 2006 Carter report to aim for universal electronic delivery of returns by IT literate groups by 2012.

HMRC have accepted the recommendations of the Carter report that, from 2007/08, the filing deadline for paper returns should be shortened to 31 October, but that the deadline for electronic returns should remain 31 January.

If precise figures are not available when the return is submitted, best estimates should be used. Where provisional figures are used, box 23.2 should be ticked and an acceptable explanation for the delay, together with an estimated date by which the final figure will be provided, entered in the additional information box. If the figures are not available within the one year time limit for taxpayer amendments or HMRC enquiries (see notes 6 and 12), HMRC will accept an 'error or mistake' claim (see Example 42) to reduce the tax payable, or will issue a discovery assessment under TMA 1970 s 29 (see note 14) to recover any additional tax payable.

If HMRC receive an unsatisfactory return it will be rejected. This includes:

–　　non-standard return form

–　　unsigned return

–　　relevant supplementary pages not enclosed with the return

–　　a return containing unjustified provisional figures.

If HMRC send back an unsatisfactory return between 18 January and 31 January following the tax year, then in cases of genuine oversight they normally allow 14 days for the return to be resubmitted without imposing a penalty.

Where a taxpayer starts a business or joins a partnership, it may not be possible to submit accurate information relating to the business as the first year-end is after the relevant 5 April. The procedure for provisional figures set out above should be used. For partnerships see Example 41 note 9.

(b)　*Calculation of tax payable*

Taxpayers do not have to work out their own tax and HMRC will make the calculations if the return is sent in by 30 September following the end of the tax year (eg by 30 September 2007 for 2006/07). If filed electronically that date is extended to 30 December (30 December 2007 for 2006/07), HMRC's calculation then being treated as a self-assessment. Calculations of amounts on which the tax is based must, however, be done by the taxpayer, for example capital allowances and capital gains. Taxpayers may ask HMRC to check valuations used in calculating their capital gains before they send in their returns.

HMRC will still calculate the tax for returns received after 30 September/ 30 December if required, but will not guarantee to advise the amounts due in time for the taxpayer to avoid interest (and possibly a surcharge). As far as employees are concerned, even if they are working out their own tax, they must meet the 30 September/30 December deadline if there is a tax underpayment of up to £2,000 that they wish to have collected through the PAYE scheme rather than being required to pay it on 31 January following the end of the tax year. If the 30 September deadline is missed but HMRC receives the paper return by the end of November, they will still try to collect the underpayment through PAYE but cannot guarantee to do so.

Where a taxpayer with employment income settled an underpayment in excess of £500 by payment in the previous year then the HMRC system will not code out underpayments in excess of £500 in the current year. Care should be taken to warn clients of this problem if they fail to file their return by 30 September and therefore have to pay the balance of tax due on 31 January following.

Taxpayers need not include pence on the return, and income and gains may be rounded *down* and tax paid/dividend tax credits rounded *up*. If an entry in a particular box covers several different items, it is the *total* figure that should be rounded. The tax calculation may also be rounded, although not the resulting payments on account. If the tax is calculated either by HMRC or by commercial software, it will be calculated in pounds and pence, and software packages also show income and gains in pounds and pence.

Several errors have been identified in HMRC's computer program for calculating tax and interest, so it is advisable to check the figures.

(c) *Trust and estate returns*

To minimise delays in winding up estates and trusts and distributing estate or trust property, HMRC will, on request, issue tax returns before the end of the tax year of death, or of winding up an estate or trust, and will give early confirmation if they do not intend to enquire into the return.

The death of the taxpayer does not automatically cancel the payments on account due for that year based upon the previous year's liabilities. It is necessary to compute the likely liabilities to the date of death, then make a claim on form SA 303 to reduce the payments on account to the expected liability.

(d) *Partnerships*

In addition to partners completing their own self-assessment returns, a partnership is required to file a partnership return, together with a partnership statement (TMA 1970 ss 12AA, 12AB). A partner's individual return shows only the partner's share of income and gains, the details being in the partnership return. See Example 41 for the detailed provisions.

(e) *No tax liability for year*

If a taxpayer receives a return, and he has no tax liability, HMRC takes the view that the return must even so be completed. Since most penalties under self-assessment cannot exceed the tax payable, the only penalty which would be effective in securing the return would be the £60 daily penalty, only payable after a Commissioners' direction (TMA 1970 s 93(3)). See note 11 for more detail on penalties. If the return is not completed, it would, however, be advisable to notify HMRC that there was no income.

2. *Self-employment and 'Standard Accounts Information'*

When completing the self-employment pages of the tax return, the profit or loss is required to be shown in 'Standard Accounts Information' (SAI) format (see Example 15 for an illustration), and for taxpayers who have a balance sheet, the balance sheet details must also be provided (in SAI format). This does not apply to those whose turnover is less than £15,000, who are not required to submit a balance sheet and need only show their turnover, purchases and expenses, and net profit (but see note 12 re the increased possibility of an HMRC enquiry).

Where more than one accounting period relates to the basis period for the year (for example where the accounting date has changed), a separate set of self-employment pages must be completed for each account.

Accounts need not be sent in with returns (with the exception of very large partnerships and partnerships with only corporate partners – see Example 41 note 5). Taxpayers may send whatever supporting information with their returns they consider is necessary in order to make a full disclosure, but unless the relevance of any additional material is pointed out, this will not stop HMRC later trying to make a discovery assessment (see Example 43). The return forms include various blank spaces for additional information (known as 'white space'), and it would be sensible to use the white space to refer to any additional information that is being sent with the return.

3.   *Retaining records*

Even though accounts etc need not be submitted with returns, taxpayers must retain their records for a statutory period. Traders and those with letting income must keep the records until the fifth anniversary of the 31 January next following the relevant tax year. Other taxpayers must retain records until the first anniversary of that 31 January date. So for 2005/06 the time limit for traders and landlords is 31 January 2012 and for other taxpayers 31 January 2008. If HMRC enquires into the return (see note 12), the records must be retained until the enquiry is completed if later than the normal retention date (TMA 1970 s 12B).

Where a claim is made other than in a return (see Example 42), records relating to the claim must similarly be retained until any HMRC enquiry into the claim is completed, or until HMRC is no longer able to start such an enquiry (TMA 1970 Sch 1A para 2A).

A penalty of up to £3,000 per tax year may be charged for non-compliance.

4.   *Information from employers*

Employers must provide employees with appropriate information relating to their earnings to enable the employees to complete their tax returns. Forms P60 (pay and tax details) must be supplied by 31 May, and forms P11D/P9D (details of expenses payments and benefits, including calculations of cash equivalents) by 6 July.

Employers sometimes make PAYE 'tax equalisation' arrangements for foreign national employees (see Example 9 explanatory note 19). There is a special Help Sheet IR 212 to assist such employees and their advisers in the completion of their tax returns, and see also Revenue Tax Bulletins of October 1997, June 1998, June 2002 and February 2006.

5.   *Notification of liability if no return received*

Anyone who is liable to income tax or capital gains tax and does not receive a notice under TMA 1970 s 8 must notify HMRC that he is so chargeable within six months from the end of the tax year, ie by 5 October 2007 for 2006/07 (TMA 1970 s 7). There is a penalty of up to the amount of tax payable as at 31 January following for non-notification.

There is no liability to notify if the individual has no capital gains or liability to higher rate tax, and tax on all income has been accounted for under PAYE, or by deduction at source, or by tax credits on dividends. Employees will not usually have received their coding notices by 5 October, but if they have a copy of form P11D they may assume HMRC is aware of its contents unless they have reason to believe otherwise.

Tax returns will not normally be issued unless income exceeds £2,500, providing the tax due can be dealt with through PAYE.

6. *HMRC corrections and taxpayer amendments*

HMRC has nine months from the date a return is received to correct obvious errors in the return (TMA 1970 s 9ZB), and taxpayers may make amendments within a year from the filing date (TMA 1970 s 9ZA), but if the return is selected for further enquiry – see note 12 – amendments made between the time HMRC gives notice that they intend to enquire into the return and the time the enquiries are completed only take effect on the completion of the enquiry (TMA 1970 s 9B). HMRC will accept an amendment from a taxpayer's agent unless they believe the taxpayer may not have authorised it. HMRC's right to correct a return extends to making consequential corrections within nine months after a taxpayer amendment.

The taxpayer has an explicit right under TMA 1970 s 9ZB to reject an HMRC correction to a return, providing notice of rejection is given within thirty days (similar rights being given in relation to partnership returns by s 12ABB – see Example 41 note 8). In practice any rejection outside that period will be accepted if it is as a result of an HMRC error.

If an amendment results in extra tax payable, the due date of payment for the extra tax is 30 days after the amendment or, where relevant, the date of completion of an HMRC enquiry (TMA 1970 Sch 3ZA), although interest on overdue tax runs from the original due date for the return.

7. *Payments on account*

Under TMA 1970 s 59A, provisional payments on account are due half-yearly on 31 January in the tax year and 31 July following. The payments on account are equal to half of the *net* income tax and Class 4 national insurance liability of the previous tax year (ie after deducting PAYE tax relating to that year, tax deducted from interest etc, dividend tax credits and tax deducted from subcontractors' payments). Payments on account are not required where more than 80% of the previous year's tax liability was covered by tax deducted at source and dividend tax credits, or where the previous year's net tax and Class 4 NI was less than £500.

At any time before the 31 January filing date for the return, a taxpayer who believes he would otherwise overpay tax may make a claim (on form SA 303) for the payments on account not to be paid, or to be reduced. Care needs to be taken in working out appropriate payments on account for a taxpayer whose PAYE coding includes a previous year's underpayment or, in the future, a recovery of overpaid tax credits. The tax return provides for claims to reduce payments on account to be made in the return itself, but it has been reported that such claims may not be properly processed, so it is advisable to send in form SA 303.

Following a claim, if either or both of the payments on account have already been made, the appropriate amount will be repaid, with repayment supplement from the payment date. If, however, the final tax figures for the year show that all or part of the reduction in the payments on account should not have been made, interest will be charged on the shortfall from the original due dates. In addition to being charged interest, a taxpayer who fraudulently or negligently reduces his payments on account is liable to a penalty not exceeding the shortfall in payment (TMA 1970 s 59A(6)).

HMRC will calculate payments on account for taxpayers who do not calculate their own tax. Taxpayers receive regular statements of account (forms SA 300) showing amounts due, amounts paid, and interest charges/repayment supplement where relevant. Statements will be issued when a new charge will become due within 35 days, every two months where an overdue amount is between £32 and £500 and every month where an overdue amount is £500 or more. HMRC will provide summary information, excluding interest on unpaid tax, on a client's statement of account at key dates in the year to agents for whom HMRC has the taxpayer's authority (on form 64-8) to send copy information.

8. *Balancing payments/repayments*

Under TMA 1970 s 59B, the total income tax, Class 4 NI and capital gains tax due for the tax year is compared with the amount already paid and the balance is payable or repayable on or before the following 31 January. If, however, a taxpayer had given notice of liability by 5 October following the tax year as indicated in note 5, and did not receive a notice to complete a return until after 31 October, the balancing payment is due three months from the date of the notice. In either case, the first payment on account for the next tax year is due at the same time.

Although the balancing payment for a tax year is due for payment at the same time as the latest date for sending in the return, the payment is sent to the HMRC accounts office and the return to the tax office.

Where a return shows an overpayment, it will be refunded if the appropriate box is ticked in the return, but overpaid payments on account are not refunded automatically. A letter requesting a refund of the payments on account should be sent.

9.   *Interest on overdue tax/Class 4 national insurance and repayment supplement*

Interest on overdue payments on account and balancing payments runs from the due date of payment to the date the tax is paid (TMA 1970 s 86), and repayment supplement from the payment date to the date the repayment order is issued (TA 1988 s 824) (see Example 43 part B note 11 for the date when payment is regarded as having been made). There is no liability to tax on repayment supplement (ITTOIA 2005 s 749).

Class 4 national insurance contributions and student loan repayments that are collected along with income tax also attract interest and repayment supplement as appropriate. Where a taxpayer has deferred Class 4 contributions (see Example 47), any amount that ultimately becomes payable is collected by the national insurance contributions office (NICO) and interest is not payable. If a taxpayer has overpaid Class 4 contributions because of exceeding the annual maximum, the refund is made by NICO and no adjustment is made to the amount self-assessed, so there is no effect on payments on account, interest etc.

The provisions in note 7 for charging interest in relation to payments on account apply where the payments have been reduced below half the previous year's liability. Except in relation to such a reduction, interest is not charged on any amount by which the payments on account fall short of the final net income tax liability for the year. If, however, the payments on account *exceed* the final income tax liability, repayment supplement is paid from the dates the payments were made. Since the first payment on account for the following year is due at the same time as the balancing adjustment, there will not usually be a repayment, but this does not affect the entitlement to repayment supplement. If a surcharge or penalty is repaid, repayment supplement is added to that repayment. For further points relating to interest and supplement calculations see Example 43.

10.   *Surcharges*

Surcharges apply as follows (in addition to interest) if the balancing payment for a year is more than 28 days late (TMA 1970 s 59C):

5% of the unpaid amount if the balance of tax due is not paid by 28 February.

A further 5% if not paid by 31 July.

The taxpayer may appeal against a surcharge, and the Appeal Commissioners may set the surcharge aside if the taxpayer has a reasonable excuse. HMRC has the power to mitigate or remit the surcharge.

Where additional tax is payable following an amendment to a return, the tax is due 30 days after the amendment, and surcharge arises only if the tax is paid more than 28 days after the 30 day period, and further surcharge only if the payment is not made within a further 5 months.

Surcharge is due for payment within 30 days after the date on which it is imposed, and it attracts interest from that date in the same way as the tax itself if it is paid late (s 59C(6)).

11.   *Penalties for late returns*

If returns are made late, automatic penalties will be charged as follows (TMA 1970 s 93):

£100 if the return is not made by 31 January (or the filing date for the return if later), plus a further £60 a day if HMRC has applied for and received a direction from the General or Special Commissioners to charge the daily penalty. Following the case of Steeden v Carver (1999) a late filing penalty will not be charged for returns received up to midnight on 1 February.

Further £100 if the Commissioners have not imposed the daily penalty and the return is not made by 31 July (or six months from the filing date if later).

Further penalty of an amount equal to the tax that would have been payable under the return if it is not made by next 31 January, or by one year from the filing date if later (not applicable to partnership returns).

HMRC stated in their February 2002 Tax Bulletin that they will be making increasing use of daily penalty proceedings.

The *fixed* penalties cannot exceed the amount of tax that remains outstanding at the return due date, and cannot be charged if a repayment is due. Where this applies, any fixed penalty already paid, or the appropriate part thereof, will be refunded (TMA 1970 s 100).

The taxpayer may appeal against a penalty, and the Appeal Commissioners may set it aside if the taxpayer has a reasonable excuse. Interest is charged on unpaid penalties as it is on unpaid tax (TMA 1970 s 103A).

In a reasonable excuse case the onus is on the taxpayer to show that the excuse should be considered reasonable and that excuse must exist throughout the period of default. A reasonable excuse for late filing of a tax return could include:

– Fire or flood at the Post Office that handled the return, or prolonged industrial action within the Post Office.

– Loss of records through fire, flood or theft.

– Very serious illness such as coma, stroke, major heart attack or serious mental or life threatening illness.

– Death of a close relative or domestic partner.

Although HMRC does not consider reasonable excuse cases for VAT relevant for direct tax, such cases may well influence the decision of the Commissioners.

The following reasons are unlikely to be acceptable:

– Pressure of work.

– Failure of a tax agent, although this excuse was held to be reasonable in an appeal against a surcharge (Rowland v HMRC, 2006).

– Lack of information, unless due from a third party and actively pursued.

– Considering the tax form too difficult.

HMRC previously imposed penalties in some cases not only where a return was late, but where a return filed on time was not correct and complete (for example, where the return contained estimated figures). Following an appeal against their practice, they now accept that the inclusion of provisional or estimated figures does not enable them to impose a late filing penalty (unless reasonable care was not taken with the figures, or final figures could have been obtained before the return was sent in), although it will be a factor to take into account in deciding whether to open an enquiry.

12.   *HMRC enquiries into return and claims made separately from return*

HMRC has a year after the filing due date, eg to 31 January 2009 for a 2006/07 return filed by 31 January 2008, to open an enquiry. If the return or an amendment to it is made after the due date, then the time limit is a year from the time the return or amendment is delivered plus the period to the next quarter day, ie the next 31 January, 30 April, 31 July or 31 October) (TMA 1970 s 9A).

Otherwise the tax as calculated will normally stand unless there has been inadequate disclosure or fraudulent or negligent conduct. (Similar rules apply to partnership returns – see Example 41.) Lord Carter's review recommends that the enquiry deadline should be based on the date of filing the return.

When HMRC has opened an enquiry, they have the power under TMA 1970 ss 19A and 20 to require the taxpayer and third parties to produce relevant documents to them (see Example 45 part (a) and explanatory note 4).

Following completion of the enquiry, HMRC will issue a closure notice informing the taxpayer of their conclusions and any amendments they have made to the return. The taxpayer has 30 days to appeal against the conclusions stated and amendments made by HMRC, and the appeal and postponement procedures dealt with in Example 43 apply. (TMA 1970 ss 28A, 31).

HMRC has similar powers to enquire into claims made separately from the return (TMA 1970 Sch 1A.5) (for claims procedures see Example 42). The time limit for opening an enquiry into such a claim is the same as for an enquiry into an amendment to a return, and the same procedures apply for the taxpayer to appeal against HMRC amendments when the enquiry is completed. There is, however, no provision for tax to be postponed.

HMRC may select cases for enquiry at random, and are not required to state whether the enquiry is a random one or whether they suspect something is wrong. There is no statutory relief for accountancy fees, although HMRC has confirmed that if an enquiry results in no addition to profits, or only in an adjustment to the year of enquiry that does not arise out of negligent or fraudulent conduct, accountancy expenses relating to the enquiry will be allowed (see Example 15 explanatory note 3). If it is considered that an enquiry has been unnecessarily prolonged, taxpayers may ask the Commissioners to direct that it should be closed, and they may also complain to the Adjudicator or Ombudsman, each of whom has the power to recommend compensation.

HMRC has substantially increased the number of enquiries into returns for businesses that have completed three line accounts showing turnover just below £15,000 in successive years (see note 2), because the number of such businesses has increased significantly since the opportunity to submit three line accounts was introduced from 1996/97.

13. *HMRC determinations of tax due*

HMRC has the power to determine the amount of tax due if a return is not submitted and their determination is treated as a self-assessment until superseded by an actual self-assessment (TMA 1970 s 28C). A determination under s 28C cannot be made more than five years after the filing date for the return, and a superseding self-assessment can only be made within the time limit, or if later within 12 months after the determination.

14. *HMRC assessments*

Under self-assessment, HMRC will not normally issue assessments themselves except for 'discovery assessments' under TMA 1970 s 29 to prevent a loss of tax in cases of fraudulent or negligent conduct, or where there has been inadequate disclosure (see Example 43). There are still some other limited occasions when assessments will be raised outside the self-assessment system, for example:

Under TA 1988 s 350 to collect tax deducted at source from an annual payment such as patent royalties where the payer has insufficient taxable income to cover the payment – see Example 1 explanatory note 12.

Under FA 1990 s 25 to recover tax deemed deducted from a gift aid payment to charity where the payer has insufficient income tax or capital gains tax chargeable to cover the tax – see Example 91.

Under TA 1988 s 307 to withdraw relief under the enterprise investment scheme – see Example 94.

Under TCGA 1992 s 153A to withdraw capital gains rollover relief provisionally given in respect of business assets – see Example 83.

Tax under HMRC assessment is due for payment thirty days after the issue of the assessment (TMA 1970 s 59B(6)). Interest is, however, payable from 31 January following the tax year to which the assessment relates, regardless of when the assessment is issued (TMA 1970 s 86).

The appeal and postponement procedures outlined in Example 43 apply to all HMRC assessments.

15. *Company self-assessment*

Self-assessment applies to companies for accounts ending after 30 June 1999.

16. *Electronic submission of returns (ELS) and filing by internet (FBI)*

Accountants and tax agents approved by HMRC may submit tax returns in respect of individuals, partnerships and trustees electronically or filing by internet (FBI) (TMA 1970 s 115A & Sch 3A). The Electronic Lodgement System (ELS), was withdrawn at the end of 2005/06.

Filing by internet is available to taxpayers and agents who have registered with HMRC. For agents initial registration is via the HMRC website using the agent's code. Then the agent registers via the government gateway at www.gateway.gov.uk. The service can only be used for clients for whom a valid form 64-8 is registered against that agent. The agent is required to keep a copy of the filed tax return and accompanying schedules which must have been approved by the client, ie signed before submission.

Although FBI will handle most tax returns where more than one copy of certain pages are required, eg capital gains, then it will be necessary to forward the extra pages by post.

Users of FBI have the facility to view the client's self-assessment statement of account on line. This enables agents to see the same information as HMRC staff in respect of liabilities and allocation of payments. Agents can also check when repayments are issued, view the previous year's tax account and check the filing status (ie which returns have been filed for self-assessment and when) on-line.

It is government policy to increase electronic filing, and HMRC has been recommended to aim for electronic filing by computer literate groups by 2012. In FA 2002 ss 135 and 136, HMRC has been given power to make regulations *requiring* taxpayers to use electronic communications for the delivery of information, subject to a penalty of up to £3,000 for failing to do so. Initially this power has been used in relation to PAYE returns (see Example 9 part A note (12)), but the legislation paves the way for a much wider use of internet filing in the future.

17. *Post-transaction rulings*

HMRC has a system of 'post-transaction rulings' under which taxpayers may seek HMRC's views on transactions *after* they have occurred but *before* submitting their tax returns (see Revenue Code of Practice 10 – information and advice).

18. *Certificates of tax deposit*

Individuals, partnerships, personal representatives, trustees or companies may purchase certificates of tax deposit, subject to an initial deposit of £500, with minimum additions of £250. The certificates may be used to pay any tax except PAYE, VAT, tax deducted from payments to subcontractors and corporation tax. The only purpose for which companies may use tax deposit certificates is to pay income tax due under the quarterly accounting system. A certificate purchased in the name of a partnership can only be used against partnership liabilities.

Interest at a variable rate accrues daily for a maximum of six years. A lower rate of interest applies if the deposit is withdrawn for cash rather than used to cover tax liabilities. The interest accrued at the time the deposit is used or cashed is charged to tax as savings income.

The certificates are a way of ensuring that funds are available to meet tax payments when due. They also prevent interest charges on tax in dispute, because interest on overdue tax is not charged when the certificates are used to pay tax, except to the extent if any that the deposit was made after the due date of payment for the tax.

19. *Short tax return*

From 2004/05 the short tax return has been used nationally for taxpayers whose affairs are straightforward. These include employees and pensioners with limited investment income and those self-employed with turnover below £15,000. The return does not include the facility to self-calculate so really needs to be completed by 30 September for HMRC to perform the calculations before the following 31 January. There is an option to file the short return over the telephone using voice recognition software. A short tax return cannot be used by a company director, those receiving trust income or those who require supplementary pages. A short return will not be issued on demand or to taxpayers who failed to file on time in the previous tax year. A taxpayer whose affairs have changed such that they are not eligible for a short return must request a full return.

20. *Disclosure of use of tax avoidance schemes*

Taxpayers who use tax avoidance schemes are required to include on their tax return the registration number of the scheme. If the scheme has been acquired offshore or developed in-house then taxpayers will be required to provide details of the scheme directly to HMRC.

Outline the self-assessment provisions that apply to partnerships.

Requirement to send in partnership returns

1. Self-assessment applies to partnerships as well as to sole traders in that partnerships must complete partnership returns (TMA 1970 s 12AA). There is, however, no assessment on the partnership itself, and each partner brings his profits into his own personal self-assessment.

2. The responsibility for completing the return is usually that of a representative partner to whom it is sent, but it may be issued in the name of the partnership, in which case the partners may nominate a partner to complete it. If the partner originally responsible for filing returns is no longer available, provision is made for a successor to be nominated by the partners, or if they do not do so, by HMRC.

    The due date for filing the partnership return is 31 January following the tax year or, if later, three months after the day on which notice to complete a return is given. There are different rules for partnerships with corporate partners (see Example 26 explanatory note 8).

Penalties for late partnership returns

3. Automatic penalties are charged for late returns as follows, the penalties being charged on the partners themselves and not on the partnership (TMA 1970 s 93A):

    Fixed penalty of £100 for *each partner* who was a member of the firm during the period covered by the return;

    Unless HMRC has applied for a daily penalty, a further fixed penalty of £100 per partner if the return is still outstanding six months after the filing date.

    For more substantial delays, HMRC may apply to the Commissioners for a daily penalty of up to £60 per relevant partner, which will be charged from the date the Commissioners issue the relevant direction.

    Appeals against the imposition of penalties may be made by the representative partner.

    The penalty provisions are similar to those relating to personal returns. There is, however, no tax geared penalty since no tax is payable by the partnership as such. On the other hand, there is no provision as there is for individual returns for fixed penalties to be restricted where the tax due on the partnership profits is minimal.

Business profits

4. Partnership returns show details of trading or professional profits for the accounting period ended in the tax year to which the return relates. If more than one account was made up to a date in that tax year, separate sets of trading pages should be completed for each account, unless there was a temporary change in the accounting date such that the two sets of accounts together added up to the normal 12 month period. In that event the figures could be combined and shown as a single set of figures (see note 9). As far as changes of accounting date are concerned, the same rules apply for partnerships as for individuals (see Example 28), and the individual partners are bound by the accounting periods adopted by the partnership. See Example 25 explanatory note 3 for the particular problems of self-assessment where there is a partnership merger.

5. Accounts details must normally be shown in the partnership return in 'Standard Accounts Information' (SAI) format (see Example 15). Where the annual partnership profits are below £15,000, however, only the turnover, expenses and net profit need be shown. If profits are above £15 million (or all members of the partnership are companies), accounts must be submitted (and the SAI need not be completed). Otherwise accounts need not be sent in unless HMRC ask for them. As for individual traders, records relating to returns must be kept until the fifth anniversary of the 31 January next following the relevant tax year (TMA 1970 s 12B).

    Any expenses paid personally by partners and capital allowances on partners' own cars *must* be included in the *partnership* return and cannot be separately claimed in the partners' own personal returns. Such items must be included before apportioning the profit between the partners, with the share of the relevant partner then being adjusted appropriately. If expenses incurred individually are not shown in the partnership accounts, it will be necessary to reconcile the accounts figures with those shown in the partnership return. To avoid the possibility of discrepancies leading to an HMRC enquiry, it would be appropriate to file both the accounts and the details of the adjustments with the partnership return.

Charges from which tax is deducted are shown under 'Other expenses' in the SAI and are disallowed in calculating the trading profit. If they are *trade* charges, however, such as an annuity to a former partner, they are shown in the partnership statement (see note 7) and allocated between the partners, each individual partner then being able to claim a deduction for his share in his personal return. It is provided in TMA 1970 s 12AB(1)(a)(iv),(b) that the partnership statement should show charges and the division thereof in relation to *periods of account*. The self-assessment partnership tax return, however, states that the amount to be shown in the return is the amount paid in the *tax year*, the partnership statement then showing the allocation between the partners. This is, in fact, the information required by each partner in order to claim the appropriate relief in his own personal return.

Non-trading income

6. The return includes details of income other than from the trade or profession and of disposals of partnership chargeable assets. The details provided normally relate to the accounting year ended in the tax year. Details of *taxed* income and of disposals of chargeable assets (and charges on income – see note 5) are, however, shown for the tax year itself rather than for the accounting year ended in the tax year, in order that the partners have the information they need to complete their own returns.

    The return states that the taxed income of the relevant accounting periods should be apportioned to arrive at the figure for the tax year. A straight time apportionment would, however, give anomalous results if tax rates changed. It is acceptable, and probably more appropriate, to enter the taxed income actually received in the tax year itself. Similarly, where profit shares change, the partners' actual shares of the taxed income may be shown rather than time apportioning the total for the tax year.

Partnership statement

7. The partnership return must be accompanied by a statement showing the names, addresses and tax references of everyone who was a partner at some time in the year, the dates of joining or leaving where relevant, each partner's share of profits, losses and charges on income, and tax deducted or credited (TMA 1970 s 12AB). There is a short version of the partnership statement for partnerships with only trading or professional profits and taxed interest and a full version for partnerships with other types of income and/or capital gains. In the latter case, the statement shows each partner's share of the proceeds for chargeable assets, each partner calculating his gain or loss according to his own circumstances.

Amendments and HMRC enquiries

8. The rules for amending individual returns broadly apply to partnership returns and statements, ie the partners may notify amendments within 12 months (TMA 1970 s 12ABA) and HMRC may correct obvious errors within nine months, the partnership having the right to reject the correction (TMA 1970 s 12ABB) (see Example 40 for further details). Under TMA 1970 s 12AC, HMRC may notify their intention to enquire into a return or amendment within 12 months from the filing date (or for late returns, a year from the time the return or amendment was filed plus the period to the next 31 January, 30 April, 31 July or 31 October as the case may be). As with individual returns, the partnership return may be amended within the permitted twelve month period while an enquiry is in progress, but amendments that affect amounts stated in the return will not take effect until the enquiry is completed, and only then if they are accepted by HMRC (TMA 1970 s 12AD).

    If HMRC enquire into a partnership return, this automatically means that the enquiry extends to partners' personal returns, since the personal returns must reflect any changes to the partnership return. An enquiry into a personal return relating to non-partnership matters does not affect the other partners. HMRC will notify each partner when they open and close an enquiry, but the partner responsible for the return must keep the other partners aware of how the enquiry is progressing.

Under TMA 1970 s 30B, HMRC may amend a partnership statement outside the twelve month enquiry period if they discover that profits have been understated because of the fraudulent or negligent conduct of a partner, or because of inadequate information.

Under TMA 1970 s 31, the partnership may appeal within thirty days of receiving a closure notice from HMRC against the conclusions stated and amendments made in the notice, or within thirty days of being notified of an HMRC 'discovery' amendment under s 30B.

Partners' personal returns

9. Each partner is required to complete supplementary partnership pages in his personal return. As with the partnership return, the personal return contains a short version of the partnership pages if the partnership has only trading profits and taxed interest. The income shown in the personal return must agree with that shown in the partnership statement. In some circumstances, however, the partner will not receive the relevant information in time to give the correct figures in his personal return.

    For example, if an established partnership makes up accounts to 31 December and a new partner joins on 1 January 2007, the new partner will be taxed in 2006/07 on his profit to 5 April 2007, but his profit share will form part of the profit shown on the 2007/08 partnership statement. In these circumstances, he would have to include an estimate of the relevant figure in his 2006/07 return, and notify the exact figure as soon as it was known.

    Say that following the admission of the new partner, an existing partner left the partnership on 31 March 2006. He would have a basis period for 2006/07 covering the 15 months from 1 January 2006 to 31 March 2007, and he would similarly have to include an estimate of the three months' profits to 31 March 2007 in his 2006/07 return. (He would be entitled to deduct any available overlap relief from the profits of the 15 months' period to the date he left the firm.)

    It would be possible for the partnership to prepare intermediate accounts to 31 March 2007 without permanently changing its accounting date, because a change of accounting date does not take effect unless notice is given to HMRC (see Example 28). It might then be possible for the partnership to let the incoming/retiring partner know his exact profit share for the three months to 31 March 2007. If this were done, the accounts to 31 March 2007 would even so not be shown in the 2006/07 partnership statement but would be combined with those of the nine months to 31 December 2007 and shown as a single set of figures in the 2007/08 partnership statement.

10. Class 4 national insurance contributions are included in partners' personal returns. The personal tax return makes provision for a partner to indicate that he is excepted from contributions or that contributions have been deferred. See Example 47 for detailed notes on national insurance contributions.

11. Partners are individually responsible for paying their own tax. If a partnership pays the bill on behalf of the partners, the partners' names, tax reference numbers and amounts applicable to each partner must be provided. HMRC would prefer the partners' individual payslips to be forwarded as well.

Limited liability partnerships (LLPs)

12. An LLP is taxed as a partnership and will receive a partnership tax return as if the members were partners carrying on a business in partnership. Accordingly all of the rules set out above apply to an LLP.

    Where an existing partnership incorporates as an LLP during an accounting period, then a single partnership return can be made for the tax year. This will apply even if there is a change of accounting date.

Outline the procedure for making claims and elections, both for individuals and companies.

Claims procedure for income tax and capital gains tax

The procedure for making claims and elections and for giving notices was made more formalised from 1996/97. TMA 1970 s 42 now provides that where notice to submit a return has been given, claims must normally be made in the return or an amendment to the return, which means that the time limit for making the claim is normally twelve months from the filing date for the return. S 42(1A) requires claims to be quantified when made.

Where it is not possible to include a claim in a return, a separate claims procedure is laid down in TMA 1970 Sch 1A, under which similar provisions apply as for entries in returns, ie HMRC have nine months from the date of the claim to correct obvious errors and the taxpayer has twelve months to amend it. HMRC may enquire into a claim made outside a return, or amendment to such a claim, within the period ending 12 months after 31 January following the tax year to which the claim relates, or if later, the quarter day (31 January, 30 April, etc) next following 12 months after the date of the claim. Unless another time limit is stipulated in the legislation, the time limit for claims made outside the return is five years from the 31 January filing date for the return (TMA 1970 s 43).

S 42 and the Schedule 1A claims procedures do not apply to capital allowances claims by traders, which are still required by CAA 2001 s 3(3)(a) to be made in a return or amendment to a return.

Where HMRC enquire into a return or claim, as a result of which they make amendments to the return or claim, the taxpayer may appeal against the amendments within 30 days of being notified of them (TMA 1970 ss 31, 31A and Sch 1A.9).

Claims for relief involving two or more years

Schedule 1B to TMA 1970 deals with claims that involve two or more years. It provides that references to claims include references to elections and notices. It does not apply to claims to treat payments made under gift aid to be deemed paid in the preceding tax year under FA 2002 s 98 (see Example 91).

Where relief is claimed for a loss incurred or payment made in one tax year to be set against the income of an earlier year, then although the tax adjustment resulting from the claim is calculated by reference to the tax position of the earlier year, the claim is treated as relating to the later year and is given effect in relation to that later year.

These provisions also apply to carrying back post-cessation receipts (see Example 16 part (c)(ii) claims for averaging farming profits (see Example 33)), profits of creative artists (see Example 23), and carrying back personal pension premiums (see Example 38).

For claims to carry back losses and personal pension premiums, the recalculated tax will be lower than that originally payable. Farmers' and creative artists' averaging claims may result in the earlier year's tax being reduced or increased. Claims to carry back post-cessation receipts result in the tax of the earlier years being increased. Since the claim is *given effect* in relation to the later year, however, it is the view of HMRC that interest on underpaid tax or supplement on overpaid tax runs from the balancing payment date for the later year, ie 31 January following that later year. In relation to repayment supplement this has now been made explicit in the legislation (TA 1988 s 824).

When recalculating the tax position of the earlier year following a carryback claim, any relevant claims for allowances, reliefs etc, may be made or revised, for example transferring surplus married couple's allowance. On the other hand, the carryback may mean that pension premiums paid in the earlier year are no longer covered by the revised relevant earnings, in which case the relief must be reduced and excess personal pension contributions would have to be refunded. See HMRC's Tax Bulletin of August 2000 for further comments.

Claims for coding adjustments under PAYE

Taxpayers may make claims for coding adjustments (for example when someone born before 6 April 1935 gets married) either in their tax returns or separately from the return. A claim made in-year may subsequently be reflected in a tax return. Where no such return is issued the claim will normally become final 22 months after the end of the tax year (for example by 31 January 2009 for a 2006/07 claim) and cannot be reopened by HMRC unless there has been fraudulent or negligent conduct or incomplete disclosure. HMRC has confirmed that they will apply the same time limits where coding claims are carried forward automatically, or are implemented on the basis of preliminary information from the taxpayer, even though HMRC may strictly enquire into such claims at any time up to 5 years 10 months after the end of the tax year (Tax Bulletin October 1996).

Claims procedure for companies

Under corporation tax self-assessment, which applies to accounting periods ending after 30 June 1999, the provisions for claims and elections are similar to those for income tax self-assessment. The general provisions are in FA 1998 Sch 18 Part VII. Unless there is a specific provision giving a longer or shorter period, the time limit for making claims is six years from the end of the accounting period. Where a discovery assessment is made, other than one arising from the taxpayer's fraud or negligence, provision is made for claims, elections, notices etc to be made, revoked or varied within one year after the end of the company accounting period in which the assessment is made.

Where possible claims must be included in the corporation tax return (CT 600) or in an amended return and the claims will be given effect in the company's self-assessment. This means that claims must normally be made within two years from the end of the accounting period. If HMRC enquire into the return the time limit is extended to thirty days after the time when the the profits or losses of the period are finally determined. The provisions of TMA 1970 Sch 1A mentioned under the income tax self-assessment provisions above also apply to companies in respect of claims that cannot be included in a return. The time limit for an HMRC enquiry into a claim made outside a return is the quarter day (31 January, 30 April, etc) next following 12 months after the date of the claim.

The group relief claims provisions are in FA 1998 Sch 18 Part VIII. The provisions enable group relief claims to be made without being accompanied by copy notices of consent to surrender, and enable one company to act on behalf of the group in making claims and surrenders and amending returns where the group is dealt with mainly within one tax district.

The six year time limit for claims does not apply. Group relief claims must be made by the latest of one year after the filing date for the return, thirty days after the completion of an HMRC enquiry into the return, thirty days after notice of HMRC amendments to the return following an enquiry, and thirty days after the final determination of an appeal against such an amendment.

The order in which claims are treated as made for the purpose of determining amounts previously surrendered or claimed in respect of group or consortium relief for overlapping periods is dealt with in TA 1988 s 403A(6)(7).

Capital allowances claims are dealt with in FA 1998 Sch 18 Part IX and CAA 2001 s 3(3)(b). The six year time limit does not apply and claims are subject to the same time limits as stated above for group relief. If the effect of a claim following an enquiry is to reduce the allowances available for a later period for which a return has been submitted, the company has thirty days from the settlement of the enquiry to make any necessary amendments to that return, failing which amendments will be made by HMRC.

Late claims

HMRC has discretion to admit late claims by companies. They have stated that this will only be done in exceptional circumstances, for example where the delay was due to circumstances beyond the company's control, or where an HMRC error was a major reason for the delay, and not where claims are late because the company has changed its mind or because a different combination of claims would be more advantageous.

Error or mistake claims

A taxpayer can claim a repayment of tax under the 'error or mistake' provisions of TMA 1970 s 33 (individuals) or FA 1998 Sch 18.51 (companies), where an error or mistake has been made in a *return*. Relief is not available in respect of mistakes in claims included in the return, for which the normal time limits apply. Nor is it available where there has been an error as to the basis on which tax ought to have been computed if the return was made in accordance with the practice prevailing at the time. This prevents the error or mistake procedure being used to reopen assessments where there is a court decision against HMRC. There are similar provisions enabling claims to be made in respect of errors or mistakes in partnership statements (TMA 1970 s 33A). Where the partnership statement is amended, HMRC will notify partners of the changes to be made to their self-assessments.

The time limit for an error or mistake claim by individuals is five years from 31 January following the relevant tax year. The time limit for companies is six years from the end of the company accounting period.

Whereas prior to June 2003 HMRC regarded any interest, surcharge or penalty for the claim year as unaffected by the claim, they now accept that these charges too should be mitigated, in line with the relief granted under the claim.

Supplementary Notes

Time limits and late claims

1. There are many exceptions to the normal time limits for claims and it is essential that the time limit for the relevant claim is complied with. Although HMRC usually has discretion to admit late claims, they will only exercise that discretion in exceptional circumstances. See SP 5/01 for HMRC's approach to late company claims for loss relief, capital allowances and group relief.

Requirements for valid claims

2. The requirements for making a valid claim have often not been clear-cut, and it was only as a result of losing a case on what a group relief claim needed to contain that HMRC specified the minimum information required. Group relief claims are now made in accordance with specific statutory provisions.

   As far as income tax loss claims are concerned, a loss claim may be made by indicating the source of the loss, the year of loss and either the year of claim or the statutory reference under which the relief is claimed. Providing that claim is made within the relevant time limit, the supporting accounts may follow later.

3. Many claims are required by the provisions of the legislation to be made in writing. This has been varied by FA 1998 s 118, which enables HMRC to direct that specified income tax claims may be made by the use of a telecommunications system. This applies to claims by individuals or their agents (but not to claims by partners, trustees or personal representatives). HMRC has issued a statements of practice SP2/03 and SP3/03 giving details of claims that may be made and information that may be given by telephone. There is the possibility of allowing claims to be made by internet at a later stage (and claims and elections are included within the information that HMRC may require to be made electronically at some future time under the provisions of FA 2002 s 135 – see Example 40 note 16).

Error or mistake claims

4. See Example 40 note 1(a) re the use of error or mistake claims when provisional figures have been included in a return.

A. Explain the procedure for making assessments in respect of income tax and capital gains tax and the extent to which an assessment (including a self-assessment) is capable of being amended, and whether an assessment, once determined, is capable of being re-opened either by the taxpayer or by HMRC.

B. Outline the provisions for charging interest on overdue income tax and capital gains tax and and paying repayment supplement on overpayments of those taxes.

C. Bill has taxable income for 2006/07 of £37,415, made up as follows:

	£	£
Business profits		51,980
Untaxed interest	1,470	
Taxed interest (tax deducted £1,800)	9,000	10,470
		62,450
Less: 100% initial alllowance: conversion of flat over shop		(20,000)
		42,450
Less: Personal allowance		(5,035)
		37,415

Bill paid a personal pension premium of £1,950 (net) during the year.

The investment on the conversion of the flat was made on 31 March 2007, and no rental income was receivable for 2006/07. On 15 January 2008, before filing his tax return, he made a gift aid donation of £1,560 (net), having made an election to carry the gift back to 2006/07.

Bill made payments on account of his 2006/07 tax and Class 4 national insurance liability of £6,850 each on 15 February 2007 and 30 September 2007, based on the net tax and Class 4 liability for 2005/06 of £13,700.

He submitted his 2006/07 tax return at the end of January 2008, claiming relief for the initial allowance of £20,000, and including the claim to carry back to 2006/07 the January 2008 gift aid payment. The repayment due to Bill was made on 21 April 2008.

(a) Calculate the tax and Class 4 national insurance contributions due for the year 2006/07, indicating the net amount repayable after taking into account the first payment on account for 2007/08 due on 31 January 2008.

(b) Calculate the interest on overdue tax originally chargeable, and the interest and repayment supplement adjustments following the submission of the return.

Interest on overdue tax and repayment supplement are to be taken as 6.5% and 2.25% respectively throughout.

D. Petersen's original net tax payable for 2003/04 was £25,000, so that 2004/05 payments on account of £12,500 each were payable on 31 January 2005 and 31 July 2005. A discovery assessment relating to 2003/04 was issued on 1 December 2007 for additional tax of £15,000.

State the consequences of the issue of the discovery assessment on tax payable for 2003/04 and 2004/05, and the position relating to interest on overdue tax, on the assumption that on 31 January 2006 a balancing payment had been made for 2004/05 amounting to:

(a) £20,000

(b) £5,000.

A. **Assessments**

Self-assessment

1. Under self-assessment, it is the responsibility of the taxpayer to assess his own tax liability. Although HMRC will make the calculations for him, this still counts as a self-assessment. If a taxpayer does not submit a return, HMRC has the power to determine the tax payable, but this determination is still treated as a self-assessment until superseded by the taxpayer's own self-assessment. For details see Example 40 note 13.

2. HMRC has the absolute right, without giving any reason, to enquire into any return within 12 months after its submission (TMA 1970 ss 9A, 12AC). The enquiry procedure does not, however, enable HMRC to issue *assessments* if they consider the taxpayer's self-assessment to be insufficient. Their remedy is to make amendments to the return (see Example 40 note 12).

HMRC assessments

3. There are only limited circumstances in which HMRC will issue assessments themselves, other than under the TMA 1970 s 29 'discovery' procedure dealt with in note 9 below (see Example 40 note 14 for the main occasions when such assessments will be issued).

4. The provisions of s 29 enable HMRC to issue an assessment if they discover that profits have escaped assessment, or an assessment has become insufficient, or excessive relief has been given. If a return has been submitted, HMRC's powers under s 29 may only be used in cases of fraudulent or negligent conduct, or where they could not reasonably have been expected to be aware of the situation in time to deal with it under the enquiry procedures. See Example 40 note 1(a) for the use of the discovery procedure when provisional figures have been included in a return. Similar 'discovery' provisions apply under TMA 1970 s 30B to enable HMRC to amend partnership statements. The time limits for discovery assessments are five years from 31 January following the tax year to which the assessment relates (s 34), extended to 20 years from that 31 January date in cases of fraudulent or negligent conduct (s 36).

Appeals and postponement applications

5. Under TMA 1970 ss 31 and 31A, a taxpayer has thirty days to appeal against any HMRC conclusions stated or amendments made at the end of an enquiry, jeopardy amendments made during the course of an enquiry (see Example 46 supplementary note 5), 'discovery' amendments to partnership statements (see Example 41 note 8) and any assessments which are not self-assessments. Appeals may be made within the same thirty day period against HMRC amendments to claims made outside the return (TMA 1970 Sch 1A).

    The Inspector may accept a late appeal made without unreasonable delay after the thirty days if he is satisfied that there was a reasonable excuse for not bringing the appeal within the time limit. If the Inspector is not prepared to do so, the taxpayer can ask for his late appeal to be admitted by the General, or sometimes the Special Commissioners (TMA 1970 s 49).

    An appeal against a national insurance issue may be made, within 30 days of the decision, to the General, or sometimes the Special, Commissioners (Social Security Contributions (Transfer of Functions etc.) Act 1999 Part II).

    There is no prescribed form of appeal, although a tax assessment is usually accompanied by a form on which an appeal and, if appropriate, postponement application may be made.

6. An appeal does not alter the due date of payment of tax unless an application is made for postponement (TMA 1970 s 55). Under self-assessment the postponement provisions apply only to amendments to self-assessments made by HMRC as a result of an enquiry into the return and to HMRC assessments.

    The time limit for making a postponement application is also within thirty days after the date of the assessment/amendment as the case may be. Late applications for postponement may be made if changed circumstances since the original postponement application or lack of it result in the taxpayer having grounds for believing that he has been overcharged. It is not sufficient in a postponement application to say that the tax may be excessive. The application must state by how much the taxpayer believes he has been overcharged and the specific reasons for that belief (TMA s 55(3)).

Where application is made for tax to be postponed, the due date for that *not postponed* becomes thirty days after the Commissioners' decision on the postponement and against which no appeal is pending. If the inspector agrees the postponement without recourse to the Commissioners, the due date for the tax not postponed becomes thirty days after the inspector's agreement to the postponement provided that no appeal is made against the postponement decision (TMA 1970 s 55).

7. When the appeal is settled, any tax and, if relevant, Class 4 NIC found to be due but previously postponed and any additional amounts become payable thirty days after the inspector issues to the appellant notice of the total amount payable (TMA 1970 s 55).

8. If an assessment or HMRC amendment to a self-assessment is not appealed against within the time limit (or within any further time allowed by HMRC), the assessment will stand. Where an appeal is made, it may be heard by the General or Special Commissioners, whose decisions on questions of fact are normally binding on both parties, but with a right of further appeal on a point of law to the High Court, Court of Appeal and, where leave is granted, House of Lords. To assist appellants the General Commissioners have a website which explains how the appeals procedure works. See www.courtservice.gov.uk/tribunals/gcit/index.htm. Once an appeal has been determined, it is final and conclusive (TMA 1970 ss 46(2), 56). TMA 1970 s 54 provides that an appeal can be settled by agreement between the taxpayer and HMRC before going to the Commissioners, in which case the agreement is treated as if the appeal had been determined by the Commissioners.

The case of Pepper v Hart (HL 1992) led to a change in the way legislation may be interpreted by the courts. The House of Lords held in that case that the intentions of Parliament in introducing the legislation could be looked at where the legislation was obscure, or led to an absurdity, providing the material relied on consisted of clear ministerial statements and other parliamentary material relevant to understanding those statements.

Discovery assessments

9. Following the introduction of self-assessment, HMRC can make a 'discovery' where there has not been full disclosure and

(a) the loss of tax is the result of fraudulent or negligent conduct by the taxpayer or his agent, or

(b) the Inspector could not reasonably be expected to have been able to identify the circumstances giving rise to the loss of tax either before the end of the normal enquiry period, or by using the information made available to him

(TMA 1970 s 29(4) and (5)).

Information is treated as made available if

(a) it is contained in the tax return or supporting accounts, statements or documents supplied; or

(b) it is contained in any claim made; or

(c) it is contained in any document, accounts or particulars supplied in relation to an enquiry into a return or claim; or

(d) it is information which could reasonably be expected to be inferred from the above; or

(e)   it is information notified in writing by the taxpayer.

References to a return mean the return under review and either of the two previous returns. Information supplied by an agent is deemed to be supplied by the taxpayer (TMA 1970 s 29(6) and (7)).

Accordingly HMRC cannot make a discovery if the relevant information has been supplied to them with the tax return (or the previous two returns) and, based upon the Olin Energy Systems Ltd case mentioned below, a reasonably competent inspector would have been aware of the relevant matter from the information supplied. It is thought that this will apply whether or not the taxpayer has brought the specific point to the attention of HMRC.

As far as discovery assessments are concerned, a discovery can be made by a different inspector from the one who made the assessment, and can apply where it is decided that the law has been incorrectly applied, as well as when new facts emerge. It was held in the case of Cenlon Finance Co Ltd v Ellwood 1962, however, that a discovery cannot be made in respect of a specific point which has been dealt with in reaching an agreement on an appeal under TMA 1970 s 54. It was further held in the case of Scorer v Olin Energy Systems Ltd 1985 that even where there has been no specific agreement, HMRC cannot make a discovery where the information provided and on which an agreement under s 54 was based was such as to bring home to an ordinarily competent inspector the nature of what had been claimed. In the Olin case, brought forward losses of a ship-chartering trade were clearly shown in the computations submitted as being set against profits of a manufacturing trade. It was, however, held in the case of R v HM Inspector of Taxes, ex parte Bass Holdings Ltd (QBD 1992) that the Olin decision does not apply if a written agreement does not reflect what the parties actually agreed. In the Bass case group relief had mistakenly been deducted twice.

It has also been held, in the case of Gray v Matheson (ChD 1993), that a s 54 agreement is not binding where *incorrect information* has been supplied, even though there was no culpability on the taxpayer's part. The facts of the case were that there had been an investigation of two years' accounts, and in the next two years a significantly lower gross profit percentage was shown, reverting to the previous level in the following year. The Court held that it was consideration of the events both before and after the two 'low' years that led the inspector to make a discovery, and that the Olin decision was not relevant.

HMRC issued a detailed statement of practice (SP 8/91) covering discovery assessments, in which they indicated that they do not consider the Olin decision applies where:

(i)   Profits or income have not been charged because of fraudulent or negligent conduct

(ii)   The inspector has been misled or misinformed

(iii)   There is an undiscovered arithmetical error in a computation

(iv)   There is an error which cannot be claimed to be unintended, such as a double deduction of a particular item.

The principles established by the Olin and Cenlon cases strictly only apply where there has been an appeal against an assessment, or an appeal against a decision relating to a claim under TMA 1970 s 42 (see Example 42) but HMRC stated in SP 8/91 that they will stand by an agreement on a specific point, even where there was no appeal. Where a point was not specifically agreed, or was not fundamental, they will still not make a discovery assessment providing all relevant facts were disclosed and the taxpayer could reasonably have believed that the inspector's view was correct. Nor will they seek adjustments where their view of the law is changed as a result of a Court decision.

In the case of Langham v Veltema (2004) the taxpayer was advised that the value of a house transferred to him by his employer was £100,000. He used this figure in his self-assessment tax return which was received and acknowledged by HMRC as needing no correction on

9 September after the tax year. Later the issue of valuation was raised by HMRC and a revised amount of £145,000 was agreed with the taxpayer's agent. HMRC raised a discovery assessment on the taxpayer for £45,000. The courts upheld HMRC's appeal. Given the facts it would not have been reasonable to expect the Inspector to have been aware that the valuation of the property in September 1998 was unreliable.

By revenue statement of 23 December 2004, updated in January 2006, it is recommended that taxpayers who use a valuation in completing their tax return should state in the Additional Information box

–   that a valuation has been used, and

–   who carried out the valuation giving the name and qualification and stating that they are an independent suitably qualified valuer.

If a taxpayer has adopted a different view of the law from that published by HMRC the Additional Information space should state that HMRC guidance has not been followed.

If the return includes exceptional items the entry in the Additional Information space should give full details of the exceptional entries.

If this guidance is followed then the return should become final at the end of the 12-month enquiry period if HMRC does not open an enquiry (or open and close an enquiry). A 'discovery' would not then arise unless the information provided was incorrect because of fraud or negligent conduct by the taxpayer.

Equitable liability

10.   Once the time limits for appealing against assessments, or for substituting a taxpayer's own self-assessment for an HMRC determination under self-assessment, have expired, the tax assessed or determined becomes legally due. HMRC has, however, stated that where income tax (including PAYE tax) or capital gains tax is higher than it would have been if all the relevant information had been submitted at the proper time, they may be prepared to accept an amount equal to what the correct liability would have been, providing the taxpayer's affairs are brought fully up to date, although this should rarely be necessary under the self-assessment system. This practice is known as 'equitable liability' (see Revenue's Tax Bulletin August 1995).

National insurance contributions

11.   HMRC considers that there is no time limit on their power to *assess* Class 1, 1A and 2 national insurance contributions, although they usually only go back six years. (Class 4 contributions are subject to the income tax rules (SSCBA 1992 s 16).)

The Limitation Act 1980 prevents any action to recover amounts due after six years from the date on which the liability arose. It does not, however, apply to Crown proceedings to recover 'any tax or duty or interest on any tax or duty'. It is apparently accepted by HMRC that national insurance is not a tax or duty, so that the Limitation Act places a time-bar on an action for recovery of national insurance contributions. HMRC considers, however, that the six years runs from the date the liability is discovered rather than from when the contributions fell due.

If the person liable to pay the contributions acknowledged the liability or made any payment in respect of it, a new six-year period would start from that time. Any payment made on account of arrears should therefore specify to which years it relates, without referring to the earlier years, since that would constitute an 'acknowledgment'.

HMRC may still *assess* and endeavour to collect arrears for all years, but they would not be able to enforce the assessments in proceedings once the six-year limit had elapsed.

B.   **Interest on overdue tax and repayment supplement**

Due date of payment of tax

1.   The dates on which tax is payable under self-assessment are dealt with in Example 40. In most cases, equal payments on account are due on 31 January and 31 July in the tax year, based on the net tax, Class 4 national insurance liability and student loan repayments of the previous year, and a balancing payment, which includes any capital gains tax payable, is due on 31 January following the tax year (or three months after receiving notice to complete a return for certain late issued notices – see Example 40 note 8).

2.   Where a self-assessment is amended after, or less than 30 days before, the due date for the balancing payment for the year, tax is payable or repayable 30 days after the notice of amendment is given.

3.   Where HMRC issues an assessment, the due date of payment for the tax is 30 days after the issue of the assessment (TMA 1970 s 59B(6)). Most HMRC assessments will be discovery assessments under TMA 1970 s 29 (see part A).

4.   The payments on account that are regarded as being due for any tax year take into account any subsequent amendments to the previous year's tax liability resulting from taxpayer amendments, or amendments following HMRC enquiries, or HMRC discovery assessments (TMA 1970 s 59A(4A)(4B)(5)). If a non-discovery HMRC assessment is made, it does not affect payments on account.

5.   Special provisions apply where a claim is made that involves more than one tax year (TMA 1970 Sch 1B). These are dealt with in Example 42. See note 10 below re the effect on interest and repayment supplement.

Interest on overdue tax

6.   Under TMA 1970 s 86, interest is normally charged on tax and (by SSCBA 1992 Sch 2.6) Class 4 national insurance paid late from the date the payment was due to the date the tax is paid, ie from 31 January in the tax year and 31 July following for payments on account, and from 31 January following the tax year for the balancing payment.

       Interest also runs from 31 January following the tax year to which the assessment relates for assessments issued by HMRC (unless otherwise provided) regardless of when the assessment was issued (see Example 40 note 14). For amendments to self-assessments, interest runs from 31 January following the relevant tax year. Note that the tax itself is payable by a different date (see notes 2 and 3 above).

       It is understood that when calculating interest on overdue tax, a denominator of 366 days is always used regardless of whether or not a leap year is involved. A denominator of 365 days is understood to be used for repayment supplement calculations. This practice works in favour of the taxpayer. Supplement is dealt with in note 9 below.

7.   In addition to being charged on unpaid tax, interest is payable on late paid surcharges and penalties (see Example 40 notes 10 and 11).

       Any interest charged under these provisions is not an allowable deduction for tax purposes (TMA 1970 s 90).

8.   Discovery assessments, in addition to carrying interest as indicated in note 6, also affect payments on account. TMA 1970 s 59A(4B) provides that the payments on account that should have been made for the next following year are increased accordingly, subject to a claim under TMA 1970 s 59A(3)(4) to eliminate or reduce them because they exceeded the tax payable for that following year. The effect is that if, even after taking into account the revised payments on account, a balance of tax would remain payable for the following year, interest would be payable on the increase in each payment on account from the due date to 31 January following the later

year. If the revised payments on account would produce an overpayment for the following year, the taxpayer could apply for them to be reduced so as to prevent the overpayment occurring, and the interest chargeable would be reduced or eliminated accordingly. This is illustrated in part D of the example.

Repayment supplement

9.   Tax-free repayment supplement under TA 1988 s 824 (income tax) and TCGA 1992 s 283 (capital gains tax) is paid to both residents and non-residents on overpaid tax relating to payments made direct to HMRC (and also on any overpaid surcharge and penalties) from the date the amount was paid until the date the repayment order is issued. If, however, a taxpayer pays more than the amount that is legally due at the payment date, the overpayment does not attract supplement.

Where there is a refund of tax deducted at source, supplement runs from 31 January following the relevant tax year. Tax deducted at source includes PAYE tax, except that amounts deducted in respect of previous years are excluded.

As indicated in note 6 above, a denominator of 365 is used in making supplement calculations even if a leap year is involved.

Claims involving more than one year

10.   Special provisions apply to claims involving more than one year (see Example 42). Where such claims result in an *increase* in tax for the earlier year (for example through farmers' averaging), any additional tax payable is regarded as relating to the later year and is due for payment on 31 January following that later year. Where a claim *reduces* the tax for the earlier year (for example through farmers' averaging, or where losses or gift aid donations are carried back), *effect is given* to the claim in relation to the later year, by repayment or set-off, or by an increase in the amount to be deducted in arriving at the balancing payment for the year under s 59B, or 'otherwise'. HMRC takes the view that this enables amounts repayable to be offset against tax that has not yet been paid for the earlier year. They used to do this regardless of whether the payment for the earlier year was already due, or due at some time in the future. Following representations they have agreed to relax this position for claims to carry back losses. Now if the earlier year's tax is not yet due, the set-off need not be made and repayment can be claimed up to the amount of the earlier year's tax. This treatment must be specifically requested, through the self-assessment account. Effectively the 35-day rule no longer applies (see Tax Bulletin June 1997). Interest due on the tax for earlier years will cease from the date of the claim. Thus an early claim can stop interest accruing against a taxpayer even if no supplement would be due if the same amount was repaid. Supplement will only be relevant if the claim is given effect after the 31 January following the later year, supplement then running from that 31 January date (TA 1988 s 824).

Date when payments regarded as made

11.   Payments of tax and national insurance contributions are treated as made as follows for the purpose of calculating interest or repayment supplement:

Tax payments made at local offices are credited on the date of payment.

The payment date for postal payments is the day they are received by HMRC, except those received following a day when the HMRC office was closed, which are treated as received on the first day the office was closed.

Payments by electronic funds transfer (BACS/CHAPS) are treated as paid one working day before HMRC receive them.

Payments by bank Giro or Girobank is the date payment is made at the bank or post office.

It is understood that PC and telephone banking payments are treated as made on the date the bank make the transfer.

Tax/national insurance payable by employers

12. As far as late payments by employers of tax, NI and other amounts due under PAYE are concerned, interest is charged from 19 April after the end of the tax year if the amount due is not paid by that date (TA 1988 s 203(2)(d) & SI 1993/744 reg 51, SI 2001/1004 Sch 4.17).

    Large employers (250 or more employees) are required to make their monthly payment of PAYE/NI and subcontractors' tax electronically (SI 2003/2682 part 10 chapter 3). The full amount must reach HMRC by the last bank working day before the 23rd of the month. Thus for September 2006 the payment due on 22 October 2006 (Sunday) must reach HMRC by 20 October 2006.

    Electronic payments include BACS direct credit, CHAPS (Clearing House Automated Payment System), Internet banking, BillPay and telephone banking. The extended payment date also applies to medium/smaller employers who pay electronically. CHAPS is a same day transfer facility whereas most other electronic methods require three bank working days for clearance (Revenue directions 5 April 2004).

    If a large employer fails to pay by the due date then a default notice will be issued. A surcharge will then be payable from the third default notice within the surcharge period. The surcharge period starts with the due date for payment for the first period in default and ends at the end of the year in which the taxpayer has not been in default in respect of any payment. The surcharge applies to the net total of tax due for the year and is at the following rate per default:

No of defaults within surcharge period	%
1 – 2	Nil
3 – 5	0.17%
6 – 8	0.33%
9 – 11	0.58%
12 or more	0.83%

    The surcharge is payable 30 days after the issue of the surcharge notice (SI 2003/2682 regs 199–204).

    Class 1A contributions on employee benefits are due for payment by 19 July following the tax year to which they relate (eg contributions re 2005/06 should be paid by 19 July 2006). Interest is charged on late payments (SI 2001/1004 reg 76). The amount due is shown by the employer on form P11D(b).

    Where Class 1B contributions are payable under a PAYE Settlement Agreement (as to which see Example 9 explanatory note 9), they are due for payment by 19 October following the tax year in respect of which the payment was due and interest runs from that date (SI 2001/1004 Sch 4.17).

Fixing interest and repayment supplement rates

13. Interest on overdue tax and NI is based on a reference rate (which is a rounded average of the base rates of six main banks) plus 2.5%. Repayment supplement is based on the same reference rate, but reduced by 1 and further reduced by the lower rate of tax of 20%. This gives effective rates from 6 September 2005 of 6.5% on underpaid tax and 2.25% on overpaid tax.

C. **Bill – tax position for 2006/07**

(a) **Tax and Class 4 national insurance contributions due**

			£	£
Tax on income of £37,415: Non-savings income	2,150	@ 10%	215	
	24,795	@ 22%	5,455	
Savings income – part	8,855	@ 20%	1,771	
	35,800*			
– balance	1,615	@ 40%	646	
	37,415		8,087	

* Basic rate limit increased by gross pension contribution of £2,500

Class 4 NICs (33,540 – 5,035) @ 8%	2,280		
(51,980 – 33,540) @ 1%	184	2,464	10,551
Less: Tax deducted at source			1,800
Tax due for direct payment			8,751
Less: Payments made on account (2 @ £6,850)			13,700
Tax repayable			4,947

Further repayment due in respect of
gift aid donation carried back
to 2006/07 by extending the higher rate tax band
applicable to savings income by £1,615 (being less than
the gross donation of £2,000), saving tax on £1,615 at
20%

	323
	5,272
Less: Used to cover first payment on account for 2007/08 due 31.1.08 (half of £8,751)	4,375
Net amount repayable 21 April 2008	897

Notes

1. The conversion of redundant space above business premises entitles Bill to an initial allowance of 100% of the expenditure, subject to a number of conditions. If the building had already been let, the allowance would have been given primarily against the letting income and then against other income. Since the building is not tenanted in 2006/07, Bill can claim relief for the UK property loss against his income of that year. For the detailed provisions see Example 21.11E.

2. Class 4 national insurance contributions are calculated on trading income after taking into account balancing charges and capital allowances relating to the trading activities, but not allowances on non-trading activities, or the personal pension premium (Sch 2.3).

(b)   **Interest on overdue tax and repayment supplement**

£

Interest originally charged on payments on account:

		£
On 1st instalment of £6,850 from 31.1.07 to 14.2.07 =	15 days	
On 2nd instalment of £6,850 from 31.7.07 to 29.9.07 =	61 days	
	76 days @ 6.5%	92.46
Payments on account actually due were (½ x 8,751) = £4,376 each, with interest on £4,376 for (15 + 61) days @ 6.5%		59.06
Interest repayable		33.40

Repayment supplement on overpaid payments on account of (6,850 − 4,376) = £2,474 each:

		£
On 1st instalment − 15.2.07 to 21.4.08 =	432 days	
On 2nd instalment − 30.9.07 to 21.4.08 =	204 days	
	£2,474 for 636 days @ 2.25%	96.99
Offset by part of repayment used to cover 31.1.08 payment on account = £4,375 @ 2.25% for 81 days from 1.2.08 to 21.4.08		21.79
Repayment supplement due		75.20

No repayment supplement is due in respect of the refund of £323 relating to the carried back gift aid donation (see part B note 10). Nor does it reduce the 2006/07 or 2007/08 tax for the purpose of calculating payments on account. If tax relief for the payment would be at higher rates in 2007/08, it would probably have been better to claim relief for the donation in that year, thereby reducing the 2008/09 payments on account.

D.   **Petersen − discovery assessment and interest on overdue tax**

Before the discovery assessment was made, the position was:

2003/04	Net tax payable	£25,000
2004/05	31 January payment on account	£12,500
	31 July payment on account	£12,500
(a)	Balancing payment (giving total 2004/05 tax of £45,000)	£20,000
(b)	Balancing payment (giving total 2004/05 tax of £30,000)	£5,000

The tax of £15,000 under the 2003/04 discovery assessment would be due for payment on 31 December 2007, but interest would run from 31 January 2005 to the date the tax was paid. The revised tax for 2003/04 is £40,000.

In the case of (a) (ie 2004/05 balancing payment of £20,000), the amounts that should have been paid by way of payments on account for 2004/05 would be increased by £7,500 to £20,000 each, and interest thereon would run from the half yearly due dates of 31 January 2004 and 31 July 2005 to 31 January 2006 (the underpayments of £7,500 each being effectively paid as part of the balancing payment of £20,000).

In the case of (b) (ie 2004/05 balancing payment of £5,000), the effect of increasing the payments on account to £20,000 each would be to give an overpayment of £10,000 for the year, so that a claim could be made to reduce the additional amounts payable to £2,500 each. As with (a), interest thereon would run from the half yearly due dates of 31 January 2005 and 31 July 2005 to 31 January 2006.

Your firm has recently been appointed as advisers to Sparks Manufacturing Ltd. Following your appointment the accountant of the company has informed you that HMRC is shortly to carry out a PAYE investigation and he has asked that your firm review the procedures in operation prior to the HMRC visit. The following information is relevant:

(1) The company employs 36 full-time and 10 part-time workers. These include 3 full-time office staff, one sales representative and the directors, who are Mr and Mrs Sparks. Mr and Mrs Sparks own all the shares in the company.

(2) The manufacturing workers are paid weekly in cash, and earnings are variable depending on hours worked. Any production bonuses are paid on a month by month basis.

(3) The office staff are paid monthly by cheque. The sales representative is paid gross on a commission basis and is treated as self-employed. His commission is in excess of £40,000 per annum.

(4) Mr and Mrs Sparks receive monthly standing order payments of £500 each. Any additional amounts for expenses are drawn by cheque on a monthly basis.

(5) The accountant applies PAYE and national insurance to the wages and bonus payments made to the full-time employees with the exception of Mr and Mrs Sparks and the salesman.

(6) Part-time employees are all production workers, who each receive £83 per week gross. The production bonus for part-time workers in April 2006 amounted to £100 each and was paid gross.

(7) The company does not hold signed forms P46 for the following part-time workers:

(a) Mrs Acorn (aged 35) – a married lady with no other employment.

(b) Mrs Beech (aged 63) – in receipt of a state pension based upon her husband's contributions and with no other employment.

(c) Mr Chestnut (aged 19) – a student.

(d) Mr Dallow (aged 40) – a milkman.

It is understood that all part-time workers were first employed on 6 April 2004 when the evening shift commenced.

(8) The company pays £18 per week to each of its full-time employees and £10 per week to each of its part-time employees as subsistence payments. These amounts do not appear on the tax cards (P11) and the full-time employees have received them since 6 April 2001 and the part-time workers since they joined the company.

(9) The company provides a car first registered 1997 (1298 cc) with fuel to the foreman, who travels 10,000 business miles per year. The list price of the car when new was £23,200. The foreman's salary in 2005/06 was £18,000.

(10) Miss Fallow, secretary to the managing director, also has a car provided for her own use with all fuel paid for by the company. The current car is two years old (1298 cc) and had a list price of £10,200 when new and a CO_2 emissions figure of 149. In 2005/06 she travelled approximately 1,000 business miles. Her salary in that year was £8,400.

(11) Mr Sparks, whose salary is shown in the company accounts as £40,000 per annum, is provided with a 2500 cc car which had a list price of £26,000 and a CO_2 emissions figure of 272 when new in 2005. He travels 25,000 business miles each year. Mrs Sparks only attends directors' meetings and is paid £4,700 per annum. She is provided with a 2 year old car (1988 cc, CO_2 figure 249) which had a list price of £19,500 when new. Business mileage is minimal. Fuel is provided for both cars.

Mr Sparks has a mobile telephone with 'hands free' operation in his car. The telephone bills in 2005/06 amounted to £1,200 plus VAT. From the bills it would appear that 40% of the calls are non-business.

(12) Mr Jones, the accountant, uses his own car (1998 cc) for business purposes and is paid 75p per mile.

(13) Miss Fallow prefers to buy her own petrol, which is reimbursed to her through petty cash.

The other car users and the sales representative have obtained petrol on company credit cards, the amounts for 2005/06 being as follows (amounts excluding VAT):

	£
Foreman	1,480
Sales representative	2,040
Mr Sparks	3,880
Mrs Sparks	300

As car parking is limited at the factory, 5 season tickets for the car park in the next street are purchased by the company for £2,000 per annum plus VAT each for use by the above.

All VAT on the above items has been recovered in full without any adjustments for private usage.

(14) The following expenses have been drawn in the year 2005/06 (amounts shown net of 7/47 VAT where appropriate):

	Subsistence £	Entertaining £	Round Sum £	Motoring £	Home telephone £
Sales representative	2,460	428	–	–	940
Foreman	820	–	–	–	280
Mr Sparks	–	–	10,500	–	770
Mrs Sparks	–	–	4,300	–	–
Mr Jones	–	1,842	–	1,452	320
Miss Fallow	–	–	–	460	–

(15) Forms P11D have been completed only for Mr Sparks and Mr Jones showing the figures above and Mr Sparks's car.

(16) Sparks Manufacturing Ltd arranged a golf weekend for its customers in 2005/06 and invited ten managing directors to join Mr Sparks and the sales representative for the event. The total cost was £12,000.

The firm also gives its suppliers Christmas hampers, the size of which reflects the value of transactions undertaken in the year. At Christmas 2005 the cost of the hampers varied from £50 to £500.

Set out the implications of the above in respect of PAYE, national insurance, VAT and corporation tax as regards Sparks Manufacturing Ltd, and the effect on the individual's taxable earnings under the following headings:

(a) Part-time employees

(b) Directors' remuneration

(c) Cars and fuel

(d) Other benefits

(e) Sales representative

Without calculating precise figures, indicate the possible basis on which a settlement with HMRC might be negotiated for the period to 5 May 2006, and any steps which could be taken to minimise the liability.

(a) *Part-time Employees*

Part-time employees are subject to PAYE and national insurance in the same way as other staff. For those employees for whom form P46 is held showing that this is the main or only employment, no PAYE or national insurance liability or reporting requirement arises unless their weekly pay equals or exceeds the following limits:

	PAYE	NI (lower earnings limit)
	£	£
2004/05	91	79
2005/06	94	82
2006/07	97	84

Their current weekly pay inclusive of subsistence payments is £93 a week, and they receive a variable monthly bonus. The cumulative pay inclusive of bonuses needs to be checked to ensure that the PAYE limit has not been exceeded. (If it had been, forms P46 should have been sent to HMRC.) The same check needs to be made for national insurance, but on a non-cumulative basis. As far as national insurance is concerned, there is clearly a liability in the weeks when bonus payments are made, and a reporting requirement throughout.

For those employees who have not signed form P46, or where it is not possible to obtain a signed P46 certifying that this is the main or only employment, income tax at the basic rate of tax should be deducted from all remuneration (see below re Mrs Beech). Failure to do so could result in HMRC grossing up the amount paid for the tax not deducted and then applying PAYE/NI to the grossed up equivalent.

It would appear that the company has been in breach of its obligations under the PAYE/NI scheme since April 2004. It will be necessary to agree a settlement with HMRC for that period. The penalty for failing to submit form P46 is the same as that for not submitting or not giving employees copies of forms P11D and P9D, ie an initial penalty of up to £300 per form, plus up to £60 a day if the form is still not submitted or copy provided (TMA 1970 s 98(1)). There is a penalty of up to £3,000 for fraudulently or negligently submitting incorrect forms P11D, P9D and P46 (TMA 1970 s 98(2)). With regard to any tax and national insurance underpaid, HMRC may issue a determination of the amount due under SI 2003/2682 reg 80. Interest is charged on unpaid tax and national insurance from 14 days after the end of the tax year (except to the extent that the collector has required an amount to be paid by an employee) without the need for a formal determination.

It is probable that the HMRC auditors would compute the liability for the month of April 2006 and then apply that amount for the previous two years. In the case of employees without code numbers it is their policy to gross up the amount paid for basic rate tax.

The company should compute the actual liability for the twenty five month period. It is possible that for a number of weeks the actual remuneration (inclusive of subsistence) would be under the lower earnings limit for national insurance and therefore no liability to employer's or employees' contributions would arise. The company should also obtain signed forms P46 wherever possible. In the case of Mrs Acorn this could mean that the remuneration would not be grossed up. In the case of Mr Chestnut a form P38(S) should be obtained and retained for three years as he is a student. Again, it is unlikely that any income tax liability would arise. Since Mrs Beech receives a pension, if the company obtains a form P46 from her now, it will have to be sent to HMRC in any event and tax at the basic rate deducted from her pay. If the company obtains a certificate of age for Mrs Beech for national insurance purposes, no employee's national insurance would be payable, although employer's contributions would still be due. It seems almost certain that basic rate tax and appropriate national insurance contributions will be applicable to Mr Dallow.

If this matter is disclosed to HMRC and correct procedures are put in place, then it is possible that a settlement could be negotiated based upon the correct liability plus interest and notional penalties.

(b) *Directors' Remuneration*

It is not clear whether the monthly standing order is intended to be remuneration or withdrawals from directors' current accounts.

PAYE and national insurance are not relevant unless the amounts are on account of remuneration (see Example 9 explanatory note 11).

In the case of Mr Sparks it would appear that the remuneration of £40,000 per annum, when credited to his director's current account net of PAYE/NI, would be sufficient to provide funds for his withdrawals. If, however, the round sum drawings by Mr Sparks have not been charged to his director's current account, they would give rise to a liability. In that event, the amount drawn should be grossed up and PAYE applied to that gross figure. As Mr Sparks will already have paid the maximum higher rate employees' national insurance contributions, only employer's liability will apply to that grossed up figure plus 1% employees' contributions since 6 April 2003.

Similar comments apply to Mrs Sparks. However, it is almost certain that Mrs Sparks will not have a credit balance on her director's current account and therefore if the round sum drawings are not in anticipation of earnings and they have been charged to her director's current account, the beneficial loans rules and the provisions of TA 1988 s 419 will apply (see below). If the round sums have not been charged to the account, PAYE and national insurance must apply on each and every withdrawal. Unless there is evidence that the payment to Mrs Sparks is made by Mr Sparks as part of their personal relationships, it is not likely that HMRC would treat the withdrawal by Mrs Sparks as coming from the remuneration of Mr Sparks.

Directors' national insurance contributions are computed on a yearly pay period basis and liability strictly only arises when the cumulative drawings for the tax year exceed the lower earnings limit. National insurance liability will of course arise on the total amount when the annual lower earnings limit is reached, thus giving a material liability in that month for employer and director.

Should the company pay the PAYE liability due in respect of Mr and Mrs Sparks in any settlement, then that amount will be treated as a further benefit in kind taxable on the director unless it is charged to the director's loan account (ITEPA 2003 s 223). Any settlement by the company of a national insurance liability in respect of employee contributions applicable to the director will again be treated as a benefit in kind giving rise to further PAYE liabilities, again unless charged to the director's loan account.

If a director's account becomes overdrawn, then there will be a potential benefit in kind liability in respect of the interest due on that loan under ITEPA 2003 Part 3 Chapter 7. In addition, the company will have a charge to tax at 25% on the loan under TA 1988 s 419.

To avoid the problems with s 419 and the beneficial loans rules (and also possible contravention of the Companies Acts), it is suggested that regular monthly salaries should be drawn which are subject to PAYE and national insurance contributions. All round sum allowances should be stopped. Mr and Mrs Sparks should draw actual expenses against vouchers.

The VAT position of round sum allowances should be checked. If any input tax has been recovered because of purported VAT inclusive expenditure in the round sum allowances this must be declared to HMRC and repaid.

If the above was put into force then it is possible that Mrs Sparks would receive remuneration under the national insurance limit and contributions would not be payable. In addition, it should be suggested to her that fuel should not be provided for her car as the benefit in kind cost appears to be greater than the value of fuel provided (a similar comment will apply for VAT and Class 1A national insurance contributions – see (c)).

A form P11D should have been completed for Mrs Sparks as she is a director. The penalty for failure to provide that information is as stated in part (a). If the company had sent in form P11D(b), which confirms that forms P11D have been submitted for all relevant employees, this will probably be regarded as fraudulent or negligent conduct triggering the penalty of up to £3,000 in addition to the penalty for not sending in the form P11D.

HMRC may contend that the car provided to Mrs Sparks is in fact provided by reason of Mr Sparks's employment. Such a contention should be disputed on the grounds that ITEPA 2003 s 169 applies, ie that the car was provided to Mrs Sparks by reason of her directorship and that it is normal commercial practice for a director to be provided with a motor vehicle. Although the charge is the same amount as would be charged on Mr Sparks, it is likely that Mrs Sparks's tax rate will be lower than her husband's.

It is possible that HMRC could argue that the remuneration paid to Mrs Sparks is excessive for her duties as a director. The remuneration for 2005/06 could be considered to be:

Salary	4,700
Round sum allowance	4,300
Benefit in kind – Car 35% x 19,500	6,825
Fuel 35% x 14,400	5,040
	£20,865

plus the PAYE/NI on that amount, unless charged to Mrs Sparks's director's account.

It is therefore possible that a disallowance will occur in the Schedule D Case I computation of the company.

The company should have paid Class 1A national insurance contributions in respect of the directors' cars (see (c)).

(c) *Cars and Fuel*

Clearly, both the foreman and Miss Fallow are employees not excluded from the benefits code (they are not in lower-paid employment by virtue of ITEPA 2003 s 217) when the benefits charges for cars are added to their respective salaries.

Again forms P11D should have been provided to HMRC in respect of the foreman, Miss Fallow and probably the sales representative (see (e)), so that penalties may arise.

The company should have paid Class 1A national insurance contributions each year in respect of the cars and fuel provided to employees, including the directors' cars. Records should be available in respect of the business mileage travelled to 5 April 2004 to show that the correct contributions have been paid.

It would appear that no VAT adjustments have been made for private fuel. The company should apply the scale charges in respect of private fuel at the relevant rate. It would appear that there would be two cars at the lower rate (foreman and Miss Fallow), one car at the middle rate (Mrs Sparks) and one car at the higher rate (Mr Sparks). In addition, there will be a scale charge in respect of the sales representative if he is an employee. If he is not, VAT will be due on the full value of the supply to him, including the supply of the car.

Providing the company makes a voluntary declaration to HMRC of the underpaid VAT there will be no penalties. Interest will be chargeable where appropriate.

The company should consider the financial viability of providing cars. The combined tax, VAT and national insurance charges on employer and employee may well be greater than the benefits actually obtained, particularly for Miss Fallow.

Similar comments apply to the provision of fuel to all employees and directors. For Mr and Mrs Sparks the fuel charge for 2005/06 is 35% of £14,400 = £5,040 each. If fuel is to be withdrawn, the charge for a tax year will be reduced according to the period for which fuel is provided (unless free fuel is provided again later in the same tax year).

Mr Jones is paid a mileage allowance. If that amount exceeds the mileage allowance payment in ITEPA 2003 s 230 then it should be treated as remuneration. The figure of 75p per mile exceeds 40p per mile and therefore PAYE and NI should have been applied to the excess of 35p per mile (ie 1,936 miles @ 35p = £677). For 2000/01 and 2001/02 the authorised mileage allowance rate for tax for Mr Jones's car was 45p for the first 4,000 business miles and 25p thereafter, the 45p rate applying to all miles for NI. From 2002/03 the rates changed to 40p per mile up to 10,000 miles and 25p thereafter, the 40p rate applying to all miles for NI. If Mr Jones's mileage allowance is restricted to the authorised rate, it would no longer have to be taken into account for PAYE and NI.

(d)   *Other Benefits*

Telephones

The provision of a mobile phone to Mr Sparks and private use thereof is not subject to an income tax charge. However, VAT is payable on the non-business use of the mobile. This would appear to be 40% × (1,200 × 17.5%) = £84 per year. This amount must be declared to HMRC and repaid assuming full input tax deduction had occurred. The home telephone expenses for Mr Sparks and Mr Jones have already been shown on forms P11D. From 2006/07, an income tax charge could apply to the mobile phone, if the company provides more than one per employee.

They should also be shown for the foreman and the sales representative (if he is an employee). It is then up to the individual employee to make an ITEPA 2003 s 336 claim for actual business calls. The balance will be liable to PAYE. For national insurance purposes, identified business calls (but not part of the rental) may be excluded from the amount on which contributions are payable, or alternatively if there is an agreement with HMRC as to the business proportion for tax purposes, it is acceptable for NI purposes. The required adjustment for the telephones will be applied for all relevant years. Although the income tax liabilities are technically those of the individual employees it is possible that the company will wish to settle them, as it has been in breach of its obligations under PAYE/NI in not submitting forms P11D. The penalties and interest within any such settlement would not be an allowable deduction for Schedule D purposes, but the tax and national insurance would be allowed in the year of payment if the amounts paid by the company in respect of the telephone bills had been grossed up to calculate that tax and national insurance.

Entertaining

The amounts to be shown on forms P11D should be inclusive of VAT. If any input tax has been recovered on such sums then it must be repaid to HMRC. Interest will be charged but not penalties if voluntary declarations are made to HMRC. No deduction is allowed for Schedule D Case I purposes.

Car Parking

As the car parking is purchased directly by the company there will be no PAYE or national insurance liabilities on these amounts.

Subsistence

Subsistence will be an important part of the settlement. Subsistence payments in cash to employees are pay, and PAYE and NI are due at the appropriate rates. Similar payments are due for earlier years back to 2001. For example, 36 employees x £18 per week x 48 weeks = £31,104 per annum which at 22% + NI of 21.8% = £13,623 per annum for two years (based on 2002/03 NI rates) and £31,104 at 22% + NI of 23.8% = £14,245 for 2003/04, 2004/05 and 2005/06. In so far as the amount related to employees' PAYE and NI, it would not be deductible for Schedule D Case I purposes, leaving a reduction only for employer's national insurance. (Although the company may have a claim against the employees for that amount it may prefer not to pursue that claim, or be unsuccessful in recovery of the tax and NI due from the workers.) HMRC could, however, argue that the amounts were net payments and therefore should be grossed up, in which case it would normally be agreed that the whole of the PAYE and NI would be deductible for Schedule D Case I in the accounting period when it was paid, but the settlement of the PAYE/NI irregularities would, of course, have been higher.

It should be noted that if the company had an in-house canteen with subsidised or free meals or arrangements had been made with a local caterer to provide similar meals then no liability would arise. In those circumstances a dispensation should be obtained from HMRC. Although VAT would be due on amounts paid by employees, any costs involved would give rise to deductible input tax.

To minimise the costs, calculations should be made to ensure that the actual liabilities are applied rather than global calculations, eg go back and exclude days for which allowances were not paid to employees because of illness, holidays etc. Also confirm any days for which subsistence allowance was genuinely due, eg days out of the factory. Check if any employee was lower paid or on lower national insurance rates, thus avoiding liability or having a lower liability.

The treatment of the subsistence paid to the sales representative depends on whether he is classified as employed or self-employed. If he is an employee the position is as described above. In the unlikely event that HMRC agrees that he is self-employed (see (e)), the subsistence payments to him will represent part of his fees. Unless he is VAT registered and has submitted a VAT invoice, no VAT input tax should have been recovered on the subsistence, and if any has been, it should be repaid to HMRC. Any subsistence provided and paid for directly by a business for self-employed agents etc is disallowed as entertaining expenditure (C & E v Shaklee International 1981).

Third party benefits

Where an employer has *arranged* for a third party to provide benefits to employees the employer is required to include the benefits on forms P11D. If third party benefits are provided other than by arrangement with the employer, the third party is required to provide written details of the cash equivalent of the benefits to the employees concerned by 6 July following the relevant tax year, ie by 6 July 2006 for 2005/06 (SI 2003/2682 reg 95). The third party is not required to provide details to HMRC unless they call for a return under TMA 1970 s 15.

The third party benefits provisions do not apply to corporate hospitality, ie entertainment/hospitality provided by someone who is not the employer or a person connected with the employer, where the employer/connected person has not arranged or procured the provision of the benefit, and it is not provided in return for particular services performed or anticipated to be performed by the employee in the course of his employment (ITEPA 2003 s 265).

Nor do they apply to benefits covered by ITEPA 2003 s 324. This excludes gifts from third parties that do not exceed a VAT inclusive value of £250 (£150 to 5 April 2003) to any individual in a tax year.

The golf weekend will be covered by the corporate hospitality provisions unless HMRC argue that the benefit was provided as a result of specific services performed or to be performed by the managing directors in their companies, eg to give special favour to contracts with Sparks Manufacturing.

The provision of Christmas hampers up to a value of £250 would be covered by concession A70 (now ITEPA 2003 s 324). Suppliers receiving hampers would only be chargeable if they received them as employees. In this case hampers in excess of that value would need to be notified. The same penalty applies for not notifying third party benefits as for not providing employees with forms P11D/P9D.

If Sparks Manufacturing do not wish the recipients to pay tax on the benefit, they may arrange with the Incentive Valuation Unit of HMRC to pay tax on the grossed-up value of the award under the Taxed Award Scheme. In that event the recipients would receive information under the Taxed Award Scheme rules rather than the third party benefits reporting requirements.

Sparks Manufacturing will not be able to claim a deduction for VAT or Schedule D Case I for the golf weekend or the hampers.

Any amounts paid or reimbursed to Mr Sparks (and the sales representative if an employee) in respect of the golf weekend should be included on forms P11D. A s 336 claim can then be made in respect of the whole amount, since it represents a specific payment for entertaining (which has been disallowed for Schedule D Case I purposes).

National insurance on benefits in kind

From 6 April 2000 employer's Class 1A national insurance contributions are payable on all taxable benefits (except certain childcare provision). The rate of Class 1A contributions for 2000/01 was 12.2%, reduced to 11.9% for 2001/02 and 11.8% for 2002/03. The rate is 12.8% for 2003/04 onwards. Benefits are shown separately from expenses on form P11D for 2000/01 and later years. No liability arises for non-directors who are lower paid, for whom P9D is used. The liability is computed for all relevant directors/employees and summarised on form P11D(b). A separate payslip is then used to pay the Class 1A liability to the Accounts Office by 19 July following the tax year. Interest is charged on late payments and a penalty may be levied of £100 per 50 employees (or part thereof) for each month (or part thereof) the return is late.

Strictly the employer is liable to Class 1A national insurance on any benefits received by an employee from a third party. However, HMRC will not impose that charge on the employer provided the third party has paid the Class 1A liability. This can be done as part of the provision of a Taxed Incentive Award.

Sparks Manufacturing Ltd should carefully check the completion of forms P11D to ensure that benefits are shown separately from expenses, and that Class 1 national insurance has been paid on round sum payments and the settlement of employees' pecuniary liabilities. No Class 1A liability arises on any amount liable to Class 1, or exempt from tax (eg one mobile telephone per employee). Liability is as follows:

Subsistence	Class 1 on profits
Cars and fuel	Class 1A on scale charges
Mileage payments	Class 1 on profit
Mobile telephones	No charge (one per employee)
Reimbursed petrol	Class 1 (on profit if business usage identified)
Car parking	No charge
Entertaining	No charge
Round sums	Class 1 on full amount
Home telephone	Class 1 (on rent and private calls provided business calls identified)

Sparks Manufacturing Ltd may also wish to pay the employers' Class 1A national insurance due on the golf weekend if HMRC succeeds in treating the amount as taxable.

(e)   *Sales Representative*

The status of this worker should be clarified. The information provided suggests at point 1 that he is an employee, but at point 3 that he is treated as self-employed. The facts suggest that he is under the control and direction of the company. He would appear to be an integral part of the business and does not appear to be taking commercial risks. He draws all expenses from the company and is provided with benefits such as subsistence allowance, car parking space etc. He would appear to work only for the company. It is therefore most likely that he will be treated as an employee throughout.

Reclassification can strictly take place from the date of the commencement of the employment, but if the position has been clearly disclosed to HMRC in earlier years, reclassification from a later date may be negotiated, particularly if the sales representative has prepared and submitted accounts and agreed and paid all of his tax liabilities to date. In computing the liability HMRC should take into account the personal allowances of the employee and any potential s 336 expenses claims. The Class 2 national insurance contributions paid by the sales representative should be credited against his employee's national insurance liability. Any Class 4 national insurance contributions and trading income tax paid will be repaid to the employee. As the sales representative still works in the business, negotiations should take place for part or all of those amounts to be repaid to the company, or indeed set off in the settlement by agreement between the sales representative and the company. Strictly the company has no legal right to recover from the sales representative national insurance contributions for previous years.

If he were to be classified as an employee, the sales representative would be assessed on benefits in kind in the normal way.

The provision of personal services through a limited company or partnership became liable to PAYE/NI on a deemed salary from 6 April 2000. If the sales representative attempts to retain his self-employed status by use of a partnership (or limited company) it is likely to be ineffective. However, in those circumstances Sparks Manufacturing Ltd would have no liability for any PAYE/NI arising on a reclassification. The case of Cable & Wireless plc v Muscat found there to be an implied contract of employment between the company and an individual working via both his own limited company and an employment agency. It is unlikely that the sales representative's self-employed status can be maintained.

Generally

The company clearly has material liabilities to HMRC in respect of failure to operate PAYE and national insurance in earlier years. These amounts should be quantified as soon as possible and declared to HMRC before the commencement of the visit. The company should regularise its position as follows: place the sales representative on the PAYE records unless it can be specifically established with HMRC that he is self-employed; cease paying subsistence and replace with canteen facilities (or add subsistence to pay for payroll purposes); apply PAYE and NI to part time staff; regularise the position of Mr and Mrs Sparks and their monthly drawings; prepare and submit outstanding forms P11D for all relevant employees, also providing the directors and employees with copy P11Ds for 2005/06; give third parties written details of benefits provided in 2005/06; obtain signed forms P46/P38S for all part-time workers; use Mileage Allowance Payment Rate for the accountant.

In addition, the VAT implications of all transactions mentioned above should be reviewed. A voluntary disclosure should be made to HMRC as soon as possible. If the net disclosure is under £2,000 this can be made by adjustment to the next VAT return. If the figure is in excess of £2,000 a written declaration must be made to HMRC showing the liability divided between VAT accounting periods so that interest may be calculated for the last three years.

The company should cease paying round sum allowances and should only reimburse expenses against actual vouchers. VAT input tax can then be recovered with the exception of that on entertaining. In the case of motoring, VAT will only be recoverable on the petrol element of the allowance paid to Mr Jones. It should be confirmed that VAT has only been recovered on the business proportion of telephone bills, not the total bill. Note that the European courts have ruled that the recovery of input VAT by an employer on company expenses where the expense was incurred by the employee is against EU rules. In Notice 700/64 HMRC states that input tax may be recovered in respect of business use if supported by a VAT invoice. Output tax must be accounted for in respect of private use.

It is probable that there will be significant settlements to be agreed with HMRC in respect of past breaches. Full co-operation and correction of past errors will be strong mitigating factors when negotiating the level of liability and penalties thereon.

Explanatory Notes

PAYE audits

1.   HMRC has power to visit employers' premises to undertake PAYE tax and national insurance inspections (Income Tax (PAYE) Regulations 2003 (SI 2003/2682 reg 97) and Social Security (Contributions) Regulations 2001 (SI 2001/1004 Sch 4)).

Employers are required to produce to HMRC investigators all records relating to the calculation of emoluments, and the deduction of tax and national insurance therefrom. It is common for an audit to reveal areas of non-compliance with the regulations by the employers, and in that event HMRC will require settlement for the current and previous six years, with the addition of interest and penalties depending on the nature of the irregularities. HMRC may agree to accept the amount due by instalments. The example illustrates most of the points to be considered in a PAYE/NI investigation.

2. Where HMRC consider that the employer has been guilty of fraudulent or negligent conduct, a penalty of up to 100% of the underpayment could be charged, but this will be subject to mitigation along the lines indicated in Examples 45 and 46. HMRC leaflet IR 109 indicates their approach to negotiating PAYE settlements.

Year-end returns

3. As far as employers' returns are concerned, year-end forms P35 and P14 are due to be submitted by 19 May after the end of the tax year (ie within 44 days), although the tax is due for payment by 19 April. TMA 1970 s 98A imposes penalties in respect of late submission (although by Revenue Concession B46 a penalty will not be charged if the forms are received on or before the last business day within the seven days following 19 May). It is possible for HMRC to proceed instead under TMA 1970 s 98, in which case the penalties are the same as for forms P11D etc as outlined in part (a) of the example.

Under s 98A, there are automatic penalties for late year-end forms P35 and P14 as follows:

(a) A non-mitigable amount of £100 a month or part month for every 50 employees (and an additional £100 where the number of employees is not a multiple of 50), for up to 12 months, plus

(b) If the returns are outstanding for more than 12 months, an amount not exceeding the amount unpaid at the original due date (ie 19 April following the year to which the returns relate).

These penalties are imposed by a determination made by an inspector under TMA 1970 s 100 and no proceedings before the Commissioners are necessary.

Similar penalties apply for late year-end forms P11D(b) (SI 2001/1004 Sch 4.22).

Where the statutory penalty exceeds the total tax and national insurance due, it will normally be reduced to that amount or to £100 whichever is greater.

The s 98A penalties based on number of employees cover both tax and national insurance. Where the returns are outstanding for more than twelve months, a penalty may be imposed up to the amount of national contributions unpaid at the original due date, in addition to the penalty on the unpaid tax (Social Security Contributions and Benefits Act 1992 Sch 1.7).

4. The time limit for sending in forms P11D, P11D(b) and P9D is 6 July after the end of the tax year. The penalties outlined above will normally be imposed if the forms are not filed with HMRC by 19 July. Employers must provide employees with copies of forms P11D and P9D by 6 July following the tax year (see Example 9), and the penalties that apply for failing to provide such copies are outlined in part (a) of the example. HMRC will not normally impose penalties for failure to provide copy forms P11D unless the amount involved is significant or the employer persists in failing to comply. As indicated in part (d) of the example, similar penalties apply for not notifying third party benefits.

Determinations of tax due

5. Under SI 2003/2682 reg 78 HMRC has power to estimate the monthly payments due if no payment is made or they are not satisfied with the tax paid. The specified amount must be paid within seven days of the issue of the notice unless the employer can satisfy HMRC that a lower amount is due.

6. Where an officer considers that tax and national insurance due under PAYE has not been paid, he may issue a formal determination of the amount due (SI 2003/2682 reg 80). Where a regulation 80

determination is made, interest automatically runs on late paid tax and national insurance from 19 April after the end of the tax year (income tax SI 2003/2682 reg 82, national insurance SI 2001/1004 Sch 4.17).

Employees' national insurance position on PAYE settlements

7.   Where an employer negotiates a settlement with HMRC and pays a sum representing tax that should have been deducted from the employees' earnings it is contended that the employer is thereby meeting a pecuniary liability of the employee and that contributions are due on the payment. The cases of CIR v Woollen (1992) and CIR v Nuttall (1990) suggest that this is not correct, since the employee is not party to such an agreement and HMRC's right to recover the amounts from the employee has been subsumed within the overall amount payable by the employer.

PAYE Settlement Agreements (PSAs)

8.   Some employers negotiate annual voluntary settlements with HMRC in respect of the tax liability on certain expenses payments and benefits to employees, which are referred to as PAYE settlement agreements (ITEPA 2003 Part 11 Chapter 5). From 6 April 1999, a new class of national insurance contributions, Class 1B, was introduced, under which contributions are payable on the benefits etc taxed under a PSA plus the tax thereon, to the extent that there would have been a national insurance liability under Class 1 or Class 1A. For details see Example 9 explanatory note 9.

Recovery of underpaid tax and national insurance from employee

9.   Where an employer has to account for tax and national insurance contributions that he has failed to deduct, his rights of recovery from the employee are limited. However, the case of Kleinwort Benson Ltd v Lincoln City Council (1998 4 AER 513) now allows recovery where money was wrongly paid under a mistake of law, such as incorrectly treating an employee as self-employed. For other recoveries from an employee the case of Bernard and Shaw Ltd v Shaw 1951 held that recovery was restricted to later payments of remuneration. As far as national insurance is concerned, the regulations provide that recovery can be made only by deducting it from pay in the same year, and then not exceeding an extra amount in each pay period equal to the normal deduction for that period (SI 2001/1004 Sch 4.6, 4.7). In any event, most employers would find it difficult to recover amounts from their employees, and may well suffer all or most of the payment themselves.

Childcare vouchers

10.   See Example 10 at note 24 for details of the income tax and national insurance treatment of childcare vouchers provided by an employer.

See also Example 5 at note 7 for the interaction of tax credit claims with the provision of childcare vouchers.

Personal service companies

11.   This legislation is covered in detail in Example 88.

Grenville is an antique dealer, and he has accounts professionally prepared to 31 October each year. The accounts for the year ended 31 October 2005, forming the basis of his self-assessment return for the tax year 2005/06, were submitted to HMRC, together with the return, on 30 September 2006.

Grenville is married, his wife assisting minimally in the business, for which she has consistently received a wage just below the income tax threshold. She has no other income.

On 28 February 2007 Grenville received a formal notice from HMRC under TMA 1970 s 9A(1) stating that they had decided to enquire into his 2005/06 self-assessment, and calling for the following documents and information:

1. The business records for the accounting year to 31 October 2005.

2. Grenville's private bank statements and building society account books covering the tax year ended 5 April 2006.

3. An explanation of the source of £20,000 described in the accounts as capital introduced.

4. An analysis of the deduction in arriving at the accounts profits for wages, casual labour and porterage.

Grenville is concerned at the apparent extent of HMRC's powers in pursuing its enquiry and in particular the implied ability of the officer to examine his private financial records.

He says that he can explain and prove the capital introduced, since it was from his wife's bank current account, but confides in you that when the officer sees his own private bank and building society accounts he is bound to be curious about large deposits and withdrawals, which Grenville acknowledges are for business transactions which have not been recorded in the business books and hence not reflected in the profits.

Advise Grenville:

(a) of the consequences of failing to comply with the officer's request for information and documents, and what protection he has if he finds that request unreasonable;

(b) given that the information and documents are provided, how the officer's enquiry is likely to proceed; and

(c) to what extent the officer may extend his enquiry to cover the self-assessment for 2004/05 (which was filed on 31 December 2005, tax having been paid appropriately) and to 2003/04 and earlier years.

(d) state what action you, as a tax adviser, must take to comply with money laundering regulations.

(a) **HMRC's request for information and documents**

If Grenville fails to comply with the request for information and documents, HMRC is able formally to demand these under TMA 1970 s 19A, the initial request to Grenville with the formal notice of enquiry being an opportunity for him to provide what HMRC requires without their using their formal powers.

Grenville cannot object to the officer enquiring into the return, but if he finds the request for information and documents unreasonable, he has the right to appeal to the Appeal Commissioners within 30 days from the date of the s 19A notice. If the Commissioners confirm the notice, the taxpayer has 30 days from their decision to produce the required documents. If during the progress of the enquiry the taxpayer feels that HMRC has no reasonable grounds for continuing it and that it should therefore be concluded, he can ask the Commissioners to direct HMRC to issue a closure notice (TMA 1970 s 28A(4)).

(b) **Enquiry procedure**

Upon seeing Grenville's bank and building society accounts, HMRC will undoubtedly come to the conclusion which Grenville predicts, and he would be advised at the time of submitting them to point out to HMRC the irregularities in his business records and accounts.

Despite Grenville's ability to explain the £20,000 capital introduced and to prove the source from which it has come, HMRC can also be expected to question how his wife, given her evident income, could have accumulated that amount of money in her current account.

They cannot directly ask Grenville about this unless his wife gives her specific permission for them to do so and for Grenville to disclose such information about her affairs to them, but they can serve a formal notice on her under TMA 1970 s 20(3) which empowers HMRC to ask for documents in the possession or power of one person which might affect the taxation liability of another.

The implication here is that the wife's current account, like Grenville's own personal bank and building society accounts, had been used for business transactions and Grenville and his wife should be advised to agree a way forward with HMRC under which the omitted profits can be ascertained.

Although the business records have been discredited, they may still be useful in piecing together what has happened, for example by seeking to match the recorded expenditure on purchases, restoration costs, hotels, credit card payments showing where petrol and meals have been purchased, with sales and stock records.

An overall reconsideration of personal and business finances over an agreed period, embracing the accounts results, those of the specific matching exercise referred to in the previous paragraph, and the transactions through Mrs Grenville's account, will go a long way to calculating meaningful profits.

In the course of its investigation, HMRC will be concerned to prove the veracity of the recorded business expenditure, particularly in the areas highlighted by their request for information, there being a danger that amounts paid away for casual labour and porterage should really have gone through the payroll or otherwise have been reported to HMRC under the procedures for providing information about monies paid to the employees of others.

When the enquiry is completed Grenville will be invited to make an offer to HMRC in consideration of its not taking proceedings against him, the amount of the offer comprising the tax and interest plus a penalty.

Where income or gains have been understated, the maximum penalty is 100% of the unpaid tax and Class 4 national insurance (TMA 1970 s 95).

This is mitigated by the disclosure of the taxpayer and his cooperation in calculating the underpaid duties. Further mitigation is possible, depending on the size and gravity of the offence (see explanatory notes 20 and 21).

For example, a protracted underdisclosure will attract less mitigation than a one-off offence, and one involving alteration of documents will be regarded as more serious than a suppression of cash sales.

If HMRC accepts the taxpayer's offer, a binding contract is concluded, breach of which through nonpayment by the taxpayer enables HMRC to take action for recovery of the amount outstanding.

(c) **Extending enquiry to earlier years**

Except where a return is filed late, HMRC may only open an enquiry under TMA 1970 s 9A into the amount of a taxpayer's self-assessment within the period ending 12 months after the filing date (31 January next but one after the tax year – and hence 31 January 2007 for Grenville's 2004/05 assessment). It is therefore too late to open an enquiry into the 2004/05 return. Even though the time for opening an enquiry has expired, however, HMRC has the power to issue an assessment themselves (under TMA 1970 s 29) in cases of fraudulent or negligent conduct, or where there has been inadequate disclosure by the taxpayer. The time limit for such assessments in cases of inadequate disclosure is five years from 31 January following the tax year (TMA 1970 s 34), extended to 20 years where there is fraudulent or negligent conduct (TMA 1970 s 36). For years before 1996/97 HMRC has similar powers to issue assessments, the time limits being six years and 20 years after the end of the relevant tax year.

If, therefore, their enquiries into the 2005/06 self-assessment indicate that the self-assessments for 1996/97 to 2004/05, and the assessed profits for earlier years, are likely to have been inadequate, they can raise discovery assessments for those years to the best of the officer's judgment under TMA 1970 s 29.

Grenville and his advisers should agree with HMRC a suitable way of attempting to calculate the profits for a mutually acceptable number of years working back from 2005/06.

(d) The tax practitioner, whether qualified or not, is bound by the money laundering regulations which came into force on 1 March 2004. These regulations require them to make reports not only of money laundering transactions, but also of the existence of any proceeds of crime. By under declaring income, Grenville has obtained a monetary advantage in retaining funds that he otherwise would not have, and these are the proceeds. The proceeds of crime include the proceeds of tax evasion, bribery or any costs saved by failure to comply with regulatory requirements where failure to comply is a criminal offence – in this case the failure appears to be deliberate, and could be the subject of prosecution if HMRC so chose.

The fact that the tax authorities are aware of the matter does not obviate the need to make a report as soon as possible. The Tax practitioner must report the matter to the firm's Money Laundering Reporting Officer (MLRO). The MLRO must then consider whether to report, and whether to make a full report or a Limited Information Value Report (LIVR).

There is no indication that these omissions were unintentional, or particularly small (there is no de minimis limit for reporting), so clearly a report must be made. As there is good evidence for the identity of the person holding the proceeds of crime, and the whereabouts of the proceeds of crime themselves, a full report must be made.

The report must, therefore, be made as soon as reasonably possible to SOCA on a Suspicious Activity Report (SAR). This can be done online, or mailed by first-class post.

Explanatory Notes

Conduct of an enquiry

1. Example 46 deals with the method of computing overall income or income omitted from tax returns, and the way in which a settlement will usually be concluded with HMRC. In making that calculation, allowance must be made for VAT on additional sales for which a liability exists.

HMRC's sources of information

2. HMRC might already be in possession of information about Grenville and his affairs, and some of the documents or information called for may be to test that he is being completely open in providing them following the officer's challenge.

3. There are a number of statutory provisions requiring persons to disclose income or transactions of others.

    Those producing most information to HMRC are the requirements for banks and building societies to provide details of interest credited to depositors; for those paying commissions to provide details of the payee and amount, for example insurance and finance companies; for insurance companies to provide details of chargeable events arising out of the surrender or partial surrender of life assurance policies; and returns by solicitors and others of income arising on funds under their control. Government Departments, public bodies, and the National Savings and Investments are also required to provide information. With the approval of a Special Commissioner, HMRC is able, where serious tax default is suspected, to require information without naming the suspected individuals, eg asking sponsors of tax avoidance schemes that are not legally effective to give details of those who used the scheme.

    Information is also obtained from other government departments such as HMRC Capital Taxes, Department for Work and Pensions, the Land Registry and in respect of holdings of Government Stocks. The exchange of information between government departments is strictly controlled, but FA 1997 s 110 extended the rules relating to the disclosure of information by the Department for Work and Pensions to HMRC, so that there are now general powers for information to be exchanged between both departments.

4. In addition to the persons that are required to provide information mentioned in note 3, HMRC has a general power under TMA 1970 s 20 to obtain information from third parties, with the consent of a General or Special Commissioner, and under this provision an accountant may be required to make available his working papers relating to a client's tax affairs, except for audit papers and tax advice (TMA 1970 s 20B). In April 2006, HMRC was granted a disclosure order by the Special Commissioners under this legislation, requiring a major bank to disclose details of offshore accounts held by customers with UK addresses. The power extends beyond documents to other things. This could include computers. HMRC has issued Statement of Practice 5/90 outlining how their powers are used in this area. See also their Tax Bulletin of April 2000 concerning claims to professional or legal privilege. This should be read in conjunction with the case of Morgan Grenfell & Co Ltd (2002) which confirmed that documents subject to legal professional privilege are excluded from the scope of those powers.

    From 28 July 2000, HMRC also has the power to ask a circuit judge to issue an order to a person requiring him to deliver documents to HMRC in the case of suspected serious fraud. The documents are those which may contain evidence of the suspected fraud. A person receiving such an order must deliver the specified documents within 10 days or such longer period specified in the order (TMA 1970 s 20BA & Sch 1AA). It is a criminal offence to falsify or destroy documents called for under ss 20 and 20BA (TMA 1970 s 20BB).

    In Grenville's case, HMRC could have obtained information on Grenville's affairs as a result of looking at working papers relating to someone else.

5. A considerable amount of information available to the public generally is also used by HMRC to check the accuracy of returns, such as share registers, planning applications, press and media coverage, entries in telephone and trade directories, and details of new company formations not only in so far as the new company is concerned, but the other business activities of the personnel involved which may be apparent from the documents submitted to the Companies Registry.

    HMRC also has a vast amount of information at their disposal from the files of other taxpayers, for example, loans, capital acquisitions and disposals, and they glean considerably more in meetings with taxpayers and in examining their business records, when the affairs of others with whom they have been concerned are bound to come under scrutiny and comparisons are made between the records of businesses which deal with each other.

In Grenville's case, HMRC might well have been alerted to the apparent irregularities in his affairs through investigating the affairs of another trader with whom he has done business, or indeed by having had a concentrated look at his particular trade in his geographical area. For example, they might have seen the records of an auction house and, by a combination of those and other means, have formed the view that declared profits were inadequate.

Finally, HMRC, like other authorities, receive information from informants and someone suspecting Grenville's underdeclarations might well have provided HMRC with information which has assisted them in formulating their views.

Completion of enquiry

6. In addition to examining bank and building society accounts, HMRC will require a certified statement of assets and liabilities before agreeing Grenville's liabilities, to ensure that all of these have been included in considering the calculation of profits.

   Grenville will also be asked to sign a certificate of complete disclosure and of bank and building society accounts operated.

7. From a combination of the certified statements at note 6 above, the independent information which they hold and the detailed workings, HMRC will be as satisfied as in the circumstances it is possible to be that all income and gains have been taken into account.

8. The enquiry will usually be settled by HMRC accepting an offer from the taxpayer (contract settlement), or for some self-assessment enquiries, by HMRC issuing a closure notice under TMA 1970 s 28A setting out HMRC's conclusions and the amendments to the self-assessment. For details of the settlement procedure see notes 20 to 22.

Criminal proceedings

9. Whilst the usual practice of HMRC is to seek a pecuniary settlement with the taxpayer, it should always be borne in mind that they could take criminal proceedings in the case of provable fraud, being quite distinct from the civil proceedings for the recovery of unpaid tax, interest and penalties.

   Furthermore, the Court of Appeal held in R v W and Another (1998) that the Crown Prosecution Service could prosecute a taxpayer even where HMRC had decided not to do so. The Revenue stated, however, in their Tax Bulletin of June 1998 that this will ordinarily only occur where tax evasion is incidental to allegations of non-fiscal criminal conduct, which was the case in R v W.

   A new criminal offence of fraudulent evasion of income tax came into force from 1 January 2001 (FA 2000 s 144). It applies where, in relation to things done or omitted on or after that date, someone is knowingly concerned in the fraudulent evasion of income tax by himself or someone else.

   From 2 October 2000 the Human Rights Act 1998 applies, which introduces further rights and protections for a client in criminal matters. The definition of 'criminal' includes offences that can give rise to a penalty which is punitive. It is thought that any case where HMRC imposes a penalty, as opposed to only recovering the unpaid tax plus interest, could be classified as criminal under the Human Rights Act 1998.

   It may be argued in such cases that HMRC needs to prove its case beyond all reasonable doubt (instead of on the basis of balance of probability), that the taxpayer is not required to incriminate himself, that the onus of proof is on HMRC and that only admissible evidence may be used to prove the case.

   In practice taxpayers may prefer to negotiate a settlement rather than risk the possibility that HMRC may take a criminal prosecution.

Any appeal to the Commissioners could be considered a civil matter, eg determining the facts of a case such as employment status, or a criminal matter. In the latter case it would be best practice for the matter to be fully discussed with HMRC to get them to disclose their skeleton arguments and to give the taxpayer's advisers full access to any evidence.

In the matter of a deceased taxpayer, the Human Rights Act confirms that criminal liability ceases at the date of death. This will prevent HMRC imposing tax geared penalties on the personal representatives for actions of the taxpayer prior to death.

Enquiries under self-assessment – income tax and capital gains tax

10. The time limit for submitting a return is 31 January following the end of the tax year (eg 31 January 2007 for 2005/06). HMRC has an absolute right, without giving any reason, to enquire into any return within 12 months after its submission, ie by 31 January 2008 for a 2005/06 return (TMA 1970 ss 9A, 12AC). Under TMA 1970 s 28C, HMRC is able to 'determine' the tax due where a return is not submitted, and this is treated as a self-assessment unless and until superseded by an actual self-assessment. The time limit for the determination is five years from the 31 January following the tax year, and a superseding self-assessment can only be made within that period or, if later, within 12 months after the determination.

11. HMRC assessments will still be issued (under TMA 1970 s 29) in cases of fraudulent or negligent conduct, or where there has been inadequate disclosure by the taxpayer, as indicated in part (c) of the example. In cases of fraudulent or negligent conduct HMRC has the power to issue a discovery assessment even though the time limit for opening an enquiry into a return has not expired. See HMRC's Tax Bulletin August 2001 for the circumstances in which this might be done.

12. As far as interest on overdue tax is concerned, interest automatically runs from the due dates of the payments on account and balancing payments and there is no provision for interest to be mitigated (TMA 1970 s 86). (For years before self-assessment, ie 1995/96 and earlier, interest is also charged under s 86 and runs from 31 January following the relevant tax year.) Where there is an HMRC discovery assessment under TMA 1970 s 29, the provisional payments required for the following tax year will be regarded as being increased accordingly (TMA 1970 s 59A(4B)). Interest will therefore be charged not only on the underpaid tax for the tax year to which the discovery assessment relates but also on the amounts by which the next year's provisional payments fell short of what they should have been. The interest on the shortfall in the provisional payments will run to the date when the balancing payment fell due (ie normally 31 January following the end of the tax year).

13. A taxpayer can only amend his self-assessment within 12 months after the 31 January filing date for the return. If a taxpayer's original return was made fraudulently or negligently, amending it within the twelve month period will not prevent a penalty being charged under TMA 1970 s 95, although the voluntary disclosure will be taken into account when mitigation of the penalty is being considered, as indicated in note 21.

    TMA 1970 s 28A provides that returns are not amended by a taxpayer on completion of an HMRC enquiry. Amendments required by HMRC are made by them in a closure notice issued to the taxpayer (see note 22).

14. HMRC enquiries under self-assessment may either be *full enquiries* to check the return as a whole or *aspect enquiries* that concentrate on one or more specific aspects of the return, although aspect enquiries may turn into full enquiries if the initial enquiry casts doubt on the accuracy of the whole return. Most enquiries into business returns will be full enquiries, while most enquiries (other than random enquiries) into non-business returns will be aspect enquiries. The opening of an enquiry does not mean that HMRC has already identified a reason for dissatisfaction with the return, but the vast majority of enquiries will be opened because of the potential risk that the returns concerned are incorrect or incomplete. (See Example 40 note 12 re the targeting by HMRC of small businesses that have submitted three line accounts showing turnover just below £15,000 in successive years.) About 1 in 1,000 returns will be selected for full enquiry at random. The scale of the enquiry will, however,

reflect the circumstances of the case and the degree of risk of error or omission. Trivial or remote risks will not be pursued, nor will HMRC seek information that can be verified from their own records.

Enquiries under self-assessment – corporation tax

15.   Self-assessment applies to companies for accounting periods ending after 30 June 1999.

The same provisions apply as for income tax for the company to amend the return and HMRC similarly have the power to enquire into the return within 12 months after the end of the accounting period, eg for an accounting period ending 31 January 2007 for which a return is filed by 31 January 2008, an enquiry can be opened on or before 31 January 2009. HMRC may also issue determinations of the tax due if no return is submitted, such determinations being superseded by an actual self-assessment if it is made not later than five years after the filing date for the return or 12 months after the determination if later. HMRC may still make discovery assessments, and they may also make 'discovery determinations' where a return incorrectly states an amount that affects another period or another company.

HMRC may only make discovery assessments and discovery determinations where there is fraudulent or negligent conduct or HMRC was given inadequate information.

The time limits for assessments in respect of accounting periods ending on or before 30 June 1999 are six years after the end of the accounting period (TMA 1970 s 34), extended to 20 years where there is fraudulent or negligent conduct (TMA 1970 s 36). Under corporation tax self-assessment, the six year time limit remains the same but the 20 year time limit is increased to 21 years, both provisions being contained in FA 1998 Sch 18.46.

Level of penalties and interest

16.   In all cases HMRC has power to determine penalties at less than the maximum levels (TMA 1970 s 102) and this power is reflected in the offer procedure. The interest element will rarely be less than the maximum.

There is, however, a 'tax only' settlement procedure for smaller cases. Where adjustments to the latest figures returned are £1,000 or less, HMRC's approach is normally only to adjust those figures. Settlements between £1,000 and £2,000 are also normally agreed on a tax only basis, but covering earlier years within the normal time limits as well as the current year.

Whether interest is payable then depends upon the dates of the issue of assessments and when tax payments have been made.

17.   HMRC will normally indicate to a taxpayer in Grenville's position that his disclosure and co-operation in establishing the amount of unpaid tax will be to his advantage in determining the amount eventually required from him and in the circumstances he should be advised to make a complete disclosure to HMRC and to co-operate fully in ascertaining the tax underpaid for earlier years.

Depending upon the level of profits there might also be liability for Class 4 national insurance contributions, and if so, this will have to be included in the amount due to HMRC.

18.   Interest will run at the prescribed rate on the unpaid tax (and Class 4 national insurance contributions) for the years concerned, and in order to restrict it, Grenville should be advised to make a meaningful payment on account to HMRC.

Appeals against estimated assessments

19.   It is usual for the taxpayer to lodge appeals against estimated assessments raised by HMRC. HMRC will usually resist any application to postpone the charge for tax and Class 4 national insurance unless a meaningful payment on account of liabilities to be agreed is made.

Contract procedure for settlement of enquiry

20.　When the unpaid tax and Class 4 national insurance contributions have been ascertained, Grenville will be invited to make an offer to HMRC in consideration of their not issuing formal assessments or additional assessments for its recovery and not formally determining the interest and penalties, and upon his doing so and the Board of HM Revenue and Customs accepting that offer, there is a legally binding contract upon which HMRC can rely if Grenville does not make payment.

　　The amount of the offer will usually have to be for at least the unpaid tax and national insurance contributions plus interest and an appropriate uplift to cover the penalty element.

21.　The amount of this uplift will depend upon a variety of factors, but HMRC will usually start at the maximum 100% equivalent of unpaid tax and national insurance and reduce the penalty loading by an appropriate percentage for

　　–　disclosure by the taxpayer (taking into account whether it is prompted or spontaneous, complete, or inevitable in view of information in HMRC's hands) – usually up to 20%.

　　–　co-operation by the taxpayer – usually up to 40%.

　　Someone in Grenville's position will usually be represented by a tax adviser who will prepare a report which seeks to quantify the irregularities and calculate the tax lost. The co-operation of the taxpayer embraces that of his representative and conversely the lack of it or the inefficiency of the representative will reflect in the mitigation of the penalty.

　　The reduction available for the remaining 40% depends on the size and gravity of the irregularities, in which connection not only the amount of the loss to HMRC but also the period over which it arose and the action or inaction of the taxpayer are taken into account.

Settlement of self-assessment enquiry by s 28A notice

22.　The legislation provides that at the end of an enquiry HMRC will issue a closure notice stating their conclusions and showing the revisions to the taxpayer's self-assessment and the additional tax due (TMA 1970 s 28A). The taxpayer then has thirty days in which to appeal in writing against conclusions stated or amendments made by the closure notice, giving the grounds of appeal (TMA 1970 ss 31, 31A).

　　Where penalties are being sought HMRC will usually look for a contract settlement rather than using the s 28A procedure.

Taxpayer amendments notified in the course of an enquiry

23.　A taxpayer may give HMRC notice of an amendment to the self-assessment return (within the permitted twelve months after the filing date for the return) whilst an enquiry is in progress. The amendment will not restrict the scope of the enquiry but may be taken into account in the enquiry. If it affects the tax payable, it will not take effect unless and until it is incorporated into the s 28A closure notice issued to the taxpayer (see note 22 above) (TMA 1970 s 9B).

Referral of questions to Special Commissioners during enquiry

24.　At any time during an enquiry, any question in connection with the subject matter of the enquiry may be referred to the Special Commissioners for their determination. To do so, the referral must be made in writing jointly by the taxpayer and HMRC. Either party may withdraw from the referral process providing they give notice before the first hearing of the matter by the Special Commissioners. The determination will be binding on both parties as if it were a decision on a preliminary issue under appeal (TMA 1970 ss 28ZA–28ZE and ss 31A–31D for companies).

Class 4 national insurance contributions

25.　Class 4 national insurance contributions are included for interest and penalty purposes where they arise because of failure to supply information or the supply of erroneous information. From 6 April 1999, criminal proceedings may be taken for fraudulent evasion of national insurance contributions (SSAA 1992 s 114).

Acceptance of offer at local level

26. The tax district dealing with the enquiry has power to accept an offer by a culpable taxpayer up to certain limits of size and gravity, but above those limits the offer has to be referred to a head office department who will consider it, taking into account the recommendations of the tax district and endeavouring to preserve national consistency.

Civil Investigation of Fraud

27. A new civil procedure for dealing with cases of suspected serious fraud is set out in HMRC's Code of Practice 9 (COP9), which takes effect from 1 September 2005. Following the merger of Inland Revenue and Customs and Excise, the separate powers of each of the original departments were retained, and will be replaced in future by new powers which are currently the subject of consultation.

However, in the case of suspected serious fraud a new procedure will be adopted by HMRC as a whole, covering both direct and indirect taxes. The procedure remains very similar to the 'Hansard' regime that it replaces, with the exception that the threat of prosecution for the original offence (but not necessarily offences coming to light during the course of the procedure) is removed, and interviews will no longer be tape-recorded.

The Commissioners reserve complete discretion to pursue criminal investigations, and will refer cases to the Revenue and Customs Prosecution Office (RCPO) before commencing the COP9 'Civil Investigation of Fraud' procedure. The COP9 procedure will not lead to prosecution for the original offence, but other related offences might be reported to SOCA and lead to prosecution. The procedure gives the taxpayer the opportunity to make a complete disclosure of all irregularities in direct and indirect taxes. In the case of direct taxes, HMRC will propose a settlement covering tax, interest and penalties, which will form part of a legal contract if accepted. In the case of indirect taxes, an assessment will be issued. If the disclosures are found to be materially incorrect, then prosecution can follow.

The previous 'Hansard' procedure was carried out by the former Special Compliance Office. This has been replaced by Special Civil Investigations Office, but the COP9 procedure will not be restricted to SCI investigators. It is possible that the disclosure orders obtained against banks will result in wider use of this procedure.

Amending claims on completion of enquiries

28. Where an assessment is issued to make good any loss of tax, the taxpayer can make, revise or withdraw claims which would otherwise be out of time. Following Finance Act 2003 that right is extended to situations where a return is amended at the end of an enquiry. Claims affecting another person's liability will require the written consent of that other person. The ability to amend claims does not extend to rebasing elections for capital gains tax, surrender of married couple's allowance or children's tax credit, and is restricted to the additional tax payable by the assessment or amendment.

Tax Credits

29. From 2003/04 onwards any adjustment to income may have a corresponding effect upon the income for tax credits. Likewise an enquiry and adjustment for 2001/02 could affect a tax credits computation. The fact that tax credits are based on joint income will complicate the enquiry procedures in the event of a joint claim. The Tax Credits Act 2002 ss 19 and 20 give HMRC appropriate enquiry and discovery powers. It is understood that where a taxpayer under enquiry has made a tax credits claim that both enquiries will be undertaken at the same time by the same officer. Separate opening and closing letters and 'offer' letters will be required. Normally enquiries for the years 2002/03 or earlier years will not affect tax credits. Where the enquiry is for 2003/04 or later years, as for Grenville, then any adjustment to income will affect the tax credits claim made for 2003/04, 2004/05 and 2005/06 and the provisional awards for 2006/07. The tax credit cost of any settlement could be higher at 37% than the combined income tax (22%) and national insurance (8%) liabilities. The tax credits settlement would not attract interest (unless the claim was fraudulent) and

any penalties are not tax based. The maximum penalty is £3,000 for providing incorrect information fraudulently or negligently, or £300 for failure to provide information. In both instances the penalty can be reduced depending upon the seriousness of the issue, amounts involved, co-operation and disclosure. For further details see Code of Practice 23 and 27 (COP 27) on Enquiries, leaflet WTC4 Tax Credits Penalties and HMRC Manual CCM 10380 in respect of Penalties and Interest.

The Money Laundering Regulations – Tax Practitioners

30. Money laundering regulations, which had long applied to banks and other financial institutions, were extended to accountancy and tax advice activities on 1 March 2004. Interim guidance for accountants was issued by the Consultative Committee of Accountancy Bodies (CCAB) in March 2004 to assist in complying with the requirements of the Proceeds of Crime Act 2002 and the Money Laundering Regulations 2003.

The purpose of the regulations is to require relevant businesses to make reports to SOCA of any knowledge or suspicions of money laundering activity. However, this is limited to knowledge or suspicions required in the course of business for employment, not knowledge acquired through personal social connections.

Firms affected must appoint an individual as the Money Laundering Reporting Officer to receive money laundering reports from staff, and to make reports to SOCA. All staff must be trained in the recognition and reporting of potential money laundering transactions, and how to verify the identity of new clients. The firms must establish appropriate internal procedures to detect and prevent money laundering. There are a number of further important requirements, and significant criminal penalties for principals and employees for breaching money laundering regulations. The CCAB guidance has recommendations on complying with the regulations, which can be downloaded from www.c-cab.org.uk.

Firms, and their staff, are affected by money laundering regulations if they provide accountancy services, insolvency services, tax advice, or the services of formation or management of a company. This applies as much to unqualified accountants and tax advisers as to qualified individuals, applies outside the UK as well as within the UK, and applies to accountants generally, not just within the profession.

The form of identification to be obtained is not specified by the Act, but is determined by the firm's own policies via a risk-based approach. The guidance given to them by the Joint Money Laundering Steering Group (originally intended for banking and financial services), is often followed.

The offences to be reported include any criminal activity giving rise to proceeds, and, in particular, these are not limited to terrorism or drug dealing. The proceeds of crime, termed 'criminal property', include the proceeds of tax evasion, bribery, or costs saved by failure to comply with regulatory requirements (where the failure to comply is a criminal offence). There is no de minimis limit for the value of the proceeds of crime to be reported, so even the smallest transactions may require a report.

Reports must be made as soon as reasonably possible to SOCA on a Suspicious Activity Reports (SAR), and can be made online at www.soca.gov.uk/financialIntel/index.html. The details to be reported are specified on this site.

A Limited Intelligence Value Report (LIVR) may be made where, individually, the information in the report is likely to be of limited value (the report is required in case correlation of many such reports yields useful information). A LIVR is never appropriate for serious crimes such as terrorism or drugs offences, but might be used for small discrepancies arising from mistakes rather than dishonest behaviour, or where the identity of the criminal is not known.

Accountants and tax advisers in practice are expected to make reports on clients in circumstances where failure to comply with tax regulations has led to underpayment of tax, or late payment. HMRC indicates that around a fifth of SARs received identify a new subject of interest and a quarter lead to new enquiries in relation to direct taxation matters.

Legal privilege

In a relatively narrow range of circumstances, such as litigation or giving legal advice where making a report to SOCA would compromise the client's rights to legal privilege, qualified accountants have the same legal privilege as the legal profession allowing them to claim protection from reporting suspicious transactions. An example of a circumstance where an accountant would enjoy legal privilege, would be where he is working as an expert witness for a firm of lawyers. This applies only to money laundering, not offences under the Terrorism Act 2000.

Feckless, a married man with three children all born between 1989 and 1996, has been in business on his own account as a retailer of fruit and vegetables at shows, carnivals and race meetings since May 2000. HMRC had sent him self-assessment forms for the years 2000/2001 onwards, but he had not submitted them, and in their absence HMRC had determined the tax for each tax year up to 2004/05 in amounts which increased each year, Feckless having paid the tax and the fixed penalties for failing to make returns.

As a result of reading in the press in May 2007 that some £50,000 had been stolen from Feckless's house, HMRC wrote to him pointing out that although the determinations for earlier years had been made in amounts which were HMRC's then best estimates of what he should have paid, they were entitled to increase such estimates if they were discovered to be inadequate, the reported theft of such a large cash hoard suggesting that they were. The officer invited Feckless to provide HMRC with a statement showing his overall financial position, seeking thereby to ascertain his trading profit since he commenced in business, and enabling assessments in correct amounts for all years to replace the determinations.

A friend who had limited experience in this area produced for Feckless the following statement which purported to calculate the profits figures covering the period to 30 April 2006 and resulting tax position for the tax years 2000/01 to 2006/07:

'Assets at 30 April	2000 £	2001 £	2002 £	2003 £	2004 £	2005 £	2006 £
Cash hoard	50,000	50,000	50,000	50,000	50,000	50,000	–
Cash at bank – current account	100	3,900	7,600	11,300	13,900	19,900	47,100
Stock (minimal since everything sold at the end of a day)	–	10	10	15	15	20	20
Wife's jewellery (received from deceased relative) at original value	6,000	6,000	5,000	3,000	–	–	–
Freehold house at cost net of £150,000 mortgage	–	–	–	–	20,000	20,000	20,000
	56,100	59,910	62,610	64,315	83,915	89,920	67,120
At previous 30 April		56,100	59,910	62,610	64,315	83,915	89,920
Increase/(Decrease)		3,810	2,700	1,705	19,600	6,005	(22,800)
Expenses							
Rent (before buying house)		4,338	4,338	4,338	4,169	–	–
Mortgage interest		–	–	–	720	10,440	10,440
Housekeeping		5,156	5,156	5,156	5,156	5,156	5,156
Miscellaneous		1,200	1,200	1,200	1,200	1,200	1,200
		10,694	10,694	10,694	11,245	16,796	16,796
Total of wealth increase + expenses		14,504	13,394	12,399	30,845	22,801	(6,004)
Income							
Sale of jewellery		–	(1,000)	(2,000)	(3,000)	–	–
Betting winnings		(650)	(800)	(1,000)	(1,200)	(1,500)	(2,000)
Net increase/(decrease)		13,854	11,594	9,399	26,645	21,301	(8,004)

Total increases over the five trading years to 30 April 2005 are £82,793, giving an average income over that period of £16,558 per annum.

Loss of £8,004 for the year to 30 April 2006 establishes a nil profit for the tax year 2006/07 and the loss may be deducted from the 2005/06 profit of £16,558, reducing it to £8,554.'

Feckless submitted this statement to HMRC accompanied by completed self-assessments for 2000/01 to 2005/06 in which estimated figures of turnover, purchases and business expenses were included to net off to the averaged profit figures.

HMRC has issued formal notices of enquiry into the self-assessments for all years, saying that there are many anomalies and areas which the statement does not properly or sufficiently address, setting out their areas of concern and listing the information and documents that they require in order to resolve them.

(i)   Without preparing an amended statement, set out what you believe HMRC's reaction to the content of the statement will have been and say what further information and evidence you feel will have been asked for.

(ii) Apart from an amended statement, amended self-assessments for 2000/01 to 2005/06 and eventually the self-assessment for 2006/07, what other certificates etc will HMRC require at the conclusion of its enquiry?

(iii) Since Feckless had not put in false returns, as distinct from accepting HMRC determinations, is HMRC correct in suggesting in the summer of 2007 that it can amend the tax payable for 2000/01 when the time limit for replacing a determination for that year expired on 31 January 2007 (five years after the filing date for 2000/01, which was 31 January 2002)?

(iv) How might the statutory procedure for amending the self-assessments be adapted in the present circumstances?

(i) **Officer's reaction to statement, and information etc required to take matter forward**

Cash hoard

1.1 Whilst the theft might be evidence of the cash stolen, what evidence is there that it was consistent over the years?

1.2 How did a hoard of £50,000 arise in 2000 before business commenced? It is far more likely to have arisen over the trading period.

1.3 What evidence is there that the stolen cash hoard represented all the cash? Certificate required of present cash count. Was it kept in one place and in what sort of container? What is the result of insurance company investigations if a claim for loss was made?

1.4 The amount stolen should be included in the statement for 2006. Its omission accounts for the apparent decrease in wealth for that year and before considering any other points, turns the loss of £8,004 into a profit of £41,996, which makes a nonsense of the figures Feckless has used for turnover, purchases and expenses in the calculation of the result for the year to 30 April 2006 contained in the self-assessment for 2006/07.

Bank accounts

2.1 Banker's certificate required, not only to confirm current account balances but also as a check on other transactions and matters included by banks in the standard certificate required by HMRC, eg accounts at other branches (including abroad), securities held etc.

Bank statements required for examination. Particular deposits, withdrawals, indications of transfers to/from other accounts, and the pattern of transactions may lead to other relevant points.

Trading stock

3.1 Stock very low despite the nature of the trade. More information required on how the trade is operated.

3.2 Are purchase invoices and dates of shows etc available? If so this will give some idea if stocks are, albeit exceptionally, carried.

3.3 Such invoices will also give some idea of the potential profit achievement if, for example, a trading pattern, attempted profit margin, wastage etc, can be established.

Jewellery

4.1 What evidence is there that jewellery was inherited or received by way of gift, as distinct from being purchased, for which funds would be required?

4.2 If purchased, then as with the cash at 1.2, how could it have been accumulated before trading started? HMRC is likely to suggest that it did not exist, or if it did, that it was acquired after trading started. Also, what evidence of sales?

4.3 Contents insurance policy required to confirm/contradict the point.

4.4 It has, in any event, been included twice – once as a movement in assets and once more as income.

4.5 Alternatively the income figure may represent the profit on sale. Determine actual cost and sale proceeds, profits and likely gain, or exceptionally does this constitute a further trading source?

House mortgage etc

5.1 Consistent mortgage interest implies that house purchase was financed on a fixed mortgage. Confirm by reference to statements or adjust for capital repayments.

5.2 Copy of mortgage application form required since this may indicate the level of income reported to the lender. How was that income calculated?

5.3 Costs of buying house and of furnishing it to be incorporated.

5.4 The fixed mortgage suggests that capital repayments are being dealt with by an endowment or personal pension policy. No premiums are indicated in the yearly expenditure.

5.5 Has there been any house improvement expenditure and how financed? Was the property previously occupied as a 'sitting tenant'?

Living expenses

6.1 Housekeeping is low for a family of this size.

6.2 Further, it will have risen over the years with the cost of living and will not have been consistent.

6.3 Sample costs required at present time, which will then be worked backwards using appropriate index and taking into account known changes in circumstances.

Miscellaneous expenses

7.1 What is covered under miscellaneous expenses?

7.2 What should be covered, given the habits of the family; such as smoking, drinking, gambling, entertaining and holidays?

Betting winnings

8.1 Absolute proof required of betting winnings.

8.2 In absence of absolute proof, the inclusion of the winnings has admitted the activity and since it usually costs money, an additional expense instead of an item of income will arise.

8.3 The inspector will in all probability contend that proved winnings have, in any event, been cancelled by undisclosed losses, thus cancelling the winnings and involving further cash payments.

Wife and children

9.1 Child benefit will have been received in respect of the children, mitigating the position.

9.2 The statement includes certain items relating to wife, eg jewellery. It does not include wife's income or expenses (eg personal expenditure, hairdresser, clothes, motoring costs of her vehicle). Although the officer has not opened an enquiry into the wife's affairs, clearly they interlink with those of Feckless. In practice the officer may ask for voluntary disclosure of the assets, liabilities, income and expenses of Mrs Feckless, only resorting to issuing a tax return to her (so that a formal enquiry notice may be issued) if she will not cooperate.

National insurance and tax payments

10.1 Self employed Class 2 national insurance contributions have not been included as an outgoing.

10.2 The tax and Class 4 national insurance paid on the determinations has not been included as an outgoing.

Arriving at increases/decreases

11.1 The increases/decreases cannot be averaged. Each year must stand on its own.

11.2 The only decrease in this case has already been eliminated (see 1.4), but should one arise it may suggest further expenditure on assets, extraordinary items or living expenses, in the latter case with persuasive influence on other years.

11.3 An increase may be used as an indication that other years should show a similar increase, or be persuasive as to profitability.

The 2004 increase arises directly as a result of the house purchase. It is undoubtedly not applicable solely to that year. Where were the funds previously held and did any of them arise before the business started?

Fixed assets of the business

12.1 The statement does not include anything for fixtures, fittings or vehicles. Presumably there will be some. When acquired and for how much?

(ii) **Other certificates etc required**

Apart from a new statement and (subject to (iv) below) amended self-assessments, reflecting the above points, HMRC will require from Feckless a certificate of complete disclosure, a certified statement of assets and liabilities at a date approximating to that on which the inspector concluded his enquiry and a certified list of bank and building society accounts operated throughout the period covered by the enquiry.

(iii) **HMRC's position re 2000/01**

In order to replace the determination for 2000/01 which is outside the normal statutory time limit, HMRC would have to prove negligent or fraudulent conduct. They would undoubtedly succeed in their contention that the acceptance of determinations lower than what would be compatible with living standards and accumulation of wealth amounts to negligent conduct, their grounds being that the reasonable man must have known that his trading was more successful than the profits which would have been necessary to produce the tax and Class 4 NIC payable under the determinations. As a result, not only will Feckless have to pay the additional tax and Class 4 national insurance contributions for those years, but the unpaid amounts will attract interest from 31 January following the relevant tax year, with a consequential effect on the payments on account for the next tax year and hence interest thereon from those earlier dates.

(iv) **Adaptation of the statutory procedure for amending the self-assessments**

In consideration of their not taking proceedings against him, Feckless will be invited by HMRC to make an offer to them embracing tax, interest and a penalty loading for the tax years 2000/01 to 2005/06. A binding contract ensues upon acceptance by HMRC, hence the expression a 'contract settlement'.

The amendments to the original 2000/01 to 2005/06 self-assessments will then be dealt with by HMRC internal procedures without any action from Feckless.

The self-assessment for 2006/07 will be able to be made in the correct amount and filed under the normal procedures.

Supplementary Notes

National insurance and VAT

1. If Class 2 national insurance contributions have not been paid (see (i) 10.1 above), Feckless will have an additional liability for the unpaid amount. He will be required to pay the contributions at the highest rate applicable over the relevant period plus a penalty of £100 for failure to notify. There is no provision for charging interest on unpaid Class 2 contributions.

As far as VAT is concerned, any amount due to HMRC is available to reduce the calculated trading profits so long as the VAT liability is agreed before the settlement of the direct tax with HMRC. Since all sales may well have been zero-rated, Feckless may have registered for VAT as all returns would give rise to refunds. In that event, copies of VAT returns submitted may assist in allocating income and expenditure to accounting periods.

If wrong VAT returns have been submitted, a further settlement will be necessary under civil fraud procedures, with turnover and expenditure figures being estimated using similar techniques to those for calculating trading profits.

Negligence assessments

2. Under the self-assessment provisions, a taxpayer's self-assessment is final unless HMRC enquire into the return (see note 3 below), except where there is fraudulent or negligent conduct or inadequate disclosure, in which case HMRC may issue assessments under TMA 1970 s 29. The time limit for HMRC assessments is five years from 31 January following the tax year, extended to 20 years in cases of fraudulent or negligent conduct.

3. Under self-assessment, HMRC may serve formal notice on the taxpayer that they are enquiring into the accuracy of his tax return within twelve months after the 31 January filing date (that is by 31 January 2008 for 2005/06), extended appropriately where, as in this example, the self-assessment is filed late.

2006/07 self-assessment

4. Given that the taxable profits are calculated on the basis of a comparison of assets and liabilities, taking into account other sources of income and personal/private expenditure, it is unrealistic to require the inclusion of individual figures in the self-assessment, since they could only be estimated and would serve no purpose.

Jeopardy amendments

5. HMRC has the power to issue 'jeopardy amendments' to a self-assessment to create an additional tax charge during the course of an enquiry if they think there is likely to be a loss of tax if they do not make an immediate amendment (TMA 1970 s 9C). This power should only be used when HMRC believe or suspect that the taxpayer intends to dispose of assets, or become non-resident or bankrupt, or is about to go to prison.

    A well advised taxpayer will normally make a substantial payment on account at an early stage in the enquiry, thus negating the need for HMRC to consider a jeopardy amendment to the self-assessment.

Tax credits

6. If Feckless has made a claim for tax credits for the years 2004/05 to 2006/07 then the tax credits office should be notified that the declared profits are incorrect and amended details for 2004/05 (year to 30 April 2004) to 2006/07 (year to 30 April 2006) filed with them. This may not affect the tax credit claim if payment had been at the family rate of £545 for each year and the amended joint tax credit income does not exceed £50,000 for each year. Otherwise an overpayment will arise and possibly penalties for incorrect returns. In those circumstances an enquiry should be opened by the tax credits office and a settlement agreed at the same time as for income tax. See also Example 45.

7. HMRC was created by the Commissioners for Revenue and Customs Act (CRCA) 2005, taking over the functions of the Inland Revenue and HM Customs and Excise. These two departments had different procedures and powers, which were ring-fenced and brought forward into the new HMRC. The procedures and powers described above are principally those of the former Inland Revenue.

    On 30 March 2006 a consultation document was issued entitled 'HMRC on the Taxpayer: Modernising Powers, Deterrents and Safeguards – a consultation on the developing programme of work'. This was the second consultation document for the review of powers.

    The intention of the document is to explore a system for replacing the existing powers inherited from the legacy departments with a new system applicable to HMRC as a whole. The document proposes a risk-based approach to be adopted by HMRC. It suggests that on one end of the scale it would support compliant taxpayers, while progressing through various stages of compulsion for less compliant taxpayers. The proposals are still at an early stage, and no definite proposals for the new system, nor a timetable for its implementation, are available.

(a)   There are various classes of contributions for national insurance purposes. Indicate the circumstances in which a liability arises under each class.

(b)   State how earnings are defined for national insurance purposes, the payments that may be excluded and the way in which benefits in kind are treated.

(c)   J Bond is a Member of Parliament and his salary is £60,000. He also carries on business as a management consultant and for the year ended 30 June 2006 his taxable profits were £22,000. His wife is employed by him as a research assistant for his Parliamentary duties and receives a salary of £5,000 per year. She is also employed by him in his management consultancy business for which she receives a salary of £5,000 per year.

Advise him and his wife of their national insurance position and calculate their national insurance liabilities for 2006/07.

(d)   Mrs Williams and her son are the directors of Tation Ltd, which trades as a restaurant employing four waitresses. She has asked you to explain how contributions are charged on directors' earnings and also to state whether the following items must be included in gross pay for the purposes of Class 1 contributions of the waitresses:

(i)   Tips and gratuities

(ii)   Benefits in kind

(iii) Payment of bills.

Draft a memorandum to answer the points raised by Mrs Williams.

(e)   (i)   Set out the national insurance consequences for the employer and employee of contracting out of the State Second Pension (S2P).

(ii)   Set out how national insurance contributions are collected.

(a)   **Classes of national insurance contributions**

National insurance contributions are payable under six categories as follows:

Class 1 contributions (SSCBA 1992 ss 5-9)

These relate to employed persons and are subdivided into primary contributions (payable by employees) and secondary contributions (payable by employers). A liability arises whenever earnings exceed the relevant limit in any earnings period (SSCBA 1992 s 5). For 2006/07 the relevant limit is known as the earnings threshold, and it is fixed at the same amount as the PAYE threshold. For employees there is also a lower earnings limit, with a 'nil contributions' band for earnings between that limit and the earnings threshold. Even though no contributions are payable on that band of earnings, employers are required to report earnings at or above the lower earnings limit in order that the employee may retain entitlement to social security benefits. There is an upper earnings limit for employees' contributions at 11% but no upper limit for employers' contributions which are paid at 12.8% on all earnings over the primary earnings threshold. On earnings above the upper earnings limit employees pay 1% contributions from 2003/04.

The employees' contributions are deducted by the employer from earnings and paid with the employer's contributions and the PAYE tax to the HMRC Accounts Office by the 19th of the following month, unless payment is made quarterly.

Payment may be deferred until 22nd of the month (or the last working day before that date if the 22nd is a non-working day) if payment is made electronically.

The current (2006/07) earnings limits are:

	Weekly	*Monthly*	*Annual*
Lower earnings limit (LEL)	£84	£364	£4,368
Earnings threshold (ET)	£97	£420	£5,035
Upper earnings limit for employees (UEL)	£645	£2,795	£33,540

An earnings period is the interval at which earnings are normally paid. Thus if pay is paid weekly the first limits apply, if two-weekly twice the first limits and so on. If pay is paid at intervals of less than one week then the weekly limit applies. If the employee is a director then the annual limit applies (except in the year of appointment, where a pro rata limit applies, based on the weeks from the week of appointment to the end of the tax year). Contributions for directors may, however, be payable provisionally according to the normal pay period, with an annual adjustment if necessary (SI 2001/1004 reg 8(6) – see part (d)).

Contributions are payable by employees on or after their 16th birthday until they are of retirement age (normally 65 years for a man and 60 for a woman). An employer has no liability to pay contributions for an employee under 16 but full secondary contributions are payable for persons over retirement age. In some circumstances, employees' contributions are credited rather than paid, such credits counting towards satisfying the contribution conditions for certain benefits, in particular the basic state pension (see under Class 3).

Certain married women elected on or before 11 May 1977 to pay reduced rate (Table B) contributions in exchange for limited benefits. The employer still pays full secondary contributions. If a reduced rate election lapses or is revoked it cannot be revived (see explanatory note 11).

The liability is calculated on the earnings of a given pay period from a given employer (subject to anti-avoidance rules relating to uneven payments and pay from another business which is 'in association' with the employer – see explanatory note 10). There is now no maximum Class 1 national insurance liability for employed earners. Those earning over £33,540 in one or more employments have to pay 1% on that excess. For those with more than one employment (or with employment and self-employment) there are complex rules to ensure that they do not pay excessive contributions (see below under Maximum contributions payable). There is no maximum for employers' secondary contributions. 'Earnings' broadly means amounts paid in cash/cheques or paid on the direction of the employee. Payments in kind do not count as pay for Class 1 contributions unless the asset concerned is specifically included (see part (b)). The assets included are mainly assets that can be readily converted into cash. From 6 April 2000 employers' Class 1A contributions are payable on virtually all taxable benefits that are not within the Class 1 charge (see below).

The rates of contributions for 2006/07 are:

Employer's contributions

Earnings up to earnings threshold (ET):	–	Nil
Excess above ET	–	12.8%

Employee's contributions

The employee's contributions (full rate) are:

Earnings up to earnings threshold (ET)	Nil
Earnings between ET and upper earnings limit (UEL)	11%
Earnings above UEL	1%

Married women's reduced rate contributions are:

No liability if earnings do not exceed ET.

Earnings between ET and UEL	4.8%
Earnings above UEL	1%

The rebate for contracted-out contributions on earnings between the lower and upper earnings levels is:

Salary related schemes	1.6%	Employees
	3.5%	Employers
Money purchase schemes	1.6%	Employees
	1.0%*	Employers

* HMRC pays an age-related rebate into the scheme – see part (e)(i).

Any contracted-out rebate due to an employee is first deducted from any primary national insurance liability of that employee for that period. In so far as the rebate exceeds the national insurance liability of the pay period it is retained by the employer. The rebate due to the employer is recovered by deduction against any national insurance payable for the tax year or is paid to the employer by HMRC.

Class 1A contributions (SSCBA 1992 s 10)

Class 1A national insurance contributions are payable by employers (not by employees) in respect of the provision of any taxable benefits (except certain childcare provision) to a P11D employee or director.

The amounts on which the contributions are payable are the cash equivalents of the benefits as measured for income tax purposes, reduced by any employee contribution. For 2006/07 the contributions are at the rate of 12.8% of the cash equivalents and are payable annually in arrear by 19 July, after the taxable benefits have been calculated by the employers for P11D purposes. The summary of the Class 1A amounts shown on P11Ds plus the calculation of the contributions due is shown on form P11D(b). The payment is sent to the Accounts Office using a special payslip.

If the business ceases, then the liability for Class 1A contributions arises 14 days after the tax month of succession or cessation, eg if an employer ceases in October 2006 then Class 1A contributions for the period 6 April 2006 to the date of cessation will be payable with the October national insurance payment on 19 November 2006. If the date of cessation is any day up to 5 July then the liability includes the Class 1A amount due for the preceding tax year. The same provisions apply to a predecessor employer if a business changes hands, but only in respect of employees not continuing with the successor. The successor takes over the liability for employees who continue in the business.

No Class 1A liability arises on any amount already charged to Class 1 or 1B, or not liable to income tax as employment income, or benefits provided exclusively for business use. However Class 1A contributions are due on the full amount of benefit where there is mixed business and private use. Insignificant private use is ignored for this purpose.

The main benefits chargeable to Class 1A contributions are:

Cars and fuel
Vans
Beneficial loans
Living accommodation
Private medical insurance
Gifted assets
Taxable gifts from third parties (chargeable on the provider)
Goods and services provided for private use
Taxable relocation expenses.

Class 1B contributions (SSCBA 1992 s 10A)

Employers are able to settle the tax and national insurance liability on minor and irregular benefits by making a lump sum payment under a PAYE Settlement Agreement (PSA) (see Example 9 explanatory note 9). Class 1B contributions are payable on all items in the PSA that would otherwise be liable to Class 1 or Class 1A contributions and on the tax payable under the agreement. The rate of contributions is the employers' secondary rate of 12.8%. The Class 1B contributions are payable with the tax on the agreement on 19 October following the relevant tax year, eg 19 October 2007 for 2006/07.

Class 2 contributions (SSCBA 1992 ss 11, 12)

Class 2 contributions are payable by 'self-employed earners', which means those who are gainfully employed other than as employed earners (SSCBA 1992 s 2). The Class 2 net is wider than for Class 4, because it relates to 'businesses', whereas Class 4 is restricted to trades, professions and vocations. Class 2 contributions are due at the flat rate of £2.10 per week for 2006/07. Contributions are payable within 28 days of receiving a bill for the previous quarter from the HMRC National Insurance Contributions Office (NICO), or by monthly direct debit. A liability arises whenever a person is self-employed in any week if they are over 16 and under pension age. A person who is also employed is liable to pay both Class 1 and Class 2 (and possibly also Class 4) contributions.

If the earnings from self-employment are expected to be below £4,465 in 2006/07 or were below the limit of £4,345 in 2005/06 and circumstances have not materially altered, then application may be made for a certificate of exception. Exception cannot apply from a date earlier than 13 weeks before the date of the application but waiver of Class 2 contributions may be granted by concession. The certificate needs to be renewed each year.

If exemption has not been granted, and earnings prove to be below the exemption limit then application for repayment of Class 2 contributions must be submitted before the next following 31 January, ie 2006/07 refund applications must be made by 31 January 2008.

Earnings for this purpose are the net earnings from self employment shown in the accounts. If any income from *employment* is included in the accounts figures it is disregarded (SI 2001/1004 reg 45), but care should be taken to exclude any other non-trading income (such as rents) from the accounts, otherwise HMRC may contend that it is part of the earnings.

If no Class 2 contributions are paid in a year then benefits (eg retirement pension) may be reduced. A voluntary Class 3 contribution could be paid to safeguard the benefits but from 6 April 2000 benefits can be safeguarded at a Class 2 cost of only £2.10 a week. As with Class 1 contributions, in some circumstances contributions are credited rather than paid, such credits counting towards satisfying the contribution conditions for certain benefits, in particular the basic state pension (see under Class 3). Neither Class 2 nor Class 3 contributions give rise to an entitlement to jobseeker's allowance.

A woman with a valid reduced rate contribution certificate (see Class 1 above) need not pay Class 2 national insurance contributions.

Class 3 contributions (SSCBA 1992 ss 13, 14)

Class 3 contributions are voluntary so there is no obligation to pay them. The contributions give an entitlement to basic retirement pension and widow's benefits. Payment could be made by those not liable for other contributions, eg non-employed, self-employed with small earnings, persons taking early retirement or moving abroad etc, to maintain a full national insurance record. Anyone who is registered as unemployed or is receiving jobseeker's allowance is credited with Class 1 contributions at the lower earnings limit and does not have to pay Class 3 contributions to maintain a full contributions record. An unemployed man aged 60 to 64 is credited with Class 1 contributions whether or not he is registered as unemployed. Class 1 credits are also usually given to those aged 16 to 18 who would otherwise not have paid enough contributions, and also for certain periods of full-time training lasting up to 12 months, but not for longer courses such as university degree courses. Credits are also given to those claiming incapacity benefit, maternity allowance, invalid care allowance or disability working allowance.

The Class 3 rate for 2006/07 is £7.55 per week. Payment is as for Class 2, that is by quarterly bill or monthly direct debit.

Class 4 contributions (SSCBA 1992 ss 15–18)

These contributions do not provide any benefits. The liability is calculated on trading profits, as agreed for income tax, after adjusting for capital allowances, balancing charges, trading losses and trade charges but before retirement annuity premiums and personal pension premiums. Where trading losses have been relieved against non-trading income for income tax purposes, they still reduce the first available current or later trading profits for Class 4 contributions (SSCBA Sch 2.3(4)).

Class 4 contributions are paid as part of payments on account and balancing payments under self-assessment. The rates for 2006/07 are:

Profits up to	£5,035	@ Nil
Profits between	£5,035 – £33,540	@ 8%
Profits in excess of	£33,540	@ 1%

The Class 4 contributions relate to a tax year, so the limits remain the same where more than one account is made up to a date within the tax year, or where the trader is involved in more than one business. Husband and wife are charged separately. A liability does not arise in any tax year in which the taxpayer is aged under 16 (and holds a certificate of exception) or over 65 (60 for a woman) at the commencement of the year, or in which he is not resident in the UK for income tax.

If income taxed as trading income is also liable to Class 1 national insurance contributions (eg sub postmasters, accountant as a director) then the amount liable to Class 4 contributions is reduced by the amount on which Class 1 contributions have been paid.

Maximum contributions payable

Maximum Class 1 and 2

Where a person has more than one 'employment' (and in this context that includes self-employment) the annual maximum of Class 1 and Class 2 contributions depends on the number of jobs, and how much is earned in each of those jobs. Each earner will therefore have his, or her, own individual maximum.

The computations are complex, involving eight steps, but basically each earner will be required to pay at 11% on 53 times the difference between the primary earnings threshold and the upper earnings limit (£548 (£645 – £97) × 53 = £29,044 @ 11% = £3,194.84), plus 1% of the *aggregate* of all 'employed earner's' earnings which fall between the primary and upper earnings limits insofar as they exceed £29,044, plus 1% of all 'employed earner's' earnings above the upper limit. (The fact that the regulations take 53 times the difference between the upper earnings limit and the primary threshold means that the normal annual upper limit (£33,540) is effectively superseded. This is reflected in HMRC's leaflets CA72A and CA72B where contributors are invited to apply for refund if they have paid Class 1 at the standard rate on annual earnings of at least £34,185.)

Employees who think that they may have overpaid should complete a refund claim form CA 5610 by applying to NICO, Refunds Group, Benton Park View, Newcastle-upon-Tyne, NE98 1ZZ. The provisions determining the annual maxima are in SI 2001/1004 and work as follows:

An individual has three 'employments', A, B and C, receiving salaries of £40,000, £10,000 and £2,000. Steps 1 and 2 of Reg 21 of SI 2001/1004 require the calculation of the **£3,194.84** as above (Step 1 calculates the £29,044, Step 2 takes 11%). Step 3 aggregates the earnings of each employed earner's employment which fall between the primary earnings threshold and the upper earnings limit, in this case:

A	28,505	(33,540 – 5,035)
B	4,965	(10,000 – 5,035)
C	–	(all below 5,035)
	33,470	

Step 4 deducts from this figure 53 times the difference between the upper limit and the earnings threshold, that is the £29,044 of Step 1, leaving £4,426 (33,470 – 29,044). Step 5 takes 1% of this figure, giving **£44.26**.

Step 6 takes the earnings of each employed earner's employment in so far as it exceeds the upper earnings limit, in this case just employment A, £40,000 less £33,540 = £6,460 and Step 7 takes 1% of that figure **£64.60**. The annual maximum for Class 1 for this individual becomes £3,303.70, the sum of Steps 2, 5 and 7 (£3,194.84 + £44.26 + £64.60).

Where an individual has Class 2 liability, and therefore more than one 'employment' the same procedure applies but the maximum calculated will be compared with the sum of their Class 1 and 2 payments, see the main example below and Example X in the Table below.

Maximum Class 1, 2 and 4

Where a person has employment and is also self-employed and paying Class 4, there is also a maximum amount of contributions to be paid at the main Class 1 and Class 4 rates (11% and 8%).

Contributors should apply for a refund if they pay more than:

- £2,389.60 at the Class 1 (11%) rate, Class 2 and Class 4 (8%) rate in 2006/07, or

- £3,194.84 at the Class 1 (11%) rate and Class 2 in 2006/07.

The computation of the Class 4 refund is even more complex than the calculation for Class 1. It is a nine step process with three different 'Case' scenarios applying after the fourth step (see Reg 100 of 2001/1004). The method is best demonstrated by working through the steps in one main example and then giving summary figures for three further examples (X, Y and Z) in a Table below.

Take the situation of someone employed on a salary of £36,000, with self-employed profits of £40,000. Their national insurance liability before applying any annual maxima will be:

	£
Class 1, assumed paid monthly, (2,795 – 420) @ 11% × 12	3,135.00
(3,000 – 2,795) @ 1% × 12	24.60
	3,159.60
Class 2, £2.10 × 52	109.20
	3,268.80
Class 4, (33,540 – 5,035) @ 8%	2,280.40
(40,000 – 33,540) @ 1%	64.60
	5,613.80

Steps 1, 2 and 3 involve computing the £2,389.60 maximum of Class 2 and 4 (52 × £2.10 = £109.20 plus (33,540 – 5,035) 28,505 × 8% = £2,280.40). Step 4 then requires the deduction of the Class 1 contributions at the main rate plus the total Class 2 contributions actually paid, in this case a total of £3,244.20 (£3,135.00 + £109.20).

	£
Steps 1, 2 and 3	2,389.60
Step 4	(3,244.20)
	(854.60)

If a negative figure is achieved, the result of this step is nil, the maximum amount of Class 4 payable at the main rate is nil and four more steps have to be applied to compute the 1% liability. This is a Case 3 scenario. (See below for Case 1 and 2 scenarios.)

Step 5 involves taking the figure at Step 4 and multiplying it by 100/8. In this case the answer is still nil. Step 6 involves deducting the lower profits limit from the smaller of the actual profits and the upper profits limit. In this case, the latter applies:

	£
Step 6	33,540
Lower profit limit	(5,035)
	28,505

Step 7 requires Step 5 to be deducted from Step 6, in this case leaving £28,505 and Step 8 takes 1% of that figure ie £285.05.

Step 9 calculates the extra Class 4 that is due on profits over £33,540 (40,000 – 33,540 @ 1%), in this case £64.60 and the maximum Class 4 payable by this taxpayer is the sum of Steps 4, 8 and 9 ie £349.65 (Nil + £285.05 + £64.60). This is, of course, 1% of all the profits over the lower profits limit ((40,000 – 5,035) @ 1% = £349.65). This taxpayer should apply for a refund of Class 4 of £1,995.35 (£2,345.00 less £349.65).

This individual would also be entitled to a refund of Class 1 or 2 as the following application of the eight step process shows:

		£
Steps 1 and 2		3,194.84
Step 3, Employment income (33,540 – 5,035)	28,505	
Step 4	(29,044)	
Step 5, 1% of	–	Nil
Step 6, Employment income (36,000 – 33,540)	2,460	
Step 7, 1% of £2,460		24.60
Step 8		3,219.44
Class 1 and 2 paid		3,268.80
Refund due of Class 2		49.36
Refund of Class 4 as above		1,995.35
Total refund		2,044.71

The Table below shows three further examples:

- Another case 3 scenario but where the Class 4 is only paid at the main rate (Example X);

- A Case 1 scenario – that is where the result at Step 4 is positive and exceeds the aggregate of Class 1 (11%) rate plus Class 2 plus Class 4 (8%) rate. For Case 1 the Steps 5 to 9 are unnecessary (Example Y); and

- A Case 2 scenario where the surplus at Step 4 does not exceed the NI paid at main rates, and Steps 5 to 9 become necessary to determine the total Class 4 maximum.

Example X has also been chosen to show no repayment of Class 1 and 2. The Table assumes all salaries paid monthly.

	X (Case 3) £		Y (Case 1) £		Z (Case 2) £
Class 1, salary £30,000	2,745.60	Class 1, salary £9,600	501.60	Class 1, salary £9,600	501.60
Class 2	109.20		109.20		109.20
Class 4, profits £8,000	237.20	Class 4, profits £15,035	800.00	Class 4, profits £29,035	1,920.00
Total NIC	3,092.00		1,410.80		2,530.80
Steps 1, 2 and 3	2,389.60		2,389.60		2,389.60
Main rate Class 1 + Class 2	2,854.80		610.80		610.80
Step 4	Nil		1,778.80		1,778.80
Step 5	Nil		$1,779 \times 100/8$	22,235 £	
Step 6, deduct lower profit limit	8,000.00				29,035.00
	5,035.00				5,035.00
	2,965.00				24,000.00
Step 7, deduct Step 5	–				22,235.00
	2,965.00				1,765.00
Step 8, take 1% of Step 7	29.65				17.65
Step 9 not applicable	–				–
Max Class 4 sum of Steps 4, 8 and 9	29.65		1,778.80		1,796.45
Class 4 refund due	207.55		Nil		123.55

Under Y, Step 4:

This figure exceeds all the NI paid at the main rates (£1,410.80) so the computation ends and the max Class 4 NI is £1,778.80

Example X would not give rise to a refund of Class 1 or 2 as the following application of the eight step process shows:

		£
Steps 1 and 2		3,194.84
Step 3, Employment income (30,000 – 5,035)	24,965	
Step 4	(29,044)	
Step 5, 1% of	Nil	Nil
Step 6, Employment income (30,000 – 33,540)	Nil	
Step 7, 1% of	Nil	Nil
Step 8		3,194.84
Class 1 and 2 paid		2,854.80
Refund due		Nil

Where contributions are paid at the contracted out rate or married woman's reduced rate then they are recomputed at the standard rate in order to compare with the above limits.

If self-employed earnings are expected to be below the exemption limit of £4,465 then exemption should be claimed. For information re exemption contact the Class 2 Self-Employment Contact Centre on 0845 91 54655.

It is possible to apply for deferment of Class 1, 2 and 4 contributions.

If an individual has more than one employment and expects to pay primary Class 1 contributions on earnings of at least £645 per week, or equivalent, throughout the whole tax year in any one employment or combination of employments they can apply for deferment. Again the position is complex and reference should be made to HMRC's leaflets CA72A (in respect of deferral of Class 1 contributions) or CA72B (in respect of deferral of Class 2 and 4 contributions) which give some useful examples.

A person who is both employed and self-employed may apply to defer payment of Class 2 and/or Class 4 contributions. If successful in the application for deferment, assessment and collection of Class 2 and Class 4 contributions will be made by Deferment Services who will do their calculations after the end of the year, taking into account the profits and gains and the contributions already made. The extra 1% Class 4 will be paid with income tax through the self-assessment form. Leaflets CA72A and CA72B contain the necessary deferral forms which can also be downloaded from HMRC's website. Other useful forms are:

SE1 Starting your own business
CA04 Class 2 and Class 3 NI – direct debit, the easier way to pay

The address for Deferment Services is HMRC NICO Deferment Services, Benton Park View, Newcastle upon Tyne, NE98 1ZZ. Telephone: 0845 9157141.

Interest on late paid contributions

Late paid Class 1 contributions attract interest from 19 April after the end of the tax year in which the contributions were due for payment. Late paid Class 1A contributions attract interest from 19 July after the end of the tax year. Late paid Class 1B contributions attract interest from the due date of payment, ie 19 October following the tax year in respect of which the contributions were due. (SI 2001/1004 Sch 4.17.)

There is no provision for charging interest on late paid Class 2 contributions.

Penalties

Liability to Class 2 must be notified no later than three calendar months after the calendar month of commencement. A penalty of £100 applies for failure to notify. This will not be imposed if a successful claim for exemption is available.

Failure to notify liability to Class 1A by 19 July on form P11D(b) gives rise to a penalty of £100 per month (or part thereof) per 50 employees (or part thereof), restricted to the Class 1A liability.

Provisions that had been intended to impose penalties for inaccurate Class 1 NIC returns, even where the correct amount had been paid, have been deferred.

Various breaches of the national insurance legislation may lead to criminal proceedings.

(b)   **Earnings for Class 1 national insurance contributions**

Meaning of earnings

Earnings for Class 1 national insurance contributions are defined in s 3 of the Social Security Contributions and Benefits Act 1992 as including 'any remuneration or profit derived from an employment'. The amount of a person's earnings for any period is computed in accordance with Part 2 of the Social Security (Contributions) Regulations SI 2001/1004. That statutory instrument provides that a liability arises on earnings paid, or treated as paid, in an earnings period (reg 2). The amount paid is the gross earnings from the employment.

Payments that do not count as earnings

SI 2001/1004 Sch 3 lists certain payments that do not count as earnings, with a vast number of exclusions from the provisions, and with the Schedule running to ten separate parts. This represents a minefield for employers struggling to know what does and what does not constitute earnings, and there are even longer lists in the Employer's Further Guide to PAYE and NICs (CWG2). Most of the exclusions, however, relate to items that are exempt from income tax. Some particular exclusions are as follows:

Payments in kind, unless specifically included – see below. (Virtually all taxable benefits that escape Class 1 liability are liable to employers' Class 1A contributions where they are provided to P11D employees and directors – see part (a).)

Tips or gratuities not paid directly or indirectly by the employer and where the payment is not directly or indirectly allocated by the employer to the earner, providing the payments are not from a trust where the beneficiaries are employees or of an amount in excess of amount that a non-connected person might give if from a connected person (SI 2004/173).

Any payments by way of a pension.

An employer's contribution to an employee's personal pension.

A payment by shares or options over shares which form part of the ordinary share capital of the employer company or its holding company, where the shares or options are either obtained under an approved scheme or are not readily convertible assets.

Any value added tax chargeable on earnings.

Redundancy payments.

Any specific and distinct payment of, or contribution towards, expenses actually incurred by an employed earner in carrying out his employment.

Payments in kind treated as earnings

The following are exceptions to the 'payments in kind' exclusion and are treated as earnings (SI 2001/1004 reg 25 & Sch 3 Parts II, III and IV):

Stocks and shares, and warrants and options in respect of stocks and shares, that are readily convertible assets (other than as indicated above) (see Example 9 explanatory note 12 and Example 87)

Unit trusts and units in collective investment schemes (eg enterprise zone trusts)

Commodity futures and other futures and hedging contracts

Options to acquire or dispose of:
        an asset falling under any other heading
        currency
        gold, silver, palladium or platinum

Assets capable of being sold on a recognised investment exchange (ie an investment exchange recognised under the Financial Services and Markets Act 2000) or on the London Bullion Market

Money debts

Gemstones and certain fine wines

Assets (including vouchers) which are readily convertible assets (see Example 9 explanatory note 12)

Any voucher capable of being exchanged for any of the assets listed above and any other non-cash vouchers other than those falling within SI 2001/1004 Sch 3 Part V (see below).

Certain life insurance policies including
        Life and annuity policies
        Linked long term policies
        Capital redemption policies
        Other policies with any of the foregoing elements

Contributions made by employers to unregistered pension schemes

Benefits received by an employee who makes a restrictive covenant with his employer (SSCBA 1992 s 4 – see Example 12 part (a)).

The exceptions from the voucher charging rules mainly mirror income tax provisions. They include transport vouchers for non-P11D employees working for passenger transport undertakings, vouchers exchangeable for sports or recreational facilities, vouchers exchangeable for meals on the employer's premises, the first 15p per day of luncheon vouchers, and childcare vouchers up to £55 per week for children up to age 16. Non-cash vouchers are valued as for tax purposes, but unlike the tax position, they must be dealt with on a weekly basis rather than at the year-end.

In addition to Class 1 contributions, employers (but not employees) have to pay Class 1A national insurance contributions at 12.8% on taxable benefits provided to P11D employees and directors that are not within the Class 1 charge.

(c)   **Mr and Mrs Bond – national insurance position**

J Bond has employment liable to Class 1 contributions and self employment liable to Class 2 and 4 contributions. As the total payments exceed the likely maxima, application should be made in advance for deferment of Class 2 and 4 liabilities. The small technical liability that will arise because the maximum is based on 53 weeks' contributions may not then be collected, giving a total liability of £3,399.60 under Class 1 paid monthly rather than £3,463.44 paid after refunded Class 2 (see computation below).

If deferment is not applied for then the payments would have been:

		£
Class 1, salary paid monthly, (2,795 – 420) @ 11% x 12		3,135.00
(5,000 – 2,795) @ 1% x 12		264.60
		3,399.60
Class 2		109.20
Class 4, profits (22,000 – 5,035) @ 8%		1,357.20
Total NIC		4,866.00

Class 4 refund computation

	£
Steps 1, 2 and 3	2,389.60
Main rate Class 1 + Class 2	3,244.20
Step 4	Nil
Step 5	Nil
Step 6,	22,000.00
deduct lower profit limit	5,035.00
	16,965.00
Step 7, deduct Step 5	–
	16,965.00
Step 8, take 1% of Step 7	169.65
Step 9 not applicable	–
Max Class 4, sum of Steps 4, 8 and 9	169.65
Class 4 paid	1,357.20
Class 4 refund due	1,187.55

Mr Bond would also be entitled to a refund of Class 2 as the following application of the eight step process shows:

		£
Steps 1 and 2		3,198.84
Step 3, Employment income (33,540 – 5,035)	28,505	
Step 4	(29,044)	
Step 5, 1% of	Nil	Nil
Step 6, Employment income (60,000 – 33,540)	26,460	
Step 7, 1% of	26,460	264.60
Step 8		3,463.44
Class 1 and 2 paid		3,508.80
Refund due		45.36
Total refund (45.36 + 1,187.55)		1,232.91

Mrs Bond has two employments, but both are with J Bond. The earnings must therefore be aggregated (unless it would be impracticable to do so, because for example earnings were worked out at different pay points), giving a liability for primary (employee's) Class 1 contributions (assuming paid equally throughout the year) of:

	£	
5,035 @ nil	–	
4,965 @ 11%	546.15	(if tables are used £546.48)
10,000		

J Bond will have a liability as employer to pay secondary contributions of £10,000 – £5,035 = £4,965 @ 12.8% = £635.52 (£635.88 using tables), which will be allowed in computing his earnings/profits in the year of payment.

(d) **Memorandum for Mrs Williams re national insurance liabilities**

Treatment of directors' earnings

Contributions are charged on directors' earnings on an annual basis. An employer may, however, use the normal pay period rules to compute the weekly or monthly contributions provided that the liability is recomputed at the end of the year (or when a director leaves) by reference to the annual limits.

This special treatment prevents irregular payments of bonuses, commissions etc, being used to give reduced contributions because of the monthly upper limit. Where a regular salary is paid, the overall amount will be the same.

For example, if an employee is paid £36,000 at £3,000 a month, his monthly contributions will be (261.25 + 2.05 =) £263.30, making £3,159.60 in the year and the employer will pay contributions on the excess of the monthly pay of £3,000 over the earnings threshold of £420, ie £2,580 @ 12.8% = £330.24, giving £3,962.88 for the year. If a director is paid the same amount and the annual basis is used, the *total* amount payable is the same, but the position will be as follows:

Cumulative pay		Employee's contribution		Employer's contribution	
Mth	£		£		£
1	3,000		–		–
2	6,000	5,035 @ nil	–	5,035 @ nil	–
		965 @ 11%	106	965 @ 12.8%	123
3	9,000	3,000 @ 11%	330	3,000 @ 12.8%	384
4 to 11	33,000	24,000 @ 11%	2,640	24,000 @ 12.8%	3,072
12	36,000	540* @ 11%	59	3,000 @ 12.8%	384
		2,460 @ 1%	24		
Total contributions payable			3,159		3,963

*   1% contributions on (36,000 – 33,540) = £2,460, therefore 11% contributions due on (3,000 – 2,460) = £540.

Treatment of payments/benefits for waitresses

(i) *Tips and gratuities*

If Tation Ltd collects the tips and divides them between the employees or controls the way in which they are divided, then they are earnings liable to Class 1 national insurance (providing the total earnings exceed the lower limit in an earnings period). If Tation Ltd does not control the division of the tips but leaves that to the employees, the amounts are not liable to national insurance, even if collected in the main till with other takings. Any amount paid directly from the customer to staff does not attract national insurance. This also applies if the donor is connected to the employer provided that the tip does not exceed an amount an unconnected person might have given.

Any amounts collected by the employer and paid to staff under a legal obligation or as part of the national minimum wage are liable to national insurance regardless of who shares out the money.

For further details and examples on tips etc see HMRC booklet E24 (reissued in 2006). To determine the tax, national insurance and VAT treatment it is necessary to divide tips into the following categories

–   mandatory service charges,

–   discretionary service charges,

–   gratuity paid to the employer (eg by debit/credit card),

–   gratuity put into a staff box, or

   –   cash gratuity handed directly to a member of staff.

A tip, freely given, is outside the scope of VAT. If a customer is required to pay a service charge that amount is standard rated.

For PAYE the employer must deduct tax from all amounts paid to the employee. If a member of staff distributes the tips, this is known as a tronc and the troncmaster is responsible for deducting PAYE.

The individual member of staff is responsible for declaring tips received, and paying tax on amounts received. This may be done by way of a code number adjustment or direct payment of tax due.

For mandatory service charges, and where an employer has a continuing involvement in tips distributed by an employee, PAYE must be deducted by the employer.

(ii) *Benefits in kind*

The basic rule for national insurance is that Class 1 contributions are not payable on benefits in kind. Instead they are chargeable to Class 1A contributions of 12.8% payable by the employer. However, where a benefit can be converted to cash merely by surrendering the asset (see explanatory note 6), or represents the settlement of a debt of the employee (see (iii)), or is a round sum payment or expense with a profit element, then Class 1 contributions are due.

(iii) *Payment of bills*

If an employer pays bills relating to the employee, the treatment depends on who made the contract. If the employer made the contract it is a payment in kind; if the employee made the contract the employer's payment is the settlement of a pecuniary liability of the employee and is therefore earnings for Class 1 national insurance.

For example, if Tation Ltd paid an employee's telephone bill the payment would be earnings (because the contract was between the employee and the telephone company) whereas if Tation Ltd was the subscriber for the telephone installed at the employee's home, Class 1 contributions would not be payable. However, because there is both private and business use of the line Class 1A contributions would be due on the total bill if the employee is a P11D employee or director.

If the company reimbursed an employee for the cost of parking near the restaurant, Class 1 contributions would be payable, but not if the company contracted directly with the car parking company. In that event there would also be no Class 1A charge, as the benefit is not taxable. If the company contracted with a supplier for the supply of meat and then gave the meat to its employees the gift would not be earnings for Class 1 but would be a taxable benefit liable to Class 1A contributions if provided to a P11D employee or director. Whereas if the employee went to the same supplier and ordered meat, giving the bill to the company for settlement, it would be earnings for Class 1.

Reimbursements of expenses incurred in the course of the employment are not earnings or benefits provided the expenses are identified and quantified. Round sum allowances are earnings and are fully liable to Class 1 national insurance unless they represent no more than a reasonable estimate of actual costs incurred and the employer has a written agreement with HMRC to enable them to make such payments free of tax and national insurance. An advance may be made against expenses providing the actual expenses are identified and any surplus repaid (or treated as earnings).

HMRC may grant a dispensation to enable certain payments to be regarded as covering expenses incurred by the employee in carrying out his duties, and such a dispensation is also accepted for national insurance purposes. Where an employee is away from home overnight on business, contributions are not chargeable on payments or reimbursements of personal expenses up to £5 a night (£10 if outside the UK).

(e)   (i)   An employee may be contracted out of the State Second Pension scheme (S2P) in one of two ways:

1.   An employer may provide a registered approved salary related or money purchase pension scheme in return for paying reduced national insurance contributions on employees' earnings between the lower and upper earnings levels. From 6 April 1997 (for the purposes of contracting out of SERPS (which applied until 5 April 2002) or S2P) salary related schemes must broadly provide retirement benefits that are equivalent to or better than the state scheme. (Pension rights built up before that date had to provide a 'guaranteed minimum pension' for each individual member.) Under a money purchase scheme, employers must make guaranteed minimum contributions.

2.   Alternatively, the employee may take out a registered personal pension plan and elect to contract out of SSP. In that case full contributions are paid by both employee and employer and the HMRC National Insurance Contributions Office (NICO) makes a refund payment directly to the pension provider. NICO also pays in an additional amount equivalent to tax relief on the employee's share of the contracting out rebate, grossed up at the basic rate of tax.

All contracting out rebates of Class 1 contributions for both personal pension plans and contracted-out money purchase schemes (but not final salary schemes) are age-related. The minimum rebate is 2.6%. The age at which the maximum rebate of 10.5% is reached is currently 55.

For 2007/08 onwards, the combined rebates for money purchase schemes start at 3%, increasing to 7.4% at age 48 in 2007/08 and 2008/09, 49 in 2009/10 and 2010/11 and 50 in 2011/12 and over. The rebate for contracted-out salary related schemes is 5.1% (employer 3.5%, employee 1.6%). From 2007/08, the employer rebate will increase to 3.7%. Employers with a contracted-out money purchase scheme pay a rebated national insurance contribution for scheme members based on the lowest age-related rebates level of 2.6% (employer 1%, employee 1.6%). From 2007/08, the employer figure will rise to 1.4%.

For personal pension plans the rebates are biased to give lower earners a higher rebate. This is done by applying different percentages to different bands of earnings. For 2006/07 the first band covers earnings between the lower earnings limit and a stipulated 'low earnings threshold' of £12,500 (SI 2006/500) per annum, the next covers earnings between £12,500 and £28,800 and the third covers earnings between £28,800 and the upper annual earnings limit of £33,540. The rebate rate on the first band of earnings is double that on the third band. This is offset by a reduced rebate rate on the second band. The overall effect for those earning above £28,800 is to give a rebate of 4.2% for those under 18, increasing to 10.5% at age 55 or over.

The relevant information is recorded on year-end forms P14 and HMRC pays the age-related rebate top-up when they receive the forms P14.

(ii)   National insurance contributions are normally collected as follows (subject to what is said in part (a) about deferment of contributions):

Class 1   Employees' (primary) contributions are deducted from earnings when paid, and together with the employers' (secondary) contributions, they are paid over to HMRC by the employer with the PAYE deductions either monthly or, if total payments average less than £1,500 a month and the employer so wishes, quarterly.

Class 1A   Employers' contributions on taxable benefits are paid to HMRC annually in arrears by the 19 July following the tax year.

Class 1B	Employers' contributions payable under a PAYE Settlement Agreement (PSA) on benefits liable to NI plus the tax thereon are paid to HMRC together with the tax on the PSA annually in arrear on 19 October.
Class 2 & *Class 3*	Direct to NICO by quarterly bill payable within 28 days after the bill is issued, or by direct debit monthly in arrears.
Class 4	Provisional half yearly payments are made to HMRC on 31 January and 31 July in respect of all income tax and Class 4 national insurance due, with any remaining balance on the following 31 January.

Explanatory Notes

Liability to pay national insurance contributions

1. HMRC frequently assess arrears of contributions for several years where, for example, someone has been reclassified as employed rather than self-employed. Although they have the right to assess arrears for as many years as they wish, their rights to *enforce payment* for more than six years may be restricted by the Limitation Act 1980, providing liability has not been admitted in writing.

    See Example 13 explanatory note 2 for the special rules regarding the employment status of entertainers and explanatory note 3 for the treatment of contributions paid in the mistaken belief that a worker was an employee.

2. Where there is a dispute about national insurance contributions, there is a right of appeal to the appeal commissioners on a question of fact or law relating to a decision of HMRC, with further rights of appeal on points of law to the High Court, Court of Appeal or House of Lords.

Structural changes to state pension scheme

3. The State Earnings Related Pension Scheme (SERPS) has been replaced by the State Second Pension (S2P) from 6 April 2002. The new scheme gives enhanced benefits to lower earners (below £12,500 per annum), carers and long-term disabled. As a consequence the rebate payable on contracting out by way of a personal pension plan (but not by way of a money purchase scheme) has been biased to give lower earners a higher rebate as indicated in part (e)(i) of the example (SI 2001/1354 and SI 2006/1009 for years after 2006/07).

Alignment of tax and national insurance legislation

4. There are already many areas where the national insurance legislation has been aligned with the income tax legislation, and this process is continuing. There are still some differences in treatment, however, for example where an employee receives a mileage allowance for business use of his own car, national insurance contributions are not payable on allowances that do not exceed the Mileage Allowance Payment Rates for up to 10,000 miles (40p), whatever the mileage (for details see Example 10 explanatory note 20).

    For details of HMRC dispensations and the treatment of incidental personal expenses see Example 10 explanatory notes 11 and 12. For the national insurance position on relocation allowances see Example 10 explanatory note 7.

5. Following the transfer of the Contributions Agency to HMRC, the Department for Work and Pensions has retained responsibility for benefit entitlement including pension credits, but not for tax credits, statutory sick pay, statutory maternity pay or contracted-out pension schemes. Appeals on those matters are, however, to an appeals tribunal set up under the Social Security Act 1998.

Benefits that can be surrendered for cash

6. The employer's further guide to PAYE and NICs CWG2 gives detailed notes on what is included in pay both for tax and national insurance.

It is the view of HMRC that even where a benefit is transferred from the employer to the employee it does not come within the definition of a benefit in kind if it can be converted into cash by mere surrender, rather than requiring to be sold, and they give as an example premium bonds. Class 1 national insurance contributions would therefore be payable on such benefits.

Cars – benefits or cash

7. Where an employee has a choice between the use of a car and additional salary, the employee's tax and national insurance position is based on what he actually gets – either salary or the use of the car (ITEPA 2003 s 119).

Directors and other special classes of employees

8. Special rules apply for certain classes of employees – for example see booklet:

Directors	CA 44
Foreign going mariners and deep sea fishermen	CA 42
Persons working in the UK for overseas employers or embassies	CA 65
Social Security abroad	NI 38

See part (d) of the example for the special annual earnings period rules for directors.

9. Where payment by a company of a director's personal bills is charged to the director's loan or current account, the payment does not count as earnings for national insurance unless the payment represents drawings in anticipation of earnings. This will occur where the overdrawn loan account is settled by way of a bonus. The liability then arises at the time the loan account became overdrawn.

Associated employers etc

10. Class 1 national insurance contributions are payable on earnings from one employment in one earnings period without regard to any other payment of earnings (Social Security Contributions and Benefits Act 1992 s 6(4)). However where two or more employers 'carry on business in association' or where more than one job is held with the same employer, earnings are aggregated to compute the liability for that earnings period unless it is not reasonably practical to do so (Social Security Contributions and Benefits Act 1992 Sch 1.1). See the Revenue's Tax Bulletin of August 2000 for their views on the meaning of 'not reasonably practicable'. It has been assumed that the two employments of Mrs Bond in part (c) of the example would be aggregated as both jobs are with J. Bond. If however the research post was with her husband's political party then her liability in respect of each employment would be:

£

5,000 @ nil   –

giving a reduction of £546.15, and the employer's liability would also be reduced to nil compared with £635.52.

Married women's reduced rate contributions

11. Married women who pay reduced contributions cannot claim contributory benefits, but they can claim retirement pension (at a reduced level) and widow's benefit on their husband's contributions. A woman widowed after 5 October 2010 will, however, inherit only half of her late husband's SERPS/S2P entitlement. Those widowed between 6 October 2002 and 5 October 2010 will inherit between 60% and 90% of the spouse's SERPS/S2P entitlement. Women lose the right to pay reduced contributions on divorce (effective immediately after the decree absolute) or widowhood (effective from the end of the tax year, or if the husband died between 1 October and 5 April, from the end of the next tax year). The right is also lost if a married woman neither pays Class 1 contributions nor has self-employed earnings for two consecutive tax years.

Contracted-out contributions

12. When contributions are paid at contracted-out rates the actual contributions are revalued to their full rate equivalent in order to test whether the maximum contribution levels have been exceeded. The order of repayment of excess contributions is:

Class 4
Class 2
Class 1 (full rate)
Class 1 (contracted-out rate, contributions in respect of salary-related schemes being refunded before contributions in relation to money purchase schemes)

therefore contracted out contributions will not normally be repaid unless there is more than one such employment. In that case the appropriate actual excess will be refunded (not the full rate calculated contribution).

Liability for outstanding national insurance contributions of employees

13. From 6 April 1999 a company director or other culpable officer (including any shareholder who exercises management powers) will be personally liable under SSA 1992 s 121C for the arrears of a company in respect of national insurance contributions if a notice is issued under this section. The arrears must arise through the officer's fraud or neglect and the amount payable will include interest. The officer may appeal against the notice to the appeal commissioners, with the burden of proof on HMRC as agent for the Secretary of State.

Employer's liability to Class 1 contributions re unapproved share option schemes

14. When an employee exercises an unapproved share option in a company where the shares are marketable (ie a readily convertible asset), then a PAYE/NI liability arises on the taxable value realised by exercise of the option. This gives the employer a liability on an amount that cannot be determined in advance by the employer and the timing of the liability depends on the actions of the employee. To prevent unexpected national insurance costs affecting the employer, in respect of unapproved options granted on or after 6 April 1999 that have not yet been exercised, the employer and employee may jointly elect that the liability will be that of the employee. Furthermore, in computing the income tax payable by the employee the national insurance Class 1 secondary contributions paid by the employee on behalf of the employer will be deductible from the taxable amount (ITEPA 2003 s 478), for example: Gain on exercise of option liable to income tax £10,000. Employer's NIC paid by employee £1,280. Tax due (10,000 − 1,280) = £8,720 @ say 40% = £3,488, giving the employee an effective marginal rate of tax of 47.68% (ie 1,280 + 3,488 = £4,768 paid out of £10,000).

Holsworthy Ltd, which has no associated companies, commenced trading as a manufacturer of adhesives in 1960. It has always drawn up its accounts to 31 December. It is not a close company.

For the year to 31 December 2006 the net profit before taxation was £5,467,185. The following information has been provided (VAT having been adjusted appropriately in the figures given):

1. The following items of investment income have been included in the profit:

    Interest receivable   £

    Lundy Building Society   85,000
    Interest on 10% loan note (issued by Worth plc)   68,000
                                                                      153,000

    The amounts actually received in the year to 31 December 2006 were building society interest of £87,000 in March 2006 and interest on Worth plc loan note of £65,000 on 31 May 2006.

    UK dividends of £18,000 (20,000 including tax credits of £2,000) were received in November 2006, and are reported in the accounts in accordance with FRS 16.

    Rent

    Rent received is shown as £24,800. £12,800 of this amount was rent received from a house behind the factory which is let furnished. The company paid £1,200 insurance premium for the house on 1 January 2006 and this has been included in the general charge for insurance. The tenant pays the council tax and water rates.

    The remaining £12,000 was received in respect of a block of garages let on tenant's repairing leases. In the accounts a deduction has been made for £2,000 of rent arrears on the garages. The company has not yet taken any steps to recover the overdue rent.

2. In January 2006 the company had sold its 6% stake in an unquoted trading company which it had acquired in October 1991, resulting in a chargeable gain (after indexation allowance) of £5,330. A freehold investment property which cost £121,018 (including legal costs of purchase) in December 1989 was sold for £289,370 in February 2006. Indexation allowance for the period December 1989 to February 2006 was 63.5%. The profit figure of £5,467,185 is before taking these transactions into account.

3. On 30 August 2006 Holsworthy Ltd acquired leasehold factory premises at Milford Parva to be used in its trade. The term of the lease is 30 years. No premium was payable. In June 2006, the company had vacated its former leasehold factory premises at Milford Parva. The lease still had four years to run from the end of June 2006 and the company was likely to find it difficult to assign the lease in the foreseeable future. The annual rent was £100,000. In addition to the annual rent, a provision of £200,000 was made at 31 December 2006 and charged against profits (in accordance with Financial Reporting Standard Number 12) for the company's future rental obligations under the lease (less its estimated income from sub-letting).

4. An analysis of the salaries and wages account shows that the following payments were made during the year:

                                                                            £
    Removal expenses of new employee   8,700
    Expenses of employee seconded to Housing Charity   15,400
    Misappropriation of funds by former employee   12,000
    Ex gratia payment to former director to settle claims made by him on the company   20,000
    Statutory redundancy payments   70,000

5. An analysis of legal charges shows that the following amounts have been expended:
                                                                            £
    Debt recovery   3,200
    Sale of property February 2006   10,360

	£
Lease of factory at Milford Parva	15,780
Fine for breach of Health and Safety at Work Regulations	3,700
Penalty for infringement of a patent	12,800
Legal costs of (successful) defence of action for breach of contract	3,890
Preparation of service agreement for sales manager	1,600

6.   The entries in the bad debts account may be summarised as follows:

	£
Debts written off	35,000
Debts recovered	(15,000)
Decrease in specific bad debt provision	(8,000)
Increase in general bad debt provision	9,000
Charge to profit and loss account	21,000

7.   Sundry expenses include the following items:

	£
Fees for apprentice training course at technical college	2,500
Contribution to Milford Parva Enterprise Agency	3,000
Donation to Political Party	4,000
Gift Aid donation to Oxfam June 2006	5,000
Gift Aid payment to local charity (gross amount – paid January 2006)	2,000
Trade association subscription	400
Debit interest on quarterly instalments of corporation tax for 2005	4,360

8.   Entertaining and gifts were made up as follows:

	£
Entertaining and gifts – UK customers	138,940
– Foreign customers	24,480
Staff dinner	42,460
Pocket diaries for UK customers (company's name embossed thereon) costing £3.75 each	13,125
	219,005

9.   Depreciation charged for the year on the factory and plant and machinery amounted to £521,000. In addition, goodwill of £300,000 was written off to profit and loss account. This related to goodwill costing £2,100,000 that was acquired on the purchase of the Sven Glue Co Ltd business and assets in January 2002. The company is amortising the goodwill equally over seven years. Capital allowances of £756,400 are available on assets used in the factory.

10. Loan interest payable charged against the profit was £200,000. The loan was £2,000,000 borrowed from the trustees of the company's self-administered pension fund to provide additional finance for the trade on 1 October 1998, on which interest at 10% per annum was payable half yearly on 31 March and 30 September.

11. Patent royalties of £42,000 per annum (gross) were charged against the profit. These were paid to Barmouth plc half yearly in June and December.

12. A final dividend of £800,000 for the year ended 31 December 2005 was paid in June 2006 and an interim dividend of £500,000 for the year to 31 December 2006 was paid in January 2007.

13. Holsworthy Ltd had no surplus ACT or surplus franked investment income brought forward at 1 January 2006.

(a) Compute the corporation tax liability for the year to 31 December 2006.

(b) Show how the company would account for the taxation liabilities arising out of the information given. (Note: The company was liable to pay its tax under the quarterly payment regime in 2005.)

(a)   **Computation of Corporation Tax liability for year to 31 December 2006**

		£	£
Net profit per accounts			5,467,185
Less: Interest receivable		153,000	
UK dividends		18,000	
Rent (24,800 income less 1,200 expenses)		23,600	
Capital allowances on plant and machinery		756,400	951,000
			4,516,185
Add: Legal expenses re sale of property			10,360
Legal expenses re lease of factory			15,780
Fine for breach of Health and Safety at Work Regulations			3,700
Penalty for infringement of patent			12,800
Increase in general bad debt provision			9,000
Donation to Political Party			4,000
Donation to Oxfam			5,000
Gift Aid payment to local charity			2,000
Entertaining and gifts (other than staff dinner and diaries) (219,005 − 42,460 − 13,125)			163,420
Depreciation and amortisation of goodwill (521,000 + 300,000)			821,000
Schedule D Case I Trading Profit			5,563,245
Schedule A Rent (footnote 1)			22,320
Schedule D Case III Interest *receivable*			
Worth plc 10% loan note interest			68,000
Building society interest			85,000
Chargeable gains (footnote 2)			86,476
Total profits			5,825,041
Less charges on income (gross amounts paid):			
Gift aid donations (paid gross) (5,000 + 2,000)			(7,000)
Profits chargeable to corporation tax			5,818,041
Corporation tax thereon (see explanatory note 12):			
£5,818,041 @ 30% (FY 2005 and FY 2006 both 30%)			1,745,412

Footnotes

		£	£
1.	Schedule A business – rental income (12,800 + 14,000)		26,800
	Less: insurance (house)	1,200	
	wear and tear allowance (house – 10% of 12,800)	1,280	
	provision for rent arrears (garages)	2,000	4,480
			£ 22,320

2.   The chargeable gains are (see explanatory note 10):   £   £

On sale of unquoted trading company shares January 2006   5,330
On sale of freehold investment property February 2006:
Sale proceeds   289,370
Less: Costs of sale   10,360
                                                                       279,010

Cost of property – December 1989   121,018

Gain before indexation allowance   157,992
Less: Indexation allowance £121,018 x 63.5%   76,846   81,146
                                                                                    86,476

(b)   **Accounting for taxation liabilities arising out of information given**

   (i)   *Treatment of dividends*

   As the tax credit of £2,000 is a notional amount rather than an actual amount of tax deducted from the dividend, FRS 16 requires the accounts to report the amount received of £18,000.

   For purposes of tax, such as calculating total income for income tax or calculating marginal rates of corporation tax, the dividend is treated as a tax-credit inclusive amount of £20,000 (10% x 20,000 =) £2,000 (see Example 1 explanatory note 8).

   (ii)   *Accounting for income tax deducted when paying interest and charges (TA 1988 Sch 16)*

   From 1 April 2001, companies no longer deduct tax from annual interest and patent royalties etc. where they believe the recipient is chargeable to UK corporation tax. From 1 October 2002, this also applies to payments to exempt bodies, such as the pension fund. Holsworthy Ltd does not therefore deduct tax from payments to the pension fund trustees after 30 September 2002. Since 1 April 2000, qualifying gift aid donations are paid on a 'gross' basis. See explanatory note 11 for further details.

   (iii) *Accounting for corporation tax on profits*

   As the company paid its 2005 tax liability under the quarterly instalment payment ('QIP') regime and its profits chargeable to corporation tax for the year ended 31 December 2006 exceed £1,500,000, the corporation tax payable of £1,745,412 per part (a) will be accounted for under the QIP regime. Thus 25% of the estimated liability is payable on each of 14 July 2006, 14 October 2006, 14 January 2007 and 14 April 2007 (see explanatory note 15).

   During 2006, the company paid tax on account of its 2005 corporation tax liability. The last two 25% instalments of the 2005 liability were paid on 14 January 2006 and 14 April 2006. The debit interest of £4,360 on the QIPs arises due to insufficient tax being paid on the QIP basis compared with the relevant proportion of the final liability which should have been paid. Such interest is an allowable deduction against profits for corporation tax purposes.

Explanatory Notes

Scope of corporation tax

1.   Corporation tax is charged on the *profits* of *companies* (TA 1988 s 6). Profits means both income and chargeable gains (see note 10 below). Corporation tax is not, however, charged on dividends and other distributions received from other UK companies (known as franked investment income), subject to what is said in note 4(ix) about share dealers (TA 1988 s 208).

The definition of company for corporation tax purposes is 'any body corporate or unincorporated association'. This would include a members' club, which is liable to corporation tax on its income from non-members, such as investment income and guests' fees. (Income from members, eg subscriptions, is not taxed under the 'mutuality' principle.) Registered community amateur sports clubs, broadly amateur sports clubs open to the whole community which require their surpluses to be reinvested in the club, enjoy a number of special tax exemptions (see Example 91 for the detailed provisions).

The definition specifically excludes a partnership, a local authority or a local authority association. Most unit trusts fall within the definition (TA 1988 ss 468 and 832). LLPs are treated as partnerships unless and until they go into formal liquidation, from which time they are taxed as companies. See Example 26 part (b) for details.

UK resident companies are charged on their worldwide profits. Non-resident companies carrying on a trade in the UK through a permanent establishment are charged on income arising from the permanent establishment and on capital gains on the disposal of assets in the UK used for the purposes of the trade or attributable to the permanent establishment.

Certain companies, called close companies, are subject to special restrictions. A close company is broadly one under the control of five or fewer shareholders or of its directors. See Example 55 for details.

Chargeable accounting periods

2. The basis of the charge to tax is the profits of a 'chargeable accounting period'. This normally means the period for which a company makes up accounts, as in the case of Holsworthy's year to 31 December 2006. Where a period of account exceeds twelve months, however, it has to be split into one or more chargeable accounting periods of twelve months, and a chargeable accounting period comprising the remainder of the period. For detailed notes on chargeable accounting periods see Example 51.

Calculation of profits

3. In computing a corporation tax liability, the principles of income tax broadly apply in determining the taxable profits (TA 1988 s 9). Different rules apply, however, to interest paid and received, profits and losses on a company's capital transactions relating to loans, foreign exchange and certain financial instruments (see note 5) and (from 1 April 2002) expenses and gains on most intangible fixed assets including goodwill (see explanatory note 4(vii) and (viii)).

    HMRC accept that accounts prepared in accordance with generally accepted accounting practice (GAAP) form the starting point for tax purposes; in particular GAAP determines the period in which receipts and expenses are recognised, in the absence of a specific statutory rule (see note 4(i)). The expression 'generally accepted accounting practice' has now been brought into the tax legislation (TA 1988 s 836A), and FA 1998 s 42 has been amended to require accounts to be computed in accordance with GAAP, subject to any adjustment required or authorised by law.

    However, by virtue of FA 2004 s 50, the results of accounting periods beginning on or after 1 January 2005 which are drawn up in accordance with international accounting standards (where these differ from GAAP) will be accepted for tax purposes. See note 16 for introduction of International Accounting Standards.

4. The general income tax rule in TA 1988 s 74 for dealing with trading expenses in computing Schedule D Case I profit is that, unless they are covered by a specific statutory provision, expenses must be wholly and exclusively for the purposes of the trade. In addition they must not involve committing a criminal offence, such as paying a bribe or protection money (including, from 1 April 2002, payments overseas that would be illegal if paid in the UK), nor be paid in response to threats, menaces, blackmail and other forms of extortion (TA 1988 s 577A as amended by FA 2002 s 68). Any VAT input tax on legal expenses in court proceedings relating to illegal acts may, however, be recovered providing the criminal payment relates directly to the business (C & E v Rosner, 1993). Applying the rules to this example:

(i)   *Rents and provision for lease rental obligations*

Rent is clearly expenditure incurred for trade purposes, even after a company has vacated its premises. CIR v Falkirk Iron Co Ltd 1933 held that rent payable on premises which had ceased to be occupied was an allowable deduction as the rent obligation arises from the lease which is taken out for trading purposes. Furthermore, it was decided that provision for future rental obligations on vacated premises was acceptable under GAAP in Herbert Smith (a Firm) v Honour 1999.

Following the High Court's decision in that case, HMRC conceded that there was no longer a (judge-made) rule which prevented provision being made for future expenditure in accordance with GAAP, and this has now been made statutory as indicated in note 3 above. In particular, accounting provisions required under Financial Reporting Standard (FRS) Number 12 are accepted for tax purposes. Broadly, FRS 12 requires provision to be made where the business has a current (legal or constructive) obligation as a result of a past event; it is probable that expenditure will be required to satisfy it; and the provision can be reliably estimated. FRS 12 would require provision to be made for future net rental obligations where the company is unable to assign the lease or can only sub-let it at a lower rent. By entering into the lease, the company has incurred the legal obligation to pay the rents – the lease becomes an onerous contract since the unavoidable costs of meeting the obligations exceed the benefits to be received under it. This applies to Holsworthy's rent provision in this example.

(ii)   *Salaries and wages, loss of money lent to staff, redundancy payments*

The basic requirement is that the payments must be wholly and exclusively for the purposes of the trade. The removal expenses for the new employee satisfy this rule and are allowable. For the tax treatment of the employee see Example 10 explanatory note 7.

The expenses of an employee seconded to a charity would not usually satisfy the 'wholly and exclusively for the trade' rule, but they are specifically allowable by TA 1988 s 86.

The loss of money lent to directors and employees would normally be allowed as a non-trading debit under the 'loan relationship' rules (as the lending would not be connected with or arising out of the trade). No relief would be given if the debtor was a connected person (FA 1996, Sch 9.6 – see Example 62 explanatory note 7). The amount written off would normally be charged on the employee under the general charging provisions of employment income or under ITEPA 2003 s 188 for employees earning £8,500 or more and directors, s 188 applying to such employees even after they have left) or under the special provisions for close companies (see Example 57). The ex gratia payment will be allowed to the company providing it is wholly and exclusively for the trade, and will be charged on the director under the 'golden handshakes' provisions (see Example 12).

Misappropriations of funds by staff are an allowable expense provided they are the sort which one might expect to be an ordinary risk of the trade. Such losses are distinguished from those arising as a result of misappropriations by persons in controlling positions such as directors, which have been held in various cases to be not allowable – eg Curtis v Oldfield Ltd 1925, Bamford v ATA Advertising Ltd 1972.

In the case of an ongoing business, redundancy and other termination payments would normally be incurred as part of a rationalisation programme and would be allowed under general principles as expenditure incurred wholly and exclusively for the purposes of the trade (TA 1988 s 74). Statutory redundancy payments are specifically deductible as a trading expense (TA 1988 s 579). HMRC also allow *contractual* redundancy payments made on cessation of trade, following the Privy Council's decision in Hong Kong CIR v Cosmotron Manufacturing Co Ltd 1997. The rationale is that such payments are made under a pre-existing obligation to employees taken on for the purposes of the trade (HMRC Tax Bulletin February 1999).

The Cosmotron decision does not cover ex-gratia or non-contractual redundancy payments made on cessation. Under TA 1988 s 90, however, an amount of up to three times the statutory redundancy payment is specifically allowed provided it would otherwise have satisfied the 'wholly and exclusively' rule.

(iii) *Legal charges*

Capital items, ie the charges on the sale of the property and the acquisition of the lease, are not allowable (TA 1988 s 74). Fines and penalties for breaches of the law, and costs connected therewith, are not allowable. The costs of defending a civil action for breach of contract are wholly and exclusively for the purposes of the trade and are allowable, whether the action is successful or not.

In the case of McKnight v Sheppard 1999, the House of Lords held that legal expenses incurred by a stockbroker in an (unsuccessful) defence against Stock Exchange disciplinary proceedings for gross misconduct were to avoid the destruction of his business and satisfied the 'wholly and exclusively' rule, although the fines imposed by the Stock Exchange were not allowable, since they represented a loss which did not arise out of the trade.

(iv) *Bad debts*

In relation to ordinary trading transactions with customers and suppliers, bad debts written off and specifically provided for are allowable (TA 1988 s 74). A general bad debts provision, or increase therein, is not. (Bad debt provisions are not covered by FRS 12 (see note (i) above) as they reduce the value of an asset (the debtors).) Bad debts which do not relate to ordinary trading transactions are dealt with under the rules for 'loan relationships' (see note 5).

(v) *Sundry expenses*

Where expenses of training courses are met by the employer, they are allowable to the employer as part of the benefits provided to staff, and they are not assessable on the employees providing certain conditions are met (see Example 10 explanatory note 33). Employers may also deduct the cost of retraining employees who are about to leave or have just left their present jobs (TA 1988 s 588).

Contributions to approved local enterprise agencies, training and enterprise councils, Scottish local enterprise companies and 'business link' organisations are specifically allowable (TA 1988 ss 79 and 79A).

Charitable and political donations are not allowable as trading expenses, unless exceptionally they satisfy the 'wholly and exclusively' rule. Charitable donations are, however, normally allowable under the Gift Aid rules as deductions from *total* profits (see note 11).

As far as trade association subscriptions are concerned, most trade associations have agreed with HMRC to pay tax on the excess of their receipts over their allowable expenditure and the subscriptions are accordingly allowed to the payer. Any other subscriptions would be considered under the 'wholly and exclusively' rule.

Under corporation tax self-assessment (CTSA), interest on overdue and overpaid tax is taken into account in calculating taxable profits (see Example 52 explanatory note 7). However for accounting periods ended on or before 30 June 1999, interest on overdue tax was specifically disallowed (TMA 1970 s 90) and interest on overpaid tax was not assessable (TA 1988 ss 825 & 826).

(vi) *Entertaining and gifts*

With regard to entertaining and gifts, all expenditure in relation to customers, both home and overseas, is disallowed, except for gifts that are not food, drink, tobacco or gift vouchers, that carry a conspicuous advertisement and that cost not more than £50 per person in each accounting period, which applies to the pocket diaries in this example (TA 1988 s 577). The disallowance does *not* apply to anything provided for staff, unless it is incidental to entertaining customers. The cost of staff entertaining is allowed in calculating taxable profits providing it is wholly and exclusively for the trade. Staff entertaining may, however, result in a tax and national insurance charge on employees earning £8,500 per annum or more and directors under the benefits provisions (see Example 10 explanatory note 31), unless the conditions for staff entertaining are fulfilled and the expenditure in a tax year does not amount to more than £150 per head.

Relief may be claimed for gifts of machinery, plant and trading stock to schools and other educational establishments (TA 1988 s 84). Similarly, relief is available under TA 1988 s 83A for gifts in kind to a charity or heritage body (within TA 1988 s 507(1)).

Under these provisions, nothing has to be brought into account either as a trading receipt if the item is from trading stock or as disposal proceeds for capital allowances if it has been used in the donor's trade. Under s 84 (educational establishments), but not under s 83A (charities), relief must be specifically claimed within one year from 31 January following the tax year in which the gift was made for income tax and within two years from the end of the relevant accounting period for companies. For gifts made on or after 1 April 2002, relief is also given for trading stock consisting of medical supplies donated for humanitarian purposes to developing countries (together with transportation and delivery costs) (FA 2002 s 55).

VAT-registered traders donating used or obsolete items have to account for VAT only on the current value of such items, not on their original cost.

See note 11 re relief as a charge on income for gifts of stocks and shares and land.

(vii) *Depreciation of factory and plant etc and amortisation of goodwill*

Depreciation is a capital item and is disallowed. (Most but not all assets qualify instead for capital allowances.)

Amortisation of purchased goodwill is deductible as a Schedule D Case I expense under the FA 2002 intangible fixed assets regime provided it relates to goodwill acquired *on or after* the 1 April 2002 commencement date (FA 2002 Sch 29.118). Thus no relief is available for the goodwill purchased in January 2002. This goodwill is dealt with under the capital gains regime, with the amount paid being deducted in computing any capital gains on a future disposal of the goodwill. See Example 65 for details of the FA 2002 intangible fixed assets rules.

(viii) *Patent royalties*

Before 1 April 2002 patent royalties were charges on income deductible from total profits (see explanatory note 11). From that date patent royalties are dealt with under the intangible fixed assets rules in FA 2002 Sch 29. The broad effect of these rules is to provide Schedule D Case I tax relief for all expenses, losses, profits etc relating to such assets, normally based on the amounts reflected in the accounts. This means that patent royalties are deductible as a trading expense instead of as a charge on income. Thus, in this example, full relief can be taken for the patent royalties of £43,000 already charged against Holsworthy's profits, with no further tax adjustment being required.

(ix) *Non-trading income*

Non-trading income is excluded from the Schedule D Case I computation. It is then brought in appropriately elsewhere, except dividends received from other UK companies, which are not chargeable to corporation tax.

For share dealers, dividend income and manufactured payments that are treated as dividends are trading income rather than investment income and are included in trading profits (exclusive of tax credits).

UK rental income of companies is computed as a single figure under the 'UK property business rules' that apply to individuals. Allowable deductions are broadly those that apply to business profits, hence a provision may be made for unpaid rents as indicated in the example. Rent from sub-letting *part* of business premises (not land) that is *temporarily* surplus to requirements may for convenience be included in the trading income providing it is comparatively small. For detailed notes on the treatment of rents see Example 98.

Interest from banks and building societies is received by companies in full without deduction of tax (TA 1988 ss 477A & 481). The same applies to interest on UK government stocks, unless application is made for net payment (TA 1988 s 50 – see Example 6 part (a)). Following changes in FA 2001 and FA 2002, companies will also receive most other interest in full (see explanatory note 11). In the rare cases where investment income is received net of income tax, the gross amount is nonetheless included in the profits chargeable to corporation tax. The income tax suffered is taken into account in the Schedule 16 quarterly income tax accounting (see note 13) or set off against the corporation tax payable. The corporation tax treatment of interest is dealt with in explanatory note 5 below.

Loan relationships

5. Special rules apply to a company's 'loan relationships', which essentially means all money debt except where it relates to amounts outstanding on trading transactions for goods and services (FA 1996 ss 80 to 105 and Schs 8 to 15). Interest payable that relates to a trade is brought into account in calculating the Schedule D Case I result. Non-trading interest payable and all sources of interest receivable both in the UK and abroad (and any profits/losses on non-trading loans) are aggregated and an overall profit is charged under Schedule D Case III (unless the company's trade includes moneylending, in which case the relevant amounts are Case I income). If there is an overall loss (a non-trading deficit) relief is available similar to that for trading losses (see Example 63).

    Under the loan relationships rules, interest is brought into account according to the amounts payable and receivable, ie on the accruals basis.

    For detailed notes on the loan relationships provisions see Example 62.

Pre-trading expenditure

6. Pre-trading expenditure, other than interest (and elected research and development expenditure – see below), incurred by a company within seven years before the start of the trade that would have been allowable if incurred after commencement is treated as paid on the first day of trading (TA 1988 s 401).

    Where interest is paid before the trade starts, it is deducted on an accruals basis in calculating the non-trading profit or loss under Schedule D Case III. This does not apply if the company makes a claim, within two years after the end of the period in which the deduction was given, to bring the interest in as a trading expense of the first trading period. In order to be deductible in that period the trade must start within seven years after the end of the accounting period in which the interest would otherwise have been deducted under Schedule D Case III (s 401(1AA)–(1AC)).

    Where a small/medium-sized company incurs qualifying research and development (R&D) expenditure before it begins to carry on the relevant trade, it may elect to treat 150% of the expenditure as if it were a trading loss (see Example 51 explanatory note 9). Where an R&D election is made, the amount cannot be treated as a pre-trading expense.

Capital allowances

7. When the trading profit has been ascertained using the above principles, capital allowances are then deducted as a trading expense and balancing charges included as a trading receipt (CAA 2001 s 2).

Value added tax

8. For a fully VAT-registered company, VAT does not normally enter into the profits and expenditure for corporation tax, except as follows:

    (a) Non-recoverable VAT on cars forms part of the allowable cost for capital allowances.

(b)   Scale VAT charges for private fuel provided to employees are included in motoring expenses.

There may be other non-recoverable VAT, for example on repairs, refurbishments and other expenses relating to domestic accommodation provided for directors, and it will form part of the allowable expense against the profit (subject to the normal rules for allowable expenses). Non-recoverable VAT on entertaining is disallowed along with the entertaining expenditure itself (but see Example 15 explanatory note 7 re staff entertaining).

A partly exempt or non-VAT registered company includes VAT as part of allowable expenses or capital costs, subject to the disallowance of VAT on business entertaining. Some approximation may be necessary for partly exempt companies in allocating the VAT to the various items of expenditure, and this will be accepted by HMRC providing it is reasonable.

National insurance contributions

9.   Companies are required to pay Class 1 secondary national insurance contributions at 12.8% in respect of their employees' earnings in excess of £97 a week (from 6 April 2006). (Employees' Class 1 primary contributions are also payable on earnings in excess of £97 a week. For 2006/07 the main charge runs out at the upper earnings limit of £645 a week, £33,540 a year, and a charge of 1% applies to earnings above this limit.) Earnings for Class 1 contributions comprise cash pay and certain benefits in kind that can be readily converted into cash. Employers (but not employees) also pay Class 1A contributions at 12.8% on most taxable benefits in kind that do not attract Class 1 contributions, and also Class 1B contributions at 12.8% in relation to PAYE settlement agreements (see Example 9 for details). The contributions are an allowable expense against the profits.

See Example 47 for the detailed provisions on national insurance.

Chargeable gains

10.   Company chargeable gains are calculated using capital gains tax principles, but are then charged to corporation tax rather than to capital gains tax (TA 1988 s 6, TCGA 1992 ss 1 and 8). References in the capital gains legislation to years of assessment are treated as references to accounting periods. If losses exceed gains, the excess is carried forward to set against later gains (see Example 96 explanatory note 11).

In 1999, the Government confirmed that the existing capital gains rules will continue to apply for companies, including the ability to calculate indexation relief beyond April 1998. (The FA 1998 changes, notably the introduction of taper relief, the freezing of indexation allowance and the abolition of share pooling, only apply to individuals and trusts.) However, companies have seen an increasing amount of capital assets being removed from the capital gains regime (where they are only broadly taxed on a 'realisation' basis) and taxed instead in accordance with profits and losses recognised in the accounts. Recent examples of this tendency to bring company tax computations into line with the accounts include the FA 1996 loan relationships rules (see note 5 above) the FA 2002 rules governing intangible fixed assets (see note 4 (vii) above) and the adoption of IAS by listed companies.

Charges on income and interest

11.   Charges on income are deductible from total profits (both income and capital profits) so far as paid in the chargeable accounting period (TA 1988 s 338). There is an exception to the rule that charges must be paid in the accounting period for companies who are wholly owned by a charity that donates the whole of their taxable profits to the charity (see Example 91 explanatory note 7 for details).

Charges on income used to comprise many types of transaction commonly found in corporation tax. They now principally comprise the following.

•   Qualifying donations made by companies under gift aid, including covenanted payments. See Example 91.

•   The market value (plus incidental costs) of certain gifts of stocks and shares to charity and qualifying interests in land (TA 1988 s 587B).

From 16 March 2005 annuities and other annual payments were removed from the scope of charges on income. Annuities and other annual payments are treated as management expenses (see companies with investment business, Example 63). Companies will rarely make any payments within the 'annuities or other annual payments' category.

Before 1 April 2001, companies deducted income tax from most payments of charges, covenants and annual interest (but not from interest paid to banks or building societies or short interest). Payments by companies under gift aid, most interest, and most patent royalties are now paid gross (without deduction of tax).

Companies and local authorities pay patent royalties and annual interest on a gross basis (without deducting tax) where they believe the recipient to be a UK-resident company, local authority or a UK permanent establishment of a non-resident company (TA 1988 ss 349A–349D). Interest is also paid gross on quoted Eurobonds which means interest-bearing securities issued by a company and listed on a recognised stock exchange (TA 1988 s 349(4)).

In other cases, such as where the recipient is an individual, a non-exempt trust or a non-resident company, the amounts continue to be subject to deduction of tax at the relevant rate. (If the payment is made overseas with the benefit of a double tax treaty, a 'nil' or reduced rate of withholding may apply.)

Companies may still *receive* patent royalties net of tax where the payer is an individual.

Corporation tax rates

12. The rate of corporation tax is fixed for years ended 31 March which are called financial years. Financial years are identified by the calendar year in which they start. Thus the year ending 31 March 2007 is called the financial year 2006. The rates for the financial year 2006 are a small companies' rate of 19% where profits do not exceed £300,000 and a full rate of 30% where profits exceed £1,500,000. The full rate for the financial year 2007 is 30% (announced in advance for instalment payment purposes).

   Where company accounting periods do not coincide with financial years, the profit for corporation tax is apportioned over the years concerned to determine the rates at which tax is payable (TA 1988 s 8), unless the rate is the same for both years. This apportionment is done in days rather than months.

Quarterly income tax returns (TA 1988 Sch 16)

13. A company has to make a return under TA 1988 Sch 16 to account for any income tax it has deducted in each relevant calendar quarter from payments to individuals or non UK residents. If the company has suffered income tax on any of its income (for example if it has received patent royalties from an individual), the income tax suffered will be set off against the income tax to be accounted for. Where tax is deducted, the rate of tax deducted from interest is 20% and the rate of tax deducted from relevant charges on income is 22%. The return under Sch 16 must be made within fourteen days after the end of the return period on form CT 61.

   If the income tax suffered exceeds income tax to be accounted for and income tax has been paid over to HMRC on an earlier return in the same accounting period, a repayment will be made, but not exceeding the amount of the earlier payments.

   At the end of an accounting period, if income tax suffered on relevant payments received exceeds income tax to be accounted for on relevant payments made, the excess is deducted from the corporation tax payable for that accounting period. If the excess of income tax suffered should *exceed* the corporation tax payable, the excess is *repayable*.

Corporation tax self-assessment (CTSA)

14. For accounting periods ended after 30 June 1999, the CTSA system applies, under which companies are required to send in a statutory corporation tax return CT 600, together with full accounts and

computations, within twelve months after the end of the accounting period, and are liable to penalties if they do not (FA 1998 Sch 18 paras, 3, 11, 14 and 17).

Payment of corporation tax

15. Although the corporation tax self-assessment return CT600 must be filed within twelve months of the year end, corporation tax must be paid within nine months and one day of the end of the accounting period (except for large companies that must pay by instalments). Interest on corporation tax unpaid after nine months was reduced from 7.5% to 6.50% from 6 September 2005.

Quarterly instalments

In Holsworthy's case the company qualifies as large and the tax must be paid in four equal instalments as follows:

Instalment	Due	Date	Percentage
Instalment 1	6 months + 13 days after start of AP	14/07/06	25%
Instalment 2	3 months after instalment 1	14/10/06	25%
Instalment 3	3 months after instalment 2	14/01/07	25%
Instalment 4	3 months plus 14 days after end of AP	14/04/07	25%

The number of instalments will be reduced if the accounting period is less than nine months in length.

A company qualifies as large if its profits (including non-group franked investment income) exceed £1.5 million, as scaled-down for shorter accounting periods and for the number of associate companies (see 49.4 note 3).

A company is not large if:

(a)   its tax liability does not exceed £10,000 (as scaled-down for shorter accounting periods); or

(b)   its profits for the accounting period do not exceed £10 million (as adjusted for shorter accounting periods), *and* it was not large (disregarding the £10 million exclusion) in the previous accounting period.

Holsworthy's profits were below £10 million, but it was large in the previous year, and its profit is above £1.5 million so quarterly payments are required. A company will not be large in the previous period if it did not exist or have an accounting period in any part of the previous 12 months, or if it was not a large company for an accounting period that fell within or ended in the previous 12 months.

Estimating quarterly instalment payments (QIPs)

It is the company's responsibility to state on the self-assessment return CT600 that it is liable to make QIPs. It is also its responsibility to estimate the amount of the QIP, which involves estimating the profit for the year before the year has ended. Because the instalments are estimated the amount paid will rarely match the final liability, and interest is charged or paid on underpaid or overpaid instalments. Interest runs from the date of the first instalment, and is charged at 5.5% on underpayments, and credited at 4.25% on overpayments (from 15 August 2005; the rates are changed frequently).

Interest on unpaid instalments is deductible, and interest on overpaid instalments is assessable in calculating profits for tax.

Payments can be made at any time, and a system exists for reclaiming overpayments made during the year. Group payment arrangements can be made by groups of companies, with the effect that over and underpayments by a group member can be offset.

Introduction of International Accounting Standards (IAS)

16. FA 2004 s 51 paved the way for the introduction of IAS, and has been followed by further details in FA 2005 and F (No 2) A 2005.

Publicly traded companies will be required to adopt IAS, and will be most affected by the transition. It is thought that smaller companies will choose not to adopt IAS in the immediate future, but the alignment of UK GAAP and IAS will produce a similar effect in the next few years. Companies that do not have hedging transactions, intangibles or securities to which FRS 26 or IAS 39 applies may find that differences arising on transition are small.

Amendments made to existing legislation by the Finance Act 2005 ensure that full IAS or EC-adopted IAS will both be acceptable as GAAP for tax purposes. Accounts of group companies prepared under IAS in other jurisdictions will therefore be acceptable for UK tax purposes.

FA 2005 contained detailed changes to existing legislation to accommodate IAS terminology and statements, to recognise debits and credits taken direct to reserves, and to broaden the definition of a group from its previous basis in UK GAAP.

Where the transition from UK GAAP to IAS gives rise to a prior year adjustment, the legislation provides that the adjustment will be recognised for tax purposes in the year to which the accounts relate, not the prior year. Where the period of account containing the prior year adjustment is more than 12 months long, anti-avoidance provisions ensure that the prior year adjustment is taxed in the first period of account after the change is recognised.

Special provisions allow securitisation companies to be taxed in accordance with UK GAAP for a further year, as uncertainties over tax treatment could be particularly damaging to the sector. Draft regulations outlining a special regime for securitisation companies have been issued.

A.   (a)   Able Limited, a company with no associated companies, has been trading for ten years and has always prepared accounts annually to 31 March. The accounts for the year to 31 March 2007 show profits chargeable to corporation tax of £310,000. There is no franked investment income.

            Compute the corporation tax payable.

B.   Baker Ltd, a UK trading company with no associated companies, produced the following results for the year ended 31 March 2007:

Income and gains:	£	£
Adjusted trading profit		244,000
Rental income		15,000
Bank deposit interest receivable		5,000
Capital gains: 25 September 2006	35,000	
28 March 2007	7,000	42,000
(There were capital losses of £8,000 bf at 1 April 2006)		
Dividends from UK companies (13,500 + tax credits 1,500)		15,000
Charges paid (gross):		
Gift Aid donation to charity		7,000
Dividend paid:		
24 July 2006		52,000

     (a)   Compute the corporation tax payable by Baker Ltd for the above accounting period.

     (b)   Comment on the effect on the company's tax liability of the sale of the asset on 28 March 2007, resulting in the capital gain of £7,000.

C.   Cakes Ltd, a company with no associated companies, has traded for several years, making up accounts to 31 March each year.

     During the year ended 31 March 2006, Cakes Ltd's tax adjusted trading profits were £9,000. Its only other income was dividends received of £450. No dividends were paid during the year.

     (a)   How much corporation tax was payable by Cakes Ltd for the above period?

     (b)   Show what the corporation tax would have been if the trading profits had been £11,500 instead of £9,000.

     (c)   How much corporation tax is due on a profit for tax of £9,000 for year ended 31/3/07?

Corporation tax rates and marginal relief limits and fractions from 1 April 2004 to 31 March 2007 have been as follows:

Year ended 31 March	*2005*	*2006*	*2007*
Full rate	30%	30%	30%
Small companies' rate (marginal relief limits £300,000 to £1,500,000 throughout)	19%	19%	19%
marginal relief fraction	11/400	11/400	11/400
Starting rate (marginal relief limits £10,000 to £50,000 throughout)	0%	0%	N/A
marginal relief fraction	19/400	19/400	N/A

D.   Doily Ltd, a company with no associated companies has made up its accounts to 30 September for many years, and had undistributed reserves brought forward of £100,000 at 1 October 2004.

     Recent results have been:

Year Ended	Profit	Dividend	
30 September 2004	£nil	£10,000	(paid 30 September 2004)
30 September 2005	£10,000	£nil	
			(paid 31 March 2006)
30 September 2006	£24,000	£10,000	

(a) Calculate the corporation tax payable for the two years 30 September 2005 and 2006.

(b) Calculate the corporation tax payable to the year 30 September 2006, on the basis that the dividend was paid on 1 April 2006.

(c) Comment on the effect of a dividend of £50,000 paid on 1 October 2006.

A. (a) **Able Limited**

Corporation Tax Computation – year ended 31 March 2007

Profits chargeable to corporation tax (and also for small companies' rate since there is no franked investment income)	£ 310,000
Corporation tax thereon @ 30%	93,000
Less: $(1,500,000 - 310,000) \quad \times \dfrac{310,000}{310,000} \quad \times \dfrac{11}{400}$	32,725
Corporation tax payable	£ 60,275

Looked at in marginal rate terms, this represents:

£300,000 @ 19%	57,000
10,000 @ 32.75%	3,275
	60,275

B. (a) **Corporation tax payable by Baker Ltd for year to 31 March 2007**

	£
Schedule D Case I trading profit	244,000
Schedule A business rental income	15,000
Schedule D Case III bank interest	5,000
Chargeable gains net of allowable losses (42,000 – 8,000)	34,000
Total profits	298,000
Less charges on income:	
Gift Aid donation	7,000
Profits chargeable to corporation tax (I)	291,000
Add franked investment income (tax credit inclusive dividends)	15,000
Profits for small companies' rate (P)	306,000
Corporation tax payable on £291,000 @ 30%	87,300
Less: $(1,500,000 - 306,000) \times \dfrac{291,000}{306,000} \times \dfrac{11}{400}$	31,225
	56,075

(b) **Corporation tax effect of the sale of the asset on 28 March 2007**

The sale of the asset on 28 March 2007 at a gain of £7,000 took the company's profits above the small companies' rate lower limit of £300,000 and thus attracted tax to the extent of the excess, ie £6,000, at over 32%. If the gain had not been made, the profits for small companies' rate would have been £299,000 and the corporation tax on the profits of £284,000 would then have been @ 19%, ie £53,960, compared with £56,075, a reduction of £2,115. The overall rate of tax on the gain of £7,000 therefore works out at just over 30%. In addition, deferring the gain to 1 April 2007 would have given a cash flow advantage because corporation tax would then have been payable one year later.

C.   **Corporation tax payable by Cakes Ltd for year to 31 March 2006**

		£
(a)	Schedule D Case I trading profit	9,000
	Profits chargeable to corporation tax	9,000
	Add: Franked investment income	
	Dividend received 450 x 100/90	500
	Profits for corporation tax starting rate	9,500
	Corporation tax payable on 9,000 @ 0%	nil

(b)   *If trading profits had been £11,500*

	£
Profits chargeable to corporation tax	11,500
Add: Franked investment income	500
Profits for corporation tax starting rate	12,000
Corporation tax on 11,500 @ 19%	2,185

$$\text{\textit{Less}: } (50,000 - 12,000) \times \frac{11,500}{12,000} \times \frac{19}{400} \qquad (1,730)$$

	£
Corporation tax payable	455
Tax payable on extra £2,500 of profit (455 – nil)	455

Looked at in marginal rate terms, this represents:

	£
500 @ 0% (taking profits to £10,000 starting rate limit)	–
2,000 @ 22.75%	455
	455

If there had been no franked investment income, the marginal rate on the £2,000 excess above £10,000 would have been 23.75% (see explanatory note 8).

(c)   Both the small companies starting rate, and the non-corporate distribution rate, are abolished as of 1 April 2006. A profit of £9,000 for year ended 31/3/2007 will therefore be taxed at 19% = £1,710.

D.   **Corporation Tax payable by Doily Ltd**

(a)   *Year to 30 September 2004*

		£
Profit for corporation tax		nil
Corporation tax on £nil at 0%		Nil
Lesser of profit of nil or distribution of £10,000 = £nil	At non-corporate distribution rate (19% – 0%) = 19%	Nil
Corporation tax due		Nil
Non-corporate distribution carried forward		£10,000

The amount chargeable at the non-corporate distribution rate could not exceed the profit for the period. Where the distribution paid in the period exceeded the profit, the excess was carried forward.

Year to 30 September 2005

		£
Profit for corporation tax		10,000
Corporation tax on £10,000 at 0%		Nil
Non-corporate distribution brought forward £10,000	At non-corporate distribution rate (19% – 0%) = 19%	1,900
Corporation tax due		1,900

Had profits been retained in the company, the starting rate of corporation tax of 0% would have applied to the first £10,000 of profit, and no tax would have been payable. However, a dividend had been paid after 1 April 2004 and had not been matched with previous profits for corporation tax. This constituted a non-corporate distribution brought forward, which had to be matched against subsequent profits benefiting from the small companies starting rate.

This caused the corporation tax to rise from £nil to £1,900, which was the maximum increase that the non-corporate distribution rate regime could cause in any one year.

Had the dividend been paid on 6 April 2005 instead of 30 September 2004, the company's position would have been the same, but the dividend would have fallen into the 2005/06 personal income tax year.

Year to 30 September 2006

As the rates of corporation tax changed during the period of account, profits must be apportioned into the correct financial year, and the rates for that financial year applied to the proportion of profit.

				£
Profit for corporation tax for the year				24,000
Six months to 31 March 2006				12,000
Corporation tax on £12,000	@	19%		2,280
Less £25,000 – £12,000 = £13,000 x 19/400				(618)

i.e. (50,000 × 6/12 – 12,000 × 19/400) [handwritten]

(apportioned for short period of account)	
Corporation tax before non-corporate distribution rate	1,662
Underlying rate of corporation tax £1,662 /£12,000 = 13.85%	

Because there is a distribution, and the underlying rate is less than the non-corporate distribution rate, the difference between the non-corporate distribution rate and the underlying rate is applied to the lesser of the distribution, or the profits of the company for the period.

Note that the figure of £1,662 can be arrived at by subtracting six months of the nil rate band (£10,000 x 6/12) from profit (£12,000 – £5,000 = £7,000), and multiplying the resulting £7,000 by the marginal rate of 23.75% to give £1,662.

Non-corporate distribution element

Lesser of profits £12,000 and distribution £10,000 = £10,000	£515

Non-corporate distribution rate 19% less underlying rate of 13.85% = .0515%	£2,177

Note: This can be reconciled as £12,000 x 19% = £2,280 less £2,000 (£12,000 – £10,000) x .0515% = £103.

The proportion of profit falling into the financial year 2006 (the financial year ending on 31 of March 2007) is taxed as follows:

Profit for corporation tax for the year			£24,000
6 months 1 April 2006 to 30 September 2006			£12,000
Corporation tax on £12,000	@	19%	£2,280

As the small company rate was abolished with effect from 1 April 2006, no adjustments are required. Profits in the range from £1 to £300,000 are taxed at the same rate of 19%.

Tax for the period 1 October 2005 to 31 March 2006	£2,177
Tax for the period 1 April 2006 to 30 September 2006	£2,280
Tax payable	£4,457

(b) Calculation of tax on the basis that the dividend was paid on 1 April 2006.

The calculation is the same for (a), but the dividend is paid after the abolition of the non-corporate distribution rate. As a result, the profits of 1 October 2005 to 31 March 2006 can be taxed at the then small companies rate, giving the following total:

Tax for the period 1 October 2005 to 31 March 2006	£1,662
Tax for the period 1 April 2006 to 30 September 2006	£2,280
Tax payable	£3,942

Had the dividend been paid after the abolition of the non-corporate distribution rate, the savings of the small companies rate for the year ended 31 March 2006 could have been retained.

(c) Effect of a dividend of £50,000 paid on 1 October 2006.

The non-corporate distribution regime had provisions for carrying forward excess dividends. These provisions ceased with the abolition of the non-corporate distribution rate, and distributions paid after 31 March 2006 have no effect on the rate of corporation tax of the paying company.

Explanatory Notes

Small companies' rate

1. Corporation tax is payable on both capital profits and income profits (other than franked investment income).

   A reduced rate of corporation tax known as the 'small companies' rate' (TA 1988 s 13) applies to a UK resident company where the *profits* (as defined below) are less than what is called the lower relevant maximum amount. A lower 'starting rate' applied from 1 April 2000 to 31 March 2006 where profits fall below the 'first relevant amount' of £10,000, with marginal relief where profits were between £10,000 and £50,000 (s 13AA) (but see note 7 where there are associated companies). The starting rate was 10% for the financial years 2000 and 2001, but it was reduced to 0% for the financial years 2002, 2003, 2004 and 2005 (see explanatory note 8 below). The small companies' rate and starting rate did not apply to the profits of a 'close investment-holding company' (see Example 55 for definition of close investment-holding company). (See also Example 50 for the non-corporate distribution rate.)

   The small companies' rate and full corporation tax rate are fixed for financial years, the financial year 2006 being the year to 31 March 2007. The rates for the financial year 2006 are 19% and 30% respectively. The full rate of 30% also applies for the year to 31 March 2008 (announced in advance for the purposes of companies paying tax under the quarterly instalment payment regime).

Meaning of 'profits'

2.   'Profits' for starting and small companies' rates means corporation taxable profits (including chargeable gains) plus franked investment income.

     Franked investment income is not, however, included in profits for the starting and small companies' rate if it comes from a UK-resident 51% subsidiary or from a fellow UK 51% subsidiary of a parent company (s 13 and s 13ZA).

Marginal small companies' rate relief

3.   Marginal small companies' rate relief is available where profits are above the lower limit but below an upper limit. Since financial year 1994 the lower and upper limits have been £300,000 and £1,500,000, with marginal relief fractions as shown on page 49.1.

     The limits are scaled down pro rata where there are associated companies and for accounting periods of less than 12 months (see explanatory note 7). Where there are different relevant maximum amounts and/or different rates of tax for different parts of the same accounting period, the profits are apportioned between those parts. If the marginal relief fraction changes, the same proportions are applied in calculating the marginal relief, as shown in part A(b) of the example.

     Where an accounting period is split in this way because of a change in the upper and lower limits, it is treated as two separate periods in applying the rules outlined below for associated companies (FA 1994 s 86(3)). After the starting rate was abolished, the accounts straddling 1 April 2006 are similarly treated as two separate accounting periods (FA 2006 ss 26(9) to (11)). The accounting period is not, however, regarded as two separate periods where the rate changes, the legislation merely requiring profits to be apportioned as necessary (TA 1988 s 8(3)).

4.   Where marginal relief applies, tax is calculated at the full rate on the corporation taxable profits, but is then reduced by:

$$(M - P) \ \text{x} \ \frac{I}{P} \ \text{x relevant fraction}$$

     where M is the upper limit for marginal relief, I is the 'basic profits', which means profits chargeable to corporation tax, and P is profits as defined for small companies' rate purposes, ie including franked investment income (see explanatory note 2).

5.   The effect of the marginal relief is to charge *all* of the corporation tax profits at a gradually increasing rate, which reaches the full tax rate at the upper limit. Looked at in terms of marginal rates, the effective tax charge on each £1 of income and/or chargeable gains between the lower and upper limits is 32.75% for the financial year 2006. This marginal rate applies where profits do not include franked investment income.

     Thus Able Ltd in part A(a) of the example, would have paid tax at 19% if profits had been £300,000, amounting to £57,000. The tax payable on its profits of £310,000 is £60,275, so the extra £10,000 of profits has resulted in extra tax of £3,275, ie 32.75%.

6.   If profits include franked investment income, the marginal rates on income and/or chargeable gains are somewhat lower.

Thus in the year to 31 March 2007:

	£	£
Profits (P):		
Income and/or chargeable gains (I)	290,000	
Franked investment income (FII)	10,000	
	300,000	
Tax on I £290,000 @ 19%		55,100
Profits (P):		
I	300,000	
FII	10,000	
	310,000	
Tax on I £300,000 @ 30%	90,000	
Less: $(1{,}500{,}000 - 310{,}000) \times \dfrac{300{,}000}{310{,}000} \times \dfrac{11}{400}$	31,669	58,331
Tax on extra £10,000 of income and/or chargeable gains (= 32.31%)		3,231

Associated companies

7. If a company has associated companies, the lower and upper limits are reduced proportionately and they are also reduced proportionately if the accounting period is less than twelve months. An associated company (including a non-resident associated company) is counted even if it is associated for only part of the accounting period. One way of avoiding the adverse effect of this rule would be to commence a new accounting period before a new associated company was acquired.

An associated company that has not carried on any trade or business throughout the accounting period is ignored. In Jowett v O'Neill & Brennan Construction Ltd 1998, an associated company that had substantial money on deposit on which it received interest was held not to be carrying on business. However, in Land Management Ltd v Fox 2002, a company which let property, made and held investments, advanced an interest-bearing loan to a connected company, as well as placing funds on deposit at the bank, was held to be carrying on a business. As far as holding companies are concerned, HMRC will disregard a non-trading holding company only if it has no assets other than shares in 51% subsidiaries, it has no income or gains other than group income that it has distributed to its own shareholders, and it has no expenses entitling it to a deduction for charges on income or management expenses (SP 5/94).

Companies are 'associated' for small companies' rate (and starting rate) purposes if one has control of the other or both are under the control of the same person or persons (TA 1988 s 13(4)). 'Control' is defined in TA 1988 s 416 – see Example 55 explanatory notes 3 and 4.

If a person or group of persons can control one company, but cannot control another company without the addition of another person or persons, the companies are not associated. If, for example, A owns 51% of company X and 40% of company Y, and B owns 20% of each of X and Y, the companies are not associated, because A controls X on his own, but controls Y only with B.

Although the rights of defined relatives are taken into account in deciding whether two companies are controlled by the same persons (see Example 55 explanatory note 4(b)(ii)), HMRC ignore relatives other than the spouse (and from 5 December 2005, civil partners – see Example 55 note 4) and minor children for small companies' rate purposes unless there is substantial commercial interdependence between the companies (HMRC concession C9). Concession C9 also indicates other circumstances in which the strict definition of 'control' will not be applied for small companies' rate purposes. The House of Lords decision in R v IRC ex parte Newfields Development Ltd (2001) confirmed that HMRC can attribute any shares held by associates to an individual irrespective of whether that individual is a shareholder in the company. For an illustration of the associated companies rules see Example 61 part A.

Corporation tax starting rate

8. A lower corporation tax starting rate applied from 1 April 2000 (TA 1988 s 13AA). The starting rate was 10% for both the years ended 31 March 2001 and 31 March 2002, but it was reduced to a 'zero rate' for the years ended 31 March 2003 to 2006 as indicated on page 49.1. The starting rate applied when profits (defined in the same way as for small companies' relief – see explanatory note 2) did not exceed £10,000 (known as the 'first relevant amount'). Thus, with the introduction of a 0% starting rate, the first £10,000 of company profits (provided they do not exceed £50,000, and there are no non-corporate distributions or associated companies) are completely exempt from tax. The starting rate was abolished from 1 April 2006.

    Where a company's profits fell between £10,000 and £50,000 (known as the 'second relevant amount'), the profits were charged at the small companies' rate, which was then reduced by:

    $$(R2 - P) \ \times \ \frac{I}{P} \ \times \text{ relevant fraction}$$

    where R2 was the second relevant amount and I and P were as defined for small companies' rate. The relevant fractions are shown on page 49.1. The marginal rates on profits falling between £10,000 and £50,000 were 22.5% for the year ended 31 March 2002 and 23.75% for the years ended 31 March 2003, 2004, 2005 and 2006. Accounting periods straddling 1 April 2002 were apportioned to determine the respective rates applicable.

    From 1 April 2006, where profits are between £1 and £300,000, the small companies' rate applies.

    The marginal relief limits are scaled down as for small companies' rate where the company has associated companies or an accounting period of less than 12 months.

Planning points

9. The effect of profits lying in the marginal tranche for small companies' rate purposes should be borne in mind, particularly:

    (i)   Where there are alternative ways of obtaining relief, such as carrying back or carrying forward losses, or transferring losses to another group company.

    (ii) When considering at what time capital expenditure qualifying for capital allowances should be incurred.

    (iii) When considering the timing of large items of revenue expenditure.

    (iv) When considering the timing of capital disposals.

    Every £1 by which profits are increased or reduced within the *marginal tranche* presently costs or saves tax at 32.75% (small companies' rate), reduced to some extent where there is franked investment income. This is shown in part B of the example in relation to the capital disposal by Baker Ltd and in part C (b) in relation to the additional profit assumed for Cakes Ltd.

Claims for relief

10. HMRC issued Statement of Practice 1/91 stating that small companies' rate and marginal relief are not applied automatically and the company must make a claim. The same applies to the starting rate. The claim may be made merely by an appropriate indication on the corporation tax computation or return, the return including a box for this purpose. Except for unincorporated associations the claim should state the number of associated companies in the accounting period, or that there are none, as the case may be.

Non-corporate distribution rate — introduction

11. The non-corporate distribution rate was abolished with effect from the 31 March 2006. These notes are given to assist with computations affecting dividends paid before 1 April 2006. To assist small businesses, the 2002 Budget introduced a rate of corporation tax of 0% on the first £10,000 of profits liable to corporation tax. No such assistance was provided to unincorporated businesses. If a

business making a profit of £14,615 was incorporated, a salary of £4,615 (the then PAYE threshold) could be paid without PAYE liability, profit would be reduced to £10,000 with the result that no corporation tax fell due, and this profit could be extracted as dividends free of tax in the hands of the basic rate taxpayer. If the business was not incorporated a liability to tax and national insurance of £2,774 arose. In addition, employees of limited companies with modest earnings are not required to make payments on account, and CIS deductions may be offset against a company's PAYE liability, with no corresponding relief for an unincorporated business. These anomalies were the driver for a spate of incorporations.

12. Since this was an initiative to assist small businesses it could not be reversed. Instead the complex measures of the non-corporate distribution rate were introduced as a corrective measure. This ensured that a minimum rate of corporation tax of 19% was charged when a company made distributions to non-company shareholders, while lower rates of corporation tax continue to apply where profits were retained. Following its abolition, all profits in the range £1–£300,000 are taxed at 19%. As the combined rate of tax and national insurance is 30% on profits in the range of £7,000–£37,000 for an unincorporated business (which also has to make payments on account), trading through a limited company still remains an attractive option.

Basic principle

13. The relevant legislation is found in FA 2004 s 28 and Sch 3.

14. Companies with profits below the lower limit for the purposes of the small companies' rate (£50,000 in the case of a non-associated company) were penalised by a higher corporation tax charge if they distributed all or any of their profits by way of dividend to individual or trust shareholders. This non-corporate distribution rate applied to dividends paid between 1 April 2004 and 31 March 2006.

The conditions for the non-corporate distribution rate, which was set at 19% for the financial years 2004 and 2005, are found in s 13AB of TA 1988. TA 1988 s 13AB(1) states that the regime is in point where:

(a) a company made a distribution to a person other than a company; and

(b) the 'underlying rate' of corporation tax which applied to the profits of that company was less than the non-corporate distribution rate.

15. Where a company falls within TA 1988 s 13AB:

(a) the amount of its taxable profits which matched the amount of the non-corporate distribution were chargeable, for the years ended 31 March 2005 and 2006, at the 19% rate; and

(b) the rest of the company's taxable profits were chargeable at the underlying rate.

16. TA 1988 s 13AB(4) introduces TA 1988 Sch A2 which supplements the section. In particular, TA 1988 8ch A2:

(a) defines the terms 'non-corporate distribution' and 'underlying rate';

(b) provides the rules for matching company profits and non-corporate distributions; and

(c) provides for non-corporate distributions to be allocated to other companies in certain circumstances.

Non-corporate distributions

17. A non-corporate distribution is any distribution made by a company to a person beneficially entitled to the distribution who is not a company (TA 1988 Sch A2.2). A distribution to a partnership is treated as if it were made directly to the partners, even if the partnership is treated as a legal person or as a body corporate in the country or territory in which it is based. Thus Scottish partnerships, for example, are dealt with in the same way as partnerships formed elsewhere in the UK.

Underlying rate

18. The underlying rate of corporation tax is found by calculating the company's liability on its profits chargeable to corporation tax (but ignoring the impact of TA 1988 s 13AB) and expressing this figure as a percentage of the taxable profits (TA 1988 Sch A2.3). Apart from any relief which is taken into account in calculating the company's corporation tax charge (eg marginal starting rate relief), other reliefs such as double taxation relief are ignored for this purpose.

A short corporation tax form 'CT600 (new)' is available on HMRC website with a layout that facilitates the calculation of the non-corporate distribution rate.

Matching rules

19. Where the total distributions made in an accounting period do *not* exceed the company's taxable profits, the non-corporate distribution rate is applied to that part which equates to the dividends paid to individuals and trustees (TA 1988 Sch A2.4).

Where the total distributions made in an accounting period *exceed* the company's taxable profits, the non-corporate distribution rate is applied to the proportion of the profits given by the following fraction (TA 1988 Sch A2.5);

$$\frac{\text{Non-corporate distributions}}{\text{Total distributions}}$$

In other words, if all the dividends go to individuals and trustees, all the profits of that period will be subject to the non-corporate distribution rate.

Allocation to other companies

20. Where a company is a member of a 51% group and its total distributions exceed its taxable profits, the excess of the non-corporate distributions over the matched figure of profits must be allocated, as far as possible, to other group members (TA 1988 Sch A2.7).

This allocation must be made in accordance with the following rules:

(a) Excess non-corporate distributions of a distributing company cannot be allocated to another company unless that other company has what are known as 'available profits' for the accounting period in question. Available profits are defined as the excess of the recipient company's taxable profits over *its* non-corporate distributions.

(b) The maximum allocation of excess non-corporate distributions is found by taking that company's available profits (see (a) above) and multiplying them by the following fraction:

$$\frac{\text{Distributing company's non-corporate distributions}}{\text{Distributing company's total distributions}}$$

Thus, if 90% of a distributing company's dividends are non-corporate distributions, the maximum allocation will be 90% of the recipient company's available profits.

(c) These two rules apart, the allocation can be made to suit the respective companies' tax preferences. It should be borne in mind that, when a distribution is allocated to a recipient company, that company is treated as if *it* had paid the dividend in question.

(d) If an allocation is not made within nine months after the end of the distributing company's accounting period, HMRC are free to determine the relevant allocation themselves (TA 1988 Sch A2.10(2))

21.   There are special provisions dealing with the situation:

(a)   where the two companies do not have coterminous year ends (TA 1988 Sch A2.8); and

(b)   where the two companies cease to be in the same 51% group but nevertheless remain under the control of the same person(s) (TA 1988 Sch A2.9).

Carry-forward of non-corporate distributions

22.   Any excess non-corporate distributions are carried forward by the company paying the dividend (TA 1988 Sch A2.13). They are then treated as if they were non-corporate distributions made in the next accounting period (in addition to any non-corporate distributions actually made in that next accounting period). Thus, if a company which only has individual shareholders made profits of £10,000 for the year ended 31 March 2005 and if it paid a dividend of £18,900 on 15 September 2004, the excess non-corporate distributions of £8,900 (£18,900 – £10,000) was deemed to have been made during the year ended 31 March 2006. The company will pay 19% corporation tax on its profits up to £8,900 for the year ended 31 March 2006.

As the rate of 19% applies to all companies with profits under £300,000 from 1 April 2006, the amount of dividend paid does not affect the rate after that date.

Your firm has acted for Captain H. Blower for many years, preparing rental income computations and personal tax returns. After a distinguished career in the forces, he started trading in executive cars in April 2005, under the name EEC (Extremely Expensive Cars). Accounts prepared by the bookkeeper, showing a profit of £40,000, have proved remarkably accurate, and give rise to a tax bill of £15,045 in respect of the car dealing business, after taking into account £20,000 of other income.

The following note of 12 December 2006 addressed to the senior partner who is on holiday, has just been found amongst the accounting records, and passed to you on 15 December 2006 to deal with.

'Jim, what a great round of golf last weekend – I'll get even with you next time!

I had a fantastic first year, not just because of good profits, but I just love driving those wonderful cars. The hard bit is parting with them when I get to the customer. I have a good customer base now, although some of them make my jaw drop. One customer bought an old Audi from me for £14,995 in cash, which was a pretty steep price, and then I saw it advertised for sale at £7,500 a week later. And then he gave me an unbelievable price on my Aston Martin! Well, it takes all types to make a world. Anyway, I feel the time has come to transfer the business to a limited company. It does not have much in the way of assets, other than the Aston Martin, but I hope to buy a transporter next summer. Apparently, I can save tax by transferring the goodwill of EEC cars to the company, and closing it after a couple of years, and pay tax at only 10%. The rental income business is paying the bills, so I could put as much money as you advise from the car business into a pension. I set up the company myself on 3 February 2005, and immediately put £5,000 into a company deposit account, so it receives trivial amounts of interest every month. I put a couple of cars deals through it on 3 November 2006 to start it trading, and then on 10 November 2006 issued a second share to my wife, who is also a director. I have just put in Form 225 to extend the year end to get extra time for filing the accounts and I am changing the name to European Executive Cars Limited. You probably do not know the answer to this, or would not know how to do it, but should my company adopt the new International Accounting Standards if it is allowed to? I would like to do so if it saved any tax. So, this will wait until you have recovered from your holiday. Have a good trip.

Rodney'

Research on Companies House website shows that the directors are indeed as stated, and that the company was formed on 3 February 2005.

(a)   Draft notes for a meeting with the captain, explaining the compliance and tax issues that the note raises for the limited company.

(b)   State what action you, as a tax adviser, need to take to comply with statutory requirements.

Disregard VAT & Excise Duty.

(a) **Notes for a meeting with Captain H. Blower**

Money laundering

The captain has been a client for many years and has met the firm's procedures for existing clients.

Company filing dates

As the captain's private company was formed on 3 February 2005, its accounting reference date (ARD) will be 28 February. For a newly formed company, the accounts must be filed within 22 months of the date of incorporation (not ten months from the ARD), that is by midnight on 3 December 2006. The accounts are therefore already overdue.

Extending the company's year end will not extend the date of filing of the accounts. Furthermore, the application must be made within the timescale for filing the accounts. As the application to extend the year end will be received after the due date for filing the accounts, it will be rejected. The company's ARD remains 28 February.

Company name

Companies House controls the use of 'sensitive words and expressions'. Examples are words such as 'British', 'International' or 'European' which may imply greater size and scope than the company actually possesses. A list can be found in the guidance section on company names in the Companies House website. The change of name application will be rejected unless the company can show that their scope of trading within Europe is sufficient to justify it.

Charge to corporation tax

For incorporations after 22 July 2004, the company must give notice to HMRC within three months of coming into charge to corporation tax, in this case of the company acquiring the deposit account which earns interest. If this has not been done, the company faces a penalty of at least £300. Notification should be made as soon as possible.

As the company receives interest, it is within the charge to corporation tax, and not dormant. The normal tax payment and tax filing deadlines apply to it. As a period of account for corporation tax cannot exceed one year, there are two periods of account: 3 February 2005 to 2 February 2006; and 3 February 2006 to 28 February 2006. Any tax on these accounting periods should have been paid by 3 November 2006 and 29 November 2006 respectively, after which interest would run, but after costs and fees it is unlikely that any tax would fall due. Although the payment deadline is nine months, the filing deadline for the tax return CT600 (of which two are required, one for each accounting period) is twelve months. A tax return is required for each period, failing which a penalty of £100 each will apply. The filing deadline is 28 February 2007 for both returns (see note 5(b)), so these penalties can easily be avoided.

Consideration should be given to shortening the current accounting period (year ending 28 February 2007). The due date for filing the accounts for this year will be 28 December 2007 (not 31 December 2007), so an application to shorten the accounting period may be made at any time up to that date. An accounting period may not be less than six months in length, so it would be possible to shorten the accounting period to 31 October 2006, which would give an eight-month period.

The amount of tax for this period will be non-existent or minimal, as trading does not commence until November 2006. The effect of shortening the non-trading accounting period to 31 October 2006 will be to place the trading activity and profits into a year ending 31 October 2007, with the due date for filing accounts of 31 August 2008, and deferring the due date of corporation tax to 31 July 2008. It would also allow the company to claim capital allowances for any capital expenditure it incurred up to 31 October 2007.

Form 42

At the time the company was formed, and when the captain received his shareholding, HMRC required a return of details of all such share issues on Form 42, giving details of the shares and the transferees. This report should have been filed by 6 July 2005, and the company could face a penalty of £300 for failure to comply. However, it is HMRC's policy to issue two warnings for failure to report before imposing penalties.

It should not be necessary to make a report of this transaction, because the revised guidance issued by HMRC in April 2006 no longer requires a report of the issue of shares to the founder before commencement of trade. This guidance clarifies that a report still needs to be made on issue to directors after commencement of trade. A report must therefore be made by 6 July 2007 of the issue shares to Mrs Blower on 10 November 2006. We recommend making the report immediately, to avoid having to remember this date, as the report may be made annually or on issue by issue basis.

Transfer of goodwill

The recognition of goodwill in the accounts at fair market value is a proper transaction for both tax and accounting purposes. Achieving an acceptable valuation is a matter of extreme uncertainty.

Because the goodwill introduced generates a liability as a credit to the director's loan account it has no effect on the value of the company, nor are there tax implications in extracting the fair value.

Goodwill can be classified into three kinds (see HMRC Manual):

(i) Personal goodwill – the trader's name and reputation.

(ii) Inherent goodwill – the location of the business.

(iii) Free goodwill – the brand name, customers, business reputation and super-profits.

Personal goodwill cannot be transferred as it is personal to the individual. Inherent goodwill goes with the property, and can only be transferred if an interest in the property is transferred. HMRC accept that free goodwill of a sole trader business may be transferred to the owner's new limited company. If EEC cars has contracts, premises, salesmen and a business separable from the proprietor himself, then there may be goodwill to transfer. If the whole process of buying, selling and delivery is done by the captain himself, this may be regarded as evidence that goodwill is not separable from him as an individual. The fact that a couple of deals can easily be put through another legal entity is unlikely to be helpful, unless there is some special reason for singling out these particular transactions.

It seems unlikely on the face of it that goodwill can be valued at a substantial figure. If it is placed on the company at over-value, HMRC may seek to treat the excess as a dividend, or even to tax it under PAYE as an inducement to take up employment.

It is possible to agree the value of goodwill with HMRC, via a post-transaction valuation check, but by definition this happens only after the transaction has been completed. The request for a post-valuation check should be made well before the deadlines for filing the personal or corporation tax returns, to allow them to reflect the agreed figure.

The value for goodwill that is agreed will be the disposal value for capital gains tax. That amount will be credited to Director's Current Account and can be withdrawn with no further tax liability. To minimise the CGT payable, the goodwill should not be transferred until EEC cars has been trading for a full two years and therefore able to take advantage of business property taper relief of 75%.

Even if goodwill is transferred, there is no tax advantage to the company. The Loan Relationship rules do not allow depreciation for tax of assets acquired from a connected person. The capital gain on disposal by the sole trader will suffer tax whether or not the company can claim relief. If the business has independent goodwill, which can later be sold, then the initial value of goodwill forms the base cost which will reduce the chargeable gain in the company on a sale of trade and assets out of the company.

Tax avoidance

The UK has no General Anti-Avoidance Rule (GAAR), and the captain may arrange his tax affairs in such a way as to minimise tax liability, subject to specific laws.

However, the client believes that he could save tax by transferring goodwill in the company, taking very low remuneration, and then liquidating the company to take advantage of the 75% business property taper relief on unquoted shares. The anti-avoidance rule of ICTA 1988 s 703 (cancellation of tax advantages in transactions in securities) is likely to allow HMRC to cancel such an advantage. There is also the danger that surplus assets in the company would cause it to lose business property status for taper relief, in which case any gain would be taxed at up to 40%.

If the issue of one share to the captain's wife is to divert income to her by means of dividends, then care must be taken with the settlements legislation (as described in 58.4). The settlements legislation involves a bounteous transfer, and in this context a high value placed on goodwill as a result of future earnings would be unhelpful. However, there is no obstacle to transferring shares in the course of ordinary family relationships, nor to the receipt of income by their owners from companies that generate profits independently of the main earner. If the transfer of the business to the limited company goes ahead, the shareholdings and a dividend policy will have to be examined with great care.

Pension payments

Pension payments are deductible against company profits in the same way as salary, and they do not bear the NIC charge. If contributions are made by the company to a personal pension scheme they will be treated as the settlement of a pecuniary liability and will be liable to tax and NIC. The premiums will then be limited to 100% of remuneration and are paid net of basic rate tax. Higher rate tax relief will be available to the individual.

If the company sets up a registered pension scheme, then contributions are not limited and are paid gross. If the amount added to the benefits of an individual exceed the annual limit, £215,000 for 2006/07, then the excess is liable to the annual allowance charge of 40%, payable by the individual. Although the company may pay exceptionally high pension contributions, it will obtain tax relief only on the amount that is expended wholly and exclusively for the purposes of the trade. This is measured in the same way as other deductions, which are also deductible only insofar as they are expended wholly and exclusively for the purposes of the trade. One informal guideline is that an amount that would have been taxed as profit on a sole trader will generally be allowable as remuneration for a controlling director. HMRC guidance on the deductibility of pension payments states that the proportion of pension to salary in the overall remuneration package will be disregarded. On this basis, it would appear that the captain's remuneration could be paid entirely as pension, and the company would still obtain a tax deduction for the remuneration.

The guidance also states that large or exceptional pension contributions are likely to attract attention, particularly if they were made on behalf of a controlling director. It is likely that such a high proportion of pension would attract scrutiny.

Other matters

As a sole trader, the captain has to make payments on account on 31 January 2007 and 31 July 2007. The payment on 31 January 2007 will therefore be £22,568, being £15,045 for 2005/06 plus the first payment on account of 2006/07. The payment on account system accentuates the fluctuations in tax liabilities for sole traders with uneven profits. The transfer of a trade to a limited company will reduce the tax liability for 2006/07. Care should be taken to make payments on account of an amount sufficient to cover the tax liability on the income retained in the captain's own name. The reduction should be claimed by completing form SA303, and submitting it to HMRC. The payment of salary subject to PAYE tends to increase the overall tax bill because of higher payroll NIC burdens, however the fact that PAYE is paid during the tax year can prevent the build-up of unmanageable tax liabilities.

The Aston Martin should not be brought into the limited company since the scale charges, which are based on its list price when new and not the advantageous price paid for it, are likely to be prohibitive. A claim of 40p per mile (25p after 10,000 miles per annum) should be made for actual business miles travelled by the captain for the company. As a sole trader, the captain receives a tax deduction on the proportion of motor expenses related to business use, and bears the actual cost of private mileage out of taxed profit.

High value dealer

As EEC does not have a clear policy of not accepting cash for sales of €15,000 or over, it is classed as a high value dealer, and should have registered with HMRC. They monitor compliance with money laundering regulations for money service businesses and high value dealers. There are requirements to observe policies on identification and record keeping, to check Bank of England 'financial targets' for MSBs, and to make reports to SOCA on suspicious transactions.

EEC should have registered as soon as practicable after commencing trade, and both it and the company must now register as soon as possible. Penalties for non-compliance with these regulations are up to £5,000 for each failure to comply, and there are clearly major failures.

Accounting Standards

UK GAAP is converging with IAS, and the two standards are treated as equal as a basis for preparing accounts for UK tax. For a company without intangibles, financial assets or derivatives, the differences are likely to be small. All companies are entitled to adopt IAS for accounting periods beginning after 1 January 2005. Our firm is of course able to prepare IAS accounts, but at present IAS has no equivalent to the Financial Reporting Standard for Smaller Entities (FRSSE), so adoption will involve additional work, and a higher level of fees.

(b) **Disclosure of Tax Avoidance Schemes (DOTAS)**

The DOTAS rules are aimed principally at marketable tax avoidance schemes, and are specifically not intended to apply to routine advice. The advice that our firm will be giving will be aimed at allowing the taxpayer to benefit from the reliefs intended by tax legislation and will not involve any abuse of artificial transactions intended to exploit loopholes in the law. The captain can be reassured that there is no requirement to make a disclosure under the DOTAS rules in respect of our advice.

To comply with the money laundering regulations, our firm has set up procedures for identifying clients, for training staff to detect signs of money laundering, for reporting to the Money Laundering Reporting Officer (MLRO) and for the MLRO to report to SOCA.

The details of the identification procedures were decided by us. The firm may have decided that it was not necessary to obtain identification for existing clients as at 22 March 2004. We should, however, obtain identification in respect of the start of EEC Ltd, as this is the start of a new type of business relationship. We should obtain identification details of the ownership of the limited company and of its directors. It may well be that the senior partner is able to identify both directors, for instance by means of home visits, but this is only valid if it is recorded. There is an obligation to retain the records of identification for five years after the business relationship ceases.

The training the firm has received in money laundering enables us to detect the likelihood of serious incidences of money laundering. It would appear that the captain's customers have bought cars for cash, both in the case of the Audi and the Aston Martin, and then resold them (accepting a loss) in exchange for bankable funds from a reputable source, a classic form of money laundering. This must be reported immediately to the MLRO, who will probably wish to make a report to SOCA as a matter of urgency.

It is an offence under the money laundering regulations to 'tip off' a suspect, subject to a maximum term of imprisonment of five years, or a fine, or both. The captain is not the suspect, but under no circumstances must any member of our staff let him, or anyone else, know that a report may be/has been made to ensure compliance with this regulation. We may continue to act for him as normal, indeed there is an obligation on us to do nothing to tip him off that our suspicions have been aroused.

The captain's failure to register as a high value dealer is a compliance failure that could potentially lead to prosecution. As such, it should be reported to the MLRO, who will probably decide to make a report – particularly since, had he registered, the HMRC guidelines supplied with the registration pack would have alerted the captain to what was going on. This makes it all the more important that he notifies HMRC voluntarily as soon as possible, before an enquiry is opened in response to information from SOCA.

Explanatory Notes

Company formation

1.   A company is formed by registration with Companies House, website http://www.companieshouse.gov.uk/ from whom full details and statutory forms may be downloaded.

A new company must:

- file a Memorandum and Articles of Association, showing its objects and authorised share capital;

- give names, addresses and other details of its directors, company secretary and members;

- specify a registered office. The registered office of the company will be either in England and Wales, or in Scotland, and the country cannot subsequently be changed.

Details of limited companies, and their accounts, are placed in the public domain by filing with Companies House, and can be obtained on payment of a fee. There are procedures and forms for changing the details, and an annual return confirming that details remain unchanged must be filed each year. Many forms, documents and returns can be filed on-line.

A new company comes into existence when the Registrar of Companies issues a certificate of incorporation, which may be achieved within 24 hours for a private company. There are a number of restrictions on names.

The types of private company available are:

- limited by shares;

- limited by guarantee; or,

- unlimited.

These companies may have only one member, although both a director and a company secretary are required.

A public limited company (PLC) has a higher level of regulation commensurate with access to financial markets. It must have at least two members, two directors, and a qualified company secretary. The minimum issued share capital is £50,000.

A Societas Europeae (SE), is a European company. These have been available since 8 October 2004, but very few have been formed in UK. They have regulations similar to those of the PLC, and a special tax regime to facilitate trading within Europe. They may be formed by merger, as a holding company or as a subsidiary, and can also be formed by a PLC transforming into an SE. There are requirements for worker participation.

Accounting reference date

2.   The company must specify its accounting reference date, which must not exceed 18 months, nor be shorter than six months. As the accounting period for corporation tax may not exceed one year, longer periods of account may have to be split.

An accounting reference date may not be extended more than once in every five years unless specific circumstances apply.

Companies House filing deadlines

3.   Under company law, public companies must normally file accounts with the Registrar of Companies not later than seven months after the end of the accounting period, the time limit for private limited companies being ten months. There are automatic penalties for late filing, the penalties for public companies ranging from £500 if accounts are up to three months late, to £5,000 if accounts are more than twelve months late, and for private companies from £100 to £1,000. The Companies Registry interpretation of seven or ten months is that the accounts are due by the same day of the month as that in which the company's account ends, eg accounts to 28 February 2007 should be filed by 28 September/28 December 2007.

Duty to give notice of coming within charge to corporation tax

4.   Under FA 2004 s 55, a company must give notice to HMRC of the start of its first accounting period, or of a period in which it becomes chargeable to corporation tax after a period of dormancy. The notice must specify the date the accounting period began, and the following.

(a)   the company's name and its registered number;

(b)   the address of the company's registered office;

(c)   the address of the company's principal place of business;

(d)   the nature of the business being carried on by the company;

(e)   the date to which the company intends to prepare accounts;

(f)   the full name and home address of each of the directors of the company;

(g)   if the company has taken over any business, the name and address of that former business and, the name and address of the person from whom it was acquired.

Notice must be given within three months of coming into charge, subject to a penalty of £300.

This duty applies to companies only, not to partnerships or unincorporated associations.

Corporation tax self-assessment

5.   Corporation tax is administered on the self-assessment system, and a guide to HMRC's views is found at http://www.hmrc.gov.uk/ctsa/index.htm.

The self-assessment provisions are contained in FA 1998 s 117 and Sch 18, with minor and consequential amendments in Schedule 19 and also in FA 1999 Sch 11 and FA 2001 Sch 29. The provisions relating to payment dates and interest are in TMA 1970 ss 59D, 59DA, 59E, 87 and 87A, and TA 1988 ss 826, 826A.

Returns for corporation tax must be made on prescribed forms within time limits, and must be accompanied by accounts and computations. A company only satisfies its filing obligation when it delivers the completed corporation tax return form (and relevant supplementary pages) together with a copy of its accounts and tax computations.

The most important supplementary pages are:

CT600A	For loans made to participators of close companies.
CT600B	For tax liabilities of controlled foreign companies.
CT600C	For claims to and surrenders of group and consortium relief.
CT600E	Charities and Community Amateur Sports Clubs.
CT600G	Corporate Venturing Scheme.
CT600J	Disclosure of tax avoidance schemes.

Corporation tax returns may be filed on-line, in which case it is possible to view the filing and payment status on-line.

The return must be made on the standard form CT600, or for small companies, may be made on the short form if it contains boxes for all the entries that the company requires. It does not contain boxes for group transactions of CFCs, but will be sufficient for many small standalone companies trading within the UK.

The company tax return CT600 contains a self-assessment of the amount of tax payable, including the tax on loans or advances by close companies' participators and tax relating to controlled foreign companies. This self-assessment creates the charge to tax.

Filing dates

6.   HMRC issue a notice to deliver a corporation tax return (CT603) between three and seven weeks after the end of the return period. This is accompanied by a return Form (CT600), unless the company's agents use an approved substitute form. (Tax agents receive a monthly listing (CT603A list) detailing their client companies to whom a CT603 has been sent.) The CT603 notice should be for the period that HMRC believes to be an accounting period of the company. Where the period specified in the notice does not correspond with the company's accounting period, a return is usually required for any period that ends within the specified notice period.

Dormant companies do not usually receive a notice to complete a corporation tax return, but if they do, then technically a nil return is required. The company should write to inform the inspector that the company is dormant and ask whether the return is required. It is important not to ignore the notice, otherwise penalties may arise.

A notice to deliver a corporation tax return might specify a period that does not coincide with the company's accounting period. If so, the company has to make a return for any accounting period(s) ending in the specified period. If a period of account started but none ended within the specified period, a nil return has to be made for the period up to the date the period of account started. If the specified period is less than twelve months and falls wholly within an accounting period of the company, a return does not have to be made but the inspector should be notified. If the company is outside the scope of corporation tax throughout the specified period (eg because it is non-resident and not trading in the UK, or because it is dormant), a nil return should be filed.

The return must usually be filed within one year of the end of the accounting period for corporation tax, failing which penalties will be incurred.

If a *period of account* exceeds twelve months but does not exceed 18 months, the due date for filing the returns for the accounting periods within that period of account is twelve months from the end of the period of account, if later than the normal due date. If a period of account exceeds 18 months, the due date is 30 months after the beginning of the account, or the normal due date if later. For example, if accounts are made up for the 18 months from 1 October 2004 to 31 March 2006, the returns for the accounting periods to 30 September 2005 and 31 March 2006 are both due by 31 March 2007. If the accounts were made up instead for the 21 months from 1 October 2004 to 30 June 2006, the return for the accounting period to 30 September 2005 would still be due by 31 March 2007 (30 months after the start of the account). The return for the nine months to 30 June 2006 would be due by 30 June 2007 (twelve months after the end of the account).

A flat rate penalty of £100 is charged if the return is no more than three months late, and £200 if more than three months, but these rise to £500 and £1,000 if the returns are late for more than three accounting periods in a row.

In addition, if the company does not file a return within 18 months of the end of the accounting period and has not paid the right amount of tax, a tax related penalty of 10% is imposed. This rises to 20% if the return is late by 24 months or more.

Payment of tax

7.   Companies with profits below the small companies' rate upper limit (£1,500,000) pay corporation tax nine months and one day after the end of the accounting period (TMA 1970 s 59D).

Large companies (for this purpose meaning companies with profits at or above the upper limit for small companies' relief, ie £1.5 million) are required to pay their corporation tax by equal quarterly instalments (under SI 1998/3175 issued under TMA 1970 s 59E). The upper limit is reduced pro rata where there are associated companies and for accounting periods of less than twelve months – see Example 48.

Claims and elections

8. General provisions on claims are in FA 1998 Sch 18 paras 9, 10 and Part VII. All claims must be for a specified amount and must be made where possible in a return or amendment to a return, although there is an overall time limit for most claims of six years from the end of the accounting period. Claims for group relief (Part VIII) and capital allowances (Part IX) can only be made in a return or amendment to a return. Where it is not possible to make claims on a return the provisions of TMA 1970 Sch lA apply (see Example 42).

   Unless HMRC otherwise allows, the time limit for capital allowances claims is the latest of twelve months after the filing date for the return, 30 days after the completion of a HMRC enquiry, 30 days after the issue of a HMRC amendment following an enquiry, and 30 days after the date when any appeal against such an amendment is finally determined. See Example 63 explanatory note 8 regarding group relief claims.

HMRC corrections and taxpayer amendments

9. HMRC have nine months from the date a return is received to correct obvious errors in the return, and companies can make amendments within a year from the filing date. If the return is selected for further enquiry, amendments within the permitted twelve-month period will not restrict the scope of the enquiry but may be taken into account in the enquiry. If an amendment affects the tax payable for the current or another period, or by another company, it will not take effect unless and until it is incorporated in the closure notice issued to the company at the end of the enquiry (see note 12).

HMRC enquiries

10. Under FA 1998 Sch 18.24, unless a CT600 return is filed late, HMRC must initiate an enquiry into the return by the first anniversary of the filing date, ie within two years after the end of the relevant accounting period. Thus, for a period ending on 31 December 2006, the filing date is 31 December 2007 and the enquiry window closes on 31 December 2008. See Example 45 explanatory note 24 regarding referring questions to the Special Commissioners during an enquiry, and see Example 42 regarding HMRC enquiries into claims made separately from the return.

Keeping records

11. Companies are required to keep sufficient records to make a correct and complete return. These records must be kept for six years from the end of the accounting period, and there is a penalty of up to £3,000 per accounting period for failing to comply.

   Submitted CT600 returns are subject to a detailed checking system. HMRC are likely to start an enquiry where there is a potential risk of the return being incorrect, or where additional information is needed to satisfy them that the tax treatment adopted is correct. A small number of enquiries are made on a random basis. An enquiry may either be an aspect enquiry raising one or more specific queries in relation to the return, or it may be a full enquiry including a comprehensive review of the accounts and underlying records. HMRC have wide powers to request further information, documents etc for the purpose of their enquiry.

   HMRC Code of Practice 14 (COP 14) provides useful information about HMRC's approach to enquiries under CTSA. For example, it states that where relevant records are required for examination by HMRC they should be provided within a reasonable time. A request may be made to examine them at the company's premises, as this may be more convenient. Similarly, HMRC may request a meeting with relevant officers or employees of the company and their professional adviser. The company may be asked to comment on HMRC's notes of the meeting (noting any disagreement) and sign them.

A company may be invited to make a payment on account during the enquiry process to mitigate its potential interest exposure, although it is not legally obliged to pay any additional tax until HMRC invite it to amend its self-assessment.

A closure notice will be issued by HMRC when they conclude their enquiry, together with their findings. HMRC undertake to agree their findings with the company before inviting an amended return in accordance with their proposed adjustments. If the company disagrees and does not amend the return within the relevant 30-day window, HMRC make their own amendments, which can then be subject to the appeals process. (If the return or an amendment to it is made after the due date, the enquiry window runs from a year from the time the return or amendment is delivered plus the period to the next quarter day, ie the next 31 January, 30 April, 31 July or 31 October.) If an enquiry is not opened within the time limit, the tax as calculated will normally stand unless there is a HMRC 'discovery assessment' (see note 15 below).

Interest and penalties regarding overdue and overpaid tax

12.   Interest on overdue and overpaid corporation tax (including tax on close company loans to participators) is deductible/taxable as non-trading interest under the 'loan relationships' provisions (see Example 62). If interest on overpaid tax is received or receivable by a company in liquidation in its final accounting period, however, the interest is not included in taxable profits if it does not exceed £2,000. The rates of interest are adjusted to reflect the fact that the interest is taken into account in computing taxable profits, but the rate on underpaid tax is still much higher than that on overpaid tax.

It is understood that regardless of when leap years occur HMRC use a denominator of 366 in all calculations of interest on overdue tax and a denominator of 365 for interest on overpaid tax, which in each case gives a slight benefit to the taxpayer company.

HMRC determinations and assessments

13.   As with income tax self-assessment, HMRC are able to determine the tax payable in the absence of a return, and this will count as a self-assessment until superseded by an actual self-assessment. Note that losses and other negative amounts are subject to self-assessment and are thus incorporated within the figure of tax payable under HMRC determination. HMRC may still make discovery assessments under the self-assessment regime (FA 1998 Sch 18.41). They may also make 'discovery determinations' where a return incorrectly states an amount that affects another period or another company, see 43.4.

Penalties

14.   The corporation tax self-assessment legislation levies penalties for failing to notify liability, failing to deliver a return and fraudulently or negligently delivering incorrect returns. Companies under HMRC enquiry will also be subject to penalties for failing to produce documents.

The penalty for failing to notify the HMRC where no notice to deliver a return is received is an amount not exceeding the corporation tax remaining unpaid after twelve months (FA 1998 Sch 18.2). Where a company is unable to supply final figures by the due date, 'best estimates' may be used, providing the basis of the estimates is stated when the return is submitted, and providing the correct figures are supplied as soon as they are available. An incorrect return or late filing penalty would then not normally be charged.

Form 42 – employment-related securities – reportable events

15.   Finance Act 2003 Sch 22 introduced rules requiring a report to be made to HMRC of securities issued in connection with employment. These details must to be returned on Form 42 or a suitable alternative.

The circumstances under which a report is required have been the source of much confusion. At the time the legislation was originally enacted, it was thought to affect complex unapproved share schemes, in which employees were remunerated by shares or securities. HMRC then issued guidance making it apparent that, in their view, the reporting requirement was of far wider scope, and affected the routine transactions of ordinary trading companies, flat management companies, and clubs that issue shares. The regulations apply to all companies including those with simple shareholding structures.

Revised guidance was issued in April 2006 (available from HMRC website at www.hmrc.gov.uk), reducing the number of situations in which a report was required, particularly in the case where founder shareholders acquire shares from a formation agent.

Reportable events must be notified to HMRC, on Form 42, by 6 July following the year in which the securities were issued, failing which penalties commencing at £300 per reportable event per employee may be charged.

Reportable events include acquisitions, transfers and disposals of securities, rights issues or alteration in the values and rights of securities. Securities include shares, debentures, loan stock, bonds, certificates of deposit, warrants, futures, units in collective investment schemes and rights under contracts for differences, all in connection with employment.

A report of the issue of such securities is required unless one of the exemptions applies. It is emphasised that Form 42 is concerned with the transfer of shares in connection with employment. Transfers of shares in the normal course of domestic, family or personal relationships do not have to be reported. However, it is up to the transferor to determine whether the transfer is being made for purely personal reasons, and to be able to demonstrate this. HMRC specifically states that it will accept that shares passing to children involved in the business will be considered as being made in the normal course of family relationships. However, if any element of remuneration is shown to be present, a report would be required (and the transfer would be liable to income tax and national insurance).

For companies incorporated in the year ended 5 April 2006, the transfer of founder shares to the owners of the new company need not be reported provided:

- all the initial shares are obtained at nominal value; and

- the shares are the only form of security that is obtained; and

- their shares are not acquired by reason of another employment; and

- the shares are acquired by a person who to be a director of the company, or by somebody with a family relationship with the director (provided the transfer is in the normal course of family relationships, rather than by reason of employment).

Similarly, if prospective directors or other family members acquire additional shares before trading commences, Form 42 will not be required. However, if additional shares are issued after the company commences trading, then Form 42 is required but only for the shares issued after commencement of trade.

A report is only required if a reportable event occurs in the tax year, unless HMRC has issued a Form 42 return, in which case it must be filed whether there was a reportable event or not. A Form 42 report is not required for HMRC approved share schemes and options, as these have their own specific reporting requirements. For Enterprise Management Incentives (EMI), the grant of options up to the EMI limit of £100,000 will be reported on a special scheme form, while the excess over £100,000 must be reported on Form 42.

The requirement affects not just current employees but directors and office holders, prospective employees, and former employees where the event was within seven years of the ex-employee leaving.

A separate Form 42 may be submitted for each reportable event, or all reportable events for the year may be submitted on a single Form 42 by 6 July. For companies incorporated in the year ended 5 April 2005 that have issued only unrestricted shares, a simplified form (Form 42 (2005) (New Companies)) is available on HMRC's website.

For unrestricted shares, the information required is the name of the employee, the employer's name, the description of the shares, date of transfer, number of shares, market value, price and whether PAYE was applied.

It is important to consider Form 42 reporting requirements whenever a security is transferred.

Goodwill on incorporation

16. The goodwill attaching to a business at the date of incorporation may have substantial tax consequences for capital gains tax, income tax, and corporation tax, in the year of incorporation and in subsequent years.

Where a sole trader or partner disposes of goodwill to a company that they control, the transfer is one between connected persons, so takes place at market value for tax purposes. A capital gain arises in this case for the individual (which may be sheltered by reliefs, such as taper relief (see Example 89), while an intangible asset and director's loan account will be established in the company's records. The transfer of goodwill is exempt for stamp duty purposes.

The key difficulty is establishing the value of goodwill and to what it is attributable. In view of the reliefs available, it is desirable to place as high a value as can be justified on goodwill, but excess valuation may be challenged by HMRC. The overvalue may give rise to income tax, national insurance contributions, or corporation tax, depending on the circumstances.

Where, as in the case of the skills of individual tradesman, the goodwill is inseparable from the individual, it is not capable of being transferred to the company. It is essential to demonstrate that goodwill attaches to the business rather than the owner, using the evidence of location of business premises, an organisation separate from the owner, brands, contracts or customer lists.

The disposal of goodwill must be reported in the capital gains tax section of the individual's self-assessment return, where it may well qualify for 75% taper relief, and where the annual exemption of £8,800 may be available. As a result, a valuation of up to £35,200 will potentially incur no tax liability.

The company's balance sheet will show an intangible asset but, because it was acquired from the connected person, no tax relief will apply to amortisation. The company may pay for the goodwill, but often will credit its value to a director's loan account. The cost recorded for goodwill can in future be used as the base cost in the event of sale of the trade, while the corresponding director's loan may provide a means of extracting funds without incurring a tax liability.

Sale of goodwill at overvalue

17. HMRC offers a free post-transaction value check service, but as its name implies it can only be requested after the event.

If it proves that goodwill was transferred at overvalue, under exceptional circumstances it is possible to unwind the transaction, and have the individual repay the company or reduce the directors' loan account. This is only possible where goodwill was formally valued by a named qualified valuer, who was given adequate information. If the reduction in the loan account causes it to become overdrawn, income tax will be due on the benefit, and tax may become payable under ICTA 1988 s 419. In most cases it is likely to give rise to a tax charge, either as income of employment, or as a distribution.

If excess goodwill is shown to be an inducement for the individual to join the company, or to represent payment for future services, it will be treated as income of employment under ITEPA 2003 s 62. The company is required to account for income tax and national insurance contributions under PAYE regulations, failing which penalties and interest will apply. It may, under certain circumstances, represent a benefit reportable on Form PllD.

Where there is no evidence that the excess goodwill represents earnings from employment, particularly when transferred before the company commences trade, the excess will be treated as a distribution. If the distribution does not cause the individual to exceed the higher rate band, no further tax will arise on the individual.

The money laundering regulations – tax practitioners

18. Money laundering regulations, which had long applied to banks and other financial institutions, were extended to accountancy and tax advice activities on 1 March 2004. Interim guidance for accountants was issued by the Consultative Committee of Accountancy Bodies (CCAB) in March 2004 to assist in complying with the requirements of the Proceeds of Crime Act 2002 and the Money Laundering Regulations 2003.

The purpose of the regulations is to require relevant businesses to make reports to SOCA of any knowledge or suspicions of money laundering activity. However, this is limited to knowledge or suspicions acquired in the course of business or employment, not knowledge acquired through personal social connections.

Firms affected must appoint an individual as the money laundering reporting officer (MLRO) to receive money laundering reports from staff, and to make reports to SOCA. All staff must be trained in the recognition and reporting of potential money laundering transactions, and how to verify the identity of new clients. The firm must establish appropriate internal procedures to detect and prevent money laundering. There are a number of other important requirements, and significant criminal penalties for principals and employees for breaching money laundering regulations, which can be found in the CCAB guidance. This can be downloaded from www.ccab.org.uk.

Firms, and their staff, are affected by money laundering regulations if they provide accountancy services, insolvency services, tax advice, or the services of formation or management of a company. This applies as much to unqualified accountants and tax advisers as to qualified practitioners, applies outside the UK as well as within the UK, and applies to accountants generally, not just within the profession.

The form of identification to be obtained is not specified by the Act, but is determined by the firm's own policies via a risk-based approach. The guidance given them by the Joint Money Laundering Steering Group (originally intended for banking and financial services), is often followed. The offences to be reported include any criminal activity giving rise to proceeds, and in particular are not limited to terrorism or drug dealing. The proceeds of crime, termed criminal property, include the proceeds of tax evasion, bribery, or costs saved by failure to comply with regulatory requirements (where the failure to comply is a criminal offence). There is no de minimis limit for the value of the proceeds of crime to be reported, so even the smallest transactions may require a report. Reports must be made as soon as is reasonably possible to SOCA on a suspicious activity reports (SAR), and can be made online at www.soca.gov.uk/financialIntel/index.html. The details to be reported are specified on this site.

A limited intelligence value report (LIVR) may be made where, individually, there is likely to be limited intelligence value in the report (the report is required in case correlation of many such reports yields useful information). A LIVR is never appropriate for serious crimes such as terrorism or drugs offences, but might be used for small discrepancies arising from mistakes rather than dishonest behaviour, or where the identity of the criminal is not known.

Accountants and tax advisers in practice are expected to make reports on clients in circumstances where failure to comply with tax regulations has led to underpayment of tax or late payment. HMRC indicates that around a fifth of SARs received identify a new subject of interest and a quarter lead to new enquiries in relation to direct taxation matters.

Legal privilege

19. In a relatively narrow range of circumstances, such as litigation or giving legal advice where making a report to SOCA would compromise the client's rights to legal privilege, qualified accountants have the same legal privilege as the legal profession allowing them to claim protection from reporting suspicious transactions. This applies only to money laundering, not offences under the Terrorism Act 2000.

Money laundering – HMRC responsibilities

20.   HMRC have the responsibility for administering the money laundering regulations in respect of:

  •   money service businesses;

  •   high value dealers.

These businesses have similar obligations to make reports of suspicious dealings under the Money Laundering Regulations 2003 as described above, but in addition are required to register with HMRC. Failure to register or to comply with money laundering regulations may lead to prosecution by HMRC, or penalties of up to £5,000. Businesses must register as soon as possible on commencing the above activities, which need not be their sole or main activities.

A money service business (MSB) is a business that carries out the activities of:

  •   bureau de change; or

  •   transferring a customer's money (money transmission); or

  •   third party cheque cashing.

Banks and businesses regulated by the FSA do not need to be registered under the MSB scheme.

The registration number issued to the MSB forms part of its identity, which it will use in its dealings with banks and other MSBs. A register of all businesses not covered by the FSA register will be created. It will cover bureaux de change, money transmitters and third party cheque cashers.

A high value dealer (HVD) is any business that does not have a clear policy of not accepting payments over €15,000 per transaction in cash.

While the obligations for these businesses are fundamentally the same as those for tax advisers, HMRC's website has further details of what it expects of these businesses. It summarises the procedure that is to be put in place by the acronym CATCH which stands for:

  •   Control your business by having anti money laundering systems in place;

  •   Appoint a nominated officer;

  •   Train your staff;

  •   Confirm the identity of your customers; and

  •   Hold all records for at least five years.

HMRC may visit these businesses to monitor compliance.

HMRC has provided additional guidance on identification, which is required for each transaction over €15,000, or at the start of a regular basis of trading. This is a combination of primary identification such as passport, identity card or for driving licence and secondary identification, such as credit cards, bank statements, utility bills. In addition, MSB's are required to check the Bank of England website to ensure their customers are not listed as financial targets.

The new regime is designed to help ensure businesses comply with their responsibilities under anti-money laundering law. All money service businesses (MSBs) other than those already regulated by the Financial Services Authority (FSA) will be required to register with Customs and Excise. HMRC have the power to inspect premises, records and currency of MSBs to ensure that such businesses understand their responsibilities and are complying with the law.

Countering tax avoidance

21.   There is no general anti-avoidance rule in the UK although a consultative document on GAAR was published in 1998. Historically, taxpayers have been entitled to rely on a strict interpretation of tax law to minimise their taxes, and professional advisers have been entitled to assist them in doing so.

This principle has been changed by the decision of the European Court of Justice on 21 February 2006 concerning a VAT repayment claimed by the Halifax bank, which had set up a separate company to maximise a claim to VAT on the construction of a call centre. The court confirmed that it was not permissible to exploit the VAT provisions abusively, but instead that the purpose of the legislation had to be established and taken into account. As this decision affects indirect taxes, its application to direct taxes is yet to be clarified.

In the Halifax case, however, the court stated that the fact that a company was trying to minimise tax was not in itself a sufficient reason to look through the arrangements. In an opinion dated 2 May 2006, an advocate general of the European Court of Justice gave the opinion that establishing a subsidiary in another EC state so as to take advantage of a more favourable tax regime was legitimate, and anti-avoidance provisions such as the UK's CFC rules should be targeted at 'wholly artificial arrangements'.

There are many measures for non-compliance with existing tax law, which are covered in context throughout this publication. The government's and HMRC's anti-avoidance campaign is concerned with situations where weaknesses or anomalies in the law are exploited abusively to give unintended advantages, particularly where artificial transactions are concerned.

Tax avoidance is addressed in two main ways:

- specific anti-avoidance rules;

- the disclosure of tax avoidance schemes (DOTAS).

Specific anti-avoidance rules

22. There are a very large number of specific anti-avoidance provisions throughout tax legislation, designed to prevent exploitation of specific rules to give unintended tax advantages. It is not possible to give a comprehensive list, but examples include: the dividend stripping rules; the transfer pricing rules; rules concerning transactions in land; and the controlled foreign companies (CFC) rules.

Recently introduced rules include Transactions involving Arbitrage (F(No 2)A 2005), Corporate Capital Losses and Sale of Lessor Companies (both FA 2006). These involve entering into transactions that do not necessarily have any commercial purpose independent of tax minimisation.

FA 2006 introduced retroactive legislation effective from 2 December 2004 against avoidance using employment-related securities. This amends the detail of existing legislation whose intention was already clear.

Tax avoidance seeks to remain within the existing law, while manipulating or abusing it to obtain tax advantages that it was not intended to confer, and often involves artificial transactions or entities whose main purpose is to obtain tax advantages. Because anti-avoidance law is intended to ensure that existing law achieves its purpose, it may be brought to bear on transactions carried out for purely commercial reasons, or on persons who believed they were complying fully with the law.

Avoidance and anti-avoidance gives rise to considerable uncertainty for many taxpayers who are not seeking to abuse the tax system.

In the Garnet v Jones case, the company was acting in a way that most of the tax and accountancy profession believed to be fully compliant with tax law. HMRC used the anti-avoidance provision of s 660A, originally dating back to the 1930s, to cancel the tax advantage obtained by paying dividends. See Example 58 for comments on the Garnet v Jones case.

Taxpayers are advised to bear anti-avoidance legislation in mind, to ensure that they do not fall foul of it even with structures or transactions that have no tax avoidance purpose. For example, in the field of personal taxes, the setting up of any trust is likely to have tax consequences, and gifts made to assist relatives may well fall foul of the pre-owned assets charge.

Disclosure of Tax Avoidance Schemes (DOTAS)

23. The Disclosure of Tax Avoidance Schemes rules aim to deter the use of schemes that are abusive or involve artificial transactions, or exploit loopholes that parliament did not intend, by allowing HMRC to detect and close them down more quickly, perhaps with retrospective effect.

    The provisions are not intended to prevent tax advisers from advising their clients of the tax reliefs intended by legislation, nor to prevent taxpayers minimising their taxes within the framework of the tax legislation, provided that by sticking to the letter of the law they are not abusing the purpose of the law.

    The Disclosure of Tax Avoidance Schemes regime began on 1 August 2004, when it was limited to financial products and arrangements connected with employment. From 1 August 2006, any arrangements providing a tax advantage in income tax, corporation tax or capital gains tax may need to be disclosed as tax avoidance schemes.

    The definition of arrangements and of tax advantage is drawn very widely, but a number of 'hallmarks' limit the number of schemes that need to be disclosed. The hallmarks for a promoter's scheme, which are found in The Tax Avoidance Schemes (Prescribed Descriptions of Arrangements) Regulations 2006 (SI 2006/1543), are as follows.

    * Hallmark 1(a): Confidentiality from other promoters.

    * Hallmark 1(b): Confidentiality from HMRC.

    * Hallmark 3: Premium fee.

    * Hallmark 4: Off-market terms (involving financial products).

    * Hallmark 5: Standardised tax products.

    * Hallmark 6: Loss schemes.

    * Hallmark 7: Leasing arrangements.

    If arrangements exist that provided tax advantage, and one or any of these hallmarks apply, the promoter must notify HMRC within five days of the scheme becoming available. The scheme will be issued with an eight-digit reference number, which the users must show on their tax returns. If the scheme is not disclosed by the promoter, for example if the promoter is offshore, the user must make the disclosure within 30 days. The maximum penalty for initial failure to disclose is £5,000, plus £600 per day thereafter.

    Schemes meeting the hallmark tests may not constitute avoidance, but might still need to be disclosed. HMRC guidance 'Disclosure of Tax Avoidance Schemes (Income Tax, Corporation Tax, Capital Gains Tax and Stamp Duty Land Tax)'. The main guidance states that it may be necessary to disclose schemes that HMRC is already aware of, or schemes that are not considered as avoidance.

    The advice provided to the client in this example is in reaction to specific circumstances, and is not a scheme. It does not cause any hallmarks to apply, and is therefore not notifiable. The legislation is aimed at schemes of far wider scope, and larger potential tax saving.

    The rules for an in-house scheme are different, with the following hallmarks.

    * Hallmark 2: Confidentiality from HMRC.

    * Hallmark 3: Premium fee.

    * Hallmark 7: Leasing arrangements.

    An in-house scheme is only notifiable if it is intended to give a tax advantage to a business that is not a small or medium-sized enterprise.

    Additional exemptions from disclosure apply to the leasing hallmark, one of which is that schemes providing an advantage to SMEs need not be disclosed.

International information and gathering powers

24. FA 2006 sections 174–177 provide for the cancellation of existing agreements to exchange information with overseas tax authorities, and replace them with arrangements giving increased powers to collect and disclose information. In addition, it provides for the possibility of recovery of foreign tax debts through UK courts, and therefore the recovery of UK tax debts in foreign courts.

These powers will probably have a greater effect on tax fraud rather than tax avoidance. Furthermore, in 2006, HMRC obtained disclosure orders against Barclays bank requiring them to disclose details of all offshore accounts held by customers with UK addresses and details of holders of credit cards linked to offshore accounts. It is thought that other banks will be targeted. This move does not change existing law, but has the effect of policing it more stringently.

Accounting Standards, tax law and IAS

25. The relationship between accounting practice and law is stated in FA 1998 s 42: 'the profits of the trade, profession or vocation must be computed in accordance with generally accepted accounting practice subject to any adjustment required or authorised by law . . .'

Generally Accepted Accounting Practice (GAAP) is defined in FA 2004 s 50 as follows: 'UK generally accepted accounting practice means generally accepted accounting practice with respect to accounts of UK companies (other than IAS accounts) that are intended to give a true and fair view . . .' The same section specifies that this definition applies to individuals, non-UK companies and entities other than companies.

HMRC expect GAAP to be applied in the computation of all business profits. For example, they clearly expect UITF 40 to be applied in the case of all companies whether adopting the FRSSE or not, and all other entities. In this respect IAS is as acceptable as UK GAAP.

As GAAP is increasingly codified and becoming more uniform, there is a trend to align profits for tax with accounting profits. Furthermore, it is the intention of the ASB to align UK GAAP with IAS, which is already similar to it in many respects. The International Accounting Standards Board (IASB) is working with the US FASB on the global convergence of accounting standards. The European commission has adopted most international accounting standards, with some exceptions from IAS 39. FA 2004 s 50 makes it clear that accounts will be regarded as complying with generally accepted accounting practice whether full IAS standards, or EEC approved standards, are used.

European law required listed companies to use IAS for accounting periods commencing on or after 1 January 2005 for the consolidated accounts. However, all UK companies and limited liability partnerships may adopt IAS for their consolidated and individual accounts from that date. Listed companies will have to adopt IAS under European law, larger companies may choose to adopt IAS, while other companies will continue to comply with GAAP, which is actively being aligned with IAS.

It is the intention of the legislation that companies drawing up their accounts under either set of standards should receive broadly equivalent tax treatment. This will of course be increasingly achieved as IAS and GAAP converge in the next few years.

While it is government policy to align tax and accounting profits, there will continue to be departures from the accounting rules, whether from IAS-based accounts or from UK GAAP. There are a great many departures, arising from public policy, in the areas of anti-avoidance, the distinctions between capital and revenue, fiscal incentives or valuation rules. Examples are given in context throughout the publication, and particularly in Example 48.

Securitisation companies regime

26. A systematic departure from taxing profit as reported by use of IAS was made in the case of securitisation companies.

Securitisation companies typically involve financial assets generating an income stream, matched by liabilities by which these assets were acquired. For example, a batch of commercial property mortgages generating rents receivable may be transferred to a securitisation company, which funds the purchase price by issuing marketable bonds, allowing the transfer or company to raise further borrowings for more productive assets. The margin between the income receivable and the costs of funding the borrowings may be very fine.

Under IAS, there is a danger that the financial assets would be valued by fair value accounting, while the corresponding funding liabilities would be valued at amortised cost. This could produce unpredictable tax liabilities that the company would have no means of paying out of its narrow margin. This might well have the effect of destabilising a major source of finance.

Although many of these companies would be required to adopt IAS Finance Act 2006 s 101 provides that these companies will be taxed on the basis that UK GAAP still applies. The draft regulations 'The Taxation of Securitisation Companies Regulations 2006' envisage that, for accounting periods commencing on or after 1 January 2007, these companies will be taxed effectively on their small amount of retained profits.

51.1 CORPORATION TAX COMPUTATION – 18-MONTH ACCOUNT, RESEARCH & DEVELOPMENT TAX RELIEF, SHADOW ACT, COLLECTION OF INCOME TAX FROM COMPANIES

Tweeters Ltd has traded as a manufacturer of specialist hi-fi speakers since 1968 and has no associated companies. Accounts have previously always been prepared for years ended 31 March. The following information relates to the period of account for eighteen months ended 30 September 2006.

(a) Trading profits as adjusted for tax purposes but *before* making any adjustment for capital allowances are summarised as follows:

	£
Trading profits after finance costs	2,371,770
Add: Depreciation	120,000
Disallowable legal costs	5,780
Charitable donations to CAFOD (see (e) below)	36,000
Entertaining	15,250
	2,548,800
Less: Investment income	(77,600)
Additional 50% on research and development expenditure of £120,000	(60,000)
Adjusted trading profits before capital allowances	2,411,200

As research and development (R&D) expenditure of £120,000 (all eligible under FA 2000 Sch 20) has been written off in the period, a further £60,000 deduction has been made to bring the overall R&D tax credit up to 150% of the qualifying R&D expenditure. Tweeters Ltd qualifies as a medium-sized company for Sch 20 purposes.

(b) The written down value of the plant and machinery allowances pool at 31 March 2005 was £300,000. On 21 September 2005 plant which had cost £100,000 in February 1989 was sold for £196,800 and plant costing £70,000 was acquired on 10 September 2006. Tweeters Ltd qualifies as a medium-sized company for Companies Act purposes.

(c) Investment income was:

			£
(i)	Bank deposit interest received		
	30 June 2005	3,000	
	31 December 2005	2,500	
	30 June 2006	5,500	11,000
(ii)	Building society interest received 1 January 2006		2,000
(iii)	Gross debenture interest receivable from Dovedale plc (£100,000 at 8.4% per annum) (received half yearly on 1 March and 1 September)		12,600
(iv)	Dividends from UK companies		
	May 2005 (27,000 + tax cr 3,000)	30,000	
	May 2006 (18,000 + tax cr 2,000)	20,000	50,000

The opening and closing accruals in respect of (i) to (iii) were as follows:

	At 1.4.05 £	At 30.9.06 £
Bank interest	1,100	3,000
Building society interest	1,400	1,500
Debenture interest	700	700

(d) Interest at 10% per annum is paid on 1 July each year on a loan of £200,000 from Mr Woofer. Mr Woofer is a controlling shareholder of Tweeters Ltd and lent the money to provide additional working capital for trading purposes.

(e) Gift Aid donations were paid to CAFOD (a UK charity) on 30 April each year amounting to £18,000 per annum (gross amounts).

(f) A dividend of £800,000 was paid on 1 March 2006.

(g) The company had surplus ACT brought forward at 1 April 2005 of £100,800 which was the amount of ACT remaining unrelieved on a purchase of its own shares in June 1998.

(h) Indexation allowance for the period February 1989 to September 2005 is 72.7%.

(1) Calculate the company's corporation tax liability for eighteen months ended 30 September 2006.

(2) State the main conditions required for an R&D tax relief claim under FA 2000.

(3) Calculate the corporation tax payments due for that period (based on the final liability), stating the relevant due dates of payment. (In recent years Tweeters Ltd has always paid tax at the main rate.)

(4) Show any amount required to be reported on Form CT 61 (quarterly return of income tax) for the eighteen months to 30 September 2006.

(1)   Corporation Tax Liability

	£	12 months to 31.3.06 £	6 months to 30.9.06 £
Schedule D Case I			
Trading profits (see note 3) (365:183 days)		1,606,000	805,200
Less: Capital allowances: plant and machinery			
Year to 31 March 2006			
WDV at 31 March 2005	300,000		
Sale proceeds 21 September 2005			
(elimination from pool is limited to cost)	(100,000)		
	200,000		
WDA 25%	(50,000)	(50,000)	
	150,000		
6 months to 30 September 2006			
WDA 25% × 6/12	(18,750)		(18,750)
Addition 10 September 2006	70,000		
FYA 40%	(28,000) 42,000		(28,000)
WDV cf	173,250		
		1,556,000	758,450
Schedule D Case III (see note 7)			
Bank deposit interest		8,600	4,300
Building society interest		1,400	700
Debenture interest		8,400	4,200
Chargeable gain:			
Plant sale proceeds (March 2006)	196,800		
Less: Cost	100,000		
Unindexed gain	96,800		
Less: Indexation allowance			
100,000 @ 72.7%	72,700		
Gain after indexation allowance		24,100	
		1,598,500	767,650
Less charges on income:			
Gift Aid donations paid		(18,000)	(18,000)
Profits chargeable to corporation tax		1,580,500	749,650
Corporation tax thereon:			
FY 2005 1,580,500 at 30%		474,150	
FY 2006 749,650 at 30%*			224,895
Surplus ACT recoverable (see note 21)		100,800	–
Mainstream corporation tax liability		373,350	224,895

* Profits for small companies' rate are £749,650 plus FII £20,000 = £769,650, therefore marginal small companies' rate does not apply.

(2)   **Main conditions for a FA 2000 research and development tax relief claim**

Small and medium-sized companies (see below) are able to claim special research and development (R&D) tax relief equal to 150% of their qualifying research and development expenditure provided they spend more than £10,000 in an accounting period (reduced pro rata for periods of less than 12 months). This means, in effect, that an additional 50% trading deduction is given (making 150% in all). For these purposes, R&D is as defined in accordance with generally accepted accounting practice (particularly SSAP 13) as qualified by the DTI guidelines on the topic entitled 'Guidelines on the meaning of Research and Development for Tax Purposes', adopted by SI 2004/712.

The R&D tax relief is given as a Schedule D Case I deduction for the accounting period. In the example, the deductions given in the 12 months to 31 March 2006 and 6 months to 30 September 2006 represent 150% of the amounts allowable as a deduction in computing Tweeters Ltd's trading profits (the trading deductions in each period being the time-apportioned amounts of the R&D expenditure).

The main conditions for the special R&D relief under FA 2000 are as follows:

- The claimant company is a medium-sized enterprise under the EU regulations. This means that the company (together with any company in which it controls more than 25% of the capital or voting rights) has:

  - fewer than 250 employees *and*

  - annual turnover not exceeding Euro 50 million (approx. £33.5 million), *or*

  - gross balance sheet totals not exceeding Euro 43 million (approx. £28.8 million).

  A company ceases to qualify as a medium-sized enterprise if it fails the above definition for two consecutive periods.

- The R&D expenditure is of a revenue nature (ie not capital expenditure, although 100% R&D capital allowances may be available on capital expenditure – see Example 20 explanatory note 25).

- The expenditure relates to the company's trade, an extension of that trade, or a trade that will be derived from the R&D.

- The expenditure relates only to staffing costs (as defined in Sch 20.5), consumable stores, software and certain utility costs such as power, fuel and water (see FA 2004 s 141) or to R&D contracted out to someone else.

- Any intellectual property created from the R&D, such as know-how, patents etc, vests in the company or jointly with the company and others.

- The R&D does not relate to activities that have been contracted out to the company by any person (but see explanatory note 10 re separate relief for work contracted out by a qualifying large company).

- The R&D spending is not subsidised by the State or any other party (the R&D tax relief being ignored for this purpose).

To assist companies not yet in profit, companies may 'surrender' their unused relief to obtain a cash tax credit equal to up to 24% of the actual R&D cost. See explanatory note 9 for further details.

The definition of R&D expenditure is complex. Claimants need to be sure that their expenditure falls within it before making a claim. Claims must be made, amended or withdrawn on the company's corporation tax return, within one year of the anniversary of the filing date.

(3)   **Corporation tax payments**

	Year to 31.3.06 £	6 months to 30.9.06 £
Mainstream corporation tax payable as in (1)	373,350	224,895
Due dates of payment (see note 23):		
14 October 2005	93,337	
14 January 2006	93,337	
14 April 2006	93,338	
14 July 2006	93,338	
14 October 2006	–	112,447
14 January 2007	–	112,448
	373,350	224,895

In practice, Tweeters Ltd would make instalment payments based on its *estimated* tax liability for the relevant periods, making appropriate adjustments to the payments when it had finalised its self-assessed liability. HMRC would compare the estimated payments with the payments which should have been made based on the final liability and calculate the appropriate (underpaid) debit interest or (overpaid) credit interest up to the normal nine month due date when the normal interest rates apply. The interest will be reflected on the company's statement. See note 23.

(4)   **Accounting for income tax (TA 1988 Sch 16)**

Period	Date due		Tax deducted from interest etc paid		Payable to Inland Revenue
			Tax rate		
		£		£	£
Year ended 31.3.06					
Qr to 30.6.2005 no return required					
Qr to 30.9.2005	14.10.2005	20,000	20%	4,000	4,000
Qr to 31.12.2005 no return required					
Qr to 31.3.2005 no return required					
					4,000
6 mths ended 30.9.06					
Qr to 30.6.2006 no return required					
Qr to 30.9.2006	14.10.2006	20,000	20%	4,000	4,000

Explanatory Notes

Chargeable accounting periods

1.   Full notes on the computation of profits for corporation tax are in Example 48.

2.   (a)   Corporation tax rates are fixed for financial years (defined as the year beginning 1 April), but corporation tax assessments are made by reference to chargeable accounting periods, and the

profits arising in an accounting period are apportioned on a time basis between the financial years in which the accounting period falls in order to determine the rate of corporation tax applicable (TA 1988 s 8(3)).

(b)   An accounting period of a company begins whenever:

    (i)   the company, not then being within the charge to corporation tax, comes within it, whether by the company becoming resident in the UK or acquiring a source of income, or otherwise, or

    (ii)   an accounting period of the company ends without the company then ceasing to be within the charge to corporation tax (TA 1988 s 12(2)).

(c)   An accounting period of a company ends on the first occurrence of any of the following (TA 1988 s 12(3)(7)):

    (i)   twelve months after the beginning of the accounting period

    (ii)   an accounting date of the company or, if there is a period for which the company does not make up accounts, the day before the date from which accounts are made up

    (iii)   the company beginning or ceasing to trade or to be, in respect of the trade or (if more than one) of all the trades carried on by it, within the charge to corporation tax

    (iv)   the company beginning or ceasing to be resident in the UK

    (v)   the company ceasing to be within the charge to corporation tax

    (vi)   the commencement of winding-up of the company (following which accounting periods end at twelve monthly intervals until the completion of the winding-up).

Since the period for which Tweeters Ltd has made up accounts exceeds twelve months, the eighteen month period ended 30 September 2006 must be divided into two chargeable periods, the year to 31 March 2006 and the six months to 30 September 2006.

Allocating profits and losses to accounting periods

3.   TA 1988 s 72 provides that where it is *necessary* in order to arrive at profits for Schedule D Case I, II or VI to apportion profits/losses to specific periods, the apportionment is made according to the days in the respective periods. In exceptional circumstances, a more accurate measure of profits may be obtained other than by time-apportionment, in which case time-apportionment is not *necessary* (Marshall Hus & Ptnrs Ltd v Bolton 1981).

4.   Except for interest, in respect of which there are special rules (see note 7) and (from 1 April 2002) income from intangible fixed assets, such as patent royalties (see Example 65), a company's other sources of income are dealt with in the chargeable period in which they arise, using income tax principles. Capital gains and losses are dealt with in the chargeable period in which the disposal is made (TCGA 1992 s 8). Where gains and losses on disposal relate to a company's 'loan relationships' they are included in calculating income rather than capital gains (see Example 62). The same applies to gains and losses on intangible fixed assets, although a special rollover relief applies where intangible fixed assets are replaced.

5.   For capital allowances purposes, additions and disposals are dealt with in the chargeable accounting period in which they occur.

6.   Charges on income (the charitable Gift Aid donations in this example) are deducted in the chargeable period in which they are paid, not as they accrue (TA 1988 s 338(1)).

Treatment of interest paid and received

7. Interest paid and received is normally taken into account on an accruals basis (see Example 62 for details). If the interest relates to the trade (which, except for financial businesses, will usually apply only to interest *payable*), it is incorporated within the Schedule D Case I result of the period of account, which is time apportioned over the chargeable accounting periods if the period of account exceeds twelve months. As far as non-trading interest is concerned, the same treatment would normally be used to arrive at the amounts included in the Schedule D Case III profit or deficit, unless the amounts involved were material and time-apportionment would not give a fair result.

In this example, the loan interest paid will already be deducted in arriving at the trading profits. The non-trading interest received over the period to 30 September 2006 is arrived at as follows and has been time-apportioned as shown:

	£	*To 31.3.06* £	*To 30.9.06* £
Bank interest (11,000 – 1,100 + 3,000)	12,900	8,600	4,300
Building society interest			
(2,000 – 1,400 + 1,500)	2,100	1,400	700
Debenture interest (12,600 – 700 + 700)	12,600	8,400	4,200

Research and development (R&D) tax reliefs

8. Where *any* trader either incurs revenue expenditure on research and development related to his trade, or pays a sum to an approved scientific research association, university, college or research institute to be used for that purpose, the expenditure is deductible as a trading expense of the accounting period in which it is incurred (TA 1988 ss 82A, 82B).

9. The special 150% tax deduction for R&D revenue expenditure by small/medium-sized (SME) companies summarised in part (2) of the example was introduced in FA 2000 s 69 and Sch 20.

For pre-trading R&D expenditure, the company may elect to treat the 150% deduction as a trading loss for that pre-trading period and it will not then be treated as incurred on the first day of trading under the normal rules (see Example 48 explanatory note 6).

Where the effect of the deduction is to give a trading loss, the normal company loss reliefs will apply. Where a trading loss is attributable to the 150% R&D relief, this part of the loss can be 'surrendered' for a tax repayment (ie R&D credit) from HMRC equal to 16% of the surrendered loss (which equates to 24% of the corresponding R&D expenditure). However, the R&D credit is restricted to the total amount of the company's PAYE and Class 1 national insurance payments for the relevant accounting period (excluding deductions for working families' tax credits and disabled persons' tax credits). For this purpose the PAYE/NI for the tax months (to 5th of each month) ending in the accounting period would be taken. Say, for example, a company spent £120,000 on R&D (on revenue account) so the R&D tax deduction at 150% was £180,000. The PAYE/NI for the period was £16,000. In this case the maximum potential R&D tax refund would be £28,800 (= 24% of £120,000) but the R&D tax credit repayment would be restricted to £16,000. The repayment represents a trading loss of £100,000, leaving an unused loss available to carry forward of £80,000 (£180,000 less £100,000).

10. A similar R&D tax relief is available for 'large' companies (ie non-SME companies – see note 9 above). Large companies may claim an enhanced R&D tax deduction equal to 125% of qualifying R&D expenditure (the rules are contained in FA 2002 Sch 12). Although similar to the SME provisions, the relief for large companies is given at a lower rate and there is no corresponding provision allowing for a cash repayment in loss-making situations.

Where a company carries out R&D on its own behalf, the qualifying rules include the same provisions as for SMEs in relation to the qualifying threshold of £10,000 per 12-month period, the requirement for the expenditure not to be capital in nature and to be incurred on staffing costs, consumables, software or utility costs, and for the company to be a trading company.

The principal difference from the SME relief relates to subcontracted R&D, as it is possible for a subcontractor to claim under the 'large' company rules even where it will not be the owner of the intellectual property developed, and also for the relief to be claimed by a small/medium-sized subcontractor working for the large company. There are also provisions giving the enhanced relief where a large company makes contributions to special defined bodies or individuals conducting R&D which is relevant to the trade of the company concerned.

11. A special 50% relief is available to companies from 22 April 2003, over and above the normal or enhanced R&D deductions dealt with in notes 8 to 10 above, in respect of qualifying expenditure on research and development relating to vaccines and medicines for TB, malaria, HIV and AIDS, and contributions to independent research into such vaccines or medicines (FA 2002 Sch 13).

Quarterly accounting for income tax

12. A company has to make a return under TA 1988 Sch 16 to account for any income tax it has deducted in the return period from patent royalties (see Example 48 explanatory note 13), interest and any charges on income (such payments being referred to as 'relevant payments'), subject to a set-off for any income tax suffered on taxed income. The return must be made within fourteen days after the end of the return period on form CT 61.

The return periods are the calendar quarters to 31 March, 30 June, 30 September and 31 December. If a company's accounting period does not end on one of those dates, however, the company must make up returns to each of those dates and also a return ending on the last day of the accounting period.

Taxed receipts and payments are brought into the quarterly accounting system according to when they are received and paid. Where, looking at the cumulative position during a chargeable accounting period, too much income tax has been accounted for owing to later receipts of taxed income, the excess payments to HMRC are repayable upon completion of the appropriate CT 61 return form. HMRC will not, however, repay sums in excess of those already paid to them in the accounting period. Such excesses can be used to cover the company's liability on later payments in the same accounting period, any balance being treated as indicated in note 13. The rate of tax deducted from interest is 20%. The rate of tax deducted from other taxed amounts such as patent royalties is the basic rate, presently 22%.

As demonstrated in part (4) of the example, considerably fewer CT61 returns are now required, as a result of changes made in recent Finance Acts (see Example 48 explanatory notes 11 and 13 for details). Thus in the example Tweeters Ltd receives its debenture interest from Dovedale plc gross, but must withhold 20% tax from its loan interest payments to Mr Woofer, since tax must still be deducted from interest payments to individuals (other than on quoted Eurobonds). Companies are still required to deduct tax on payments of annual interest, patent royalties and any annual payments where they are made to individuals, trustees (other than trustees of exempt bodies), or non-residents (such as overseas group or associate companies), and will suffer tax if they receive payments such as patent royalties from individuals. Investment companies, in particular, should obtain beneficial cash flow and compliance administration advantages as a result of receiving (virtually all) their taxed UK investment income gross (although their ability to recoup tax credits on UK dividend income was lost after 2 July 1997).

Excess income tax suffered

13. If at the end of an accounting period more income tax has been suffered on taxed income than the company is liable to account for in respect of its taxed payments, the excess income tax is set off against the corporation tax bill for the relevant accounting period (see note 14). If it should *exceed* the corporation tax bill, then the balance will be *repaid to the company*. Since the majority of UK

source investment income is now paid on a 'gross' basis, such situations are likely to be comparatively rare. However, in such cases, companies claim repayment of excess income tax suffered when they send in their corporation tax returns (TA 1988 s 7).

14. Companies are not *required* to set off income tax suffered against income tax payable under the Schedule 16 quarterly return procedure, and may if they wish set the whole amount against the corporation tax payable for the relevant accounting period (TA 1988 s 7(2) and Sch 16 paras 5 and 7). In most cases, it will only be *excess* income tax suffered that is set against corporation tax payable. The relevant accounting period in which excess income tax suffered is set off is that in which the related income is taken into account (TA 1988 s 7(2)).

Abolition of ACT

15. Before 6 April 1999, companies accounted for ACT on a quarterly basis under TA 1988 Sch 13 on the excess of franked payments (dividends paid or distributions made plus ACT) over franked investment income (dividends received plus tax credits). The ACT/tax credit rate at that time was 25% of the cash amount (20% of the tax credit inclusive figure). Although ACT is no longer payable for distributions on or after 6 April 1999, shareholders still receive tax credits, but at a reduced rate of 1/9th of the dividend (equal to 10% of the tax credit inclusive amount). For the income tax treatment see Example 1 explanatory note 8.

16. ACT paid was set off against the corporation tax payable, subject to a maximum set-off limit of 20% of the profits chargeable to corporation tax. (The 20% rate has applied since 1 April 1994, higher rates applying before that date.)

Surplus ACT arising in periods up to 5 April 1999 could be carried back and set against the liability of accounting periods *commencing* in the previous six years, setting against the latest period first (TA 1988 s 239). Claims for carry back had to be made within two years after the end of the chargeable accounting period in which the surplus arose.

Any surplus ACT which remains unrelieved after a carry back claim, or for which a carry back claim has not been made, may be carried forward and regarded as ACT paid in a later accounting period. Unrelieved ACT at 5 April 1999 can, however, only be set off in a later period under the shadow ACT system (see notes 18 to 22).

Whether relief for ACT is under the carry back or carry forward provisions, in no accounting period can a company exceed the maximum permitted ACT set-off.

17. If franked investment income exceeded franked payments, a company had surplus franked investment income to carry forward to frank a later distribution. Franked investment income received after 5 April 1999 could not be used to reduce the ACT liability on pre-6 April 1999 distributions, even if it would otherwise have been in the same return period (eg if a dividend was paid on 1 April 1999 and a dividend was received on 10 April 1999, both would be in the quarter to 30 June 1999, but the ACT payable would not take the franked investment income into account). See explanatory note 20 for the treatment of surplus franked investment income in the shadow ACT system.

An accounting period was regarded for ACT purposes as ending on 5 April 1999 and the return to that date was the last return period for which ACT had to be paid under Schedule 13. For accounting periods that straddled 6 April 1999, the profits were split proportionately and the old ACT rules applied to the period up to 5 April 1999 and the shadow ACT rules outlined below to the remainder of the period.

Shadow ACT regulations and recovery of surplus ACT

18. Companies with surplus ACT at 5 April 1999 cannot set it off against mainstream tax other than under the shadow ACT system (FA 1998 s 32). The detailed regulations are contained in SI 1999/358 (the references below being to these regulations). The shadow ACT regime basically enables companies to recover surplus ACT brought forward at 6 April 1999 on a similar basis to the old

ACT offset system. Shadow or 'pretend' ACT is calculated at the rate of 25% on post 5 April 1999 dividends and other distributions (see note 20 below) and is regarded as set off, subject to the maximum offset limit (20% x taxable profits) in priority to the actual surplus ACT brought forward. To the extent that there is ACT offset capacity remaining, part or all of the actual surplus ACT can be set off and recovered against a company's corporation tax liability. As indicated in note 21, all of Tweeters Ltd's surplus ACT of £100,800 (at 1 April 2005) can be offset against its corporation tax liability, as this is within the ACT offset capacity remaining after the prior offset of shadow ACT on the March 2006 dividend. If the shadow ACT exceeds the maximum offset, this is allocated in various ways as outlined below.

19. Shadow ACT is generated on non-qualifying as well as qualifying distributions (as to which see Example 56), to prevent loan notes etc being used to avoid paying dividends. Shadow ACT exceeding the maximum set-off for the current period is carried back for up to six years (but not to accounting periods beginning before 6 April 1999) and treated as set off in those years, latest first. The carried back shadow ACT will displace any actual set-off of surplus ACT in (broadly) the immediately preceding accounting period, but not in any earlier accounting period in the carryback years. Any shadow ACT that cannot be carried back is carried forward (reg 12).

Special provisions apply to (broadly) 51% groups (reg 6). Where a group company has excess shadow ACT after its own offsets, the parent company is required to allocate the excess to other group members. If the parent company fails to do so, HMRC can impose its own allocation, although this would be disregarded if the parent company then made its own allocation (reg 13).

HMRC can issue assessments to recover corporation tax where an earlier set-off of surplus ACT is displaced by shadow ACT. Companies may, if they wish, opt out of the shadow ACT system and forgo the possibility of recovering their surplus ACT.

20. Under the shadow ACT system, the rate of ACT remains at 25% of the dividend payment or distribution. Where the company has franked investment income, the tax credit included therein is at the rate of 1/9th of the dividend received from 6 April 1999. Shadow ACT is then calculated as 20% of the excess of franked distributions (ie dividends paid plus 25% ACT) over nine-eighths of the franked investment income (ie dividends received plus 1/9th tax credit) (reg 11). So long as tax credits remain at the same rate, this can more simply be calculated by taking 25% of the excess of the tax-credit exclusive amounts, ie:

Post-5 April 1999 dividends

Paid	1,600	+ (25%) 400	= Franked distribution	2,000
Received	720	+ (1/9) 80 = 800 x 9/8	= Franked investment income	900
	880			1,100

Shadow ACT is:			
25% x 880 =	£220	20% x 1,100 =	£220

If the franked investment income in the above calculation had exceeded the franked distributions, the excess would be carried forward and taken into account in the next shadow ACT calculation. If a company had surplus franked investment income at 5 April 1999, it would similarly be taken into account in calculating shadow ACT, but since it would include a tax credit of 25% rather than 1/9th, the 9/8ths calculation would not apply.

In this example, Tweeters Ltd has surplus ACT brought forward at 1 April 2005 of £100,800. (This would be the amount of ACT remaining after making the appropriate ACT offsets for the six years ended 31 March 2005, the period from 6 April 1999 to 31 March 2005 being dealt with under the shadow ACT regime.)

21. The full amount of £100,800 can be recovered in respect of the twelve months to 31 March 2006, as calculated below:

	£	£
Surplus ACT at 1.4.2005		100,800
12 months to 31.3.06		
Max offset capacity		
£1,580,500 @ 20%	316,100	
Shadow ACT		
Dividend paid (March 2006)	800,000	
Less: Dividend received (May 2005)	(30,000)	
Excess of dividend paid over dividend received	770,000	
Shadow ACT @ 25%	192,500	
Therefore surplus ACT offset within remaining capacity (316,100 – 192,500 = 123,600)		(100,800)

22. The shadow ACT regulations contain various anti-avoidance provisions which seek to ensure that companies cannot recover their surplus ACT by 'unacceptable' means, such as where franked investment income is replaced by interest income, the main purpose being to reduce shadow ACT (reg 7) or where there are 'unallowable' arrangements to pass on the value of surplus franked investment income (reg 8).

There are also rules which mirror the ACT anti-avoidance provisions repealed from 6 April 1999. Thus, surplus ACT cannot be carried forward beyond a change in ownership if there is a major change in the nature of the company's trade or business within three years (either side of the ownership change) (reg 16). Similarly, surrendered ACT carried forward in a subsidiary is blocked when a parent company is taken over and there is a major change in the conduct of its business within three years (reg 17).

Payment of corporation tax

23. Corporation tax self-assessment applies to both accounting periods in this example. As Tweeters Ltd is a 'large' company paying tax at the full rate for both periods, it is liable to pay its (self-assessed) corporation tax for these periods under the quarterly instalment payment (QIP) regime.

For the twelve months to 31 March 2006, the company must pay its corporation tax in four equal instalments on 14 October 2005, 14 January 2006, 14 April 2006 and 14 July 2006.

For the following accounting period (six months to 30 September 2006), the company must pay the full amount of tax of £224,895 in two equal instalments as follows:

1st instalment   (6 mths and 13 days after 1.4.2005)   14 October 2006
Final instalment (3 mths and 14 days after 30.9.2005) 14 January 2007

In practice, Tweeters Ltd would pay instalments based on its *estimated* liability at the due dates, with interest being charged or credited on underpayments or overpayments as compared with the final liability.

Capital gains rollover relief

24. If the plant sold in this example is fixed plant, the company may claim rollover relief in respect of the chargeable gain if the proceeds are reinvested in other business assets acquired within one year before and three years after the date of disposal (see Example 83 for details).

If, on the other hand, the plant sold (or the replacement plant) is not fixed plant but moveable plant, then rollover relief is not available.

Research spin-out companies

25. FA 2005 ss 20–22 introduced into statute provisions relating to research spin-out companies, but unfortunately Tweeters Limited is unable to make use of this very specialised relief. It applies in the context of scientific research organisations (SROs) (which may comprise universities, NHS trusts, or the Ministry of Defence), who share intellectual property (IP) with their employees by setting up spin-out companies to exploit the IP. Employees receive shares in the newly formed company, which constitute remuneration from employment liable to income tax and NIC. The relief serves to defer the tax charge to the time of disposal of the shares, when the value will be known, and funds will have been generated. The relief works by deeming the value of the IP to be nil provided the employee receives shares before the transfer of the IP or within 183 days of the transfer.

Streetfield Limited, which has no associated companies, had made up its accounts to 30 September since its incorporation in 1978, but decided after the accounting year to 30 September 2004 to make up a six-month account to 31 March 2005.

The results of recent periods were:

	Year ended 30.9.04 £	6 mths ended 31.3.05 £	Year ended 31.3.06 £
Adjusted trading profit (loss)	91,000	84,500	(210,000)
Schedule D Case III			
Interest on debenture stock of Lane plc	2,000	1,000	2,000
Capital gains	–	–	20,500

Having reorganised the business following its difficult trading period, the company has recently secured a major new contract and a (taxable) trading profit of some £320,000 is anticipated for the year to 31 March 2007. The company will continue to receive the debenture interest.

Corporation tax rates during the period have been as follows:

Year ended 31 March	2004	2005	2006	2007
Full rate on profits over £1,500,000	30%	30%	30%	30%
Small companies' rate on profits up to £300,000	19%	19%	19%	19%
Effective marginal rate on profits between £300,000 and £1,500,000	32.75%	32.75%	32.75%	32.75%
Starting rate on profits up to £10,000	0%	0%	0%	19%
Effective marginal rate on profits between £10,000 and £50,000	23.75%	23.75%	23.75%	N/A

(a) Illustrate the alternative ways in which relief may be obtained for the trading loss of the year to 31 March 2006, stating the time limits within which any claims must be made. The company did not make any non-corporate distributions.

(b) Indicate what the position would be if the company had made a Gift Aid donation to a charity of £1,000 gross on 31 March each year.

(a) **The loss claims available in respect of the loss of the year to 31 March 2006 are as follows:**

1. The adjusted trading loss of £210,000 can be carried forward under TA 1988 s 393(1) to set against future profits of the *same trade* (not any other income nor chargeable gains). If the anticipated trading profit of £320,000 is made in the year to 31 March 2007, relief for the loss will be obtained in that year, reducing the corporation tax payable on 1 January 2008.

    If this alternative is adopted, Streetfield Limited will have profits chargeable to corporation tax for the year ended 31 March 2006 of £22,500 taxable at the small companies' rate of 19% less marginal starting rate relief.

2. Alternatively a claim may be made under s 393A to set the loss against the *total profits* of the same accounting period, viz.

Trading loss for year ended 31 March 2006	210,000
Set against total profits before charges of same accounting period	22,500
Leaving a balance unrelieved of	£ 187,500

    which may be carried forward under s 393(1).

    On its own, there would only be a small tax saving from this claim, because there is only £22,500 profit chargeable to corporation tax in the year to 31 March 2006, the tax on which amounts to £2,969 (10,000 at 0% and 12,500 at 23.75%). The claim against any current profits is, however, a prerequisite if the company wishes to claim under the provisions of note 3 below.

3. After a claim has been made under 2 above, then alternatively to carrying the unrelieved trading loss of £187,500 forward it may be carried back to set against the *total* profits of accounting periods ending wholly or partly within the previous twelve months, latest first. Results are apportioned where, as in this example, an accounting period falls only partly within the twelve-month period. Any unrelieved balance is then carried forward. S 393A provides that when losses are carried back, the set-off in the earlier period(s) is restricted so as not to interfere with relief for *trade* charges (but non-trade charges are not protected).

    The carryback claim is as follows:

	£	£
Unrelieved loss of year to 31 March 2006 as above		187,500
Set against total profits of six months to 31 March 2005:		
Trading profits	84,500	
Loan interest	1,000	
		(85,500)
Set against one half of total profits of year to 30 September 2004:		
Trading profits	91,000	
Debenture interest	2,000	
	93,000	
Loss set-off (see explanatory note 5)	(46,500)	(46,500)
Leaving taxable profits of	46,500	
Loss carried forward under s 393(1)		55,500

4. Losses that are carried forward under s 393(1) are set off automatically against later trading profits without the need for a claim. The time limit for making current and carryback claims under s 393A is two years after the end of the loss period, ie by 31 March 2008, or within such further period as HMRC may allow.

5.   (i)   The anticipated results for the year to 31 March 2007 are:

Schedule D Case I	320,000
Schedule D Case III (say)	2,000
	£322,000

The company therefore expects to have £22,000 profits in the marginal small companies' rate tranche. Since there would be a loss carried forward of £55,500 after the carryback claim, the benefit of setting off losses against profits chargeable at the higher marginal corporation tax rate shown on page 52.1 would be available whichever loss claim is made, and the balance of carry forward loss relief would be at the small companies' rate of 19%. The rate of tax saved through the carryback loss claims would be saving tax at just over (part of profits now qualify for 0% starting rate) 19% for the six months' offset against the year ended 30 September 2004 and at 19% for the six-month period to 31 March 2005. Although there is only a small tax saving from the current year claim (see explanatory note 2), carrying the maximum loss back will save tax.

   (ii)   The other factors to be considered in relation to the loss claims are the time when the tax saving will occur and whether any repayments will be boosted by tax-free interest.

   (iii)   To the extent that the loss is carried forward, the relief will reduce the corporation tax payable on 1 January 2008. Relief against current or earlier profits will either result in tax not yet paid being discharged, or in tax being repaid.

From a cash flow and interest point of view, therefore, it will obviously be better to claim the maximum possible carryback of the loss.

   (iv)   Any repayment for the earlier years would attract interest, if any, from 1 January 2007, except for the six months to 31 March 2005, for which interest would run from 1 January 2006 (see explanatory note 7).

(b)   **If Streetfield Ltd had paid £1,000 gross annually on 31 March to a charity under Gift Aid**

A Gift Aid donation to charity is a charge on a company's income, but can only be deducted where there are profits available to cover it. (Excess charges may, however, be surrendered under the group relief provisions whether they are trade charges or non-trade charges – see Example 63 explanatory note 5.) Where losses are carried back, it is only trade charges that are protected, not non-trade charges. Few payments are now treated as trade charges, so they will be encountered only infrequently.

Streetfield Ltd would obtain full relief for the Gift Aid donations if it made the carry forward claim, sufficient profits being available in both the loss year to 31 March 2006 and the following year to cover the non-trade charges. If the loss was set against the current and previous profits as indicated above, there would be £1,000 unrelieved in the loss year to 31 March 2006 and in the six months to 31 March 2005. In the year to 30 September 2004, the donation would be covered by the profits of £46,500 remaining after the loss claim.

Explanatory Notes

Loss relief against current and previous profits under TA 1988 s 393A

1.   This example outlines the reliefs available to a single company in a continuing business in respect of trading losses and excess charges on income. Under corporation tax self-assessment, all 'negative amounts', including trading losses, included in the CT 600 return become final in the same way as a self-assessment, subject to HMRC's ability to enquire into a return or make a discovery.

2.   Relief for trading losses may be claimed under TA 1988 s 393A against profits of whatever description in the current and carryback periods. Before F(No2)A 1997 the carryback period was

three years. This was reduced to one year by F(No2)A 1997 s 39, except for companies ceasing to trade, for whom the three-year carryback still applies for losses of the last twelve months' trading (see Example 53). The loss is set against the profits of accounting periods ending wholly or partly within the carryback period of twelve months or three years preceding the loss period, latest first. Where an accounting period falls only partly within the carryback period, relief is given against a proportionate part of the profits (see explanatory note 5). The length of the loss period does not affect the carryback period.

Current and carryback claims under s 393A must be made within two years after the end of the loss period, or within such further period as HMRC may allow. See Statement of Practice 5/01 for the circumstances in which HMRC may accept late claims.

Carrying losses forward under TA 1988 s 393

3. Where relief is not claimed under s 393A, or part of a loss remains unrelieved, the loss is carried forward automatically under s 393(1) without the need for a claim.

Unrelieved charges

4. In respect of the accounting period in which a trade ceases, s 393A(7) provides that any unrelieved trade charges of that accounting period may be included in the loss available to be carried back. For an illustration of loss claims on cessation of trading see Example 53. F (No 2) A 2005 provides that only qualifying charitable donations and gifts of assets to charities may be deducted as charges. Annuities and other annual payments that would previously have been deducted as charges must now be treated as management expenses (see Example 63).

5. Where there is a change of accounting date during the carryback period, as shown in this example, s 393(2) provides that the reduction to be made in the profits of a period falling only partly within the carryback period shall not exceed the appropriate proportion of those profits, as indicated in explanatory note 2 above.

    Where there are charges on income, s 338 provides that they are allowed as a deduction against the total profits for the period as reduced by any other relief from tax, other than group relief. S 393A(8) provides that relief is not to be given for a trading loss in the carryback period 'so as to interfere with any relief under s 338 in respect of payments made wholly and exclusively for the purposes of that trade'.

Other loss claims

6. Losses may be the subject of a group relief claim for a company that is a member of a 75% group – for details see Example 63. That example also deals with the treatment of excess charges on income and excess management expenses of an investment company.

Interest on repayments

7. Where tax is repaid following a loss claim, interest on the repayment normally runs from nine months and one day after the loss period (except for a repayment relating to an account falling wholly within the 12 months before the loss period, for which interest runs from nine months and one day after that earlier period).

    Hence in this example, interest on repayments would run from 1 January 2007, except for any repayment for the six months to 31 March 2005, on which interest would run from 1 January 2006, as indicated in the example at part (a) note 5(iv).

    A 'large' company which is subject to the quarterly instalment payment rules may also generate repayments following the carryback of losses. However, even in such cases, interest will accrue only from the relevant nine months and one day due dates (TA 1988 s 826(7D)(7E)).

    Interest on underpaid and overpaid tax is taken into account in calculating profits chargeable to corporation tax.

Relief for non-trading losses

8. Companies may generate non-trading losses on other activities. The relief available for such losses depends on the nature of the loss, as summarised below for the most important categories:

    (a) Capital losses – offset against capital gains of the same accounting period, with any unrelieved loss being carried forward to reduce capital gains in future periods (see Example 73 explanatory note 1).

    (b) Non-trading foreign exchange/loan relationships deficit – a claim can be made to relieve such deficits in various ways (see Example 63 part A).

    (c) Property business losses on leased UK property – TA 1988 s 392A provides that losses on a UK property leasing business can be offset against the company's total profits of the same period and/or included in a group relief claim under TA 1988 s 403ZD. Any surplus property business loss is carried forward against future total profits (provided the property business continues). A company with investment business can carry forward an unrelieved property business loss (*after* the property business has ceased) as a management expense under TA 1988 s 75 (TA 1988 s 392(3)). See Example 98.

    (d) Schedule D Case V losses relating to an *overseas* property letting business must be carried forward for future offset against profits of the same overseas property business (TA 1988 s 392B) (see Example 98 explanatory note 12).

    (e) Schedule D Case VI losses can only be relieved against current or future Schedule D Case VI income.

Calamity Limited, a family-owned close company, ceased trading on 30 June 2006.

It was incorporated many years ago and the company has had no income other than from the trade. The company has paid a charitable Gift Aid donation of £1,000 per annum. The last payment under Gift Aid was made in December 2005. A summary of recent adjusted trading results is as follows:

		£
Year ended		
31.12.02	Profit	150,000
31.12.03	Profit	143,000
31.12.04	Profit	35,000
31.12.05	Loss	65,000
6 months to 30.6.06	Loss	53,500

On 31 August 2006 the company's factory was sold, a balancing charge of £48,000 and a chargeable gain of £15,000 arising. The final accounting period is to 31 December 2006.

Assuming that the company claims relief for losses in the most appropriate way:

(a)   Show the tax position in relation to the balancing charge and chargeable gain.

(b)   Show the final amounts chargeable to corporation tax for each of the chargeable periods shown, after loss relief claims, together with the amounts of unrelieved losses and charges, if any.

(c)   Give the latest dates by which the loss claims could be made by Calamity Limited.

(a)   **Tax position on balancing charge and chargeable gain**

The balancing charge of £48,000, together with the chargeable gain of £15,000, totalling £63,000, will be taxed at 30% (see explanatory note 5), giving tax payable of £18,900. The balancing charge is, however, treated in the same way as a post-cessation receipt under TA 1988 s 105 (CAA 2001 s 354), so that brought forward losses may be set against it.

Taking into account the rate of tax payable on the balancing charge, and the other circumstances of the period concerned, as shown in part (b) below, it would be better to carry forward the loss of the six months to 30 June 2006 against the balancing charge than claiming carryback relief under s 393A, ie:

	£
Relief under TA 1988 s 393A	
Loss of 6 months to 30.6.06 of £53,500, set against profits of year to 31.12.03, saving tax of 53,500 @ 19% (profits of year to 31.12.04 having been eliminated by loss carried back from the year to 31.12.05)	10,165
Relief wholly under CAA 2001 s 354	
Unrelieved loss 53,500 carried forward and set against balancing charge, saving tax of 48,000 @ 30% and leaving unrelieved loss of £5,500	14,400
Additional saving with CAA 2001 s 354 relief	4,235

(b)   **Final amounts chargeable to corporation tax, after loss claims:**

Taking into account (a) above, the position is as follows:

Accounting period to	Case I profit £	Chargeable gains £	Trading losses* £	Non-trade charges** £	Chargeable to corporation tax £
31.12.06	48,000	15,000	(48,000)	–	15,000
30.6.06	–		–	–	–
31.12.05	–		–	–	–
31.12.04	35,000		(35,000)	–	–
31.12.03	143,000		(30,000)	(1,000)	112,000
31.12.2002	150,000			(1,000)	149,000

* *Losses are relieved as follows:*

	1.1.05 – 30.6.05 £	1.7.05 – 31.12.05 £
Year to 31.12.05 (see explanatory notes 1 and 2)		
Trading loss (£65,000)	32,500	32,500
Set against profits of previous year/three years, net of trade charges (s 393A):		
Year to 31.12.04 (£35,000)	(32,500)	(2,500)
Year to 31.12.03 (balance)		(30,000)
6 months to 30.6.06		
Trading loss		53,500
Set against balancing charge of period to 31.12.06		48,000
Leaving loss unrelieved of		5,500

** *Unrelieved non-trade charges*

Non-trade charges are deducted after trade losses and, if there are no profits to cover them, no relief is available. The payments under Gift Aid for the years to 31 December 2004 and 31 December 2005 are therefore unrelieved.

(c) **The latest date for making the s 393A claim** to carry back the loss of the year ended 31 December 2005 is 31 December 2007 (or such further period as HMRC may allow) (TA 1988 s 393A). The loss carried forward is automatically set against the balancing charge without the need for a claim.

Explanatory Notes

Terminal loss relief

1. Relief for losses in the final period of trading is claimed under the normal rules and there is no separate provision for claiming relief for terminal losses as there is for income tax. Although the normal loss carryback period under TA 1988 s 393A is one year, there are two provisions that extend the relief available for the loss of the last 12 months of trading.

   First, losses in that 12 months may be carried back for a full three years (TA 1988 s 393A subsections (2A), (2B)) (subject to what is said in note 6). Where an accounting period falls partly within the last 12 months, the three year carryback applies to the appropriate proportion.

2. In Calamity Ltd's case, the loss of the 12 months ended 31 December 2005 must be apportioned between:

   6 months to 30 June 2005, which is available for carryback against the previous year only (TA 1988 s 393A(2))

   6 months to 31 December 2005, which falls within 12 months of the cessation date, and can therefore be carried back against the previous three years' profits (s 393A(2)-(2B)).

   The loss for the final 6 months to 30 June 2006 could also be carried back for up to three years (as part of the loss of the last 12 months), but it is more beneficial to carry the loss forward to relieve the balancing charge.

3. The carryback provisions of TA 1988 s 393A restrict the set-off in an earlier accounting period so as not to interfere with earlier relief for *trade* charges, but relief for non-trade charges is not protected, as shown in the example.

Trade charges

4.   A number of payments that were treated as trade charges in the past are now tax deductible. Trade charges will now be encountered only rarely.

Capital gains and balancing charges after cessation of trade

5.   The capital gain after the cessation of trading illustrates the possible danger of disposing of capital assets after the cessation of a trade.

Trading losses of the *same accounting period only* are available for set-off against capital gains. Since the cessation of trade marks the end of an accounting period (TA 1988 s 12), any losses of the final trading period are automatically prevented from being allowed against gains arising on the subsequent disposal of the company's assets, resulting in practical difficulties since invariably the assets have to be retained until after the cessation of trading. If the asset is an industrial or enterprise building or hotel, there may well be a balancing charge as well as a capital gain when it is disposed of. Under CAA 2001 s 354 unrelieved trading losses may be set against such a balancing charge, as shown in the example. But there can be no set-off against capital gains.

Furthermore, once the trade has ceased, Calamity Ltd becomes a close investment-holding company and must therefore pay tax at the full corporation tax rate of 30% regardless of the level of its profits. The protection available for the *first* accounting period during a company's liquidation is not applicable here (see Example 59, explanatory note 5).

If, however, the *contract* for sale of the assets was made prior to the cessation of trading, with *completion* taking place after the cessation, the date of disposal would be the contract date (TCGA 1992 s 34), so that the chargeable gains would then arise in the final trading period and be available to offset any trading losses of that period and the close investment-holding company problem would also be avoided.

Although a balancing charge effectively represents delayed trading profits, and is treated in the same way as a post-cessation receipt under TA 1988 s 105, enabling unrelieved amounts to be set against it (see Example 16 part (c)(ii)), the provisions of ITTOIA 2005 s 257 which enable post-cessation receipts to be carried back and treated as received on the date the trade ceased do not apply. There is also no provision for regarding the trade as being carried on in the period in which the balancing charge is received, so that the balancing charge suffers tax at 30%.

Because of this anomaly, more tax is saved in the example by not claiming s 393A relief for the final period to 30 June 2006 and instead carrying forward the loss of £53,500 in the period to 30 June 2006 to set against the balancing charge. The greater tax saving is achieved despite the fact that £5,500 of the loss remains unrelieved.

Company reconstructions without a change of ownership

6.   Under TA 1988 s 343, where a trade is transferred from one company to another, and at some time within one year before the transfer and two years after the transfer the same persons have a 75% ownership, the trade is treated as being transferred to the successor company rather than being discontinued for the purposes of carrying forward capital allowances. This prevents the predecessor carrying trading losses back three years, and enables the successor to take over the unrelieved losses of the predecessor. Where, however, the successor does not take over all the predecessor's assets and liabilities, and the liabilities of the predecessor immediately after the transfer exceed the market value of its assets (including any consideration received or receivable for the transfer of the trade), the trading loss transferred to the successor is reduced by the excess.

The successor also takes over the predecessor's capital allowances computations. First year allowances on plant and machinery are claimed by whoever incurred the expenditure and balancing adjustments are made on the company carrying on the trade at the time of the disposal. Writing down allowances are split on a time basis.

A. Domo Ltd is a UK trading subsidiary of a large multinational group, which has over twenty active UK and overseas trading companies. The majority of Domo Ltd's business is carried on from the UK but it also has a branch in Norland, a country which imposes taxation at the rate of 35% on the profits of companies resident there and profits arising there. Domo Ltd also has a number of trade-related investments.

The following information relates to Domo Ltd for the year ended 31 March 2007:

	£
Trading income – UK trade	180,000
– Norland branch (before deducting tax suffered in Norland)	30,000
Investment income	
Dividend on a holding of 15% of the ordinary (voting) shares in Fiord Norland Ltd (after deducting 15% withholding tax)	11,050
Interest receivable on a holding of 12% of the debentures of Lake Norland Ltd (after deducting 20% withholding tax)	12,000
Dividend on a holding of 8% of the ordinary shares of Valley Norland Ltd (after deducting 15% withholding tax)	10,200
Net capital profit on land in Norland bought for £20,000 in 1997, sold in March 2007 for £37,000 – tax suffered in Norland £5,950 (UK indexation allowance to be taken as 25%)	11,050
Gift Aid donation paid to NSPCC	5,000
Dividend paid – January 2007 – final for year ended 31 March 2006	152,000

The company did not have any unrelieved amounts brought forward at 1 April 2006.

Compute the corporation tax payable by Domo Ltd for the year ended 31 March 2007 after all reliefs.

B. Jones Ltd is a member of an international group of thirty companies and its only investment is a 40% holding in Shelley SA, a company resident in Ruritania. This is a country with which the UK does not have a double taxation agreement. In June 2006, Jones Ltd received in cash a dividend of 108,000 Ruritanian Dollars (R$), which had suffered a 10% Ruritanian withholding tax. The rate of exchange is R$1 = £1.25.

The dividend resolution did not indicate the accounting period for which it was paid. The Ruritanian accounts of Shelley SA for the three years to 31 October 2004, 2005 and 2006 are set out below.

Shelley SA – trading and profit and loss account

	Year ended 31.10.04 R$	Year ended 31.10.05 R$	Year ended 31.10.06 R$
Operating profit before tax	205,000	350,000	400,000
Unrealised exchange gain/(loss) on investments	100,000	(80,000)	70,000
Taxation			
Current tax	(40,000)	(60,000)	(80,000)
Deferred tax	(15,000)	(20,000)	(20,000)
(Under-)/over-provision for previous year	10,000	(5,000)	(5,000)
Profit after taxation cf	260,000	185,000	365,000

	Year ended 31.10.04 R$	Year ended 31.10.05 R$	Year ended 31.10.06 R$
Profit after taxation bf	260,000	185,000	365,000
Unrealised exchange items transferred (to)/from non-distributable capital reserve	(100,000)	80,000	(70,000)
Transfer to statutory non-distributable reserve for contingencies	(30,000)	(30,000)	(30,000)
Transfer to general reserve	(25,000)	(45,000)	(60,000)
Dividend paid in the year	–	–	(300,000)
Retained profit/(loss) per accounts	R$ 105,000	R$ 190,000	R$ (95,000)
Actual tax paid for the year	R$ 45,000	R$ 65,000	R$ 80,000

For its year ended 31 March 2007, Jones Ltd has adjusted profits taxable under Schedule D Case I of £200,000 (before deducting (non-trade) interest payable of £150,000). It also paid a dividend of £80,000 in January 2007. There were no unrelieved amounts brought forward at 1 April 2006.

(a)   Compute the income assessable under Schedule D Case V arising from the dividend, and

(b)   Calculate the corporation tax payable by Jones Ltd for the year ended 31 March 2007.

A. **Domo Ltd – Mainstream Corporation Tax for year ended 31 March 2007**

	Total	UK	Schedule D Case I Norland Branch (Note 1)	Sch D Case III Lake Norland (Note 2)	Schedule D Case V Fiord Norland (Note 3)	Valley Norland (Note 4)	Foreign chargeable gains (Note 5)
	£	£	£	£	£	£	£
Trading profit	210,000	180,000	30,000				
Debenture interest	15,000			15,000			
Foreign dividends	32,000				20,000	12,000	
Chargeable gains	12,000						12,000
	269,000	180,000	30,000	15,000	20,000	12,000	12,000
Less charges – Gift Aid donation (see note 6)	(5,000)	(5,000)					
Profits chargeable to CT (and also for small companies' rate since no FII)	264,000	175,000	30,000	15,000	20,000	12,000	12,000
Corporation tax payable @ 30% (see notes 7 and 8)	79,200	52,500	9,000	4,500	6,000	3,600	3,600
Less double tax relief * restricted to UK tax	(23,400)		(9,000)*	(3,000)	(6,000)*	(1,800)	(3,600)*
Corporation tax payable	55,800	52,500	–	1,500	–	1,800	–
Foreign tax unrelieved							2,350
Unrelieved foreign tax carried forward (or carried back in relation to the Norland branch)			1,500		2,950		

Notes

1. Norland branch profits foreign tax – 30,000 @ 35% =   £ 10,500

   The excess double tax of £1,500 suffered on the Norland branch income (ie £10,500 less £9,000 maximum offset) can be carried back for set-off against UK tax suffered on the Norland branch income of the three years to 31 March 2006, any balance being carried forward to set against future Norland branch income.

2. Debentures in Lake Norland – 12,000 + (20/80) 3,000 withholding tax =   £15,000

3. *Related qualifying foreign dividend (QFD)*

   Shares in Fiord Norland (holding carries at least 10% voting power):

	£
Dividend (net)	11,050
Withholding tax (15/85)	1,950
	13,000
Underlying tax (35/65)	7,000
Schedule D Case V income	20,000

Following FA 2001, the calculation of Schedule D Case V income includes all foreign taxes, whether relievable or not. The maximum relievable foreign tax (known as the 'mixer cap') is 30% of the sum of the dividend plus the underlying tax.

Calculation of eligible unrelieved foreign tax credit

The tax suffered on the Fiord Norland dividend exceeds the 30% mixer cap restriction, and gives rise to eligible unrelieved foreign tax (EUFT). However, the amount of foreign tax which is eligible for relief cannot exceed 45% of the gross dividend (the 45% restriction applying to both underlying and withholding tax). The EUFT is the amount by which the 45% cap on the dividend (or, if less, the actual foreign tax suffered) exceeds the double tax relief offset, as shown below.

	£	£
Lower of :		
45% cap		
Sch D Case V income – £20,000 x 45% (upper limit)	<u>9,000</u>	
Total foreign tax suffered		
Withholding tax	1,950	
Underlying tax	<u>7,000</u>	
	<u>8,950</u>	
Foreign tax suffered on dividend		8,950
Less: Actual DTR restriction		<u>(6,000)</u>
EUFT		<u>2,950</u>

This EUFT could be used to offset the UK tax suffered on any other qualifying foreign dividends (QFDs) in the same period (year ending 31 March 2007), but in this case there are none. The excess EUFT may be carried back for offset against the UK tax on QFDs for the years ended 31 March 2006, 2005 and 2004. Otherwise it must be carried forward for future offset. It should be noted that the excess EUFT on the Fiord Norland dividend cannot be applied against the residual UK tax on the dividend from Valley Norland, since this must be held in a separate EUFT pool as it attracts relief for withholding tax only (the Valley Norland shares carrying less than 10% voting power).

4. *Unrelated qualifying foreign dividend*

Shares in Valley Norland
10,200 + withholding tax (15/85) 1,800 = £12,000

5. Chargeable gain:

Sale proceeds March 2007		37,000	
Cost – 1997	20,000		
Indexation allowance 25%	<u>5,000</u>	<u>25,000</u>	£12,000

6. Gift Aid donations are treated as a charge on income and paid gross.

7. The small companies' rate is not available to Domo Ltd as it is associated with twenty active companies (active non-resident companies count for the purpose of this test).

B. (a) **Jones Ltd – Schedule D Case V income arising from June 2006 dividend**

Jones Ltd's dividend from Shelley SA before withholding tax is $108,000 \times \dfrac{100}{90} = R\$120,000$

The total dividend paid by Shelley SA is $120,000 \times \dfrac{100}{40} = R\$300,000$.

Since the dividend is not paid out of a specified period (see explanatory note 4), it is treated as coming first out of the distributable profits of the year to 31 October 2005 (being the last accounts before June 2006 when the dividend was received) then the previous year as follows:

	Year to 31.10.05 R$		Year to 31.10.04 R$
Retained profits per accounts	190,000		105,000
Add transfer to general reserve	45,000		25,000
	235,000		130,000
Attributable to dividend (R$ 300,000) (1st)	235,000	(balance)	65,000
Actual tax paid	65,000		45,000

	R$
Underlying tax:	
Year to 31.10.05 40% x 65,000	26,000
31.10.04 40% x ($\frac{65,000}{130,000}$ x 45,000)	9,000
	35,000
Dividend inclusive of withholding tax	120,000
	155,000
Overseas tax borne (35,000 + 12,000)	47,000

Converted to sterling at R$1 = £1.25 =	58,750
Dividend received R$108,000 converted at R$1 = £1.25 =	135,000
Schedule D Case V income (including overseas tax £58,750)	£ 193,750

(b)   **Corporation tax payable by Jones Ltd for year to 31 March 2007**

	Total £	Schedule D Case I £	Schedule D Case V £
UK and foreign profits	393,750	200,000	193,750
Non-trading deficit (interest payable)	(150,000)	(150,000)	
Profits chargeable to corporation tax	243,750	50,000	193,750
Corporation tax payable @ 30%*	73,125	15,000	58,125
Less double tax relief (restricted to UK tax)	(58,125)		(58,125)
Mainstream corporation tax	15,000	15,000	–

The excess foreign tax suffered on the dividend from Shelley SA of £625 (£58,750 – £58,125) represents EUFT relievable against the UK tax on future dividends received from Shelley SA (see explanatory notes 6 and 7).

*   Small companies' rate not applicable in view of the number of associated companies, overseas companies counting for this purpose.

Explanatory Notes

Interest received

1.   Interest received from abroad by individuals is taxed as income from foreign securities as interest income under Chapter 2 of Part 6 ITTOIA 2005. This does not apply to companies, for whom both

UK and foreign interest is taxed according to the 'loan relationships' provisions (see Example 62). Unless received by a financial business as trading profits, it is taxed under Schedule D Case III, as shown in part A of the example.

The 'loan relationships' rules provide for interest received to be brought into account on an accruals basis rather than on the amount arising in the period. As a result, foreign tax may be apportioned to an earlier accounting period than that in which it was suffered. Thus in part A of the example, the debenture interest receivable from Lake Norland Ltd of £12,000 after 20% withholding tax may include interest accrued but not received at 31 March 2007. The withholding tax taken into account for double tax relief would include the tax suffered on the accrued amount.

Double taxation relief

2.   Where a company suffers tax twice on the same profits, whether they are income profits or capital profits, relief may be claimed either under the provisions of a double tax treaty (TA 1988 s 788) or unilaterally (s 790) for a credit against the UK tax charged. Double tax treaties specify which taxes are covered by the agreement. Most treaties are based on the OECD model agreement, but each is separately negotiated between the respective countries, and there are often points specific to the particular treaty. HMRC have issued Statement of Practice 7/91 concerning their approach to identifying relevant foreign taxes where unilateral relief applies.

3.   FA 2000 s 103 and Sch 20 introduced far-reaching changes to the double tax relief system. These changes targeted the use of offshore mixer companies which were previously used to ensure that maximum double tax relief was obtained on a UK company's various sources of overseas income, also enabling lowly taxed income from controlled foreign companies to be repatriated with little or no extra tax, thus avoiding a UK tax charge on undistributed profits. Extensive detailed anti-avoidance legislation of a very technical nature exists, and continues to be issued, to combat schemes giving a UK tax advantage in this area.

Double tax relief is computed on a 'source by source' basis. For each source, the relief given is at the lower of the UK tax (based on the most beneficial allocation of losses etc) and the overseas tax attributable to the income or gain.

A measure of relief is available for unrelieved foreign tax relating to *overseas branch income* arising in accounting periods ending on or after 1 April 2000 and for *dividends received from overseas companies* from 31 March 2001 (see explanatory notes 6 and 7). The relief enables any unused double tax relief credit to be carried back against the UK tax on the same source of foreign income for up to three years (but not to periods before 1 April 2000 in relation to branch income or before 31 March 2001 in relation to dividends) and then carried forward indefinitely against future UK tax from the same foreign source (TA 1988 ss 806A to 806M).

S 806C provides that the relief may be claimed by a non-resident company in respect of foreign tax suffered on dividends by a UK branch or agency other than in the non-resident company's home state. A claim to relieve unused foreign tax must be made within six years after the end of the accounting period in which the amount arose.

Clearly, if the overseas tax rate suffered on the foreign income is consistently higher than the UK rate, these rules are likely to be of little assistance.

Relief for underlying tax and relevant profits

4.   Normally, only direct overseas taxes are taken into account, but underlying tax on overseas *dividends* may be taken into account if the UK company controls not less than 10% of the voting power in the foreign company. Relief may also be claimed for underlying tax paid by other companies in a chain where the 10% control test is met at each stage in the chain and dividends are paid by one company to the other (TA 1988 s 801). There are anti-avoidance provisions to prevent companies exploiting these provisions (see explanatory note 8).

The underlying tax is that part of the foreign tax on the relevant profits that is attributable to the dividend. The relevant profits are as follows:

(a)   If the dividend is paid for a specified period, the profits of that period, or

(b)   The profits of the last set of accounts ended before the dividend became payable.

If (a) or (b) applies, but the total dividend exceeds those profits, the excess is treated as coming out of earlier undistributed profits, latest first (TA 1988 s 799).

Thus, in part B of the example, the dividend (being for an unspecified accounting period) is treated as being paid out of the last accounting period (31 October 2005) which *ended* before it was paid in June 2006. The balance of 'unmatched' dividend is then allocated to the prior accounting period to 31 October 2004. Prior to 31 March 2001 it was possible for the dividend resolution to specify the profits from which it was paid to determine the relevant profits and underlying tax for double tax relief purposes.

5.   The relevant profits are the foreign company's *distributable* profits, not profits for tax purposes (Bowater Paper Corporation Ltd v Murgatroyd 1970). This ruling has now been codified into TA 1988 s 799(5)(6), which provides that the distributable profits are based on the foreign company's accounts drawn up under the law of that country. Those accounts must only include reserves, provisions for bad debts or contingencies permitted under the law of the company's home State. HMRC take the view that:

(i)   Realised gains on exchange differences are distributable profits. Unrealised exchange gains are not, unless they are in fact used for a dividend or are treated by the foreign company as distributable profits.

(ii)   Realised capital profits are also distributable profits.

(iii)   Deferred tax, and any under- or over-provisions for tax in earlier years may be taken into account in computing distributable profits (but not in computing the actual rate of underlying tax).

Some countries, including Jersey and Guernsey, operate a system under which tax is accounted for when a dividend is paid ('company tax deducted'), and is thus shown on the dividend voucher, but that tax may then be refunded depending on the company's ultimate tax position. HMRC require the actual underlying tax to be computed and relief is restricted to that amount (SP 12/93).

Current system of double tax relief for overseas dividends

6.   FA 2000 s 103 and Sch 30 (as amended by FA 2001) introduced radical changes to the system of double tax relief for dividends received from overseas resident companies. The revised provisions apply to dividends paid after 30 March 2001.

TA 1988 s 799, as amended by FA 2000, provided for the rate of overseas taxes suffered on a dividend to be 'capped' where the total amount suffered exceeded 30%. S 799 has been further amended by FA 2001 so as to retain the previous method of calculating a Schedule D Case V dividend without capping the underlying tax to the 30% rate (see note 3 of part A of the example). The 'capping' formula will apply when computing the amount of excess double tax which can be applied as eligible unrelieved foreign tax (EUFT) against the tax suffered on other eligible overseas dividends in the offshore pooling calculation (see explanatory note 7).

Broadly, the rate of underlying tax attributed to an overseas dividend is capped at a rate equal to the main UK corporation tax rate (currently 30%). This is achieved through the so-called 'mixer cap' formula (which applies irrespective of whether dividends have been paid through an overseas dividend mixing company!). The formula was revised in FA 2001 and is shown in note 3 to part A of the example.

Eligible unrelieved foreign tax (EUFT)

7.   Where an overseas company (or overseas intermediate holding company) pays a dividend which has suffered withholding tax and/or underlying tax at a total rate exceeding 30% of the 'gross' dividend, an amount of EUFT arises.

The EUFT can then be applied to relieve the overseas tax on other eligible overseas dividends in the same period under the so-called 'onshore pooling' calculation. For this purpose only certain dividends can be pooled (referred to as qualifying foreign dividends – QFDs). A QFD will broadly be a dividend from any overseas resident company *except* dividends that have been paid by a controlled foreign company in pursuance of an acceptable distribution policy.

Having calculated the EUFT on all dividends (this will be the amount of £2,950 included in note 3 to part A of the example), the respective amounts are included in a single pool of EUFT and effectively used against QFDs. The EUFT pool must be split between separate *underlying tax* and *withholding tax* pools. Dividends will enter the withholding tax pool if they do not attract relief for underlying tax (broadly dividends from companies in which less than 10% of the voting rights are held).

The total EUFT is initially offset against the pooled QFD (TA 1988 s 806D). Any excess EUFT can be carried back for up to three years on a last in first out basis (TA 1988 s 806E) or carried forward indefinitely. EUFT that cannot be carried back may be surrendered to another company in the same 75% group (TA 1988 s 806H and SI 2001/1163). The claimant company may treat the surrendered EUFT as its own EUFT for the purposes of the carry back/carry forward rules. The group relief option is available only in respect of unrelieved foreign tax on dividends and not for unrelieved foreign tax on overseas branch income.

Anti-avoidance provisions

8.   There are anti-avoidance provisions in TA 1988 s 801A to prevent group companies, particularly financial companies, artificially increasing the amount of underlying tax they are entitled to by means of an avoidance scheme. The provisions limit relief for underlying tax by reference to the rate of corporation tax payable by the UK company on the dividend which it receives.

There are also rules in TA 1988 ss 798, 798A, 798B and 803 to prevent banks and other financial traders getting excessive relief for foreign tax paid on overseas interest that is part of their trading profits. FA 2005 and F (No 2) A 2005 contain many detailed technical anti-avoidance provisions targeted at schemes notified under the anti-avoidance regime, affecting much of the detail of the CFC and DTR rules.

Treatment where double tax relief not claimed

9.   Where no credit is claimed for the overseas tax, the foreign profits are taken into account net of the overseas tax (s 811).

If, for example, profits, including overseas profits, were to be reduced to nil by trading losses, so that no UK tax was payable, there would be no credit available for the foreign tax. By including the foreign profits net of overseas tax, the offset of losses would be reduced, leaving the losses available to set against other profits as shown below:

	£
UK profits	60,000
Overseas branch profits (£50,000 less foreign tax paid £20,000)	30,000
	90,000
Trading losses (part of £130,000)	(90,000)
Profits chargeable to corporation tax	–
Losses available against other profits	40,000

If the overseas branch profits had been brought into account before overseas tax, giving total profits of £110,000, no foreign tax credit would have been available since no corporation tax is payable, and the unrelieved losses would be only £20,000 instead of £40,000.

Treatment of charges on income etc

10.   Where there are charges on income, management expenses, group relief, or other amounts which can be offset against profits of more than one description, the company is able to use them in the most

advantageous manner for double tax relief (s 797(3)). Domo Ltd in part A can accordingly offset the charges paid against UK profits in priority to foreign income and gains, leaving a higher amount of foreign profits to absorb double tax credits. The non-trade interest (loan relationship non-trading 'deficit') can be set against the UK trading profits rather that the overseas trading profits, as shown for Jones Ltd in part B of the example.

Set-off of ACT

11. If the company has surplus ACT brought forward, this will be recoverable under the shadow ACT regime. This means that, broadly, shadow ACT on current dividends must be set off after double tax relief. The set-off is limited in respect of *each source* of profit to the appropriate percentage (currently 20%) of the profits chargeable to corporation tax, or the amount of tax remaining after double tax relief whichever is less (Shadow ACT regulations (SI 1999/358) reg 12(4)). If excess offset capacity remains after the offset of shadow ACT, surplus ACT brought forward can be recovered up to that amount.

Under the pre-6 April 1999 ACT regime, many companies with significant overseas income built up an ever-increasing amount of surplus ACT on dividends because of the prior offset of double tax relief, which invariably eliminated the UK tax on the overseas income. The shadow ACT system does not improve their position, since notional ACT on current dividends must still be offset in priority to the recoverable surplus ACT brought forward.

Later adjustments to foreign tax paid

12. If the amount of foreign tax payable is later adjusted, the amount of double tax relief claimed will be similarly adjusted. If an adjustment to foreign tax results in too much relief having been claimed, HMRC must be notified within one year after the adjustment (TA 1988 s 806).

A.   Bray Motors plc has an authorised and issued share capital of 10,000,000 ordinary shares of £1 each, and its shares are listed and regularly dealt in on the Stock Exchange.

The present shareholdings in the company are as follows:

	Shares
John Bray (the company's founder, now retired)	2,550,000
Colin Rawson (a private investor)	1,000,000
Lawrence Jones (the company's managing director)	600,000
Globe Autos Ltd (a close company)	470,000
Alan Brooks (a private investor)	460,000
James Baker (the company's financial director)	370,000
Ace Car Hire Ltd (not a close company)	370,000
Brian Pritchard (a private investor)	360,000
Edward Hay (a private investor)	340,000
340 private investors, none of whom own more than 20,000 shares	3,480,000
	10,000,000

All the shares are beneficially owned.

None of the shareholders is related to or associated with any other shareholder.

The company owns a trade investment of 5,000 shares in Marsh Alternators Ltd, an unquoted company with an authorised and issued share capital of 100,000 ordinary shares of £1 each.

The other shares in the company are currently owned as follows:

	Shares
Norman Marsh	8,000
Trustees of a settlement made by Norman Marsh for his grandchildren	19,000
Henry Simpson (Norman Marsh's cousin)	3,000
Gerald Black (no relation to any of the above)	5,000
Ellen Black (Gerald's wife)	1,500
Tom Black (Gerald's son)	4,000
Nigel Clement (Gerald Black's nephew)	3,000
Walter Metcalfe (Nigel Clement's partner in a garage business)	2,500
Richard Court (no relation to any of the above)	3,500
Keith Court (Richard's brother)	1,500
35 other shareholders, none of whom owns more than 2,000 shares and none of whom is related to or associated with any other shareholder	44,000
	95,000

All the shares are beneficially owned.

The directors of Marsh Alternators Ltd are Gerald Black and Richard Court.

Set out the reasoning as to whether the close company provisions are applicable to:

(i)   Bray Motors plc

(ii) Marsh Alternators Ltd.

B.   Indicate the circumstances in which a close company is within the definition of a 'close investment-holding company' and state the consequences.

C.   Cook is about to acquire shares in a publicly quoted company for £350,000 out of his own funds, giving him around a 2% equity stake. The shares currently yield a dividend of £28,000 pa and the prospects of significant capital appreciation in the future are excellent. At the end of 10 years, Cook may decide to sell some or all of the shares. It has been suggested to Cook by a friend, Dodge, that instead of buying the shares himself he should form a new investment company, Cook Limited. Cook would subscribe for 350,000 £1 shares in Cook Limited, which would then use the cash to buy the shares. Dodge has told Cook that he could draw out director's remuneration of up to £10,000 pa and that Cook Limited could deduct this against the dividend income and that the balance of £18,000 would only attract a small amount of tax because of the 'nil' starting rate of corporation tax. Dodge has also said that Cook could save tax on his director's earnings by paying premiums into a personal pension scheme.

State whether the advice which Cook has received from Dodge is correct.

A. (i) **Bray Motors plc**, whilst controlled by five participators, is a quoted company in which 35% of the shares are held by the public and not more than 85% are held by the principal members, viz:

Name	Shares	Control Test 5 largest participators	Public ownership Test 35%	Principal Members Test 5 largest over 5% (500,000 shares)
John Bray	2,550,000	2,550,000		2,550,000
Colin Rawson	1,000,000	1,000,000		1,000,000
Lawrence Jones (director)	600,000	600,000		600,000
Globe Autos Ltd (close company)	470,000	470,000	470,000	
Alan Brooks	460,000	460,000	460,000	
James Baker (director)	370,000			
Ace Car Hire Ltd (open company)	370,000		370,000	
Brian Pritchard	360,000		360,000	
Edward Hay	340,000		340,000	
340 private investors	3,480,000		3,480,000	
Total Shares	10,000,000	5,080,000	5,480,000	4,150,000
Percentage	100%	50.8%	54.8%	41.5%

Therefore Bray Motors plc is *not* a close company.

(ii) **Marsh Alternators Limited** is controlled by five participators together with their associates, viz:

5 largest holdings		Holding including associates
Norman Marsh	8,000	
Trustees of settlement for grandchildren	19,000	27,000
Gerald Black	5,000	
His wife	1,500	
His son	4,000	10,500
Nigel Clement	3,000	
His partner	2,500	5,500
Richard Court	3,500	
His brother	1,500	5,000
Bray Motors Ltd		5,000
		53,000
Others: H Simpson	3,000	
35 other shareholders	44,000	47,000
		100,000

Marsh Alternators Ltd is therefore a close company.

B. A close company is a close investment-holding company in an accounting period *unless* throughout that period it exists wholly or mainly for one or more of the following purposes:

   (i)   Carrying on a trade on a commercial basis (including dealing in land, shares or securities)

   (ii) Investing in land or buildings for letting to third parties (ie other than to persons connected with the company or their spouses or relatives)

   (iii) Acting as a holding company for one or more companies each of which qualifies under (i) or (ii) above.

A company that makes loans to qualifying companies in the same group, or holds property or provides other services for those companies, qualifies for exclusion, as does a holding company that itself carries on a trade, or acts as the top company in a group and merely holds shares in a subsidiary that has qualifying subsidiaries (TA 1988 s 13A(1)–(3)).

Where a close company goes into liquidation, it is not treated as a close investment-holding company for the accounting period commencing with the winding-up if it was a qualifying company in the previous accounting period (but this may not help if the company ceased trading some time before going into liquidation – see Example 59 explanatory note 5).

The main consequence of being a close investment-holding company is that, regardless of the level of the company's profits, corporation tax is charged at the full rate, ie it is not entitled to the benefit of the corporation tax small companies' rate, or marginal relief (TA 1988 ss 13(1)(b) and 13AA(8)).

A further important restriction is that interest relief on loans taken out to acquire ordinary share capital of a close company is not given if the company is a close investment-holding company or becomes such a company (TA 1988 s 360(1)(2)).

C. Since Cook Limited would be controlled by Cook, it would be a close investment-holding company. As such it was not able to take advantage of the 'nil' starting rate (abolished with effect from 1 April 2006) or the small companies' rate, regardless of the level of its profits. The full rate (currently 30%) is payable. If, however, the only source of profits was the dividends on the shares, that income would be franked investment income which is not chargeable to corporation tax. There would therefore be no profits out of which to pay any director's fees.

As far as director's remuneration is concerned, the remuneration would have to be wholly and exclusively for the purposes of the company's business. If the only activity of the company was to hold the shares in the public company it is clear that Cook's directorship would not involve much commitment and it is unlikely that anything more than a nominal amount would be allowed as director's fees. Any amounts that were allowed would be subject to payment of national insurance contributions by the company and also by Cook.

From 6 April 2006, pension contributions paid by the company would be limited for practical purposes by the individual's annual and lifetime allowances (see Example 37). As an individual, Cook may contribute the higher of £3,600 or 100% of earnings, and if a higher rate taxpayer he may claim higher rate tax relief. He would retain basic rate tax relief at 22% out of the payment, the pension provider recovering that amount from HMRC, and if Cook is a higher rate taxpayer, he would claim the extra higher rate relief in his self-assessment return. However, the amount that the company can claim for a tax deduction is limited by the wholly and exclusively test, and is likely to be nominal.

In the long term, the capital appreciation on the shares may lead to double taxation, if the company is liquidated when the shares are sold. The capital gain on the disposal of the shares would be charged to tax at the full corporation tax rate. (Given that Cook Limited would only hold a 2% interest in the shares, it would not be entitled to the substantial shareholdings exemption on the disposal – see Example 65.) Cook could either extract the company's chargeable gain as a dividend prior to the liquidation, receiving the balance of the proceeds by way of capital distribution, or leave the gain as part of the funds paid out on the liquidation. If the company sold the shares for, say, £550,000 and, assuming indexation allowance of £50,000 for the company and 10 years' (maximum) non-business asset taper relief of 40% for Cook, the comparative position using the current corporation tax rates is set out below. (It is assumed that there is no retained income in the company at this point.)

If accounting profit (reserves) paid out as dividend prior to liquidation

	£
Gain (£550,000 less cost £350,000)	200,000
Corporation tax @ 30% on capital gain of £150,000 (£200,000 less indexation)	45,000
Cash dividend (= reserves)	155,000
Tax credit 1/9	17,222
Cook's income for tax purposes	172,222
Tax thereon @ say 32½%	55,972
(of which £38,750 is payable after deducting tax credit)	
Balance of proceeds paid out in liquidation (= share capital) (550,000 less tax and dividend amounting to 200,000)	350,000
Cost of Cook's shares in Cook Limited	350,000
Chargeable gain	–
Surplus on share sale, net of tax (£505,000 – £350,000 – £38,750)	116,250

If investment shares sold and company liquidated

	£
Sale proceeds for investment shares	550,000
Corporation tax on gain	45,000
Capital distribution to Cook	505,000
Cost of Cook's shares in Cook Limited	350,000
Chargeable gain before taper relief	155,000
Non-business asset taper relief at 40% (10 years)	62,000
Cook's chargeable gain after taper relief	93,000
Capital gains tax @ 40% (assuming annual exemption already used)	37,200
Surplus on sale of shares net of tax (£505,000 – £350,000 – £37,200)	117,800

If Cook held the investment shares personally, his surplus on sale would be £152,000, calculated as follows:

	£
Sale proceeds	550,000
Cost of investment shares	350,000
Chargeable gain before taper relief	200,000
Non-business asset taper relief at 40% (10 years)	80,000
Cook's chargeable gain	120,000
CGT @ 40% (assuming annual exemption used elsewhere)	48,000
Surplus on sale (£550,000 – £350,000 – £48,000)	152,000

This demonstrates the impact of the 'double taxation' which arises where appreciating assets are held within an (investment) company.

Explanatory Notes

Definition of close company

1. A close company is one under the control of five or fewer participators or of participators who are directors (TA 1988 s 414).

2. A *participator* is a person having a share or interest in the capital or income of the company (TA 1988 s 417(1)), the most common form of participator therefore being a shareholder although the legislation does not restrict the definition to a shareholder. The word 'person' includes both an individual and a company.

3. *Control* means exercising, or able to exercise, or entitled to acquire control over, the company's affairs, and in particular, but without prejudice to the general meaning of the foregoing, possessing or entitled to acquire the greater part of the share capital, or issued share capital, or of the voting power in the company (TA 1988 s 416(2)).

    An entitlement to receive now or in the future the greater part of the income if the whole income were to be distributed, or the greater part of the assets of the company that were available for distribution among the participators on a winding-up, also denotes control.

Participator's associates etc

4. In determining whether five or fewer participators (or participators who are directors) control a company, the rights of certain other persons must be regarded as those of the participator, namely:

    (a) His nominee (TA 1988 s 416(5))

    (b) His associates, being (TA 1988 ss 416(6) and 417(3) & (4))

         (i)   a business partner

         (ii) his spouse or civil partner (see below), parent or remoter forebear, child or remoter issue, brother or sister

         (iii) trustees of any settlement made by the participator or the relatives in 4(b)(ii) above

         (iv) where the participator has an interest in shares or obligations of the company that are in a trust or deceased's estate, the trustees and personal representatives and, if the participator is a company, any other company interested in those shares or obligations. (This provision covers, inter alia, trusts for occupational pensions and employee benevolent funds.)

    (c) Any company or companies of which the participator or he and his associates have control (TA 1988 s 416(6)).

    The Civil Partnership Act 2004 came into effect on 5 December 2005, allowing same-sex couples to register as civil partners. The detailed amendments to existing legislation of SI 2005/3229 operate to give civil partners parity in tax treatment with married couples for IHT, CGT and income tax as well as corporation tax from that date. The rights and holdings of civil partners' shares will be taken into account in determining both close company status and associated company status.

Close company exclusion where public holdings are 35% or more

5. There is an exclusion from close company status if shares in the company carrying not less than 35% of the voting power (and not carrying a fixed rate of dividend with or without further rights to participate in profits) are *held by the public* (see note 6 below) and such shares have within the preceding twelve months been listed on and the subject of dealings on a recognised stock exchange (TA 1988 s 415(1)). This exclusion does not, however, apply where the voting power possessed by the principal members exceeds 85%, the principal members being the five persons possessing the greatest percentage of the voting power, each owning over 5% (TA 1988 s 415(2) and (6)). Where

there are no such five persons, because two or more possess equal percentages, all those with equal percentages are counted, eg two with 20% and five with 10% = seven principal members together holding 90%.

6. Shares are regarded as held by the public if they satisfy one of the following tests (unless they are excluded by the next following paragraph):

    (a) If held by a non-close company

    (b) If held on trust for an approved superannuation fund

    (c) If not held by a principal member.

    Public holdings *exclude* a holding by a director or his associate or by a company under their control, or by a company associated with the company concerned, or a holding by certain funds for the benefit of past and present employees, directors or their dependants (for example occupational pension funds, employee share trusts and benevolent funds). Companies are 'associated' if, within twelve months previously, one has control of the other or both are under the control of the same person or persons (TA 1988 s 416(1)). See Example 49 explanatory note 7 for further details.

    The holding of a non-close company counts as a public holding and is included in the 35% rule, but if the non-close company has one of the five largest vote carrying holdings it also counts as a principal member and is therefore included in the 85% rule.

    eg voting power in quoted company held as follows:

	(a)	(b)
Two directors equally	60%	60%
Non-close company	10%	30%
Members of public (none holding over 5%)	30%	10%
	100%	100%

    In both cases the public holdings are 40%.

    In example (a) the principal members hold 70% and the company is accordingly *not* a close company.

    In example (b) the principal members hold 90% and the company *is* a close company.

Other exclusions from close company status

7. There are certain other exclusions from close company status:

    (a) a non-resident company

    (b) a registered industrial and provident society within the meaning of TA 1988 s 486

    (c) a building society

    (d) a company controlled by the Crown, unless it could be treated as a close company on the ground of being under the control of persons acting independently of the Crown

    (e) a company controlled by a company which is not a close company (other than by reason of non-residence), or by two or more companies none of which is a close company, where it cannot be treated as a close company except by taking as one of the five or fewer participators requisite for its being so treated a company which is not a close company

    (f) a company which could only be close by taking as a participator entitled to receive the greater part of its assets on a winding-up, a loan creditor which is a non-close company (other than by reason of non-residence).

    (TA 1988 s 414).

Consequences of being a close company

8.   Where a company is within the definition of a close company, the following provisions apply:

(a)   Any benefits derived by a participator, other than an employee earning £8,500 per annum or more, or a director, are regarded as distributions of profits rather than deductions from trading profits (see Example 57).

(b)   If a close company makes a loan to a participator, the company has to pay tax at 25% on the amount of the loan, subject to certain exceptions (TA 1988 s 419 – see Example 57 and also (e) below).

(c)   The small companies' rate is not available if the company is also a close investment-holding company (TA 1988 ss 13(1)(b) and 13AA(8)).

(d)   If the company transfers an asset at undervalue, the shareholders will suffer an appropriate reduction in the capital gains base cost of their shares, unless the shortfall has already been taken into account for income tax (TCGA 1992 s 125 and HMRC concession D51).

(e)   Under the 'loan relationships' rules for companies (see Example 62), where the parties to a loan are a close company and a participator or associate of a participator, the following provisions apply:

(i)   For accounting periods starting after 30 September 2002, the company is not denied a deduction for a loan written off unless the loan is to a controlling shareholder (see Example 62 explanatory note 7). See Example 57 explanatory note 11 for the treatment of individuals where loans to them have been written off.

(ii)   Where the company has borrowed from a participator or his associate, interest paid by the company more than twelve months after the period in which it would otherwise be treated as accruing cannot be deducted until it is paid, unless the participator or associate is a company that has included the interest in its profits on an accruals basis (Sch 9.2). For accounting periods starting after 30 September 2002, this rule has been extended to borrowings from a company controlled by a participator, or in which a participator holds a 40% or more interest (new Sch 9.2 – see Example 62 explanatory note 7(b)).

(iii)   Where the close company has borrowed from the participator or associate on a discounted security (ie where the difference between issue price and redemption price is more than 0.5% per year or more than 15% overall), relief for the discount is not given until the security is redeemed (Sch 9.18), but for accounting periods starting after 30 September 2002 this rule ceases to apply where the holder of the security is within the loan relationships rules, ie is taxed on the discount.

See also Example 70 note 4 re the apportionment of gains of non-resident companies that would have been close companies if they had been UK resident.

(f)   When shareholders dispose of their shares, taper relief for capital gains tax may be lost (for pre-17 April 2002 sales) where there has been a 'relevant change of activity' and restricted (for post-16 April 2002 sales) where the company is not 'active' (see Example 74 part (a)(i) under *Anti-avoidance provisions*).

Other points

9.   For detailed provisions on personal pension scheme contributions see Example 38. Capital gains tax is dealt with in Examples 73 to 85.

You have been appointed to act professionally for Morrissey Ltd, a close company which was formed a month ago and which has an issued share capital of £50,000 divided into 50,000 ordinary shares of £1 each.

The managing director, Mr Morrissey, has only a general knowledge of corporation tax and is particularly anxious that you should explain to him:

 (i)   What is meant by a 'distribution';

 (ii)   Whether the fact that it is not intended that the company should declare any dividends during the first few years of its existence, but rather to retain any profits in the business, would have any taxation effects;

 (iii)   Whether the granting of a loan by the company to any of its shareholders would be affected by taxation;

 (iv)   How the company might be affected from a taxation point of view if it had to go into liquidation.

Mr Morrissey stresses to you that it should be borne in mind that the company's operations will be confined to the UK, its income will only be derived from its trading profits and from the letting of property owned by it and it is not intended that the company's issued share capital should be altered in any way nor any other shares or securities issued. The profits are not expected to exceed the upper limit for small companies' rate.

Write to Mr Morrissey setting out the information requested by him.

10 Upping Street
Downtown

21 July 2006

Mr Morrissey
Morrissey Ltd
Downtown Industrial Estate
Downtown

Dear Mr Morrissey,

Thank you for your letter of 1 July asking me for information on the taxation treatment of certain matters affecting your company. The answers to the points raised by you are as follows:

(i) *Meaning of the term distribution*

The term distribution has a very wide meaning for corporation tax, and that meaning is extended in the case of companies controlled either by their directors or by five or fewer participators (broadly shareholders). Such companies are termed close companies and Morrissey Ltd falls within the definition.

Many of the provisions relating to distributions are concerned with share issues, redemptions etc, and since your company is not contemplating any changes in its share capital they will not apply. The term distribution in your case will therefore cover:

(a) Any dividends paid in cash

(b) Any distribution of assets in a non-cash form, and any benefit provided for shareholders or their associates (such as the use of cars, provision of living accommodation, entertainment etc). This will not usually apply where the assets or benefits are provided to a director, or to an employee earning £8,500 per annum or more. Directors and employees earning £8,500 per annum or more are charged to tax on the provision of assets and benefits as employment income and the company suffers a Class 1A national insurance contributions charge of 12.8%. The expense of the provision is deductible by the company in arriving at its profits so long as it can be shown to be wholly and exclusively for the purposes of the trade.

(ii) *Effect of retaining profits rather than paying dividends*

The fact that the company does not intend to make any distributions within the first few years will not have any immediate taxation effects and will undoubtedly assist with your cash flow and working capital requirements.

The payment of dividends does not normally affect the company's corporation tax payments. However, for dividends paid between 1/4/04 and 31/3/06, if the company's taxable profits were less than £50,000 and the dividend was paid to individual shareholders, the amount of the profits which 'matched' the dividend paid were subject to corporation tax at a flat rate of 19% (this is known as the 'non-corporate distribution rate') rather than the lower rates which would otherwise have been payable if the distribution had not been made.

Some companies are required to pay corporation tax in instalments, but only where their profits exceed a specified limit, presently £1,500,000 (which is not expected to apply in your case). It should be mentioned that, as and when dividends are paid, the shareholders will receive a tax credit equal to one ninth of the dividend (ie 10% on the grossed up amount of the dividend). Shareholders will only suffer an additional tax liability if they are higher rate taxpayers, the additional tax being equal to 25% of the cash dividend received (22.5% on the grossed up amount).

If the company's profits can be retained and subsequently taken in a 'capital' form, this is likely to prove more beneficial for tax purposes. Subject to certain anti-avoidance provisions, all shareholdings in unlisted trading companies (and also non-trading companies for shareholder employees who do not have a material interest in the company, which broadly means more than 10% of the shares, votes or profits) qualify for business asset taper relief, which is given as a reduction in computing gains arising on the sale of the shares. For close company shareholders who are higher rate taxpayers, the taper relief, if available, would reduce the tax on gains to an effective rate of 10% after just two years of share ownership. The fact that the company receives letting income may, however, deny taper relief at the business asset rate (other than to employee shareholders with less than a 10% interest as indicated above) because it must be shown that any non-trading purposes have no substantial effect on the extent of the company's activities. HMRC may regard the letting as having a substantial effect if the letting receipts exceeded 20% of the combined trading and letting income, but this depends on the company's particular circumstances. The maximum taper relief on non-business assets is available only after ten years, and the effective tax rate on gains for a higher rate taxpayer is 24%. In the company's case, the opportunities for shareholders to take capital profits are relatively limited, for example, on receiving a capital sum on a liquidation (see (iv) below) or on selling shares back to the company on retirement (provided they have been held at least five years and certain other conditions are satisfied). Such considerations would not usually be expected to dictate the company's dividend policy during its early years, although reduction of surplus cash balances by payment of dividend would reduce an obstacle to qualifying for full business property taper relief later.

(iii) *Loans to shareholders*

If the company makes loans to shareholders (other than loans of £15,000 or less to full-time directors or employees who do not own more than 5% of the share capital) the company will have to pay tax at 25% of the loan, repayable by HMRC as and when the loan is repaid by the shareholder to the company. This is a 'stand-alone' tax charge and is not deductible from the corporation tax payable on profits.

If the company should release or write off such a loan, the company can reclaim the tax paid. However, a shareholder who controls the company is connected with the company under the special rules for loans. This means that if the amount released relates to a controlling shareholder, it cannot be deducted from the company's profits for corporation tax purposes.

As far as the shareholder is concerned, any amount released is grossed up at the dividend tax credit rate of 10%, ie by 100/90, and treated as income. It would, however, only be liable to the higher dividend tax rate of 32½% (less the lower rate credit of 10%) where taxable income exceeded the basic rate limit (currently £33,300). Any higher rate liability is effectively 22½% of the gross amount released.

There will be no other effect on a shareholder who receives a loan from the company unless he earns £8,500 or more, or is a director. In that event he will be charged to tax under the employment-related loans provisions. This means that he will be deemed to have received extra remuneration equal to interest on the loan at the prevailing official rate less any interest which he actually pays to the company (which will be computed and returned on his P11D form). This will not apply if the total loans outstanding in a tax year to that shareholder or anyone connected with him do not exceed £5,000. If the loan is one on which interest (if charged) would have been available for income tax relief, no taxable benefit arises.

You should also note that the company will have to pay Class 1A national insurance contributions at 12.8% on the taxable benefit arising from non-qualifying loans.

(iv) *Tax consequences of liquidation*

If the company goes into liquidation, the commencement of the winding-up will denote the end of an accounting period and commencement of another for corporation tax. If the company ceases trading prior to the commencement of liquidation the cessation of trading also triggers the end of a corporation tax accounting period.

The cessation will require balancing adjustments to be made in respect of capital allowances claimed and if trading losses arise in the final twelve months that are not covered by other profits of the same period, relief may be claimed against the total profits of the three previous years, latest first. Profits may arise in the final trading period in the form of chargeable gains on the disposal of assets, but it would be necessary for the contract for the disposal to be made before the cessation of trade to enable trading losses in the final accounting period to be set off against those gains. Brought forward trading losses cannot be set against other sources of income or gains.

To the extent that the company retains income and capital profits, a double tax charge will inevitably occur on liquidation. The company will have paid corporation tax at the time the profits were made, and unless they have been distributed to the shareholders as a dividend before the liquidation, the retentions will swell the amounts received by the shareholders in the winding-up. Amounts paid out to the shareholders during the liquidation will be chargeable to capital gains tax, after deducting their base value for the shares, any capital gains tax reliefs, including the relevant taper relief and any available personal annual exemption. If the shares have qualified for full business asset taper relief, it will normally be important to ensure the gain is not materially diluted for taper relief purposes. If practicable, the capital distribution should be made as soon as possible after the cessation of trade/start of the winding-up as this will reduce the part of the gain relating to the post-trading period which attracts relief at the lower non-business asset taper rate.

I shall be happy to provide any additional information you require, or to discuss further with you the matters dealt with above.

Yours sincerely,

John Smith

Explanatory Notes

Distribution – general meaning

1.   For companies in general the term 'distribution' means (TA 1988 ss 209–211):

   (a)   Any dividend paid by the company, including a capital dividend

   (b)   Any other distribution out of the company's assets, whether in cash or not, except a repayment of capital or an amount for which new consideration is given

   (c)   Any bonus issue of securities or redeemable shares issued in respect of shares or securities of the company (excluding scrip dividends – see note 6)

   (d)   Any excess of market value of benefit received where assets or liabilities are transferred to shareholders over any new consideration given (except for intra-group transfers)

   (e)   Where share capital (other than fully paid preference share capital) is repaid, bonus issues made at the same time or subsequently. This does not apply to non-close listed companies where the bonus issue is not redeemable share capital and takes place more than 10 years after the repayment of capital

   (f)   Interest payments on securities in certain circumstances, eg where the interest exceeds a normal commercial rate (defined in FA 1996 s 103(3A)) or varies with the company's profits. This does not, however, catch interest on 'ratchet loans' (ie loans where the rate increases as profits deteriorate and vice versa). The legislation is intended only to apply where interest effectively represents a share in profits. The provisions are complex and are subject to anti-avoidance provisions in TA 1988 s 212 which prevent interest payments from one company to another being artificially turned into franked investment income in the receiving company's hands because of the distribution provisions. For companies in a 75% group, no matter where resident, the amount of interest treated as a distribution is the excess, if any, of the amount paid over what would have been paid between unconnected companies. This rule is aimed at preventing 'thin capitalisation' of UK companies (ie financing a UK company predominantly by loan capital rather than share capital). There are special transfer pricing measures to counter thin capitalisation in cases where there is less than 75% control (see Example 69).

2. Distributions in a winding-up do not count as income distributions and are subject to capital gains tax (as a 'deemed' disposal of shares under TCGA 1992 s 122).

3. The distribution provisions are relaxed in relation to demergers (see Example 67) and the purchase by a company of its own shares (see Example 60).

Qualifying and non-qualifying distributions

4. Non-qualifying distributions are bonus issues of redeemable shares or securities, either issued directly or issued out of bonus redeemable shares or securities received from another company (TA 1988 s 14). The shareholder is liable where appropriate to the excess of the dividend rate upper rate of 32½% over the dividend income ordinary rate of 10% on the grossed up amount of the distribution. The company is required to notify HMRC within fourteen days after the end of the quarter in which the non-qualifying distribution is made (TA 1988 s 234). When the shares are redeemed the redemption is a qualifying distribution but tax paid at excess rates on the non-qualifying distribution may be set against any tax due at excess rates on the later qualifying distribution (TA 1988 s 233).

Distribution – extended meaning for close companies

5. For close companies the term distribution has an extended meaning (TA 1988 s 418). It covers the provision of benefits to participators and their associates, except those provided to directors and employees earning £8,500 or more, which are already assessable as employment income (see Example 10). The calculation of the amount of the distribution in respect of benefits to participators is made in the same way as for benefits to directors and employees earning £8,500 or more (TA 1988 s 418(4)). For further details on directors' loans see Example 57. Close company liquidations are dealt with in Example 59.

Scrip dividends

6. As indicated in note 1(c), scrip dividends, ie dividends taken in the form of shares rather than in cash, are not treated as distributions. Thus no ACT was due on scrip dividend shares issued before 6 April 1999 and they do not give rise to any shadow ACT after 5 April 1999 (TA 1988 s 230).

    Where an individual takes a scrip dividend, he is deemed to have received income equal to the 'appropriate amount in cash', grossed up at the dividend income rate of 10%. The 'appropriate amount in cash' means the amount of the cash option, unless it is substantially different from the market value of the shares, 'substantially' being interpreted by HMRC as 15% or more either way (Statement of Practice A8). In practice HMRC will ignore a difference of up to 17% in any case not involving avoidance. If the difference is substantial, the appropriate amount in cash is the market value of the shares on the first day of dealing. Basic rate taxpayers have no liability on the scrip dividend, but the notional credit is not repayable. Those liable to higher rate tax pay tax at 22½% (32½% less 10%) on the grossed up amount as for cash dividends (ITTOIA ss 409–414).

    The gross equivalent of scrip dividends is income of a deceased's estate when such shares are issued to personal representatives. It is also income of discretionary and accumulation trusts (other than trusts in which the settlor has retained an interest), the trustees being liable to tax, for 2004/05 onwards, at the same 32½% rate as individuals (less the 10% credit). See Example 79 explanatory note 3 for the position of life interest trusts and notes on the capital gains position generally.

    Where scrip dividends are issued to a company, or a trust in which the settlor retains an interest, they are capital rather than income, with a capital gains base cost of nil.

    Companies have to make separate quarterly returns of any scrip dividends issued (TA 1988 s 250).

Loans written off

7. See Example 55 explanatory note 8 part (e) for the treatment of loans written off for companies and Example 57 for the treatment of individuals.

Non-corporate distribution rate

8.   For details on the 19% non-corporate distribution rate, see the explanatory notes on Example 50.

Capital gains tax taper relief

9.   For detailed notes on taper relief for capital gains tax see Example 74 part (a)(i). See HMRC's Tax Bulletin of December 2002 for their views on the meaning of trading company for taper relief purposes.

Misses Stiff and Starch are the only directors of Oaks in Charnwood Ltd, which owns a large country property from which it carries on the business of rest home for the elderly.

They live on the premises in order properly to attend to the residents, sharing with their lifelong friend Miss Gentle (who is employed as resident matron) a private suite, the annual rental equivalent of which has been agreed with HMRC at £3,600 for the whole suite. The suite was fully refurnished at the company's expense on 7 April 2006 at a cost of £6,000 and the cost of lighting, heating, cleaning, repairs and maintenance in 2006/07 was £3,000 for the whole suite. Neither the directors nor Miss Gentle make any contribution to the company for this accommodation.

The equal shareholders are Misses Stiff and Starch together with Miss Stiff's brother, Donald. Although Donald does not live at the rest home he has his meals there daily, the cost of the meals being £2,000 in the year ended 31 March 2007. Donald has not contributed anything towards this cost. Misses Stiff and Starch each pay to the company an amount representing the cost of their own meals.

Miss Gentle is paid a salary of £9,000 per annum. As well as living on the premises, she has the use of a 1900 cc company car with an original list price of £12,000 (CO_2 emissions figure 169 grams per kilometre) and the annual running expenses borne by the company amount to £1,200. Miss Gentle reimburses to the company the cost of petrol provided for her private motoring. The annual mileage is 10,000, of which 2,600 relates to private motoring.

Miss Gentle has an interest-free loan from the company of £4,300, the whole amount of which was outstanding during 2006/07. On 6 April 2006 the company had released her from repaying £700, the original loan having been £5,000 in 1998, to help her to furnish a seaside cottage which she intends to use as a retirement home.

The directors each receive a salary of £24,000 per annum under the PAYE system.

No dividends have been paid during the year.

During the year ended 31 March 2007, the company made private payments for the directors which were charged to their current/loan accounts, as follows (there being nil balances on the accounts at the beginning of the year):

	Stiff £	Starch £
30 June 2006	3,600	–
30 September 2006	2,500	950
31 December 2006	1,000	600
31 March 2007	2,500	450
	9,600	2,000

The directors have the use of company cars. Miss Stiff's is a Volvo 70 series (CO_2 emissions figure 240 grams per kilometre), that had a list price when new of £24,320, and Miss Starch's is a Volkswagen Golf (petrol CO_2 emissions figure 162 grams per kilometre) list price when new £19,270. Miss Stiff travels extensively on the business of the company and in 2006/07 recorded 20,000 business miles. Miss Starch's total mileage was 15,000, of which 5,000 was for business purposes. The company provides all the motor running expenses.

The corporation tax adjusted profit for the year ended 31 March 2007, before any adjustment arising out of Donald's meals, was £20,650.

Apart from her income from Oaks in Charnwood Ltd, Miss Gentle has gross building society interest of £6,000 per annum.

(a) Calculate the corporation tax payable by the company for the year ended 31 March 2007.

(b) State the amounts of directors' assessable emoluments for 2006/07 in respect of each of Miss Stiff and Miss Starch and calculate the national insurance contributions liability payable by the company on their emoluments.

(c) Calculate the total income tax payable by Miss Gentle for 2006/07.

(d) State the taxation position resulting from the balances on the directors' current/loan accounts with the company from time to time.

(e) State what the consequences and procedure would be if it was discovered that, during the year to 31 March 2007, Misses Stiff and Starch had each irregularly retained for themselves company income of £7,500, which had not been reflected in the company accounts.

The official rate of interest is set at 5% for 2006/07.

(a) **Corporation tax computation – year ended 31 March 2007**

	£
Profit chargeable to corporation tax (20,650 + 2,000 for Donald's meals)	22,650

(The cost of the directors' and employees' benefits will already have been charged in arriving at the profit and is allowable)

Corporation tax thereon: 22,650 @ 19%, payable 1 January 2008	4,304

(b) **Directors' assessable emoluments – 2006/07**

	Miss Stiff £	Miss Starch £
Remuneration for year ended 31 March 2007	24,000	24,000
Use of company car:		
car benefit –		
Volvo 70 (CO_2 = 240) 24,320 x 35%	8,512	
Volkswagen Golf (CO_2 = 162) 19,270 x 19%		3,661
car fuel benefit –		
Volvo (£14,400 × 35%)	5,040	
Volkswagen (£14,400 × 19%)		2,736
Annual rental equivalent of accommodation		
(1/3rd each x 3,600)	1,200	1,200
Value of furnishings (20% x 6,000 x 1/3)	400	400
and services (3,000 x 1/3)	1,000	1,000
Beneficial loan interest (see (d))	216	–
	40,368	32,997

Company's national insurance liability re directors – 2006/07

	£	£
Employer's Class 1 NIC (24,000 – 5,035) @ 12.8%	2,427	2,427
Employer's Class 1A NIC 16,368/8,997 @ 12.8%	2,095	1,152
Total employer's NIC	4,522	3,579

(c) **Miss Gentle – tax payable 2006/07**

	£
Salary – Oaks in Charnwood Ltd	9,000
Use of company car (CO_2 = 169) 12,000 x 20%	2,400
Amount of loan released	700
	12,100
Benefit of furnishings, heating and lighting etc	
(1,000 + 400, but limited to 10% of other emoluments)	1,210
Emoluments from Oaks in Charnwood Ltd	13,310
Building society interest	6,000
	19,310
Less: Personal allowance	5,035
Taxable income	14,275

		£
Tax thereon: On non-savings income	2,150 @ 10%	215
	6,125 @ 22%	1,348
On savings income	6,000 @ 20%	1,200
	14,275	
Income tax payable		2,763

Miss Gentle will not be charged to tax on the benefit of the interest-free loan, since it does not exceed £5,000. She is, however, charged on the loan released, as indicated above.

(d) **Tax position on directors' loans**

Tax charge under TA 1988 s 419

The company will have to pay tax on the amount of the directors' overdrawn accounts at 31 March 2007 amounting to 25% x £11,600 = £2,900. The tax is payable by 1 January 2008, interest being charged from that date if the tax is not paid (TA 1988 s 419). The tax is not payable if the loan is repaid within that time (see explanatory note 9).

The company must report the loans made during the year ended 31 March 2007 on supplementary page CT 600A on its self-assessment corporation tax return for the year. If it fails to do so, it will have made an incorrect return. As such action would invariably be negligent, the company would be liable to a tax-related penalty, the maximum amount being the amount of tax understated. For these purposes no account is taken of s 419 tax which is refundable or relievable due to the loan being repaid (FA 1998 Sch 18.89).

There would be no assessment on the directors, but if the company released or wrote off the loans or any part of them, then that part released or written off would be included in the director's taxable income, grossed up at 10%. Basic and starting rate taxpayers would have no liability, but higher rate taxpayers would have to account for tax at the difference between the dividend income upper rate, currently 32½% and the dividend income ordinary rate of 10% on the grossed up equivalent of the loan (ITTOIA 2005 s 416). The effective rate is therefore currently 22½% of the 'gross' amount released, ie 25% of the cash amount. (This charge takes priority over the release of loans taxed as a benefit under ITEPA 2003 s 188.)

If the directors repay all or part of the loans *after* the s 419 tax falls due, the company may claim repayment of the appropriate part of the tax paid (TA 1988 s 419(4)). The tax will be due for repayment nine months after the end of the accounting period in which the loan is repaid, and the repayment will attract interest from that date (see explanatory note 10). If the loan is released or written off, the company may reclaim the tax in the same way as for loans repaid (see explanatory note 11).

Charge on directors under employment-related loans rules

Notwithstanding the operation of TA 1988 s 419 HMRC will also apply the employment-related loans rules contained in ITEPA 2003 ss 173–191 by calculating the notional interest chargeable as a benefit.

There will be no charge on Miss Starch, since the total amount outstanding at any time in the year did not exceed £5,000 (ITEPA 2003 s 180). There will, however, be a charge on Miss Stiff. The normal method of calculation (ITEPA 2003 s 182) is to take the average of the opening and closing overdrawn balances at the beginning and end of the tax year (or from the date the account was overdrawn to the date the loan was repaid, as the case may be), multiply by the complete months for which the loan was outstanding and divide by 12, then multiply by the official rate of interest. This gives the following result:

Average balance for period 1 July 2006 – 5 April 2007 $\dfrac{3,600 + 9,600}{2}$ = £6,600

6,600 x 9/12 (9 months) @ 5% = £248

The 'alternative' method shows a lower amount of interest payable, ie £216 (see explanatory note 6). Miss Stiff may elect to be assessed on the lower figure.

(e)   **Irregular extractions of company funds**

The profits of the company would be increased by £15,000, and the tax payable adjusted accordingly.

Misses Stiff and Starch would also be treated as having had an advance of £7,500 each from the company, totalling £15,000, on which a tax charge at 25% amounting to £3,750 would be payable to HMRC (TA 1988 s 419). This £3,750 would be repayable by HMRC to the company following the repayment by Misses Stiff and Starch to the company of the £15,000 irregularities (TA 1988 s 419(4)). The underpaid corporation tax and tax under s 419 would attract interest and penalties. Where a corporation tax return is shown to understate the true tax liability, owing to fraud or negligence, the company is subject to a tax-related penalty. The maximum penalty chargeable is the total tax understated. For these purposes, any understated s 419 tax is treated as a full tax liability (with no credit offset given for any repayment of the loan after the nine months due date) (FA 1998 Sch 18.89).

HMRC's policy in negotiated settlements is to abate any penalty to an appropriate percentage of the tax lost by reason of the offence. (The factors taken into account include the extent of the taxpayer's disclosure of the irregularities, the extent of the taxpayer's co-operation and the gravity of the offences.) HMRC would usually seek from the company an offer embracing the tax and interest with a loading for penalties, based on a percentage of the corporation tax and tax under s 419 (see explanatory note 9).

Because of the irregularities which had been discovered, HMRC would undoubtedly seek to satisfy themselves that no other irregularities, extractive or otherwise, had occurred. They would do this by an in-depth examination of the company records and of the personal finances of the directors, in the latter case satisfying themselves in particular that all personal bank/building society lodgments, asset purchases and personal and private expenditure were properly explained and accounted for.

HMRC are strictly entitled to assess Misses Stiff and Starch on employment-related loan interest under ITEPA 2003 s 175 in respect of the advances of £7,500 each. They have announced they will not do so where the extractions also involve liabilities to corporation tax and under s 419 with interest and penalties thereon.

Explanatory Notes

Close company benefits in kind to participators

1.   The provision of Donald's meals is a distribution and thus cannot be deducted in computing trading profits (TA 1988 s 418(4)). Whilst the benefits in kind treatment extends to services provided for the family or household of a director (or employee earning £8,500 or more), family or household for this purpose is defined as spouse and from 5 December 2005, civil partners; sons and daughters and their spouses/civil partners; parents; and servants, dependants and guests; the term does not therefore include a brother or sister (TA 1988 s 168(4)). Hence in this example the meals are treated as a distribution to Donald as a shareholder and not as a benefit to his sister.

Provision of living accommodation

2.   Miss Gentle is not assessable on the value of the benefit arising from her living accommodation since she is a representative occupier, ie one whose duties require her to live on the premises for their

proper performance (ITEPA 2003 s 99(1)). Directors are not entitled to the representative occupier exemption unless they are full-time directors owning not more than 5% of the shares. Misses Stiff and Starch do not come within this exemption and are chargeable (ITEPA 2003 s 99(3)). The legislation now covers the position where directors/employees share the use of living accommodation – by virtue of ITEPA 2003 s 108, the total benefits charges will not exceed the amount that would have been chargeable on a single employee.

The value of living accommodation is based on the old gross annual value for rating purposes. Employers are asked to estimate rateable values for new property and also where there are significant changes to existing property, and their estimates will be agreed by HMRC with assistance from the District Valuer.

There is specific legislation to prevent salary sacrifice schemes being used to reduce the tax charge for the provision of living accommodation (ITEPA 2003 s 109).

Residential care homes are classed as domestic dwellings for council tax, with the liability for payment of the tax being that of the owner, ie Oaks in Charnwood Ltd in this example, rather than the residents. Had the property been mixed business/private property instead of a care home, with Misses Stiff, Starch and Gentle having to live there to do their jobs, and the company had paid the council tax on the domestic accommodation, Misses Stiff and Starch would have been assessable on the benefit relating to them, but Miss Gentle would have escaped tax under the representative occupier provisions.

3. For a P11D employee, the representative occupier exemption does not extend to the provision of furnishings and the cost of lighting, heating, cleaning, repairs and maintenance. The normal calculation of the benefit is the expense of providing the services and where an asset like furniture is made available, 20% of the cost (ITEPA 2003 s 205(3)(b)), but for a representative occupier the assessable benefit is limited to 10% of the emoluments excluding the expenditure in question (ITEPA 2003 s 315). Emoluments for this purpose are after deducting allowable expenses, occupational pension scheme contributions and retirement annuity premiums, but no provision is made for the deduction of personal pension contributions.

The provision of care in residential homes for the elderly is exempt from VAT. If Oaks in Charnwood had been liable to VAT, it would not have been able to claim a set-off for input tax on repairs, refurbishments and other expenses relating to domestic accommodation provided for directors and their families (VATA 1994 s 24(3)). Any such non-recoverable input tax would be deducted as an expense in computing profit. As a non-registered business, Oaks in Charnwood will have included any VAT it has suffered in all its expenditure taken into account for tax purposes, any VAT relating to business entertaining being disallowed along with the entertaining expenditure itself.

Provision of cars and fuel

4. Directors and employees earning £8,500 or more are assessable on the benefit of private use of a motor car (ITEPA 2003 s 120).

The assessable benefit is (from 6 April 2002) based on a percentage of the relevant car's list price, the percentage being graduated according to the carbon dioxide (CO_2) emissions rating of the relevant car (the emissions figure for a car being rounded *down* to the nearest 5 grams per kilometre). The relevant CO_2 ratings for the various company cars are given in the example. In practice, details of CO_2 ratings can be obtained from the *New Car Fuel Consumption and Emission Figures* booklet published by the Vehicle Certification Agency – also found on the internet at www.vcacarfueldata.org.uk. For detailed notes on the company car benefit regime (including the relevant CO_2 ratings tables) and the related VAT and national insurance position, see Examples 10 and 11.

From 2003/04 onwards, where employees have private petrol paid for by their employer (whether directly or by reimbursement), the same percentage which applies to the car's list price is also applied to a statutory figure of £14,400 (ITEPA 2003 ss 149–153).

Benefit charge on interest-free or cheap loans

5. Where a company makes a loan either interest-free or at a rate below the 'official rate' to an employee earning £8,500 per annum or more or to a director (or to their relatives, meaning spouse, parents and remoter forebears, children and remoter issue, brothers and sisters, and the spouses of any of these relatives) the benefit is charged to tax under ITEPA 2003 ss 173–191 on the shortfall of the interest charged compared with the official rate. The official rate is normally set in advance for the whole of the tax year (5% for 2006/07), although this policy is subject to review if market rates change significantly during the year.

    There is no tax charge on loans made to employees on commercial terms by employers who lend or supply goods and services on credit to the general public. No employment-related loan charge arises if the loan is a qualifying loan, ie where the interest on the loan (irrespective of whether it is actually paid) would qualify for income tax relief (for example, a loan taken out to buy shares in a close company or a loan used for trading purposes – see Example 1 explanatory note 13) (ITEPA 2003 s 178). Nor is there any charge if the total of all non-qualifying loans to any person or those connected with him do not exceed £5,000 at any time in the tax year (ITEPA 2003 s 180). If there are qualifying loans and non-qualifying loans, there is no charge on the non-qualifying loans if they do not exceed £5,000 in total at any time in the tax year.

    If the loan is for a qualifying purpose for interest relief (see Example 1 explanatory note 13), the tax relief due on the interest paid reduces the tax chargeable.

6. The normal method of calculation of the beneficial loan interest is shown in part (d) of the example. An employee may elect for the interest to be calculated using the alternative method. The alternative method may also be used if the inspector so requires (ITEPA 2003 s 183). The time limit for the employee or inspector to make such an election is one year from 31 January following the relevant tax year. To calculate the interest under the alternative method, the amounts outstanding for each day in the tax year for which the interest rate is the same are added together, divided by 365 (or 366 in the case of a leap year) and multiplied by the official rate. The amounts arrived at for each rate are then added together. The interest for Miss Stiff on the alternative method is therefore calculated as follows:

1.7.06 – 30.9.06	3,600 x 92 days	=	331,200			
1.10.06 – 31.12.06	6,100 x 92 days	=	561,200			
1.1.07 – 31.3.07	7,100 x 90 days	=	639,000			
1.4.07 – 5.4.07	9,600 x 5 days	=	48,000	$\dfrac{1,579,400}{365}$	x 5%	£ 216

    This is less than the amount calculated on the normal basis (£248).

7. Employers must show the cash equivalents of employment-related loans on forms P11D, a copy of the P11D being given to employees (see Example 9). Where there are several loans, the loans are not aggregated to calculate the benefits. Employers who are close companies may, however, elect to aggregate non-qualifying employment-related loans in the same currency that are outstanding at the same time in the tax year (ITEPA 2003 s 187).

Class 1A NIC charge on taxable benefits

8. Employer's Class 1A national insurance contributions are chargeable on all taxable benefits in kind provided to P11D employees and directors (except for certain childcare benefits and apart from those already subject to the normal Class 1 charge, such as loans written off, readily convertible assets and the payment of personal bills). The Class 1A NIC charge is based on cash equivalents calculated under the taxable benefits provisions. See Example 47 for details.

Loans by close companies to participators

9. If a close company makes a loan or advances any money to a participator, there are tax implications for the company under TA 1988 s 419, as indicated in part (d) of the example. These are, in addition

to the employment-related loans, rules where the participator is a director or £8,500+ employee. A loan is treated as made where the participator incurs a debt to the close company, or to a third party who assigns the debt to the close company. The provisions of s 419 do not apply to:

(a)   a loan made in the ordinary course of a moneylending business;

(b)   a debt for goods or services unless more than six months' credit or a longer credit period than normal is given; and

(c)   a loan of up to £15,000 to a full-time employee/director owning not more than 5% of the ordinary share capital.

As indicated in part (d) of the example, under self-assessment, loans to participators are reported on the supplementary form CT 600A with the corporation tax return CT 600, which must be submitted within twelve months from the end of the company's accounting period.

The 25% tax charge on the loan is due nine months and one day after the end of the accounting period in which the loan is made (TA 1988 s 419), and interest is charged from that date if the tax is not paid on time. Tax is not payable if the whole of the loan is repaid within the nine month period. Companies show the tax on s 419 loans in their tax returns as part of the total tax due, but can claim an offsetting deduction if the loan has been repaid before the return is filed.

Repayment of loans after tax paid

10.   When all or part of the loan is repaid after the tax has been paid, the company may claim repayment of the appropriate amount of tax, the time limit for the claim being six years after the end of the accounting period in which the loan is repaid (TA 1988 s 419(4)). However, this tax is not repayable until nine months after the end of the accounting period in which the loan is repaid and interest on the repayment runs from that date (TA 1988 s 826(4)).

Thus in part (d) of the example, if the directors repaid the loans on or before 1 January 2008 the company would not have to pay tax on the loans under TA 1988 s 419. If the loans were repaid in (say) February 2008, ie in the year to 31 March 2008, the company should have paid the tax by 1 January 2008 (interest being charged from that date if it had not) and would not be entitled to repayment until 1 January 2009, interest on the tax repayable running from that date.

Loans written off

11.   If a loan or overdrawing is written off by a company, the effect on both the lender and the borrower needs to be considered.

As far as the lender company is concerned, writing off loans is normally allowable under the 'loan relationships' rules unless the parties are connected. A close company used to be connected with participators in the company and their associates and so the loan relationship rules did not permit a deduction if a loan to such persons was written off. From 1 October 2002, the 'connected' test does not apply to *all* participators but only to controlling shareholders (see Example 62 for the detailed provisions). The company may recover the tax paid on loans written off in the same way as for loans repaid (TA 1988 s 419).

The release of a loan due to a 'non-connected' company gives rise to a taxable credit in the borrower's books, except where the release is part of a relevant compromise or arrangement (FA 1996 Sch 9.5(3)). A released debt for expenditure previously deducted against the borrower's trading profits produces a taxable receipt under TA 1988 s 94. (This debt would fall outside the loan relationship regime as it represents an amount due for the supply of goods and services and not the lending of money (FA 1996 s 81).)

For close companies, the treatment for a shareholder of loans written off (including a shareholder who is a director or employee) is as indicated in part (d) of the example. Thus s 419 loans written off are treated as being net of the dividend income ordinary rate of 10% (ITTOIA 2005 s 416), effectively being taxed in the same way as dividends.

If the write-off of the loan is not caught by the close company rules for loans to shareholders, and it has been obtained by reason of the borrower's employment (such as the loan to Miss Gentle, who is not a shareholder but is an employee), then whether the employee is a P11D employee or not, and whether or not the loan is at a rate of interest below the 'official rate', the director or employee is treated as having received an equivalent amount of remuneration at that time (which also attracts NIC). This does not apply to loans written off on death. Nor does it apply if the write-off occurs after the employee has left, except for P11D employees.

Irregular extraction of company funds

12.   Extractive irregularities are not treated as additional remuneration. They are not subject to tax on the directors. Instead, the directors are accountable to the company for their repayment, corporation tax then being payable on the additional profit if the extractions arise from suppressed income or overstated expenses. Tax at 25% is also payable by the company pending repayment by the directors to the company of the amounts extracted. Since interest and penalties are calculated on both the corporation tax and the s 419 liabilities which arise out of the same irregularities, the interest and penalty cost is that much greater than in the case of identical irregularities by sole traders and partners.

Tank Engines Ltd trades as a manufacturer of toy train and railway sets, and draws up accounts to 31 March each year. It has a dormant subsidiary company, Toby Ltd. There are no other associated companies. Following a successful advertising campaign, the company is making substantial profits and expects that its profits for the current year to 31 March 2007 will be around £1,200,000. (Its total asset value at the year end is expected to be around £6,000,000.)

Mr Thomas (aged 52) is the company's managing director and owns 800 of the company's 1,000 £1 ordinary shares. The other 200 shares are held by the trustees of an accumulation and maintenance trust set up for the benefit of Mr Thomas's children, Annie and Clarabel.

Following this year's exceptional trading performance, Mr Thomas wishes to extract £200,000 for himself either as a bonus or dividend. He already draws a monthly salary of £4,000. Mr Thomas is a member of the company's pension scheme (which he joined in July 1982).

Mr Thomas also plans a £50,000 bonus for each of his other directors, Mr Gordon and Mr Toby. Both directors have intimated that they would like a small shareholding in Tank Engines Ltd as they have both worked for the company for over 10 years and would welcome a sense of proprietorship. Mr Thomas is agreeable to this provided they take no more than 5% of the company's total shareholding.

Mr Thomas also wishes to pass some income to his wife, who does not work for the company and has little personal income. He realises that he cannot pay her a significant salary and therefore wishes the company to issue her with sufficient non-voting preference shares to provide her with an annual dividend of £10,000.

Mr Thomas has asked you to comment on his proposals at a meeting before the company's year end on 31 March 2007. Prepare a detailed briefing paper for Mr Thomas to consider at the meeting.

Mr Thomas – Bonus v dividend

1. The decision to take £200,000 either as a bonus or dividend depends on a number of factors. A key consideration is usually the combined tax and national insurance (NIC) cost for each option. In this case, the company's anticipated profits fall within the marginal small companies' rate band of £300,000 to £1,500,000 for the year to 31 March 2007 and so the marginal rate is 32.75%.

    The marginal limits are not reduced by reference to the dormant subsidiary company. Although this is an associated company, it is disregarded as it is not carrying on a trade or business in the relevant accounting period (TA 1988 s 13(4)).

    As Mr Thomas draws a salary of £48,000 per annum, he is above the upper earnings limit for NIC purposes (£33,540 for 2006/07). Thus he will only be liable for the additional 1% charge on any bonus. Employer's NIC would be paid on the bonus at the rate of 12.8%.

2. A comparison between the bonus v dividend routes shows the following:

	Bonus £		Dividend £
Profits to be extracted	200,000		200,000
Less: Employer's NIC 200,000 x 12.8/112.8	(22,695)		
Corporation tax 200,000 @ 32.75%			(65,500)
Bonus/dividend payment	177,305		134,500
Less: PAYE/NIC on bonus 177,305 @ 41%	(72,695)		
Dividend		134,500	
Tax credit 1/9th		14,944	
		149,444	
Dividend income tax @ 32.5%		48,569	
Tax credit		(14,944)	(33,625)
Net cash available	104,610		100,875

    The payment of a £200,000 bonus rather than a dividend would leave Mr Thomas with (104,610 – 100,875 =) £3,735 additional cash.

3. PAYE is deducted at the time of the bonus payment. If the bonus was paid in March 2007, the PAYE tax would be due by 19 April 2007 (or 22 if paid electronically). In the case of a dividend, the tax would be paid in accordance with Mr Thomas's self-assessment payment position. Assuming Mr Thomas's only income for the previous year was his salary, the dividend upper rate tax on a dividend paid in March 2007 would not fall due until 31 January 2008. A dividend would thus offer a small cash flow saving.

    If the bonus is provided in the accounts and paid (or made available) within nine months after the year end (ie by 31 December 2007), it can still be deducted against the company's taxable profits for the year ended 31 March 2007.

4. From 6 April 2006, pension contributions may be made based on the lesser of the cumulative lifetime limit of £1,500,000 or the annual limit of £215,000 for 2006/07. These are contribution limits, not the limits for tax relief, which are lower for practical purposes. Where paid by an individual, tax relief will be obtained on an amount of the greater of £3,600 or 100% of earnings. The payment of a bonus will therefore increase the potential amount of higher rate tax relief available to Mr Thomas on additional pension contributions. If contributions are paid by an employer, they will be tax deductible provided they are expended wholly and exclusively for the purpose of the trade.

5. Other factors to consider would include the following:

    (i)   The fact that dividends are payable rateably to all shareholders may not provide a fair basis for rewarding the 'working' shareholder, Mr Thomas. If, for example, a dividend of £200,000 was declared, 20% would be received by the trustees of the accumulation and maintenance trust, leaving Mr Thomas with only £160,000. As an alternative, a dividend of £250,000 could be proposed, with the trustees of the accumulation and maintenance trust waiving their entitlement to the trust's dividend of £50,000 (20% x £250,000) before it becomes payable, but waiver of dividends could give rise to an HMRC enquiry.

(ii) Share valuations – while dividend payments may influence *minority* share valuations for capital tax purposes, they would not usually be a factor in determining *controlling* shareholding valuations, which tend to be based on earnings and/or net asset values.

6. Based on the above considerations, it is recommended that the £200,000 should be taken out as a bonus. It gives greater post-tax funds and also enhances potential tax relief for Mr Thomas on additional pension contributions of the year.

Mr Gordon and Mr Toby – bonus

7. The net cost to the company of paying £100,000 out as bonuses (£50,000 each) to Mr Gordon and Mr Toby would be:

	£
Bonuses (50,000 x 2)	100,000
Employer's NIC @ 12.8%	12,800
Gross cost	112,800
Corporation tax relief @ 32.75%	(36,942)
Net cost	75,858

The bonuses would rank for tax relief if paid during the year ended 31 March 2007 or if provided in the accounts to 31 March 2007 and paid within nine months of the year-end.

Mr Gordon and Mr Toby – shares in Tank Engines Ltd

8. Any issue or transfer of shares in the company to Mr Gordon and Mr Toby would be regarded as obtained by virtue of their employment. Each director would have an amount of employment income equal to the difference between the market value of the shares less the amount they paid for them (see explanatory note 7). In this instance, the market value of the shares would be based on the value of a very small minority holding and hence would be heavily discounted. Assume that, based on its past maintainable earnings, Tank Engines Ltd is worth £4,000,000. A shareholding of (say) 2½% might be valued at (say) £25,000 (ie £4,000,000 x 2½% x 25% (75% discount)). Each director would have to pay around £25,000 for his shares in order to avoid any taxable benefit.

If the shares constitute 'readily convertible assets' (ie where there are trading arrangements in existence enabling the director to obtain cash for his shares now or at a future date), the tax would be payable through the PAYE system (ITEPA 2003 s 696) and NICs would also be chargeable (see explanatory notes 7 and 8). If the shares are not readily convertible assets, no NICs would be due.

In addition, the company would have to complete Form 42 which is headed 'Employment-related securities and options: reportable events under s 421J ITEPA 2003' and submit to IR Share Schemes before 7 July 2007.

9. Consideration should be given to granting share options under the enterprise management incentive (EMI) scheme. This would enable the directors to be granted options to acquire shares exercisable at any time (within ten years). No income tax (or NIC) charge arises if the option enables the shares to be acquired at an amount equal to their market value at the date the option is *granted*. The total initial market value of the shares (based on the value at the date of the grant) held under EMI options granted by the company cannot exceed £3 million at the date of any grant (see Example 87 for details). Tank Engines Ltd will therefore not have any difficulty in meeting this requirement. Tank Engines Ltd should also satisfy the various qualifying conditions for establishing an EMI scheme. It is an independent (non-controlled) company and carries on an acceptable manufacturing trade. The

balance sheet total of its gross assets is well within the maximum permissible amount. The EMI scheme is much more attractive than an approved company share option plan as it gives complete flexibility with regard to the timing of the exercise of the options. Furthermore, business asset taper relief automatically accrues from the date the option is granted and the procedure enabling the value of shares to be agreed with Shares Valuation Division (promptly) at the time of the grant gives certainty of tax treatment. EMI share option agreements must be notified to HMRC within 92 days of the option grant.

Providing a dividend income of £10,000 for Mrs Thomas

10. As a 75% plus controlling shareholder, Mr Thomas could arrange for Tank Engines Ltd to issue non-voting preference shares carrying the relevant dividend coupon to give Mrs Thomas a dividend of £10,000. However, following the case of Young v Pearce 1996 (see Example 2 part (b)(iii)), it is likely that such arrangements would be treated as a settlement by Mr Thomas in favour of his wife. This would mean that the dividend income on the shares would be taxed on Mr Thomas as settlor (TA 1988 s 660A(1)(2)).

11. If, however, shares which carried substantive rights (such as voting rights and an entitlement to capital surpluses on a winding up, as well as dividend income) were issued or transferred to Mrs Thomas, this should escape the settlement provisions, since the shares would be an outright gift which carried other significant rights apart from a right to income (s 660A(6)).

    Mr Thomas could transfer part of his existing (ordinary) shareholding to his wife. Alternatively, he could arrange for the company to create another class of ordinary shares (but carrying the same rights as the existing ordinary shares). This would provide greater flexibility with regard to future dividends, for example enabling dividends to be declared on the new class of shares. Mr Thomas could provide the necessary funds to enable his wife to subscribe for the new class of shares.

12. Over a number of years, HMRC have sought to apply the settlements legislation contained in TA 1988 s 660A(1)(2) to dividends paid to the spouse of the main earner in certain circumstances. HMRC issued guidance, and a number of illustrations of their view, in Tax Bulletin issues 64 (April 2003) and 69 (February 2004). The case of Jones v Garnett (the Arctic Case) was won by HMRC at a hearing of the Special Commissioners and in the High Court, but lost in the Court of Appeal. HMRC are to appeal to the House of Lords, and the tax treatment of small husband and wife businesses will depend on the outcome of this case in the short term.

    HMRC argument concerns the situation where profits derive principally from the work of the main owner, and where the main earner takes remuneration at less than the market rate. This allows funds to accumulate, to be paid subsequently as dividend, resulting income being transferred to the other spouse in proportion to shareholding. It is HMRC's view that this arrangement confers bounty and constitutes a settlement, so that the income remains that of the settlor. If this view is correct, the income will remain that of the main earner, not that of the other spouse (which is typically taxed at a lower rate).

    HMRC consider that the settlements legislation applies to a wide range of small companies and partnerships, but that 'it does not apply to income from those companies and partnerships that have normal commercial arrangements.' As Mr Thomas takes a full salary, the shares have full rights and asset backing, and the company's income does not derive principally from work he performs personally, Tank Engines Limited should not be affected by the Arctic case.

Explanatory Notes

Bonus v dividend

1. The detailed comparisons between bonus and dividend payments are set out in notes 1 to 6 of the example. Even if substantial dividends are being contemplated, it is recommended that a basic level of remuneration is paid following the National Minimum Wage Act 1998 unless a director does not

have an 'explicit' contract of employment with the company. If he does have an explicit contract he would fall within the minimum wage rules and must pay himself at least £5.35 per hour (£5.05 per hour prior to 1 October 2006). See HMRC's Tax Bulletin of December 2000 for their detailed comments on the minimum wage legislation. Dividends are disregarded for minimum wage purposes. Similarly, benefits in kind are ignored, except living accommodation. Regular remuneration also builds up an NIC contribution record (to secure full state benefits), provides the basis for any redundancy entitlement, and assists with mortgage applications etc.

2. Where the shareholder's marginal rate of tax is 40%, the overall tax/NIC cost of paying a bonus will be lower if the company pays tax at the marginal small companies' rate of tax (32.75% for the year ended 31 March 2007). If the company pays tax at the full or small companies' rate (30% and 19% respectively for the year ended 31 March 2007), greater tax/NIC savings are obtained by paying a dividend. Taking £200,000 as the amount to be extracted (as in the example) but assuming the company paid tax at 19%, the net cash available for a bonus would still be £104,610, as in note 2 of the example.

The net cash available by paying a dividend would be £121,500 (a saving of £16,890 over the bonus) calculated as follows:

	£
Profits to be extracted	200,000
Corporation tax @ 19%	(38,000)
Cash dividend	162,000
Tax credit 1/9th	18,000
	180,000
Dividend income tax at 32.5%	(58,500)
Net cash available	121,500

Even if the company paid tax at 30%, the net cash available by paying a dividend would be £105,000 (a saving of £390 over the bonus).

3. For shareholders paying tax at the basic rate, and liable to additional employees' NIC, separate calculations are required in each case to determine whether a bonus or dividend should be paid, although the comments in note 1 regarding payment of a basic level of remuneration are likely to be particularly appropriate.

Pension contributions from 6 April 2006

4. From 6 April 2006 pension contributions will be based on a lifetime limit, with an annual contribution equal to earnings for the year. The company will therefore be able to make very substantial contributions.

If Mr Thomas agreed to take £100,000 subject to PAYE, and £100,000 as a pension contribution, the situation would be:

	Bonus £200,000	**Bonus £100,000 Pension £100,000**
Earnings subject to PAYE	200,000	100,000
Employer's NIC @ 12.8/112.8	(22,695)	(11,348)
Bonus payment	177,305	88,652
PAYE and NIC @ 41%	(72,695)	(36,347)
Net cash are available	104,610	52,305
Contribution to pension fund		100,000
Value extracted	104,610	152,305
Tax borne	95,390	47,695

The reduction in current year taxes would be £47,695, but the pension will be subject to PAYE when drawn (although perhaps at a lower rate). To be tax deductible for Tank Engines Ltd, the pension contribution, as other remuneration or costs, must be expended wholly and exclusively for the purpose of the trade. HMRC guidance specifically states that the contribution is looked at in the context of the overall remuneration package, not a stand-alone amount. The proportion of pension contribution to other remuneration is not considered for this purpose.

The normal situation is that contributions will be tax deductible, unless there is an identifiable non-trade purpose. As Tank Engines Ltd is a profitable trading company, and paying this remuneration out of profit, there should be no objection from HMRC, in spite of the tax saving arising from the salary sacrifice.

Dividend waivers

5. To be effective for income tax purposes, dividend waivers must be made before the dividend becomes due and payable. For this purpose, an interim dividend does not become due and payable until it is actually paid – the directors could rescind the dividend at any time before it is paid. However, a final dividend becomes payable at the company's annual general meeting when it is declared, unless the resolution specifies a later date (Hurll v CIR, 1922; Potel v CIR, 1970).

6. A dividend waiver would only be treated as a settlement for income tax purposes where the necessary element of bounty was present (CIR v Plummer (1979)). HMRC would argue that 'bounty' would have been conferred if the company's distributable profits could not have supported the dividend without the waiver, ie where the waiver enables one or more shareholders to receive a greater dividend than would otherwise be the case. In such cases, HMRC would only apply the settlement legislation where dividends are waived to increase the dividend payable to the settlor's spouse, children or the trustees of an accumulation and maintenance trust for the settlor's children (TA 1988 s 660A). There is no transfer of value for inheritance tax purposes, provided a dividend waiver is made within twelve months before the right to the dividend accrues (IHTA 1984 s 15). The detailed inheritance tax provisions are in the companion to this book, Tolley's Taxwise II 2006/07.

Giving shares to employees

7. Except for shares acquired under HMRC-approved schemes (as to which see Example 87), a tax charge arises on shares given to employees unless full market value is paid for them. The taxable amount is the market value of the shares less the amount (if any) paid for them and this is chargeable under the normal 'money's worth' provisions of ITEPA 2003 s 62, although as it is not a payment in cash it is not chargeable through PAYE unless the shares are readily convertible assets. Since it is chargeable under s 62, it is outside the 'cash equivalents' benefits charging provisions for P11D employees and directors. The employer is, however, required under SI 1993/744 reg 46 to make a return within 92 days after the end of the tax year. Employees need to report the relevant details in their tax returns (see Example 87 under *Self-assessment* for further details). Gifts of shares in an employer company that are not readily convertible assets are not chargeable to either Class 1 or Class 1A national insurance contributions (SI 2001/1004 reg 40 and Sch 3 Part IX para 2).

8. Unquoted shares are unlikely to be readily convertible assets unless there are arrangements which exist or might in future exist enabling them to be realised in cash. This might be the case where there is a planned sale or flotation of the company or where an employee share trust is available to buy the shares. The wide subjective nature of the definition can be difficult to apply.

The Steamdriven Computer Co Ltd has faced a declining market in recent years. It is expected to make a net *unadjusted* trading loss of £17,750 in the six months ending on 31 March 2007. Results for the previous three years (*before* any adjustments for tax purposes) have been as follows:

	Trading Profits £	Bank Interest receivable £
Year ended 30 September 2004	10,000	–
Year ended 30 September 2005	3,000	–
Year ended 30 September 2006	4,000	400

The projected balance sheet at 31 March 2007 on a going concern basis is as follows:

	£	£
Fixed assets		
Office premises (at valuation)		120,000
Fixed plant and machinery	50,000	
Less: Depreciation	(35,000)	15,000
		135,000
Current assets		
Trading stock		39,000
Cash		500
		39,500
Less: Creditors (excluding any corporation tax of year to 30 September 2006, which will be discharged by loss claim)		(4,000)
Net current assets		35,500
Total assets		170,500
Financed by:		
Share capital		10,000
Retained profits		135,500
		145,500
10% Debenture		25,000
		170,500

The projected profit and loss account for the 6 months to 31 March 2007, again on a going concern basis, is as follows:

	£	£
Sales		91,000
Opening stock	42,000	
Purchases	60,000	
Less: Closing stock	(39,000)	(63,000)
Gross profit		28,000
Less: Staff and administrative costs	42,200	
Depreciation	2,500	
Debenture interest	1,250	
Bank interest	(200)	(45,750)
Net loss		(17,750)

Mr Ludd, who owns 99.9% of the company's issued share capital, proposes that the company should sell all of its assets on 31 March 2007 for cash to an unconnected third party for a total amount of £143,000, attributable as follows:

	£
Goodwill	–
Office premises	107,000
Plant and machinery	2,000
Trading stock	34,000
	143,000

Immediately after the assets are sold, the company would cease trading and the liquidation of the company would commence. The company would pay all of its liabilities at cessation and the liquidator would distribute the balance of cash to its shareholders shortly afterwards. Mr Ludd is unsure whether the cash should be distributed before or after 6 April 2007.

The company is expected to receive any repayments of corporation tax, including any arising out of its trading loss, by 7 June 2007. It is estimated that these amounts will just be sufficient to cover the liquidator's fees so that no further cash will be distributed to the company's shareholders.

The following information is also available:

(i) The 10% Debenture was issued in March 1975 to finance the company's trading activities. Interest is payable and has always been paid half yearly on 30 September and 31 March. The interest has been deducted in arriving at the profit figure shown.

(ii) All of the plant and machinery was acquired on 1 April 2000. The company has claimed maximum writing-down allowances (but no other allowances) in respect of this expenditure.

(iii) In computing depreciation for accounts purposes, the company uses a straight-line basis and applies the same depreciation rate to all of the plant and machinery.

(iv) The company has no associated companies and has not paid dividends for several years.

(v) The disposal of the office will give rise to a nil gain/nil loss position for capital gains purposes.

(vi) Mr Ludd inherited his shares in the company in March 1982, when they had a probate value of £10,000.

(vii) Mr Ludd, who is single and aged 46, will have total income of £60,000 in 2006/07 and around £10,000 in 2007/08. He plans to retain all of his existing capital assets (except his shares in the company) for the foreseeable future.

Assume that all staff and administrative expenses are fully allowable. Indexation allowance from March 1982 to April 1998 was 104.7%.

On the basis of the estimated figures:

(a) Compute the final corporation tax liabilities of the company in respect of the periods commencing 1 October 2003 and ending 31 March 2007.

(b) Compute the total amount which should be repaid to the company by the Revenue on 7 June 2007.

(c) Advise Mr Ludd as to which method of distributing cash by the company is preferable.

(a)   **Final corporation tax liabilities for periods from 1 October 2003 to 31 March 2007**

	Yr to *30.9.04* £	*Yr to* *30.9.05* £	*Yr to* *30.9.06* £	*6 mths to* *31.3.07* £
Profit per accounts	10,000	3,000	4,000	
Add: depreciation (see workings)	5,000	5,000	5,000	
Less: capital allowances (see workings)	(3,955)	(2,967)	(2,225)	
Schedule D Case I	11,045	5,033	6,775	–
Schedule D Case III				
Bank interest			400	200
Total profits	11,045	5,033	7,175	200
Less: loss relief under s 393A				
(totalling £23,453)	(11,045)	(5,033)	(7,175)	(200)
Profits chargeable to corporation tax	–	–	–	–
Unrelieved loss (25,123 per workings – 23,453)				£1,670

There are no charges on income in this example. Debenture interest is treated as a trading expense (see note 4). Had there been any charges in the final trading period, the loss would have been set off *before* those charges.

Workings

Capital allowances computation:

		£
WDV at 30.9.2003 (50,000 less 25% pa on reducing balance for 4 years)		15,820
Yr to 30.9.04	WDA 25%	3,955
		11,865
Yr to 30.9.05	WDA 25%	2,967
		8,898
Yr to 30.9.06	WDA 25%	2,225
		6,673
6 mths to 31.3.07	Sale proceeds	2,000
	Balancing allowance	4,673

Loss to 31 March 2007:	£
Net loss per accounts	(17,750)
Depreciation	2,500
Bank interest	(200)
Capital allowances	(4,673)
Loss on sale of stock (39,000 – 34,000)	(5,000)
Loss available for relief under TA 1988 s 393A	(25,123)

Depreciation:

Cumulative figure of £35,000 on balance sheet represents £5,000 per annum on a straight line basis from 1 April 2000 to 31 March 2007.

(b) **Amount repayable to company on 7 June 2007**

No tax is payable for the 6 months to 31 March 2007, so interest is not relevant. Interest on a repayment for the year to 30 September 2006 would run from 1 July 2007, and for the years to 30 September 2005 and 30 September 2004 from 1 January 2008 (the payment date for the loss period). Since the repayment is made on 7 June 2007, it does not attract any interest.

	£
Year to 30 September 2004:	
11,045 @ 19%	2,098
Less: (50,000 – 11,045) × 19/400	(1,850)
	248

The corporation tax on the profits of £5,033 for the year to 30 September 2005 and on the profits of £7,175 for the year to 30 September 2006, was zero. The loss claim of £200 for the six months to 31 March 2007 would result in only a minimal saving of £19, following abolition of the nil rate band from 1 April 2006.

(c) **Advice to Mr Ludd on how cash should be distributed**

If all the cash is distributed before 6 April 2007, Mr Ludd will have a chargeable gain in 2006/07 as follows.

	£
Available funds in company:	
Proceeds of sale of assets	143,000
Add cash in hand	500
Less amounts used to pay creditors and debenture holders (4,000 + 25,000)	(29,000)
Distributable to shareholders	114,500
Mr Ludd's share of distributions (99.9%)	114,386
Cost of shares March 1982	(10,000)
Indexation allowance to April 1998 104.7%	(10,470)
Gain before taper relief	93,916
Maximum business asset taper relief @ 75%	70,437
Gain before annual exemption	23,479
Less: Annual exemption	(8,800)
	14,679

The gain of £14,679 would be taxed at 40%, giving rise to a tax liability of £5,872. (Strictly, a small part of the £93,916 gain (maximum 5 days after cessation of trade) would not be eligible for business asset taper and attracts non-business asset taper instead, but the effect is immaterial – see below for the detailed calculation for post 5 April 2007.)

If the capital distribution is delayed until, say, 7 April 2007, Mr Ludd will not benefit from any additional (business) taper relief. Based on the 'strict' diluted taper calculation his chargeable gain would be £14,559, as follows:

	£
Gain before taper relief (as above)	93,916
Less: maximum business asset taper relief (10 years' relief for non-business asset proportion – see below)	(70,367)
Gain after taper relief	23,549
Less: Annual exemption (say)	(9,000)
Chargeable gain	14,549

Although a 2007/08 gain will be virtually identical to one arising in 2006/07 (there being no taper relief advantage), Mr Ludd would still benefit from having the gain taxed at a lower tax rate. Based on current rates, the gain of £14,549 would (in 2007/08) be taxed at 20%, giving a liability of £2,910. The gain would fall within the available basic rate band.

Note: The capital distribution should be paid on (or immediately after) 6 April 2007 to ensure that there is no material dilution of business asset taper relief. If there are (say) 7 non-trading days, then the above gain of £93,916 would strictly be apportioned as follows:

	Days	Gain £		Taper relief £
Business asset 6.4.98 – 31.3.07	3,282	93,716	75%	70,287
Non-business asset 1.4.07 – 7.4.07	7	200	40%	80
	3,289	93,916		70,367

Clearly, Mr Ludd should arrange for the capital distribution to be paid on (say) 7 April 2007 rather than before 6 April 2007, as this produces a tax saving of £2,962 (£5,872 – £2,910) and delays the CGT payment by twelve months. A further saving could be made by paying a sufficient amount before 6 April 2007 to absorb Mr Ludd's 2006/07 annual exemption of £8,800.

Explanatory Notes

Chargeable accounting periods

1. TA 1988 s 12 provides that a chargeable accounting period ends on the earliest of the following (see Example 51 explanatory note 2(c)):

    Twelve months from its commencement

    An accounting date of the company

    Cessation of trading

    Commencement of winding-up.

Trading losses

2. Trading losses carried forward are only available against future profits of the *same trade* (TA 1988 s 393(1)). If any chargeable gains had arisen in the liquidation period, therefore, the losses could not have been set against them. Had the trade premises been an industrial building, trading losses could have been carried forward to set against a balancing charge on the building. For an illustration see Example 53. That example also deals with the rules for including trade charges of the last twelve months of trading in the loss available for relief under TA 1988 s 393A.

Interest on overpaid tax

3. For detailed notes on the dates from which interest runs when tax is repaid following loss claims, see Example 52 explanatory note 7.

    Under self-assessment, interest on underpaid and overpaid tax is taken into account in calculating taxable profits. If interest on overpaid tax is received or receivable by a company in liquidation in its final accounting period, however, the interest will not be included in taxable profits if it does not exceed £2,000. The actual tax repayments in this example did not attract any interest.

Loan interest payable

4. Interest on a loan for the purposes of the trade is deducted on an accruals basis in arriving at the Schedule D Case I profit. For detailed notes see Example 62.

Close investment-holding companies

5. Where a company is a close investment-holding company, it is liable to tax at the full corporation tax rate, no matter how small its profits are (TA 1988 s 13A). (For detailed notes see Example 55.)

    Companies that are trading or property investment companies are excluded from the definition of close investment-holding company, but clearly there is a problem when a company goes into liquidation following the cessation of its trade. S 13A(4) provides that a company that is wound up will not be treated as a close investment-holding company in the accounting period commencing with the winding-up if it was outside the definition in the previous accounting period. But the cessation of a trade itself triggers the end of an accounting period, and there will often be an interval between that cessation and the passing of the winding-up resolution, in which case the company in liquidation will not be helped by this provision. It would be relevant, however, if a company's trade had been continued by a receiver up to the date of the winding-up resolution, or if a company had let properties and the lettings continued after the cessation of the trade, enabling the company to escape close investment-holding company status in the period leading up to the winding-up resolution.

    In this example, the disposal of the assets after the cessation of trading does not give rise to any chargeable gains, nor is any income received, so that the problem of being a close investment-holding company does not arise. For an illustration see Example 53.

Liquidation distributions

6. Once a liquidation has commenced, sums can only actually be paid to shareholders by the liquidator as a capital distribution payment in respect of their shares. Any surplus over the indexed cost of the shares (or indexed 31 March 1982 value as the case may be) is subject to capital gains tax, after taking into account available reliefs and exemptions, including taper relief and the annual exemption, as shown in the example.

    Any distributions before the commencement of the liquidation carry a tax credit equal to 10% but with no tax liability for the shareholders unless their income exceeds the basic rate limit, and then only at the excess of dividend income upper rate tax of 32% over 10%. This represents an effective tax rate for a shareholder liable at the higher rate of 25% of the cash dividend.

    The present 75% rate taper relief for assets that qualify as business property applies from 6 April 2002 providing the shares have been held for just two complete years. Although the 'two-year' requirement is introduced from that date, the ownership period before that date can be counted (as far back as the original taper base date of 6 April 1998, where appropriate). For higher rate taxpaying shareholders entitled to the full 75% taper relief, their effective CGT rate becomes 10% (40% x tapered gain of 25%). At this rate it will generally be more tax-efficient to extract the company's reserves as a capital gain rather than a dividend.

    It is crucial to ensure the shares qualify for taper relief at business asset rates as opposed to non-business asset rates. At non-business asset rates a dividend or even bonus through PAYE may be more beneficial. As an example taking assets held for nine years:

	Business taper	Non-business taper	Dividend
Distribution available	1,000,000	1,000,000	1,000,000
Taper Relief – 9 years	75%	35%	N/A
Capital gain/income	250,000	650,000	1,000,000
Tax rate (after credit)	40%	40%	25%
Tax	100,000	260,000	250,000

    In this case a dividend would be more tax-efficient than a capital gain reduced by non-business property rates. Full business asset taper relief can be lost or reduced if significant non-business assets are held in the company. The shares or assets being sold need be held only two years, but the company's status for all years since 6 April 1998 are considered in qualifying for business asset taper relief. See Example 74 for details.

Before the introduction of the present taper relief regime, it was generally beneficial to extract the anticipated capital gain before liquidation as a normal dividend chargeable to income tax. The effective 25% tax rate often produced a saving on the CGT payable on a capital distribution.

As noted in part (c) of the example, the longer the period between cessation of trade and the capital distribution, the greater will be the reduction in the gain qualifying for the business assets rate of relief.

For detailed notes on the various capital gains reliefs and exemptions see the relevant capital gains examples.

7.   Under HMRC Concession C16, a distribution of assets by a company to its shareholders, the company then being dissolved as a defunct company, will usually be regarded as having been made under a formal winding-up. Consequently, it will not be regarded as income in the hands of the shareholders, providing appropriate assurances are given to HMRC by the company and the shareholders. This is a useful way of proceeding when the company is not insolvent. The procedure for voluntary striking-off is in the Companies Act 1985 ss 652A to 652F.

Share capital and other non-distributable reserves cannot strictly be repaid on a dissolution, although it appears that HMRC and Registrar of Companies accept this in practice. Many advisers suggest a prudent approach of proceeding by voluntary liquidation if the company's share capital exceeds a certain amount, say, £10,000. A voluntary liquidation also offers greater protection for shareholders, as a Court can only restore a dissolved company after liquidation within two years after an application by the liquidator or any other interested person (Companies Act 1985 s 651). In contrast, where a company has been struck-off, an 'aggrieved' member or creditor can apply to the Court to restore the company, which can normally be done at any time within 20 years from the publication of the striking off notice (s 653).

Administration Orders and Voluntary Arrangements

8.   Under the Insolvency Act 1986, Administration Orders and Voluntary Arrangements may be used (inter alia) to obtain a more advantageous realisation of a company's assets than would occur on a winding-up. HMRC have a unit to handle voluntary arrangements, known as the Voluntary Arrangements Service.

It is HMRC view that an administrator is not normally personally liable for tax liabilities, although as the company's agent he is an 'employer' for PAYE/NIC purposes and may have some liability if the company does go into liquidation. If the administrator arranged to sell shares in subsidiaries, the arrangements would block entitlement to group relief (TA 1988 s 410(1)(b)).

When a company goes into administration, after 14 September 2003 (EA 2002 s 248) this will mark the start of a new accounting period. Thereafter, the normal 12-month rule will apply. The date when a company comes out of administration will represent the end of an accounting period (FA 2003 Sch 41.1).

If a Voluntary Arrangement is made based on 'a proposal to the company and its creditors for a composition in satisfaction of its debts or a scheme of arrangement of its affairs', a compromise in satisfaction of debt would constitute a release of the debt, but the debtor does not have to treat such a debt as a taxable receipt and the creditor may claim a deduction for the release of the debt (TA 1988 ss 74(j) and 94 and FA 1996 Sch 9.5 – see Example 62 explanatory note 6).

FA 2005 Sch 4 para 8 inserts a definition of 'statutory insolvency arrangement' into ICTA 1988 s 884(1). A statutory insolvency arrangement is an arrangement under British insolvency laws or the Companies Act, or a corresponding arrangement in countries outside the United Kingdom.

A. Fitzwilliam Ltd is an unquoted trading company in which 80% of the share capital is owned by members of one family. The remaining shares are currently owned by Hilton, who is not related in any way to the other shareholders.

Hilton, a longstanding employee, now wishes to retire from work and to dispose of all or a part of his shareholding. The other members do not have funds which they could use to purchase his shares, but the company has sufficient funds to purchase at least part of his holding.

List the points that you would discuss with the secretary of Fitzwilliam Ltd on the taxation implications of the purchase of shares from Hilton by the company in 2006/07.

B. You act as tax adviser for Bliss Limited (which operates a successful marriage bureau) and its managing director, Mr Crippen. The company has made tax-adjusted trading profits in excess of £250,000 pa over the previous five years. It has now built up a substantial reserve of cash, since its policy has been not to pay out any dividends. The company has not made any chargeable gains in recent years and has always made up its accounts to 30 April. Mr Crippen informs you that he and Mr Bluebeard, his fellow shareholder, are in serious disagreement about the future strategy of the company and that this is having a very harmful effect on the running of the business. It has therefore been decided that Mr Bluebeard should no longer be involved in the management of the company and that the company will purchase all of his shares from him.

Further relevant information is as follows:

(a) Mr Bluebeard is 66 years old and has worked in the company as a full-time director since it was incorporated on 1 January 1988, when he acquired 30% of the ordinary shares at par for £50,000. The company has agreed to buy the shares back at their market value of £662,000 on 7 April 2006.

(b) All of Bliss Limited's assets are in use for the purposes of its trade.

(c) Mr Bluebeard, who is single, has a private income of £55,000 pa and has made no capital disposals in 2006/07.

Set out the amounts and dates of payment of the tax liabilities which would be incurred by both Bliss Limited and Mr Bluebeard in respect of the share purchase, on the assumption that:

(i) the purchase does not qualify for the special treatment in TA 1988 ss 219–229,

(ii) the purchase does qualify for the special treatment.

A.   **Fitzwilliam Ltd – points to discuss with secretary on taxation implications of purchase of shares from Hilton by the company**

Treatment of share purchase as capital gains disposal

1.   Under the provisions of TA 1988 ss 219–229, the purchase of its own shares by an *unquoted* trading company will not be treated as a distribution but as a capital gains tax disposal by the shareholder providing certain conditions are satisfied, as follows:

   (a)   Hilton must be resident and ordinarily resident in the UK.

   (b)   He must have owned his shares for at least five years.

   (c)   The company must either acquire the whole of Hilton's shareholding or his holding must be 'substantially reduced', which means that the holding *after* the purchase as a fraction of the reduced share capital must not exceed 3/4 of the corresponding fraction before the purchase. In Hilton's case this means that he must not be left with more than 15% of the reduced share capital.

   (d)   The purchase must be made wholly or mainly to benefit the company's trade and not to enable Hilton to participate in profits without receiving a dividend or for tax avoidance reasons.

   (e)   The purchase must not be part of a scheme or arrangement under which, although Hilton's shareholding is initially substantially reduced, his interest at a later stage will be such as to breach the 'substantially reduced' requirement.

2.   The company may apply for an HMRC clearance that the proposed purchase will not be treated as a distribution.

3.   Within 60 days of paying for the shares the company must provide details to the local HMRC.

4.   If the purchase is treated as a disposal for capital gains tax, any gain will be reduced by 75% business asset taper relief (for more than 2 years' ownership) and the annual exemption of £8,800 unless Hilton has already used it.

Treatment of share purchase as income distribution

5.   If the purchase does not satisfy the requirements in 1 above, the excess of the price paid by the company over the amount originally subscribed for the shares will be treated as a distribution. Hilton will receive a tax credit equivalent to the dividend income ordinary rate (10%) and will be liable if applicable at the excess of the dividend income upper rate (32.5%) over the dividend income ordinary rate (10%) on the amount of the distribution plus the tax credit. For capital gains purposes, Hilton would effectively be regarded as having disposed of his shares for the amount originally subscribed for them, since the price he receives will be reduced by the net distribution amount on which he pays income tax. Assuming the base cost of the shares was equal to their subscription price, there would be no capital gain and no allowable loss.

B.   **Amounts and dates of payment of tax liabilities which would be incurred by Bliss Limited and Mr Bluebeard in respect of the share purchase**

   (i)   *If the purchase does not satisfy the provisions of TA 1988 ss 219–229*

   The excess of the payment of £662,000 by Bliss Ltd on 7 April 2006 over the amount subscribed for the shares of £50,000, ie £612,000, is treated as a distribution.

   Mr Bluebeard is regarded as having received dividend income of £612,000 + (1/9th) £68,000 = £680,000 on 7 April 2006. This will form part of his taxable income for 2006/07. The tax credit will cover Mr Bluebeard's dividend income ordinary rate liability and he will be liable to tax at a further 22½% (32½% − 10%), amounting to £153,000, which will be payable with his balancing payment under self-assessment on 31 January 2008.

Since the tax credit of £68,000 is not repayable, Mr Bluebeard cannot recover it by making tax-efficient investments, although, if he uses the cash from the share purchase to make such investments, he would be able to recover other tax paid.

He will also be treated as having disposed of his shares for capital gains tax, the position being:

	£
Disposal proceeds April 2006	
(662,000 less 612,000 charged as income)	50,000
Cost January 1988	50,000
	–

No gain or loss therefore arises.

(ii) *If the purchase does satisfy the provisions of TA 1988 ss 219-229*

Bliss Limited will be treated as having bought the shares from Mr Bluebeard for £662,000. The purchase will not result in a tax liability for the company.

Mr Bluebeard will be liable to capital gains tax for 2006/07 on:

	£
Sale proceeds April 2006	662,000
Cost January 1988	(50,000)
Indexation allowance to April 1998 $\dfrac{162.6 - 103.3}{103.3} = 57.4\%$	(28,700)
	583,300
Less: Maximum business asset taper relief @ 75%	(437,475)
Annual exemption	(8,800)
Chargeable gains for 2006/07	137,025
Capital gains tax thereon @ 40% (Mr Bluebeard's income being above basic rate limit)	£ 54,810

Due for payment 31 January 2008

Explanatory Notes

Purchase of own shares by unquoted company

1. The provisions of TA 1988 ss 219 to 229 enable the purchase by an unquoted trading company of its own shares ('purchase' requiring the consideration to be in money) to be effectively treated in certain circumstances as a disposal by the shareholder for capital gains tax rather than the receipt of a distribution attracting an income tax liability. The provisions are designed to facilitate the raising of equity capital by the smaller unquoted trading company by helping it to buy out a shareholder, or substantially reduce his shareholding, where this benefits the trade. They can also be used to make it easier for a company to help a shareholder to meet an inheritance tax liability where it cannot otherwise be met without undue hardship although such cases are now rare, given the availability of 100% business property relief on all unquoted shareholdings.

2. Where an unquoted trading company or the unquoted holding company of a trading group (75% subsidiaries) buys back its own shares (or redeems them or makes a payment for them in a reduction of capital) in order to benefit a trade (excluding dealing in shares, securities, land or futures), the transaction will *not* be treated as a distribution (attracting dividend income upper rate tax where appropriate). Instead, there is a disposal for capital gains tax. (Where there is an arrangement the

main purpose of which is simply to get undistributed profits into a shareholder's hands without incurring the 'distribution' tax liabilities capital gains treatment will be denied.)

3. In order for the transaction to be treated as a capital gains tax disposal and not a distribution the very detailed requirements of the legislation must be complied with. These are broadly as follows:

   (i) The company must be an unquoted trading company or holding company of a trading group (companies on the Alternative Investment Market being treated as unquoted). The company does not qualify if its trade is dealing in shares, securities, land or futures.

   (ii) The shareholder must be resident and ordinarily resident in the UK.

   (iii) The shares must normally have been owned by the shareholder for at least five years but where the shares are in an estate (or have been inherited) the period is reduced to three years, and ownership by the deceased (and the estate) counts towards the three years. If during the five years the shares had been transferred to the shareholder by his spouse with whom he still lives, the spouse's ownership is treated as the shareholder's ownership.

   (iv) The shareholder must either dispose of his entire interest in the company or his interest must be 'substantially reduced'. This means that the fraction he owns of the (reduced) issued share capital immediately after the purchase must not exceed 75% of the corresponding fraction he owned immediately before the purchase and also that he would not be entitled to more than 75% of the share he was previously entitled to of the company's distributable profits. HMRC have indicated that a purchase would rarely be regarded as for the benefit of a company's trade unless virtually the whole of the shareholder's interest was disposed of. Furthermore, in order to ensure the 'trade benefit' test is satisfied, any existing directorship with the company must be severed and a director cannot continue to act for the company in a consultancy capacity. The 75% rule would permit a purchase to be made in stages, or a small number of shares to be retained for sentimental reasons. (HMRC Statement of Practice 2/82).

   (v) The shareholder must not immediately after the purchase be connected with the company (ie be able to control it, or be in possession of more than 30% of the voting power, share capital, combined share capital and loan capital etc).

   (vi) There are provisions dealing with cases where the company is a member of a group, and interests held by associates after the purchase have to be taken into account. Associates include husband or wife, minor children, trustees of a settlement created by the shareholder and a wide range of other relationships.

   (vii) The capital gains treatment is not applied if there are arrangements under which any of the tests could cease to be satisfied.

   (viii) The company must send a return to HMRC within sixty days after the purchase stating that the payment has not been treated as a distribution.

4. The redemption, repayment or purchase of its own shares by an unquoted trading company or unquoted holding company of a trading group is also not treated as a distribution where the payment (net of any capital gains tax arising) is used to pay inheritance tax charged on a death, but only where the inheritance tax cannot otherwise be paid without undue hardship and is paid within two years of the death.

5. A company may apply for clearance before a transaction is undertaken.

6. If the above provisions do *not* apply, then part of a payment for the purchase by a company of its own shares will be treated as a dividend income distribution. The amount of the distribution is the excess of the payment over the amount originally subscribed for the shares (even though the vendor may not be the original subscriber) (TA 1988 s 209(2)(b)).

7. Insofar as the company is concerned, the purchase of the shares must be covered by the proceeds of a new issue or by a transfer from distributable reserves (although any premium on the redemption

must be taken from reserves). Any legal costs and other expenditure incurred by a company in purchasing its own shares will not be allowable against the company's profits.

Capital gains taper relief

8. Where assets have been held for a full two years, and qualify as wholly business assets, the maximum 75% business asset taper relief is available. For a 40% taxpayer, this corresponds to an effective rate of tax (ignoring other CGT reliefs) of 10%. Given that a buy-back of shares which is treated as a distribution is effectively taxed at 25% of the net distribution, many shareholders will wish to ensure that their sale back to the company is structured as a capital gains transaction within TA 1988 s 219 so far as this is practicable.

    This will certainly be the case where they qualify for 'undiluted' business taper relief (ie they also qualified under the original FA 1998 rules in the two year period to 5 April 2000), as is demonstrated in Mr Bluebeard's sale of shares back to Bliss Limited on 7 April 2006. In such cases, it will clearly be very important to ensure that the numerous conditions set out in explanatory note 3 above are satisfied.

9. Other factors will also affect the choice of route. These include the availability of capital losses, high March 1982 value for the shareholding, and restrictions on qualifying for business property taper relief as opposed to non-business property relief.

    Business property relief may not be available for certain years. For example, before 6 April 2004 a property let to a company or partnership, did not qualify as business property, whereas the same property let to a sole trader would have qualified. In the case of shares, holding of surplus funds by the company can prevent the shares qualifying for business asset taper relief. Although only two years are needed to qualify for taper relief, if the asset has been held longer, its use in all years since 1998 are considered in establishing the proportion of business to non-business taper relief available.

    This underlines the need to prepare draft comparative tax calculations before the buy-back in order to determine the best route. The capital route is usually the most advantageous, but consider the loss of business property taper relief for two years where the asset has been held for three:

		Capital Distribution	*Dividend*
Funds		300,000	300,000
1 Year Business taper	£100,000 @ 50%	(50,000)	
2 Years non-business	£200,000 @ 0%		
Annual exemption		(8,800)	
Taxable		241,200	300,000
Tax @ 40%/25%		96,480	75,000

    Availability of business property rates is crucial to the decision. It is essential to be sure of the status of the assets for business property taper relief in performing the calculation.

    If the outgoing shareholder satisfies the conditions for CGT treatment but the distribution treatment is likely to give a lower tax liability, then one of the CGT conditions must be breached, for example by lending back part of the buy-back consideration immediately after the sale of the shares so as to remain 'connected' with the company by having more than 30% of the company's issued share capital and loan capital (see explanatory note 3(v)).

Effect on Mr Bluebeard of application of TA 1988 s 219

10. The amounts of tax payable by Mr Bluebeard in B (i) and (ii) are £153,000 and £54,810 respectively.

11. The fact that the purchase in part B of the example is made on 7 April 2006 moves it into the tax year 2006/07 instead of 2005/06. This is advantageous if the purchase does not satisfy the provisions of TA 1988 ss 219–229, as Mr Bluebeard's higher rate tax liability is deferred. If the conditions of TA 1988 ss 219–229 are satisfied, a similar cash flow advantage arises for capital gains tax.

Returning funds to shareholders

12.   A number of quoted companies have returned funds to shareholders by means of redeemable 'B' shares. One of the main reasons is to replace share capital with borrowing, interest on which, unlike dividends, is allowable against profits. Additionally, the denial of tax credit repayments makes interest-bearing investments a more attractive investment to tax-exempt institutions, such as pension funds, particularly if the securities are convertible so that there is an opportunity of sharing in growth.

A.

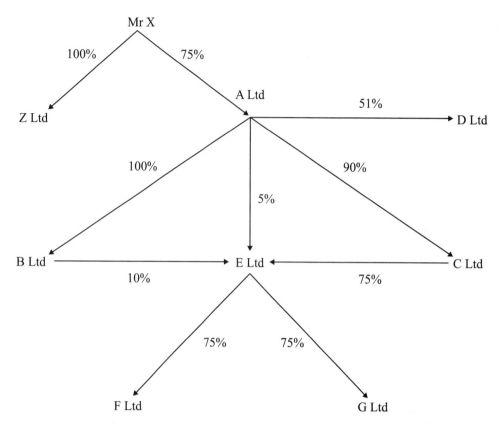

This diagram outlines ownership of various companies. They are resident in the United Kingdom and none deals in shares.

From the diagram above calculate the percentage ownership in each case and explain the relationship for taxation purposes amongst the companies and the taxation position in regard to:

(i)   small companies' rate of corporation tax;

(ii)   deduction of tax from payments passing between them;

(iii)   assets transferred for the purposes of capital gains.

B.   The directors of Spitch Ltd, the parent company of a trading group, intend that the company should purchase an interest in Wick Ltd, a manufacturing company, in the autumn of 2006. The proposal is that Spitch Ltd will acquire either 70% or 80% of the issued share capital of Wick Ltd.

Wick Ltd has accumulated unrelieved trading losses brought forward, and it is expected that the company will continue to incur losses for the next few years. Wick Ltd also has unused surplus ACT of £150,000 carried forward.

It is intended that, after the purchase, freehold property owned by Wick Ltd, which is surplus to that company's requirements, will be transferred to Spitch Ltd at market valuation (which is substantially above cost) and used subsequently by Spitch Ltd for the purpose of its trade.

Draft a memorandum in note form of the taxation consequences (including stamp duty taxes) of the proposals.

A.   **Relationship for tax purposes among group of companies**

D Ltd is a 51% subsidiary of A Ltd.
B Ltd is a 100% subsidiary of A Ltd.
C Ltd is a 90% subsidiary of A Ltd.
E Ltd is owned as follows:

Directly by A Ltd	5 %
Through B Ltd 100% x 10%	10 %
Through C Ltd 90% x 75%	67.5%
	82.5%

Therefore E Ltd is the 82.5% subsidiary of A Ltd.

F Ltd and G Ltd are each 75% owned by E Ltd, who in turn is 82.5% owned by A Ltd, therefore F Ltd and G Ltd are 75% x 82.5% = 61.875% subsidiaries of A Ltd.

Mr X controls:

100% of Z Ltd
75% of A Ltd

Through A Ltd –

75% of 51%	= 38.25% of D Ltd
75% of 100%	= 75% of B Ltd
75% of 90%	= 67.5% of C Ltd
75% of 82.5%	= 61.875% of E Ltd
75% of 61.875%	= 46.4% of F Ltd and G Ltd

(i)   **Taxation position in relation to small companies' rates**

The upper and lower limits for small companies' rate are scaled down according to the number of 'associated companies' in the accounting period, including companies who have been associated for only part of the period as well as overseas associated companies, but excluding dormant companies.

For small companies' rate purposes, two companies are associated if one controls the other or the same person or persons control both (TA 1988 s 13(4)). See Example 49 explanatory note 7 for further details. The rights of a company controlled by a person are attributed to that person. Although Mr X indirectly owns only 38.25% of the share capital of D Ltd, and 46.4% of each of F Ltd and G Ltd, the rights of A Ltd are attributed to him, because he controls A Ltd. Since all of the six companies D Ltd, B Ltd, C Ltd, E Ltd, F Ltd and G Ltd are controlled by A Ltd, they are regarded as controlled by Mr X. Mr X therefore controls Z Ltd plus the other seven companies for small companies' rate purposes, so that the upper and lower limits are divided by eight for each company.

(ii)   **Taxation position in relation to deduction of tax from intra group payments**

As all the companies in the group are UK-resident, tax will not be deducted from any payments of interest and patent royalties between them. Tax is still required to be deducted from some payments in other circumstances, although there are now very few payments to which this applies. For the detailed provisions see Example 48 part (b) and explanatory note 11.

(iii)   **Taxation position in relation to assets transferred for the purposes of capital gains**

Assets transferred between connected persons (which includes companies in a group) are normally deemed to be transferred at open market value for capital gains purposes (TCGA 1992 ss 17 & 18). Assets are, however, transferred on a no loss/no gain basis in a group of companies between a UK-resident parent company and its 75% UK-resident subsidiaries and also any UK resident 75% subsidiaries of those 75% subsidiaries, but excluding a company that is not an 'effective 51% subsidiary' (ie where the parent company is not entitled both to more than 50% of any profits available for distribution to equity shareholders and more than 50% of the assets available to equity shareholders on a winding-up) (TCGA 1992 ss 170 & 171). A company is a 75% subsidiary of another company if the other company owns, directly or indirectly, not less than 75% of its ordinary share capital (TA 1988 s 838).

A non-UK resident parent or subsidiary company can be included in establishing the required group relationship for capital gains purposes. A non-UK resident company can also be the principal company of the capital gains group. (Previously the capital gains group could only comprise UK-resident companies and required a UK-resident principal company at the 'top' of the group ownership structure.) However, despite the removal of the UK residence requirement, companies can only benefit from the reliefs provided they are UK-resident or in relation to assets that would be chargeable to UK corporation tax under TCGA 1992 s 10B (ie capital assets that have been used or will be used for the purposes of a UK trade carried on by a non-resident through a permanent establishment). For example, the no gain no loss transfer rule under TCGA 1992 s 171(1) (dealt with below) would only operate on a transfer between UK-resident companies or in relation to assets used for the purposes of a UK permanent establishment trade carried on by a non-resident company (TCGA 1992 s 171(1)(1A)). F (No 2) A 2005 ss 51–65 introduce reliefs facilitating formation of a Societas Europaeas by merger.

The inclusion of 75% subsidiaries of 75% subsidiaries means that the group relationship between a parent and a sub-subsidiary can be less than 75%. In this example B Ltd, C Ltd and E Ltd are 75% subsidiaries of A Ltd, and F Ltd and G Ltd are 75% subsidiaries of E Ltd. All these companies are also effective 51% subsidiaries of A Ltd. Hence, all the companies controlled by A Ltd except D Ltd form a 75% group for capital gains purposes.

In the case of a transfer to which s 171(1) TCGA 1992 applies, the transferee takes over the base cost of the transferor, inclusive of any indexation allowance due at the date of transfer, but not so as to create or increase a loss when the transferee disposes of the asset (TCGA 1992 s 56). The rule about indexation allowance not creating or increasing a loss does not apply to indexation allowance already incorporated into base cost as a result of no gain/no loss transfers made before 30 November 1993 (TCGA 1992 s 55(7)(8)).

For disposals on or after 6 April 1988, an irrevocable election may be made for all assets that were owned on 31 March 1982 to be treated as acquired at their market value on that date. Where the election is made, indexation allowance is given on that 31 March 1982 value. Where the election is not made, the asset is still treated as acquired at its 31 March 1982 value in calculating the gain or loss on disposal unless using original cost (or 6 April 1965 value for assets acquired before that date) would give a lower gain or lower loss. (For most taxpayers, the time limit for making the election will have expired. For the detailed provisions see Example 77.) Indexation allowance in this event is always given on the higher of 31 March 1982 value and cost (or 6 April 1965 value if that value is used to calculate the gain or loss under the pre-31 March 1982 rules) (TCGA 1992 ss 35 & 55).

Where an asset acquired before 31 March 1982 is transferred on or after 6 April 1988 to another group company, then when the acquiring company disposes of the asset outside the group, the indexation allowance is still calculated using the 31 March 1982 value where this is beneficial, but the indexation allowance included in the base cost on the intra-group transfer is excluded from the allowable cost on the eventual disposal (TCGA 1992 s 55). If the intra-group transfer was made before 30 November 1993, indexation allowance up to the date of the transfer may be used to create or increase an allowable loss when the transferee company disposes of the asset, as indicated above.

Unless a 31 March 1982 rebasing election had been made, however, the value of the asset on the intra-group transfer would be its original cost plus indexation allowance to the date of the transfer. On a subsequent disposal outside the group, the transferee company is treated as holding the asset on 31 March 1982 (TCGA 1992 Sch 3.1) and can use the 31 March 1982 value of the asset with full indexation based thereon. The transferee company would therefore do two computations, using the deemed acquisition cost (as adjusted for indexation) and 31 March 1982 value, and take the lower gain or lower loss. In practice, this intermediate step would usually be ignored as 31 March 1982 value will normally give a lower gain or loss – the transferee company will simply calculate the gain by reference to 31 March 1982 value with full indexation from March 1982 to date.

Example:	£
Asset cost 1980	100,000
31.3.82 value	120,000

	£
Irrevocable election for 31 March 1982 value not made. Transferred intra-group May 1989 when asset valued at	170,000
Deemed to be transferred at cost of £100,000 plus indexation allowance of 44.8% calculated on 31.3.82 value of £120,000 = £53,760, giving	153,760
Sold April 2006 by transferee company for	310,000

Indexation allowance from March 1982 to April 2006 – 147.36%

The position on sale is as follows (based on 31.3.82 value since using cost would clearly give a higher gain):	£	£
Sale proceeds April 2006		310,000
Value at 31 March 1982	120,000	
Indexation allowance 147.36% x £120,000 31.3.82 value	176,832	296,832
Gain		£ 13,168

If the sale proceeds had been £110,000, then the indexation allowance of £53,760 accrued up to the time of the intra-group transfer in May 1989 would be allowed as part of the cost in computing the allowable loss, but the lower loss would in fact be arrived at by using the 31 March 1982 value as follows:

	Using cost £	*Using 31.3.82 value* £
Sale proceeds	110,000	110,000
Deemed cost	(153,760)	
31.3.82 value		(120,000)
Giving loss of	(43,760)	(10,000)
Allowable loss would therefore be		£10,000

The provisions of s 171 deeming intra-group transfers to be on a no loss/no gain basis do not apply where there is a share for share exchange between group companies (s 171(3)). However, from 1 April 2002, the disposal may be eligible for the substantial shareholdings exemption (SSE) in TCGA 1992 s 192A and Sch 7AC (introduced by FA 2002), even though the disposal is to a fellow group company. Where the share for share exchange rules disapply s 171, the transferor's capital gains position is protected by the SSE (assuming all the relevant conditions are met) since Sch 7AC.4(1)(b) also overrides the application of the capital gains 'no disposal' treatment under the reorganisation provisions of TCGA 1992 s 127. Thus the transferor's base cost for the new 'replacement' shares is market value (and *not* the original cost of the 'transferred' company's shares).

Where the SSE is not available (for example, where the transfer occurred before 1 April 2002 or where the transfer does not satisfy all the relevant SSE conditions), the transferor company is treated as acquiring the replacement shares at the original cost of the shares for which they were exchanged (TCGA 1992 ss 127 and 135), and the transferee company is treated as acquiring the transferred shares at market value (s 17(1)). This, of course, assumes that HMRC accept that the share exchange was motivated by bona fide commercial reasons, for which clearance may be obtained in advance under TCGA 1992 s 138, if appropriate. Nor do the no gain/no loss rules apply if shares are exchanged for a new issue of loan notes which constitute qualifying corporate bonds. The provisions of TCGA 1992 s 116 require the gain or loss at the time of such an exchange to be calculated and held over until the bonds are disposed of (see Example 80 explanatory note 4), but the exchange is not treated as a disposal of the shares (s 116(10)). For s 171 to apply there must be both a disposal and an acquisition (TCGA 1992 s 171(1) – see Revenue's Tax Bulletin December 1996). Once again, as noted above, the SSE can override the 'no disposal' rule in appropriate cases (TCGA 1992 Sch 7AC.4(1)(a)).

There are anti-avoidance provisions where a company leaves a group within six years after acquiring an asset from another group company on a no loss/no gain basis (TCGA 1992 s 179).

There are wide-ranging anti-avoidance provisions in TCGA 1992 ss 177A, 177B and Schedules 7A, 7AA and FA 2006 to eliminate the benefit of 'capital loss' buying or 'capital gain' buying. The provisions effectively prevent group companies deriving a tax benefit by bringing together gains and losses that have accrued while the relevant assets were in unrelated ownership. For further details see Example 64 explanatory note 3(b).

B. **Taxation consequences of proposal for Spitch Ltd to acquire 70% or 80% of issued share capital of Wick Ltd**

(1) Unless Spitch Ltd acquires at least 75% of the share capital of Wick Ltd it will not be able to take advantage of either the group relief provisions for trading losses or the group capital gains provisions.

(2) If Spitch Ltd acquires 75% or more of Wick Ltd's share capital and is entitled to 75% of Wick Ltd's profits and 75% of its assets on a winding-up, trading losses of Wick Ltd arising after the acquisition will be able to be transferred to Spitch Ltd under the group relief provisions, providing Spitch Ltd has sufficient profits in the relevant corresponding accounting period to cover the losses it wishes to transfer.

(3) Similarly, 75% share capital ownership and entitlement to more than 50% of profits and of assets on a winding-up will enable Spitch Ltd to acquire by transfer the freehold property from Wick Ltd on a no loss/no gain basis for capital gains purposes (TCGA 1992 s 171). This will also enable any capital losses realised by Wick Ltd or Spitch Ltd after the takeover to be offset against capital gains made by the other company provided a joint election is made under TCGA 1992 s 171A. The election enables a 75% group member disposing of a chargeable asset outside the group to *deem* that it had first been transferred to a fellow 75% group member which has capital losses (or indeed other amounts) available for offset against the gain. For corporation tax purposes, the deemed transferee group member is treated as having sold the asset to the third party and will record the capital gains computation on its tax return even though the actual disposal is made by the original group company.

(4) A similar 'tax neutral' basis applies for intangible fixed assets transferred between group companies under the intangible fixed assets regime (FA 2002 Sch 29.55 and 29.140). For these purposes, the 'group' definition is based on 75% ownership of subsidiaries and is very closely modelled on the one used for capital gains purposes (see FA 2002 Sch 29.46 to 29.54). These rules enable intangible fixed assets, such as goodwill, intellectual property etc. acquired by the *group* after 31 March 2002 to be transferred at their original cost to the group company, irrespective of the actual consideration passing between the companies (and recorded in their accounts).

(5) Previously, assets normally passed between group members in a 75% ownership relationship without attracting stamp duty under FA 1930 s 42. (The stamp duty 'group' requirements were satisfied where the parent company (directly or indirectly) held at least 75% of the ordinary share capital (as well as *at least* 75% of the profits available for distribution to equity holders and assets available on a winding up). There were anti-avoidance rules in FA 1967 s 27 which prevented stamp duty intra-group transfer relief being given in certain specified cases, such as where there were arrangements for the transferee company to leave the group at the date of the intra-group transfer. Furthermore, for transfers after 15 April 2003, a stamp

duty degrouping charge applied where land was transferred (or a lease had been granted or surrendered) and the transferee company left the group within three years after the transfer. In effect, the stamp duty relief obtained on the intra-group transfer was clawed back (FA 2003 s 126). Note that the clawback avoidance device of dropping property into a subsidiary and then selling the *parent* company of that subsidiary has been stopped. In large part, the provisions of FA 2003 s 62 and Sch 7 have continued the group relief exemption for stamp duty land tax where land and buildings are transferred.

(6)   As far as Wick Ltd's brought forward trading losses are concerned, it will not be possible for these to be carried forward for use against profits subsequently made by Wick Ltd, unless the change of ownership can steer clear of the 'blocking' provisions of TA 1988 ss 768 and 769.

(7)   Where there is a change in ownership of a company, s 768 prevents losses being carried forward to a period after the change, and s 768A prevents losses being carried back to a period before the change, if either:

    (a)   within a period of three years during which a change of ownership occurs there is also a major change in the nature or conduct of the trade; or

    (b)   the change in ownership occurs after the scale of activities of a company has become small or negligible and before any considerable revival.

Similar provisions apply to prevent surplus ACT being carried forward under the post-5 April 1999 shadow ACT rules (SI 1999/358 reg 16).

(8)   Although a major change in the nature or conduct of the trade is widely defined and includes a major change in the types of property dealt in, the services or facilities provided, or customers and outlets, it is sometimes possible to steer clear of the three year rule in 7(a) by keeping the trade ticking over at its current level for three years and not making any significant changes in customers, outlets etc during that time. But there is no three-year time limit for 7(b) and so if Wick Ltd's scale of activities has already sunk to a low level, a revival at any time would bring the provisions of ss 768 and 768A (and the shadow ACT rules) into effect.

(9)   As Wick Ltd has surplus ACT brought forward, it will be subject to the shadow ACT regulations (SI 1999/358). Care will therefore need to be taken with reg 16, which prevents surplus ACT being carried forward (and therefore used to obtain a reduction of corporation tax) if a major change in the nature of Wick Ltd's trade occurs within three years (either side) of its acquisition by Spitch Ltd, or there is a considerable revival in its trade in the circumstances noted in (7) above.

Provided Wick Ltd can avoid the above anti-avoidance rule, it may offset its actual surplus ACT against corporation tax under the shadow ACT rules. It will only obtain an offset, however, if it can generate taxable profits and its consequential ACT offset capacity (ie 20% of its taxable profits) is not covered by shadow ACT allocated by Spitch Ltd on its own dividends.

None of the surplus ACT in Wick Ltd can be offset against the tax arising on a gain attributable to the disposal of the freehold property (transferred from Spitch Ltd) within three years of the acquisition of Wick Ltd by Spitch Ltd (SI 1999/358 reg 18).

(10)   Any dividends paid by Wick Ltd to Spitch Ltd do not give rise to shadow ACT (unless Wick Ltd has franked investment income and an election is made to treat an identical amount of any dividend it makes as a franked payment).

(11)   For small companies' rate purposes, the relevant upper and lower limits are divided by the number of associated companies and Spitch Ltd and Wick Ltd will be associated companies for this purpose, since Spitch Ltd will control Wick Ltd.

Explanatory Notes

Statutory provisions relating to groups

1. The main provisions relating to groups of companies and the required group relationships are as follows:

Group relief for losses etc	75% groups	(TA 1988 ss 402 to 413)
Group capital gains	75% groups	(including 75% sub-subsidiaries) (TCGA 1992 ss 170 to 184)
Group intangible fixed assets	75% groups	(including 75% sub-subsidiaries) (FA 2002 Sch 29.46 to 29.71)
Group stamp duty relief	75% groups	FA 2003 Sch 7

Under the provisions of TA 1988 s 806H, regulations have been introduced in relation to double taxation relief to enable unrelieved foreign tax on dividends to be surrendered within a group (SI 2001/1163 – see Example 54 explanatory note 7).

Change in ownership of a company

2. There are various anti-avoidance provisions that apply when there is a change in ownership of a company coupled with a major change in the nature or conduct of the trade or business, as follows:

TA 1988

ss 767A & 767AA	Avoiding payment of corporation tax (see explanatory note 6)
ss 768 & 768A	Carrying trading losses forward and back (see part B note (7))
s 768B	Carrying excess management expenses etc forward (see explanatory note 4)

TCGA 1992

ss 177A, 177B & Schs 7A, 7B	Set-off of pre-entry losses and use of pre-entry gains when a company joins a group (see Example 64 explanatory note 3(b))

Shadow ACT regs (SI 1999/358)

Reg 16	Carrying ACT forward on a change of ownership after 5 April 1999
Reg 17	Carrying forward ACT surrendered to a subsidiary on a change of ownership after 5 April 1999
Reg 18	Setting off ACT carried forward on a change in ownership against tax on a gain on an asset transferred intra-group

The shadow ACT rules in SI 1999/358 regs 16, 17 and 18 replicate the original statutory provisions of TA 1988 ss 245, 245A and 245B which applied in relation to ACT offsets under the pre-6 April 1999 regime.

The rules for deciding whether a change of ownership has occurred are in TA 1988 s 769, which provides that true economic ownership is taken into account. Revenue Statement of Practice SP 10/91 indicates their interpretation of 'a major change in the nature or conduct of a trade or business'.

Small companies' profits

3. When calculating a company's profits for small companies' rate purposes, dividends received from a 51% subsidiary company (or from a fellow 51% subsidiary of the same holding company) or by a member of a consortium from its consortium (trading or holding) company are left out of account (TA 1988 s 13). See Example 49 explanatory note 7 for the treatment of group holding companies in calculating the number of associated companies for small companies' rates.

Change in ownership of company with investment business

4. Provisions similar to those in TA 1988 s 768 outlined in note (7) of part B to the example apply to companies with investment business (for accounting periods beginning before 1 April 2004,

investment companies only comprised those companies whose business consists wholly or mainly of making investments and whose income is mainly derived therefrom – TA 1988 s 130). Unrelieved management expenses, interest and charges of a company with investment business and, from 1 April 2002, unrelieved non-trading losses on intangible fixed assets, may not be carried forward where, within the six years beginning three years before the change of ownership, there is a major change in the nature or conduct of the business; or the business revives at any time, after having become small or negligible; or after the change there is a significant increase in the company's capital.

Similarly, unrelieved management expenses, interest etc of an acquired company with investment business cannot be used to reduce capital gains arising on the disposal of an asset routed through that company by a member of the purchasing group. This restriction only applies to disposals within the three years following the takeover of the company with investment business.

(TA 1988 ss 768B, 768C, 768E and Sch 28A).

Relieving surplus ACT under the shadow ACT regime

5.   Where a group company buys a company with unrelieved ACT and transfers assets to it shortly before they are sold, ACT in respect of distributions made before the company is purchased cannot be set against tax on gains on assets transferred intra-group on a no gain no loss basis if they are disposed of within three years of the change in ownership, as noted in part B(9) of the example (SI 1999/358 reg 18). These rules mirror those of TA 1988 s 245B which prevented the set-off of ACT in the same circumstances on a pre-6 April 1999 takeover.

Schemes to avoid corporation tax liabilities

6.   TA 1988 s 767A contains provisions to counteract schemes under which a company's trading assets are transferred to another group company prior to the sale of the company and the new owners strip the company of the remaining cash assets, leaving the company unable to pay its corporation tax. (Such action may result in criminal proceedings on the basis that it may involve conspiracy to defraud HMRC.)

Corporation tax liabilities arising before the sale of the company may in prescribed circumstances be collected from the previous owners. There are also provisions in TA 1988 s 767AA which enable unpaid corporation tax liabilities arising after a sale to be collected from the previous owners if it could reasonably have been inferred at the time of the sale that the tax liabilities were unlikely to be met. HMRC have specific powers in TA 1988 s 767C to obtain information re changes in ownership.

Capital gains

7.   Part B of the example indicates that Wick Ltd is still incurring losses. If it transfers its freehold property to Spitch Ltd *before* it becomes its 75% subsidiary, a chargeable gain will arise, but trading losses of the *same accounting period* will be able to be set off against the gain, and the cost of the property to Spitch Ltd will be the higher market value at the time of transfer. This would enable some of the Wick Ltd current trading losses to be utilised more quickly and put Spitch Ltd in a better position on a future sale of the property.

Had the property been standing at a loss at the time of the intra-group transfer, the loss could not be used to offset a capital gain made by Spitch Ltd after the transfer. For details see Example 64 explanatory note 3(b).

8.   See Example 85 part (2) and explanatory notes 1 and 2 for further notes on the capital gains position on intra-group no gain no loss transfers, including a potential problem where the transfer was made between 31 March 1982 and 5 April 1988.

Cross references

9.   For detailed notes on group relief and on management expenses see Example 63. Other examples deal in detail with the computation of the various reliefs. See Example 64 for group capital gains

(including the election for group companies to be *deemed* to have transferred assets between them and the provisions of TCGA 1992 ss 178–180 where a company leaves a group within six years of acquiring an asset from another group company). The group aspects of rollover relief for replacement of business assets are dealt with in Example 83 explanatory note 9.

A.   You have received the following letter from Mr Wilkins, Finance Director of Systems Holdings plc, one of your major clients.

Systems House
97 Commercial Road
Birmingham

21 July 2006

J S Lower Esq
Carter, Sons & Co
Chartered Accountants
19 South Street
Birmingham

Dear Mr Lower,

Group Borrowings

The above matter was discussed at our last Board Meeting. I have been asked by the Board to prepare a report on current and future borrowing requirements of the group. The report will include a section on taxation, covering the occasions on which income tax has to be deducted at source from interest, the deductibility of interest for corporation tax purposes and the reliefs available for a loss attributable to interest payments. It would be helpful if you could provide an analysis of these tax aspects to enable me to draft the tax section of the report.

As you know, we have a number of trading and investment companies in our group all based in the United Kingdom. Our current financing comes mainly from three sources:

(1)   overdrafts and short, medium and long term loans from United Kingdom banks;

(2)   short, medium and long term loans from other United Kingdom based institutions;

(3)   intra-group loans.

It is envisaged that the same sources will supply the necessary funds in future.

I should be grateful if you would let me have your comments on the taxation implications as soon as possible.

Yours sincerely,

T.M. Wilkins

Finance Director

Reply to Mr Wilkins setting out, with reference to the relevant legislation, the taxation implications of the above.

B.   Baikal Ltd, a UK-resident company which is an unlisted company that is not a close company, has been engaged in the manufacture of agricultural equipment since the company was incorporated in 1956. It owns 60% of the share capital of Ladoga Ltd, another UK resident company, but is not connected with any other company.

In the summer of 2006, the directors of Baikal Ltd wish to borrow funds to expand the trade and are considering the methods shown below.

(1)   A mixture of long term loans and overdrafts from UK banks.

(2)   An issue of debentures, of which 70% would be taken up by a UK merchant bank and 30% by the directors. The debentures would be redeemable in 2007.

(3)   A loan for 2 years from Ladoga Ltd, which has surplus funds.

(4)   A loan by a director. This would be repayable in 11 months' time.

Indicate how interest on each of the above types of borrowing would be relieved for corporation tax, also indicating the extent to which income tax is deductible at source.

A.

Carter, Sons & Co
Chartered Accountants
19 South Street
Birmingham

11 August 2006

T M Wilkins Esq
Finance Director
Systems Holdings plc
Systems House
97 Commercial Road
Birmingham

Dear Mr Wilkins,

Group Borrowings

In reply to your letter of 21 July 2006, the treatment of interest for corporation tax purposes is part of wider provisions in FA 1996 ss 80 to 105 and Schs 8 to 15 dealing with a company's 'loan relationships'. The term 'loan relationships' essentially means all money debt (for the lending of money) except where it relates to trading transactions for goods and services. The provisions cover not only interest payable and receivable but also capital profits and losses on loans. The basic rules are as follows:

(1)   *Deductibility of interest for corporation tax purposes*

The trading companies in your group deduct interest payable from their trading profits (FA 1996 s 80(2)). The deductions are arrived at on an accruals basis rather than on the basis of the payments made.

The group's companies with investment business aggregate all non-trading interest receivable and payable (and also any profits and losses on the disposal of loans) and are taxed on the overall profit under Schedule D Case III (FA 1996 s 80(3)). As with interest relating to the trade, the interest is usually taken into account on an accruals basis. If there is an overall loss (a non-trading deficit) the rules in (3) below apply.

For both trading and non-trading loans, the amounts allowable include any expenses relating to the loans, including incidental costs of raising the loans, or of attempting to raise them even if unsuccessful (FA 1996 s 84(4)).

As far as intra-group payments are concerned, they are treated in the same way as other payments, providing the amounts have been fully taken into account (under the UK loan relationships rules) on the accruals basis by both borrower and lender. If that does not apply (for example, where the lender is an overseas affiliate), interest paid more than a year after the end of the accounting period of accrual cannot be taken into account by the payer until it is actually paid (FA 1996 Sch 9.2).

Transfer pricing applies to transactions between UK resident companies. The basic principle of the transfer pricing legislation is that all transactions involving connected persons must use arm's length prices. An adjustment is required where a transaction departs from an arm's length price and confers a tax advantage. Interest therefore needs to comply with the transfer pricing legislation to be deductible.

(2)   *Deduction of income tax at source*

Interest may be either short interest or annual interest. Short interest is interest on loans for a fixed period of less than twelve months, and it includes overdraft interest, since overdrafts are usually repayable on demand. Annual interest is interest payable on loans for a year or more.

Income tax is never deducted at source from short interest, nor from annual interest paid to banks. As far as other annual interest is concerned, since 1 April 2001 companies do not have to deduct tax from interest payments where they reasonably believe the recipient company to be a UK corporation taxpayer, ie where the lender is either a UK-resident company or a UK permanent establishment of a non-resident company (TA 1988 ss 349A to 349D). This will, of course, include interest paid to other UK-resident group members. Since 1 October 2002 companies have not had to deduct tax from interest paid to local authorities or certain tax-exempt bodies including pension funds (TA 1988 s 349B as amended by FA 2002 s 94).

Following the changes outlined above, the distinction between short and annual interest only remains important for interest paid to non-UK resident lenders, non-corporate lending institutions other than local authorities and exempt bodies, or individuals. In such cases, tax must still be deducted at source from annual interest but not short interest. Where any such interest is paid, all companies should deduct 20% income tax therefrom and account for it to HMRC (TA 1988 ss 349 and 350). The tax is accounted for on form CT 61 within fourteen days after each calendar quarter end, ie by 14 April, 14 July, 14 October and 14 January, and also within fourteen days after the end of the company's accounting period if it does not coincide with one of the calendar quarter ends (TA 1988 Sch 16). If payment to HMRC is not made on the due dates, interest is payable thereon.

(3) *Reliefs available for a loss attributable to interest payments etc*

Interest that has been deducted by trading companies in arriving at trading income as indicated above will be incorporated within any trading loss the company makes, and the normal reliefs for trading losses may be claimed. These are that the loss may be the subject of a group relief claim (see below), and any part of the loss not included in such a claim may be set against *any* profits (including chargeable gains) of the same accounting period, then against any profits of the previous year (TA 1988 s 393A). Any remaining balance may be carried forward to set against later trading income from the same trade (TA 1988 s 393(1)).

As far as companies with investment business are concerned, any loss relating to interest will be incorporated within an overall non-trading deficit on loans (see (1) above). Under FA 1996 s 83 and Sch 8, as amended by FA 2002 Sch 25, relief for all or part of the deficit may be claimed against any other profits (including capital gains) of the deficit period, or by way of group relief (see below), or against Schedule D Case III loan relationship profits of the previous year. Any part of the deficit for which relief is not claimed as indicated above will be carried forward to set against the *total* non-trading profits (including capital gains) of later accounting periods. A claim may, however, be made for all or part of any carried forward amount not to be set against the non-trading profits of the accounting period immediately following the deficit period (FA 1996 Sch 8.4 as amended by FA 2002 Sch 25). Such a claim may be desirable in order to maximise overseas income and its corresponding double tax relief.

Where losses that are attributable to interest payments arise in groups of companies (in which there is a minimum 75% parent/subsidiaries relationship), they may be surrendered to other companies in the group who have profits available in the corresponding accounting period to cover the amount surrendered (TA 1988 ss 402 to 413). The available amount may be split between two or more companies in the group.

If a loan between companies in your group was written off, no relief would be available to the lender. Conversely the borrower would not have to bring any credit into account.

(4) *Documenting transfer pricing policies*

Under corporation tax self-assessment, it is necessary to keep and maintain adequate records to support a correct and complete return. In relation to transfer pricing with connected companies, the documentation must demonstrate that carefully considered arm's length transfer pricing policies were adopted and applied. The payment of interest between group companies should therefore be reviewed together with any other group transactions as part of a transfer pricing exercise.

It will be seen from the foregoing that the tax treatment of interest is fairly complex, particularly in relation to non-trading interest and where losses are involved. If there are any points on which you would like further information or which you would like to discuss with me, please let me know.

Yours sincerely,

J S Lower

B. **Baikal Ltd – treatment of interest paid**

1. Interest on overdrafts and long term loans from UK banks is paid gross and deducted as a trading expense in arriving at the trading profit under Schedule D Case I, the amount allowable being arrived at on the accruals basis.

2. Interest paid on the debentures is paid gross to the merchant bank as the bank is a UK-resident company. The interest paid to the directors is subject to deduction of tax, with the tax being accounted for on the normal quarterly basis. The gross amount of the interest is allowed on the accruals basis in arriving at the Schedule D Case I trading profit.

3. Interest on the loan from the subsidiary company, Ladoga Ltd, is paid gross and deducted from trading profits on the accruals basis as in 1 and 2.

4. Since the loan from the director is for less than a year, it is 'short' interest and tax is not deducted at source. The interest is allowed as a trading expense under Schedule D Case I on an accruals basis.

Explanatory Notes

Loan relationships rules

1. The provisions of FA 1996 ss 80 to 105 and Schs 8 to 15 deal with profits, gains and losses (including exchange gains and losses (FA 1996 s 84A)) on a company's 'loan relationships', which essentially means all money debt (both UK and foreign), except where it relates to trading transactions for goods and services. The provisions therefore cover both simple debts and securities such as government stocks and corporate bonds. Where a company has guaranteed a debt, however, a payment under the guarantee is outside the loan relationships rules (see Example 96 explanatory note 5). Interest may not be deducted from profits other than under the loan relationships rules (TA 1988 s 337A). Certain interest is, however, treated as a distribution rather than as interest and such interest is outside these rules (FA 1996 Sch 9.1). For notes on such interest see Example 56 explanatory note 1.

Shares are not loan relationships (FA 1996 s 81(4)). For accounting periods starting after 30 September 2002 the definition of shares has been amended to exclude a share in a building society (FA 2002 Sch 25.14) and so building society permanent interest bearing shares (PIBS) are within the loan relationships rules for all purposes. (For individuals and trusts, PIBS are an exempt asset for capital gains tax as they are treated as a qualifying corporate bond in their hands (TCGA 1992 s 117(A1)(4)(5)). Before FA 2002, PIBS were outside the scope of the loan relationships rules. However, under TA 1988 s 477A(3), interest and dividends paid on the PIBS were deductible as though they were incurred under a loan relationship and their receipt in the hands of a company was taxed on the same basis. A company's capital profits and losses relating to PIBS were chargeable/allowable under the capital gains regime.

Non-resident companies who have UK income that does not arise through a UK permanent establishment pay *income tax* on that income (see Example 71). The loan relationships provisions only apply for corporation tax. The income tax provisions for interest paid and received are dealt with in the income tax examples.

References in the following notes are to the FA 1996 provisions unless otherwise stated.

2. A company's income profits include not only interest payable and receivable but also profits and losses on the disposal of loans and fees and expenses incurred. Guarantee fees incurred in connection with loan relationships are considered by HMRC to be allowable where the loan would not be granted without the guarantee being given (as is frequently the case). The basic rules are subject to various special provisions, particularly in relation to unit trusts, investment trusts and insurance companies. There are also special rules for stock market transactions such as manufactured payments and stock 'repos' (sales and repurchases of stock).

   Under FA 1996 s 84A (introduced by FA 2002 Sch 23.3), foreign exchange gains and losses on loan relationships are brought within the loan relationships rules. This is not a major computational change, as non-trade foreign exchange gains and losses were already 'pooled' with non-trade loan relationships gains and losses.

Authorised accounting methods

3. There have traditionally been two authorised accounting methods for bringing amounts of interest into the corporation tax computation – the accruals basis, under which adjustments are made for amounts in arrears and advance, and the 'mark to market' basis under which amounts are brought into account in each period at fair value (s 85). Where the accruals basis is used, interest that has been capitalised in the company's accounts is still deducted as it accrues (Schedule 9.14).

   Accounts for tax must be prepared in accordance with UK GAAP, or in accordance with IAS, which was made the full equivalent of UK GAAP by FA 2004. The trend is for UK GAAP to align with IAS, and both favour fair value accounting for financial assets and liabilities, of which 'mark to market' is an approximation. For the vast majority of loans on standard terms by commercial providers of finance, the accrual method will continue to be used, as giving the same result as fair value accounting. The adjustments made to the value of loans in the process of fair value accounting enters the corporation tax computation through the loan relationships rules.

   There are special rules for derivatives, and there is a special regime for securitisation companies.

Bringing amounts into account

4. Amounts that relate to a trade are brought into account in calculating the Schedule D Case I result (s 82). See Example 52 for details of the relief available for trading losses. Non-trading profits and losses (including foreign exchange gains and losses for accounting periods starting after 30 September 2002 – see note 2 above) are aggregated. They are then merged with any foreign exchange gains or losses for periods starting before 1 October 2002, and with financial instruments (or derivative contracts) non-trading gains and losses (pre-1 October 2002 FA 1994 s 160, post-30 September 2002 FA 2002 Sch 26.14(3)). An overall non-trading profit is charged under Schedule D Case III (s 82). If there is an overall loss (a 'non-trading deficit'), relief is available similar to that available for trading losses. The reliefs for deficits are outlined in part A of the example. The notes in part A in relation to carried forward deficits apply to accounting periods starting after 30 September 2002. The provisions for earlier periods had broadly the same effect but were framed in a more complicated way. For detailed notes see Example 63.

   Except for moneylending businesses such as banks, the amounts brought into the computation of trading profits comprise interest payable on loans for the purposes of the trade and expenses relating thereto. The non-trading amounts for non-moneylending businesses comprise interest payable on loans re investments, such as the purchase of shares in an associate/subsidiary or let property (other than qualifying furnished holiday lettings, for which the interest is treated as relating to the trade – see Example 99), interest receivable, expenses relating to non-trading loans, and any profits and losses on the disposal of loans.

In the case of indexed gilts held for non-trading purposes, taxable income is reduced each year by the index increase (or increased if the index decreases) (s 94). Other indexed securities (except those linked to a share index – see note 5) are treated in the same way as other loan stock.

Some companies may be neither trading companies nor companies with investment business (for example housing associations). Such companies were previously only able to get relief for interest in restricted circumstances. They are now entitled to relief under the provisions for non-trading profits and losses.

Loan relationships with embedded derivatives

5.   FA 1996 s 94 provides for the treatment of embedded derivatives. It addresses the situation whereby the main contract ('a host contract') is subject to the loan relationships rules, but part of the consideration is options, futures or convertible securities.

Such contracts are likely to be financial assets or liabilities, which must be accounted for by fair value accounting. The embedded derivatives may be difficult to value, and cause the value of the contract as a whole to fluctuate undesirably. These contracts must be split into their separate components, and the separate components accounted for and taxed according to the nature of the underlying component.

Loss of money lent

6.   As far as the loss of money lent is concerned, the loan relationships rules override the restrictions in TA 1988 s 74 relating to the deduction of amounts as a trading expense (s 82(7)). Writing off or releasing debts covered by the loan relationships provisions is specifically allowed by Sch 9.5 (except for loans between connected persons – see note 7). Any subsequent recoveries must be brought into account. If the borrower is a company, that company is required to bring a credit into account for the amount released, unless the release is part of a compromise or arrangement with creditors (for notes on such arrangements see Example 59 explanatory note 8). The loan relationships rules effectively extend to all companies the treatment that previously applied only to moneylending companies.

7.   Special rules apply where the parties to a loan relationship are connected in an accounting period. (For accounting periods starting before 1 October 2002, the 'connection' test was also met where the parties were connected at any time in the previous two years.) For accounting periods starting after 30 September 2002, a person (including a company) will be connected with a company only if they are able to secure that the company's affairs are conducted in accordance with their wishes, by reason of their shareholding, voting power, or rights under the company's Articles etc in the accounting period (TA 1988 s 87A). For earlier accounting periods, the 'connection' test follows the wider TA 1988 s 416 test of control and broadly applies to companies under common control, or where one controls the other, or where the lender is a close company and the debtor is a participator or associate of a participator. The special rules are as follows:

(a)   Where a company lender writes off or releases a loan to a connected person, a deduction is not allowed (Sch 9.6). If the borrower is a company, that company does not have to bring a credit into account. See Example 56 for further points relating to close company loans, including the income tax treatment of the release of loans made to close company participators. There is a special concession (C28) relating to debt/equity swaps in the course of company rescues and to investment by venture capitalists in developing companies.

(b)   Interest paid more than 12 months after the period in which it would otherwise be treated as accruing cannot be deducted until it is paid, unless the other party to the transaction is a company that has brought the full amount into account on the accruals basis under the loan relationships rules. For accounting periods starting *before* 1 October 2002, the original 'connection' test applies (as noted above). For later accounting periods, the 'late interest' rule will apply where one of the parties has control of the other (as defined in TA 1988 new s 87A – see above), or where one has a major (ie 40%) interest in the other, or in most cases where the loan is made by trustees of a retirement benefits scheme (within TA 1988 s 611). These provisions also extend to cover loans to *close* companies where the lender is a participator, associate of a participator, or a company in which that participator has a major interest (FA 1996 Sch 9.2 as amended by FA 2002 Sch 25.22).

(c)   Relief to the borrower for discount accruing on discounted securities is only allowed if the lender is taxed on the amount accrued. Otherwise relief is given when the security is redeemed (Sch 9.17). The original 'connection' test applies for accounting periods starting *before* 1 October 2002 (as noted above). For later accounting periods, this rule broadly operates where one of the companies controls or has a major interest in the other during the relevant period (using the new FA 1996 s 87A definition of control for this purpose). For close company borrowers, relief is given only at redemption even if the participator who made the loan is a company except (for accounting periods starting after 30 September 2002) where the lender is within the loan relationships rules (Sch 9.18 as amended by FA 2002 Sch 25.34 – see Example 55 explanatory note 8(e)(iii)). Securities are discounted securities where the difference between issue price and redemption price is more than 0.5% per year or more than 15% overall (Sch 13.3).

Groups of companies

8.   Transfers of loan relationships between companies in a 75% group are ignored (Sch 9.12).

Anti-avoidance provisions

9.   There are anti-avoidance provisions covering transactions not at arm's length (Sch 9.11) and loans for unallowable purposes (Sch 9.13). See also Example 61 explanatory note 4 for the provisions dealing with losses on change of ownership of a company with investment business.

Short interest

10.   The meaning and treatment of short interest is outlined in part A of the example. Where statutory interest is payable on late paid commercial debts, HMRC regard it as short interest, so that tax is not deducted at source. As interest on a money debt it will be taken into account by companies under the loan relationships rules (see Revenue Tax Bulletin August 1999). F (No 2) A 2005 inserts a definition of a commercial rate of interest into FA 1996 s 103.

Deduction of tax from interest payments

11.   The FA 2001 s 85 provisions re paying interest (and charges on income) gross between UK companies from 1 April 2001 are dealt with in Example 48 explanatory note 11. For the detailed treatment of the way tax deducted from other interest and charges is accounted for see Example 51.

Transfer pricing

12.   See Example 69 (note 13 for the FA 2004 changes) for more details on transfer pricing.

Alternative finance arrangements

13.   Certain finance arrangements are structured so as to avoid giving rise to the receipt or payment of interest to comply with Islamic law. FA 2005 ss 46–57 and Schedule 2 do not deem interest to arise, but provide that the return or yield is in every way treated as if it were interest. This extends to administrative matters such as the requirement for banks to deduct tax where appropriate, and to issue certificates.

These arrangements may be structured in a number of ways. A finance institution, instead of advancing a loan, might buy an asset for a business and resell it to that business for a profit that equates to the rate of interest. Under present law, this might be treated as capital rather than revenue transaction.

The effect of these provisions is to provide certainty that the treatment of such arrangements, which are parallel to the paying or receiving of interest, are treated for tax purposes as if they are interest. Where the recipient or payer is a company, the interest equivalent falls into the loan relationship rules.

A.   What reliefs may be obtained for excess interest and expenses of management incurred by a company with investment business and for interest and charges in excess of profits from which they can be deducted by any company, if it is:

    (i)   An unconnected company

    (ii) A member of a group.

B.   Cribbon Holdings Limited owns 75% of the equity share capital of Cribbon Inks Limited and 90% of the equity share capital of Cribbon Travel Limited. Both subsidiaries undertake trading activities but the parent does not trade. All three companies started business on 1 April 2001 and accounts are made up annually to 31 March.

The adjusted results for the year ended 31 March 2007 are as follows:

	Cribbon Holdings Ltd £	Cribbon Inks Ltd £	Cribbon Travel Ltd £
Schedule D Case I		55,500	488,000
Schedule D Case III		750	1,000
Chargeable gains		12,000	20,000
Non-trading deficit on loans	(10,000)		
Charges on income (qualifying charitable donations)	(3,000)	(2,000)	(4,000)
Management expenses	(6,850)		
Dividends received	10,800		9,765

No intra-group dividends have been paid during the year.

There were no unrelieved amounts brought forward from the year to 31 March 2006 and Cribbon Holdings Ltd did not have a Schedule D Case III loan relationship surplus for that year.

Calculate the corporation tax payable by each of the three companies in respect of the year ended 31 March 2007 on the assumption that the group wishes to minimise its taxation liability.

C.   X Ltd has four wholly owned subsidiaries, A Ltd, B Ltd, C Ltd and D Ltd, each of which makes up accounts to 31 March annually and each of which made profits of £500,000 in the year to 31 March 2006.

X Ltd makes up accounts to 31 December and made a trading loss of £400,000 in its year to 31 December 2006.

Show the maximum amounts X Ltd may surrender to each subsidiary by way of group relief in respect of its trading loss, and the most efficient way of using group relief.

D.   The issued share capital of Z Ltd is 80,000 £1 ordinary shares. In its year to 31 July 2006 it had a trading profit of £50,000. Its shares are owned by the following companies, whose trading results for the year to 31 July 2006 were:

		£	Shares in Z Ltd
A Ltd	Profit	40,000	48,000
B Ltd	Loss	(60,000)	24,000
C Ltd	Profit	10,000	8,000
			80,000

All companies are resident in the United Kingdom.

Explain what consortium relief is available in respect of B Ltd's loss.

A.   (i)   *Interest payable*

Under the loan relationships provisions of FA 1996 (see Example 62), interest payable that relates to a trade is taken into account in arriving at the trading result, so that it forms part of a trading loss for which the normal loss reliefs are available ie the loss may be set off under TA 1988 s 393A against the total profits of the same accounting period, then the total profits of the previous year, with any remaining loss carried forward against later trading income under TA 1988 s 393. The time limit for a s 393A claim is two years from the end of the loss period.

The treatment of unrelieved interest that does not relate to a trade is the same for both trading companies and companies with investment business. Non-trading interest payable is aggregated with interest receivable and any profits and losses on non-trade related loans, *including* foreign exchange or financial instruments losses and gains (see Example 62 explanatory notes 2 and 4). If there is an overall loss, ie a 'non-trading deficit', then for accounting periods starting before 1 October 2002 relief for *all or part of the loss* may be claimed as follows (FA 1996 s 83 & Sch 8):

(a)   Against any other profits (including capital gains) of the deficit period.

(b)   By way of group relief (see also (ii) below).

(c)   Against Schedule D Case III loan relationship profits of the previous year. If relief is claimed under this heading, the claim must relate to the *whole* of any deficit not relieved under (a) or (b), so far as the earlier profits permit.

(d)   Against *total* non-trading profits (including capital gains) of the next following accounting period.

The time limit for the above claims is two years from the end of the deficit period (three years for a claim under (d)) (FA 1996 s 83(6)(7)).

Any part of the deficit for which relief is not claimed under (a) to (d) is carried forward to set against total non-trading profits in periods after the next following period (FA 1996 s 83(3)). The mechanics are a little complex. If a non-trading deficit arose in 2001 (ie year ended 31 December 2001), it was automatically carried forward to 2002 if no offset claim under (a) to (d) was made for 2001. (This may have been desirable, for example, to preserve double tax relief on overseas income in 2001.) For 2002, a claim could be made to offset the deficit under (d) against the non-trading profits in 2003, failing which the deficit rolls forward to 2004, when again a claim may be made under (d) or the deficit again rolls forward, and so on.

For accounting periods starting after 30 September 2002, the complexity has been removed, while retaining the essence of the previous provisions (FA 1996 s 83 and Sch 8 as amended by FA 2002 Sch 25). For heading (b), a specific *claim* by the surrendering company is not needed. The claimant company may simply make a normal group relief claim to use the surrendering company's non-trade deficit in the same way as any other loss. Heading (d) has been deleted and any part of the deficit for which relief is not claimed under (a) to (c) is carried forward to set against total non-trading profits of succeeding accounting periods. The company may, however, make a claim for all or part of the carried forward amount not to be set against the non-trading profits of the accounting period *immediately* following the deficit period. The time limit for the claim is two years after the end of that next following accounting period (FA 1996 Sch 8.4).

See explanatory note 2 for the interaction of relief for non-trading deficits with other claims for relief, and also for points on restricting claims.

Excess charges on income and management expenses (other than interest)

Interest payable is excluded both from charges on income and from the management expenses of a company with investment business. Charges on income now almost invariably comprise qualifying charitable donations. From 16 March 2005 annuities and other annual payments are dealt with as management expenses, so the trade charges rules outlined below are normally only relevant for pre-1 April 2002 payments.

Charges on income are deducted from profits *after* all other reliefs except group relief (TA 1988 s 338). But carried back trading losses and carried back Schedule D Case III loan relationship deficits do not displace relief for *trade* charges (losses TA 1988 s 393A(8), deficits FA 1996 Sch 8.3(6)). The deduction of management expenses under TA 1988 s 75 is mandatory.

Neither excess charges nor excess management expenses can be carried back against earlier profits (with the exception of excess *trade* charges of the last twelve months when a trade ceases, which may be included in a loss carryback claim under TA 1988 s 393A and for which the carryback period is three years – see Example 53 explanatory note 1). Excess charges relating to a continuing trade are incorporated within a loss carried forward under TA 1988 s 393(9) and set against future *trading* profits. Excess management expenses of a company with investment business), together with excess charges paid wholly and exclusively for the company's business, are carried forward in accordance with TA 1988 s 75(3) and treated as though they were management expenses of the subsequent year, so that they are set off against any profits chargeable to corporation tax.

Anti-avoidance provisions

For companies with investment business, there are anti-avoidance provisions relating to amounts carried forward in respect of non-trading deficits, charges on income and management expenses if there is a change in ownership of the company (see Example 61 explanatory note 4).

(ii) Where a company is a member of a 75% group, trading losses, non-trading deficits on loans and the net surplus of charges, Schedule A business losses and management expenses over the surrendering company's gross profits may be the subject of a claim for group relief under TA 1988 s 402 (see ss 403(1)(2), 403ZA, 403ZC, 403ZD and FA 1996 s 83(2)). Excess management expenses (within a s 403ZD claim) of a company with investment business may be surrendered whether or not the *claimant* company is a company with investment business.

Group relief claims may be made only in respect of the unrelieved amount of the *current* period, and cannot include unrelieved amounts brought forward.

B. **Cribbon Holdings Ltd**

Since there are three companies in the group, the lower and upper limits for small companies' rate for the financial year 2006 are £100,000 and £500,000.

Before any claims are made, the position of each company for the year to 31 March 2007 is as follows:

	Cribbon Holdings Ltd £	*Cribbon Inks Ltd* £	*Cribbon Travel Ltd* £
Schedule D Case I	–	55,500	488,000
Schedule D Case III	–	750	1,000
Chargeable gains	–	12,000	20,000
	–	68,250	509,000
Less: Charges on income	(3,000)	(2,000)	(4,000)
Management expenses	(6,850)		
Profits chargeable to corporation tax	–	66,250	505,000
Non-trading deficit on loans	(10,000)		
Management expenses	(6,850)		
Charges on income	(3,000)		
Excess amounts for surrender (TA 1988 s 403ZD)	(9,850)		
Corporation tax payable:			
66,250 @ 19%		12,587	
505,000 @ 30%			151,500
Franked investment income			
(10,800 + (1/9) 1,200)	12,000		
(9,765 + (1/9) 1,085)			10,850

Cribbon Holdings Ltd cannot carry back any part of the non-trading deficit on loans of £10,000 to the year to 31 March 2006, since it did not have a Schedule D Case III loan relationship surplus for that year. Nor can it carry back excess management expenses and charges totalling £9,850 (see part A(i) of the example). Relief could, however, be obtained by a group relief claim, under which these amounts, totalling £19,850, could be surrendered to Cribbon Travel Ltd or Cribbon Inks Ltd or partly to one company and partly to the other.

Since the rate of tax saved on any surrender to Cribbon Inks Ltd would be only at the small companies' rate, the full excess amounts should be surrendered to Cribbon Travel Ltd, who will save tax partly at the full rate and partly at the marginal small companies' rate.

The revised tax payable by Cribbon Travel Ltd after the group relief claim will be as follows:

	£
Profits before group relief claim	505,000
Less Amounts surrendered by Cribbon Holdings Ltd (see explanatory note 1):	
Non-trading deficit on loans (TA 1988 s 403ZC)	(10,000)
Excess charges on income and excess management expenses (TA 1988 s 403ZD)	(9,850)
Profits chargeable to corporation tax (I)	485,150
Add franked investment income	10,850
Profits for small companies rate (P)	496,000
Corporation tax payable: 485,150 @ 30%	145,545
Less: Marginal relief	
$(500,000 - 496,000) \times \dfrac{485,150}{496,000} \times 11/400$	(108)
	145,437
Compared with tax originally payable of	151,500
Tax saved through group relief claim (approx 30.5%)	£ 6,063

The corporation tax payable by each company for the year to 31 March 2007 after group relief claims is as follows:

	£
Cribbon Holdings Ltd	Nil
Cribbon Inks Ltd	12,587
Cribbon Travel Ltd	145,437

In view of the minority interest, a payment from Cribbon Travel Ltd to Cribbon Holdings Ltd for the tax value of the amount surrendered would be appropriate.

Both Cribbon Holdings Ltd and Cribbon Travel Ltd have surplus franked investment income at 31 March 2007 (£12,000 and £10,850 respectively).

C.   **X Ltd and its subsidiaries – maximum group relief claims**

X Ltd's loss period corresponds as to three months with the accounting periods to 31 March 2006 of each of its four subsidiaries, the remaining 9/12ths of the loss period corresponding with the subsidiaries' accounts to 31 March 2007. X Ltd cannot surrender more *in total* than 3/12ths of its loss, ie £100,000, for use by its subsidiaries in the year to 31 March 2006. Each of the subsidiaries has more than enough profit in the corresponding part of the accounting period to 31 March 2006 to cover the amount available for surrender. If £100,000 were surrendered, say, to A Ltd, there would be no further loss available to surrender to the other subsidiaries. If less than £100,000 were surrendered to A Ltd, the remainder could be surrendered to one or more of B Ltd, C Ltd and D Ltd.

The remaining £300,000 of X Ltd's loss would be similarly treated in relation to the accounts of the subsidiaries for the year to 31 March 2007.

D.   (i)   Consortia are often appropriate to specific projects and joint venture structures and the group relief provisions extend to them in defined circumstances. A claim under these provisions is called a consortium claim (TA 1988 s 402(3)). Before FA 2000, group/consortium relief was available only to UK-resident companies but it has now been extended as indicated below.

(ii)   A company is owned by a consortium if three-quarters or more of its ordinary share capital is beneficially owned between them by companies, including, from 1 April 2000, non-resident companies, of which none beneficially owns less than one-twentieth of that ordinary share capital.

These companies are called the *members* of the consortium (TA 1988 s 413(6)).

(iii)   Despite the wider post-FA 2000 definition of a consortium, until 6 April 2006 consortium relief claims or surrenders could only be made by UK-resident companies or by non-resident companies in relation to the losses of a UK permanent establishment trade (and only if they were not relievable in the overseas country against profits not taxable in the UK). Similarly, a UK-resident company can also obtain relief for trading losses of an overseas permanent establishment (provided those losses cannot be deducted for overseas tax purposes against profits not subject to UK corporation tax) (TA 1988 ss 402(3A)(3B), 403D and 403E).

From 6 April 2006, FA 2006 introduced limited relief for losses of subsidiaries in EC. See note 4.

Group relief for consortia which satisfy the above criteria is available where *either* the surrendering company *or* the claimant company is a *member* of a consortium and the other is:

(a)   a trading company which is owned by the consortium and which is not a 75% subsidiary of any company, or

(b)   a trading company:

(i)   which is a 90% subsidiary of a holding company which is owned by the consortium; and

      (ii)   which is not a 75% subsidiary of a company other than the holding company, or

(c)   a holding company which is owned by the consortium and which is not a 75% subsidiary of any company.

A holding company is defined for these purposes as a company whose business consists wholly or mainly in holding shares in 90% trading subsidiaries, irrespective of where they are resident (TA 1988 s 413(3)(b)).

Losses surrendered to a consortium company member are limited according to the percentage of ordinary share capital the member company owns, and losses surrendered by a consortium company member to a consortium-owned company are similarly limited to the fraction of the profits of the consortium-owned company that the loss making consortium member owns (TA 1988 s 403C).

Where a company is both a member of a group and is either a consortium-owned company or one of the joint owners of a consortium, a loss may be surrendered partly as group relief and partly as consortium relief, and consortium relief can flow through the consortium member to and from other companies in the consortium member's group (TA 1988 ss 405 and 406).

TA 1988 ss 403A to 403C prevent companies obtaining relief earlier than would otherwise be available by having different year-ends for the various group/consortium companies (see part C of the example and explanatory note 7).

A surrendering company does not have to claim other loss reliefs available to it in priority to a group relief surrender, but where the surrendering company is owned by a consortium, the trading loss available for surrender is deemed to be reduced to the extent that the surrendering company has profits chargeable to corporation tax in the same accounting period against which a s 393A claim *could* be made, regardless of whether such a claim is actually made (TA 1988 s 403ZA(3)).

(iv)   In the example Z Ltd is owned as to:

A Ltd	48,000	shares
B Ltd	24,000	shares
C Ltd	8,000	shares
	80,000	

A Ltd, B Ltd and C Ltd are members of a consortium and Z Ltd is owned by the consortium. As a member of the consortium, B Ltd may surrender its trading loss of £60,000 in the year to 31 July 2006 against the profits of a trading company owned by the consortium (Z Ltd) in the proportion which it owns the shares of Z Ltd.

The position is therefore:

Loss of B Ltd	£ 60,000

Available for set off against profit of Z Ltd:

$\dfrac{24,000}{80,000}$ x the profit of Z Ltd (£50,000)   £ 15,000

The balance of B Ltd's loss after the surrender of whatever amount up to £15,000 is chosen will be carried forward against its own future trading profits under TA 1988 s 393(1) or relieved against its own other profits under s 393A, or under the group relief provisions if B Ltd itself is a group member.

Had the companies had different year-ends, the amount that B Ltd could have surrendered would have been restricted to the *lowest* of the *unused* part of its available loss for the overlapping period, the *unused* part of Z Ltd's profits for the overlapping period and the proportion of the loss of the overlapping period equal to the proportion B Ltd owns of Z Ltd's shares (TA 1988 s 403C). Similar provisions apply where a loss is surrendered *by* a consortium owned company *to* a consortium member. (See explanatory note 7 for the meaning of the *unused* part of a profit or loss.)

As the accounting period is for the year ended 31 July 2006, the claim for consortium relief must normally be made within one year after the filing date for the claimant company's tax return for the year ended 31 July 2006 (unless a later date is appropriate – see explanatory note 8) (FA 1998 Sch 18.74), and requires the consent of each member of the consortium as well as that of the surrendering company.

Explanatory Notes

Reliefs available for losses and deficits

1. The reliefs available to a single trading company in respect of trading losses and excess charges on income are outlined in Example 52. This example deals additionally with non-trading deficits on a company's loan relationships, excess charges on income and excess management expenses of companies with investment business and with the loss relief available to groups and consortia.

   TA 1988 s 403(3) requires charges on income, Schedule A losses and management expenses to be aggregated and only the *excess* amount over the surrendering company's gross profits of the same period can be group relieved. (For these purposes, the gross profits are *before* deducting any current trading losses, excess capital allowances and any other losses or deficits (TA 1988 ss 403ZD and 403ZE).) On the other hand, s 403(2) allows trading losses, excess capital allowances and non-trading deficits on loans to be surrendered whether or not the surrendering company has profits available to cover them.

   In part B of the example, therefore, Cribbon Holdings Ltd could not have surrendered the management expenses and charges on income totalling £9,850 if it had had any other profits. In contrast, the non-trading deficit of £10,000 could be surrendered even if the company had profits against which it could have been set.

Non-trading deficits

2. The FA 1996 provisions for dealing with a non-trading deficit on a company's loan relationships (hereafter described as a Schedule D Case III loss) are outlined in part A of the example. Where there are other claims for relief, relief for the Schedule D Case III loss against the other profits of the *same* accounting period is given *after* relief for brought forward trading losses but *before* relief for current or carried back trading losses, carried back Schedule D Case III losses or for charges on income. The fact that partial claims may be made, however, enables profits to be left in charge where appropriate, for example to cover non-trade charges or to maximise double tax relief.

   The carry-back relief for Schedule D Case III losses is given against the Schedule D Case III loan relationship profits of the set-off period *after* relief for a Schedule D Case III loss incurred in the set-off period or in an earlier period, relief for trade charges, group relief, and current or carry-back relief for trading losses.

3. Interest is excluded from the management expenses of a company with investment business and is instead brought into account in calculating Schedule D Case III loan relationship profits and losses (TA 1988 s 75(1A)). The overall rules for dealing with unrelieved interest are considerably more flexible than they were before the loan relationships rules were introduced.

Group and consortium relief

4. The group relief provisions are contained in TA 1988 ss 402–413.

   Two companies are members of a group if one is a 75% subsidiary of the other or both are 75% subsidiaries of a third company. (75% subsidiary means holding, directly or indirectly, 75% of the ordinary share capital, entitled to 75% or more of any profits available to equity holders and of any assets available to equity holders on a winding-up (TA 1988 ss 413 and 838).) From 1 April 2000, the group relationship can be traced through any company (irrespective of its residence), although as indicated in part D(iii) of the example only UK-resident companies or UK permanent establishments of non-resident companies could benefit from group relief claims and surrenders. This relaxation was beneficial to multinational groups as they previously had to ensure that any UK subsidiaries acquired (perhaps through the purchase of another group) had to be located in a UK sub-group relationship. This often meant that they had to change their shareholding structures through a reorganisation. It is now possible, for example, for two or more UK-resident subsidiaries owned directly by a US holding company to make group relief claims between themselves. From 6 April 2006, FA 2006 Sch 1 sets out arrangements for a limited form of group relief for EC-resident subsidiaries and consortium companies.

Group relief where the surrendering company is not resident in the UK

On 13 December 2005 the Court of Justice of the European Communities gave its decision in the case of Marks & Spencer plc v Halsey, a case concerning the surrender of losses of European subsidiaries that had been running for some years. As a result, limited group relief for European subsidiaries is introduced from 1 April 2006, subject to significant restrictions. The details are set out in Schedule 1 to the Finance Act 2006.

Relief is given by extending the existing group relief provisions to cover qualifying overseas losses. The surrendering company must be in charge to tax under the law of another EEA territory (this comprises the countries of the European Union plus Iceland, Liechtenstein and Norway). It need not be resident in these countries, but it may instead be chargeable to tax through a permanent establishment. The claimant company must be UK resident. The surrendering company must be a 75% subsidiary of the UK-resident claimant company, or both the surrendering and claimant companies must both be subsidiaries of a third UK-resident company.

Losses will not be available for surrender by way of group relief unless they meet four conditions, which are:

- The equivalence condition,

- The EEA tax loss condition,

- The qualifying loss condition, and

- the precedence condition.

The equivalence condition

The loss must be equivalent in all material respect to an amount of a kind that, for purposes of s 403, would be available for surrender for UK group relief.

The EEA tax loss condition

The loss must first be calculated in accordance with the tax law of the country in which the subsidiary is resident for tax purposes. There are detailed provisions to isolate this loss from losses incurred in the UK, or from sources of income that would be exempt from tax.

The qualifying loss condition

UK tax relief is only available if all possibilities for overseas tax reliefs for the current period, previous period and for subsequent periods have been exhausted, after every effort has been taken to secure them.

The precedence condition

The loss must be offset against all available profits of group companies in any overseas territory in priority to being group relieved against UK profits.

If the loss meets these four conditions, and is potentially available for group relief, it must be recalculated in accordance with UK tax law. Schedule 1 gives details of the basis on which it is to be recalculated.

The amount available for group relief is the lower of the loss computed according to UK tax principles, and the loss computed according to overseas tax principles. If either computation yields a profit, then there is no loss for group relief.

The provisions for consortia are outlined in part D of the example.

5.   The items eligible for a group or consortium relief claim are as follows:

   (a)   Trading losses (providing trade is conducted on a commercial basis with a view of profit). Foreign trading losses under Schedule D Case V are not eligible (TA 1988 s 403ZA), but most overseas permanent establishment losses will fall within Schedule D Case I (the permanent establishment being controlled from the UK).

   (b)   Excess capital allowances on plant and machinery leased other than in the course of a trade or Schedule A letting business (see Example 18 part (b) (s 403ZB)).

   (c)   Non-trading deficits on loan relationships (s 403ZC).

   (d)   Charges on income (trade and non-trade charges), Schedule A business losses, and management expenses to the extent that the aggregate amount exceeds the surrendering company's gross profits (s 403ZD).

   As indicated in part A(ii) of the example, group relief cannot include any unrelieved amounts brought forward.

6.   Group relief is given as a deduction from the claimant company's total profits *before* reduction by any relief derived from a later accounting period (eg by carry-back of losses under s 393A) but *after* reducing by any other relief, including relief for charges.

   The loss company does not have to make use of the loss reliefs available to it to reduce the amount surrendered, but note the point in D(iv) in the example in relation to consortium claims.

Overlapping accounting periods

7.   Where the accounting periods of the surrendering and claiming companies do not coincide, the amount that may be surrendered to any company is the lower of the *unused* part of the surrendering company's available loss for the overlapping period and the *unused* part of the claimant company's profits for the overlapping period (TA 1988 s 403A). (For consortium claims, a further limit is imposed by s 403C based on the proportion of the trading company's shares owned by the consortium member, as indicated in part D of the example.) The 'unused' part of the profit or loss is the amount remaining after taking previous group relief (or consortium relief) claims into account. Apportionments are normally made on a time basis, but may be made on a 'just and reasonable' basis, if appropriate (s 403B).

Group relief claims

8.   The self-assessment group relief claims provisions are in FA 1998 Sch 18 Part VIII (these apply to accounting periods ending after 30 June 1999).

   All claims, or changes to claims, for group relief must be made in the corporation tax return (CT 600) or in an amended return and the amount claimed must be quantified (ie not formulaic) at the time of the claim. Written notices of consent to surrender must be made to the relevant HMRC office at the same time as, or before, the claim. Claims need not be for the full amount available. They must be preceded or accompanied by written notice of consent from the surrendering company (and for consortium claims, the consent of each consortium member as well). Notices of consent may only be amended by a 'withdrawal notice' and replaced by a new notice of consent. Such changes must be made on an amended return if the tax return has already been filed.

If all, or substantially all, of a group's tax returns are made to the same HMRC office, the group may make special arrangements whereby all group relief claims are deemed to include surrenders (ie there is no need to provide copy notices of consent to surrender), and amendments to returns may be made by a single joint amended return, although individual group companies must each make a separate return initially (FA 1998 Sch 18.77 and SI 1999/2975).

The time limits for group relief claims are the latest of one year after the filing date for the return, thirty days after the completion of an HMRC enquiry into the return, thirty days after the notice of HMRC amendments to the return following an enquiry, and thirty days after the final determination of an appeal against such an amendment.

The order in which claims are treated as made for the purpose of determining amounts previously surrendered or claimed in respect of group or consortium relief for overlapping periods is dealt with in TA 1988 s 403A(6)(7).

HMRC will only consider late group relief claims in exceptional circumstances, for example where the delay was due to circumstances beyond the company's control, or where a HMRC error was a major reason for the delay (FA 1998 Sch 18.74).

Payment for group relief

9.   No payment for group relief amounts need be made by the claimant company to the surrendering company. However, payment can be made up to the full amount surrendered without it being taken into account in computing profits or losses of either company for corporation tax purposes, nor is it regarded as a distribution or a charge on income (TA 1988 s 402).

In some cases, a payment will clearly be appropriate, for example where subsidiaries are not wholly owned or in the case of consortia.

There are provisions to deny or restrict an allowable loss for capital gains purposes where there has previously been a 'depreciatory transaction' within a group of companies (TCGA 1992 s 176). The amount of a payment, or lack of a payment, for group relief could constitute a depreciatory transaction, but HMRC will not usually seek to apply the provisions so long as any payments do not exceed the tax advantage obtained.

Anti-avoidance provisions

10.   There are various anti-avoidance provisions in relation to groups, including those in TA 1988 ss 403A to 403C outlined in note 7. Other rules include provisions to prevent companies forming groups on a temporary basis to take advantage of the group relief provisions (TA 1988 s 410), and denying group relief where the surrendering company is a dual resident investing company (s 404).

Group relief is also not available for that part of any accounting period during which arrangements exist under which one of the companies could leave the group (TA 1988 s 410). See Statement of Practice SP3/93 and concession C10 for the way HMRC interpret and apply the provisions relating to 'arrangements'.

Ivon Products plc is a quoted engineering company with an issued share capital of £2,380,000 in ordinary shares of £1 each. It has two subsidiary companies, being the owner of the whole of the issued share capital of Dylan (RGW) Ltd and 65% of the issued share capital (which consists solely of ordinary shares) of Terrence Supplies Ltd. Dylan (RGW) Ltd is a property letting business, letting commercial units to third parties. Terrence Supplies Ltd is a wholesale supplier.

The accounts of Ivon Products plc for the year ended 31 March 2007 show a trading profit of £576,190 and investment income of £39,260. Further information available is shown below.

1.   Expenses charged in arriving at trading profit include the following:

	£
Depreciation	41,350
Health club subscriptions –	
re managing director of Ivon Products plc	450
re managing director of Dylan (RGW) Ltd	380
Architect's fees for proposed new factory	2,400
Cost of levelling adjacent ground for use as company car park	2,265
Patent application fees re new patent	250
Legal fees – Debt collection	955
New service agreements	1,045
Planning application for new factory	4,160
Patent royalties	25,880

2.   The capital allowances for the year were £16,160 on plant and machinery (including £10,000 on acquisitions during the year) and £21,900 on industrial buildings.

3.   The amount shown for patent royalties takes into consideration accrued royalties of £5,380 on 31 March 2006 and £3,605 on 31 March 2007.

4.   Investment income consists of the following items, all of which were received during the year:

	£
Interest on government stocks (received gross) 30 September 2006 and 31 March 2007 (no interest accrued due at 31 March 2006 or 2007)	5,760
Dividend from Terrence Supplies Ltd	21,450
Dividends from other United Kingdom companies (excluding tax credit) received 1 January 2007	8,100
Building society interest received 31 March 2007 (no interest accrued due at 31 March 2006)	3,950
	39,260

5.   During the year ended 31 March 2007, Ivon Products plc paid a final dividend of 5p per share for the year ended 31 March 2006 on 1 July 2006, and an interim dividend of 4p per share for the year ended 31 March 2007 on 1 December 2006.

6.   On 31 March 2006, Ivon Products plc had surplus advance corporation tax to carry forward of £300,000.

7.   On 1 February 2007, the managing director of Ivon Products plc exercised an option under the company's approved share option plan. He acquired 20,000 shares in Ivon Products plc for 150p each at a time when the share price was listed at 625p. The company's results have not been adjusted to reflect this transaction.

The following figures relate to the subsidiaries for the year ended 31 March 2007:

	Dylan (RGW) Ltd £	Terrence Supplies Ltd £
Schedule A profit	24,610	
Schedule D Case I profit		103,150
Interest on local authority stocks (gross amount) (£2,425 received 30 September 2006 and £2,425 received 31 March 2007)		4,850
Dividend paid 1 December 2006 (including that to Ivon Products plc)		33,000

The directors of Ivon Products plc are currently negotiating the sale of the company's shares in Dylan (RGW) Ltd and it is expected that the transaction will be completed in December 2007. The principal asset of Dylan (RGW) Ltd is a freehold building originally bought by Ivon Products plc for £72,000 in 1981 and transferred to Dylan (RGW) Ltd for £100,000 in December 2002, when its market value was £220,000. The market value of the building was considered to be £80,000 at 31 March 1982 and its current value is approximately £285,000. (The building has always been let to third parties.) Assume indexation allowance from March 1982 to December 2002 was 116.8%.

(a)   Calculate the mainstream corporation tax payable by Ivon Products plc for the year ended 31 March 2007.

(b)   Calculate the mainstream corporation tax payable by each subsidiary for the same year.

(c)   Explain how the surplus advance corporation tax brought forward in Ivan Products plc is dealt with, also showing how the dividends paid in the year to 31 March 2007 are treated.

(d)   Explain the taxation implications of the proposed sale of shares in Dylan (RGW) Ltd and suggest an alternative transaction which might be more efficient for corporation tax purposes.

(a) **Mainstream corporation tax payable by Ivon Products plc for year to 31 March 2007**

		£	£
Trading profit per accounts			576,190
Add:	Depreciation		41,350
	Health club subscription re managing director of Dylan (RGW) Ltd		380
	Architect's fees for proposed new factory		2,400
	Cost of levelling adjacent ground for use as company car park		2,265
	Costs of planning application		4,160
			626,745
Less:	Managing director's share acquisition (see explanatory note 2)	(95,000)	
	Capital allowances – Plant and machinery pool	(16,160)	
	Industrial buildings	(21,900)	(133,060)
Schedule D Case I Trading profit			493,685
Schedule D Case III Interest on government stocks		5,760	
	Building society interest		3,950	9,710
Profits chargeable to corporation tax			503,395
Corporation tax payable thereon @ 30%			151,018

(small companies' rate not applicable since upper limit for a company
with two associated companies is £500,000 for financial year 2006)

Less: ACT offset (see workings in (c) below)	(49,154)
Mainstream corporation tax payable	101,864

(b) **Mainstream corporation tax payable by Dylan (RGW) Ltd for year to 31 March 2007**

Schedule A business profit	£ 24,610
Corporation tax payable thereon @ 19%	£ 4,676

Mainstream corporation tax payable by Terrence Supplies Ltd for year to 31 March 2007

	£
Schedule D Case I trading profit	103,150
Schedule D Case III interest on local authority stocks	4,850
Profits chargeable to corporation tax	108,000

Corporation tax payable thereon (marginal small companies' rate applies, lower
limit being £100,000 and upper limit £500,000 for financial year 2006)

	£
108,000 @ 30%	32,400
Less: $(500,000 - 108,000) \times \dfrac{11}{400}$	(10,780)
Mainstream corporation tax payable	£ 21,620

(c) **Treatment for Ivon Products plc of surplus ACT brought forward of £300,000 and shadow ACT arising on dividends paid in year to 31 March 2007**

The surplus ACT brought forward of £300,000 must be recovered under the shadow ACT regulations. Broadly, this means that it can only be offset (and hence repaid) after the shadow ACT on current dividends paid (net of non-group dividends received) has been fully deducted in Ivon Products plc (within the normal 20% set-off limit) (see explanatory note 4).

The position relating to the shadow ACT arising in the period to 31 March 2007 is as follows:

			£	£
Final dividend	2,380,000 x 5p			119,000
Interim dividend	2,380,000 x 4p			95,200
				214,200
Dividend received				8,100
Net distributions				206,100
Shadow ACT @ 25%				51,525
Maximum ACT offset for period:				
£503,395 @ 20%				100,679
Less: Shadow ACT offset				(51,525)
Surplus ACT brought forward			300,000	
Offset in year – balance			(49,154)	49,154
Surplus ACT carried forward			250,846	

Thus, at 31 March 2007, Ivon Products plc has a surplus of actual ACT carried forward for future offset of £250,846, with no surplus shadow ACT carried forward.

(d)   **Taxation implications of proposed sale of shares in Dylan (RGW) Ltd**

The substantial shareholdings exemption (SSE) is potentially available in respect of gains on post-31 March 2002 disposals of subsidiaries and associated companies provided the investing company holds at least a 10% equity stake for a minimum period of twelve months within the two years before the disposal. The detailed provisions are in Example 65. However, in this example, Ivon Products plc would not be entitled to the SSE on the disposal of its 100% shareholding in Dylan (RGW) Ltd because Dylan (RGW) Ltd would not satisfy the 'trading company' requirement in TCGA 1992 Sch 7AC.19.

Furthermore, when Dylan (RGW) Ltd ceases to be a subsidiary of Ivon Products plc in December 2007, this will trigger a TCGA 1992 s 179 'degrouping' charge, ie Dylan (RGW) Ltd will be deemed to have sold the freehold building acquired from Ivon Products plc in December 2002 when it was acquired from that company, the deemed sale proceeds being the market value at that time. A gain of (220,000 – 80,000 =) £140,000 less indexation allowance @ 116.8% of £80,000, ie £93,440 = £46,560 will therefore be deemed to be made by Dylan (RGW) Ltd in December 2002. Although computed as if the asset had been disposed of in December 2002, the gain is regarded as arising at the beginning of the accounting period in which Dylan (RGW) Ltd leaves the group, and will be charged at the corporation tax rate applicable to that accounting period (see explanatory note 5).

It is possible for the degrouping 'gain' to be allocated to the parent company and its 75% subsidiaries under TCGA 1992 s 179A. The departing subsidiary and the group member(s) to whom the gain is allocated must make a joint election under s 179A within two years after the end of the departing subsidiary's accounting period in which the degrouping gain arose. The ability to reallocate degrouping gains in this way enables the degrouping charge to be allocated to other (75%) group members that may have available capital losses etc to shelter the degrouping gain. In this example, the only prospective recipient of the potential degrouping gain is Ivon Products plc but it does not have any reliefs available to reduce it, although it might agree to take over the liability as part of the sale negotiations. (Terrence Supplies Ltd is only a 65% subsidiary and is not eligible for any s 179A allocation.)

FA 2002 also allowed degrouping gains to be eligible for business assets rollover relief under TCGA 1992 s 152 where the subsidiary leaves the group after 31 March 2002 (TCGA 1992 s 179B and Sch 7AB). However, TCGA 1992 s 152(1) as modified by Sch 7AB provides, amongst other things, that the relevant asset giving rise to the degrouping charge must have been used for trading purposes by the degrouped subsidiary and by the group transferor company. In this example, the freehold property has always been used for letting (the rents being taxed under Schedule A) and hence rollover relief is not possible.

Thus, if no s 179A allocation is made, Dylan (RGW) Ltd will have to pay the tax, and the s 179 liability will presumably be taken into account in determining the sale price of the shares.

The market value of the premises less an allowance for the potential tax liability (appropriately discounted) on an eventual sale of the premises may also no doubt be reflected in the sale price of the shares, so that Ivon Products plc would effectively have borne tax on the increase in value of the premises through a reduction in the price it receives for its shares in Dylan RGW Ltd. Since Ivon Products plc will also have a tax liability on any profit on sale of its shares in Dylan (RGW) Ltd, it is effectively bearing tax twice on the increase in value of the premises.

Explanatory Notes

Adjustments to trading profits and treatment of interest

1. The subscription paid by Ivon Products plc on behalf of the managing director of its subsidiary, Dylan (RGW) Ltd, does not relate to the company's own trade and is therefore not allowable.

    Both managing directors would have the subscriptions included in their employment income and it is irrelevant that the managing director of the subsidiary did not have the subscription paid by his own employer. It arises from his employment and is taxable as part of his emoluments.

    Whilst the architect's fees and car park levelling costs are capital expenditure and thus not allowed in calculating trading profits, they would qualify as expenditure for industrial buildings relief purposes when the factory and car park are brought into use.

    The costs of the planning application, on the other hand, while similarly disallowed as capital expenditure, will not be taken into account for capital allowances purposes since they are not expenditure on the *construction* of the building.

Corporation tax relief for employee share acquisitions

2. For accounting periods beginning on or after 1 January 2003, companies are able to claim, subject to various qualifying conditions, a statutory corporation tax relief for amounts equivalent to:

    (a) the difference between market value and the consideration given (if any), where shares are awarded to employees; and

    (b) the difference between market value and the consideration given, where there has been the exercise of an approved, unapproved or EMI share option.

    The company's deduction is given against its profits for the accounting period in which the employee acquires the shares.

    The underlying policy objective of the provision is to recognise the increasing use of shares as part of an employee's remuneration package. The aim is to match relief for the company with the taxation of the income on the employee. In order to achieve this, eligibility for the relief is dependent on the employee being liable to income tax on his acquisition (or that he would be were it not for the fact that the acquisition is from a tax-relieved share scheme).

    The shares acquired must meet the following requirements:

    (a) They must be part of the company's ordinary share capital.

    (b) They must be fully paid-up.

    (c) They must not be redeemable.

    (d) They must be:

(i) shares of a class listed on a recognised stock exchange; or

(ii) shares in a company which is not controlled by another company; or

(iii) shares in a subsidiary of a listed company.

The reduction is computed as follows:

	£
Market value of shares acquired (20,000 at 625p each)	125,000
Less: Consideration given for shares (20,000 at 150p each)	(30,000)
	£95,000

Group provisions available to Dylan (RGW) Ltd and Terrence Supplies Ltd

3. The main provisions in relation to groups of companies are outlined in Example 61. The group capital gains provisions apply between a parent and its 75% subsidiaries and also any 75% subsidiaries of those 75% subsidiaries (TCGA 1992 ss 170 and 171), whereas the group relief provisions for trading losses apply only to a parent and its own 75% subsidiaries (subject to the rules relating to a consortium) (TA 1988 ss 402–413). From 1 April 2000, shares in 75% non-resident companies are included in determining whether a group relationship exists for both group loss relief and capital gains purposes, although only UK-resident companies or UK permanent establishments that are subject to corporation tax can benefit under these rules.

The percentage share ownership in the subsidiaries in this example enables the group to take advantage of the following provisions:

Wholly owned subsidiary – Dylan (RGW) Ltd:

(a) *Shadow ACT*

Under the shadow ACT rules (see explanatory note 4 below), dividends paid by Dylan (RGW) Ltd to Ivon Products plc do not give rise to shadow ACT.

(b) *Transfer of chargeable assets*

Either company can transfer a chargeable asset to the other without incurring a liability to corporation tax on the chargeable gain which would arise if a sale were made outside the group. Instead, the transferee company is treated as acquiring the asset from the transferor company at the base cost to the transferor company plus the indexation allowance thereon (TCGA 1992 ss 56, 170 & 171), but not so as to create or increase a loss when the transferee company disposes of the asset (TCGA 1992 s 56). Indexation allowance already built into cost on a no gain no loss transfer *before* 30 November 1993 is not affected.

As a 75% subsidiary, Dylan (RGW) Ltd can enter into an election to allocate degrouping gains under the TCGA 1992 s 179A arrangements as described in part (d) of the example.

As Dylan (RGW) Ltd is not a trading company, it is unlikely to be party to a group business assets rollover relief claim or be able to roll over any degrouping gains under TCGA 1992 s 179B and Sch 7AB. Such reliefs would, however, normally be available to a 75% *trading* subsidiary.

FA 2000 effectively introduced a system of group relief for capital losses. From 1 April 2000, a group company can treat the disposal of a capital asset to a third party as though it had been made by another group member. TCGA 1992 s 171A enables the two group members jointly to elect that the relevant asset is first *deemed* to be transferred from one to the other on a no gain no loss basis, with the transferee group member being treated as selling the asset to the third party purchaser. For s 171A purposes, it is possible to elect that appropriate (fractional) parts of the asset are deemed to have been transferred through one or more companies, thus enabling the capital losses held in such companies to be fully accessed. The conditions for a valid actual intra-group transfer must be satisfied. Both companies must make a joint election for the deemed intra-group/onward sale rule to apply within two years after the end of the chargeable accounting period of the transferor group member in which the actual sale is made.

The deemed transfer rule is generally used to obtain relief for the group's capital losses and eliminates the administrative burden and potential increased stamp duty and stamp duty land tax costs of routing disposals through a group company with capital losses. Alternatively, if it wishes to do so, the 'disposing' company can still make an actual transfer of the asset to a group 'capital loss' company first, which then makes the onward disposal to the third party purchaser. There are, however, provisions in TCGA 1992 s 177A and Sch 7A to prevent 'capital loss buying'. Where a company with realised or unrealised capital losses joins a group, those losses cannot be used against gains of another group company. The loss company may use the losses against gains on its own assets held when it entered the group or on assets acquired later from outside the group that are used in its pre-existing trade.

A variant of the above, ie 'capital gain' buying, is blocked by TCGA 1992 s 177B and Sch 7AA, which prevent a group acquiring a company with realised gains to utilise as yet unrealised group losses. Capital gains made by a company before it joins a group may only be reduced by losses made by the company before it joined the group and losses arising later in the same accounting period on assets held by the company when it joined the group. There are provisions to prevent groups circumventing the rules through the use of intermediate groups.

(c) *Capital gains rollover/holdover relief on replacement of business assets*

If one group company makes a disposal of an asset within the classes attracting rollover/holdover relief and this disposal attracts corporation tax on a chargeable gain, and another group company makes an acquisition of an asset within those classes within the permissible rollover/holdover period, the chargeable gain of the company disposing can be rolled/held over against the acquisition by the other company (TCGA 1992 s 175). See also (b) above and part (d) of the example for the rollover relief provisions in relation to degrouping gains. For detailed notes on rollover relief see Example 83.

(d) *Group relief*

Trading losses of either parent or subsidiary can be surrendered under the group relief provisions for use by the other against profits of the corresponding accounting period (TA 1988 s 402). For details see Example 63.

65% subsidiary – Terrence Supplies Ltd:

The chargeable gains provisions at (b) and (c) and the group relief provisions at (d) do not apply, so only (a) is relevant.

Shadow ACT

4. If a company had actual surplus ACT carried forward at 6 April 1999, it is recoverable under the shadow ACT regulations (SI 1999/358). The main rules are summarised in Example 51 explanatory notes 18 to 22.

A company cannot offset its actual surplus ACT until its available ACT set-off has first been regarded as used up by shadow ACT, and if the available set-off has been fully covered by shadow ACT, no actual set-off is possible. Shadow ACT is treated as having been paid at the rate of 25% on the value of net distributions paid (after deducting distributions received).

In part (c) of the example, the shadow ACT is less than the maximum ACT offset in Ivon Products plc, hence the remaining offset capacity of £49,154 can be applied against the actual surplus ACT brought forward. The company can therefore recover this amount by deduction against its corporation tax liability. On the other hand, if the shadow ACT had exceeded the available offset, the surplus *shadow ACT* would be carried back against the previous six years on a last in first out basis, but only to accounting periods beginning from 6 April 1999. (Accounting periods straddling 6 April 1999 are treated as two separate periods for ACT offset purposes.) Thus prior year offsets are confined to periods dealt with under the shadow ACT rules. Any actual ACT offset in the previous year only is displaced by a carryback of shadow ACT – the company would have to repay the tax offset and it would be resurrected as surplus ACT carried forward (SI 1999/358 reg 12).

For a parent company and its 51% subsidiaries, any remaining surplus shadow ACT must be allocated between those subsidiaries. In this example, Ivon Products plc has fully offset its current shadow ACT of £51,525 against its tax liability and hence there is no shadow ACT to be carried back or allocated to its 51% subsidiaries.

Intra-group dividends do not give rise to shadow ACT in the paying company and are not taken into account as franked investment income in the recipient company. This is subject to an exception where a group company has received franked investment income from outside the group. The group company may elect (within two years after the end of the relevant accounting period) to pay an intra-group dividend of an equivalent amount as a franked dividend. This would not give rise to shadow ACT in the paying company but the recipient company would have franked investment income to reduce shadow ACT on its own dividends.

Any surplus shadow ACT remaining after the carryback and maximum group surrender is carried forward to the next accounting period in the company generating the shadow ACT.

Capital gains position when company leaves a group

5. Where a company leaves a group and continues to hold an asset which it acquired from another group member within the previous six years, the company leaving is treated as having sold the asset when it was acquired from the other group member at its market value at that time and immediately reacquired it at that value. A chargeable gain or allowable loss is deemed to arise accordingly. The time when the gain or loss is deemed to arise under these provisions is either at the beginning of the accounting period in which the company leaves the group, or, if later, at the time the asset was acquired from the other group member (TCGA 1992 s 179). If, for example, Dylan (RGW) Ltd had left the group on 15 December 2007, the gain on the asset transferred intra-group within the six years to 15 December 2007 would be worked out according to the actual transfer date of December 2002, but would be deemed to arise on 1 April 2007.

    Although the legislation provides that the liability falls on the subsidiary acquiring the asset (ie Dylan (RGW) Ltd in this example), as noted in part (d) of the example, following FA 2002 an election may be made to allocate all or part of post-31 March 2002 s 179 gains to one or more members of the 'vendor' group (TCGA 1992 s 179A). Also from 1 April 2002, degrouping gains on business assets can be rolled over under the normal rollover relief rules against qualifying expenditure by the vendor group or the departing subsidiary (TCGA 1992 s 179B and Sch 7AB).

    In the absence of a s 179A reallocation election or s 179B rollover claim, the gain will arise on the acquiring company in the normal way. However, in all cases, following the s 179 charge, the base cost of the relevant asset is uplifted to market value by virtue of the deemed reacquisition.

31 March 1982 rebasing and share pooling elections for capital gains

6. TCGA 1992 s 35 provides that for disposals on or after 6 April 1988, taxpayers may make an irrevocable election within a two year time limit to treat all chargeable assets they owned on 31 March 1982 (other than plant and machinery) as having been acquired at their market value on that day. If the election is not made, the 31 March 1982 value is still used to calculate the gain or loss unless using the previous computational rules would show a lower gain or loss, in which case the lower figure is taken. For the detailed provisions on rebasing see Example 77.

7. In relation to a group of companies, an irrevocable rebasing election under TCGA 1992 s 35(5) (to treat all chargeable assets as acquired on 31 March 1982 at their market value on that day) may normally only be made by the parent company, and it applies to all companies in the group, the time limit of two years from the end of the accounting period of disposal applying to the first relevant disposal on or after 6 April 1988 by any group company (TCGA 1992 Sch 3.8). A company that had already made a disposal and for which the two year time limit had already expired before the

company joined the group is not covered by the election. A company that joins the group after the group election has been made may still make its own election in respect of its first post 5 April 1988 disposal if the time limit has not expired.

Similar provisions apply in relation to share pooling elections under TCGA 1992 Sch 2.4 to bring pre-6 April 1965 acquisitions of quoted shares into the 1982 holdings (see Example 78 explanatory note 4 and Example 85 explanatory note 3). The two-year time limit runs from the end of the company accounting period in which a disposal is made after 31 March 1985 by any company in the group.

8. To obtain greater certainty with 31 March 1982 valuations of land and buildings for self-assessment, companies and groups holding a substantial property portfolio at that date (ie current total valuation of all relevant properties more than £30 million or 30 relevant properties or more) can ask HMRC's District Valuer to agree the valuations in advance for rebasing purposes. For notes on these provisions, and also another scheme relating to valuations for large property portfolios, see the Revenue's Tax Bulletin of February 2002.

Further anti-avoidance provisions

9. Group relief cannot be claimed for that part of an accounting period in which arrangements exist whereby one of the companies could leave the group during or after the end of the accounting period (TA 1988 s 410). This would have restricted a group relief claim between Ivon Products plc and Dylan (RGW) Ltd in the year to 31 March 2007 if the sale offer had been accepted in that year, group relief only being available for the part of the accounting period up to the date that the acceptance of the offer brought 'arrangements' into existence. (See Example 63 explanatory note 10.)

10. In this example, Ivon Products plc cannot claim the valuable benefit of the substantial shareholdings exemption (SSE) on the disposal of its wholly owned subsidiary, Dylan (RGW) Ltd, for the reason given in part (d) of the example. This means that the normal raft of anti-avoidance provisions that potentially bite on a sale of a subsidiary must be considered. Broadly, these provisions prevent companies reducing or eliminating capital gains on the sale of a subsidiary by reducing its value before the sale. If the subsidiary distributes what are effectively unrealised gains to the parent company, the parent company will be deemed to have received additional consideration up to the amount attributable directly or indirectly to the 'chargeable' value-shift. There will be no adjustment in respect of distributions that could be made wholly out of normal distributable profits and reserves (TCGA 1992 ss 31–33). Thus a normal pre-sale dividend will still be effective in reducing the capital gain arising on the sale of a subsidiary (since the 'taxable' sale price will be reduced by the amount of the 'tax-free' dividend). The special value-shifting rules broadly apply to dividends paid out of profits which have not been taxed – for example, the book profit arising on an intra-group transfer of an asset under TCGA 1992 s 171.

    Before 9 March 1999, multinationals could also circumvent the special 'value-shifting' charge by arranging to transfer the subsidiary to an *overseas* group company before it was sold on to the ultimate purchaser. TCGA 1992 s 31A counters such arrangements for subsidiaries transferred after 8 March 1999. If the subsidiary is sold by the overseas group company (within six years of its transfer from the UK group company) a charge now arises in respect of the value stripped out of the subsidiary.

11. The ownership definitions for groups to be entitled to group relief and group capital gains treatment are drawn so as to prevent advantage being taken of those provisions when the subsidiary company is in reality under different ownership.

The Hogwarts Group manufactures and sells pharmaceutical products and develops potential drugs, making up accounts to 31 December each year. All companies in the group pay tax at the main rate of 30% and there are no brought forward trading or capital losses.

The corporate structure of the Hogwarts Group shown below (indicating the relevant percentage of ordinary share capital and voting rights held for each holding) has remained the same for many years.

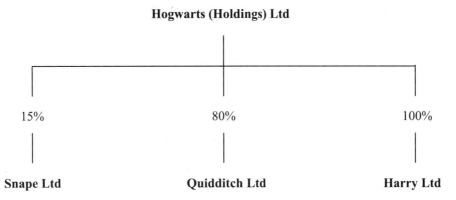

Hogwarts (Holdings) Ltd

15%	80%	100%
Snape Ltd	**Quidditch Ltd**	**Harry Ltd**

All the above companies carry on pharmaceutical trades except Harry Ltd, which specialises in the development of herbal remedies. The remaining 85% of Snape Ltd's ordinary share capital is held by Leviosa Spa, a listed Italian resident company. 20% of Quidditch Ltd is owned by Rowling plc.

The group is currently considering an offer to sell the entire share capital of Harry Ltd to Wizard plc. Harry Ltd was incorporated as a subsidiary of Hogwarts (Holdings) Ltd in 1975 with 100,000 £1 ordinary shares (issued at par). It is estimated that Harry Ltd's shares were worth about £500,000 at 31 March 1982. At that date, the value of Harry Ltd's goodwill was £300,000. Harry Ltd has never acquired capital assets from other members of the group.

The sale of Harry Ltd is likely to take place on 31 December 2006 and legal Heads of Agreement for a share sale were finalised some weeks earlier. The expected sale consideration is £4 million. The current balance sheet value of Harry Ltd's net assets is around £1.5 million, which effectively places around £2.5 million on the value of Harry Ltd's goodwill, patents and other intellectual property.

However, Wizard plc have just indicated that they would now prefer to buy Harry Ltd's trade and assets (including goodwill) and would be willing to pay an additional £200,000 (ie total consideration of £4,200,000) to secure this deal structure. Mr Dumbledore, the finance director of Hogwarts (Holdings) Ltd, still believes, however, that the disposal should proceed as a sale of the entire share capital of Harry Ltd.

(a)   As tax adviser to the Hogwarts Group, you have been asked by Mr Dumbledore to prepare a brief memorandum for him, indicating the most advantageous method of sale for the group. He has also requested that the memorandum explains why the purchaser is likely to prefer to buy the trade and assets from Harry Ltd. (Assume that the rise in the retail prices index from March 1982 to December 2006 is 150%.)

To: Mr Dumbledore – Finance Director, Hogwarts (Holdings) Ltd

From: Ron Weasley

Re: Sale of Harry Ltd

Date: 31 October 2006

1. *Introduction*

You have asked me to consider the most advantageous method of structuring the sale of the business carried on by Harry Ltd. The basic choice is whether the deal should be structured as a sale of the group's 100% shareholding in Harry Ltd or a disposal of Harry Ltd's trade and assets (including goodwill etc).

2. *Recommendation*

In my view, for the reasons given below, the group should sell the shares in Harry Ltd for £4 million and should not accept Wizard plc's current proposal for the group to sell Harry Ltd's trade and assets (including goodwill) for £4.2 million.

3. *Substantial shareholdings exemption (SSE)*

TCGA 1992 Sch 7AC provides a valuable capital gains exemption for *companies* that sell their substantial shareholdings in trading companies – this is known as the substantial shareholdings exemption (SSE). For these purposes, substantial means at least 10% of the ordinary share capital (and other economic rights such as at least a 10% entitlement in profits available for distribution) (Sch 7AC.8).

Based on my understanding of the group's activities etc, the proposed sale of Harry Ltd's shares should qualify for the SSE. This avoids a potential tax liability on a share sale of around £837,000, calculated as follows:

	£000
Sale proceeds (estimated)	4,000
Less: 31 March 1982 value	(500)
Indexation (March 1982 to date) £500,000 x 150%	(750)
Capital gain	2,750
Corporation tax thereon at 30%	825
Net proceeds (£4,000,000 less £825,000)	3,175

On the basis that the SSE is available, the group should expect to receive the £4 million free of tax. There are no other tax charges to consider as Harry Ltd has not received any chargeable assets by way of intra-group transfer within the previous six years.

It is clearly important to ensure that the relevant conditions for obtaining the SSE will be satisfied. Briefly, these are:

(a) The investing company (ie Hogwarts (Holdings) Ltd) must be a sole trading company or a member of a trading group throughout the 'qualifying period' which *begins* at the start of the relevant 12-month 'substantial shareholding' period (see (b) below) and *ends* when the substantial shareholding is sold. It must also be a sole trading company or trading group member immediately after the disposal.

(b) The relevant shareholding investment must qualify as a 'substantial shareholding' held *throughout* a 12-month period starting not more than two years before the shares are disposed of. (It is possible to 'look through' any no gain/no loss transfer (such as an intra-group transfer) and include the *transferor's* period of ownership for the purpose of satisfying this test.)

(c) The company in which the shares are held (ie Harry Ltd) must be a qualifying trading company or qualifying holding company of a trading group throughout the 'qualifying period' defined in (a) above and immediately after the disposal.

4. *Trading group requirement*

For the purpose of the above rules, a trading company or trading group is one whose activities do *not* to any 'substantial' extent include *non-trading* activities. Based on my understanding of the group's activities, I do not see any particular difficulty here. Taken together, all the activities of the group relate to trading. Although the shareholding in Snape Ltd might appear to be treated as an investment activity, it should qualify as a 'trading' activity under the special rules for joint venture companies. Broadly, these provisions enable the corporate shareholder of a trading joint venture company to be treated as carrying on an appropriate part of the joint venture company's trading activity. This beneficial treatment is only available where the relevant shareholding is at least 10% *and* at least 75% of the shares in the joint venture company are held by five or fewer persons (irrespective of their tax residence status), which is the case in relation to the group's holding in Snape Ltd.

5. *Wizard plc's preference for an asset-based deal*

Given that the value placed on Harry Ltd includes a substantial premium for its goodwill and related intellectual property, I suspect that Wizard Ltd is keen to benefit from the tax reliefs available for post-31 March 2002 purchases of intangible fixed assets.

Broadly, under the Finance Act 2002 intangible fixed assets regime, Wizard plc would obtain a tax 'write-off' on the £2.5 million it would pay for Harry Ltd's goodwill and intellectual property. The value of this tax relief would depend on the timing of the amortisation of the goodwill/intellectual property in Wizard plc's accounts. For example, if such assets were written off over five years, the value of Wizard plc's tax relief is likely to be £150,000 each year (being £500,000 at 30%), some £750,000 in total (before discounting for the timing of the related cash flow). Furthermore, the purchase of such assets would be free of stamp duty, whereas Wizard plc would be liable to stamp duty at 0.5% on the entire amount paid for the shares in Harry Ltd.

Clearly, an asset deal would be very attractive to Wizard plc and would provide them with a significant financial advantage, even allowing for their proposed 'sweetener' payment of £200,000. On the other hand, an asset deal would be expensive for Harry Ltd. At the very least, Harry Ltd would incur a tax charge on the sale of its goodwill/ intellectual property of just over £525,000, calculated as follows:

	£000
Sale proceeds (estimated)	2,500
Less: 31 March 1982 value	(300)
Indexation (March 1982 to date) £300,000 x 150%	(450)
Capital gain	1,750
Corporation tax thereon at 30%	525

In addition, it is likely that Harry Ltd would incur further tax liabilities, for example due to a clawback of capital allowances and profit on the sale of its trading stock.

As the group would be able to sell the *shares* in Harry Ltd on a tax-free basis, this remains the best deal structure. This would also be sensible from a commercial viewpoint since all pre-sale contingent risks and liabilities associated with Harry Ltd's business and tax affairs would, in effect, be assumed by Wizard plc (subject to the negotiated warranties and indemnities). Under an asset-based deal, these risks would generally remain with the group.

Explanatory Notes

Substantial shareholdings exemption (SSE)

1. FA 2002 Sch 8 introduced an important capital gains exemption enabling companies to sell their shareholdings in qualifying companies (where they hold a substantial interest) on a tax-free basis.

Similarly, as the gains are not chargeable, no tax recognition is given for capital losses realised in such cases. The substantial shareholdings exemption (SSE) is not restricted to shareholdings in UK-resident companies and applies equally to gains arising on the sale of non-resident subsidiaries and other eligible investments. The Government's main policy objective was to increase the UK's attractiveness as a location for multinational groups, since the SSE enables them to restructure and sell their subsidiaries without triggering a tax charge.

2. Companies wishing to rely on the substantial shareholdings exemption (SSE) must pay careful attention to the numerous qualifying conditions and various anti-avoidance provisions in TCGA 1992 Sch 7AC. The main conditions are stated in paras 7–9, 18 and 19 of the Schedule, which are summarised in note 3 of the example.

Trading company and trading group requirements

3. It will be seen from note 3 in the example that both the investing company/group and the company being sold must satisfy the strict 'trading company/group' definitions laid down in the legislation, which are identical to those which apply for capital gains tax business asset taper relief. This means that, in the case of a singleton company, it must be 'a company carrying on trading activities whose activities do not include to a substantial extent activities other than trading activities' (TCGA 1992 Sch 7AC.20). A company is treated as carrying on trading activities if it is carrying them on in the course of, or for the purposes of, its trade. This also includes an intended acquisition of a significant interest in the share capital of a trading company/group (from a third party). Activities carried out for the purposes of preparing to trade also count.

    In practice, HMRC apply a 20% 'benchmark' for determining whether a company has a *substantial* level of non-trading activities. Where a company has 'non-trading' activities or investments, HMRC may look at a range of possible measures depending on the facts of the particular case, such as contribution to profits, assets employed, expenses and management time (see Example 74 explanatory note 13).

4. A 'trading group' is defined in much the same way as a sole trading company (TCGA 1992 Sch 7AC.21). The definition of 'group' follows TCGA 1992 s 170 (see Example 61, part A), except that the qualifying holding requirement is 51% (as opposed to 75%).

    A trading group is one where, taking all the activities of the group together, it carries on trading activities, ignoring any non-substantial non-trading activities. The legislation requires all the activities of the group to be taken together. This ensures that any intra-group transactions are effectively ignored. For example, property leased to another 51% group member is not regarded as an investment/non-trading activity.

    The special rule for joint venture companies referred to in note 4 of the example is covered by Sch 7AC.23 and 7AC.24.

Interaction of SSE with other exemptions

5. The SSE takes priority over the normal capital gains reorganisation provisions, such as TCGA 1992 s 127. This means that the normal 'no disposal' treatment is disapplied, and that, for example, the SSE applies (where the relevant conditions are met) on a share-for-share exchange. This is particularly helpful if the shares received on the exchange do not qualify for SSE (for example, they represent a holding of less than 10%). The new shares would be treated as being acquired for market value at the date of sale, so the benefits of the SSE would be 'locked-in' at that point (Sch 7AC.4). On the other hand, corporate no gain no loss transfers (such as intra-group disposals under TCGA 1992 s 171 or corporate reconstruction transfers under TCGA 1992 s 139) take priority over the SSE (Sch 7AC.6).

Secondary SSE

6. Where the vendor company satisfies the conditions for the main SSE referred to above, and owns an 'asset related to shares' (ie options over or securities convertible into such shares), any gain arising on

such a related asset is tax-exempt (Sch 7AC.2). Sch 7AC.3 also permits relief to be claimed in circumstances where the trading company/holding company requirement is not satisfied at the time of sale but would have been met at any time in the previous two years. This may apply, for example, where the company invested in receives a post-liquidation capital distribution.

Anti-avoidance

7. A special anti-avoidance rule is contained in Sch 7AC.5 to prevent the SSE being abused in certain prescribed cases.

FA 2002 intangible fixed assets regime

8. For many years, the UK tax system has struggled to deal with the so-called new economy businesses. Before 1 April 2002, the capital cost of most intangible fixed assets did not attract any tax relief against trading profits, although capital allowances were available on patents and know-how (see Example 20 explanatory notes 24 and 26). From that date, a new regime applies for companies in respect of goodwill, intellectual property and other intangible assets, including fishing and agricultural quotas. For the treatment of computer software see Example 20 explanatory note 3.

Scope of the intangible fixed assets regime

9. As indicated in explanatory note 8, the intangible fixed assets regime in FA 2002 Sch 29 applies from the 1 April 2002 'commencement date'. However, the transitional provisions are designed to ensure that only intangible fixed assets which were acquired from an unrelated third party or internally created after 31 March 2002 qualify for relief under the regime. Special rules apply where the intangible fixed assets were owned before 1 April 2002 but additional expenditure is incurred on them after that date.

   The effect of the 1 April 2002 commencement date is that intangible fixed assets held on 1 April 2002 (or acquired from a related party who held them on that date), known as 'old regime' assets, continue to give rise to capital gains on their subsequent sale. For example, if a company that started trading in 1990 sells its trading goodwill, this will generate a capital gain (with indexation relief).

   The related party provisions are in Sch 29.92 to 29.101. Companies are related where one controls the other or the same person controls both. In the case of a close company, a person will be related to the company if the person is a participator or associate of a participator in that company.

10. In broad terms, companies can generally obtain tax relief for intangible fixed assets purchased (other than from related persons) or created from 1 April 2002 onwards, referred to as 'new regime' assets. This means that expenditure on purchased goodwill, patents, trade marks, copyrights, know-how, licences, brands, names, logos, customer lists, designs, commercial formats etc now qualifies for tax relief. These rules only apply for corporation tax purposes and thus to UK-resident companies and UK permanent establishments. (The existing capital gains tax rules continue to apply to individuals.)

11. The tax relief for intangible assets will be given under Schedule D Case I for trading companies, Schedule A for property businesses and Schedule D Case VI where there are non-trading amounts (Sch 29.30 to 29.34). If there is a non-trading loss, relief may be claimed within two years after the end of the accounting period to set the loss against the total profits of the same period. Any loss not relieved in that way and not surrendered by way of group relief will be carried forward to set against later non-trading profits (Sch 29.35).

Alignment with accounting treatment

12. The intangible assets rules follow the increasing trend of aligning the tax treatment with that adopted in the accounts. The timing of the tax relief for new regime assets will therefore follow the rules in Financial Reporting Standard (FRS) 10, which deals with goodwill and other intangibles, including intellectual property. FRS 10 requires such assets to be amortised or written off against profits based on the useful working life of the asset. An appropriate goodwill 'write-off' may also be made where

its value has been 'impaired'. Thus overall these rules provide the advantage of tax-deductible amortisation and 'impairment review' write-downs where none existed before.

The accounting treatment adopted will therefore influence the timing of the tax relief for purchased goodwill or intellectual property, being based on the amount amortised in the accounts, as illustrated in note 5 of the example (Sch 29.7 to 29.9). However, as an alternative, companies may elect to claim tax relief at the rate of 4% of the goodwill/ intellectual property cost per year (Sch 29.10 and 29.11).

Where the accounting treatment does not properly reflect generally accepted accounting practice (GAAP), it will be replaced for tax purposes by a treatment that accords with that practice. This is most likely to apply to UK permanent establishments of companies incorporated outside the UK, since they are not required to comply with UK GAAP. However, for accounting periods beginning on or after 1 January 2005, accounts drawn up in accordance with international accounting standards, whether those adopted by the European Commission or full IAS, will be accepted as the equivalent of UK GAAP. (FA 2004 s 50).

Profits on sale of intangible fixed assets and 'income' rollover relief

13. Any profits on the sale of goodwill and other intangible property will be treated as income rather than capital gains (Sch 29.13 and 29.14). However, the tax can be deferred under an 'income' style rollover relief, provided the proceeds are reinvested into other new regime intangible fixed assets within the normal 'reinvestment window' starting one year before and ending three years after the gain arises (Sch 29.37 to 29.45).

   The rollover relief for intangible fixed assets is modelled on the existing capital gains rollover relief, and is extended to cover intangible fixed assets transactions by 75% group members (Sch 29.56). Profits arising on the disposal of such assets are deferred to the extent that the proceeds are reinvested in intangible fixed assets. The relief is reduced where only part of the proceeds are reinvested. The base cost of the 'replacement' intangible fixed asset is reduced by the original profit. Thus, as the relief reduces the base cost for tax deduction purposes, there will be a mismatch with the accounting treatment. Separate computations will be required to calculate the tax deduction for each period and keep track of the post-rollover relief base cost applying for tax purposes.

   There is a special rule designed to give some neutrality between asset and share-based acquisitions. In such cases, profits on intangible fixed assets may be rolled over against any new regime intangible fixed assets *owned by an acquired 75% subsidiary*. The broad effect of this special rule is therefore to look through the shareholding investment in the 75% subsidiary to its underlying *new regime* intangible fixed assets. The profits will be deducted from the carrying values of the relevant intangible fixed assets owned by the subsidiary at the date of its acquisition.

   Under transitional rules, capital gains on old regime goodwill and fishing and agricultural quotas will qualify for the Sch 29 rollover relief when reinvested into new regime intangible fixed assets (Sch 29.130). Under further transitional rules in Sch 29.132, old regime goodwill and quotas disposed of on or after 1 April 2002 may be rolled over under the capital gains rules against certain pre-1 April 2002 acquisitions of goodwill or quota or under the Sch 29 rules or partly under the capital gains rules and partly under the Sch 29 rules (see Example 83 explanatory note 16 for details).

Treatment of groups

14. Intra-group transfers of new regime assets are made on a no gain/no loss ('tax-neutral') basis in broadly the same way as the capital gains rule in TCGA 1992 s 171 (see Sch 29.55). The same 75% group definition also applies (Sch 29.46 to 29.54).

15. An income-based degrouping charge applies if new regime intangible fixed assets are transferred on a tax-neutral basis between group companies and the transferee company leaves the group within six years, still owning the transferred asset (Sch 29.58 to 29.67). The mechanics of the intangible fixed assets degrouping charge and the related exemptions are identical to those used for group capital

gains purposes. Thus, for example, the degrouping charge can be rolled over or reallocated within the group (see Example 64 part (d) for detailed coverage of the capital gains rules).

Treatment of royalties etc

16. The intangible fixed assets regime applies equally to payments made for the use of both old and new regime intangible fixed assets. Hence, royalties payable and receivable are taxed on the amount reflected in the accounts. Special transitional rules ignore any royalties previously recognised for tax purposes (see Example 48 explanatory note 4(viii)).

Fred Nietz, the managing director of Chase Ltd, has approached your firm for advice.

Chase Ltd, a UK company that has been trading for 30 years making up accounts annually to 31 March, is a subsidiary of a large UK-resident company. The present market conditions have hit Chase Ltd particularly hard and it is essential that substantial investment in new machinery be made. The directors of the parent company are unwilling to authorise this expenditure and instead propose to sell the company.

Fred and his colleagues are interested in acquiring the business of Chase Ltd and have arranged the necessary finance for the acquisition and for the new machinery.

Chase Ltd has unrelieved trading losses of £200,000 and a property worth £440,000 which was acquired from the parent company in July 2002 at its cost price of £220,000 when its market value was £370,000. The parent company had bought the property in February 1991. Assume indexation from February 1991 to July 2002 was 30.3%.

Write a memorandum to the Tax Partner, outlining the tax matters to be considered in effecting the buy-out either:

(a)   through a direct purchase of the shares held by the parent company, or

(b)   by forming a new company which would acquire the trade and assets of Chase Ltd,

and indicating any income tax points that should be brought to the attention of Fred Nietz and his colleagues.

31 August 2006

To Tax Partner

From **Alan White**

Chase Ltd – Proposed management buy-out

I have considered the proposed buy-out of Chase Ltd by Fred Nietz, managing director, and his colleagues and outline below the tax matters to be considered.

Acquisition by direct purchase of shares held by parent company

1. The parent company would almost certainly favour a sale of the shares in Chase Ltd, since any capital gain should be entirely exempt under the substantial shareholdings exemption (SSE) rules in TCGA 1992 Sch 7AC. (All the relevant SSE conditions appear to be satisfied.) Furthermore, the parent company would not have any balancing charge on the sale of the assets, and any contingent commercial and tax liabilities will effectively be assumed by the purchaser. The latter is subject to any limitations imposed by warranties and indemnities under the share sale agreement, but these are often restricted in management buy-out situations as managers are assumed to be aware of the company's previous commercial and financial obligations and possibly its tax compliance history (see 2(c) below).

    On the other hand, the parent company might consider an asset sale if this would facilitate the acquisition provided there were no material tax costs. For example, the trading losses brought forward are available against any balancing charges and the proceeds could be paid up to the parent as a 'tax free' intra-group dividend or, alternatively, loaned by Chase Ltd (which would of course in those circumstances still be a group member) to other group companies.

2. A share purchase/sale has several disadvantages for the buy-out team:

    (a) It may be more difficult to raise finance for the purchase of the shares than it would be for the purchase of machinery, for example through hire purchase.

    (b) There would be a crystallisation of the held-over gain on the property acquired from the parent company in July 2002 (the degrouping charge). Chase Ltd would be deemed to have made a gain of (£370,000 – £220,000) = £150,000 less indexation allowance of 30.3%, (ie £66,660) = £83,340, in July 2002. The gain would be regarded as arising at the beginning of Chase Ltd's accounting period in which the shares were purchased (likely to be 1 April 2006).

    Such degrouping gains can be allocated to the parent company or any of its 75% subsidiaries by making a TCGA 1992 s 179A election. This would enable the gain to be sheltered by any capital losses etc in those companies. Alternatively it can be rolled over under the business assets rollover rules – either against qualifying expenditure in the parent company's group (under TCGA 1992 s 179B) or within Chase Ltd itself (for example, to the extent that the new machinery qualified as *fixed* plant or machinery). The replacement qualifying assets must be purchased within the normal reinvestment period beginning one year before and ending three years after the gain occurs. (Note that post-31 March 2002 acquisitions of goodwill do not count as a qualifying business asset for capital gains regime rollover relief.)

    If the gain (and hence the liability) remains within Chase Ltd, it would be necessary to ensure that the purchase price of the shares was reduced to take account of this tax charge. The gain cannot be reduced by brought forward trading losses, but if losses were still being made, the losses of the same accounting period could be offset against it.

    (c) There may be other latent capital gains and other liabilities of which Fred Nietz is not aware, because of decisions taken at parent company level and because of statutory non-compliance or HMRC making an enquiry under corporation tax self-assessment, which may extend to earlier years.

Whilst the buy-out team should seek to obtain suitable warranties and indemnities from the parent company as part of the agreement to purchase, these are often restricted (for the reasons outline in 1 above). Furthermore, the transaction is inevitably far more complicated, costly in legal fees and time-consuming.

(d)   There is a possibility that the brought forward losses plus any further losses not relieved against other profits may be forfeited because of the provisions of TA 1988 s 768. This section prevents losses being carried forward following a change of ownership if either:

   (i)   Within a period of three years there is both a change of ownership and also a major change in the nature or conduct of the trade, or

   (ii)   The change in ownership occurs after the scale of activities of a company has become small or negligible and before any considerable revival.

In the particular circumstances of this buy-out, Fred Nietz and his colleagues could argue a strong case against the application of s 768, since it appears unlikely that the trade has sunk to a negligible level. Furthermore, the injection of new machinery should be held not to constitute a major change in the nature or conduct of the trade, particularly having regard to SP10/91, under which HMRC confirm that the section will not be applied to investment necessary to keep pace with new technology etc. HMRC apply this particular section very harshly, however, and the carry forward losses may be vulnerable to forfeiture. If any (discounted) payment is sought for the losses (as part of the share price), this should only be paid on a deferred basis as and when the future loss offsets are effectively agreed.

There would, however, be no possibility at all of the losses being available for carry forward if the trade and assets were purchased instead of the shares.

Acquisition by forming new company to acquire trade and assets of Chase Ltd

1.   This method will probably be the preferred method for the buy-out team because it is more straightforward and does not have the disadvantages of the share purchase which have been indicated. Although it is unlikely that a significant amount would be paid for Chase Ltd's goodwill (owing to its recent trading losses etc), it is worth noting that the new company can now secure a trading deduction for goodwill (along with intellectual property), based on the amount amortised in its accounts each year. The stamp duty land tax on the chargeable assets purchased may, however, be more expensive than a share purchase. (Shares only attract stamp duty at 0.5% and would be based on the *net* value of the company (ie reduced by debt).) If the total consideration (which includes assumed liabilities) for the chargeable assets, such as property (£440,000) and fixed plant, exceeds £500,000, stamp duty land tax will be levied at 4%. Chargeable consideration between £250,000 and £500,000 attracts stamp duty land tax of 3%. Stock and moveable plant should not attract a stamp duty charge. Goodwill and intellectual property transfers (such as trade marks, patents, etc) are specifically exempt from stamp duty.

2.   The buy-out team would be able to claim capital allowances on the plant transferred, as well as on the new purchases. The allowances for the first accounting period would be at 40% instead of 25% (assuming that the new company qualified as medium-sized – see explanatory note 6). Industrial buildings writing down allowances (if applicable) would be at a higher rate because of the clawback of allowances on the vendor, with the residue of expenditure being divided over the remaining tax life of the building.

3.   The sale of assets as far as the parent company is concerned may be more difficult to achieve, bearing in mind that a 'share sale' of Chase Ltd is exempt from tax under the SSE rules noted above. However, the following points may be relevant in trying to negotiate an 'asset deal':

(a)   Although there would be a balancing charge on the disposal of the assets on which capital allowances had been claimed, this could be offset by the brought forward trading losses of £200,000; if not used before sale, these losses would have to be discounted on a share sale because of the provisions of TA 1988 s 768 mentioned above. If a profit still remained, the tax thereon would be at a maximum rate of 30% if it occurred in the year to 31 March 2007 (unless profits fell in the marginal small companies' rate band, in which case the tax rate on profits within the band would be 32.75%).

(b)   There would be a capital gain on the disposal of the property but a large part of this will crystallise in any event on a share sale (under the degrouping rules) and would have to be taken into account in the price for the shares. There may be the possibility of rolling over the gain (on a direct disposal) against other acquisitions of the group. Alternatively, the property could be retained and leased to the new company formed by the purchasers.

(c)   The parent company would be able to extract the book profit on the sale of the assets (less any corporation tax thereon) by way of a tax-free intra-group dividend. The overall tax arising on the sale may therefore be minimal if the balancing charge on the assets can be mitigated by the brought forward trading losses and the property gain can be rolled over.

Overall, the parent company is likely to seek to sell the shares in Chase Ltd because of the SSE exemption and the much greater commercial protection. In practice, it would only accede to sale of Chase Ltd's trade and assets if it can be structured on a broadly 'tax-neutral' basis.

Other considerations

If the parent company sold Chase Ltd to an outside party, then unless the staff were taken over (under the transfer of undertakings rules on an asset sale) it would be involved in heavy redundancy payments and possibly union problems. If staff transfer under TUPE, as will almost certainly be the case in an asset sale, both seller and buyer are vulnerable to unfair dismissal and other staff claims. This favours share sale unless indemnities are obtained from the buyer.

Income tax points to be brought to the attention of Fred Nietz and his colleagues

1.   It appears that the new venture, whether through Chase Ltd or a new company, will be a close company. Fred Nietz and his colleagues will therefore be able to obtain interest relief on money borrowed to buy their shares or lent to the company for the company to buy the assets, providing they either each own more than 5% of the share capital, or own some share capital and work full-time in the management of the company (TA 1998 s 360).

But the funds provided as share capital will be locked into the company, whereas money provided on loan can be withdrawn when the company is able to repay it. If money is borrowed to lend to the company, interest relief is restricted if the loan is repaid by the company without a corresponding reduction in the loan to the buyout team.

2.   HMRC take the view that where employees buy out the company or business for which they previously used to work, they do so in pursuance of an opportunity offered to them as employees of that company or of a new company formed to take over the business. There is a contrary argument that where a new company is formed to purchase the target company or its assets and trade, the management buy-out team acquire the shares in the new company as founders.

Clearly, the risk exists that HMRC will look for any 'benefit' derived from the managers' employment. This would arise where the parent company has sold the company or business to the management team below an arm's length price. There are likely to be practical difficulties in demonstrating that a commercial price has been paid by the management team in the absence of comparable bids for the company from third parties. A discount may be appropriate on a management buy-out if the deal can be completed quickly and with fewer warranties (see above).

Many buy-out teams typically form a new company to acquire the shares or trade and assets, as this is more efficient for financing and facilitates bank and institutional lending and investment. If management acquire their shares in the new company on preferential terms (for example, compared with shares issued to institutions etc), it may be argued that an employment income charge arises.

This is a notoriously difficult area in practice. Under self-assessment, appropriate disclosure is required (to avoid any accusation of negligence). A fully justified case should be disclosed on the return where no taxable amount is being reported.

3.   If a new company is formed, and at some future date the shares are disposed of at a loss, the capital loss will be able to be set off against income of the year of disposal or the previous year (or both years, if the loss is large enough) (TA 1988 s 574). This relief is only available where shares have been subscribed for and so would not be available if the management team directly purchased the existing shares in Chase Ltd from the parent company.

4.   Whether the existing shares are purchased or new shares subscribed for, any new capital could be raised from non-working shareholders through the enterprise investment scheme. On an assets purchase, all the share capital put up by non-working shareholders would qualify whereas only new capital would qualify on a share purchase (but see explanatory note 4).

        If the management team formed a new company to acquire the *shares* in Chase Ltd, then the non-working shareholders could subscribe for shares in the new company and obtain enterprise investment relief, provided the trade and assets of Chase Ltd were hived-up to the new company on acquisition (under TA 1988 s 343 and TCGA 1992 s 171).

        For EIS shares in a close company, it is not possible to get tax relief on interest paid on a loan to buy the shares. Another possible source of funding is a venture capital trust (see explanatory note 4).

Explanatory Notes

Different forms of management buy-out

1.   The example describes the features of two of the main forms of management buy-outs.

        Although a direct purchase of Chase Ltd's shares is contemplated here by the management team, it is more common for the acquisition to be made by a new company formed by the management team. This makes for easier and more efficient financing. Bank borrowing etc is through the new company, which can be repaid out of the post-acquisition cash flows of the acquired trade. If the managers borrowed personally to finance the acquisition, they would have to pay tax on monies taken out to finance the repayment of the bank borrowing.

        A third possibility where the buy-out team already owns shares in the company is to utilise the provisions enabling a company to purchase its own shares without the payment being treated as a distribution. The provisions are covered in Example 60. Yet another variation is for assets to be hived down into a new company, using the reorganisation provisions of TA 1988 s 343, and for the shares in the new company to be sold to the buy-out team.

Substantial shareholdings exemption

2.   From 1 April 2002, groups can sell their trading subsidiaries (or indeed any shareholding investment in which they hold at least 10% of the equity) free of tax under the substantial shareholdings exemption (SSE) rules. This means that they will invariably be seeking to structure their 'business' disposals as a sale of shares. On the other hand, if a significant amount is being paid for goodwill (which is *not* the case in this example), a corporate purchaser would clearly prefer an asset deal. This is because, from 1 April 2002, they can claim tax relief on the cost of the goodwill (and any intellectual property), usually based on the amount amortised in the accounts under generally accepted accounting practice (see FA 2002 Sch 29). These tax rules mean that the 'fiscal tension' between vendors and purchasers is probably greater than ever and the structure of each transaction will have to be negotiated on a case-by-case basis. The relative negotiating strength of each party usually determines the outcome.

Taper relief

3.   The management team will wish to ensure that they will be able to enjoy the full benefit of business asset taper relief on an exit, for example, on a trade sale of the business or the company buying back their shareholding on retirement. All the shareholders should be able to accrue taper relief at the business asset rate. (Chase Ltd is an unlisted trading company and Newco would be an unlisted holding company of a trading group.)

The managers' capital gain on eventual disposal would therefore be reduced by a maximum of 75%. The 75% reduction applies after only two complete years' ownership. The company's activities should be regularly reviewed to ensure that no investment activities are started which would jeopardise the shareholders' taper relief (see Example 74 for the detailed provisions).

Sources of finance

4. Financing a buy-out can be a major problem. It is helped by the provisions of the enterprise investment scheme linked with the provisions enabling a company to buy its own shares. This means that the company may buy back an investor's shares after the five-year period has elapsed, but it is not possible for guaranteed exit arrangements to be provided at the outset (TA 1988 s 299B).

    A newly formed company may qualify under the enterprise investment scheme (EIS) rules where it is formed to buy the trade and assets *or* the shares in Chase Ltd. (HMRC would accept that the share subscription proceeds were applied for trading purposes if the trade and assets of Chase Ltd were transferred to the new company on acquisition – see below.) The management team could not, however, obtain any EIS relief as they would be 'connected' with Chase Ltd and the new company under TA 1988 ss 291(2) and 291A.

    Bank borrowing and any institutional finance can be conveniently structured through a new company, which then makes the acquisition.

    A direct purchase of the existing shares in Chase Ltd would not qualify for EIS relief but the subsequent issue of new shares (for new assets and new working capital) would attract relief.

    Another possible source of funding is from a venture capital trust. HMRC commented in their Tax Bulletin of August 1995 on the circumstances in which such a trust may provide funding for a management buyout. Even where the buyout company acquires shares in the existing company rather than its assets, HMRC will accept that shares issued by the buyout company to the venture capital trust will be a qualifying holding if the trade of the acquired company is hived up to the buyout company as soon as possible after the buyout.

    For details of the enterprise investment scheme and venture capital trusts see Example 94.

Other points

5. See the Revenue's Statement of Practice 10/91 for their interpretation of a 'major change in the nature or conduct of a trade'.

6. See Example 20 explanatory note 2 for the 40% first year allowance available for expenditure on plant and machinery incurred by small and medium-sized companies.

Pluto Ltd owns 100% of Socrates Ltd and 100% of Aristotle Ltd. All companies are UK-resident, and each company carries on a different trade associated with the chemical industry.

The shareholding in Pluto Ltd is held equally by three families, each of which has a different view as to how the group could be more effectively controlled and managed. Owing to the differing views of the families, it is clear that the companies in the group could be better managed by each of the families taking control of one particular trade currently carried on by the companies in the group.

This objective may be achieved through a reorganisation at the end of December 2006 by either:

(i)   Pluto Ltd distributing the shares in the subsidiary companies directly to the family shareholders interested in gaining control of that particular company's trade, or

(ii) Pluto Ltd transferring the shares in the subsidiary companies to new companies especially formed for that purpose. These new companies would then issue shares to the respective shareholders of Pluto Ltd.

Under either alternative, the shares held in Pluto Ltd by the families who are to acquire Socrates Ltd and Aristotle Ltd will be cancelled, leaving the members of the third family as the only shareholders in Pluto Ltd.

State what reliefs (if any) are available to the shareholders of Pluto Ltd if the proposals at (i) or (ii) above were implemented and what conditions must be satisfied for those reliefs to apply.

Comment on any other tax implications.

Reliefs available to shareholders of Pluto Ltd and conditions to be satisfied for those reliefs to apply

There are various tax problems associated with a company break-up such as that planned for Pluto Ltd, and some of the problems are dealt with under the demerger provisions of TA 1988 ss 213–218, as follows:

(1) Distributions that are exempt distributions as defined are not treated as income in the hands of the shareholders. An exempt distribution is defined as (s 213(3)):

  (a) a distribution consisting of the transfer by a company to *all or any* of its members of shares in one or more companies that are its 75% subsidiaries; or

  (b) a distribution consisting of the transfer by a company to one or more other companies of a trade or trades, or of shares in one or more companies which are its 75% subsidiaries, and the issue of shares by the transferee company or companies to *all or any* of the members of the distributing company.

(2) Both the distribution of the subsidiaries' shares directly to the individual shareholders as proposed in Pluto Ltd's alternative (i) and the transfer of the subsidiaries' shares to the relevant new companies as proposed in alternative (ii) would come within the definition of exempt distributions (s 213(3)). The distributing company will often be a holding company distributing one or more trades or shares in 75% subsidiaries. In some cases, a singleton trading company may distribute one or more of its trading divisions via a demerger distribution. The shares in the new companies would be issued to the requisite family shareholder groups in Pluto Ltd. Since the distributions would be exempt distributions, there would be no income tax implications for the shareholders.

(3) An exempt distribution under part (a) of the definition is also not treated as a capital distribution for capital gains purposes, but as a company reorganisation under the provisions of TCGA 1992 ss 126–131 (TCGA 1992 s 192). This covers the distribution of the subsidiaries' shares in alternative (i), so that there would be no capital gains tax consequences for the shareholders and their taper relief would not be affected. Under the second alternative, the issue of shares in the new companies in exchange for the Pluto Ltd shares would not be treated as a CGT disposal under the shareholder reconstruction provisions in TCGA 1992 s 136 (reconstruction involving issue of securities) – the shareholders would effectively retain their existing taper relief base date (being treated as acquiring the new shares at the same time and cost as their old shares).

(4) As far as corporate gains are concerned, Pluto Ltd will make a capital gains disposal when it distributes its 100% holdings in Socrates Ltd and Aristotle Ltd. From 1 April 2002, it is important to note that the substantial shareholdings exemption (SSE) could apply to the disposal of a qualifying shareholding (see Example 65 explanatory notes 1 to 7). However, where the disposal falls to be dealt with under the TCGA 1992 s 139 corporate capital gains reconstruction relief provisions (which provide for 'no gain/no loss' treatment), these will prevail over the SSE (FA 2002 Sch 8.6(1)(a)). The SSE should be available to exempt any gain arising on the direct 'demerger' disposal of the shares to the individual shareholders under alternative (i) as this would not rank for s 139 relief. This is because one of the pre-conditions for s 139 relief is that the disposal is to another *UK-resident company* (or of an asset which is to be used in a UK permanent establishment trade carried on by a non-resident). Alternative (ii) will meet this requirement as the transfer of the shares in the 100% subsidiaries (treated as the transfer of a business for TCGA 1992 s 139 purposes) is to the relevant two new *companies*. Thus, under this route, the shares in the subsidiaries will be transferred on a no gain/no loss basis (ie at their indexed base cost) under s 139 and not under the SSE provisions.

(5) The provisions in TCGA 1992 s 179 for the crystallisation of capital gains on a company leaving a group do not apply when a company ceases to be a member of a group as a result of an exempt demerger distribution. There will therefore be no charge on Aristotle Ltd and Socrates Ltd when they leave the group under either alternative (i) or (ii), in respect of any assets that have been transferred to them on a no gain no loss basis by any group company within the previous six years. Similarly, a 'degrouping charge' under the intangible fixed assets provisions (see Example 65 explanatory note 15) will not apply to an exempt distribution (FA 2002 Sch 29.61).

In order for the above treatment to apply the following conditions must be satisfied:

(i) All the companies concerned must be UK-resident at the time of the distribution.

(ii) The distributing company must be a trading company or member of a trading group and each subsidiary must be either a trading company or the holding company of a trading group.

(iii) The shares transferred by the distributing company and, where relevant, issued by the transferee company, must be non-redeemable and must constitute all or substantially all (considered by HMRC to mean around 90% or more) of the ordinary share capital, and confer all or substantially all of the voting power in the company concerned.

(iv) The distributing company must remain a trading company or member of a trading group unless the demerger involves two or more 75% subsidiaries and the parent company is wound up without there being any net assets available for distribution (other than to cover liquidation costs and any negligible share capital remaining – Revenue concession C11).

(v) Where a trade is transferred the distributing company must not retain more than a minor interest in the trade (which HMRC interpret as around 10% or less).

(vi) The only or main activity of any transferee company must be to carry on the trade or hold the shares transferred to it.

(vii) The distribution must be wholly or mainly to benefit some or all of the trading activities previously carried on by a single company or group and subsequently by two or more companies or groups.

(viii) The distribution must not be part of a tax avoidance scheme, or a scheme to enable other persons to obtain control of one of the companies, or a scheme for the purpose of the cessation or sale of a trade. Where a payment other than a bona fide commercial payment is made to the shareholders within five years after an exempt distribution it is treated as miscellaneous income in their hands, the paying company may not deduct it for corporation tax and the 'demerger' capital gains reliefs (such as protection from the TCGA 1992 s 179 de-grouping charge but not the general TCGA 1992 ss 136 and 139 reconstruction reliefs) are withdrawn.

It appears that either of the alternatives proposed by Pluto Ltd would satisfy the required conditions, but there is provision for advance clearance of a demerger transaction and it is obviously sensible for the clearance to be obtained. Furthermore, the shareholder capital gains tax relief under TCGA 1992 s 136 and the company reconstruction capital gains relief under TCGA 1992 s 139 are dependent on the transaction being for bona fide commercial purposes, for which advance clearance can be sought under TCGA 1992 s 138 and s 139(5) respectively. (A statutory clearance is not required for SSE disposals under FA 2002 Sch 8.)

The demerger provisions do not provide relief for all the tax consequences of a demerger. Under both routes, the anti-avoidance rules that prevent the carry forward of trading losses or shadow ACT on a change of control may be triggered if there is a major change in the nature or conduct of the trades (TA 1988 s 768 and shadow ACT rules in SI 1999/358 reg 16). HMRC have, however, indicated in Statement of Practice 13/80 that these matters will be given sympathetic treatment. Pluto Ltd's disposal of the shares in the subsidiaries to the shareholders under the first alternative should be exempt under the SSE provisions (as indicated above).

Stamp duties must always be considered when structuring a demerger. A direct demerger distribution to shareholders (first alternative) does not give rise to any stamp duty or stamp duty land tax liability. An indirect demerger distribution by a holding or 'stand alone' company should obtain relief under FA 2003 Sch 7.8, restricting the tax to ½% on the dutiable assets transferred. This relief is particularly beneficial if chargeable assets (such as property) are being transferred as a demerger distribution of a trade (where the shareholdings are being split). Goodwill was exempted from charge with effect from 23 April 2002. Since alternative (ii) involves the transfer of shares which only attract a ½% stamp duty charge, there would be no need to rely on the FA 2003 Sch 7.8 transfer of undertaking relief in this case.

There is the possibility of problems occurring under both alternatives by reason of TA 1988 s 703 (cancellation of tax advantage from transactions in securities). A clearance procedure is, however, available (s 707).

Supplementary Notes

Aim of demerger provisions

1. The aim of the demerger legislation, according to the then Chancellor, was to enable businesses grouped inefficiently under a single company umbrella to be run more dynamically and effectively by being demerged and being allowed to pursue their separate ways under independent management. It is accordingly not relevant where the aim is for a company to be liquidated or sold.

Company reconstructions

2. The shareholder and company reconstruction reliefs in TCGA 1992 ss 136 and 139 respectively both require a 'scheme of reconstruction'.

   Under the statutory rules, of TCGA 1999 Sch 5AA a scheme of reconstruction contains the following key elements:

   ● Only the ordinary shareholders of the relevant business must receive ordinary shares under the scheme, ie no one else must be entitled to receive new shares

   ● The proportionate interests of the shareholders before and after the reconstruction must remain the same

   ● The business previously carried on by the 'original' company or companies must be carried on by one or more successor companies *unless* the scheme is carried out under a compromise or arrangement under Companies Act 1985 s 425 (or equivalent).

Other statutory demerger routes

3. A further type of statutory demerger covered by the 'exempt distribution' provisions involves the transfer of a trade or trades to one or more new companies in consideration of the transferee company/companies issuing shares to all or any of the distributing company's shareholders. Such a demerger would normally be covered by the TCGA 1992 s 139 corporate reconstruction provisions, so that the relevant assets such as 'old regime' goodwill (see Example 65 explanatory notes 9 and 13) and property would be transferred on a no gain no loss basis (see note (4) in the example). A similar 'tax neutral' treatment applies to the transfer of goodwill under the intangible fixed assets regime in FA 2002 Sch 29 (FA 2002 Sch 29.84). It is possible to have a variant of this basic transaction, since TA 1988 s 213(12) enables the demerger distribution of the trade and assets to be made by a 75% *subsidiary company* to the new company (although this would not qualify for the FA 2003 Schs 7–8 stamp duty reduction). Where the subsidiary makes a demerger distribution of the trade and assets, this must be followed by a further demerger distribution by the parent company of that subsidiary company's shares (their value would invariably be minimal due to the prior demerger distribution).

   It should be noted that it is not possible to transfer the trade and assets directly to the shareholders, although, as seen in alternative (i) in the example, this is permissible for a transfer of shares in a 75% subsidiary. The general thrust of the demerger rules requires the trades and underlying assets to remain in the corporate sector.

   Where a demerger proceeds as a transfer of a trade and assets, the distributing company will be treated as ceasing to carry on the relevant trade, with the normal tax consequences, such as the forfeiture of brought forward trading losses and the potential crystallisation of balancing charges on the transfer of plant. These particular adverse effects could be eliminated if the transfer of the trade fell within the scope of the TA 1988 s 343 corporate trade succession provisions, which require, amongst other things, that there is 75% common ownership at shareholder level before and after the transfer. For post-16 April 2002 disposals, the taper relief entitlement for shareholders under this type of demerger would not be affected. Under the capital gains reconstruction provisions referred to in part (3) of the example, their new shares would be treated as having being acquired at the same time as their old shares. Previously, their taper relief 'clock' would have been reset. This is because the commencement of trade by the 'transferee' company would have triggered a 'relevant change of activity' within TCGA 1992 Sch A1.11, but these provisions were substantially altered from 17 April 2002 and no longer bite in such cases (see Example 74, part (a)(i) under *Anti-avoidance provisions*).

Non-statutory demerger using Insolvency Act 1986 s 110

4. It is possible to demerge businesses or 75% subsidiaries without using the statutory demerger provisions in TA 1988 ss 213-218. This route would involve winding up the relevant company, with the liquidator then distributing the businesses or subsidiaries under the procedure laid down in s 110 of the Insolvency Act 1986. These are often known as 'non-statutory' demergers and may be used where it is not possible to satisfy a particular condition in the statutory demerger code, for example where an investment business (such as property letting, which is not a trade) is being demerged by way of a partition between different groups of shareholders. It is necessary for the transfers (which are generally for no consideration other than the assumption of liabilities) to take place in the course of a winding up to prevent the shareholders from suffering an income tax charge under the distribution provisions (TA 1988 s 209(1) proviso). The shareholders' and corporate capital gains reconstruction reliefs under TCGA 1992 ss 136 and 139 will also apply here.

Demergers and trusts

5. Although, as indicated in the example, demergers usually have neither income tax nor capital gains tax consequences for shareholders, there are particular problems for trustees. For details see Example 80 explanatory note 3.

Harrison Group Limited is considering making an offer for the whole of the ordinary share capital of Jayes Limited (a close company making electrical components).

The finance director of Harrison Group Limited has asked you to write a memorandum indicating the various taxation indemnities and warranties which should be incorporated in the purchasing agreement.

Draft a reply to the finance director, explaining the thinking behind the inclusion of these aspects in the agreement, the meaning of each of the terms, their purpose and significance.

Incorporate into your reply five areas that you consider should be the subject of a tax warranty and five areas that would be dealt with by a deed of indemnity.

Memorandum to the finance director of the Harrison Group Limited (Harrison) in connection with the possible offer for the whole of the ordinary share capital of Jayes Limited (Jayes)

Since Harrison proposes to acquire the share capital of Jayes as distinct from purchasing its assets on a going concern basis and continuing the trade, any actual or contingent liabilities and potential claims against Jayes will not be affected by the sale of shares.

In the event of claims of whatever nature arising against Jayes, Harrison will be affected in that the price which it is proposed to pay for the Jayes shares may, with the benefit of hindsight, be thought excessive, quite apart from the effect on the continuing trading of Jayes, depending upon the nature, seriousness and size of the claim.

The known liabilities and defined contingent liabilities will of course be taken into account in fixing the purchase price for the shares, but it is the unknown claim in respect of which care has to be exercised in a transaction of this sort.

Such claims are not limited to taxation matters, and can arise for example through product guarantees, breach of trade descriptions, property liabilities (such as contaminated land), employee matters and so on. Together with those relating to taxation, they will be the subject of a series of indemnities and warranties in the purchase agreement. The objective is to ensure that Harrison, as the new owner of the shares, is protected against claims which are made against Jayes relating to a period before the shares were acquired.

It should be remembered that the value of the indemnities and warranties is only as good as the ability of the vendors of the shares to make payment in the event of a claim, quite apart from the considerable professional costs which are usually involved. The vendor may therefore take out appropriate insurance to cover the potential liability (although it can be relatively costly). This arrangement would be beneficial to Harrison as it would have the comfort of knowing that in the event of a claim being necessary, the funds will be forthcoming if the claim is proved. If the vendor refuses to take out insurance cover, the purchaser may insist on a proportion of the sale proceeds being retained for (say) a year to meet potential liabilities. (There is a view that most problems surface after the first audit by the purchaser's auditors.)

There is usually a de minimis provision in the purchase agreement so that insignificant claims are not raised, and an overall ceiling on the liability of the vendors which is normally no greater than the price paid to them for their shares.

The indemnities and warranties in the purchase agreement will be drafted so as to be as wide and comprehensive as possible. There will be a blanket tax indemnity covering diminution in the value of the Jayes shares as a result of any unprovided tax liability arising from the period prior to the purchase of the shares.

Having said that, it is usual in the purchase agreement to set out specific points on which indemnities and warranties are given.

Defining the terms:

The deed of indemnity (also known as the 'tax covenant') is an undertaking to compensate for loss or expense flowing from the matters contained in the deed.

A warranty is something contractually guaranteed, breach of which justifies a claim for damages but from which loss will not necessarily flow so that no claim will arise under the deed of indemnity.

Drawing attention to the matters which the purchaser wishes to cover by warranties does, however, minimise the risk of a claim eventually arising, since the vendor of the shares is alerted to possible areas where a loss may arise because of events before the share sale. Most vendors will take the opportunity to take any appropriate corrective action before the sale. They will invariably make appropriate disclosure to the purchaser (in the 'letter of disclosure'). The purchaser is then deemed to take that point into account in negotiating his purchase, no claim then arising under the warranties for a loss flowing from that point. It will normally be difficult for the 'disclosure' to protect the vendor against any liability under the deed of indemnity.

Typical tax areas to be dealt with by the deed of indemnity are:

1.   That there is no liability for corporation tax (including tax payable under TA 1988 s 419 (loans to participators)) for periods of account ended prior to the share sale, beyond that provided in the accounts.

2.   That there is no liability for PAYE, national insurance (or tax deductions from subcontractors, if appropriate) for periods of account ended prior to the share sale, beyond that provided in the accounts.

3.   That there is no liability for VAT for periods of account ended prior to the share sale, beyond that provided in the accounts.

4.   That, except as provided in the accounts for the latest period ended before the share sale, no liability arises under TA 1988 Schedules 13 and 16 (accounting for advance corporation tax (to 6 April 1999) and for income tax on company payments which are not distributions).

5.   That the company has not caused any diminution of its assets which is such that an apportionment of that diminution could be made amongst its participators for inheritance tax purposes, with the liability to pay falling on the company (IHTA 1984 s 94).

The share sale will inevitably not coincide with the last available accounts. The indemnity will have to be extended to cover the period from those last accounts to the date of completion of the share sale but will not apply to tax liabilities arising on transactions in the ordinary course of the business since the accounts date (other than interest, penalties, or a surcharge). (Many standard 'deeds of indemnity' specify certain tax 'anti-avoidance' provisions and capital asset disposals as *not* being in the ordinary course of business.) Alternatively, if completion accounts are being drawn up, the deed of indemnity will be aligned to cover liabilities not provided for in the completion accounts.

Typical areas covered by the warranties will be:

1.   That there has been proper compliance with PAYE, national insurance (and subcontractors tax deduction if appropriate) regulations. (If not, a liability may arise which is not covered by the creditors in the accounts.)

2.   That the accounts, tax computations and returns submitted to HMRC have been correct. That no disagreement exists between the company and HMRC. That all pre-self assessment returns and computations including (where relevant) those on the last prepared accounts prior to the share sale have been agreed. That no disclosure which should have been made has not been made, and that there are no outstanding appeals or enquiries.

      That the correct tax has been paid by the due date. Where the company is paying tax in instalments, that tax has been paid in the appropriate instalments and there are no circumstances which could give rise to penalties for deliberately failing to pay instalments.

3.   That the VAT regulations have been properly complied with, and that no dispute exists with HMRC as to the rate and incidence of output tax and the eligibility to claim input tax (again, a liability not provided in the accounts may arise).

4.   That the base value for capital gains purposes of any assets appearing in the accounts is not less than the figure in the balance sheet. (It will be if there has been business assets rollover relief, giving a potentially higher tax liability than the commercial profit on sale.)

5.   That there is no potential capital gains liability arising from the investment of asset proceeds in wasting assets and thus having given rise to capital gains holdover relief, the tax on which will become payable at latest ten years from the earlier sale unless replaced by rollover relief.

Chiltern Tools (UK) Ltd is a small company resident in the UK. It holds

(a)   80% of the ordinary shares in Paradise Measuring (West Indies) Ltd, which is resident in a Caribbean country with which there is no double tax treaty. (HMRC have agreed that control is not exercised from the UK so as to make it a UK resident company.)

(b)   100% of Chiltern Tools (Europe) Ltd which is UK resident. This company is primarily engaged in retail distribution world-wide of precision scientific measuring instruments. The parent company charges rent and management charges to the subsidiary.

The stock-in-trade of each company is manufactured in various countries. Each company finds its own markets but various transactions take place between them. In the year to 31 August 2006, Chiltern Tools (UK) Ltd bought 8,000 items from Paradise for sale in UK markets.

The amount paid by Chiltern was based on the ultimate selling price of the items in the UK, which ranged between £75–£200, subject to an agreed deduction to reflect Chiltern's profit margin.

Chiltern's corporation tax computation and return for the year ended 31 August 2006 was submitted in July 2007 reflecting the above purchases from Paradise without any further adjustment.

In December 2007, HMRC opened an enquiry into the return for the year ended 31 August 2006 and queried the basis on which the transfer price of the items purchased from Paradise had been determined.

(a)   State whether each company is within the scope of the transfer pricing rules, and outline their tax obligations.

(b)   Detail the procedure for HMRC's enquiry and the specific information which Chiltern requires to satisfy HMRC's queries.

(c)   State how Chiltern may obtain greater certainty on the acceptability of the transfer pricing used on its future transactions with Paradise.

(d)   Explain how HMRC could extend its enquiries to earlier periods if they felt that non-commercial transfer pricing was operated by the two companies in those years.

(a)   Small and medium-sized companies are exempt from transfer pricing rules in respect of transactions with related businesses that are based in the UK or in any country with which the UK has a double taxation treaty containing a suitable non-discrimination article. As there is no such treaty in respect of Paradise Measuring (West Indies) Ltd, the rules apply to Chiltern Tools (UK) Ltd. In determining whether a company qualifies for the small or medium status, all connected companies must be aggregated. Provided that the companies are not large when aggregated, Chiltern Tools (Europe) Ltd will not be caught by transfer pricing rules in respect of transactions with its parent company. Chiltern Tools (Europe) Ltd would be caught by the transfer pricing rules in respect of any transactions with Paradise Measuring (West Indies) Ltd.

Of course, the usual rule that expenses are deductible from profit only in so far as they are expended wholly and exclusively for the purposes of the trade will apply to both companies.

Chiltern Tools (UK) Ltd must declare its profit for tax after making any adjustments necessary to bring its transactions with Paradise Measuring (West Indies) Ltd on to an arm's length basis. Chiltern Tools (Europe) Ltd, if the group qualifies as small, will declare on page one of the company tax return form CT600 that it qualifies for the SME exemption for transfer pricing. In the event that its profits would be reduced by the compensating adjustment under transfer pricing (see note 14), it would be able to waive the exemption.

(b)   **HMRC enquiry procedure and specific information required to satisfy HMRC**

HMRC have the right to make an enquiry into the company's tax return without giving any reason. A notice must be issued by HMRC, indicating their intention to enquire into the return, within the 12-month period following the filing date (for returns submitted on time) (FA 1998 Sch 18.24). The enquiry can extend to anything contained in the return. In Chiltern's case, the enquiry is specifically in relation to its application of the transfer pricing provisions of TA 1988 s 770A and Sch 28AA (given that Chiltern has direct control of Paradise – see TA 1988 Sch 28AA.1(1) and 4(1)).

The determination of an arm's length transfer price is based on OECD guidelines and Chiltern is required to show that the amount paid for the items purchased from Paradise is justifiable on this basis. Given that no adjustment was made in the return, the amount paid to Paradise must be an arm's length price not giving rise to a UK tax advantage. A UK tax advantage would only occur if the amount actually paid exceeded the arm's length price, reducing Chiltern's UK taxable profits. (HMRC could also attack the transaction under TA 1988 s 74 on the grounds that the excess amount was not laid out wholly and exclusively for the purposes of the trade.)

A vital part of Chiltern's defence is to demonstrate that a reasonable and honest attempt has been made to apply a commercially justifiable arm's length price and, furthermore, good quality documentation has been prepared and retained to support this. Chiltern should have the following information to support the transfer pricing policy with regard to its purchases from Paradise:

–   The nature of the transactions between the two companies, showing the terms, amounts, unit prices and payment terms. Transactions of the same or similar nature can be aggregated.

–   The transfer pricing methodology used, demonstrating how an arm's length transfer price was arrived at. As Chiltern is primarily acting as distributor, the discounted resale price method could easily be applied by the parties in this case. For each line of items, the ultimate UK sale price would be taken, reduced by an appropriate 'gross margin' for Chiltern.

If Chiltern adds little value to the product, the gross margin would be determined by its selling and other costs, stock and bad debt risks, and its expected profit. Chiltern's gross profit margins earned on similar items purchased from third party suppliers would be useful here. If Chiltern had 'third party' comparable information for similar transactions undertaken by competitors and gross profit margins for similar distributorships, this would give additional support.

HMRC would expect the 'connected' companies to have used their commercial knowledge and judgement to apply an arm's length transfer pricing policy on their transactions. The documentary evidence should indicate that a considered effort was made to satisfy the arm's length requirements of TA 1988 Sch 28AA.

Obviously, there may be a range of prices which may be reasonably justifiable. HMRC may disagree that the price charged for certain items meets the arm's length standard. However, transactions between the same connected companies may be evaluated together to determine whether a UK tax advantage arises. If an adjustment is conceded, HMRC would do this as part of its 'closure notice' procedure, inviting Chiltern to amend its return on completion of its enquiry. Provided the above procedures have been followed, Chiltern should not be regarded as negligent and thus should not be liable to any penalty under FA 1998 Sch 18.20. An interest charge only would arise from the tax payment date(s).

(c) **Obtaining greater certainty on the acceptability of transfer prices set on future transactions**

Chiltern could apply to HMRC for an advance pricing agreement (APA) under FA 1999 s 85. The APA would cover the transfer pricing basis to be used on its future transactions with Paradise. Provided the transfer prices are set in accordance with the APA, they are treated as satisfying the arm's length standard in TA 1988 Sch 28AA and will be accepted by HMRC while the APA remains in force. This therefore provides Chiltern with certainty about its transfer pricing position before it files its return.

In practice, the company would approach HMRC's International Division to discuss how an APA would apply to the relevant transactions. Chiltern's formal application to HMRC would then deal with the transfer pricing basis which would be applied to the purchases from Paradise so as to satisfy the arm's length requirements of the legislation, the issues on which clarification is sought from HMRC and Chiltern's understanding about how they should be implemented.

HMRC can revoke an APA from a particular time or where the company fails to comply with one of the conditions laid down in the APA, such as the requirement to provide information and reports.

(d) **Statutory powers of HMRC to extend their enquiries to earlier years**

If the results of HMRC's enquiry in (a) revealed significant problems, they may raise discovery assessments under TMA 1970 s 29 (FA 1998 Sch 18).

HMRC's 'discovery' powers enable them to raise estimated assessments on companies where they believe tax to be understated, and the onus is then on the taxpayer company to dispute the assessment through the appeal procedure.

Explanatory Notes

1. The transfer pricing legislation applies to transactions, or series of transactions, between businesses that are connected, or are under common control. If one business is in a position to directly or indirectly participate in the management, control or capital of the other, the rules will apply. Similarly, if the third party participates in the management, control or capital of a number of businesses, those businesses are connected. The rules will also apply to businesses which are under the control of a number of 'major participants'. A major participants is defined as one who has at least 40% of the holdings of the enterprise.

    The system requires arm's length transfer pricing on transactions between commonly controlled businesses, both UK – resident and non-resident. Transactions between a joint venture enterprise controlled by two participants (each having at least a 40% interest) and one or both of those participants are also caught.

    The basic principle of the transfer pricing legislation is that all transactions involving connected persons must use arm's length prices. An adjustment to the potentially advantaged person's profits or losses is required where any part of the arrangements involving a transaction or series of transactions departs from the arm's length standard and confers a tax advantage (ie where the price charged gives a lower taxable profit or a higher allowable loss than would have resulted if an arm's length price had been used). An arm's length price is considered to be doing business on terms and conditions which independent parties would adopt, expecting both businesses to make a profit.

If the actual provision (ie term of the contract) made between the 'connected' parties creates a tax advantage (when compared with the arm's length provision), the enterprise must compute its profits for corporation tax using arm's length prices (TA 1988 Sch 28AA.1). (A tax advantage arises where the actual provision creates lower profits or greater losses than would have applied under an arm's length basis (TA 1998 Sch 28AA.5).) Any difference giving rise to a tax advantage should be corrected by making an appropriate adjustment in the tax return.

2. There are three main methods of arriving at an arm's length price for goods and services supplied between connected parties:

   (i)   Evidence of prices in similar transactions between independent parties dealing at arm's length.

   (ii) Discounted resale prices of goods and services.

   (iii) Cost plus approach.

   Evidence of prices on comparable transactions between unconnected buyers and sellers is often hard to come by. The companies may have no near competitors selling similar products. Even where there are similar transactions the question is complicated by such matters as the terms of the transaction, after sales service, warranties, discounts etc. And often the information will be unavailable because it is confidential to the parties concerned.

   The discounted resale price approach has the advantage of starting from the actual price at which the goods are sold, but the determination of an appropriate discount taking into account the respective contributions of the various parties concerned is extremely difficult.

   The cost plus approach is similarly fraught with all sorts of difficulties relating to the manner in which the companies operate their allocation of central and other costs, the size of the profit mark-up and so on.

3. The transfer pricing rules apply to all forms of transaction, including non-trading and financial transactions. Thus, where a UK-resident company makes an interest-free loan to a non-resident subsidiary, the loan would be the transaction and a commercial rate of interest would have to be charged on the loan. However, where a UK subsidiary pays excessive interest on a loan from an overseas group company, the excess interest is disallowed. (Interest may be deemed to be excessive not simply because of the rate charged but also in terms of the size of the loan, for example where the UK company is thinly capitalised.)

4. HMRC's specialist transfer pricing division deals with large and complex cases involving multi-nationals. Other transfer pricing enquiries are dealt with at district level, with appropri-ate support.

Documenting transfer pricing policies

5. Under corporation tax self-assessment, taxpayers must keep and maintain adequate records to support a correct and complete return. In relation to transfer pricing with connected companies etc, the documentation must demonstrate that carefully considered arm's length transfer pricing policies were adopted and applied. The precise form of the documentation would depend on the complexity of the transactions involved (see HMRC's Tax Bulletin of September 1998 for the information HMRC would expect to see documented).

   To reduce or eliminate the administrative burden, most small and medium-sized businesses will largely be exempt from the new transfer pricing rules. The adjectives 'small' and 'medium-sized' are defined using EU criteria. These definitions apply to an employee headcount ceiling and a financial ceiling to a business or, where that business is part of a group, to the group.

   A small business is one with fewer than 50 employees and either an annual turnover or a balance sheet asset total not exceeding €10,000,000 (approximately £6,700,000).

A medium-sized business is one with fewer than 250 employees and either an annual turnover not exceeding €50,000,000 (approximately £33,500,000) or a balance sheet asset total not exceeding €43,000,000 (approximately £28,800,000).

Small and medium-sized businesses benefit from the transfer pricing exemption in respect of transactions with related businesses which are based in the UK or in any country with which the UK has a double taxation treaty containing a suitable non-discrimination article. Tax treaties drafted on the OECD model contain such a clause, but each treaty must be checked individually.

Notwithstanding the exemption, HMRC have power to require transfer pricing adjustments to be made in exceptional cases involving medium-sized businesses. Such an instruction will only be issued where the amount of tax involved is 'significant'. There is no equivalent power for HMRC to issue a similar notice to a small business.

6.   The documentation should exist at the latest by the time the corporation tax return is made. It is not necessary to prepare fresh documentation for each return period, provided the original information supports a correct and complete return. If significant transactions are not documented, the taxpayer may be found negligent and penalties would be applied to any adjustment made under FA 1998 Sch 18.20.

7.   The normal self-assessment rules for retaining records apply (see Example 40 note 3 for income tax).

Use of Advance Pricing Agreements

8.   As noted in part (b) of the example, Advance Pricing Agreements (APAs) under FA 1999 ss 85 to 87 can be used to achieve greater certainty about the transfer pricing policies used in transactions between connected companies. APAs are particularly useful for very complex transactions where there are considerable difficulties or doubts in determining the method by which the arm's length principle should be applied. An APA is likely to be much more efficient than a retrospective examination of transfer pricing policies.

An APA is a binding written agreement between the company and HMRC for determining the transfer pricing method before the return is submitted. HMRC's detailed policy and procedures relating to applications for APAs are set out in SP 2/99. Provided the terms of the APA are complied with, it will be binding on HMRC and the company for the period covered by the APA. The company is expected to propose the initial term for the APA over which the relevant transfer pricing method(s) will remain appropriate – -this is expected to be between three and five years. The APA will apply to accounting periods beginning after the application has been made, but may also be effective for a period which has ended before agreement has been reached.

9.   An APA may be used to determine:

(a)   transfer pricing between separate companies where issues arise as to the determination of the arm's length provision under the legislation;

(b)   transfer pricing between parts of the same company operating in different countries where it is necessary to determine the taxable income arising in each country, as follows:

–   The attribution of income to a UK permanent establishment (where there is no double tax treaty)

–   The attribution of income arising outside the UK within a UK-resident company (where there is no double tax treaty)

–   Income attributable to any permanent establishment where a double tax treaty is in force.

10.   A 'bilateral APA' enables the transfer pricing basis to be agreed by the UK HMRC and the relevant overseas tax authority and is therefore preferred. This can only be obtained where there is a double tax treaty between the UK and the relevant overseas country which contains a mutual agreement procedure (see note 12).

UK companies providing the same service or facility (for example, licensing know-how or brand names) in several countries may wish to seek APAs with the various overseas tax administrations using a so-called multilateral APA. There is no formal mechanism for negotiating multilateral APAs and this will strictly represent a series of bilateral APAs. In some cases, whilst the arrangements may appear to be the same, there can be individual variations requiring a different transfer pricing basis to be adopted. Multilateral APAs are especially useful for allocating the profits of a global activity or operation carried out in various UK and overseas permanent establishments so as to avoid double taxation.

11.   A 'unilateral APA' only provides agreement with HMRC on the UK tax treatment of transfer pricing. It does not necessarily provide an agreed basis with the overseas tax jurisdiction and may therefore give rise to double taxation. A UK company would, however, choose a unilateral APA where it considers the 'bilateral APA' process to be unnecessarily long or complicated.

It should be noted that HMRC only intend to enter into APAs to resolve difficult transfer pricing problems which involve significant doubt and may decline applications where the transfer pricing can be readily established (such as where reliable market comparables exist). Consequently, Chiltern Tools (UK) Ltd may not be successful in obtaining an APA on its UK distributorship of precision tools as there should be comparable 'benchmark' transactions within the industry etc.

Once the policies have been agreed by HMRC, then provided the relevant transactions are priced in accordance with the APA, they will be accepted by HMRC as satisfying the arm's length requirement.

An APA is nullified if the taxpayer fraudulently or negligently provides false or misleading information when negotiating an APA and a penalty of up to £10,000 can also be imposed.

Procedures for corresponding transfer pricing adjustments

12.   Transfer pricing adjustments in one country clearly have consequences in relation to tax charged in the other country, and transfer pricing is one of the matters dealt with in double taxation agreements. The OECD model agreement and various guidelines provide for a profits adjustment where transfers between associated enterprises result in profits that are not at a proper commercial level. Countries in the European Union have established a mechanism for resolving transfer pricing disputes between member states, following the ratification by member states of the Arbitration Convention, which came into force on 1 January 1995. TA 1988 s 815B requires effect to be given in the UK to agreements and decisions under the Convention. See also the HMRC's Tax Bulletin of October 1996 for their transfer pricing procedures in the light of the OECD guidelines and the Arbitration Convention and the mutual agreement procedure enabling countries with double tax treaties to consult one another to resolve transfer pricing issues and if possible to prevent any adjustments resulting in unrelievable double taxation.

13.   **Payments of interest**

The transfer pricing rules perform the same function as the 'thin capitalization' rules in force in many countries to counter excessive amounts of interest being charged between parent companies and other group members funding subsidiaries with higher levels of debt than would have been available on an arm's length basis. In determining whether the interest payment is greater than that which would have been made in the absence of a special relationship or connection, the following criteria should be considered:

(a)   the extent of the borrowing company's overall indebtedness;

(b)   whether the loan or the amount of the loan would have been made to the borrowing company if arm's length conditions had applied; and

(c)   whether the rate of interest charged and the other terms of the loan were on a commercial basis.

Loans which are made between companies under common control, whether UK-resident or not, will be subject to restrictions. Where a loan exceeds the amount that would have been provided by an unconnected lender, the interest on the 'excessive' part of the borrowing is disallowed as a tax deduction. Similarly, the lending company is only taxed as if it had received an arm's length amount of interest. F(No 2)A 2005 Sch 7 para 13 introduces the definition of 'a commercial rate of interest' into FA 1996 s 103(3A).

Anti-avoidance provisions of F(No 2)A 2005 s 40 counters tax advantages derived from financing arrangements set up by parties acting in concert up to six months before a control relationship exists. This is intended to counter coordinated avoidance action by investors who (although not connected parties according to the normal definition) share control of the company. Although any of the parties concerned may be minority owners, interest paid to all by them is not considered to be at arm's length the rate, and relief are excessive interest can be denied.

14. **Corresponding adjustments**

The intention is the transfer pricing should not cause double taxation of the same profits. As far as cross-border transactions are concerned, double taxation treaties already contain procedures for addressing this. For domestic transactions, the same outcome will be achieved by allowing a compensating reduction in the profits of one party to a transaction where there had been a transfer pricing adjustment to increase the profits of the other party.

'The legislation provides for "balancing payments". These enable a business with the benefit of a compensating reduction in profits to pass the cash effect of the benefit back to the related business which suffered the disallowance.'

The directors of your company have decided to set up a trading operation in a country outside the European Economic Area where the rate of corporation tax is 10%. They are considering two alternative approaches:

(a)   To run the overseas operation as a permanent establishment of the UK company

or

(b)   To run it as a foreign-registered subsidiary of the UK company.

Prepare detailed notes on the UK taxation implications of each of the alternative proposals as a basis for a report to the directors.

UK tax implications of operating as an overseas permanent establishment compared with operating through an overseas subsidiary

Setting up an overseas permanent establishment or an overseas subsidiary

1. The establishment of either an overseas permanent establishment or an overseas subsidiary will involve foreign tax being suffered on the profits, because the company will be moving from trading *with* the country concerned to trading *in* it. Overseas countries generally impose tax where business is carried on through a permanent establishment in their country. Most double tax treaties have a similar definition to the OECD model, which states that a permanent establishment includes a place of management, a branch, an office, a factory, a workshop and a mine, oil or gas well, quarry or any other place of extraction of natural resources (subject to certain exclusions). The way in which the foreign tax may be relieved is dealt with below.

UK corporation tax liability re overseas permanent establishment

2. If a trade is carried on through an overseas permanent establishment of a UK-resident company, the company is liable to corporation tax on all the profits of the permanent establishment. The liability will be under Schedule D Case I unless, exceptionally, the trade is carried on *wholly overseas*, in which case the charge would be under Schedule D Case V. It would be difficult to establish that the operation was carrying on its trade wholly overseas unless it was clearly managed and controlled in the overseas country. There would in any event be little point in trying to establish a Case V source rather than a Case I source because a company's profits are measured under Case V using Case I principles (TA 1988 s 70) but relief for Case V losses is confined to Case V rather than being allowable against profits generally as with Case I (TA 1988 s 391).

   For accounting periods ended on or after 1 April 2000, any trading loss etc incurred by such an overseas operation can only be group 'relieved' provided it is *not* relievable against taxable overseas profits of any other company under the law of the relevant foreign jurisdiction (TA 1988 s 403E). This would exclude, for example, any loss which is offset in a consolidated tax return or surrendered under foreign group relief provisions. Under the group relief provisions as amended by FA 2000, the loss can be surrendered to a UK-resident holding company, or any 75% UK-resident subsidiary (irrespective of whether the requisite 75% ownership is traced through a UK or foreign resident company), or against the profits of a UK permanent establishment of a non-resident 'group' member.

UK corporation tax liability re overseas subsidiary

3. If a trade is carried on through a non-UK resident subsidiary, the parent company would be liable to tax on amounts received from the subsidiary by way of interest, dividends etc. Profits that are accumulated in the overseas country would be subject to overseas tax. Furthermore, there are provisions in TA 1988 ss 747 to 756 and Schs 24 to 26 relating to 'controlled foreign companies'. These rules enable UK companies to be taxed on the profits of a foreign company if it is (broadly) under overall UK control and pays tax in its country of residence of less than three-quarters the amount that a UK-resident company would pay, which would clearly apply in this case. The provisions will not be applied if the foreign company satisfies one or more of certain tests (for example it pursues an acceptable distribution policy, carries on exempt activities or was established for genuine commercial reasons and not tax avoidance). Furthermore, the CFC rules do not apply if the foreign company's profits for a 12-month period were less than £50,000. Under the acceptable distribution policy, the required distribution level is 90% of *taxable* profits net of capital gains and foreign tax. In order to avoid being caught by these provisions it would be necessary to ensure that the overseas company met one of the various CFC 'let-out' provisions (and even then the company may still be subject to the CFC provisions if the country in which the company is located has been specified in regulations as being one in relation to which the CFC exemptions do not apply – see explanatory note 10).

   If the overseas subsidiary makes losses rather than profits, these generally cannot be relieved against the UK company's profits. UK transfer pricing legislation operates to ensure that transactions between the companies must take place at arm's length value. If the subsidiary is operating in the EEA area (that is the European Community plus Iceland, Liechtenstein and Norway), and a 75% group relationship exists, then losses may in certain circumstances be group relieved against UK profits. All foreign tax relief for tax credits must be sought and used in priority to group relief against UK profits, and other restrictions apply. Losses made by a subsidiary outside the EEA area cannot be group relieved against UK profits, and would only attract relief under the tax provisions of that overseas country.

Capital gains

4. Capital gains made by an overseas permanent operation are chargeable to corporation tax. Gains made by a non-resident subsidiary are not so chargeable, except where they come within the provisions of TCGA 1992 s 13 (which apply where the company would be 'close' if it had been UK resident). This section provides for a non-resident company's gains to be apportioned to the UK-resident 'participators' as defined in TA 1988 s 417 (participators mainly being shareholders, but the term is more widely defined – see Example 55 explanatory note 2) and charged to UK capital gains tax, unless the apportioned gain is not more than 10% of the total gain. Such apportioned gains do not qualify for taper relief. For gains arising after 6 March 2001 the section does not apply to gains attributed to an exempt approved pension scheme. Nor does it apply if the gains relate to UK PE or overseas business assets (subject to certain provisions).

Where the gain is distributed within the *earlier* of three years from the end of the accounting period in which it arose or four years from when the gain arose, the capital gains tax suffered on the apportionment is deducted in calculating income tax or capital gains tax liabilities on the distribution.

Any amount not so relieved forms part of the capital gains cost of the shares (whether or not the gain was distributed within the prescribed period). If the overseas subsidiary is resident in a country whose double tax treaty with the UK exempts residents from a UK capital gains charge, this may prevent s 13 applying.

5. There would be no disposal for capital gains on the transfer of assets to a permanent establishment (being an 'internal' transfer), whereas a chargeable disposal would arise on the transfer to a non-resident subsidiary (as the assets are being removed from the charge to UK tax). The no loss/no gain provisions of TCGA 1992 s 171 (transfers within a 75% group) would not apply, because they do not cover transfers to non-resident companies (except where they are to be used for the purposes of a UK permanent establishment trade).

Establishing non-resident status

6. There may be a problem with an overseas subsidiary in establishing that it is actually not resident in the UK.

If the parent company exercised control of its activities in a management rather than a shareholding sense then the subsidiary could be held to be UK resident. The subsidiary must in any event be incorporated abroad since if it is incorporated in the UK it will be regarded as UK-resident no matter where it is managed and controlled (unless held to be non-resident under the provisions of a double tax treaty) (FA 1988 s 66).

If the company established a permanent establishment initially and then incorporated it

7. The conversion of a permanent establishment into an overseas subsidiary would result in a notional discontinuance of the trade for the parent company (TA 1988 s 337) and stock would accordingly have to be valued at open market value. There would also be balancing adjustments for capital allowances purposes on the relevant assets transferred to the subsidiary, which may result in significant balancing charges.

8. The parent company could make a claim to defer the charge to tax on the net capital gains arising on the transfer of assets to the subsidiary if the following conditions were satisfied (TCGA 1992 s 140):

(a)   All the assets of the permanent establishment (other than cash) used for the trade (or part of the trade, if the whole trade is not transferred) must be transferred.

(b)   The consideration must be wholly or partly shares or loan stock in the transferee company, and the parent company must hold at least 25% of the ordinary share capital of the transferee company (which in a holding/subsidiary relationship it will). If the consideration is only partly shares and loan stock, only part of the gain may be deferred.

The deferred gain would crystallise as and when the parent company disposed of the shares or stock. It would also crystallise if the transferee company disposed of the assets within six years after the transfer.

9.   Treasury consent is required if the subsidiary is to issue shares or debentures, or if the UK company is to transfer some of its shares in the subsidiary (see below).

Clearances to be obtained from the UK authorities

Certain transactions by an overseas resident subsidiary company, such as the issue and transfer of shares and securities, require the consent of the Treasury (TA 1988 ss 765 to 767). Breach of the section involves fines and/or imprisonment of appropriate company officers.

The Treasury have given general consent in respect of certain transactions. In other cases special consent is required. The Treasury will want to establish that there are sound commercial reasons for the transaction and that tax avoidance is not its sole or main objective.

Relief available in respect of foreign tax paid and shadow ACT offset

Relief for foreign tax paid either by a permanent establishment or by a subsidiary is available against the UK corporation tax paid on the permanent establishment or dividend income, subject to the overriding restriction that it cannot exceed the amount of UK corporation tax payable. In arriving at that UK tax, charges on income and interest payable may be deducted in the most favourable manner to leave foreign income as high as possible (TA 1988 s 797). (From 1 April 2000, any unrelieved foreign tax relating to an overseas permanent establishment may be carried back for up to three years and then carried forward indefinitely against the UK tax on the same source of income. This requires a claim to be made within six years of the end of the relevant accounting period (TA 1988 ss 806L and 806M). The same three-year carryback/indefinite carry forward rule applies to double tax relief on dividends received on or after 31 March 2001 (ss 806A to 806K).) See also Example 54 explanatory note 7 re surrendering foreign tax attributable to dividends within a group of companies.

Dividends paid by companies after 5 April 1999 do not give rise to ACT. This is of considerable benefit where the company is distributing dividends received from an overseas subsidiary or foreign branch profits, as no surplus ACT can arise. Surplus ACT remaining at 6 April 1999 can only be recovered under the shadow ACT rules. Post-5 April 1999 dividends give rise to shadow ACT which is (notionally) offset before actual surplus ACT. The normal ACT offset limit is 20% of profits but there is an exception for foreign income. The shadow ACT regulations mirror the pre-6 April 1999 ACT offset rule for foreign income – so that the ACT offset is restricted to the residual UK tax on the foreign income *after* double tax relief (or if lower, 20% of the foreign income). These rules therefore still pose a problem for companies trying to recover structural surplus ACT built up by the previous distributions of foreign income.

As and when dividends are received from an overseas subsidiary, double tax relief is available in respect of the underlying tax on the profits out of which the dividend is paid, in addition to the withholding tax on the dividend, providing the parent company owns at least 10% of the voting power in the subsidiary (TA 1988 ss 799, 800 & 801). (For further details of double tax relief, see Example 54.)

Where relief is not claimed by way of tax credit, foreign tax suffered may be deducted in arriving at the income chargeable to UK tax, which may be more beneficial if there are UK trading losses (TA 1988 s 811).

Explanatory Notes

Factors affecting choice between overseas permanent establishment and overseas subsidiary

1.   The main UK tax considerations in the choice between an overseas permanent establishment and an overseas subsidiary are explained in the example. The UK position must be considered alongside the taxation position in the overseas country. There are also many commercial factors, such as the local 'commercial' perception of dealing with a local company rather than a permanent establishment of a UK company.

   Following the introduction of the substantial shareholdings exemption (SSE) from 1 April 2002, UK companies may prefer operating their overseas business through a separate subsidiary, if it is likely to be sold at some stage. The SSE is available on the sale of shares in a trading subsidiary etc and the exemption is available on shareholdings in both UK and overseas resident companies (see Example 65). Also, there is no requirement that the subsidiary's trade is carried on in the UK. In contrast, the sale of the trade and assets (including goodwill) of an overseas permanent establishment would be subject to UK (and possibly overseas) tax. (Some protection of the UK tax base from possible exploitation of the exemption has been introduced by FA 2002 s 90, amending TA 1988 s 747 – see explanatory note 6.)

   Other overseas taxes must be considered, such as indirect (VAT or sales type) taxes, property taxes (which can be expensive), employee taxes and social security.

   Many overseas tax authorities have thin capitalisation rules which prevent excessive debt being used to finance the overseas company (to secure as much tax deductible interest as possible). From the UK company's viewpoint, it would not be efficient for interest charged on debt (fully taxed in the UK) to create surplus losses overseas.

   The method of financing the overseas permanent establishment or company also requires careful consideration, for example local 'third party' borrowing is tax-efficient for a permanent establishment of the UK company (as 'interest' on internal funds from the UK head office would not be tax-deductible).

Residence of a company

2.   FA 1988 s 66 provides that companies incorporated in the UK on or after 15 March 1988 are resident here, no matter where they are managed and controlled (subject to what is said in explanatory note 6).

3.   Prior to 15 March 1988 the following general principles had been established:

   (a)   A company resides where its real business is carried on, ie where the central management and control is situated (De Beers Consolidated Mines v Howe 1906).

   (b)   The place of incorporation is a factor to be considered but is not conclusive (Calcutta Jute Mills v Nicholson 1876).

   (c)   The place where directors meet is an important indicator (Cesena Sulphur v Nicholson 1876) but again it is not conclusive.

   (d)   Control as a shareholder does not amount to management and control (Kodak Ltd v Clark 1901). (But where a parent company usurped the functions of its subsidiary company's board, or the subsidiary's board merely rubber stamped the parent company's decisions without independently considering them, HMRC would draw the conclusion that the subsidiary's residence was the same as that of the parent company.)

   (e)   A company may have dual residence, but this requires some substantial business operations in each country (Bullock v Unit Construction Co Ltd 1959).

Where dual residence is concerned, many double tax treaties provide that the company is deemed to be resident where its place of effective management is situated. The treaty may also have a 'tie breaker' clause under which a company is held to be resident in only one of the two countries (see explanatory note 6).

4. The case law provisions outlined in explanatory note 3 (a) to (e) are still relevant to decide where companies incorporated abroad are resident (subject to what is said in explanatory note 6). If they are regarded as UK-resident and if they wish to migrate, they will have to give HMRC notice of their intention and make HMRC-approved arrangements for payment of tax (FA 1988 s 130 – see SP 2/90). This will include tax on unrealised gains, except on UK assets of a permanent establishment which remains here (TCGA 1992 s 185). Deferment is possible in respect of foreign assets of a foreign trade if the company is a 75% subsidiary of a company remaining resident in the UK and the two companies so elect within two years. The parent company is then charged to tax on the net gains on the deemed disposal as and when the subsidiary disposes of the assets (within six years), or ceases to be a subsidiary (at any time) (TCGA 1992 s 187).

5. Certain UK incorporated companies were treated as non-resident at 15 March 1988 or had applied to be so treated at that date and obtained Treasury consent subsequently. Such UK companies will not be treated as UK-resident unless they cease business or cease to be liable to overseas tax, in which case they will be treated as UK-resident from that time. If, however, they transfer their central management and control to the UK, they will be treated as resident from the time of the transfer (FA 1988 Sch 7).

Dual resident companies

6. Where there is a tie-breaker clause in a double tax agreement that provides for a company to be resident in another country and *not* in the UK, FA 1994 s 249 provides that the company is non-resident for *all* UK tax purposes (preventing, for example, the surrender of losses by way of group relief). From 1 April 2002, the provisions of FA 1994 s 249 are disregarded in deciding whether a company is a 'person resident in the UK' for the controlled foreign company rules dealt with in explanatory notes 9 and 10. This exception does not, however, apply to companies treated as not resident in the UK immediately before that date (TA 1988 s 747 as amended by FA 2002 s 90).

Dual resident companies that are *not* regarded as non-UK resident under a tie-breaker clause are not within FA 1994 s 249. However, if they are *investing* companies they are subject to some specific anti-avoidance provisions, the main ones being the following:

(a) The company cannot surrender losses, non-trading deficits on loans, charges etc under the group relief provisions (TA 1988 s 404 & Sch 17).

(b) Where an asset is sold to such a company by a company under the same control, the sale may not be treated as being at written down value for capital allowances (CAA 2001 s 570).

(c) An asset may not be transferred intra-group to such a company on a no loss no gain basis for capital gains purposes (TCGA 1992 s 171).

(d) Rollover relief on replacement of business assets cannot be claimed within a group where the new asset is acquired by such a company (TCGA 1992 s 175).

Matters requiring Treasury consent

7. TA 1988 ss 765 to 767 provide that it is unlawful without Treasury consent:

(a) For a UK-resident company to cause or permit a non-UK resident company it controls to issue shares or debentures.

(b) For a UK company to transfer shares in a non-resident company it controls, other than to enable a director to obtain qualification shares.

The Treasury have given general consent to certain transfers, for example permitting transfers under (b) to another UK company that is a member of the same 75% group. Transfers not covered by a general consent require special consent.

Transactions between companies in member states of the European Economic Area (ie the European Union plus Iceland, Liechtenstein and Norway) do not require Treasury consent under s 765, but the company may be required to report the transaction to HMRC within 6 months (under regulations contained in SI 1990/1671). There are penalties of up to £3,000 for non-compliance with the reporting requirements (TA 1988 s 765A).

Capital gains on transfer of business within EU

8. For businesses operating in the European Union, TCGA 1992 s 140C provides an alternative to the relief available under s 140 outlined in note 8 of the example. Under the EU Mergers Directive, local tax is not payable on a transfer of a business between companies resident in member states. TCGA 1992 s 140C provides for a UK-resident company to claim relief on the transfer of a non-UK trade carried on through a permanent establishment located in a country in the EU to a company in another member state in exchange for shares or securities in the other company. The transfer must be for bona fide commercial reasons and not part of tax avoidance arrangements (s 140D). Where the conditions are satisfied, the net capital gains are charged to tax, but the tax is reduced by the local tax that would have been paid in the country where the permanent establishment is located had it not been for the Mergers Directive (s 140C(5) and TA 1988 s 815A).

    Under the provisions of the Distributions Directive (90/435/EEC), most EU companies do not deduct withholding tax from dividends to parent companies in other EU countries, although many countries have imposed a minimum time for the parent to have held shares in the subsidiary before this applies ('subsidiary' in this context requiring not more than 25% ownership by the 'parent'). F (No 2) A 2005 ss 51–58 introduce reliefs to facilitate the tax neutral formation of the Societas Europaeas (SE) from 1 April 2005.

    Where a permanent establishment was converted into a subsidiary before 6 April 1988 and capital gains tax was deferred under the provisions of TCGA 1992 s 140 (see note 8 in the example), then if the deferred gain related wholly or partly to an asset acquired before 31 March 1982, and it crystallises on or after 6 April 1988, one half of the gain is exempt from tax (TCGA 1992 Sch 4.4). If the conversion took place on or before 31 March 1982, however, and the date when the liability would crystallise is on or after 6 April 1988, the deferred gain is wholly exempt from tax (TCGA 1992 Sch 4.4(5)).

Controlled foreign companies

9. The controlled foreign company legislation of TA 1988 ss 747 to 756 is aimed at preventing UK companies diverting profits to overseas tax havens or preferential tax regimes. The rules are particularly intended to counter the establishment in low tax areas of companies interposed between UK supplier and foreign customer, or vice versa, captive finance and insurance companies, and companies established to accumulate dividends from other foreign subsidiaries. Where the low tax area is an EU country, the UK provisions may well conflict with EU law.

    As a general rule, if the local corporation tax rate is 10%, it would be efficient for the overseas trade to be run through a separate overseas company, as those profits would be insulated from the higher UK tax rate until remitted. However, this would be subject to the application of the controlled foreign company rules noted below.

    A controlled foreign company (CFC) is a company which is resident outside the UK, controlled by persons resident in the UK, and subject to a 'lower level of taxation'. (See explanatory note 6 for the provisions treating a company that is non-resident under a 'tie breaker' clause in a double tax agreement as a 'person resident in the UK' for the CFC rules.) This broadly means less than 75% of the tax that a UK resident company would pay. (However, the use of 'designer-rate' schemes which permit potential CFCs to pay just the right amount of overseas tax to avoid the 'lower level of tax' condition is prevented by TA 1988 s 750A.) A non-resident company can only be a CFC if the UK company has at least a 25% 'interest' in it, which normally coincides with voting shares (see TA 1988 s 749B – loan creditors do not have an interest).

The UK 'control' definition includes joint venture 'CFC' companies where at least 40% of the shares etc are held by a UK company and at least 40% (but not more than 55%) are held by a foreign person.

10. A controlled foreign company is not subject to a CFC tax liability under TA 1988 s 747 if it satisfies one of certain specified exemptions for the relevant accounting period. In order to protect the UK from harmful tax practices, however, TA 1988 s 748A enables HMRC to issue regulations preventing any of the exemptions applying to controlled foreign companies operating in specified overseas jurisdictions, so that all such companies would be within the provisions. Such regulations cannot take effect without the express consent of Parliament. S 748A applies to accounting periods beginning on or after 24 July 2002. The specified exemptions are as follows:

(a) the company pursues an acceptable distribution policy (see below), the distributions being made at a time when the company is not resident in the UK, or

(b) the company is engaged in exempt activities (broadly trading activities with third parties, but subject to various conditions), or

(c) the company is publicly quoted in its country of residence, with at least 35% of the voting power held by the public (plus other conditions which are similar to the close company exclusion rules), or

(d) the company's profits do not exceed £50,000 (proportionately reduced if the accounting period is less than twelve months), or

(e) the company does not exist wholly or mainly to reduce UK tax by diverting profits from the UK, and any reduction was either minimal or incidental (the 'motive' test).

The acceptable distribution level is 90% of *taxable* income profits, ie excluding capital gains and foreign tax. (For these purposes, the taxable income is calculated using UK tax principles.) The dividend from the CFC must be paid within 18 months after the end of the CFC's accounting period (and, in HMRC's view, received by the UK company within the 18 month period). Many multinational groups route an 'acceptable distribution policy' ('ADP') dividend through an intermediate 'dividend averaging' company (usually based in the Netherlands) to arrange for sufficient double tax relief to cover the UK tax on the dividend. However, TA 1988 s 806C provides that from 31 March 2001 'ADP dividends' paid by a CFC company (which does *not* satisfy any of the exemptions in (b) to (e) above) cannot be 'mixed' with any other dividends.

A UK-resident company that is treated as non-resident under a double tax treaty is treated as non-resident for *all* UK tax purposes (FA 1994 s 249), subject to the exception outlined at the beginning of this note. It is not possible for the 'acceptable distribution' test to be satisfied by paying large dividends to such a company, because it is provided that the test is not satisfied unless the dividends are charged to corporation tax in the receiving company's hands.

Some groups previously exploited a 'loophole' in the CFC legislation by transferring a UK trading company to a CFC. Dividends from the UK subsidiary would then be passed through the CFC and would count towards the acceptable distribution test. (They would not be relevant income in the CFC on UK principles (see TA 1988 s 208).) Since the underlying profits were subject to UK corporation tax, the acceptable distribution dividend was not taxed again in the hands of the UK holding company. From 17 March 1999, however, dividends which are paid by a CFC consisting of 'tax exempt' dividends from a UK company no longer count towards the ADP test (TA 1988 Sch 25.2(1B)). Anti-avoidance is strengthened by F (No 2) A 2005 s 44 which prevents excluded income from UK sources distorting the lower level of tax test, and takes account of local credits/repayments from 2 December 2004.

Companies are excluded from the CFC provisions if they are resident and carrying on business in a country listed in the 'Excluded Countries' regulations (SI 1998/3081).

Self-assessment provisions

11.   For accounting periods ending after 30 June 1999, UK (holding) companies must 'self-assess' their corporation tax liabilities in respect of CFCs. Where the UK company pays its tax in instalments (as will often be the case) the tax relating to CFCs must also be included in the estimated tax payable.

Full details of all CFCs must be disclosed on the supplementary page CT 600B of the corporation tax return CT 600. If the CFC's profits are covered by an acceptable distribution policy or satisfy one of the other exemptions (see below), an appropriate note is made. For each *non-exempt* CFC, the company must report its chargeable profits (less creditable tax) and the UK tax due.

Companies which *may not* be CFCs (for example, because they are not subject to a lower level of tax) but would clearly be covered by an exemption can also be shown on the return. This saves the UK company the cost of working out whether the company is, in principle, a CFC and preserves its disclosure position.

Under self-assessment, the UK corporation tax payable in respect of a non-exempt CFC is based on the UK company's share of the CFC's income profits (which must be at least 25% as indicated in explanatory note 9), as computed for UK corporation tax purposes. If the CFC is carrying on a trade, it is treated as though it were a UK resident carrying on a trade wholly abroad, using Schedule D Case V rules. The UK corporation tax on the CFC's income is then reduced by the appropriate share of 'creditable tax', which comprises double tax relief for overseas tax, including local tax payable in the CFC's country of residence and any actual UK tax charged on any part of the CFC's profits.

To give companies greater confidence in determining their self-assessment position and liabilities in respect of CFCs, HMRC introduced a comprehensive CFC clearance system for companies and their advisers. Clearances generally apply indefinitely provided the underlying facts and the law remain the same. HMRC work to a 28-day turnaround target provided all the necessary information is included in the clearance application. Full details are given in HMRC's CFC guidance notes.

Transfer pricing

12.   Transactions between UK-resident and non-resident companies under common control are subject to the self-assessment transfer pricing provisions. Transactions for goods, services, financing etc between the UK company and its overseas subsidiary company must be based on arm's length prices or consideration. The UK company's tax computation and return must incorporate arm's length income and expenditure on transactions with 'connected' overseas companies (with an appropriate transfer pricing adjustment if necessary to reflect this). If the UK company fails to reflect arm's length transfer pricing on its return, it is likely to be liable to significant penalties and interest. (The UK transfer pricing legislation is based on OECD principles and most overseas jurisdictions have similar tax rules.) See Example 69 for the detailed provisions.

The profits of an overseas permanent establishment would be fully liable to UK tax. The overseas jurisdiction would normally have powers to ensure that the profits arising in the permanent establishment are established on an arm's length basis, for example under the 'associated enterprises' article of a double tax treaty.

Double tax relief

13.   The calculation and application of double tax relief is dealt with in Example 54.

Anti-avoidance

14.   The interaction of rules of different jurisdictions has provided an opportunity for many tax-avoidance schemes of a technical nature, and many have been notified under the avoidance disclosure regime. Many of the CFC and DTR regulations are the subject of detailed technical anti-avoidance provisions, contained in FA 2005 and F (No 2) A 2005.

International Tax Enforcement Arrangements

15.   FA 2006 paves the way for a major strengthening in international tax enforcement arrangements. At present a number of agreements, for instance under double tax treaties, allow for the exchange of information between the UK and overseas tax jurisdictions, typically limited to direct taxes.

The Act increases the United Kingdom's ability to make agreements with other territories concerning mutual assistance on the enforcement of taxes, and also enables the UK to ratify the 1988 Council of Europe – OECD convention on Mutual Administrative Assistance in Tax Matters. HMRC and other government department are empowered to collect information on liabilities to income tax, corporation tax and capital gains tax, for the purposes of assisting with quantifying the liability to foreign taxes.

As well as facilitating the exchange of information relating to foreign taxes, it also empowers HM Treasury to make regulations to facilitate the recovery in the UK of foreign tax debts. The rules specifying the procedure for recovery of foreign tax debts will be made by statutory instrument at the date to be announced.

Bergplatz SA, a company resident in Switzerland for tax purposes, has decided to set up a business in the UK manufacturing plastic food containers under the name Boris. The anticipated profits of the branch are likely to be around £100,000 for the first few years.

Draft notes briefing the tax partner as to the major UK tax considerations that should be borne in mind in determining whether to operate through a permanent establishment or subsidiary company, and consider whether a European Company (SE) would be possible or advantageous.

(Comment on the specific provisions of the UK/Switzerland double tax agreement is not required.)

31 August 2006

To: Tax partner

From: A D Viser

Bergplatz SA: UK permanent establishment or subsidiary – major UK tax considerations

Operating through UK permanent establishment

1.   If the Boris manufacturing operation is carried on through a UK permanent establishment, Bergplatz SA will be liable to corporation tax on the permanent establishment's trading profit and on any income from property or rights used or held by the permanent establishment. It will also be liable to corporation tax on any capital gains on the disposal of property or rights held by the permanent establishment and assets situated in the UK used for the trade or by the permanent establishment (TA 1988 ss 11 and 11AA and TCGA 1992 s 10B). If there are any sources of UK income that are not connected with the permanent establishment the company will be liable to income tax at the basic rate thereon.

There will be no tax consequences when the permanent establishment makes remittances to Bergplatz.

Assuming Bergplatz SA has no UK subsidiaries, the legislation enabling UK permanent establishments of non-resident companies to take advantage of the group relief provisions for losses and the capital gains provisions for tax neutral intra-group transfers and group rollover relief on replacement of business assets is not relevant.

2.   It is provided by TA 1988 ss 13 and 13AA that a non-resident company is not entitled to the benefit of the small companies' rate of corporation tax, and must pay the full rate, currently 30%. This will not apply, however, if the UK/Switzerland double tax treaty contains a non-discrimination clause. Even if it did not, there is a strong possibility that a Swiss resident company (being an EU resident) could argue that the UK's restriction of the small companies' corporation tax rate is in breach of EU law (especially following the taxpayers' success in Metallgesellschaft Ltd v CIR and Hoechst AG v CIR (2001), where the UK's exclusion of groups with non-resident parent companies from the provisions enabling subsidiaries to pay dividends without accounting for ACT was held to be discriminatory). If ss 13 and 13AA did apply, the whole of Bergplatz SA's profits would be taken into account in deciding whether the small companies' rate was available on the branch profits.

3.   Where a permanent establishment pays interest for the purposes of the trade, it is deductible as a trading expense (on an accruals basis) (FA 1996 s 82). The borrowing would be taken out by Bergplatz for the purpose of the UK permanent establishment's trade. In contrast any interest charged to the permanent establishment by Bergplatz as a result of an internal transfer of funds would not be allowable since a permanent establishment is not a separate entity. As a general rule, third party borrowing is advised in order to ensure that competent interest deductions can be made by non-banks.

There will be no deduction for royalties paid by the permanent establishment to Bergplatz SA – see explanatory note 1 for the treatment of royalty and interest payments.

4.   If the permanent establishment suffers any foreign taxes, double taxation relief may be claimed for both direct and underlying foreign tax paid other than in Bergplatz SA's home state, ie Switzerland (TA 1988 s 794).

5.   A permanent establishment of a non-resident company is outside the definition of close company in TA 1988 s 414. Close trading companies do not, however, suffer any major tax disadvantages, so this exclusion has little practical importance.

Operating through UK subsidiary

6.   If Boris is set up as a UK subsidiary, then in order for the subsidiary to be regarded as UK-resident, it must either be incorporated in the UK (FA 1988 s 66) or its place of central management and control

must be in the UK. Unless this applies, the subsidiary would be treated as a non-resident company and its tax treatment would be the same as that described above for a permanent establishment.

7. If the subsidiary is regarded as UK-resident, then it will be fully liable to UK corporation tax on its worldwide profits in the same way as any other resident company. It should therefore be able to take advantage of the small companies' rate of corporation tax on its anticipated profits (currently 19% on profits up to £150,000 if the subsidiary's only associated company is Bergplatz).

8. The general right to repayment of dividend tax credits to non-residents ceased on 6 April 1999, but this does not affect tax credits repayable under some of the UK's double tax treaties (F (No 2) A 1997 s 30(5)(9)). Dividends paid by a UK subsidiary of a Swiss parent company continue to enjoy repayment of part of the tax credit (under the UK/Switzerland double tax treaty). However, with the lower tax credit of 10%, the amount refunded is now only 0.278% of the net cash dividend (before 6 April 1999, the amount repaid was 6.875% of the dividend paid). The treaty refund must be claimed direct from HMRC's Centre for Non-Residents (CNR).

9. Interest paid by a UK subsidiary for the purposes of a trade is normally deductible as a trading expense. In order to prevent thin capitalisation, interest paid to a non-resident parent company by a UK subsidiary is not, however, deductible to the extent that it exceeds the amount that would have been paid between unconnected companies.

Converting a branch to a subsidiary

10. If Boris is set up in the first place as a permanent establishment, it may subsequently be converted into a UK-resident subsidiary. The transfer of the trade from the non-resident parent to the UK-resident subsidiary will not have any adverse effect on trading results because the acquiring company will take over the losses, capital allowances etc (TA 1988 s 343). Stock can be transferred at the amount paid rather than open market value, providing that amount is taken into account in the subsidiary's profit computation and an election is made by both companies under TA 1988 s 100(1C) within two years after the transfer.

11. As far as capital gains are concerned, where a non-resident company transfers the whole or part of a UK permanent establishment business to a UK resident company in the same group (as defined in TCGA 1992 s 170), the chargeable assets are automatically transferred on a no loss no gain basis (TCGA 1992 s 171).

Societas Europaeas (SE)

12. As Switzerland is not in the EEC, and Societas Europaeas (SE) must have their head office in a member state, Bergplatz SA cannot form an SE. The purpose of the SE is to allow businesses operating in several member states to combine their operations into a single entity without tax cost. The resulting SE would be subject to the tax regime of the country in which its head office is registered. An SE has corporate governance obligations similar to a PLC's, and is required to make provision for employee participation. The minimum issued share capital for an SE is €120,000 including at least £50,000 in sterling in the UK.

Even if Bergplatz SA is operating in a number of EC countries on a large scale, it cannot group those activities into an SE because the commercial bodies forming an SE must have their registered offices in the EU.

Explanatory Notes

Taxation of non-UK resident companies

1. The basis of charge to corporation tax in respect of accounting periods beginning on or after 1 January 2003 is found in FA 2003 ss 148–156 and Schs 25–27 and is as follows:

    (a) A non-UK resident company is to be subject to corporation tax by reference to a 'permanent establishment' in the UK rather than a branch or agency in the UK.

(b) There are specific rules for quantifying the profits attributable to a permanent establishment. For this purpose, the permanent establishment must be treated as a separate enterprise dealing independently with the non-UK resident company.

(c) Mechanisms in the UK tax system for the assessment, collection and recovery of tax, as well as for interest on unpaid tax, will apply to the permanent establishment as a representative of the non-UK resident company.

As was previously the case, a non-UK resident company carrying on a non-trading business in the UK (eg property investment) will not be subject to corporation tax, but may remain liable to income tax on any UK source profits.

What is a permanent establishment?

Non-UK resident companies are chargeable to corporation tax if they carry on a trade in the UK through a permanent establishment. A non-UK resident company will have a permanent establishment in the UK if:

(a) there is a fixed place of business in the UK through which the company's business is carried on; or

(b) company business is carried on in the UK by an agent acting on the company's behalf.

Some examples of a fixed place of business are:

(a) a place of management;

(b) a branch;

(c) an office;

(d) a factory or workshop;

(e) an installation or structure for the exploration of natural resources; and

(f) a building site or construction project.

However, a non-UK resident company will not be treated as having a permanent establishment if its UK activities are 'only of a preparatory or auxiliary character'. This includes:

(a) the use of facilities for the purpose of storage, display or delivery of goods or merchandise belonging to the company;

(b) the maintenance of a stock of goods or merchandise belonging to the company for the purpose of storage, display or delivery;

(c) the maintenance of a stock of goods or merchandise belonging to the company for the purpose of processing by another person; and

(d) purchasing goods or merchandise, or collecting information, for the company.

Where a non-UK resident company previously had a UK branch or agency, it will almost certainly have a permanent establishment under the revised rules. Since the definition of a permanent establishment is somewhat wider than that of a branch or agency, a number of non-UK resident companies not previously subject to corporation tax may subsequently be caught by the revised regime.

Determination of profits attributable to a permanent establishment

One of the difficulties with the previous rules for UK branches or agencies was the absence of clear guidelines for the determination of attributable profits. The new legislation provides a specific basis for the calculation of such profits. However, it should be noted that this can be overridden where there is a treaty between the UK and the non-UK resident company's home jurisdiction which contains a business profits article – ICTA 1988 s 788(3) specifies that treaty provisions take precedence over domestic law.

Under ICTA 1988 s 11(2A), the profits attributable to a permanent establishment for corporation tax purposes are:

(a)   trading income arising directly or indirectly through, or from, the permanent establishment;

(b)   income from property or rights used or held by the permanent establishment; and

(c)   chargeable gains arising on the disposal of assets used in, or for the purposes of, the trade carried on through the permanent establishment or on the disposal of assets used or held by the permanent establishment.

The main assumption to be made in the determination of the relevant profits is to treat the permanent establishment as though it were a separate and distinct enterprise, engaged in the same activities under the same conditions and dealing independently with the rest of the non-UK resident company of which it is a part. This is referred to as the 'separate enterprise principle' and it reflects the wording of Article 7(2) of the OECD Model Tax Convention.

In applying this principle, transactions between the permanent establishment and any other part of the non-UK resident company are deemed to take place on an arm's length basis, unless the non-UK resident company provides the permanent establishment with goods or services which it does not supply to third parties in the ordinary course of its business. In that case, the arm's length rule is not applicable and the quantum of the permanent establishment's expense is the actual cost incurred by the non-UK resident company. In addition, expenses incurred for the purposes of the permanent establishment (even if not incurred or reimbursed by the permanent establishment itself) are deductible, as long as they would have been allowable if incurred by a company resident in the UK.

Two further assumptions underlying the separate enterprise principle are that the permanent establishment is to be treated as having:

(a)   the same credit rating as the non-UK resident company; and

(b)   such equity and loan capital as it could reasonably be expected to have if it were an independent enterprise.

The law then prohibits deductions in arriving at profits chargeable to corporation tax in excess of those which would have arisen on those assumptions.

No deduction is available to a permanent establishment for royalties and similar payments made to any part of the non-UK resident company for the use of intangible assets held by the non-UK resident company (although contributions to the costs of creating such assets are allowable). It is difficult to reconcile this stipulation with the separate enterprise principle – in particular, it is unclear why a permanent establishment, which is treated for tax purposes as an independent entity, should not be allowed to deduct an arm's length charge for the use of an intangible asset.

Similarly, no deduction is available for payments of interest or other financing costs by a permanent establishment to other parts of the non-UK resident company, unless they are payable in respect of borrowings by a permanent establishment in the ordinary course of a financial business such as banking or money-lending carried on by it. On the other hand, a permanent establishment should be entitled to tax relief in respect of interest incurred on its own external borrowings.

There are a number of other special rules for the permanent establishments of overseas banks.

Assessment, collection and recovery of corporation tax (FA 1995 s 126 and Sch 23)

The UK representative of a non-UK resident company is required to deal with all matters connected with the payment of corporation tax (including interest on unpaid tax) as if any obligations and liabilities of the non-UK resident company were its own.

The UK representative is defined as the permanent establishment in the UK through which the non-UK resident company carries on its trade. Should the permanent establishment cease to trade in the UK, it will continue to be the non-UK resident company's UK representative in relation to the profits attributable to the permanent establishment. The UK representative is treated as a distinct and separate person from the non-UK resident company.

Factors affecting choice of UK business medium

2. The main points to be taken into account are explained in the example or in note 1 above, but see notes 7 and 8 below re group relief and no loss no gain transfers for capital gains purposes.

3. For notes on the country of residence for a company see Example 70.

4. Transactions between Bergplatz and a UK-resident subsidiary will be subject to the transfer pricing provisions. Similarly, transactions between Bergplatz and its UK branch must take place on an arm's length basis. For details see Example 69.

5. The decision on whether to operate through a permanent establishment or subsidiary needs to take into account the taxation position in Switzerland. If a permanent establishment makes losses, it may be possible to offset them against the profits of Bergplatz in Switzerland. Permanent establishment profits, on the other hand, may suffer further tax in Switzerland. In contrast, the profits of a UK subsidiary would be insulated from tax in Switzerland until they are repatriated there, usually by means of a dividend.

6. From a company law point of view, there is very little difference in that a UK subsidiary would be subject to the accounts and filing provisions of the Companies Acts, whilst a foreign company with a UK permanent establishment would have to register with the Registrar of Companies and supply information, including the company's accounts, on a regular basis.

Group provisions

7. Where a non-resident company carries on a trade in the UK through a permanent establishment and is itself a member of a group which includes other UK-resident companies or UK branch activities, then it may participate in various 'group reliefs'. It may surrender to other UK-resident members of the group its trading losses etc attributable to its UK trading activities under TA 1988 s 402(3A)(3B). However, any part of a trading loss that is relievable against non-UK profits (not chargeable to UK corporation tax) for foreign tax purposes is excluded from the loss available for surrender (TA 1988 s 403D). This rule applies irrespective of whether an actual foreign tax offset has been claimed – the fact that a loss is potentially relievable is sufficient. Similarly, the UK permanent establishment may claim group relief from other UK-resident members of the group against its profits which are chargeable to UK corporation tax. It is important to note that, following the relaxation in the UK residence requirement for certain group relationships, it does not matter if the non-resident company holding the UK permanent establishment is owned by another non-resident company.

8. A UK permanent establishment can also transfer chargeable assets used in the UK trade to other 75% UK resident subsidiaries and vice versa under the no gain no loss rule in TCGA 1992 s 171. The normal degrouping charge under TCGA 1992 s 179 will arise if the recipient company leaves the group within six years of the intra-group transfer while still holding the asset. The UK permanent establishment can also participate in group rollover relief in respect of assets which have been or are to be used for the purposes of the UK trade under the provisions of TCGA 1992 s 175.

    See Example 54 explanatory note 3 re double tax relief in respect of foreign tax suffered by a UK permanent establishment of a non-resident company.

Treatment of permanent establishment's income

9. Where interest is paid by any UK resident to a UK permanent establishment and the permanent establishment's profits are liable to UK tax, tax does not have to be deducted at source from the interest under TA 1988 s 349(2)(c), even though the permanent establishment is operated by a non-resident company.

10. Where income is charged to income tax rather than corporation tax, for example where a non-resident company's only UK income is property income, it is not subject to the 'loan

relationships' provisions of FA 1996 and interest may be deducted where appropriate, despite the TA 1988 s 337A prohibition of a deduction for interest other than under the loan relationships provisions.

Capital gains

11. There are various capital gains provisions relating to non-residents.

Non-residents are charged on gains if they carry on a trade, profession or vocation through a UK permanent establishment (TCGA 1992 s 10B).

Rollover relief for replacement of business assets is available only where the replacement asset is within the charge to UK tax, ie acquired for the purpose of the UK trade (TCGA 1992 s 159). Group rollover relief may also be available (see explanatory note 8) and assets can be transferred to other UK-resident companies or UK permanent establishments under the no gain no loss rule in TCGA 1992 s 171.

Where an asset ceases to be a chargeable asset, either because the UK permanent establishment's business ceases, or because the asset is removed from the UK charge to tax, the asset is treated as disposed of and reacquired at market value, thus triggering a tax charge (TCGA 1992 s 25).

TCGA 1992 s 25 does not apply to the transfer of a UK permanent establishment by a non-resident company to another company under TCGA 1992 s 171 (intra-group disposal) or s 139 (company reconstruction). Nor does it apply to the transfer of a UK trade from one company resident in an EU country to another EU resident company in exchange for securities (including shares). Providing the conditions are satisfied, such transfers are made on a no loss no gain basis (TCGA 1992 s 140A).

Recovery of unpaid tax from other group companies etc

12. There are provisions in TCGA 1992 s 190 to the effect that if a non-resident company operating through a UK permanent establishment fails to pay the corporation tax on a chargeable gain within six months after the due date, the tax may be recovered from another company in the same 51% group or from a controlling director.

There are separate provisions in FA 2000 s 98 and Sch 28 enabling *any* corporation tax due from a non-resident company that remains unpaid after six months to be collected from another company in the same group or (to the appropriate extent) from a member of a consortium owning the non-resident company.

Societas Europaeas (SE)

13. The concept of the European company was created by Council Regulation (EC) No 2157/2001 of 8 October 2001, and made possible in the UK by SI No 2326/2004. The effective date of this was 8 October 2004, and it has been possible to set up this new legal entity since December 2004. Most of the tax provisions relating to it have effect from 1 April 2005.

The SE is intended for large organisations with operations in a number of member states. The legislation covering the formation and governance of SEs has many parallels with that of Plcs, and accounting requirements are the same as a Plc's. The SE is required to have a minimum amount of subscribed share capital to the equivalent of at least €120,000 (including at least £50,000 in the UK). Its accounts can be kept in any currency.

An SE cannot be registered and brought into existence until either an agreement has been reached for employee involvement in company decisions, or until it is confirmed that the standard rules of the jurisdiction for employee involvement apply. It will be possible for an SE registered in one member state to move to another, unlike a Plc.

It is envisaged that SEs will be formed by merger of the existing companies in different member states, by transformation of a PLC into an SE, or by the formation of subsidiaries by companies registered in the EC. The commercial bodies forming an SE must have their registered offices in the EU, and a presence in more than one member state.

FA 2005 ss 51–65 amended existing tax legislation to ensure that a UK company's decision to merge with a company in another member state to form an SE is not disadvantaged or driven by tax considerations. These sections deal with chargeable gains, intangibles, loan relationships, derivative contracts, capital allowances and stamp duty reserve tax, giving certainty to the tax treatment of a number of transactions, and making them tax neutral. They are designed to allow UK businesses to take advantage of the new corporate vehicle if they so wish.

Woodhouse Eaves Limited is a manufacturing company preparing accounts to 31 March, but its system of management accounting enables it accurately to predict its result for the year after the result shown by the three quarters' accounts to 31 December is known.

Harold and Frank are the only two directors, owning between them the entire issued share capital. There are no associated companies.

The company has a money purchase pension scheme for the directors and a designated stakeholder pension scheme for the workforce.

The trading profit for the year ending 31 March 2007, after deducting capital allowances, is expected to be £400,000, and to be higher in the following year.

Earlier profits have been depleted by the capital allowances resulting from a substantial plant investment programme, but the profits for corporation tax purposes for the year to 31 March 2006 were £130,000. The company has not paid any dividends for that year and does not anticipate paying a dividend in 2007. The company paid £20,000 to the pension scheme for the directors in the year to 31 March 2006.

It has been suggested to Harold and Frank that substantial increased payments could be made to the pension scheme for the directors.

There is not expected to be any lack of cash within the company following the completion of the plant investment programme and the directors feel that this would be a good opportunity to make up for the years where they have not been contributing significant amounts to a pension scheme, by not only paying the first of the intended regular annual contributions but also a substantial additional amount.

Illustrate how relief for the contributions in the year to 31 March 2007 will be given, assuming the payment of an annual premium of £260,000 and an additional contribution of an equivalent or a smaller amount.

Provided a pension scheme is registered by HMRC through the HMRC Savings, Pensions, Share Schemes (IR SPSS), a contribution paid by the employer is deductible in computing the trading profits of the chargeable period in which it is paid (FA 2004 s 196).

In addition to normal contributions, companies may make special contributions to a registered scheme, for example to provide benefits for back service, to augment benefits already secured or to make up an actuarial deficiency in the fund. Where large contributions are paid, HMRC may require that the deduction in computing profits is to be spread forward over a period of years (FA 2004 s 197). Forward spreading is not, however, required for excess contributions that, in total, are less than £500,000 or that do not exceed 210% of the amount contributed in the previous chargeable period. Any amount in excess of 110% of the amount contributed in the previous chargeable period is known as the 'relevant excess contribution'. Relevant excess contributions are normally spread evenly over a period of up to four years as follows, commencing in the year of payment:

Relevant excess contributions	*Spread over*
£500,000 or more but less than £1,000,000	2 years
£1,000,000 or more but less than £2,000,000	3 years
£2,000,000 or more	4 years

(See note 2 below for periods of other than one year)

Once determined, the period of spread will not be varied because of subsequent fluctuations in contribution(s) or the payment of further large contributions in later years. If the trade ceases relevant excess contributions that have not been allowed by the time the trade ceases will normally be allowed in that period, or by election re-apportioned over the period since they were paid. (FA 2004 s 198).

The position if a regular contribution of £260,000 and an additional contribution of the same amount is paid in the year to 31 March 2007 will be:

	£	£
Anticipated profit for the year		400,000
Pension scheme contributions:		
Normal	260,000	
Additional	260,000	520,000
Resulting trading loss		(120,000)
Carry back against profits of year to 31 March 2005		120,000

If the additional contribution was more than £262,000, it would reduce the amount allowed against the profits of the year to 31 March 2007 to one half of the relevant excess contribution plus 110% of the amount contributed in the previous year. A pension contribution of (£260,000 + £265,000) £525,000 would give an allowable deduction of:

		£
Paid in year to 31 March 2006		20,000
Paid in year to 31 March 2007		525,000
Less 110% of year to 31 March 2006		22,000
'relevant excess contribution' which exceeds:		503,000
210% of year to 31 March 2006	£42,000	
and	£500,000	
Allowed in year to 31 March 2008 – one half		251,500
		251,500
110% of year to 31 March 2006		22,000
Allowed in year to 31 March 2007		273,500

In order to qualify for relief, the pension contributions must be paid in the relevant period and not merely provided for in the accounts.

The tax saved as a result of making the contribution would be:

	£	£
Year to 31 March 2007		
300,000 @ 19%	57,000	
100,000 @ 32.75%	32,750	89,750
Year to 31 March 2006		
Tax on original profit, 130,000 @ 19%	24,700	
Tax on revised profit, 10,000 @ 0%	–	
Repayment		24,700
Total saving		114,450

giving effective rate of tax relief on £520,000 of 22.01% (114,450/520,000).

The company needs to consider the anticipated marginal tax rates in deciding when to make additional contributions. For periods before 31 March 2006 the first £10,000 of profits is taxed at a nil rate. The 19% band runs to £300,000 with a marginal rate of 32.75% on the next £1,200,000. See Example 52 for comparisons of different loss claims.

Although a premium of £520,000 is extremely tax efficient for Woodhouse Eaves Limited the same cannot be said when considering the tax position of the two directors, Harold and Frank.

Assuming that neither director makes any other pension contribution in the year to 5 April 2007 and that the payments are allocated equally between the two directors then each will have a 'pension input' in respect of the Woodhouse Eaves Ltd scheme of:

		£
½ × £520,000	=	260,000
Annual limit for 2006/07		215,000
Excess		45,000
Liable to an 'annual allowance charge' of 40%	=	£18,000

Which would require a bonus (assuming the director is liable to tax at 40%) of:

		£
Gross bonus		30,508
Less tax at 40%	12,203	
NI at 1%	305	12,508
Net to meet tax liability		18,000

and the employer would have a further liability to employer NI of 12.8% × £30,508 = £3,905 giving a cost to the company of (£30,508 + 3,905 =) £34,413 for each director, reduced by the value of the corporation tax relief.

	£	
Cost of bonus (2 × £34.413)	68,826	
Loss carried back to y/e 31 March 2006	10,000	@ 0%
Loss carried forward to y/e 31 March 2008	58,826	@ 32.75%

It would be more sensible to restrict the additional pension contributions so that the 'total pension input' for each director does not exceed £215,000.

On total contributions of £430,000 the corporation tax position would be:

			£
Anticipated profit for the year			400,000
Pension scheme contributions			430,000
Resulting trading loss			30,000
Carry back against profits of year to 31 March 2006			30,000

		£	
The tax then saved would be:			
Year to 31 March 2007			
300,000 @ 19%		57,000	
100,000 @ 32.75%		32,750	89,750
Year to 31 March 2006			
Tax on original profit	130,000 @ 19%	24,700	
Tax on revised profit	100,000 @ 19%	19,000	5,700
Total saving			94,450

giving effective rate of tax relief on £430,000 of 21.97%, without giving £36,000 of additional tax liability in the hands of the directors or the costs of extracting funds from the company to meet that additional liability.

Explanatory Notes

Occupational pensions from 6 April 2006

1. From 6 April 2006 the previous tax provisions relating to occupational and personal pension schemes have been replaced by a single scheme for all registered pension schemes. The limits on contributions, the earnings cap, the 2/3rds of final remuneration limit for occupational schemes, and the lump sum restrictions are no longer relevant. Occupational schemes are able to offer flexible retirement, enabling employees to draw benefits while continuing to work for the employer (FA 2004 part 4). See Example 37 for the new provisions.

2. Individuals are able to contribute to as many schemes as they wish. There are no provisions for carrying contributions back or forward. Pension providers are able to invest in most types of investment, excluding residential property and tangible moveable property if the policyholder or member can influence the investment decisions of the fund (FA 2004 Sch 29A inserted by FA 2006). The minimum pension age will rise from 50 to 55 on 6 April 2010 (earlier retirement still being permitted on ill health grounds).

    The new regime has two key features:

    -   A single lifetime allowance restricting the amount of pension savings that can benefit from tax relief, set at £1.5 million for 2006/07, rising to £1.6 million for 2007/08, £1.65 million for 2008/09, £1.75 million for 2009/10 and £1.8 million for 2010/11. If benefits are withdrawn in excess of the allowance, tax will be charged on the excess at 55%.

    -   An annual allowance for 'total pension inputs', ie contributions paid to money purchase schemes and/or increases in accrued benefits under defined benefit (final salary) schemes. The allowance starts at £215,000 for 2006/07 and increases at £10,000 a year for each of the next four years, reaching £255,000 for 2010/11. If total pension inputs exceed the annual allowance, tax is charged at 40% on the excess.

    Both the lifetime and annual allowances will be reviewed every five years.

    There is no limit on the contributions an individual may make, but tax relief is only given on contributions up to the higher of 100% of relevant earnings and £3,600 (the £3,600 limit applying to a scheme where contributions are paid net of basic rate tax).

All schemes (subject to their own rules) will be able to offer a tax-free lump sum of up to 25% of the fund, subject to an overriding maximum of 25% of the lifetime allowance.

The limit on contributions by employers is the requirement that the expenditure is incurred wholly and exclusively for the purpose of the business. This will normally mean that all contributions paid in the chargeable period will be deductible (FA 2004 s 196). (See HMRC manuals at BIM 46001 for further guidance)

In order for pension contributions paid to be allowable they must form part of a normal remuneration package. They are not considered as a stand-alone amount. It follows that a salary sacrifice will not prevent a tax deduction. Contributions will be allowable if the overall salary package is a normal commercial amount.

It is likely that HMRC will disallow any amount identifiable as relating to a non-trade purpose, for example as part of arrangements to dispose of a business where the payment represents part of the sale proceeds, or of exceptional size. This would be of issue if the employer was not carrying on a trade eg property holding company.

The main focus of disallowances is likely to be in respect of directors who are controlling shareholders or their relatives/friends, and where the salary package has been significantly increased, eg where funds previously taken as dividends are now taken as a pension contribution.

In the case of Harold and Frank they run a highly profitable trading company. HMRC would normally accept a remuneration package of any amount that could be funded by the efforts of the controlling directors. It follows that a total package, that includes a bonus for earlier years, even though paid mainly as a pension will be a commercial amount incurred 'wholly and exclusively' for the purpose of the business. It is unlikely that a pension contribution of £520,000 or less would be challenged in this set of circumstances.

Where large contributions are made the relief may be spread. This applies where contributions are made in two consecutive chargeable periods and the amount paid in the current period exceeds 210% of the amount in the previous period. The excess over 110% is known as the 'relevant excess contribution' and is then subject to the following rules (FA 2004 s 197)

(1) If the excess is less than £500,000   no restriction applies.
(2) If the excess is between £500,000 and £999,999   – ½ allowed in current period
                                                                 ½ allowed in following period.
(3) If the excess is between £1,000,000 and £1,999,999   – ⅓ allowed in current period
                                                                 ⅓ allowed in next period
                                                                 ⅓ allowed in following period.
(4) If the excess is £2,000,000 or more   – ¼ allowed in current period
                                                                 ¼ allowed in each of the following
                                                                 three periods.

Where the previous and current chargeable periods are not of equal length the amount paid in the previous chargeable period is adjusted by applying the fraction

$$\text{Contribution in previous period} \times \frac{\text{Days in current chargeable period}}{\text{Days in previous chargeable period.}} = \text{relevant contribution}$$

If the employer ceases trading before relief has been fully given for the spread contributions then the unrelieved contributions are deductible in the period of cessation or spread evenly over the period that starts on the first day of the current chargeable period (ie the period of actual payment) and ends on the date of cessation (FA 2004 s 198).

For detailed notes on the new pensions regime and transitional rules to preserve existing rights see Example 37.

Self-administered schemes

3. Employers may use an insurance company to provide a registered pension scheme.

    Employers can instead (or also) establish under trust a registered self-administered scheme, using an insurance company to cover death in service benefits, but receiving the pension premiums into a fund under the control of trustees, one of whom must be an appropriately qualified person, referred to as the pensioneer trustee. This may be done in conjunction with an insurance company, actuary or professional trustees.

    This gives the employers flexibility over the investment of the fund pending its being required to pay the retirement benefits, but the employer must always remember that the fund is under the control of the trustees and that it must be sufficiently liquid at the right time to provide the retirement benefits.

    The insurance company in the first case, and the pensioneer trustee in the second, will structure the scheme and register it with HMRC.

Pension splitting on divorce

4. The legislation was changed from 1 December 2000 to enable a share in pension rights to be transferred on divorce (FA 1999 s 79 and Sch 10). See Example 37 explanatory note 23 for details.

Self-assessment

5. Trustees of registered pension schemes, other than insured schemes, are within the scope of self-assessment, and trustees are required to notify HMRC by 5 October following the tax year if they have a liability to tax and do not receive a return. The same self-assessment rules and time limits apply to trusts as for individuals. Pension fund trustees may complete returns on an accounting year basis and accounts should accompany the return.

    Self-assessment does not apply to scheme administrators (although they may be the same people as the trustees), who have separate responsibility for notifying liability on various chargeable events. HMRC will issue assessments to collect the tax due.

    See Revenue Tax Bulletin February 1999 for further details.

Other pension points

6. As all schemes now operate under the same legislation the notes appended to Example 37 apply equally to company pension schemes. For detailed notes on:

Pension inputs	See explanatory note 2
Annual allowance —	
excess contributions	note 3
Tax relief on members' contributions	note 4
Lifetime limit	note 5
Unsecured pensions	note 6
Alternatively secured pensions	note 7
Transitional provisions	note 8
Unapproved retirement benefit schemes	note 9
Death in service benefits	note 10
Commutation of trivial pensions	note 11
Retirement annuity contracts and personal pension contracts	note 12
Relief for pension premiums	note 13
National insurance contributions	note 14
Personal losses	note 15
Contracting out of S2P	note 16
SERPS	note 17
Employer contributions	note 18
Commission on pension policies	note 19

73.1 BASIS OF CHARGE, PERSONS LIABLE, EXEMPTIONS CONNECTED PERSONS, CHARGEABLE AND EXEMPT ASSETS

(a)   Give a brief outline of the basis of charge to capital gains tax, stating:

   (i)   the main persons chargeable to capital gains tax, and how it is charged;

   (ii)   how gains are measured;

   (iii)   what events trigger a charge to tax.

(b)   Explain the effect of a taxpayer's country of residence on his liability to capital gains tax.

(c)   Explain the tax treatment of an individual who is temporarily resident outside the UK.

(d)   (i)   State, in the context of capital gains tax, what is meant by the term 'connected persons'.

   (ii)   Explain what special considerations apply when computing the chargeable gain or allowable loss arising on a disposal between a brother and his sister (both being adult).

(e)   Capital gains tax is assessed on chargeable gains accruing to a person on the disposal of assets.

   (i)   Indicate which assets are exempt from capital gains tax.

   (ii)   Explain, where an asset is disposed of under a contract, how the date of the disposal is determined.

   (iii)   Explain how the date of a capital gains tax chargeable event is fixed where there is not a disposal under a contract.

(a)   **Basis of charge to capital gains tax**

    (i)   *Who is liable to tax*

Individuals, personal representatives and trustees are liable to capital gains tax. This is a separate tax from tax on income, although for individuals it is calculated by adding taxable gains as the 'top slice' of the income tax calculation.

Taper relief is given to relieve gains for periods after 5 April 1998. Taper relief reduces the taxable gain remaining after all other reliefs. This includes indexation allowance where the asset was acquired prior to April 1998. The amount remaining chargeable after taper relief is then reduced by an annual exemption.

Charities are exempt from tax on gains, provided that they use the money for charitable purposes. Pension funds are exempt from tax on gains realised for the benefit of pensioners.

Certain investment vehicles such as authorised unit trusts and investment trusts, open-ended investment companies and venture capital trusts are exempt from tax on gains made on their investment assets.

Companies pay corporation tax on gains, not capital gains tax. For details of the differences, see Example 85.

    (ii)   *How gains are measured*

Capital gains tax (or corporation tax on chargeable gains) is a tax on increases in value, not on cash profits. If a disposal or acquisition is made other than as a bargain at arm's length, the market value of the asset is used instead of any actual consideration (TCGA 1992 s 17). This means that the gain which has accrued during a person's ownership is charged when they dispose of the asset, even if they paid nothing for it (on a gift or inheritance) or receive nothing for it (on a gift).

    (iii)   *Chargeable events*

The following events trigger a charge to tax on gains:

1.   Disposal or part disposal of the asset by sale at arm's length, sale at undervalue, or gift (s 21).

2.   Exchange of one asset for another.

3.   Capital sums derived from an asset (s 22), for example insurance proceeds arising when an asset is damaged.

4.   Creation of rights over an asset (s 21(2)(b)).

The following events do not trigger a charge to tax on gains:

1.   Disposal of an asset which is exempt.

2.   Disposal by an exempt person.

3.   Gifts to charity and registered community amateur sports clubs (from 6 April 2002) (s 257 and FA 2002 s 58 and Sch 18).

4.   Disposals between spouses (s 58) or companies within a 75% group (s 171).

5.   Disposals on death (s 62).

6.   Reorganisation of share capital (ss 127–136).

In addition, many reliefs apply to reduce or defer the charge in certain circumstances.

(b) **Effect of residence on capital gains tax liability**

An individual is liable to capital gains tax if he is resident or ordinarily resident in the UK (TCGA 1992 s 2). If he is also domiciled in the UK he is liable on all gains wherever they arise. If domiciled abroad he is liable on gains arising in or remitted to the UK (s 12). For the meaning of residence, ordinary residence and domicile see Example 8. Non-residents who are not ordinarily resident in the UK are not liable to capital gains tax unless they carry on business in the UK through a permanent establishment. In that event they are liable to tax on gains arising on the disposal of business assets in the UK (s 10), and they are also liable if the assets are removed from the UK, or if the permanent establishment business ceases (s 25) (see Example 71).

(c) **Temporary non-residence**

Special rules apply to those who become 'temporarily' non-resident (TCGA 1992 s 10A). Someone who has been resident or ordinarily resident in the UK for any part of at least four of the previous seven tax years, and becomes not resident and not ordinarily resident for less than five tax years, will be liable to tax on gains on assets owned before they left the UK. All such gains in the tax year of departure will be taxed for that year, and assessments in respect of such gains may be made up to two years after the 31 January following the tax year of return. Later gains on such assets during the period of absence will be taxed in the year when the person again resumes UK residence. Losses will be allowed on the same basis as gains are taxed. Gains on assets acquired while the individual was resident abroad that are realised in the years between the tax year of departure and the tax year of return are exempt (subject to certain anti-avoidance provisions). With effect from 16 March 2005, F (No 2) A 2005 introduced anti-avoidance measures which counter the use of double tax treaties to establish CGT non-residence for short periods of absence.

Under Revenue Concession D2, it is possible in certain circumstances to split the tax year, and to regard the taxpayer as resident for part and not resident for part. Where this treatment applies, gains in the non-resident part are not charged, and losses in the non-resident part are not allowed. Split year treatment applies:

- to those leaving the UK, only if they have been not resident in the UK for four of the last seven years (ie they are not caught by the provision on gains realised abroad, as described above);

- to those coming to the UK, only if they have been not resident in the UK for the whole of the five tax years up to the tax year of return.

This means that the split year treatment is generally available (on both arriving and leaving) to foreign people coming to the UK and leaving after a brief period; but it is not generally available (on either leaving or arriving) to UK residents who go abroad for a brief period and then return. Such a person must wait until 6 April following departure to make a disposal on which the gain will be exempt (albeit possibly subject to a charge on re-entry), and must make disposals by 5 April before returning (and will then escape tax if the assets disposed of were not owned at the time of departure).

The re-entry charge was introduced for taxpayers who became non-resident on or after 17 March 1998. Revenue Concession D2 was also more generous before that date.

(d) **Connected persons**

(i) The term 'connected persons' for capital gains tax is defined as follows (TCGA 1992 s 286):

A person is connected with his or her spouse/civil partner, with his or his spouse's/civil partner's close relatives (ie brothers, sisters, ancestors, lineal descendants) and relatives' spouses/civil partners, and with business partners and their spouses/civil partners and relatives (except in relation to normal commercial acquisitions and disposals of partnership assets).

If a person is trustee of a settlement, he is connected with the settlor (if an individual) and with any person connected with the settlor. The transfer of property into settlement is a connected persons transaction, because the trustees become connected with the settlor at the time the settlement is created. After the settlor's death, the trustees are no longer connected with those who were connected with the settlor.

Companies under the same control are connected with each other and with the person controlling them.

(ii) In computing the chargeable gain or allowable loss arising on a disposal between adult brother and sister, the disposal is deemed to be at open market value (TCGA 1992 ss 17 and 18).

If the disposal is by way of gift and it gives rise to a chargeable gain, and either the asset is a qualifying business asset or the gift is a transfer which is immediately chargeable to inheritance tax, a claim may be made for the gain not to be charged, but to be treated as reducing the acquisition cost of the donee, so that the donee's base cost is the cost to the donor plus the indexation allowance to date or to April 1998 if earlier. (This relief is not confined to connected person transactions (TCGA 1992 ss 165 and 260 – see Examples 82 and 84 for details and certain restrictions introduced by Finance Act 2004).) Taper relief will be based on the *donee's* period of ownership (see Example 74 part (a)(i)).

If the disposal gives rise to an allowable loss, the loss may not be set against general gains, but only against a gain made on a later transaction with the same connected person (see Example 96 explanatory note 11 for the order in which losses may be used up) (TCGA 1992 s 18).

(e) **Exemptions; date of disposal**

(i) Assets which will not give rise to capital gains tax on disposal (and for which no relief is available for capital losses) are as follows (references are to TCGA 1992):

1. Private motor cars (s 263) (see explanatory note 10).

2. Foreign currency for an individual's own spending and maintenance of assets abroad (s 269).

3. British Government securities and qualifying corporate bonds (s 115).

4. Life policies in the hands of the original holder or beneficiaries (s 210).

5. Chattels (ie tangible movable property) with a predictable useful life not exceeding fifty years, except where they are used in a business and capital allowances have been or could have been claimed (s 45). Plant and machinery is always regarded as having a predictable life of less than 50 years (even if it is a collector's item that is in fact much older) (s 44) (see explanatory note 10).

6. Decorations for valour acquired otherwise than for money or money's worth (s 268).

7. Bettings, pools and lottery winnings and winnings from games with prizes (s 51).

8. Compensation or damages for personal or professional wrong or injury (s 51) (see explanatory note 13).

9. Compensation for mis-sold personal pensions (FA 1996 s 148) (see Example 72 explanatory note 20).

10. National Savings Certificates and premium bonds (s 121). (The terminal bonus under a Save As You Earn contract is also exempt from all taxation (s 271(4) & ITTOIA 2005 ss 702–703).)

11. The taxpayer's only or main residence (ss 222–226). Part of the gain may be chargeable in certain circumstances – for details see Example 82.

12. Gifts of assets that are considered by the Treasury to be of pre-eminent national, historic or scientific interest, but breach of any conditions imposed will nullify the exemption (s 258).

13. Gifts to charities and registered community amateur sports clubs (from 6 April 2002) (s 257 and FA 2002 s 58 and Sch 18) (see Example 91).

14. Gifts of land to registered housing associations (s 259).

15. Shares in respect of which business expansion scheme relief has been given and not withdrawn (s 150).

16. Shares which qualified for enterprise investment scheme relief which have been held for three years (five years where shares issued before 6 April 2000), although losses remain allowable (s 150A).

17. Investments held through a Personal Equity Plan or Individual Savings Account (s 151).

18. Shares in a qualifying venture capital trust (s 151A).

19. A company's 'substantial shareholding' in another company (from 1 April 2002 – see Example 65).

(ii) Where an asset is disposed of under a contract, the date of disposal is the contract date, unless the contract is conditional, in which case the date of disposal is the date when the condition is satisfied (TCGA 1992 s 28).

(iii) Where a gain is charged on a capital sum derived from an asset, the time of disposal is the date of receipt of that sum (s 22(2)).

If an asset is destroyed without compensation, the disposal occurs on the date of destruction (s 24(1)).

An estate duty case (Re Rose) established that a gift of shares takes place when the donor has done everything necessary to make the gift happen (in this case, handing over a signed transfer form and the share certificate).

Explanatory Notes

Scope of capital gains tax

1. Capital gains tax was introduced on 6 April 1965 to charge tax on gains arising on the disposal of assets on or after that date. Companies are charged to corporation tax on their gains rather than capital gains tax as indicated in part (a) of the example (see Example 48 explanatory note 10).

Technically, the charge covers all assets unless the *gain* is specifically exempt, and the assets themselves are not classified as either chargeable or exempt. It is, however, more usual and convenient to use the terms chargeable assets and exempt assets. The main body of capital gains legislation is the Taxation of Chargeable Gains Act 1992 (TCGA 1992) and references are to that Act unless otherwise stated.

In general the same rules apply for calculating allowable capital losses as for chargeable gains (ss 15, 16). Where losses exceed gains of the same chargeable period the excess is carried forward to set against later gains. Special rules apply to losses on transactions between connected persons, as indicated in part (d)(ii) of the example. For the treatment of losses carried forward and the interaction with the annual exemption and taper relief see Example 74. See also Example 96 explanatory note 11.

2. Where an asset is not a chargeable asset, then neither a chargeable gain nor allowable loss can arise (ss 15, 16). All forms of property, including options, debts and intangible property, any currency

other than sterling, and assets created by the person disposing of them, eg goodwill, are chargeable assets unless they are specifically exempt, either wholly or in part (s 21) or, in the case of companies, are covered by the loan relationships rules (see Example 62) or intangible assets rules (see Example 65). Special provisions apply to taxpayers other than companies in respect of the loss of money lent. For details see Example 96 explanatory note 5.

3.   Taxpayers other than companies may reduce gains by taper relief and an annual exemption. Different rates of taper relief apply to business and non-business assets. Until FA 1998, indexation allowance was available to reduce gains. From April 1998 no further indexation allowance is available to taxpayers other than companies. Taper relief, indexation allowance and the annual exemption are dealt with in Example 74.

Meaning of 'disposal'

4.   A gift of an asset is normally treated as a disposal at open market value (see Example 84 explanatory note 1). A disposal includes a part disposal, and there is also a disposal when a capital sum is derived from an asset even though no asset is acquired by the person paying the capital sum, the time of disposal being the time when the capital sum is received (s 22). This particularly applies to compensation, including insurance proceeds, for loss of or damage to an asset (subject to what is said in Example 96 explanatory notes 6 and 7), and to compensation for surrendering rights. Where, however, *statutory* compensation is paid, for example to business tenants under the Landlord and Tenant Act 1954, it is exempt (see Revenue's Tax Bulletin April 1996 for the circumstances in which such an exemption will apply). Certain other compensation is exempt (see items 8 and 9 of part (e)(i) of the example and explanatory note 13).

Cashbacks

5.   HMRC has stated its view on the treatment of 'cashbacks' offered as inducements to purchase goods, services or financial products (for example in connection with a mortgage or car purchase). Such payments are not regarded as deriving from an asset and are exempt from capital gains tax. An income tax liability may, however, arise if the payments are received by a business, or by an employee by reason of his employment (SP 4/97).

Building society and other mergers, conversions etc

6.   Payments to account holders on building society *mergers* are regarded by HMRC as being income payments and are paid net of 20% tax. Following the cases of Foster v Williams and Horan v Williams heard by the Special Commissioners in 1997, HMRC accepts that the treatment of cash payments on building society *takeovers and conversions* is that amounts received by *depositors* (and presumably by borrowers) are wholly exempt from tax, and gains on amounts received by *shareholders* are taxable but may be reduced by any available indexation allowance on the account balance. The gain does not, however, qualify for taper relief (s 214C). Where account balances have fluctuated frequently, the calculation of the indexation allowance is very complicated. HMRC will, if asked, use their computer programs to produce the figures for taxpayers who are unable to produce the figures for their tax returns themselves. Calculations are not, however, necessary, where the payment is covered by the annual exemption (taking into account any other capital gains in the tax year).

Where *shares* are received in a building society conversion or takeover, there is no capital gains liability at that time and they are treated as acquired for the amount paid for them. Where they are issued free, there is no allowable cost for a future disposal and therefore no indexation allowance (s 217), but taper relief is available, based on the time since the shares were acquired (Sch A1.18).

Some mutual insurance companies have also converted into companies, and the tax treatment depends on the facts of the particular case (see Revenue's Tax Bulletin April 1998). For both building society and insurance company conversions, it was possible to avoid future capital gains tax on shares issued on the conversion by transferring the shares to a personal equity plan, but only up to 5 April 1999. Shares cannot be transferred in this way into an Individual Savings Account – see Example 93 part (a) note 8.

Where shares are issued to the members of the mutual organisation, and are then exchanged for loan notes, the capital gain is 'frozen' at the date of the exchange and deferred until the loan notes are encashed. Because taper relief is given only for the period since the shares were acquired, none will be available, because the shares are only owned for the short period between their creation and the exchange. However, the encashment of the loan notes over a period of years enables the holder to set several annual exemptions against the capital gain.

Connected persons

7. All transactions between connected persons, or not at arm's length, are regarded as being made at open market value. This does not apply to transactions between spouses/members of a registered civil partnership which are not normally chargeable (see Example 76), nor to normal commercial transactions between partners, where HMRC will accept the value placed thereon by the partners, eg goodwill on admission of a new partner, where this is dictated by commercial terms and not because of the family relationship between the partners.

8. In general, market value means the price that might reasonably be expected on a sale in the open market (s 272). Quoted securities are valued at the *lower* of one-quarter up from the lower of the quoted prices and halfway between the lowest and highest recorded bargains. Unit trust holdings are valued only at the bid price, not 'quarter up' (s 272(5)). In valuing unquoted securities it is assumed that all relevant information is available to the prospective purchaser (s 273). Where the value of an asset has been ascertained for inheritance tax on a death, that value is regarded as the market value at death for capital gains tax (s 274), and whoever acquires the asset acquires it at that value. See Example 76(c) for further consideration of this rule.

9. Where someone disposes of assets on different occasions within a period of six years to one or more persons connected with him, and their value taken together is higher than their separate values, then the disposal value for each of the transactions is a proportionate part of the aggregate value, and all necessary adjustments will be made to earlier tax charges (ss 19 & 20).

See Example 96 explanatory note 11 re the possible effect on connected persons of the self-assessment rules for setting off losses brought forward.

Exemptions

10. The exemption for private motor cars applies to 'a mechanically propelled road vehicle constructed or adapted for the carriage of passengers, except for a vehicle of a type not commonly used as a private vehicle and unsuitable to be so used'. It therefore covers veteran and vintage cars (except one-seater models), and is available whether or not the cars are used in a business. So profits on the disposal of cars are either trading profits if the seller is carrying out 'an adventure in the nature of trade' or are exempt. A one seater car that is not covered by the 'cars' exemption, and also any other 'plant or machinery', would be exempt as a wasting chattel if it was disposed of by an investor rather than a trader, even if it was a collector's item (ss 44 & 45). The chattels exemption therefore covers items such as antique clocks and watches.

11. For details on British Government securities and qualifying corporate bonds see Example 81.

12. Where chattels are used in a business, and/or are non-wasting chattels, gains are exempt if the chattel is sold for £6,000 or less (s 262). For details see Example 75 explanatory note 6.

13. There is a complete exemption for 'compensation or damages for any wrong or injury suffered by an individual in his person or in his profession or vocation'. HMRC considers that 'in his person' has a wide definition extending beyond physical injury, so that damages or compensation for 'distress,

embarrassment, loss of reputation or dignity' such as unfair discrimination are not chargeable. The same exemption applies to wrong or injury suffered in a professional capacity, such as libel or defamation.

Where compensation is for personal injury, and it is received by way of periodical payments, or where interest is payable on the compensation, such payments are income rather than capital, but they are similarly exempt from income tax – ITTOIA 2005 ss 731, 732, 751.

Strictly, any right to compensation or damages not covered by the exemption is taxable. By Concession D33, however, damages are treated as derived from any underlying assets (and therefore exempt, taxable or partly taxable depending on the extent to which the underlying asset is exempt or taxable). For example, compensation for professional negligence that resulted in damage to a building would be treated as outlined in Example 96 explanatory note 6. By Concession D50, certain compensation from foreign governments for property lost or confiscated is exempt.

Contracts

14.   In the case of Jerome v Kelly (HL 2004), the House of Lords had to examine the effect of the contract disposal rule in TCGA 1992 s 28. Mr Jerome made a disposal of land which, for the purposes of illustration, can be simplified as follows:

-   in tax year 1, J signed a contract to sell the land, for delivery in tax year 3;

-   in tax year 2, J assigned the land (subject to the contract for sale) to a foreign trust;

-   in tax year 3, the trustees completed the sale and received the consideration.

HMRC assessed the gain on disposal on J in tax year 1. He appealed, contending that s 28 could only fix the time of disposal, but it could not change the identity of the person who made that disposal – in this case, the trustees. In the High Court, Park J agreed with this argument, and suggested that HMRC should have assessed J on his disposal to the trustees in year 2.

The Court of Appeal restored the traditional understanding of the effect of s 28. The asset was disposed of under a contract; the signing of that contract fixed not only the time of disposal, but also the identity of the seller.

The House of Lords' view was that s 28(1) was no more than a timing provision and did not deem the contract to be a disposal. Furthermore, Parliament should not be attributed as having intended to impose a liability on someone who would not be treated as having made a disposal under the scheme for taxing the disposal of assets held on trust. They allowed the taxpayer's appeal and held that the disposal was made by the foreign trust.

Subject to further legislative changes, this may leave scope for some limited post-transaction planning in cases where there is a period between entering into a contract for disposal and the executing of the contract (completion). For example, a husband agrees a contract and then realises that his wife has unrelieved losses brought forward. The husband could transfer the land subject to the uncompleted contract.

Date of disposal

15.   A Special Commissioner's hearing, A & S Smith v CIR SpC 388, considered whether a contract was conditional on giving vacant possession. Mr & Mrs Smith owned a farm where they carried on their business as farmers. They received an offer and payment for the farm in 1991. However they remained in occupation until 31 October 1999. They paid rent from 1 February 1992. The letter of offer placed an obligation on the sellers 'to flit and remove from the subjects (ie farm property) at 1 February 1992 or such other date on which the sellers are entitled to take occupation of their new farm . . .'. The taxpayers tried to argue that this made the contract conditional, so the time of disposal was when the condition (the purchase of the new farm) was satisfied. The Commissioner rejected this argument.

(a)   (i)   Indicate the annual exemption available for 2006/07, outline the provisions of TCGA 1992 s 2A and Sch A1 relating to taper relief, and indicate how the two interact where there are losses brought forward.

    (ii)   Show how taper relief should be allocated assuming that the following gains arise in a tax year and that there are allowable losses of £10,000:

Gains net of indexation allowance	*Taper relief available*
£	
4,000	–
15,000	10%
20,000	50%

    (iii)   Show the treatment of the following gains and losses (which are after taking indexation allowance into account) for a taxpayer who had no losses brought forward at 6 April 1998:

	Gains	*Losses*	*Annual exemption*
	£	£	£
1998/99	3,000	6,000	6,800
1999/2000	6,800	1,000	7,100
2000/01 to 2005/06		Gains covered by exemption	
2006/07	14,000*	1,200	8,800

    *   taper relief of 50% available

    What would the position in 2006/07 have been if the losses brought forward had been £7,000?

(b)   An individual has chargeable gains for 2006/07 of £18,500. Show the amount of capital gains tax payable in the following instances, his income in each case not including any savings income:

  (i)   His taxable income after personal allowances is £14,800.

  (ii)   His taxable income after personal allowances is £24,800.

  (iii)   His taxable income after personal allowances is £37,000.

  (iv)   His taxable income before personal allowances is £4,000 and the personal allowances available amount to £5,035.

(c)   An individual has disposed of an asset for £400,000, creating a chargeable gain of £350,000. Assuming that this gain will be taxed at 40%, amounting to £140,000, state how the tax will be paid if:

  (i)   the contract was dated 31 March 2006,

  (ii)   the contract was dated 6 April 2006,

  (iii)   the contract was dated 31 March 2006, and the consideration will be payable in four instalments of £100,000 each on 31 March 2006, 31 March 2007, 31 March 2008 and 31 March 2009.

(d)   Three employees of XYZ plc, a quoted trading company, acquired shares in the company as follows:

  (i)   Kim acquired a 6% holding on 1 January 1998;

  (ii)   Chris acquired a 1% holding on 1 January 1998;

  (iii)   Alex acquired a 1% holding on 6 April 2000.

Explain the taper relief available to each employee if they make a gain on disposal of their shareholdings on 6 April 2002, 6 April 2004, and 6 April 2006.

(e)   Alan acquired a building on 6 April 1999, and rented it out to an unconnected partnership which carried on a trade. On 6 January 2004, the partnership incorporated its business, and carried on as an unquoted trading company after that. On 5 October 2006 Alan sold the building for £300,000 more than its original cost.

Explain the taper relief available to Alan, assuming that he has no other reliefs to set against this gain.

(f)   Beatrice sold her trading company on 30 September 2006 in a deal which gave her £1m in cash immediately, with a promise of 20% of the profits earned over the next four years, payable on 31 March 2011. The company had been set up in 1990 for £1. Set out the capital gains tax consequences if the following figures apply to the right to receive more proceeds as valued in 2006, and the amount of the further proceeds actually received in 2011:

	2006 value	Received 2011
(i)	£200,000	£900,000
(ii)	£900,000	£900,000
(iii)	£900,000	£200,000

(g)   What (in principle, without calculations) would the situation be if Beatrice was instead given £1m of shares in the purchasing company in 2006, with a promise of more shares to the value of 20% of the profits over the next four years, so she received further shares in 2011?

What would the situation be if the right to more consideration was in the form of loan stocks rather than shares? Would it make a difference if Beatrice continued to be employed by the company?

(h)   Cuthbert is a 100% shareholder in Dextrose Limited. The principal activity of the company is the provision of computer services. Cuthbert takes a modest salary from the company and the occasional dividend. However, most distributable profits in the company have been accumulated and left on deposit with the bank.

The company's average taxable profits from its trading activities amount to £40,000 (from a turnover of £50,000). In the year ending 31 December 2006, its interest income is £15,000.

Discuss the status of the company's shares for taper relief purposes.

Annual exemption and taper relief

(a)   (i)   **Outline of legislation**

Annual exemption

Individuals are entitled to an annual exemption of £8,800 for 2006/07. Personal representatives are entitled to an exemption of the same amount on disposals in the tax year of death and the next two tax years (but not thereafter). Unless the settlor has retained an interest in the trust, trustees are entitled to an annual exemption of £4,400, or £8,800 if the trust is a trust for the disabled. Except for pre 7 June 1978 trusts, or pre 10 March 1981 disabled trusts, the annual exemption is divided equally between trusts created by the same settlor, subject to a minimum exemption of £880 for each trust. Where the settlor has retained an interest in the trust, the trust's gains are treated as his gains and the trust's annual exemption is not available (see explanatory note 4). No annual exemption is available to companies.

If chargeable gains for a fiscal year do not exceed the annual exemption, and total proceeds from chargeable disposals do not exceed four times the annual exemption (£35,200 for 2006/07), it is not necessary to complete the detailed capital gains pages of the personal tax return. These limits were substantially increased to this level in FA 2003 as a simplification measure. Although it is obvious how this will benefit HMRC, the taxpayer will only know whether they do not need to report a gain if they know how much the total is, so the benefits seem especially weighted towards HMRC. Personal representatives and trustees also potentially benefit from these rules.

Introduction of taper relief

Taper relief reduces gains on the disposal of assets on a sliding scale according to the *complete* number of years up to a maximum of 10 that the asset has been held from acquisition or from 6 April 1998 if later (TCGA 1992 s 2A & Sch A1). Except where the anti-avoidance provisions mentioned below apply, or for business assets disposed of after 5 April 2000, an extra year is added to the qualifying period for any asset owned before 17 March 1998. For example, if a business asset was acquired in January 1998 and disposed of in June 1999, the qualifying period was two years, even though the asset was only owned for eighteen months. If the asset was disposed of in June 2000, the qualifying period would still be two years, because the extra year does not apply to business assets disposed of after 5 April 2000, but the rate of taper relief is higher (see below).

Taper relief is not available to companies. They continue to claim indexation allowance. Indexation allowance is given to individuals, personal representatives and trustees on assets held on 5 April 1998 in respect of periods of ownership up to that date.

Rates of taper relief

A higher rate of taper relief applies to business assets than to other assets. After maximum taper relief only 25% of gains is chargeable for business assets compared with 60% for other assets. Using the 2006/07 rates of 10%, 20% and 40%, this gives minimum tax rates of 10% on business assets for a higher rate taxpayer and 5% for a basic rate taxpayer and 2.5% for a starting rate taxpayer, and 24%, 12% and 6% respectively on non-business assets. Note that these reduced rates for 1998/99 onwards should not be compared directly with the situation before April 1998, because the rates of tax then applicable (which at that time were the non-savings rates of income tax) applied to a gain adjusted for inflation, so the charge at a higher percentage was on a smaller amount.

For disposals between 6 April 2000 and 5 April 2002, the taper relief period for business assets was reduced, increasing the rate of taper relief available, but the 'extra year' was no longer counted for business assets. The taper rates were 12.5% for one year's ownership, 25%

for two years, and 50% for three years (the maximum possible taper period which could have accrued up to 5 April 2002, because periods before 6 April 1998 did not count).

For disposals from 6 April 2002 onwards, the taper rates for business assets are 50% for one year and 75% for two years (FA 2002 s 46). The maximum period that is taken into account remains, however, ten years. This is important where an asset has not been a business asset throughout its period of ownership, and it is necessary to apportion the gain into different elements according to qualifying and non-qualifying periods over the last ten years (or the period from 6 April 1998, if shorter). This is covered in more detail below.

The taper relief scales are shown on page (xiv).

Definition of business asset

Following FA 2000, FA 2001 and FA 2003, the definition of business asset was widened. Points 1 and 3 apply for disposals on or after 6 April 2000. Point 2 relates to disposals after 6 April 2004. For individuals, the following assets qualify as business assets from these dates:

(1) Shares in a *qualifying company*, which means:

   (i) A company in which the shareholder works as an employee or director, provided that the shareholding does not exceed 10% of the share capital (a *material interest* – see explanatory note 11). In this case it does not matter whether the company is a trading company or not.

   (ii) An unquoted company (including a company whose shares are traded on the Alternative Investment Market) which is a trading company or the holding company of a trading group.

   (iii) A trading company, or the holding company of a trading group, in which the shareholder owns at least 5% of the voting rights.

   In all cases the expression 'shares' includes securities (TCGA 1992 Sch A1.22) (see explanatory note 12).

(2) Assets used for the purposes of a trade carried on by:

   • an individual; or

   • a partnership of which an individual is a partner; or

   • trustees/personal representatives; or

   • an unlisted trading company or holding company of a trading group; or

   • a partnership whose members include a qualifying company.

(3) Assets held for use in the employment by an employee working for a trading employer.

It is possible for the tests for shares to overlap. For example, an employee who owns a 6% holding of an unquoted trading company qualifies on all three counts. Test (1)(iii) will rarely apply on its own. Because (1)(ii) applies to unquoted holdings whatever the size of the company, (1)(iii) is effectively only relevant to quoted companies. It is rare for individuals to own 5% of a quoted company, particularly if they are not directors or employees. If they were, (1)(i) would also apply.

Test (1)(ii) is generally the important test for owners of a family company. They cannot qualify under (1)(i) because they are likely to own a material interest. For them, therefore, it is important that the company is treated as a trading company (see explanatory note 13).

The rules outlined above are adapted to apply to shares and other assets held by trustees and personal representatives. For example, (1)(ii) and (iii) are also business assets for trustees. The equivalent of (1)(i) and (3) applies to trustees if a beneficiary with an interest in possession is an employee (provided that the interest is not a mere fixed annuity and is not time limited).

Where a legatee disposes of shares or other assets acquired from the personal representatives, the asset is deemed to have been a business asset for the vendor legatee for any period during which it qualified as a business asset for the personal representatives.

Before 6 April 2000, for a company to be a qualifying company the taxpayer either had to hold at least 25% of the voting rights, or had to be a full-time officer or employee holding at least 5% of the voting rights, and under heading (3) an employee had to be a full-time employee. See part (d) of the example for the consequences of the changed definition in relation to employees and see explanatory note 13 for further comments on qualifying companies.

Point (2) therefore allows business asset treatment for an asset used in trade of anyone other than a quoted company which is not the individual's employer. Before 6 April 2004, for an asset to qualify under point (2) it had to be used in a trade carried on by the individual alone or in partnership, or by a qualifying company as defined at point (1) (or by a subsidiary of a qualifying company). See above for definition of a qualifying company before 6 April 2000.

Landlords

A possibly unintended effect of the changed definition in 2000 was that if an asset other than shares is used by *any* unquoted trading company, the company is the taxpayer's qualifying company and the asset qualifies as a business asset. Taper relief was therefore available to a landlord with an unquoted trading company tenant with which the landlord had no connection, but not if the tenant was a partnership in which the landlord was not a partner.

From 6 April 2004, business assets taper relief was extended to property used by any unincorporated trading business (ie run by a sole trader, partnership or trust). This change was announced in the 2003 Budget, but did not take effect for nearly a year. The period up to 5 April 2004 remains 'non-business' unless the tenant is an unquoted trading company, and the apportionment described below will be necessary.

This change makes investment in commercial property considerably more attractive from a CGT viewpoint, than investment in residential property which remains a non-business asset.

Example

Matthew purchases a shop, which he lets to a sole trader, and a semi-detached house (not his residence) on 1 May 2004 for £250,000 each. In two and a half years he sells both for £400,000 each. His gains will be:

	Shop	*House*
Proceeds	400,000	400,000
Less cost	(250,000)	(250,000)
	150,000	150,000
Less taper 75%/0%	(112,500)	–
	37,500	150,000
Annual exemption	(8,800)	(8,800)
	28,700	141,200
Tax @ 40%	11,480	56,480

It will be necessary to monitor the tenant in occupation. Say property is let to an unquoted trading company that decides to sublet to a non-qualifying user such as a subsidiary of a quoted company, or a tenant, decides to float and become a plc.

Where an asset owned personally by a partner/director is used in the partnership or company business, the payment of rent does not prevent the asset being a business asset.

Point (2) applies to all assets other than shares – not just real property. Intellectual property can be held by an individual and licensed to another qualifying person for exploitation and the same treatment will apply.

In the Special Commissioner's hearing, Patel v Maidment, the taxpayer tried to argue that as the letting of property was taxed as a business he should (amongst other things) be entitled to business asset taper relief on the property. The Special Commissioner's decision upon examining the legislation was that business asset taper relief did not apply to all business assets, but rather to trading assets. Thus the taxpayer was not entitled to business asset taper relief which is only available where the property is used for qualifying trading purposes.

Adjustments for changes in use and mixed use

Where an asset has not been a business asset throughout the period of ownership, the gain is split on a time apportionment basis according to the usage over the last *ten* years (or since 6 April 1998 if shorter) and the gains are regarded as arising on separate business and non-business assets. The total period after 5 April 1998 for which the asset is regarded as held is not, however, affected. These rules have to be applied where an asset qualifies as a business asset only from 6 April 2000 or 6 April 2004 (see part (d) for an illustration and see also explanatory notes 8 to 10). Where there is mixed use of an asset, the appropriate fractions of the gain are deemed to relate to separate business and non-business assets.

Unlike the indexation provisions, taper relief takes into account the whole of the expenditure on an asset from the time of its original acquisition, despite the fact that enhancement expenditure may have been incurred on it at a much later date.

Anti-avoidance provisions

There are anti-avoidance provisions to deny the accrual of taper relief during periods in which the owner is not exposed to the risk of fluctuations in value, for example where the economic ownership has been transferred to someone else while the original owner retains nominal title. These provisions were originally very widely drawn, and included the worrying rule that the taper relief 'clock' would be reset to zero if a close company had a 'relevant change of activity' (TCGA 1992 Sch A1.11). This included the commencement of a trade or the commencement of an investment activity. It was therefore possible that the sale of a trade followed by investment of the proceeds would not only change the status of the company from business asset to non-business asset, but the benefit of all accrued taper relief to date would be lost.

The Sch A1.11 rule was repealed in FA 2002 with effect for disposals on or after 17 April 2002. It was replaced by a new rule (TCGA 1992 Sch A1.11A) which disregards any period for which the company is not 'active' (which is defined to include carrying on any kind of business, preparing to do so, or winding up the affairs of a business that the company has ceased to carry on). This is much more closely targeted at the intended mischief, which would be the holding of a dormant 'off the shelf company' for some years before introducing assets into it and immediately (apparently) qualifying for taper relief greater than would be available on starting a new activity from scratch. Under the new rule, a new company is treated in the same way as a dormant company, and the sale of a trade and investment of the proceeds will only change the status of the asset from business to non-business rather than changing the calculation of the qualifying period. This new rule is considered in some detail, with a number of useful examples, in the Revenue's Tax Bulletin of October 2002.

Position on change of ownership, postponed gains, holdover and rollover

In relation to transfers between spouses/civil partners, the taper period applies to the combined period of ownership (see Example 76, in particular part (b)). For gifts holdover relief, only the holding period of the new owner is taken into account.

Where gains are postponed, the taper period runs to the time of disposal of the original asset. This applies in relation to temporary non-residents (see Example 73 part (c)), company reorganisations and takeovers (see Example 79 explanatory note 1 and Example 80 explanatory note 1), holdover relief on replacement of business assets (see Example 83), and gains deferred under the venture capital trust scheme (see Example 94). This means that where a gain had already been postponed before 6 April 1998, no taper relief will be available on the deferred gain when it crystallises. These provisions also apply to gains deferred under the enterprise investment scheme, except that there are special provisions in TCGA 1992 Sch 5BA which allow taper relief to be given on the combined period of ownership where there are successive investments in EIS companies. For details see Example 94 part (a) note 14.

Where gains have reduced the cost of a replacement asset (such as with business assets rollover relief – see Example 83), taper relief will depend on how long the *replacement* asset has been owned. The time for which the asset which gave rise to the rolled over gain was owned is not taken into account. This can lead to significant increases in capital gains tax payable if there is a disposal shortly after a rollover or gifts relief holdover claim, or an incorporation. This aspect of the rules has been much criticised as anomalous and unfair, and a limited solution has been introduced in relation to incorporation relief by FA 2002 s 49 (see Example 89 for details). In respect of business assets, the fact that maximum taper relief is restored once the new asset has been owned for only two years greatly reduces the problem, but care still needs to be taken before claiming such reliefs in case the later qualifying period will be very short.

Where relief is given and interaction with annual exemption

The taper relief is applied to the gains that are chargeable to tax (ie after deducting any available reliefs), net of allowable losses in the same tax year and also net of losses brought forward from earlier years or carried back from the year of death. Losses are set against gains so as to give the lowest tax charge, which means setting them first against any gains on which no taper relief is available, then against gains with less taper relief before gains with more taper relief (see (ii) below). As indicated above (under *Adjustments for changes in use and mixed use*), on the disposal of an asset that has not been a business asset throughout the period of ownership, the gains are regarded as arising on separate business and non-business assets. This enables them to be looked at separately for the purposes of offsetting losses.

Where reliefs are applied to particular gains (such as gifts relief), the relief is given before taking into account taper relief on that asset. Where there may be an element of choice in applying a relief to different gains (eg deferral relief in respect of investments in enterprise investment scheme shares or venture capital trust shares where there are different disposals in the qualifying period), the choice of which gain to defer should take into account the effect on taper relief (see Example 94 part (a) notes 13 and 14 for details of deferral relief).

The annual exemption reduces chargeable gains after taking into account taper relief, so that the annual exemption may be wasted. Brought forward losses are not set against gains covered by the annual exemption. If the gains exceed the annual exemption, however, any brought forward losses that are used against gains must be set off *before* taper relief as indicated above, so the annual exemption may still be effectively wasted, as shown in (iii) below.

(ii) **Allocation of taper relief**

Gains £	Taper relief %	Optimum loss set-off £	Taper relief £	Net gains £
4,000	–	(4,000)	–	–
15,000	10%	(6,000)	(900)	8,100
20,000	50%	–	(10,000)	10,000
39,000		(10,000)	(10,900)	18,100

Setting losses off in the order shown maximises the available taper relief. TCGA 1992 s 2A(6) requires this order to be used.

(iii) **Treatment of losses brought forward**

		£
1998/99	Net losses for the year carried forward	(3,000)
1999/2000	Net gains for the year of £5,800 are covered by the annual exemption, leaving losses carried forward as before	(3,000)
2006/07	Gains before taper relief (14,000 – 1,200)	12,800
	Less losses brought forward	(3,000)
		9,800
	Less 50% taper relief	(4,900)
		4,900
	Less annual exemption (restricted)	(4,900)
	Chargeable gains	Nil

The law requires the offset of losses brought forward in this way, even though taper relief on its own would reduce the chargeable gains to less than the annual exemption. The effect of the law is that the annual exemption will preserve losses brought forward, but taper relief will not do so. The only way to avoid wasting relief in this circumstance is to realise more gains against which the losses brought forward (and the current losses) can be offset, leaving the gain of £14,000 to be reduced by 50% taper relief.

If losses brought forward had been £7,000, ie £4,000 higher, the gains before taper relief would be reduced to the level of the annual exemption by the offset of £4,000 of the loss. £3,000 of the loss would not be used and would be carried forward, but taper relief would be irrelevant because the gains would be covered by annual exemption. The loss would be used up against a gain that would otherwise be covered by taper relief.

Rates of tax

(b) Chargeable gains of £18,500 are reduced by the annual exemption of £8,800, leaving £9,700 chargeable to tax. The amount of capital gains tax payable is as follows:

(i) Basic rate band available £18,500, therefore tax payable is £9,700 @ 20% = £1,940.

(ii) Basic rate band available £8,500, therefore tax payable is:

8,500 @ 20%	1,700
1,200 @ 40%	480
	£ 2,180

(iii) Since income exceeds the basic rate limit, the gains are charged @ 40%, therefore tax payable is £9,700 @ 40% = £3,880.

(iv) Unused personal allowances may not be used to reduce the gain, but the starting rate band is available, so the tax payable is:

2,150 @ 10%	215
7,550 @ 20%	1,510
9,700	£ 1,725

Payment of tax, including payment by instalments

(c)   (i)   Disposal in 2005/06: tax payable in one sum on 31 January 2007. Capital gains tax has no effect on payments on account for the following year, which are only based on income tax liabilities.

Capital gains tax unpaid at 31 January 2007 will, however, attract interest from that date; any tax remaining unpaid at 28 February 2007 will attract surcharge. See Example 40 for further details on payment of tax, interest and surcharge under self-assessment.

(ii)   Disposal in 2006/07: tax payable in one sum on 31 January 2008. A delay of 6 days in executing the contract delays payment of the tax by 12 months.

(iii)   Since the instalments are payable over a three year period, the taxpayer may opt to pay the tax by such instalments as HMRC allow (see explanatory note 5). Interest is charged only on instalments paid late. HMRC's practice is to set the instalments at 50% of the consideration received to date, although the taxpayer may be able to negotiate better terms depending on the circumstances. Otherwise it is likely in this example that the instalments will be £50,000 due on each of 31 January 2007 (the normal due date) and 31 March 2007 and £40,000 due on 31 March 2008.

Taper relief – employee shareholdings

(d)   For disposals after 5 April 2000, all shares held by employees (if not a material interest – see explanatory note 11) qualify for the business assets rate of taper relief. However, where the shareholding was owned before 6 April 2000 as a non-business asset, the eventual gain has to be time-apportioned and tapered separately according to the business and non-business rules.

(i)   Kim qualified for the business assets taper relief both before (assuming he is a full-time worker) and after 5 April 2000. For disposals on and after 6 April 2002 the maximum 75% rate of business assets taper relief is available after two qualifying years provided the asset has been a qualifying business asset throughout the period of ownership, as in this case.

(ii)   Chris owned the shares as a non-business asset for two years from 6 April 1998 to 5 April 2000. The proportion of the gain attributable to this period will only enjoy the lower rates of taper relief, but will qualify for the extra year because the shares were owned on 17 March 1998.

Disposal 6 April 2002

Business: 4 years 2/4 x 75% =	37.5%
Non-business: 5 years 2/4 x 15% =	7.5%
Taper applied to whole gain:	45.0%

Disposal 6 April 2004

Business: 6 years 4/6 x 75% =	50.00%
Non-business: 7 years 2/6 x 25% =	8.33%
Taper applied to whole gain:	58.33%

Disposal 6 April 2006

Business: 8 years 6/8 x 75% =	56.25%
Non-business: 9 years 2/8 x 35% =	8.75%
Taper applied to whole gain:	65.00%

Note that the 'extra year' does not affect the apportionment of the gain, which is taken over the period from 6 April 1998.

The existence of the non-business period will prevent Chris from enjoying the full 75% relief until the shares have been owned as a business asset for 10 years, ie until 6 April 2010. Although this seems unfair and illogical (given that he has owned a business asset for two years), the Government has confirmed that there is no intention to change this rule.

(iii) Alex will always own the shares as a business asset (until and unless employment ceases). Taper relief will be 75% from 6 April 2002 onwards (see (a)(i) above).

Taper relief and business/non-business use

(e) Alan has owned the building for 7 years and 6 months. For 4 years and 9 months, it was a non-business asset (because it was rented to a partnership in which Alan was not a partner). It then became a business asset (because renting to an unquoted trading company qualifies – see (a)(i) above). If the business had continued as a partnership it would have become a business asset on 6 April 2004 (see 74.5 above).

Strictly, the apportionment of the gain should be worked out in days, but months will be used for simplicity. The gain will be treated as follows:

	£
Non-business: 4.75/7.5 x £300,000 = £190,000,	
taper relief 25% (7 years)	142,500
Business: 2.75/7.5 x £300,000 = £110,000,	
taper relief 75% (more than 2 years)	27,500
Total chargeable gain	170,000

Earn-outs

(f) The earn-out deal is treated as two separate disposals. The 'right to more' is valued and forms part of the proceeds for the first disposal, and this value is then the base cost for the second disposal. As the 'right to more' is an asset in its own right, it receives taper relief independently of the shares disposed of, and is unlikely to be a business asset.

The three scenarios produce the following gains and losses:

	(i) £'000	(ii) £'000	(iii) £'000
2006/07			
Proceeds: cash plus right	1,200	1,900	1,900
Taper relief: 75%	(900)	(1,425)	(1,425)
Chargeable gains	300	475	475
2010/11			
Proceeds: more cash	900	900	200
Cost	(200)	(900)	(900)
Gain/(loss)	700	Nil	(700)
Taper (if no other reliefs): 10%	(70)		
Chargeable gain	630		
Total chargeable	930	475	see below

Under TCGA 1992 s 279A, Beatrice could make an election in respect of the 2010/11 disposal to treat the loss of £700,000 as realised instead in 2006/07. This would have the effect of reducing the gain of that year to £1,200,000 before taper relief, and the CGT would be recalculated and repaid on that basis. The election is complicated if there are other reliefs which have already been used against the gain in the earlier year. See explanatory notes 14 and 15.

(g) If Beatrice was given securities and a right to more in 2006/07, she would be treated as receiving two different securities, unless she elected to be treated as making a disposal. The transaction would be a 'share-for-share exchange' within TCGA 1992 s 135. Strictly, the base cost should be split between the actual shares received and the deemed security, so that the cost of the 'more shares' relates to the amount allocated to the deemed security. In this case, the cost is insignificant, so this is not important.

If the right to more was in the form of a right to qualifying corporate bonds, it would again in theory be necessary to value that right so that the base cost could be split between the shares and the deemed security. When the QCBs are issued in satisfaction of the deemed security, a gain must be calculated on the basis of the value of the loan stocks at that time, and the gain will be attached to the loan stocks and charged when they are disposed of. In this case, because the cost is insignificant, the 'frozen gain' on issue of the loan stocks will simply be equal to their value.

See explanatory note 16 for the implications of Beatrice continuing to be an employee.

(h) Shares held by an individual in an unlisted company are business assets for taper relief purposes if:

   (i)   the company is trading; or

   (ii)   the individual:

        •   is an employee of the company; and

        •   does not hold more than 10% of the shares.

Because Cuthbert owns more than 10% of the shares in Dextrose Limited, the shares will qualify as business assets if and only if Dextrose Limited qualifies as a trading company.

Whilst the company is clearly conducting a trade, this is not always sufficient. TCGA 1992 Sch A1.22A defines as a trading company 'a company carrying on trading activities whose activities do not include to a substantial extent activities other than trading activities'.

This definition has applied since 17 April 2002. Between 6 April 1998 and 16 April 2002, a different definition applied. However, HMRC assert that the effect of the two versions of the legislation is the same.

There is no statutory definition of what constitutes 'substantial'. However, HMRC regard 20% non-trading activities as sufficient to make a company a non-trading company.

In Tax Bulletin 60 (December 2002), HMRC suggested that they would consider the following guides as to whether a company's non-trading activities were substantial:

   (i)   turnover from the respective activities;

   (ii)   the asset base of the company – considering both the market value and the historical cost;

   (iii)   expenses incurred and time spent by employees of the company in undertaking its activities.

HMRC will consider all of these activities and, where they give conflicting results, will weigh them up before giving an overall result.

Applying the HMRC guidance to the facts of Dextrose Limited gives the following results:

   (i)   Under the turnover test, Dextrose Limited's non-trading income represents £15,000/£65,000 of the company's turnover – this is more than 20%.

   (ii)   It is probable that Dextrose Limited has few assets on its balance sheet other than cash balance. However, the company should also consider any inherent goodwill in the business although much of this might belong to Cuthbert rather than the company itself.

   (iii)   Only the activity and expenditure test is clearly favourable to Cuthbert Limited since there will be only a negligible amount of time or money spent on generating the interest income.

HMRC are known to want to treat such companies as non-trading companies – especially once the cash reserves become relatively significant. However, the matter is still very much in doubt. If one were to refer to the legislation, one will see that the focus is on the activities of the company. Whilst the turnover levels (and, to a lesser extent, the balance sheet) are indicative of what a company is doing, overall, it must be the actual time and money spent by the company on the various activities that must be determinative of the issue. Consequently, it is suggested that Cuthbert's shares should constitute business assets for the purposes of taper relief.

Explanatory Notes

Rates of tax – individuals

1. For individuals, gains are charged at the rates which would apply if they were the top slice of income and were savings income other than dividends, ie 10%, 20% or 40% (TCGA 1992 s 4). Personal allowances, charges on income etc cannot be set against chargeable gains. This is illustrated in part (b) of the example.

2. See Example 95 explanatory note 6 for the capital gains tax calculation where there is a gain on a life assurance policy that is charged to income tax.

Rates of tax etc – trustees and personal representatives

3. The capital gains tax rate for all trusts and for personal representatives is 40% (TCGA 1992 s 4(1AA)) from 6 April 2004 (previously 34%).

4. Special provisions apply under TCGA 1992 ss 77–79 where both a settlor and the trustees of the settlement are resident or ordinarily resident in the UK and the settlor or spouse/civil partner and/or a dependent child has or may have a present or future interest in the income or property of the settlement, or enjoys a benefit from the settlement (eg free use of property or an interest-free loan). The trust's annual exemption is not available and chargeable gains of the settlement (net of any taper relief available to the trustees) are treated as the settlor's and taxed at his marginal rate of tax. No taper relief is available to the settlor. When taper relief was first introduced, the settlor could not reduce any such gains by his own losses. His annual exemption was, however, first used against any trust gains charged on him before applying the rules relating to brought forward losses, so that his brought forward losses reduced his own untapered gains only to the extent that such gains remained after setting off any balance of the annual exemption not used against the trust gains (TCGA 1992 s 2). Any tax payable by the settlor on trust gains may be recovered from the trustees.

The above provisions do not apply to gains in a tax year in which the settlor dies. In addition, if the interest or benefit relates to the spouse (and not the settlor) the provisions do not apply to gains made in the tax year in which the spouse dies or the settlor and spouse divorce.

The treatment of gains taxed on settlors has been changed for 2003/04 and later years (FA 2002 s 51 and Sch 11 amending TCGA 1992 ss 2 and 77). The trust gains are no longer reduced by taper relief before being attributed to the settlor. If the settlor's personal losses exceed his personal gains, the balance of losses will be set against the attributed trust gains. Taper relief will then apply to the amount remaining, the rate of taper relief on the trust gains being that which would have applied to the trustees. Settlors could *elect*, not later than 31 January 2005, for the revised treatment to apply for any or all of the years 2000/01, 2001/02 and 2002/03. The trustees would have to join in the election if it would result in an increase in the total tax that they would have to reimburse to the settlor for those years.

There are also provisions similar to those stated above for attributing gains of offshore trusts to settlors, and similar changes have been made by FA 2002 in relation to the treatment of the settlor's losses. The detailed provisions are in the companion to this book, Tolley's Taxwise II 2006/07.

Payment by instalments

5.   Where the consideration, or part of the consideration, is payable over a period exceeding eighteen months from the date of disposal, then at the taxpayer's option, capital gains tax may be paid by such instalments as HMRC allow over a period not exceeding eight years and ending not later than the time of the last instalment (TCGA 1992 s 280). No specific provision is made for interest on overdue tax, so interest would be payable on any instalment that was paid late. HMRC's practice is illustrated in part (c) of the example.

Capital gains tax may also be paid by instalments on certain gifts where gains on the gifts cannot be deferred under the gifts relief provisions. The gifts concerned are gifts of land, or a controlling holding of shares or securities in a company, or minority holdings of shares or securities in a company that is not quoted on a recognised stock exchange. Companies whose shares are traded on the Alternative Investment Market (AIM) are treated as unquoted. Tax may be paid by ten annual instalments. Interest is, however, charged on the full amount outstanding, the interest being added to each instalment (TCGA 1992 s 281).

6.   For a further illustration of the instalment option and for the detailed provisions on gifts relief, see Example 84.

7.   Where consideration is due after the time of disposal, provision is made for a gain to be adjusted if part of the consideration becomes irrecoverable (TCGA 1992 s 48). It was held by the Court of Appeal in Goodbrand v Loffland and Bros North Sea Inc (1998) that where the consideration was in foreign currency (in this case American dollars) payable by instalments over several years, s 48 did not cover a loss arising as a result of the sterling equivalent of the consideration being much lower than expected because of exchange rate fluctuations.

In effect, the company made a chargeable gain based on the sterling equivalent of the contract price, as calculated on the date of the contract; it then made a separate loss on realisation of the contract debt (an exempt asset, not being a 'debt on a security') in later years.

Taper relief and change of status to/from business or non-business asset

8.   The effect of a change of an asset's status from business to non-business (or vice versa) is described in part (a) of the example and illustrated in parts (d) and (e). Unfortunately, the generous extension of business status to many more shareholdings from 6 April 2000 has made this complicated calculation increasingly common.

9.   It has been suggested that the denial of 75% relief to someone in the position of the employee in (d)(ii) (or a person owning shares in an AIM trading company from before 6 April 1998) is unfair and cannot be intentional. As it is unlikely that the law will be changed, it is an unfortunate 'penalty' for owning shares over a longer period.

10.   Until 10 December 2003 it was possible to restart the taper relief 'clock', for example by transferring the business asset to a trust for the benefit of the settlor and holding over the gain under TCGA 1992 s 165 (or s 260), so that no tax was paid on the transfer. The trustees were then entitled to taper relief based upon their period and use of the asset. In the right circumstances this enabled the trustees to sell the asset two years later with full business asset taper relief. This has effectively been blocked by FA 2004 as it is no longer possible to hold over gains where the settlor has an interest in the trust (see Example 84).

It is possible to cause the clock to restart in certain other circumstances (eg a transfer of the asset to anyone other than a spouse/civil partner, incorporation of the business under s 162, demergers, certain reorganisations) however the alternatives are not as attractive commercially.

Business assets taper relief – material interests

11.   FA 2001 s 78 and Sch 26 removed, with retrospective effect from 6 April 2000, the requirement that an employee shareholding has to be held in a trading company (or holding company of a trading

group) in order to qualify for business assets taper relief. However, the requirement remains for anyone who has a 'material interest' in the company (for this purpose, more than 10% of the shares, votes, distributable profits or assets on a winding up, owned personally or by connected persons). This means that employees who own a few shares in a quoted employer do not have to worry about the statutory definitions of 'trading company' and 'holding company' before claiming the benefit of the higher rate. See explanatory note 13 for more detail on the definition of a trading company.

Taper relief – meaning of 'securities'

12.   TCGA 1992 Sch A1 para 22 states that 'shares' for the purposes of taper relief includes securities, but securities are not defined. HMRC gave their views in their Tax Bulletin of June 2001. They consider that a security within TCGA 1992 s 132 (which provides that 'security includes any loan stock or similar security . . . of any company, . . .whether secured or unsecured') is a security for taper relief. They also accept that an 'earn-out' right that is the subject of a valid election under TCGA 1992 s 138A (see explanatory note 16 below) is also a security for taper relief. At that time, however, HMRC asserted that a loan note that was not 'marketable' and therefore was not a debt on a security, and would not count as a chargeable asset for taper relief purposes.

FA 2002 Sch 10.8 has provided that, with effect from 17 April 2002, debentures which are issued by a company as part of a takeover (and which are therefore regarded as securities for capital gains purposes under TCGA 1992 s 251(6)) are also regarded as securities for taper relief purposes. This clarifies the situation for loan stocks issued in a takeover or reorganisation, but HMRC's original view may still apply to loan notes issued in other circumstances.

This point is only significant when the loan stocks are chargeable assets for CGT, ie are not 'qualifying corporate bonds'. See Example 80 explanatory notes 4 and 5 for a discussion of qualifying corporate bonds.

Taper relief: trading company or holding company of a trading group

13.   The original definition of 'trading company' (TCGA 1992 Sch A1.22) required that the company should exist 'wholly for the purpose of carrying on one or more trades', or else should have non-trading purposes that were 'capable of having no substantial effect on the extent of the company's activities'. A holding company of a trading group was similarly defined – its activities had to consist wholly or mainly in holding shares in its 51% subsidiaries, and the group's activities would be considered in the same way as those of an individual company.

HMRC gave some information about how these definitions would be interpreted in their Tax Bulletin for June 2001. In particular, the expression 'capable of having [a] substantial effect' would be considered relevant if non-trading purposes represented over 20% of whatever measure HMRC thought relevant – assets in the balance sheet, revenue in the profit and loss account, or even management time spent on the activity. The Tax Bulletin article also considered in detail the significance of 'purpose' – it was possible to have non-trading activities that were incidental to a trading purpose, and so satisfy the 'wholly' test rather than the 'no substantial effect' test.

The definition of trading company has been changed by FA 2002 Sch 10 with effect from 17 April 2002. The old definition still applies to periods up to that point, so it is possible for a company to change its status on 17 April 2002 without changing its activities. However, such a change will be rare. It is likely that most companies that would be regarded as trading under the old definition will still be regarded in the same way under the new version.

The new definition concentrates on the 'activities' of the company rather than its 'purposes'. The Tax Bulletin of December 2002 updated HMRC's approach for the new definition, and it appears that it will in practice be very similar. The main effect of the change appears to be the removal of a defence for the company: it can no longer argue that non-trading activities are incidental to a trading purpose, and therefore substantial non-trading assets or revenues are more likely to lose business assets status.

The Tax Bulletin article suggested that it should be possible for the company to ask its inspector of taxes for a ruling on trading status for an accounting period which has finished. This is a sensible idea: the corporation tax inspector is more likely to be able to make an informed decision based on each accounting period than the income tax inspectors of the individual shareholders on the occasions that they make a disposal. The company might usefully ask its inspector for the ruling each year, and put a note in the accounts. Although inspectors may have been reluctant to respond to this request at the outset, it is increasingly becoming a useful procedure.

Earn-outs

14. An 'earn-out' is the usual expression used to describe the type of deal in part (f) of the example, which involves 'contingent variable' consideration. This is dealt with in accordance with the decision in the case Marren v Ingles HL 1980, 54 TC 76:

   • the initial disposal is treated as a sale for consideration in two parts – the 'right to more' has to be valued as at the date of the contract (ie building in estimates of the likelihood of receiving something, the likely amounts, and the timing);

   • the receipt of further consideration is a further disposal for CGT – the base cost of the 'right to more' is the value brought into account on the first disposal, and the 'more' is the proceeds.

This can have unfortunate results. The most basic problem is the difficulty of valuing the contingent right, which is by its nature speculative. Strictly, the value of the earn-out right does not constitute 'consideration receivable by instalments', so there is not a clear right to payment of tax by instalments, but this may be negotiated with the inspector, as the situation is very similar to the receipt of fixed instalments and may cause the same hardship. Nevertheless, if a high value is placed on the earn-out right, it may create a cash-flow difficulty for the vendor.

If an over-optimistic value is placed on the 'right to more' (perhaps to obtain the benefit of more business assets taper relief), it is possible to pay extra CGT on the first disposal and then incur a loss on the second. Before the Finance Act 2003 this could not be offset against the gain in the earlier year.

On the other hand, the first disposal generally qualifies for business assets taper relief. The second disposal generally does not. This might encourage the vendor to argue for a more optimistic valuation for the earn-out right. Part (f) of the example illustrates how much more tax may be payable overall as a result of placing a low value on the earn-out right.

15. Finance Act 2003 introduced a significant relief to reduce the disadvantage of overvaluing the earn-out right. Where the 'second disposal' takes place on or after 10 April 2003, it will be possible to elect for a loss on the second disposal to be treated as if it had been realised in the same year as the first disposal, so allowing offset against the gain on that first disposal. The rules, in TCGA 1992 ss 279A to 279D, are very complicated, because they determine the interaction between this loss and gains, other losses of the year of the first disposal, losses brought forward and relieved in that year, trust gains attributed to the settlor, and all the other details of CGT. But the essence of the relief is that the loss on the second disposal will reduce the gain on the first disposal, so that it will be charged to tax as if exactly the right value (without any discounting for time) was placed on the earn-out right at the time of the first disposal. It should be noted that this special loss carry-back relief is only available to individuals and trustee vendors (not companies).

16. Where the 'right to more' is only a right to securities (of a variable amount) in the purchaser, the first and second disposals are treated as 'share-for-share exchanges' (provided normal rules in TCGA 1992 s 135 are met). It is recommended that advance clearance is obtained on this point. The 'right to more' being treated as if it were a security itself. This is not available if there is any possibility that the further consideration could be taken in cash.

The first disposal still requires a valuation of the 'right to more', because the original cost has to be split between the immediate consideration (whether shares or cash) and the deemed security. The portion of the cost which is allocated to the deemed security is then carried forward and transferred to the shares which are issued in satisfaction of the earn-out right.

Prior to FA 2003 it was necessary to elect for 'security treatment'. It is now automatic unless the vendor chooses for it not to. It is most likely to be beneficial.

If the earn-out right is treated as a security, it qualifies for taper relief as such. If the vendor continues to work for the company, business assets taper will accrue without interruption. If the vendor does not work for the company (and it is other than an unquoted trading company), the 'deemed security' will be a non-business asset, and the calculation of taper relief may require time apportionment.

If the earn-out right is eventually exchanged for qualifying corporate bonds, a charge to CGT is calculated at that point (with taper relief accruing up to that date) and attached to the bonds (as described in Example 80 explanatory note 4). Even if the eventual consideration will be exempt qualifying corporate bonds (QCBs), the deemed security is not a QCB and is regarded as chargeable to CGT. See also FA 2003 s 161.

Employment related securities

17. The introduction of the complex employment related securities regime in FA 2003 Sch 22 has created some uncertainties in relation to the tax treatment of earn-outs satisfied by loan notes and/or shares in the acquirer. Where the right is obtained by reason of employment or prospective employment, the receipt of the earn-out loan notes or shares would be subject to an income tax charge and, where appropriate, national insurance contributions.

HMRC has confirmed that where an earn-out fully represents consideration for sale of the target company's shares (as it will normally do) the income tax charges above will not apply. However, where all or part of an earn-out relates to value provided to an employee as a reward for services over a performance period, this remuneration element would constitute taxable earnings.

HMRC has issued guidance on the key factors for determining whether an earn-out is further sale consideration rather than remuneration. Where the earn-out is a mixture it is necessary to make a just and reasonable apportionment. Where certainty is required an application can be made under Code of Practice 10 to Employee Shares & Securities Unit, HM Revenue and Customs, Room G52, 100 Parliament Street, London, SW1A 2BQ (see Example 40 note 17).

Cross references

18. For the detailed provisions relating to the indexation allowance see Example 75, the private residence exemption Example 82, and gifts holdover relief Example 84. The taxation of trusts and estates is dealt with in detail in the companion to this book, Tolley's Taxwise II 2006/07. See Example 77 explanatory note 10 for relief for a capital loss against *income* where it relates to the disposal of shares subscribed for in a qualifying unquoted trading company.

(1) A acquired a chargeable business asset in April 1983 at a cost of £10,000. In September 1983 the value of the asset was increased by enhancement expenditure of £5,000 and the value was further increased in June 1996 by enhancement expenditure of £15,000. Show the capital gain or loss arising on the asset, assuming that the asset was sold on 10 May 2006 for (a) £50,000 or (b) £28,000, and that no claim to rollover or holdover relief is available.

Without making calculations, indicate what the position would have been if the facts had related to A Ltd rather than an individual.

(2) (i) On 1 January 1988 D purchased an antique for £2,600 and on 20 April 2006 sold it at auction for £7,200, incurring selling expenses of £720.

(ii) On 1 January 1988 E purchased a picture for £7,000 and sold it on 20 April 2006 for £4,850.

(iii) On 1 January 1995 F purchased a set of antique candlesticks for £4,800 and sold part of the set to a collector on 20 April 2004 for £2,600. On 20 April 2006 he sold the remainder to the same person for £4,600.

D, E and F are private collectors. Show the capital gains or losses arising in each case.

(3) Explain what determines wasting assets (other than short leases) for capital gains tax purposes, and state the taxation implications on the disposal of such assets.

(4) G, a property owner, acquired a fifty-one year lease for £60,000 on 16 March 2003. On 16 March 2007 he assigned the lease to Y for £77,000. Show the capital gain or loss arising.

(5) John Gregory owned a farmhouse which had been let to tenants for many years. On 1 January 2006 he granted an option to Jack Price, on payment of £10,000, to acquire the property for £215,000. The option could be exercised at any time between 1 May 2006 and 31 December 2006. Finding himself unable to finance the purchase, Jack sold the option to Jimmy Matthews on 30 June 2006 for £15,000. Jimmy exercised the option on 31 December 2006.

Set out the taxation implications of the transactions described above.

The retail prices index figures for the calculation of indexation allowance are as follows:

April 1983	84.28
September 1983	86.06
January 1988	103.3
January 1995	146.0
June 1996	153.0
April 1998	162.6

(1)   **A – treatment of enhancement expenditure** (see explanatory notes 1 and 5)

(a)

Sale proceeds 10 May 2006		50,000
Less: Cost April 1983	10,000	
Enhancement expenditure September 1983	5,000	
Enhancement expenditure June 1996	15,000	30,000
Unindexed gain		20,000

Less: Indexation allowance to April 1998

On cost April 1983

$$£10,000 \times \left(\frac{162.6 - 84.28}{84.28} \right) = 92.9\%$$ 9,290

On enhancement expenditure September 1983

$$£5,000 \times \left(\frac{162.6 - 86.06}{86.06} \right) = 88.9\%$$ 4,445

On enhancement expenditure June 1996

$$£15,000 \times \left(\frac{162.6 - 153.0}{153.0} \right) = 6.3\%$$ 945   14,680

Chargeable gain 2006/07 (before taper relief)   £ 5,320

The gain of £5,320 would be aggregated with A's other gains and losses for the year and would qualify for business assets taper relief of 75% (amounting to £3,990 if the gain was not reduced by losses) for a qualifying period of over two years. Gains net of taper relief would then be reduced by the annual exemption of £8,800.

(b)

Sale proceeds 10 May 2006		28,000
Less: Cost April 1983	10,000	
Enhancement expenditure September 1983	5,000	
Enhancement expenditure June 1996	15,000	30,000
Allowable loss 2006/07 (no indexation or taper for a loss)		£ 2,000

If the facts had related to A Ltd, the position in (b) would have remained the same but indexation allowance in (a) would have run to May 2006, when the retail prices index stood at 197.7 compared with 162.6 at April 1998. The indexation allowance would have been increased accordingly. Taper relief would not have been available.

(2) **2006/07 gains on sales of chattels in April 2006** (see explanatory notes 6 and 7)

(i)	£	(ii)	£	(iii)	£
Sale by D (7,200 – 720)	6,480	Sale by E		F's two transactions are treated as	
Cost Jan.1988	2,600	deemed to be	6,000	one since the set has been sold to	
Unindexed gain	3,880	Cost Jan.1988	7,000	the same person	
Indexation allce					
2,600 x 57.4%*	1,492			Thus:	£
Gain	2,388			1st sale	2,600
				2nd sale	4,600
					7,200
				Cost Jan.1995	4,800
				Unindexed gain	2,400
				Indexn allce 4,800 x 11.4%**	547
				Gain	1,853
Limited to (7,200 – 6,000) =				This is less than 5/3 x £1,200	
£1,200 x 5/3	£ 2,000	Allowable loss £ 1,000		= £2,000, so gain is	£ 1,853

$$* \quad \text{Index increase} \left(\frac{162.6 - 103.3}{103.3}\right) = 57.4\%$$

$$** \quad \text{Index increase} \left(\frac{162.6 - 146.0}{146.0}\right) = 11.4\%$$

35% taper relief is available to reduce the gain in (i), if no other reliefs (eg capital losses) are offset against it.

HMRC manuals state (Capital Gains Manual 76637–8) that the gain in (iii) is apportioned between the two tax years of disposal in proportion to the sale proceeds, so 26/72 = £669 would be assessed in 2004/05 (with 25% taper) and the remaining £1,184 would be assessed in 2006/07 (with 35% taper). See explanatory note 7.

(3) **Wasting assets**

Wasting assets are defined in TCGA 1992 s 44 as assets with a predictable useful life not exceeding fifty years, subject to the following:

(a)   Freehold land is never a wasting asset

(b)   Plant and machinery is always treated as a wasting asset.

The cost of a wasting asset is deemed to waste away on a straight line basis over its useful life (TCGA 1992 s 46), unless the asset has been used in a trade, profession or vocation and capital allowances have been or could have been claimed on it, in which case the rules for straight line depreciation do not apply (TCGA 1992 s 47).

Where the wasting asset is a chattel, ie tangible movable property, then unless it is used in a business it is not a chargeable asset for capital gains purposes, so that no chargeable gain or allowable loss can arise (TCGA 1992 s 45). Gains on business chattels are exempt if the chattel is sold for £6,000 or less. (For further points on business chattels see explanatory note 6.)

Since wasting chattels are either exempt or are business chattels to which the straight line rules do not apply, the provisions of s 46 will apply only to intangible property, such as options (see part (5) of the example and also explanatory note 10). (Special rules apply to short leases – see part (4) of the example and explanatory note 8.)

(4) **G – assignment of short lease** (see explanatory note 8)

	£
Sale proceeds – 16 March 2007	77,000

Cost March 2003 £60,000 x $\dfrac{\text{Years unexpired on sale } 47}{\text{Years unexpired on acquisition } 51}$

	£
Substituting percentages £60,000 x $\dfrac{98.902}{100}$	59,341
Chargeable gain 2006/07	17,659

10% taper relief (or 75% if the lease qualified as a business asset) is available to reduce this gain if no other reliefs (eg capital losses) are offset against it.

(5) **Tax implications of option transactions**

John Gregory

Since the option was exercised in a later tax year than that in which it was granted, John Gregory will initially have been liable to tax on the option proceeds of £10,000 in 2005/06 (less the annual exemption if available).

The option then being exercised, the price paid for the option is incorporated with the proceeds for the farmhouse to form a single transaction. (The tax originally charged will be taken into account in the amount of tax payable on the second transaction.)

John Gregory will therefore be liable to capital gains tax on the disposal in December 2006, his proceeds being the £10,000 received on granting the option plus the proceeds of £215,000 for the farmhouse. This will be reduced by the cost of the farmhouse plus indexation allowance to April 1998 (after which indexation allowance is no longer available). 35% taper relief will be available since the farmhouse is a non-business asset and it has been owned for seven complete years at the date of disposal plus one year before 6 April 1998 which counts as part of the qualifying period. Any capital allowances given to Gregory will not be deducted from the cost in computing the gain (whether or not they have been withdrawn by means of a balancing charge).

Jack Price

Since Jack Price did not exercise the option, the disposal of it is treated as a separate chargeable transaction. The option is a wasting asset and its cost wastes away on a straight line basis over its life, ie from 1 January 2006 to 31 December 2006. The allowable cost is restricted according to how much of that life has expired. The depreciated cost is set against the disposal proceeds of £15,000. Taper relief is not available since the option was held for only six months. The position is therefore as follows:

	£
Sale proceeds 30 June 2006	15,000
Depreciated cost 10,000 x $\dfrac{6}{12}$	5,000
Chargeable gain 2006/07	10,000

Jimmy Matthews

Since Jimmy Matthews exercised the option, the purchase of the option and of the farmhouse will be treated as a single transaction. Taper relief will be based on the period of ownership from the time the option was exercised (TCGA 1992 Sch A1.13).

Explanatory Notes

Introduction and application of capital gains tax legislation

1.   Capital gains tax was introduced on 6 April 1965 to charge tax on gains arising on the disposal of assets on or after that date by individuals, trustees and personal representatives. The gains of companies are computed under capital gains principles but are then charged to corporation tax rather than capital gains tax. The law was consolidated in the Taxation of Chargeable Gains Act 1992, to which all references in this example relate. For details of exempt assets see Example 73.

Major structural changes were made by FA 1998, although these changes do not affect companies, for whom there are no plans at present to change the existing rules.

Before FA 1998 the broad effect of the legislation was to calculate gains and losses on each chargeable asset, allowing an indexation allowance for inflation as detailed in notes 4 and 5 (but since 30 November 1993 not so as to increase allowable losses), aggregating the results and reducing net chargeable gains by an annual exemption, which was not, however, available to companies.

For individuals, trustees and personal representatives, FA 1998 froze indexation allowance at April 1998 and introduced a taper relief instead. Gains and losses are calculated on each chargeable asset, taking indexation allowance into account to April 1998 if the asset was acquired before 1 April 1998. The results are then aggregated to give the net chargeable gains or allowable losses for the tax year. Net chargeable gains are then reduced by any available taper relief, and finally by the annual exemption. Taper relief is given on the disposal of business assets that have been owned for at least one complete year and on the disposal of non-business assets that have been owned for at least three complete years after 5 April 1998. For assets acquired before 17 March 1998 an extra year is added, but this extra year does not apply to disposals of business assets from 6 April 2000 onwards (see Example 74 part (a)(i)). Unlike indexation allowance, taper relief is based on the time the asset has been owned, regardless of the dates of any later enhancement expenditure, as shown in part (1) of the example.

If losses exceed gains the excess is carried forward to set against later chargeable gains, subject to anti-avoidance provisions in relation to groups of companies (see Example 64 explanatory note 2(b)).

For further details on taper relief and the annual exemption see Example 74.

Allowable expenditure

2.   The allowable expenditure that may be taken into account in computing gains and losses is (s 38):

   (i)   Cost of the asset plus incidental costs of acquisition

   (ii)   Enhancement expenditure, ie additional capital expenditure reflected in the asset at the time of disposal

   (iii)   Incidental costs of disposal.

Incidental costs of acquisition or disposal are fees etc for services of surveyors, valuers, auctioneers, accountants, agents or legal advisers, costs of transfer or conveyance (including stamp duty), advertising to find a seller or a buyer, and costs of making valuations or apportionments, including expenses of ascertaining market value, but not, in HMRC's view, any costs incurred in *agreeing* a valuation. (Under self-assessment, individuals, trustees and companies may ask HMRC to check valuations used to calculate gains and losses before they send in their returns, and any values agreed in this way will not later be challenged unless information relating to the valuations has been withheld.)

No loss no gain disposals

3.   Married couples and civil partners are taxed independently on their capital gains, with separate annual exemptions, and losses of one spouse/civil partner may not be netted off against gains of the other. Assets may, however, be transferred from one spouse/civil partner to the other on a no gain/no

loss basis (see Example 76). Certain other disposals may also be made on a no loss/no gain basis. For the detailed provisions and the effect on the use of 31.3.82 value see Example 85 at explanatory notes 1 and 2.

Indexation allowance

4.   No allowance was made for the effects of inflation until 1982, when an *indexation allowance* was introduced to reduce the gain that would otherwise arise. The indexation allowance applies to disposals on or after 6 April 1982 (1 April 1982 for companies).

Various changes, which can still be relevant where past gains have been held over and therefore affect current disposals, have been made as follows:

(i)   *Disposals before 6.4.85 (1.4.85 for companies)*

Indexation allowance given from 31.3.82 onwards, based on cost (or 6.4.65 value if appropriate).

Not given for first 12 months of ownership.

Could reduce or eliminate a gain but could not create or increase a loss.

(ii)   *Disposals between 6.4.85 and 5.4.88*

12 months' restriction and losses restriction removed.

Taxpayer could *elect* to calculate indexation allowance on 31.3.82 value.

(iii)   *Disposals between 6.4.88 and 29.11.93*

Irrevocable election could be made to calculate gains and losses using 31.3.82 value for virtually all assets. Otherwise calculations were made under both pre March 1982 and post March 1982 rules, but in each case calculating indexation allowance on the higher of the cost (or 6.4.65 value) and 31.3.82 value (s 55(2)).

(iv)   *Disposals between 30.11.93 and 5 April 1998*

No change to rebasing rules, but indexation allowance could not create or increase a loss (except for limited transitional relief in 1993/94 and/or 1994/95).

(v)   *Disposals on or after 6 April 1998*

Except for companies, no further indexation allowance arises after April 1998, taper relief possibly being available instead. Any indexation allowance available cannot create or increase a loss, as in (iv).

5.   The indexation allowance is calculated by applying to each item of expenditure the increase in the retail prices index between the month when the expenditure was incurred, or March 1982 if later, and the month of disposal of the asset, or, when relevant, April 1998 if earlier.

The formula used for this calculation is

$$\frac{RD - RI}{RI}$$

where RD is the index for the month of disposal or April 1998 as the case may be and RI the index for the month in which the expenditure was incurred (or March 1982 if later). If the index for the month of disposal is less than that for the month the expenditure was incurred, the indexed rise on that item of expenditure is nil. The index increase is expressed as a decimal and rounded (up or down) to three decimal places (s 54).

The retail prices index was established at base 100 in January 1974. It was re-referenced to base 100 again at January 1987 (January 1987 on the old base being 394.5). In most published tables of indices (including the one in this book) the figures for months before January 1987 have been re-referenced to the new base, so that the standard formula may be used in all cases.

Chattels

6.   Chattels (ie tangible movable property) that are wasting chattels (ie with a predictable life of fifty years or less) are exempt from capital gains tax unless they are business chattels on which capital allowances have been or could have been claimed (s 45). Where capital allowances have been claimed but then withdrawn because the taxpayer was not entitled to them, plant and machinery qualifies for exemption from capital gains tax as a non-business wasting chattel (Burman v Westminster Press Ltd 1987). The main examples of non-wasting chattels are antiques, works of art and collectors' items (subject to what is said in Example 73 explanatory note 10 about collectors' items that are machinery).

Gains on business chattels and non-wasting chattels are exempt if the sale proceeds (before deducting any selling expenses) are £6,000 or less (s 262). Where the proceeds exceed £6,000 the chargeable gain is not to exceed 5/3rds of the excess of the proceeds (before deducting selling expenses) over £6,000 (s 262(2)).

Where a loss arises on the disposal of business or non-wasting chattels, then if the proceeds are less than £6,000 they are deemed to be £6,000 in calculating the allowable loss (s 262(3)). Hence in part (2)(ii) of the example, although E's actual loss is (7,000 – 4,850) = £2,150, his allowable loss is only £1,000.

Note that it is only *movable* plant and machinery that is within the chattels rules. Fixed plant and machinery is fully chargeable to capital gains tax if sold at a capital profit, but the gains arising qualify for rollover relief if the assets are replaced (rollover relief not being available on movable plant and machinery). In the more usual case where fixed plant and machinery is sold for less than cost, an allowable loss will not arise. For further details on plant and machinery and rollover relief see Examples 83 and 96.

7.   Where two or more assets which have formed part of a set owned by one person are disposed of by him to the same person or connected persons, then for the purpose of applying the chattels rules in explanatory note 6, the transactions are regarded as one transaction, as illustrated in part (2)(iii) of the example (s 262(4)).

The resulting gain is then apportioned between the tax years concerned in proportion to the sale proceeds of each part of the set, increasing the gains of an earlier year. It is not clear how this would work in practice under self-assessment, because once 31 January 22 months after the tax year had passed, the only way in which HMRC could increase the tax would be by means of a discovery assessment. The legislation contains no time limit on its operation, although it is perhaps unlikely that a set would be sold piecemeal to the same person over a very long period.

HMRC has commented on the position regarding fine wines and shotguns in their bulletins. While a pair of shotguns may or may not be a set depending upon circumstances, bottles of wine would constitute a set if they are from the same vineyard and vintage year. Manuscripts and collections of books are likely to form a set where they are 'similar, complementary and worth more together than separately' (CG 76632).

The chattels exemption is relatively generous. Where a collection of goods represents a number of separate assets that are individually exempt (proceeds below £6,000) there will be no tax to pay even if the total proceeds are much higher. Care is required to ensure that the collection does not constitute a set.

Short leases

8.   Where a lease with fifty years or less to run is disposed of, part of the cost is deemed to have wasted away. Wasting assets generally are deemed to waste away on a straight line basis, as stated in part (3) of the example, but where the wasting asset is a lease, the part of the expenditure that is deemed to have wasted away is determined on a curved line basis according to the Table in Schedule 8

(reproduced on page (x)). The allowable expenditure for the purpose of calculating the indexation allowance is the depreciated amount. For a detailed illustration see Example 100.

Part disposals

9.   Where part only of an asset is disposed of, the cost of the part disposed of is the proportion of the overall cost that the sale proceeds bear to the sale proceeds plus the market value of what remains unsold (s 42). Any available indexation allowance is calculated on the apportioned part of the cost and not on the cost of the whole asset.

Any expenditure which is, on the facts, wholly attributable to what is disposed of, or wholly attributable to what is retained, is not apportioned. If, for example, conversion expenditure was incurred on a property in order to divide it into two self-contained flats, and it could be shown that some part of the expenditure was properly relevant only to the first flat or only to the second flat, that part of the expenditure would be attributed to the relevant part and would not be apportioned.

Special provisions apply to a part disposal of land. For details see Example 96 explanatory note 3.

Options

10.   Special rules apply to options connected with employment (see Example 87). For companies, currency or interest rate options and options relating to loans (for example re government securities and qualifying corporate bonds) are dealt with in calculating the company's income under the rules for derivative contracts in FA 2000 Sch 26 (see Example 62 explanatory notes 2 and 4). Options to acquire or dispose of intangible fixed assets are dealt with for companies in calculating income under the intangible assets rules (see Example 65).

There are anti-avoidance provisions in TA 1988 s 127A & Sch 5AA and ITTOIA 2005 ss 555–569 imposing an income tax or corporation tax charge on profits realised from schemes involving commodity or financial futures or options that effectively produce a *guaranteed* return. The provisions do not apply if the profits are already taxed as trading income, or to a company's transactions if they are within the derivative contracts legislation referred to above, or to authorised unit trusts.

The capital gains rules apply to other options, and the treatment depends on the type of option (ss 143-148). The following options are not treated as wasting assets:

(a)   Quoted options to subscribe for new shares

(b)   Traded options to buy or sell shares or other financial instruments quoted on a recognised stock exchange or futures exchange and 'over the counter' financial options

(c)   Options to acquire assets for use by the option holder in his business.

When such options are disposed of or abandoned, therefore, the full cost is taken into account in calculating the chargeable gain or allowable loss.

Other options are treated as wasting assets, so that their cost wastes away on a straight line basis over their life (s 46). If such options are abandoned no allowable loss can arise. The forfeiture of a deposit is treated as the abandonment of an option.

Whether an option is treated as a wasting asset or not, it is generally treated as a separate chargeable asset, so that the full amount of the consideration for the option is treated as a chargeable gain. This separate treatment does not apply if the option is exercised. In that case the price paid for the option is incorporated with the cost of the asset to form a single transaction both as regards the seller and the buyer, as shown in the example for John Gregory and Jimmy Matthews, and taper relief runs from the date of the exercise of the option (Sch A1.13). If John Gregory had occupied the land for the purposes of a trade, he would have been entitled to taper relief of 75%, since he has owned the asset for more than two complete years after 5 April 1998. (A lessor of tied premises is treated as occupying the land – s 156(4).) If he had acquired a qualifying replacement asset within the relevant time limits, he could have claimed business assets rollover relief (see Example 83). Taper relief would then have been given according to the period of ownership of the *replacement* asset.

Where a call option is exercised and settled in cash, rather than by delivery of the asset, the grantor of the option is treated as having disposal proceeds equal to the price paid by the grantee for the option, less the cash payment made by the grantor, and the grantee is treated as having disposal proceeds equal to the cash received from the grantor less the indexed cost of the option (but with indexation restricted so as not to create or increase a loss) (s 144A).

In Garner v Pounds Shipowners & Shipbreakers Ltd (HL 2000), a company received some £400,000 for the grant of an option over land it owned, and applied £90,000 in removing a restrictive covenant over the land. Although the prospective purchaser had requested this, the option was not exercised, and the £400,000 was assessed as a gain. The House of Lords held that this was correct: the £90,000 was a cost of improving the land which was still owned, and was neither an allowable cost nor a deduction from proceeds in the computation of the gain on the option.

11. In relation to shares the above provisions are modified to bring options within the rules for matching disposals with acquisitions. From 6 April 1998 the share pooling provisions apply only to companies, and indexation allowance for periods after April 1998 are only given to companies.

The rules that apply to companies (and to individuals pre 6 April 1998) are that purchased options of the same series will be pooled if an acquisition is not matched with a disposal on the same day or within the next nine days, and indexation allowance will then be available. If an option is exercised, the shares acquired will merge with any existing pool of shares of the same class in the same company, and the indexed cost of the option will form part of the pool cost.

For disposals by individuals on or after 6 April 1998, the matching rules are outlined in Example 78 explanatory note 6. The amount paid for an option will still be merged with shares acquired if the option is exercised, but the acquisition will be a separate asset rather than merging with a share pool, taper relief running from the date the option is exercised as indicated in explanatory note 10.

For individuals, the disposal of an option to buy or sell gilt-edged securities or qualifying corporate bonds is exempt (subject to what is said in explanatory note 10). For companies, such options are taken into account in calculating profits under the 'loan relationships' rules (see Example 62).

12. The case of Mansworth v Jelley CA 2002 STC 53 led to a major revision of the way in which shares acquired by employees under share option schemes are treated, and a change in the law. The consequences of the case are considered in Example 87, but the most important CGT aspects are as follows:

TCGA 1992 s 120 increases the base cost of shares acquired under an unapproved employee option scheme by any amount on which the employee has paid income tax. This was intended to avoid a double charge to tax on the same amount. So, if an employee exercised unapproved options at £1 when the shares were worth £10, it was thought that £9 would be chargeable to income tax and the CGT base cost was £1 + £9 = £10.

Mr Jelley was exempt from the income tax charge by virtue of his residence status, but he was chargeable to CGT on the disposal of the shares. He was assessed on a gain taking into account only the amount he had actually paid for them (£1, in the above example). HMRC therefore appeared able to withdraw the income tax exemption by charging CGT instead. He argued that the acquisition of the shares was 'not at arm's length', and he should therefore be treated as acquiring the shares at their market value (£10 in the example). The Court of Appeal agreed.

HMRC then issued a statement (8 January 2003) acknowledging that the effect of the judgment, combined with TCGA 1992 s 120, was that people exercising unapproved options and paying income tax (unlike Mr Jelley) should add the income tax charge to the market value to arrive at the base cost. In the example, this would give a figure of £19. Many substantial gains, which had been declared and taxed, would become losses as a result.

13. HMRC issued further guidance on 17 March. The guidance deals with the manner in which the change of treatment can be given effect in earlier years. In brief summary:

    • If a gain or loss was reported in a self-assessment year which is still regarded as 'open' (HMRC enquiry in progress, or not yet at the end of the 'enquiry window' of 12 months from the normal filing date) then the taxpayer is free to amend the figures in all circumstances.

    • If a gain was reported in a self-assessment return for a closed year, any claim to reduce the gain (including to zero) will have to be made under TMA 1970 s 33 ('error or mistake relief'), and HMRC will resist it on the basis that the original return was made in accordance with the practice prevailing at the time. HMRC may succeed with this argument.

    • If a loss was reported in a self-assessment return for a closed year, HMRC's original guidance was that they would resist any claim to increase the amount of the loss for the same reason. This guidance was revised in August 2003. A 1998/99 capital loss could be revised provided it was claimed by 31 January 2005.

    • Where a loss was not reported (possibly because a gain was reported on the same disposal), the time limit for claiming a capital loss under self-assessment applies: five years from the normal filing date for the year of disposal, for example 31 January 2003 for 1996/97. HMRC states that they will accept claims for losses that are made within this time limit, and will repay tax accordingly even for closed years. It seems that a distinction is drawn between changing the figures on the return in order to obtain relief (where HMRC thinks that s 33 applies) and simply obtaining relief for a loss (where HMRC thinks that it does not).

    This is a brief summary of a complex argument, and HMRC's own statements do not make the position either clear or uncontroversial. These principles may also be relevant to other situations in which a previous understanding of the law is overturned by a Court decision, and they are not limited to the particular circumstances of unapproved share option schemes.

14. Not surprisingly, the Finance Act 2003 included a provision reversing the effect of Mansworth v Jelley and restoring the previous understanding that the base cost for CGT was the exercise price (plus any amount charged to income tax). This means that someone in Mr Jelley's position would now have to pay CGT on the amount that 'ought to be exempt'.

    However, the change only applies where the options are exercised after 9 April 2003. This means that losses arising on past disposals are still valid, and relief may still be claimed for them, subject to the time limits above. It also means that shares acquired before and retained since 9 April 2003 continue to have the unexpectedly high base cost, and may produce CGT allowable losses on sale, even if they produce apparent gains.

    The Finance Act 2003 changes operated by disapplying the market value rule in s 17 in relation to transactions with options (TCGA 1992 s 144ZA).

    However, this section opened the way to avoidance in cases where the market value rule was intended to prevent such manipulation. Therefore, the Finance Act 2003 amendments were themselves revised by F (No 2) A 2005 with effect from 2 December 2004.

Agricultural buildings

15. For the interaction of agricultural buildings allowance and capital gains tax see Example 22 explanatory note 7.

(a)   (i)   Explain the special capital gains tax rules which affect a husband and wife.

        (ii)   Explain how these rules apply to couples who are registered as civil partners under the Civil Partnership Act 2004.

        (iii)   Explain how these rules apply to other cohabiting couples.

(b)   Indicate the position in relation to taper relief in respect of the following:

    1.   Husband runs his business from premises owned by his wife, who does not work in the business. She acquired the premises in 1991. In December 1999 she transfers the premises to her husband and in June 2006 he sells them at a substantial gain.

    2.   Husband has been a full-time working director for twenty years of an unquoted trading company in which he owns 4% of the voting shares. His wife, who does not work in the business, has also owned 4% of the voting shares for a similar period. She transfers her shares to her husband on 6 June 1999 and he sells the entire holding on 6 June 2006.

    3.   Facts as in (2), except that husband gives his shares to wife on 6 June 1999 and she sells the entire holding on 6 June 2006.

(c)   Explain the capital gains tax implications of a taxpayer's death.

(a) (i) **Capital gains tax position of husband and wife**

Since 6 April 1990, married couples have been taxed independently in respect of their capital gains, each being entitled to the annual exemption, which is £8,800 for 2006/07. Any unrelieved losses brought forward from 1989/90 by either spouse can only be set against that spouse's gains.

Where property is owned jointly by husband and wife, gains and losses are calculated according to the underlying beneficial ownership. (See Example 2 part (b)(iii) for the different forms of joint ownership, ie as joint tenants or tenants in common.) Where a couple have a joint holding of shares in a company, and either or both also own shares individually, HMRC does not regard a spouse's share in the joint holding as being held in a different capacity from the individually owned shares. This is important when applying the special rules for matching disposals with acquisitions (see Example 81 part (1) for an illustration).

Transfers between husband and wife who are living together are not chargeable to capital gains tax (unless the asset is disposed of or acquired as trading stock, in which case the transfer is deemed to be at open market value (TCGA 1992 s 58)). In order to give effect to this provision there is deemed to be an unindexed gain equal to the available indexation allowance, so that the net result is no gain/no loss and the acquiring spouse acquires the asset at original cost plus indexation allowance to date or to April 1998 if earlier. Indexation allowance added on an inter-spouse disposal on or after 30 November 1993 cannot, however, create or increase a loss on disposal. If there was an inter-spouse disposal before that date, the indexation up to the inter-spouse disposal is able to create or increase a loss on a subsequent disposal by the recipient spouse.

If, for example, an asset that had cost £10,000 was transferred from husband to wife in September 1993 at an indexed cost of £13,000, and the wife disposed of it in June 2003 for £11,000, the position would be as follows:

Sale proceeds June 2003		11,000
Cost	10,000	
Indexation allowance to September 1993	3,000	13,000
Allowable loss		£2,000

No further indexation allowance would be added to the indexed figure of £13,000 for the period September 1993 to April 1998, since the disposal already shows a loss.

For assets owned before 31 March 1982 taxpayers were able to make a 'rebasing election' to use 31 March 1982 values of the assets for calculating gains and losses. For details, and for the calculations when the rebasing election was not made, see Example 77. For inter-spouse transfers, if the transferor spouse acquired the asset before 31 March 1982, the position for disposals by the transferee spouse on or after 6 April 1988 is that the disposal will not be covered by a general 31 March 1982 rebasing election unless it was made by whichever spouse held the asset at 6 April 1988. Effectively the calculation is made as if one spouse had owned the asset throughout (TCGA 1992 s 55, Sch 3.1 & 3.2).

Taper relief applies to disposals after 5 April 1998, different rates of relief applying to business and non-business assets. The relevant period for taper relief when assets have been transferred between spouses is the combined period of ownership. Where the asset has not been a business asset throughout the ownership of both spouses, special rules apply. For details and an illustration see part (b) of this example and explanatory note 4.

The inter-spouse exemption applies throughout the year of separation, but not in later years. Since husband and wife are connected persons up to the date of divorce (TCGA 1992 s 286), transfers between them after 5 April following separation but before divorce are deemed to be made at open market value (TCGA 1992 s 17). The gifts holdover relief (see Example 84) is usually available on transfers of qualifying assets.

Tax Bulletins 66 and 68 revise HMRC's views on transfers between spouses on divorce. Prior to this, they viewed transfers as part of a divorce settlement being for money or money's worth and therefore hold-over relief was not available. Following G v G [2002] EWHC 1339 (and effective for claims made after or unsettled at 31 July 2002 in cases where there is recourse to the courts and a court makes an order):

- for ancillary relief under the Matrimonial Causes Act 1973 which results in a transfer of assets from one spouse to another, or

- formally ratifying an agreement reached by the divorcing parties dealing with the transfer of assets.

They now accept that the transfer does not give consideration and therefore a claim for hold-over relief should not be restricted on the grounds that actual consideration has been given.

One consequence is that transferring ownership of the rights conferred by a life insurance policy under a court order is not for money or money's worth and no gain can arise. In the past insurers may have issued chargeable event certificates reporting gains as a result of assignments on divorce and the 2002/03 self assessment tax guide was incorrect. It may therefore be possible to amend earlier self assessment tax returns to reflect the change and further details about which returns can be amended are given in Bulletin 68.

Married couples may have between them at any time only one residence that qualifies as their main residence for relief under the rules in TCGA 1992 ss 222 to 226B.

(ii) Following a statutory instrument under the provisions of Finance Act 2005 s 103, members of a registered civil partnership have been subject to capital gains tax in the same way as married couples since 5 December 2005.

Similarly, when a civil partnership relationship ends, the parties may transfer assets to each other on a nil-gain nil-loss basis at any time until the end of the year in which they cease to live together.

(iii) Other couples are not subject to any of the above rules. In particular, transfers between such couples can generate chargeable gains and/or losses (subject to the rules in TCGA 1992 s 17 concerning transactions otherwise than at arm's length). Each member of such couples can own their own main residence.

An attempt for non-married couples to obtain the same taxing rights as married couples failed in the Special Commissioners (*Holland* v CIR (2002) SpC 350) on the basis that the difference in rules did not interfere with a couple's human rights. It remains to be seen whether the tax 'penalties' of being married are susceptible to a similar challenge.

(b) **Taper relief and inter spouse transfers** (see explanatory notes 4 to 6)

1. Since the premises were used in the business by the husband throughout his wife's and his own ownership, the business assets rate of taper relief is due on the whole of the chargeable gain on disposal. The qualifying period is over two years, so the taper relief is 75%. See explanatory note 4.

2. The post April 1998 period of ownership includes eight complete years and for non-business assets there is an extra year in the qualifying period because the shares were owned before 17 March 1998, giving nine qualifying years in all. In order for a period of post 5 April 1998 ownership of *shares* by a spouse prior to an inter-spouse transfer to qualify for the business assets rate of taper relief, the company must have been the qualifying company of the *transferee* spouse throughout the relevant period. As the husband did not hold the requisite

5% voting shares (required for a full-time employee shareholding up to 5 April 2000) until the wife transferred her shares to him, the proportion of the gain from 6 April 1998 to 5 June 1999 (ie 14/98ths) will qualify only for the non-business assets taper relief, amounting to 35% for an nine-year qualifying period (including the extra year for pre 17 March 1998 ownership). The remaining 84/98ths of the gain will qualify for business assets taper relief of 75% for the qualifying period of over two years.

Had the husband owned 5% or more of the shares before the transfer from his wife, the business assets rate of taper relief would have applied to the whole of the gain on disposal, and the rate of relief for the whole gain would have been 75%. (From 6 April 2000 *any* shareholding in an unquoted company, and *any* shareholding of an employee who owns up to 10%, is a business asset for taper relief – see Example 74 part (a)(i). See also explanatory notes 4 and 5.)

3. If he had transferred the shares to her, the qualifying period would have been the same. However, as she was not a full-time employee, the shares would not have been a business asset for her until 6 April 2000. As an unquoted trading company is involved, from that date the shares are a business asset even for a non-employee (she also qualifies on the 5% test). Her taper relief will therefore be 24/98ths at 35% and 74/98ths at 75%.

(c) **Capital gains tax implications of a taxpayer's death**

No capital gains tax charge arises on death (TCGA 1992 s 62). If prior to his death the deceased has made losses in excess of gains in that tax year, they may be carried back and set against gains assessable in the three previous tax years, latest first. As with brought forward losses, the set-off is made only against any gains not covered by the annual exemption in the carryback years (s 62), but the interaction with taper relief may cause the annual exemption to be wasted in the same way as illustrated in Example 74 part (a)(iii).

Following the reduction of earlier gains, tax will be refunded accordingly, with interest if appropriate. Although the repayment is *calculated* by reference to the tax position of the earlier year(s), interest on the repayment runs from 31 January following the tax year of death (TMA 1970 Sch 1B).

If the gains of the year of death exceed the losses of that year they are taxable in the usual way and the full annual exemption is available.

The personal representatives or legatees are treated as acquiring the assets at the market value at the date of death (TCGA 1992 s 62). If an asset qualifies as a business asset by reference to the deceased's personal representatives, it will qualify as a business asset by reference to a legatee of the deceased during the period from the date of the deceased's death and the assets being assented to the legatee. Market value normally means open market value (s 272). Where, however, the probate value has been *ascertained* for inheritance tax, that value is taken as the market value for capital gains tax (s 274). Inheritance tax will not be ascertained where no tax is payable on the estate, for example because of exemptions and/or the inheritance tax nil rate band. When personal representatives dispose of assets at values in excess of the values at death, gains arising are charged to CGT (after deducting any available taper relief for the period from the date of death), but the personal representatives may claim the annual exemption in respect of disposals by them in the tax year of death and in each of the two following tax years (TCGA 1992 s 3(7)). If any losses arise, they may only be set against gains of the personal representatives and cannot be transferred to the beneficiaries. Personal representatives pay tax on gains at the rate of 40% from 6 April 2004 (previously 34%).

For inheritance tax, where land is sold within three years after death, a claim may be made by those liable to pay the tax to substitute the sale proceeds for the value at death (IHTA 1984 ss 190, 191). A similar claim is available in the fourth year after death if the property is sold at a lower value than its value at death (IHTA 1984 s 197A). Such a claim is normally relevant where land is sold at a loss. In the case of Stonor & Mills (Dickinson's Executors) v CIR (SpC 288, 2001), no inheritance tax was payable on the estate because of the nil rate band and exemptions. The executors sold freehold properties from the estate for significantly more than the probate value. They tried to claim under IHTA 1984 s 191 to substitute the sale proceeds for the probate value, thus increasing the capital gains tax base cost and eliminating the gains. It was held that, since no one was liable to pay any tax on the estate, no one was entitled to make a s 191 claim.

Personal representatives are allowed to treat a proportion of the costs of obtaining probate as allowable expenditure. SP 2/04 sets out HMRC's policy on this and a simplified calculation using a sliding scale.

If the personal representatives distribute assets to the legatees, this is not treated as a disposal, and the legatee is deemed to take over the base cost at the date of death.

Where within two years after a death the persons entitled to the estate vary the way in which it is distributed, and include a statement in the deed of variation that it is to take effect for capital gains tax, the variation is not regarded as a disposal by those originally entitled but as having been made by the deceased at the date of death so that no capital gains tax charge arises on any increase in value between the dates of death and variation for those who give up all or part of their entitlement (TCGA 1992 s 62(6)–(9)) and the beneficiary receiving the chargeable asset does so for tax purposes at the value at the date of death. In Marshall v Kerr (1994), the House of Lords decided that this deeming provision only has the effect of exempting gains on the variation itself. A trust established by a variation is treated for capital gains tax as settled by the person who made the variation, not by the deceased. Before 1 August 2002 it was necessary to make a separate election to HMRC within six months after executing the deed of variation for it to be ignored for capital gains tax (and, if desired, for inheritance tax).

For disposals before 10 December 2003, personal representatives did not enjoy the benefit of private residence relief unless they qualified under ESC D5. Since this date, the concession has been given statutory effect. The concession/new legislation is necessary as personal representatives are not trustees and do not enjoy the benefit of the relief in TCGA 1992 s 226 (trust disposal of a property occupied by beneficiary).

Personal representatives can now claim private residence relief if any persons who lived in the property both before and after the relevant death were entitled to at least 75% of the net proceeds of sale. A specific claim for relief is required by the personal representatives.

For example, Mr X owned a house and following his death his widow and children occupied the house until it was sold by the personal representatives. Mrs X and children were entitled to over 75% of the net proceeds (proceeds less costs allowable under TCGA 1992 s 38(1)(c)). Any gain arising between date of death and the sale of the house would be exempt under the private residence rules.

Explanatory Notes

Transfers between spouses and civil partners

1. Disposals between spouses/civil partners are not charged to capital gains tax because they are treated as made at a 'no loss, no gain' price. In effect, the transferee takes over the original owner's base cost, plus indexation to April 1998 if the asset was owned before that time (TCGA 1992 s 58).

2. For taper relief purposes in general, the transferee is allowed to count the original owner's period of ownership, including the extra year if the original owner held a non-business asset on 17 March 1998 (TCGA 1992 Sch A1.15).

3. As a result of these two provisions, it is common practice to regard the transferee as simply taking over the transferor's original acquisition cost and acquisition date. However, this is not correct, and will give a misleading answer where the rules for share identification apply.

Example

H has owned 1,000 shares in ABC plc since 1988. Their indexed cost at April 1998 is £5,000. W acquired 2,000 shares in the same company for £18,000 on 10 June 1998. H gave his shares to W on 25 December 1999, following which W sold 1,000 shares for £20,000 on 10 June 2006. The shares are non-business assets for taper relief.

W's acquisition from H is separately identified on 25 December 1999, and is not regarded as something acquired by W in 1998. Her disposal is therefore identified with these shares and not with any of her own purchase; but:

● the shares have a base cost of £5,000;

● 35% taper relief is available against the gain of £15,000, because W can count H's qualifying period.

Business and non-business assets rates of taper relief and transfers between spouses and civil partners

4. Where an asset other than shares or securities has been transferred between spouses/civil partners, it is treated as a business asset for taper relief for that part of the period of post 5 April 1998 ownership of the *transferor* during which it was in qualifying business use by *either* of them. The rate of relief for the period of ownership of the *transferee* will depend on the use by *that spouse/civil partner* (see part (b)1. of the example).

   Where shares or securities are transferred, the business assets rate of taper relief applies only to that part of the combined period of ownership after 5 April 1998 during which the company was the qualifying company of the *transferee*, as illustrated in part (b)2. of the example. From 6 April 2000 an unquoted company is a qualifying company by reference to an individual whether or not the individual is a shareholder or employee (see Example 74 part (a)(i)). Had the husband and wife in part (b)2. of the example acquired their shares on or after 6 April 2000, therefore, the shares would have qualified for business assets taper relief from the date of acquisition for both of them.

   Note that the available rate of taper relief depends on the *total* number of complete years in the qualifying period (including the extra year for pre 17 March 1998 ownership if relevant), but the gain is split on a time basis according to the periods of business/non-business use after 5 April 1998.

5. The rules on transfers of shares between spouses and civil partners mean that the taper *period* is preserved, but the *status* of the gain can be changed for the whole of the period. This can reverse long-standing planning techniques such as dividing assets between spouses and civil partners to use two annual exemptions. For example, if a husband acquired shares in his employer quoted company on 5 April 2005 and sold them on 5 April 2007 when they were showing a gain of £34,000, he would be taxed on only £8,500 (after 75% business assets taper relief and subject to annual exemption). If he gave half the shares to his wife first and they both sold their shares on 5 April 2006, his wife not being an employee of the company, he would be taxed on £4,250, but she would be taxed on the full £17,000, since the company was not a qualifying company for her before the transfer. If the company was unquoted, however, it would also be a qualifying company for the wife throughout the period (even though she owned no shares to begin with), as indicated in note 4, so that both would be entitled to the full business assets taper relief on the sale.

6. Where shares are acquired under an EMI option scheme (as to which see Example 87 part (6)), the *employee* enjoys taper relief from the *grant of the option* to the sale of the shares. A transfer of shares to a spouse/civil partner between the time of exercising the option and sale would result in the taper relief being given only from the date of exercise.

Cross-references

7. See Example 81 for an illustration of points concerning shareholdings of married couples and civil partners. For detailed provisions on inheritance tax and the taxation of personal representatives see the companion to this book, Tolley's Taxwise II 2006/07.

(1) B, who had not previously disposed of any chargeable assets since 5 April 1988, has made various disposals in 2006/07 showing the following chargeable gains and allowable losses:

	Without general rebasing election £	*If general rebasing election made* £
Quoted shares:		
In Richmond plc	12,500	12,500
In Putney plc	–	(2,500)
In Fulham plc	2,200	2,900

The only other chargeable assets he owned on 31 March 1982 were ten holdings of quoted investments, all except one having a market value at that date in excess of their cost. The exception was a shareholding acquired for £4,000 in 1979 that had a market value of £3,650 on 31 March 1982 and is currently worth £10,000. All shareholdings are non-business assets.

Consider whether B should make a general rebasing election, and state the time limit for making the election.

(2) C, who had not disposed of any of his assets since 5 April 1988, sold an investment property on 10 April 2006 for £150,000 which had cost £1,000 on 10 April 1940. The costs of purchase and sale were £185 and £3,000 respectively. The value was £15,000 at 6 April 1965 and £48,200 at 31 March 1982. Show the chargeable gain or allowable loss on the disposal of the property.

(3) H purchased a house for £44,000 on 5 January 1974 and on 5 July 1977 paid £12,000 to convert the house into two self-contained flats. On 27 April 2006 he sold the upper floor flat for £65,000 but declined an offer of £77,000 for the ground floor flat. He recognised that £77,000 was the market value, but preferred to let that flat in the expectation that the value would increase during the next few years. At no time did H live in the house. The market value of the whole at 31 March 1982 was considered to be £60,000. Show the capital gain or loss arising.

(4) J had to close his business down on 31 March 2007 because of continuing losses. He had commenced trading on 28 March 1961. No goodwill had been purchased. At 6 April 1965 goodwill was considered to be worth £18,000, and at 31 March 1982 £15,000. By the date of cessation of trading it was worthless, so that the disposal proceeds were nil. Show the capital gain or loss arising.

(5) Facts as in (4), but on commencement of trading on 28 March 1961 J had paid £20,000 for goodwill.

(6) Ebenezer, who has not made a general 31.3.82 rebasing election, had acquired the following shares in Scrooge Ltd, an unquoted company:

6 April 1960	100	shares for	£2,600
6 October 1963	50	shares for	£700
26 May 1984	200	shares for	£10,000

The market value of the first two purchases totalling 150 shares was:

at 6 April 1965	£3,750	(£25 each)
at 31 March 1982	£4,500	(£30 each)

On 6 April 2000 he sold 300 shares for £26,850, his holding of 350 shares being valued at £89.50 each at that date. Owing to very difficult trading conditions, Scrooge Ltd went into liquidation in 2005. Ebenezer was informed by the liquidator on 5 January 2007 that no distribution would be made to shareholders.

Show the capital gains or allowable losses arising on the disposals in 2000/01 and 2006/07.

(7) In December 2006 Mrs Upjohn sold 25,000 £1 ordinary shares in an unquoted company for 75p each. The sale was at arm's length for full consideration. Mrs Upjohn had subscribed for the shares

for cash at par when the company was formed in 1981 and the company has been a trading company throughout this period. The value of the shares on 31 March 1982 was 80p. No general 31.3.82 rebasing election has been or is being made.

Mrs Upjohn has a considerable investment income, her marginal income tax rate in 2006/07 on taxable income of around £40,000 being 40%. Mrs Upjohn has no earned income.

Calculate the allowable loss and state how it may be treated.

(1)   **B – Effect of general rebasing election** (see explanatory note 1)

In respect of the disposals already made in 2006/07, the effect of making a rebasing election would be to reduce the net chargeable gains as follows:

Gains without rebasing election (12,500 + 2,200)	14,700
Net gains with rebasing election (12,500 – 2,500 + 2,900)	12,900
Net reduction in chargeable gains	£ 1,800

35% taper relief is available against these gains. Although this makes the reduction in taxable gains only 65% x £1,800 = £1,170, it brings the net taxable gains (£8,385 against £9,555) below the annual exemption. It therefore eliminates the tax otherwise payable.

The rebasing election also affects all other chargeable assets owned by B on 31 March 1982. If he makes the election he will therefore have an increased gain when he disposes of the holding that cost £4,000 in 1979. The maximum extent of the disadvantage if the shares are sold at a profit will be (4,000 – 3,650 =) £350 plus indexation allowance to April 1998, reduced by taper relief as appropriate. There will be no disadvantage if the shares are sold at a loss, because the allowable loss will be based on the lower 31 March 1982 value with or without the election, indexation allowance not being available to increase losses.

If, for example, he sold the shares in May 2007 for proceeds of (a) £10,000, (b) £3,850 or (c) £3,500, indexation allowance to April 1998 being 104.7%, the position would be:

Indexation allowance:

On cost of £4,000 @ 104.7% = £4,188

On 31.3.82 market value of £3,650 @ 104.7% = £3,822

		Without general rebasing election £	£	If general rebasing election made £
(a)	Proceeds	10,000	10,000	10,000
	Less: Cost	(4,000)		
	31.3.82 value		(3,650)	(3,650)
	Unindexed gain	6,000	6,350	6,350
	Indexation allowance	(4,188)	(4,188)	(3,822)
	Gain	1,812	or 2,162	
	Chargeable gain	1,812		2,528

The increase in the gain with the rebasing election is £716, being £350 + 104.7%. Unless reduced by allowable losses, the gain would be reduced by 40% taper relief to £1,517, a net increase of £430 (£716 × 60%).

(b)	Proceeds	3,850	3,850	3,850
	Less: Cost	(4,000)		
	31.3.82 value		(3,650)	(3,650)
	Unindexed gain (loss)	(150)	200	200
	Indexation allowance (restricted)			(200)
			No gain no loss	–

			£	£	£
(c)	Proceeds		3,500	3,500	3,500
	Less: Cost		(4,000)		
	31.3.82 value			(3,650)	(3,650)
	Loss		(500) or	(150)	
	Allowable loss			(150)	(150)

In view of the immediate reduction of £1,170 in his taxable gains, B should make the election. The election will give the additional benefit of eliminating the need to make comparative calculations on his future disposals. The time limit for making the election is one year from 31 January following 2006/07 (in which he made his first post 5 April 1988 disposal), ie by 31 January 2009.

(2) **C – asset acquired before 6 April 1965** (see explanatory note 2)

(a) The gain using time apportionment is as follows:

		£
Sale proceeds – 10 April 2006		150,000
Less: Costs of disposal		3,000
		147,000
Less: Cost – 10 April 1940	1,000	
Costs of purchase	185	1,185
		145,815
Less: Indexation allowance to April 1998 on 31 March 1982 value*		
£48,200 x 104.7%		50,465
Overall gain		95,350

Time apportionment:

$$£95,350 \times \frac{41 \text{ years after } 6.4.65}{61 \text{ years from } 6.4.45 \text{ to } 10.4.05}$$

(6.4.45 being earliest acquisition date for time apportionment)

Gain using time apportionment   £ 64,088

The taxpayer had the right to elect to use 6 April 1965 value to compute his gain, but clearly there would now be no question of making an election where the 31 March 1982 value exceeded the 6 April 1965 value.

(b) The gain using 31 March 1982 value is:

	£
Net sale proceeds – 10 April 2005	147,000
Less: 31 March 1982 value	48,200
Unindexed gain	98,800
Less: Indexation allowance as above*	50,465
	£ 48,335

*   If, exceptionally, original cost (or 6 April 1965 value if that value had been used to determine the result) had been higher than 31 March 1982 value, the higher figure would be used to make the indexation calculation.

The chargeable gain arising in 2006/07 is therefore £48,335, being the lower of the gains of £48,335 and £64,088. Since the asset had been owned for eight complete years after 6 April 1998, increased by one year because it was acquired before 17 March 1998, the gain will be reduced by taper relief of 35%, amounting to £16,917 providing the gain is not reduced by allowable losses.

C could avoid making the computation under (a) if he elects for the capital gains and losses on *all* assets held at 31 March 1982 to be calculated by reference to their 31 March 1982 values. In that event, indexation allowance to April 1998 would always be based on the 31 March 1982 value of any asset disposed of, whether it was higher or lower than cost or 6 April 1965 value.

(3) **H – part disposal** (see explanatory note 4)

		£
The gain using 31 March 1982 value is:		
Sale proceeds – 27 April 2006		65,000

$$\text{31 March 1982 MV £60,000} \times \frac{65,000}{65,000 + 77,000} = \qquad 27,465$$

	£
Unindexed gain	37,535
Indexation allowance on 31 March 1982 value: 27,465 x 104.7%	28,756
Gain chargeable 2006/07	8,779

The gain computed using original cost (£44,000 + £12,000 = £56,000) will clearly be higher, so the MV 82 computation will be used.

Taper relief of 35% will reduce the gain unless other reliefs (eg capital losses) are offset against it.

(4) **J – effect of rebasing election on allowable losses** (see explanatory note 2)

(a) *If J had not made a rebasing election*

Since the goodwill was worthless on disposal of the business, and no goodwill had ever been purchased, there is no allowable loss using original cost. An election for 6 April 1965 value (in this case £18,000) could be made, but it could not produce a loss greater than the loss over the whole period of ownership, which in this case is nil.

Although a computation using 31 March 1982 value would produce an allowable loss because of the value of the goodwill at 31 March 1982, the lower of the losses under the two methods is taken, so there would still be no allowable loss.

(b) *If J had made a rebasing election*

The goodwill would be deemed to have been acquired for £15,000 on 31 March 1982, so that J would have an allowable loss in 2006/07 of that amount (not, however, increased by any indexation allowance).

(5) **J – goodwill purchased for £20,000**

If J had paid £20,000 for the goodwill, it would make no difference to the calculations in (4) if J had made a rebasing election, because J would have been treated as acquiring the goodwill for £15,000 on 31 March 1982. If he had not made a rebasing election, the position would be as follows:

(a) Position using original cost:

	£
Sale proceeds 31 March 2007	–
Cost 28 March 1961	20,000
Overall loss	20,000

$$\text{Time apportioned £20,000} \times \frac{42}{46}$$

	£
Giving allowable loss of	18,261

No election would be made to use 6 April 1965 value of £18,000 since using cost shows a larger loss.

(b)   Position using 31 March 1982 value:

	£
Sale proceeds 31 March 2007	–
31 March 1982 value	15,000
Allowable loss	15,000

J's allowable loss in 2006/07 would therefore be £15,000.

(6)   **Ebenezer – disposal of unquoted shares**

Sale of 300 shares on 6 April 2000 is deemed to be:

Sale of 200 shares out of post-1982 pool (shares acquired 26 May 1984).
Sale of 50 shares acquired 6 October 1963.
Sale of 50 out of 100 shares acquired 6 April 1960.

	£	Chargeable Gains £
Sale of 200 shares @ £89.50 each	17,900	
Indexed pool cost*	18,271	Nil

(loss not allowed as due to indexation)

	Using cost/6.4.65 value**		Using 31.3.82 value**
	£	£	£
Sale of 50 shares @ £89.50 each	4,475	4,475	4,475
Cost 6 October 1963	700		
6 April 1965 value		1,250	
31 March 1982 value			1,500
	3,775	3,225	2,975
Less: Indexation allowance 104.7% x £1,500 (31 March 1982 value being higher than cost/6 April 1965 value)	1,571	1,571	1,571
	2,204		

Time apportionment
$$\frac{6.4.65 - 6.4.2000}{6.10.63 - 6.4.2000} = \frac{35}{36\frac{1}{2}} \times 2,204$$

Gain using time apportionment	2,114		
Gain if election made for 6 April 1965 value		1,654	
Gain using 31 March 1982 value			1,404 1,404
Sale of 50 shares @ £89.50 each	4,475	4,475	4,475
Cost 6 April 1960 (100 for 2,600 x ½)	1,300		
6 April 1965 value		1,250	
31 March 1982 value			1,500
	3,175	3,225	2,975
Less: Indexation allowance (on 31 March 1982 value £1,500 x 104.7% as above)	1,571	1,571	1,571
cf	1,604	1,654	1,404 1,404

		£	£	£	£
bf		1,604	1,654	1,404	1,404

Time apportionment

$$\frac{6.4.65 - 6.4.2000}{6.4.60 - 6.4.2000} = \frac{35}{40} \text{ x } 1,604$$

	£	£	£	£
Gain using time apportionment	1,404			
Gain if election made for 6 April 1965 value		1,654		
Gain using 31 March 1982 value			1,404	1,404
Total chargeable gains on disposal in 2000/01				2,808

* *Post-1982 pool*		Shares	Unindexed pool value £	Indexed pool value £
May 1984 bought		200	10,000	10,000
Indexation allowance	$\frac{94.78 - 88.97}{88.97} = 6.5\%$			650
At 6 April 1985		200	10,000	10,650
April 2000 sold		(200)		
Indexed rise to April 1998	$\frac{162.6 - 94.78}{94.78} = 71.56\%$			7,621
				18,271
Applicable to sale			(10,000)	(18,271)

Disposal of remaining 50 shares on 5 January 2007 is treated as follows:

	Using cost/6.4.65 value**		Using 31.3.82 value**
	£	£	£
Disposal proceeds 5 January 2007	–	–	–
Cost 6 April 1960	1,300		
6 April 1965 value		1,250	
31 March 1982 value			1,500
Overall loss	1,300		

Time apportioned

$$\frac{6.4.65 - 5.1.07}{6.4.60 - 5.1.07} = \frac{41\frac{3}{4}}{46\frac{3}{4}} \text{ x } 1,300$$

Loss	1,161	1,250	1,500

Election will be made for 6 April 1965 value giving an allowable loss in 2006/07 of £1,250, being lower than the loss of £1,500 using 31.3.82 value. (The allowable loss with a 6 April 1965 election could not have exceeded the loss over the whole period of ownership (but without time apportionment), ie £1,300.)

** Calculations have been shown in columnar form for convenience. If the calculation using cost/6.4.65 value had resulted in no gain no loss (for example if election for 6 April 1965 value had shown a loss and time apportionment a gain) the calculation based on 31 March 1982 value cannot apply, so strictly the calculation need not be made in those circumstances. If Ebenezer had made a 31 March 1982 rebasing election, the cost/6.4.65 value calculations would not have applied and the allowable loss would have been £1,500.

(7)   **Mrs Upjohn – loss on unquoted shares in trading company**

	Using cost	*Using 31.3.82 value*
	£	£
Sale proceeds December 2006 for 25,000 unquoted shares	18,750	18,750
Cost 1981	25,000	
31 March 1982 value		20,000
	(6,250)	(1,250)
Allowable loss, being the lower of the two		(1,250)

For which relief may be claimed against Mrs Upjohn's income in 2006/07, giving tax relief at 40% amounting to £500.

Explanatory Notes

Rebasing election

1.   The original capital gains tax base date of 6 April 1965 has been generally moved forward to 31 March 1982 so that only gains or losses accrued since 31 March 1982 are brought into account (TCGA 1992 s 35 & Sch 3), and inflation is recognised from that time by the introduction of the indexation allowance, which has, however, been frozen at April 1998 except for companies (see Example 75 notes 1 and 4).

A taxpayer may make an irrevocable election for the capital gains and losses on *all* assets held at 31 March 1982 (with the following exceptions) to be calculated by reference to 31 March 1982 values (s 35(5)) (known as a rebasing election). The irrevocable election does not apply to plant and machinery, or an asset held in connection with a trade or part thereof involving working a source of mineral deposits, or an oil licence, providing in each case capital allowances had been or could have been claimed (Sch 3.7).

The time limit for making the election for companies is within two years after the end of the company accounting period in which the first disposal takes place on or after 6 April 1988 of an asset held on 31 March 1982 (s 35(6)); the time limit for individuals, trustees and personal representatives is one year from 31 January following the tax year. For many taxpayers the time limit has already expired. The disposal of an asset on which a gain would not usually arise, but which is nonetheless potentially a chargeable asset (such as a private residence), strictly triggers the time limit for making the election. HMRC have, however, indicated in Statement of Practice 4/92 that they will normally ignore such disposals in applying the time limit, and will exercise their discretion to extend the time limit in some other circumstances. The statement also states that certain people, such as trustees and partners, need to make separate elections in their various capacities.

The rebasing election is favourable or neutral for assets whose 31 March 1982 value is higher than cost, but will usually be unfavourable if an asset's 31 March 1982 value is below cost. This is because in addition to the base cost itself being lower, indexation allowance is based on that lower value, as shown in part (1) of the example. It is not possible to make the election for some assets and not for others.

If the rebasing election has not been (and is not being) made, two calculations are made, one based on the original cost and the other based on the 31 March 1982 value. In these calculations indexation allowance is the *same* in each computation and is based on the higher of cost (or 6 April 1965 value if that value is being used in the computation – see note 2) and 31 March 1982 value. If both computations show gains, the chargeable gain is the lower of the two. If both show losses, the allowable loss is the lower of the two. If one shows a gain and the other a loss, the result is treated as neither a gain nor loss. Where under the rules for assets held on 6 April 1965 the disposal would be treated as taking place at no gain/no loss (see note 2), rebasing does not apply.

Unlike the position with assets owned before 6 April 1965, a taxpayer cannot avoid getting 31 March 1982 valuations for his assets by not electing for rebasing, because the 31 March 1982 value has to be used in the calculation anyway (but see Example 75 explanatory note 2 re getting valuations checked by HMRC). The election does have the benefit of making it possible to establish allowable costs for all assets, whereas there may be insufficient information available to provide the historical cost figures. For those taxpayers for whom a rebasing election is not out of time, the taxpayer's overall portfolio of assets must be reviewed in order to decide whether the election should be made.

Assets held on 6 April 1965

2. The rules for quoted securities held on 6 April 1965 are dealt with in Examples 78 and 79.

   Where an asset other than quoted securities or land with development value was acquired before 6 April 1965, then in making the calculations based on cost, only the time proportion of the gain falling after 6 April 1965 is chargeable. Any period of ownership before 6 April 1945 is ignored in the time apportionment calculation (TCGA 1992 Sch 2.16(6)). The gain is reduced by the indexation allowance before the time apportionment calculation is made. The calculation using 31 March 1982 value will almost invariably show the lower gain and the time apportionment calculation will now rarely be used.

   The taxpayer (but not HMRC) can *elect* to have the gain under the pre-1982 rules computed using the 6 April 1965 value of a particular asset as the cost instead of using time apportionment, but this election if made is irrevocable (Sch 2.17). The legislation provides that where the election is made the assets are treated as sold and reacquired by the taxpayer on 6 April 1965. Hence the 6 April 1965 value replaces the original cost and the costs of acquisition, with the indexation allowance being calculated on the 6 April 1965 value or 31 March 1982 value as appropriate. If the election would otherwise substitute a loss for a gain then there is deemed to be no gain or loss, and the election cannot give an allowable loss greater than the loss (without time apportionment) over the whole period of ownership (Sch 2.17(2)).

   Unless the irrevocable election is made to use 31 March 1982 value for all assets, the rebasing rules in note 1 do not apply if a lower loss or gain, or a no loss/no gain result, would arise using cost/6 April 1965 value. It may therefore be necessary to make three calculations for pre 6 April 1965 acquisitions of quoted securities and land with development value, unless the cost/6 April 1965 calculation gives a no loss/no gain result, in which case the calculation based on 31 March value is not made. In many cases it will not be necessary to look at the 6 April 1965 market value option, so that the time apportioned gain or loss is compared with the result using 31 March 1982 value, as shown in part (2) of the example.

3. The time apportionment rules are relevant when making calculations for unquoted securities acquired before 6 April 1965. Various special rules apply. The rules are illustrated in part (6) of this example.

4. See Example 75 explanatory note 9 for the rules relating to part disposals. That note also deals with the possibility of some of the conversion expenditure, such as that in part (3) of this example, relating wholly to the part disposed of. Where the 31 March 1982 value is used to calculate the gain on a part disposal, it is apportioned in the same way as the original cost.

Unquoted shares

5. Where a rebasing election has been made, or where all acquisitions have been made since 6 April 1965, unquoted shares are treated in almost exactly the same way as quoted shares, disposals being

identified with acquisitions according to the rules in Example 78 explanatory note 6. The only difference is that when the cost of a holding has to be split after a capital event (eg a scrip or rights issue of a different class of shares):

- a quoted holding is split according to the values on the first dealing day after the event;

- an unquoted holding is split according to the values (to be agreed with HMRC on the occasion of the first disposal after the event.

6. Where a rebasing election has not been made and there are pre-6 April 1965 acquisitions of unquoted shares, the identification rules in Example 78 explanatory note 6 apply subject to the following differences:

- there is no 'pooling election' for unquoted shares – the pre-6 April 1965 holdings are always kept separate from the 1982 pool;

- time apportionment applies in calculating the gains on unquoted shares in the same way as for assets in general, but time apportionment does not apply to quoted shares.

Thus the sale of 300 shares by Ebenezer on 6 April 2000 in part (6) of the example is identified first with the post-1982 pool acquired in May 1984, then with the shares acquired in 1963 and then with those acquired in 1960.

7. Shares which were quoted on a recognised stock exchange on 6 April 1965 (or had been at any time in the previous six years), and units in unit trusts whose prices were published regularly, are treated as quoted shares at 6 April 1965 for this purpose (TCGA 1992 Sch 2.1). Shares and securities dealt in on the Alternative Investment Market (AIM) are treated as unquoted. Note that from 6 April 2000 *any* holding of shares in an unquoted trading company counts as a business asset for taper relief. Before that date the shareholder either had to hold 25% or more of the voting rights or had to be a full-time officer or employee holding 5% or more of the voting rights (see Example 74 part (a)(i)).

Valuation of unquoted shares

8. The value of unquoted shares depends on what percentage of the shares is held. When valuing the holdings of married couples or civil partners, each is looked at separately. They are not valued as a proportion of the joint holding, as they are for inheritance tax. Although for identification purposes shares held on 31 March 1982 may need to be regarded as a number of separate assets, all the shares held by one person are taken together in order to determine the overall value of the holding on that day, which is then split pro rata over the various separate acquisitions (Revenue Statement of Practice 5/89). Where 31 March 1982 values are needed and several shareholders with similar holdings agree, HMRC Shares Valuation will begin valuation negotiations before receiving a formal request from the tax office.

Where there has been a transfer of unquoted shares between spouses or civil partners, or a no gain no loss transfer within a group of companies, after 31 March 1982 (see Example 85 explanatory note 1), and the transferor held a larger holding at 31 March 1982 than the transferee is regarded as having held, the 31.3.82 value of the shares in the transferee's hands may be lower than their value in the hands of the transferor. By Revenue Concession D44, the transferee may claim to have the 31.3.82 value of his shares calculated as the appropriate proportion of the transferor's 31.3.82 holding.

Reorganisations relating to pre 6 April 1965 unquoted shares

9. For unquoted shares acquired before 6 April 1965, there are special provisions where there is a reorganisation of the share capital. These provisions prevent time apportionment being used if the reorganisation took place before 6 April 1965, and only permit time apportionment up to the time of the reorganisation if it occurs after 6 April 1965 (TCGA 1992 Sch 2.19). Since in most cases the 31 March 1982 value of such shares will greatly exceed the 6 April 1965 value, these provisions will rarely be relevant. However, they would increase the allowable loss where an asset becomes worthless and no general rebasing election has been made (see Unilever (UK) Holdings Ltd v Smith, CA (2002) STC 15).

Loss on unquoted shares in trading company

10. Where an individual makes a loss on the disposal of shares he has *subscribed for* in money or money's worth in an *unquoted* qualifying *trading* company (and see below re quoted companies), he may claim *income tax relief* under TA 1988 s 574 instead of relief against capital gains. (The relief does not apply to shares acquired some other way, for example by transfer from another shareholder, unless the transferor subscribed for the shares and the transfer is a lifetime transfer to his or her spouse/civil partner.) Relief may be claimed against the net total income of the tax year in which the disposal is made or the previous year (or both, if the loss is large enough). Relief for the capital loss takes priority over a claim under TA 1988 s 380 or s 381 in respect of an income loss. The *tax saving* flowing from carrying back the loss against an earlier year's income is computed by reference to the tax position of the earlier year, but the claim is *given effect* in the tax year of loss (see Example 42).

The time limit for the claim is one year from 31 January following the tax year of loss (ie by 31 January 2009 for Mrs Upjohn's 2006/07 loss in part (7) of the example).

The rules for identifying which shares have been disposed of are the same as those that apply for the enterprise investment scheme (EIS) and venture capital trust scheme (VCT). For details of those schemes see Example 94.

Under the rules which have applied since 6 April 1998, a qualifying trading company is a UK resident company none of whose shares, stocks, debentures or other securities are marketed to the general public and which

(a)   either   (i)   is an eligible trading company at the time of disposal,

          or   (ii)   has ceased to be an eligible trading company within three years of that time and has not since been an excluded company, an investment company or a trading company that is not an eligible trading company; and

(b)   either   (i)   has been an eligible trading company for a continuous period of six years up to the time in (a) above,

          or   (ii)   has been an eligible trading company for less than six years but has not previously been an excluded company, an investment company or a trading company that is not an eligible trading company.

An eligible trading company is defined by reference to the EIS definition in TA 1988 s 293 (TA 1988 s 576(4A)). Furthermore, in line with the revised conditions for EIS shares (see Example 94 part (a) note 3), s 574 relief will be available for a loss on *quoted* shares, providing they were unquoted at the time they were issued and there were no arrangements at that time for the company to cease to be unquoted. This applies to shares issued on or after 7 March 2001, and shares issued before that date but after 5 April 1998 where the company ceases to be unquoted on or after 7 March 2001.

An excluded company is a company dealing in land, in commodities or futures or in shares, securities or other financial instruments, or a company not operated on a commercial basis, or a company that is the holding company of a non-trading group, or a building society or registered industrial and provident society.

Although the company itself must qualify as an EIS company, the shares disposed of do not have to be shares on which EIS relief was given. It is therefore possible for a person to qualify for s 574 relief even if they are connected with the company, or even on a share subscription of over the EIS subscription limit of £400,000 (before 2006/07, £200,000). The EIS-based conditions do not apply to shares subscribed for before 6 April 1998.

A disposal does not qualify for relief under these provisions unless it is:

(a)   at arm's length for full consideration, or

(b)   a distribution in a winding up (or when the disposal occurs on the dissolution of a company without a distribution being made), or

(c)   a deemed disposal under TCGA 1992 s 24(2) where the shares have become of negligible value.

(TA 1988 ss 574–576).

In relation to (c), HMRC will accept a loss claim of less than £100,000 without referring the case to its Shares Valuation specialists if the company is UK registered, is not a plc and is either in liquidation or has ceased trading (see CG13131).

11.   The use of s 574 relief means that the full value of any loss is relieved. If the loss had been set off against capital gains (or carried forward) it could have lost some of its value as losses are set off against gains *before* the deduction of taper relief.

(1)   Jeremy sold 5,500 shares in Penny Pincher plc on 15 August 2006 for £41,250, his previous dealings in the shares having been as follows:

10 November 1986	bought	3,000	shares for	£6,100
16 July 1988	bought	1,000		£3,060
25 May 1990	sold	2,000		£9,125
15 July 1993	bought	3,500		£14,210
25 March 2005	bought	500		£2,675
30 March 2005	sold	2,000		£12,700
15 June 2006	bought	3,000		£18,000

Calculate his chargeable gains on the disposals on 30 March 2005 and 15 August 2006.

(2)   Pickles had the following dealings in the shares of Chutney plc:

10 May 1983	bought	2,000	shares for	£8,000
14 July 1983	bought	1,000		£5,300
18 October 1984	bought	500		£2,300
21 February 1985	bought	500		£2,250
13 June 1996	sold	2,500		£16,500
17 July 1996	bought	1,000		£9,500
19 September 2006	sold	2,000		£17,700

(a)   Show the workings on the post-1982 pool and calculate the gain or loss on the September 2006 disposal.

(b)   State how the computation would be affected if Pickles bought another 1,000 Chutney plc shares for £8,950 later in September 2006.

(3)   Inwood has made the following acquisitions of ordinary shares in the quoted company, Butterfield plc:

Date	Number of shares	Cost £
2 June 1963	1,000	500
8 February 1965	680	907
14 July 1980	2,100	5,880
13 October 1980	750	2,325
15 April 1983	1,275	3,697
26 March 1985	600	2,550
18 March 1994	1,000	8,000
29 March 1998	1,000	11,100
20 April 1998	3,000	33,750
26 August 1998	2,000	23,900

The market value of Butterfield plc shares was £1.30 per share at 6 April 1965 and £2.75 at 31 March 1982.

Show how Inwood's shares in the company are treated for capital gains purposes

(a)   on the basis that an irrevocable 31 March 1982 rebasing election has been made,

(b)   on the basis that no general rebasing election has been made but that a pooling election was made under TCGA 1992 Sch 2.4 in respect of pre-6.4.65 acquisitions of quoted shares,

(c)   on the basis that neither a general rebasing election nor a pooling election under TCGA 1992 Sch 2.4 has been made.

(4)   On 5 April 1982 Anthony owned 30,000 shares in Trollope plc, the total cost of which was £15,290. The 31 March 1982 value was 80.3p per share. The following transactions have taken place since that date:

30 April 1991	sold	9,000	shares for	£24,055
8 May 1993	sold	16,000	shares for	£40,366
16 September 2006	sold	5,000	shares for	£3,950

Show the result of the disposals with and without a 31 March 1982 rebasing election.

Show also the result of the September 2006 disposal if the proceeds had been (i) £2,200, or (ii) £10,500.

The following indexation figures may be used:

	RPI	*From Mar 82*	*To Apr 98*
Mar 82	79.44	–	104.7%
Apr 83	84.28	6.1%	92.9%
May 83	84.64	6.5%	92.1%
Jul 83	85.30	7.4%	90.6%
Oct 84	90.67	14.1%	79.3%
Feb 85	91.94	15.7%	76.9%
Mar 85	92.80	16.8%	75.2%
Apr 85	94.78	19.3%	71.6%
Nov 86	99.29	25.0%	63.8%
Jul 88	106.7	34.3%	52.4%
May 90	126.2	58.9%	28.8%
Apr 91	133.1	67.5%	22.2%
May 93	141.1	77.6%	15.2%
Jul 93	140.7	77.1%	15.6%
Mar 94	142.5	79.4%	14.1%
Jun 96	153.0	92.6%	6.3%
Jul 96	152.4	91.8%	6.7%
Mar 98	160.8	102.4%	1.1%
Apr 98	162.6	104.7%	–

Treat all shares as non-business assets.

(1)   **Jeremy: post-1982 pool, chargeable gains on disposals in 2004/05 and 2006/07**

500 of the 2,000 shares sold on 30 March 2005 are identified with the purchase on 25 March 2005 (acquisitions since 6 April 1998, most recent first). The remaining 1,500 shares come out of the post-1982 pool. The sale on 15 August 2006 is identified first with the shares acquired after 5 April 1998 and then with the post-1982 pool. The position is therefore as follows:

Post-1982 pool

			Shares	Unindexed Pool value £	Indexed Pool value £
November 1986	Bought		3,000	6,100	6,100
July 1988	Bought		1,000		
Indexed rise	106.7 − 99.29				
	99.29				455
Add new expenditure to both pools				3,060	3,060
			4,000	9,160	9,615
May 1990	Sold		(2,000)		
Indexed rise	126.2 − 106.7				
	106.7				1,757
					11,372
Proportion applicable to sale	2,000			(4,580)	(5,686)
	4,000				
			2,000	4,580	5,686
July 1993	Bought		3,500		
Indexed rise	140.7 − 126.2				
	126.2				653
Add new expenditure to both pools				14,210	14,210
			5,500	18,790	20,549
March 2005	Sold		(1,500)		
Indexed rise to April 1998*	162.6 − 140.7				
	140.7				3,198
					23,747
Proportion applicable to sale	1,500			(5,125)	(6,476)
	5,500				
			4,000	13,665	17,271
August 2006	Sold		(2,500)		
Proportion applicable to sale	2,500			(8,541)	(10,794)
	4,000				
Pool values cf			1,500	5,124	6,477

* The rounded percentage from the table, 15.6%, may also be used.

	£	£
Disposal on 30 March 2005		
Sale proceeds 500 shares (500/2,000 x 12,700)	3,175	
Cost 25 March 2005	(2,675)	500
Sale proceeds 1,500 shares (1,500/2,000 x 12,700)	9,525	
Indexed pool cost as above	(6,476)	3,049
Total chargeable gain on disposal		3,549

25% taper relief will be available on the gain of £3,049 on the indexed pool in 2004/05 (seven-year qualifying period, including the 'bonus year' for pre-17 March 1998 ownership). The relief will be £762, unless other reliefs (eg capital losses) are set against the gain first. Such reliefs would be set first against the gain of £500 which qualifies for no taper relief.

	£	£
Disposal on 15 August 2006		
Sale proceeds 3,000 shares (3,000/5,500 x 41,250)	22,500	
Cost 15 June 2006	(18,000)	4,500
Sale proceeds 2,500 shares (2,500/5,500 x 41,250)	18,750	
Indexed pool cost as above	(10,794)	7,956
Chargeable gain		12,456

The taper relief on the pool gain of £7,956 in 2006/07 would be 35% (nine-year qualifying period), amounting to £2,785, unless reduced by losses etc, such reliefs being set first against the gain of £4,500 that does not qualify for taper relief.

(2) **Pickles: post-1982 pool, gain or loss on September 2006 disposal**

(a) Holding at 6 April 1985, which provides the opening figures for the post-1982 pool, comprised:

		Shares	Cost £	Indexation allowance to April 1985		£
May 1983	Bought	2,000	8,000	$\dfrac{94.78 - 84.64}{84.64}$	= 12%	960
July 1983	Bought	1,000	5,300	$\dfrac{94.78 - 85.3}{85.3}$	= 11.1%	588
October 1984	Bought	500	2,300	$\dfrac{94.78 - 90.67}{90.67}$	= 4.5%	104
February 1985	Bought	500	2,250	$\dfrac{94.78 - 91.94}{91.94}$	= 3.1%	70
		4,000	17,850			1,722

Post-1982 pool		*Shares*	*Unindexed pool value* £	*Indexed pool value* £
At 6 April 1985		4,000	17,850	19,572
June 1996	Sold	(2,500)		12,022
Indexed rise	$\dfrac{153.0 - 94.78}{94.78}$			
				31,594
Proportion applicable to sale	$\dfrac{2,500}{4,000}$			
			(11,156)	(19,746)
cf		1,500	6,694	11,848

Post-1982 pool			*Shares*	*Unindexed pool value* £	*Indexed pool value* £
bf			1,500	6,694	11,848
July 1996	Bought		1,000		
Indexed rise nil since July 1996 index at 152.4 is less than June 1996 index					
Add new expenditure to both pools				9,500	9,500
			2,500	16,194	21,348
September 2006	Sold		(2,000)		
Indexed rise to April 1998*	$\dfrac{162.6 - 152.4}{152.4}$				1,429
					22,777
Proportion applicable to sale	$\dfrac{2,000}{2,500}$			(12,955)	(18,222)
Pool values cf			500	3,239	4,555

September 2006	Sale proceeds 2,000 shares		
	Less: Cost	17,700	
		(12,955)	
		4,745	
	Less: Indexation allowance 18,222 – 12,955 = 5,267, but restricted to	(4,745)	–
	Therefore no allowable loss.		

* The rounded percentage from the table, 6.7%, may also be used.

(b)   The disposal of 2,000 shares would be identified first with purchases of the same class in the next 30 days. This would give rise to an allowable loss of £100 (£8,850 – £8,950). Only 1,000 shares would come out of the pool, still giving rise to neither a gain nor a loss. This would leave a balance of 1,500 shares in the post-1982 pool.

(3)   **Inwood's holding of Butterfield plc shares – matching rules** (see explanatory note 6)

(a)   *If irrevocable 31 March 1982 rebasing election has been made*
       Holding consists of:

Post-5 April 1998 acquisitions		*Shares*	*Cost* £	
20.4.98		3,000	33,750	
26.8.98		2,000	23,900	

Post-1982 pool		*Shares*	*Unindexed pool value* £	*Indexed pool value* £
15.4.83		1,275	3,697	3,697
Indexed rise to April 1985 12.5%				462
26.3.85		600	2,550	2,550
Indexed rise to April 1985 2.1%				54
At 6.4.85		1,875	6,247	6,763
18.3.94	Bought	1,000		
Indexed rise	$\dfrac{142.5 - 94.78}{94.78}$			3,405
Add new expenditure to both pools			8,000	8,000
		2,875	14,247	18,168
29.3.98	Bought	1,000		
Indexed rise	$\dfrac{160.8 - 142.5}{142.5}$			2,333
Add new expenditure to both pools			11,100	11,100
		3,875	25,347	31,601
Indexed rise to April 1998*	$\dfrac{162.6 - 160.8}{160.8}$			354
		3,875	25,347	31,955

Pre-1982 pool				
2.6.63		1,000		
8.2.65		680		
14.7.80		2,100		
13.10.80		750		
		4,530	@ £2.75 each = £12,458	

* The rounded percentage from the table, 1.1%, may also be used.

When any disposals are made of Butterfield plc shares, they will be identified first with acquisitions after 5 April 1998, latest first, then with Inwood's post-1982 pool and then with the pre-1982 pool, after adjusting the latter for indexation allowance to April 1998. If any further shares are purchased, they will be included with the post-5 April 1998 acquisitions and matched with later disposals on a last in, first out basis.

Shares in a post-1982 pool or pre-1982 pool are treated as a single asset, the shares in the post-1982 pool being treated as acquired when the pool came into being and those in the pre-1982 pool as acquired on 31 March 1982 (see explanatory note 4). The fact that shares were added to the post-April 1982 pool between 17 March 1998 and 5 April 1998 does not therefore affect the entitlement to one year's extra taper relief by reference to the whole of the post-1982 pool, providing in the case of the post-1982 pool that it was in existence before 17 March 1998, which applies in Inwood's case.

If any scrip or rights shares are issued, they will be added pro rata to and be deemed to be part of each post-5 April 1998 acquisition, the post-1982 pool and the pre-1982 pool. Although treated as acquired when the original shares were acquired, rights shares that relate to pre-6 April 1998 holdings will not attract any additional indexation allowance. The gain eligible for taper relief will, however, be calculated by reference to the date of acquisition of the original shares, so that for the pre-6 April 1998 holdings an extra year will be added to the taper period even though rights shares were bought at a later date. See Example 79 for an illustration of these rules.

(b) *If no general rebasing election made but pooling election made under TCGA 1992 Sch 2.4*

The post-5 April 1998 acquisitions and post-1982 pool will be as in (i).

The pre-1982 pool will be:	*Shares*	*Cost*	*31.3.82 value* @ £2.75
		£	£
Pre-6.4.65 shares @ £1.30	1,680	2,184	
14.7.80	2,100	5,880	
13.10.80	750	2,325	
	4,530	10,389	12,458

Purchases, including scrip and rights shares, will be treated as in (a). Disposals will be identified first with the post 5 April 1998 acquisitions, latest first, then with the post-1982 pool, then with the pre-1982 pool. Two calculations must be made in respect of each disposal out of the pre-1982 pool, one based on cost and the other based on 31 March 1982 value, with indexation allowance in both calculations being based on 31 March 1982 value (since it is higher than cost).

(c) *If neither a general rebasing election nor pooling election under TCGA 1992 Sch 2.4 made*

The post-5 April 1998 acquisitions and post-1982 pool will be as in (i).

The pre-1982 pool will be:	*Shares*	*Cost*	*31.3.82 value* @ £2.75
		£	£
14.7.80	2,100	5,880	
13.10.80	750	2,325	
	2,850	8,205	7,838

In addition there will be the two pre-6 April 1965 acquisitions, each of which will be treated as a separate asset.

Purchases will be treated as in (a), except that the pre-6 April 1965 acquisitions will each attract the appropriate number of scrip and rights shares.

After matching disposals with the post-5 April 1998 acquisitions and the post- and pre-1982 pools, they will be matched with the shares acquired on 8 February 1965 and lastly the shares acquired on 2 June 1963. When the pre-6 April 1965 shares are disposed of, three calculations will need to be made, two comparing the outcome of the disposal using either cost or 6.4.65 value and the third using 31 March 1982 value, but in each case basing indexation allowance on the 31 March 1982 value (since higher than both cost and 6.4.65 value). If, however, the computation using cost and 6.4.65 value showed a no gain no loss result, that result would stand and the 31 March 1982 calculations would not be made.

(4)   **Anthony and Trollope plc – pre-1982 pool**

Anthony's holding comprises a pre-1982 pool, the cost of each share being (£15,290/30,000) = 50.97p.

If no rebasing election made

		£	£
30.4.91	Sale proceeds 9,000 shares	24,055	24,055
	Cost (9,000 @ 50.97p)	4,587	
	31.3.82 value (9,000 @ 80.3p)		7,227
		19,468	16,828
	Indexation allowance 67.5% x 7,227	4,878	4,878
	Gain	14,590	or 11,950
	Chargeable gain is therefore subject to taper relief at 35% of £4,183		11,950
8.5.93	Sale proceeds 16,000 shares	40,366	40,366
	Cost (16,000 @ 50.97p)	8,155	
	31.3.82 value (16,000 @ 80.3p)		12,848
		32,211	27,518
	Indexation allowance 77.6% x 12,848	9,970	9,970
	Gain	22,241	or 17,548
	Chargeable gain is therefore subject to taper relief at 35% of £6,142		17,548
16.9.06	Sale proceeds 5,000 shares	3,950	3,950
	Cost (5,000 @ 50.97p)	2,548	
	31.3.82 value (5,000 @ 80.3p)		4,015
		1,402	(65)
	Indexation allowance to April 1998 104.7% x 4,015 = £4,204, but restricted to	1,402	–
		–	(65)

Therefore no gain no loss.

If rebasing election made

Disposal on 16 September 2006 would show loss of £65. Gains on remaining two disposals would be unchanged since they are already calculated using 31 March 1982 value.

Result of 16.9.05 disposal if proceeds were (i) £2,200 or (ii) £10,500

(i)   *Disposal proceeds £2,200*

Without a rebasing election there would be an allowable loss of (2,548 – 2,200 =) £348, being smaller than the loss using 31 March 1982 value. With a rebasing election the allowable loss would be (4,015 – 2,200 =) £1,815.

(ii)   *Disposal proceeds £10,500*

Since 31 March 1982 value is higher than cost, the chargeable gain both with and without a rebasing election would be (10,500 – 4,015 – 4,204 =) £2,281. Except to the extent that it was reduced by allowable losses, the gain would be eligible for taper relief of £798, ie at the 35% rate for nine complete years' ownership, an extra year being added to the taper period for pre-17 March 1998 acquisitions.

Alternative layout

It is possible to use the same approach for the pre-1982 pool as for the post-1982 pool, although indexation calculations should be rounded to three decimal places, because it is only on the post-1982 pool that they are not. (In practice indexation calculations on the post-1982 pool may often be calculated using rounded figures from published indexation tables, and it is considered unlikely that HMRC would object, provided that the approach were used consistently.) The layout is the same as for the post-1982 pool if the irrevocable rebasing election has been made. If it has not, pool values for both cost and 31 March 1982 value must be shown. This approach is particularly helpful in dealing with the sale of rights nil paid, as shown in Example 79 part (3). Some small differences may arise compared with the statutory method because of rounding. Using this example for illustration, the position would be as follows:

If no rebasing election made

	Shares	Cost	Indexed cost	31.3.82 value (80.3p)	Indexed 31.3.82 value
		£	£	£	£
At 5.4.82	30,000	15,290	15,290	24,090	24,090
30.4.91 Sold	(9,000)				
Indexn $\dfrac{133.1 - 79.44}{79.44}$					
= 67.5% × 24,090			16,261		16,261
			31,551		40,351
Re sale		(4,587)	(9,465)	(7,227)	(12,105)
	21,000	10,703	22,086	16,863	28,246
8.5.93 Sold	(16,000)				
Indexn $\dfrac{141.1 - 133.1}{133.1}$					
= 6% × 28,246			1,695		1,695
			23,781		29,941
Re sale		(8,155)	(18,119)	(12,848)	(22,812)
	5,000	2,548	5,662	4,015	7,129
16.9.06 Sold	(5,000)				
Indexn $\dfrac{162.6 - 141.1}{141.1}$					
= 15.2% × 7,129			1,084		1,084
			6,746		8,213
Re sale		(2,548)	(6,746)	(4,015)	(8,213)

Sale on 30.4.91

Since the proceeds exceed the indexed figures, there is a gain (before taper relief) of (24,055 – 12,105 =) £11,950, being less than the gain using cost. This is exactly the same as the figure reached by the statutory method.

Sale on 8.5.93

Since the proceeds again exceed the indexed figures, there is a pre-taper gain of (40,366 – 22,812 =) £17,554, based on 31.3.82 value (the gain was £17,548 using the statutory method).

Sale on 16.9.06

There is a loss of (4,015 – 3,950) = £65 using 31.3.82 value, and no gain no loss using cost (the unindexed gain of 3,950 – 2,548 = £1,402 being reduced to nil by indexation allowance), therefore the result is no gain no loss. Again, this is the same result as that given by the statutory method.

If rebasing election made

The cost and indexed cost columns would not be relevant, so there would be only three columns as for a 's 104' indexed post-1982 pool holding. The disposal on 16 September 2006 would show a loss of (4,015 – 3,950 =) £65. Gains on the remaining two disposals would be unchanged.

Result of 16.9.06 disposal if proceeds were (i) £2,200 or (ii) £10,500

(i) *Disposal proceeds £2,200*

The allowable losses would be the same as under the statutory method, ie £348 without a rebasing election and £1,815 with a rebasing election.

(ii) *Disposal proceeds £10,500*

With or without a rebasing election, there would be a chargeable gain of (10,500 – 8,213) = £2,287 (compared with £2,281 under the statutory method) on which 35% taper relief of £800 would be available.

Although the columnar method where there is no rebasing election appears complicated, the gain or loss on any disposal may be easily identified. If the proceeds lie anywhere between the lowest and highest figures, there is neither a gain nor loss. If they do not, a chargeable gain is calculated using the *highest* of the four figures, and an allowable loss is calculated using the *lowest* of the four figures. Using the three proceeds figures in the example, £3,950 is between £2,548 and £8,213 so there is neither gain nor loss. £2,200 is below £2,548 so the allowable loss is £348. £10,500 is above £8,213 so the chargeable gain before taper relief is £2,287.

Explanatory Notes

Basic rules re shares and loan stock

1. All references in this example are to TCGA 1992 unless otherwise stated. The treatment of corporate shareholders differs in some respects from that for other shareholders. Notes 4 to 7, and Examples 79 to 81, deal with the position of non-corporate shareholders, with the position of corporate shareholders being dealt with in Example 85.

    The general principles of capital gains tax dealt with in other examples apply to all chargeable assets, including quoted securities, but because of the special problems of frequent purchases and sales, scrip and rights issues, takeovers etc, there are additional provisions relating only to securities. The rules for shares are different from the rules for interest bearing stocks, although from 6 April 1998 the same rules are used for matching disposals with acquisitions in the case of non-corporate shareholders, as indicated in note 6.

    In general, references to 'quoted' securities have been replaced by references to 'listed' securities (FA 1996 Sch 38) and shares referred to as unquoted shares are normally those that are not listed on a recognised stock exchange. The terms quoted and unquoted are, however, still retained in some parts of the legislation and for convenience they are used in this publication. Securities on the Alternative Investment Market (AIM) are unquoted. This example deals with the basic points relating to quoted shares. Examples 79, 80 and 81 deal with some of the more complex areas and also with interest bearing stocks.

    Foreign stocks and shares are broadly subject to the same provisions as UK stocks and shares, and any provisions relating to quoted securities apply to foreign securities that are listed on a stock exchange recognised by HMRC (TA 1988 s 841). In 2001, HMRC adopted a new interpretation of the expressions 'listed' and 'quoted' (IR Press Release 28 November 2001). This mainly affects foreign securities, and will not change the status of AIM shares.

Securities held on 6 April 1965

2. The treatment of shares (and loan stock) that had quoted market values on a recognised stock exchange at 6 April 1965 is different from the treatment of shares (and stocks) that were unquoted at that date (Sch 2). For later share acquisitions up to and including 5 April 1998 the same rules apply to all shares of the same class in the same company (s 104). The treatment of unquoted shares is dealt with in Example 77.

Stamp duty and stamp duty reserve tax

3. Transactions in securities are subject to stamp duty or stamp duty reserve tax. See Example 86 for details.

Share pooling for non-corporate shareholders

4. Before FA 1998, shares of the same class in the same company were subject to a pooling system, except for certain pre-6 April 1965 acquisitions. There are two separate pools for each class of shares, one relating to shares acquired between 6 April 1965 and 5 April 1982, referred to in the legislation as the 1982 holding (s 109) but referred to in this book as the pre-1982 pool, and the other relating to shares acquired between 6 April 1982 and 5 April 1998, now referred to in the legislation as the s 104 holding but referred to in this book as the post-1982 pool.

Shares acquired under an employee share scheme and subject to restrictions are treated as shares of a different class from unrestricted shares until the restrictions are lifted. See Example 81 explanatory notes 1 to 3.

Shares acquired on or after 6 April 1998, except for scrip and rights shares, are not pooled and are treated as separate, free-standing assets (s 104).

The way in which the legislation developed (which may still be relevant if a share history has to be reconstructed from a list of transactions) was as follows:

(a) *6.4.65 to 5.4.82*

Shares of the same class in the same company were pooled, ie treated as a single asset, growing with purchases and diminishing with sales, so that an average price was used as the cost of disposals.

The pool excluded shares already owned on 6 April 1965, but in respect of *quoted* shares the taxpayer could make an election (under what is now Sch 2.4) to include them in the pool at their quoted price on that day. Two pooling elections could be made, one in respect of all 6 April 1965 holdings of fixed interest securities and preference shares, and the other in respect of all other quoted securities held on that day. If such pooling elections were not made, the shares were dealt with as separate, free-standing assets according to the date they were acquired. This separate treatment still applies unless a rebasing election is made (see (c) and note 7(b)).

(b) *6.4.82 to 5.4.85*

Indexation allowance was introduced, but because it was subject to various restrictions, shares acquired between 6.4.81 and 5.4.85 were treated as separate free-standing assets.

(c) *6.4.85 – 5.4.98*

Following the removal of the original restrictions on indexation, the shares referred to in (b) were merged to form the post-1982 pool, except for shares acquired between 6.4.81 and 5.4.82, which were merged with the pre-1982 pool.

No shares are added to the pre-1982 pool, other than as a result of scrip or rights issues (see Example 79 explanatory note 1) (or as a result of a pooling election after 5 April 1985 to include pre-6 April 1965 shares in it).

From 6.4.88 a 'rebasing' election could be made to use only 31 March 1982 value, and ignore original costs, for virtually all assets held on that day (see Example 77 explanatory note 1).

(d) *6.4.98 onwards*

Shares acquired on or after 6 April 1998 are treated as separate, free-standing assets, except for scrip and rights shares (see Example 79 explanatory note 1).

Freezing of indexation allowance and introduction of taper relief

5. Indexation allowance is not given to non-corporate shareholders on any acquisitions on or after 6 April 1998 and no further indexation allowance is given after April 1998 on earlier acquisitions (s 110A). Taper relief is given instead of indexation from that time according to the complete years the shares have been owned, with an extra year added for shares acquired before 17 March 1998, unless the shares qualify as business assets (see Example 74 part (a)(i)). As indicated in part (3) of the example, the pre- and post-1982 pools are regarded as single assets, with the post-1982 pool treated as acquired when it first came into being (s 106A), so that providing this was before 17 March 1998 acquisitions between 17 March 1998 and 5 April 1998 still count for the extra year's taper relief.

See Example 75 explanatory note 4 for the changes in the rules for indexation allowance that have taken place since 6 April 1982.

Matching disposals with acquisitions

6. Disposals of shares of the same class in the same company by non-corporate shareholders on or after 6 April 1998 (17 March 1998 in relation to heading (b)) are matched with acquisitions as follows (s 106A):

(a) Acquisitions on the same day as the disposal

(b) Acquisitions within 30 days after the disposal, earliest first (but see the note below)

(c) Previous acquisitions after 5 April 1998, latest first

(d) The post-1982 pool

(e) The pre-1982 pool

(f) Pre-6 April 1965 acquisitions that are not included in the pre-1982 pool, latest first

(g) Acquisitions more than 30 days after disposal, earliest first.

All acquisitions on the same day are normally treated as a single asset. This is subject to special rules where some of the acquisitions are acquired under an approved employee share scheme – see Example 81 explanatory note 3.

The matching rules apply not only to shares but also to loan stock that is not exempt from capital gains tax, although for loan stock there is no post-1982 pool and heading (d) relates to securities acquired between 6 April 1982 and 5 April 1998, which would be matched with disposals on a latest first basis. Loan stock used to be subject to different matching rules from those applicable to shares. See Example 81 explanatory note 7 for details.

The above matching rules apply despite the fact that some of the shares were otherwise identified by the disposal, but shares disposed of by a person in one capacity are not identified with shares held in another capacity (s 106A). This means that shares held by trustees or personal representatives are not identified with shares they own personally. It does not, however, in the view of HMRC, treat shares held by a husband and wife/civil partners jointly as held in a different capacity from shares held by them separately. See Example 81 part (1) for an illustration of this point.

Where shares are held in an individual savings account (ISA) or personal equity plan (PEP) they are regarded as held in a different capacity from other shares held (see Example 93).

The 30-day rule in (b) above prevents 'bed and breakfast' transactions, where shares are sold and bought back on the following day in order either to use the capital gains exemption or to produce losses to reduce chargeable gains. For married couples (or civil partners) it would, however, be possible for the spouse to repurchase the shares on the market (but not directly from the other spouse).

In the case of Davies v Hicks (2005), the 30-day rule was successfully used by a trust which was about to become non-resident in the UK. To avoid an exit charge on the trust, the trustees sold its shareholding shortly before ceasing to be UK resident. When it had become non-resident (and within 30 days of the original disposal), the shares were reacquired by the non-resident trustees. The shares disposed of were then matched with the shares subsequently reacquired and so a considerable gain was eliminated. The non-resident trustees consequently acquired the original base cost of the shares.

This scheme was blocked with effect from 22 March 2006 by FA 2006 which provides that the 30-day rule does not apply in respect of any acquisition by a person who is not UK resident (and not treated as resident under a tax treaty).

The Revenue's Tax Bulletin of April 2001 contains a review of their understanding of the identification rules, and comments on a number of published planning schemes which make use of the 'bed and breakfasting' rule. HMRC does not believe that the identification of 'same day share transactions' overrides the many provisions of TCGA 1992 which trigger a gain or loss by deeming a 'disposal and immediate reacquisition' of an asset.

The Tax Bulletin of August 2001 included further examples of how HMRC resolves the difficult interaction of share identification, inter-spouse disposals (now also relevant for civil partners) and taper relief. This is analysed in two articles in Taxation, 18 October 2001, which point out a number of difficulties which HMRC's approach leaves unresolved. More recently this issue is touched upon in 'merging and diverging interests' (Taxation, 22 May 2003).

Calculating gains and losses for non-corporate shareholders

7.   Gains and losses are calculated as follows:

Post-1982 pool

(a)   There are two pool values, one representing the actual qualifying expenditure and the other an indexed pool of expenditure, no further indexation being added, however, after April 1998 (s 110). To arrive at the initial figures for shares already on hand at 6 April 1985, indexation allowance was calculated on each separate acquisition from the month of purchase to April 1985, and the indexed pool of expenditure at 6 April 1985 was the total qualifying expenditure plus the total of all the calculated indexation allowances.

Where a post-1982 pool first came into being after the April 1985 date, the unindexed pool value and the indexed pool value were initially the same amount, as shown in part (1) of the example.

Every time there is an 'operative event' on the holding (ie an event which results in the qualifying expenditure being reduced or increased), then before dealing with that event, the indexed pool value is increased by:

$$\frac{RE - RL}{RL}$$

where RE is the retail prices index for the month in which the event occurs, and RL is the retail prices index for the month when the last event occurred (or the month the pool was created if there have been no previous acquisitions or disposals).

The first operative event after 5 April 1998 is the last occasion on which the indexation adjustment will be made, indexation being given only up to April 1998 as shown in the example. Thereafter the unindexed and indexed pool figures will be adjusted only for disposals and for scrip and rights issues. It is possible to calculate the final indexation in anticipation of that operative event, as shown in part (3)(a). However, it is still necessary to identify separately the cost and indexed cost, because indexation cannot create or increase a loss.

The index increase is expressed as a decimal (and unlike the normal indexation allowance calculation, there is no stipulation for this to be rounded to three decimal places, although as indicated in part (4) of the example, HMRC would probably not object if rounded figures from published indexation tables were used). If RL exceeds RE the indexed rise is nil and the indexed pool value remains the same. When the next purchase or sale occurs, however, RL in that calculation is the index for the month of the previous operative event, even though no index adjustment took place.

In part (2) of the example, therefore, the indexed pool is uplifted at June 1996 using an index figure of 153.0. In July 1996, the index figure is 152.4, so RL exceeds RE and no adjustment is made. In September 1998 the uplift is calculated using the index at the last event, ie that of 152.4 for July 1996, even though the pool value to which the uplift is added was established using an index figure of 153.0.

After the index adjustment has been made to the indexed pool, the new expenditure is then added to both pool values.

Where a disposal occurs, a proportionate deduction is made from both pools, the indexation allowance on the disposal being the difference between the two pool values.

If a receipt is not treated as a disposal (eg on a capital distribution or sale of rights – see Example 79 note 2), the amount received is deducted from both pool values.

The operation of the indexed pool is shown in parts (1) and (2) of the example, and the treatment of capital distributions and rights issues is dealt with in Examples 79 and 80.

Pre-1982 pool

(b)   Where a general rebasing election has been made (see note 4(c)), the pre-1982 pool is regarded as having been acquired at 31 March 1982 value. If the rebasing election has not been made, the gain or loss is still calculated using 31 March 1982 value unless using cost would show a lower gain or loss. If one method shows a loss and the other a gain, the transaction is treated as giving neither gain nor loss. If, however, the calculation using cost already shows neither a loss nor a gain that result is not disturbed.

The indexation allowance is calculated by taking the increase in the retail prices index between March 1982 and the month of disposal, but with no further index increases being added after April 1998. The calculation is based on 31 March 1982 value, unless there has not been a rebasing election and using the cost would give a higher figure (s 55). (For the application of this provision in relation to certain no loss/no gain disposals see Example 85 explanatory note 1.)

The statutory rules for dealing with the pre-1982 pool require complex adjustments to be made where rights shares are concerned. The approach shown in part (4) of this example and in Example 79 produces virtually the same figures as the strictly correct method but using the same method as is used for the post-1982 pool. It is considered that it would be acceptable to HMRC. Note, however, that unlike the post-1982 pool, indexation calculations are rounded to three decimal places. The figure is frequently shown as a percentage, and in this event the percentage increase needs to be shown to one decimal place. After April 1998, the indexation on the March 1982 figures will be 104.7%.

Unless the rebasing election has been made, the pre-1982 pool and shares acquired before 6 April 1965 (if also not covered by a pooling election) still have to be regarded as separate assets for identification purposes because of the rules for working out gains and losses. If the rebasing election has been made, however, the pre 6 April 1965 shares are merged with the pre-1982 pool, since all the shares will be treated as sold and reacquired on 31 March 1982 with the same 31 March 1982 value.

Pre-6 April 1965 acquisitions

(c)   Unless either a pooling election or a general rebasing election has been made, each pre 6 April 1965 acquisition is treated as a *separate asset*, so that a separate calculation must be made when it is disposed of, and disposals are linked to acquisitions on a last in, first out basis. Two computations are necessary.

The first computation compares the proceeds both with the original cost and with the market value at 6 April 1965, taking indexation allowance into account in both cases. The indexation allowance is based on the higher of the value of the shares at 31 March 1982 and either the cost or 6 April 1965 value as the case may be. If the results using both figures show a gain the lower gain is taken. If both figures produce a loss the lower loss is taken. If one figure produces a gain and the other a loss the transaction is treated as giving rise to neither gain nor loss (Sch 2.2).

The second computation compares the proceeds with the 31 March 1982 value of the shares, but the indexation allowance is nonetheless based on the higher of the 31 March 1982 value and either the cost or 6 April 1965 value whichever was used to arrive at the result in the first computation. If, however, the first computation had already resulted in no gain no loss, that result stands and the second computation is not made.

Partly paid shares

8.   Where a company issues partly paid shares, the subsequent calls qualify for any available indexation allowance from the date the shares were issued, unless they are paid more than 12 months later, in which case they qualify from the date they are paid (s 113). This does not apply where the shares are already fully paid, but are then sold with the price payable by instalments, as in the case of the privatisation issues, which qualified for indexation allowance on the full purchase price from the date of issue even if sold when some instalments had not been paid, providing any unpaid instalments were added to the disposal proceeds in the computation on the sale. Any privatisation issue vouchers that were used to reduce bills were deducted from the allowable cost. Any free shares acquired later were added to the holding and treated as acquired at market value on the first day of dealing in them.

Unit trusts, investment trusts and open-ended investment companies (OEICs)

9.   Authorised unit trusts and investment trusts are exempt from tax on their gains (s 100). Disposals by those who invest in such trusts are usually chargeable to tax in the normal way. Those who invest in unit and investment trusts through monthly savings schemes used to be able to simplify the post-1982 pool calculations by being treated as if they had made a single annual investment in the seventh month of the trust's accounting year, but this no longer applies. Each monthly contribution must now therefore be separately identified.

The 2003 Budget Press Releases included a statement that the rules are unwieldy when applied to savings plans, and a promise that a clearer explanation of how to operate them is being developed. Presumably it will use some of the simplifying effects of the post-indexation regime. Under taper relief, when units are disposed of, the monthly acquisitions can be grouped together in bands of 3 years (no taper) and single years after that (5%, 10% etc). The effect of separate identification will therefore be quite similar to the previous rule. However, if any individual month's acquisition shows a loss, that should be separately identified for offset against gains with the lowest taper.

From 28 April 1997, open-ended investment companies (OEICs) are permitted under UK law. The shares in OEICs may be continuously created or redeemed, depending on investor demand. They are treated in essentially the same way as unit trusts, and existing unit trusts may convert into OEICs if they wish.

Cross reference

10.   See Example 96 explanatory note 8 for the treatment of shares that have become of negligible value.

Stock lending, repos, etc

11.   In line with the Government's intention to maintain the competitiveness of the UK in world financial markets, there are various special rules designed to facilitate stock market transactions such as stock lending, manufactured payments and 'repos' (ie sale and repurchase transactions where the repurchase price is fixed, fluctuations in market value being borne by the original holder) (TA 1988 ss 727, 727A, 730A, 736A, 737A to 737E, TCGA 1992 ss 263A to 263C, FA 2003 Sch 38).

(1)   (i)   In 1972 Kevin bought 2,000 ordinary shares in Collins plc for £12,000. The shares were quoted at £8.80 each on 31 March 1982. Collins plc made a scrip issue of one ordinary share for every four held in December 1985 and a further scrip issue of one for one in May 2005. In July 2006 Kevin sold 2,500 of his shares for £20,840. Kevin has not made a general 31.3.82 rebasing election.

Calculate the chargeable gain or allowable loss arising.

(ii)   Show the position if Kevin had acquired the 2,000 shares in July 1983, all other particulars remaining the same (but references to 31 March 1982 being irrelevant).

(2)   Before 31 March 1982 Sharon acquired the following shares in Digby plc:

Number of shares	Date acquired	Cost
		£
2,000	11.4.79	8,000
1,500	8.1.81	9,000

The shares were quoted at £6.25 each on 31 March 1982. A further 2,000 shares were acquired in February 1984 for £16,500. In November 1986 Digby plc made a rights issue of 1 ordinary share for every 10 held, at £6 each. Sharon took up her rights in full. She sold 2,600 shares in October 2006 for £19,500 and a further 3,000 shares in March 2007 for £24,000. Sharon has not made a general 31.3.82 rebasing election.

Calculate the chargeable gain or allowable loss arising on the disposals and, without making calculations, state what the position would have been if the rights issue had been made in June 1999, all other particulars remaining the same.

(3)   On 1 November 1981 Charlton purchased 10,000 Marietta plc shares at £1 each. The shares were quoted at £1.20 each on 31 March 1982. On 20 January 2006 the company made a rights issue of one share for every five held at £1 per share. The shares were quoted at £3 immediately after the rights issue. Charlton did not take up the shares and sold his rights for 80p per share. On 24 April 2006 he sold 2,000 shares for £5,500.

What is his capital gains tax position on the sale of the rights and on the subsequent sale of the shares, assuming he had not made a general 31 March 1982 rebasing election?

(4)   In January 1998 the Tinpot Co plc offered its shareholders a scrip option of a cash dividend of 5p per share or 1 share for every 30 held. The shares were quoted at £1.60 each on the first day of dealing. A second scrip option was offered in May 2006 on the basis of a cash dividend of 3p per share or 1 share for 60. The shares were quoted at £2.20 each on the first day of dealing.

Mr Eager, who has made a general rebasing election, has a 1982 holding of 9,000 Tinpot shares with a 31 March 1982 value of £12,600. Show the effect on his holding if he took up both scrip offers.

(5)   On 27 June 2006 Julian sold 5,000 quoted ordinary shares in Verdon plc for £31,250. Before the sale he owned 14,600 such shares, the history of his holding being as follows:

		£
March 1979	Bought 4,500 shares for	3,520
September 1980	Bought 1,500 shares for	3,050
November 1982	Bought 2,000 shares for	4,130
April 1984	Received a 1 for 2 scrip issue	
May 1988	Rights offer of 1 for 5 at £2 a share. One half of the rights sold nil paid for proceeds of £3 a share and other half of rights shares taken up. Ex rights price was £4.80 a share.	
July 1989	Bought 2,400 shares for	12,000
March 1994	Sold 1,000 shares for	3,500

The market value of the shares in issue at 31 March 1982 was £2.10 per share.

Julian had made a general rebasing election in respect of assets held at 31 March 1982.

Calculate the chargeable gain or allowable loss arising on the sale of the rights shares in May 1988, the 1,000 shares in March 1994 and the 5,000 shares in June 2006.

The following retail price indices may be used:

Mar 82	79.44
Jul 83	85.30
Feb 84	87.20
Apr 85	94.78
Nov 86	99.29
Apr 98	162.6

(1) **Kevin – scrip issues** (see explanatory note 1)

(i) The original cost of the shares was £6 each and the 31.3.82 value £8.80 each. Provided that the computation using 31.3.82 value shows a gain, the alternative computation using cost need not be carried out. Following the first scrip issue in December 1985 Kevin's holding in Collins plc is increased to (2,000 + 500 =) 2,500 shares. The 31.3.82 value of £8.80 per share before the scrip issue is therefore adjusted to (8.80 x 4/5 =) £7.04. Following the second scrip issue in May 2005 the holding becomes 5,000 shares and the 31.3.82 value per share becomes (£7.04 x ½ =) £3.52.

	£
The position is as follows:	
Sale proceeds 2,500 shares July 2006	20,840
31.3.82 value 2,500 @ £3.52 (being higher than cost of £6,000)	8,800
	12,040
Indexation allowance to April 1998 – on 31.3.82 value of 2,500 x £3.52 = £8,800 x 104.7%	9,214
Chargeable gain (which will be reduced by 35% taper relief provided that it is not offset by capital losses or other reliefs)	2,826

(ii) Kevin's shares would constitute a post-1982 pool as follows:

	Number of shares	Unindexed pool value £	Indexed pool value £
July 1983	2,000	12,000	12,000
Indexation allowance $\dfrac{94.78 - 85.3}{85.3} = 11.1\%$			1,332
At 6 April 1985	2,000	12,000	13,332
December 1985 scrip issue 1 for 4	500		
May 2005 scrip issue 1 for 2	2,500		
(no indexation adjustment since pool value not increased)			
	5,000		
Sold July 2006	(2,500)		
Indexed rise to April 1998 $\dfrac{162.6 - 94.78}{94.78}$			9,540
			22,872
Applicable to sale $\dfrac{2,500}{5,000}$		(6,000)	(11,436)
Carried forward	2,500	6,000	11,436
Sale proceeds			20,840
Indexed pool cost			(11,436)
Chargeable gain (subject to 35% taper relief as before)			£ 9,404

(2)   **Sharon – rights issue** (see explanatory note 1)

Sharon's holding in Digby plc is as follows:

Post-1982 pool		Number of shares	Unindexed pool value £	Indexed pool value £
February 1984		2,000	16,500	16,500
Indexation allowance $\dfrac{94.78 - 87.2}{87.2} = 8.7\%$				1,436
At 6 April 1985				17,936
November 86 Rights issue 1 for 10		200		
Indexed rise $\dfrac{99.29 - 94.78}{94.78}$				853
Add new expenditure to both pools			1,200	1,200
		2,200	17,700	19,989

Pre-1982 pool	Number of shares	Cost of original shares £	Cost of rights shares £	Total cost £
11.4.79	2,000	8,000		8,000
8.1.81	1,500	9,000		9,000
	3,500			
Nov 86 Rights issue 1 for 10	350		2,100	2,100
	3,850	17,000	2,100	19,100

Value of 3,500 shares at 31.3.82 @ £6.25 is £21,875.

The sale of 2,600 shares in October 2006 is identified with the 2,200 shares in the post-1982 pool and with 400 out of the 3,850 shares in the pre-1982 pool. The sale of 3,000 shares in March 2007 comes out of the remaining 3,450 shares in the pre-1982 pool. The position is therefore as follows.

Post-1982 pool		Number of shares	Unindexed pool value £	Indexed pool value £
At November 1986		2,200	17,700	19,989
Sold October 2006		(2,200)		
Indexed rise to April 1998 $\dfrac{162.6 - 99.29}{99.29}$				12,746
				32,735
Applicable to sale			(17,700)	(32,735)
Sale proceeds $\dfrac{2,200}{2,600} \times 19,500$				16,500
Cost				(17,700)
Allowable loss				(1,200)

Pre-1982 pool

October 2006 sale

The position using cost is:		£	£
Sale proceeds 400 shares $\dfrac{400}{2,600}$ x 19,500			3,000
Cost $\dfrac{400}{3,850}$ x 17,000		1,766	
Cost of rights $\dfrac{400}{3,850}$ x 2,100		218	1,984
Unindexed gain			1,016

Indexation allowance (on 31.3.82 value, being higher than cost)

$\dfrac{400}{3,850}$ x 21,875 = 2,273 x 104.7%   2,380

Indexation allowance on cost of rights (see above) from November 1986

$\dfrac{162.6 - 99.29}{99.29}$ = 63.8% x 218   139

                                       2,519

but restricted to	1,016
No loss using cost	–

The position using 31 March 1982 value is as follows, although it need not in fact be calculated since the calculation using cost shows neither loss nor gain, and the alternative calculation cannot replace that result either with a loss or a gain:

	£	£
Sale proceeds as above		3,000
31.3.82 value $\dfrac{400}{3,850}$ x 21,875	2,273	
Cost of rights as above	218	2,491
Unindexed gain		509
Indexation allowance as above but restricted to		509
No loss using 31.3.82 value		–

There is therefore neither gain nor loss.

The total allowable loss on the disposal is therefore £1,200.

After the disposal Sharon's pre-1982 pool is as follows:

	Number of shares	Cost of original shares £	Cost of rights shares £	Total cost £
Before sale October 2006	3,850	17,000	2,100	19,100
Shares sold	400	1,766	218	1,984
Leaving	3,450	15,234*	1,882	17,116

* The 31.3.82 value of the 3,450 shares is (21,875 – 2,273) = £19,602 plus £1,882 for the rights shares, giving a total 31.3.82 value of £21,484.

March 2007 sale

		£	£
The position using cost is:			
Sale proceeds 3,000 shares			24,000
Cost $\dfrac{3,000}{3,450}$ x £15,234		13,247	
Cost of rights $\dfrac{3,000}{3,450}$ x £1,882		1,637	14,884
Unindexed gain			9,116

Indexation allowance on 31.3.82 value

$$\frac{3,000}{3,450} \text{ x £19,602} = \text{£17,045 x 104.7\%} \qquad 17,846$$

Indexation allowance on cost of rights from November 1986

$$\frac{162.6 - 99.29}{99.29} = 63.8\% \text{ x } 1,882 \qquad \begin{array}{r} 1,201 \\ \hline 19,047 \end{array}$$

but restricted to	9,116
No loss using cost and calculation using 31.3.82 value not relevant	–

After the March 2007 disposal Sharon's pre-1982 pool is as follows:

	Number of shares	Cost of original shares £	Cost of rights shares £	Total cost £
After October 2006 sale as above	3,450	15,234	1,882	17,116
Shares sold	3,000	13,247	1,637	14,884
Leaving	450	1,987*	245	2,232

* The 31.3.82 value of the 450 shares is (19,602 – 17,045) = £2,557 plus £245 for the rights shares, giving a total 31.3.82 value of £2,802.

Using the non-statutory method outlined in Example 78 part (4), the position on the pre-1982 pool would be as follows:

	Number of shares	Unindexed pool cost	Indexed pool cost	Unindexed 31.3.82 value	Indexed 31.3.82 value
		£	£	£	£
11.4.79	2,000	8,000			
8.1.81	1,500	9,000			
At 31.3.82	3,500	17,000	17,000	21,875	21,875
Nov 86 Rights issue 1 for 10	350				
Indexed rise*					
$\dfrac{99.29 - 79.44}{79.44} = 25\%$			5,469		5,469
Add new expenditure to both pools		2,100	2,100	2,100	2,100
	3,850	19,100	24,569	23,975	29,444
Sold October 2006	(400)				
Indexed rise to April 1998*					
$\dfrac{162.6 - 99.29}{99.29} = 63.8\% \times 29,444$			18,785		18,785
			43,354		48,229
Applicable to sale $\dfrac{400}{3,850}$		(1,985)	(4,504)	(2,491)	(5,011)
	3,450	17,115	38,850	21,484	43,218
Sold March 2007	(3,000)				
Applicable to sale $\dfrac{3,000}{3,450}$		(14,883)	(33,783)	(18,682)	(37,581)
cf	450	2,232	5,067	2,802	5,637

* Since 31.3.82 value is above cost, the indexed rise is calculated on the 31.3.82 value, and the same figure appears in both the cost and the 31.3.82 value columns.

Since the proceeds of £3,000 for the October 2006 sale lie between £1,985 and £5,011 there is neither gain nor loss. The same applies on the March 2007 sale, where the proceeds of £24,000 lie between £14,883 and £37,581.

The benefit of the non-statutory approach is that it is not necessary to keep the cost and 31 March 1982 values separate from the cost of the rights because the indexation adjustment has already been made. It is particularly beneficial following the FA 1998 changes, because the final indexation adjustment is made at April 1998 and subsequent sales are dealt with by simply taking the appropriate proportions, as shown for the March 2007 sale.

The non-statutory approach also means that a standardised treatment is used for both the post-1982 pool and the pre-1982 pool. If a rebasing election had been made, only three columns would be required.

If rights issue had been made in June 1999

Although the rights shares would be added to the post- and pre-1982 pools as shown, no indexation allowance would be due on the rights shares. A final indexation adjustment to April

1998 would be made to both pools prior to adding in the rights shares. If the statutory method was being used for the pre-1982 pool, the indexation adjustment to April 1998 would be made at the time of each subsequent sale, calculated on the cost of the shares sold, excluding the appropriate number of rights shares.

(3)　**Charlton – sale of rights nil paid** (see explanatory note 1)

The proceeds of the sale of rights in January 2006 are 2,000 @ 80p = £1,600. Since this is less than £3,000, even though more than 5% of the value of the holding (10,000 shares @ £3 = £30,000 + rights proceeds £1,600 = £31,600, of which £1,600 is 5.06%) the rights sale will not be treated as a part disposal but will be regarded as reducing the cost and 31 March 1982 value of the holding for the purposes of later disposals.

If the strict statutory method is used, every time a disposal is made out of the holding, indexation allowance has to be calculated without taking into account the rights sale proceeds, and a negative indexation adjustment has to be made in respect of the rights proceeds. The non-statutory method shown below automatically adjusts for the small rights proceeds, in the same way as on a post-1982 holding. This is particularly beneficial following the freezing of indexation allowance at April 1998, because a final indexation adjustment is made at that date.

	Number of shares	Unindexed pool cost	Indexed pool cost	Unindexed 31.3.82 value	Indexed 31.3.82 value
		£	£	£	£
1 November 1981	10,000	10,000	10,000	12,000	12,000
January 2006 Sale of rights Indexed rise from March 1982 to April 1998 104.7% x 12,000			12,564		12,564
Deduct rights sale proceeds		(1,600)	(1,600)	(1,600)	(1,600)
	10,000	8,400	20,964	10,400	22,964
April 2006 sold Applicable to sale 2,000	(2,000)				
10,000		(1,680)	(4,193)	(2,080)	(4,593)
	8,000	6,720	16,771	8,320	18,371

Proceeds of £5,500 are compared with £4,593 (highest of four figures), giving a gain of £907 (subject to 35% taper relief unless offset by capital losses).

If all or part of Charlton's 2005/06 capital gains exemption was available, he could have treated the January 2006 sale of rights as a part disposal if he had wished. Instead of all the pool figures being reduced by £1,600, the deductions would be based on the proportions of the respective cost figures that the cash received bore to the total value of the holding, ie 1,600/31,600, as follows:

Amount of deduction	£
From unindexed pool cost	506
From indexed pool cost	1,142
From unindexed 31.3.82 value	608
From indexed 31.3.82 value	1,244

This would leave higher base costs carried forward, and the chargeable gain would be (1,600 – 1,244 =) £356, which would be reduced or eliminated by taper relief and the available annual exemption.

(4)   **Mr Eager – scrip dividend options** (see explanatory note 3)

On the first scrip offer, Mr Eager could take a dividend of (30 x 5p =) £1.50 or a share worth £1.60 for every 30 shares held. The difference of 10p represents 6.25% of the value of the share, so the 'appropriate amount in cash' is the cash dividend. On the second scrip offer, the choice is between a dividend of (60 x 3p =) £1.80 and a share worth £2.20 for every 60 shares held. The difference of 40p represents 18.18% of the value of the share, so the 'appropriate amount in cash' is the first day price of the shares.

The scrip shares acquired in January 1998 are added in to the pre-1982 pool in the same way as ordinary scrip shares. The scrip shares acquired in May 2006 are treated as a separate, free-standing post 5 April 1998 acquisition. The position is therefore as follows:

Tinpot Co plc

Pre-1982 pool	*Shares*	*Unindexed 31.3.82 value* £	*Indexed 31.3.82 value* £
Holding at January 1998	9,000	12,600	12,600
Indexed rise from March 1982 100.8%			12,701
			25,301
Scrip option shares (@ 1.50 cash option value)	300	450	450
Holding (to be indexed to April 1998)	9,300	13,050	25,751

Post-5 April 1998 shares	*Number*	*Cost* £
Scrip option shares acquired May 2006 (@ £2.20 first day price)	155	341

(5)   **Julian – Part sale of rights shares in May 1988, sales of 1,000 shares in March 1994 and 5,000 shares in June 2006**

At the date of the rights issue in May 1988 the holding comprises:

Pre-1982 pool (non-statutory method)	*Shares*	*Unindexed 31.3.82 value* £	*Indexed 31.3.82 value (£2.10)* £
March 1979 Bought	4,500		
Sept 1980 Bought	1,500		
	6,000	12,600	12,600
April 1984 Scrip issue 1 for 2	3,000	–	–
	9,000	12,600	12,600
Indexed rise to May 1988 33.7%			4,246
	9,000	12,600	16,846

Post-1982 pool	*Shares*	*Unindexed pool value* £	*Indexed pool value* £
Nov 1982 Bought	2,000	4,130	4,130
April 1984 Scrip issue 1 for 2	1,000		
Indexation allowance to April 85			
$\dfrac{94.78 - 82.66}{82.66} = 14.7\%$			607
At 6 April 1985	3,000	4,130	4,737
Indexed rise to May 1988 $\dfrac{106.2 - 94.78}{94.78}$			571
	3,000	4,130	5,308

Value of holdings in May 1988:	*Pre-1982 pool* £	*Post-1982 pool* £
9,000/3,000 shares @ ex rights price of £4.80 each	43,200	14,400
1,800/600 rights shares worth £3 each nil paid,		
half sold, half retained	5,400	1,800
	48,600	16,200

5% of (48,600 + 16,200) £64,800 = £3,240, which is less than rights sale proceeds of (1,200 @ £3) = £3,600, so sale of rights is treated as part disposal. Cost of part disposed of is:

Pre-1982 pool

Unindexed value $12,600 \times \dfrac{2,700}{48,600} = £700$. Indexed value $16,846 \times \dfrac{2,700}{48,600} = £936$

Post-1982 pool

Unindexed value $4,130 \times \dfrac{900}{16,200} = £229$. Indexed value $5,308 \times \dfrac{900}{16,200} = £295$

The sale of 1,000 shares in March 1994 is identified with the post-1982 pool.

The sale of 5,000 shares in June 2006 is identified first with the post-1982 pool, then with the pre-1982 pool.

The sale and acquisition of rights shares in May 1988 and sales in March 1994 and June 2006 are therefore dealt with as follows:

Post-1982 pool at May 1988 as above

	Shares	*Unindexed pool value* £	*Indexed pool value* £
	3,000	4,130	5,308
Applicable to sale of rights		(229)	(295)
Rights shares purchased	300	600	600
cf	3,300	4,501	5,613

	Shares	Unindexed pool value £	Indexed pool value £
bf	3,300	4,501	5,613
July 1989 Bought	2,400		
Indexed rise			
$\dfrac{115.5 - 106.2}{106.2}$			
			492
Add new expenditure		12,000	12,000
	5,700	16,501	18,105
March 1994 Sold	(1,000)		
Indexed rise			
$\dfrac{142.5 - 115.5}{115.5}$			
			4,232
			22,337
Applicable to sale (1,000/5,700)		(2,895)	(3,919)
	4,700	13,606	18,418
June 2006 Sold	(4,700)		
Indexed rise to April 1998			
$\dfrac{162.6 - 142.5}{142.5}$			
			2,598
Applicable to sale		13,606	21,016

	Shares	Unindexed 31.3.82 value £	Indexed 31.3.82 value £
Pre-1982 pool at May 1988 as above	9,000	12,600	16,846
Applicable to sale of rights		(700)	(936)
Rights shares purchased	900	1,800	1,800
	9,900	13,700	17,710
June 2006 Sold	(300)		
Indexed rise to April 1998			
$\dfrac{162.6 - 106.2}{106.2} = 53.1\%$			9,404
			27,114
Applicable to sale (300/9,900)		(415)	(822)
cf	9,600	13,285	26,292

On sale of 1,200 rights shares May 1988 (sold for more than indexed cost):

Sale proceeds 300 shares in post-1982 pool	900
Indexed cost as above	295
Gain	£ 605
Sale proceeds 900 shares in pre-1982 pool	2,700
Indexed cost as above	936
Gain	£ 1,764
Total gain on May 1988 sale of rights	£ 2,369

On sale of 1,000 shares March 1994 (proceeds between unindexed and indexed cost):

Sale proceeds 1,000 shares in post-1982 pool	3,500
Unindexed cost as above	2,895
Unindexed gain	605
Indexation allowance (3,919 − 2,895) = 1,024, but restricted to	(605)
No gain no loss	–

On sale of 5,000 shares June 2006 (sold for more than indexed cost):

Sale proceeds 4,700 shares in post-1982 pool (4,700/5,000 x £31,250)	29,375
Indexed cost as above	21,016
Gain	£ 8,359
Sale proceeds 300 shares in pre-1982 pool (300/5,000 x £31,250)	1,875
Indexed cost as above	822
Gain	£ 1,053
Total gain on June 2006 sale of shares (eligible for 35% taper relief)	£ 9,412

Explanatory Notes

Scrip and rights issues

1. A reorganisation of a company's capital (eg by scrip or rights issue) is not treated as a disposal of the original shares or acquisition of a new holding. The new shares stand in the shoes of the old as regards acquisition date and cost, but for indexation purposes any payment for rights shares is regarded as incurred on the date when it was actually incurred and not when the original shares were acquired (TCGA 1992 ss 126–131), so that indexation allowance is not given on rights shares acquired after 5 April 1998 as illustrated in part (2) of the example. On the other hand, when such rights shares form part of pre-6 April 1998 acquisitions and the shares do not constitute business assets, their cost is taken into account in computing the gain eligible for the extra year's taper relief.

   If on the reorganisation the shareholder receives any cash from the company, that cash is regarded as a capital distribution and is accordingly dealt with as detailed in note 2 below (s 128(2)). The value of the holding is worked out by taking the ex rights value of the existing shares plus the proceeds of the sale of rights. Where a shareholder sells some of his rights and takes up the balance, the value of the holding at the time of the sale includes the 'nil paid' value of the rights retained (see part (5) of the example). In part (3) of the example, since the £1,600 cash received is less than £3,000, even though more than 5% of the value of the holding, it is regarded as 'small' and therefore reduces the base cost of the holding instead of being treated as a part disposal (unless Charlton chooses the part disposal treatment). Part (5) of the example illustrates rights proceeds that are not 'small'.

Capital distributions

2. Where a company makes a capital distribution it is treated as a disposal of an interest in the shares (TCGA 1992 s 122) and a chargeable gain or allowable loss arises accordingly, unless the distribution is regarded as 'small'. HMRC will accept a distribution as small if it is *either* not more than 5% of the value of the shares *or* not more than £3,000, and they will consider on their merits cases where the taxpayer wants an amount to be treated as small even though it exceeds both these limits. Where the capital distribution is small then instead of being treated as a part disposal it is regarded as reducing the base cost of the holding. HMRC will not, however, object if someone wants to treat the receipt as

a part disposal, which may be to their advantage if a gain would be covered by the annual exemption, or if a loss would reduce an existing chargeable gain, as illustrated in part (3) of the example. A small capital distribution must be treated as a part disposal if it exceeds the allowable expenditure, or if the allowable expenditure is nil (as is the case with demutualisation shares). Where there is allowable expenditure that is less than the 'small' capital distribution, the amount chargeable may be reduced by that expenditure, leaving the holding with no allowable cost for future disposals.

For indexation purposes, the treatment of a 'small' capital distribution that relates to a post-1982 pool is covered by the provisions in Example 78 explanatory note 7(a). If the 'small' capital distribution relates to a pre-1982 pool or to pre-6 April 1965 shares, the legislation provides that the original cost of the holding (or 31 March 1982 value where appropriate) is indexed from March 1982 and the reduction from base cost is indexed from the date the capital sum is received (TCGA 1992 s 57). These adjustments are not necessary, however, if the pre-1982 pool is maintained in the same way as the post-1982 pool, as indicated in Example 78 explanatory note 7(b). This is illustrated in part (3) of the example in relation to a nil paid sale of rights (which is treated as a capital distribution – see note 1).

Some companies return capital to shareholders by linking the payment to a consolidation of the shares in order to avoid a reduction in earnings per share. The cash received in such instances represents a capital distribution that is subject to the rules outlined above. Other companies have merely paid special dividends to shareholders, such dividends being treated as income and having no capital gains consequences.

Some companies have carried out a reorganisation of share capital into 'ordinary shares' and 'B shares', followed by a purchase of the B shares through a broker or redemption of the B shares by the company. Although this seems to be a transparent scheme to circumvent the treatment of a purchase of own shares as a dividend, it appears that HMRC generally allow the share split to be treated as a capital reorganisation, and the redemption of the B shares to be a pure capital disposal for the shareholders.

Scrip dividend options

3. Where scrip shares are offered by a UK resident company as an alternative to a cash dividend, the capital gains tax cost for an individual, personal representatives, or trustees of a discretionary trust (other than one in which the settlor retains an interest) is the 'appropriate amount in cash'. That means the amount of the cash option, unless it is substantially different from the market value of the shares (TCGA 1992 s 142), 'substantially' was previously interpreted by HMRC as 15% or more either way (Statement of Practice A8). HMRC also ignored differences of up to 17% in any cases not involving deliberate avoidance. SP A8 also stated that the 15% calculation was based on the market value of the shares, but in fact HMRC accepted calculations based on the cash dividend instead. From 6 April 2005, however, SP A8 has been legislated for and its provisions are now found in ITTOIA 2005 s 412. That refers to a 15% figure and this is applied to the market value. However, it remains to be seen whether HMRC will continue to relax the rules in accordance with former SP A8 in certain cases. If the difference is substantial, the appropriate amount in cash is the market value of the shares on the first day of dealing. This is illustrated in part (4) of the example.

    For shares acquired before 6 April 1998, the 'appropriate amount' is treated in the same way as a purchase of rights shares, ie the shares increase existing holdings proportionately, and the deemed cost attracts indexation allowance from the month of issue. This does not apply to a 'bare trust', ie where someone is absolutely entitled as against the trustees (or would be but for being an infant or a person under a disability). For bare trusts, the scrip shares are treated as acquired for the 'appropriate amount in cash' by the beneficiary directly, so that they are not treated as an addition to an existing holding (TCGA 1992 s 142).

    For shares acquired on or after 6 April 1998, scrip option shares are treated as a separate, free-standing acquisition in all cases where the shares are taxed as income (see Example 56 explanatory note 6), and not just for bare trusts (s 142).

Where scrip option shares are issued to a corporate shareholder or to a discretionary trust in which the settlor retains an interest, they are capital rather than income, with a capital gains base cost of nil (because the 'income' treatment in TA 1988 s 249 only applies where an *individual* is beneficially entitled to the shares, or when the shares are issued to personal representatives or trustees of discretionary trusts – see Example 56 explanatory note 6). This means that the whole of their value will be reflected in a capital gain on disposal, with no cost or indexation allowance.

The position of life interest trusts is not clear, and the offers by many companies some years ago of enhanced scrip options led to particular problems for such trusts. The Revenue issued a Statement of Practice (SP 4/94) giving their views. They consider that it is up to the trustees, taking into account trust law and the position of the particular trust, to decide whether the scrip shares constitute capital or income. They will not seek to challenge what the trustees have done if they have treated the scrip dividend in one of the following ways:

(a)   The scrip dividend belongs to the income beneficiary;

(b)   The scrip dividend belongs to the trust capital;

(c)   The scrip dividend is added to capital, but the income beneficiary is compensated for the loss of the cash dividend he would have had.

The effect of alternative (a) would be that the trustees would be treated as holding the shares as bare trustees, the beneficiary thus being treated as having acquired the shares directly. Under alternatives (b) and (c) the treatment would be the same as for a corporate shareholder, ie there would be no income tax implications and the shares would be treated as acquired at nil cost for capital gains tax. Different provisions apply to Scottish life interest trusts.

Some companies have replaced scrip dividend options with dividend reinvestment plans (DRIPs), under which shareholders may use their dividends to acquire shares bought on the stock market by the company on their behalf. Such schemes avoid the reduction in value of existing shares caused by issuing scrip dividend shares. Shareholders taking DRIPs have higher costs than for scrip dividends, because they have to pay brokers' fees and stamp duty reserve tax. Since the abolition of the repayable tax credit in April 1999, and the treatment of scrip dividend options as market purchases from April 1998, DRIPs are now taxed in exactly the same way as scrip dividend options (higher rate income tax on the cash dividend forgone, and a purchase of shares for CGT at the same amount).

Part sale of rights

4.   Part (5) of the example illustrates the treatment of a rights issue where the shareholder sells some of the rights nil paid and takes up the balance. The value of the unsold holding at the time of the sale includes the 'nil paid' value of the rights retained as well as the ex rights value of the existing shares.

5.   Rights shares are sometimes issued partly paid. In that event, the unpaid amount is added both to the sale proceeds when the shares are sold and to the cost (s 128). The unpaid amount is indexed from the date of acquisition of the rights shares unless it is due more than 12 months later, in which case it is indexed from the payment date (s 113). If therefore partly paid shares are sold more than 12 months before the balance is due, the balance would not qualify for indexation allowance even though it is included in the allowable expenditure. Indexation allowance is not available on rights shares acquired by non-corporate shareholders after 5 April 1998.

(1)   (i)   On 1 May 1981 Larkin purchased 6,000 ordinary shares in Maine plc at a price of £2 each. On 1 November 1981 there was a scrip issue of 1 for 2. The market value of the shares at 31 March 1982 was £1.30 each, giving £11,700.

           On 1 March 2004 there was an offer of £0.50 cash plus two ordinary shares of Street plc for each Maine plc share held.

           The offer was accepted and following acceptance Street plc's shares were quoted at £2.50 each.

           Larkin has not made a general 31.3.82 rebasing election.

           Calculate the chargeable gain, and show the position if Larkin then disposes of the Street plc holding in December 2006 for £49,500.

    (ii)   What would the position in part (i) have been if Larkin's purchase had been in May 1982, with the scrip issue taking place in November 1986?

(2)   Pamela bought 2,000 shares in Fielding plc for £3,300 in February 1984. In November 1986 Fielding plc made a rights issue of 1 preference share for every 10 ordinary shares held, at £1.20 each. Pamela took up her rights in full. The opening market values on the first day of dealing ex rights were £2 for the ordinary shares and £1.40 for the preference shares. The ordinary shares were sold for £8,000 in September 2006.

        Show the capital gains treatment of the rights issue and calculate the capital gain or allowable loss on the disposal of the ordinary shares.

(3)   Victoria owned 20,000 shares in Forum Follies plc which she purchased in May 1998 for £50,000. In November 2006 Exciting Enterprises plc acquired all the share capital of Forum Follies plc. Under the terms of the takeover shareholders in Forum Follies received 3 ordinary shares and 1 preference share in Exciting Enterprises plc plus £1 cash for every 2 shares previously held in Forum Follies plc. Immediately after the takeover the ordinary shares in Exciting Enterprises were quoted at £3 each and the preference shares at £1.50 each. Victoria then sold the preference shares, receiving £15,000, in June 2007.

        Calculate Victoria's gains for 2006/07 and 2007/08.

(4)   Neville owned a pre-1982 pool of 10,000 ordinary shares in Bateman plc. The 31 March 1982 value of the shares was 310p and Neville had made a general rebasing election. On 10 January 2004 a demerger took place in which shareholders received 1 Newbee plc ordinary share for each Bateman plc share. First day prices were Bateman plc ordinary 630p, Newbee plc ordinary 625p. On 15 June 2006 Neville sold his Newbee plc shares for £65,000. He retained his holding of Bateman plc shares.

        Show the treatment of the demerger and of the sale of the Newbee plc shares.

(5)   Michael Stewart received £250,000 on 10 July 2006 from Big plc when that company repaid all its issued 9% loan stock at par. Mr Stewart had received the loan stock (which is a qualifying corporate bond) in June 1987 in exchange for his 100,000 shares of £1 each in Small Ltd when Big plc acquired Small Ltd. Mr Stewart had acquired his shares in Small Ltd for £125,000 in November 1983. The shares were worth £250,000 in June 1987.

        Show Mr Stewart's tax position at the time of the takeover and at the time of the repayment of the loan stock.

The following retail price indices may be used:

Mar 82 79.44; May 82 81.62; Nov 83 86.67; Feb 84 87.20; Apr 85 94.78; May 86 97.85; Nov 86 99.29; June 87 101.9; Apr 98 162.6

The index increase from March 1982 to April 1998 was 104.7%.

Treat all shares as non-business assets.

(1) **Larkin – takeover** (see explanatory note 1)

   (i) *Maine plc*

		£
6,000	shares purchased 1981 @ £2	12,000
3,000	scrip issue 1 for 2 in 1981	–
9,000		12,000

Takeover by Street plc March 2004	£
18,000 Street plc shares (2 for 1) @ £2.50	45,000
Cash (50p per share for 9,000 shares)	4,500
Total value received	49,500

Since the cash of £4,500 exceeds £3,000 and also exceeds 5% of the total value received (£2,475) it is likely to be treated as a part disposal as follows:

		Using cost £	Using 31.3.82 value £
Proceeds March 2004		4,500	4,500
Cost	$\dfrac{4,500}{49,500}$ x £12,000	1,091	
31.3.82 value	$\dfrac{4,500}{49,500}$ x £11,700		1,064
		3,409	3,436
Indexation allowance to April 1998 on cost (being higher than 31.3.82 value) £1,091 x 104.7%		1,142	1,142
		2,267	2,294

Chargeable gain in 2003/04 is the lower of the two (eligible for 20% taper relief unless reduced by losses)	£ 2,267

Sale of Street plc shares December 2006		Using cost £	Using 31.3.82 value £
Sale proceeds		49,500	49,500
Cost (12,000 – 1,091 allowed on takeover by Street plc)		10,909	
31.3.82 value (11,700 – 1,064 allowed on takeover by Street plc)			10,636
		38,591	38,864
Indexation allowance to April 1998 on cost (being higher than 31.3.82 value) £10,909 x 104.7%		11,422	11,422
		27,169	27,442

Chargeable gain in 2006/07 is the lower of the two, ie	£ 27,169

The Street plc shares are treated as being identical to the Maine plc shares. They are therefore treated as owned since before 17 March 1998, and the disposal in December 2006 qualifies for 35% taper relief.

As shown in Example 78 part (4), the pre-1982 pool could be handled in the same way as the post-1982 pool. Since Larkin had not made a general rebasing election, again there would have to be computations for both cost and 31 March 1982 value, and in this case the indexed rise would be calculated on the cost figure since it is higher than 31 March 1982 value.

		Number of shares	Unindexed pool value £	Indexed pool value £
(ii)	*Post-1982 pool*			
1 May 1982 bought		6,000	12,000	12,000
Indexation allowance to April 1985 $\frac{94.78 - 81.62}{81.62} = 16.1\%$				1,932
At 6 April 1985		6,000	12,000	13,932
1 November 1986 scrip issue 1 for 2		3,000		
		9,000		
1 March 2004 Takeover (2 shares for 1)		x 2		
Indexed rise to April 1998 $\frac{162.6 - 94.78}{94.78}$				9,969
		18,000	12,000	23,901
Cash on takeover treated as part disposal.				
Cost of part disposed of is: $\frac{4,500}{49,500}$			(1,091)	(2,173)
		18,000	10,909	21,728
December 2006 Sold		(18,000)		
Applicable to sale			(10,909)	(21,728)

Proceeds March 2004 as in (i)		4,500
Indexed pool value		2,173
Chargeable gain in 2003/04 (20% taper as before)		£ 2,327
Proceeds December 2006		49,500
Indexed pool value		(21,728)
Chargeable gain in 2006/07 (35% taper as before)		£ 27,772

(2)   Pamela and Fielding plc – rights shares of a different class

Where rights shares of a different class are acquired, the existing holding is first indexed to the date of the rights issue (or April 1998 if earlier), the amount paid for the rights is added, and the respective pool values are then split according to the ex rights values of the different classes of shares on the first day that prices are quoted, as follows:

The respective values of the shares ex rights are:

10 ordinary shares @ £2	20.00
1 preference share @ £1.40	1.40
	£ 21.40

The pool values are therefore split in those proportions, ie .93458 to the ordinary shares and .06542 to the preference shares. The treatment of the transactions is as follows:

Fielding plc	Ord shares	Unindexed pool value £	Indexed pool value £
Feb 1984	2,000	3,300	3,300
Indexn to April 1985			
$\dfrac{94.78 - 87.2}{87.2}$			
= 8.7%			287
At 6.4.85	2,000	3,300	3,587
Nov 86			
Indexed rise			
$\dfrac{99.29 - 94.78}{94.78}$			171
Rights 1:10	200	240	240
	2,200	3,540	3,998
Exclude re pref .06542	(200)	(232)	(262)
Leaving re ord .93458	2,000	3,308	3,736
Sold September 2006	(2,000)		
Indexed rise to April 1998			
$\dfrac{162.6 - 99.29}{99.29}$			2,382
			6,118
Re sale		(3,308)	(6,118)
Sale proceeds September 2006			8,000
Indexed cost			(6,118)
Chargeable gain 2006/07 (eligible for 35% taper relief)			£ 1,882

Fielding plc	Pref shares	Unindexed pool value £	Indexed pool value £
At Nov 86	200	232	262

(3) **Victoria: takeover – gain on Forum Follies shares 2006/07**

Value received on takeover by Exciting Enterprises plc is:

Ordinary shares 30,000 @ £3	90,000
Preference shares 10,000 @ £1.50	15,000
Cash	10,000
	£ 115,000

Since the cash of £10,000 exceeds 5% of £115,000 (£5,750), it is likely to be treated as a part disposal of the holding.

The holding's base cost of £50,000 is split 90:15:10 as follows:

Ordinary shares	39,130
Preference shares	6,522
Cash	4,348
	£ 50,000

The new shares stand in the shoes of the old as follows:

Forum Follies plc	*Shares*	*Cost*
		£
May 1998 Bought	20,000	50,000
Nov 2006 takeover		
Cost of part disposal (cash)		(4,348)
Balance to Exciting Enterprises holdings:		45,652
Being: Ordinary		39,130
Preference		6,522
		45,652

Exciting Enterprises ord	*Shares*	*Base cost*
		£
November 2006 from Forum Follies	30,000	39,130

Exciting Enterprises pref	*Shares*	*Base cost*
		£
November 2006 from Forum Follies	10,000	6,522

The cash treated as a part disposal gives a chargeable gain (eligible for 30% taper relief) of (10,000 – 4,348) =	£ 5,652

2007/08	
Proceeds	15,000
Base cost	(6,522)
Gain	8,478

The gain arising is eligible for 35% taper relief (subject to losses and other reliefs).

(4) **Neville – demerger of Bateman plc and Newbee plc**

Subject to some special rules for trusts (see explanatory note 3), the demerger is treated in a similar way to a scrip issue of a different class, and since there is no cash element there is no indexation uplift at the time of the demerger. The value of the holding is split according to first day prices, as follows:

Bateman plc $\dfrac{630}{1,255}$ = .501992

Newbee plc $\dfrac{625}{1,255}$ = .498008

Original 31.3.82 market value was 310p. Therefore respective 31.3.82 market values following demerger are:

Bateman plc 310p × .501992 = 155.62p
Newbee plc 310p × .498008 = 154.38p

Neville's tax position is as follows:

Pre-1982 pool Bateman plc			*Shares*	*31.3.82 value*	*Indexed 31.3.82 value*
				£	£
At 31.3.82			10,000	31,000	31,000
10.1.04 To Newbee plc	(.498008)			(15,438)	(15,438)
Bateman plc cf	(.501992)		10,000	15,562	15,562

Pre-1982 pool Newbee plc		*Shares*	*31.3.82 value*	*Indexed 31.3.82 value*
			£	£
10.1.04 From Bateman plc demerger		10,000	15,438	15,438
June 2006 sold		(10,000)		
Indexed rise to April 1998 $\dfrac{162.6 - 79.44}{79.44}$				
= 104.7%				16,164
				31,602
Applicable to sale			(15,438)	(31,602)
Sale proceeds				65,000
Indexed cost				(31,602)
Chargeable gain 2006/07 (eligible for 35% taper relief)				33,398

(5) **Michael Stewart – Tax position in relation to Big plc loan stock received on takeover**

Position at time of takeover

Deemed proceeds, being value of Small Ltd shares June 1987 (see explanatory note 4)		250,000
Cost of shares November 1983	125,000	
Indexation allowance to April 1985 to establish post-1982 pool:		
$\dfrac{94.78 - 86.67}{86.67}$ = 9.4%	11,750	
	136,750	
Indexation allowance to June 1987		
136,750 x $\dfrac{101.9 - 94.78}{94.78}$	10,273	147,023
Gain held over until disposal of loan stock		£ 102,977

On the repayment of the loan stock on 10 July 2006 the held over gain is chargeable, so that there is a chargeable gain in 2006/07 of £102,977. No taper relief is available, because taper relief on such a deferred gain is based on ownership of the original asset (here, all before April 1998).

Explanatory Notes

Takeovers

1. Where shares or debentures in a new company are received for shares or debentures held in a company which has been taken over, the takeover is treated as if the two companies were the same

company and the exchange were a reorganisation of its capital (TCGA 1992 s 135) (known as 'paper for paper' treatment). Any cash received is therefore treated as a capital distribution as explained in Example 79 explanatory note 2. The part disposal element in Larkin's case in part (1) of this example is accordingly £4,500 and the gain is calculated by reference to the ratio that the cash bears to the cash plus market value of the shares received in exchange for the original shares (TCGA 1992 s 129). Since the cash is more than £3,000 and more than 5% of the value received, it is not 'small' and is not therefore treated as reducing the base cost of the holding, although HMRC has indicated that they will negotiate if the taxpayer considers that a larger receipt should be treated as 'small' in the circumstances.

See Example 74 explanatory notes 14–16 for consideration of 'earn-out' elements in a paper-for-paper takeover.

See part (5) of the example for the position where part of a takeover package takes the form of qualifying corporate bonds and see Example 81 explanatory note 10 for further comments.

Reorganisations: rights and scrip shares of a different class

2. The treatment of rights shares of a different class from the existing shares is shown in part (2) of the example. An indexation uplift is made to the holding before the cost of the rights is added in (but not after April 1998 for non-corporate shareholders), and the unindexed and indexed figures are then split between the different classes of shares according to the market values on the first day that prices are quoted following the issue (TCGA 1992 s 130).

    Similar treatment applies where different classes of shares are received as a result of a takeover, as illustrated in part (3) of the example.

    For a scrip issue of a different class the treatment is the same as for a rights issue, except that no indexation uplift is made because no additional expenditure is incurred.

Demergers

3. Demergers that are 'exempt distributions' normally do not have either income tax or capital gains tax consequences for the shareholders, although there may be a taper relief problem in some circumstances (see Example 67). The capital gains tax treatment is shown in part (4) of the example. Effectively the demerger is treated like a scrip issue of a different class of shares, the unindexed and indexed values of the shares being split between the demerged holdings according to market values on the first day that prices are quoted after the demerger.

    Demergers can cause problems for trusts. In relation to the demerger of ICI and Zeneca, it was held in the case of Sinclair v Lee (1993) that the demerger represented a capitalisation by ICI of part of its distributable profits and thus the Zeneca shares were a capital distribution in the hands of the trustees.

    This is not necessarily the case for all demergers. Where shares in a 75% subsidiary are distributed direct to the shareholders (a 'direct demerger'), the HMRC view is that although the shares are exempt from income tax under the 'exempt distribution' rules, they are nonetheless income of the trust, because under company law they are a dividend paid out of accumulated profits. The treatment then differs according to whether the trust is a discretionary trust or a life interest trust (see Revenue's Tax Bulletin October 1994). The tax consequences for trusts of the different types of demerger are dealt with in the companion to this volume, Tolley's Taxwise II 2006/07, at Example 49.

Reorganisations: qualifying corporate bonds

4. For details of the rules relating to qualifying corporate bonds, see Example 81 explanatory notes 4 to 6. Sometimes on a reorganisation of share capital or on a takeover, qualifying corporate bonds may be converted into, or exchanged for, shares or vice versa. If qualifying corporate bonds are exchanged for shares, the normal reorganisation provisions dealt with in note 1 above do not apply, and the shares are deemed to be acquired at their market value at the date of the exchange. If shares are

exchanged for qualifying corporate bonds, the shares are treated as disposed of for their market value immediately *before* the exchange, the gain or loss at that date is calculated and is then 'frozen' until the qualifying corporate bonds (or part thereof) are disposed of, when the frozen gain or loss crystallises accordingly, as illustrated in part (5) of the example (TCGA 1992 s 116). The same applies where a security changes its status from non-qualifying to qualifying corporate bond. The frozen gain or loss does not crystallise on a transfer between spouses, or intra-group (see also Example 61 part A), but it is 'inherited' by the person acquiring the bonds, so that it will crystallise on disposal by that person. (Where the shares were acquired before 31 March 1982 and the exchange took place before 6 April 1988, one half of the frozen gain is exempt from tax – see Example 83 at explanatory note 11.) Where a frozen gain crystallises, it is possible for an individual to defer it again by subscribing for shares in a qualifying unquoted trading company under the enterprise investment scheme provisions (but not VCT after 6 April 2004) (see Example 94).

For companies, under the rules for 'loan relationships', any gain or loss arising on the disposal of qualifying corporate bonds in exchange for shares on or after 1 April 1996 is brought into account in calculating income. Where shares are exchanged for qualifying corporate bonds, either before or after 1 April 1996, the 'frozen gain or loss' treatment applies, with the frozen gain or loss on the shares being brought in as a *capital* gain or loss when the bonds are disposed of (s 116(16)).

If the qualifying corporate bonds fall in value, the effect of the 'frozen gain' treatment may be that the taxpayer is charged on a gain even though in fact he has made a loss. This problem can be overcome by giving the bonds to a charity. The frozen gain will not then crystallise, nor are there any tax consequences for the charity when it disposes of the bonds (TCGA 1992 s 257, Revenue Interpretation 23).

If a frozen gain on qualifying corporate bonds has not crystallised by the time the taxpayer dies, the gain escapes tax. It is not chargeable on the personal representatives, nor on any beneficiary. If, however, there is a frozen gain accruing to the personal representatives themselves, the gain crystallises on disposal (but not on transfer to a beneficiary, the crystallisation in those circumstances being further deferred until the beneficiary disposes of the loan stock).

5. A number of companies have arranged takeovers to include the issue of 'non-QCB loan stock' (convertible into shares or a foreign currency). This is intended to extend the taper relief period for those taking the stock, because chargeable loan stock is treated in the same way as shares for CGT (so 'share-for-share' treatment would apply). In their Tax Bulletin for June 2001, the Revenue expressed the view that many of these loan notes are 'simple debts' and not 'marketable securities', and so do not extend the taper period. HMRC has reversed this view for loan stocks issued as part of a takeover or reorganisation, but it remains a possible argument where the stocks came into existence in different circumstances.

(1) On 30 September 2006 Mr McCarthy, who works for Mack plc, a quoted company, acquired 5,000 shares in the company for £25,000 with the proceeds of an approved SAYE share option scheme run by the company. The market value at the date of acquisition was £37,500. He and his wife (who does not work for the company) already had a joint holding of 20,000 shares in the company which had been held since before 17 March 1998. The indexed value to April 1998 was £128,000. Mr and Mrs McCarthy decide to sell half the joint holding on 31 October 2006, realising £76,800. Show the capital gains treatment of the sale.

(2) Alex acquired shares in his employer company (a quoted trading company) as follows:

		Number of shares	*£*
June 1997	Allocation from approved profit sharing scheme (APSS)	800	3,200
June 1998	Allocation from APSS	750	3,600
June 1999	Allocation from APSS	650	4,000
August 1999	Exercised share options	1,000	4,100
June 2000	Allocation from APSS	560	5,000
June 2001	Allocation from APSS	500	5,200
June 2002	Allocation from new approved share incentive plan (SIP)	400	6,000
June 2003	Allocation from SIP	500	5,000
August 2003	Exercised share options	1,500	9,000
June 2004	Allocation from SIP	450	4,500
June 2005	Allocation from SIP	550	5,500
June 2006	Allocation from SIP	600	7,000
		8,260	

The company's approved profit sharing scheme released each allocation of shares to Alex three years after the allocation date. The value shown is the market value on each allocation date. The SIP shares will be restricted for five years.

The company's SAYE-related share option scheme enabled Alex to buy shares in 1999 and 2002 at the prices shown. The values of the shares on the exercise dates were £6,200 in 1999 and £25,000 in 2002.

On 31 December 2006, Alex transferred 1,500 shares to his civil partner, Chris, and on 1 January 2007 they each sold 1,500 shares for their full market value of £22,500.

Set out the capital gains tax position of Alex and Chris (who does not work for the company).

(3) In what circumstances will an investment by an individual constitute a 'qualifying corporate bond'?

The following retail price indices may be used:

June 1997	157.5
April 1998	162.6

(1)   **Mrs & Mrs McCarthy – joint and separate holdings**

Even though Mr and Mrs McCarthy have disposed of some of the shares held jointly, for capital gains purposes HMRC does not regard Mr McCarthy as holding his 50% proportion of those shares in a different capacity from those he owns individually. His sale will therefore be identified with the shares acquired by him under his company's share option scheme. The position on the sale of 10,000 shares is therefore as follows:

Mr McCarthy

Sale proceeds 5,000 shares October 2006 (½ x 76,800)	38,400
Cost September 2006	25,000
Chargeable gain (reduced by annual exemption if available)	£ 13,400

Mrs McCarthy

Sale proceeds 5,000 shares October 2006	38,400
Cost pre April 1998 (¼ x 128,000)	32,000
Chargeable gain (reduced by 35% taper relief and annual exemption if available)	£ 6,400

The remaining 15,000 shares will be regarded for capital gains purposes as owned as to 10,000 by Mr McCarthy and 5,000 by Mrs McCarthy, all acquired before 17 March 1998.

(2)   **Alex and Chris**

Shares held within an employee share scheme trust are not identified with 'unrestricted' shares (TCGA 1992 s 104(4)). The allocations in June 2002, 2003, 2004, 2005 and 2006 are therefore not identified with the disposal. The shares which have been released from the APSS are treated as acquired on the allocation date for their market value; shares acquired under an approved option scheme are treated as acquired on the date the option is exercised for the amount paid for them.

Alex's holding on 31 December 2006 is therefore:

Post-1982 pool

	Number of shares	Cost £	Indexed cost £
June 1997	800	3,200	3,200
Indexn. to April 1998			
$\dfrac{162.6 - 157.5}{157.5}$			104
Closing pool 5 April 1998	800	3,200	3,304

Post 5.4.98 acquisitions

	Number of shares	Cost £
June 1998	750	3,600
June 1999	650	4,000
August 1999	1,000	4,100
June 2000	560	5,000
June 2001	500	5,200
August 2003	1,500	9,000

Transfer to Chris 31 December 2006

For identification purposes, the transfer to Chris is treated as any other disposal. He therefore acquires the latest shares acquired by Alex, ie the August 2003 shares.

Disposals 1 January 2007

		£
Chris's gain is:	Proceeds	22,500
	Cost	9,000
	Gain (before taper relief)	13,500

Although he can count Alex's ownership period for taper relief, the status of the shares is based upon Chris's own personal circumstances, and unlike Alex he is not an employee of the company. Therefore, he is treated as disposing of a non-business asset which he is treated as having owned for between three and four years. Therefore 5% taper relief is due.

Alex's own gain is based on the 500 shares acquired in June 2001, 560 shares acquired in June 2000 and 440 of the 1,000 shares acquired in August 1999. The gains are:

	£
Proceeds for 500 shares	7,500
Cost June 2001	(5,200)
Gain A	2,300
Proceeds for 560 shares	8,400
Cost June 2000	(5,000)
Gain B	3,400
Proceeds for 440 shares	6,600
Cost August 1999 440/1,000 x 4,100	(1,804)
Gain C	4,796

The qualifying period for taper relief is gain A five years, gain B six years and gain C seven years (for either business or non-business assets). The shares became business assets on 6 April 2000, and the time-apportioned fraction of gain C attributable to the period since that date will enjoy 75% taper relief. The non-business proportion will attract taper relief at 25%. Assuming the acquisitions were at the *beginning* of each month, the overall period of ownership was 1.8.99 – 1.1.07 = 89 months for the August 1999 acquisition, of which the business assets proportion (working in round months) is 6.4.00 – 1.1.07 = 81 months. The gains are therefore:

	£
Gain A	2,300
Less: 75%	(1,725)
	575
Gain B	3,400
Less: 75%	(2,550)
	850
Gain C	4,796
Less: 75% × 81/89 × 4,796	(3,274)
25% × 8/89 × 4,796	(108)
	1,414

This calculation assumes that no other reliefs (such as capital losses) are available against these gains, as they would reduce the taper relief.

After the disposal, Alex would still own 560 shares acquired in August 1999 with a base cost of £2,296, 650 shares acquired in June 1999 at a cost of £4,000, 750 shares acquired in June 1998 at a cost of £3,600, and 800 shares in the post-1982 pool, with a cost of £3,200 and an indexed cost of £3,304.

(3)   **Qualifying corporate bonds**

Qualifying corporate bonds (QCBs) are defined in TCGA 1992 s 117 as sterling loan stock purchased or issued on commercial terms after 13 March 1984, including bonds that are convertible into other qualifying corporate bonds but excluding bonds that are convertible into shares or other kinds of securities and securities linked to a share index. The interest bearing stocks that are outside the definition, therefore, are those denominated in a foreign currency, those that are convertible into shares or linked to a share index, and non-commercial loans. Corporate bonds purchased before 14 March 1984 are also outside the definition.

QCBs are exempt from the charge to capital gains tax. Profits on some QCBs (relevant discounted securities) are chargeable to income tax; on most other QCBs, an income tax accrued income scheme charge has to be calculated on disposal.

A loan stock which is a 'debt on a security' and which is not a QCB is a chargeable asset for capital gains tax, and will give rise to gains, losses, indexation allowance and taper relief in the normal way. A loan stock which is a 'simple debt' may not be chargeable to CGT – see Example 80 explanatory note 5 and Example 74 explanatory note 12. Various points on non-exempt loan stocks are set out in explanatory notes 7 and 8.

Explanatory Notes

References in these notes are to TCGA 1992 unless otherwise stated.

Shares acquired under HMRC approved schemes

1.   Unless they are subject to any special restrictions, shares acquired under approved SAYE and discretionary share option schemes are treated in the same way as other acquisitions. They are regarded as acquired on the date the option is exercised for the amount paid for them, plus the amount, if any, paid for the option. The amounts paid attract indexation allowance from the date of payment, but not after April 1998.

2.   Shares acquired under an approved profit sharing scheme (APSS) or approved share incentive plan (SIP) are in each case regarded as being of a different class from other shares held by the employee while they are retained by the trustees (s 104(4)). APSS shares are treated as acquired by the employee at market value at the date they are allocated to him and indexed from that date (until April 1998). After the three year period of retention, the shares are no longer kept separate from the employee's other holdings and are either added to pre 6 April 1998 holdings or treated as free-standing acquisitions depending on the date they were allocated to the employee, the acquisition value being cost plus any available indexation allowance. They are effectively inserted into the acquisitions record retrospectively, even though disposals may have already occurred which would have been identified with them if they had not been kept separate. SIP shares are treated as acquired at market value on the date they are withdrawn from the plan (as long as they have remained within it for at least five years), so if they are disposed of immediately after withdrawal no capital gains tax arises. If they are disposed of at a later time, taper relief runs from the date they were withdrawn from the plan.

3.   The rules for matching disposals of shares with acquisitions are dealt with in Example 78 explanatory note 6. Parts (1) and (2) of this example illustrate the application of the rules to disposals between married couples and civil partners, and also the identification rules for shares acquired under employee share schemes. Example 78 explanatory note 6 indicates that all acquisitions of shares of the same class in the same company on one day are normally treated as being a single asset. This rule has been varied for shares acquired by employees on or after 6 April 2002 under an approved share option scheme (TCGA 1992 ss 105A, 105B introduced by FA 2002) (see Example 87 parts (1), (2) and (6) for details of such schemes). Where some of the same day acquisitions are from an approved share option scheme they may have a lower capital gains cost than the other

acquisitions, which would reduce the average cost of any shares disposed of, and if there was a part disposal of the holding the capital gain would be correspondingly higher. In respect of scheme shares acquired on or after 6 April 2002 on the same day as other shares, the taxpayer may make a written election, on or before 31 January in the next but one tax year after the tax year in which he first makes a disposal of any of the same day acquisitions (eg by 31 January 2009 in respect of a disposal in 2006/07), to have the scheme shares and the other shares treated as two separate assets, the non-scheme shares being treated as disposed of first. The effect of the election could be to reduce immediate gains on a part disposal, although the remaining shares would have a lower capital gains tax cost. For detailed notes on the various share schemes see Example 87.

Qualifying corporate bonds

4.   Most interest bearing stocks issued by UK companies come within the definition of qualifying corporate bonds. Before FA 1996, both individual and company investors were exempt from tax on gains (and could not normally claim relief for losses) on qualifying corporate bonds and government stocks. This no longer applies as far as company investors are concerned from 1 April 1996 (subject to one or two special provisions), and all profits and gains on a company's 'loan relationships' are brought into account along with interest payable and interest receivable in arriving at the company's income profits. For the detailed provisions see Example 62. The *capital gains* exemption still applies and is extended as far as companies are concerned to any securities that would previously have been outside the definition of qualifying corporate bond, subject to what is said below (s 117(A1)).

5.   A company's gains and losses on the disposal of convertible securities and securities linked to a share index are still dealt with under the capital gains rules (such securities being outside the definition of qualifying corporate bond and therefore within the capital gains charge – see note 7) (FA 1996 ss 92, 93).

     A company's holdings of 3½% Funding Stock 1999/2004 and 5½% Treasury Stock 2008/12 are still covered by the capital gains exemption, although interest on the stocks is within the loan relationships rules (FA 1996 s 96).

6.   The exemption from capital gains tax for investors other than companies still applies, so that there are neither chargeable gains nor allowable losses on government securities and qualifying corporate bonds.

Non-exempt loan stock

7.   Where interest bearing stocks are not exempt as qualifying corporate bonds, the post-1982 pooling provisions do not apply, and each acquisition on or after 6 April 1982 is treated as a separate asset (s 104). If a rebasing election has been made to treat all assets owned on 31 March 1982 as acquired at the market value on that date, all securities of the same class in the same company owned on that date may be regarded as a single asset. Even if the rebasing election has not been made, the same treatment applies for quoted securities if an election was made for acquisitions before 6 April 1965 to be pooled with later acquisitions (s 109). If there has been neither a rebasing election nor an election to pool pre 6 April 1965 quoted securities, those securities are treated as separate assets.

     Before FA 1998, disposals were not matched with acquisitions according to the rules for shares. They were matched with acquisitions in the following order (s 108), subject to provisions for matching securities bought for delivery on or before the delivery date for the disposal:

     Those acquired in the previous 12 months on a first in first out basis
     Earlier acquisitions since 5.4.82, on a last in first out basis
     The pool of acquisitions from 6.4.65 to 5.4.82
     Non-pooled pre 6.4.65 acquisitions, last in first out

     No indexation allowance was available if the securities were disposed of within the nine days after the date they were acquired (s 54(2)).

8.   These matching rules still apply for companies in respect of those securities that remain within the capital gains charge (see note 5 and also note 9 re building society permanent interest bearing shares).

Where securities are dealt with under the loan relationships provisions, there are no special rules for matching disposals with acquisitions and any consistent basis adopted for accounting purposes is acceptable. For individuals the matching rules for disposals of non-exempt loan stock after 5 April 1998 are the same as those for shares, except that, as indicated above, there is no post-1982 pool and under heading (d) of the matching rules, securities acquired between 6 April 1982 and 5 April 1998 will be identified on a last in first out basis (see Example 78 explanatory note 6).

An instance where the rules for non-exempt loan stock apply is on the disposal of stock bought before 14 March 1984. It is not possible to circumvent the rules by making a no gain no loss transfer after 13 March 1984, for example from husband to wife.

Unusual loan stocks

9. Increasingly, corporate financiers are designing unfamiliar financial instruments with which to carry out transactions. The terms of the instrument need to be compared carefully with the legislation to determine the correct tax treatment.

    For example, a 'special stock unit' with a set redemption date and premium was issued as part of the Royal Bank of Scotland takeover of National Westminster Bank. This was treated as a share; it was chargeable if the shareholder sold it, but the premium on redemption would be charged to income tax as a dividend.

    An index-linked government stock is exempt from capital gains tax, but an index-linked stock issued by a company is an 'excluded indexed security' rather than a 'relevant discounted security'. It is therefore chargeable to capital gains tax rather than to income tax.

    Some building societies have issued permanent interest bearing shares (PIBS), which are treated as QCBs for the purposes of capital gains tax, and are therefore exempt in the hands of an individual or trustee. For corporation tax purposes, since PIBS are shares, they were previously outside the 'loan relationships' rules (except in relation to interest received), so a gain or loss on disposal was within the scope of corporation tax on gains (s 117(A1)(4)(5)). For accounting periods beginning on or after 1 October 2002, the loan relationships definition of shares excludes building society shares (FA 1996 s 103 as amended by FA 2002), so PIBS are wholly within the loan relationship rules from that date and the capital gains rules do not apply (see Example 62 explanatory note 1).

10. Because of the different treatment of takeovers where QCBs and non-QCBs are received in exchange for shares (see Example 80 explanatory notes 1 and 4), close attention has to be paid to the following choice:

    ●   exchange shares for QCBs: calculate the gain at the date of exchange, 'freezing' it until the QCB is disposed of, and fixing the taper relief at that date; or

    ●   exchange shares for non-QCBs: no disposal at the date of exchange; a gain is only calculated when the bonds are disposed of, and the whole ownership period counts for taper relief.

    The non-QCB route is preferable if the loan stocks become worthless, because the gain is never charged and the loss is allowable. The longer taper period will also be attractive if the loan stock qualifies for the business assets rate (if the issuing company is an unquoted trading company, or if the holder is an employee of the issuer). However, if the seller is disposing of a business asset with significant accrued taper relief (as will often be the case), and the loan stock would be a non-business asset (for example because the buyer is a quoted company or a non-trader and the seller will not be an employee), it is probably better to fix the existing high level of business assets taper relief by taking QCBs.

    As can be seen in the case of Weston v Garnett (Inspector of Taxes) [2005] EWCA Civ 742, it is important that the loan note is really a QCB. In this case the loan notes were found to be non-QCBs as they carried the right (albeit indirect) to conversion into shares.

    See Example 80 explanatory note 5 and Example 74 explanatory note 12 for HMRC's views on takeovers involving 'non-QCB loan stock'.

(1) Show the capital gains position in the following instances:

(a) Miss Fielding sold a freehold house in Southampton on 28 March 2007 for net proceeds of £252,220. She had bought the house for £15,000 on 1 October 1970 and immediately occupied it as her sole residence; between 1 October 1972 and 1 April 1986 the house was let while she was employed in Suffolk, where she lived in rented accommodation. She resumed occupation of the house on 1 April 1986 but moved to a different permanent residence on 27 March 1988, the house then being let until the date of sale. The value of the house at 31 March 1982 was £70,000. Miss Fielding has made a general rebasing election.

(b) Galsworthy bought a freehold house on 1 April 1983 for £27,000 including expenses of purchase. He lived in the house until 30 September 1997 when he took a job as a caretaker and had to live on his employer's premises. He therefore let the house until he sold it on 30 June 2006 for £352,100 after deducting expenses of sale, his employer moving him to a branch in another part of the country so that he could not resume residence.

(c) On 1 January 1971 Hardy purchased for £8,000 a flat which he used as his only residence. On 30 June 1975 he purchased a house which became his main residence and from that date his widowed mother occupied the flat free of any consideration. His mother vacated the flat on 31 March 1986 and he let it continuously at a commercial rent from that date until he sold it for £240,000 on 30 September 2006. The value on 31 March 1982 was considered to be £52,000. No general 31.3.82 rebasing election has been made.

Comment on the position that would have applied if Hardy's mother had left the property on 31 December 1981 and it had been let from that date until sold.

(d) On 30 June 2006 Compton sold a freehold house in Hampshire for net proceeds of £273,260. He had bought the house for £2,800 on 1 October 1954 and the history of his ownership is summarised below:

1.10.54	Occupied house as sole residence.
1. 4.80	House let on taking up employment abroad. He returned to England on 1 January 1983, but started his own business in Liverpool and lived in rented accommodation, continuing to let his own house.
1. 7.87	Resumed occupation of own house on retiring from business.
1. 1.89	Moved to Sussex and purchased a house which became his main residence from this date, the Hampshire house being let until it was sold.

The market value of the Hampshire house was £6,500 on 6 April 1965 and £90,000 on 31 March 1982.

(e) Harold married Georgina on 6 April 1994. Both had been married before, and both owned houses. Harold had bought his house in April 1982, and lived in it with his wife, who died in 1990. Georgina and her first husband bought their house in June 1986, but divorced in 1994, after the husband had moved out in January 1993. The house was subject to an order along the lines of Mesher v Mesher, which provided that it would be held on trust for Georgina and her former husband until their children reached the age of 18 (in October 2006), when it would be sold, and the proceeds divided equally.

Harold moved into Georgina's house in April 1994, and they have lived there ever since, during which time Harold's own house has been let out. In October 2006, they sold both houses, and bought a third. The gain on Harold's house after indexation allowance was £400,000; the gain on Georgina's house was £200,000, of which her share was £100,000. Harold had kept his own house in his own name.

(f) Stanley's father died in 1990, and Stanley decided to provide a home for his mother. He bought a house for £160,000 and placed it into a trust in which his mother had a life interest, with reversion to Stanley on her death. In 1998, the trustees sold the first house for £260,000, and bought another for the same sum. In 2006, Stanley's mother died, when the second house was worth £440,000. It will be sold as soon as possible and the proceeds returned to Stanley.

(g) Gordon sold his house for £500,000 on 30 September 2006. He bought it for £220,000 in April 1999. He has always used 20% of his house exclusively for business purposes, and has made claims for income tax relief for that proportion of the running costs (including council tax and mortgage interest). Calculate the chargeable capital gain on disposal.

(h) On 31 January 2003, James transferred a house to the trustees of a discretionary trust and claimed to hold over the gain of £200,000 that would otherwise accrue. The beneficiaries of the trust are his children, Gemma and Sue. The terms of the settlement permit the trustees to allow certain persons to occupy the house. The trustees allow Gemma to do so, and she occupies the house as her only residence on 31 January 2003.

On 31 August 2006, Gemma vacates the house. The trustees then sell the property on 30 September 2006 giving rise to a gain (including the held over gain) of £250,000. Calculate the trustees' entitlement to private residence relief.

(2) In addition to his London house (which he has owned and occupied since 1989) Nash has just bought a house in the country. Nash has stated that it is his intention in approximately five years to give his London house to his nephew and then live solely in his new house in the country. He now divides his time equally between the two houses and expects this arrangement to continue until he gives his London house to his nephew. The London house is currently worth about 20% more than he paid for it. Nash has a substantial part of his income charged at 40% and regularly makes gains in excess of the annual exempt limit. Advise Nash what he should do.

(1)

(a) **Miss Fielding**

Property was occupied from 31.3.82 as follows:

31.3.82-31.3.86	4 yrs	Let while working away (resident before and after)
1.4.86-27.3.88	2 yrs	Owner occupied
28.3.88-28.3.07	19 yrs	Let up to sale
	25 yrs	

Exempt proportion:

Owner occupation	2 yrs
Allowable period of absence while working elsewhere in UK	4 yrs
Last 3 yrs	3 yrs
	9 yrs

	£	£
Sale proceeds March 2007		252,220
31 March 1982 value	70,000	
Indexation allowance to April 1998 104.7%	73,290	143,290
Gain		108,930
Less exempt proportion 9/25		39,215
		69,715
Less residential lettings exemption		
Lower of £40,000 and exempt gain of £39,215		39,215
Chargeable gain (subject to 35% taper relief)		30,500

(b) **Galsworthy** has no chargeable gain. Either actual (to September 1997) or deemed (6 years for place of work, last 3 years) owner occupation throughout. See explanatory note 4.

(c) **Hardy**

The gain will clearly be based on 31 March 1982 value of £52,000 rather than the cost of £8,000.

		£	£
Flat sale proceeds 30 September 2006			240,000
31 March 1982 value		52,000	
Indexation allowance to April 1998 104.7%		54,444	106,444
			133,556
Less:	Exempt re dependent relative occupation		
	(31.3.82 to 31.3.86) 4/24.5 x 133,556	21,805	
	Exempt re last three years' ownership		
	3/24.5 x 133,556	16,354	
	Residential lettings exemption	16,354	54,513
Chargeable gain (subject to 35% taper relief)			79,043

The exemption for the let period is the smaller of £40,000 and the amount exempt through *owner* occupation. Occupation by a dependent relative does not qualify as stated at paragraphs CG64718/ 65562 of HMRC's Capital Gains Tax Manual. However, this view has been challenged – see Taxation 'Bill defeats Revenue argument' 13 May 2004 and Readers' Forum 'Last 36 months' 27 January 2005. On the revised understanding of the legislation, the residential lettings exemption reduces the overall gain by £38,159 (£21,805 + £16,354) rather than just £16,354.

If Hardy's mother had left the property on 31 December 1981, the exemption for occupation by a dependent relative would not be available since there would have been no occupation on or after 31 March 1982 qualifying for exemption.

(d) **Compton**

Property was occupied from 31.3.82 as follows:

	Period of ownership on and after 31.3.82		Note	Actual or deemed owner occupation		Chargeable period	
	Yrs	Mths		Yrs	Mths	Yrs	Mths
31.3.82-1.1.83		9	(i)		9		
1.1.83-1.7.87	4	6	(ii)	4	6		
1.7.87-1.1.89	1	6	(iii)	1	6		
1.1.89-30.6.06	17	6	(iv)	3		14	6
	24	3		9	9	14	6

(i)   Employed abroad, house let, resident before and after.

(ii) Working away from home, house let, resident before and after, therefore covered for first four years because of absence through working away in UK and for remaining 6 months as part of period of up to 3 years for any reason.

(iii) Owner occupied.

(iv) Let prior to sale (partly covered by exemption for last three years of ownership).

Chargeable proportion of gain is therefore $\dfrac{14.5 \text{ years}}{24.25 \text{ years}}$

The gain using cost is:

	£
Net sale proceeds 30 June 2006	273,260
Cost 1.10.1954	2,800
	270,460
Indexation allowance to April 1998 on 31 March 1982 value £90,000 x 104.7%	94,230
Overall gain	176,230

Time proportion $\dfrac{6.4.65 - 30.6.06}{1.10.54 - 30.6.06} = \dfrac{41.25}{51.75} \times 176{,}230$

Gain   £ 140,473

The election for 6 April 1965 value will clearly give a higher gain than using 31 March 1982 value, so it is not considered.

The gain using 31.3.82 value is:

Net sale proceeds – 30 June 2006		273,260
31 March 1982 value	90,000	
Indexation allowance (as before)	94,230	184,230
Gain		£ 89,030

The chargeable gain before owner occupier relief is the lower of £140,473 and £89,030, ie £89,030. This would also be the gain if a general 31.3.82 rebasing election had been made.

Chargeable proportion of gain $\dfrac{14.5}{24.25} \times 89{,}030$ 53,234

Residential lettings exemption is lower of £40,000 and
amount equal to gain exempt through owner occupation,

ie £89,030 x $\dfrac{9.75}{24.25}$ (35,796)

Chargeable gain (subject to 35% taper relief) £ 17,438

(e) **Harold and Georgina**

Harold's house has been his only or main residence at some point during his ownership. While he is married to Georgina, only one of the two houses can be the exempt residence, and his house has been let out since the marriage; accordingly, that house is chargeable. However, the last three years of ownership qualify for exemption, and the additional lettings relief is also available. The chargeable gain on Howard's house is therefore:

Actual occupation: 12 years; deemed occupation: 3 years; total ownership: 24.5 years

	£
Chargeable gain: 9.5/24.5 x £400,000	155,102
Lettings exemption: lowest of £155,102; £244,898; £40,000	40,000
Taxable gain 2006/07 (before 35% taper relief)	115,102

The Mesher order results in a transfer into trust. Any gain on this transfer is normally covered by TCGA 1992 s 225. The sale of Georgina's house is therefore exempt from CGT, because the house has been occupied throughout as the only or main residence by a beneficiary of the trust (Georgina and the children) and there has been no previous transfer subject to gift relief. The shares of the proceeds paid out to both Georgina and her former husband are exempt from CGT.

(f) **Stanley**

The sale in 1998 is exempt under TCGA 1992 s 225. The trust is one in which the settlor retains an interest (as Stanley is entitled to the reversion), but this only means that Stanley is assessable on any gains that would normally be assessed on the trustees. As the trustees would not be assessed on a gain on the disposal of the house, neither is Stanley.

The reversion to settlor on the death of the life tenant is exempt from inheritance tax (IHTA 1984 s 54) (because her interest was created before 22 March 2006), so the return to his own estate does not create an inheritance tax charge for Stanley. However, TCGA 1992 s 73 provides that the normal 'uplift to probate value' does not apply on such a reversion to settlor, so the base cost of the second house to Stanley is the trustees' deemed cost of £260,000, not the current market value of £440,000.

The gain is realised by Stanley. Therefore, subject to selling costs, a gain of £180,000 will be realised subject to taper relief of up to 30% (or 35%) if the house was acquired before 16 March 1998.

(g) **Gordon**

		£
Sale proceeds September 2006		500,000
Cost April 1999		(220,000)
Gain before OMR exemption		280,000
OMR exemption: 80%		(224,000)
Gain before taper relief		56,000
Taper relief:		
Business proportion of gain (20%) at 75%	11,200	(8,400)
Non-business proportion of gain (80%) at 25%	44,800	(11,200)
Chargeable gain		36,400

See explanatory note 12 for an explanation of the taper relief calculation.

(h) **James**

Anti-avoidance legislation was introduced from 10 December 2003 to prevent exploitation of the interaction between private residence and hold-over relief to avoid CGT. Therefore because the trustees' allowable expenditure was reduced as a result of the claim to gift relief, they cannot cover the whole gain by private residence relief. But because the gift relief related to a transfer before 10 December 2003 the transitional rule applies.

31.1.03 to 9.12.03 = 313 days
31.1.03 to 30.9.06 = 1,339 days

Entitlement to private residence relief:

313/1,339 × 250,000   58,439

Private residence relief is not available in respect of the 1,026 days from December 2003 to September 2006. The transitional rule specifically prevents any period on or after 10 December 2003 from qualifying for relief as part of the final three years exemption.

(2) **Nash** needs to elect which of his two residences is his main residence qualifying for exemption from capital gains tax. The election must be made within two years from the date of acquisition of the second property. The election can subsequently be varied, and any variation will take effect not earlier than two years before HMRC is notified that Nash wishes to vary the election.

The gift to the nephew of the London house will be treated for capital gains tax as a sale at open market value. If Nash elects for the London house to remain as his exempt house for capital gains tax, then no chargeable gain or allowable loss will arise when he disposes of it, but the intervening period will result in a chargeable gain or allowable loss on the country property when it is disposed of, for the part of the period of ownership for which it is not Nash's main residence for capital gains tax (unless it is not disposed of in Nash's lifetime).

If Nash elects for his country property to be his main residence, then no chargeable gain or allowable loss will arise on its eventual disposal. As a result, a proportion of any eventual gain on the London house may become chargeable. The last three years of ownership will, however, always be counted as a qualifying period of residence, which will make the chargeable fraction quite small (perhaps 2/22). Indexation allowance to April 1998 (about 40%) and taper relief according to the complete years of ownership after April 1998 (the maximum 40% for a sale after 5 April 2007) would help to reduce or eliminate the chargeable gain.

Depending on the likely date of disposal of the country house and the probable gain, Nash might wish to elect for the London house to be his main residence for two further years (ie until three years before its likely sale) and then elect for the country house to be his main residence.

It is also worth ensuring that the country house is treated as Nash's main residence for some period in the period of ownership (as little as one day). This will ensure that the last three years of ownership will qualify for the exemption.

Explanatory Notes

More than one residence

1.   References in this example are to TCGA 1992. The gain on the disposal of an individual's only or main residence is exempt from tax, wholly or in part. Where an individual has two or more residences he may *elect* which is to be his exempt residence for capital gains tax and this need not be the residence which is in fact his main residence. (It must, however, be or have been his *residence*. An investment property in which he had never lived would not qualify.) If no election is made the matter is determined by the facts of the case. The right to make an election would revive if a taxpayer had a

change of residence, or acquired a third residence, but the period covered by the election would only date from the time that the new or additional property was acquired if the time limit had previously expired. If householders realise losses rather than gains when selling properties, such losses are not allowable losses unless and to the extent that there is a non-exempt period of ownership.

Following Griffin v Craig-Harvey (1993), it is generally taken to be the case that an initial election must be made within two years of a taxpayer acquiring a second residence. If this time limit is missed, no election may be made at all unless there is a subsequent change in the taxpayer's number of residences. Whilst it is therefore advisable for tax advisers to make protective elections within the two-year period, it has since been suggested that Griffin v Craig-Harvey was wrongly decided (see the *Personal Tax Planning Review*, 2005, 10(1), 27–38). If this view is correct it would mean that elections might be made at any time backdated (if necessary) by up to two years whether or not one was owned during the initial two-year period.

The provisions enabling a main residence election to be varied with retrospective effect for two years could be beneficial to someone who has had two residences for some years and plans to sell the one that is not the elected main residence. An election could be made for the property that is to be sold to be the main residence with effect from two years before the date HMRC was notified of the change. A further election could then be made one week after the first election reverting back to the original main residence, again with retrospective effect for two years. The effect would be to obtain the exemption for the last three years' ownership of the property that is being sold (see note 3), and possibly the extra lettings exemption as well, at the cost of only one chargeable week in respect of the original main residence. This is confirmed in the HMRC's Capital Gains Tax Manual.

Nash's gift to his nephew in part (2) of the example would be regarded as made at open market value, since it would not be an arm's length bargain (s 17). If the nephew had been a connected person, then under s 18 any loss arising could have only been set against a gain on a later transaction with the nephew, but a nephew is not within the definition of relative in s 286 (see Example 73 part (d)(i)).

An election is not required where someone owns a residence and has a second residence that he/she neither owns nor leases (eg accommodation with relatives, or a hotel room). A tenancy of a property would, however, need to be taken into account even if the right of occupation had no capital value (see Revenue's Tax Bulletin October 1994).

2. For a married couple or civil partners living together, there can only be one main residence for both, and if they own two or more residences between them (either jointly or separately) the main residence election must be made by both (s 222(6)). If only one member of the couple is the property owner, only that person would make the election. If on marriage/registration of a civil partnership each owned a residence, the two year period for electing which was the main residence would start at the date of marriage/registration. No election is necessary in the case of Harold and Georgina in part (e) of the example, because Harold does not live in his house following his marriage. When one spouse/civil partner inherits the residence on the other's death, then although the survivor's acquisition value for capital gains is the market value at death, the period of ownership of the other (since 31 March 1982), and therefore any non-residence during that period, is taken into account to compute any chargeable gain on disposal by the survivor (s 222(7)).

Periods of non-residence

3. Where there have been periods of non-residence then the non-resident fraction of the total period of ownership since 31 March 1982 is the chargeable part of the gain (or allowable part of the loss).

    Where there is a delay of up to a year (extended in some circumstances to not more than two years) in taking up residence, because land has been bought on which a house is being built, or because of alterations or redecorations, or because of completing the arrangements to sell a previous property, the period of non-residence will count as a period of residence by Revenue Concession D49, and the exemption on any other qualifying property during that period will not be affected.

Providing a property has been an individual's only or main residence at some time during his total period of ownership (whether before or after 31 March 1982), the last three years of ownership always count as a period of residence (s 223(1)). Certain other absences also count as residence, if preceded and followed (not necessarily immediately before and after) by a period of actual residence and providing relief is not being claimed for another main residence during the absence. These are (ss 222 & 223):

(a)   Up to three years for any reason

(b)   Any absence throughout which the individual is employed abroad

(c)   Up to four years during which the individual is prevented from living in the house because of the distance from his place of work or because his employer requires him to live elsewhere. 'Place of work' covers both employment and self-employment, hence the exemption for Compton in part (d) of the example covering four years of the period from 1.1.83 to 1.7.87 when he was working too far away to live in his own house.

By Revenue Concession D4 absences under headings (b) and (c) do *not* require a later period of actual residence if an individual cannot resume residence because the terms of his *employment* require him to work elsewhere. The concession does not apply to an absence under (c) where the individual is self-employed, so a later period of actual residence is necessary for such an absence to qualify.

If someone is going to occupy rented accommodation while away, then the rented property would be treated as a residence (see note 1). HMRC would probably be prepared to accept a main residence election for the owned property, so that the rules for allowable periods of absence would apply.

Job-related accommodation

4.   If a person who lives in job-related accommodation (eg caretaker, like Galsworthy in part (b) of the example) owns a house that he intends in due course to occupy as his only or main residence, he is regarded as being in occupation of his house during the time he lives in the job-related accommodation (s 222(8)). This provision also applies to self-employed people living in job-related accommodation.

Galsworthy either lived in the property himself or lived in job-related accommodation throughout the period from 31 March 1982 to the date of sale. Providing he had intended to live in the house again after taking the caretaker's job, his period of non-residence would count wholly as a period of residence. Even if he had not intended to resume residence at some later date the period of non-residence would still have counted as residence, because it is covered by the allowance of the last three years of ownership plus up to four years of absence while required by one's employment to live elsewhere. (A later period of actual residence is not necessary for an employment-related absence – see note 3.)

Residence occupied by a dependent relative

5.   The exemption for owner occupied property extends to one residence occupied *rent free* by a dependent relative as his/her sole residence, but only where the relative occupied the property on or before 6 April 1988. The exemption is not available where a dependent relative first occupies a property on or after 6 April 1988. If there are periods of non-residence, the same rules apply as outlined in note 3. But if the property ceases to be the sole residence of the dependant, either before or after 6 April 1988, subsequent periods of residence on or after that date by that or any other relative do not qualify for relief (s 226).

The legislation defines a dependent relative but imposes no income restriction, so that the relative need not be financially dependent on the owner of the residence. By Concession D20 HMRC do not regard payments of council tax by the relative or payments towards the upkeep of the property as breaching the 'rent free' requirement providing the owner is not left with a surplus over his outgoings.

Divorce and separation

6. When spouses or civil partners separate, the matrimonial home ceases to be the main residence of the party who leaves it. His or her share of any calculated gain on a subsequent sale is therefore chargeable to the extent that it relates to the period of non-residence, subject to any available exemptions or reliefs. The last three years of ownership always count as a period of residence, even if a new qualifying residence has been acquired. If the property is disposed of more than three years after an individual leaves it, part of the calculated gain is assessable, but only in the proportion that the excess period over three years bears to the total period of ownership since 31 March 1982, against which any available taper relief and annual exemption (currently £8,800) may be used. There is a Concession (D6) covering absences exceeding the final three-year period, but only where the property is eventually transferred to the spouse/civil partner remaining in it as part of the financial settlement, and an election for a new qualifying residence has not been made by the individual moving out in the meantime.

    A better arrangement, using a Court Order and the rule for settlements, is illustrated in part (e).

Residential lettings exemption

7. There is a further relief for owner-occupiers who at any time during their period of ownership have let all or part of the property as residential accommodation (s 223(4)). The gain attributable to the letting is reduced by the lower of:

    (a) An amount equal to the part of the total gain that is exempt because of the owner occupation, and

    (b) £40,000.

    The relief is illustrated in parts (a), (c), (d) and (e) of the example.

    This relief in relation to letting residential accommodation also applies where a residence is occupied under the terms of a settlement but not where a residence is occupied by a dependent relative. Hence in part (c) of the example the part of the gain attributable to the dependent relative's occupation is not taken into account in the calculation of the residential lettings relief.

    'Residential letting' is not defined in the legislation. HMRC took the view that the letting must have some degree of permanence, but they lost a case on the point in the Court of Appeal (Owen v Elliott 1990), where it was decided that the exemption was available to the owners of a small private hotel who occupied the whole of the property during the winter months, with one or two guests, but moved to an annexe during the summer.

    The exemption can be claimed only if the property qualifies as the capital gains tax exempt residence for at least part of the period of ownership, so it cannot be claimed on a property which, although the taxpayer lives in it sometimes, has never been his only or main residence for capital gains tax. Subject to that, it can be claimed where all of the property has been let for part of the period of ownership, or part of the property has been let for all or part of the period of ownership.

Property acquired before 31 March 1982

8. Where the residence was acquired before 31 March 1982, it is only periods of residence and non-residence on and after that date that determine how much, if any, of the gain is chargeable (although the last three years' ownership is exempt in any event providing there has been owner occupation at any time during the full period of ownership). The gain before the owner occupier relief is first ascertained, by comparing the calculation using cost/6.4.65 value with that using 31.3.82 value in the usual way (unless a general 31 March 1982 rebasing election has been made). (For detailed notes on the alternative calculations see Example 77, in particular explanatory note 2, re the time apportionment calculation for property acquired before 6 April 1965.) The period of non-residence after 30 March 1982 as a fraction of total ownership after that date is then the chargeable part of the gain, as shown in parts (a), (c) and (d) of the example.

Sale of land after sale of residence

9.   The private residence exemption includes land that is for 'occupation and enjoyment with the residence as its garden or grounds up to the permitted area' (s 222(1)(b)), the permitted area being (inclusive of the site of the house) up to half a hectare, which is approximately 1¼ acres, or such larger area as is appropriate to the size and character of the house. The exemption applies even if some of the land is sold separately. But the land must satisfy the conditions *at the time of disposal*, so that in Varty v Lynes 1976 it was held that land sold *after* the sale of the house did not qualify since it did not form part of the residence at that time.

Meaning of 'residence'

10.   There have been several cases on what constitutes a residence. In Batey v Wakefield 1981 a caretaker's bungalow physically separate from the main house was included within the exemption. In Markey v Sanders 1987 the court held that for a group of buildings to be treated as a single residence they must be capable of being regarded as a single building, so a large, separate staff bungalow some distance from the main house did not qualify. But in Williams v Merrylees 1987 a staff lodge even further away from the house than the Markey v Sanders bungalow was held to be part of a single entity and included within the private residence exemption. The High Court in the case of Lewis v Rook 1990 similarly held that a gardener's cottage some distance away from the house occupied by the elderly woman owner was part of the main residence, but this was overruled in the Court of Appeal in 1992. There are clearly very fine distinctions in some of these decisions, and the way in which questions of fact are presented to and decided by the Commissioners is very important. HMRC issued a statement in their Tax Bulletin of February 1992 indicating what they take into account in arriving at the exempt area of land with a dwelling house, and how they deal with buildings separate from the main house. They have made further comments in their Tax Bulletins of August 1994 and August 1995.

In the case of Longson v Baker 2000 the taxpayer appeared to convince the inspector that an area of just over 1 hectare was 'reasonably required' for a person who bought a house for its stables and riding opportunities. However, his claim for 7½ hectares was rejected by the inspector, Special Commissioners and High Court. The High Court judge stated that 'reasonably required' was an objective test, and the taxpayer's subjective liking for horses was irrelevant. This suggests that the inspector may have been too generous in allowing more than the minimum.

11.   A different point was at issue in Goodwin v Curtis, in which the Court of Appeal decided in 1998 that a short period of occupation of a property while it was up for sale did not constitute residence, even though it was accepted that there was no trading motive (as to which see note 16). The Court held that the General Commissioners were entitled to conclude that the occupation did not have a sufficient degree of permanence to have the quality necessary for residence.

Part use for business

12.   Where part of a residence is used exclusively for business purposes, the provisions for exempting all or part of the gain relating to the only or main residence (including the exemption for the last three years of ownership) do not apply to the business proportion of the gain, but rollover relief is available on the business proportion if the property is replaced.

13.   An article in Taxation (7 August 2003 – Splitting up the home) argues that it may be possible to obtain the benefit of the last three years exemption if say the business ceases one year before the property is sold or if say a doctor was able to move his surgery to a different part of the property for the last six months before sale. This is on the basis that the last three years exemption applies in any case except where part has been used throughout for business purposes.

14.   If the gain is not rolled over and is chargeable, it appears that the taper relief is not applied only at the business assets rate. This would seem logical, as the chargeable gain has arisen because part of the house is being treated as a business asset, so the chargeable gain appears to arise on something that ought to qualify for business assets taper. However, HMRC's view is that the chargeable gain arises on the disposal of a single asset (the house). This single asset has been partly used for business

purposes and partly for non-business purposes, and the taper relief rules require an apportionment. In part (g) of the question, therefore, Gordon receives business assets taper on only 20% of the gain on the house, and non-business assets taper on the remaining 80% of the chargeable gain. Of course, this is a much less favourable treatment than simply regarding the gain as arising on a purely business asset, but it appears to be what the law requires. The only way to secure the more favourable treatment appears to be to argue (if the facts support it) that the business part is genuinely a separate asset, for example a different building within the curtilage of the property. If it is the common situation of an office within the main residence, it is unlikely that this would succeed.

Relocation of employee

15.   Where an employee is relocated and sells his home either to his employer or to a relocation company, with a right to share in any profits when the employer or relocation company later sells the home, then by Revenue Concession D37, the employee is exempt from capital gains tax on the later amount to the same extent as he was exempt on the original sale, providing the later sale occurs within three years. (Part of the original gain may have been chargeable because the home had not always been the main residence, or had been let, etc, in which case the same proportion of the later amount will be chargeable.) See Example 10 explanatory note 7 for the income tax position in relation to employee relocation.

Intention to resell at a profit

16.   The capital gains tax exemption does not apply if the residence was acquired with the intention of reselling at a profit, and if expenditure has been incurred on the property wholly or partly to make a gain on sale, an appropriate part of the gain is not exempt (s 224(3)). In practice HMRC ignores costs of obtaining planning permission or of removing restrictive covenants. A series of profitable sales may in exceptional circumstances be challenged as trading, as in the case of Kirkby v Hughes (ChD 1992), where a builder had bought and sold three houses that he had renovated while living in them (see Example 13 for the criteria for deciding when a trade is being carried on).

Restriction of private residence relief where holdover relief is claimed

17.   Where the base cost of a property is reduced by an earlier holdover relief claim under s 260 (whenever made), no private residence relief can be claimed on a subsequent disposal (by the trustees or an individual) after 9 December 2003. The rules only apply where the gain is affected by an earlier holdover relief claim.

Transitional rules permit a claim to residence relief for disposals after 10 December 2003 in respect of the period before this date on a time apportioned basis. Therefore, had the trustees triggered a disposal for CGT on say 1 January 2004 they would have suffered the disallowance of relief for only 22 days and the qualifying gain would have increased to $313/335 \times 250,000 = £233,582$ thus reducing the taxable gain.

If the holdover claim is withdrawn in respect of an earlier disposal, it is treated as if it had never been made (new s 226A(6)). Also, if a holdover claim is made subsequently, the gain on disposal is recomputed. All necessary adjustments are made to the assessments.

In the future, the transferor could refrain from claiming holdover relief on the transfer and pay tax on any gains up to that point. Private residence relief could then apply to any subsequent gains during the period in which the property was a beneficiary's or donee's main residence. If the property does not show any significant taxable gain it may be worth paying tax on this transfer if that enables subsequent gains to be sheltered by the valuable residence relief.

Trustees of settlements

18.   For disposals on or after 10 December 2003 it is necessary for trustees to make a claim for private residence relief when they dispose of property which has been occupied by a beneficiary under the settlement as that person's qualifying residence.

Inheritance tax

19.   The exemption from inheritance tax on the death of Nash's mother (in part 2 of the example) would not have applied if she had acquired her interest in possession after 22 March 2006 following changes to the inheritance tax rules in FA 2006.

(a) Norris purchased a freehold building for £40,000 in June 1982 for use in his trade of ironmonger and sold it in October 1986 for £60,000. At the same time he rented accommodation in another part of the country and acquired the goodwill of a greengrocery business for £56,000, claiming rollover relief appropriately. The goodwill was sold in January 2007 for £100,000.

    (i) Calculate the chargeable gains arising as a result of these transactions.

    (ii) Calculate the chargeable gains that would have arisen if the freehold building had been acquired in 1972 instead of in June 1982, the market value being £54,000 at 31 March 1982, and all other particulars remaining the same. From 6 April 1985 to 5 April 1988, gains on pre-March 1982 purchases were calculated using original cost, with the taxpayer having the right to elect to calculate indexation allowance on the March 1982 value.

(b) Assume that Bartlett has realised a gain of £100,000 on a business asset he has owned for two years after 6 April 1998, the gain qualifying for full taper relief of 75%. He has invested sufficient in both a non-depreciating asset and a depreciating asset to cover the whole of the gain. He is thinking of retiring in a few years' time. Show the effect of claiming (i) rollover relief and (ii) holdover relief if he retires and sells the business one complete year after he acquired the relevant replacement asset.

(c) Your client, Medway Ltd, has been offered £1,000,000 for a freehold factory it is considering disposing of in October 2006. It acquired the factory in October 1943 for £40,000 and it had been valued for insurance purposes at £136,000 in April 1965 and £380,000 in March 1982. The factory site does not have any development value. The company has not made a 31 March 1982 rebasing election.

    1. Compute the chargeable gain which will arise if Medway Ltd disposes of the factory (assuming indexation allowance from March 1982 to October 2006 to be 150%).

    2. Indicate to the company the capital gains consequences of each of the following alternative courses of action it is considering taking following the sale, and give any advice you consider to be relevant:

        (i) acquiring a larger freehold factory in 2006 for £1,040,000.

        (ii) acquiring a smaller freehold factory in 2006 for £900,000 and using the remainder of the proceeds as working capital.

        (iii) using the proceeds to pay a premium of £1,040,000 for a 40 year lease of a new factory (it is possible that a freehold warehouse will be bought in about five years' time for an estimated cost of £1,080,000).

        (iv) acquiring a 40 year lease of a new factory for a yearly rental of £56,000 and a nil premium and loaning the sale proceeds to Newtown Ltd (a subsidiary in which Medway Ltd holds between 70% and 80% of the ordinary share capital) to be used by Newtown Ltd to acquire a freehold shop costing £1,020,000.

        (v) acquiring a new lease for a nil premium (as in (iv) above) and investing the proceeds in working capital. A 100% subsidiary, Parkland Ltd, that was acquired by Medway Ltd in 1985, will dispose of a holding of shares giving rise to an allowable loss for capital gains purposes of £100,000. Medway Ltd wishes to set the loss of Parkland Ltd against its chargeable gain.

(d) On 30 March 2007 Rochester disposed of his property in Darke Road, comprising a house and workshop in the garden, for £225,150. He purchased the property on 1 May 1975 for £5,000 and its value at 31 March 1982 was £58,000. Throughout his period of ownership the house was his principal private residence and the workshop was used for his printing business. 20% of the value of the property relates to the workshop.

On 20 April 2006 Rochester had purchased a house, with a workshop annexe, in Howells Road for £250,000. Both the house and workshop were kept empty until 30 March 2007 when his family and the printing business occupied the premises. 15% of the value of this property relates to the workshop.

Calculate the chargeable gain arising, assuming that Rochester had made a 31 March 1982 rebasing election and that he claims rollover relief on the gain on the workshop.

(a) **Norris – rollover relief**

(i)

	£	£
Sale proceeds – freehold building – October 1986		60,000
Cost June 1982	40,000	
Indexation allowance $\dfrac{98.45 - 81.85}{81.85}$ = 20.3%	8,120	48,120
		11,880
Less: rollover relief claimed re amount reinvested in replacement		7,880
Chargeable gain (assuming no other acquisitions of business assets within rollover period; £60,000 proceeds less £56,000 reinvested)		4,000
Second sale proceeds – goodwill – January 2007		100,000
Cost October 1986	56,000	
Less: Rolled over gain	(7,880)	48,120
Unindexed gain		51,880
Less: Indexation allowance to April 1998 $\dfrac{162.6 - 98.45}{98.45}$ = 65.2% x 48,120		31,374
Chargeable gain (again assuming no other acquisitions of business assets within rollover period)		20,506

Taper relief depends on the period of ownership of the *replacement* asset, but as the goodwill has been owned for over two years, business assets taper relief at 75% will be available, amounting to £15,380 (providing the gain is not reduced by allowable losses).

The gains on the two assets are therefore £4,000 in 1986/87 and £20,506, tapered to £5,126, in 2006/07.

If rollover relief had not been claimed, there would have been a gain of £11,880 on the disposal of the freehold building, but indexation allowance would have been given on £56,000 for the goodwill instead of £48,120, amounting to £36,512, giving a chargeable gain of £7,488 (taper relief £5,616). The combined gains would therefore have been £19,368, with taper relief of £5,616.

(ii)

	£	£
Sale proceeds – freehold building – October 1986		60,000
Cost 1972		40,000
Unindexed gain		20,000
Less: Indexation allowance on election for 31 March 1982 value £54,000 x 23.9%		12,906
		7,094
Less: Used in replacement		3,094
Chargeable gain (assuming no other acquisitions of business assets within rollover period; £60,000 proceeds less £56,000 reinvested)		4,000

	£	£
Second sale proceeds – goodwill – January 2007		100,000
Cost – October 1986	56,000	
Less: Rolled over gain (see explanatory note 11)		
3,094 x ½ =	(1,547)	54,453
Unindexed gain		45,547
Less: Indexation allowance £54,453 x 65.2% as in (i)		35,503
Chargeable gain (again assuming no other acquisitions of business assets within rollover period)		10,044

Taper relief of 75% would be available as in (i), amounting to £7,533 (subject to reduction if there are allowable losses).

(b) **Bartlett – interaction of rollover/holdover relief and taper relief**

   (i) *Gain rolled over into non-depreciating asset*

   The gain of £100,000 will be incorporated in the gain on the disposal of the replacement asset by reducing the base cost of that asset, but it will be reduced by taper relief of only 50%, relating to the period of ownership of the *replacement* asset, leaving £50,000 chargeable.

   (ii) *Gain held over against depreciating asset*

   The gain of £100,000 will be held over until the sale of the depreciating asset but it will qualify for full taper relief of 75%, relating to the period of ownership of the *original* asset, leaving £25,000 chargeable.

(c) **Medway Ltd – alternatives for deferring gains**

   1. *Chargeable gain that will arise on disposal of factory*

	Using cost	Using 31.3.82 value
	£	£
Sale proceeds October 2006	1,000,000	1,000,000
Cost October 1943	(40,000)	
31 March 1982 value		(380,000)
	960,000	620,000
Indexation allowance (on 31.3.82 value)		
150%* x 380,000	(570,000)	(570,000)
Overall gain	390,000	

   * Assumed figure given in example

   Time proportion
   $$\frac{6.4.65 - \text{October } 2006}{6.4.45** - \text{October } 2006} = \frac{41½}{61½} \quad \text{x } 390,000$$

	263,171	50,000

   ** Earliest date for time apportionment

   The chargeable gain will be £ 50,000

If a general 31.3.82 rebasing election had been made the gain would have been the same, ie £50,000. The election for 6.4.65 value would clearly give a higher gain than 31.3.82 value, so it is not considered. There is no taper relief for a company, which still enjoys indexation allowance after April 1998.

(c)   2.   (i)   If a larger freehold factory were acquired in 2006 for £1,040,000, the gain of £50,000 need not be charged and could instead be rolled over to reduce the base cost of the new factory for capital gains purposes to (1,040,000 – 50,000 =) £990,000 (ie indexed 31 March 1982 value £950,000 plus £40,000 further expenditure).

       (ii)   If a smaller freehold factory were acquired for £900,000 in 2006, with the remainder of the proceeds used as working capital, then the whole of the gain would be realised and included in the profit for corporation tax purposes.

The rolled over gain would thus be reduced to nil giving a base cost for the replacement factory of £900,000.

       (iii)   If the proceeds were used to pay a premium of £1,040,000 for a 40 year lease of a new factory, then since the replacement asset would be a depreciating asset (life 60 years or less at the time of acquisition) the gain could not be rolled over, but it would be held over and assessment deferred until the earliest of:

A   Date of disposal of the leasehold factory

B   Time when leasehold factory ceased to be used for the purposes of the trade

C   Ten years from the date of acquisition of the leasehold factory

unless another qualifying non-depreciating asset, such as the freehold warehouse that may be purchased in about five years' time, was acquired at or before the time that one of these three chargeable occasions occurs. In that case the deferred gain could be deducted from the acquisition cost of the third asset for capital gains tax purposes.

       (iv)   If the proceeds were not used by Medway Ltd to acquire qualifying assets but were instead loaned to its subsidiary Newtown Ltd, which in turn used the loan to acquire a freehold shop costing £1,020,000, the capital gains treatment would depend on how much of Newtown's ordinary share capital Medway owns. If Medway owns 75% or more of Newtown's ordinary share capital then Medway's gain could be rolled over against Newtown's acquisition, so that Newtown's base cost for capital gains tax would be (1,020,000 – 50,000 =) £970,000 (ie £950,000 indexed 31 March 1982 value of old factory plus £20,000 further expenditure). If Medway does not own 75% of Newtown's share capital then rollover relief would not be available and the gain of £50,000 would be immediately assessable (subject to the acquisition of qualifying assets by Medway within three years after the sale of its factory, in which event rollover relief could be claimed).

       (v)   Since the requisite 75% or more parent/subsidiary relationship exists between Medway and Parkland, they form a group for capital gains purposes. Parkland could therefore transfer the shareholding to Medway on a no loss no gain basis under TCGA 1992 s 171 and Medway could then make the disposal outside the group, so that Medway would be able to set the loss arising of £100,000 against the chargeable gain of £50,000 on the sale of the factory, provided Medway disposes of the shareholding before the end of the accounting period in which it disposes of the factory.

Under TCGA 1992 s 171A, there is no need for actual transfer of the shareholding from Parkland to Medway. S 171A provides that Parkland may make the disposal of the shareholding and the two companies may elect, within two years after the end of the accounting period in which the asset was disposed of outside the group, to be treated as if the shareholding had been transferred by Parkland to Medway immediately before the disposal, and s 171 is deemed to have applied to the deemed transfer, so that the gain would be regarded as made by Medway. This virtually amounts to the group surrender of capital gains or losses. See Example 64 explanatory note 3(b) for more detailed comments.

Additional points to note in relation to the various alternatives are as follows:

1. Rollover relief has the effect of reducing the capital gains base cost of the replacement asset, so that when the replacement is sold, indexation allowance is effectively forfeited on the rolled over amount for the intervening period. This does not apply where gains are held over as a result of acquiring depreciating assets, because the capital gains cost of the replacement is unaltered. On the other hand the maximum deferral time is ten years, so the point when tax becomes payable may be much sooner. (If the depreciating asset is a lease, the cost of the lease will be depreciated once the unexpired life is 50 years or less, reducing the indexation allowance accordingly if the lease is disposed of.)

2. If alternative (iv) were adopted (Medway owning 75% or more of Newtown's share capital), then a larger gain would be charged on Newtown when it disposed of the shop. Since Newtown is not a wholly owned subsidiary a compensating financial adjustment would need to be made between the companies in respect of any additional tax arising.

3. The claim for 'deemed transfer' in (v) above can transfer the loss or the gain. It is therefore possible to match the gain and loss in the same company, and also to choose which of the two will pay the tax. If one would have a lower marginal corporation tax rate, this would give a further advantage.

(d) **Rochester – business use of private residence**

		£
Sale proceeds 30 March 2007 Darke Road house		225,150
31 March 1982 value		58,000
		167,150
Indexation allowance to April 1998		
£58,000 x 104.7%		60,726
Gain before reliefs		106,424
Less private residence exemption 80%		85,139
Gain on workshop 20%		21,285
Less rolled over against replacement acquired within previous year:		
Proceeds relating to old workshop		
20% x 225,150	45,030	
Amount reinvested in new workshop		
15% x 250,000	37,500	
Amount not reinvested	7,530	
Total gain on workshop	21,285	
Rolled over gain	13,755	13,755
Chargeable gain		£ 7,530

It is assumed that the workshops are used exclusively for business purposes.

It seems likely that the workshop and house are treated, both on the old property and on the new, as a single asset. If this is the case, the base cost of the new house for CGT purposes will be (£250,000 – £13,755 =) £236,245. When the new house is sold, a gain calculated using this base cost will be 15% chargeable by reason of business use.

The gain immediately chargeable will qualify for taper relief, but only 20% of this will enjoy the business assets rate (see Example 82 explanatory note 14). The chargeable gain will therefore be:

		£
Gain calculated above		7,530
Business asset proportion, taper at 75%	1,506	(1,130)
Non-business asset proportion, taper at 35%	6,024	(2,108)
Chargeable gain		4,292

If the new workshop could be regarded as a separate asset which cost 15% x £250,000 = £37,500, that separate asset would have a base cost of (£37,500 – £13,755 =) £23,745.

If the old workshop could be regarded as a separate asset which was independent of the house, it would only receive business assets taper, and the chargeable gain would be (25% x £7,530 =) £1,882.

Explanatory Notes

Assets qualifying for rollover/holdover relief

1.   References in this example are to TCGA 1992 unless otherwise stated. Traders may claim rollover/holdover relief for business assets under s 152 when both the assets disposed of and those acquired are within the following classes (s 155):

Land, buildings and fixed plant and machinery ('fixed' is considered to mean fixed on a permanent or semi-permanent basis to the premises)

Ships, aircraft, hovercraft, satellites, space stations and spacecraft

Goodwill*

Milk and potato quotas* (see note 12)

Ewe and suckler cow premium quotas*

Fish quota*

Lloyd's syndicate rights

* Since 1 April 2002 these assets have been dealt with for companies under the intangible assets rules – see note 16.

The acquisition must be made within one year before or three years after the disposal. The fact that the replacement may be acquired up to one year before the disposal does not, however, permit a gain on the sale of part of an asset within 12 months after its acquisition to be rolled over against the acquisition cost (Watton v Tippett, CA 1997). HMRC has discretion to extend the time limits, and would probably exercise their discretion where there was a firm intention to acquire qualifying assets within the stipulated period but the taxpayer was prevented from doing so by circumstances beyond his control (Tax Bulletin November 1991). However, as shown in R v CIR ex p Barnett the discretion to allow a late claim was solely in the hands of the Revenue (now HMRC) and the Commissioners (although making certain helpful findings in the taxpayer's favour) had no jurisdiction to review it. The disposal and acquisition do not have to be within the same class of asset, and the replacement asset need not be used in the same trade where one person carries on two or more trades either successively or at the same time. HMRC regards two trades as having been carried on successively if there is an interval between them not exceeding three years (SP 8/81). Disposals during the interval qualify for relief, appropriately adjusted for the period of non-business use. Gains may be rolled over or held over by reference to acquisitions during the interval, providing the assets acquired are not used or leased for any purpose during that time and are brought into use in the successor trade on its commencement.

The relief is not confined to a single disposal and a single acquisition. The gain on one asset could be rolled over or held over against several replacement assets, or gains on several assets could be rolled or held over against a single replacement. Concession D22 provides that capital expenditure on improvements to existing qualifying assets may be treated as expenditure on new assets. (The initial cultivation costs of short rotation coppice (net of any woodland grants) count as improvement expenditure under this heading.)

To prevent abuse of the concession, and other concessions deferring gains, ss 284A, 284B provide that where a gain has been deferred under a concession first published before 9 March 1999, or a later replacement concession with substantially the same effect, then if, when the asset is disposed of, the person disposing of it seeks to avoid bringing the gain into charge on a disposal on or after 9 March 1999, he is treated as having made a chargeable gain equal to the deferred gain in the tax year or company accounting period in which the disposal takes place. The person on whom the charge arises could be the same taxpayer or another taxpayer to whom the asset had been transferred with the benefit of capital gains deferral.

Reinvesting the proceeds

2. (i) To get full relief the full amount of the proceeds must be reinvested. Where only part of the proceeds is reinvested, the chargeable gain is deemed to be reinvested last (s 153). This means that if the amount paid for the replacement asset is less than the sale proceeds for the old asset, the difference represents a realised gain, in respect of which relief is not available. If the difference exceeds the chargeable gain then rollover/holdover relief is not available at all. Where several disposals take place at the same time but the total proceeds are not fully reinvested, the disposals in respect of which relief is claimed may be chosen so as to maximise the benefit of the claim. For example if two assets were sold for a total of £200,000, being £130,000 and £70,000 respectively, showing total gains of £70,000 (£25,000 and £45,000 respectively) and replacement assets were acquired costing £120,000, relief could be claimed in respect of the second asset, the proceeds of £70,000 having been reinvested, even though looking at the combined position it appears that no part of the gains has been reinvested.

   (ii) The relief is available if a gain arises on a gift of a qualifying asset, providing the deemed proceeds are matched by reinvestment in qualifying assets.

Rollover relief

3. The rolled over gain on the disposal is deducted from the cost of the new asset(s). Indexation allowance up to the time of disposal or, for individuals, up to April 1998 if earlier, is taken into account in arriving at the gain and thus effectively forms part of the base cost of the replacement asset, as shown in part (a)(i) of the example, where the base cost of the goodwill is £48,120, being £40,000 original cost of the freehold building plus £8,120 indexation allowance on its disposal. In part (a)(ii) the goodwill has a base cost of £54,453, being £40,000 cost of the freehold building plus indexation allowance of £12,906 plus the half of the deferred gain, £1,547, that is excluded under the provisions of Sch 4 (see note 11).

   The effect of the rollover relief is to give a lower base cost for the replacement asset(s), which means that indexation allowance is effectively forfeited on the rolled over amount for the intervening period to the time the replacement asset is sold, as shown in part (a)(i) of the example. Taper relief for non-corporate taxpayers (see note 6) is, however, given by reference to the period of ownership of the *replacement* asset, so that in part (a)(i) of the example it operates to Norris's benefit, because the rolled over gain of £7,880 on the 1986 disposal is included in the amount that qualifies for 75% taper relief.

4. If, exceptionally, the gain on a qualifying asset acquired before 6 April 1965 is arrived at by using time apportionment rather than 6 April 1965 value or 31 March 1982 value, and the full proceeds are not reinvested in qualifying replacement assets, the whole of the non-reinvested gain would not be chargeable because it would be restricted by time apportionment (s 153(1)).

If, for example, in part (c)1. of the example the time apportioned gain of £263,171 had been the lowest gain, and £100,000 of the proceeds of sale had not been reinvested as in 2(ii), only 41½/61½ x £100,000 = £67,480 would be immediately chargeable and the remainder of the chargeable gain would be rolled over.

For detailed notes on time apportionment in relation to assets acquired before 6 April 1965 see Example 77.

Holdover relief on depreciating assets

5. If the replacement asset is a wasting asset (ie with a life of 50 years or less), or an asset that will become a wasting asset within ten years (called a depreciating asset), the gain cannot be deducted from the cost thereof, but a claim may be made for it to be held over and deemed not to arise until the earliest of the following three dates, thus deferring calculation of the tax (and payment) to that time:

    (i)   The date of disposal of the replacement asset

    (ii) The time when the replacement asset ceases to be used for the purposes of the trade

    (iii) Ten years from the date of acquisition of the replacement asset.

    If, however, another qualifying non-depreciating asset is purchased not later than the earliest of the three dates, the gain may instead be deducted from that purchase (s 154). The rules are illustrated in part (c)2.(iii) of the example.

    Since a heldover gain is not deducted from the cost of the replacement asset, it does not affect that cost for indexation allowance purposes. On the other hand, taper relief for non-corporate taxpayers is given by reference to the period of ownership of the asset on which the heldover gain arose. Contrast this with rollover relief – see note 3 above.

Taper relief

6. Taper relief replaces indexation allowance for non-corporate taxpayers from April 1998 (see Example 74 part (a)(i) for details). As indicated above, taper relief is given by reference to length of time the *replacement* asset has been owned where gains are rolled over, and by reference to the period of ownership of the asset to which the heldover gain relates where gains are held over against depreciating assets.

    It is important to remember that taper relief is only given after all reliefs have been claimed. It is therefore the untapered gain that is deducted from the cost of the new asset, and the full proceeds that must be invested in the new asset. Only where replacement is in the form of a depreciating asset, and the gain on the original asset remains identifiable, is any taper relief available in respect of the first period of ownership. This could be particularly unfair where a trader has regularly replaced business premises over a long period, and retires shortly after such a replacement: rollover relief will have the effect of charging the gains of the whole period at once, but taper relief will only be given for that final short period.

    Care will need to be taken to ensure that claims are appropriate in the light of anticipated future events, and it may well be sensible to delay rollover/holdover claims in order to have as much information as possible on which to base decisions. Part (b) of the example illustrates one scenario where holdover relief would be preferable to rollover relief.

    However, the acceleration of business assets taper relief from 6 April 2002 means that maximum taper will be enjoyed provided that the 'final' asset (on which the series of gains will at last be chargeable without further rollover) is owned for at least two years.

Rollover/holdover relief claims

7. Because of the length of time that may elapse before an asset is replaced, the position for corporation tax for accounting periods ended on or before 30 June 1999 (which also applied for capital gains tax

for years before 1996/97) was that gains should be assessed at the normal time, but with the company having the opportunity to claim to postpone the tax on production of satisfactory evidence of its intention to acquire a qualifying replacement. Should the intended replacement then not materialise, interest on the tax that should have been paid will be charged from the normal due date. Corporation tax claims should be made within six years from the end of the company accounting period to which the claim relates (TMA 1970 s 43).

Under s 153A, applicable from 1996/97 for non-corporate taxpayers and for accounting periods ending after 30 June 1999 for companies, provisional claims for rollover relief may be made in tax returns before reinvestment takes place, the provisional claims being replaced by actual claims when the conditions are satisfied. If the reinvestment does not take place, the provisional claim ceases to have effect three years from 31 January following the tax year of disposal, or four years from the end of the accounting period of disposal for companies, and all necessary adjustments will then be made to earlier assessments. Where a holdover claim is being replaced by a rollover claim as a result of the later acquisition of a non-depreciating asset (which could in fact be up to thirteen years after the disposal giving rise to the gain that has been held over), it is thought that the claim to switch from holdover to rollover relief would need to be made at or soon after the time of acquisition of the non-depreciating asset, and in any event in the next tax return. The capital gains tax time limit for claims from 1996/97 is five years from 31 January following the relevant tax year.

Death of taxpayer

8.   If a taxpayer dies before a rolled over gain crystallises, the gain escapes tax as a result of the death. The same does not strictly apply where a gain has been held over under the provisions in note 5 above, but by Concession D45 the death of the taxpayer does not trigger the held-over gain.

Groups of companies

9.   Where two or more companies form a 75% group (parent company and subsidiaries in which the parent owns 75% or more of the ordinary share capital), all the trades in the group are treated as a single trade for rollover/holdover relief and the relief may be claimed no matter which group company makes the disposals and which the acquisitions (s 175). (A non-trading company that holds assets for trading companies in its group is included in these provisions under s 175(2B).)

Disposals from one group company to another are made on a no loss/no gain basis, as indicated in part (c)2.(v) of the example. Where, however, a company joined a group after 31 March 1987, and had realised or unrealised capital losses at 16 March 1993, the losses cannot be used against gains of another group company arising on or after 16 March 1993. In part (c)2.(v) of the example, therefore, Medway Ltd would not have been able to use an intra-group transfer (whether actual under s 171 or deemed under s 171A) to obtain the use of Parkland Ltd's loss on the shareholding if Parkland had joined the group after 31 March 1987 and the shareholding had been standing at a loss at 16 March 1993.

Further anti-avoidance provisions deny rollover relief where the replacement asset is acquired on a no loss no gain basis (s 175(2C)). These provisions would prevent Medway Ltd in part (c) of the example avoiding the gain on the disposal of the factory by acquiring a qualifying business asset from Parkland Ltd on a no loss no gain basis. To obtain the relief, a new asset must be brought into the group.

For detailed notes on the group capital gains provisions see Examples 61 and 64. See also note 14 to this example re compulsorily purchased land.

Assets owned personally and used by company

10.   Rollover/holdover relief is also available on the disposal and replacement of an asset owned personally and used in the owner's partnership or personal trading company (ie a trading company in which he owns 5% or more of the voting rights). The payment of rent does not affect the position (s 157).

Where personally owned assets are used in a personal company, the old and new assets must be acquired by the same individual, and used by the same personal company (and not for example by a new company following the liquidation of the first company). If the personal company is a holding company, use of an asset by a subsidiary does not qualify, because the subsidiary does not qualify as a personal company.

Effect of 31 March 1982 rebasing provisions on rolled over and heldover gains

11.   If a qualifying asset was disposed of at a gain before 31 March 1982 and a replacement asset was acquired before that date against which the gain was rolled over, the effect of the FA 1988 rebasing provisions is that the rolled over gain escapes tax, because it is not taken into account in arriving at the 31 March 1982 value of the replacement asset. The same result would not occur if the pre 31 March 1982 disposal had produced a gain to be held over as distinct from rolled over, but it is provided by Sch 4.4(5) that any such gain also escapes tax (see below in last paragraph of this note).

If a qualifying asset acquired pre 31 March 1982 is disposed of on or after 6 April 1988, the 31 March 1982 value may be used to calculate the gain to be rolled over or held over.

But if a rollover or holdover had occurred after 31 March 1982 and before 6 April 1988 (as in part (a)(ii) of the example, where the building acquired in 1972 was disposed of in 1986), then only the cost of the asset and not the March 1982 value was deducted in calculating the gain (despite the indexation allowance being calculated on the March 1982 value if the taxpayer had made an appropriate election). In these circumstances, any increase in value at 31 March 1982 of the asset giving rise to the deferred gain forms part of the deferred amount, since the gain has not been reduced by the increase in value up to 31 March 1982.

It is accordingly provided in Sch 4 that a claim may be made (normally within one year from 31 January following the tax year or two years after the end of the company accounting period in which the relevant event occurs) for only one half of any deferred amount to be charged to tax in these circumstances, where the deferred amount is attributable directly or indirectly, in whole or in part, to a gain on the disposal before 6 April 1988 of an asset acquired before 31 March 1982. This applies in the following situations:

(a)   Under the following provisions, where the deduction made in the base cost of a replacement asset acquired after 31 March 1982 and before 6 April 1988 is halved:

    (i)   Where a replacement asset is acquired after receipt of compensation or insurance money (s 23(4) and (5))

    (ii)   Where a replacement asset is acquired on the disposal of a business asset, as in this example (see (a)(ii)) (s 152)

    (iii)   Where shares are acquired on transfer of a business to a company (s 162)

    (iv)   Where a gain is held over on a business asset acquired by gift (s 165)

    (v)   Where replacement land is acquired on compulsory acquisition of other land (s 247)

    (vi)   Where a gain is held over on an asset acquired by gift under the former general gifts relief (FA 1980 s 79).

(b)   Under the following provisions, where gains that have been postponed on a disposal before 6 April 1988 are halved when they crystallise (or, in the case of the first four items, possibly exempted altogether, as indicated in the last paragraph of this note):

    (i)   Where securities are acquired in exchange for a business acquired by a non-resident company (s 140)

    (ii)   Where gilts are acquired on compulsory acquisition of shares (s 134)

(iii)   Where a depreciating asset is acquired on compulsory acquisition of land (ss 247 and 248(3))

(iv)   Where a depreciating asset is acquired as replacement for a business asset, as in part (c) 2. (iii) of this example (s 154)

 (v)   When a company leaves a group, in respect of an asset acquired from another group company (s 178)

(vi)   Where a gain held over under the gifts relief provisions crystallises under ss 67(6) and 168 on emigration of the donee

(vii)   Where there is a reorganisation involving the acquisition of qualifying corporate bonds (s 116(10) and (11)).

By Sch 4.4(5) where a gain (or loss) would otherwise crystallise on or after 6 April 1988 in relation to any of the items (i) to (iv) above, and it is *directly* attributable to the disposal of an asset on or before 31 March 1982, then it is not brought into account at all.

Milk quota

12.   Milk quota was introduced in 1984. HMRC considers that quota is a separate asset from the land to which it relates, and if the owner had the quota allotted in 1984 he will have no base cost, and thus will get no indexation allowance if he disposes of the quota (Tax Bulletin February 1993). Those who have an acquisition cost get indexation allowance in the normal way, but not taking into account any part of the cost of the land. Even though HMRC regards quota as a separate asset, they usually considered that retirement relief was not available on the disposal of quota unless land was disposed of as well, because a disposal without land is not 'part of the business'. This view was upheld in Wase v Bourke 1995. See note 16 for the treatment of quota in the hands of companies from 1 April 2002.

Where compensation is paid to producers (called SLOM producers) as a result of their not being allocated milk quota in 1984, the Revenue consider it to be income, and that it should be taken into account when the legal entitlement arises and when the amount payable can be quantified with reasonable certainty (Tax Bulletin May 1994).

Capital allowances

13.   The reduction of the base values of assets for capital gains tax does not affect the income tax figures. Capital allowances would still be available, for example, on the amount of £1,040,000 (less the cost of the land) paid for the freehold factory in part (c)2.(i) of the example, whereas the base figure for capital gains tax is £900,000. And in (c)2.(iii), Medway would be able to claim a deduction against its profit each year for the part of the £1,040,000 premium that was assessed on the landlord as extra rent. For details see Example 100 part (h).

Rollover relief and compulsory purchase

14.   Although rollover relief is not normally available on investment property (except for furnished holiday lettings – see Example 99 explanatory note 6), s 247 allows relief to be claimed where property is disposed of under a compulsory purchase order, and a replacement is acquired within one year before and three years after the disposal. The relief is not available if the replacement property is the taxpayer's capital gains tax exempt dwelling at any time within six years after acquisition (s 248). Companies in a 75% group can claim this relief if one company makes the disposal and another company acquires the replacement. 'Compulsory purchase' includes purchase of the freehold by a tenant exercising his right to buy (SP 13/93).

Where *part* of a holding of land is compulsorily purchased, small proceeds may be treated as reducing the capital gains cost of the holding rather than being treated as a part disposal (s 243). 'Small' is not defined but is taken by HMRC to mean not more than 5%.

Rollover relief and grants towards replacement assets

15. Where a grant is received towards the cost of an asset, it is generally required to be deducted from the expenditure allowable for capital gains tax (TCGA 1992 s 50). The case of Wardhaugh v Penrith Rugby Union Football Club (Ch D 2002) considered whether this had any effect on a rollover relief claim. The club sold some land for £315,000, realising a gain of £204,000; it bought a new clubhouse for £600,000, and received a grant of £409,000 from the Sports Council towards this expenditure. The Revenue argued that the grant should reduce the expenditure on the new asset to £191,000 for rollover purposes, which would leave £124,000 of the gain in charge to tax. The High Court held that s 50 operates only in calculating the gain on a disposal, and is independent of s 152 which restricts rollover relief for partial reinvestment. Accordingly, the full gain could be held over against the expenditure of £600,000. This has the surprising effect of establishing a negative cost for the asset (as it would be reduced by the rollover claim and by the s 50 deduction). The Revenue did appeal this decision, but the appeal was dismissed in June 2003.

New rules for intangible fixed assets

16. From 1 April 2002, companies receive deductions from revenue profits for the cost of goodwill and fish and agricultural quotas purchased. Accordingly, goodwill and quotas purchased from that date cease to be a capital gains rollover asset for companies (unless acquired from related parties) and the sale of such goodwill and quota is subject to taxation as a trading profit. There is a separate rollover relief for that trading profit where the proceeds are used to buy other intangible assets: this operates in a similar way to capital gains rollover, but is independent of it, and there is no interaction between the two reliefs.

There was a transitional period during which a disposal on or after 1 April 2002 of goodwill or quota acquired before 1 April 2002 could be rolled over:

- under the capital gains rules against a purchase of goodwill or quota before 1 April 2002, and within the 12 months before the sale (ie the normal reinvestment time limit), or

- under the intangible assets rules (see Example 65), or

- partly under the capital gains rules and partly under the intangible assets rules.

Apart from this transitional provision, capital gains will not be rolled over against the purchase of intangible assets, and gains on intangible assets will not be rolled over against property within the capital gains rollover classes.

Goodwill and quotas purchased by a sole trader or partnership remain chargeable assets for CGT, and remain eligible for rollover relief.

For the detailed provisions of the intangible assets legislation see Example 65.

(a)   On 1 March 2002 Fordwich, aged 57, acquired a 20% shareholding in a trading company. 85% of the company's chargeable assets are chargeable business assets. He gave 5% of the shares to his son on 1 May 2006, and the gain arising before taking any available reliefs into account was £80,000.

Show how much of the gain, if any, is chargeable to tax assuming all available reliefs are claimed.

(b)   Quincey invested £35,000 in April 1987 in unquoted shares in his friend's trading company (the shares representing a 4% holding). On 5 July 2006 Quincey sold the shares to his sister for £55,000. She agreed to pay the purchase price in ten equal instalments commencing July 2006. The market value in July 2006 was £85,000. Quincey had made other chargeable disposals in 2006/07 which used the annual exemption, and he had no allowable losses brought forward.

Show the capital gain arising and state how this may be treated.

(c)   In January 2007 Harry transfers a painting to a discretionary trust and claims gifts relief. The asset was bought in March 2001 for £200,000 and was worth £500,000 at the date of transfer. Harry does not have an interest in the settlement at the date of transfer.

The asset is sold by the trustees in March 2007 for £502,000. The trustees also dispose of another asset realising a loss of £275,000.

Calculate the trustees' capital gain.

Explain what the consequences would be if Harry acquired an interest in the settlement in May 2007.

(a) **Fordwich – gift of shares to son 1 May 2006**

Since 15% of the company's chargeable assets are not business assets, only 85% of the gain qualifies for gifts relief under TCGA 1992 s 165. If the existence of that level of non-business assets means that the company is not regarded as 'trading' for taper relief purposes, gifts relief is not available at all after 5 April 2004 (but 15% is unlikely to be regarded as 'substantial' on its own – further information is required about the importance of the non-business assets to the operations of the company).

The chargeable gains therefore become:

	£
Gain before reliefs	80,000
Gifts relief (85%)	(68,000)
Chargeable gain before taper	12,000
Taper relief (75%, assuming non-trading is insubstantial)	(9,000)
Chargeable gain after taper	3,000

The son's base cost of the shares would be the market value at the date of gift, less the £68,000 held over. Taper relief for the son would depend only on his period of ownership (commencing 1 May 2006) and on the company's trading or non-trading status during that same period.

(b) **Quincey – sale of shares at undervalue to sister, payment by instalments**

Quincey's sister is a connected person, therefore sale is deemed to be at open market value (see note 1).

	£	£
Deemed sale proceeds – July 2006 (replacing £55,000 received)		85,000
Cost April 1987	35,000	
Indexation allowance to April 1998 $\frac{162.6 - 101.8}{101.8} = 59.7\%$	20,895	55,895
Chargeable gain		29,105

Quincey's shares qualify as a business asset for taper relief from 6 April 2000 (see Example 74 part (a)(i)). The gain would therefore be reduced by taper relief based on the business/non-business use over the 99 months from 6 April 1998 to 5 July 2006 as follows (the *rate of relief* for the non-business proportion being based on nine qualifying years, including the extra year for pre 17 March 1998 ownership):

Business:	75/99 x 75% = (more than 2 qualifying years)	56.8%	
Non-business:	24/99 x 35% = (8 qualifying years plus one bonus year)	8.5%	
Taper relief on gain of 29,105 @		65.3%	£19,006

The taper relief would therefore reduce the gain to £10,099, and it would be further reduced by the annual exemption of £8,800 to £1,299.

£20,000 of the gain, ie the £55,000 consideration less £35,000 cost, relates to the actual consideration received and £9,105 to the 'gift' element of the deemed consideration.

Quincey and his sister may elect for the 'gift' element of the gain, ie £9,105, to be treated as reducing the sister's acquisition cost (see note 4). In that event, taper relief on that part of the gain will be given on eventual disposal according to the sister's period of ownership. As far as the remaining gain of £20,000 is concerned, taper relief at 65.3% of £20,000 amounts to £13,060, so that the taxable gain will be (20,000 − 13,060) = £6,940. If the annual exemption is not available and tax is due, there are two alternative provisions enabling the tax on this gain to be paid by instalments.

Since part of the consideration is due more than 18 months after the date of disposal, Quincey may opt to pay the tax by such instalments as HMRC allows over a maximum of eight years (TCGA 1992 s 280). Interest will be charged only on instalments paid late.

Alternatively, he may elect to pay the tax by ten annual instalments, but with interest on the full amount outstanding being added to each instalment. Furthermore, if the shares were later disposed of for valuable consideration (whether by the sister or by someone else) the full amount of tax outstanding at that time would be payable immediately (TCGA 1992 s 281). See note 10.

Of course, as the tax on £6,940 is only £2,776 (if Quincey is a higher rate taxpayer and his annual exemption is not available), it may be simpler to pay all the tax on the normal due date.

(c)   **Trustees' capital gain 2006/07**

Asset from Harry

		£
Proceeds		502,000
Less trustees' base cost		
MV January 2007	500,000	
Less gain held over	(300,000)	(200,000)
Gain		302,000
Less loss		(275,000)
Capital gain		27,000

Tax due thereon is payable by 31 January 2008.

Harry acquiring an interest in the settlement in May 2007

Holdover relief is no longer available for gifts to settlor interested trusts from 10 December 2003. This applies where the trust is settlor interested at the date of the gift or within the claw-back period (see explanatory note 14).

Harry is therefore assessed to tax on the gift in January 2007 in the tax year 2007/08 (the year he acquired an interest in the settlement) as follows:

	£
Market value (January 2007)	500,000
Less cost	(200,000)
Gain	300,000
Taper relief 5 yrs (only to January 2007) 15%	(45,000)
Capital gain	255,000

The trustees' gain is recomputed on the basis that gifts relief was not due on Harry's transfer to them.

		£
Proceeds		502,000
Less trustees' base cost		
MV January 2007	500,000	
Less gain held over	−	(500,000)
Gain		2,000
Less loss		(275,000)
Capital gain		−

The excess losses of £273,000 would be carried forward and any tax paid in January 2008 would be repaid.

Explanatory Notes

Gifts and disposals to connected persons

1. A gift of a chargeable asset is regarded as a disposal at open market value (except for transfers between spouses/civil partners) (s 17), and the chargeable gain or allowable loss is computed in the usual way, with indexation allowance being taken into account to reduce or eliminate a gain for periods up to April 1998, and gains being reduced by any available taper relief thereafter (see note 12). Where the parties are connected persons, then not only gifts but all transactions between them are deemed to be at market value (except for husband/wife transactions). For detailed notes on connected persons and how market value is arrived at see Example 73. See also Example 55 explanatory note 8(d) for the effect of a transfer at an undervalue by a close company.

Holdover relief on pre 14 April 1989 gifts

2. Before FA 1989, where a gain arose on a gift, then provided that the gift was made by an individual or trustees, and the donee was either an individual resident or ordinarily resident in the UK, or trustees who on a subsequent disposal would be liable to UK capital gains tax, a claim could be made for the gain which would otherwise be chargeable to be held over and treated as reducing the base acquisition cost of the donee (FA 1980 s 79). The relief applied to gifts from and to individuals after 5 April 1980, extended to include gifts to trustees after 5 April 1981 and to gifts by trustees after 5 April 1982. This general gifts relief was abolished by FA 1989 for disposals on or after 14 March 1989, but many assets will still be owned against which such gains have been held over. See note 13 for the availability of taper relief.

3. For disposals on or after 14 March 1989 more restricted gifts relief provisions are now contained in ss 165 and 260. Company donors do not qualify for gifts relief, but the donee of a s 165 gift may be a company (except for gifts of shares – see note 4). See note 13 for the availability of taper relief.

Holdover relief for gifts of business assets under s 165

4. S 165 broadly provides for individuals to claim that gains on gifts of the following assets be held over and treated as reducing the base acquisition cost of the donee:

    (a) Assets used in the donor's business or in his personal trading company (ie a company in which he holds not less than 5% of the voting rights), or used by a company in a trading group of which the holding company is the donor's personal trading company.

    (b) Farm land and buildings that would qualify for inheritance tax agricultural property relief (broadly all farming land providing certain conditions as to length of ownership and occupation are satisfied, including farm land held as an investment providing it has been owned for seven years and occupied for agriculture throughout that period).

    (c) Shares or securities in unquoted trading companies, or unquoted holding companies of trading groups. (Shares on the Alternative Investment Market qualify for relief.)

    (d) Shares or securities in the donor's personal trading company or personal holding company of a trading group.

    A gift of shares or securities to a company does not qualify for s 165 relief (s 165(3)(b)).

    Where agricultural property has development value, the gain qualifying for relief under (b) is not restricted to the agricultural value, even though inheritance tax agricultural property relief is so restricted.

    It should be noted that heading (d) enables relief to be claimed on a gift out of a 5% holding of shares in a *quoted* company. A holding of *any* size qualifies for relief under (c). If the holding (of quoted or unquoted shares) is 5% or more, however, relief is restricted to the business assets proportion of the gain (Sch 7.7). In part (b) of the example, Quincey owns only 4% of the shares, so his relief is not restricted. In part (a) of the example, the relief *is* restricted, because Fordwich owns 20% of the shares in his company.

Relief under s 165 is also available for disposals by trustees, heading (a) above being amended so as to relate to assets used in a trade carried on by the trustees or a life tenant and heading (d) relating to holdings in quoted companies carrying at least 25% of the voting power.

Claims for s 165 relief are made jointly by the donor and donee, unless the *donees* are trustees, in which case the claim is made by the donor alone.

Holdover relief under s 260

5. S 260 provides for holdover relief on gains on the following gifts by individuals or trustees:

    (a) Certain gifts of heritage property (works of art, historic buildings etc)

    (b) Gifts to funds for the maintenance of heritage property

    (c) Gifts to political parties

    (d) Gifts that are *immediately* chargeable to inheritance tax, or would be apart from the annual exemption or nil rate threshold. (This mainly covers gifts to certain trusts. For detailed provisions see the companion to this book, Tolley's Taxwise II 2006/07.)

As with claims for relief under s 165 (see note 4), claims for relief are made by the donor and donee jointly, unless the *donees* are trustees, in which case the claim is made by the donor alone.

Effect of gifts relief on inheritance tax

6. For both ss 165 and 260, any inheritance tax payable on the gift is deductible in arriving at the chargeable gain on a later disposal (but not so as to create a loss), and this applies where inheritance tax is payable at some later time, for example because the donor dies within seven years. All necessary adjustments will be made to the earlier computation. But if a gift does not qualify for gifts relief and capital gains tax is payable, there is no direct inheritance tax relief for the capital gains tax paid if the gift becomes chargeable to inheritance tax because of the donor's death within seven years (although the capital gains tax paid has reduced the wealth of the donor and therefore the amount liable to inheritance tax on his death). The detailed inheritance tax provisions are in the companion to this book, Tolley's Taxwise II 2006/07.

Assets disposed of at an undervalue

7. Gifts relief under both ss 165 and 260 is also available where assets are not given outright but are disposed of for less than their value, but if the actual consideration is greater than the original cost of the assets, so that the donor has in fact realised some of the gain in cash, then the chargeable gain which may be held over is restricted by the excess of the actual proceeds over cost, as shown in part (b) of the example.

Effect of non-residence

8. Gifts relief is not available if the donee is not resident and not ordinarily resident in the UK, or would not be chargeable to tax on a gain as a result of being regarded as non-resident under a double tax treaty (ss 166 and 261). Relief under s 165 is not available if the donee is a foreign controlled company (s 167).

The held-over gain is charged to tax if the donee becomes not resident and not ordinarily resident in the UK within six years after the end of the tax year in which the gift was made (s 168). This can have significant implications for taper relief. Assume Georgie gave a long-held business property to her son Sam in May 2004 and the gain of £180,000 was held over. In March 2007 Sam emigrated to Australia. The held-over gain of £180,000 would crystallise in 2006/07 with tax due on 31 January 2008. No taper relief is available in these circumstances. If Sam did not pay this tax within 12 months, it can be collected from the donor, ie Georgie. This compares to the situation if no hold-over claim had been made. Georgie would have been charged the tax on only:

	£
Gain	180,000
Taper (75%)	(135,000)
	45,000

Gifts relief claims

9. No specific time limit is stipulated for the gifts relief claims, so that the normal time limit of five years ten months in TMA 1970 s 43 will apply.

   HMRC has stated that in most circumstances it will not be necessary to agree market values at the time of a gifts relief claim. Establishing the market value at the date of the gift can normally be deferred until the donee disposes of the asset (Statement of Practice 8/92 and *Tax Bulletin* April 1997). There is a standard claim form for holdover claims. The form is included in HMRC Helpsheet IR 295. Under self-assessment the claim is separate from the return, although it will often be sent in with the return.

Paying tax by instalments

10. Where gifts relief is not available, or does not cover the full amount of the gain, any tax arising may be paid by ten annual instalments on gifts of land, a controlling holding of shares or securities in a company, or minority holdings of shares or securities in an unquoted company. Interest is, however, charged on the full amount outstanding and is added to each instalment (s 281). The other instalment option outlined in part (b) of the example is only available where the consideration is payable by instalments over a period of more than 18 months (see Example 74 explanatory note 5 for details).

Effect of 31 March 1982 rebasing provisions

11. Where the occasion of the claim for gifts relief under s 165, or the now withdrawn FA 1980 s 79, arose before 31 March 1982 with the subsequent disposal on or after 6 April 1988, 31 March 1982 market value may be substituted for the base acquisition cost, thus removing the heldover gain from the reckoning on a disposal after 5 April 1988.

   Where the heldover gain relates in whole or in part to a period before 31 March 1982 and the occasion of the claim arose between 31 March 1982 and 6 April 1988, the heldover gain is halved when brought into charge on or after 6 April 1988 (see Example 83 explanatory note 11). This also applies where a gain crystallises under s 168 on emigration of the donee.

Taper relief

12. Indexation allowance is no longer available other than to companies for periods after April 1998. Instead, non-corporate taxpayers may claim taper relief from 6 April 1998, as indicated in Example 74 part (a)(i).

13. As far as gifts holdover relief is concerned, taper relief is not available to reduce the donor's gain and is given by reference to the donee's period of ownership and use of the assets as indicated in parts (a) and (b) of the example.

   Where the donor qualifies for substantial taper relief, a decision must be taken between paying tax now on the tapered gain, or paying tax later on a gain without the benefit of the period up to the date of the gift. The acceleration of taper relief on business assets from 6 April 2002 significantly reduces this problem. As long as the transferee will hold the asset as a business asset for two complete years, maximum taper relief of 75% will be enjoyed in spite of the lost period.

FA 2004 restriction of gift relief to settlor interested trusts

14. Prior to 10 December 2003, gift relief was often used to restart the taper relief clock to avoid apportionment provisions, as part of an IHT avoidance arrangement and to use tax reliefs within a trust (eg other losses or entitlement to private residence relief) to eliminate a chargeable gain.

As shown in part (c) above, holdover relief is no longer available where the trust is settlor interested either at the date of the gift or any time before the sixth anniversary of the start of the tax year following the one in which the disposal was made (the claw-back period). This applies to gifts under both s 165 (business assets) or s 260 (IHT).

For the holdover claim to fail, the following conditions must be satisfied (new TCGA 1992 s 169B onwards):

(a)   The disposal must be to a trust;

(b)   The disposal can be from a trust to a trust or from an individual to a trust and either

   (i)   the trust is settlor interested or there is an arrangement (which is widely defined) under which an interest could be acquired by the settlor; or

   (ii)   the trust is one which benefits an individual who in the past (whenever) has made a holdover claim in respect of which that asset thereby now has a reduced base cost.

Interest is widely defined at new TCGA 1992 s 169F and includes where either the settlor or spouse (s 169F(4)) obtains a benefit directly or indirectly from such property. Subsection (5) provides that an interest of a settlor (or spouse/civil partner) can be ignored in limited circumstances involving the death of particular parties.

Point (b) above is intended to prevent the rules being avoided using a chain of transfers, eg Connor settles assets on trust A from which he is excluded (claiming holdover relief) which then transfers the asset to trust B from which he is not excluded.

The claw-back provisions provide that a chargeable gain arises at the time the settlement becomes a settlor interested settlement equal to the held-over gain, and the trustees' allowable expenditure is increased by the amount of the held-over gain. Taper relief is only available up to the date of transfer to the trust, not the deemed accrual of the gain.

There are limited exclusions from these rules for certain disabled trusts and historic buildings.

(1)   (a)   Outline the principal differences between the tax treatment of capital gains made by individuals and those made by companies.

      (b)   Kaput Ltd owns a 100% subsidiary, a 60% subsidiary and a 40% stake in a consortium company. All the companies are UK resident. Comment on the implications of these shareholdings for the taxation of Kaput Ltd's capital gains, including the implications of transactions between the companies.

(2)   Fancy Trading Ltd has a UK subsidiary, Plain Trading Ltd, in which it holds 80% of the issued share capital. Both companies make up accounts annually to 31 December. No general 31.3.82 rebasing election has been or is being made in respect of the group.

On 30 April 2006 Plain Trading Ltd sold 10,000 50p ordinary shares in Twisty Ltd, a non-quoted company, for £38,370. It had acquired the shares in May 1986 from Fancy Trading Ltd for £1.50 each. Fancy Trading Ltd had acquired the shares at par in January 1980, and they were valued at £1.55 each on 31 March 1982.

Show the capital gains position on the sale in April 2006 and indicate what the position would have been if the proceeds had been only £6,000.

The following indexed rises may be used:

March 1982 – May 1986:   23.2%

March 1982 – April 2006: 147.4%

(1) (a) **Principal differences between the tax treatment of capital gains made by individuals and companies**

    (i) Individuals are charged separately to capital gains tax on gains (albeit at marginal income tax rates), while companies treat chargeable gains as another source of profits chargeable to corporation tax.

    (ii) Individuals enjoy an annual exemption for gains (£8,800 for 2006/07), but companies do not.

    (iii) From April 1998 onwards individuals cease to accrue indexation allowance, and start to accrue taper relief instead; companies continue to accrue indexation allowance and do not receive taper relief.

    (iv) Many capital gains reliefs and exemptions are not relevant to companies (eg only or main residence, incorporation relief, gifts relief).

    (v) There is no 'exit charge' when an individual becomes non-UK resident, but a company becoming non-UK resident is deemed to dispose of all its chargeable assets at their market value on the date it becomes foreign resident (unless the assets remain within the charge to corporation tax through being used by a UK permanent establishment of the company).

    (vi) The tax treatment of loan stocks and foreign currencies is different for companies. Under the 'loan relationships' provisions, most loan stocks and currency exchange differences are dealt with for companies as income under Schedule D Case III. Individuals and trustees would pay:

- income tax on the whole profit on a 'relevant discounted security';

- capital gains tax on some loan stocks which are qualifying corporate bonds (QCBs) for corporation tax but not so for capital gains tax (eg stocks redeemable in a foreign currency);

- income tax on accrued income on disposal of most QCBs;

- capital gains tax on exchange profits on foreign currency assets (but foreign currency liabilities are outside the scope of capital gains tax).

For the detailed corporation tax provisions on loan relationships see Example 62.

    (vii) For acquisitions on or after 1 April 2002 from unrelated parties, goodwill and fishing and agricultural quotas are not chargeable assets for companies. Gains and losses on such assets are taken into account under the 'intangible assets' provisions. For the details see Example 65.

    (viii) For disposals on or after 1 April 2002, companies are exempt from tax on the disposal of a substantial shareholding (broadly 10% of ordinary share capital) in a trading company. For details see Example 65.

    (ix) Since 5 December 2005, companies have been subject to specific anti-avoidance measures not relevant for capital gains tax. These measures are intended to prevent companies from claiming relief in respect of capital losses:

      1. that arise in the course of a transaction where the realisation of the loss was a main or the main purpose;

      2. where there is a change in the ownership of a company and a main or the main purpose for the change in ownership is to secure a tax advantage; or

3.   where a capital gain has arisen but it would ordinarily have been charged as income but for a tax avoidance scheme entered into in order to convert the income into a gain so as to offset capital losses.

(b)   Kaput Ltd and its 100% subsidiary are a group for capital gains purposes. This means that any assets chargeable to tax on gains are transferred between them on a 'no loss no gain' basis (see explanatory note 1), and a gain on the disposal of a business asset by one can be rolled over against the acquisition of a qualifying asset by the other (see Example 83).

Kaput Ltd and its 60% subsidiary do not qualify for the above treatment. They are connected persons, so transactions between them are routinely taxed at open market value. A loss on a disposal by one to the other can only be offset against gains on disposals to the same person.

Kaput Ltd is not connected with the consortium company. A transaction which is not at arm's length would have to be adjusted to market value, but losses on disposal should be allowed against other gains.

(2)   **No gain no loss transfers – disposal of shares in Twisty Ltd 30 April 2006**

Plain Trading Ltd will be treated as having acquired the shares in Twisty Ltd at their cost to Fancy Trading Ltd, ie £5,000 plus indexation allowance to May 1986 of 23.2% x £5,000 = £1,160, giving a total acquisition cost of £6,160. (Although an election could have been made to base the indexation allowance on the intra-group transfer on the 31.3.82 value of £15,500, this would not usually have been done, since as the law then stood, it would not have affected the calculation when the asset was transferred outside the group.)

The position on the sale on 30 April 2006 is as follows:

		Using cost			*Using 31.3.82 value*
		£			£
Sale proceeds		38,370			38,370
Deemed value on intra-group transfer May 1986	6,160				
Less: indexation allowance included therein	1,160				
	5,000				
31.3.82 value – 10,000 @ £1.55				15,500	
Indexation allowance on 31.3.82 value 147.4% x 15,500	22,847	27,847	22,847	38,347	
		10,523			23
Chargeable gain is the lower of the two, ie					23

Note that for companies indexation allowance continues to be available after April 1998 (and taper relief does not apply).

If the sale proceeds had been £6,000

Although indexation allowance cannot normally create or increase a loss on a disposal on or after 30 November 1993, this does not apply to the indexation allowance up to the time of the intra-group transfer in May 1986. It is not clear, however, whether HMRC would be prepared to allow the calculation to be based on the 31.3.82 value of £15,500, giving indexation allowance of 23.2% of £15,500 = £3,596, since the election to use 31.3.82 value on such a transfer had to be made within two years from the end of the relevant accounting period (ie by 31.12.88) or within such further period as HMRC allows. If HMRC did allow this, the proceeds of £6,000 would be compared with an indexed cost of £8,596, giving an allowable loss of £2,596. If they will not allow 31.3.82 value to be used to calculate the indexation allowance, only 23.2% x £5,000, ie £1,160, could be added to the cost of £5,000, making £6,160, and the allowable loss would be £160 (being less than the loss using 31.3.82 value of £15,500).

Explanatory Notes

No gain no loss disposals

1. References in this example are to TCGA 1992 unless otherwise stated. S 56 provides that on a disposal which would be treated as a 'no gain, no loss' disposal under the normal rules, an unindexed gain equal to any available indexation allowance is deemed to arise, thus giving a net result of no gain, no loss. These provisions apply to:

   (a) Transfers on company reconstructions (s 139)

   (b) Transfers (or deemed transfers) within a 75% group of companies (ss 171, 171A)

   (c) Transfers between spouses/civil partners (s 58)

   (d) Replacement of business assets (s 152).

   If, however, there is a loss when the asset is eventually disposed of, it is reduced by any indexation allowance added at the time of the no gain/no loss transfer (s 56(3)). This does not apply if the transfer was made before 30 November 1993, indexation allowance up to the time of such a transfer being available as part of an allowable loss (s 56).

   If, for example, a husband acquired an asset in January 1987 and transferred it to his wife in August 1997, the wife would be treated as having acquired the asset at the cost to the husband plus indexation allowance from January 1987 to August 1997. When she disposed of the asset, indexation allowance would be given from August 1997 to April 1998, but if a loss arose, the allowable loss could not be increased by indexation allowance, and would be based on the original unindexed cost to her husband.

   In part (2) of the example, Plain Trading Ltd is treated as acquiring the shares in Twisty Ltd at their cost to Fancy Trading Ltd in 1980 plus indexation allowance to the time of the intra-group transfer in May 1986. This can create a loss as it occurred before November 1993.

2. The rebasing provisions of s 35 enable gains and losses on assets acquired before 31 March 1982 to be calculated using 31 March 1982 value. Where an asset owned on 31 March 1982 was transferred before 6 April 1988 under specified no loss/no gain provisions, and is then disposed of on or after 6 April 1988, Sch 3.1 provides that the eventual transferor is treated as having owned the asset on 31 March 1982. The gain or loss on that eventual disposal is therefore computed using either 31 March 1982 value or original cost whichever shows the lower gain or loss (unless a general 31 March 1982 rebasing election has been made). In making the calculation based on cost, indexation allowance can be given on 31 March 1982 value, but in order to prevent double counting the indexation allowance included in the acquisition cost has to be excluded (s 55(5)(6)).

   In part (2) of the example, therefore, the calculation based on cost excludes the indexation allowance made on the intra-group transfer from Fancy Trading Ltd to Plain Trading Ltd.

   The provisions to prevent double counting would also apply if the original acquisition by the first person had been before 31 March 1982 and the no gain/no loss transfer had been after 5 April 1988. For an illustration see Example 61 part A.

   There is a problem as indicated in part (2) of the example where intra-group transfers took place between 31.3.82 and 5.4.88. Up to 31.3.85 indexation allowance was based on cost, and from 1.4.85 to 5.4.88 it could be based on 31.3.82 value only if an appropriate election was made. Although 'rolled up indexation' on a no gain no loss transfer between those dates may be treated as part of cost under s 56, it is not clear whether the indexation calculation can be made using the 31.3.82 value where that would be beneficial to the taxpayer.

The main instances to which these provisions apply are those in (a), (b) and (c) of explanatory note 1, ie transfers on company reconstructions, within a 75% group and between spouses/civil partners.

For 75% groups of companies, the general 31.3.82 rebasing election is made by the principal company in the group, and it applies to all group companies (subject to provisions to deal with companies joining and leaving the group – see Example 64 explanatory note 6) (Sch 3.8 & 3.9).

Corporate shareholders

3. Before FA 1998, the rules for post- and pre-1982 pools and pre 6 April 1965 acquisitions were broadly the same for individuals and companies. Some minor differences were that indexation allowance for companies applied from 1 April 1982 rather than 6 April 1982, the post-1982 pool came into being from 1 April 1985 rather than 6 April 1985, and there were some differences in the rules for matching disposals with acquisitions. The freezing of indexation allowance from April 1998 and introduction of taper relief do not apply to companies, so that the pooling rules and indexation provisions continue.

   Disposals are matched with acquisitions as follows, except for scrip and rights shares (including scrip dividend options – see Example 79 explanatory note 3), which are treated as acquired when the original shares were acquired, and loan stock (see Example 81 explanatory note 7):

   (a)   Acquisitions on the same day as the disposal

   (b)   For disposals before 5 December 2005: where the company owns 2% or more of the issued shares of a particular class, acquisitions in the previous month (latest first) then acquisitions in the following month (earliest first)

   (c)   Where (b) does not apply, acquisitions within the previous nine days (and no indexation allowance is available on the disposal)

   (d)   The post-1982 pool

   (e)   The pre-1982 pool

   (f)   Pre 6 April 1965 acquisitions that are not included in the pre-1982 pool, latest first

   (g)   Acquisitions after disposal (other than those taken into account in (b)), earliest first.

   The rules outlined above (except (b) and the scrip dividend option rules) applied to unincorporated shareholders as well as companies before 6 April 1998.

   The abolition of rule (b) with effect from 5 December 2005 was a consequence of the introduction of the specific anti-avoidance rules referred to in part 1(a)(ix) of the example. On the basis that artificial losses do not now qualify as allowable losses, the anti-bed and breakfasting provision previously found in s 106 was thought no longer necessary.

Capital gains provisions for groups of companies

4. The capital gains treatment of groups of companies is dealt with in more detail in Examples 61 and 64. See also Example 83 part (c) for rollover relief aspects.

A.   Briefly describe when a liability will arise to:

(a)   stamp duty land tax

(b)   stamp duty

(c)   stamp duty reserve tax.

B.   A wealthy client, Mr Argenton, has been involved in a number of transactions during the year ended 5 April 2007:

8 May 2006	He purchased the total issued share capital of a company from Mr Copperfield; the consideration was a £1 nominal cash payment together with the release of a loan of £50,000 which Mr Argenton had originally made to Mr Copperfield.
7 August 2006	He sold land and standing timber, with a value of £450,000, to a timber merchant.
9 September 2006	As trustee of his family's accumulation and maintenance settlement, he arranged for the transfer of trust shares having a value of £75,000 to his eldest daughter. The transfer was made upon his daughter reaching the age of 25 and was in accordance with the terms of the settlement.
10 January 2007	A gift of £350,000 cash was made to his eldest son to help with a property purchase.
15 January 2007	Mr Argenton subscribed in cash for £250,000 nominal value 5 year convertible loan stock 8%. The issue was by his wholly owned investment company.
20 March 2007	Mr Argenton had previously loaned £250,000, interest free, to a friend's property development company. As part of a reconstruction scheme for that company, he agreed to receive 2,500,000 10p shares issued by the company in satisfaction of the debt.

Provide Mr Argenton with a memorandum that sets out the stamp duty liabilities of each transaction.

C.   (a)   Explain what is meant by the process known as 'adjudication' in relation to stamp duty, indicating when it is used, the consequences that flow from it and the remedies available to a dissatisfied taxpayer.

(b)   Brown Ltd is the parent company of a diverse group. As part of an exercise to rationalise the group investment structure, all shareholdings in both group and non-group companies are being transferred to Brown Ltd.

The following transactions took place on 31 December 2006:

(i)   Blue Ltd, a wholly owned subsidiary, transferred its shares in Black Ltd (its own wholly owned subsidiary) to Brown Ltd for £50,000.

(ii)   Brown Ltd owned 70% of Colourless Ltd, which in turn owned all the capital of Rainbow Ltd. All shares in Rainbow Ltd were transferred to Brown Ltd for £100,000. (The remaining 30% of Colourless Ltd was not owned by the group.)

(iii)   Rainbow Ltd contracted to sell 200 shares in Indigo plc, a quoted company, to Brown Ltd for £3,000. Before the contract was completed, Brown Ltd transferred its beneficial interest in the shares to a third party for £2,900 on 21 January 2007.

Outline the stamp duty and stamp duty reserve tax consequences of these transactions.

A.   (a)   **Stamp Duty Land Tax** (FA 2003 ss 42–124 and Schs 3–19)

Stamp duty land tax (SDLT) was introduced from 1 December 2003 to tax transactions involving UK land and buildings. It applies to transactions completed or substantially completed on or after 1 December 2003 where the contract was entered into after 10 July 2003. It applies whether or not a document is used. It applies regardless of where the contract is executed and is not dependent on UK residency. The charge arises when the transaction is 'substantially performed' (ie when consideration paid or purchaser, or someone connected with the purchaser, takes possession) or on completion.

SDLT applies to consideration in money or money's worth. If there is a contingency it is charged on the assumption that the full amount is payable. The tax is then adjusted when the contingency occurs or it is clear that it will not occur. VAT is included unless the vendor/landlord has not opted to tax the land/building at the time of sale/granting of the lease (see explanatory note 3).

Where the consideration is uncertain (for example, where it is based on future turnover), or unascertained (for example, based on a set of accounts which have not been finalised), then a reasonable estimate is made. The purchaser may apply to defer payment in respect of contingent and uncertain consideration. There is no such provision for unascertained consideration.

If a company acquires land from a connected person consideration is deemed to be not less than market value.

From 22 July 2004 the acquisition of land by a partnership from a partner or an incoming partner, or, the acquisition of land by a partner or former partner from a partnership or from another partner is liable to SDLT.

Land transactions on marriage breakdown, variations following death, assents and appropriations by personal representatives and certain leases granted by registered social landlords are exempt from SDLT.

The rates of SDLT are based upon chargeable consideration.

For transactions after 22nd March 2006, the exempt limit for Residential Property is increased from £120,000 to £125,000, so that the rates are:

Rate	Other land in the UK		Land in disadvantaged areas	
	Residential	Non-Residential or Mixed	Residential	Non-Residential or Mixed
Zero	£125,000	£150,000	£150,000	£150,000
1%	£125,001–250,000	£150,001–250,000	£150,001–250,000	£150,001–250,000
3%	£250,001–500,000	£250,001–500,000	£250,001–500,000	£250,001–500,000
4%	Over £500,000	Over £500,000	Over £500,000	Over £500,000

Where a lease is granted, there are two potential elements which are chargeable to SDLT.

The first is the premium payable on the grant. This is subject to SDLT in the same way as on a sale. However, if the annual rental under the lease exceeds £600 per year, the zero rate band does not apply, instead the 1% rate applies to the premium (FA 2003 Sch 5.9)

The second element is the rental payable during the term of the lease. This is subject to SDLT at the following rates

Rate (%)	Net present value of rent	
	Residential	Non-residential or Mixed
Zero	First £125,000	First £150,000
1%	Excess over £125,000	Excess over £150,000

Note that where the net present value of rent on a residential property exceeds £125,000, the 1% rate does not apply to the whole of the rental but only applies to the excess above £125,000 (the 'slice' system of charging tax). This is unusual in the context of stamp duty land tax where the rate usually applies to the whole of the consideration (the 'slab' system).

The 'net present value of rent' is defined in FA 2003 Schedule 5 para 3 and is effectively the aggregate of the rent payable over the term of the lease, discounted by the 'temporal discount rate' which has been set initially at 3.5% per year.

A land transaction is a chargeable transaction for SDLT, unless it falls within an exemption. The most important exemptions are:

(a)   transactions where there is no chargeable consideration for the disposal (ie gifts);

(b)   transactions in connection with divorce;

(c)   variations of wills etc. after death.

No land transaction return is required if one of the exemptions apply.

SDLT on property with a mortgage based on unconventional principles (eg Islamic rules) will be the same as that payable on a property with a conventional mortgage.

If two pieces of land are exchanged, there will be two separate SDLT transactions. The chargeable consideration for each transaction is the market value of the land acquired by each purchaser and SDLT will be payable accordingly. There are special reliefs for certain exchanges of residential property. These include the situation where a house-building company acquires a dwelling in part exchange for the disposal of a newly constructed dwelling. The old dwelling must have been the only or main residence of the individual disposing of it and he must intend to occupy the new dwelling as his only or main residence. The effect of the relief will usually be that no SDLT is payable on the old dwelling.

A return and payment of SDLT must be made by the purchaser within 30 days of the effective transaction date. The tax is self-assessed. A return is required for every 'notifiable transaction' even if no tax is chargeable because of a relief. A return is also required within 30 days of any event altering the SDLT liability eg confirmation of consideration or contingency, withdrawal of any relief such as SDLT group relief.

In order to register the land transaction the purchaser must produce a certificate showing compliance with SDLT. The certificate will be issued by HMRC, or the purchaser (self-certification) where a return is not required in respect of the transaction.

(b)   **Stamp Duty**

Stamp duty is a duty on documents completed in the UK relating to UK transactions involving shares and marketable securities. No duty arises on transactions which are carried out orally (FA 1999 ss 112–113 and Schs 13–16).

If an instrument that is liable to be stamped is not so stamped, it cannot be used as evidence in civil proceedings. Therefore, a failure to have a document properly stamped could lead to legal problems in the case of a dispute. A company secretary will not register a transfer of shares or securities if the document has not been properly stamped.

Although stamp duty is not directly enforceable, interest and penalties can be levied for a failure to ensure that documents are properly stamped. (The interest and penalty rules are set out at note 9).

The administration and collection of stamp duty is the responsibility of HM Revenue and Customs (Stamp Taxes).

The Stamp Act 1891 s 5(a) requires that full details of the facts and circumstances relating to an instrument are provided in order to allow the correct stamp duty to be calculated. Failure to do so can lead to a fine of up to £3,000.

There are two types of duty payable. Duties can be 'fixed' – ie, a fixed amount is charged irrespective of the consideration paid for the transfer of the shares. Alternatively, duties can be 'ad valorem' which means that the duty will be a percentage of the consideration passing. Some instruments – most notably instruments which transfer shares by way of a gift where no consideration is payable – are not stampable, provided that the appropriate exemption certificate is completed. These instruments are listed in SI 1987/516.

Stamp duty depends upon the heading under which a transaction falls, ie

(1)   Share and convertible loan stock transactions (including purchase by a company of its own shares, takeovers, mergers, demergers, and schemes of reconstruction and amalgamation, except where there is no real change in ownership)   ½%

(2)   Shares converted into depositary receipts or put into duty free clearance systems (see part (c))   1½%

(3)   Most bearer instruments (excluding those in foreign currency – but see part (c))   1½%

Where a fixed duty is charged, the amount of the duty is £5. (FA 1999 Sch 13.16).

Duty is calculated as a strict percentage, and then rounded up to the nearest multiple of £5 (FA 1999 s 112).

Stamp duty is not payable when a company issues new shares to its shareholders, for example on the initial creation of the company or when new shares are subscribed for.

Where shares are repurchased by a company, ad valorem duty at a rate of 0.5% is payable on the Form 169 delivered to the Registrar of Companies.

The consideration payable by the purchaser to the vendor will usually be in the form of cash. However 'consideration' can take other forms such as other shares and marketable securities, the release of debt or liability or a dividend in specie.

Therefore stamp duty cannot be avoided by the purchaser paying for the new shares in non-cash form. Effectively the value of the non-cash assets offered in exchange for the shares is treated as consideration and is subjected to ad valorem stamp duty.

Sometimes the consideration for a transfer of shares may be uncertain at the time of the transaction. The stamp duty payable depends on how the deal is structured. If the contingent amount is fixed then that amount is also subject to stamp duty. The same rule applies if the variable amount has a maximum limit, stamp duty is then payable on the maximum amount. However, if the variable amount only has a minimum limit then stamp duty is only payable on the minimum amount. If the variable amount has no maximum or minimum limit then there will be a fixed charge of £5 in relation to the potential extra consideration.

If shares are exchanged, then two share transfers will be executed. Both will be liable for ad valorem duty. Each will be liable to stamp duty by reference to the value of the shares transferred by the other document.

In both cases, the transaction may be documented as a sale of the higher value shares. The transfer of the higher value shares will be liable to ad valorem duty but the transfer of the shares in consideration will be liable only to a fixed £5 duty as a transfer of any other kind. To qualify as a sale of the higher value shares, there must be a cash element to the sale which is more than nominal.

There is an exemption from stamp duty where shares pass between two companies in a group. A group is where one company owns 75% of the shares of another, or both are under the 75% ownership of another company. This is sometimes referred to as 'stamp duty group relief' (FA 1930 s 42). The instrument of transfer must be adjudicated (see below at C). The exemption does not apply if, at the time the instrument is executed, arrangements are in existence which mean that any other person can gain control of the transferee company (FA 1967 s 27).

There are special exemptions from duty for financial intermediaries trading in UK securities and in connection with stock borrowing and sale and repurchase arrangements (FA 1986 ss 80A to 80C). These exemptions apply to transactions on a UK or European Economic Area exchange, a recognised foreign exchange and other specified markets. The Treasury can extend these reliefs to multilateral trading facilities (MTFs). Exemption also applies where a mutual insurance company transfers its business to a conventional company (FA 1997 s 96), and to transfers of units in unit trusts or shares in open-ended investment companies (OEICs – see explanatory note 7) (FA 1999 Sch 19), although the latter are now charged to stamp duty reserve tax (see below).

A stamp duty (and stamp duty reserve tax) exemption also applies where the trustees of an approved share incentive plan (previously referred to as an all-employee share ownership plan) transfer shares to the employees as partnership shares or dividend shares (FA 2001 s 95 – see Example 87 part (3)).

(c)   **Stamp Duty Reserve Tax**

Stamp duty reserve tax is charged under the provisions of FA 1986 ss 86 to 99 on transactions in *chargeable securities* (broadly, stocks, shares, loan capital, and units under a unit trust scheme (as to which see below) (FA 1986 s 99)) which are not charged to stamp duty, for example, sales of renounceable letters of allotment. The rate of tax is ½%. Transactions under the paperless system for transferring securities (CREST), are subject to stamp duty reserve tax on the agreement to transfer, rather than stamp duty (FA 1996 s 186). Stamp duty continues to be charged on securities transferred outside the CREST system. Stamp duty reserve tax does not apply to gilt edged stocks, traded options and futures, non-convertible loan stocks, foreign securities not on a UK register, depositary interests in foreign securities, purchases by a charity, transfers of units in foreign unit trusts, and the issue of new securities. See also part (b) for the exemption for shares transferred to employees under approved share incentive plans.

There are special exemptions for financial intermediaries (FA 1986 ss 88, 88B, 89AA) which apply to transactions on a UK or European Economic Area exchange, or on a recognised foreign exchange. If a person who has qualified for exemption then transfers securities to a fellow group member, the normal exemption on intra-group transfers does not apply and stamp duty reserve tax is payable (FA 1986 s 92). The Treasury is empowered to extend reliefs to a market that is not a recognised exchange, but is a multilateral trading facility (MTF).

An anti-avoidance measure charges stamp duty reserve tax at ½% on transfers of foreign currency bearer shares and of sterling or foreign currency bearer loan stock that is convertible or equity related. The charge does not apply if the securities are listed on a recognised stock exchange and the transfer is not made as part of a takeover (FA 1986 s 90).

A further anti-avoidance measure charges stamp duty reserve tax at 1½% on the issue or transfer by a UK company of foreign currency bearer instruments into a depositary or clearance service in connection with a merger or takeover of any company and on the issue or transfer into a depositary or clearance system of foreign currency bearer instruments that would otherwise be exempt from duty, unless they are subscribed for cash and carry a right to a dividend at a fixed rate or are loan capital (FA 1986 ss 95 & 97).

From 6 February 2000 stamp duty reserve tax replaced stamp duty on transfers of units in a unit trust and shares in open-ended investment companies (OEICs). The rate is ½%, but this can be reduced where within the same or following calendar month similar units are issued.

Liability to stamp duty reserve tax arises at the date of the agreement (or, if the agreement is conditional, the date the condition is satisfied) (FA 1986 s 87). For transactions via an exchange (in particular CREST transactions), the tax is payable on a date agreed with HMRC (or if there is no agreed date, the fourteenth day after the transaction). For other transactions the due date is the seventh day of the month following the date of the transaction and the person liable to pay the tax (ie the broker, dealer or purchaser) must give notice of the charge to HMRC on or before that date. If stamp duty is paid after reserve tax has been paid, the reserve tax is refunded (plus interest on refunds over £25, the interest being free of income tax).

Stamp duty reserve tax also applies to securities converted into depositary receipts or put into a duty free clearing system, and the rate of tax on these transactions is 1½% (FA 1986 ss 93-97). The tax is only payable, however, to the extent that it exceeds any ad valorem stamp duty on the transaction, and where the ad valorem duty exceeds the amount of reserve tax, no reserve tax is payable. There are exemptions for exchanges of securities between associated companies (FA 1930 s 42, FA 1986 s 88 – see explanatory note 6). Clearing systems may elect to pay stamp duty or stamp duty reserve tax in the normal way on their transactions, and in that event the 1½% charge when securities are put into the system does not apply (FA 1986 s 97A).

B. **Memorandum for Mr Argenton**

8 May 2006	The true consideration for the purchase of the company's share capital is £1 plus the loan of £50,000 = £50,001. The rate of stamp duty on shares is ½% rounded up to the nearest £5. Accordingly the duty payable is £255.
	If the shares are actually worth less than £50,001 then the transfer may be submitted for adjudication and duty paid at the above rate on the actual value of the shares (FA 1980 s 102(2)).
7 August 2006	The sale of land and standing timber is a transfer of property valued in excess of £250,000 but less than £500,000 and therefore attracts SDLT at the rate of 3%, ie £450,000 x 3% = £13,500, unless Mr Argenton had elected to waive his exemption for VAT (see explanatory note 3). If the sale was subject to VAT, the VAT would amount to 17½% of £450,000 = £78,750, making total consideration of £528,750. SDLT payable is therefore £528,750 × 4% = £21,150. The purchaser is liable for the tax (FA 2003 s 85).
9 September 2006	The trustees are transferring property in accordance with the trust deed. That transaction is exempt from duty in accordance with the Stamp Duty (Exempt Instruments) Regulations 1987 (SI 1987/516) – Category F. No duty is payable providing the appropriate certificates are signed.
10 January 2007	Stamp duty is a tax on shares. SDLT is a tax on land and buildings. As cash does not fall into these categories no duty is payable.
15 January 2007	Mr Argenton is not liable to stamp duty on the issue of loan stock because it is specifically exempt under FA 1986 s 79(2). (That section also exempts the *transfer* of loan stock unless it carries a right either of conversion into shares or to more than a commercial rate of return, but see part A(c) re the charge to stamp duty reserve tax on the transfer of certain bearer loan stock.)
20 March 2007	No liability arose on the granting of the loan, and the issue of new shares to Mr Argenton in satisfaction of the debt is also exempt from duty. (The exemption from duty on issues of shares does not apply where they are issued as consideration for a sale, subject to what is said in explanatory note 6. Nor does it apply to bearer shares – FA 1963 s 60.)

C. (a) **Adjudication**

Adjudication is the process whereby HMRC (Stamp Taxes) assess the amount of duty, if any, payable on a document, including adjudication as to the amount of any penalty payable for late stamping (as to which see explanatory note 8). Additionally, if after adjudication an unstamped or insufficiently stamped document is not duly stamped within 30 days, a penalty of up to £300 may be charged.

Adjudication may be voluntary or compulsory. Any person may ask HMRC to adjudicate as to whether a document is chargeable to stamp duty, and if so, to state the duty payable. If HMRC decide that no stamp duty is payable the document will be stamped to that effect. Once stamped a document is admissible in evidence (Stamp Act 1891 s 12).

The Registrar of Companies may require adjudication for an allotment of shares where the terms have not been put in writing (Companies Act 1985 s 88(4)).

Adjudication may also be required where consideration needs to be established in order to determine the duty payable, eg where shares are issued as consideration for a transaction.

If a taxpayer is dissatisfied with the decision of HMRC he may appeal against it. Appeals must be made within 30 days and the duty plus any interest or penalty must be paid first. Appeals relating to late stamping penalties go first to the Special Commissioners and other appeals to the High Court.

With effect from 1 December 2003 SDLT is a self-assessed tax with HMRC powers to enquire into the return. From that date stamp duty is no longer chargeable on a document unless it relates to shares, or until 22 July 2004, partnership acquisitions where the relevant partnership property includes an interest in land.

(b) **Transactions by Brown Ltd group of companies**

(i) Providing the documents are submitted for adjudication, the transfer by Blue Ltd to Brown Ltd of shares in Black Ltd will be exempt from stamp duty as Blue Ltd is a wholly owned subsidiary of Brown Ltd (FA 1930 s 42).

(ii) Stamp duty of ½% of £100,000, ie £500 will be payable as Brown Ltd owns only 70% of Colourless Ltd.

(iii) The agreement to sell shares in Indigo plc is not itself dutiable, and therefore the transfer of the beneficial interest in that contract by Brown Ltd will avoid stamp duty but not stamp duty reserve tax. This will be charged on Brown Ltd, ie ½% x £3,000 = £15.

The actual share transfer will be between Rainbow Ltd and the third party and that document will attract stamp duty of £15, ie ½% x £2,900 = £14.50, rounded up to nearest multiple of £5.

Explanatory Notes

SDLT legislation

1. From 1 December 2003 SDLT applies to transactions in UK land and buildings and stamp duty only applies to documents relating to stocks and marketable securities and the issue of bearer instruments. SDLT also applies to the acquisition of a partnership which holds UK land.

SDLT, stamp duty, and stamp duty reserve tax are dealt with by HMRC (Stamp Taxes).

Adjudication

2. The process of adjudication is outlined in part C(a) of the example. Where a document bears an adjudication stamp this is normally conclusive evidence of stamping.

Section 12 of the Stamp Act 1891 provides for HMRC to 'adjudicate' on any executed instrument if requested to do so. HMRC can be asked to adjudicate on a number of points such as:

(a)   whether the instrument is stampable;

(b)   the amount of duty;

(c)   whether a late stamping penalty is payable;

(d)   what penalty is correct and appropriate.

If HMRC decides that an instrument is not chargeable to stamp duty, then it will be stamped to show this. Otherwise it will be stamped with the amount adjudicated and the relevant amount should be paid as appropriate. Adjudication is the only way to formally determine the amount of stamp duty due. Adjudication is compulsory for certain instruments, such as transfers of shares to charities, specifically exempt transfers (eg, intra group transfers) and transfers in satisfaction of a debt.

If a person is unhappy with the adjudication, he has 30 days to bring an appeal. However, an appeal can only be brought on payment of the stamp duty plus any penalty in conformity with HMRC's decision and any interest that would be payable following the adjudication.

Value added tax

3.   Where property that is conveyed or leased is property on which the option may be taken to charge VAT (broadly all land and buildings except domestic, relevant residential or non-business charity buildings) then SDLT is payable on the value *plus VAT* if the option is exercised. The availability of a claim to recover input tax will not alter the charge to SDLT.

Chargeable consideration does not include any VAT that may become payable as a result of an election to waive exemption after the effective date. This means that, for example, if a landlord 'opts to tax' *after* granting a lease, the VAT payable will not form part of the chargeable consideration.

The notice to waive exemption from VAT (option to tax) is not liable to SDLT, and SDLT itself is never liable to VAT.

On the sale of the land and standing timber in part B on 7 August 2006 the option to charge VAT may have been available. If Mr Argenton did not exercise the option before sale, SDLT is not payable on the VAT that might have become due. If, on the other hand, the option was exercised at any time before completion, then SDLT would be payable on the VAT inclusive value.

If the transaction is part of a sale of a business, then VAT is not chargeable under the transfer of a going concern provisions. If this is expected to be the case, it may well be that the provisions relating to contingent consideration will apply.

Mortgaged property

4.   Care must be taken with transfers of mortgaged property, as the value for SDLT is the sum of the price paid plus the outstanding loan (see CIR v City of Glasgow Bank 1881, a case decided under stamp duty). This also applies where there is no actual consideration; duty is payable on the value of the debt taken over (see Revenue Statement of Practice SP6/90).

This is particularly relevant where the transaction is between connected persons, eg a mortgaged property held in the name of one spouse is transferred into joint names, or into the name of the other spouse, or from joint names to a single name.

Where the transferor covenants to pay the debt and the transferee does not assume any liability for it, no consideration has been given. The transfer is then not liable to SDLT as no chargeable consideration is provided by the purchaser (FA 2003 Sch 3.1 and Sch 4.1).

If, however, the transferee agrees to pay the debt or to indemnify the transferor against his personal liability to the lender that will constitute valuable consideration liable to SDLT. A covenant or agreement may be in writing or implied.

The above rules do not affect any statutory exemption from SDLT, eg transfers to a charity or a charitable trust (FA 2003 Sch 8) and certain transfers from one party to the other in connection with a divorce or separation (FA 2003 Sch 3.3).

Transfer to connected company

5.　Special rules apply where the purchaser is a company and either:

(a)　the vendor is connected with the company; or

(b)　some or all of the consideration for the transaction is the issue or transfer of shares in a company with which the vendor is connected.

An example would be where land is transferred from a sole trader or partnership to a company on incorporation. In this case, the chargeable consideration is the market value of the land at the date of the transaction. This rule applies even if the land is gifted to the company, as the exemption in FA 2003 Sch 3.1 is disapplied (FA 2003 s 53).

Transfers between associated companies and company reconstructions

6.　Transfers of property between associated companies and on company reconstructions are exempt from SDLT (FA 2003 Sch 7). Group relief applies where one company is the parent of the other company, or both are subsidiaries of a common parent, and the parent company owns in each case not less than 75% of the ordinary share capital of the subsidiary, and is entitled to 75% or more of the profits and on a winding up 75% or more of the assets (Sch 7.1). Exemption also applies to the grant of a lease by one group company to another group company or an agreement for a lease between group companies. There are anti-avoidance provisions in Sch 7 paragraph 3 to prevent these provisions being used to avoid SDLT when property, or an economic interest in it, passes out of the group.

Group relief may be withdrawn if the purchaser company ceases to be a group member within three years, in certain circumstances. The tax that would originally have been paid becomes chargeable. It becomes payable 30 days after the event which causes the withdrawal of the group relief.

SDLT group relief must be claimed in a land transaction return and a further return made if the relief is withdrawn.

A reduced rate of duty of ½% applies where a company acquires the whole or part of an undertaking of another company in exchange for shares (Sch 8.1). This is subject to anti-avoidance provisions where the undertaking includes UK land (FA 2003 Sch 9).

As indicated in part A(c) of the example, there is an exemption from stamp duty reserve tax for certain transfers of securities between associated companies.

Transfer to a limited liability partnership

7.　There is an exemption from stamp duty land tax where land is transferred to a limited liability partnership (LLP) in connection with its incorporation.

Three conditions must be satisfied:

(a)　the effective date of the transaction is not more than one year after the incorporation of the LLP;

(b)　the partners in the old partnership and the new LLP are the same and the transferor is one of those partners;

(c)　the interests of the partners in the old and new partnerships are the same or any change in the interests is not part of a tax avoidance scheme (FA 2003 s 65).

Interest and penalties

8.　From 1 December 2003 SDLT is subject to a regime similar to income tax self-assessment with penalties for failure to deliver a return, for a fraudulent or negligent return, failure to keep or preserve records, failure to comply with notices to provide documents or information and criminal sanctions for fraudulently evading SDLT. Interest is paid on overpaid tax and charged on overdue SDLT at the same rates as for income tax.

Penalties for stamp duty and stamp duty reserve tax may apply where documents are submitted late for stamping (SA 1891 s 15B). There are separate interest and penalty provisions in relation to bearer instruments.

If documents are not presented for stamping within 30 days, the maximum penalty for documents presented up to one-year late is £300 or the amount of the duty if lower. For documents submitted outside the one year period the maximum penalty is £300 or the amount of the duty if more. The penalties are subject to mitigation where there is a reasonable excuse. For documents executed abroad the 30 days and one-year periods run from the date the document is brought into the UK. There is a penalty of up to £300, or up to £3,000 in cases of fraud, for administrative offences.

Interest is chargeable where a document liable to ad valorem duty is not stamped within 30 days of execution. The interest is rounded down to a multiple of £5, and is not chargeable if it amounts to £25 or less. For documents executed abroad, the interest runs from 30 days after execution, not the date the document is brought into the UK. Where stamp duty or late stamping penalties have been overpaid, interest is payable on repayments amounting to £25 or more from 30 days after execution or from the date of payment of the duty or penalty if later. The rates of interest are the same as for income tax, ie from 6 September 2006 7.5% (previously 6.5%) on underpayments and 3% (previously 2.25%) on overpayments.

Executing a document outside the UK does not delay payment if it relates to UK shares, because the transaction is caught by stamp duty reserve tax (FA 1986 s 86(4)), even if made outside the UK between non-resident parties.

Interest is charged on overdue stamp duty reserve tax at the same rate as for income tax from 14 days after the transaction date for transactions on an exchange and otherwise from 7 days after the end of the month of the transaction, and there are various penalties for defaults, including a mitigable penalty of £100, plus £60 a day following a declaration by the General or Special Commissioners, where the appropriate notice of liability has not been given and the tax has not been paid. Interest is payable on repayments from the payment date at the same rate as for income tax.

Variable or contingent consideration

9. Where all or part of the consideration (or rent) payable on a land transaction is not in money or money's worth then market value at the effective date of the transaction is used. However, this rule only applies in the absence of any contrary provision. 'Market value' is determined using the capital gains tax rules in TCGA 1992 (FA 2003 s 118 and Sch 4.7). There is no discount for postponed consideration (Sch 4.3). Where, however, the consideration is ascertainable but not fixed, SDLT is paid on the basis that any contingent amount will be payable. Where consideration is uncertain SDLT is paid on the amount that could reasonably be certain to be received (FA 2003 s 51). Where the value is based upon an annuity payable for more than 12 years the value is restricted to the twelve highest annual payments (FA 2003 s 52).

    Special rules apply to leases in the case of variable or uncertain rent (see FA 2003 Sch 17A.7).

Outline the provisions relating to the acquisition of shares by employees and directors and the special rules relating to the following worker participation schemes:

(1)   SAYE share option schemes

(2)   Company share option plan (CSOP) schemes

(3)   Share incentive plans

(4)   Corporation tax relief on employee shares

(5)   Enterprise management incentives

Acquisitions of shares by employees and directors

The legislation relating to the acquisition of shares by employees and directors is complex and wide ranging. Although favourable tax treatment is given to the approved employee share schemes, there are very detailed statutory provisions for each scheme. The costs of establishing all employee share schemes are, however, allowable deductions for corporation tax and see also below under **Corporation tax relief on employee shares**. The legislation was entirely rewritten by Income Tax (Earnings and Pensions) Act 2003 which took effect on 6 April 2003, though the purpose of this was simply to make it more intelligible, and only minor changes were made to the law itself. Less than two weeks after this Act took effect, however, much of the legislation was again completely rewritten in what became FA 2003, this time making major changes to the law, in particular tightening up the many anti-avoidance provisions. Under all the approved schemes, employers are required to provide annual returns to HMRC. Detailed information must also be provided when chargeable events occur in relation to shares. Penalties apply if the company fails to comply. Employees must similarly ensure that appropriate details are included in their tax returns (see below under **Self-assessment**).

The legislation in ITEPA 2003 s 421J goes further and requires notification, by 6 July following the fiscal year, of *all* acquisitions of shares and securities by a director/employee. (This includes past and prospective employments (s 421B).) Thus acquisition of an initial subscriber share by a company formation agent is not reportable, but all subsequent transfers of shares or an issue of new shares will be reportable if the shareholder is or will be a director or employee. The report should be on form 42 sent to the Share Scheme Unit. HMRC will not impose penalties if the information is provided by letter to the local Inspector with the CT 41 G (notification of a company coming within the charge to corporation tax (FA 2004 s 55)). In 2005, a simplified form became available for use by newly formed companies and their advisers. However, by 2006 HMRC announced that most subscriptions to shares in newly formed companies would not need to be the subject of a return, provided that trade had not commenced. The notification must be given by the responsible person. In the case of the initial subscriber share notification is required by either the company formation agent or by the company. In the case of subsequent transfers or issue of shares ITEPA 2003 s 421L provides that notification is to be given by either the employer or the person from whom the shares were acquired.

There is a penalty not exceeding £300 for failure to file by the due date which can be increased by up to £60 per day for continued failure.

A return is not required if it can be ascertained that there was no element of remuneration and the transfer was made by an individual and the right or opportunity was made available in the normal course of the domestic, family or personal relationships of that person (s 421B(3)).

Except in relation to the approved schemes, the legislation applies to 'securities' rather than just to shares, so that it includes debentures, loan stock and other securities issued by companies, and a wide range of other financial instruments, including government and local authority loan stock. The approved schemes deal only with 'shares' as defined. The definition includes stock, except for CSOP schemes (although CSOP scheme shares may be exchanged for stock or other securities on a reorganisation). The term 'shares' is used below for convenience, but the wider scope of the provisions should be borne in mind.

The main provisions of the current schemes and other relevant legislation are as follows.

Shares that are readily convertible into cash

Where shares are acquired by employees other than under approved schemes, or are subject to a tax charge under the rules of an approved scheme, employers must charge tax and Class 1 national insurance contributions under the 'notional pay' provisions of PAYE if the shares are 'readily convertible assets', ie they may be sold on the Stock Exchange or arrangements exist for them to be traded (see Example 9 explanatory note 12). These provisions apply to shares acquired directly and through the exercise of unapproved options that were granted on or after 27 November 1996. They also apply where a share option is assigned or released, or a risk of forfeiture of shares is lifted, or shares are converted into shares of a different class (see below). The national insurance legislation for options granted on or after 6 April 1999 charges Class 1 contributions when the options are exercised. (See Example 47 note 14 for the optional treatment of the employee paying the employer's secondary Class 1 liability.) The tax provisions relating to convertible shares and shares liable to forfeiture are mirrored for national insurance purposes for shares or interests in shares acquired on or after 9 April 1998. If shares are not readily convertible assets, neither Class 1 nor Class 1A national insurance contributions are payable.

From 10 July 2003, shares and other securities that would not otherwise be readily convertible assets are treated as such (except for the purposes of the share incentive plan rules) unless they are shares (or stock) that attract a corporation tax deduction under the provisions at (4) below. When the major changes made by FA 2003 to unapproved schemes came into effect on 1 September 2003, PAYE and national insurance were extended to chargeable events within those new provisions. Where the chargeable event takes the form of a receipt of money, or of an asset which is a readily convertible asset, PAYE etc applies regardless of whether or not the scheme shares are themselves readily convertible assets.

See Example 58 explanatory note 7 for the treatment of shares issued free or below market value to employees where the shares are not readily convertible assets.

Directors or employees with a 'material interest'

Under all approved employee share schemes, employees or directors with a material interest in the company cannot participate if the company is a close company (see Example 55). 'Material interest' is determined by the percentage of the company's ordinary share capital owned or controlled by the employee and his or her associates. Associates are normally close relatives, but also include trustees of trusts under which the employee might benefit. Shares held by a trust set up for the benefit of employees will, however, usually be ignored in determining whether an employee has a material interest.

The relevant percentages are more than 30% for enterprise management incentives, more than 25% for share incentive plans, SAYE schemes, CSOP schemes and approved profit sharing schemes, and more than 5% for employee share ownership trusts. Before 10 July 2003, the percentage for CSOP schemes was 10%. (The limits for enterprise management incentives and employee share ownership trusts apply to all companies, not just close companies.)

Restrictions on sale etc

Shares issued under approved share option or profit sharing schemes may be subject to a restriction in the company's articles of association requiring employees to sell them when they leave their employment, thus enabling companies to retain some control over holdings of their shares. Employee-controlled companies may use a class of shares of which the majority is held by directors or employees and gives them control of the company.

Options

Favourable tax treatment is given under ITEPA 2003 Part 7 Chapters 7 & 8 for approved SAYE and CSOP schemes and under ITEPA 2003 Part 7 Chapter 9 and Sch 5 for enterprise management incentives (EMI). Granting an option at a discount under an approved share option scheme does not have any capital gains effect for the employer. The employer is regarded as having received disposal proceeds equal to the amount, if any, that the employee pays for the option (TCGA 1992 s 149A), rather than market value, which usually applies to non-arm's length transactions (see **Capital gains tax** below and Example 73 explanatory note 7). As far as the employee is concerned, there is an *income tax* charge if the discount relates to an option under a CSOP scheme (see (2) below). Capital gains tax taper relief on shares acquired both under approved and unapproved options runs from the time the option is exercised (see Example 75 explanatory note 10), except for EMI, for which the taper relief period runs from the time the option is granted.

Where the option does *not* arise under an *approved* scheme, an income tax charge arises on the difference between the open market value at the time of exercising the right and the cost of the shares, including any amount paid for the option (ITEPA 2003 s 476). As indicated above, tax and national insurance contributions will be collected through PAYE if the shares are readily convertible into cash.

Where a right to acquire shares other than under an approved scheme is assigned or released, an income tax charge arises on the consideration received less the cost of acquisition of the rights. A charge to income tax also arises when any benefit is received or gain is realised because the option holder allows the option to lapse, or grants someone else an option over the shares. As indicated above, tax and national insurance contributions will be charged under PAYE if the shares are readily convertible into cash.

These tax charges apply on the exercise, assignment or release of the option by any associated person and not just by the employee (ie the person by reason of whose employment the option was granted). 'Associated persons' include the person to whom the option was granted (if not the employee), persons connected with the employee (or with the grantee) and members of the same household as the employee (or grantee). To some extent, this was always the case but the scope of the charge is narrower before the appointed date (ie 1 September 2003) in that it applies only where the person exercising, assigning or releasing the option is connected with the employee.

A tax charge also arises on the amount or market value of any benefit received, in money or money's worth, by the employee (or an associated person) in connection with the option, which might include, for example, sums received for varying the option or as compensation for its cancellation.

Whatever the reason for a tax charge, any amount paid for the option itself is deductible in determining the taxable amount. From 1 September 2003, expenses incurred in connection with the exercise, assignment, release or receipt of benefit are also deductible.

For capital gains tax, the amount taxed as income on exercise of an unapproved employee share option counts as part of the cost of acquisition of the shares (as does anything paid for the option itself). The position was temporarily thrown into disarray, however, by the Court of Appeal decision in Mansworth v Jelley in December 2002 and, in particular, the Revenue's reaction to it. It was decided in that case that the appellant could deduct for capital gains purposes the market value of the shares at the time he acquired them and not just their actual cost. In a statement on their website on 8 January 2003, the Revenue announced that following this judgment taxpayers could deduct *both* the market value of shares acquired *and* the amount charged to income tax. This was illogical and likely to result in a capital loss being incurred for tax purposes, even though in reality no such loss had occurred. For options exercised after 9 April 2003, FA 2003 restored the position to what it was understood to be before Mansworth v Jelley. For options exercised on or before that date though, the Revenue's interpretation of Mansworth v Jelley still applies. The decision in Mansworth v Jelley did not affect options exercised under approved SAYE and CSOP schemes in accordance with the rules of those schemes, but it does apply to options exercised under enterprise management incentive schemes in the same way that it applies to unapproved options.

For the purposes of the above provisions, no income tax liability arises on the *grant* of an option, unless exceptionally the option is granted at a discount under a CSOP scheme. Before that date, if an option was capable of being exercised more than ten years after it was granted, a charge arose at the time the right was *granted* on the excess of the then market value of the option shares over the price which, under the option, had to be paid for the shares. For years before 2002/03 the *tax paid* when the option was granted was deducted from any tax arising when the option was exercised. From 2002/03 the *amount chargeable to tax* when the option is granted is deducted from the amount chargeable to tax on exercise (ITEPA 2003 s 478).

Partly paid shares

If shares are issued at a price equal to the current market value, with the price being paid by agreed instalments, no charge will arise under the general charging provisions since full market value is being paid, and this will apply even though the market value has increased by the time the shares are paid for. Any growth in value of the shares is liable only to capital gains tax. A director or an employee who acquires shares other than under the approved schemes and does not pay the full price for shares immediately is, however, regarded as having received an interest-free loan equal to the deferred instalments, on which tax is charged at the beneficial loans interest rate, unless the total of all beneficial loans outstanding from that director or employee in the tax year, including the deferred instalments, does not exceed £5,000. The loan is regarded as being repaid as and when the instalments are paid. Any amount written off is taxed as employment income at that time; any amount so charged is deductible for capital gains tax purposes when the shares are disposed of (ITEPA 2003 ss 192–197, 446Q–446W). In relation to shares acquired before 16 April 2003, these charges did not apply to lower-paid employees (ie those earning less than £8,500 per annum).

Anti-avoidance rules

Various anti-avoidance provisions apply to employment-related shares and securities. These do not apply in relation to shares that comply with the provisions of approved schemes, but enterprise management incentive schemes are not regarded as approved schemes for this purpose. The FA 2003 charges mean that advantages gained not just by the employee but by 'associated persons' are brought fully within the charge to tax. 'Associated persons' include the person who acquired the shares (if not the employee), persons connected with the employee (or with the person who acquired the shares) and members of the same household as the employee (or person who acquired the shares). There are exemptions from some of the rules below where the shares are acquired under a public offer, or are shares in an employee-controlled company or where the event in question affects all the company's shares of the same class and the majority of them are held by outside shareholders; these exceptions apply in respect of restricted shares, convertible shares and post-acquisition benefits.

In addition, the Paymaster General announced on 2 December 2004 that share-related avoidance schemes discovered after that date could be blocked with retrospective effect going back to that date. This threat was carried out in Finance Act 2006 with changes being made to ITEPA 2003 s 420 which took effect from 2 December 2004.

Restricted shares

If shares have certain restrictions or conditions attached to them, including risk of forfeiture, their value will be less than their true unrestricted value, which reduces the charge to tax on acquisition. To counter this, a chargeable event occurs when the restrictions are lifted or, if earlier, when the shares are disposed of. The charge is calculated using a complex formula which is designed to tax the effect the restriction had on the value of the shares at the time it was lifted. In cases where the shares may be forfeited within five years, the normal charge on acquisition is removed, but tax is still chargeable when the risk of forfeiture is lifted. There is no charge once seven years have expired after the employment ceases and no charge on death. These provisions apply from 1 September 2003 but only affect shares acquired on or after 16 April 2003. (ITEPA 2003 ss 422–432 and FA 2003, Sch 22.3.)

The previous rules are contained in ITEPA 2003 ss 422–434 as originally enacted and ss 449–452 as originally enacted and still affect shares acquired before that date. Under the original ss 422–434, the charge to tax when a risk of forfeiture is lifted, or on earlier disposal, is on the market value of the shares at that time less anything paid for them and less amounts previously charged to tax when they were acquired or subsequently. The original ss 449–452 charge tax where the value of shares increases because of the creation or removal of restrictions or the variation of rights relating to the shares or to other shares in the company.

Whilst the new rules might be said to be broadly comparable with the old, they can result in very different amounts being taxed at different times. Various elections are now available which have the effect of charging amounts earlier than would otherwise be the case but possibly by reference to lower market values at that earlier time. Valid elections in such cases take the form of an irrevocable agreement between employer and employee, made within 14 days after a chargeable event; there is no requirement that they be submitted to HMRC or that the approval of HMRC be sought. One such election possibility is to waive the exemption on acquisition (for shares subject to early forfeiture) in order to limit the potential charge on a subsequent chargeable event; this was not possible under the old rules.

Any amount charged to income tax forms part of the acquisition cost of the shares for capital gains tax purposes. Where the shares are held in trust until such time as the risk of forfeiture or other restriction is removed, they are usually treated as acquired at that time, rather than any earlier time, though this does depend on the exact terms of the agreement.

Convertible shares

Where shares are convertible into shares of a different class or description, or may become convertible if conditions are met, any tax due on acquisition is computed by reference to what their market value would be without the conversion right. When they are converted, or on any other chargeable event (which could be a disposal, a release of the conversion right or a receipt of a benefit), the value of the conversion right is taxed at that time at its then value, with a deduction allowed for anything payable by the employee for the conversion itself. These provisions apply from 1 September 2003 and, except for the way tax is charged on acquisition, apply to all shares from that date regardless of when they were acquired. (ITEPA 2003 ss 435–444 and FA 2003 Sch 22.4.)

The previous rules were contained in ITEPA 2003 ss 435–446 as originally enacted. Under those rules, convertible shares were taxed on conversion at their value at that time, less anything paid for them on acquisition or conversion and any amounts charged to tax when they were issued. There was no special rule for computing tax on acquisition.

Amounts charged to income tax form part of the acquisition cost of the shares for capital gains tax purposes.

Post-acquisition benefits

Tax is chargeable on the amount or market value of any *benefit* received by virtue of the ownership of the shares. Apart from the extension of the charge to benefits received by associated persons (see above), the new rules, which apply from 16 April 2003, are fairly similar to the old (ITEPA 2003 ss 447–450).

Shares with artificially depressed market value

From 16 April 2003, if the market value of employment-related shares is depressed by 10% or more by means of non-commercial transactions, the reduction in value is charged to income tax as employment income. This applies at acquisition, and also applies in conjunction with the rules above for restricted shares and convertible shares to prevent the reduction of tax charges on chargeable events under those rules. In addition, in the case of restricted shares only, if any such non-commercial transaction has occurred in the previous seven years, a charge arises on 5 April in the tax year as if the restrictions had been lifted on that date. For national insurance purposes, these provisions apply from the appointed date (ie 1 September 2003) (ITEPA 2003 ss 446A–446J).

Shares with artificially enhanced market value

Also from 16 April 2003, provisions are introduced to ensure that where in any tax year the market value of employment-related shares is enhanced by 10% or more by means of non-commercial transactions, the increase in value is charged to income tax as employment income on 5 April in that year or, if earlier, on disposal. For national insurance purposes, these provisions also apply from 1 September 2003 (ITEPA 2003 ss 446K–446P).

Shares disposed of for more than market value

When employment-related shares are disposed of for more than their market value, the excess is chargeable to income tax rather than capital gains tax. In relation to shares disposed of before 16 April 2003, this charge did not apply to lower-paid employees (ie those earning less than £8,500 per annum) (ITEPA 2003 ss 198–200, 446X–446Z).

Priority allocations in public offers

Where shares are offered to the public, a priority allocation is often made to employees and directors. Where there is no price advantage, a benefit will not be deemed to arise because of the right to shares in priority to other persons so long as the shares that may be allocated do not exceed 10% of those being offered, all directors and employees entitled to an allocation are entitled on similar terms (albeit at different levels), and those entitled are not restricted wholly or mainly to persons who are directors or whose remuneration exceeds a particular level (ITEPA 2003 Part 7 Chapter 10).

Where employees are offered a discount compared with the price paid by the public, the employees will pay income tax on the discount, but the benefit of the priority allocation will still escape tax. The employee's base cost for capital gains tax is the amount paid plus the discount that was charged to tax.

Detailed points on the various approved employee share schemes are as follows:

(1)   **SAYE share option schemes**

SAYE share option schemes are permitted under ITEPA 2003 ss 516–520 and Sch 3. No income tax charge arises when the option is granted nor on exercise of the option where the cost of the shares is paid out of the proceeds of a linked SAYE scheme.

The SAYE contributions themselves are saved with National Savings and Investments, a building society or a bank (usually by way of a deduction from pay). The present maximum monthly contribution is £250 and the minimum stipulated contribution may not exceed £10. There is no tax relief on the contributions, but any interest and bonuses received are tax-free. This applies whether or not the employee exercises the option to take up the shares.

The employee is given the option to buy shares after either three, five or seven years, at a price which must not normally be less than 80% of the market value of the shares at the time the option is granted. The total price to be paid must not exceed the proceeds of the SAYE contract. The scheme must be available to all directors and employees within a qualifying period of not more than five years' service and it must not have features that discourage eligible employees from participating or which exclude part-time employees. If an employee dies before completing the contract, his personal representatives may exercise the option within 12 months after the date of death.

Employees who leave because of injury, disability, redundancy or retirement must be allowed to exercise the option within six months thereafter. Those who leave for any other reason will not normally be allowed to exercise the option unless they have been in the scheme for at least three years. An employee who has been transferred to an associated company which is not participating in the scheme may nonetheless be permitted by the scheme rules to exercise the option within six months after the date his savings contract matures, or, if he leaves because of injury, disability, redundancy or retirement, within six months of leaving. Employees may also exercise scheme options if the company or part of the business which employs them is sold or otherwise leaves the group operating the scheme, even though they have been in the scheme for less than three years, but in these circumstances any gain arising is charged to income tax. Regardless of the treatment of the option, the SAYE contract itself may be continued by an employee after he leaves, by arrangement with the savings body, so that the benefit of receiving tax-free interest and bonuses at the end of the contract is retained. Payments will then be made direct to the savings body.

(2)   **Company share option plan (CSOP) schemes**

Under the provisions of ITEPA ss 521–526 and Sch 4, shares acquired by employees under an *approved company share option plan* do not attract an income tax charge when the option is granted unless the price to be paid for the shares under the option plus the price paid for the option itself is less than the market value of a similar quantity of shares at the time the right to acquire is granted. In that event an income tax charge arises on the difference in the year the option is granted, the amount charged to income tax then forms part of the cost of the shares for capital gains tax when the option is exercised (TCGA 1992 s 120(6)).

There is also no income tax charge when the option is exercised if the scheme conditions are complied with. Options may only be exercised between three and ten years after they are granted. (Prior to 9 April 2003 there was a further requirement that they must not be capable of being exercised more frequently than once in three years.)

Employees who leave because of injury, disability, redundancy or retirement will be allowed to exercise the option within the three year period without a charge to income tax.

For directors to participate they must be full time working directors (ie working at least 25 hours per week), but part time employees qualify. The value (at the time of the grant) of shares on which a person holds options must not exceed £30,000. (The limit for options granted under the rules applicable before 17 July 1995 is the greater of £100,000 and four times the employee's employment earnings, excluding benefits and after deducting contributions to an employer's pension scheme, for the current or previous tax year.)

If a disposal takes place other than under the approved scheme conditions an income tax charge arises at that time, but any discount already charged to tax when the option was granted is excluded.

ITEPA 2003 Sch 3 Part 7 and Sch 4 Part 6 permit participants in a SAYE scheme or CSOP scheme to exchange existing share options for options over shares in a company that takes over the employer company, so long as an election is made within six months.

(3) **Share incentive plans**

Under ITEPA 2003 s 488 and Sch 2 an employer can introduce a plan that enables the company to give shares to its employees and obtain a tax deduction for the market value of those shares in the accounting period in which the shares are awarded. Furthermore the plan enables an employee to buy shares in its employing company out of gross income. Such plans were previously referred to as all employee share ownership plans. They are now referred to as share incentive plans. A share incentive plan must provide benefits to all employees who are eligible and liable to UK tax on employment income. An employee does not have to accept an offer to join the plan. The plan must not contain features which discourage participation (eg loss of other rights for joining). All employees must participate on similar terms, although those terms may vary by reference to remuneration, length of service, hours worked or performance targets, but not so as to give preferential treatment to directors or higher paid employees.

The plan may contain a qualifying period for participation but this must not exceed 18 months. From 11 May 2001, where an employee within a group works for more than one group company, employment with any group company can count towards the qualifying period. The employee must not have a material interest in the employing company (see page 87.3) or receive shares under another share scheme from the same or a connected company in the same year, except, where a group restructures and the employee transfers to another company within the group. Then the employee, subject to one overall limit may receive shares under share schemes run by both companies.

The shares available under the plan can be of four types:

1. *Free shares*

An employee can be given shares worth up to £3,000 in a tax year, valued as at the date of the award. The gifted shares are held within a trust and no tax liability arises on the grant while the shares are so held. Free shares must normally be kept in the trust for a stipulated period, which may be not less than three nor more than five years. If an employee ceases employment, the shares are removed from the trust and the scheme may provide for such shares to be forfeited.

2. *Partnership shares*

An employee may be given the opportunity to buy shares (known as partnership shares) by way of a salary deduction. The maximum deduction is 10% of salary as defined by the scheme (excluding benefits in kind) to a limit of £1,500 in a year, with a minimum no greater than £10 per deduction. The deduction reduces gross salary before PAYE/NI is applied (but does not reduce net relevant earnings for pension purposes or income for tax credits). The money must either be used to buy shares within 30 days or accumulated for up to one year and then used within 30 days of the end of the period to acquire shares. The price may then, however, be by reference to the lower of market value on the first day of the accumulation period or the date of acquisition. If the employee leaves during the accumulation period, the amount deducted (net of PAYE/NI) is returned to him. The employee may withdraw the shares from the plan at any time (although this may result in a tax charge as indicated below).

3. *Matching shares*

An employer can offer up to two free matching shares for each partnership share purchased. They must be awarded on the same day and on the same basis as the partnership shares and be of the same class. They are held in trust on the same terms as other free shares.

4. *Dividend shares*

The scheme may provide, or an employee may elect, for dividends to be reinvested into shares whilst they are held in trust, to a maximum of £1,500 per tax year. Reinvested dividends do not carry a tax credit. The shares purchased will have the same rights as the shares on which the dividend is paid and are not subject to forfeiture. Such shares must be acquired within 30 days of the payment of dividend. Any dividend so invested is not liable to higher rate tax as long as the reinvested shares are held in trust, which must be for a period of at least three years. If the shares are withdrawn within that period, eg on leaving employment, dividend upper rate tax is payable (after taking into account a tax credit at the rate in force when the shares are taken out of the plan).

General provisions

The shares used in the plan must be ordinary shares that are fully paid up and not redeemable. They can be listed, or shares in a company not controlled by another company, or shares in a non-close company which is under the control of a company listed on a recognised stock exchange. The shares may have restrictions such as pre-emption, right of forfeiture or on voting rights, subject to the detailed provisions of the legislation. The shares must not be in a service company.

Tax provisions

No tax charge arises on the acquisition of the shares by the plan. An income tax charge (and a Class 1 national insurance charge if the shares are readily convertible assets) can, however, arise if free, partnership or matching shares are removed from the plan within three years, based on the value on removal. On removal between three and five years, the charge is on the lower of the value on removal and the value of the original award. Dividend shares removed from a plan within three years are taxable as dividend income as indicated above, based on the original dividends reinvested. See also under *Partly paid shares* and *Restricted shares etc* on pages 87.4 and 87.5 for the charge on directors and P11D employees where employers have guaranteed a sale price.

No tax arises on the death of the employee, or on withdrawal after five years. Furthermore, no charge arises if the shares cease to be subject to the plan because of injury or disability, redundancy, transfer under the Transfer of Undertakings (Protection of Employment) Regulations, change of control of the employing company or retirement on or after retirement age (not earlier than 50).

As far as capital gains tax is concerned, there is no liability if the shares are kept in the plan until sold. If they are removed and sold later, the capital gain will be the increase in value after they are withdrawn. Taper relief will apply from the date of withdrawal.

From 12 May 2001 partnership or dividend shares transferred to employees under the plan are exempt from stamp duty and stamp duty reserve tax (see Example 86 part A(b) and (c)).

Capital gains tax rollover relief (TCGA 1992 s 236A & Sch 7C)

Where existing shareholders (other than companies) transfer ownership of shares they hold in an unquoted company to an approved share incentive plan that holds (either immediately or within twelve months after the transfer) 10% of the company's shares, gains arising on the shares transferred may be treated as reducing the acquisition cost of replacement chargeable assets acquired within six months after the disposal (unless the chargeable assets are shares on which enterprise investment scheme income tax relief is given (see Example 94) and subject to some special provisions relating to dwelling houses).

Shares in qualifying employee share ownership trusts

Shares may be transferred into a share incentive plan from an existing qualifying share ownership trust without the trust or company suffering a tax charge. Such shares must be used as either free or matching shares.

(4)   **Corporation tax relief on employee shares**

Companies were encouraged to promote employee share ownership through a trust set up for this purpose known as a qualifying employee share ownership trust (QUEST). Payments made by the employer to set up the trust and to acquire shares to distribute to its employees obtained corporation tax relief so long as certain stringent conditions were met. These trusts were expensive to operate and are being replaced with less restrictive arrangements.

In general, from 1 January 2003, an employer will receive corporation tax relief of an amount equal to the difference between the market value of the shares at the time the employee exercises a share option and the price the employee pays. The relief is given in the accounting period in which the option is exercised and the shares acquired. The relief applies to CSOP and EMI options (which are tax free) and unapproved options or outright share acquisitions where the employee is subject to income tax.

The shares must be ordinary shares, and the company either a listed company, or a stand-alone company (or the holding company of a group).

Shares for a SIP have always given a corporation tax deduction as set out above (87.8 para (3)).

(5)   **Enterprise management incentives (EMI)**

A further share option scheme is known as the enterprise management incentives scheme (EMI) (ITEPA 2003 ss 527-541 and Sch 5). The scheme enables employees to be awarded share options worth up to £100,000 each in a qualifying company. Each employee may be awarded a different amount without restriction. The grant and exercise of the option is tax free (except to the extent, if any, that the option price is less than the value of the shares at the time the option was granted). When the shares are sold, the excess of the proceeds over the price paid (plus any amount charged to income tax) is a chargeable gain, but taper relief is given at the business assets rate and the taper relief period runs from the *date of grant of the option*.

In order to qualify, the EMI must satisfy the detailed requirements of the legislation. These include:

(a)   The employing company must be one that would qualify under the rules for the Enterprise Investment Scheme (EIS) (see Example 94). For options granted on or after 1 January 2002, however, the EIS gross assets rule is amended for EMI to a limit of £30 million (£15 million for options granted earlier) on the company's (or if relevant, group's) gross assets.

(b)   From 11 May 2001, the maximum value of shares in respect of which unexercised options exist must not exceed £3 million.

(c)   The option must be granted for commercial reasons to recruit or retain an employee and not for tax avoidance purposes.

(d)   The individual must work at least 25 hours per week for the company (or if less, 75% of his working time – in both employment and self-employment if applicable) and must not, with associates, have a material interest in the company (ie 30% or more of the ordinary share capital).

(e)   An employee may not hold unexercised options in respect of shares with a total value of more than £100,000 when the options were granted. Once that limit is reached, any further options granted within three years of the date of the last qualifying option are not qualifying options, regardless of whether the earlier options have then been exercised or released. Any unexercised options under CSOPs (see part (2)) count towards the £100,000 limit.

(f)   The general requirements relating to the option must be met, eg notice must be given to HMRC within 92 days of the grant of the option in the form specified, together with a declaration that the information is complete and correct and that the employee is an eligible employee.

If a disqualifying event occurs after an EMI option has been granted, but before it is exercised, the holder of the option has 40 days from the date of the event in which to exercise the option without losing the scheme benefits. If the option is exercised after that time, then income tax is charged under ITEPA 2003 Part 7 Chapter 5 s 476 on the difference between the market value of the shares on the date of exercise and their market value immediately before the disqualifying event (s 532).

Disqualifying events include (s 533):

–   The company becoming a 51% subsidiary, or under the control of another company,

–   The company ceasing to meet the trading activities test,

–   The employee ceasing to be an eligible employee,

–   A variation in the terms of the option so that the market value of the shares is increased,

–   An alteration to the share capital without prior HMRC approval,

–   Certain conversions of shares into shares of a different class,

–   The company having qualified on the basis that it was preparing to trade, but not doing so within two years of the grant of the option.

Capital gains tax

Shares acquired under approved SAYE or CSOP schemes are regarded for capital gains tax as acquired at the price paid (plus the amount, if any, paid for the option), and when they are disposed of, any gain is accordingly chargeable (subject to any available indexation allowance, taper relief and any unused annual exemption). For SAYE schemes, approved profit sharing schemes and share incentive plans, shares can be transferred free of capital gains tax within 90 days of emerging from the scheme, or within 90 days after the end of the three year period, if earlier, into an Individual Savings Account (ISA) up to the annual ISA limit. Any income and gains within the ISA will then be tax-free (see Example 93). There is no similar provision for EMI shares. From 6 April 2001 shares acquired under SAYE schemes and share incentive plans may be transferred into personal pension schemes and tax relief obtained thereon (see Example 38 explanatory note 26). This has continued after A-Day (FA 2004 s 195). For the interaction of the employee share scheme provisions with the capital gains tax rules for matching disposals with acquisitions, including special rules from 6 April 2002 where shares acquired under SAYE share option schemes, company share option plans and enterprise management incentive schemes are acquired on the same day as other shares, see Example 81 explanatory notes 1 to 3.

See 87.4 above for the impact of the decision in Mansworth v Jelley.

Self-assessment

Details of taxable events in relation to share schemes and share related benefits must be shown in tax returns (in the Share Schemes section) and any tax due must be included in the self-assessment. This does not apply to approved profit sharing schemes, since any tax due is collected by the employer or the trustees through PAYE, and is therefore included in pay in the Employment pages of the return. Where shares have been taxed as notional pay under PAYE (see page 87.2), the relevant amounts will be included in the pay figures in the Employment pages of the return, but they must also be included in the Share Schemes pages. The detailed provisions are in HMRC Helpsheet 218.

Employees who do not get tax returns must notify HMRC by 5 October after the end of the tax year if they have income or gains that have not been fully taxed (see Example 40 note 5). If the only untaxed amounts relate to shares or share options and the total tax due is less than £1,000, employees may ask to have the tax collected through their PAYE codings. When the extra tax due is £1,000 or more tax returns must be completed. Employers do not have to give details of taxable amounts on forms P11D, but since the scheme rules require them to give details to HMRC, they should be able to provide the relevant figures. Trustees of profit sharing schemes are required to provide the relevant information.

As noted at 87.2 above a return of all employment-related securities and options issued, transferred, or disposed of, is required for each fiscal year normally using Form 42. The return will be made by the employer by 6 July following the fiscal year or by the person from whom the securities or option was acquired (ITEPA 2003 s 421L).

A.   Explain the rules that deem a salary to be liable to PAYE and national insurance where services are provided through an intermediary, set out who is liable to pay the tax, the relieving provisions to mitigate double tax liabilities and the restrictions on the use of any loss created.

B.   Margaret Johnson, a design engineer, provides her services to her clients via M J Engineering Ltd, a company owned equally by Margaret and her partner John Allen. (Margaret and John live together as husband and wife.) M J Engineering Ltd has always made up its accounts to 31 December each year. The latest accounts, before taking into account personal services adjustments, include:

	£	Yr ended 31 Dec 2006 £	£	Yr ended 31 Dec 2007 £
Turnover		46,000		54,000
Less: Salary – John Allen (administrator)	7,210		8,100	
Travelling	5,340		6,086	
Training and courses	450		780	
Use of home as office	620		660	
Telephone, internet and sundries	1,120		1,234	
Bank and professional costs	1,710		1,930	
Capital allowances – computers	1,240		410	
Director's salary – Margaret Johnson	6,000		6,000	
National insurance	1,730		1,950	
Pension payments	5,000	30,420	5,000	32,150
Profit for year		15,580		21,850

On 5 May 2006 M J Engineering Ltd declared a dividend of £10,800.

M J Engineering Ltd had paid PAYE/NI on deemed salary plus employer's NI of £16,200 for the year 2005/06 in April 2006. The resulting loss had been carried back to the accounting year ended 31 December 2005. No dividend was paid in 2005/06. The deemed salary, net of employee's tax and NI, for 2005/06 was £9,844.

In the tax year 2006/07 M J Engineering Ltd received £48,200 (net of VAT) from clients in respect of work done by Margaret. In performing her duties she had travelled in 2006/07 14,800 miles in her own car and was paid 40p per mile mileage allowance by M J Engineering Ltd. Margaret's P11D for 2006/07 shows:

	£	
Use of home as office	640	
Excess mileage allowance (4,800 miles @ 15p per mile)	720	
Telephone (bill in name of employee)	700	(one half re business)
Private medical insurance	400	
	2,460	

M J Engineering Ltd had paid a pension contribution for Margaret of £3,000 on 6 December in each year. The use of Margaret's home as an office has been agreed as an allowable expense against her employment income.

Assume that PAYE tax has been paid on Margaret's salary and taxable benefits, less her personal allowance of £5,035.

Compute the amount liable to PAYE/NI for Margaret Johnson in the name of M J Engineering Ltd for 2006/07, together with amounts liable to corporation tax. Set out the amount of dividend taxable on Margaret for 2006/07 if the appropriate election is made.

A. **Provision of personal services through an intermediary when legislation applies**

Where an individual (known as 'the worker') personally provides services for another person (known as 'the client') and the contractual arrangements involve one or more third parties (known as the 'intermediary'), in such a way that if the services of the worker had been provided directly to the client the worker would be an employee of the client, then the legislation in ITEPA 2003 Part 2 Chapter 8 applies. From 10 April 2003 the legislation also applies if the client is an individual who is not in business (eg provision of care to an older person directly and provision of services by domestic workers such as nannies or butlers). It does not apply to any contract where the worker does not directly or indirectly have any interest in the intermediary (eg a non-connected employee of the intermediary).

Deemed salary payment

Where the personal services legislation applies, deemed salary is calculated for the work done by the worker for the client and compared with actual salary and non-cash benefits from the intermediary (net of VAT and net of allowable expenses). Any shortfall of actual salary and benefits is treated as a single payment, made on the last day of the tax year, liable to tax as employment income and to Class 1 national insurance contributions. The PAYE tax and NIC are payable by the intermediary by 19 April following the end of the tax year. The amounts are included on the worker's P60 and therefore appear on the worker's personal tax return on the employment pages. The deemed salary, together with employer's Class 1 national insurance thereon, becomes a deduction for trading income for the intermediary in the period of account in which the last day of the tax year falls. The deemed salary is not included as income for tax credits.

Effect on dividend payments

In so far as the deemed salary, net of PAYE and employee's national insurance, is paid out as a dividend, the intermediary company may make a claim, by 31 January following the tax year in which the dividend is paid, for the dividend to be treated as covered by the deemed salary and not therefore liable to income tax. Such dividends would however count as income for tax credits. Dividends treated as covered by the deemed salary are not taken into account when working out the liability to non-corporate distribution rate of corporation tax.

Trading losses

If the deduction of deemed salary gives rise to a loss in a trade and the intermediary is a company, then normal loss rules apply, ie the loss may be carried back one year, or carried forward, and can be used in a terminal loss claim.

If the intermediary is a partnership, then the deduction can only reduce the trading profits to nil – it cannot create a loss. Any excess is unrelieved. Furthermore, in computing the trading income of a partnership the maximum deduction for expenses relating to actual earnings is restricted to the amount deductible in computing the deemed salary (including the 5% of relevant earnings deduction – see below).

Amounts taken into account

The earnings taken into account in computing the deemed salary are the total amounts of the cash and non-cash benefits received in the tax year by the intermediary in respect of engagements to which the personal services legislation applies for that worker. The amount includes any sub-contractor's tax deducted but excludes any VAT. The exclusion of VAT applies even if the flat-rate scheme is used. Irrecoverable VAT relating to allowable expenses met by the intermediary would be allowable as part of the expenses in the same way as if the intermediary was not VAT registered.

Computation of deemed salary

To compute deemed salary the following formula is used:

		£
Amounts received from relevant engagements by the intermediary		X
Less: 5%		X
		X
Add: any other payments or benefits received by the worker in respect of relevant engagements, not otherwise chargeable as employment income of the worker, but which would be so chargeable if the worker had been an employee of the client		X
		X
Less: Expenses paid by the intermediary that would have been deductible against employment income if paid by the worker (as an employee of the client). This includes reimbursed expenses	X	
Capital allowances that could have been claimed by the worker	X	
Pension contributions paid by the intermediary for the worker	X	
Employer's Class 1 national insurance paid and Class 1A or 1B national insurance payable for the worker	X	X
		X
Compared with amounts actually received by the worker from the intermediary in the tax year (which do not represent items for which a deduction has already been given above):		
Taxable actual salary	X	
Taxable benefits in kind and exempt mileage allowances	X	X
Maximum deduction from trading income		X

The amount computed is deemed salary plus employer's Class 1 national insurance contributions. If the employer's NI nil band of £5,035 (for 2006/07) has already been used for the worker then deemed salary will be:

	£
Deemed salary including employer's NIC (as above)	X
Less: 12.8/112.8 x deemed salary including employer's NIC*	X
Deemed salary to enter on worker's PAYE tax card (P11)	X

* If the nil band has not been fully used any excess is deducted from this amount first.

There is a template to calculate deemed payments at www.hmrc.gov.uk/ir35/ir35.xlt

More than one intermediary

If more than one intermediary exists, then all intermediaries have a joint and several liability for the PAYE/NI in so far as the intermediary has received any payment or benefit for the worker. However, the relevant earnings may be reduced by any amount included as relevant earnings by subsequent intermediaries to prevent double counting, leaving the prime liability with the last intermediary in the chain.

Benefits received directly from client

If the worker receives benefits or other amounts directly from the client (eg provision of a company car by client to worker) then the deemed salary is increased by that amount without a 5% deduction.

B.   **M J Engineering Ltd**

Computation of deemed salary for 2006/07 for Margaret Johnson

		£
Amounts received		48,200
Less: 5% allowance		2,410
		45,790
Less: Expenses – Use of home as office	640	
Business use of telephone	350	
Pension contribution for M Johnson	3,000	
Employer's NI for M Johnson		
Class 1 ((6,000 + 700*) – 5,035) @ 12.8%	213	
Class 1A (on medical insurance 400) @ 12.8%	51	
Salary	6,000	
Taxable benefits and exempt mileage allowances (400 + 350 + 720 + 5,200)	6,670	16,924
Excess amount		28,866
Less: Employer's Class 1 NIC therein (12.8/112.8 x £28,848)		3,276
Deemed salary		25,590

* Re telephone – no NI on mileage allowance since permitted NI rate for 2006/07 is 40p per mile regardless of miles travelled.

PAYE/NI liability on deemed salary in name of Margaret Johnson

Actual salary	6,000
Taxable benefits (2,460 – 990)	1,470
Deemed salary	25,590
	33,060
Less: Personal allowance	5,035
Total taxable earnings	28,025

Tax has already been charged on salary and benefits of (6,000 + 1,470 – 5,035 =) £2,435, leaving £30,865 of basic rate band available. Employee's and employer's NI has already been charged on excess of salary and benefits of £6,700 over the earnings threshold of £5,035, so that the employee's and employer's NI rates payable are 11% (up to upper earnings limit of £33,540) plus 1% on the excess and 12.8% respectively.

		£
Tax on deemed salary:		
25,590 @ 22%		5,630
NI on deemed salary:		
Employee	25,590 @ 11%	2,815
Employer	25,590 @ 12.8%	3,276
Payable by M J Engineering Ltd by 19 April 2007		6,091

Amounts liable to corporation tax:

			Year to 31.12.06 £	Year to 31.12.07 £
Profit per accounts			15,580	21,850
Less: Personal services			(16,200)	(28,866)
Loss for year carried back			(620)	
Loss for year carried forward				(7,016)

Taxable dividend 2006/07:			Margaret Johnson £	John Allen £
Dividend (50% x £10,800)			5,400	5,400
Deemed salary – 2006/07		25,590		
Less: Tax	5,630			
Employee's NI	2,815	8,445		
Net		17,145		
Brought forward from 2005/06		9,844		
		26,989		
Offset after claim for relief –				
Worker		(5,400)	(5,400)	
Others		(5,400)		(5,400)
			–	–
Available to offset future dividends		16,189		

Explanatory Notes

Liability under personal services legislation

1. *Companies*

   The legislation only applies to workers who have, together with associates, a material interest in the intermediary company or who receive or could receive payments or benefits from the intermediary company which are not salary but could reasonably be taken to represent remuneration for services charged to the client by the intermediary.

   Material interest means the ability, alone or with associates, to control more than 5% of the ordinary share capital, or to receive more than 5% of distributions, or to be entitled to more than 5% of assets on winding up. For this purpose the worker does not need any holding in his own name for the holdings of associates to be included. An associate is any relative or business partner. Relative means husband or wife, parent or remoter forebear, child or remoter issue, brother or sister. A man and a woman living together as husband and wife are deemed married and are therefore associates. The interests of the associates of business partners are included with their own interest. Trustees of settlements made by the taxpayer or any relative are also included. A company is connected with another person if that person has (together with associates) control of the company.

   See Tax Bulletin 60 (August 2002) for the Revenue's view on the application of the personal service company legislation to Composite Service Companies.

2. *Partnerships*

   Again the legislation applies to any worker whose payments or benefits from the partnership represent the amount charged for the worker's services to the client. Otherwise a partner is only caught by the legislation if one of the following tests is satisfied:

–   The worker (together with his/her relatives) is entitled to 60% or more of the profits of the partnership, or

–   Most of the profits of the partnership arise from the provision of personal services to a single client (including the client's associates), or

–   The profit share of the worker is based on the income generated by that worker in the provision of personal services.

3. *Individuals*

The legislation can apply where the intermediary is an unincorporated body of which the worker is a member or where the intermediary is an individual (but the worker cannot be an intermediary for himself). This only applies if the amount receivable by the worker from the intermediary can reasonably be taken to represent remuneration for services provided by the worker to the client.

Classification as an employee

4. The legislation only applies if the worker would have been an employee of the client if the services had been provided directly to the client. See Examples 13 and 44 part (e) for detailed notes on the points relevant to determine status as an employee. There have been several cases specifically on the issue of whether the personal service company legislation applies, and most contain discussion on employment status. Readers are referred to PCG v IRC [2002] STC 165, Hewlett Packard v O'Murphy [2002] IRLR 4 EAT, FS Consulting Ltd v McCaul [2002] STC (SCD) 138, Lime-IT Ltd v Justin [2002] SpC 342, Synaptek Ltd v Young [2003] STC 543 and Future Online Ltd v Faulds (2004) Sp C 406.

It should be noted that in the case of Cable and Wireless v Muscat in October (2005, an individual working through an employment agency, also using a service company, was held to be an employee, and entitled to employee rights. This decision might make the IR35 legislation unworkable and a response from HMRC is awaited.

Exclusions

5. The legislation does not apply to non-resident entertainers or sportsmen, who are subject to deduction of tax under ITTOIA 2005 ss 13 and 14.

6. If the worker would not be liable to tax on UK employment income if directly employed by the client, eg the worker is non-resident and the services are provided outside the UK, then the legislation does not apply. However, if the worker is resident in the UK, the services are provided in the UK and the client carries on business in the UK, the intermediary is treated as carrying on business in the UK wherever actually resident. See Tax Bulletin 64 (April 2003) for more detail on the service company legislation and international issues.

Expenses

7. The deductions allowable are those met by the intermediary that would have been deductible from the taxable earnings of the worker if he or she had been employed by the client and met the expenses from his or her earnings. They include all items deductible under Chapters 1 to 5 of Part 5 of ITEPA 2003 (eg expenses incurred wholly, exclusively and necessarily, travel expenses, professional fees, employees' liabilities and indemnity insurance, agency fees paid by entertainers and fixed allowances). They specifically include amounts originally met by the worker but reimbursed by the intermediary (ITEPA 2003 s 54(3)) and, where the intermediary provides a vehicle which is chargeable as a benefit in kind on the worker, approved mileage allowances which the worker could have claimed if he or she had been employed by the client and used his or her own car for business (ITEPA 2003 s 54(4)). The benefit in kind itself (representing the private use of the car) would be deductible as part of the taxable salary and benefits provided by the intermediary to the worker. If the worker uses their own car in reality (as in this example) ITEPA 2003 s 54(7) preserves the relief for the approved mileage allowances by allowing the exempt amounts to be included in the amounts deducted as salary or benefits.

No deduction is allowed for training costs borne by the intermediary, as no claim is generally possible for such costs under Chapters 1 to 5 of Part 5 of ITEPA 2003.

8. Because all contracts undertaken by the worker for the intermediary relate to his/her employment with the intermediary, this means that most client premises will be temporary workplaces (see Example 13 explanatory note 6) and therefore travelling costs will be allowed from the worker's home to that temporary workplace.

Capital allowances

9. Only capital allowances claimable by a worker can be deducted, ie those claimable under CAA 2001 s 262, being plant and machinery necessarily provided for use in the performance of the duties. It is likely that Margaret's computer, whilst helping her to better perform her duties, would fail this test and no deduction would be allowed.

Employees of the intermediary

10. No deductions are allowed for salaries or other administrative costs in computing deemed pay. This does not prevent a deduction for Schedule D for companies.

    If the employee provides relevant services to the client, but does not have a material interest etc in the company then the amount charged to the client is excluded from the computation of deemed pay. If an invoice is rendered for the services of more than one individual, the amount must be apportioned between the individuals and only the earnings of an individual (with a material interest etc) are taken into account.

Dividends

11. To prevent double taxation, dividends may be offset by net deemed salary if a claim is made by the intermediary company by 31 January following the tax year in which the dividend is paid. The relief is given primarily against distributions of the current year and then distributions of subsequent tax years, with relief firstly against the dividends paid to the worker and then against other dividends paid for that year. This claim also prevented the dividend covered by deemed salary from being treated as a non-corporate distribution for the calculation of corporation tax before its abolition in 2006.

Actual pay

12. The deduction for actual pay is the payments or benefits received in a tax year by the worker from that intermediary which are chargeable as employment income. Consequently any payments made after 5 April 2006 cannot be deducted in 2005/06, even if the amount relates to earnings in that year which have been charged to tax as deemed salary. Instead the amount will be deducted as actual pay in the year of payment. This could result in actual pay in a subsequent year exceeding the computed deemed pay. There is no relief for the excess. Care should be taken to distribute any amount charged as deemed salary by way of dividend, with an appropriate claim for relief being made.

Computation of deemed salary other than at 5 April

13. If a worker ceases to be connected with an intermediary during the tax year, then the deemed salary is treated as paid immediately before that event (and the deduction for the payment is based on the day before the event occurred). For partnerships this applies when a partner (or employee) ceases to hold that position. For companies it applies if the worker ceases to be a member (shareholder), director or employee. Thus if a worker resigns as a director during the tax year, a computation of deemed salary is due to that date, with payment of the relevant PAYE/NICs. All receipts, expenses etc to the end of the tax year will be included in the computation, even though the payment is regarded as made at the earlier date (and the company's deduction will be based on that date). From 6 April 2002 a similar provision applies where a company ceases to trade, the computation being prepared at the date of cessation with a deduction in the final accounting period.

Accounting year end

14. As part B of the example shows, the deemed salary deduction from income can occur in a different accounting period from that in which the earnings arise and are charged to tax. To prevent losses arising that can only be carried forward, and which might never be relieved, it is advisable to use a 5 April year end for any intermediary caught by these rules.

HMRC opinions

15. It is possible to get an opinion from HMRC as to whether a particular contract is caught by the IR35 provisions. The address is IR35 Unit HM Revenue & Customs, North East Metropoliton Area, Fountain Court, 119 Grange Road, Middlesburgh TS1 2XA. There is also a dedicated helpline for IR35 matters 0845 303 3535, and two useful leaflets IR2003 'Supplying services. How to calculate the deemed payment' and IR175 'Supplying services through a limited company or partnership'. There is also a dedicated part of HMRC website at www.hmrc.gov.uk/ir35/index.htm.

Edzell was the sole proprietor of an aircraft maintenance business until he transferred it as a going concern to a limited company on 30 April 2006.

Since founding the business in 1980 Edzell has always made up accounts to 5 April in each year.

The profits, as adjusted for income tax purposes but before capital allowances, have been calculated as £48,753 for the year to 5 April 2006 and £3,340 for the final period to 30 April 2006.

The written down values of plant and machinery for capital allowances purposes after allowances for the year ended 5 April 2005 were as follows:

	£
Plant and equipment pool	3,506
Motor car	5,925

Subsequent plant and machinery additions have comprised a new testing machine at a cost of £2,700 on 16 June 2005 and a new aircraft tractor at a cost of £13,181 on 31 March 2006. (The business qualifies as 'small' for capital allowances purposes.)

Edzell has always declared business use of the car at 90%, based on reasonable apportionment.

The maximum capital allowances have always been claimed as early as possible.

A freehold aircraft hangar was acquired in 1981 at a cost of £30,000 and industrial buildings allowances equal to that amount have been claimed so that the written down value is nil.

The market values of the assets at the time of the transfer of the business to the company were:

	£
Goodwill	87,500
Freehold aircraft hangar	80,800
Plant and equipment (not including any fixed plant)	20,000
Motor car	5,000
Net current assets including debtors of £15,000 (but excluding cash)	12,700
	206,000

Edzell has never made any payment for goodwill. No other asset except the aircraft hangar was transferred at a market value greater than cost, and none of the plant and equipment cost more than £6,000.

For capital allowances purposes, both Edzell and the company have elected to transfer the assets at their written down value.

The transfer was satisfied by the issue to Edzell of all of the authorised share capital of 100,000 ordinary shares of £1 each of Famosa Ltd (a company formed specifically for the purpose of the transfer) and the payment to him of £60,000 cash.

(a)   Show Edzell's capital allowances and taxable profits for his last two accounting periods as a sole trader and comment on what the position would have been if Edzell had made up a final account from 6 April 2005 to 30 April 2006.

(b)   Calculate Edzell's chargeable gain arising on the transfer of the business to Famosa Ltd and the capital gains tax base value of his shares in Famosa Ltd.

In this connection, the values of the goodwill and aircraft hangar at March 1982 can be taken as £25,000 and £30,000 respectively.

(c)   State the effect on both Edzell and Famosa Ltd, had the election to transfer the assets for capital allowances purposes at their written down value not been made.

(d)   State the national insurance consequences of transferring the business to the company.

(a) **Edzell's capital allowances computation and taxable profits for final two accounting periods**

Capital allowances computation

		Plant pool £	Motor car (10% private) £		Total allowances £
WDV at 6.4.05			3,506	5,925	
2005/06 (6.4.05 – 5.4.06)					
WDA 25%			(877)	(1,481)	(90% = 1,333)	2,210
Qualifying for FYA:					
New testing machine	2,700				
New aircraft tractor	13,181				
	15,881				
FYA 40%	(6,352)	9,529			6,352
		12,158	4,444		8,562
2006/07 (6.4.06 – 30.4.07)					
Deemed transfer at tax written down value (see explanatory note 9)		12,158	4,444		–

The aircraft hangar would be transferred to the company at its written down value of nil.

Taxable profits

		£
2005/06	48,753 less capital allowances 8,562	40,191
2006/07	(capital allowances nil)	3,340

If Edzell had made up a final account from 6 April 2005 to 30 April 2006, capital allowances would be computed for that period of account. Since it is the period of discontinuance of Edzell's trade, neither first year nor writing down allowances would have been available and the computation would have been as follows:

	Plant £	Motor car £	Total allowances £
6.4.05 – 30.4.06			
WDV at 6.4.05	3,506	5,925	
Additions:			
New testing machine	2,700		
New aircraft tractor	13,181		
	19,387		
Deemed transfer at tax written down value	19,387	5,925	–

The taxable profit of the final period would have been increased by £8,562 in respect of the capital allowances that would no longer be given and the written down values transferred to the company would be increased by £7,229 on the plant pool and £1,481 in respect of the motor car, a total of £8,710. This is £148 more than the capital allowances that have been claimed, because the capital allowances on the car were restricted by that amount in respect of the private use proportion. They will not be restricted in the company's computation, but Edzell will be taxed on the benefit of private use of the car under the employment income rules.

The taxable profits would be assessable as follows (see explanatory note 10):

2005/06	365/390 × (48,753 + 3,340 =) 52,093	£48,753
2006/07	25/390 × 52,093	£ 3,339

(b) **Edzell's chargeable gain on transfer of business to Famosa Ltd**

	Goodwill £	Aircraft hangar £
Market value on transfer to company	87,500	80,800
Market value at March 1982	(25,000)	(30,000)
Indexation allowance to April 1998 on March 1982 values		
Goodwill £25,000 x 104.7%	(26,175)	
Hangar £30,000 x 104.7%		(31,410)
Chargeable gains before rollover relief	36,325	19,390

	55,715
Less: rolled over against base cost of shares in Famosa Ltd (see explanatory note 1)	39,487
Chargeable gain before taper relief	16,228
Business asset taper relief – 75%*	(12,171)
Chargeable gain 2006/07 (subject to annual exemption)	4,057

*   Providing the gain is not reduced by allowable losses.

Edzell is not entitled to taper relief in respect of the gain rolled over against the base cost of the Famosa Ltd shares. As and when he disposes of the shares, taper relief will be based on the time for which the shares have been owned.

The remaining assets do not attract a capital gains liability, since none is transferred at a value in excess of cost (and there would not have been any capital gains in any event, since both the motor car and the items of plant and equipment each valued at less than £6,000 are exempt).

The capital gains tax base value of the shares in Famosa Ltd is 146,000 – 39,487 = £106,513.

(c) **If the election to transfer assets at written down value for capital allowances purposes had not been made**

As Famosa Ltd gives full 'market value' consideration, this would determine the disposal proceeds for plant and machinery allowance purposes (CAA 2001 s 61). For the purposes of industrial buildings allowances, on a transfer between connected persons, CAA 2001 s 568 normally deems the transfer to be made at open market value in any event, unless an election is made under CAA 2001 s 569. Famosa Ltd would therefore be deemed to have acquired the assets at market value. This would result in balancing charges on Edzell as follows:

	Plant	Motor car		Aircraft hangar
WDV	10,569	4,444		–
Market value 30.4.06 (but not exceeding cost)	20,000	5,000		30,000
Balancing charges	£ 9,431	£ 556	x 90% = £ 500	30,000

Giving an increase in 2006/07 assessable profits of	£ 39,931

(d) **Edzell's national insurance position**

As a sole trader, Edzell will have been liable to pay weekly flat rate Class 2 contributions of £2.10 during 2005/06. He will also have been liable to pay Class 4 contributions of 8% of his profits between £4,895 and £32,760. In addition, contributions have been payable at 1% on profits above the upper profits limit. This gave him a national insurance liability for 2005/06 of Class 2 £109 + Class 4 £2,303 = £2,412. The equivalent figures for 2006/07 are Class 2 £2.10 per week and Class 4 8% of profits between £5,035 and £33,540, together with an uncapped 1% payable on all profits above £33,540.

The national insurance position (using 2006/07 rates) if the business is transferred to the company is as follows. As a company director Edzell will be liable to pay Class 1 employee's contributions at the rate of 11% on his earnings between £97 and £645 per week, with an uncapped 1% charge on any earnings in excess of £645 per week. (Strictly a director has an annual earnings period – see Example 47 part (d).) In addition, the company, as his employer, will have to pay contributions at 12.8% on remuneration exceeding £97 per week (£5,035 per year), with no upper ceiling on the earnings on which contributions are payable. Furthermore, most taxable benefits in kind (including company cars, private fuel, living accommodation) also attract company Class 1A national insurance contributions at the rate of 12.8%. The company's contributions will, however, be allowable expenses against the profit for corporation tax.

Edzell will be able to control how much of the profit is left in the company and how much to draw as remuneration. In relation to Famosa Ltd, for the financial year to 31 March 2007 profits up to £300,000 will be taxed at the small companies' rate of 19%.

Since there is no upper limit for the employer's contributions, it is not possible to work out an overall maximum of national insurance contributions. But if Edzell had no other income and drew remuneration in 2006/07 of £38,335 to cover the starting and basic rate bands of £33,300, £38,335 and and personal allowance of £5,035 (and taking the position as if he had been employed for the full year for simplicity), the position would be:

Employee's contributions

£548 (645 – 97) x 11% x 52 weeks	3,135	
£4,795 (38,335 – 33,540) × 1%	48	3,183

Employer's contributions

£33,300 (38,335 – 5,035) x 12.8%	4,262	
Less corporation tax relief @ say 19%	(810)	3,452
Net national insurance cost		£ 6,635
Compared with the liability of a self-employed person earning £38,335		£ 2,437

Clearly there is a much higher national insurance liability operating through a company than as a sole trader. A greater range of state benefits is, however, available to Edzell as an employee, particularly jobseeker's allowance and earnings-related retirement pension.

The national insurance disadvantage of operating through the company could be reduced (or avoided altogether) if Edzell drew a lower salary and received higher dividends, on which national insurance contributions are not payable. Taken with the fact that the corporation tax rate at 19% is 3% lower than the basic rate of income tax, this could give a lower tax/national insurance bill than the sole trader format. Payment of dividend now comes under closer scrutiny, but this company is not affected by IR35, and the settlements legislation does not apply. The company may still pay dividends.

Explanatory Notes

Rollover relief under TCGA 1992 s 162 on transfer of business to company

1. Where a business is transferred to a company as a going concern, together with all assets of the business other than cash, wholly in exchange for shares in the company, the chargeable gains arising

on the assets transferred are deducted from the cost of the shares. As indicated in part (b) of the example, taper relief is not available on the gain to be rolled over, and will be given when the shares are disposed of (see Example 74 part (a)(i) for detailed notes on taper relief).

Partial relief is available where the consideration is only partly satisfied by shares in the new company, using the fraction:

$$\frac{\text{Value of shares in new company}}{\begin{array}{c}\text{Value of whole consideration received in}\\\text{exchange for the business}\end{array}} \quad \text{x} \quad \text{Chargeable gains on assets transferred}$$

(TCGA 1992 s 162)

The relief under s 162 is automatic and a claim is not necessary. However, for post-5 April 2002 disposals, it is possible to disapply s 162 relief by making a TCGA 1992 s 162A election – this would normally be done to benefit from additional taper relief where the shares in the company are sold shortly after the incorporation (see explanatory note 2 below). Certain reliefs take priority over relief under s 162, such as rollover relief for replacement assets under s 152, because the relief is given by reducing the *consideration* for a disposal. But s 162 relief cannot be ignored where, for example, gains would be covered by the annual exemption. To avoid the problem, the appropriate part of the consideration equal to available reliefs and exemptions could be left on director's loan account, so that a gain would be immediately realised.

Where the transfer to the company occurred between 31 March 1982 and 6 April 1988 and the deferred gains relate in whole or in part to a period before 31 March 1982, the deferred gains are halved when brought into charge on or after 6 April 1988 (see Example 83 explanatory note 11).

Where gains have been held over following the acquisition of a depreciating asset (see Example 83), those gains will crystallise when the depreciating asset is transferred to the company, but technically they do not arise on the disposal of the asset and cannot therefore be deferred under s 162.

The total market value of assets transferred by Edzell to Famosa Ltd in the example was:

Goodwill	87,500
Freehold aircraft hangar	80,800
Plant and equipment	20,000
Motor car	5,000
Net current assets including debtors of £15,000 (but excluding cash)	12,700
	£ 206,000

The chargeable gain can therefore be rolled over against the base cost of the shares in the proportion:

$$\frac{146,000 \text{ (consideration received as shares)}}{206,000 \text{ (total consideration)}}$$

which is $\dfrac{146}{206}$ x £55,715   £ 39,487

Stamp duty land tax is chargeable on the market value of the land and buildings transferred under the sale of business agreement:

Freehold aircraft hangar   £ 80,800

However, because the premises are business premises, the rate of tax is 0% where the consideration given for the hangar is £150,000 or less (FA 2003 s 55).

Note that goodwill and debtors are exempt from stamp duty, which is especially beneficial for the incorporation of profitable businesses under TCGA 1992 s 162.

Electing under TCGA 1992 s 162A to disapply s 162 relief

2. The incorporation of a business can adversely affect the proprietor's taper relief. Under s 162, the 'untapered' gains are rolled over and the proprietor's taper relief clock is reset to start afresh (in relation to the shares). No taper 'credit' is given for the pre-incorporation holding period of the property, goodwill etc.

    TCGA 1992 s 162A election (introduced by FA 2002 s 49) can assist in recapturing the taper relief 'lost' on incorporation if the shares are sold shortly afterwards. The s 162A election does this by removing the automatic application of s 162 relief to the various gains. The gains thus become chargeable and would qualify for taper relief, which would be at the full 75% rate for two complete years of ownership. Calculations would normally be required in each case to determine whether a s 162A election would be beneficial.

    Where the shares acquired on incorporation are sold by the end of the tax year *following* the tax year of the incorporation, the s 162A election must be made by the 31 January after the end of that *following* tax year (the normal time limit for amending a self-assessment return), ie by 31 January 2009 for a 2006/07 disposal. In all other cases (ie where the shares are still retained at the end of the tax year following the tax year of incorporation) the time limit is extended by a further year (to 31 January 2010 for a 2006/07 disposal).

Retaining some assets and claiming gifts holdover relief under TCGA 1992 s 165 on others

3. The gain on the aircraft hangar could have been avoided if it had been retained by Edzell personally and let to the company. If rent were charged for the hangar, this would not prevent full business asset taper relief being available if there was a gain when the hangar was disposed of, as the hangar would be used in the trade by Edzell's 'qualifying company' – a rent charge does not restrict the relief (FA 1998 Sch 20.5(2)(b)).

    If the hangar was not transferred, Edzell would have a chargeable gain on the goodwill, since the relief described in note 1 where assets are transferred to the company is only available where the *whole assets* of the business (other than cash) are transferred.

    Even in that case, however, the gain on the goodwill could be deferred if Edzell assigned the goodwill to the company under the business gifts holdover relief provisions of TCGA 1992 s 165 for its value at 31 March 1982 (plus the unused part of his capital gains tax annual exemption if appropriate, grossed up by 75% business asset taper relief). This relief is not affected by his retaining the premises.

    (A holdover election under TCGA 1992 s 165 is not available on the transfer of shares in an unquoted trading company etc to a company, although this will rarely be relevant on a business incorporation.)

    Thus, if Edzell had not used his capital gains tax exemption of £8,800, he could sell the goodwill for its 31 March 1982 value of £25,000 plus the annual exemption grossed up by 75% business assets taper relief, ie (8,800 x $^{100}/_{25}$ =) £35,200, giving a total transfer value of £60,200. This would give him a credit of that amount to his director's account with the company and would be an exempt gain for him as follows:

		£
Deemed sale proceeds		87,500
31 March 1982 value	25,000	
Indexation allowance to April 1998	26,175	51,175
		36,325

Less: Gain immediately chargeable, being excess of actual proceeds over 31 March 1982 value (but covered by taper relief of 75% of £35,200 (= £26,400), leaving a gain of £8,800 covered by the annual exemption) ... 35,200

Gain held over ... 1,125

The company would have a base cost of £86,375 as follows:

Market value on acquisition		87,500
Less: Heldover gain		1,125
		£ 86,375
Being: Paid to Edzell		60,200
Indexation allowance		26,175
		£ 86,375

Under this arrangement, Edzell is only credited in the accounts of the company with £60,200, and the company's capital gains cost is that amount plus indexation allowance of £26,175, ie £86,375, rather than the market value of £87,500. The company will continue to be entitled to indexation allowance on the amount of £86,375 (the replacement of indexation allowance with taper relief from April 1998 applying only to non-corporate taxpayers).

Taper relief is not available on the gains held over under TCGA 1992 s 165 since the relief is only given on chargeable gains. It is important to note that the individual proprietor's or partner's taper relief clock starts again based on the date the shares were acquired (or if later, when the company starts to trade). The consequential loss of the taper period should be taken into account when an incorporation is being considered, particularly if there is a strong likelihood of the business being sold in the next two years.

Where gifts holdover relief is claimed, HMRC require the shares to be subscribed for separately from the document for the transfer of the gifted assets.

Alternative strategy of selling goodwill at its market value

4.   In many cases, the sole trader's goodwill will have accrued the maximum business asset taper rate of 75%. Hence it should be possible to sell the goodwill to the company for its fair market value at a relatively low tax cost – ie effective CGT rate of 10% with no stamp duty (for post-22 April 2002 transfers). This would enable a further 'credit' to be booked to the proprietor's loan account. In this way, proprietors can use appropriate repayments of their loan account (in effect created at an effective CGT rate of 10%) to replace salary/dividends (taxed at a much higher rate, including NICs on salary payments), possibly for a number of years. Such an arrangement is likely to be beneficial, but care must be taken to avoid overvalue – see Example 50.

In this example, assuming Edzell retained the hangar, the capital gain on the goodwill would be a modest £281, being:

	£
Capital gain	36,325
Less: Taper relief @ 75%	(27,244)
Annual exemption	(8,800)
Taxable gain	281

Deferral relief under the enterprise investment scheme

5.   A possible further alternative may be to 'incorporate' using the enterprise investment scheme (EIS) provisions of TCGA 1992 s 150C and Sch 5B (although the small gain, assuming that only goodwill is transferred, would not make it practicable in this particular case). The scheme enables a taxpayer who has made a chargeable gain to defer it to the extent that he subscribes for shares in cash in a qualifying unquoted trading company within one year before and three years after the disposal of the asset giving rise to the gain. There are, however, very detailed and complex conditions in order for deferral relief to be available (see Example 94) and it is not clear that the incorporation of a business may be structured in such a way as to enable the relief to be claimed, for example, shares must be subscribed for in cash and there are restrictions on receiving value. If it was used in Edzell's case, the same gain would be deferred in respect of the goodwill as for gifts holdover relief (ie without taper relief), but the capital gains base cost of the goodwill for the company would be its full value of £87,500.

Tax relief for amount paid for goodwill

6.   Goodwill is included in the 'intangible fixed assets' provisions introduced by FA 2002 s 84 and Schs 29, 30, applicable from 1 April 2002 (see Example 65). Profits and losses on such assets are taken into account in calculating income profits, and provision is made for goodwill to be amortised in the accounts. On the incorporation of a business on or after 1 April 2002, however, where the unincorporated business held the goodwill at 1 April 2002, the company would not be entitled to any tax relief for the subsequent amortisation of the purchased goodwill in the company's books, as it would be acquired from a 'related party' (Sch 29.118). It should be possible for an acquiring company to obtain Schedule D Case I tax relief on the amount paid for sole trade/partnership goodwill to the extent that the goodwill arises, or is acquired by the sole trade/partnership from an unrelated third party, after 31 March 2002. The relief would be based on the amount written off in the accounts each year.

Share premium account

7.   The example illustrates that, when a business is transferred to a limited company as a going concern, wholly or partly for consideration to be satisfied by shares in the company, it will usually not be possible to issue *a number* of shares corresponding exactly with that part of the consideration to be satisfied in shares, since the final value of the business will not be known until after the event. Thus in this example the part of the consideration of £206,000 to be satisfied by shares is £146,000 and the nominal value of the shares allotted is £100,000.

The remaining £46,000 will be dealt with in the accounts of the company through a share premium account.

Income tax basis periods

8.   Since Edzell has always made up accounts to 5 April, his basis periods coincide with his accounting periods and there is no overlap relief. Had his annual accounts been made up to another date, any overlap relief would have been deducted from the assessable profit of the last *tax year* (see Example 32 explanatory note 5). If, instead of making up a final 25-day account to 30 April 2006 as in the example, he had made up accounts for the period from 6 April 2005 to 30 April 2006, then under the change of accounting date rules in TA 1988 s 62A, the accounting date would normally have been treated as having changed in *2005/06*, with the basis period for that year being 12 months to the new date, ie 12 months to 30 April *2005*. A change of accounting date is not, however, effective if the taxpayer does not notify the change to HMRC. It is confirmed in the Revenue's booklet SAT 1 at paragraph 1.77 that if such an account had been made up, the 2005/06 taxable profit could be calculated by reference to the old date of 5 April. The profits of the last period of account (calculated *after* capital allowances, which because of the transfer to the company would in this case be nil, as indicated in the example) would therefore have been time-apportioned as to 365/390 to 2005/06 and 25/390 to 2006/07. Any available overlap relief would have been deducted from the 2006/07 profit, and if it created a loss the normal loss reliefs would have been available.

Capital allowances and election to transfer at written down value

9.   The capital allowances basis periods are the same as the income tax basis periods. If the final account had been made up for the period 6 April 2005 to 30 April 2006, then as indicated in the comments in part (a) of the example, this would result in no first year or writing down allowances being available in the final period (CAA 2001 ss 46, 55, 65). Where the final accounting period to cessation includes significant capital expenditure, it may be beneficial to draw up accounts to an earlier date prior to cessation (or, as in this example, not to extend the normal accounting period to include a short final period) to enable first year allowances etc to be claimed. Alternatively, it may be possible to crystallise a large balancing allowance on cessation by selling the pooled plant (including the newly acquired items) at less than the tax written down value (and not making an election to transfer at tax written down value) (s 61). This treatment would not apply to non-pooled assets, such as expensive cars (s 79) and short life assets (s 88).

Where the consideration allocated to plant and industrial buildings exceeds its tax written down value, a balancing charge would arise. This can be avoided as shown in the example by an election under CAA 2001 ss 266, 267 (plant and machinery) or ss 569, 570 (industrial buildings) where the purchaser and the seller are connected persons (see Example 18 part (c)). A written notice to HMRC is required not later than two years after the transfer date. The company assumes the written down values of the assets, which are treated as sold in the period to the date of transfer at an amount that gives neither a balancing allowance nor a balancing charge.

The 40% (50% for acquisitions between 6 April 2006 and 5 April 2007) first year allowance for expenditure on plant (excluding cars and certain other assets) is not available to the company on assets acquired from Edzell because it is controlled by Edzell and first year allowance is therefore blocked by CAA 2001 ss 214, 217 (connected persons etc).

Relief for trading losses

10.   If there had been unrelieved trading losses, Edzell could have obtained relief in respect of them against income from the company under TA 1988 s 386 (see Example 32 explanatory note 7). An alternative way of relieving brought forward losses may arise if no election is made to transfer assets at written down value for capital allowances, so that they would be transferred at market value. If this gave rise to balancing charges (such as those indicated in part (c) of the example), the result would be to increase the profits against which the losses could be set.

Value added tax

11.   Since the business is to be transferred as a going concern, the effect for value added tax purposes is that the transfer will not be treated as a supply of goods or services and no VAT will be payable on the assets transferred (assuming that the option to tax in respect of the building had not been exercised by Edzell, or Famosa Ltd had also made the election before the transfer). Famosa Ltd will accordingly have no input tax to reclaim.

The local HMRC office must be notified within thirty days of the transfer, and at the same time Edzell and Famosa Ltd may jointly apply for Edzell's VAT registration number to be re-allocated to the company. Edzell's personal registration will then be cancelled and the company will stand in his shoes for VAT purposes.

Jefford has recently received a substantial legacy and is planning to buy an established hotel in a seaside resort. His wife will help him in running the business. He is expecting modest profits at the outset but hopes that his plans for the business will enable it rapidly to become highly successful.

He is not sure whether to operate the business as a sole trader/partnership or as a limited company.

Outline the considerations he should take into account in making his choice.

Operating as a sole trader/partnership or as a limited company

(a) *Sole trader/partnership*

If the unincorporated format is chosen it would probably be appropriate for Mrs Jefford to be a partner from the outset, since she is helping to run the business. This will enable profits to be shared so as to make the best use of available allowances and lower tax rates. However, it should be borne in mind that the settlements legislation s 660A applies to partnerships as well as to companies. It is important to be able to demonstrate the reality of Mrs Jefford's involvement in the business, to counter any challenge that the partnership constitutes a settlement. If she were an employee, her wages would have to be justifiable as 'wholly and exclusively for the purposes of the trade' and the national insurance cost would be significantly higher (as illustrated in (b) if the business is run through a company).

For 2006/07, sole traders and partners pay income tax at 40% on income (after personal allowances) in excess of £33,300, whether profits are retained in the business or withdrawn. Tax on income below that level is at the basic and starting rates.

National insurance contributions are payable as follows for 2006/07:

Class 2 £2.10 per week

Class 4 8% of profits between £5,035 and £33,540, with an additional 1% payable on all profits over £33,540.

The tax and Class 4 national insurance contributions on the profits plus the tax on any other income is payable by half-yearly instalments on 31 January in the tax year and 31 July following (based on the net tax/Class 4 NI payable for the previous year), with a balancing payment on the following 31 January, eg 31 January and 31 July 2007 and 31 January 2008 for 2006/07.

If accounts were made up to 31 March annually, the profits taxable in 2006/07 would be those of the year/period to 31 March 2007. If the accounting date was 30 April, the 2006/07 profits would be those for the year/period to 30 April 2006. Choosing a 30 April year-end means that the taxable profits of one year are broadly those of the previous year, which is an advantage if profits are rising, although there is a compensating disadvantage of bunching of profits when the business ceases (see Example 17 for further details).

(b) *Limited company*

For the year ended 31 March 2007, company profits (which are after deducting directors' remuneration) below £300,000 are taxed at 19%. Lower rates of tax applied to profits below £50,000 in the 2000 to 2005 financial years, making limited companies even more attractive at that time.

Mr and Mrs Jefford would be liable to income tax as employees on any amounts drawn from the company (except to the extent that the drawings were to reduce loans made by them to the company) and the remuneration would attract employer's and employee's national insurance contributions as follows:

Employer

For 2006/07, employers pay no contributions on the first £97 per week (£5,035 per annum) but pay 12.8% on the earnings (and taxable benefits in kind) above that amount, with no upper ceiling. The contributions reduce profits chargeable to corporation tax.

Employee

For 2006/07, employees pay no contributions on the first £97 per week and 11% on earnings between £97 and £645 per week. Earnings in excess of this upper earnings limit (equivalent to £33,540 per annum) are subject to a 1% charge. Employees earning between £84 and £97 a week do not pay contributions but their rights to benefits are protected (see Example 47 part (a)).

The time lag between earning profits and paying the tax would be nine months for company profits (provided the company's profits do not exceed £1,500,000), with tax and national insurance on directors' fees being payable as and when remuneration is paid or credited. If the company did not pay the remuneration within nine months after the end of the period of account, it would be deducted in calculating corporate taxable profits in the accounting period in which it was *paid*, thus increasing the tax liability of the earlier accounting period and reducing that of the period in which paid.

(c) *Comparison of alternatives*

The rates of corporation tax payable by a company tend to be lower than the rates of income tax on the same profits payable by partners or sole traders. For example, profits of up to £300,000 are taxed at 19% in a limited company, whereas for 2006/07 for a sole trader the effective rate (excluding NIC) would be approximately 23% at £50,000 profit, or 37% at £300,000. The whole profits of a sole trader or partnership are taxed, whether drawn out or reinvested, while in the limited company proprietors/employees are taxed (possibly at higher rates) on dividend/salary taken. If funds are required for reinvestment, and are not drawn as salary or dividend, then the profits retained by the company are taxed only at the rate of corporation tax (not potentially higher rate income tax), facilitating growth. However, if all funds are to be extracted, in many circumstances the tax burden will be substantially similar, while the NIC cost is very much higher on salaries taken from a company.

In the case of fluctuating profits, the sole trader/partner may waste allowances or basic rate bands in a bad year, while paying higher rate tax in a good year, although averaging arrangements exist for farmers and authors. A limited company may pay a constant justifiable salary, which is deductible for corporation tax and may generate losses, to use up bands and allowances each year. The losses may be relieved against future profits, subject to loss relief rules.

The administration of cash flow tends to be simpler in a limited company, but tax liabilities may arise earlier, as some taxes are paid by PAYE monthly or quarterly, and the corporation tax is due nine months after the year end. The sole trader/partner's situation is complicated by the requirement to make payments on account. In the case of fluctuating profits there may be no requirement to make a payment on account one year, followed by the need to pay two years' worth of tax within six months the following year. If the profits for the year ended 31 March 2006 (for example) did not give rise to payments on account, and for the year ended 31 March 2007 produced a tax liability of £10,000 (for example), £15,000 (£10,000 + POA £5,000) would fall due on 31 January 2008, and £5,000 on 31 July 2008. The difficulties of finding a large lump sum have to be compared to the advantages of any deferral of payment.

In addition, if the business is required to operate the CIS scheme, deductions suffered by a company can be offset against its PAYE liability, whereas for sole traders they are set against the year's liability unless a special claim is made.

The national insurance cost is significantly higher for limited companies than for the self-employed – see 90.2(a). If profit is drawn as salary, the NIC cost will tend to negate the potential saving offered by the difference between corporation tax rates and income tax rates.

NIC cost may be controlled by paying a relatively low salary, liable to NIC, supplemented by dividends, which are not liable to NIC, but this is increasingly being prevented by HMRC interpretations, or uncertainties of tax law. The tax credit on dividends covers the shareholder's basic rate liability (but is not tax deductible so the profit has been taxed on the company at 19%), and the higher rate of 32.5% (less tax credit of 10%) is charged only to the extent that the recipient is a higher rate taxpayer. The dividends save national insurance, but not do not make significant income tax savings unless they use additional bands and allowances of individuals who would not have been entitled to be paid salary.

From 6 April 2000 the 'IR35' rules obliged certain companies to pay salary and NIC in place of dividends, see Example 88. The workers of these companies are taxed on substantially their whole income, as are the self-employed, but with fewer deductible expenses, and much higher NIC cost.

From April 2003 HMRC issued guidance on the application of the settlements legislation to dividends paid other than to the company's main earner – see 58.4. If the guidance is not in point, and the dividends can be paid according to shareholdings, the limited company format is likely to result in a lower tax cost. The simplified pensions regime, which commenced on 6 April 2006 may offer opportunities for tax efficient investment. Sole traders or employees may contribute up to 100% of salary, a much higher percentage than was previously possible. A limited company may set up a company pension scheme, contributing higher amounts still if it wishes. However, to obtain a corporation tax deduction, the amounts paid must be expended wholly and exclusively for the purposes of the trade.

Contributions paid by the self-employed save higher rate tax, but not NIC. Company contributions, provided they are paid wholly and exclusively for purposes of the trade, save both NIC and corporation tax. HMRC guidance states that, in determining whether contributions are wholly and exclusively for purposes of the trade, it will look at the overall remuneration package, not the proportion that pension bears to salary. The application of this practice has not been tested, but it appears that a combination of salary, pension and dividend should result in a lower tax cost for limited companies than for the self-employed.

As Jefford expects the business to become highly successful, the limited company can help control tax by ensuring higher rate tax is paid only on profits taken out of the company, which he may be able to control. As the business is a hotel, profits would derive from Mrs Jefford's efforts as well as his, so it should be possible for her to receive dividends as well as salary, using her bands and allowances, as well as controlling NIC cost (see 58.4 for considerations of the settlement legislation). The couple's willingness to make pension contributions also needs to be ascertained, as a company pension scheme would allow tax-efficient pension provision in the company.

(d)   *Illustrative computations*

The following illustrations show that the point at which the company format will give a lower tax bill than the partnership depends on the extent to which profits are left in the company or drawn as profits/dividends.

Illustration 1

Say business profits before tax and national insurance are £90,000 and there are no other sources of income. Assume Mr and Mrs Jefford each drew a salary of £38,335, which after the personal allowance of £5,035 leaves £33,300 to use the basic and starting rate bands. The comparative position for 2006/07 is (see overleaf):

		Partners £	Company director	£
Profits/remuneration		90,000	38,335 x 2	76,670
Personal allowances		(10,070)		(10,070)
Taxable income		79,930		66,600
Tax thereon:	4,300 @ 10%	430		430
	62,300 @ 22%	13,706		13,706
	13,330 @ 40%	5,332		
	79,930	19,468		
Class 2 NI		218		
Class 4 NI		4,688	Employees' NI	6,367
Total personal tax and NI		24,374		20,503
Company's tax and NI:				
Profits			90,000	
Less: Directors' remuneration			(76,670)	
Company's NI thereon @ 12.8% on (76,670 – 10,070)			(8,525)	8,525
Taxable profits			4,805	
Tax thereon (£4,805 @ 19%)			913	913
			3,892	
Total tax and NI liabilities		£ 24,374		£ 29,941

The partnership format shows an overall tax/NIC saving of £5,567. However, any further increase in profits would be subject to 41% in the partnership against 19% in the company up to £300,000. Thus, if profits increased by £12,000, tax under the partnership format would rise by £4,920 (= £12,000 @ 41%), whereas tax under the company format would increase by £2,280. The rate differential is 22% where the company's taxable profits are below £300,000.

There would be further higher rate tax liabilities on the company retentions of £3,892 if they were paid out as dividends.

Illustration 2

Say profits were only £40,000 and, under the company format, each spouse took a salary of (say) £7,500, with the balance as a dividend. The position would then be:

		Partners £	Company director		£
Profits/remuneration		40,000	7,500 x 2		15,000
Dividends (19,739 as below + (⅑) 2,193)					21,932
Personal allowances		(10,070)			(10,070)
Taxable income		29,930			26,862
Tax thereon:	4,300 @ 10%	430	4,300 @ 10%		430
	25,630 @ 22%	5,639	630 @ 22%		139
	29,930	6,069	21,932 @ 10%		2,193
			26,862		2,762
Tax credit on dividends					(2,193)
					569
Class 2 NI		218	Employees' NI (7,500 – 5,035)		
Class 4 NI (20,000 – 5,035) @ 8% x 2		2,394	@ 11% x 2		542
Total personal tax and NI		8,681			1,111
Company's tax and NI:					
Profits			40,000		
Less: Directors' remuneration			(15,000)		
Company's NI thereon @ 12.8% on (15,000 – 10,070)			(631)		631
Taxable profits			24,369		
Tax thereon (see working below)			(4,630)		4,630
Profits paid out as dividend			19,739		
Total tax and NI liabilities		£ 8,681			£ 6,372
Saving through company format		£ 2,309			

Working

		£
Profits before remuneration		40,000
Salaries	15,000	
Employer NI Contributions	631	(15,631)
Profit for tax		24,369
Tax at 19%		4,630

(e)   *Other considerations*

1.   Sole traders and partners are fully liable for the debts of the business and can ultimately be made bankrupt. The liability of company shareholders is limited to the amount, if any, unpaid on their shares. This protection is not, however, as valuable as it seems because lenders, landlords and sometimes suppliers often require directors to give personal guarantees. There are also major compliance requirements for companies under the Companies Acts. Companies whose turnover is not more than £5.6 million (and balance sheet total of not more than £2.8 million) need not have their accounts audited (although many banks may still insist on it), but there are administration costs in filing annual returns and keeping minutes of meetings. It is possible to form a limited liability partnership, which will broadly give partners the same

protection as members of limited companies, although it will also involve similar accounts and filing requirements (see Example 26 part (b) for details).

2. Certain social security benefits, in particular jobseeker's allowance and earnings-related retirement pension, are not available to the self-employed.

3. More generous loss reliefs are available to individuals than to companies in the early years of a new business (see Example 30).

4. The capital gains cost to shareholders of receiving retained profits as capital distributions or a capital gains structured purchase of own shares under TA 1988 s 219 has been reduced substantially by the enhanced business asset taper relief rules introduced by FA 2000 and FA 2002. For example, a capital realisation of retained profits which have been subject to (say) 19% small companies' rate can be extracted at an overall tax rate of just over 27% after just two years' worth of business asset taper relief, as demonstrated below:

	£	Tax £
Profit	100,000	
Corporation tax @ 19%	(19,000)	19,000
Retained profit = gain	81,000	
Taper relief @ 75%	(60,750)	
Capital gain	20,250	
CGT @ 40%		8,100
Total tax		27,100
Effective rate		27.1%

The effective rate would be even lower if other reliefs are available.

5. Some family companies have in the past paid remuneration at around the national insurance threshold, either just below to avoid paying national insurance at all or just above to protect entitlement to contributory benefits. (Benefits can now be protected without paying any contributions, since there is a 'nil' band of contributions on earnings between £84 and £97 a week, as indicated in part (b) of the example.) This is only possible if the family members are directors, because it is necessary for family companies to comply with the National Minimum Wage Act 1998 (see Example 58 explanatory note 1). At the post-October 2006 minimum rate of £5.35 per hour, a weekly wage of £97 represents less than 19 working hours. The DTI have confirmed that proprietorial directors will only be subject to the minimum wage rules if they have an *explicit* contract of employment with the company. If they are engaged in normal work in their capacity as a director, they will not fall within these regulations, since the regulations do not apply to office holders of the company. See the Revenue's Tax Bulletin of December 2000 for further comments.

6. Although PAYE on payment of salaries may involve higher NI contributions than apply to sole trader profits, salary payments can facilitate use of rate bands and allowances between years of fluctuating profits. Furthermore, the PAYE is paid regularly, and removes the wide swings of the payment on account system that causes difficulties to sole traders.

7. CIS deductions paid by a company can be set against its PAYE liability monthly or quarterly, while those of sole traders cannot.

A.   (a)   Fred, who is a married man aged 81, has the following income in 2006/07:

	£
State pension	6,105
Occupational pension (no tax deducted under PAYE)	2,305
Building society interest taxed at source (gross amount)	2,100
Dividends (including tax credits)	3,100

He paid £1,560 net to a charity under a gift aid declaration. Show the amount of income tax repayable to Fred for 2006/07.

(b)   Set out the differing ways in which tax efficient donations may be made to charities.

B.   (a)   The Blackhills Rugby Club has registered as a Community Amateur Sports Club (CASC) with effect from 1 April 2002. Its income and expenditure in the year ended 31 March 2007 comprise:

			£	
Income:	Membership fees		9,800	
	Donations under gift aid (including tax)		6,000	
	Bar takings – members	18,600		
	– non-members	5,400	24,000	
	Letting of club house		2,600	
	Building society interest		200	42,600
Expenditure:	Purchases for bar		12,600	
	Expenses of running club house		8,400	
	Maintaining pitches		4,800	
	Travelling costs of teams		8,100	
	Costs of members' 'night out'		4,800	
	Other costs of running club		1,900	40,600

Compute any amounts liable to corporation tax for the year ended 31 March 2007, assuming appropriate claims for relief are made.

(b)   Show the effect on part (a) if Blackhills Rugby Club had sold part of its land in the year to 31 March 2007 for £200,000, resulting in a potential chargeable gain of £63,000.

(c)   John, a 40% taxpayer, was a member of Blackhills Rugby Club. He pays a membership fee of £50 per year and has made a further donation to the club of £50 under gift aid. Set out the effect on John's tax liability in 2006/07.

A. (a) **Fred – Income tax repayment 2006/07**

		Income £	Income tax paid £
State pension		6,105	
Occupational pension		2,305	–
Building society interest (gross amount)		2,100	420
Dividends (including non-repayable credits £310)		3,100	
		13,610	420
Personal allowance (75 and over)		7,420	
Taxable income		6,190	
Income tax thereon:			
On non-savings income			
(6,105 + 2,305 – 7,420)	990 @ 10%	99	
On savings income (non-dividend)	1,160 @ 10%	116	
	940 @ 20%	188	
On dividends	3,100 @ 10%	310	
	6,190	713	
Less: Age related married couple's allowance (restricted – see below)		273	
		440	
Less: Tax credits on dividends		310	130
Repayment due			290
Tax retained on gift aid payment 1,560 + (22/78) = 2,000 @ 22%			£440

Personal allowances, including married couple's allowance, are restricted to ensure that the amount of income tax (and capital gains tax) charged is no less than the amount deducted from the gift aid donation.

Surplus married couple's allowance available for transfer to wife:

	£	Tax saving @ 10% £
Allowance due	6,135	614
Used	2,730	273
Transfer to wife	3,405	341

(b) **Tax-efficient giving to charity**

Gifts to charity by individuals

Where an individual wishes to make a donation to a charity, tax relief can be obtained provided certain steps are taken. The gift can be made in a number of ways:

(i)   Payroll giving

(ii) Direct gift to charity with an appropriate declaration (gift aid)

(iii) Gift of stocks and shares or land and buildings

A company can also make tax allowable gifts to a charity, including gifts of stocks and shares or land and buildings, without completing a declaration.

Payroll giving

Employees can authorise their employer to deduct an amount from their pay to be given to charity (ITEPA 2003 ss 713–715). This reduces their pay for tax and tax credit purposes (but not for national insurance contributions). Tax relief is therefore given at the employee's highest marginal rate on the donation. The payroll deduction is passed to an HMRC approved payroll giving agency, who will pay the amount to the nominated charity (after deducting an administration fee, typically 5%). Voluntary payments to the agency by the employer to cover running costs are allowed against the employer's taxable profits (TA 1988 s 86A).

Gift aid donations by individuals (FA 1990 s 25)

A gift to charity by an individual qualifies for relief at the payer's highest tax rate if a gift aid declaration is made, providing the donor is within the scope of UK tax, ie a UK resident, or a Crown employee serving overseas, or a non-resident making the payment out of income or capital gains chargeable to UK tax. The gross gift is also deductible in computing income for tax credits.

The declaration can be made for the specific gift, or for all gifts to that charity, and can be made in writing or orally. A donor giving orally need only give his name and address. The charity must, however, then keep an auditable record of the declaration, retaining a copy for inspection by HMRC. A written declaration must contain (SI 2000/2074):

- the donor's name and home address

- the charity's name

- a declaration that the donation is to be treated as a gift aid declaration

- a note explaining that the donor must pay income tax or capital gains tax equal to the tax deducted from the donation

- date of declaration

- donor's signature.

A written record of an oral donation needs to contain the same information as a written declaration (except the donor's signature) and must in addition state that the donor may cancel the declaration within 30 days. Such a cancellation would be retrospective. Donors may cancel a declaration at any time, and all subsequent donations are not then gift aid payments.

Payments under a gift aid donation are treated as being net of basic rate tax. The charity can recover the tax deducted providing it can show an audit trail between the gift and the donor. This can be a cheque, standing order, direct debit or by physical evidence of cash giving, eg an envelope.

Higher rate relief is obtained by increasing the basic rate band by the gift plus the tax thereon. The tax on a cash gift of £3,900 is 22/78 x 3,900 = £1,100, giving a gross gift of £5,000. The basic rate band would be (33,300 + 5,000 =) £38,300. The rate of tax saved depends on the rate payable on the top slice of the taxpayer's income. For illustrations of the various marginal rates see Example 4 part (c). The basic rate band is not extended when computing top slicing relief on life policy gains (see Example 95).

Where necessary, personal allowances are restricted to ensure that sufficient tax is paid to cover the tax on the donations, as illustrated in part (a) of the example. If there is still insufficient tax, HMRC will issue an assessment to recover the shortfall.

In computing the tax that has been charged on the donor's income, notional tax on scrip dividends and on life policy gains is excluded, but the tax taken into account is before deducting relief for married couple's allowance or relief for maintenance payments (see Example 1 explanatory note 6). Any unused married couple's allowance can be surrendered to the spouse.

Tax credits

A gift which obtains relief under FA 1990 s 25 is deductible from income for tax credits. For claimants who are within the threshold taper of 37% this increases the value of reliefs and reduces the net cost of a gift of £100 to £41. To achieve this result the taxpayer makes an actual gift of £78 (which is net of £22 tax, ie £100 gross).

Income for tax credits is reduced by the gross gift of £100 giving an increase in tax credits of £100 × 37% = £37.

	£
Gift to charity	78
Increase in tax credits	37
Actual cost	41

If the claimant is within the threshold taper of 6.67% a similar effect occurs. However as income may be liable to the higher rate the net cost of a gross gift of £100 would then be £53.33 again with an actual payment of £78 ie:

	£	£
Gift to charity		78.00
Higher rate relief (40–22)	18.00	
Increase in tax credits	6.67	24.67
Actual cost		53.33

See Example 5 for details of tax credits.

The relief for a gift carried back for tax purposes, but relieved on a current year basis for tax credit purposes can be even more dramatic. The carryback to 2005/06 could give relief at the higher rate whereas relief in 2006/07 could give tax credits relief at 37%.

	Net cost if 37% taper applies in 2006/07 £
Gift to charity	78
Higher rate relief 2005/06	(18)
Increase in tax credits 2006/07	(37)
Actual cost	23

Benefits from charities

A charity may make a token gesture to show its appreciation for a donation. The maximum benefits that a donor can receive are:

Aggregate donations in tax year £	*Maximum aggregate value of benefits*
0 – 100	25% of aggregate donations
101 – 1,000	£25
1,001 – 10,000	2.5% of aggregate donations
10,001 +	£250

The provision of free or reduced price admission for the donor (or family) to the property of a heritage or wildlife conservation charity (such as the National Trust) is disregarded (this provision is only disregarded from 6 April 2006) provided the right applies for at least one year or the gift is at least 10% more than the normal admission price (FA 1990 s 25(5H) as added by F(No 2)A 2005).

Transactions with substantial donors

To counter perceived abuses of the charities' exemptions involving benefits provided to substantial donors, from 22 March 2006, FA 2006 ss 54–58 restricts tax reliefs for charities and individuals in certain circumstances.

The legislation targets payments made by a charity to substantial donors or persons connected with them. A substantial donor is a person donating gifts on which tax relief was received of at least £25,000 in a year, or £100,000 over a period of six years. The donor remains a substantial donor for tax purposes for five years after making such donations.

The transactions affected are sales or leases of property, provision of services, and loans or investments between the charities and the donors. Transactions of the type that truly independent parties would have entered into are not affected, nor are arm's length transactions, provided they do not form part of an arrangement to avoid tax. A company wholly owned by the charity cannot be a substantial donor.

The value or monetary equivalent of such transactions will be treated as non-charitable expenditure, and the charity's reliefs will be restricted, according to the method shown in part B.

Gift aid donations by companies (TA 1988 s 339)

Companies may make tax-efficient gift aid donations in a similar way to individuals, although they are not required to make gift aid declarations. The same limits apply as for individuals where the company receives a benefit from the gift. Company donations will not be relieved if they are conditional or the company or a connected person receives one or more benefits from the donation and their value exceeds the relevant limits in TA 1988 s 339(3DA). From 1 April 2000 companies no longer deduct tax from gift aid donations, including covenanted payments. Tax relief is obtained by treating the payment as a charge against profits for corporation tax (see Example 48 explanatory note 11).

Gifts of shares or land and buildings

Under TA 1988 s 587B, tax relief is available for gifts to charity by individuals or companies of shares or securities listed or dealt in on a recognised stock exchange (which includes shares on the Alternative Investment Market), units in authorised unit trusts, shares in open-ended investment companies and interests in offshore funds. From 6 April 2002 (1 April 2002 for a gift by a company) the relief is extended to a gift of a freehold or leasehold interest in UK land (s 587C). The relief is equal to the market value of the security or land on the date of disposal plus costs, less any consideration received. This relief is in addition to the capital gains relief, which treats the disposal as giving rise to neither gain nor loss. An individual deducts the relief from his total income, saving tax at his top tax rate, and a company deducts the relief as a charge against profits (see Example 48 explanatory note 11). Care must be taken if relief is given against dividend income, as the top rate of tax includes the non-repayable tax credit of 10%. Relief for a higher rate taxpayer may therefore be restricted to 22½%, with a non-repayable credit of 10%.

No deduction is given for tax credits for gifts of shares or land and buildings.

Gifts in kind by traders

See Example 48 explanatory note 4 for the allowance of salary payments for employees seconded to charity and business gifts to charity of trading stock and plant and machinery.

Tax-efficient giving

An individual who wishes to give to charity needs to consider the tax implications of the gift. If he has quoted securities pregnant with gains, then a gift of such securities will not give rise to a capital gains liability and in addition will attract relief at his highest rate (say 40%, but possibly only 22½% if the top slice of income is dividend income, as indicated above). Alternatively, if the individual can get his employer company to make the donation then the amount is paid out of funds that have not borne national insurance contributions.

For regular giving an indefinite gift aid declaration should be made to the charity. All gifts should be recorded and entered on the individual's tax return, so that the charity may recover the basic rate tax and the donor may obtain higher rate relief if appropriate. For one-off gifts the charity should be able to provide a gift aid declaration in the form of an envelope into which the gift is placed. Donors should maintain a record of the gift and report it on their tax return.

B. (a) **Blackhills Rugby Club – corporation tax liability year ended 31 March 2006**

As Blackhills Rugby Club is a registered Community Amateur Sports Club (CASC) under FA 2002 s 58 and Sch 18, its income is exempt from corporation tax as follows, the exempt amount being restricted to the extent that its expenditure of £40,600 includes non-qualifying expenditure (see explanatory note 10):

	£
Trading income (exempt limit £30,000 – mutual trading with own members ignored)	5,400
Property income (exempt limit £20,000)	2,600
Gift aid income	6,000
Building society interest	200
	14,200
Less: Restriction re non-qualifying expenditure on members' night out $14,200 \times \dfrac{4,800}{42,600}$	1,600
Exempt income	12,600

Corporation tax is not payable on membership fees, so the only chargeable profits are the proportionate amount of non-qualifying expenditure of £1,600 and tax thereon at 19% is £304.

(b) **Effect on (a) of sale of land with gain of £63,000**

If Blackhills Rugby Club has a potential chargeable gain of £63,000 from the sale of land, which is used for qualifying purposes, this would be added to the amount on which exemption is claimed in (a) above, but the restriction of the exemption because of the non-qualifying expenditure would increase to:

$$(14,200 + 63,000 =) \quad \frac{77,200}{105,600} \times 4,800 = £3,509$$
$$(42,600 + 63,000 =)$$

The chargeable amount of £3,509 would be taxed at 19%, resulting in a tax charge of £667.

(c) **Tax treatment of John in respect of payments to Blackhills Rugby Club**

Membership fees cannot be treated as gifts for gift aid, so John will only be eligible for higher rate tax relief on £64, being £50 gift aid payment plus basic rate tax retained of £14. This will reduce John's higher rate tax liability by £64 @ 40% = £26, less tax retained £14 = £12.

Explanatory Notes

Paying sufficient tax to cover tax on gift aid payments

1. A taxpayer may offset allowances and reliefs against income of different descriptions in the most advantageous way unless the legislation provides otherwise (TA 1988 s 835). See Example 4 explanatory note 5.

    A taxpayer is entitled to retain the basic rate income tax deducted from gift aid payments providing he pays at least that much tax. Fred in part (a) of the example must therefore have £440 of tax chargeable. Income tax or capital gains tax charged in the year can be used to cover that amount. If, however, the tax charged would otherwise be lower than the tax retained, personal allowances are restricted to keep a sufficient amount in charge (FA 1990 s 25).

    If Fred had not made a gift aid payment, he would have claimed full married couple's allowance as follows:

	£	£
Tax as at 91.2 above	713	420
Less: MCA	614	
	99	
Less: Tax credits on dividends (restricted)	99	–
Repayment due		420

    The effect of the payment to charity has been to decrease Fred's repayment, but to fully utilise the tax credits on dividends and to enable surplus married couple's allowance to be transferred to his wife:

	£
Value of transferred married couple's allowance	341
Less: Reduction in repayment (420 – 290)	130
Further dividend tax credits now used (310 – 99)	211

    Without the charitable payment Fred would be required to offset his married couple's allowance of £614 before using non-repayable tax credits (see Example 4 explanatory note 5) and as the resultant tax would be less than the tax credits, an amount would be unrelieved. If, however, Fred was aware of that position before the commencement of the tax year he could elect jointly with his wife for her to claim married couple's allowance of £3,405, ie:

	£	£
Tax at 91.2 above	713	420
Less: MCA (6,135 – 2,350 to wife =)		
3,785 @ 10%	379	
	334	
Less: Tax credits on dividends	310	24
Repayment due		396
MCA claimed by wife 2,350 @ 10%		235
		631

    The effect would be that none of the dividend credits would then be wasted.

2. If restricting personal allowances still leaves insufficient tax in charge to cover the charitable payments, HMRC will issue an assessment to recover the shortfall. For example if Fred's net gift had been £15,600, with tax retained of (22/78 =) £4,400, his tax position would be:

		Income £	Income tax paid £
Income as before		13,610	420
Tax thereon:	2,150 @ 10%	215	
	6,260 @ 22%	1,377	
	2,100 @ 20%	420	
	3,100 @ 10%	310	
	13,610	2,322	
Less: Tax credits on dividends		310	2,012
Tax payable under self-assessment			1,592
Tax retained on gift aid payment			4,400
Tax charged			2,322
Tax to be collected by HMRC assessment			2,078

Full married couple's allowance of £6,135 would be available for transfer to Fred's wife.

3. The tax available for offsetting tax relief under the enterprise investment scheme or venture capital trust scheme, or foreign tax credits, is after the deduction of the tax deemed to be retained on charitable payments.

4. If, after restricting personal allowances to nil, insufficient tax has been paid, then in computing the amount of the excess to be assessed, the tax charged does not include notional tax (on non-qualifying distributions, scrip dividends and life policy gains), tax at the basic rate on patent royalties and other annual payments, and tax treated as deducted when a loan to a close company participator is released.

Settlor-interested trusts

5. Where a trust is caught by the anti-avoidance legislation in ITTOIA 2005 part 5 Chapter 5, the trust income is deemed to be that of the settlor in certain circumstances. If such a trust gives money to a charity, ITTOIA 2005 s 628 provides that the amount taxable on the settlor is reduced by the amount (plus tax) given to the charity. The rate of tax recoverable by the charity depends on the tax payable by the trust. A charge on a settlor is also prevented where an interest free loan is made to a charity (ITTOIA 2005 s 620).

For detailed notes on the taxation of trusts see the companion to this book, Tolley's Taxwise II 2006/07.

Exemption for trading activities

6. Where a charity carries on a trade as part of its charitable purpose (for instance, employing beneficiaries of the charity in producing goods) any profits will usually be exempt from tax. Before 22 March 2006, such charities risked losing tax relief on all profits if some of its activities did not qualify as charitable. From that date, profits may be apportioned between those generated by the primary purpose of the charity, and those generated by other activities.

Where trading is to raise funds, the profits are taxable unless the turnover does not exceed £5,000 or, if greater, the lower of £50,000 and 25% of the charity's gross income (FA 2000 s 46).

Revenue Concession C4 exempts profits for certain small-scale fund-raising events. Fund raising events are exempt providing there is no distortion of competition with commercial providers and there are no more than 15 events of the same kind in one location in a year.

Small events do not count towards the limit providing aggregate takings for such events do not exceed £1,000 a week.

Trading subsidiaries

7. If the trading activities are likely to exceed the above limits, it is advisable to set up a wholly owned trading subsidiary, which will be liable to corporation tax on its profits. Any gift aid payments to the charity parent will, however, be deductible as a charge before computing the corporation tax due. (This arrangement effectively converts trading profits which would fall to be taxed in the hands of the charity into tax exempt investment income (see TA 1988 s 505).) A gift aid payment made by a wholly owned trading subsidiary to its charity parent can be treated as paid in an accounting period falling wholly or partly within the nine months before the payment was made (TA 1988 s 339).

   Before 22 March 2006 this did not apply to payments made by a company wholly owned by more than one charity. These were treated as distributions, and so did not achieve corporation tax relief for the paying company. ICTA s 339 is amended from 22 March 2006 to ensure that such payments benefit from gift aid relief.

Gift aid donations in 2003/04 and later years

8. Where on or after 6 April 2003 an individual makes a gift aid donation before 31 January in the tax year and before the tax return for the previous tax year has been filed, an election may be made to deem the donation to be made in the previous tax year. The carryback is not effective for tax credit purposes. The gift aid payment will still be deducted from the tax credits income on a current year basis. This is *not* treated as a claim affecting the earlier year under TMA 1970 Sch 1B but as a payment of the earlier year. The tax liability of the earlier year is reduced accordingly, as well as the payments on account for the current year.

   For example a taxpayer who was a higher rate taxpayer in 2005/06 makes a gift aid payment of £780 on 31 May 2006. This is included, by election, in his 2005/06 tax return filed on 30 September 2006. The effect on his tax liability and payments will be:

	£
Reduction in 2005/06 higher rate tax	
780 x 100/78 = 1,000 @ (40 − 22)%	180
Reduction in 2005/06 payment on account	90
Saving on payment due 31 January 2007	270
Saving on payment due 31 July 2007	90
Additional amount due 31 January 2008 (being savings in payments on account)	180

9. From April 2004 taxpayers are able to nominate a charity to receive all or part of any tax repayment due to them. To nominate a charity the taxpayer must enter its charity code. This is available by ringing 0845 9000 444 or from the HMRC website at www.hmrc.gov.uk/charities/charities-search.htm. That repayment will itself be a gift aid donation to be included for tax relief on the tax return for the year in which the payment is made to the charity. Any election made by a taxpayer will not affect the timing of any repayment due to the recipient charity.

Amateur sports clubs

10. Under FA 2002 s 58 and Sch 18, tax exemptions are available to registered community amateur sports clubs (CASCs) similar to those available for charities. In order to register as a CASC, a club must be open to the whole community without discrimination, have reasonable membership fees, be organised on an amateur basis and have as its main purpose the provision of facilities for and promotion of participation in one or more eligible sports. To date over 3,750 clubs have registered with HMRC.

    This requires the club to be non-profit making, providing ordinary benefits for its members and their guests and using surplus funds for the purposes of the club. On dissolution any surplus must be paid to another CASC or eligible sports ruling body or a charity. Ordinary benefits are:

- provision of sporting facilities

- provision and maintenance of sports equipment

- provision of suitably qualified coaches or coaching courses

- insurance and medical cover

- reimbursement of travel expenses of players and officials for away matches

- post-match refreshments for players and match officials

- sale of food and drink associated with the sporting activities.

The club may pay staff, who may be members of the CASC, on an arm's length basis.

Once registered, a club is exempt from tax on trading income (before expenses) not exceeding £30,000, property income (before expenses) not exceeding £20,000, interest and gift aid income, and capital gains, providing in each case the whole of the income or gains as the case may be is applied for qualifying purposes (ie providing facilities for, and promoting participation in, one or more eligible sports, as designated by statutory instrument) and claims for the exemptions are made.

If expenditure is incurred for non-qualifying purposes, the total amount of exempt income and gains is reduced by the proportion of non-qualifying expenditure to total income and gains. The effect on exempt income is illustrated in part B(a) of the example, where the cost of the members' night out is non-qualifying expenditure, as its main purpose is not that of providing facilities for participating in sport, resulting in part of the exempt income becoming chargeable income. Where there are exempt gains, as in B(b) the non-exempt amount is increased.

11. From 6 April 2002 registered CASCs are treated as charities for gift aid payments by individuals, and can recover the basic rate tax on donations but not membership fees. The reliefs for gifts of shares and land and buildings (see part A of the example) and business gifts of stock or plant (see Example 48 explanatory note 4) also apply, as do the capital gains tax and inheritance tax charitable gifts exemptions.

12. If a CASC ceases to hold an asset for qualifying purposes (without disposing of it), or ceases to be registered, the club will be treated as having disposed of and reacquired the asset at market value. The resultant gain will be chargeable to corporation tax.

Your notes of a meeting with new clients Mr Powell and Mrs Powell, both aged 48, include the following points:

(i)   Your new clients have two children aged 15 and 19 (both in full time education – no income).

(ii)   Mr Powell owns 60% of the share capital of P Transport Ltd, the remainder being held by Mrs Powell. The company was formed four years ago, and specialises in continental transport and storage. Its profits for the year ending 31 March 2007 are expected to amount to £330,000 after remuneration of:

	Mr Powell	Mrs Powell
	£	£
Salary	22,000	3,000
Bonus (to be paid August 2007)	38,000	–
	60,000	3,000

Both Mr and Mrs Powell work full time in the business. Mr Powell is a director and Mrs Powell is a book-keeper and also company secretary. The business is estimated to be worth £1,500,000 as a going concern. Although the company normally has a small credit balance at the bank, it has overdraft facilities of £100,000.

P Transport Ltd is based in an enterprise zone. The company anticipates needing additional storage facilities in the near future. A suitable site in the zone would cost in the region of £160,000 and the required building £500,000. Bank finance would be available for this project.

Your clients have suggested that the new building could be held either:

●   by the company for its own use, or

●   by Mr and Mrs Powell personally, but let to the company, or

●   by a self-administered pension fund, again let to the company.

(iii)   Mr Powell has a retirement annuity policy with an annual premium of £2,000. He does not have any life assurance cover.

(iv)   Mr and Mrs Powell have a joint building society account containing £2,000, a house in joint names worth £440,000 (with a £75,000 mortgage) and no other assets except a director's account with the company to which Mr Powell's bonuses have always been credited and which currently stands at £60,000.

(v)   Both Mr and Mrs Powell have made wills leaving their estate to the other or, if there is no surviving spouse, equally to their children.

They have changed their adviser because they are unhappy with the lack of tax planning advice they have been receiving.

Prepare, giving reasons for the points chosen, a memorandum of tax planning points to discuss with Mr and Mrs Powell.

(a) **Children**

Both

Could they be paid by the company for legitimate services rendered in holidays, weekends etc? Watch the national insurance cost and compliance with PAYE and employment regulations. Could the amount be enhanced by the company making pension contributions for them, contributing up to £3,600 each per year?

Elder aged 19

See (b) below for possible transfer of shares to the elder child, the dividends on which would be covered by the available basic rate band.

Younger aged 15

Any income produced on funds provided by parents (but not capital gains in a bare trust) would be taxed on the parent not on the child until the child reaches age 18 or marries before that date (ITTOIA 2005 s 629). This is subject to a de minimis exemption whereby each parent can provide funds to produce income of up to £100 per annum. This de minimis exemption is only available if the child's total income from that parent does not exceed that amount. It does not cover the first slice of a larger sum.

If money is being provided by the parents for savings, invest in sources that do not produce income, eg investment bonds, or are not liable to income tax, such as national savings certificates including children's bonus bonds. Share transfers could be made as in (b), which would be effective for inheritance tax, but income from dividends would for the time being be treated as the parents' income. Premiums of up to £270 per annum may be paid by the parents for a qualifying friendly society policy for the child without breaching the parental settlement rules.

(See Example 2 part (c)(ii) for notes on bare trusts.)

(b) **Shareholdings in P Transport Ltd**

Any transfer of shares by Mr or Mrs Powell should take into account the following:

(i) They need to retain control of the company between them if they are to continue to qualify for 50% business property relief for inheritance tax purposes on any property owned by them and rented to the company. The shares themselves qualify for 100% business property relief, no matter how small the holding.

(ii) For capital gains tax, any chargeable gains on the transfer of shares could be held over by the use of business assets gifts holdover relief (TCGA 1992 s 165 – see Example 84), or by use of deferral relief under the Enterprise Investment Scheme (EIS) (TCGA 1992 Sch 5B – see Example 94). Their shareholdings should not, however, fall below the required level for the gifts relief (which is not less than 5% of the voting power). This could give rise to capital gains tax on a subsequent sale after all such relief has been used (see Example 84).

(iii) As P Transport Ltd is an unquoted trading company, the shares in the company will qualify for business assets taper relief (see Example 74 part (a)(i)). Any building owned by Mr and Mrs Powell and let to the company will also qualify for business assets taper relief. However, if gifts relief is claimed, the gain held over is not reduced, and taper relief can only be claimed by reference to the donee's period of ownership.

For relief claimed under the deferral provisions of the EIS, the taper period runs to the time of disposal of the original asset. The gain is then suspended behind the EIS investment and becomes chargeable net of taper relief when the EIS investment is sold or disposed of. Taper relief is not taken into account in arriving at the gain to be deferred, ie the amount of EIS investment must cover the gain before taper relief.

(iv) Mr & Mrs Powell need to be aware of the HMRC views on transfer of shares to children, and its interaction with the anti-avoidance legislation in ITTOIA 2005 Part 5 Chapter 5 (see Tax

Bulletin 64). This legislation applies if the purpose of the transfer is to divert income to another and tax is saved. For the rules to apply the transfer must be:

– bounteous, or

– not commercial, or

– not at arm's length, or

– in the case of a gift between spouses wholly or substantially a right to income.

The provisions are unlikely to apply in this case if the gift of shares to a child is part of a strategy of involving the child in the business with a view to eventual succession to the company, provided that no dividend waivers occur to increase the income on the child's shares, and the shares are given absolutely.

Subject to the above, share transfers to the children will ensure that future growth is in the hands of the next generation, that dividends are at once treated as the income of the elder child and in three years' time will be treated as that of the younger child, and that the children are given some incentive within the business.

A return of the issue of shares in connection with employment is required on Form 42 by 6 July following the tax year in which it is made. HMRC guidance makes it clear that the return it is not required in the cases of transfers arising through personal or family relationships, and cites the example for the shares being transferred to children working in the business as an illustration of this.

Transfers now rather than later will avoid any risk that the 100% business property relief for inheritance tax is reduced by subsequent legislation, and if the shares cease to qualify for business property relief, the seven year period during which a transfer is only potentially exempt will have begun that much sooner. On the other hand, lifetime transfers are subject to capital gains tax and although the gains may be deferred they would not arise at all if the shares were still held when the parents died. However, providing the children had held the shares for at least two years at the time of disposal, capital gains tax taper relief at 75% will be available, as well as their own annual exemptions (£8,800 for 2006/07) and starting and basic rate tax bands. Note that if 100% inheritance tax business property relief remained available, there would be no charge either to capital gains tax or inheritance tax if the shares were held until death.

A shareholding by a self-administered pension fund could also be considered, subject to the same considerations and also depending upon what other involvement the fund is to have with the company (since HMRC imposes limits on the fund's participation in company shares/loans back). Furthermore the trustees of the fund may not be happy with a holding of unquoted shares which they may find difficult to realise. For further comments on self-administered schemes see (e) below.

(c) **Profits of P Transport Ltd**

The projected profits are within the marginal tranche for small companies' rate (TA 1988 s 13). The anticipated £30,000 excess over £300,000 would therefore attract corporation tax @ 32.75% = £9,825, compared with the small companies' rate of 19%, giving additional tax on that slice of the profits of £4,125.

If profits could be sensibly reduced by £30,000 or more the tax saved on the £30,000 would be £9,825. (See (e) and (f) below for ways in which profits might be reduced, in addition to the possibility of paying increased remuneration.)

(d) **Remuneration to Mr and Mrs Powell**

Although charged in arriving at the company's taxable profits in the accounting periods to which they relate, any bonuses to Mr and Mrs Powell are taxed on them in the tax years when they are received. The August 2007 bonus of £38,000 would therefore be taxed on Mr Powell in 2007/08, and the bonus paid to him in 2006/07, if any, would be taxed in 2006/07. For the purpose of the calculations which follow it has been assumed that a similar bonus was paid in August 2006.

Increasing Mrs Powell's remuneration

Since Mrs Powell works full time in the company and is also company secretary, a substantial increase in her remuneration could be justified and is in any event necessary to satisfy the requirements of the national minimum wage. If her earnings were substantially increased and Mr Powell's correspondingly reduced, then higher rate tax would be saved. The saving in higher rate tax would, however, be partly offset by increased employee's national insurance contributions at 11%, since Mr Powell is only paying contributions of 1% on his earnings above £33,540 for 2006/07, whereas his wife would pay contributions on the extra remuneration above £5,035. (Employer's contributions are at 12.8% whether remuneration is paid to husband or wife, on earnings above £97 per week (£5,035 per annum).) Increased remuneration could be used to support a personal pension contribution (see (f) below). See also (e) below re the alternative possibility of the company starting a self-administered pension scheme.

Paying dividends instead of remuneration

The company could consider paying dividends. In 2006/07 the dividends would be taxable at Mr and Mrs Powell's respective marginal rates of 32½% and 10% unless substantially increased remuneration were paid to Mrs Powell in 2006/07. The comparative amounts of tax and national insurance on remuneration and dividends would depend on whether the company had taken steps to reduce its profits to within the small companies' rate limit of £300,000 (see (c) above). Assuming that Mr Powell was taking remuneration of £33,540 or more and thus paying national insurance contributions of 1% on his earnings above £33,540 as an employee, the comparative position for him in 2006/07, using a profit figure of £1,000 and a marginal tax rate of 40% for illustration, would be:

		£	£
Paying extra remuneration:	Company profit		1,000
	Remuneration	886	
	Employer's national insurance 12.8%	114	1,000
	Profits chargeable to corporation tax		–
	Gross remuneration		886
	Income tax at 40%	354	
	Employee's NIC @ 1%	9	363
	Net of tax amount		£ 523

		£	£
Paying dividend:	Company profit	1,000	1,000
	Corporation tax at 19%/32.75%	190	327
	Dividend to shareholders	810	673
	Tax credit at 1/9	90	75
	Shareholders' income	900	748
	Income tax at 32½%	292	243
	Net of tax amount	608	505

It would therefore be more tax efficient for Mr Powell to take extra remuneration if the company was liable at the marginal small companies' rate and to take dividends if it was liable at the small companies' rate.

Any dividends paid would be taxed separately on each of Mr and Mrs Powell, so the amount saved through paying dividends instead of remuneration to Mrs Powell would be the employer's and employee's national insurance contributions plus the saving in Mr Powell's higher rate liability unless her revised income exceeded the basic rate threshold. Mrs Powell would receive a net of tax dividend of £810 out of £1,000 company profits if the profits were taxed at the small companies' rate and her income was wholly within the basic rate limit.

Depending upon the tax rates in future years and other planning considerations (eg need to have remuneration to be able to make desired level of pension payments), dividends could be a suitable method of using the basic rate band available to Mrs Powell without having to justify services provided by her in order to substantiate her level of remuneration. She should, however, receive a salary that is sufficiently high to satisfy the national minimum wage (eg 35 hours per week @ £5.05 (£5.35 per hour from October 2006) minimum wage rate = £9,191 per annum) and also to fully utilise her personal allowance. The tax credits on dividends are no longer repayable. The payment of dividends would normally affect the value of the company's shares, but where a company is closely controlled by the family, other bases of valuation would also be considered, such as assets or earnings.

See also the notes in Example 27 on HMRC's current view on husband and wife companies and the settlement provisions of ITTOIA 2005 ss 625–626.

(e) **Acquisition of new storage facilities**

The building cost of £500,000 would attract a 100% initial allowance if the building is new and in an enterprise zone, but unfortunately the opportunity to make such an investment expires on October 2006, so it is unlikely to be practicable. Otherwise it would qualify only for writing down allowances at 4% of cost per annum. In neither case would there be any relief for the land (CAA 2001 s 272).

If the building is acquired by the company, the available allowances would reduce the company's taxable profits, and indeed if a loss were thereby created, that loss could be carried back against the profits of the previous year.

Mr and Mrs Powell could acquire the building personally and obtain the same allowances, firstly against rent income and then other income of the tax year of purchase and then the following tax year (TA 1988 s 379A). If they acquired the building and let it to the company, inheritance tax business property relief of 50% would be available on an eventual transfer of ownership, so long as between them they continued to control the company. The charging of rent would not affect their entitlement to business assets taper relief, provided they are accepted as incurred wholly and exclusively for the purposes of the trade.

The rental income arising is free of NI contributions, and taxed on Mrs Powell in proportion to her ownership of the property. If eventually a capital gain arises, the CGT regime for individuals, including 75% business property taper relief, is much more favourable than for companies.

Acquisition through self-administered pension fund

If purchase in an enterprise zone is not practicable, and even if it is, a purchase by a self-administered pension fund has much to commend it. The contributions to the fund from company profits would be allowable in calculating the company's corporation tax, provided they are accepted as incurred wholly and exclusively for the purposes of the trade. Furthermore, the rent paid to the pension fund by the company would be allowable in computing company profits but not taxable in the pension fund so long as the fund had HMRC approval, and the ability of the pension fund to acquire the land effectively gives tax relief on the land purchase, since the pension fund first has to be put in funds out of pre-tax company profits.

From 6 April 2006, the amount that the fund may borrow is limited to 50% of the fund value for new loans, but the effective maximum that the company can contribute to the fund in the 2006/07 year is £215,000. However, it is unlikely that the company would obtain a tax deduction on an amount as large as £215,000, as discussed under paragraph (f) below. Any excess over £215,000 would result in an annual allowance charge of 40% on the excess on Mr Powell.

The fund could take out appropriate life assurance cover on Mr and/or Mrs Powell in order to provide a capital sum with which to pay death in service benefits to the dependants in the event of the death of one or the other whilst they were still working for the company. This could be an important consideration in view of the present lack of life cover.

One difficulty of purchasing property through a self-administered pension fund is the need to provide liquid funds to acquire an annuity on retirement. This can be minimised by deferring the purchase of an annuity until an age not later than 75 and paying the pension from the income produced by the scheme assets until that age. In addition, it might be that the children will have joined the firm and become members of the pension fund. From their contributions liquid funds could be available to purchase the annuities for Mr and Mrs Powell, so that the need to sell the property at a later date is removed.

For detailed notes on company pension schemes see Example 72.

(f) **Pension provision for Mr and Mrs Powell (TA 1988 ss 618-655)**

See (e) above for the possibility of the company starting a self-administered pension scheme to provide pensions for Mr and Mrs Powell.

Mr Powell already has a retirement annuity policy but neither Mr nor Mrs Powell has a personal pension policy. Points to consider in relation to each of them are as follows.

Mr Powell

It will not be possible to make further contributions to the existing policy in 2006/07 in respect of the period if the company embarks upon a self-administered scheme of which Mr Powell is a member.

Mrs Powell

If Mrs Powell's remuneration is increased as suggested in (d) above, any increased remuneration could be used to support a personal pension premium of £5,035, £3,600, or 100% of her earnings of 2006/07, if greater.

From 6 April 2006, pension contributions may be made on the basis of annual and lifetime contributions for company schemes (£215,000 for 2006/07), or up to the greater of £3,600 or 100% of earnings for individual contributions. Individuals who make contributions within the limits will obtain tax relief.

Thus, Mr Powell may make a personal contribution to a registered pension scheme of up to 100% of his gross earnings by 5 April 2007, possibly by drawing out the balance on his director's loan account to fund it. The contributions will be paid net, but will attract higher rate tax relief.

Prior to 6 April 2006, the maximum amount that could be contributed to a pension was based on a much lower proportion of salary. Therefore, in order to make the pension contribution it was necessary to pay a comparatively high salary, subject to PAYE and employer's NI contributions. This, together with the indifferent stock market performance of the past few years, provided a disincentive to pension contributions.

The relatively high statutory contribution limits that apply from 6 April 2006 are likely to mean that many small businesses will be able to contribute as much as they can afford to the company schemes (individual schemes' contributions are limited to 100% of salary). Unlike salary, pension contributions do not involve the payment of PAYE or NI contributions, and unlike dividends they are (under certain circumstances (see below) deductible for corporation tax.

If a bonus of £30,000 were paid for Mr Powell, to reduce corporation tax by £9,825 (£30,000 @ 32.75%), the relative tax implications of salary and pension contribution would be:

	Salary £	Pension £
Gross	29,703	30,000
NI Contributions at 1%	297	nil
Income tax at 40%	11,881	nil
Cash available	17,822	nil
Corporation tax saving	9,825	9,825
Total tax (cost)/saving	(2,353)	9,825

If Mr Powell is not in need of funds, he may well find a pension contribution of £30,000, at a cost of £20,175 (£30,000 – £9,825), extremely attractive. He might also be tempted to make pension contributions for other family members instead.

The pension contribution must be paid by the year-end, whereas an accrued bonus may be paid up to nine months after, to obtain a tax deduction.

If in the past his salary level was determined by his wish to make pension contributions, he may now be tempted to reduce the salary and corresponding NI contributions, and increase dividends instead without NI contribution cost. This could act as a driver towards dividends, a trend that HMRC will be keen to counter.

Where statutory contribution limits do not limit the payment of contributions, HMRC's refusal to allow a full tax deduction is likely to do so instead. The fact that there are high allowable limits for contributions does not necessarily mean that contributions paid by businesses will be deductible against profits. Contributions paid by businesses are deductible only if expended wholly and exclusively for the purposes of the employer's trade.

However, HMRC guidance specifies that it is the remuneration package in total that is considered for the wholly and exclusively test, and that the proportion of pension contributions to salary will not be relevant in the case of ordinary employees.

It is extremely likely that the deductibility of pension contributions against employers' tax will be a subject of contention as the new rules come into force, and pension contributions are made taking them into account. The rules of the deductibility of pension contributions are the same as those for the deductibility of salaries, but whereas the existence of PAYE deductions discourages excessive salary, there is no such disincentive for owner managers in providing for retirement. It is probable that the rules on deductibility of remuneration will, in practice, be refined.

In the past there has been no objection to salaries at any level paid to owner-directors out of annual profits of their company, and no indication has been made that this attitude will change. Indeed, it would be hard to reconcile (for example) the IR35 rules with any limitation on payment of annual profits as remuneration. This would seem to open the way to salary sacrifice schemes.

Large or unusual contributions by controlling directors are likely to be the subject of HMRC scrutiny, and uncertainty on the part of the taxpayer and tax adviser. Although the proportion of contribution to salary should not be an issue, a particularly high proportion will presumably raise the question as to whether it was paid for purposes of the trade, or for purposes of saving tax.

HMRC has published in its Business Income Manual in BIM46001: Specific Deductions: Registered Pension Schemes, which provides guidance on deductibility of contributions in various circumstances, and the following paragraphs summarise the key points of this guidance.

Contributions, if tax deductible, are deductible in the period they are paid only, unless spread by tax law (which occurs if there is an increase of over 210% in contributions and the contribution exceeds £500,000, see Example 37). If the accounts charge is different to the contribution paid, the computation must be adjusted to make it reflect the amount paid.

Contributions will always be treated as revenue expenditure, not capital expenditure.

Contributions forming part of a normal remuneration package will be tax deductible. The contribution is looked at in the context of the overall remuneration package, not a stand-alone amount. The proportion of pension contribution to other remuneration is not considered for this purpose, so salary sacrifice schemes for ordinary employees should not jeopardise the tax deduction. The annual contribution limits must be borne in mind, and individuals who are able to sacrifice a material amount of salary may be controlling directors, in which case the circumstances will be scrutinised separately.

The normal situation is that contributions will be tax deductible, except if there is an identifiable non-trade purpose, or a contribution of exceptional size.

One example would be a contribution made as part of arrangements for going out of business. It will be important to demonstrate that payments made towards cessation of a business are for the purposes of the trade. The guidance clearly specifies that payments made to fund shortfalls in company schemes under Pensions Act 1995 s 75 arise from obligations of the trade, and if made after cessation of trade are deductible as post-cessation expenses. If such a payment is made in the accounting period following cessation of trade, it will be treated as an expense of the final trading period.

The main focus of HMRC scrutiny is likely to be on directors, who are also controlling shareholders, or employees who are close relatives or friends (not defined) of the business proprietors or controlling directors.

If their total remuneration package (of which contributions are part) is similar to that of unconnected employees in genuinely similar work, then the contributions will be accepted as wholly and exclusively for the purposes of the trade. If not, the existing guidelines on amounts purporting to be remuneration of directors in BIM47105 will be followed, seeking to disallow all or some of the contribution.

Amongst the considerations to be borne in mind, according to HMRC's BIM46001, are:

"To find out whether the payment was made for the purposes of the taxpayer's trade it is necessary to discover the taxpayer's object in making the payment. The general rule is that establishing the object behind making the payment involves an inquiry into the taxpayer's subjective intentions at the time of the payment.

The 'purposes of the trade' means 'to serve the purposes of the trade'.

The 'purposes of the trade' are not the same as 'the purposes of the taxpayer'.

The 'purposes of the trade' does not mean 'for the benefit of the taxpayer'.

The 'purpose for making the payment' is not the same as 'the effect of the payment.'

This clearly allows wide scope for judgment and dispute, and may lead to initial uncertainty. It may become necessary to provide proof that certain employees are not friends. Any proposal to make large or unusual contributions for proprietors, controlling directors or their friends or relatives will need to be carefully considered.

Company contributions to personal pension schemes

An alternative possibility is for the company to make payments into personal pension policies for Mr and Mrs Powell. Provided such payments are made within the accounting year, ie by 31 March 2007, a corporation tax deduction is available. The payments would save both employer's and employees' national insurance contributions. The earnings on which contributions may be based will again be those of the basis year as indicated above, with a minimum allowable amount of £3,600. Any contributions paid by Mr and Mrs Powell will have to be taken into account to compute the maximum payable.

(g) **Personal investment**

The company apparently has adequate cash resources taking into account its overdraft limit. The withdrawal of the £60,000 standing to the credit of Mr Powell's loan account would involve the company in paying additional bank interest, but this would be tax relievable against its corporate profits, and Mr and Mrs Powell could personally use the £60,000 for tax-efficient investment, including utilising available retirement annuity/personal pension premium limits.

With tax relief for mortgage interest on house purchase loans no longer being available, it would also be sensible to consider reducing the house mortgage.

(h) **Wills**

Whilst leaving their estates to the other and failing that to the children ensures that no inheritance tax is payable on the first death (IHTA 1984 s 18), it wastes the tax free threshold (currently £285,000, subject to any chargeable transfers within the seven years before death).

They should therefore consider leaving an appropriate amount to the children and/or a discretionary trust on the death of the first of Mr and Mrs Powell, and so ensure that the tax free threshold of the first to die is not wasted. Care must be taken to ensure that the survivor is adequately provided for, but this should be possible with the company from which earnings can accrue, and from the pension fund.

In any event, a survivorship clause is essential, denying the entitlement of the surviving spouse unless he/she survives the other by a stipulated period not exceeding six months (IHTA 1984 s 92). There is no point in the survivor inheriting the estate of the other in the unfortunate event of deaths in quick succession.

In considering both the wills and the proposed lifetime transfer of shares in P Transport Ltd for the benefit of the children, it is important to emphasise to the clients the practical dangers if a surviving parent were left with a minority interest in their own company.

Care should also be taken to determine the possible source of any bequest to a discretionary fund or child on the first death. If that legacy were to include shares then a specific bequest is advisable to ensure that the relevant business property relief is given in full against that bequest. If the gift were to be part of residue with the balance to the spouse then the provisions in IHTA 1984 s 39A would apply to restrict the available relief. For detailed notes on inheritance tax see the companion to this book Tolley's Taxwise II 2006/07.

(i) **Pre-owned assets**

Although not immediately of concern to Mr and Mrs Powell, they should be made aware of the income tax implications of inheritance tax planning involving the gift of property and the subsequent use or enjoyment of that property by the donor. The provisions are contained in FA 2004 Sch 15.

With effect from 6 April 2005 a free-standing income tax charge will apply to the benefit of using a property, chattel or intangible asset that was formerly owned by the taxpayer. A similar charge will apply to the use of such property at low cost or to the use of such assets purchased with funds provided by the taxpayer.

The income tax charge will not apply

(i)   To property given away before 18 March 1986 (FA 2004 Sch 15.3(2), 15.6(2) and 15.8(2)).

(ii)   If the property was transferred to a spouse or civil partner (or to a former spouse/civil partner under a Court Order) (Sch 15.10(1)(c)). This also applied where the property is held in trust and the spouse/civil partner or former spouse/civil partner has an interest in possession (Sch 15.10(1)(d)).

(iii) If the property remains within the estate of the former owner for inheritance tax, or the 'Gift with Reservation' rules apply, then the income tax charge does not apply (Sch 15.11).

(iv)   If the property was sold by the taxpayer at an arm's length price (Sch 15.10(1)(a)).

(v)   Where the assets of an estate have been redirected by a deed of variation (IHTA 1984 ss 142–147) then the deed of variation applies to the asset from date of death for the pre-owned asset rules (Sch 15.16).

(vi)   To property transferred into an interest in possession trust for the benefit of the former owner. This is excluded from the income tax charge because the property remains in the estate of the donor for inheritance tax purposes. However the exemption ceases when the interest in possession comes to an end (Sch 15.10).

(vii)   Where the gift is of property and the former owner has given part of their interest to someone with whom they share occupation or the former owner needs to move back into the gifted property following changes in circumstances (Sch 15.11(1)). These rules are the same as gift with reservation rules for inheritance tax.

(viii) Where the gift was in money and the gift had been made at least seven years before the donor first had use or enjoyment of the property acquired with the funds (Sch 15.10(1A)(c)).

(ix)   If the disposal was an outright gift covered by an annual exemption, small gifts exemption or was for the maintenance of the family (Sch 15.10(1)(d)(e)).

(x)   To the use of property that has been used in a commercial equity release scheme.

The pre-owned asset charge does not apply in any fiscal year

(a)   Where the former owner is not resident in the UK, or

(b)   Where the former owner is resident in the UK but domiciled elsewhere for inheritance tax purposes, the charge then applies only to UK property, or

(c)   Where the former owner was previously domiciled outside the UK for inheritance tax purposes the charge does not apply to property disposed of before becoming domiciled in the UK (Sch 15.12).

The income tax charge applies to the use of land or enjoyment of land, chattels and intangible assets. For the charge to apply to land the taxpayer must occupy the land (wholly or with others) and either the disposal condition, or the contribution condition must apply (Sch 15.3(1)).

Occupation is a very wide term and could even include usage for storage or sole possession of the means of access linked with occasional use of the property. Incidental usage is not considered to be occupation. This could include

–   Stays not exceeding two weeks each year (one month if the owner is present and it is the owner's residence).

–   Social visits that do not include overnight stays.

–   Domestic visits eg babysitting the owner's children.

–   Temporary stays eg for convalescence after medical treatment or to look after the owner whilst they are convalescing.

However if the property is a holiday home which is only used on an occasional basis by the owner then even occasional visits by the donor could be deemed to be occupational.

The disposal condition is that after 17 March 1986 the taxpayer owned the relevant property or property the disposal of which has directly or indirectly funded the relevant property and has disposed of all or part of that interest otherwise than by an excluded transaction (see above).

The contribution condition is that the taxpayer has since 17 March 1986 contributed directly or indirectly to the purchase of the relevant property otherwise than by an excluded transaction (see note 8 above).

The charge for land is calculated by taking the appropriate rental value less any amount that the chargeable person is legally obliged to pay the owner of the relevant land in the period in respect of its occupation. The appropriate rental value is

$$R \times \frac{DV}{V} \text{ where}$$

R is the rent that might reasonably be expected to be obtained on a year-to-year letting where the tenant pays all rates, charges and council taxes and the landlord bears the cost of repairs, maintenance and insurance.

DV is the contribution that can reasonably be attributed to the cost of the relevant property. If the property, or a property that this property replaced, was previously owned by the taxpayer, its value on valuation date. If the taxpayer only owned, or disposed of, a part of the land, the relevant proportion of its value.

Example — gift of property

For example, John gave a property worth £100,000 to his son Peter in 1994. Peter sold the property for £350,000 in 1999 buying a further property for £400,000. John moves into the relevant property in 2006 when it is worth £1,000,000. The contribution that could reasonably be attributed to the gifted property would be

$$\frac{350,000}{400,000}$$

(being the proportion of the cost of the relevant property funded by John's gift).

That proportion is then applied to the value of the property as at the valuation date of £1,000,000.

$$\frac{350,000}{400,000} \times 1,000,000 = 875,000$$

Contrast this with an example where cash was given.

Example — gift of cash

Mrs Jones, a wealthy widow, wishes to reduce her estate's liability to inheritance tax. In order to do so she gives Catherine, her only daughter, £500,000 in cash in May 2004. Her daughter then buys a property in Cornwall in February 2005 for £700,000. Mrs Jones visits this property and in 2006 decides that she would like to live there each summer, taking up residence on 6 April 2007. For the remainder of the year Mrs Jones continues to live in her London residence. Although Mrs Jones is aged 72 she is in good health and would be expected to live for another 15+ years. She is a 40% income taxpayer. For 2007/08 the annual rental value of the Cornwall property would be £36,000 pa and its open market value on 6 April 2007 is £900,000. Mrs Jones has no legal obligation to contribute towards the costs of that property.

Mrs Jones has provided funds of £500,000 which have been used to buy the Cornwall property she now occupies. The appropriate rental value is

$$£36,000 \times \frac{500,000}{900,000} = £20,000$$

which gives an income tax liability of

£20,000 @ 40% = £8,000 per annum from 6 April 2007.

In this example the gift of cash is compared with the current value of the property, whereas it would appear that if property is given then the DV value is increased by the increase in value of the property between gift and commencement of enjoyment. Although the legislation is unclear in the case of a cash gift it is difficult to see how any increase in the value attributed to the investment decisions of the recipient can be said to be reasonably attributed to the donor of the cash.

V is the value of the relevant land at the valuation date.

Valuation date is set out in SI 2005/724 para 2 as being 6 April in the relevant year, or if later the first day in the year on which enjoyment of the asset occurs.

The first valuation date occurs when use commences, and thereafter the valuation date is the first valuation date for a further four years. The subsequent valuation date is the fifth anniversary date, five years then the tenth anniversary date and so on.

The income tax payable is calculated by adding the appropriate rental value to the taxable income of the donor.

In the case of chattels the charge is based upon 5% pa of the value of the chattel at valuation day with similar rules to land applying to replacement chattels and cash.

For intangibles a charge only arises where they are held within a settlement and the settler retains an interest. Again the liability is based upon 5% pa of the value at valuation date.

Where the asset is only enjoyed for part of a year the charge is reduced accordingly. There is no charge if open market rent is paid for use of the asset, and the charge is reduced by payments made under a legal obligation for the use of the asset.

If the aggregate notional value of the benefit before contribution does not exceed £5,000 then there is no charge (Sch 15.13).

Although the legislation provides that the value of the property shall be the price which the property might reasonably be expected to fetch if sold in the open market at that time (Sch 15.15) under SI 2005/724 valuations will take place when use commences and on each fifth anniversary.

There are provisions preventing a double charge to income tax under both the benefit in kind rules and the pre-owned asset rules (Sch.15.18).

Where a taxpayer is potentially chargeable to income tax by reference to their enjoyment of any land, or chattels, or intangible property for the first time, then they may make an election, the effect of which is that the asset is deemed to be in their estate for inheritance tax and therefore no income tax charge arises. This is a deeming provision, the asset does not actually form part of their estate and therefore there is no uplift in value for capital gains tax when death occurs (Sch 15.20).

If the taxpayer permanently ceases to have occupation or use and enjoyment of the asset then the gifts with reservation rules apply so that a potentially exempt transfer is deemed to have occurred at the cessation of use. If more than seven years have elapsed since last enjoyment of the asset then no charge arises.

The election is required by 31 January following the end of the fiscal year of first use. If use first commences in 2005/06 or earlier the election is required by 31 January 2007 (Sch 15.21–23).

Where the whole of the asset would not be attributed to the donor then a similar restriction will apply to the chargeable amount ie chargeable proportion of asset value is

$$\text{Value} \times \frac{DV}{V}$$

where DV and V have the meaning set out in note 11 above.

Value is at death (if use continues) or at cessation of use if within seven years of death.

The charge is intended to penalise users of inheritance tax avoidance schemes, such as the double trust home loan scheme (the intention of which is to remove the value of the principal private residence from the donor's estate but to enable continued use of the property), or, where the full consideration for the use of the asset is negligible as compared with the open market value of the asset.

However, the charge will also apply to situations where a taxpayer would not expect a charge to arise: for example where a donor gives away assets, eg cash, and then in the future uses property acquired with those assets without paying a full commercial consideration, and does not fall within any of the exceptions for inheritance tax or pre-owned asset exceptions. Previously if the gift was in cash then provided it was made at least seven years before the death of the donor there were no tax consequences. Now an income tax charge can arise.

Example

John gave £300,000 in cash to his daughter, Wendy, on the occasion of her marriage in 2000. She used £200,000 to buy a picture. In May 2005 Wendy moves to Australia on a temporary contract for three years. She leaves the picture with John who hangs it in his hall. The open market value as at May 2005 is £500,000. Wendy returns in May 2008 reclaiming possession of the picture. John is still alive in 2016. Assume an Official Rate of 5% throughout, and that John pays tax at 40%.

There will be a pre-owned asset charge on John of

Valuation day is May 2005.

The picture was funded by John's gift of £200,000.

The charge for 2005/06 is

$$11/12 \times 5\% \times 500,000 \times \frac{200,000}{500,000} \left(\frac{DV}{V}\right) = 9,166 @ 40\% = £3,666$$

The charge for 2006/07 and 2007/08 will be

$$5\% \times 500,000 \times \frac{200,000}{500,000} = 10,000 @ 40\% = £4,000$$

For 2008/09 the calculation is

$$1/12 \times 5\% \times 500,000 \times \frac{200,000}{500,000} = 834 \text{ ie NIL}$$

(Amounts below £5,000 are not charged)

There is no inheritance tax charge. John had a potential exempt transfer in respect of the cash gift for seven years, ie until 2007. Wendy took full bona fide possession and enjoyment of the cash in 2000. The picture cannot be included in John's estate, he does not and never did own that asset. Because the picture is not included in the estate of John for inheritance tax it is not excluded from the pre-owned asset charge. An income tax charge arises because John has the use of property purchased with funds provided by him (and used by him within seven years of the gift of cash).

The charge could be avoided by John electing, by 31 January 2007, to include the picture in his estate for inheritance tax. Providing John is still alive seven years after the picture is returned (May 2015) then there will be no charge to tax.

See also companion book, Tolley's Taxwise II 2006/07, for inheritance tax provisions.

93.1 INDIVIDUAL SAVINGS ACCOUNTS, PERSONAL EQUITY PLANS, TAX EXEMPT SPECIAL SAVINGS ACCOUNTS AND CHILD TRUST FUNDS

Outline the taxation treatment of individual savings accounts (ISAs) and child trust funds and also the ongoing taxation treatment of existing personal equity plans (PEPs).

(a) **Individual Savings Accounts (ISAs)**

1. Individual Savings Accounts (ISAs) were introduced from 6 April 1999 to replace TESSAs and PEPs. Taxpayers were not required to switch TESSAs and PEPs into the new ISAs. TESSAs opened before 6 April 1999 were allowed to run their course and the capital from a maturing TESSA could be transferred to a TOISA (TESSA only Individual Savings Account). Transfers of existing PEP investments to a new manager is allowed.

2. ISAs are available to individuals aged 18 or over who are resident and ordinarily resident in the UK. Someone who becomes non-resident may retain the tax-exempt benefits of existing ISAs but no further investments may be made. Joint accounts are not permitted. ISAs are guaranteed to run for ten years, although there is no statutory minimum period for which the accounts must be held. There is no lifetime limit on the amount invested.

    From 6 April 2001, a person aged 16 or 17 can open a cash mini ISA. Care must be taken to ensure that the funds to open such an ISA did not originate from the child's parents. In that case the income from the ISA would be taxable on the parent under the settlements provisions if, with other such income, it exceeded £100.

3. The ISA regulations are in SI 1998/1870. The annual investment in an ISA may be split into two components:

    (i) cash

    (ii) stocks and shares.

    Cash

    The following investments qualify for the cash component:

    (a) Bank and building society deposit or share accounts (or European equivalent);

    (b) Units in a money market fund;

    (c) Units in a money market only fund of funds;

    (d) Designated National Savings.

    Stocks and shares

    The qualifying investments for the stocks and shares component can be:

    (a) Shares issued in any country and quoted on a recognised stock exchange;

    (b) Securities with at least five years to run (when acquired by the ISA) issued in any country and quoted on a recognised stock exchange;

    (c) Government Securities of UK or European Economic Area countries (or strips thereof) with at least five years to run when acquired by the ISA;

    (d) Units in authorised unit trusts or OEICs (open-ended investment companies) which do not hold more than 50% of value of their investments in securities with less than five years to run;

    (e) Shares in qualifying investment trusts (again the 50% rule in (d) above applies);

    (f) Units or shares in UCITS (undertakings for collective investments in transferable securities), subject to the 50% rule in (d);

    (g) Depositary interests, including CREST depositary interests;

    (h) Cash held pending investment.

4. The maximum investment for years up to 2009/10 is £7,000, of which not more than £3,000 can be invested in cash. (The whole amount may be invested in stocks and shares if the saver

wishes – see note 5.) There is no minimum subscription. Although there is no minimum holding period for the ISA, it is not possible to withdraw and reinvest at will. Once the investment in a component reaches the limit for the year, no further investment in the component may be made in that year, regardless of withdrawals.

5. Savers will have a choice of managers each year, and may make their annual investment through a single manager (called a maxi ISA) or may choose separate managers for each of the two components of the account (mini ISAs). If the latter choice is taken, the maximum investment in the shares mini ISA is £4,000 per annum, whether or not the full available amount has been invested in the cash component.

6. The annual investments in TESSAs taken out before 6 April 1999 did not affect the ISA limits and the capital (but not interest) from TESSAs maturing after 5 April 1999 could be paid into the cash component of an existing maxi ISA, or into an existing cash mini ISA, or into a separate TESSA only ISA, within six months of maturity. The TESSA account cannot, however, be transferred if the TESSA account holder has become non-resident and/or not ordinarily resident in the UK.

7. ISAs are free of income tax and capital gains tax, and where ISA investments are in shares, dividend tax credits (at 1/9th of the cash dividend) were reclaimable for the tax years to 5 April 2004. Where the ISA investment is in securities rather than shares, the 20% tax deducted is reclaimable by the ISA manager. Where interest arises on cash held for reinvestment in a stocks and shares ISA, the account manager has to account for tax at 20% to HMRC. There is, however, no effect on the investor, who is neither treated as having received taxable income nor entitled to a tax refund.

   If tax relief on an ISA is found to have been wrongly given, HMRC may make an assessment on either the account manager or the investor.

8. Shares received from approved profit sharing and savings-related share option schemes and share incentive plans (see Example 87) may be transferred within 90 days into the stocks and shares component of the ISA free of capital gains tax, so long as, together with any other investments, they are within the annual subscription limit. There is no separate single company limit as there was for PEPs, and there is no facility to transfer shares acquired under a public offer or following demutualisation of a building society or insurer. The shares component of an ISA is kept separate from any other holdings of the investor for the purpose of the capital gains rules for matching disposals with acquisitions.

9. The Treasury has introduced an optional 'CAT standard' for ISAs based on reasonable Charges, Access and Terms. To use the standard the component must satisfy the following conditions:

	Cash	Shares
Charges	None	Up to 1% (1½% from 6 April 2005 for first 10 years) of net assets plus stamp duty and dealing charges
Access	Withdrawal within 7 days; minimum amount £10 or less	Minimum £500 a year or £50 a month
Terms	Interest no lower than 2% (1% from 6 April 2005) below base rate, upward changes to be reflected within one month, no other restrictions	Units/shares to be single priced, and at least 50% to be invested in EU shares/securities

In addition the component must:

– use plain English

-    not link with any other product (no bundling)

-    undertake to maintain the CAT standard for existing customers.

10. An investor in an ISA can transfer his investment to another manager. The transfer must be of the whole of the current year's subscription and/or the whole or any part of a previous subscription.

(b) Personal Equity Plans

1. Following the introduction of ISAs, investment in Personal Equity Plans is not possible after 5 April 1999, but all PEP investments already made by that date may continue to be held in addition to investments in ISAs, and investors can still switch fund managers and investments (see supplementary note 7). The PEP regulations are in SI 1989/469.

2. PEP investors could subscribe to a general plan and/or to a single company plan using different managers (if required) in each year. Transfers were allowed, and from 6 April 2001 a single company plan could be transferred to a general plan with the same or a different manager. The transfer could be in cash or securities.

3. Any capital gains and dividends are entirely tax-free, and remain so for as long as the investment is held within the plan. On the other hand, any losses arising on disposals within a plan are not allowable losses.

4. The capital gains exemption on the plan investments does not give an investor any extra tax saving to the extent that the gains would have been covered by the annual exemption, currently £8,500, if realised outside the PEP.

5. Plan managers were able to reclaim tax credits on dividends until 5 April 2004 and either reinvest the credits and the dividends or pass them on to shareholders tax-free, so the exemption from income tax is beneficial to all taxpayers, although depending on the amount invested, the benefit may be significantly reduced by the plan manager's charges.

6. From 6 April 2001 the ISA rules on investments, transfers and administration are applied to PEPs. Furthermore, if the scheme rules permit, an investor can transfer part of a PEP to another manager. Previously the whole of the fund had to be transferred.

7. Where someone holds shares in a company both within and outside a PEP, the capital gains rules are modified so that the PEP shares are treated as held in a different capacity from those held outside the PEP.

8. A planholder may withdraw either cash or all or part of the investments themselves, with no loss of the tax advantages obtained. If investments are withdrawn, their base cost for capital gains tax is their market value at the date of withdrawal.

9. When the planholder dies, the personal representatives are treated as acquiring the plan at its market value at the date of death. The tax exemption ceases on death.

(c) Child Trust Fund

The arrangements for the Child Trust Fund (CTF) were established by SI2004/1450, 2422, and 3369, and apply to children born on or after 1 September 2002.

Every child born on or after 1 September 2002 is eligible for the Child Trust Fund, provided:

-    Child Benefit has been awarded for them;

-    they are living in the United Kingdom (or are children of Crown Servants or personnel in the Armed Forces); and

-    they are not subject to immigration controls.

Special arrangements exist for children in care, where child benefit is not awarded, to ensure that they can benefit from the child's trust fund accounts.

There is no requirement to claim for CTF. Eligibility for the CTF follows the award of child benefit. When the child benefit award has been made, a voucher for £250 is sent to the parent or guardian. The voucher should be presented to a CTF provider (accounts are offered by many banks, building societies, friendly societies and other investment companies), who will open an account on behalf of the child. Accounts available are:

– savings accounts, investing contributions in cash, earning interest;

– accounts investing in the equity of listed companies, which participate in the risks and rewards of the stock market, and which are subject to various levels of fees; and

– stakeholder accounts, offered by all providers, investing in the equity market, but limited in risk and limited to charges of 1.5% of funds.

If an account is not opened by the time the voucher expires (which appears to happen in approximately one third of cases) a stakeholder account will be opened by HMRC on the child's behalf.

Only one account may be opened, there is no facility to open multiple accounts to spread types of investment.

Where the parents' or guardians' income is below the Child Tax Credit threshold (£14,155 for 2006/07) the government will contribute a further £250 on opening the account, and on the child's seventh birthday.

The account is administered by the parent or guardian until the child is 16, when the child must take over the administration, partly to achieve the financial education aims of CTF.

The funds in the account belong to the child. Interest arising on the account will not be taxed on the parents, even if they provided the funds, in contrast to other sorts of investment that they might make on the child's behalf. Parents or others may make contributions to the child's trust fund to the limit of £1,200 a year. For purposes of the CTF a year begins with the child's birthday, except the first period of which runs from the opening account to the child's birthday. In the first period, the amount that may be contributed is not apportioned according to the length of the period, so full £1,200 may be contributed.

There is no access to the funds until the child is aged 18, at which time the child (and no one else) has access to them. There is then no restriction as to the use of the money.

The income generated within the CTF will have no affect on family benefit or tax credits during the time that the CTF account is open.

Early access to funds is allowed in the case of terminal illness of the child, on which HMRC has issued guidance.

Supplementary Notes

ISAs

1.   The legislation relating to ISAs is now contained in ITTOIA 2005 Part 6 Chapter 3 and related regulations.

2.   The aim of ISAs is to encourage more people to save. The low level of the cash component will not, however, enable substantial tax-exempt amounts to be built up and stocks and shares are inappropriate investments for those who do not already have a firm base of low risk investments. Non-taxpayers cannot benefit from a tax-free account, and as far as the stocks and shares component is concerned, basic rate taxpayers receive no income tax savings from April 2004 and have their

investment reduced by account charges. In the same way as for PEPs, the capital gains exemption is not relevant to those with modest portfolios whose gains would be covered by the annual exemption.

3. ISAs can, however, be an alternative to a personal pension plan where the ISA investment could be funded by taking income from a company by way of a dividend rather than remuneration, thus saving national insurance contributions (see Example 92 part (d)). The advantage is most marked where the taxpayer is a basic rate payer only. Although no tax relief is obtained on the ISA investment, the fund is tax-free (apart from non-repayable dividend tax credits from April 2004), and withdrawals may be made tax-free and without any restrictions.

4. Care must be taken with investors who use a cash ISA as a current account. Although the balance in the fund may be below the maximum of £3,000, investments into the fund in any year must not exceed the yearly limit. This is particularly relevant in the first year, because any withdrawals will be of that year's investment.

5. Those who are resident in the Channel Islands or Isle of Man are not UK resident for tax purposes. Those employed by the Crown overseas are, however, treated as performing duties in the UK and are eligible to invest in ISAs. From 6 April 2001 their spouses are also eligible. If an investor becomes non-resident he may retain the ISA but cannot make any further contributions unless and until he becomes resident again. Account managers should be notified immediately when an account holder dies, as the investments are no longer exempt.

6. Prior to 5 April 2005 it was possible to hold a limited amount of funds (up to £1,000 per year) within a life insurance component. To qualify the following conditions must have been satisfied:

    (a) The policy must be on the life of the ISA investor only.

    (b) It must be non-assignable.

    (c) It must be written as a long term policy.

    (d) It must cease when removed from the ISA.

    The policy must not:

    (a) be an annuity, personal portfolio bond or a pension,

    (b) have an ongoing obligation to require payments of premiums,

    (c) be connected to any other policy,

    (d) be used to provide a loan.

    From 6 April 2005 no new investment is possible into the life insurance component.

PEPs

6. The Personal Equity Plan regulations are contained in ITTOIA 2005 ss 694–701 and SI 1989/469. If someone becomes non-resident, they retain the tax-exempt benefits of existing plans. Plan managers need to be notified promptly when a planholder dies, because the investments are then no longer tax exempt.

7. PEP investors (or plan managers on their behalf) are able to switch from one qualifying investment to another without any capital gains tax effect. It is also possible to arrange with the plan manager to transfer a plan to a different plan manager, but there are costs involved.

8. Where money is held on deposit with banks or building societies prior to being invested by the plan managers, interest is received in full rather than tax being deducted from it at source. If such interest is reinvested in the PEP, it is exempt from income tax, but if it is withdrawn it is taxable in full (at the 20% savings rate) unless it does not amount to more than £180 in any tax year.

94.1 ENTERPRISE INVESTMENT SCHEME; VENTURE CAPITAL TRUSTS; CORPORATE VENTURING RELIEF; COMMUNITY INVESTMENT TAX RELIEF

(a) Compare the tax reliefs available under the provisions relating to enterprise investment schemes and venture capital trusts.

(b) Outline the tax reliefs available to a company under the corporate venturing scheme.

(c) Set out the relief available for qualifying investments in disadvantaged communities.

(a) **Enterprise investment schemes and venture capital trusts**

The enterprise investment scheme (EIS) rules are contained in TA 1988 ss 289 to 312 (income tax) and TCGA 1992 ss 150A to 150D and Schedules 5B and 5BA (capital gains tax). The rules for venture capital trusts (VCTs) are in TA 1988 ss 332A, 842AA and Schedules 15B, 28B (income tax) and TCGA 1992 ss 151A, 151B and Schedule 5C (capital gains tax). Both schemes give income tax relief and EIS gives capital gains tax relief where gains are reinvested.

Main provisions applying to both schemes

Qualifying conditions

1. The provisions for both enterprise investment schemes and venture capital trusts require investment in qualifying unquoted trading companies, the first being by direct subscription in the company and the second by acquiring shares in a venture capital trust, which is a quoted company which invests in qualifying unquoted trading companies. Shares on the Alternative Investment Market (AIM) are regarded as unquoted shares for these provisions.

2. Both schemes are available to non-residents, but relief is given only against UK tax liabilities.

3. The respective definitions of a qualifying company are broadly the same, and in each case the definitions exclude companies that deal in land, leasing companies, companies that provide finance, legal or accountancy services, property development, farming and market gardening, forestry and timber production, hotels and nursing or residential care homes (TA 1988 s 297 & Sch 28B, TCGA 1992 s 164I). The total gross assets of the company (and, where relevant, other companies in the same group) must not exceed £7 million immediately before the issue of the shares, nor £8 million immediately afterwards. Before 6 April 2006, these limits were £15m and £16m respectively. Those higher limits continued to apply in respect of shares issued after 5 April 2006 if they were subscribed for before 22 March 2006.

   In relation to groups of companies, a parent company qualifies providing the group's activities *as a whole* are qualifying activities. The test does not have to be satisfied by each group company. A subsidiary company can be a qualifying subsidiary if it is a 51% subsidiary except for property management or research and development subsidiaries which have to be 90% owned.

   For EIS, at the time of the issue of the shares there must not be any arrangements for the company to become quoted, or to become a subsidiary of a quoted company. The VCT provisions allow a VCT to continue to include shares in a company that becomes quoted in its qualifying holdings for a period of five years.

   A clearance procedure is available to enable companies to obtain *provisional* approval from HMRC that their shares qualify for EIS relief.

Guaranteed exit arrangements and guaranteed loans

4. EIS relief is denied where there are arrangements at the time of an individual's investment that protect or guarantee the investment, or set up disposal arrangements for the benefit of the investor.

   Similarly, loans or securities that are guaranteed are excluded from a VCT's qualifying holdings (see note 19), and at least 10% of the total investment in any company must be ordinary, non-preferential shares. The VCT shares must be acquired for bona fide commercial purposes and not as part of a scheme or arrangement whose purpose is tax avoidance (TA 1988 Schedule 15B.1(9)).

Income tax reliefs

5.   EIS gives income tax relief at 20% on shares *subscribed for* up to £400,000 (prior to 6 April 2006 £200,000, and before 6 April 2004 £150,000). The relief is withdrawn if the shares are not held for at least three years (five years for shares issued before 6 April 2000) unless this occurs through the death of the holder.

VCT gives income tax relief at the rate of 30% on shares *subscribed for* up to £200,000 (prior to 6 April 2004 £100,000). The 30% rate has applied since 2006/07. Previously, the rate was 20% although it was temporarily increased to 40% for the two tax years 2004/05 and 2005/06. The relief is deducted from the total bill for income tax. It is not a requirement to have income in to charge at 40%. In addition dividends on VCT shares *acquired* not exceeding £200,000 (prior to 6 April 2004 £100,000) are exempt from tax (the tax credits are not repayable). The shares must be held for at least five years. For shares issued before 6 April 2006, the waiting period was three years (as for EIS).

See also notes 6, 8 and 21.

Shares acquired by subscription or otherwise

6.   The difference between subscribing for shares and acquiring them some other way, for example by purchase from another shareholder or as a gift, should be noted. The income tax relief for EIS and VCT shares and capital gains deferral relief for EIS only apply to shares *subscribed for*, and the capital gains exemption only applies to shares on which income tax relief was given (although income tax relief is regarded as having been given even if the individual's income tax liability was insufficient to enable him to benefit from the full income tax reduction available). The VCT dividend exemptions apply to shares *acquired* up to the £200,000 (£100,000 to 5 April 2004) limit in any year.

Claims

7.   Claims for EIS income tax or capital gains tax deferral relief cannot be made until a certificate EIS 3 has been received from the company, issued on the authority of an officer of the board, stating that the relevant conditions have been satisfied. A company applies for such authority on form EIS 1, but this cannot be done until at least four months after the relevant trade has commenced (which may be up to two years after the company obtains the share subscriptions). The officer's authority will be given on form EIS 2. The claim by the investor may be included in tax returns or amendments to returns if the certificate is received in time. Otherwise claims are made on the form incorporated in the EIS 3 certificate from the company. The overall time limit for claiming the relief is five years from 31 January following the tax year in which the shares are issued.

Claims for VCT relief may similarly be made in tax returns and are subject to the same time limit.

EIS and VCT certificates should be retained as part of the taxpayer's records.

Further points relating to EIS shares

Conditions for income tax relief

8.   EIS income tax relief is given where a 'qualifying individual' subscribes for 'eligible shares' in a qualifying company carrying on or intending to carry on a qualifying business activity, as outlined in note 3 above. The subscription must be wholly in cash and all the shares must be issued to raise money for a qualifying business activity. 80% of the money raised needs to be used for the qualifying activity within 12 months of the issue of the shares or of the commencement of the trade, with the remainder being used within a further 12 months.

A qualifying individual is one who is not *connected* with the company (connected broadly meaning having 30% or more control, or being or having been a director or employee). The investor may, however, become a paid director after the shares are issued. The connected persons rules do not apply to the EIS deferral relief (see note 18).

Eligible shares are new ordinary shares that are not redeemable for at least three years. If any of the requirements for a 'qualifying individual' or 'qualifying company' are breached during a 'relevant period' – broadly, in the three years after the issue of the shares or commencement of trading if later (five years for qualifying individuals for shares issued prior to 6 April 2000) – the relief is withdrawn. The relief is subject to detailed anti-avoidance provisions, including the 'guaranteed exit' provisions in note 4. If the anti-avoidance provisions apply and relief has already been granted, it will be withdrawn and interest will be charged from the end of the tax year in which it took effect if given through PAYE and otherwise from the date on which it was granted.

Minimum subscription

9.   The minimum subscription to any one company is £500, except where the investment is made through an investment fund approved by HMRC.

Carryback to previous year

10.   A claim may be made for one-half of the amount subscribed before 6 October in any tax year to be carried back for relief in the previous tax year, up to a maximum carry-back of £50,000 (before 2006/07, £25,000). The relief will then be given by reference to the tax payable for the earlier year, but it will be *given effect* in relation to the later year (TMA 1970 Sch 1B – see Example 42).

Withdrawal of income tax relief

11.   Income tax relief is not available (or if already given, is withdrawn) if an individual is or becomes connected with the company within the two years before or three years after the shares were issued or trading commenced if later.

There are provisions for withdrawing relief if value is received from the company within the period of one year before the shares are issued or trading commenced if later than three years after that date. It is provided that receipts of insignificant value are ignored. Amounts not exceeding £1,000 will normally be regarded as insignificant. The relief withdrawn where value (other than an insignificant amount) is received is equal to lower rate tax on the lower of the value received and the amount on which relief was given. 'Value received' includes the repayment of loans that had been made to the company before the shares were subscribed for, provision of benefits, purchase of own shares from other shareholders, and purchase of assets for less than market value. It does not, however, include dividends that do not exceed a normal return on the investment. If a shareholder waives his dividend, thus increasing the dividend of an EIS shareholder, that waiver will cause the EIS shareholder to have received value in excess of a normal return.

The cessation of trade will trigger a withdrawal of relief, unless the company commences winding up at the time of the cessation, or as promptly as the circumstances permit, and the winding up is for bona fide commercial reasons and not for tax avoidance purposes. Similarly, the appointment of an Administrative Receiver does not cause the relief to be lost, providing this is done for bona fide commercial reasons and not for tax avoidance purposes.

Income tax relief is also withdrawn if the shares are disposed of within three years after the shares are issued or after trading commenced if later. Where shares are sold at arm's length the clawback of income tax relief is restricted to the lower of the relief originally given or tax at the lower rate on the sale proceeds. If the disposal is not at arm's length the relief is withdrawn completely. Interest on overdue tax normally runs from the date on which the conditions are broken.

12.   TA 1988 s 307 provides for the withdrawal of income tax relief to be effected by an assessment for the tax year for which the relief was given (see Example 40 note 14 for the issue of assessments outside the self-assessment system).

Capital gains deferral relief

13.   All or part of the gains on the disposal of *any* assets (and gains triggered after 5 April 1998 under the now withdrawn reinvestment relief provisions) may be deferred to the extent that qualifying EIS shares are *subscribed* for. There is no limit on the amount that may be deferred under the EIS (although the shares must be eligible shares – see note 8). The period during which the shares must be issued is between one year before and *three* years after the gain arises.

       Deferred gains become chargeable on the disposal of the shares, other than to a spouse/civil partner (the gain or loss on the disposal itself being dealt with separately). Deferred gains also become chargeable if the investor becomes non-resident within three years of acquiring the shares. Deferred gains are not triggered if the investor (or spouse to whom the shares have been transferred) dies. EIS deferred gains are triggered if the shares cease to be eligible shares, or the company ceases to qualify within three years. Shares are treated as ceasing to be eligible shares if the investor receives value (other than an insignificant amount) from the company within one year before or three years after the shares are issued or trading commenced if later.

       When deferred gains are triggered, further deferral is possible into qualifying EIS shares.

14.   Taper relief is not taken into account in arriving at the gain to be deferred, but when the deferred gain is triggered, the taper relief is based on the period of ownership of the asset that gave rise to the deferred gain (see Example 74 part (a)(i)). If the deferral occurred before 6 April 1998, therefore, no taper relief is available. Where an investor has a choice of gains which may be deferred, clearly it is better to defer gains with the lowest entitlement to taper relief.

       Further deferrals do not affect the taper relief available, which is still based on the period of ownership of the asset that gave rise to the deferred gain. This does not apply in respect of EIS shares on which either or both of the EIS income tax relief or capital gains deferral relief have been given, where the shares were issued after 5 April 1998 and disposed of after 5 April 1999. Where there are successive investments in such EIS shares, taper relief is based on the cumulative period of ownership of the EIS shares. This means that the taper relief period in respect of the respective deferred gains arising on the disposal of the first and each successive holding of EIS shares will run from the time that holding was acquired to the time when replacement EIS shares are disposed of without the proceeds being invested in another EIS investment. Any gaps between shares being disposed of and new shares being issued are, however, excluded. The taper relief in respect of an asset on which a gain was deferred when the *first* EIS holding was acquired is still based on the period of ownership of that asset (TCGA 1992 s 150D and Sch 5BA).

Capital gains exemption on disposal of shares

15.   Gains on disposal of EIS shares *subscribed for* up to the £400,000 (£200,000 to 5 April 2006 and £150,000 to 5 April 2004) limit per year (as distinct from deferred gains held over by reference to those subscriptions/acquisitions) are exempt, but only after three years. Relief is available for losses on EIS shares (see note 16).

       Where gains are chargeable, they are eligible for deferral in the same way as any other gains (see note 13 above) and in that event the taper relief position would be as indicated in note 14.

16.   If the disposal results in a loss, relief is available for the loss whether the disposal is within or outside the three-year period, but in calculating a loss, the allowable cost is reduced by the

amount of EIS income tax relief that has not been withdrawn. A loss may be relieved either against chargeable gains, including deferred gains triggered by the disposal, or against income (see Example 77 explanatory note 10).

17.   Where shares have been acquired at different times and some or all of the shares attract EIS relief, disposals are matched with shares acquired earlier rather than later. Where shares were acquired on the same day, disposals are identified first with shares to which neither EIS income tax relief nor capital gains deferral relief is attributable, then with shares to which deferral relief but not income tax relief is attributable, then with shares to which income tax relief but not deferral relief is attributable, and finally shares to which both reliefs are attributable. The normal capital gains tax identification and pooling rules do not apply.

Capital gains deferral relief

18.   As indicated in note 13, gains may be deferred whether or not income tax relief was available on the EIS shares (thus enabling owner/directors to obtain deferral relief where they subscribe for shares). In order for deferral relief to be available the subscription for the shares must be wholly in cash, the issue must not be part of arrangements to avoid tax, and the shares must be issued to raise money for a qualifying business activity and must be used for that purpose within 12 months. Deferral relief is not available where there are guaranteed exit arrangements (see note 4).

Unlike the income tax provisions (see note 11), where a deferred gain is triggered because an individual receives value (other than an insignificant amount) from a company, the whole of the deferred gain is brought into charge (less any available taper relief), regardless of how much value is received.

Further points relating to VCT shares

Qualifying holdings for VCTs

19.   The venture capital trust (VCT) provisions apply from 6 April 1995. To be eligible for VCT relief an investor needs to be aged 18 or over.

VCTs are quoted companies holding at least 70% of their investments in shares or securities that they have subscribed for in qualifying unquoted companies (see note 3) trading wholly or mainly in the UK, at least 30% of the VCT's total investments being in ordinary shares and no single holding being more than 15%. See also note 4 regarding guaranteed loans and the requirement for at least 10% of the total investment in any company to be ordinary, non-preferential shares.

The VCT must not retain more than 15% of its income from shares and securities and companies in which it invests must satisfy the gross assets test in note 3.

To be a qualifying holding the company in which the VCT has invested must use 80% of the money invested for the purpose of the company's trade within 12 months of the issue of the shares to the VCT or of the commencement of its trade if later, with the remainder being used within a further 12 months.

VCT's capital gains exemption

20.   VCTs are exempt from tax on their capital gains. Accordingly there is no relief for capital losses. There are anti-avoidance provisions to prevent the exemption being exploited by means of intra-group transfers, or by transferring a company's business to a VCT or to a company that later becomes a VCT (TCGA 1992 ss 101A–101C).

Withdrawal of income tax relief

21.   The income tax relief will be withdrawn to the extent that any of the shares in the VCT are disposed of within five (for shares acquired before 6 April 2006, three) years (other than to the

holder's spouse/civil partner, or after the holder's death). Where shares are acquired from a spouse/civil partner, the spouse/civil partner is treated as if he or she had subscribed for the shares. The relief will also be withdrawn if the VCT loses its qualifying status within the five (or three) year period. As with EIS relief, the legislation provides for relief to be withdrawn by an assessment (TA 1988 Sch 15B.4).

Investors' capital gains exemption

22. The capital gains exemption on the disposal of VCT shares applies to shares acquired up to the £200,000 (£100,000 to 5 April 2004) limit in any year, whether acquired by subscription or otherwise. There is no minimum period for which the shares must be held. Relief is not available for capital losses.

23. Any disposals of shares in a VCT are matched first with any shares acquired before the trust became a VCT. To decide whether other disposals relate to shares in excess of the £200,000 (£100,000 to 5 April 2004) limit in any year, disposals are identified with shares acquired earlier rather than those acquired later. Where shares are acquired on the same day, shares in excess of the limit are treated as disposed of before qualifying shares. Any shares not identified with other shares under these rules qualify for the VCT capital gains exemption on disposal, and they are not subject to the normal capital gains rules for matching disposals with acquisitions.

    If a VCT loses its qualifying status, shares eligible for the CGT exemption are treated as disposed of at market value (any gain being covered by the exemption) and immediately reacquired at market value. They are then brought within the normal capital gains rules for matching disposals with acquisitions.

Merger of VCTs

24. Regulations take effect from 27 March 2002 to enable VCTs to retain their tax approval when they merge and also to treat them as being approved when they are in the course of winding-up. This enables investors to retain their entitlement to tax reliefs in these circumstances.

Capital gains deferral relief prior to 6 April 2004

25. VCT investment attracted capital gains tax relief on reinvested gains until 5 April 2004. The rules were similar to the EIS relief set out at notes 13–17 above except the VCT shares must have been issued within the period of one year before to one year after the date on which the gain arose. Any gain so deferred will be triggered if the VCT loses its approval.

(b) **Corporate venturing scheme (CVS)**

FA 2000 s 63 and Sch 15 introduced a corporate venturing relief aimed at encouraging companies to invest in small, unquoted, higher risk trading companies and to form wider corporate venturing relationships. HMRC has produced a booklet IR2000 giving details of the scheme. Financial companies that invest by way of business are not eligible to claim the relief. The relief applies to qualifying shares issued on or after 1 April 2000 and before 1 April 2010 in a qualifying company (defined as for EIS and VCT). The company must not be a 51% subsidiary of another company except where the holding company is itself a CVS company. Companies may obtain advance clearance that their shares will qualify.

As with EIS and VCTs, the companies invested in must have gross assets before the investment no greater than £7 million and £8 million afterwards. Before 6 April 2006, these limits were £15m and £16m respectively. Those higher limits continued to apply in respect of shares issued after 5 April 2006 if they were subscribed for before 22 March 2006.

Investing companies are entitled to 20% corporation tax relief on amounts invested in new ordinary shares of a qualifying small company providing the investing company has received from the small company a certificate of compliance that the requirements for investment relief are met. The relief will be given against the corporation tax payable for the accounting period in which the shares are issued. The relief will be withdrawn if the company disposes of the shares within three years, or in certain other circumstances.

It is provided that 80% of the money invested in the small company has to be used for the purposes of the company's trade within twelve months of the issue of the shares or of the commencement of the trade if later, with the remainder being used within a further 12 months. The activities must be carried on by the company that issued the shares or a 90% subsidiary of that company.

When the shares are disposed of, then whether or not the corporation tax relief is withdrawn as a result of the disposal, tax on any capital gain arising may be deferred to the extent that the gain is reinvested in another corporate venturing scheme holding within one year before or three years after the disposal. If capital losses arise on disposals, then instead of setting the losses against capital gains, relief may be claimed for the amount of the loss (net of the corporation tax relief obtained) against the corporate venturer company's income of the current or previous accounting period.

Relief is not available if the corporate venturer company, alone or with connected persons, controls the small company. Connected persons include the corporate venturer's directors but not its employees. The corporate venturer company's holding must not exceed 30%, and at least 20% of the small company's share capital must be held by individuals. There is no minimum investment requirement.

Relief is not lost if the small company becomes quoted during the three year qualifying period providing there were no prior arrangements to do so.

(c) **Community investment tax relief**

Community investment tax relief has been introduced by FA 2002 s 57 and Schedules 16 and 17, effective from 23 January 2003. The relief applies where an individual or company makes an investment in a Community Development Finance Institution (CDFI) accredited under the scheme. The CDFI must use its funds to finance small businesses and social enterprises working in or for disadvantaged communities. The investment may be by loan or by subscription for shares or securities in the CDFI. The relevant conditions have to be satisfied for five years from the date of investment.

Loans to CDFIs

A loan must be for at least five years, but the amount can be advanced over the first 18 months. No repayments can be made in the first two years following the investment date and repayments cannot exceed 25% of the loan by the end of the third year, 50% by the end of the fourth year and 75% at the end of the fifth year. There cannot be any pre-arranged protection against risk other than normal commercial banking conditions.

The amount eligible for relief in the year of investment will be the average balance outstanding over the first 12 months. For the second year it will be the average balance between 12 and 24 months, and for the remaining three years the lower of the average balance for the investment year or for the 18 to 24 month period. Thus in the fourth year it would be the lower of the average balance for the periods 36–48 months or 18–24 months.

Investment in shares and securities

A subscription for shares or securities must be fully paid in cash, with no rights for redemption within five years. Again there cannot be any pre-arranged protection against loss.

Conditions to obtain tax relief

The investor will require a tax relief certificate. The investor must not control the CDFI, or if a partnership, be a partner in the CDFI. Investments must be held by investors in their own names for their own beneficial interest and not as part of a scheme or arrangement to avoid tax.

Relief for individuals

Tax relief is given for five tax years commencing in the tax year in which the investment is made. The relief in each year is the smaller of 5% of the invested amount and such amount as reduces the investor's tax liability to nil. The relief is deducted from the investor's tax liability after giving relief for chargeable event gains on life policies and EIS/VCT relief. Sufficient tax must, however, be left in charge to cover gift aid payments.

Relief for companies

Tax relief for companies is available for the accounting period in which the investment is made and the accounting periods in which the next four anniversaries of the investment date fall. The relief in each period is 5% of the invested amount, restricted to the corporation tax liability of the period. The relief is given after marginal small companies' rate or starting rate relief and corporate venturing relief but before double tax relief.

Withdrawal of relief

If a loan is disposed of, or repaid in excess of the allowable amount, then no claim can be made for that tax year or accounting period. In the case of shares and securities, they must be held on the relevant anniversary date. The CDFI must have accreditation at each of the anniversary dates, otherwise relief is not available for that year/period.

A disposal after the death of the individual investor does not cause the withdrawal of relief. In all other circumstances the disposal of a loan (or part thereof) within the five year period causes withdrawal of relief granted on the whole amount, unless it is a permitted disposal. Permitted disposals include the repayment of the loan by the CDFI, a negligible value or total loss claim under TCGA 1992 s 24 or loss of the CDFI's accreditation. The disposal of shares or securities within five years will also cause all the relief to be withdrawn unless it is after the death of the investor, a permitted disposal (as for loans) or is a sale at arm's length for full consideration. In the latter case the relief granted will be reduced by 5% of the sale proceeds for each year of claim. A sale for more than the subscription amount would therefore result in full withdrawal of relief granted.

Relief is also withdrawn if the investor receives value (other than an insignificant amount) in the six years commencing one year before the investment date. 'Value' is exhaustively defined but it does not include a dividend on shares providing it does not exceed a normal return.

(a)   In December 2001 Joe Friend, who is a widower, attained the age of 65 and retired from his employment. He received from his superannuation fund a lump sum of £50,000 and a pension of £12,220 per annum. He immediately invested £10,000 in a single premium insurance company bond with a life of five years and the other £10,000 in a similar bond but with a life of ten years. For both bonds the compound growth had been 15% pa for the first two years and nil since. Joe has taken annual withdrawals of 5% of the initial investment in each bond. In 2006/07 Joe's other income was the state retirement pension of £7,630 and building society interest of £2,000 (gross).

Calculate Joe's tax liability on the gain arising in 2006/07.

(b)   Show what the position in (a) above would have been if Joe Friend's taxable income after allowances had been £32,753 (savings income remaining as £2,000 building society interest).

(c)   Show the effect on the position in (a) and (b) if, after receiving the proceeds from the five year bond, Joe had made a gift aid donation to charity of £1,560 in February 2007.

(a) **Joe Friend – tax liability on gain on single premium bond in 2006/07**

There is no liability on annual withdrawals from single premium bonds providing they do not exceed 5% of the initial investment.

The annual amounts withdrawn are taken into account in calculating the gain when the bond is finally cashed.

Joe Friend therefore has no liability in 2006/07 in relation to the ten year bond which he still holds. The position on the five year bond that matures in December 2006 is as follows:

		£
2002/03	Initial investment in December 2001	10,000
	15% growth in value	1,500
		11,500
	Less 5% of £10,000 withdrawn	(500)
		11,000
2003/04	15% growth	1,650
	5% withdrawn	(500)
		12,150
2004/05	0% growth	–
	5% withdrawn	(500)
		11,650
2005/06	0% growth	–
	5% withdrawn	(500)
		11,150
2006/07	0% growth	–
	Value on maturity	11,150
	Add annual withdrawals (4 x £500)	2,000
		13,150
	Less original investment	(10,000)
	Profit on bond	3,150

The bond profit is only liable to tax at the excess, if any, of higher rate tax over the lower rate of tax. But it counts as part of income for age allowance, so a tax charge may indirectly result.

Joe's income tax position in 2006/07, taking into account the bond profit, is as follows:

				£
State pension				7,630
Occupational pension				12,220
Savings income – building society				2,000
Profit on bond				3,150
				25,000
Personal allowance (age allowance not available if income exceeds £24,590)				5,035
Taxable income				19,965
Tax thereon:	Non-savings income	2,150 @ 10%	215	
		12,665 @ 22%	2,786	
	Non-dividend savings income	5,150 @ 20%	1,030	4,031
Less lower rate tax deemed to have been paid on bond profit £3,150 @ 20%				630
Tax payable				3,401

Without the bond profit tax on Joe's income would have been as follows:

				£
State pension				7,630
Occupational pension				12,220
Savings income				2,000
				21,850
Age allowance (7,280 – ½ (21,850 – 20,100))				6,405
Taxable income				15,445
Tax thereon:	Non-savings income	2,150 @ 10%	215	
		11,295 @ 22%	2,485	
	Non-dividend savings income	2,000 @ 20%	400	3,100

The bond profit has therefore resulted in a tax charge of (3,401 – 3,100) = £301 (representing the loss of tax relief at 22% on (6,405 – 5,035)).

Top slicing relief is available to reduce the rate of tax charged on the bond profit as indicated in (b) below. This is of no benefit in the above computation, because the relief applies only where a different tax rate would apply to the 'appropriate fraction' (one fifth in this example) of the bond profit. The bond profit of £3,150 falls wholly within the income of £5,150 charged at the lower rate (and no tax arises since the tax on the bond profit is covered by the notional tax treated as deducted) and the appropriate fraction would similarly fall within the lower rate band.

(b) **Joe Friend – tax liability on gain on single premium bond in 2006/07 if taxable income after allowances was £32,753**

To the extent that the bond profit falls within the basic rate band tax is charged at the lower rate. The tax thereon is covered by the notional credit, and the tax payable on the excess is (40 – 20) = 20%. The position is therefore as follows:

	£
Basic rate threshold	33,300
Income	32,753
Basic rate band remaining	547
Bond profit	3,150
Bond profit in higher rate band	2,603
Tax thereon @ 20%	520
Less: Top slicing relief (see below)	440
	80

	£
Annual equivalent of bond profit:	
1/5 x 3,150	630
Within basic rate band	547
Taxed at 20%	83

Tax on annual equivalent = £16, multiplied by 5 (policy years) = £80, therefore top slicing relief is (520 – 80 =) £440.

Tax on income of (32,753 + 3,150 =) £35,903:

		£
Non-savings income	2,150 @ 10%	215
	28,603 @ 22%	6,293
Non-dividend savings income	2,000 @ 20%	400
	32,753	6,908
Bond profit (part) (non-savings income)	547 @ 20%	109
	33,300	
Bond profit (balance)	2,603 @ 40%	1,041
	35,903	8,058
Less: Top slicing relief		(440)
Lower rate tax deemed to have been paid on bond profit	3,150 @ 20%	(630)
		6,988

(c) **If Joe Friend made gift aid payment of £1,560 net, £2,000 gross, in February 2007**

With taxable income before allowances of £25,000 as in (a)

For the purpose of computing age-related personal allowances only, taxable income may be reduced by the gross gift aid payment. Joe Friend would therefore have a revised liability of:

		£	£
Taxable income before allowances		25,000	25,000
Less: Gift aid payment (gross)		2,000	
		23,000	
Age allowance income limit		20,100	
Excess		2,900	
Personal allowance (65 to 74)		7,280	
Less: One half of £2,900		1,450	5,830
Taxable income			19,170
Tax thereon:			
Non-savings income	2,150 @ 10%	215	
	11,870 @ 22%	2,611	
Non-dividend savings income	2,000 @ 20%	400	
Bond profit (non-savings income)	3,150 @ 20%	630	3,856
	19,170		
Less: Lower rate tax deemed to have been paid on bond profit			(630)
			3,226
Amount previously payable as in (a)			3,401
Additional tax saving			175
Tax treated as deducted from gift aid payment 2,000 @ 22%			440
Total saving (effective rate 31%)			615

With taxable income before allowances of (32,753 + 5,035 =) £37,788 as in (b)

Clearly no age allowance is due and therefore income is not reduced by gift aid payments. Instead the basic rate band of £33,300 is increased by £2,000. The increase does not apply, however, when computing top slicing relief on life insurance bonds, so that the top slicing relief remains at £440 as calculated in (b). The position would therefore be:

			£
Taxable income before allowances			37,788
Bond profit			3,150
			40,938
Personal allowance			5,035
Taxable income			35,903
Tax thereon:			
Non-savings income	2,150 @ 10%	215	
	28,603 @ 22%	6,293	
Non-dividend savings income	2,000 @ 20%	400	
	32,753		
Bond profit (part)			
(non-savings income)	2,547 @ 20%	509	
	35,300		
Bond profit (balance)	603 @ 40%	241	7,658
Less: Top slicing relief as in (b)			(440)
Lower rate tax deemed to have been paid on bond profit			(630)
			6,588
Amount previously payable as in (b)			6,988
Additional tax saving			400
Tax treated as deducted from gift aid payment	2,000 @ 22%		440
Total saving (effective rate 42%)			840

Paying a personal pension premium in place of gift aid

The tax liability on the bond in (b) above could be eliminated by Joe Friend paying a pension premium in 2006/07 of £83 gross, £65 net. For the net cost of £65 the tax of £80 on the bond profit would be eliminated and there would be £83 in a pension fund. Although the treatment of pension payments is the same as for gift aid payments, ie the basic rate band is increased by the gross payment, there is no provision denying that increase when computing top slicing relief.

If Joe Friend in (c) had paid a personal pension premium of £1,560 net instead of a gift aid payment then exactly the same relief would be obtained, as total income for age allowance is reduced by gross pension contributions by FA 2004 s 192(5).

Explanatory Notes

Qualifying policies

1. Although life assurance premium relief is not available for policies taken out after 13 March 1984, there are still tax advantages for qualifying policies, in that the proceeds are tax free unless the policy is surrendered less than ten years after the policy was taken out (or, for endowment policies, before the expiry of three-quarters of the term if that amounts to less than ten years).

   The definition of qualifying policy is broadly that the policy must be on the life of the policyholder or his spouse/civil partner, it must secure a capital sum on death, earlier disability or not earlier than ten years after the policy is taken out, the premiums must be reasonably even and paid at yearly or shorter intervals and there are various requirements as to the amount of the sum assured and sometimes as to the surrender value (TA 1988 s 267 and Sch 15).

   If the policy is surrendered before the end of the ten year period (or three-quarters of term), any profit arising is charged to tax in the same way as that on a non-qualifying policy (ITTOIA 2005 s 485) (see 2 below).

Non-qualifying policies

2.   If a policy is not a qualifying policy, the proceeds are free of capital gains tax, but any profit is charged to income tax at the excess, if any, of higher rate tax over the lower rate (ITTOIA 2005 s 530) subject to top slicing relief (see 3 below). Prior to 6 April 2004 the charge to tax was the excess of higher rate (40%) over basic rate (22%).

The most common form of non-qualifying policy is a single premium bond, as in this example. In each year (ending on the anniversary of the policy) withdrawals of not more than 5% of the initial investment may be made without attracting a tax liability at that time (to a maximum of 20 years). Any excess over the 5% limit is charged to tax at the excess of higher rate tax over the lower rate, amounting to 20% in 2006/07 as indicated in part (b) of the example. The 5% limit is, however, a cumulative figure and amounts unused in any year swell the tax-free withdrawal available in a later year. Any annual withdrawals that are not taxed when made are taken into account as part of the profit when the bond matures.

Top slicing relief

3.   In calculating the tax on the bond profit, top slicing relief is available (ITTOIA 2005 s 535). The surplus on the bond is divided by the number of complete policy years that the bond has been held (or since the last chargeable event), and the amount arrived at is treated as the top slice of income to ascertain the tax rate, which is then applied to the full profit.

If there are two chargeable events in one year, top slicing relief is calculated by working out the appropriate fractions for each policy and adding them together to arrive at the amount charged as the top slice of income.

Part (c) of the example shows the effect on top slicing relief of paying gift aid donations and personal pension premiums. The provision preventing a gift aid donation from reducing income for top slicing purposes is in FA 1990 s 25(6). See Examples 91 and 38 for detailed notes on gift aid payments and personal pension premiums respectively.

Age allowance

4.   Although in many instances it is possible to cash in a bond when no higher rate tax is payable, there is a possible tax charge as a result of the withdrawal of age allowance, as illustrated in part (a) of the example. (Note that age allowance for a man aged between 65 and 74 exceeds the normal personal allowance by £2,245. Since the excess is withdrawn at the rate of £1 for every £2 by which income exceeds £20,100, the age allowance ceases to be available when income exceeds £20,100 + (2 x £2,245) = £24,590.)

Losses on single premium bonds

5.   If there should be a loss on a single premium bond, tax relief is not available, but if such a loss occurs in a year when the taxpayer is chargeable at higher rates and earlier withdrawals have been charged to tax, the lower of the amount of the deficiency on the bond and the total amount previously charged to tax on the bond will be allowed as a deduction in calculating the taxpayer's liability to tax at excess rates. The saving will be at the excess of higher rate over basic rate tax for non-savings income, the excess of higher rate over lower rate tax for non-dividend savings income and the excess of the dividend upper rate of 32½% over the dividend ordinary rate of 10% for dividend income (ITTOIA 2005 s 539).

Savings income

6.   Savings income is normally treated as the top slice of income (TA 1988 s 1A). This is, however, subject to ITTOIA 2005 s 535(4) dealing with giving relief for higher rates of tax on life policy gains, which provides that life gains are taken into account *after* savings income to compute the relief. Hence in Joe Friend's case in part (b) of the example the life policy gain was taxed as the top slice of the income regardless of how much of the income was savings income.

Where there are life policy gains and capital gains, only the appropriate fraction of the life policy gains (see note 3 above) is taken into account in calculating *higher rate tax* on the gains (TCGA 1992 s 6(3)).

Say a taxpayer's details in 2006/07 were as follows:

Income after allowances:	
Non-savings income	£6,400
Savings income – dividends	£20,000
Life policy gain – full amount	£12,000
(fraction being 1/6th, ie £2,000)	
Capital gains after annual exemption	£10,000

The position would be:

No income tax on life policy gain since income of £26,400 plus £2,000 fraction re life policy = £28,400 is below basic rate threshold of £33,300.

For higher rate tax on the capital gains, the unused part of the basic rate band is arrived at by taking into account only the *fraction* of the life policy gain, which gives (33,300 – 28,400 =) £4,900 available, so that £4,900 of the gains are taxed at 20% and £5,100 @ 40%.

Shares in life policies

7.   Except for transfers of shares in life policies between spouses/civil partners living together, where a policy is changed from joint to single names or vice versa it will be treated as a part assignment and therefore subject to the 'chargeable events' rules outlined in this example. Any gain arising will be taxed on the transferor. No tax charge will be made if the transfer is made for no consideration (ITTOIA 2005 ss 505–514).

Personal portfolio bonds

8.   There are anti-avoidance provisions in ITTOIA 2005 ss 515–526 and SI 1999/1029 relating to personal portfolio bonds. Personal portfolio bonds are broadly investment linked or index-linked policies that enable the policyholder to select the underlying investments or index. For policy years ending on or after 6 April 2000, other than the last year, there is an annual taxable gain (yearly charge) amounting to 15% of a deemed gain equal to the total of the premiums paid and the total deemed gains in earlier years, less any taxable amounts withdrawn in earlier years. The yearly charge is taxed in a similar way to the normal chargeable events rules, but top slicing relief is not relevant. The total amount of gains taxed under the yearly provisions is deducted from any gain arising when the policy terminates. If gains arising during the life of a policy are reversed when the policy comes to an end, a compensating deduction will be made from taxable income.

Most bonds taken out before 17 March 1998 are excluded from the provisions, and those who needed to change the terms of the policy to benefit from this exclusion had until the end of the first policy year after 5 April 2000 to do so. Policyholders who were not UK resident on 17 March 1998 will have at least 12 months after becoming resident to make the change.

Commissions and discounts

9.   On 27 November 1997 the Revenue published a detailed statement of practice (SP 4/97) about the taxation of commission, cashbacks and discounts and comments about the statement were published in the Revenue's Tax Bulletin of February 1998.

In general, commissions on a policyholder's own policies that would otherwise form part of trading profits or employment income are not taxed if a member of the general public would have received an equivalent amount.

In relation to a policyholder's own life policies, where commission is received, netted off or invested, the qualifying status of the policy is not affected if commission is paid under a separate commission contract. If a discounted premium is paid, it is the net premium that is taken into account to decide whether the policy qualifies.

In relation to life policy chargeable events, if commission is paid separately, the gain is calculated by reference to the gross premium. Commission invested in the policy counts as part of the premiums paid. Where a premium is paid net of commission, or a discounted premium is paid, the gain is calculated using the amount paid.

Tax credits

10.   The profit on a bond is counted as investment income for tax credits. No top slicing relief is available. Assuming that the claimants have used their £300 deduction against other investment income this could mean that a taxpayer, only liable at basic rate, would have a significant withdrawal of tax credits.

Say the claimant's tax credit details for 2006/07 were as follows:

Employment income (both full-time)	£31,200
Investment income	£300

The couple have two qualifying children (aged 3 and 5) and pay eligible childcare costs of £180 per week. Their tax credits income in 2005/06 was £36,400 and they have received £4,015 in tax credits in 2006/07. Because their income has dropped they cashed a bond giving a chargeable event gain of £5,000 (number of complete years – 5) with notional tax credit of £1,000. No income tax liability arises, however for tax credits the cost would be:

		Income with Chargeable Event Gain £	Income without Chargeable Event Gain £
Employment		31,200	31,200
Investment income (less £300)		5,000	nil
Tax credits income 2006/07		36,200	31,200
Maximum claim (per day)	£		
WTC – Basic	4.56		
– Second adult	4.49		
– 30 hours	1.86		
– 2 children £4.84 × 2	9.68		
– Family element	1.50		
Total	22.09		
Annual figure £22.09 × 365	8,062.85		
Childcare £180 × 80% × 52	7,488.00	15,551	15,551
Restricted by 37% × (36,200 – 5,220)		11,462	
(31,200 – 5,220)			9,612
		4,089	5,939
Tax credits – received		4,015	4,015
– now payable		74	1,924

Effective cost of chargeable event gain is £5,000 × 37% = £1,850 (1,924 – 74).

In the same way a claimant liable to higher rate tax and a tax credits withdrawal at 6.67% would find that the effective cost of a chargeable event gain in 2006/07 will be 20% + 6.67% = 26.67%, where income for tax credits including chargeable event gain has increased by more than £25,000 over base year.

Ellis Containers Ltd, which makes up its accounts annually to 31 July, has a wholly owned foreign subsidiary – Ellis Containers (Utopia) Ltd. Ellis Containers Ltd has not made a general 31.3.82 rebasing election.

In the year ended 31 July 2006 Ellis Containers Ltd made disposals of assets as follows:

(a)   A freehold factory which it had purchased when it was first built on 1 May 1981 at a cost of £50,000 including land of £8,000. The factory was used as such until 31 October 1987 and thereafter entirely as offices. On 30 April 2006 it was sold for £253,000 including £53,000 for the land. An initial allowance of 50% had been claimed when the building was first acquired. The market value of the factory (including land) on 31 March 1982 was £95,000.

(b)   On 31 December 2005 the company sold a building that had cost £85,000 on 6 June 1967, including £10,000 for the land. The sale proceeds were £335,000, including £75,000 for the land. The market value at 31 March 1982 was £137,000. The building had been used for industrial purposes until September 1996, then as offices until the date of sale.

(c)   On 2 April 2006 two acres of land were sold for £18,900, being part of a holding of ten acres purchased in November 1987 for £37,250. The market value of the unsold land at 2 April 2006 was £56,700. No question of dealing in land arises, and the land has never been used for the trade.

(d)   The company's freehold interest in a storage depot was sold on 1 October 2005 for £350,000. The depot was acquired in February 1988 for £170,000 and capital expenditure incurred subsequently consisted of £12,750 in June 1989 for temporary partitioning and £19,840 in August 1991 for the replacement of the partitioning by permanent dividing walls. The expenses of the sale consisted of £930 valuer's fees.

(e)   Three of the company's machines were sold in April 2006 to different businesses for a total consideration of £4,700. The machines had already been replaced three months previously as part of the company's plan to modernise its fixed plant and machinery. The three machines that were sold had all been acquired in October 1999.

Details of their cost and the proceeds of sale are as follows (£):

	Cost	Proceeds
Cutting machine	1,600	2,650
Folding machine	1,500	1,200
Binding machine	710	850

The company also sold two items of movable machinery, details being as follows:

1st machine bought December 1997 for £7,000, sold March 2006 for £4,500.

2nd machine bought June 1998 for £5,500, sold April 2006 for £4,000.

No balancing charges arose on any of the sales because the pool residue of expenditure covered the proceeds.

(f)   On 1 January 1997 the company was granted a 21-year lease of premises which it used as a showroom and for which it paid a premium of £82,500. On 30 December 2005 the company contracted to sell the lease for £94,000, completion taking place in January 2006.

(g)   In December 2005 the company's sales office building was damaged by fire. On 30 April 2006 the company received £400,000 in compensation from its insurance company. The company intends to use this sum to restore the building to its original condition. The building was purchased new in June 1992 at a cost of £500,000 including land. The insurance company estimated that after the fire the site and the damaged building were worth £320,000.

(h)   In June 2006 the company's wholly owned foreign subsidiary, Ellis Containers (Utopia) Ltd, was nationalised by the Government of Utopia and no compensation was received. Requests are continuing to be made to the Utopian authorities for compensation, but it is not expected that they will be successful. The shares in the subsidiary company were acquired in 1976 for £5,000 and were considered to be worth £100,000 in March 1982. An unsecured loan of £80,000 was made to the subsidiary in 1985 and is still outstanding. In the accounts for the year the investment and the loan have each been written down to nil.

On 31 December 2005 a newly built factory was brought into use, having been constructed at a cost of £800,000 since 1 April 2005 on land already owned. The new factory qualified as an industrial building, but was not in an enterprise zone.

The company's trading profits for the year ended 31 July 2006, as adjusted for taxation purposes but before dealing with any balancing adjustments on the sale of the old building, or allowances on the new factory, amounted to £551,820 and it had neither received nor paid any dividends.

1.   Calculate the capital gains arising before any claims for relief are made.

2.   Compute the amount upon which corporation tax is payable for the year ended 31 July 2006 after all available reliefs are claimed.

The following retail price indices should be used in answering this example:

Mar 1982	79.44	
Nov 1987	103.4	
Feb 1988	103.7	
Oct 1990	130.3	
Aug 1991	134.1	
June 1992	139.3	
Jan 1998	159.5	
Oct 1999	166.5	
Oct 2005	193.3	
Dec 2005	194.1	(rise from Mar 1982: 144.3%)
Apr 2006	196.5	(rise from Mar 1982: 147.4%)

Ellis Containers Ltd – year ended 31 July 2006

1.   **Capital gains arising before any claims for relief are made**

(a)   **Disposal of freehold factory**

	Using cost £	*Using 31.3.82 value* £
Sale proceeds April 2006	253,000	253,000
Cost 1981	50,000	
31 March 1982 market value		95,000
Unindexed gain	203,000	158,000
Indexation allowance		
£95,000 x 147.4%	140,030	140,030
	62,970	17,970

Chargeable gain is therefore £17,970

Since the disposal proceeds exceed the cost, a balancing charge arises to claw back all the industrial buildings allowances given:

Cost (excluding land)	42,000
Initial allowance 1981 (50%)	21,000
Writing down allowances 1981–1987 (7 x 4% = 28%)	11,760
Notional writing down allowances only for years 1988 onwards since in non-industrial use	–
Balancing charge to clawback allowances given	£ 32,760

(b)   **Disposal of office building**

Since the building was used for industrial purposes for the 25 years from June 1967 to June 1992, the cost of £75,000 excluding land will have been fully relieved by capital allowances, and those allowances are not withdrawn on any subsequent disposal (see Example 21 explanatory note 9).

Chargeable gain:

	Using cost £	*Using 31.3.82 value* £
Sale proceeds December 2005	335,000	335,000
Cost June 1967	(85,000)	
31 March 1982 value		(137,000)
Unindexed gain	250,000	198,000
Indexation allowance		
137,000 @ 144.3%	(197,691)	(197,691)
	52,309	309

Chargeable gain is therefore £309.

(c) **Disposal of land**

	£	£	£
Sale proceeds for 2 acres April 2006 (more than 20% of (£56,700 + £18,900) – see explanatory note 3)		18,900	

Cost of 10 acres in November 1987 = £37,250

Cost of part disposed of =

$$37{,}250 \times \frac{18{,}900}{(18{,}900 + 56{,}700)} \qquad 9{,}313$$

Indexation allowance

$$\frac{196.5 - 103.4}{103.4} = 90.0\% \qquad 8{,}382 \qquad 17{,}695$$

Chargeable gain   1,205

(d) **Sale of freehold storage depot**

	£	£	£
Sale proceeds October 2005		350,000	
Less: Sale expenses – valuation fee		930	
		349,070	
Less: Cost February 1988	170,000		
Permanent dividing walls August 1991	19,840	189,840	
Unindexed gain		159,230	

Less: Indexation allowance:

On cost February 1988

$$\frac{193.3 - 103.7}{103.7} = 86.4\% \times 170{,}000 \qquad 146{,}880$$

On permanent dividing walls August 1991

$$\frac{193.3 - 134.1}{134.1} = 44.1\% \times 19{,}840 \qquad 8{,}749 \qquad 155{,}629 \qquad 3{,}601$$

(e) **Sale of machines**

	£	£	£

Dealt with as part of capital allowances computation

	£	£	£
Proceeds deducted from pool (limited to cost)			
Cutting machine	1,600		
Folding machine	1,200		
Binding machine	710		
1st movable machine	4,500		
2nd movable machine	4,000	12,010	

Chargeable gains/allowable losses:

	£	£	£
Cutting machine proceeds April 2006		2,650	
Less: Cost October 1999		1,600	
Unindexed gain		1,050	

$$\textit{Less: Indexation allowance} \quad \frac{196.5 - 166.5}{166.5} = 18.0\% \times 1{,}600 \qquad 288 \qquad 762$$

Folding machine – Difference between cost of £1,500 and proceeds of £1,200 covered by capital allowances, therefore no allowable loss   –

                                             cf   762

	£	£
		bf 762
Binding machine proceeds April 2006	850	
Less: Cost October 1999	710	
Unindexed gain	140	
Less: Indexation allowance 18.0% x 710	128	12
		774

Both movable machines are sold for less than their cost and also for less than £6,000 each. Since the proceeds must be regarded as £6,000 to calculate an allowable loss, and since indexation allowance cannot be taken into account, there is no allowable loss on either machine.

(f) **Sale of leasehold interest in showroom**

	£	£	£
Proceeds December 2005			
– contract date is the relevant disposal date			94,000
Cost January 1998		82,500	
Less: Part of purchase price allowed as rent in computing trading profits (TCGA 1992 s 39)			
Premium paid	82,500		
Less (21 – 1) x 2% = 40%	33,000		
Assessable as rent on recipient	49,500		

$$\frac{49,500}{21} = \text{£2,357 per annum for January 1998 to December 2005 inclusive}$$

	£	£	£
		18,856	
		63,644	

Depreciated cost under TCGA 1992 Sch 8:

$$63,644 \times \frac{13 \text{ yrs when disposed of}}{21 \text{ years when acquired}}$$

Substitute TCGA 1992 Sch 8 percentages:

$$63,644 \times \frac{56.167}{74.635} \qquad\qquad 47,896$$

Unindexed gain			46,104
Indexation allowance			

$$\frac{194.1 - 159.5}{159.5} = 21.7\% \times 47,896 \qquad\qquad 10,393$$

Chargeable gain			35,711

(g) **Sales office compensation** (treated as part disposal)

	£	£
Compensation from insurance company April 2006	400,000	
Less: Cost June 1992 £500,000 x $\dfrac{\text{£400,000 proceeds}}{\text{£400,000 proceeds + £320,000 value remaining}}$	277,778	
Unindexed gain	122,222	
Less: Indexation allowance $\dfrac{196.5 - 139.3}{139.3} = 41.1\% \times 277,778$	114,167	8,055

(h) **Ellis Containers (Utopia) Ltd**

No disposal has yet been made.

2. **Amount on which corporation tax is payable after claiming reliefs**

Claims for relief may be made as follows:

Re (a), (b), (e) and (f) (see explanatory note 2)

Since the whole proceeds in each case have been reinvested in the new factory, ((a) £253,000, (b) £335,000, (e) £2,650 and £850 and (f) £94,000 = £685,500) the gains may be rolled over and treated as reducing the base cost of the factory, which will therefore have a capital gains tax base cost of:

Construction expenditure		800,000
Less: Gain on previous factory	17,970	
Gain on office building	309	
Gain on cutting machine	762	
Gain on binding machine	12	
Gain on leasehold showroom	35,711	54,764
		£ 745,236

Since the cutting and binding machines had been replaced, the small gains of £762 and £12 could have been held over until the replacement machinery is disposed of or no longer in use, or until ten years from its acquisition if sooner. It is, however, preferable to roll over the gains against the cost of the new factory, rather than deferring it for a maximum of ten years.

Re (g)

Compensation received need not be treated as a disposal if it is used to restore the asset. Instead the compensation can be deducted from the restoration cost, or indeed from the cost of the original acquisition to the extent that the compensation slightly exceeds the restoration costs (see explanatory note 6) (TCGA 1992 s 23).

Hence the calculated gain of £8,055 will not be chargeable at this time if the insurance compensation is used to reinstate the building and a claim for relief is made.

Re (h) Ellis Containers (Utopia) Ltd

A claim may be made for the shares to be regarded as worthless and consequently treated as sold and immediately reacquired for that nil value. Thus a constructive loss can be claimed at that point and if any proceeds are ever received, a gain will arise to that extent in future (TCGA 1992 s 24(2)). The allowable loss would be £5,000, being smaller than 31 March 1982 value of £100,000.

There is no relief for the unsecured loan (see explanatory note 5).

Computation of profits chargeable to corporation tax	£	£
Trading profit (assumed to be stated *after* the allowance for rent of £2,357 in item (f))		551,820
Balancing charge on factory/offices (a)		32,760
		584,580
Industrial buildings allowance on new factory		
Cost £800,000		
Writing down allowance 4%		(32,000)
		552,580
Chargeable gains after claims for relief		
Sale of land (c)	1,205	
Sale of storage depot (d)	3,601	
Shares in Ellis Containers (Utopia) Ltd (h)	(5,000)	NIL
Corporation tax payable on		552,580

Explanatory Notes

Lease premiums

1. References in these notes are to TCGA 1992 unless otherwise stated. Since the acquisition of the leasehold interest in the showroom at part (f) of the example was on the grant of a lease, so that the grantor would have a tax charge on part of the premium (by way of additional rent) as illustrated, the payer can deduct, in calculating his trading profit, over the period of the lease that part of the premium assessed on the recipient as rent. The interaction of the rent deduction permitted by TCGA 1992 s 39 with the application of the lease depreciation fraction to the cost per TCGA 1992 Sch 8 is not clear in the legislation. HMRC takes the view that the rent deduction is made *before* the depreciation factor is applied to the cost (Capital Gains Manual at CG 71201), as illustrated in the example. This is, in fact, a more beneficial treatment for the taxpayer, since the rent reduction in allowable expenditure is then 'depreciated'.

    If the premium paid had been for the *assignment* of a leasehold interest, the vendor would not normally be taxable where the payer is subject to income tax on any part of his proceeds and accordingly no part of the payment would be allowed in calculating the payer's trading profit (TA 1988 ss 34 and 87 or the equivalent rules in ITTOIA 2005). Instead, the assignee can claim the same amount of the original premium that the assignor was entitled to deduct, if the lease was originally granted for a period of less than 50 years. See Example 100 for detailed notes on lease premiums.

Rollover relief on replacement of business assets

2. Rollover relief is available in respect of the gains on the old factory, the office building, the storage depot, the cutting and binding machines and the showroom, since all six and the replacement asset – the new factory – are within the classes set out in s 155 and the replacement is acquired within the time limit of 12 months before and three years after the disposals.

    The cost of the replacement factory (£800,000) is not, however, sufficient to enable all the gains to be rolled over, so it is necessary to decide how to maximise the available relief. The position is as follows:

	Sale proceeds £	Gain £
Factory	253,000	17,970
Office building	335,000	309
Storage depot	350,000	3,601
Cutting machine	2,650	762
Binding machine	850	12
Showroom	94,000	35,711
	1,035,500	

The maximum deferral of gains is achieved by excluding the storage depot from the claim. The gain on the storage depot would still be eligible for rollover/holdover relief if £350,000 was invested in qualifying assets within three years from October 2005 (a balance of (800,000 – (1,035,500 – 350,000) =) £114,500 of the expenditure on the new factory being available towards this amount). If Ellis Containers had wanted to defer the gain, it could have claimed to postpone payment of the tax if it had declared on its tax return that it intended to incur qualifying replacement expenditure within the three years. In fact, after taking into account the loss on the Ellis Containers (Utopia) Ltd shares, none of the gain of £3,396 is chargeable to tax, and if the provisional claim was made the company would have around £3,800 unrelieved capital losses to carry forward, so a provisional claim may not be appropriate.

Part disposals of land

3. Where part only of a holding of land is disposed of (other than between spouses/civil partners, or intra-group) and the amount or value of the consideration is not more than 20% of the market value

of the land immediately before the disposal and the proceeds do not exceed £20,000, the transferor may claim that this does not constitute a disposal, but that the consideration received be deducted from allowable expenditure in computing a gain on any subsequent disposal of the land. This relief does not, however, apply where in the chargeable period in which the transfer is made, the transferor made other disposals of land, the total consideration for all disposals of land in that year exceeding £20,000 (s 242). In TCGA 1992 land, unless the context otherwise requires, 'includes messuages, tenements and hereditaments, houses and buildings of any tenure' (s 288). Section 242 expressly excludes leasehold interests with 50 years or less to run. The time limit for the claim for companies is two years from the end of the accounting period of disposal (one year from 31 January following the tax year of disposal for individuals).

On a subsequent disposal of the land the indexation allowance is calculated in the normal way and is then reduced by an indexation amount calculated on the earlier disposal proceeds from the date they were received, thus ensuring that the reduction in the base cost of the land as a result of that earlier disposal only affects the calculation of the indexation allowance from that date and not over the whole period of ownership. For non-corporate taxpayers indexation allowance is not given for periods after April 1998.

In part (c) of the example the disposal proceeds of £18,900 are more than 20% of the value before the disposal (20% of £75,600 = £15,120). Even if they had not been, the company has made other substantial disposals of property in the year thus denying relief under this de minimis provision.

Where part disposals of land are concerned, it may be costly to get a valuation of the whole estate in order to apply the part disposal formula. HMRC will allow the part sold to be treated as a separate asset, using any reasonable means of apportioning part of the total acquisition cost to the part sold. This cannot be done where earlier part disposals have followed the statutory method, unless the alternative method would have given broadly the same result for those disposals (Revenue Statement of Practice D1).

Capital allowances – temporary partitioning

4.   The cost of the temporary partitioning in the storage depot is not allowable in calculating the chargeable gain since it is not reflected in the state or nature of the asset at the time of disposal (s 38(1)).

The cost of the partitioning should, however, have qualified as plant for capital allowances if there was a business requirement for the partitions to be moved (Jarrold v John Good & Sons (1963)).

Loss of money lent

5.   For companies, the treatment of the loss of money lent is dealt with under the rules for 'loan relationships', profits and losses on disposals being taken out of the capital gains regime and brought into the calculation of a company's income profits. Where a company has guaranteed a debt, however, a payment under the guarantee is outside the loan relationships rules. The company guarantor can, if appropriate, claim relief under the provisions of TCGA 1992 s 253 outlined below.

The loan relationships rules enable companies to claim relief for the loss of money lent, except for loans between connected persons (see Example 62 explanatory note 7). Connected persons include companies under common control or where one controls the other, as is the case for Ellis Containers Ltd and its subsidiary, Ellis Containers (Utopia) Ltd. Relief is not therefore available in respect of the unsecured loan to the subsidiary.

For capital gains tax purposes, relief is not normally available in respect of the loss of money lent unless the debt is a 'debt on a security' which means loan stock or similar security, whether secured or unsecured (ss 251 and 132). (This only applies, however, to the original creditor and not to an assignee, for whom an allowable loss or chargeable gain may arise, except that an allowable loss cannot arise if the creditor and the assignee are connected persons – s 251(4).)

Furthermore, most securities fall within the definition of 'qualifying corporate bonds', which are exempt from capital gains tax (see Example 81 explanatory note 4), so that even though the debt is a 'debt on a security' the loss is not usually allowable under the general rules.

There are provisions in s 253 to enable relief to be claimed for a loss where a loan is made or a guarantee is given and the recipient of the loan is a UK resident who uses the money lent wholly for the purpose of a trade carried on by him, providing the debt is not a 'debt on a security' (s 253). Even if the loan was a debt on a security, loss relief could previously be claimed if the debt was a qualifying corporate bond, where the bond was held on, or issued on or after, 15 March 1989. The relief in this case was limited to the underlying principal of the loan or the amount subscribed for the bond, whichever was lower (ss 254 and 255). Relief under ss 254 and 255 is abolished for loans made on or after 17 March 1998 (FA 1998 s 141).

Where the relief is available, the loss is deemed to arise at the time of the claim that the loan has become irrecoverable, or at the time of the guarantee payment, provided that the debt or the rights acquired by subrogation under the guarantee payment are not assigned (s 253). If they are assigned, then providing the loan does not constitute a qualifying corporate bond, the assignee may claim relief for a loss under s 251 unless he and the debtor are connected persons. For the definition of connected persons for this purpose see Example 73 part (d). Relief under s 253, and under s 254 for pre 17 March 1998 loans, may be given as if the loss had arisen at a time not more than two years before the beginning of the tax year of claim (or for a claim by a company guarantor, not earlier than the first day of the earliest accounting period ending not more than two years before the time of the claim) where the stated conditions are satisfied (ss 253(3A) and 254(8A)). If allowed losses prove in whole or part to be recoverable, a capital gain arises on the amount recovered (or recovered from co-guarantor).

Relief is not available if the loss arises because of an act or omission by the lender, nor is it available where the claimant and borrower are husband and wife or companies in the same group.

By Revenue Concession D38, where someone acquired unquoted stock before 14 March 1989 in respect of shares or securities on a takeover, the stock then becoming a qualifying corporate bond because of FA 1989 s 139, and the stock later becomes of negligible value or gives rise to a loss, the loss may be treated as an allowable loss under s 254.

Assets damaged, lost or destroyed

6.   Where an asset is damaged but not lost or destroyed, compensation that is used to restore the asset need not be treated as a disposal. Instead it is treated as reducing the restoration cost in deciding how much of that cost is allowable expenditure on a later disposal.

No indexation allowance would be calculated at the time of restoration, so that in part (g) of the example the £400,000 compensation received would be balanced by restoration expenditure of the same amount, leaving the original cost intact for the purposes of a later disposal. If the restoration costs exceed the compensation the excess would represent additional allowable expenditure for a later disposal, indexed from the date it was incurred (after April 1998, only for companies).

If the compensation exceeds the restoration cost by a small amount ('small' regarded by HMRC as 5% of the compensation), then for assets other than wasting assets the excess may be deducted from the cost of the asset instead of being treated as a part disposal, thus eliminating any current gain but increasing the gain on a subsequent disposal. In those circumstances the available indexation allowance on a later disposal is first of all calculated on the full amount of allowable expenditure, but is then reduced by an indexation amount calculated on the small excess compensation from the date the compensation is received. This ensures that the benefit of indexation on that small amount is not lost for the period from the time the original expenditure is incurred to the date the compensation is received (ss 23 and 57). If the compensation was received before 31 March 1982 the excess over restoration cost would escape tax because it would not affect the 31 March 1982 value. If it was received after 31 March 1982 but before 6 April 1988, it is deducted in arriving at the 31 March

1982 value (but with the same indexation allowance provisions applying to ensure that indexation allowance is not lost for the period up to the receipt of the compensation) (Sch 3.4(2)).

If the compensation exceeds the restoration cost by more than 5%, or by any amount for wasting assets, a claim may be made for the part that is used to restore the asset not to be treated as a part disposal but as reducing the allowable expenditure, so that the restoration expenditure does not then count as part of the allowable cost (s 23(3)).

7.   If an asset is lost or destroyed, rather than being merely damaged as in part (g) of the example, and any insurance proceeds or compensation received are used to replace the asset within one year of receipt, a claim may be made for the old asset to be deemed to have been disposed of for such consideration as leaves an unindexed gain equivalent to the available indexation allowance, so that the net result is no loss/no gain (s 23). If a building is lost or destroyed, and a replacement is built or acquired on other land, the building may be treated as separate from the land for the purposes of this claim (s 23(6)). If the compensation received exceeds the deemed proceeds for the destroyed asset, the excess is treated as reducing the cost of the replacement (s 23(5)). Where such a reduction occurred between 31 March 1982 and 5 April 1988 and it relates wholly or partly to an asset acquired before 31 March 1982, it is reduced by half in calculating a gain on a disposal on or after 6 April 1988, under the deferred charges provisions of Sch 4 (see Example 83 explanatory note 11).

Assets of negligible value

8.   The 'entire loss, destruction, dissipation or extinction' of an asset is treated as a disposal of it, whether or not any compensation is received (s 24). Where this does not apply, but the asset has become of negligible value, a claim may be made to be treated as if the asset had been disposed of and immediately reacquired for that negligible value (s 24(2)), as is shown for the shares in Ellis Containers (Utopia) Ltd in part (h) of the example. The date of the deemed disposal is either the date of the claim or, if the claim so requires, an earlier date falling within the two years before the tax year or company accounting period in which the claim is made. The asset must have been of negligible value on that earlier date (whether or not it was of negligible value before then).

Interaction of capital allowances and capital gains

9.   For capital gains purposes, where assets have qualified for capital allowances, the allowances are ignored in computing a gain but are taken into account in computing a loss (the allowances being deducted from 31 March 1982 value when making computations based on that value). This means that capital losses will not arise, since the difference between cost and disposal proceeds is covered by the capital allowances. As far as plant and machinery is concerned, if the item is sold for more than cost, any capital allowances given will be withdrawn by taking into account sale proceeds equal to the original cost, as shown in part (e) of the example. But even if capital allowances are not withdrawn, as in the case of the office building in part (b) of the example, the capital allowances are not taken into account in computing a gain. A similar situation can arise with agricultural buildings – see Example 22 explanatory note 7.

Fixed and movable plant and machinery

10.   Gains on plant and machinery are calculated using different rules according to whether the items are fixed or movable. Gains on fixed items are chargeable, subject to a claim for rollover/holdover relief if there is qualifying replacement expenditure. It was held in the case of Williams v Evans (1982) that 'fixed' applies to both plant and machinery, so for example, mobile cranes and fork lift trucks would not qualify. Movable items are 'tangible movable property' and are subject to the chattels rules of s 262. These rules provide that a gain is not a chargeable gain if the gross sale proceeds are £6,000 or less. If the proceeds exceed £6,000 the gain is calculated in the usual way (except that it cannot exceed 5/3rds of the excess of the sale proceeds over £6,000 – see Example 75 part (2) for an illustration) and it cannot be deferred.

Claims

11.   Capital gains reliefs are not given automatically, and a claim must be made within the normal time limit under TMA 1970 s 43(1), ie within six years from the end of the chargeable period for companies (five years from 31 January following the tax year for individuals). Ellis Containers must accordingly make claims by 31 July 2012 for the reliefs in relation to replacement of business assets and the compensation used for restoration. In relation to the negligible value claim, in order to establish the loss as a loss of the year to 31 July 2006, the claim must be made not later than 31 July 2008 as indicated in note 8 above.

If brought forward losses are to be set against gains, a claim must be made under s 16(2A). Individuals will normally claim relief in their tax returns, with an overall time limit for the claim of five years from 31 January following the end of the tax year. The time limit for companies is six years after the end of the accounting period. For both capital gains tax and corporation tax, losses arising after the introduction of self-assessment (ie from 1966/97 for individuals and for accounting periods ending after 30 June 1999 for companies) will be regarded as set off before earlier losses (FA 1995 s 113(2)). This may be particularly relevant in relation to pre 1996/97 losses on transactions with connected persons, because if there was a gain on a later transaction with that person, that gain, together with other gains of the same tax year, would be eligible to be relieved by losses arising in and after 1996/97 before the earlier loss on the disposal to the connected person could be used against it.

See Example 75 explanatory notes 12 to 14 for comments on revisions to earlier returns following the Court of Appeal's decision in Mansworth v Jelley and the Revenue's responses to it.

Where a claim has been made under FA 1991 s 72 to treat an *income* loss as a capital loss, thereby reducing capital gains (see Example 29 explanatory note 1(d)), and a later claim, such as rollover relief, reduces the gains against which the loss was set, the deemed capital loss that thereby becomes unrelieved is carried forward to set against later gains, but cannot be relieved in any tax year after that in which the trade ceases (s 72(6)). Where such unrelieved losses occur, therefore, they must be separately identified in the amount of capital losses carried forward.

Convey commenced to practise on 1 May 1977.

In 1981 he took Sing into partnership, the balance sheet immediately after the admission being:

Capital accounts:		£	Fixed assets:		£
Convey	10,000		Premises – at cost		7,500
Sing	4,000	14,000			
Current liabilities:			Current assets:		
Creditors	2,000		Work in progress	4,500	
Bank overdraft	4,000	6,000	Debtors	8,000	12,500
		20,000			20,000

It was agreed that the premises, which had been acquired by Convey some time earlier, be vested in both partners, that the profit sharing ratio be two-thirds to Convey and one-third to Sing, and that they should contribute capital as agreed from time to time.

No payments or adjustments were made for goodwill or increase in value of premises on the admission of Sing, although it was acknowledged at that time that should Convey have sought a payment from Sing, the premises were worth £25,000 and the goodwill £10,000.

In April 1993 it was decided to introduce goodwill into the accounts and a value of £75,000 was agreed. The book value of the premises was not disturbed. The value of goodwill on 31 March 1982 is agreed at £30,000, the value of the premises on that day being £20,000.

From 30 April 1994 the profit sharing ratio was altered to give equal shares to Convey and Sing. Although no accounting adjustments were made the partners acknowledged that the premises were currently worth £97,500, and the goodwill £99,000.

In anticipation of the retirement of Convey, a longstanding employee, Dance, was admitted to the partnership from 1 May 2000 as an equal partner. It was agreed that at that stage no payment or accounting adjustments should be made for goodwill and premises.

Convey retired from the business on 30 April 2007, which was his 68th birthday.

Sing and Dance remained as equal partners.

It was agreed that the terms of Convey's retirement should reflect an appropriate amount for his share in the premises and goodwill, the values of which assets were acknowledged as being £420,000 each, the accounts however still showing the premises as having cost £7,500, with £75,000 included for goodwill on the basis of the 1993 valuation, the values in the accounts not having been disturbed.

The profits of the firm for the last eleven years have generally increased and the tax adjusted profits have been:

		£
Year ended 30 April	1997 (after capital allowances of £20,000)	150,000
	1998 (after capital allowances of £22,000)	168,000
	1999 (after capital allowances of £21,000)	172,000
	2000 (after capital allowances of £26,000)	201,000
	2001 (after capital allowances of £25,000)	219,000
	2002 (after capital allowances of £18,000)	240,000
	2003 (after capital allowances of £25,000)	198,000
	2004 (after capital allowances of £33,000)	360,000
	2005 (after capital allowances of £20,000)	202,000
	2006 (after capital allowances of £30,000)	255,000
	2007 (after capital allowances of £20,000)	480,000

The retail prices index for the relevant months was March 1982 79.44, April 1993 140.6, April 1994 144.2, April 1998 162.6.

The partners have made general 31 March 1982 rebasing elections in respect of partnership chargeable assets.

Show the taxation implications arising from the above assuming that Convey, on his retirement, in order to reflect the full value of the premises and goodwill, received in addition to the balance on his capital account:

(a)   £280,000 cash, or

(b)   an annuity of £46,000 per annum (having an estimated capital value of £280,000) in consideration of his past services in the partnership, or

(c)   a reduced annuity of £34,500 per annum plus a lump sum of £70,000.

Capital gains liabilities

(i) 1981 Admission of Sing ⎫ No chargeable gains.

(ii) 1993 Revaluation of goodwill ⎭ See explanatory notes 2 and 4.

(iii) **1994/95 Change in profit sharing ratio on 30 April 1994**

Convey disposes of a one-sixth share to Sing.

The property has not been revalued and is therefore at a no loss/no gain value (Sing's cost becomes one-half of the 31.3.82 market value).

The share of goodwill is deemed to be disposed of at the revaluation figure from 1993, because two-thirds of that will have been credited to Convey's capital account. Before the change Convey's share of the 31.3.82 market value is £20,000 and Sing's £10,000. The gain on the disposal by Convey is as follows:

	£
Proceeds of one-sixth share: 75,000/6	12,500
MV 31.3.82: 30,000/6	(5,000)
Indexation: Mar 82 – Apr 94 $(\dfrac{144.2 - 79.44}{79.44}) = 81.5\%$	(4,075)
Chargeable gain	3,425

This would have been covered by retirement relief of £3,425 in 1994/95.

Convey's base cost of goodwill is reduced to £15,000 and Sing's base cost of £10,000 is increased by £12,500 incurred in April 1994.

(iv) **2000/01 – Admission of Dance on 1 May 2000**

On the admission of Dance on 1 May 2000 Convey and Sing each dispose of a one-sixth share of goodwill and premises to him. The disposal of the premises takes place on a no gain/no loss basis, since there has been no earlier revaluation and no payment by Dance to the partners. Because of the earlier revaluation of goodwill, each of Convey and Sing has deemed disposal proceeds of £12,500, being amounts in their capital accounts not now represented by their share in goodwill.

Their capital gains indexed base costs of their current shares of the assets are as follows:

	Goodwill – Convey £	Goodwill – Sing £	Premises – each £
31.3.82 MV	15,000	10,000	10,000
Indexation to April 1998 $(\dfrac{162.6 - 79.44}{79.44}) = 104.7\%$	15,705	10,470	10,470
April 1994		12,500	
Indexation to April 1998 $(\dfrac{162.6 - 144.2}{144.2}) = 12.8\%$		1,600	
	30,705	34,570	20,470
One third of a half share:	10,235	11,523	6,823
Their deemed disposal proceeds are	12,500	12,500	6,823
Capital gains	2,265*	977**	–

* Covered by retirement relief

** Before taper relief of 25%, which may reduce gain to £732

After the transaction, the partners' capital gains base costs (excluding indexation for Convey and Sing) are as follows:

			Goodwill £		Premises £
Convey	(March 1982)	(15,000 – 5,000)	10,000	(10,000 – 3,333)	6,667
Sing	(March 1982)	(10,000 – 3,333)	6,667	(10,000 – 3,333)	6,667
	(April 1994)	(12,500 – 4,167)	8,333		
Dance	(May 2000)	(12,500 + 12,500)	25,000	(6,823 + 6,823)	13,646

On any future disposals by Convey and Sing, indexation allowance to April 1998 will be added to the above figures from March 1982 for Convey and from March 1982 and April 1994 for Sing. As far as disposals by Dance are concerned, the indexation allowance within his base cost for the premises will need to be identified in the event of a disposal at a loss (see explanatory note 6).

(v)   **2007/08 – Retirement of Convey on 30 April 2007**

	Goodwill £	Premises £
(a) **Cash settlement**		
(Cash being split pro rata to the agreed values since balance sheet values are not disturbed)		
Base cost for capital gains tax (see (iv))	10,000	6,667
Indexation allowance to April 1998 ($\frac{162.6 - 79.44}{79.44}$) = 104.7%	10,470	6,980
	20,470	13,647
Disposal proceeds	140,000	140,000
Gains	119,530	126,353

Total gains on goodwill and premises (before taper relief)	245,883
Less: Business assets taper relief (max) 75% (see explanatory note 7)	184,412
Chargeable gain before annual exemption	61,471

The capital gains tax base costs of goodwill and premises for Sing and Dance will each be increased by £70,000 (ie £70,000 on each of two assets for each of two partners, total £280,000), being the amount paid to Convey to acquire his share.

(b)   **Annuity**

	Goodwill £	Premises £
Base cost for capital gains tax plus indexation allowance as in (a)	20,470	13,647
Deemed disposal proceeds (see explanatory notes 4 and 6)	20,470	13,647
No gain no loss	–	–

The capital gains tax base costs of goodwill and premises for each of Sing and Dance will be increased by half (ie their share) of £20,470 and £13,647 respectively.

The annuity itself is not chargeable to capital gains tax (see explanatory note 9) but it will be assessed to income tax in the hands of Convey, and allowed as a charge against income to Sing and Dance, on which they will obtain relief at their marginal rate of tax (see under 'Income tax implications of retirement of Convey' note (b) below).

(c) Annuity plus lump sum

	Goodwill £	Premises £
Indexed base cost for capital gains tax as in (a)	20,470	13,647
Disposal proceeds (split pro rata)	35,000	35,000
Indexed gains	14,530	21,353
Less: Taper relief (75%)	(10,898)	(16,015)
Chargeable gains	3,632	5,338

Convey's total chargeable gain of £8,970 will be reduced by the annual exemption for 2007/08, if he realises no other capital gains. If he realises capital losses in the year, it will affect the calculation of his taper relief.

The capital gains tax base costs of premises and goodwill for each of Sing and Dance will be increased by half (ie their share) of £35,000 in each case.

Income tax implications of retirement of Convey

(a) The retirement of Convey on 30 April 2007 will not affect the calculation of the taxable profits of Sing and Dance. The amount assessable on Convey is his share of the profits (net of capital allowances) for the year ended 30 April 2007 less overlap relief for the period 1 May 1996 to 5 April 1997 (calculated on profits *before* capital allowances), ie:

1/3 × (500,000 – CAs 20,000 = 480,000)	160,000
Less: 340/365 × (1/2 × (150,000 + 20,000))	79,178
	£ 80,822

(b) The receipt of the annuity of £46,000 per annum would be taxable as pension income in the hands of Convey from 2007/08 onwards. The payment of £46,000 per annum is a charge on income for Sing and Dance, and is paid net of basic rate tax, so it is disallowed in computing trading profits. The gross amount paid in the *tax year* (not the accounting period) must be shown in the annual partnership statement, divided between the partners in the way profits are shared in the tax year. Each partner will show his share in his own personal tax return, and relief at the higher rate, if appropriate, would be given in calculating the tax payable (see explanatory note 12).

(c) The annuity of £34,500 would be treated in the same way as under (b) above.

Explanatory Notes

Partnership capital gains

1. The rules relating to partnership capital gains are contained in TCGA 1992 ss 59 and 286(4), supplemented by a Revenue Statement of Practice originally issued on 17 January 1975 (D12). The statement has been updated, most recently in August 2003. The latest version makes clear that the statement generally applies to the gains of limited liability partnerships (see explanatory note 14), and also contains guidance on the effect of taper relief on partnership goodwill acquired piecemeal over a number of years (see explanatory note 15).

   The position is very complex and there are areas where the approach to be taken is not clear. This is particularly so in relation to the integration of the 31 March 1982 indexation provisions with the 1975 statement. It is considered that the approach taken in this example reflects the views expressed in the practice statements.

2. Any charge to capital gains tax arises in the hands of each individual partner, not the partnership, each partner being deemed to own a proportionate part of the partnership's chargeable assets, being

his share under the partnership agreement. The amount of the partner's capital/current account is irrelevant and it is helpful in understanding the capital gains tax aspects of partnerships to remember that a partner's capital/current account arises in one of three ways:

(i) Cash (or other assets) are introduced

(ii) Profits are retained

(iii) Assets are revalued, the capital account being credited with the partner's share of the surplus (or debited with his share of the deficit).

If capital is withdrawn, it will comprise a mixture of those three items.

Clearly there is no capital gains tax on withdrawals up to the amount introduced, nor on the withdrawal of retained profits. If, however, amounts are realised (as distinct from the capital account becoming overdrawn) in excess of these two items, they must reflect an upward revaluation of assets or, by implication, a payment for goodwill.

In order for capital gains tax to arise there must be a disposal, and a mere revaluation with a credit to the partners' capital accounts in the profit sharing ratio does not constitute a disposal. A subsequent withdrawal of the capital account on retirement, however, would do so, the liability on revaluation then crystallising. It will also crystallise on the admission of a new partner or a change in profit sharing ratio, since the capital/current account of the partner whose share is being reduced then includes an amount over and above the value of his new share in the chargeable asset concerned – tantamount to his having made a disposal, his capital account containing the proceeds.

3. In relation to partnership assets a partner is not connected with his fellow partners if the transaction is a bona fide commercial arrangement. This means that unless the partners are otherwise connected, eg father and son (and even then if the same transaction could be expected to have been made were they not so connected), HMRC will accept whatever valuation is placed upon a transaction by the partners and will not substitute market value. In the same way no charge to inheritance tax will arise. Furthermore it renders the holdover relief for business gifts in TCGA 1992 s 165 unnecessary in these situations.

4. Therefore, on the admission of a partner or a change in profit sharing ratio, no charge to capital gains tax will arise unless there is or has been a revaluation of assets with a corresponding adjustment in the capital/current accounts, or payment is made for assets. The reason is that on the admission of a partner, any cash he pays into the partnership will not constitute a disposal for capital gains tax purposes on the part of the existing partners if it is credited to the incoming partner's capital account; and unless he pays the existing partners for a share in the goodwill (or other chargeable assets) it will be treated as having been disposed of by the existing partners to the incoming partner for a consideration of such amount that neither chargeable gain nor allowable loss arises for capital gains purposes, the future ownership of each chargeable asset then being in the future capital profit sharing ratio.

Bringing goodwill into the accounts

5. On the introduction of goodwill into the accounts in 1993 the accounting entries will have been:

	Goodwill	*Capital Accounts*	
	(Asset Account)	*Convey (2/3rds)*	*Sing (1/3rd)*
Valuation	£75,000	£50,000	£25,000

Upon the profit sharing ratio being altered in 1994 this is tantamount to saying that Convey has disposed of (2/3rds – 1/2 =) 1/6th of the goodwill to Sing. But his capital account still contains the credit of £50,000, so this is equivalent to his having realised £12,500 of chargeable gains – that is £50,000 credited to capital account less £37,500 which is the value of his half share of the goodwill after the change in profit sharing ratio.

The same applies on the introduction of Dance, this time both Convey and Sing making disposals. The calculations are as follows:

	Convey £	Sing £	Dance £
Amount originally credited to capital account in 1993	50,000	25,000	–
At 30 April 1994			
Disposal on change in profit sharing ratio	(12,500)		
Deemed cost of acquisition for Sing		12,500	
	37,500	37,500	
At 1 May 2000			
Deemed cost of acquisition for Dance			25,000
Disposal by Convey and Sing (since these amounts remain in their capital accounts)	(12,500)	(12,500)	
New share of goodwill in accounts is deemed to be	25,000	25,000	25,000

Effect of rebasing to 31 March 1982 values

6. Following the rebasing provisions of FA 1988, as applied to partners by SP1/89, for disposals on and after 6 April 1988 partners are able to take advantage of using 31 March 1982 value in computing gains. This effectively means that on 6 April 1988 they are deemed to hold their then shares of partnership assets acquired before 31 March 1982 at either original cost or 31 March 1982 value, whichever shows the lower gain or loss on a disposal, or, as with Convey and Sing, where a general rebasing election has been made, at 31 March 1982 value in any event. Where any no gain no loss disposals (see note 4) take place on or after 6 April 1988 they will be deemed to be for such consideration as gives a nil result after taking any available indexation allowance into account.

If no gain no loss changes in partnership sharing ratios occurred between 6 April 1985 and 5 April 1988 inclusive, the no gain no loss provisions operated *before* taking indexation allowance into account, so that allowable losses would have been created on such changes. In these circumstances, indexation allowance on disposals on and after 6 April 1988, although computed on 31 March 1982 value if appropriate, is calculated from the date when the indexation allowance was given on the no gain no loss disposal.

For disposals on or after 30 November 1993, indexation allowance cannot be used to create or increase a loss, but can be used to reduce a profit (to nil if appropriate). Accordingly the no gain no loss provisions still apply after taking any available indexation allowance into account, but the base value carried forward must be divided into cost and indexation allowance and in so far as a disposal results in a loss, indexation allowance will be reduced by the amount of loss. Therefore a loss can only arise based upon cost (including indexation allowance for any pre 30 November 1993 transactions) or market value on 31 March 1982 as appropriate.

7. Indexation allowance for individuals is no longer available for periods after April 1998, being replaced by taper relief from that time (see Example 74 part (a)(i)). An interest in an asset of a trading partnership is a business asset, for which relief is available for each complete year of ownership from 6 April 1998 to a maximum of 75% after two years where the disposal falls after 5 April 2002. The sale by Convey in April 2007 would accordingly attract the maximum relief, ie 75% of the gain after retirement relief (unless the gain was reduced by losses from other sources).

Retirement relief

8. Retirement relief is not available for disposals after 5 April 2003. Covey would have enjoyed small amounts of relief on his disposals in 1994 and 2000, because he was already over 50 at those times, but the full disposal of his interest will not qualify.

Annuity to retiring partner

9.   Where an annuity is paid on the retirement of a partner by reason of age or ill health, then capital gains tax is not chargeable on the capitalised value provided the payment is in reasonable recognition of past service and is not a lump sum equivalent or a purchased life annuity.

A reasonable amount is regarded as being the appropriate fraction of the retiring partner's average taxable profits *before* capital allowances or charges of the best three of the last seven tax years in which the partner was required to devote substantially the whole of his time to acting as a partner. The appropriate fraction depends on the complete years of service to the partnership (or a predecessor firm prior to merger) as follows:

Complete years	*Fraction*
1 – 5	1/60 per year
6	8/60
7	16/60
8	24/60
9	32/60
10	2/3 *

Convey's best three out of the last seven shares of profit in this example are as follows (his 2007/08 share being 1/3 × (480,000 + 20,000) = 166,667 less overlap relief 79,178 = £87,489):

2002/03	⅓ x £258,000	86,000
2004/05	⅓ x £393,000	131,000
2006/07	⅓ x £285,000	95,000
		£ 312,000

Average profits 1/3 x £312,000 = £104,000

Maximum annuity which can be disregarded in computing capital gains (SP D12)
* 2/3 x £104,000   = £69,333.

Lump sums and purchased annuities

10.   Where a lump sum is paid (or an annuity is *purchased* in addition to the provision of an annuity from the partnership) the whole of the capitalised value of the *annuity from the partnership* plus the lump sum is treated as a payment for chargeable assets (but the capitalised value of the annuity from the partnership does not increase the capital gains tax base cost of those partners paying the annuity – they are after all getting relief for income tax at their marginal rates on such payments). If, however, the sum of the annuity from the partnership plus 1/9th of the lump sum or purchased annuity amounts to less than the 'reasonable amount' defined in note 9, the capitalised value of the annuity from the partnership is not chargeable to capital gains tax, but the lump sum or cost of the purchased annuity remains so (SP 1/79). Note that for income tax purposes a purchased annuity is treated as savings income (TA 1988 s 1A(2)(a)(ii)) but a partnership annuity is not.

11.   The 'reasonable amount' per note 9 is £69,333. This is compared with:

Scheme (b)	Annuity	£ 46,000
Scheme (c)	Annuity	34,500
	1/9th x £70,000	7,778
		£ 42,278

Since in each case the amount is less than £69,333 the capitalised value of the annuity is not chargeable to capital gains tax, but the lump sum in (c) represents part of the disposal proceeds and is brought into the capital gains tax computation as indicated at (v)(c) on page 97.5.

Tax position of partners paying the annuity

12. Partnership annuities are charges on income as far as the paying partners are concerned, and are allocated to the partners in profit sharing ratios. It is provided in TMA 1970 s 12AB(1)(a)(iv),(b) that the partnership statement should show charges and the division thereof in relation to *periods of account*. The self-assessment partnership tax return, however, states that the amount to be shown in the return is the amount paid in the *tax year*, the partnership statement then showing the allocation between the partners. This is, in fact, the information required by each partner in order to claim the appropriate relief in his own personal return.

13. If the partners pay a 'reasonable annuity' and continue to do so, there is no gain for the retiring partner, and symmetrical income tax treatment for those paying and receiving. If, instead, the other partners purchase an annuity on the date of retirement, then there will be a gain for the retiring partner by reference to the purchase price and the cost will be added to the other partners' base costs. There is a disadvantage if the partners commence to pay an annuity and then replace it at a later date by buying an annuity. It is likely that the right to receive the annuity is a chargeable asset, and the disposal of it in consideration for the amount paid for the purchased life annuity would give rise to a capital gains tax charge (with minimal taper relief); but the other partners would not at that time acquire any asset, so the cost to them would obtain no tax relief at all.

Limited liability partnerships (LLPs)

14. LLPs can be formed under the Limited Liability Partnerships Act 2000 from 6 April 2001. For the detailed provisions see Example 27 part (b). As indicated in that example, if an LLP goes into formal liquidation it will be treated as a company from that time, and the partners' shares in the LLP will then be chargeable assets in their own right.

The 2003 version of SP D12 makes it clear that a LLP will be treated for CGT purposes as a 'normal' partnership (that is the partners will be assessed on their shares of the underlying assets and the LLP will be 'transparent') as long as the LLP is within TCGA 1992 s 59A(1) (carrying on a trade or business and not in liquidation).

Goodwill

15. It is common for partners gradually to increase their share of partnership goodwill over a number of years. It would be open for HMRC to argue that 'shares of goodwill' are 'fungible assets' subject to the share identification rules in TCGA 1992 s 104(3). The 2003 version of SP D12 states that HMRC will not take this view, but will regard a share of partnership goodwill as a single asset that is successively enhanced. This makes the computations much easier; and it also means that a partner will qualify for taper relief on a disposal based on the full length of time he or she has been interested in the goodwill, even if some of the share has been acquired within the last one or two years.

16. This does not apply where the partnership has purchased goodwill from outside, for example on the acquisition of another business. Such goodwill must be identified separately, and taper relief will run from the later of the date on which the firm acquired it and the date on which the particular partner became interested in it.

Fred Stone owns the following properties in the UK, which he lets.

Shop 1   A butcher's shop, the annual rental of which is £13,200 under a 7 year lease expiring on 29 September 2006 and the lease was renewed on that date at £18,800 per annum for 7 years.

Shop 2   A shop selling textiles, the annual rental of which is £12,000 under a 7 year lease expiring on 25 March 2008. The quarter's rent due on 25 March 2006 was not paid until 30 April 2007.

Shop 3   A shop selling light fittings. This was let to a relative of Mr Stone at an annual rental of £2,400 when a commercial rent would have been £10,000. Mr Stone's relative is responsible for all outgoings, with the exception of insurance amounting to £2,500.

Shop 4   This shop had been let at an annual rental of £14,000 until 23 June 2006 when the tenant, who had been selling clothing, informed Mr Stone that he could not afford to pay the rent and vacated the premises forthwith. Mr Stone agreed through his agent to re-let the premises from 25 March 2007 to a new tenant who would be selling pottery imported from Scandinavia. The new rental was £16,000 per annum for 10 years and Mr Stone also received a premium of £6,000 from the incoming tenant on 25 March 2007.

Mr Stone had borrowed money to buy Shops 1, 2 and 4 and the interest payable for 2006/07 was £8,200.

House 1   A furnished house let on weekly tenancies. The house had been purchased in November 2001 with the aid of a bank loan of £62,500. Interest had been paid for 2006/07 amounting to £5,000. The property was let throughout 2006/07. The all-inclusive weekly rental was £160.

House 2   A furnished house also let on weekly tenancies. During 2006/07 the property was let for 43 weeks. The all-inclusive weekly rental was £120.

The houses are not holiday accommodation and are regularly let to one tenant for lengthy periods. House 2 had been empty and available for letting during the weeks when it was not let. Council tax had been paid by the tenants, apart from the period when House 2 was not let, when the tax was paid by Fred Stone. Wear and tear of furniture is claimed at 10% of the gross rents less water supply charges.

With the exception of the houses the rents are due in advance on the normal English quarter days, 25 March, 24 June, 29 September and 25 December. Fred makes up his rental accounts to 5 April annually. Details of expenditure for the year ended 5 April 2007, as adjusted for amounts in arrears and advance, were as follows:

Insurance	
Buildings	3,122
Contents	216
Ground rent	610
Repairs and decorating (see notes)	7,145
Accountancy	370
Newspaper advertising	134
Gardeners' wages	380
Water supply charges (house 1 £230, house 2 £310)	540
Council tax	60
	£ 12,577

Mr Stone employs agents to collect the rents, except that of Shop 3. He pays them 10% of the amount collected (not applicable to the premium). Total rent collected in 2006/07 was £49,216.

Notes on repairs

1.   £3,854 was spent on putting Shop 4 into proper condition after the previous tenant had vacated it.

2.   £1,050 was spent on dry-rot remedial treatment to House 1. The dry-rot was present in the house when Mr Stone purchased it in November 2001.

3.   £1,428 was spent on re-tiling the roof of House 2.

4.   All the expenditure on the houses in respect of repairs and decorating relates to the property and not the furniture.

In 2004/05 Mr Stone gave £20,000 to his son Donald as part payment for the son's flat, Donald borrowing a further £80,000. The net interest in 2006/07 was £3,200. To help with expenses, Donald let a furnished room in the flat to a friend and received rent of £60 a week throughout the year. He did not provide any other services. Donald paid for the buildings and contents insurance on the flat amounting to £150, and spent £250 on repairs during 2006/07. He also paid a service charge of £300, water supply charges of £110 and council tax of £400 (his friend making a contribution of £100 to the council tax).

(a)   Calculate Fred Stone's net rental income for tax purposes for 2006/07.

(b)   (i)   State Donald's position in 2006/07 in relation to his rents and expenses.

        (ii)   Indicate what the position would be if Donald took up a job where he was required to live on the premises, and he let the whole flat for an annual rent of £5,500 from 6 April 2007.

(c)   Without making calculations, indicate what the position in (a) would have been if the lettings had been undertaken by a property letting company rather than Fred Stone, Shop 3 being let to a friend of a director of the company. Assume the company makes up accounts to 31 March annually and the expenditure relates to the year to 31 March 2007.

(a)   **Fred Stone's UK property income assessment 2006/07**

Rental income   £
Shop 1
    6.4.06 – 28.9.06 (176 days) @ £18,200 pa   6,365
    29.9.06 – 5.4.07 (189 days) @ £18,800 pa   9,735
Shop 2   12,000
Shop 3   2,400
Shop 4
    6.4.06 – 23.6.06 (79 days) @ £14,000 pa   3,030
    25.3.07 – 5.4.07 (12 days) @ £16,000 pa   526
Premium *   4,920
House 1 (160 x 52)   8,320
House 2 (120 x 43)   5,160
                                                                                                      _____
                                                                                                      52,456

Expenditure

Interest re Shops 1, 2, 4 and House 1 (8,200 + 5,000)		13,200
Other expenditure as listed	12,577	
Less: Shop 3 excess of insurance paid over rent received	100	12,477
Agent's commission – 10% of (52,456 – 2,400 Shop 3)		5,006
Wear and tear of furniture **		1,294

                                                                                                     (31,977)
                                                                                                      _____
                                                                                                      20,479

   *   The part of the premium to be taken as additional rent is:

        Premium   6,000
        Less 2% x (10 – 1) = 18%   1,080
                                                                                                    _____
                                                                                                    £ 4,920

  **   The wear and tear allowance is calculated as follows:

	House 1	*House 2*
Total rent	8,320	5,160
Less water supply charges	230	310
	£ 8,090	£ 4,850
10% thereof	£ 809	£ 485

(b)   (i)   **Donald's position in 2006/07**

Donald is receiving rent of 52 x £60 = £3,120 and has incurred expenses of (150 + 250 + 300 + 110 + 300 =) £1,110 plus £3,200 interest = £4,310, part of which relates to his own occupation.

Under the 'rent a room' relief provisions, he is exempt from tax on the rents, since they do not exceed £4,250. He will not, of course, obtain any additional relief for the expenses.

(ii)   If Donald let the whole property, then he would be taxed on the rental income of £5,500 less allowable expenses, including interest.

Rent a room relief cannot be claimed unless the property is the claimant's main residence at some time in the letting period, so the relief would not be available from 6 April 2007. (Had it been, Donald could have elected to pay tax on the excess of the rent over the exempt £4,250, ie on £1,250, if this was more beneficial than the normal UK property income treatment – see explanatory note 14.)

(c) **Tax position if details in (a) had related to property letting company making up accounts to 31 March**

The taxation treatment of rental income for companies is broadly the same as for individuals. There are some differences, in particular in relation to interest paid. Interest relating to let property is taken into account in computing the surplus or deficit under the 'loan relationships' rules, rather than being deducted as a business expense as for Fred Stone (see explanatory note 15).

Apart from interest adjustments, the company's rental income would be computed in the same way as for Fred Stone, with adjustments being made for rent in arrear and in advance.

Explanatory Notes

Taxation of rental income

1. The same rules broadly apply to the calculation of rental income for individuals and companies, although there are some differences. HMRC's Property Income Manual deals with the income tax treatment.

   The rules that apply to both individuals and companies are dealt with in notes 2 to 12. Rules that apply only for income tax are dealt with in notes 13 and 14 and rules that apply only for companies in notes 15 and 16.

UK property business rules for rental income

2. All UK rental income is treated as relating to a single 'UK property business'. This applies whether the income is from sizeable businesses or from letting a single property, and no matter whether the property is let furnished or unfurnished. The net income from UK furnished holiday lettings is, however, calculated as a separate amount and then added to other property income. The holiday lettings income broadly qualifies as trading income for the purpose of various reliefs – for detailed notes see Example 99. Special rules also apply under the 'rent a room' scheme for individuals letting rooms in their own home – see note 14.

   Those who run hotels or guest houses, or individuals who provide meals to lodgers or tenants in their own homes, are usually regarded as trading (although the 'rent a room' scheme may apply). HMRC considers that where let property is not the taxpayer's home, the income will rarely constitute trading income, even if managing the properties takes up virtually all of the owner's time, although where additional services are provided over and above those normally provided for let property the income from those additional services may be treated as trading income.

Calculation of rental profits

3. Under ITTOIA 2005 s 272, the profits of a UK property business are computed broadly in the same way as business profits, although the income is still unearned income rather than earned income (except for furnished holiday lettings – see Example 99).

   The main rule in relation to allowable expenses is that they must be 'wholly and exclusively' for the purposes of the business. This will include the expenses of travelling to and from the let properties, unless in the case of an individual the trip is partly for private purposes. Provision may be made for bad and doubtful debts. Interest payable is included in allowable expenses for individuals (subject to the wholly and exclusively rule). See note 15 for the treatment of interest for companies. Legal and professional costs of *renewing* a short lease (ie with a term of 50 years or less) are allowable, but not the costs of the first letting, unless it is for less than a year. A change of tenant will not usually affect this treatment (see Revenue's Tax Bulletin December 1996). Capital allowances may be claimed where appropriate (except for fixtures, furniture or plant for use in a dwelling house (CAA 2001 s 35(2)), for which a wear and tear allowance may be available – see note 6). The allowances for vehicles are restricted to the business proportion as for traders (see Example 20 explanatory note 12), although this restriction does not affect companies.

Expenditure incurred in the seven years before the business started is treated as incurred on the first day of the business (ITTOIA 2005 s 57 (individuals) and TA 1988 s 401(1B) (companies)), except for *interest* paid by a company, which is dealt with under the loan relationships rules (see note 15).

If property is let for less than a commercial rent for personal reasons (for example to a relative or friend), expenses relating to the property are restricted by the 'wholly and exclusively' rule, and are not allowed to the extent that they exceed the rent received, nor can the excess expenses be carried forward to a later year. In part (a) of the example, therefore, Fred cannot deduct the excess insurance premium on Shop 3 from his other rental income and the company in part (c) would suffer a similar restriction.

4.   Rent and expenses are calculated on the 'earnings basis', ie with adjustments for amounts in arrear and in advance. For income tax purposes, HMRC will, however, accept figures based on receipts and payments for 'small' cases, ie where the gross rental income does not exceed £15,000, providing the cash basis is used consistently and does not produce a result substantially different from the earnings basis.

The basis period is the tax year for individuals and the accounting period for companies. If individuals do not make up their UK property business accounts for the tax year, the results must be apportioned on a time basis, eg if accounts are drawn up to 30 June, the 2006/07 income would be 86/366ths of the result to 30 June 2006 and 279/365ths of the result to 30 June 2007. (In practice HMRC will accept accounts drawn up to 31 March, providing this is done consistently and does not give materially different results from the strict tax year basis.)

Repair expenditure

5.   As far as repair expenditure is concerned, under commercial accounting principles, expenditure to rectify dilapidations that occurred in a previous ownership is allowable so long as the property was in a usable state when acquired (Odeon Associated Theatres Ltd v Jones – see Example 15 explanatory note 5). Hence Fred Stone in part (a) of the example has been allowed to deduct the cost of rectifying the dry rot in House 1. The same would apply to the company in part (c).

Repair expenditure must be distinguished from capital expenditure on improvements, additions and extensions, which is not allowable (although such expenditure would qualify for capital allowances if the let property is an industrial or agricultural building, and see also notes 6 and 7).

Capital allowances and wear and tear allowance

6.   Capital allowances are available on plant and machinery used for the maintenance, repair or management of let premises, but not on items for use in dwelling houses (CAA 2001 s 35). Under CAA 2001 s 15, qualifying expenditure is dealt with in the same way as for trades (see Example 20).

By concession B47, the disallowed expenditure on furniture etc in a dwelling house that is furnished to the extent that it can be occupied without additional expenditure by the tenant qualifies for a wear and tear allowance of 10% of rents. An adjustment is made to the 10% calculation to exclude from the rent any additions, if material, for payments that would normally be borne by a tenant, such as water supply charges, as shown in the example. Council tax is usually paid directly by the tenants, but where a property is multi-occupied, the landlord pays it instead (see note 10). In that event, any addition to rent to cover the tenant's share of the council tax should be excluded when making the 10% calculation. In the past some officers allowed a deduction for very short life items, such as crockery and linen, in addition to the 10% deduction. The concession now specifically states that such items are included within the 10% figure.

In addition to the wear and tear allowance, a deduction may be claimed for the cost of replacing fixtures that are an integral part of buildings, such as baths, toilets, central heating (but excluding any 'improvement element' where the replacements are significantly better than the original items). No deduction is allowed for items a tenant would normally provide for himself in unfurnished accommodation eg cooker, washing machine, dishwasher.

As an alternative to the 10% allowance, a renewals basis may be claimed, so that no deduction is allowed when assets are acquired but when they are replaced a deduction is given for the full replacement cost.

7. Where maintenance and repairs of property are made unnecessary because of improvements, additions and alterations, no allowance will normally be given. However if assets are replaced with broadly the same asset a full deduction can be claimed for the replacement and only additional amounts will be capital eg a replacement kitchen with extra storage (only the extra storage will be disallowed). However if the asset is substantially upgraded then the whole will be disallowed. HMRC will accept that replacing single glazed windows by double glazed equivalents counts as allowable repair expenditure (both for UK property and trading businesses). Generally if the replacement is part of the 'entirety' and is like-for-like or the nearest modern equivalent the expenditure is allowed as revenue expenditure (see Tax Bulletin June 2002).

8. Capital allowances are deducted as a business expense and are thus taken into account in arriving at the UK property business profit or loss.

Premiums on leases (ITTOIA 2005 part 3 Chapter 4)

9. The premium arising on the grant of a short lease (ie for 50 years or less) by a landlord, as distinct from the assignment of such a lease from one tenant to another, is partly assessable as income, whilst the remainder forms part of a capital gains computation.

That part assessable as income is treated as additional rent and is therefore available to cover expenses (as in Shop 4 in this example) (s 277(3)).

The formula given in the legislation is devised so that the longer the term of the lease, the more of the premium falls into the capital gains computation and the less is regarded as additional rent.

The premium is reduced by 2% for each complete 12 month period of the lease except the first, in ascertaining that part to be left in as rent (s 277(4)).

Thus:

Lease for	5 yrs	10 yrs	25 yrs	40 yrs	50 yrs
Premium £ or %	100	100	100	100	100
Reduce by 2% for each year except the first (and take this part into a capital gains computation as a part disposal)	8	18	48	78	98
Include as additional rent	92	82	52	22	2

The formula for including the discounted part in a capital gains computation is dealt with in Example 100, which also deals with other aspects of the tax treatment of premiums.

Council tax and business rates

10. Council tax on let domestic property is usually paid by the tenants, but the landlord will pay when property is in multiple occupation and for periods when, as in this example, property is empty between lettings, although various periods are exempt, such as the first six months for unfurnished property.

For property that is not domestic property, such as business premises, business rates are payable, and the payments are deductible as an expense in the normal way, subject to the rules for void periods for company landlords.

UK property let by a non-resident

11. Where property is let by a non-resident, the rental income is computed in the same way as for a resident *individual* (TA 1988 s 42A, SI 1995/2902). This applies whether the non-resident landlord is an individual, or trustees, or a company, except that it does not apply to the rental income of a UK

branch of a non-resident company. 'Non-residents' for the purpose of s 42A are those whose 'usual place of abode' is outside the UK, rather than the definition used for other purposes (as to which see Example 8 part A(i)). HMRC regards an individual as having a usual place of abode outside the UK if he is away for more than six months. Companies will not be so treated if they are UK resident for tax purposes. References to non-residents in the remainder of this note should be read accordingly.

Basic rate tax on net property income is normally deducted at source, either by a UK agent handling the let property, or by the tenant where there is no agent, and paid over to HMRC 30 days after the end of each calendar quarter, with a final settling up by the non-resident landlord. Where the tenant pays VAT on the rent, tax need only be deducted from the net of VAT amount. A tenant paying rent of £100 a week or less does not have to deduct tax unless told to do so by HMRC. Neither tenants nor agents have to deduct tax at source if the non-resident agrees with HMRC's Centre for Non-Residents to complete any tax returns he receives and to include any tax due on the property income in his payments under self-assessment (TA 1988 s 42A). Non-resident landlords are required to make half-yearly payments on account unless covered by the de minimis thresholds (see Example 40). HMRC has stated that the Centre for Non-Residents will not normally issue self-assessment returns to non-resident individual landlords who have no net tax liability, although returns may still be sent occasionally to ensure that the tax position remains the same. HMRC has produced guidance on its website (see Centre for Non-Residents) covering the detailed provisions.

Overseas property lettings

12. Income from property let abroad is calculated broadly in the same way as for a UK property business (except that the rules for furnished holiday lettings do not apply, nor the income tax rules in ITTOIA 2005 ss 92–94 relating to board and lodging and travelling expenses in connection with foreign trades). In order to calculate the amount of double tax relief available, profits and losses are calculated separately for each property and then aggregated and taxed as the profits of an 'overseas property business' (ITTOIA 2005 s 268 and s 269(2) (individuals), TA 1988 s 70A (companies)). Losses are carried forward to set against later overseas lettings profits (TA 1988 s 379B (individuals), s 392B (companies)).

Provisions applicable to individuals

Relief for losses

13. If losses arise, they are carried forward to set against future property income. See Example 18 part (b) for details of the relief available to individuals for excess capital allowances included in a UK property business loss.

Rent a room relief

14. Under the 'rent a room' relief provisions of ITTOIA 2005 part 7 Chapter 1, an owner or tenant who lets furnished rooms in his home is exempt from tax on gross rent of up to £4,250 a year. This applies whether the rent would have been charged as UK property income or trading income where the services provided are such that the income would be treated as being from a trade.

The rent taken into account for the relief is the payment for the accommodation plus payments for related goods and services, such as meals, cleaning, laundry etc.

The property must have been the claimant's only or main residence at some time during the letting period in each relevant tax year. The relief cannot be claimed if part of the property is let unfurnished in the same year.

If during the basis period someone else receives rent for letting a room in the property while it is the claimant's only or main residence the available exemption is halved to £2,125. This would apply, for example, to a couple who were jointly receiving rent from tenants, or to other joint owners.

If the taxpayer has any unrelieved losses from letting the property in earlier years in which the rent a room relief did not apply, they may be set against any profit on other rented properties in the current year, any unrelieved amount being carried forward to set against later rental profits on other properties. If capital allowances have been claimed, no allowances are due for an exempt year, and any balancing charges arising are added to rents to see if the total is below the exempt limit. The taxpayer may elect for the exemption not to apply to a particular year, which could be to his advantage if he had losses for which he could otherwise claim relief. Such an election only affects the year for which it is claimed and must be made within one year after the 31 January following the relevant tax year. It can be withdrawn within the same period.

Where gross rents exceed £4,250, the taxpayer may either be charged on rents less expenses in the normal way or alternatively he may elect to be charged on the excess of gross rents over £4,250. If he elects for the alternative basis, no capital allowances are available, but any balancing charge relating to earlier allowances remains assessable. An election for the alternative basis must be made within one year after the 31 January following the relevant tax year, and remains in force until withdrawn, the same time limit applying to the withdrawal.

For the effect of letting part of the home on the capital gains tax exemption see Example 82.

Provisions applicable to companies

Treatment of interest paid and losses

15. Interest paid by a company in relation to rented property is dealt with under the 'loan relationships' rules (as to which see Examples 62 and 63). If the interest relates to a furnished holiday letting it is deducted from the letting income. See Example 48 explanatory note 6 for the treatment of interest incurred before the commencement of a trade.

16. If a loss arises, it may be set against the total profits of the same accounting period, or surrendered by way of group relief (see Example 63 explanatory note 5), any unrelieved balance being carried forward to set against future *total* profits.

Part 4 of Finance Act 2006 introduced a new regime for real estate investment trusts (REITs). These are companies which are exempt from corporation tax. Distributions from the company are taxed as property income (Schedule A in respect of corporate shareholders).

Mrs Morley is a married woman aged forty-seven. She has a pensionable salary of £30,000 per annum. Her only other source of income is rent from two houses that she purchased on 1 January 1995. One is in London and has been let furnished at a commercial rent continuously since purchase. The other is a furnished holiday house in Suffolk used partly by the family and partly for holiday letting on commercial terms. The house in Suffolk cost £100,000 and there have been no improvements since. Both properties were purchased with the assistance of bank loans, the interest paid in the year ended 5 April 2007 being £3,738 on the loan for the London house and £4,630 on the loan for the Suffolk house.

The Suffolk house has been occupied as follows:

		Year ended 5 April	
		2006	2007
Number of weeks –	let	7	20
	occupied by family	24	20
	empty, available for letting	21	12
		52	52

The income and expenditure for each property for the year ended 5 April 2007, adjusted for accruals and prepayments, was as follows:

		London £	Suffolk £
Income –	rent receivable	15,400	7,000
Expenditure –	rates		1,300
	water supply charges	730	520
	insurance	485	364
	cleaning on change of occupants	–	996
	replacement of furniture	390	777
	repairs and decorations	940	1,810
	advertising for lettings	–	263

An allowance of 10% of rent (less rates and water) has been agreed for each property to cover depreciation of furniture.

(a)   Calculate Mrs Morley's property income for 2006/07.

(b)   State the position relating to pension contributions on the income from the Suffolk house.

(c)   Mrs Morley is contemplating selling the Suffolk house in the summer of 2007, and expects the sale proceeds to be around £485,000 after selling expenses.

Calculate the amount upon which capital gains tax would be payable if the property was sold at the estimated price on 1 June 2007, that the average period of holiday lettings and availability for letting was 3/5ths, and that Mrs Morley had no other capital transactions in 2007/08 and did not have any brought forward capital losses.

(a) **Computation of Mrs Morley's UK property income for 2006/07**

		London House			Suffolk House	
Rent receivable		15,400				7,000
Less: Rates				(32/52)	800	
Water supply charges		730		(32/52)	320	
Insurance		485		(32/52)	224	
Cleaning on change of occupants		–			996	
Repairs and decorations		940		(32/52)	1,114	
Advertising for lettings		–			263	
10% wear and tear allowance						
On (15,400 – 730)		1,467				
On (7,000 – 1,120)					588	
Interest paid		3,738	7,360	(32/52 x 4,630)	2,850	7,155
			£ 8,040			(£ 155)
Total assessable income						£ 7,885

(b) **Personal pension contributions**

The income from furnished holiday lettings in the UK is treated as trading income (TA 1988 s 504A).

From 6 April 2006 the limit on contributions into pension schemes has been 100% of earnings (or £3,600 if lower). In computing earnings the loss on the Suffolk house would be set against other UK property income first and would only reduce the total earnings available if the loss exceeded the profit on the London property.

(c) **Amount potentially liable to capital gains tax if Suffolk house is sold on 1 June 2007**

	£	£
Expected sale proceeds after expenses of selling		485,000
Cost on 1 January 1995	100,000	
Indexation allowance to April 1998 @ 11.4%	11,400	111,400
Gain		373,600

of which 2/5 = £149,440 relates to the private use proportion
and   3/5 = £224,160 relates to the holiday letting.

The gain of £149,440 relating to the private proportion would be a chargeable gain, since the property is not Mr and Mrs Morley's main residence. Taper relief at 40% for a non-business asset for a ten-year qualifying period would, however, be due since the property would have been owned for nine complete years from 6 April 1998 and a further year is counted as the property was acquired before 17 March 1998. This would reduce the gain by £59,776 to £89,664.

The gain of £224,160 relating to the holiday letting would be reduced by business assets taper relief of 75%, providing the lettings proportion of 3/5ths applies to the period from 6 April 1998 to the date of disposal (see explanatory note 6), leaving a chargeable gain of £56,040. If a replacement holiday property were acquired within three years after the disposal, the gain could be rolled over and treated as reducing the capital gains tax cost of the holiday let proportion of that property. In that event taper relief would not be available to reduce the gain and taper relief on the replacement property would relate to the period of ownership of that replacement property.

If rollover relief was not available or was not claimed, the amount chargeable to capital gains tax would therefore be (89,664 + 56,040 =) £145,704, less Mrs Morley's annual capital gains tax exemption for 2007/08.

Explanatory Notes

Furnished holiday lettings (ITTOIA 2005 part 3 Chapter 6)

1. All UK property income of individuals and companies, both from furnished and unfurnished lettings, is treated as being from a single business (ITTOIA 2005 s 264). For full details see Example 98.

    To the extent that rental income relates to *qualifying furnished holiday lettings* in the UK, the income and expenses are kept separate and are treated as if the net income arose from a trade, that income being treated as earnings for pension purposes (ITTOIA 2005 s 328). Capital allowances and loss reliefs may be claimed where appropriate (ITTOIA 2005 s 327). For both individuals and companies, any overall profit or loss is included within the result of a UK property business.

    See Example 37 for pension rules applicable from 6 April 2006. See notes 6 to 8 for the capital gains position.

Qualifying conditions

2. To qualify for furnished holiday lettings treatment, the property must be available for letting as holiday accommodation on a commercial basis for a total of 140 days or more in the tax year and must be so let for at least 70 of those days. (The 70-day test may be satisfied by averaging periods of occupation of any or all of the holiday accommodation let furnished by the same person (ITTOIA 2005 s 326).) If the accommodation is in the same occupation for a continuous period of more than 31 days then the aggregate of all such long-term occupancy must not exceed 155 days in the tax year (ITTOIA 2005 s 325).

    If the property was not let as furnished holiday lettings in the previous tax year then the above tests apply for the period of 12 months from the date of first letting as qualifying furnished holiday accommodation (ITTOIA 2005 s 324).

    Where part only of the let accommodation is holiday accommodation, apportionments are made on a just and reasonable basis.

    Relief for losses on holiday lettings may be denied on the grounds that the lettings are not on a commercial basis, particularly where property is bought as a holiday home for the family. This was the decision in Brown v Richardson (June 1997 SpC 129), where it was held that lettings were made 'with a view to generating revenue to offset costs rather than with a view to the realisation of profits'. See also Walls v Livesey (1995 SpC 4) for comments on the different commerciality tests for the holiday lettings provisions (ITTOIA 2005 s 323) and for loss relief (TA 1988 s 381(4)). The Revenue gave their views on the implications of these cases in their Tax Bulletin of October 1997.

    As far as inheritance tax is concerned, business property relief may not be available, because the lettings would probably be regarded as investments (IHTA 1984 s 105(3)). The HMRC's Capital Taxes Manual indicates, however, that business property relief will probably be available where holiday lettings are very short-term and either the owner or someone acting for him is substantially involved with the holidaymakers in terms of their activities on and from the premises.

Rent a room relief

3. The 'rent a room' relief provisions outlined in Example 98 explanatory note 14 could be claimed if appropriate in respect of furnished holiday accommodation instead of the above rules if the accommodation consisted of furnished rooms in the taxpayer's only or main residence, but not where, as in this example, the holiday home is not the main home.

Capital allowances and wear and tear allowance

4. Although the furnished holiday accommodation provisions enable capital allowances to be claimed, no guidance is given as to how to switch from the 10% wear and tear or renewals basis normally used for let property, nor as to how to deal with property that is within the provisions in one tax year and not the next, such as the Suffolk house in this example, where it did not qualify in 2005/06

because it was let for only 49 days. In practice, it is considered that capital allowances will probably not be claimed and the wear and tear or renewals treatment will continue.

Council tax and business rates

5. Council tax is payable on domestic property. Self-contained holiday accommodation is, however, liable to business rates if it is available for letting for 140 days or more a year (no matter for how long it is actually let), hence the rates payable on the Suffolk house.

As far as the London house is concerned, if it is let long-term the tenant will pay the council tax. If it is no-one's only or main residence Mrs Morley will pay the council tax, which would be an allowable expense of the letting.

Any rates and other charges normally borne by a tenant, such as water supply charges, are deducted from rent before calculating the 10% wear and tear allowance.

Capital gains tax

6. The property and other chargeable assets used in the furnished holiday lettings are eligible for capital gains rollover relief if they are replaced (see Example 83) (TCGA 1992 s 241(3)).

For non-corporate taxpayers, the business assets rate of taper relief is also available (as to which see Example 74 part (a)(i)) (s 241(3)). Where, however, the property has been used for mixed holiday letting/private purposes during the period of ownership from 6 April 1998 onwards, as in this example, the gain has to be split into a non-business assets gain and a business assets gain (TCGA 1992 Sch A1.9). Similar provisions apply where there have been periods during which the property did not qualify as a holiday letting (Sch A1.3). Apportionments are to be made on a just and reasonable basis and assuming that amounts to be apportioned accrued at the same rate over the relevant period (Sch A1.21).

7. As far as Mrs Morley is concerned, rollover relief could be claimed in respect of the lettings proportion of the gain providing the full business proportion of the proceeds of sale was reinvested in the business proportion of the new property. Gains could continue to be rolled over on a succession of such sales. The interaction of rollover relief and taper relief is indicated in part (c) of the example.

8. The gain of £149,440 that would arise on the private proportion of the Suffolk house if it were sold as contemplated is fully chargeable because the house is not the main residence. If it had been, then that part of the gain would have been exempt. Where the only or main residence has been let as residential accommodation, there is an exemption equal to £40,000 or an amount equal to the owner occupier exempt gain whichever is less. The Revenue took the view that this exemption was only available if the lettings had some degree of permanence and a series of short lets would not qualify. They lost a case on the point, however (Owen v Elliott (CA 1990) – see Example 82 explanatory note 7), so it would appear that had the Suffolk house been the capital gains tax exempt residence at some time, the residential lettings exemption would be available (TCGA 1992 s 223).

Calculate the taxable income and chargeable gains that would arise in the following circumstances assuming that in no case is a general 31 March 1982 rebasing election made.

The retail prices index is shown on page (xi). Assume the index to be 200.0 for October 2006 and 201.0 for December 2006, giving index increases from March 1982 of 151.7% to October 2006 and 153% to December 2006.

(a) An individual acquired a freehold for £188,000 on 16 May 1991. On 24 June 2006 he grants a lease of the whole premises for 21 years for a premium of £120,000 and a rent of £20,000 per annum, payable quarterly in advance on usual quarter days. The value of the reversion was £256,000.

(b) A lease is granted for 60 years for a premium of £230,000, the value of the reversion being £80,000. The other circumstances are as in (a).

(c) An individual was granted a 40 year lease on 25 December 1999 at a market rental of £20,000 per annum payable quarterly in advance on the usual quarter days and paying a market premium of £50,000. The property is used as a second home. On 25 December 2006 he assigns the unexpired portion of the lease for a premium of £70,000.

(d) The individual in (c) above, instead of assigning the lease, grants a sub-lease at the same rent for 20 years from 25 December 2006 for a market premium of £49,000.

(e) On 1 July 2001 Eric Forbes granted a lease to Jeremy Poulton on payment of a premium of £7,500. The lease was for a period of 17 years and it is considered, having regard to the terms of the lease, that a premium of £120,000 could have been demanded. On 15 January 2006 Jeremy sold the lease to Peter Long for £100,000 and Peter in turn sold the lease on 18 June 2006 to John Field for £150,000.

Compute the amount, if any, chargeable to income tax for 2005/06 and 2006/07 on the assumption that none of the persons involved is a dealer in land.

(f) Rufford Ltd makes up accounts annually to 31 March. On 6 April 1964 it acquired a lease of business premises due to expire on 6 April 2009. It paid £13,860 for the assignment of the lease and incurred £300 of allowable legal and similar fees. On 6 October 2006 it assigned the lease (at arm's length) for £35,000 incurring allowable fees of £1,300. The value of the lease at 6 April 1965 was £12,500, and at 31 March 1982 was £30,000.

(g) Newco Ltd prepares accounts to 31 March. It has a wholly owned subsidiary from which on 2 December 2006 it acquired freehold property at the then market value of £500,000. The cost to the subsidiary in July 2000 was £360,000.

On 31 December 2006 Newco Ltd granted a 21 year lease over three quarters of the property to Antiques Ltd. Newco Ltd received a premium of £220,000, and the rent was £1,000 per month payable in advance on the 1st of each month.

There are three-yearly rent reviews at which point the tenant has an option to terminate the lease, the rent to be determined in the absence of agreement by arbitration. The residual value of the whole property at 31 December 2006 following the grant of the lease was £352,000.

(h) Newport, a trader who has been in business for many years, making up accounts annually to 31 December, was granted a 21 year lease of business premises on 1 July 2006 at a premium of £90,000 and a rent of £20,000 per annum payable quarterly in advance. Show the deductions to be made in respect of the lease in Newport's accounts to 31 December 2006 and indicate the tax treatment if Newport were to assign the lease in five years' time.

(a) **Grant of short lease out of freehold**

		£
Premium – 24 June 2006		120,000
Less: Discount (21 – 1 = 20 x 2%) = 40%		48,000
Additional rent		72,000
Normal rent: 24 June 2006 to 5 April 2007 (286 days)		15,671
2006/07 UK property income subject to expenses		87,671

	£
Capital proceeds (total premium 120,000 – 72,000 taxed as additional rent)	48,000

$$\text{\emph{Less:} Cost May 1991 £188,000} \times \frac{48,000 \text{ proceeds}}{\underset{120,000 \qquad 256,000}{\text{full premium + reversion}}} \qquad 24,000$$

	£
Unindexed gain	24,000

$$\text{\emph{Less:} Indexation allowance to April 1998} \quad \frac{162.6 - 133.5}{133.5} = 21.8\% \times 24,000 \qquad 5,232$$

	£
2006/07 Capital gain, with 35% taper relief available (see note 14)	18,768

(b) **Grant of long lease at a premium**

No UK property income liability on the premium since this is a long lease, but a liability on rent as (a):

2006/07 UK property income – rent (286 days)	£15,671

	£
Capital gain – premium 24 June 2006	230,000

$$\text{\emph{Less:} Cost May 1991 £188,000} \times \frac{230,000 \text{ (cash received)}}{310,000 \text{ (cash and reversion)}} \qquad 139,484$$

	£
Unindexed gain	90,516
Less: Indexation allowance 21.8% x 139,484	30,408
2006/07 Capital gain, with 35% taper relief available (see note 14)	60,108

(c) **Assignment of short lease**

Since the lease was acquired at full market value there will be no income tax liability on the premium when the assignment takes place (see note 3).

The capital gain is:	£
Premium 25 December 2006	70,000

$$\text{\emph{Less:} Cost December 1999 £50,000} \times \frac{33 \text{ years unexpired on disposal}}{40 \text{ years unexpired on acquisition}}$$

Substituting relevant percentages:

$$£50,000 \times \frac{(33 \text{ years} =) \; 90.280}{(40 \text{ years} =) \; 95.457} \qquad 47,288$$

	£
2006/07 Capital gain, with 25% taper relief available	22,712

(d) **Grant of sub-lease out of short lease**

	£	£
Premium received 25 December 2005		49,000
Less: Discount (20 – 1 = 19 x 2%) = 38%		18,620
c/f		30,380

b/f			30,380
Less: Fraction applicable to sub-lease of premium paid on acquisition –			
Premium paid		50,000	
Less: (40 – 1 = 39 x 2%) = 78%		39,000	
Additional rent		11,000	
20 (years of sub-lease)/40 (years of head lease) x 11,000			5,500
Additional rent			24,880

Normal rent: 25 December 2005			5,000	
25 March 2006	5,000			
Less in advance (79 days out of 91)	4,341		659	5,659
2006/07 UK property income subject to expenses (including rent payable £5,659)				30,539

Capital gain

Proceeds (full premium)	49,000

Less: Cost December 1999 £50,000 x $\dfrac{\text{(33 years unexpired when sub-lease granted less 13 years unexpired when sub-lease ends)}}{\text{(40 years unexpired when lease acquired)}}$

Substituting relevant percentages:

$$£50,000 \times \frac{\text{(33 years)} = 90.280 - \text{(13 years)} = 56.167}{\text{(40 years)} = 95.457}$$

$= £50,000 \times \dfrac{34.113}{95.457}$	17,868
	31,132
Less: Part of premium assessable as UK property income	24,880
2006/07 Capital gain, with 25% taper relief available (see note 14)	6,252

Note that where there is a capital gain the rent deduction cannot convert it to a loss; it can only reduce the gain to nil, so that if the gain had been say £24,000, the result would have been no gain no loss. If the capital gains calculation had resulted in a loss, then that would be the allowable loss for capital gains purposes and the taxable UK property income could not be used to increase the allowable loss.

(e) **Grant of lease at an undervalue**

Amount forgone by Eric Forbes on the grant of the lease to Jeremy Poulton on 1 July 2001 was (120,000 – 7,500 =) £112,500.

Assignment by Jeremy Poulton to Peter Long 15.1.06

Excess of premium received over premium paid (100,000 – 7,500)	92,500
Less: 2 x (17 – 1) = 32%	29,600
Chargeable on Jeremy as UK property income for 2005/06	£ 62,900

Leaving (112,500 – 92,500 =) £20,000 to be dealt with on subsequent assignments.

Assignment by Peter Long to John Field 18.6.06

Excess of premium received over premium paid (150,000 – 100,000 =) £50,000 but restricted to balance of amount forgone	20,000
Less: 32% as above	6,400
Chargeable on Peter as UK property income 2006/07	£ 13,600

Unlike other amounts charged to income tax, the amounts charged under these provisions are not excluded from the proceeds in the capital gains computation (TCGA 1992 Sch 8.6(2)), so Jeremy will have a capital gains liability by reference to proceeds of £100,000 and Peter by reference to proceeds of £150,000 (see note 3).

(f) **Rufford Ltd – assignment of lease acquired before 6 April 1965**

(i) The gain using cost/6.4.65 value is as follows:

	£
Sale proceeds 6 October 2006	35,000
Less selling expenses	1,300
	33,700

Cost 6 April 1964 (including £300 expenses) £14,160
Allow fraction equivalent to unexpired term of lease at time of disposal, ie:

2½ years unexpired at disposal

45 years unexpired at acquisition

Substitute TCGA 1992 Sch 8 percentages
2½ years is a percentage midway between 2 and 3 years)

£14,160 x $\dfrac{14.294}{98.059}$ =	2,064
	31,636
Less: Indexation allowance on 31 March 1982 value (see (ii) below)	7,761
Overall gain	23,875
Proportion after 6 April 1965 = $\dfrac{40½}{41½}$ x 20,781	
Gain	20,280

If election made to use 6 April 1965 value

Sale proceeds less selling expenses as above	33,700

Market value at 6 April 1965

$£12,500 \text{ x } \dfrac{2½ \text{ (years of lease unexpired at disposal)}}{44 \text{ (years of lease unexpired at 6.4.1965)}}$

Thus £12,500 x $\dfrac{14.294}{97.595}$ =	1,831
Unindexed gain (cf)	31,869

	£
Unindexed gain (bf)	31,869
Less: Indexation allowance (see (ii) below)	7,761
Gain	24,108
The gain is the lower	
of £23,875 and £24,108, ie	23,875

(ii)   The gain using 31.3.82 value is:

	£
Sale proceeds 6 October 2006 less selling expenses as before	33,700
31 March 1982 market value	

$$£30,000 \text{ x } \frac{2\frac{1}{2} \text{ (years unexpired at disposal)}}{27 \text{ (years unexpired at 31.3.82)}}$$

		£
Thus £30,000 x	$\dfrac{14.294}{83.816}$ =	5,116
Unindexed gain		28,584
Indexation allowance on depreciated 31 March 1982 value		
(being higher than depreciated cost £2,064) £5,116 x 151.7%*		(7,761)
Gain		20,823

Therefore the chargeable gain is £20,823 which is included in the company's total profits for the year ended 31 March 2007 and charged at the rate of corporation tax applicable to the company's profits.

(g)   **Newco Ltd – intra-group transfer and subsequent lease**

Schedule A liability on grant of lease:

	£	£
Amount received 31 December 2006		220,000
Less: Discount ((21 – 1) x 2%) of £220,000		88,000
Portion taxable as additional rent is		132,000
Rent: 1.1.07 to 31.3.07 3 months @ £1,000		3,000
Property income (subject to expenses) yr ended 31.3.07		135,000
Chargeable gain portion		88,000

Less: Allowable expenditure		
Cost to subsidiary July 2000	360,000	
Indexation allowance $\dfrac{201.0^* - 170.5}{170.5}$ = 17.9%	64,440	
Deemed acquisition cost to Newco Ltd December 2006	424,440	
Cost of part disposed of December 2006		
(no further indexation allowance since		
disposed of in same month as acquired)		
3/4 x 424,440 = 318,330 x $\dfrac{88,000}{220,000 + 352,000}$		48,974
Chargeable gain year ended 31 March 2007		39,026

*   Assumed figures

(h)   **Newport – premium paid on short lease of business premises**

	£	£
Premium payable 1 July 2006	90,000	
Less: Discount (21 – 1) x 2% = 40%	36,000	
Assessable on landlord as additional rent	54,000	

Therefore allowable to Newport $\dfrac{54,000}{21}$ = £2,572 per annum

In year to 31 December 2006:

	£
Deduction re lease premium (6 months) ½ x 2,572	1,286
Rent payable (2 quarters)	10,000
	11,286

If Newport assigned the lease in five years' time, the assignee, providing he was a business tenant, would take over the right to make the annual deductions of £2,572 in respect of the premium (ITTOIA 2005 s 61). Newport would be treated as having made a disposal for capital gains tax, the allowable cost being the premium paid of £90,000, less the total annual deductions allowed to him, less depreciation under TCGA 1992 Sch 8 (see note 11). Since the lease is a business asset, any gain arising would qualify for maximum taper relief of 75%, except to the extent that it was reduced by allowable losses (see note 14).

Explanatory Notes

Difference between grant and assignment of lease

1.   Example 98 deals with the income tax/corporation tax treatment of let property. This example deals with some additional income aspects and also the capital gains treatment of lease premiums.

2.   A *grant* of a new lease by a landlord to a tenant and an *assignment* of an existing lease from one tenant to another must be carefully distinguished for tax purposes. A grant of a new lease for a capital sum is a part disposal of the property for capital gains purposes, but part of the capital sum is charged as income if the lease is for 50 years or less, as detailed below (ITTOIA 2005 s 279). An assignment of an existing lease on the other hand is a disposal of the whole of the assignor's interest in the property and is normally subject only to a capital gains charge.

3.   If, however, the premium obtained on the *grant* of a lease for 50 years or less is less than could have been obtained, successive assignors of the lease may be liable to an income tax (or corporation tax) charge on part of the proceeds instead of the proceeds on assignment being wholly a capital gains matter. This situation will prevail until the whole of the premium originally forgone has been charged on subsequent assignments (ITTOIA 2005 s 283). The charge is calculated in the same way as additional rent would have been calculated for the grantor of the lease, using the original lease term, as illustrated in part (e) of the example. Despite the income tax or corporation tax charge, there is no deduction from the proceeds in a capital gains computation on the premium (Sch 8.6(2)). The charge under ITTOIA 2005 s 283 is treated as part of the profits of a UK property business.

Income tax treatment on grant of short lease followed by sub-lease

4.   A premium received on the *grant* of a lease not exceeding 50 years is partly taxable as additional rent. That part so taxable is the premium less 2% for each complete year of the lease except the first (ITTOIA 2005 s 279).

5.   If the lessee then sublets at a premium, he may deduct from the amount of his additional rent calculated as in note 4 above the appropriate proportion of the base premium that is taxable, being the proportion that the sub-lease bears to the head lease (ITTOIA 2005 s 288). If he sublets at a rent

rather than at a premium, he may deduct the appropriate proportion of the premium he paid from the rent on a day to day basis (ITTOIA 2005 s 292).

In part (d) of the example, half of the £11,000 'additional rent' on which the head landlord was taxed relates to the 20 year sub-lease, ie £5,500, and this would have been deducted at £275 per annum from the rent payable by the sub-tenant if he had not paid a premium.

Similar provisions apply where a premium is paid by a business tenant – see note 11.

6.   For both individuals and companies, rental income and expenses are calculated according to commercial accounting principles, with adjustments for amounts in arrear and in advance. Full details are in Example 98.

Grant of short lease out of freehold/long lease

7.   Where a short lease (ie not exceeding 50 years) is granted out of a freehold or long lease, that part of the premium not taxed as additional rent is a part disposal for capital gains purposes.

The value of the reversion (ie the right to receive the rent and possession of the premises at the end of the lease) must be taken into account in calculating the gain arising.

The denominator in that calculation includes the full premium received, not just the deemed capital portion (TCGA 1992 Sch 8.5).

The normal rules for part disposals apply to the capital gains computation (TCGA 1992 s 42). Note that the indexation allowance is calculated on the cost of the part disposed of (or on the same proportion of the 31.3.82 value if appropriate), not on the total cost. For non-corporate taxpayers indexation allowance is no longer available for periods after April 1998. It continues for companies, as shown in the example.

Grant of sub-lease out of short lease

8.   Where a short lease is granted out of another short lease, then for capital gains purposes the gain or loss is calculated on the *full premium* according to the wasting asset rules, taking as the cost figure that part of the original expenditure that will waste away during the sub-lease. The part that has wasted away is worked out on a curved line basis, the percentages appropriate to the years concerned being in TCGA 1992 Sch 8 (see page (x)). The available indexation allowance is calculated on the depreciated amount. Where the original short lease was acquired before 31 March 1982, then unless a general rebasing election has been made, the gain or loss is calculated using pre March 1982 and post March 1982 rules, with the allowable expenditure being the depreciated 31.3.82 value or depreciated cost/6 April 1965 value, and indexation allowance being on the higher of the depreciated 31 March 1982 value and depreciated cost/6 April 1965 value as the case may be. When the gain has been calculated, the part of the premium chargeable as UK property income is then deducted from the capital gain, but not so as to create a loss, nor can it be added to a loss (TCGA 1992 Sch 8.4 & 8.5).

Assignment of short lease

9.   In calculating the capital gain arising on an *assignment* of a short lease, the cost has to be depreciated on the same curved line basis as in note 8 above, and the same provisions apply in relation to the indexation allowance and assets acquired before 31 March 1982.

Intra-group transfer; term of lease

10.   (a)   The cost to be used on the acquisition by Newco (part (g)) from its subsidiary is the cost to the subsidiary plus indexation allowance (TCGA 1992 s 171). See Example 85 explanatory note 2 for the special rules which apply where the asset was originally acquired before 31 March 1982 and for the effect of the provisions preventing the use of indexation allowance to create or increase a loss on and after 30 November 1993.

(b) The term of the lease for the purpose of calculating the exclusion from Schedule A and inclusion as a chargeable gain is considered to be 21 years, even though the tenant has an option to terminate the lease at each three-yearly rent review.

If the term had been artificially extended in the lease, whilst encouraging the tenant to terminate it earlier because of harsh rent review provisions, the term for calculating the exclusion from Schedule A and inclusion as a chargeable gain would have been taken as the period for which the lease was likely to run. (TA 1988 s 38).

Income tax treatment of lease premium paid by business tenant

11. Where a business tenant pays a premium on the grant of a short lease, that part of the premium that is assessable on the landlord as additional rent is allowable to the payer as rent payable, but spread over the period of the lease rather than as a single deduction. The appropriate fraction may accordingly be deducted in arriving at trading profits as shown in part (h) of the example (ITTOIA 2005 s 61).

If the business tenant then assigns the lease, the part of the premium that has been allowed as an expense against income must be excluded from the allowable cost in the capital gains computation, as shown in Example 96 part (f). A new business tenant would then take over the right to make the annual deductions for the balance of the premium.

Surrenders and variations

12. Where a tenant surrenders a lease in exchange for a new longer lease on broadly the same terms but at a different rent, the surrender is not normally treated as a disposal and acquisition for capital gains purposes (Revenue Concession D39).

13. Where a leaseholder acquires a superior interest in the land, such as a freehold reversion, HMRC, by Concession D42, allow indexation allowance on the original cost of the lease, reduced as appropriate under Sch 8, by reference to the date of the original acquisition, even though strictly indexation should run from the date the superior interest is acquired. Indexation on the consideration for the superior interest runs from the date of its acquisition.

Taper relief

14. The freezing of indexation allowance for non-corporate taxpayers after April 1998 was linked to the introduction of taper relief, which enables gains to be reduced by up to 75% for business assets after two years and 40% for non-business assets after ten years, the taper period running from April 1998 or the date of acquisition if later. An extra year is added to the period qualifying for relief for non-business assets acquired before 17 March 1998. Taper relief starts after one complete year for business assets and after three complete years for other assets. Taper relief is not relevant for companies, for whom indexation allowance continues. For detailed notes on taper relief see Example 74 part (a)(i).

Taper relief is available on the disposals of non-business assets in parts (a) and (b) of the example as the assets were held prior to 17 March 1998 and qualified for the bonus year. However, losses (if any) have to be deducted before applying the available taper relief to chargeable gains. Newport in part (h) would qualify for full relief as indicated, again subject to the deduction of losses.

Reverse premiums

15. Where an inducement is provided by a landlord to a tenant to encourage the taking of a lease of land or buildings it is known as a reverse premium. It is provided by FA 1999 s 54 and Sch 6 that the receipt of a reverse premium is taxable in the hands of the recipient. If the taxpayer receives the amount in the course of a trade or profession then the amount is taxed in that trade. Under Accounting Standards, the amount will normally be spread over the period of the lease (or to the date of the first rent review if shorter) and taxed over that period. There are anti-avoidance rules to prevent exploitation of this principle by granting a lease on uncommercial terms between connected persons. In such cases the reverse premium is taxable in full in the period in which the lease is

granted. Where the tenant is not in business, the premium received is taxed as UK property income, again spread over the lease. No charge arises if the property is the tenant's only or main residence or if the same amount is a deduction as a contribution towards expenditure for capital allowances.

Rent factoring

16.   Some companies have entered into rent factoring schemes, which are in substance equivalent to bank loans. It has, however, been argued that the amounts received are chargeable to corporation tax only as capital gains, which may be offset by losses or reliefs. The Revenue considered that the sums were already taxable as UK property income, but the position was put beyond doubt for transactions entered into on or after 21 March 2000 (TA 1988 ss 43A to 43G). Lump sums received for giving up the right to future rental income are charged as UK property income. There are exceptions so that the provisions do not affect genuine investment in property and capital allowances based finance leasing.

INDEX

W

Y